SIMONE DE BEAUVOIR

The Second Sex

TRANSLATED BY
Constance Borde and
Sheila Malovany-Chevallier

WITH AN INTRODUCTION BY
Sheila Rowbotham

VINTAGE BOOKS
London

Published by Vintage 2010

2 4 6 8 10 9 7 5 3 1

First published as *Le deuxième sexe* by Simone de Beauvoir © 1949
by Editions Gallimard, Paris, 1949
Translation copyright © 2009 by Constance Borde and
Sheila Malovany-Chevallier
Introduction copyright © 2009 by Sheila Rowbotham

Constance Borde and Sheila Malovany-Chevallier have asserted their right
under the Copyright, Designs and Patents Act 1988 to be identified as the
translators of this work

First published in Great Britain in 2009 by Jonathan Cape

Vintage
Random House, 20 Vauxhall Bridge Road,
London SW1V 2SA

www.vintage-books.co.uk

Addresses for companies within The Random House Group Limited can be found at:
www.randomhouse.co.uk/offices.htm

The Random House Group Limited Reg. No. 954009

A CIP catalogue record for this book
is available from the British Library

ISBN 9780099499381

Ouvrage publié avec le concours du Ministère français
chargé de la culture – Centre national du livre

The new English translation of *The Second Sex* by Simone de Beauvoir
was granted a translation subsidy from the *Centre national du livre*
(French Ministry of Culture)

The Random House Group Limited supports The Forest Stewardship
Council (FSC), the leading international forest certification organisation.
All our titles that are printed on Greenpeace approved FSC certified paper
carry the FSC logo. Our paper procurement policy can be found at
www.rbooks.co.uk/environment

Typeset in Dante MT by
Palimpsest Book Production Ltd, Falkirk, Stirlingshire

Printed and bound in Great Britain by
Clays Ltd, St Ives plc

CONTENTS

VOLUME I
FACTS AND MYTHS

Part One

DESTINY

Part Two

HISTORY

Part Three

MYTHS

VOLUME II
LIVED EXPERIENCE

To Jacques Bost

There is a good principle which created
order, light, and man,
and an evil principle which created
chaos, darkness, and woman.

Pythagoras

Everything that men have written about
women should be viewed with suspicion
because they are both judge and party.

Poulain de la Barre

Foreword

Reading Simone de Beauvoir's *The Second Sex* in this new translation by
Constance Borde and Sheila Malovany-Chevallier is both a return and
a revelation. Like many others of my generation, I began reading
Beauvoir, along with the works of Sartre, when I was at school in the
late 1950s. They travelled with me through the 1960s and, as a consequence, I had assimilated so much from the two of them by the time
I wrote *Woman's Consciousness, Man's World*, in the early 1970s, that I
took them for granted. They permeated how my thinking was structured. Yet I was not aware how much of the French version had been
abridged and altered in the 1954 translation by H. M. Parshley. In an
effort to make Beauvoir's work more accessible he muffled existentialist
terms and cut out historical material.[1] Beauvoir herself did not realise
the extent of the adaptations and omissions, declaring to Margaret A.
Simons in 1983, 'I wish with all my heart that you will be able to publish
a new translation.'[2] She would have been delighted by this scrupulous
and insightful new work.

In *The Second Sex* Beauvoir is at once a thinker, a scholar and a creative
writer. Her writing communicates on several levels simultaneously,
reasoning and seducing at the same time. Like that other great advocate
of women's emancipation, Mary Wollstonecraft, she expresses concepts
with beguiling irony. On the young woman who believes she is the exception and can circumnavigate male power, Beauvoir muses, '. . . she has
been taught to overestimate her smile, but no one told her that all women
smiled' (p.670). Abstractions become deft little cameos; when the girl
making jam writes the date on the lid, '. . . she has captured the passage
of time in the snare of sugar . . .'(p.493).

Her challenge to male cultural hegemony drives the book, sweeping
up prejudice in its transcendent energy. Beauvoir writes with passion
against the physical, psychological and intellectual confinement of
women, which she believes encourages them to accept mediocrity instead

of grandeur. Each acquiescence confirms servitude, '. . . her wings are cut and then she is blamed for not knowing how to fly' (p.660). Beauvoir, having penetrated the domain of male privilege, uses her skills to expose how the cards were stacked so unfairly against women. 'Being on the fringes of the world is not the best place for someone who intends to recreate it: here again, to go beyond the given, one must be deeply rooted in it' (p.154).

However, in *The Second Sex* the woman is not simply determined by a male defined culture. She is at once invented by men and 'exists without their invention' (p.209). Hence comes the male exasperation, as dream and reality fail to converge. For my generation the excitement of Beauvoir's thesis lay both in its exposure of the con trick of blaming women for not being in accord with men's fantasies *and* in the possibility she held out of women making themselves anew. Choice is always present, albeit from a specific situation in the famous assertion, 'One is not born, but rather becomes, woman' (p.293).

The boldness of Beauvoir's subversion remains exhilarating. It was not that she was the first to notice male hegemony or seek out ways to resist it. Both are refrains in women's writing about emancipation from the seventeenth century and indeed in a few cases even earlier. They would be reiterated and linked to a broader change in society by Mary Wollstonecraft in the late eighteenth century and disseminated far beyond Europe before *The Second Sex* was ever written. But Beauvoir's sustained critique takes 'femininity' by the throat to shake out illusion, examining women's circumstances along with the cultural sleights of hand which deceive and confuse. Nothing like it had been written before.

The scope of *The Second Sex* is dazzling indeed. Beauvoir launches herself into physiology, psychoanalysis, anthropology; ancient, medieval and modern history. She whizzes her reader through myths that define 'woman' in many cultures, demonstrating how the abstract ideal is superimposed on the actual experience of women. She then brings her argument closer to home by tracing how myths of 'the feminine' pervade nineteenth- and twentieth-century literature from Edgar Allan Poe to Henry Miller. These myths have material consequences. In one of her arch, carefully controlled asides, she remarks how, '. . . one of the most ardent zealots of unique, absolute, eternal love, André Breton, is forced to admit that at least in present circumstances this love can mistake its object: error or inconstancy, it is the same abandonment for the woman' (p. 520).

Exploring 'Lived Experience' in the second part, she breezes through child development, the cultural history of fashion and clothes, sociological surveys of prostitution, girls' attitudes to boys and to education, motherhood, ageing, and, of course, sexuality. Aware of the findings of the Kinsey Report and approving of the American young who were not restricted by European Catholic mores, her frankness scandalised many contemporaries. Resistant to biological reductionism, she argues that orgasm, '. . . can be qualified as psycho-physiological because it not only concerns the entire nervous system but also depends on the whole situation lived by the subject' (p.396). Yet heterosexual pleasure is, for Beauvoir, a precarious matter, bound up with pain and the threat of possession. Writing on the honeymoon, she quotes Nietzsche's *Gay Science*: 'To find love and shame in contradiction and to be forced to experience at the same time delight, surrender, duty, pity, terror and who knows what else, in the face of the unexpected proximity of God and beast! . . . Thus a psychic knot has been tied that may have no equal' (p.498).

In contrast, and surprisingly in a text written in the late 1940s, Beauvoir remarks: 'Between women love is contemplation; caresses are meant less to appropriate the other than to recreate oneself slowly through her; separation is eliminated, there is neither fight nor victory nor defeat; each one is both subject and object . . .' (p. 441). As Toril Moi observes the chapter on lesbianism is confused, perhaps revealing the difficulty in writing it.[3] Nevertheless Beauvoir presents love between women as an option, a possibility, though not an absolute alternative to heterosexuality. She says that lesbianism '. . . is an attitude that is *chosen in situation* . . . It is one way among others for women to solve the problems posed by her condition in general and by her erotic situation in particular' (p.448).

The Second Sex shattered other taboos in its negative portrayal of marriage, its courageous defence of contraception and abortion, its references to women taking young lovers. These all provoked comment and criticism, but most disturbing to the defenders of the status quo was the *mix* of sex and philosophy. A woman theorising in sensuous language broke all the rules of containment. Beauvoir contrived to embed her theme of the woman defined by others and yet struggling for her existential freedom in the structure of the book and in her mode of communication. She merged female and male zones, and this combination disturbed as much as what she actually said.

Her own background stood her in good stead in expressing the consequences of living the double life of a woman in a man's world. She was born in 1908 into an haute bourgeois family in straitened circumstances, and her childhood was strictly controlled by her mother. She was sent to a Catholic girls' school where mothers were encouraged to attend classes, her letters were opened and censored until she was eighteen. Individual thought and autonomous privacy were thus to become precious. In contrast to her mother's dutiful propriety, her irreligious father spent his time on amateur theatricals and enjoyed a social life outside the family. The second son of a landowner, with right-wing views, he was inclined to regret that his talented daughter was not a boy. During summer holidays on her father's family estates, novels and a close friend, Elisabeth Le Coin, were her only immediate forms of escape.[4]

In the long term, the only way out of this enclosed world would be education. Despite their sharply contrasting outlooks, both parents encouraged her interest in literature, and the brilliant pupil made her way laboriously through an exacting series of examinations to the Sorbonne. Unlike Jean-Paul Sartre, she had not received an elite education; the French system, despite recent modifications, was still based on distinct corridors of gender.[5] Nevertheless, though Beauvoir observes in *The Second Sex* how women's education discourages 'the habit of independence', (p.598) she herself displayed a remarkable will towards freedom. Uncharacteristically for a young woman, she inclined to philosophy at the Sorbonne. She regarded it in heroic terms as a discipline that, '. . . went straight to essentials. I had never liked fiddling detail'. Other subjects appeared as 'poor relations'; only philosophy went 'right to the heart of truth'.[6]

At university she became friendly with a talented coterie of young men who had studied at the École Normale Supérieure, including Merleau-Ponty. In 1929 Beauvoir began an affair with the attractive married student Rene Maheu, a friend of Sartre's. When Maheu failed his exams and left Paris, a smitten Sartre began his courtship in earnest, mustering philosophy in his effort to woo her.

Sartre could not compete with the handsome Maheu in terms of looks. His trump cards were philosophy, his strength of character, which freed Beauvoir from her parents, and his encouragement of her dream of becoming a great writer. Beauvoir always insisted that the relationship that began in their early twenties was reciprocal, but she quickly instituted a division of labour, deciding Sartre possessed the original brain of a great philosopher and her destiny would be literary. Aware of her own abilities, she was less confident and assured than the charismatic and ugly young man who became her lover. Even at this stage, Sartre took his brilliance for granted while Beauvoir's was earnestly acquired. However, given the difference in their education, Beauvoir's accomplishments were actually the greater. Ironically she would find creative writing

much harder than academic work, while Sartre, with her encouragement, would write novels and plays.[7] The agrégation jury of the Sorbonne
were divided but eventually awarded Sartre first place and Beauvoir
second.[8]

The new partnership did bring with it a certain power. Judith Okely
suggests that Beauvoir's relationship with Sartre enabled her to enter
Parisian intellectual circles. The alternative way in for a woman would
have been the salon, and this she despised, even if she had possessed
sufficient wealth.[9] Moreover the 'essential' bond with Sartre, despite all
the strains of jealousy, for it was never exclusive, turned them into a
formidable bloc of two. The 'contingent' lovers were thus loners and,
because they were often younger, and sometimes students, were in a less
powerful position.

Over the next ten years the young Sartre mapped out his philosophical belief in the existence of a material world independent of consciousness, while she struggled to write her first novel. Both continued to have
affairs, in Beauvoir's case with women as well as men; their practice of
confiding in one another served as a defence against the external world.
Love, work and talk consumed their energy. Existentialism did not lend
itself to an appreciation of the social and political traumas of depression,
the rise of fascism and Stalinism, the outbreak of the Spanish Civil War.
Though it did provide a philosophical basis for rejecting the conventional
framework of morality, it did not indicate any alternative. In her memoir,
The Prime of Life (1960), Beauvoir explains how, while she had gradually
abandoned her sense of absolute autonomy, 'it was still my individual
relationships with separate people that mattered most to me'. Her aim
in life was 'happiness'. She adds: 'Then, suddenly, History burst over me
and I dissolved into fragments. I woke to find myself scattered over the
four quarters of the globe, linked by every nerve in me to each and every
individual. All my ideas and values were turned upside down.'[10]

War changed everything, yet there are few references to it in The
Second Sex. By the late 1940s the fear, the hunger, the uneasy compromises with the occupying Germans, the unsuccessful attempts at resistance had been set aside.[11] Much later, in The Prime of Life, she would
record how she scrounged for cabbages and beetroots, took to wearing
a turban because she could not have her hair done, gave up smoking –
unlike Sartre who pursued dog-ends in the gutters.[12] She also remarked
how hard it was '. . . to speak of those days to anyone who had not lived
through them', explaining how she made her fictional character Anne
in The Mandarins reflect in her stead, 'The real tragedies hadn't happened

to me, and yet they haunted my life'.[13] The war taught Beauvoir that abstractions were not sufficient: '. . . it *did* make a very great difference whether one was Jew or Aryan; but it had not yet dawned on me that such a thing as a specifically feminine "condition" existed'.[14]

When Paris was liberated in 1944 life continued to be hard. Food was scarce, her room was too cold for writing. However, 'the future had been handed back to us'.[15] Briefly the left intelligentsia imagined a wider social change; on founding the journal *Les Temps Modernes,* Sartre proclaimed a commitment to 'la littératura engagée'.[16] The wily General de Gaulle left them with the literature and took political power, but the stark minimalism of existentialism resonated with the thoughtful young whose childhood and adolescence had been dominated by war. Ironically Sartre and Beauvoir became alternative celebrities and Beauvoir was forced to write in the basement of a bar to evade interruptions.[17]

From 1946 she was working on *The Ethics of Ambiguity.* The war had made her more alert to the constraints of circumstances. Prepared to engage with Marx's thought, while distrusting the teleological momentum of dialectical materialism, Beauvoir rejected the denial of the individual's autonomy demanded by the Communist Party despite the respect it had gained for its role in the Resistance.[18] Both she and Sartre struggled to create an alternative to the polarities of Soviet Communism and American capitalism through the medium of *Les Temps Modernes.* The journal brought Beauvoir into contact with the American left-wing writer Richard Wright, who was moving away from the Communist Party. Wright brought black American writing to her for the journal in 1946, introducing her to W. E. B. Dubois' idea of the 'double consciousness', which enabled African-Americans to survive racism while internalising elements of the inferiority projected on to them by white dominance.[19] In *The Ethics of Ambiguity* Beauvoir explored the concept of the complicity of the oppressed which would be important in *The Second Sex.*[20]

While colonialism, racism and anti-Semitism were very much part of left discourse in France after the war, discussion of the emancipation of women was less visible. Feminism had not been a strong force even before the war. The Vichy regime had celebrated the eternal feminine by excluding women from many jobs and giving out long prison sentences to anyone who distributed contraceptives. In 1943, Marie-Jeanne Latour had been guillotined for performing abortions.[21] While there was a Marxist legacy in the work of Engels and Bebel on the 'Woman Question', with which Beauvoir was familiar, the contemporary French Communist Party

stressed motherhood and the family. However, there did exist an awareness of the role women had played in the Resistance. This had both
political and cultural implications. French women would finally be given
the vote in 1944, and, in 1948, the historian Edith Thomas would dedicate her study of the early socialist women, *Les Femmes de 1848* to the
women of the Resistance.

Beauvoir's trajectory was, however, from her own subjectivity. Once
The Ethics of Ambiguity was finished, she began to contemplate writing
about herself. After a discussion with Sartre, she decided this involved
thinking through what it meant to be a woman – one of those fiddling
details she had contrived to ignore. This project of exploring her own
subjectivity fused into the broader project of *The Second Sex*. She was
adamant, however, that it was not a *feminist* work (p.3). Typically women
of her generation on the left wanted to surpass feminism, which was
regarded as narrow and restricted. Indeed it was right-wing writers such
as the Americans, Marynia Farnham and Ferdinand Lundberg who held
forth about 'Woman'. Beauvoir was sufficiently irritated to mention their
diatribe against emancipation, *Modern Woman: The Lost Sex* (1947) several
times in *The Second Sex* (pp.4, 283). This contretemps with the American
right contrasted with a bemused appreciation of the more radical aspects
of American mores, deepened by her passionate love affair with the
writer, Nelson Algren, while writing *The Second Sex*.

Beauvoir was intent on producing an existentialist analysis that recognised and demolished social and cultural constraints. As Judith Okely
notes in demonstrating the myriad ways in which women became the
Other in relation to men, Beauvoir's existentialism inclined her to see
knowledge as 'arising from each individual's specific circumstance'.[22]
This led her to take into account not only surveys of women's attitudes,
but sources that disclosed subjectivity such as the autobiography of
Isadora Duncan and the diaries of Sophia Tolstoy. She used novels by
women ranging from Virginia Woolf to Colette Audry. Two of her
childhood favourites also appear, Jo in *Little Women* and Maggie Tulliver
in *Mill on the Floss*. As a girl Beauvoir had grieved over Jo's compromise
and Maggie's death.

Beauvoir's charting of women's subjectivity is, however, problematic.
Not only does she treat fiction as evidence of actuality, as Okely notes, she
universalises from individual instances chosen to support her thesis. Okely
suggests an ethnographic reading – Beauvoir is the buried case study.[23] While
this is never explicit in the text, she is mirrored in the examples taken from
life and literature. Despite the range of her reading, her source material

focuses on women in her own image, including hardly any references to working-class women or to women of colour. Beauvoir is certainly alert to non-European cultures, but she plucks examples without situating them.

The modern historical material is scrappy and at times inaccurate. She has the militant suffragettes in the British Women's Social and Political Union joining with the Labour Party, when the reverse was the case (p.145). She dismisses Jeanne Deroin and the women around the 1848 journal *La Voix des Femmes* with an hauteur that denies the significance of their ideas and their understanding of solidarity (p.133). It is as if association and collective action by women in movements had never occurred. This is not simply because these were topics outside her experience or not her field of study, but because they do not fit into her theoretical approach. Patriarchy is boss; women are losers.

Beauvoir's ingenious strategy of entering male culture in order to undermine it is comparable to the difficulty John Milton encountered with his heroic Satan in *Paradise Lost*. Her dramatic construct inadvertently invests masculine culture with a depth and allure lacking in the female Other – who are assigned the less attractive parts as those ever inferior, bungling, moany women. Beauvoir's loathing of fixed ideals of femininity made it difficult for her to ascribe value to the lives and actualities of women, even though her intention was to show how women were not only 'diminished' but 'enriched' by the 'obstacles' they had to confront.[24] This partiality affected both her theoretical approach and the subject matter of *The Second Sex*. Her impatience with Romanticism's association of woman with nature blocked any questioning of the assumed virtue, in all circumstances, of control over nature, a critique present in the utopian socialist literature she mentions.

Beauvoir's abstraction 'patriarchy' occludes how differences in the degree of women's subordination are all important; it was after all preferable to be an Anglo-Saxon woman than a Norman. Space to manoeuvre, leeway to live your life, ideas of entitlement emerge from such distinctions. An historical approach would have yielded greater ambiguities in women's predicament and differing forms of male dominion instead of the intractable structure of 'patriarchy'. Some aspects of women's lived experience such as domestic labour are hardly mentioned though they had been extensively debated by feminists, women reformers and socialists, and Beauvoir makes only passing references to how children are to be cared for. Mothering did not adapt itself easily to her theoretical approach.

Within *The Second Sex* there are, however, interesting tensions between Beauvoir's abstract conceptualisation and what she observes. During the war she had met a number of women over forty who had confided in her. At the time she did not see their accounts of their 'dependence' as significant. Her interest, nevertheless, had been 'aroused'.[25] Perhaps she remembered their stories in noting a resolve among women to be mothers while also engaging in economic, political and social life. She ponders the problems this would entail (pp.582, 741, 751). She had located a contradiction in women's predicament which would become of crucial significance in the coming decades. Moreover, at times she provides a theoretical opening that negates the accumulative pessimism of the specific instances of women as the marginal Other. 'In truth, all human existence is transcendence and immanence at the same time; to go beyond itself, it must maintain itself, to thrust itself towards the future, it must integrate the past into itself, and while relating to others it must confirm itself in itself' (p.455). This observation, made in passing in relation to marriage, intimates a new balancing of human activity that could encompass not simply gender, but the social organisation of life and culture. While Beauvoir's work contained evident flaws, her mode of enquiry also suggests opposing perceptions of what might be.

Regardless of what Beauvoir did not do in The Second Sex, her originality and intellectual courage meant that one woman had mapped out terrains of thought and enquiry that would engage many thousands in the decades to come. The first volume of the book sold twenty-two thousand copies in the first week and the two volumes went on to sell in many countries.[26] The response to The Second Sex would transform its author's life. Paradoxically, Beauvoir, the solitary walker seeking existential freedom, would be constructed by others as a mythical antithesis to women's lot. To some this meant she was frigid and a nymphomaniac, to others a feminist heroine. Beauvoir's autobiographical writings navigated a way through the misunderstandings that assailed her. She sought to create herself in these books; and so, indirectly, The Second Sex did lead to her writing about herself after all.

If she was often uncomfortable with being the epitome of the emancipated woman, good also came from her new position. After so many years as Sartre's disciple, Beauvoir's writing inspired many. Among those who visited was a shy young woman called Sylvie Le Bon. She first arrived in 1960 and gradually a deep affection grew between the two women which lasted until Beauvoir's death. About this relationship and her attraction to other women, Beauvoir, who told so much about her life, remained warily silent.[27]

When the Women's Liberation Movement appeared in France in the early 1970s, Beauvoir was there defending abortion and thinking through the ideas that were being developed in many countries.[28] She told Alice Schwarzer that 'Women should not let themselves be conditioned exclusively to male desire any more'.[29] She became a feminist because she decided it was necessary to 'fight for the situation of women here and now', though she still believed that wider socialist changes were also needed.[30] During the 1970s she became more prepared to acknowledge that women's lack of power had resulted in positive qualities such as 'patience, sympathy, irony', which men would do well to acquire.[31] But she remained suspicious of strands in feminism which exalted women's essential difference from men. 'I find that it falls again into the masculine trap of wanting to enclose us in our differences,' she told Margaret A. Simons and Jessica Benjamin in 1979.[32]

The dilemmas raised by Beauvoir would be encountered again and again in the Women's Liberation Movements that spread around the globe. To what extent are we defined by biological difference? How is women's singularity to be at once affirmed and transcended? What makes women resist and what makes women comply with subordination? *The Second Sex* demonstrated the necessity of cultural resistance that went beyond complaint and even beyond critique. Beauvoir's left libertarian message was that new ways of being women and men would be created not simply theoretically but through human action, '... freedom can break the circle' and revolt 'create new situations' (p.780).

In 1949 Beauvoir could see that women would be able to shed their old skins and cut their own clothes, only 'if there is a collective change' (p.777). But what is to be done when this achieves partial successes, only to be confounded by force of circumstance? How was she to envisage that some aspects of equality would be achieved and new forms of inequality intensify? This is the conundrum facing women today. In rediscovering *The Second Sex* a new generation will find new insights and draw their own conclusions. Beauvoir's work retains its relevance, despite the changes that have occurred in women's position since the first publication in 1949. Moreover, she illuminates an ongoing process of exploration, resistance and creation, which is as exciting now as it ever was. Her voice echoes over the decades: 'The free woman is just being born'(p.767). Her prescient vision of '... new carnal and affective relations of which we cannot conceive' (p.781) carries hope for women – and for men.

Professor Sheila Rowbotham, August 2009

1 Margaret A. Simons, *Beauvoir and The Second Sex*, Rowman & Littlefield, Lanham, Maryland, 1999, pp.61–70.

2 Simons, *Beauvoir and The Second Sex*, p.71.

3 Toril Moi, *Simone de Beauvoir: The Making of an Intellectual Woman*, Blackwell, Oxford, 1994, p.200.

4 Kate Fullbrook and Edward Fullbrook, *Simone de Beauvoir and Jean-Paul Sartre: The Remaking of a Twentieth-Century Legend*, Harvester Wheatsheaf, New York, 1993, pp.33–35.

5 Moi, *Simone de Beauvoir*, pp.41–50.

6 Simone de Beauvoir, 'Memoirs of a Dutiful Daughter', 1987, p.158, quoted in Moi, *Simone de Beauvoir*, p.31.

7 Fullbrook and Fullbrook, *Simone de Beauvoir and Jean-Paul Sartre*, pp.62–74.

8 Ibid., pp.52–61.

9 Judith Okely, *Simone de Beauvoir*, Virago, London, 1986, p.128.

10 Simone de Beauvoir, *The Prime of Life*, Penguin, London, 1965, p.369.

11 Fullbrook and Fullbrook, *Simone de Beauvoir and Jean-Paul Sartre*, pp.128–145.

12 De Beauvoir, *The Prime of Life*, pp. 503–505.

13 Ibid., p.499

14 Ibid., p.572.

15 Ibid., p.598.

16 Fullbrook and Fullbrook, *Simone de Beauvoir and Jean-Paul Sartre*, p.156.

17 Ibid., pp.157–160.

18 Simone de Beauvoir, *Pour Une Morale de L'Ambiguité*, Gallimard, Paris 1947, pp.117, 153, 204–205, 214–220.

19 Simons, *Beauvoir and The Second Sex*, pp.177–178.

20 De Beauvoir, *Pour Une Morale de L'Ambiguité*, p.137.

21 Moi, *Simone de Beauvoir*, p.187; see also Francine Muel-Dreyfus, *Vichy et L'Éternel Feminin*, Editions du Seuil, Paris, 1996.

22 Okely, *Simone de Beauvoir*, p.159.

23 Ibid.

24 De Beauvoir, *The Prime of Life*, p.572.

25 Ibid.

26 Fullbrook and Fullbrook, *Simone de Beauvoir and Jean-Paul Sartre*, p.172.

27 Simons, *Beauvoir and The Second Sex*, pp.136–142.

28 Okely, *Simone de Beauvoir*, pp.113, 155.

29 Alice Schwarzer, *Simone de Beauvoir Today: Conversations*, 1972–1982, Chatto, London, 1984, p.113.

30 Ibid., p.32.

31 Margaret A. Simons and Jessica Benjamin, 'Beauvoir Interview (1979)', in Simons, *Beauvoir and The Second Sex*, p.19.

32 Ibid., p.18.

Translators' Note

We have spent the past three years researching *Le Deuxième sexe* and translating it into English – into *The Second Sex*. It has been a daunting task, and a splendid learning experience during which this monumental work entered our personal lives and changed the way we see the world. Questions naturally arose about the act of translating itself, about ourselves and our roles and about our responsibilities to both Simone de Beauvoir and her readers.

Translation has always been fraught with such questions, and different times have produced different conceptions of translating. Perhaps this is why, while great works of art seldom age, translations do. The job of the translator is not to simplify or readapt the text for a modern or foreign audience but to find the true voice of the original work, as it was written for its time and with its original intent. Seeking signification in another's words transports the translator into the mind of the writer. When the text is an opus like *The Second Sex*, whose impact on society was so decisive, the task of bringing into English the closest version possible of Simone de Beauvoir's voice, expression and mind is greater still.

This is not the first translation of *Le Deuxième sexe* into English, but it is the first complete one. H. M. Parshley translated it in 1953, but he abridged and edited passages and simplified some of the complex philosophical language. We have translated *Le Deuxième sexe* as it was written, unabridged and unsimplified, maintaining Beauvoir's philosophical language. The long and dense paragraphs that were changed in the 1953 translation to conform to more traditional styles of punctuation – or even eliminated – have now been translated as she wrote them, all within the confines of English. Long paragraphs (sometimes going on for pages) are a stylistic aspect of her writing that is essential, integral to the development of her arguments. Cutting her sentences, cutting her paragraphs, and using a more traditional and conventional punctuation do not render

Simone de Beauvoir's voice. Beauvoir's style expresses her reasoning. Her prose has its own consistent grammar, and that grammar follows a logic.

We did not modernise the language Beauvoir used and had access to in 1949. This decision precluded the use of the word 'gender', for example, as applied today. We also stayed close to Beauvoir's complicated syntax and punctuation as well as to certain usages of language that to us felt a bit awkward at first. One of the difficulties was her extensive use of the semi-colon, a punctuation mark that has suffered setbacks over the past decades in English and French, and has somewhat fallen into disuse.

Nor did we modernise structures such as 'if the subject attempts to assert himself, the other is nonetheless necessary for him.' Today we would say 'if the subject attempts to assert her or himself . . .' There are examples where the word 'individual' clearly refers to a woman, but Beauvoir, because of French rules of grammar, uses the masculine pronoun. We therefore do the same in English.

The reader will see some inconsistent punctuation and style, most evident in quotations and extracts. Indeed, while we were tempted to standardise it, we carried Beauvoir's style and formatting into English as much as possible. In addition, we used the same chapter headings and numbers that she did in the original two-volume gallimard edition. We also made the decision to keep close to Beauvoir's tense usage, most noticeably regarding the French use of the present tense for the historical past.

One particularly complex and compelling issue was how to translate 'la femme'. In Le deuxième sexe, the term has at least two translations: 'the woman' or 'woman' and at times, 'women', depending on the context. 'Woman' in English used alone without an article captures woman as an institution, a concept, femininity as determined and defined by society, culture, history. Thus in a French sentence such as Le problème de la femme a toujours été un problème d'hommes, we have used 'woman' without an article: 'The problem of woman has always been a problem of men.'

Beauvoir occasionally – but rarely – uses femme without an article to signify woman as determined by society as just described. In such cases, of course, we do the same. The famous sentence, On ne naît pas femme: on le devient, reads, in our translation: 'One is not born, but rather becomes, woman.' The original translation by H. M. Parshley read, 'One is not born, but rather becomes a woman.'

Another notable change we made was in the translation of la jeune fille. This is the title of an important chapter in Volume II dealing with the period in a female's life between childhood and adulthood. While it is often translated as 'the younger girl' (by Parshley and other translators of French works), we think it clearly means 'girl.'

We have included all of Beauvoir's footnotes, and we have added notes of our own when we felt an explanation was necessary. Among other things, they indicate errors in Beauvoir's text and discrepancies such as erroneous dates. We corrected misspellings of names without noting them. Beauvoir sometimes puts into quotes passages that she is partially or completely paraphrasing. We generally left them that way. The reader will notice that titles of the French books she cites are given in French, followed by their translation in English. The translation is in italics if it is in a published English-language edition; it is in roman if it is our translation. We supply the sources of the English translations of the authors Beauvoir cites at the end of the book.

We did not, however, facilitate the reading by explaining arcane references or difficult philosophical language. As an example of the former, in Part Three of Volume II, 'Justifications,' there is a reference to Cécile Sorel breaking the glass of a picture frame holding a caricature of her by an artist named Bib. The reference might have been as obscure in 1949 as it is today.

Our notes do not make for an annotated version of the translation, yet we understand the value such a guide would have for both the teacher and the individual reading it on their own. We hope one can be written now that this more precise translation exists.

These are but a few of the issues we dealt with. We had instructive discussions with generous experts about these points and listened to many (sometimes contradictory) opinions; but in the end, the final decisions as to how to treat the translation were ours.

It is generally agreed that one of the most serious absences in the first translation was Simone de Beauvoir the philosopher. Much work has been done on reclaiming, valorising, and expanding upon her role as philosopher since the 1953 publication, thanks to the scholarship of Margaret Simons, Eva Lundgren-Gothlin, Michèle Le Dœuff, Elizabeth Fallaize, Emily Grosholz, Sonia Kruks and Ingrid Galster, to mention only a few. We were keenly aware of the need to put the philosopher back into her text. To transpose her philosophical style and voice into English was the most crucial task we faced.

The first English-language translation did not always recognise the philosophical terminology in *The Second Sex*. Take the crucial word 'authentic' meaning 'to be in good faith'. As Toril Moi points out, Parshley changed it into 'real, genuine, and true'. The distinctive existentialist term *pour-soi*, usually translated as 'for-itself' (*pour-soi* referring to human consciousness), became 'her true nature in itself'. Thus, Parshley's 'being-in-itself' (*en-soi*, lacking human consciousness) is a reversal of Simone de Beauvoir's meaning. Margaret Simons and Toril Moi have unearthed and brought to light many other examples, such as the use of 'alienation', 'alterity', 'subject', the verb 'to posit', by now well documented. One particularly amusing rendition was of the title of Volume II, where '*L'Expérience Vécue*' ('Lived Experience') was translated as 'Woman's Life Today', making it sound like a ladies' magazine.

The Second Sex is a philosophical treatise and one of the most important books of the 20th century upon which much of the modern feminist movement was built. Beauvoir the philosopher is present right from the start of the book, building on the ideas of Hegel, Marx, Kant, Heidegger, Husserl and others. She developed, shared and appropriated these concepts alongside her equally brilliant contemporaries, Sartre, Merleau-Ponty and Lévi-Strauss, who were redefining philosophy to fit the times. Before it was published, Beauvoir read Lévi-Strauss's *Elementary Structures of Kinship* and learned from and used those ideas in *The Second Sex*. Although the ideas and concepts are challenging, the book was immediately accepted by a general readership. Our goal in this translation has been to conform to the same ideal in English: to say what Simone de Beauvoir said as close to the way she said it, in a both challenging and readable text.

We owe a debt of gratitude to the indomitable Anne-Solange Noble of Gallimard Editions, who for years believed in this re-translation project. Anne-Solange begged, badgered and persuaded ('I shall never surrender!') until she found the editor who was willing to take on the monumental task. That exceptional person is Ellah Allfrey of Jonathan Cape, a patient and superb editor who astutely worked with us step by step for three years, strongly supported by Katherine Murphy at Jonathan Cape and LuAnn Walther of Knopf. Anne-Solange introduced us to Sylvie Le Bon de Beauvoir, Simone de Beauvoir's adopted daughter, and our relationship has been a very special one ever since that first lunch on the rue du Bac where we four toasted the moment with, '*Vive le point-virgule*' ('Long live the semi-colon')!

Ann (Rusty) Shteir, our Douglass College friend, classmate and feminist scholar, now Professor of Humanities and Women's Studies at York University, Toronto, Canada, was always available to provide source material and to solve problematic issues, often many times a week. She, like we, felt that no task was too great to repay the debt women – and the world – owe to Simone de Beauvoir. Michael Mosher and Daniel Hoffman-Schwartz were extremely helpful with philosophical language and concepts. Gabrielle Spiegel and her generous colleagues took on the esoteric research required for the History chapter, notably the passages on the French Middle Ages of which Gaby is a leading expert. James Lawler, the distinguished professor, merits our heartfelt gratitude for re-translating, specially for this edition, the Paul Claudel extracts with such elegance and grace. Our thanks to Beverley Bie Brahic for her translations of Francis Ponge, Michel Leiris and Cécile Sauvage; Kenneth Haltman for Gaston Bachelard; Raymond MacKenzie for François Mauriac and others; Zach Rogow and Mary Ann Caws for André Breton; Gillian Spraggs for Renée Vivien. Richard Pevear and Larissa Volokhonsky allowed us the special privilege of using parts of their magnificent translation of *War and Peace* before the edition appeared in 2008; their views on translation were an inspiration to us. Donald Fanger helped us with Sophia Tolstoy's diaries.

Many writers, translators and researchers, friends, colleagues, and strangers who became friends, unfailingly contributed their expertise: Eliane Lecarme-Tabone, Mireille Perche, Claire Brisset, Mathilde Ferrer, David Tepfer, Marie-Victoire Louis, Virginia Larner, Nina de Voogd Fuller, Stephanie Baumann, Jane Couchman, Catherine Legault, Robert Lerner, Richard Sieburth, Sandra Bermann, Gérard Bonal, Lia Poorvu, Leila May-Landy, Karen Offen, Sybil Pollet, Janet Bodner, our copy-editor, Beth Humphries, and our indexer, Vicki Robinson and our two proofreaders, John Garrett and Sarah Barlow.

Our husbands, Bill Chevallier and Dominique Borde, were among our staunchest and most reliable partners, living out the difficult passages with us, helping us overcome obstacles (and exhaustion), and also sharing the joy and elation of the life-changing discoveries the text holds for us.

Very special thanks go to our expert readers. Our official reader, Mary Beth Mader, authority *par excellence* in French and the philosophical language of Simone de Beauvoir, enriched our text with her insights and corrections; Margaret Simons, showing no end to her boundless generosity, 'tested' our texts on her doctoral students and came back to us with meticulous perceptions and corrections; Marilyn Yalom, Susan Suleiman and Elizabeth Fallaize, with all of the discernment for which they are renowned, explored chapters with a fine-tooth comb and gave us a heightened understanding of *The Second Sex* for which we will ever be grateful.

And now it is for English readers to discover, learn and live Simone de Beauvoir's message of freedom and independence.

VOLUME I
FACTS AND MYTHS

Introduction

I hesitated a long time before writing a book on woman. The subject is irritating, especially for women; and it is not new. Enough ink has flowed over the quarrel about feminism; it is now almost over: let's not talk about it any more. Yet it is still being talked about. And the volumes of idiocies churned out over this past century do not seem to have clarified the problem. Besides, is there a problem? And what is it? Are there even women? True, the theory of the eternal feminine still has its followers; they whisper, 'Even in Russia, *women* are still very much women'; but other well-informed people – and also at times those same ones – lament, 'Woman is losing herself, woman is lost.' It is hard to know any longer if women still exist, if they will always exist, if there should be women at all, what place they hold in this world, what place they should hold. 'Where are the women?' asked a short-lived magazine recently.* But first, what is a woman? '*Tota mulier in utero*: she is a womb,' some say. Yet speaking of certain women, the experts proclaim, 'They are not women', even though they have a uterus like the others. Everyone agrees there are females in the human species; today, as in the past, they make up about half of humanity; and yet we are told that 'femininity is in jeopardy'; we are urged, 'Be women, stay women, become women.' So not every female human being is necessarily a woman; she must take part in this mysterious and endangered reality known as femininity. Is femininity secreted by the ovaries? Is it enshrined in a Platonic heaven? Is a frilly petticoat enough to bring it down to earth? Although some women zealously strive to embody it, the model has never been patented. It is typically described in vague and shimmering terms borrowed from a clairvoyant's vocabulary. In St Thomas's time it was an essence defined with as much certainty as the sedative quality of a poppy. But conceptualism has lost ground: biological and social sciences no longer believe

* Out of print today, entitled *Franchise*.

there are immutably determined entities that define given characteristics like those of the woman, the Jew or the black; science considers characteristics as secondary reactions to a *situation*. If there is no such thing today as femininity, it is because there never was. Does the word 'woman', then, have no content? It is what advocates of Enlightenment philosophy, rationalism or nominalism vigorously assert: women are, among human beings, merely those who are arbitrarily designated by the word 'woman'; American women in particular are inclined to think that woman as such no longer exists. If some backward individual still takes herself for a woman, her friends advise her to undergo psycho-analysis to get rid of this obsession. Referring to a book – a very irritating one at that – *Modern Woman: The Lost Sex*, Dorothy Parker wrote: 'I cannot be fair about books that treat women as women. My idea is that all of us, men as well as women, whoever we are, should be considered as human beings.' But nominalism is a doctrine that falls a bit short; and it is easy for anti-feminists to show that women *are* not men. Certainly woman like man is a human being; but such an assertion is abstract; the fact is that every concrete human being is always uniquely situated. Rejecting the notions of the eternal feminine, the black soul or the Jewish character is not to deny that there are today Jews, blacks or women: this denial is not a liberation for those concerned, but an inauthentic flight. Clearly, no woman can claim without bad faith to be situated beyond her sex. A few years ago, a well-known woman writer refused to have her portrait appear in a series of photographs devoted specifically to women writers. She wanted to be included in the men's category; but to get this privilege, she used her husband's influence. Women who assert they are men still claim masculine consideration and respect. I also remember a young Trotskyite standing on a platform during a stormy meeting, about to come to blows in spite of her obvious fragility. She was denying her feminine frailty; but it was for the love of a militant man she wanted to be equal to. The defiant position that American women occupy proves they are haunted by the sentiment of their own femininity. And the truth is that anyone can clearly see that humanity is split into two categories of individuals with manifestly different clothes, faces, bodies, smiles, movements, interests and occupations; these differences are perhaps superficial; perhaps they are destined to disappear. What is certain is that for the moment they exist in a strikingly obvious way.

If the female function is not enough to define woman, and if we also reject the explanation of the 'eternal feminine', but if we accept, even temporarily, that there are women on the earth, we then have to ask: what is a woman?

Merely stating the problem suggests an immediate answer to me. It is significant that I pose it. It would never occur to a man to write a book on the singular situation of males in humanity.* If I want to define myself, I first have to say, 'I am a woman'; all other assertions will arise from this basic truth. A man never begins by positing himself as an individual of a certain sex: that he is a man is obvious. The categories 'masculine' and 'feminine' appear as symmetrical in a formal way on town hall records or identification papers. The relation of the two sexes is not that of two electrical poles: the man represents both the positive and the neuter to such an extent that in French *hommes* designates human beings, the particular meaning of the word *vir* being assimilated into the general meaning of the word 'homo'. Woman is the negative, to such a point that any determination is imputed to her as a limitation, without reciprocity. I used to get annoyed in abstract discussions to hear men tell me: 'You think such and such a thing because you're a woman.' But I know my only defence is to answer, 'I think it because it is true,' thereby eliminating my subjectivity; it was out of the question to answer, 'And you think the contrary because you are a man,' because it is understood that being a man is not a particularity; a man is in his right by virtue of being man; it is the woman who is in the wrong. In fact, just as for the ancients there was an absolute vertical that defined the oblique, there is an absolute human type that is masculine. Woman has ovaries and a uterus; such are the particular conditions that lock her in her subjectivity; some even say she thinks with her hormones. Man vainly forgets that his anatomy also includes hormones and testicles. He grasps his body as a direct and normal link with the world that he believes he apprehends in all objectivity, whereas he considers woman's body an obstacle, a prison, burdened by everything that particularises it. 'The female is female by virtue of a certain *lack* of qualities,' Aristotle said. 'We should regard women's nature as suffering from natural defectiveness.' And St Thomas in his turn decreed that woman was an 'incomplete man', an 'incidental' being. This is what the Genesis story symbolises, where Eve appears as if drawn from Adam's 'supernumerary' bone, in Bossuet's words. Humanity is male, and man defines woman, not in herself, but in relation to himself; she is not considered an autonomous

* The Kinsey Report, for example, confines itself to defining the sexual characteristics of the American man, which is completely different.

being. 'Woman, the relative being,' writes Michelet. Thus Monsieur Benda declares in *Uriel's Report*:[1] 'A man's body has meaning by itself, disregarding the body of the woman, whereas the woman's body seems devoid of meaning without reference to the male. Man thinks himself without woman. Woman does not think herself without man.' And she is nothing other than what man decides; she is thus called 'the sex', meaning that the male sees her essentially as a sexed being; for him she is sex, so she is it in the absolute. She determines and differentiates herself in relation to man, and he does not in relation to her; she is the inessential in front of the essential. He is the Subject; he is the Absolute. She is the Other.*[2]

The category of *Other* is as original as consciousness itself. The duality between Self and Other can be found in the most primitive societies, in the most ancient mythologies; this division did not always fall into the category of the division of the sexes, it was not based on any empirical given: this comes out in works like Granet's on Chinese thought, and Dumézil's on India and Rome. In couples such as Varuna–Mitra, Uranos–Zeus, Sun–Moon, Day–Night, no feminine element is involved at the outset; neither in Good–Evil, auspicious and inauspicious, left and right, God and Lucifer; alterity is the fundamental category of human thought. No group ever defines itself as One without immediately setting up the Other opposite itself. It only takes three travellers brought together by chance in the same train compartment for the rest of the travellers to become vaguely hostile 'others'. Village people view anyone not belonging to the village as suspicious 'others'. For the native

---

* This idea has been expressed in its most explicit form by E. Levinas in his essay on *Time and the Other*. He expresses it like this: 'Is there not a situation where alterity would be borne by a being in a positive sense, as essence? What is the alterity that does not purely and simply enter into the opposition of two species of the same genus? I think that the absolutely contrary contrary, whose contrariety is in no way affected by the relationship that can be established between it and its correlative, the contrariety that permits its terms to remain absolutely other, is the feminine. Sex is not some specific difference . . . Neither is the difference between the sexes a contradiction . . . Neither is the difference between the sexes the duality of two complementary terms, for two complementary terms presuppose a preexisting whole . . . [A]lterity is accomplished in the feminine. The term is on the same level as, but in meaning opposed to, consciousness.' I suppose Mr Levinas is not forgetting that woman also is consciousness for herself. But it is striking that he deliberately adopts a man's point of view, disregarding the reciprocity of the subject and the object. When he writes that woman is mystery, he assumes that she is mystery for man. So this apparently objective description, is in fact an affirmation of masculine privilege.

of a country, inhabitants of other countries are viewed as 'foreigners'; Jews are the 'others' for anti-Semites, blacks for racist Americans, indigenous people for colonists, proletarians for the propertied classes. After studying the diverse forms of primitive society in depth, Lévi-Strauss could conclude: 'The passage from the state of Nature to the state of Culture is defined by man's ability to think biological relations as systems of oppositions; duality, alternation, opposition, and symmetry, whether occurring in defined or less clear form, are not so much phenomena to explain as fundamental and immediate givens of social reality.'[*3] These phenomena could not be understood if human reality were solely a *Mitsein*[4] based on solidarity and friendship. On the contrary, they become clear if, following Hegel, a fundamental hostility to any other consciousness is found in consciousness itself; the subject posits itself only in opposition; it asserts itself as the essential and sets up the other as inessential, as the object.

But the other consciousness has an opposing reciprocal claim: travelling, a local is shocked to realise that in neighbouring countries locals view him as a foreigner; between villages, clans, nations and classes there are wars, potlatches, agreements, treaties and struggles that remove the absolute meaning from the idea of the Other and bring out its relativity; whether one likes it or not, individuals and groups have no choice but to recognise the reciprocity of their relation. How is it, then, that between the sexes this reciprocity has not been put forward, that one of the terms has been asserted as the only essential one, denying any relativity in regard to its correlative, defining the latter as pure alterity? Why do women not contest male sovereignty? No subject posits itself spontaneously and at once as the inessential from the outset; it is not the Other who, defining itself as Other, defines the One; the Other is posited as Other by the One positing itself as One. But in order for the Other not to turn into the One, the Other has to submit to this foreign point of view. Where does this submission in woman come from?

There are other cases where, for a shorter or longer time, one category has managed to dominate another absolutely. It is often numerical inequality that confers this privilege: the majority imposes its law on or persecutes the minority. But women are not a minority like American blacks, or like Jews: there are as many women as men on the earth. Often,

---

* See Claude Lévi-Strauss, *The Elementary Structures of Kinship*. I thank Claude Lévi-Strauss for sharing the proofs of his thesis that I drew on heavily, particularly in the second part, pp. 78–92.

the two opposing groups concerned were once independent of each other; either they were not aware of each other in the past or they accepted each other's autonomy; and some historical event subordinated the weaker to the stronger: the Jewish diaspora, slavery in America, or the colonial conquests are facts with dates. In these cases, for the oppressed there was a *before*: they share a past, a tradition, sometimes a religion, or a culture. In this sense, the parallel Bebel draws between women and the proletariat would be the best founded: proletarians are not a numerical minority either and yet they have never formed a separate group. However, not *one* event but a whole historical development explains their existence as a class and accounts for the distribution of *these* individuals in this class. There have not always been proletarians: there have always been women; they are women by their physiological structure; as far back as history can be traced, they have always been subordinate to men; their dependence is not the consequence of an event or a becoming, it did not *happen*. Alterity here appears to be an absolute, partly because it falls outside the accidental nature of historical fact. A situation created over time can come undone at another time – blacks in Haiti for one are a good example; on the contrary, a natural condition seems to defy change. In truth, nature is no more an immutable given than is historical reality. If woman discovers herself as the inessential, and never turns into the essential, it is because she does not bring about this transformation herself. Proletarians say 'we'. So do blacks. Positing themselves as subjects, they thus transform the bourgeois or whites into 'others'. Women – except in certain abstract gatherings such as conferences – do not use 'we'; men say 'women' and women adopt this word to refer to themselves; but they do not posit themselves authentically as Subjects. The proletarians made the revolution in Russia, the blacks in Haiti, the Indo-Chinese are fighting in Indochina. Women's actions have never been more than symbolic agitation; they have won only what men have been willing to concede to them; they have taken nothing; they have received.* It is that they lack the concrete means to organise themselves into a unit that could posit itself in opposition. They have no past, no history, no religion of their own; and unlike the proletariat, they have no solidarity of labour or interests; they even lack their own space that makes communities of American blacks, or the Jews in ghettos, or the workers in Saint-Denis or Renault factories. They live dispersed among men, tied by homes, work, economic interests and social

* See second part, p. 128

conditions to certain men – fathers or husbands – more closely than to other women. As bourgeois women, they are in solidarity with bourgeois men and not with women proletarians; as white women, they are in solidarity with white men and not with black women. The proletariat could plan to massacre the whole ruling class; a fanatic Jew or black could dream of seizing the secret of the atomic bomb and turning all of humanity entirely Jewish or entirely black: but a woman could not even dream of exterminating males. The tie that binds her to her oppressors is unlike any other. The division of the sexes is a biological given, not a moment in human history. Their opposition took shape within an original *Mitsein* and she has not broken it. The couple is a fundamental unit with the two halves riveted to each other: cleavage of society by sex is not possible. This is the fundamental characteristic of woman: she is the Other at the heart of a whole whose two components are necessary to each other.

One might think that this reciprocity would have facilitated her liberation; when Hercules spins wool at Omphale's feet, his desire enchains him. Why was Omphale unable to acquire long-lasting power? Medea, in revenge against Jason, kills her children: this brutal legend suggests that the bond attaching the woman to her child could have given her a formidable upper hand. In *Lysistrata*, Aristophanes light-heartedly imagined a group of women who, uniting together for the social good, tried to take advantage of men's need for them: but it is only a comedy. The legend that claims that the ravished Sabine women resisted their ravishers with obstinate sterility also recounts that by whipping them with leather straps, the men magically won them over into submission. Biological need – sexual desire and desire for posterity – which makes the male dependent on the female, has not liberated women socially. Master and slave are also linked by a reciprocal economic need that does not free the slave. That is, in the master–slave relation, the master does not *posit* the need he has for the other; he holds the power to satisfy this need and does not mediate it; the slave, on the other hand, out of dependence, hope or fear, internalises his need for the master; however equally compelling the need may be to them both, it always plays in favour of the oppressor over the oppressed: this explains the slow pace of working-class liberation, for example. Now woman has always been, if not man's slave, at least his vassal; the two sexes have never divided the world up equally; and still today, even though her condition is changing, woman is heavily handicapped. In no country is her legal status identical to man's, and often it puts her at a considerable disadvantage. Even when her rights are recognised abstractly, long-standing habit keeps them from being concretely manifested in customs. Economically, men and women almost form two castes; all things being equal, the former have better jobs, higher wages and greater chances to succeed than their new female competitors; they occupy many more places in industry, in politics, and so on, and they hold the most important positions. In addition to their concrete power they are invested with a prestige whose tradition is reinforced by the child's whole education: the present incorporates the past, and in the past all history was made by males. At the moment that women are beginning to share in the making of the world, this world still belongs to men: men have no doubt about this, and women barely doubt it. Refusing to be the Other, refusing complicity with man, would mean renouncing all the advantages an alliance with the superior caste confers on them. Lord-man will materially protect liege-woman and will be in charge of justifying her existence: along with the economic risk, she eludes the metaphysical risk of a freedom that must invent its goals without help. Indeed, beside every individual's claim to assert himself as subject – an ethical claim – lies the temptation to flee freedom and to make himself into a thing: it is a pernicious path because the individual, passive, alienated and lost, is prey to a foreign will, cut off from his transcendence, robbed of all worth. But it is an easy path: the anguish and stress of authentically assumed existence are thus avoided. The man who sets the woman up as an *Other* will thus find in her a deep complicity. Hence woman makes no claim for herself as subject because she lacks the concrete means, because she senses the necessary link connecting her to man without positing its reciprocity, and because she often derives satisfaction from her role as *Other*.

But a question immediately arises: how did this whole story begin? It is understandable that the duality of the sexes, like all duality, be expressed in conflict. It is understandable that if one of the two succeeded in imposing its superiority, it had to establish itself as absolute. It remains to be explained how it was that man won at the outset. It seems possible that women might have carried off the victory, or that the battle might never be resolved. Why is it that this world has always belonged to men and that only today things are beginning to change? Is this change a good thing? Will it bring about an equal sharing of the world between men and women or not?

These questions are far from new; they have already had many answers; but the very fact that woman is *Other* challenges all the justifications that men have ever given: these were only too clearly dictated by their own interest. 'Everything that men have written about women should be viewed with suspicion, because they are both judge and party,' wrote Poulain de la Barre, a little-known seventeenth-century feminist. Males have always and everywhere paraded their satisfaction of feeling they are kings of creation. 'Blessed be the Lord our God, and the Lord of all worlds that has not made me a woman,' Jews say in their morning prayers; meanwhile their wives resignedly murmur: 'Blessed be the Lord for creating me according to His will.' Among the blessings Plato thanked the gods for was, first, being born free and not a slave, and second, a man and not a woman. But males could not have enjoyed this privilege so fully had they not considered it as founded in the absolute and in eternity: they sought to make the fact of their supremacy a right. 'Those who made and compiled the laws, being men, favoured their own sex, and the jurisconsults have turned the laws into principles,' Poulain de la Barre continues. Lawmakers, priests, philosophers, writers and scholars have gone to great lengths to prove that women's subordinate condition was willed in heaven and profitable on earth. Religions forged by men reflect this will for domination: they found ammunition in the legends of Eve and Pandora. They have put philosophy and theology in their service, as seen in the previously cited words of Aristotle and St Thomas. Since ancient times, satirists and moralists have delighted in depicting women's weaknesses. The violent indictments brought against them all through French literature are well known: Montherlant, with less verve, picks up the tradition from Jean de Meung. This hostility seems sometimes founded but is often gratuitous; in truth, it covers up a more or less skilfully camouflaged will to self-justification. 'It is much easier to accuse one sex than to excuse the other,' says Montaigne. In certain cases, the process is transparent. It is striking, for example, that the Roman code limiting a wife's rights invokes 'the imbecility and fragility of the sex' just when a weakening family structure makes her a threat to male heirs. It is striking that in the sixteenth century, to keep a married woman under wardship, the authority of St Augustine affirming 'the wife is an animal neither reliable nor stable' is called on, whereas the unmarried woman is recognised as capable of managing her own affairs. Montaigne well understood the arbitrariness and injustice of the lot assigned to women: 'Women are not wrong at all when they reject the rules of life that have been introduced into the world, inasmuch as it is the men who have made these without them.' There is a natural plotting and scheming between them and us.' But he does not go so far as to champion their cause. It is only in the eighteenth century that deeply democratic men begin to consider the issue objectively. Diderot, for one,

tries to prove that, like man, woman is a human being. A bit later, John
Stuart Mill ardently defends women. But these philosophers are exceptional in their impartiality. In the nineteenth century the feminist quarrel
once again becomes a partisan quarrel; one of the consequences of the
Industrial Revolution is that women enter the labour force: at that point,
women's demands leave the realm of the theoretical and find economic
grounds; their adversaries become all the more aggressive; even though
landed property is partially discredited, the bourgeoisie clings to the old
values where family solidity guarantees private property: it insists all the
more fiercely that woman's place should be in the home as her emancipation becomes a real threat; even within the working class, men tried
to thwart women's liberation because women were becoming dangerous
competitors – especially as women were used to working for low salaries.*
To prove women's inferiority, antifeminists began to draw not only, as
before, on religion, philosophy and theology, but also on science: biology,
experimental psychology, and so forth. At most they were willing to
grant 'separate but equal status'[5] to the *other* sex. That winning formula
is most significant: it is exactly that formula the Jim Crow laws put into
practice with regard to black Americans; this so-called egalitarian segre-
gation served only to introduce the most extreme forms of discrimination. This convergence is in no way pure chance: whether it is race, caste,
class or sex reduced to an inferior condition, the justification process is
the same. 'The eternal feminine' corresponds to 'the black soul' or 'the
Jewish character'. However, the Jewish problem on the whole is very
different from the two others: for the anti-Semite, the Jew is more an
enemy than an inferior and no place on this earth is recognised as his
own; it would be preferable to see him annihilated. But there are deep
analogies between the situations of women and blacks: both are liberated today from the same paternalism, and the former master caste wants
to keep them 'in their place', that is, the place chosen for them; in both
cases, they praise, more or less sincerely, the virtues of the 'good black',
the carefree, childlike, merry soul of the resigned black, and the woman
who is a 'true woman' – frivolous, infantile, irresponsible, the woman
subjugated to man. In both cases, the ruling caste bases its argument on
the state of affairs it created itself. The familiar line from George Bernard
Shaw sums it up: 'The white American relegates the black to the rank
of shoe-shine boy, and then concludes that blacks are only good for
shining shoes.' The same vicious circle can be found in all analogous

* See Part Two, pp. 136-137

circumstances: when an individual or a group of individuals is kept in a situation of inferiority, the fact is that he or they *are* inferior. But the scope of the verb *to be* must be understood; bad faith means giving it a substantive value, when in fact it has the sense of the Hegelian dynamic: *to be* is to have become, to have been made as one manifests oneself. Yes, women in general *are* today inferior to men; that is, their situation provides them with fewer possibilities: the question is whether this state of affairs must be perpetuated.

Many men wish it would be: not all men have yet laid down their arms. The conservative bourgeoisie continues to view women's liberation as a danger threatening their morality and their interests. Some men feel threatened by women's competition. In *Hebdo-Latin* the other day, a student declared: 'Every woman student who takes a position as a doctor or lawyer is *stealing* a place from us.' That student never questioned his rights over this world. Economic interests are not the only ones in play. One of the benefits that oppression secures for the oppressor is that the humblest among them feels *superior*: in the United States, a 'poor white' from the South can console himself for not being a 'dirty nigger'; and more prosperous whites cleverly exploit this pride. Likewise, the most mediocre of males believes himself a demigod next to women. It was easier for M. de Montherlant to think himself a hero in front of women (handpicked, by the way) than to act the man among men, a role that many women assumed better than he did. Thus, in one of his articles in *Le Figaro Littéraire* in September 1948, M. Claude Mauriac – whom everyone admires for his powerful originality – could* write about women: '*We* listen in a tone [*sic!*] of polite indifference . . . to the most brilliant one among them, knowing that her intelligence, in a more or less dazzling way, reflects ideas that come from *us*.' Clearly his female interlocutor does not reflect M. Mauriac's own ideas, since he is known not to have any; that she reflects ideas originating with men is possible: among males themselves, more than one of them takes as his own opinions he did not invent; one might wonder if it would not be in M. Claude Mauriac's interest to converse with a good reflection of Descartes, Marx or Gide rather than with himself; what is remarkable is that with the ambiguous '*we*', he identifies with St Paul, Hegel, Lenin and Nietzsche, and from their heights he looks down on the herd of women who dare to speak to him on an equal footing; frankly, I know of more than one woman who would not put up with M. Mauriac's 'tone of polite indifference'.

* At least he thought he could.

I have stressed this example because of its disarming masculine naïvety. Men profit in many other more subtle ways from woman's alterity. For all those suffering from an inferiority complex, this is a miraculous liniment; no one is more arrogant towards women, more aggressive or more disdainful, than a man anxious about his own virility. Those who are not threatened by their fellow men are far more likely to recognise woman as a counterpart; but even for them the myth of the Woman, of the Other, remains precious for many reasons;* they can hardly be blamed for not wanting to light-heartedly sacrifice all the benefits they derive from the myth: they know what they lose by relinquishing the woman of their dreams, but they do not know what the woman of tomorrow will bring them. It takes great abnegation to refuse to posit oneself as unique and absolute Subject. Besides, the vast majority of men do not explicitly make this position their own. They do not *posit* woman as inferior: they are too imbued today with the democratic ideal not to recognise all human beings as equals. Within the family, the male child and then the young man sees the woman as having the same social dignity as the adult male; afterwards, he experiences in desire and love the resistance and independence of the desired and loved woman; married, he respects in his wife the spouse and the mother, and in the concrete experience of married life she affirms herself opposite him as a freedom. He can thus convince himself that there is no longer a social hierarchy between the sexes and that on the whole, in spite of their differences, woman is an equal. As he nevertheless recognises some points of inferiority – professional incapacity being the predominant one – he attributes them to nature. When he has an attitude of benevolence and partnership towards a woman, he applies the principle of abstract equality; and he does not *posit* the concrete inequality he recognises. But as soon as he clashes with her, the situation is reversed. He will apply the concrete inequality theme and will even allow himself to disavow abstract equality.[†]

---

* The article by Michel Carrouges on this theme in *Cahiers du Sud*, no. 292, is significant. He writes with indignation: 'If only there were no feminine myth but only bands of cooks, matrons, prostitutes and blue-stockings with functions of pleasure or utility!' So, according to him, woman has no existence for herself; he only takes into account her *function* in the male world. Her finality is in man; in fact, it is possible to prefer her poetic 'function' to all others. The exact question is why she should be defined in relation to the man.

† For example, man declares that he does not find his wife in any way diminished just because she does not have a profession: work in the home is just as noble, etc. Yet, at the first argument he remonstrates, 'You wouldn't be able to earn a living without me.'

This is how many men affirm, with quasi-good faith, that women *are* equal to man and have no demands to make, and *at the same time* that women will never be equal to men and that their demands are in vain. It is difficult for men to measure the enormous extent of social discrimination that seems insignificant from the outside and whose moral and intellectual repercussions are so deep in woman that they appear to spring from an original nature.* The man most sympathetic to women never knows her concrete situation fully. So there is no good reason to believe men when they try to defend privileges whose scope they cannot even fathom. We will not let ourselves be intimidated by the number and violence of attacks against women; nor be fooled by the self-serving praise showered on the 'real woman'; nor be won over by men's enthusiasm for her destiny, a destiny they would not for the world want to share.

We must not, however, be any less mistrustful of feminists' arguments: very often their attempt to polemicise robs them of all value. If the 'question of women' is so trivial, it is because masculine arrogance turned it into a 'quarrel'; when people quarrel, they no longer reason well. What people have endlessly sought to prove is that woman is superior, inferior or equal to man: created after Adam, she is obviously a secondary being, some say; on the contrary, say others, Adam was only a rough draft, and God perfected the human being when he created Eve; her brain is smaller, but relatively bigger; Christ was made man: but perhaps out of humility. Every argument has its opposite and both are often misleading. To see clearly, one needs to get out of these ruts; these vague notions of superiority, inferiority and equality that have distorted all discussions must be discarded in order to start anew.

But how, then, will we ask the question? And in the first place, who are we to ask it? Men are judge and party: so are women. Can an angel be found? In fact, an angel would be ill qualified to speak, would not understand all the givens of the problem; as for the hermaphrodite, it is a case of its own: it is not both a man and a woman, but neither man nor woman. I think certain women are still best suited to elucidate the situation of women. It is a sophism to claim that Epimenides should be enclosed within the concept of Cretan and all Cretans within the concept of liar: it is not a mysterious essence that dictates good or bad faith to men and women; it is their situation that disposes them to seek the truth to a greater or lesser extent. Many women today, fortunate to have had all the privileges of the human being restored to them, can afford the

---

* Describing this very process will be the object of Volume II of this study.

luxury of impartiality: we even feel the necessity of it. We are no longer like our militant predecessors; we have more or less won the game; in the latest discussions on women's status, the UN has not ceased to imperiously demand equality of the sexes, and indeed many of us have never felt our femaleness to be a difficulty or an obstacle; many other problems seem more essential than those that concern us uniquely: this very detachment makes it possible to hope our attitude will be objective. Yet we know the feminine world more intimately than men do because our roots are in it; we grasp more immediately what the fact of being female means for a human being, and we care more about knowing it. I said that there are more essential problems; but this one still has a certain importance from our point of view: how will the fact of being women have affected our lives? What precise opportunities have been given us and which ones have been denied? What destiny awaits our younger sisters, and in which direction should we point them? It is striking that most feminine literature is driven today by an attempt at lucidity more than by a will to make demands; coming out of an era of muddled controversy, this book is one attempt among others to take stock of the current state.

But it is no doubt impossible to approach any human problem without partiality: even the way of asking the questions, of adopting perspectives, presupposes hierarchies of interests; all characteristics comprise values; every so-called objective description is set against an ethical background. Instead of trying to conceal those principles that are more or less explicitly implied, we would be better off stating them from the start; then it would not be necessary to specify on each page the meaning given to the words 'superior', 'inferior', 'better', 'worse', 'progress', 'regression', and so on. If we examine some of the books on women, we see that one of the most frequently held points of view is that of public good or general interest: in reality, this is taken to mean the interest of society as each one wishes to maintain or establish it. In our opinion, there is no public good other than one that assures the citizens' private good; we judge institutions from the point of view of the concrete opportunities they give to individuals. But neither do we confuse the idea of private interest with happiness: that is another frequently encountered point of view; are women in a harem not happier than a woman voter? Is a housewife not happier than a woman worker? We cannot really know what the word 'happiness' means, and still less what authentic values it covers; there is no way to measure the happiness of others, and it is always easy to call a situation that one would like to impose on others happy: in particular, we declare happy those condemned to stagnation, under the pretext that happiness is immobility. This is a notion, then, we will not refer to. The perspective we have adopted is one of existentialist morality. Every subject posits itself as a transcendence concretely, through projects; it accomplishes its freedom only by perpetual surpassing towards other freedoms; there is no other justification for present existence than its expansion towards an indefinitely open future. Every time transcendence lapses into immanence, there is degradation of existence into 'in-itself', of freedom into facticity; this fall is a moral fault if the subject consents to it; if this fall is inflicted on the subject, it takes the form of frustration and oppression; in both cases it is an absolute evil. Every individual concerned with justifying his existence experiences his existence as an indefinite need to transcend himself. But what singularly defines the situation of woman is that being, like all humans, an autonomous freedom, she discovers and chooses herself in a world where men force her to assume herself as Other: an attempt is made to freeze her as an object and doom her to immanence, since her transcendence will be forever transcended by another essential and sovereign consciousness. Woman's drama lies in this conflict between the fundamental claim of every subject, which always posits itself as essential, and the demands of a situation that constitutes her as inessential. How, in the feminine condition, can a human being accomplish herself? What paths are open to her? Which ones lead to dead ends? How can she find independence within dependence? What circumstances limit women's freedom and can she overcome them? These are the fundamental questions we would like to elucidate. This means that in focusing on the individual's possibilities, we will define these possibilities not in terms of happiness but in terms of freedom.

Clearly this problem would have no meaning if we thought that a physiological, psychological or economic destiny weighed on woman. So we will begin by discussing woman from a biological, psychoanalytical and historical materialistic point of view. We will then attempt to positively demonstrate how 'feminine reality' has been constituted, why woman has been defined as Other, and what the consequences have been from men's point of view. Then we will describe the world from the woman's point of view such as it is offered to her,* and we will see the difficulties women are up against just when, trying to escape the sphere they have been assigned until now, they seek to be part of the human *Mitsein*.

* This will be the subject of a second volume.

Part One
DESTINY

CHAPTER I

Biological Data

Woman? Very simple, say those who like simple answers: she is a womb, an ovary; she is a female: this word is enough to define her. From a man's mouth, the epithet 'female' sounds like an insult; but he, not ashamed of his animality, is proud to hear: 'He's a male!' The term 'female' is pejorative not because it roots woman in nature, but because it confines her in her sex, and if this sex, even in an innocent animal, seems despicable and an enemy to man, it is obviously because of the disquieting hostility woman triggers in him. Nevertheless, he wants to find a justification in biology for this feeling. The word 'female' evokes a saraband of images: an enormous round egg snatching and castrating the agile sperm; monstrous and stuffed, the queen termite reigning over the servile males; the praying mantis and the spider, gorged on love, crushing their partners and gobbling them up; the dog in heat running through back alleys, leaving perverse smells in her wake; the monkey showing herself off brazenly, sneaking away with flirtatious hypocrisy. And the most splendid wildcats, the tigress, lioness and panther, lie down slavishly under the male's imperial embrace, inert, impatient, shrewd, stupid, insensitive, lewd, fierce and humiliated. Man projects all females at once on to woman. And the fact is that she is a female. But if one wants to stop thinking in commonplaces, two questions arise. What does the female represent in the animal kingdom? And what unique kind of female is realised in woman?

Males and females are two types of individuals who are differentiated within one species for the purposes of reproduction; they can be defined only correlatively. But it has to be pointed out first that the very meaning of *division* of the species into two sexes is not clear.

It does not occur universally in nature. In one-celled animals, infusorians, amoebas, bacilli, and so on, multiplication is fundamentally distinct from sexuality, with cells dividing and subdividing individually. For some metazoans, reproduction occurs by schizogenesis, that is dividing the individual whose origin is also asexual, or by blastogenesis, that is dividing the individual itself produced by a sexual phenomenon: the phenomena of budding or segmentation observed in fresh-water hydras, coelenterates, sponges, worms and tunicates are well-known examples. In parthenogenesis, the virgin egg develops in embryonic form without male intervention. The male plays no role or only a secondary one: unfertilised honeybee eggs subdivide and produce drones; in the case of aphids, males are absent for a number of generations, and the unfertilised eggs produce females. Parthenogenesis in the sea urchin, the starfish and the toad have been artificially reproduced. However, sometimes in the protozoa, two cells can merge, forming what is called a zygote; fertilisation is necessary for honeybee eggs to engender females and aphid eggs, males. Some biologists have thus concluded that even in species capable of perpetuating themselves unilaterally, the renewal of genetic diversity through mixing of parental chromosomes would benefit the line's rejuvenation and vigour; in this view, then, in the more complex forms of life, sexuality is an indispensable function; only elementary organisms could multiply without sexes, and even so they would exhaust their vitality. But today this hypothesis is most inexact; observations have proved that asexual multiplication can occur indefinitely without any noticeable degeneration; this is particularly striking in bacilli; more and more – and bolder and even bolder – parthenogenetic experiments have been carried out, and in many species the male seems radically useless. Moreover, even if the value of intercellular exchange could be demonstrated, it would be a purely ungrounded fact. Biology attests to sexual differentiation, but even if biology were imbued with finalism, the differentiation of sexes could not be deduced from cellular structure, laws of cellular multiplication, or from any elementary phenomenon.

The existence of heterogenetic gametes* alone does not necessarily mean there are two distinct sexes; the differentiation of reproductive cells often does not bring about a division of the species into two types: both can belong to the same individual. This is true of hermaphroditic species, so common in plants, and also in many invertebrates, among which are the annulates and molluscs. Reproduction takes place either by self-fertilisation or by cross-fertilisation. Some biologists use this fact to claim the justification of the established order. They consider gonochorism – that is, the system in which the different gonads† belong

---

* Gametes are reproductive cells whose fusion produces an egg.
† Gonads are glands that produce gametes.

to distinct individuals – as an improvement on hermaphroditism, realised by evolution; others, by contrast, consider gonochorism primitive: for those biologists, hermaphroditism would thus be its degeneration. In any case, these notions of superiority of one system over another involve highly contestable theories concerning evolution. All that can be affirmed with certainty is that these two means of reproduction coexist in nature, that they both perpetuate species, and that the heterogeneity of both gametes and gonad-producing organisms seems to be accidental. The differentiation of individuals into males and females thus occurs as an irreducible and contingent fact.

Most philosophies have taken sexual differentiation for granted without attempting to explain it. The Platonic myth has it that in the beginning there were men, women and androgynes; each individual had a double face, four arms, four legs and two bodies joined together; one day they were split into two 'as one would split eggs in two', and ever since then each half seeks to recover its other half: the gods decided later that new human beings would be created by the coupling of two unlike halves. This story only tries to explain love: the differentiation of sexes is taken as a given from the start. Aristotle offers no better account: for if co-operation of matter and form is necessary for any action, it is not necessary that active and passive principles be distributed into two categories of heterogenic individuals. St Thomas declared that woman was an 'inessential' being, which, from a masculine point of view, is a way of positing the accidental character of sexuality. Hegel, however, would have been untrue to his rationalist passion had he not attempted to justify it logically. According to him, sexuality is the mediation by which the subject concretely achieves itself as a genus. 'The genus is therefore present in the individual as a straining against the inadequacy of its single actuality, as the urge to obtain its self-feeling in the other of its genus, to integrate itself through union with it and through this mediation to close the genus with itself and bring it into existence – *copulation*.'*[1] And a little further along, 'the process consists in this, that they become in reality what they are in themselves, namely, one genus, the same subjective vitality.' And Hegel then declares that in order for the process of union to occur, there has to be differentiation of the two sexes. But his demonstration is not convincing: the preconceived idea of locating the three moments of the syllogism in any operation is too obvious here. The surpassing of the individual towards the species, by which individual

* Hegel, *Philosophy of Nature*, Part 3, section 369.

and species accomplish themselves in their own truth, could occur without the third element, by the simple relation of genitor to child: reproduction could be asexual. Or the relation to each other could be that of two of the same kind, with differentiation occurring in the singularity of individuals of the same type, as in hermaphroditic species. Hegel's description brings out a very important significance of sexuality: but he always makes the same error of equating significance with reason. It is through sexual activity that men define the sexes and their relations, just as they create the meaning and value of all the functions they accomplish: but sexual activity is not necessarily implied in the human being's nature. In *Phenomenology of Perception*, Merleau-Ponty[2] points out that human existence calls for revision of the notions of necessity and contingency. 'Existence has no fortuitous attributes, no content which does not contribute towards giving it its form; it does not give admittance to any pure fact because it is the process by which facts are drawn up.' This is true. But it is also true that there are conditions without which the very fact of existence would seem to be impossible. Presence in the world vigorously implies the positing of a body that is both a thing of the world and a point of view on this world: but this body need not possess this or that particular structure. In *Being and Nothingness*,[3] Sartre disputes Heidegger's affirmation that human reality is doomed to death because of its finitude; he establishes that a finite and temporally limitless existence could be conceivable; nevertheless, if human life were not inhabited by death, the relationship of human beings to the world and to themselves would be so deeply upset that the statement 'man is mortal' would be anything but an empirical truth: immortal, an existent would no longer be what we call a man. One of the essential features of man's destiny is that the movement of his temporal life creates behind and ahead of him the infinity of the past and the future: the perpetuation of the species appears thus as the correlative of individual limitation, so the phenomenon of reproduction can be considered as ontologically grounded. But this is where one must stop; the perpetuation of the species does not entail sexual differentiation. That it is taken on by existents in such a way that it thereby enters into the concrete definition of existence, so be it. Nevertheless, a consciousness without a body or an immortal human being is rigorously inconceivable, whereas a society can be imagined that reproduces itself by parthenogenesis or is composed of hermaphrodites.

Opinions about the respective roles of the two sexes have varied greatly; they were initially devoid of any scientific basis and only reflected social myths. It was thought for a long time, and is still thought in some primitive societies based on matrilineal filiation, that the father has no part in the child's conception: ancestral larvae were supposed to infil-trate the womb in the form of living germs. With the advent of patri-archy, the male resolutely claimed his posterity; the mother had to be granted a role in procreation even though she merely carried and fattened the living seed: the father alone was the creator. Aristotle imagined that the foetus was produced by the meeting of the sperm and the menses: in this symbiosis, woman just provided passive material while the male principle is strength, activity, movement and life. Hippocrates' doctrine also recognised two types of seed, a weak or female one, and a strong one, which was male. Artistotelian theory was perpetuated throughout the Middle Ages and down to the modern period. In the middle of the seventeenth century, Harvey, slaughtering female deer shortly after they had mated, found vesicles in the uterine horns that he thought were eggs but which were really embryos. The Danish scientist Steno coined the term 'ovaries' for the female genital glands that had until then been called 'feminine testicles', and he noted the existence of vesicles on their surface that Graaf, in 1672, had erroneously identified as eggs and to which he gave his name. The ovary was still regarded as a homologue of the male gland. That same year, though, 'spermatic animalcules' were discovered penetrating the feminine womb. But it was thought that they went there for nourishment only, and that the individual was already prefigured in them; in 1694, the Dutchman Hartsoeker drew an image of the homunculus hidden in the sperm, and in 1699 another scientist declared he had seen the sperm cast off a kind of slough under which there was a little man, which he also drew. In these hypotheses woman merely fattened a living and active, and perfectly constituted, principle. These theories were not universally accepted and discussion continued until the nineteenth century. The invention of the microscope led to the study of the animal egg; in 1827, Baer identified the mammal's egg: an element contained inside Graaf's follicle. Soon its structure could be studied; in 1835, the sarcode – that is, the protoplasm – and then the cell were discovered; in 1877 the sperm was observed penetrating the starfish egg. From that the symmetry of the two gametes' nuclei was estab-lished; their fusion was analysed in detail for the first time in 1883 by a Belgian zoologist.

But Aristotle's ideas have not lost all validity. Hegel thought the two sexes must be different: one is active and the other passive, and it goes without saying that passivity will be the female's lot. 'Because of this differentiation, man is thus the active principle while woman is the passive principle because she resides in her non-developed unity.'* And even when the ovum was recognised as an active principle, men continued to pit its inertia against the agility of the sperm. Today, there is a tendency to see the contrary: the discoveries of parthenogenesis have led some scientists to reduce the role of the male to that of a simple physico-chemical agent. In some species the action of an acid or a mechanical stimulation has been shown to trigger the division of the egg and the development of the embryo; and from that it was boldly assumed that the male gamete was not necessary for generation; it would be at most a ferment; perhaps man's co-operation in procreation would one day become useless: that seems to be many women's desire. But nothing warrants such a bold expectation because nothing warrants universalising life's specific processes. The phenomena of asexual multiplication and parthenogenesis are neither more nor less fundamental than those of sexual reproduction. And it has already been noted that this form is not a priori favoured: but no fact proves it is reducible to a more elementary mechanism.

Rejecting any a priori doctrine, any implausible theory, we find ourselves before a fact that has neither ontological nor empirical basis and whose impact cannot a priori be understood. By examining it in its concrete reality, we can hope to extract its significance: thus perhaps the content of the word 'female' will come to light.

The idea here is not to propose a philosophy of life or to take sides too hastily in the quarrel between finalism and mechanism. Yet it is noteworthy that physiologists and biologists all use a more or less finalistic language merely because they ascribe meaning to vital phenomena. We will use their vocabulary. Without coming to any conclusion about life and consciousness, we can affirm that any living fact indicates transcendence, and that a project is in the making in every function: these descriptions do not suggest more than this.

In most species, male and female organisms cooperate for reproduction. They are basically defined by the gametes they produce. In some algae and fungi, the cells that fuse to produce the egg are identical; these cases of isogamy are significant in that they manifest the basal equivalence of the usually differentiated gametes: but their analogy remains striking. Sperm and ova result from a basically identical cellular evolution:

* Ibid.

the development of primitive female cells into oocytes differs from that of spermatocytes by protoplasmic phenomena, but the nuclear phenomena are approximately the same. The idea the biologist Ancel expressed in 1903 is still considered valid today: 'An undifferentiated prog-erminating cell becomes male or female depending on the conditions in the genital gland at the moment of its appearance, conditions determined by the transformation of some epithelial cells into nourishing elements, developers of a special material.'[4] This primary kinship is expressed in the structure of the two gametes that carry the same number of chromosomes inside each species. During fertilisation, the two nuclei merge their substance and the chromosomes in each are reduced to half their original number: this reduction takes place in both of them in a similar way; the last two divisions of the ovum result in the formation of polar globules equivalent to the last divisions of the sperm. It is thought today that, depending on the species, the male or female gamete determines the sex: for mammals, the sperm possesses a chromosome that is heterogenic to the others and potentially either male or female. According to Mendel's statistical laws, transmission of hereditary characteristics takes place equally from the father and the mother. What is important to see is that in this meeting neither gamete takes precedence over the other: they both sacrifice their individuality; the egg absorbs the totality of their substance. There are thus two strong current biases that – at least at this basic biological level – prove false: the first one is the female's passivity; the living spark is not enclosed within either of the two gametes. It springs forth from their meeting; the nucleus of the ovum is a vital principle perfectly symmetrical to the sperm's. The second bias contradicts the first, which does not exclude the fact that they often coexist: the permanence of the species is guaranteed by the female since the male principle has an explosive and fleeting existence. In reality, the embryo equally perpetuates the germ cells of the father and the mother and retransmits them together to its descendants, sometimes in a male and sometimes a female form. One might say that an androgynous germ cell survives the individual metamorphoses of the soma from generation to generation.

That being said, there are highly interesting secondary differences to be observed between the ovum and the sperm; the essential singularity of the ovum is that it is supplied with material destined to nourish and protect the embryo; it stocks up on reserves from which the foetus will build its tissues, reserves that are not a living substance but an inert material; the result is a massive, relatively voluminous, spherical or ellipsoidal form. The bird's egg's dimensions are well known. The woman's egg measures 0.13 mm while the human semen contains 60,000 sperm per cubic millimetre: their mass is extremely small. The sperm has a thread-like tail, a little elongated head; no foreign substance weighs it down. It is entirely life; this structure destines it for mobility; the ovum, on the contrary, where the future of the foetus is stored, is a fixed element: enclosed in the female organism or suspended in an exterior environment, it waits passively for fertilisation. The male gamete seeks it out; the sperm is always a naked cell, while the ovum is, according to the species, protected or not by a membrane; but in any case, the sperm bumps into the ovum when it comes into contact with it, makes it waver and infiltrates it; the male gamete loses its tail; its head swells, and, twisting, it reaches the nucleus. Meanwhile, the egg immediately forms a membrane that keeps other sperm from entering. For echinoderms where fertilisation is external, it is easy to observe the rush of the sperm that surround the floating and inert egg like a halo. This competition is also another important phenomenon found in most species; much smaller than the ovum, the sperm are generally produced in considerable quantities and each ovum has many suitors.

Thus, the ovum, active in the nucleus, its essential principle, is superficially passive; its mass, closed upon itself, compact in itself, evokes the nocturnal heaviness and repose of the in-itself: the ancients visualised the closed world in the form of a sphere or opaque atom; immobile, the ovum waits; by contrast, the open sperm, tiny and agile, embodies the impatience and worry of existence. One should not get carried away with the pleasure of allegories: the ovum has sometimes been likened to immanence and the sperm to transcendence. By giving up its transcendence and mobility, the sperm penetrates the female element: it is grabbed and castrated by the inert mass that absorbs it after cutting off its tail; like all passive actions, this one is magical and disturbing; the male gamete activity is rational, a measurable movement in terms of time and space. In truth, these are merely ramblings. Male and female gametes merge together in the egg; together they cancel each other out in their totality. It is false to claim that the egg voraciously absorbs the male gamete and just as false to say that the latter victoriously appropriates the female cell's reserves because in the act that merges them, their individuality disappears. And to a mechanistic philosophy, the movement undoubtedly looks like a rational phenomenon par excellence; but for modern physics the idea is no clearer than that of action at a distance; besides, the details of the physicochemical interactions leading to fertilisation are not known. It is possible, however, to come away with a valuable indication from this meeting. There are two movements that come together in life, and life maintains itself only by surpassing itself. It does not surpass itself without maintaining itself; these two moments are always accomplished together. It is academic to claim to separate them: nevertheless, it is either one or the other that dominates. The two unified gametes go beyond and are perpetuated; but the ovum's structure anticipates future needs; it is constituted to nourish the life that will awaken in it, while the sperm is in no way equipped to ensure the development of the germ it gives rise to. In contrast, whereas the sperm moves around, the ovum is incapable of triggering the change that will bring about a new explosion of life. Without the egg's prescience, the sperm's action would be useless; but without the latter's initiative, the egg would not accomplish its vital potential. The conclusion is thus that fundamentally the role of the two gametes is identical; together they create a living being in which both of them lose and surpass themselves. But in the secondary and superficial phenomena that condition fertilisation, it is through the male element that the change in situation occurs for the new eclosion of life; it is through the female element that this eclosion is established in a stable element.

It would be rash to deduce from such an observation that woman's place is in the home: but there are rash people. In his book *Nature and Character According to Individuals, Sex and Race*,[5] Alfred Fouillée claimed he could define woman entirely from the ovum and man from the sperm; many so-called deep theories are based on this game of dubious analogies. It is never clear what philosophy of nature this pseudo-thinking refers to. If one considers laws of heredity, men and women come equally from a sperm and an ovum. I suppose that vestiges of the old medieval philosophy – that the cosmos was the exact reflection of a microcosm – are floating around in these foggy minds: it was imagined that the ovum is a female homunculus and woman a giant ovum. These reveries dismissed since the days of alchemy make a weird contrast with the scientific precision of descriptions being used at this very moment: modern biology does not mesh with medieval symbolism; but our people do not look all that closely. If one is a bit scrupulous, one has to agree that it is a long way from ovum to woman. The ovum does not yet even contain the very notion of female. Hegel rightly notes that the sexual relationship cannot be reduced to that of two gametes. Thus, the female organism has to be studied in its totality.

It has already been pointed out that for many vegetables and some primitive animals, among them molluscs, gamete specification does not lead to individual specification, as they produce both ova and sperm. Even when the sexes separate, the barriers between them are not tight like those that separate species; just as gametes are defined from an originally undifferentiated tissue, males and females develop more as variations on a common base. For certain animals – *Bonellia viridis*[6] is the most typical case – the embryo is first asexual and its eventual sexuality is determined by the incertitudes of its development. It is accepted today that in most species sex determination depends on the genotypical constitution of the egg. The virgin egg of the honeybee reproducing itself by parthenogenesis yields males exclusively; that of fruit flies in the exact same conditions yields females exclusively. When eggs are fertilised, it is to be noted that – except for some spiders – an approximately equal number of male and female individuals is procreated; differentiation comes from the heterogeneity of one of the two types of gametes: for mammals sperm possess either a male or a female potentiality. It is not really known what determines the singular character of heterogenic gametes during spermatogenesis or oogenesis; in any case, Mendel's statistical laws are sufficient to explain their regular distribution. For both sexes, fertilisation and the beginning of embryonic development occur in an identical way; the epithelial tissue destined to evolve into a gonad is undifferentiated at the outset; at a certain stage of maturation testicles take shape or later the ovary takes form. This explains why there are many intermediaries between hermaphroditism and gonochorism; very often one of the sexes possesses certain organs characteristic of the complementary sex: the toad is the most striking case of that; the male has an atrophied ovary called Bidder's organ that can be made to produce eggs artificially. Mammals also have vestiges of this sexual bipotentiality: for example the pedicled and sessile hydra, the *uterus masculinus*, mammary glands in the male, Gartner's duct in the female, and the clitoris. Even in species where sexual division is the most clear-cut, there are individuals that are both male and female simultaneously: cases of intersexuality are numerous in animals and human beings; and in butterflies and crustaceans there are examples of gynandromorphism in which male and female characteristics are juxtaposed in a kind of mosaic. Genotypically defined, the foetus is nevertheless deeply influenced by the milieu from which it draws its nourishment: for ants, honeybees and termites, how nutrition occurs makes the larva a realised female or thwarts its sexual maturation, reducing it to the rank of worker; the influence in this case pervades the whole organism: for insects the soma is sexually defined very early on and does not depend on gonads. For vertebrates, it is essentially the gonadic hormones that play a regulatory role. Many experiments have demonstrated that varying the endocrine milieu makes it possible to act on sex determination; other grafting and castration experiments carried out on adult animals have led to the modern theory of sexuality: in male and female vertebrates, the soma is identical and can be considered a neutral element; the action of the gonad gives it its sexual characteristics; some of the secreted hormones act as stimulants and others as inhibitors; the genital tract itself is somatic, and embryology shows that it takes shape under the influence of hormones from bisexual precursors. Intersexuality exists when hormonal balance has not been realised and when neither of the two sexual potentialities has been clearly accomplished.

Equally distributed in the species, and evolved analogously from identical roots, male and female organisms seem profoundly symmetrical once they are formed. Both are characterised by the presence of gamete-producing glands, ovaries or testicles, with the analogous processes of spermatogenesis and ovogenesis, as was seen earlier; these glands deliver their secretion in a more or less complex canal according to the hierarchy of the species: the female drops the egg directly by the oviduct, holds it in the cloaca or in a differentiated uterus before expelling it; the male either lets go of the semen outside or is equipped with a copulating organ that allows it to penetrate the female. Statistically, the male and female thus look like two complementary types. They have to be envisaged from a functional point of view to grasp their singularity.

It is very difficult to give a generally valid description of the notion of female; defining her as a carrier of ova and the male as a carrier of sperm is insufficient because the relation of organism to gonads is extremely variable; inversely, the differentiation of the gametes does not directly affect the organism as a whole: it was sometimes claimed that as the ovum was bigger, it consumed more living force than the sperm; but the latter is secreted in infinitely greater quantity so that in the two sexes the expenditure balances out. Spermatogenesis was taken as an example of prodigality and ovulation a model of economy: but in this phenomenon there is also an absurd profusion; the immense majority of eggs are never fertilised. In any case, gametes and gonads are not microcosms of the whole organism. This is what has to be studied directly.

One of the most noteworthy features when surveying the steps of the animal ladder is that, from bottom to top, life becomes more individual; at the bottom it concentrates on the maintenance of the species, and at the top it puts its energies into single individuals. In lower species, the organism is reduced to barely more than the reproductive apparatus; in this case, the ovum – and therefore, the female – takes precedence over everything else, since it is above all the ovum that is dedicated to the sheer repetition of life; but it is barely more than an abdomen and its existence is entirely devoured by the work of a monstrous ovulation. It reaches gigantic dimensions compared with the male; but its members are often just stumps, its body a formless bag; all the organs have degenerated to nourish the eggs. In truth, although they constitute two distinct organisms, males and females can hardly be thought of as individuals; they form one whole with elements that are inextricably linked: these are intermediary cases between hermaphroditism and gonochorism. For the entoniscid, parasites that live off the crab, the female is a kind of whitish sausage surrounded by incubating slivers harbouring thousands of eggs; in their midst are minuscule males as well as larvae destined to provide replacement males. The enslavement of the dwarf male is even more total in the *Edriolydnus*: it is attached beneath the female's operculum and is without a digestive tube of its own; it is solely devoted to reproduction. In all these cases the female is just as enslaved as the male: she is a slave to the species; while the male is fastened to his spouse, his spouse is also fastened, either to a living organism on which she feeds as a parasite, or to a mineral substratum; she is consumed by producing eggs the minuscule male fertilises. As life takes on more complex forms, individual autonomy develops with the loosening of the link uniting the sexes; but insects of both sexes remain tightly subordinate to the eggs. In the case of ephemerals, both spouses often die after coitus and laying; and in the case of rotifers and mosquitoes, the male, lacking a digestive apparatus, sometimes perishes after fertilisation, while the female can feed herself and survive: egg formation and laying take time; the mother dies as soon as the next generation's future has been assured. The privilege of many female insects comes from the fact that fertilisation is generally a rapid process while ovulation and incubation of the eggs demand a long period of time. For termites, the enormous mush-stuffed queen that lays an egg a second until she is sterile – and then is pitilessly massacred – is no less a slave than the dwarf male attached to her abdomen that fertilises the eggs as they are expelled. In bee and ant matriarchies, males are intruders that are massacred each season: at the time of the wedding flight, all the male ants escape from the anthill and fly toward the females; if they reach and fertilise them, they die immediately, exhausted; if not, the female workers refuse them entry. They kill them in front of the entrances or let them starve to death; but the fertilised female has a sad fate: she digs herself into the earth alone and often dies from exhaustion while laying the first eggs; if she manages to reconstitute a colony, she is imprisoned for twelve years laying eggs ceaselessly; the female workers whose sexuality has been atrophied live for four years, but their whole life is devoted to raising the larvae. Likewise for the bees: the drone that catches the queen in her wedding flight crashes to the ground eviscerated; the other drones return to their colony, where they are unproductive and in the way; at the beginning of the winter, they are killed. But the sterile worker bees trade their right to life for incessant work; the queen is really the hive's slave: she lays eggs ceaselessly; and the old queen dies; some larvae are nourished so they can try to succeed her. The first one hatched kills the others in the cradle. The female giant spider carries her eggs in a bag until they reach maturity: she is bigger and stronger than the male, and she sometimes devours him after coupling; the same practices can be seen in the praying mantis, which has taken shape as the myth of devouring femininity: the egg castrates the sperm and the praying mantis assassinates her spouse; these facts prefigure a woman's dream of castration. But in truth, the praying mantis only manifests such cruelty in captivity: free and with rich enough food around, she rarely makes a meal out of the male; if she does, it is like the solitary ant that often eats some of her own eggs in order to have the strength to lay eggs and perpetuate the species. Seeing in these facts the harbinger of the 'battle of the sexes' that sets individuals as such against each other is just rambling. Neither for the ants, nor the honeybees, nor the termites, nor the spider, nor the praying mantis can one say that the female enslaves and devours the male: it is the species that devours both of them in different ways. The female lives longer and seems to have more importance; but she has no autonomy; laying, incubation, and care of the larvae make up her whole destiny; her other functions are totally or partially atrophied. By contrast, an individual existence takes shape in the male. He very often takes more initiative than the female in fertilisation; it is he who seeks her out, who attacks, palpates, seizes her and imposes coitus on her; sometimes he has to fight off other males. Accordingly, the organs of locomotion, touch and prehension are also often more developed; many female butterflies are apterous whereas their males have wings; males have more developed colours, elytrons, feet and claws; and sometimes this profusion can also be seen in a luxurious vanity of gorgeous colours. Aside from the fleeting coitus, the male's life is useless, gratuitous: next to the diligence of worker females, the laziness of drones is a privilege worth noting. But this privilege is outrageous; the male often pays with his life for this useless-ness that contains the germ of independence. A species that enslaves the female punishes the male attempting to escape: it eliminates him brutally.

In the higher forms of life, reproduction becomes the production of differentiated organisms; it has a twofold face: maintenance of the species and creation of new individuals; this innovative aspect asserts itself as the singularity of the individual is confirmed. It is thus striking that these two moments of perpetuation and creation divide; this break, already marked at the time of the egg's fertilisation, is present in the generating phenomenon as a whole. The structure of the egg itself does not order this division; the female, like the male, possesses a certain autonomy and her link with the egg loosens; the female fish, amphibian and bird are much more than an abdomen; the weaker the mother-to-egg link, the less labour parturition involves, and the more undifferentiated is the rela-tion between parents and their offspring. Sometimes, the newly hatched lives are the father's responsibility; this is often the case with fish. Water is an element that can carry eggs and sperm and enables their meeting; fertilisation in the aquatic milieu is almost always external; fish do not mate: at best some rub against each other for stimulation. The mother expels the ova and the father the sperm: they have identical roles. There is no more reason for the mother to recognise the eggs as her own than the father. In some species, parents abandon the eggs, which develop without help; sometimes the mother has prepared a nest for them; some-times she watches over them after fertilisation; but very often the father takes charge of them: as soon as he has fertilised them, he chases away the female, who tries to devour them; he fiercely defends them from anything that approaches; there are those that put up a kind of protec-tive nest by emitting air bubbles covered with an isolating substance; they also often incubate the eggs in their mouths or, like the sea horse, in the folds of the stomach. Analogous phenomena can be seen in toads: they do not have real coitus; the male embraces the female and this embrace stimulates the laying: while the eggs are coming out of the cloaca, the male lets out his sperm. Very often – and in particular in the toad known as the midwife toad – the father winds the strings of eggs around his feet and carries them around to guarantee their hatching. As for birds, the egg forms rather slowly within the female; the egg is both relatively big and hard to expel; it has much closer relations with the mother than the father that fertilised it during a quick coitus; the female is the one who usually sits on it and then looks after the young; but very frequently the father participates in the nest's construction and the protection and nutrition of the young; there are rare cases – for example the passerine – where the male sits on the eggs and then raises the young. Male and female pigeons secrete a kind of milk in their crop that they feed to the fledglings. What is noteworthy in all these cases in which fathers play a nurturing role is that spermatogenesis stops during the period they devote to their offspring; busy with maintaining life, the father has no impetus to bring forth new life-forms.

The most complex and concretely individualised life is found in mammals. The split of the two vital moments, maintaining and creating, takes place definitively in the separation of the sexes. In this branching out – and considering vertebrates only – the mother has the closest connection to her offspring, whereas the father is more uninterested; the whole organism of the female is adapted to and determined by the servitude of maternity, while the sexual initiative is the prerogative of the male. The female is the prey of the species; for one or two seasons, depending on the case, her whole life is regulated by a sexual cycle – the oestrous cycle – whose length and periodicity vary from one species to another. This cycle has two phases: during the first one the ova mature (the number varies according to the species) and a nidification process occurs in the womb; in the second phase a fat necrosis is produced, ending in the elimination of the structure, that is a whitish discharge. The oestrus corresponds to the period of heat; but heat in the female is rather passive; she is ready to receive the male, she waits for him; for mammals – and some birds – she might invite him; but she limits herself to calling him by noises, displays or exhibitions; she could never impose coitus. That decision is up to him in the end. Even for insects where the female has major privileges and consents to total sacrifice for the species, it is usually the male that provokes fertilisation; male fish often invite the female to spawn by their presence or by touching; for amphibians, the male acts as a stimulator. But for birds and above all mammals, the male imposes himself on her; very often she submits to him with indifference or even resists him. Whether she is provocative or consensual, it is he in any case who *takes* her: she is *taken*. The word often has a very precise meaning: either because he has specific organs or because he is stronger, the male grabs and immobilises her; he is the one that actively makes the coitus movements; for many insects, birds and mammals, he penetrates her. In that

regard, she is like a raped interiority. The male does not do violence
to the species, because the species can only perpetuate itself by renewal;
it would perish if ova and sperm did not meet; but the female whose
job it is to protect the egg encloses it in herself, and her body that
constitutes a shelter for the egg removes it from the male's fertilising
action; there is thus a resistance that has to be broken down, and so
by penetrating the egg the male realises himself as activity. His domination is expressed by the coital position of almost all animals; the male
is *on* the female. And the organ he uses is incontestably material too,
but it is seen in an animated state: it is a tool, while the female organ
in this operation is merely an inert receptacle. The male deposits his
sperm: the female receives it. Thus, although she plays a fundamentally active role in procreation, she endures coitus, which alienates her
from herself by penetration and internal fertilisation; although she feels
the sexual need as an individual need – since in heat she might seek
out the male – she nevertheless experiences the sexual adventure in its
immediacy as an interior story and not in relation to the world and to
others. But the fundamental difference between male and female
mammals is that in the same quick instant, the sperm, by which the
male's life transcends into another, becomes foreign to it and is separated from its body; thus the male, at the very moment it goes beyond
its individuality, encloses itself once again in it. By contrast, the ovum
began to separate itself from the female when, ripe, it released itself
from the follicle to fall into the oviduct; penetrated by a foreign gamete,
it implants itself in the uterus: first violated, the female is then alienated;
she carries the foetus in her womb for varying stages of maturation
depending on the species: the guinea pig is born almost adult; the dog
close to a foetal state; inhabited by another who is nourished by her
substance, the female is both herself and other than herself during the
whole gestation period; after delivery, she feeds the newborn with milk
from her breasts. This makes it difficult to know when it can be considered autonomous: at fertilisation, birth, or weaning? It is noteworthy
that the more the female becomes a separate individual, the more imperiously the living continuity is affirmed beyond any separation. The
fish or the bird that expels the virgin ovum or the fertilised egg is less
prey to its offspring than the female mammal. The female mammal
recovers her autonomy after the birth of the young: a distance is thus
established between her and them; and starting from this separation,
she devotes herself to them; she takes care of them, showing initiative
and invention; she fights to defend them against other animals and

even becomes aggressive. But she does not usually seek to affirm her individuality; she does not oppose either males or females; she does not have a fighting instinct;* in spite of Darwin's assertions, disparaged today, the female in general accepts the male that presents himself. It is not that she lacks individual qualities – far from it; in periods when she escapes the servitude of maternity, she can sometimes be the male's equal: the mare is as quick as the stallion, the female hound has as keen a nose as the male, female monkeys show as much intelligence as males when tested. But this individuality is not asserted: the female abdicates it for the benefit of the species that demands this abdication.

The male's destiny is very different; it has just been shown that in his very surpassing, he separates himself and is confirmed in himself. This feature is constant from insects to higher animals. Even fish and cetaceans that live in schools, loosely gathered within the group, tear themselves away when in heat; they isolate themselves and become aggressive towards other males. While sexuality is immediate for the female, it is indirect in the male: he actively bridges the distance between desire and its satisfaction; he moves, seeks, feels the female, caresses her, immobilises her before penetrating; the organs for the functions of relation, locomotion and prehension are often better developed in the male. It is noteworthy that the active impulsion that produces his sperm's multiplication is accompanied by brilliant feathers, shiny scales, horns, antlers, a crest, song, exuberance; neither the 'wedding attire' he puts on in heat nor the displays of seduction are now thought to have a selective finality; but they are witness to the power of life that flourishes in him with gratuitous and magnificent splendour. This vital generosity, the activity deployed in mating and in coitus itself, the dominating affirmation of his power over the female – all of this contributes to positing the individual as such at the moment he surpasses himself. Hegel is right to see the subjective element in the male while the female remains enclosed in the species. Subjectivity and separateness immediately mean conflict. Aggressiveness is one of the characteristics of the male in heat. It cannot be explained by competition, since there are about the same number of females as males; it is rather competition that is explained by this combative will. It is as if before procreating, the male, claiming as his very own the act that perpetuates the species, confirms the reality of his individuality in his fight against his fellow creatures. The species inhabits

---

* Some chickens fight in the barnyard for a pecking order. Cows too become head of the herd if there are no males.

the female and absorbs much of her individual life; the male, by contrast, integrates specific living forces in his individual life. He is undoubtedly also subject to laws that surpass him; he experiences spermatogenesis and periodic heats; but these processes affect the organism as a whole much less than the oestrus cycle; neither sperm production nor ovogenesis as such is tiring: the absorbing job for the female is the development of the egg into an adult animal. Coitus is a rapid operation that does not reduce the male's vitality. He manifests almost no paternal instinct. He very often abandons the female after mating. When he remains near her as head of a family group (monogamic family, harem, or herd), he plays a protective and nurturing role vis-à-vis the whole community; it is rare for him to take a direct interest in the children. In those species that are favourable to the flourishing of individual life, the male's effort at autonomy – which, in the lower animals, leads to its ruin – is crowned with success. He is usually bigger than the female, stronger, quicker, more adventurous; he leads a more independent life whose activities are more gratuitous; he is more conquering, more imperious: in animal societies, it is he who commands.

In nature nothing is ever completely clear: the two types, male and female, are not always sharply distinguished; there is often a dimorphism – the colour of the coat, the placement of the mottling – that seems absolutely contingent; it does happen though that the two types are not distinguishable, their functions barely differentiated, as was seen with fish. However, as a whole and especially at the top of the animal scale, the two sexes represent two diverse aspects of the species' life. Their opposition is not, as has been claimed, one of passivity and activity: not only is the ovum nucleus active, but the development of the embryo is also a living process and not a mechanical one. It would be too simple to define this opposition as one of change and permanence: the sperm creates only because its vitality is maintained in the egg; the ovum can only exist by surpassing itself or else it regresses and degenerates. But it is true that in both these active operations – maintenance and creation – the synthesis of becoming is not realised in the same way. Maintaining means denying the dispersion of instants, thereby affirming continuity in the course of their outpouring; creating means exploding an irreducible and separate present within a temporal unity, and it is also true that for the female it is the continuity of life that seeks to realise itself in spite of separation, while separation into new and individualised forces is brought about by male initiative; he can affirm himself in his autonomy; he integrates the specific energy into his own life; by contrast, female individuality is fought by the interest of the species; she seems possessed by outside forces: alienated. This explains why sexual opposition increases rather than abates when the individuality of organisms asserts itself. The male finds more and more ways to use the forces of which he is master; the female feels her subjugation more and more; the conflict between her own interests and those of the generating forces that inhabit her exasperate her. Giving birth for cows and mares is far more painful and dangerous than for female mice and rabbits. Woman, the most individualised of females, is also the most fragile, the one who experiences her destiny the most dramatically and who distinguishes herself the most significantly from her male.

In the human species as in most others, almost as many individuals of both sexes are born (100 girls for 104 boys); embryonic evolution is analogous; however, the original epithelium remains neuter longer in the female foetus; as a result it is subjected to hormonal influence over a longer period and its development is more often inverted; most hermaphrodites are thought to be genotypically female subjects who are masculinised later: it could be said that the male organism is immediately defined as male, whereas the female embryo is reluctant to accept its femaleness; but these tentative beginnings of foetal life are not yet well enough understood for them to be assigned a meaning. Once formed, the genital apparatus is symmetrical in both sexes; the hormones of each type belong to the same chemical family, the sterols, and when all things are considered, all of them derive from cholesterol; they order the secondary differentiation of the soma. Neither their formula nor their anatomical singularities define the human female as such. Her functional evolution is what distinguishes her from the male. Man's development is comparatively simple. From birth to puberty, he grows more or less regularly; at around fifteen or sixteen years old, spermatogenesis begins and continues until old age; hormone production occurs at the same time and marks the male constitution of the soma. When that happens, the male's sex life is normally integrated into his individual existence: in terms of desire and coitus, his surpassing towards the species is an integral part of the subjective moment of his transcendence: he *is* his body. Woman's history is much more complex. At the beginning of embryonic life, the supply of ovocytes is definitively formed; the ovary contains about fifty thousand ova and each one is enclosed in a follicle with about four hundred reaching maturity. At the moment of birth the species has taken possession of her and seeks to affirm itself; on coming into the world, the woman goes through a kind of first puberty; ovocytes suddenly

grow bigger; then the ovary reduces by about one-fifth. One could say
that the child was granted a reprieve; while its organism develops, its
genital system remains more or less stationary. Some follicles swell up
without reaching maturity; the girl's growth is analogous to the boy's:
at the same age she is often bigger and heavier than he. But at puberty
the species reasserts its rights: influenced by ovarian secretions, the
number of growing follicles increases, the ovary becomes congested and
grows, one of the ova reaches maturity and the menstrual cycle begins;
the genital system attains its definitive size and form, the soma becomes
feminised, and the endocrine balance is set up. It is worth noting that
this event has all the characteristics of a crisis; the woman's body does
not accept the species's installation in her without a fight; and this fight
weakens and endangers her; before puberty, about the same number of
girls die for every 100 boys: from fourteen to eighteen, 128 girls die for
every 100 boys, and from eighteen to twenty-two, 105 girls for every
100 boys. This is the period when chlorosis, tuberculosis, scoliosis,
osteomyelitis, and such strike. Puberty is abnormally early for some
subjects: it can occur at four or five years of age. For others, it does not
begin at all: the subject is infantile, suffering from amenorrhoea or
dysmenorrhoea. Some women manifest virile characteristics: too many
secretions from the adrenal glands give them masculine characteristics.
These anomalies are absolutely not a victory of the individual over the
tyranny of the species: there is no way to escape that tyranny because
it enslaves individual life at the same time that it nourishes it; this duality
can be seen in the ovarian functions; the woman's vitality takes root in
the ovary, that of the man in the testicles: in both cases the castrated
individual is not only sterile: it regresses and degenerates; un-'formed'
and badly formed, the whole organism is impoverished and out of
balance; it can only flourish with the flourishing of the genital system;
and yet many genital phenomena are not in the interest of the subject's
individual life and even put it in danger. The mammary glands that
develop at puberty have no role in the woman's individual economy:
they can be removed at any moment in her life. The finality of many
ovarian secretions is in the egg, in its maturity, in the adaptation of the
uterus for its needs: for the organism as a whole, they are a factor of
imbalance more than regulation; the woman is more adapted to the egg's
needs than to herself. From puberty to menopause she is the principal
site of a story that takes place in her and does not concern her personally. Anglo-Saxons call menstruation 'the curse', and it is true that there
is no individual finality in the menstrual cycle. It was thought in Aristotle's

time that the blood that flowed each month, if fertilisation occurred, was to constitute the flesh and blood of the child; the truth of this old theory is that women endlessly start up the labour of gestation. For other mammals, this oestrus cycle plays itself out during one season; there is no bloody flow: only in higher monkeys and women does this cycle take place in pain and blood.* For about fourteen days one of the Graafian follicles that envelops the eggs increases in volume and ripens at the same time that the ovary secretes the hormone folliculine at the level of the follicle. Ovulation takes place on the fourteenth day: the walls of the follicle disintegrate (sometimes causing a slight haemorrhage); the egg falls into the fallopian tubes while the opening evolves into the yellow body. Then begins the second or corpus luteum phase characterised by the secretion of the hormone progestin that acts on the uterus. The uterus changes in that the wall's capillary system swells, creases and waffles, forming a kind of lacework; this is the construction of a cradle in the womb meant to receive the fertilised egg. As these cellular transformations are irreversible, this construction is not reabsorbed in cases where there is no fertilisation: in other mammals the useless debris is possibly carried off by the lymph vessels. But for woman when the endometrial lace collapses, there is an exfoliation of the lining, the capillaries open up and a bloody mass seeps out. Then, while the corpus luteum is reconstituted, a new follicular phase begins. This complex process, whose details are still quite mysterious, sets the whole body in motion as it is accompanied by hormonal secretions that act on the thyroid and pituitary glands, the central and peripheral nervous systems and thus on all the organs. Almost all women – more than 85 per cent – show signs of distress during this period. Blood pressure rises before the beginning of the flow of blood and then falls; the pulse rate and often the temperature increase; there are frequent cases of fever; the abdomen is painful; there is often constipation and then diarrhoea, an increase in the liver volume, urea retention, albumin deficiency, or micro albumin; many women have hyperaemia of the pituitary gland (sore throat), and others complain of auditory and visual problems; there is a rise in perspiration secretions accompanied by a sometimes strong sui generis odour at the beginning of and often throughout the menstrual

* The analysis of these phenomena has been advanced in the last few years by comparing the phenomena occurring in women with those in the higher monkeys, especially for the Rhesus factor. 'It is obviously easier to experiment on the latter animals,' writes Louis Gallien (*La sexualité* [*Sexual Reproduction*]).

period. Basal metabolism increases. The number of red blood cells decreases; however, the blood carries substances usually kept in reserve in the tissues, in particular calcium salts; these salts act on the ovary, on the thyroid that is overactive, and on the pituitary gland that regulates the metamorphosis of the activated uterine tissue; this glandular instability weakens the nervous system: the central nervous system is affected, often causing headaches, and the peripheral nervous system overreacts: the automatic control by the central nervous system is reduced, which relaxes the reflexes and the convulsive complexes and is manifested in great mood changes: woman is more emotional, nervous and irritable than usual and can manifest serious psychological problems. This is when she feels most acutely that her body is an alienated opaque thing; it is the prey of a stubborn and foreign life that makes and unmakes a crib in her every month; every month a child is prepared to be born and is aborted in the flow of the crimson tide; woman *is* her body as man *is* his,* but her body is something other than her.

Woman experiences an even stronger alienation when the fertilised egg drops into the uterus and develops there; gestation is, of course, a normal phenomenon that is not harmful to the mother if normal conditions of health and nutrition prevail: certain beneficial interactions develop between her and the foetus; however, contrary to an optimistic theory that is so obviously useful socially, gestation is tiring work that offers woman no benefit as an individual but that demands serious sacrifices.† In the early months, it often brings with it appetite loss and vomiting that is not observed in any other domestic female and shows the body's revolt against the species taking possession of it; the body loses phosphorus, calcium and iron, the last of these losses being very hard to overcome later; the metabolic hyperactivity excites the endocrine system; the negative nervous system is in a heightened state of excitability; the specific weight of the blood decreases and it is anaemic, like 'that of people who fast, who are starving, or who have been bled many times, and convalescents'.‡ All that a healthy and well-nourished woman can hope for after child-

* 'I am thus my body, at least inasmuch as I have experience, and reciprocally, my body is like a natural subject, like a tentative draft of my total being' (Merleau-Ponty, *Phenomenology of Perception*).
† I am taking here an exclusively physiological point of view. It is evident that maternity can be very advantageous psychologically for a woman, just as it can also be a disaster.
‡ Cf. H. Vignes in *Traité de physiologie normale et pathologique* (*Treatise on Normal and Pathological Physiology*) volume ii, edited by Roger and Binet.

birth is to recoup her losses without too much trouble; but often serious accidents or at least dangerous disorders occur during pregnancy; and if the woman is not sturdy, if she is not careful in her personal hygiene, she will be prematurely misshapen and aged by her pregnancies: it is well known how frequent this is in the countryside. Childbirth itself is painful; it is dangerous. This crisis shows clearly that the body does not always meet the needs of both the species and the individual; the child sometimes dies, or while coming into life, it kills the mother; or its birth can cause her a chronic illness. Breastfeeding is also an exhausting servitude; a set of factors – the main one undoubtedly being the appearance of a hormone, progestin – brings milk secretion into the mammary glands; the arrival of the milk is painful and is often accompanied by fever, and the breastfeeder feeds the newborn to the detriment of her own strength. The conflict between the species and the individual can have dramatic consequences in childbirth, making the woman's body distressingly fragile. One often hears that women 'have bellyaches'; true indeed, a hostile element is locked inside them: the species is eating away at them. Many of their illnesses are the result not of an external infection but of an internal disorder: false metritis occurs from a reaction of the uterine lining to an abnormal ovarian excitation; if the yellow body persists instead of being reabsorbed after menstruation, it provokes salpingitis and endometritis, and so on.

Woman escapes from the grip of the species by one more difficult crisis; between forty-five and fifty, the phenomena of menopause, the opposite of those of puberty, occur. Ovarian activity decreases and even disappears: this disappearance brings about a vital impoverishment of the individual. It is thought that the catabolic glands, thyroid and pituitary, attempt to compensate for the ovary's deficiencies; thus alongside the change-of-life depression there are phenomena of surges: hot flushes, high blood pressure, nervousness; there is sometimes an increase in the sex drive. Some women retain fat in their tissues; others acquire male traits. For many there is a new endocrine balance. So woman finds herself freed from the servitudes of the female; she is not comparable to a eunuch, because her vitality is intact; however, she is no longer prey to powers that submerge her: she is consistent with herself. It is sometimes said that older women form 'a third sex'; it is true they are not males, but they are no longer female either; and often this physiological autonomy is matched by a health, balance and vigour they did not previously have.

Overlapping women's specifically sexual differentiations are the singularities, more or less the consequences of these differentiations; these are the hormonal actions that determine her soma. On average, she is smaller than man, lighter; her skeleton is thinner; the pelvis is wider, adapted to gestation and birth; her connective tissue retains fats, and her forms are rounder than man's; the overall look: morphology, skin, hair system, and so on is clearly different in the two sexes. Woman has much less muscular force: about two-thirds that of man; she has less respiratory capacity: lungs, trachea and larynx are smaller in woman; the difference in the larynx brings about that of the voice. Women's specific blood weight is less than men's: there is less haemoglobin retention; women are less robust, more apt to be anaemic. Their pulse rate is quicker, their vascular system is less stable: they blush easily. Instability is a striking characteristic of their bodies in general; for example, man's calcium metabolism is stable; women both retain less calcium salt and eliminate it during menstruation and pregnancy; the ovaries seem to have a catabolic action concerning calcium; this instability leads to disorders in the ovaries and in the thyroid, which is more developed in a woman than in a man: and the irregularity of endocrine secretions acts on the peripheral nervous system; muscles and nerves are not perfectly controlled. More instability and less control make them more emotional, which is directly linked to vascular variations: palpitations, redness, and so on; and they are thus subject to convulsive attacks: tears, nervous laughter and hysterics.

Many of these characteristics are due to woman's subordination to the species. This is the most striking conclusion of this study: she is the most deeply alienated of all the female mammals, and she is the one that refuses this alienation the most violently; in no other is the subordination of the organism to the reproductive function more imperious nor accepted with greater difficulty. Crises of puberty and of the menopause, monthly 'curse', long and often troubled pregnancy, illnesses and accidents are characteristic of the human female: her destiny appears even more fraught the more she rebels against it by affirming herself as an individual. The male, by comparison, is infinitely more privileged: his genital life does not thwart his personal existence; it unfolds seamlessly, without crises and generally without accident. Women live, on average, as long as men, but are often sick and indisposed.

These biological data are of extreme importance: they play an all-important role and are an essential element of woman's situation: we will be referring to them in all further accounts. Because the body is the instrument of our hold on the world, the world appears different to us depending on how it is grasped, which explains why we have studied these data so deeply; they are one of the keys to enable us to understand woman. But we refuse the idea that they form a fixed destiny for her. They do not suffice to constitute the basis for a sexual hierarchy; they do not explain why woman is the Other; they do not condemn her for ever after to this subjugated role.

It has often been claimed that physiology alone provides answers to these questions: does individual success have the same chances in the two sexes? Which of the two in the species plays the greater role? But the first question does not apply to woman and other females in the same way, because animals constitute given species and it is possible to provide static descriptions of them: it is simply a question of collating observations to decide if the mare is as quick as the stallion, if male chimpanzees do as well on intelligence tests as their female counterparts; but humanity is constantly in the making. Materialist scholars have claimed to posit the problem in a purely static way; full of the theory of psychophysiological parallelism, they sought to make mathematical comparisons between male and female organisms: and they imagined that these measurements directly defined their functional abilities. I will mention one example of these senseless discussions that this method prompted. As it was supposed, in some mysterious way, that the brain secreted thinking, it seemed very important to decide if the average weight of the female brain was larger or smaller than that of the male. It was found that the former weighs, on average, 1,220 grams, and the latter 1,360, the weight of the female brain varying from 1,000 to 1,500 grams and that of the male from 1,150 to 1,700. But the absolute weight is not significant; it was thus decided that the relative weight should be taken into account. It is $\frac{1}{48.4}$ for the man and $\frac{1}{44.2}$ for the woman. She is thus supposed to be advantaged. No. This still has to be corrected: in such comparisons, the smallest organism always seems to be favoured; to compare two individuals correctly while not taking into account the body, one must divide the weight of the brain by the power of 0.56 of the body weight if they belong to the same species. It is considered that men and women are of two different types, with the following results:

For man: $W_{0.56} = 498$ $\dfrac{1,360}{498} = 2.73$

For woman: $W_{0.56} = 446$ $\dfrac{1,220}{446} = 2.74$

Equality is the result. But what removes much of the interest of these careful debates is that no relation has been established between brain weight and the development of intelligence. Nor could one give a psychic interpretation of chemical formulas defining male and female hormones. We categorically reject the idea of a psychophysiological parallelism; the bases of this doctrine have definitively and long been weakened. I mention it because although it is philosophically and scientifically ruined, it still haunts a large number of minds: it has already been shown here that some people are carrying around antique vestiges of it. We also repudiate any frame of reference that presupposes the existence of a *natural* hierarchy of values – for example, that of an evolutionary hierarchy; it is pointless to wonder if the female body is more infantile than the male, if it is closer to or further from that of the higher primates, and so forth. All these studies that confuse a vague naturalism with an even vaguer ethic or aesthetic are pure verbiage. Only within a human perspective can the female and the male be compared in the human species. But the definition of man is that he is a being who is not given, who makes himself what he is. As Merleau-Ponty rightly said, man is not a natural species: he is an historical idea. Woman is not a fixed reality but a becoming; she has to be compared with man in her becoming, that is, her *possibilities* have to be defined: what skews the issues so much is that she is being reduced to what she was, to what she is today, while the question concerns her capacities; the fact is that her capacities manifest themselves clearly only when they have been realised: but the fact is also that when one considers a being who is transcendence and surpassing, it is never possible to close the books.

However, one might say, in the position I adopt – that of Heidegger, Sartre and Merleau-Ponty – that if the body is not a *thing*, it is a situation: it is our grasp on the world and the outline for our projects. Woman is weaker than man; she has less muscular strength, fewer red blood cells, a lesser respiratory capacity; she runs less quickly, lifts less heavy weights – there is practically no sport in which she can compete with him; she cannot enter into a fight with the male. Added to that are the instability, lack of control and fragility that have been discussed: these are facts. Her grasp of the world is thus more limited; she has less firmness and perseverance in projects that she is also less able to carry out. This means that her individual life is not as rich as man's.

In truth these facts cannot be denied: but they do not carry their meaning in themselves. As soon as we accept a human perspective, defining the body starting from existence, biology becomes an abstract science; when the physiological given (muscular inferiority) takes on meaning, this meaning immediately becomes dependent on a whole context; 'weakness' is weakness only in light of the aims man sets for himself, the instruments at his disposal and the laws he imposes. If he did not want to apprehend the world, the very idea of a *grasp* on things would have no meaning; when, in this apprehension, the full use of body force – above the usable minimum – is not required, the differences cancel each other out; where customs forbid violence, muscular energy cannot be the basis for domination: existential, economic and moral reference points are necessary to define the notion of *weakness* concretely. It has been said that the human species was an antiphysis; the expression is not really exact because man cannot possibly contradict the given; but it is in how he takes it on that he constitutes its truth; nature only has reality for him insofar as it is taken on by his action: his own nature is no exception. It is not possible to measure in the abstract the burden of the generative function for woman, just as it is not possible to measure her grasp on the world: the relation of maternity to individual life is naturally regulated in animals by the cycle of heat and seasons; it is undefined for woman; only society can decide; woman's enslavement to the species is tighter or looser depending on how many births the society demands and the hygienic conditions in which pregnancy and birth occur. So if it can be said that among the higher animals individual existence is affirmed more imperiously in the male than in the female, in humanity individual 'possibilities' depend on the economic and social situation.

In any case, it is not always true that the male's individual privileges confer upon him superiority in the species; the female regains another kind of autonomy in maternity. Sometimes he imposes his domination: this is the case in the monkeys studied by Zuckermann; but often the two halves of the couple lead separate lives; the lion and the lioness share the care of the habitat equally. Here again, the case of the human species cannot be reduced to any other; men do not define themselves first as individuals; men and women have never challenged each other in individual fights; the couple is an original *Mitsein*; and it is always a fixed or transitory element of a wider collectivity; within these societies, who, the male or the female, is the more necessary for the species? In terms of gametes, in terms of the biological functions of coitus and gestation, the male principle creates to maintain and the female principle maintains to create: what becomes of this division in social life? For species attached to foreign bodies or to the substrata, for those to whom nature grants food abundantly and effortlessly, the role of the male is limited to fertilisation; when it is necessary to search, chase or fight to provide food needed for offspring, the male often helps with their maintenance; this help becomes absolutely indispensable in a species where children remain incapable of taking care of their own needs for a long period after the mother stops nursing them: the male's work then takes on an extreme importance; the lives he brought forth could not maintain themselves without him. One male is enough to fertilise many females each year: but males are necessary for the survival of children after birth, to defend them against enemies, to extract from nature everything they need. The balance of productive and reproductive forces is different depending on the different economic moments of human history and they condition the relation of the male and the female to children and later among them. But we are going beyond the field of biology: in purely biological terms, it would not be possible to posit the primacy of one sex concerning the role it plays in perpetuating the species.

But a society is not a species: the species realises itself as existence in a society; it transcends itself towards the world and the future; its customs cannot be deduced from biology; individuals are never left to their nature; they obey this second nature, that is, customs in which the desires and fears that express their ontological attitude are reflected. It is not as a body but as a body subjected to taboos and laws that the subject gains consciousness of and accomplishes himself. He valorises himself in the name of certain values. And once again, physiology cannot ground values: rather, biological data take on those values the existent confers on them. If the respect or fear woman inspires prohibits man from using violence against her, the male's muscular superiority is not a source of power. If customs desire – as in some Indian tribes – that girls choose husbands, or if it is the father who decides on marriages, the male's sexual aggressiveness does not grant him any initiative, any privilege. The mother's intimate link to the child will be a source of dignity or indignity for her, depending on the very variable value given to the child; this very link, as has already been said, will be recognised or not according to social biases.

Thus we will clarify the biological data by examining them in the light of ontological, economic, social and psychological contexts. Woman's enslavement to the species and the limits of her individual abilities are facts of extreme importance; the woman's body is one of the essential elements of the situation she occupies in this world. But her body is not enough to define her; it has a lived reality only as taken on by consciousness through actions and within a society; biology alone cannot provide an answer to the question that concerns us: why is woman the *Other*? The question is how, in her, nature has been taken on in the course of history; the question is what humanity has made of the human female.

CHAPTER 2

The Psychoanalytical Point of View

The enormous advance psychoanalysis made over psychophysiology is in its consideration that no factor intervenes in psychic life without having taken on human meaning; it is not the body-object described by scientists that exists concretely but the body lived by the subject. The female is a woman, insofar as she feels herself as such. Some essential biological givens are not part of her lived situation: for example, the structure of the ovum is not reflected in it; by contrast, an organ of slight biological importance like the clitoris plays a primary role in it. Nature does not define woman: it is she who defines herself by reclaiming nature for herself in her affectivity.

An entire system has been erected based on this outlook: we do not intend here to criticise it as a whole, but only to examine its contribution to the study of woman. Discussing psychoanalysis as such is not an easy undertaking. Like all religions – Christianity or Marxism – it displays an unsettling flexibility against a background of rigid concepts. Sometimes words are taken in their narrowest meanings, the term 'phallus', for example, designating very precisely the fleshy growth that is the male sex organ; at other times, infinitely broadened, they take on a symbolic value: the phallus would express all of the virile character and situation as a whole. If one criticises the doctrine to the letter, the psychoanalyst maintains that its spirit has been misunderstood; if one approves of the spirit, he immediately wants to limit you to the letter. The doctrine is unimportant, he says: psychoanalysis is a method; but the success of the method strengthens the doctrinaire in his faith. After all, where would the true features of psychoanalysis be found if not with psychoanalysts themselves? But among them, as among Christians and Marxists, there are heretics: more than one psychoanalyst has declared that 'the worst enemies of psychoanalysis are psychoanalysts themselves'. Many ambiguities remain to be dissolved, in spite of an often-pedantic scholastic precision. As Sartre and Merleau-Ponty have observed, the proposition 'sexuality is coextensive with existence' can be understood in two very different ways; it could mean that every avatar of the existent has a sexual signification, or that every sexual phenomenon has an existential meaning: these two affirmations can be reconciled; but often one tends to slip from one to the other. Besides, as soon as 'sexual' and 'genital' are distinguished, the notion of sexuality becomes blurred. 'The sexual for Freud is the intrinsic aptitude to trigger the genital,' says Dalbiez.[7] But nothing is murkier than the notion of 'aptitude', or of possibility: only reality can indubitably prove possibility. Not being a philosopher, Freud refused to justify his system philosophically; his disciples maintain that he thus eludes any attacks of a metaphysical sort. There are, however, metaphysical postulates behind all of his affirmations: to use his language is to adopt a philosophy. It is this very confusion that, while making criticism awkward, demands it.

Freud was not very concerned with woman's destiny; it is clear that he modelled his description of it on that of masculine destiny, merely modifying some of the traits. Before him, the sexologist Marañón had declared: 'As differentiated energy, the libido is, one might say, a force of virile significance. We can say as much for the orgasm.' According to him, women who attain orgasm are 'viriloid' women; sexual fulfilment is a 'one-way street' and woman is only at the halfway point.* Freud does not go that far; he accepts that woman's sexuality is as developed as man's; but he barely studies it in itself. He writes: 'The libido is constantly and regularly male in essence, whether in man or in woman.' He refuses to posit the feminine libido in its originality: he will thus necessarily see it as a complex deviation from the human libido in general. And this, he thinks, develops first identically in both sexes: all children go through an oral phase that fixes them upon their mother's breast, then an anal phase and finally they reach the genital phase; it is then that they become differentiated. Freud brought out a fact whose importance had not previously been recognised: male eroticism is definitively centred on the penis, while the woman has two distinct erotic systems, one that is clitoral and develops in infancy and another that is vaginal and develops only after puberty; when the boy gets to the genital phase, he completes his development; he has to move from the autoerotic attitude, where subjective pleasure is sought, to an hetero-erotic attitude that will link pleasure to

* Curiously, this theory is found in D. H. Lawrence. In *The Plumed Serpent*, Don Cipriano sees to it that his mistress never reaches orgasm: she must vibrate along with the man, and not find individualised pleasure.

an object, usually a woman; this passage will occur at puberty through a narcissistic phase: but the penis will remain, as in infancy, the favoured erotic organ. Woman, also passing through a narcissistic phase, must make man the object of her libido; but the process will be far more complex as she must pass from clitoral to vaginal pleasure. There is but one genital step for man, while there are two for woman; she runs a greater risk of not completing her sexual development, and of remaining at the infantile stage, and consequently of developing neuroses.

At the autoerotic stage, the child is already more or less strongly attached to an object: a boy is fixated on his mother and wants to identify with his father; he is afraid of this ambition and fears that his father will punish him for it by mutilating him; the castration complex emanates from the Oedipus complex; so he develops aggressive feelings towards his father, while at the same time interiorising his father's authority: thus develops the superego that censures incestuous tendencies; these tendencies are repressed, the complex is liquidated, and the son is freed from the father, whom he in fact has installed in himself in the form of moral precepts. The more defined and strongly fought the Oedipus complex is, the stronger the superego. Freud first described the history of the girl in a completely symmetrical way; later he named the feminine form of the infant complex the Electra complex; but clearly he defined it less in itself than based on a masculine model; yet he accepts a very important difference between the two: the little girl first has a maternal fixation, while the boy is at no time sexually attracted by the father; this fixation is a carryover from the oral phase; the infant then identifies with the father; but around the age of five, she discovers the anatomical difference between the sexes and she reacts to the absence of a penis by a castration complex: she imagines having been mutilated, and suffers from it; she must therefore renounce her virile pretensions; she identifies with her mother and tries to seduce her father. The castration complex and the Electra complex reinforce each other; the feeling of frustration for girls is all the more painful as, loving her father, the girl would like to resemble him; and inversely regret strengthens her love: through the tenderness she inspires in her father, she can compensate for her inferiority. The girl experiences feelings of rivalry and hostility towards her mother. Then her superego is constituted as well, repressing her incestuous tendencies; but her superego is more fragile: the Electra complex is less clear than the Oedipus complex, because her first fixation was maternal; and since the father was himself the object of this love that he condemned, his prohibitions had less force than in the case of the rival son. It can be seen that, as with her genital development, the little girl's overall sexual drama is more complex than her brother's: she might be tempted to react to the castration complex by rejecting her femininity, obstinately coveting a penis and identifying with her father; this attitude will lead her to remain at the clitoral stage, to become frigid or to turn to homosexuality.

The two essential objections to this description stem from the fact that Freud copied it from a masculine model. He assumes that a woman feels like a mutilated man; but the notion of mutilation implies comparison and valorisation; many psychoanalysts accept today that girls miss having a penis without assuming they were ever stripped of one; this regret is not even generalised among all girls; and it could not arise from a simple anatomical encounter; many little girls discover the masculine constitution very late; and if they do discover it, it is only by seeing it; the boy has a living experience from his penis that allows him to take pride in it, but this pride has no immediate correlation with the humiliation of his sisters since they only know the masculine organ in its exteriority; this growth, this delicate stalk of skin can only inspire their indifference and even disgust; the girl's envy, when it appears, is the result of a prior valorisation of virility: Freud takes this for granted when instead he should account for it.* Besides, because there is no original description of the feminine libido, the notion of the Electra complex is very vague. Even the presence of a specifically genital Oedipus complex in boys is by no means general; but, apart from very rare exceptions, it cannot be stated that the father is a source of genital excitation for his daughter; one of the great problems of female eroticism is that clitoral pleasure is localised: it is only in puberty, in connection with vaginal eroticism, that many erogenous zones develop in the woman's body; to say that in a child of ten a father's kisses and caresses have an 'intrinsic aptitude' to arouse clitoral pleasure is an assertion that in most cases makes no sense. If it is accepted that the 'Electra complex' has only a very diffuse and affective nature, then the whole question of affectivity is raised, a question that Freudianism does not provide the means to define, once it is distinguished from sexuality. In any case, it is not the feminine libido that deifies the father: the mother is not deified by the desire she arouses in her son; the fact that feminine desire is focused on a sovereign being gives it a unique character; but the girl is not constitutive of her object, she submits to it. The father's sovereignty is a fact

* This discussion will be taken up again in more detail in Vol. II, Chapter 1.

of social order: and Freud fails to account for this; he himself admits that it is impossible to know what authority decided at what moment in history that the father would prevail over the mother: according to him, this decision represents progress, but its causes are unknown. '[In this case] it cannot be the father himself, since it is only this progress that raises him to the rank of an authority,' he writes in his last work.[*8]

Adler departed from Freud because he understood the inadequacies of a system that bases the development of human life on sexuality alone: he means to reintegrate sexuality into the total personality; while for Freud all behaviour is driven by desire, that is, by seeking pleasure, Adler sees man as aiming at certain goals; he replaces drives with motives, finality and plans; he raises intelligence to such heights that for him sexuality often has only symbolic value. According to his theories, the human drama is divided into three steps: each individual has a will to power but along with it an inferiority complex; this conflict leads him to use countless ruses rather than confront real-life obstacles that he fears may be insurmountable; the subject establishes a distance between himself and the society he fears: thus develop neuroses that are disturbances of the social sense. As for woman, her inferiority complex manifests itself in a rejection out of shame of her femininity: it is not the absence of a penis that unleashes this complex but the total situation; the girl envies the phallus only as a symbol of the privileges granted to boys; the father's place in the family, the universal predominance of males, and upbringing all confirm her idea of masculine superiority. Later on, in the course of sexual relations, even the coital posture that places the woman underneath the man is an added humiliation. She reacts by a 'masculine protest'; she either tries to masculinise herself, or uses her feminine wiles to go into battle against man. Through motherhood she can find in her child the equivalent of the penis. But this supposes that she must first accept herself completely as woman, and thus accept her inferiority. She is far more deeply divided against herself than is man.

It is unnecessary to underline here the theoretical differences between Adler and Freud or the possibilities of reconciliation: neither the explanation based on drive nor the one based on motive is ever sufficient: all drives posit a motive, but motive is never grasped except through drives; a synthesis of Adlerism and Freudianism thus seems possible. In fact, while bringing in notions of aim and finality, Adler retains in full the idea of psychic causality; his relation to Freud resembles somewhat the

* Cf. *Moses and Monotheism.*

relation of energeticism to mechanism: whether it is a question of impact or force of attraction, the physicist always recognises determinism. This is the postulate common to all psychoanalysts: for them, human history is explained by an interplay of determined elements. They all allot the same destiny to woman. Her drama is summed up in a conflict between her 'viriloid' and her 'feminine' tendencies; the former are expressed in the clitoral system, the latter in vaginal eroticism; as a very young girl, she identifies with her father; she then experiences feelings of inferiority relative to man and is faced with the alternative of either maintaining her autonomy, becoming virilised – which, with an underlying inferiority complex, provokes a tension that risks bringing on neuroses – or else finding happy self-fulfilment in amorous submission, a solution facilitated by the love she felt for her sovereign father; it is he whom she is looking for in her lover or husband, and her sexual love is mingled with her desire to be dominated. Maternity will be her reward, restoring to her a new kind of autonomy. This drama seems to be endowed with its own dynamism; it continues to work itself out through all the mishaps that distort it, and every woman passively endures it.

Psychoanalysts have no trouble finding empirical confirmations of their theories: it is known that if Ptolemy's system is subtly complicated, his version of the position of the planets could be upheld for a long time; if an inverse Oedipus complex is superimposed on to the Oedipus complex and by showing a desire in every anxiety, the very facts that contradicted Freudianism will be successfully integrated into it. For a figure to be perceived, it must stand out from its background, and how the figure is perceived brings out the ground behind it in positive delineation; thus if one is determined to describe a particular case from a Freudian perspective, one will find the Freudian schema as the background behind it; but when a doctrine demands the multiplication of secondary explanations in an indefinite and arbitrary way, when observation uncovers as many anomalies as normal cases, it is better to give up the old frameworks. Today as well, every psychoanalyst works at adapting Freudian concepts to suit himself; he attempts compromises; for example, a contemporary psychoanalyst writes: 'Whenever there is a complex, there are by definition several components . . . The complex consists in grouping these disparate elements and not in representing one of them by the others.'*⁹ But the idea of a simple grouping of elements is unacceptable: psychic life is not a mosaic; it is altogether

* Baudouin, *The Child's Soul and Psychoanalysis*.

complete in every one of its moments and this unity must be respected. This is possible only by recovering the original intentionality of existence through the disparate facts. Without going back to this source, man appears a battlefield of drives and prohibitions equally devoid of meaning and contingent. All psychoanalysts systematically refuse the idea of choice and its corollary, the notion of value; and herein lies the intrinsic weakness of the system. Cutting out drives and prohibitions from existential choice, Freud fails to explain their origin: he takes them as givens. He tried to replace the notion of value with that of authority; but he admits in *Moses and Monotheism* that he has no way to account for this authority. Incest, for example, is forbidden because the father forbade it: but why did he forbid it? It is a mystery. The superego interiorises orders and prohibitions emanating from an arbitrary tyranny; instinctive tendencies exist, but we do not know why; these two realities are heterogeneous because morality is posited as foreign to sexuality; human unity appears as shattered, there is no passage from the individual to the society: Freud is forced to invent strange fictions to reunite them.* Adler saw clearly that the castration complex could be explained only in a social context; he approached the problem of valorisation, but he did not go back to the ontological source of values recognised by society, and he did not understand that values were involved in sexuality itself, which led him to misunderstand their importance.

Sexuality certainly plays a considerable role in human life: it could be said to penetrate it completely; physiology has already demonstrated how the activity of testes and ovaries is intermixed with that of the soma. The existent is a sexed body; in its relations with other existents that are also sexed bodies, sexuality is thus always involved; but as the body and sexuality are concrete expressions of existence, it is also from here that their significance can be ascertained: without this perspective, psychoanalysis takes unexplained facts for granted. For example, a young girl is said to be 'ashamed' of urinating in a squatting position, with her bottom exposed; but what is shame? Likewise, before asking if the male is proud because he has a penis or if his penis is the expression of his pride, we need to know what pride is and how the subject's aspirations can be embodied in an object. Sexuality must not be taken as an irreducible given; the existent possesses a more primary 'quest for being'; sexuality is only one of these aspects. Sartre demonstrates this in *Being and Nothingness*; Bachelard also says it in his works on Earth, Air and

* Freud, *Totem and Taboo.*

Water: psychoanalysts believe that man's quintessential truth lies in his relation to his own body and that of others like him within society; but man has a primordial interest in the substance of the natural world surrounding him that he attempts to discover in work, play and in all experiences of the 'dynamic imagination'; man seeks to connect concretely with existence through the whole world, grasped in all possible ways. Working the soil and digging a hole are activities as primal as an embrace or coitus: it is an error to see them only as sexual symbols; a hole, slime, a gash, hardness or wholeness are primary realities; man's interest in them is not dictated by libido; instead the libido will be influenced by the way these realities were revealed to him. Man is not fascinated by wholeness because it symbolises feminine virginity: rather his love for wholeness makes virginity precious. Work, war, play and art define ways of being in the world that cannot be reduced to any others; they bring to light features that impinge on those that sexuality reveals; it is both through them and through these erotic experiences that the individual chooses himself. But only an ontological point of view can restore the unity of this choice.

Psychoanalysts vehemently reject this notion of choice in the name of determinism and 'the collective unconscious'; this unconscious would provide man with ready-made imagery and universal symbolism; it would explain analogies found in dreams, lapses, delusions, allegories and human destinies; to speak of freedom would be to reject the possibility of explaining these disturbing concordances. But the idea of freedom is not incompatible with the existence of certain constants. If the psychoanalytic method is often productive in spite of errors in theory, it is because there are givens in every individual case so generalised that no one would dream of denying them: situations and behaviour patterns recur; the moment of decision springs out of generality and repetition. 'Anatomy is destiny,' said Freud; and this phrase is echoed by Merleau-Ponty: 'The body is generality.' Existence is one, across and through the separation of existents, manifesting itself in analogous organisms; so there will be constants in the relationship between the ontological and the sexual. At any given period, technology and the economic and social structure of a group reveal an identical world for all its members: there will also be a constant relation of sexuality to social forms; analogous individuals, placed in analogous conditions, will grasp analogous significations in the given; this analogy is not the basis of a rigorous universality, but it can account for finding general types in individual cases. A symbol does not emerge as an allegory worked out by a mysterious unconscious: it is the apprehension of a signification through an analogue of the signifying object; because of the identity of the existential situation cutting across all existents and the identity of the facticity they have to cope with, significations are revealed to many individuals in the same way; symbolism did not fall out of heaven or rise out of subterranean depths: it was elaborated like language, by the human reality that is at once *Mitsein* and separation; and this explains that singular invention also has its place: in practice the psychoanalytical method must accept this whether or not doctrine authorises it. This approach enables us to understand, for example, the value generally given to the penis.* It is impossible to account for this without starting from an existential fact: the subject's tendency towards *alienation;* the anxiety of his freedom leads the subject to search for himself in things, which is a way to flee from himself; it is so fundamental a tendency that as soon as he is weaned and separated from the Whole, the infant endeavours to grasp his alienated existence in the mirror, in his parents' gaze. Primitive people alienate themselves in their mana, their totem; civilised people in their individual souls, their egos, their names, their possessions and their work: and here is the first temptation of inauthenticity. The penis is singularly adapted to play this role of 'double' for the little boy: for him it is both a foreign object and himself; it is a plaything, a doll, and it is his own flesh; parents and nurses treat it like a little person. So, clearly, it becomes for the child 'an alter ego usually craftier, more intelligent and more clever than the individual't;[10] because the urinary function and later the erection are midway between voluntary processes and spontaneous processes, because it is the impulsive, quasi-foreign source of subjectively experienced pleasure, the penis is posited by the subject as himself and other than himself; specific transcendence is embodied in it in a graspable way and it is a source of pride; because the phallus is set apart, man can integrate into his personality the life that flows from it. This is why, then, the length of the penis, the force of the urine stream, the erection and the ejaculation become for him the measure of his own worth.‡ It is thus a constant that the phallus is the fleshly incarnation of transcendence; since it is also a constant that

---

* We will come back to this subject in more detail in Vol. II, Chapter 1.

† Alice Bálint, *The Psychoanalysis of the Nursery.*

‡ The case of little peasant boys who entertain themselves by having excrement contests has been brought to my attention: the one producing the biggest and most solid faeces enjoys a prestige that no other success, in games or even in fighting, could replace. Faecal matter here played the same role as the penis: it was a matter of alienation in both cases.

the child feels transcended, that is, frustrated in his transcendence by his father, the Freudian idea of the castration complex will persist. Deprived of this alter ego, the little girl does not alienate herself in a graspable thing, does not reclaim herself: she is thus led to make her entire self an object, to posit herself as the Other; the question of knowing whether or not she has compared herself with boys is secondary; what is important is that, even without her knowing it, the absence of a penis keeps her from being aware of herself as a sex; many consequences result from this. But these constants we point out nevertheless do not define a destiny: the phallus takes on such importance because it symbolises a sovereignty that is realised in other areas. If woman succeeded in affirming herself as subject, she would invent equivalents of the phallus: the doll that embodies the promise of the child may become a more precious possession than a penis.* There are matrilineal societies where the women possess the masks in which the collectivity alienates itself; the penis then loses much of its glory. Only within the situation grasped in its totality does anatomical privilege found a truly human privilege. Psychoanalysis could only find its truth within an historical context.

Likewise, woman can no more be defined by the consciousness of her own femininity than by merely saying that woman is a female: she finds this consciousness within the society of which she is a member. Interiorising the unconscious and all psychic life, the very language of psychoanalysis suggests that the drama of the individual unfolds within him: the terms 'complex', 'tendencies', and so forth imply this. But a life is a relation with the world; the individual defines himself by choosing himself through the world; we must turn to the world to answer the questions that preoccupy us. In particular, psychoanalysis fails to explain why woman is the *Other*. Even Freud accepts that the prestige of the penis is explained by the father's sovereignty, and he admits that he does not know the source of male supremacy.

Without wholly rejecting the contributions of psychoanalysis, some of which are productive, we will nevertheless not accept its method. First of all, we will not limit ourselves to taking sexuality as a given: that this view falls short is demonstrated by the poverty of the descriptions touching on the feminine libido; I have already said that psychoanalysts have never studied it head-on, but only based on the male libido; they seem to ignore the fundamental ambivalence of the attraction that the male exercises

---

* We will come back to these ideas in Volume Two; mention is made here for the sake of methodology.

over the female. Freudians and Adlerians explain woman's anxiety before male genitalia as an inversion of frustrated desire. Stekel[11] rightly saw this as an original reaction; but he accounts for it only superficially: the woman would fear defloration, penetration, pregnancy and pain, and this fear would stifle her desire; this explanation is too rational. Instead of accepting that desire is disguised as anxiety or is overcome by fear, we should consider this sort of pressing and frightened appeal that is female desire as a basic given; it is characterised by the indissoluble synthesis of attraction and repulsion. It is noteworthy that many female animals flee from coitus at the very moment they solicit it: they are accused of coquetry or hypocrisy; but it is absurd to attempt to explain primitive behaviours by assimilating them to complex ones: they are, on the contrary, at the source of attitudes called coquetry and hypocrisy in women. The idea of a passive libido is disconcerting because the libido has been defined as a drive, as energy based on the male; but one could no more conceive a priori of a light being both yellow and blue: the intuition of green is needed. Reality would be better delineated if, instead of defining the libido in vague terms of 'energy', the significance of sexuality were juxtaposed with that of other human attitudes: taking, catching, eating, doing, undergoing, and so on; for sexuality is one of the singular modes of apprehending an object; the characteristics of the erotic object as it is shown not only in the sexual act but in perception in general would also have to be studied. This examination goes beyond the psychoanalytic framework that posits eroticism as irreducible.

In addition, we will pose the problem of feminine destiny quite differently: we will situate woman in a world of values and we will lend her behaviour a dimension of freedom. We think she has to choose between the affirmation of her transcendence and her alienation as object; she is not the plaything of contradictory drives; she devises solutions that have an ethical hierarchy among them. Replacing value with authority, choice with drives, psychoanalysis proposes an ersatz morality: the idea of normality. This idea is indeed highly useful from a therapeutic point of view; but it has reached a disturbing extent in psychoanalysis in general. The descriptive schema is proposed as a law; and assuredly, a mechanistic psychology could not accept the notion of moral invention; at best it can recognise *less* but never more; at best it acknowledges failures, but never creations. If a subject does not wholly replicate a development considered normal, his development will be seen as being interrupted, and this will be interpreted as a lack and a negation and never a positive decision. That, among other things, is what

renders the psychoanalysis of great men so shocking: we are told that
this transference or that sublimation was not successfully carried out in
them; it is never supposed that perhaps they could have rejected it, and
perhaps for good reasons; it is never considered that their behaviour
might have been motivated by freely posited aims; the individual is always
explained through his link to the past and not with respect to a future
towards which he projects himself. Therefore, we are never given more
than an inauthentic picture, and in this inauthenticity, no criterion other
than normality can possibly be found. The description of feminine destiny
is, from this point of view, altogether striking. The way psychoanalysts
understand it, 'to identify' with the mother or the father is to *alienate
oneself* in a model, it is to prefer a foreign image to a spontaneous movement of one's own existence, it is to play at being. We are shown woman
solicited by two kinds of alienations; it is very clear that to play at being
a man will be a recipe for failure; but to play at being a woman is also
a trap: being a woman would mean being an object, the Other; and at
the heart of its abdication, the Other remains a subject. The real problem
for the woman refusing these evasions is to accomplish herself as transcendence: this means seeing which possibilities are opened to her by
what are called virile and feminine attitudes; when a child follows the
path indicated by one or another of his parents, it could be because he
freely takes on their projects: his behaviour could be the result of a choice
motivated by ends. Even for Adler, the will to power is only a sort of
absurd energy; he calls any project that incarnates transcendence a
'masculine protest'; when a girl climbs trees, it is, according to him, to
be the equal of boys: he does not imagine that she likes to climb trees;
for the mother, the child is anything but a 'penis substitute'; painting,
writing or engaging in politics are not only 'good sublimations': they are
ends desired in themselves. To deny this is to falsify all of human history.
Parallels can be noted between our descriptions and those of psychoanalysts. From man's point of view – adopted by both male and female
psychoanalysts – behaviour of alienation is considered feminine, and
behaviour where the subject posits his transcendence is considered masculine. Donaldson,[12] an historian of woman, observed that the definitions
'the man is a male human being, the woman is a female human being'
were asymmetrically mutilated; psychoanalysts in particular define man
as a human being and woman as a female: every time she acts like a
human being, she is said to be imitating the male. The psychoanalyst
describes the child and the young girl as required to identify with the
father and the mother, torn between 'viriloid' and 'feminine' tendencies,

whereas we conceive her as hesitating between the role of *object*, of *Other* that is proposed to her and her claim for freedom; thus it is possible to agree on certain points: in particular when we consider the paths of inauthentic flight offered to women. But we do not give them the same Freudian or Adlerian signification. For us woman is defined as a human being in search of values within a world of values, a world where it is indispensable to understand the economic and social structure; we will study her from an existential point of view, taking into account her total situation.

CHAPTER 3

The Point of View of Historical Materialism

The theory of historical materialism has brought to light some very important truths. Humanity is not an animal species: it is an historical reality. Human society is an anti-physis: it does not passively submit to the presence of nature, but rather appropriates it. This appropriation is not an interior, subjective operation: it is carried out objectively in praxis. Thus woman cannot simply be considered a sexed organism: among biological data, only those with concrete value in action have any importance; woman's consciousness of herself is not defined by her sexuality alone: it reflects a situation that depends on society's economic structure, a structure that indicates the degree of technical evolution humanity has attained. We have seen that two essential traits characterise woman biologically: her grasp on the world is narrower than man's; and she is more closely subjugated to the species. But these facts have a totally different value depending on the economic and social context. Throughout human history, grasp on the world is not defined by the naked body: the hand, with its prehensile thumb, moves beyond itself towards instruments that increase its power; from prehistory's earliest documents, man is always seen as armed. In the past, when it was a question of carrying heavy clubs and of keeping wild beasts at bay, woman's physical weakness constituted a flagrant inferiority: if the instrument requires slightly more strength than the woman can muster, it is enough to make her seem radically powerless. But on the other hand, technical developments can cancel out the muscular inequality separating man and woman: abundance only creates superiority relative to a need; having too much is not better than having enough. Thus operating many modern machines requires only a part of masculine resources; if the necessary minimum is not superior to woman's capacities, she becomes man's work equal. Today enormous deployments of energy can be commanded at the touch of a switch. The burdens that come with maternity vary greatly depending on customs: they are overwhelming if numerous pregnancies are imposed on the woman and if she must feed and raise her children without help; if she procreates as she wishes and if society helps her during her pregnancies and provides childcare, maternal duties are lighter and can be easily compensated for in the realm of work.

Engels retraces woman's history from this point of view in *The Origin of the Family**;[13] this family history depends principally on the history of technology. In the Stone Age, when the land belonged to all members of the clan, the rudimentary nature of the primitive spade and hoe limited agricultural possibilities: feminine strength was at the level of work needed for gardening. In this primitive division of labour, the two sexes already constitute two classes in a way; there is equality between these classes; while the man hunts and fishes, the woman stays at home; but the domestic tasks include productive work: pottery making, weaving, gardening; and in this way, she has an important role in economic life. With the discovery of copper, tin, bronze and iron, and with the advent of the plough, agriculture expands its reach: intensive labour is necessary to clear the forests and cultivate the fields. So man has recourse to the service of other men, reducing them to slavery. Private property appears: master of slaves and land, man also becomes the proprietor of the woman. This is the 'great historical defeat of the female sex'. It is explained by the disruption of the division of labour brought about by the invention of new tools. 'The same cause that had assured woman her previous authority in the home, her restriction to housework, this same cause now assured the domination of the man; domestic work thence faded in importance next to man's productive work; the latter was everything, the former an insignificant addition.' So paternal right replaces maternal right: transmission of property is from father to son and no longer from woman to her clan. This is the advent of the patriarchal family founded on private property. In such a family woman is oppressed. Man reigning sovereign permits himself, among other things, his sexual whims: he sleeps with slaves or courtesans, he is polygamous. As soon as customs make reciprocity possible, woman takes revenge through infidelity: adultery becomes a natural part of marriage. This is the only defence woman has against the domestic slavery she is bound to: her social oppression is the consequence of her economic oppression. Equality can only be reestablished when both sexes have equal legal

* Friedrich Engels, *The Origin of the Family, Private Property, and the State.*

rights; but this enfranchisement demands that the whole of the feminine sex enter public industry. 'Woman cannot be emancipated unless
she takes part in production on a large social scale and is only incidentally bound to domestic work. And this has become possible only within
a large modern industry that not only accepts women's work on a grand
scale but formally requires it.'

Thus woman's fate is intimately bound to the fate of socialism as seen
also in Bebel's vast work on women. 'Women and the proletariat', he
writes, 'are both oppressed.' And both must be set free by the same
economic development resulting from the upheaval caused by the invention of machines. The problem of woman can be reduced to that of her
capacity for work. Powerful when technology matched her possibilities,
dethroned when she became incapable of benefiting from them, she
finds again equality with man in the modern world. Resistance put up
by the old capitalist paternalism prevents this equality from being
concretely achieved: it will be achieved the day this resistance is broken
down. It already has broken down in the USSR, Soviet propaganda
affirms. And when socialist society is realised throughout the whole
world, there will no longer be men nor women, but only workers, equal
among themselves.

Although the synthesis outlined by Engels marks an advance over
those we have already examined, it is still disappointing: the most serious
problems are dodged. The whole account pivots around the transition
from a communitarian regime to one of private property: there is absolutely
no indication of how it was able to occur; Engels even admits that 'for
now we know nothing about it';* not only is he unaware of its historical
details, but he offers no interpretation of it. Similarly, it is unclear if
private property necessarily led to the enslavement of woman. Historical
materialism takes for granted facts it should explain: it posits the *interest*
that attaches man to property without discussing it; but where does this
interest, the source of social institutions, have its own source? This is
why Engels's account remains superficial, and the truths he uncovers
appear contingent. It is impossible to go deeper into them without going
beyond historical materialism. It cannot provide solutions to the problems we indicated because they concern the whole man and not this
abstraction, *Homo economicus*.

It is clear, for example, that the very idea of individual possession can
acquire meaning only on the basis of the original condition of the existent.

* Ibid.

For that idea to appear, it is first necessary that there be in the subject a tendency to posit himself in his radical singularity, an affirmation of his existence as autonomous and separate. Obviously this claim remained subjective, interior and without truth as long as the individual lacked the practical means to satisfy it objectively: for lack of the right tools, at first he could not experience his power over the world, he felt lost in nature and in the group, passive, threatened, the plaything of obscure forces; it was only in identifying with the whole clan that he dared to think himself: the totem, the mana and the earth were collective realities. The discovery of bronze enabled man, tested by hard and productive work, to find himself as creator, dominating nature; no longer afraid of nature, having overcome resistance, he dares to grasp himself as autonomous activity and to accomplish himself in his singularity.*[14] But this accomplishment would never have been realised if man had not originally wanted it; the lesson of labour is not inscribed in a passive subject: the subject forged and conquered himself in forging his tools and conquering the earth. On the other hand, the affirmation of the subject is not enough to explain ownership: in challenges, struggles and individual combat, every consciousness can try to rise to sovereignty. For the challenge to have taken the form of the potlatch, that is, of economic rivalry, and from there first for the chief and then for the clan members to have laid claim to private goods, there had to be another original tendency in man: in the preceding chapter we said that the existent can only succeed in grasping himself by alienating himself; he searches for himself through the world, in the guise of a foreign figure he makes his own. The clan encounters its own alienated existence in the totem, the mana and the territory it occupies; when the individual separates from the community, he demands a singular embodiment: the mana is individualised in the chief, then in each individual; and at the same time each one tries to appropriate a piece of land, tools, or crops. In these riches of his, man finds himself because he lost himself in them: it is understandable then that he can attribute to them an importance as basic as that of his life itself. Thus man's *interest* in his property becomes an intelligible relationship. But clearly the tool alone is not enough to explain it; the whole attitude of

---

* Gaston Bachelard in *Earth and Reveries of Will* carries out, among others, an interesting study of the blacksmith's work. He shows how man asserts and separates himself from himself by the hammer and anvil. 'The temporal existence of the blacksmith is both highly particular and larger than life. Through momentary violence, the worker, uplifted, gains mastery over time'; and further on: 'Those who forge take on the challenge of the universe rising against them.'

the tool-armed man must be grasped, an attitude that implies an onto-logical infrastructure.

Similarly, it is impossible to *deduce* woman's oppression from private property. Here again, the shortcomings of Engels's point of view are obvious. While he clearly understood that woman's muscular weakness was a concrete inferiority only in relation to bronze and iron tools, he failed to see that limits to her work capacity constituted in themselves a concrete disadvantage only from a certain perspective. Because man is transcendence and ambition, he projects new demands with each new tool: after having invented bronze instruments, he was no longer satis-fied with developing gardens and wanted instead to clear and cultivate vast fields. This will did not spring from bronze itself. Woman's power-lessness brought about her ruin because man apprehended her through a project of enrichment and expansion. And this project is still not enough to explain her oppression: the division of labour by sex might have been a friendly association. If the original relation between man and his peers had been exclusively one of friendship, one could not account for any kind of enslavement: this phenomenon is a consequence of the imperi-alism of human consciousness, which seeks to match its sovereignty objectively. Had there not been in human consciousness both the orig-inal category of the Other and an original claim to domination over the Other, the discovery of the bronze tool could not have brought about woman's oppression. Nor does Engels account for the specific character of this oppression. He tried to reduce the opposition of the sexes to a class conflict: in fact, he did it without real conviction; this thesis is inde-fensible. True, the division of labour by sex and the oppression resulting from it brings to mind class division in some ways: but they should not be confused; there is no biological basis for division by class; in work the slave becomes conscious of himself against the master; the prole-tariat has always experienced its condition in revolt, thus returning to the essential, constituting a threat to its exploiters; and the goal of the proletariat is to cease to exist as a class. We have said in the introduc-tion how different woman's situation is, specifically because of the community of life and interests that create her solidarity with man and due to the complicity he encounters in her: she harbours no desire for revolution, she would not think of eliminating herself as a sex: she simply asks that certain consequences of sexual differentiation be abolished. And more serious still, woman cannot in good faith be regarded only as a worker; her reproductive function is as important as her productive capacity, both in the social economy and in her personal life; there are periods in history when it is more useful to have children than till the soil. Engels sidestepped the problem; he limits himself to declaring that the socialist community will abolish the family, quite an abstract solution; everyone knows how often and how radically the USSR has had to change its family policy to balance out production needs of the moment with the needs of repopulation; besides, eliminating the family does not necessarily liberate woman: the example of Sparta and that of the Nazi regime prove that notwithstanding her direct attachment to the state, she might still be no less oppressed by males. A truly socialist ethic – one that seeks justice without restraining liberty, one that imposes responsibilities on individuals but without abolishing individual freedom – will find itself most uncomfortable with problems posed by woman's condition. It is impossible to simply assimilate gestation to a *job* or *service* like the military service. A deeper breach is created in a woman's life by requiring her to have children than by regulating citizens' occupations: no state has ever dared institute compulsory coitus. In the sexual act and in maternity, woman engages not only time and energy but also essential values. Rationalist materialism tries in vain to ignore this powerful aspect of sexuality: sexual instinct cannot be regulated; according to Freud, it might even possess an inherent denial of its own satisfaction; what is certain is that it cannot be integrated into the social sphere, because there is in eroticism a revolt of the instant against time, of the individual against the universal: to try to channel and exploit it risks killing it, because live spontaneity cannot be disposed of like inert matter; nor can it be compelled in the way a freedom can be. There is no way to directly oblige a woman to give birth: all that can be done is to enclose her in situations where motherhood is her only option: laws or customs impose marriage on her, anticonception measures and abortion are banned, divorce is forbidden. These old patriarchal constraints are exactly the ones the USSR has brought back to life today; it has revived paternalistic theories about marriage; and in doing so, it has asked woman to become an erotic object again: a recent speech asked Soviet women citizens to pay attention to their clothes, to use makeup and to become flirtatious to hold on to their husbands and stimulate their desire. Examples like this prove how impossible it is to consider the woman as a solely productive force: for man she is a sexual partner, a reproducer, an erotic object, an Other through whom he seeks himself. Although totalitarian or authoritarian regimes may all try to ban psychoanalysis and declare that personal emotional conflicts have no place for citizens loyally integrated into the community, eroticism is an experience where individuality always prevails over generality. And for democratic socialism where classes would be abolished but not individuals, the question of individual destiny would still retain all its importance: sexual different-iation would retain all its importance. The sexual relation that unites woman with man is not the same as the one he maintains with her; the bond that attaches her to the child is irreducible to any other. She was not created by the bronze tool alone: the machine is not sufficient to abolish her. To demand for woman all the rights, all the possibilities of the human being in general does not mean one must be blind to her singular situation. To know this situation, it is necessary to go beyond historical materialism, which only sees man and woman as economic entities.

So we reject Freud's sexual monism and Engels's economic monism for the same reason. A psychoanalyst will interpret all woman's social claims as a phenomenon of 'masculine protest'; for the Marxist, on the other hand, her sexuality only expresses her economic situation, in a rather complex, roundabout way; but the categories clitoral or vaginal, like the categories bourgeois or proletarian, are equally inadequate to encompass a concrete woman. Underlying the personal emotional conflicts as well as the economic history of humanity there is an exis-tential infrastructure that alone makes it possible to understand in its unity the unique form that is a life. Freudianism's value derives from the fact that the existent is a body: the way he experiences himself as a body in the presence of other bodies concretely translates his existential situ-ation. Likewise, what is true in the Marxist thesis is that the existent's ontological claims take on a concrete form based on the material possi-bilities offered to him, particularly based on those that technology opens to him. But if they are not incorporated into the whole of human reality, sexuality and technology of themselves will fail to explain anything. This is why in Freud prohibitions imposed by the superego and the drives of the ego appear as contingent facts; and in Engels's account of the history of the family, the most important events seem to arise unexpectedly through the whims of mysterious chance. To discover woman, we will not reject certain contributions of biology, psychoanalysis or historical materialism: but we will consider that the body, sexual life and tech-nology exist concretely for man only insofar as he grasps them from the overall perspective of his existence. The value of muscular strength, the phallus and the tool can only be defined in a world of values: it is driven by the fundamental project of the existent transcending itself towards being.

Part Two
HISTORY

CHAPTER I

This world has always belonged to males, and none of the reasons given for this have ever seemed sufficient. By reviewing prehistoric and ethnographic data in the light of existentialist philosophy, we can understand how the hierarchy of the sexes came to be. We have already posited that when two human categories find themselves face-to-face, each one wants to impose its sovereignty on the other; if both hold to this claim equally, a reciprocal relationship is created, either hostile or friendly, but always tense. If one of the two has an advantage over the other, that one prevails and works to maintain the relationship by oppression. It is thus understandable that man might have had the will to dominate woman: but what advantage enabled him to accomplish this will?

Ethnologists give extremely contradictory information about primitive forms of human society, even more so when they are well informed and less systematic. It is especially difficult to formulate an idea about woman's situation in the pre-agricultural period. We do not even know if, in such different living conditions from today's, woman's musculature or her respiratory system were not as developed as man's. She was given hard work, and in particular it was she who carried heavy loads; yet this latter fact is ambiguous: probably if she was assigned this function, it is because within the convoy men kept their hands free to defend against possible aggressors, animals or humans; so their role was the more dangerous one and demanded more strength. But it seems that in many cases women were robust and resilient enough to participate in warrior expeditions. According to the accounts by Herodotus and the traditions of the Amazons from Dahomey as well as ancient and modern testimonies, women were known to take part in bloody wars or vendettas; they showed as much courage and cruelty as males: there are references to women who bit their teeth into their enemies' livers. In spite of this, it is likely that then as now men had the advantage of physical force; in the age of clubs and wild animals, in the age when resistance to nature was at its greatest and tools were at their most rudimentary, this superiority must have been of extreme importance. In any case, as robust as women may have been at that time, the burdens of reproduction represented for them a severe handicap in the fight against a hostile world: Amazons were said to mutilate their breasts, which meant that at least during the period of their warrior lives they rejected maternity. As for ordinary women, pregnancy, giving birth and menstruation diminished their work capacity and condemned them to long periods of impotence; to defend themselves against enemies or to take care of themselves and their children, they needed the protection of warriors and the catch from hunting and fishing provided by the males. As there obviously was no birth control, and as nature does not provide woman with sterile periods as it does for other female mammals, frequent pregnancies must have absorbed the greater part of their strength and their time; they were unable to provide for the lives of the children they brought into the world. This is a primary fact fraught with great consequence: the human species's beginnings were difficult; hunter, gatherer and fishing peoples reaped meagre bounty from the soil, and at great cost in effort; too many children were born for the group's resources; the woman's absurd fertility kept her from participating actively in the growth of these resources, while it was constantly creating new needs. Indispensable to the perpetuation of the species, she perpetuated it too abundantly: so it was man who controlled the balance between reproduction and production. Thus woman did not even have the privilege of maintaining life that the creator male had; she did not play the role of ovum to his spermatozoid or womb to his phallus; she played only one part in the human species's effort to persist in being, and it was thanks to man that this effort had a concrete result.

Nonetheless, as the production-reproduction balance always finds a way of stabilising itself – even at the price of infanticide, sacrifices, or wars – men and women are equally indispensable from the point of view of group survival; it could even be supposed that at certain periods when food was plentiful, his protective and nourishing role might have subordinated the male to the wife-mother. There are female animals that derive total autonomy from motherhood; so why has woman not been able to make a pedestal for herself from it? Even in those moments when humanity most desperately needed births – since the need for manual labour prevailed over the need for raw materials to exploit – and even in those times when motherhood was the most venerated, maternity was not enough for women to conquer the highest rank.* The reason for this is that humanity is not a simple natural species: it does not seek to survive as a species; its project is not stagnation: it seeks to surpass itself.

The primitive hordes were barely interested in their posterity. Connected to no territory, owning nothing, embodied in nothing stable, they could formulate no concrete idea of permanence; they were unconcerned with survival and did not recognise themselves in their descendants; they did not fear death and did not seek heirs; children were a burden and not of great value for them; the proof is that infanticide has always been frequent in nomadic peoples; and many newborns who are not massacred die for lack of hygiene in a climate of total indifference. So the woman who gives birth does not take pride in her creation; she feels like the passive plaything of obscure forces, and painful childbirth a useless and even bothersome accident. Later, more value was attached to children. But in any case, to give birth and to breast-feed are not *activities,* but natural functions; they do not involve a project, which is why the woman finds no motive there to claim a higher meaning for her existence; she passively submits to her biological destiny. Because housework alone is compatible with the duties of motherhood, she is condemned to domestic labour, which locks her into repetition and immanence; day after day it repeats itself in identical form from century to century; it produces nothing new. Man's case is radically different. He does not provide for the group in the way worker bees do, by a simple vital process, but rather by acts that transcend his animal condition. *Homo faber* has been an inventor since the beginning of time: even the stick or the club he armed himself with to knock down fruit from a tree or to slaughter animals is an instrument that expands his grasp of the world; bringing home freshly caught fish is not enough for him: he first has to conquer the seas by constructing dugout canoes; to appropriate the world's treasures, he annexes the world itself. Through such actions he tests his own power; he posits ends and projects paths to them: he realises himself as existent. To maintain himself, he creates; he spills over the present and opens up the future. This is the reason fishing and hunting expeditions have a sacred quality. Their success is greeted by celebration and triumph, man recognises his humanity in them. This pride is still apparent today when he builds a dam, a skyscraper, or an atomic reactor.

* Sociology no longer gives credit to Bachofen's lucubrations.

He has not only worked to preserve the given world: he has burst its borders, he has laid the ground for a new future.

His activity has another dimension that endows him with supreme dignity: it is often dangerous. If blood were only a food, it would not be worth more than milk: but the hunter is not a butcher: he runs risks in the struggle against wild animals. The warrior risks his own life to raise the prestige of the horde – his clan. This is how he brilliantly proves that life is not the supreme value for man but that it must serve ends far greater than itself. The worst curse on woman is her exclusion from warrior expeditions; it is not in giving life but in risking his life that man raises himself above the animal; this is why throughout humanity, superiority has been granted not to the sex that gives birth, but to the one that kills.

Here we hold the key to the whole mystery. On a biological level, a species maintains itself only by re-creating itself; but this creation is nothing but a repetition of the same Life in different forms. By transcending Life through Existence, man guarantees the repetition of Life: by this surpassing, he creates values that deny any value to pure repetition. With an animal, the gratuitousness and variety of male activities are useless because no project is involved; what it does is worthless when it is not serving the species; but in serving the species, the human male shapes the face of the earth, creates new instruments, invents and forges the future. Positing himself as sovereign, he encounters the complicity of woman herself: because she herself is also an existent, because transcendence also inhabits her and her project is not repetition but surpassing herself towards another future; she finds the confirmation of masculine claims in the core of her being. She participates with men in festivals that celebrate the success and victories of males. Her misfortune is to have been biologically destined to repeat Life, while in her own eyes Life in itself does not provide her reasons for being, and these reasons are more important than life itself.

Certain passages where Hegel's dialectic describes the relationship of master to slave would apply far better to the relationship of man to woman. The Master's privilege, he states, arises from the affirmation of Spirit over Life in the fact of risking his life: but in fact the vanquished slave has experienced this same risk, whereas the woman is originally an existent who gives *Life* and does not risk *her* life; there has never been combat between the male and her; Hegel's definition applies singularly to her. 'The other [consciousness] is the dependent consciousness for which essential reality is animal life, that is, life given by another entity.'

But this relationship differs from the relationship of oppression because woman herself aspires to and recognises the values concretely attained by males. It is the male who opens up the future towards which she also transcends; in reality, women have never pitted female values against male ones: it is men wanting to maintain masculine prerogatives who invented this division; they wanted to create a feminine domain – a rule of life, of immanence – only to lock woman in it. But it is above and beyond all sexual specification that the existent seeks self-justification in the movement of his transcendence: the very submission of women proves this. Today what women claim is to be recognised as existents just like men, and not to subordinate existence to life or the man to his animality.

Thus an existential perspective has enabled us to understand how the biological and economic situation of primitive hordes led to male supremacy. The female, more than the male, is prey to the species; humanity has always tried to escape from its species's destiny; with the invention of the tool, maintenance of life became activity and project for man, while motherhood left woman riveted to her body like the animal. It is because humanity puts itself into question in its being – that is, values reasons for living over life – that man has set himself as master over woman; man's project is not to repeat himself in time: it is to reign over the instant and to forge the future. Male activity, creating values, has constituted existence itself as a value; it has prevailed over the indistinct forces of life; and it has subjugated Nature and Woman. We must now see how this situation has continued and evolved through the centuries. What place has humanity allotted to this part of itself that has been defined in its core as Other? What rights have been conceded to it? How have men defined it?

CHAPTER 2

We have just seen that women's fate is very harsh in primitive hordes; in female animals the reproductive function is limited naturally and when it occurs, the particular animal is more or less released from other toil; only domestic females are sometimes exploited to the point of exhaustion of their forces as reproducers and in their individual capacities by a demanding master. This was undoubtedly the case of woman at a time when the struggle against a hostile world demanded the full employment of community resources; added to the fatigues of incessant and unregulated procreation were those of hard domestic duties. Nevertheless, some historians maintain that precisely at that time, male superiority was the least marked; which means that this superiority is lived in an immediate form, not yet posited and willed; no one tries to compensate for the cruel disadvantages that handicap woman; but neither does anyone try to break her down, as will later happen in paternalistic regimes. No institution actually ratifies the inequality of the sexes; in fact, there are no institutions: no property, no inheritance, no legal system. Religion is neutral; the totems that are worshipped are asexual.

It is when nomads settled the land and became farmers that institutions and law appeared. Man no longer has to limit himself to combating hostile forces; he begins to express himself concretely through the figure he imposes on the world, thinking the world and thinking himself; at that juncture, sexual differentiation is reflected in the group structure, and it takes on a particular character: in agricultural communities, woman is often vested with extraordinary prestige. This prestige is explained essentially by the new importance that children assume in a civilisation based upon working the land; by settling a territory, men begin to appropriate it. Property appears in a collective form; it demands posterity from its owners; motherhood becomes a sacred function. Many tribes live under a communal regime: this does not mean that women belong to all the men in the community; it is no longer thought today that promiscuous marriage was ever practised; but men and women only have a religious, social and economic existence as a group: their individuality remains a purely biological fact; marriage, whatever its form – monogamy, polygamy, polyandry – is itself nothing but a secular incident that does not create a mystical link. For the wife it is in no way a source of servitude, as she remains an integral part of her clan. The clan as a whole, gathered under the same totem, mystically shares the same mana and materially shares the common enjoyment of a territory. But in the alienation process mentioned before, the clan grasps itself in this territory in the guise of an objective and concrete figure; through the permanence of the land, the clan thus realises itself as a unity whose identity persists throughout the passage of time. Only this existential process makes it possible to understand the identification that has survived to this day among the clan, the gens, the family and property. In the thinking of nomadic tribes, only the moment exists; the agricultural community replaces this thinking with the concept of a life rooted in the past and incorporating the future: the totem ancestor who gives his name to the clan members is venerated; and the clan takes an abiding interest in its descendants: it will survive through the land he bequeaths to them and that they will exploit. The community conceives of its unity and wills its existence beyond the present: it sees itself in its children, it recognises them as its own, and it accomplishes and surpasses itself through them.

But many primitives are unaware of the father's role in the procreation of children who are thought to be the reincarnation of ancestral larvae floating around certain trees, certain rocks, in certain sacred places, and descending into the woman's body; in some cases, they believe she must not be a virgin if this infiltration is to take place; but other peoples believe that it also takes place through the nostrils or mouth; at any rate, defloration is secondary here and for mystical reasons the prerogative is rarely the husband's. The mother is clearly necessary for the birth of the child; she is the one who keeps and nourishes the germ within her and so the life of the clan is propagated in the visible world through her. This is how she finds herself playing the principal role. Very often, children belong to their mother's clan, bear her name and share her rights, particularly the use of the land belonging to the clan. So communal property is transmitted through women: through them the fields and their harvests are reserved to members of the clan, and inversely it is through their mothers that members are destined to a given piece of land. The land can thus be considered as mystically belonging to women:

their hold on the soil and its fruits is both religious and legal. The tie that binds them is stronger than one of ownership; maternal right is characterised by a true assimilation of woman to the land; in each, through its avatars, the permanence of life is achieved, life that is essentially generation. For nomads, procreation seems only an accident, and the riches of the earth are still unknown; but the farmer admires the mystery of fertilisation that burgeons in the furrows and in the maternal womb. He knows that he was conceived like the cattle and the harvests, and he wants his clan to conceive other humans who will perpetuate it in perpetuating the fertility of the fields; nature as a whole seems like a mother to him; the earth is woman, and the woman is inhabited by the same obscure forces as the earth.* This is part of the reason agricultural work is entrusted to woman: able to call up the ancestral larvae within her, she also has the power to make fruit and wheat spring from the sowed fields. In both cases it is a question of a magic conjuration, not of a creative act. At this stage, man no longer limits himself to gathering the products of the earth: but he does not yet understand his power; he hesitates between technical skill and magic; he feels passive, dependent on Nature that doles out existence and death by chance. To be sure, he recognises more or less the function of the sexual act as well as the techniques for cultivating the soil: but children and crops still seem like supernatural gifts; and the mysterious emanations flowing from the feminine body bring forth into this world the riches latent in the mysterious sources of life. Such beliefs are still alive today among numerous Indian, Australian and Polynesian tribes, and become all the more important as they match the practical interests of the collectivity.† Motherhood relegates woman to a sedentary existence; it is natural for her to stay at home while men hunt, fish and go to war. But primitive people rarely

---

* 'Hail, Earth, mother of all men, may you be fertile in the arms of God and filled with fruits for the use of man,' says an old Anglo-Saxon incantation.

† For the Bhantas of India, or in Uganda, a sterile woman is considered dangerous for gardens. In Nicobar, it is believed that the harvest will be better if it is brought in by a pregnant woman. In Borneo, seeds are chosen and preserved by women. 'One seems to feel in women a natural affinity with the seeds that are said by the women to be in a state of pregnancy. Sometimes women will spend the night in the rice fields during its growth period' (Hose and MacDougall). In India of yore, naked women pushed the plough through the field at night. Indians along the Orinoco left the sowing and planting to women because 'women knew how to conceive seed and bear children, so the seeds and roots planted by them bore fruit far more abundantly than if they had been planted by male hands' (Frazer). Many similar examples can be found in Frazer.

cultivate more than a modest garden contained within their own village limits and its cultivation is a domestic task; Stone Age instruments require little effort; economics and mystical belief agree to leave agricultural work to women. Domestic work, as it is taking shape, is also their lot: they weave rugs and blankets, they shape pottery. And they are often in charge of barter; commerce is in their hands. The life of the clan is thus maintained and extended through them; children, herds, harvests, tools and the whole prosperity of the group of which they are the soul depend on their work and their magic virtues. Such strength inspires in men a respect mingled with fear, reflected in their worship. It is in women that the whole of foreign Nature is concentrated.

It has already been said here that man never thinks himself without thinking the Other; he grasps the world under the emblem of duality, which is not initially sexual. But being naturally different from man who posits himself as the same, woman is consigned to the category of Other; the Other encompasses woman; at first she is not important enough to incarnate the Other alone, so a subdivision at the heart of the Other develops: in ancient cosmographies, a single element often has both male and female incarnations; thus for the Babylonians, the Ocean and the Sea were the double incarnation of cosmic chaos. When the woman's role grows, she comes to occupy nearly the whole region of the Other. Then appear the feminine divinities through whom fertility is worshipped. A discovery made in Susa shows the oldest representation of the Great Goddess, the Great Mother in a long robe and high coiffure, which other statues show crowned with towers; excavations in Crete have yielded several effigies of her. She can be steatopygous and crouched, or thin and standing, sometimes clothed, and often naked, her arms pressed beneath her swollen breasts. She is the queen of heaven, a dove is her symbol; she is also the empress of Hades, she comes out slithering, symbolised by a serpent. She can be seen in mountains, woods, the sea and in springs. She creates life everywhere; if she kills, she resurrects. Fickle, lascivious and cruel like Nature, propitious and yet dangerous, she reigns over all of Asia Minor, over Phrygia, Syria, Anatolia, and over all of western Asia. She is known as Ishtar in Babylon, Astarte to Semitic peoples, and Gaea, Rhea, or Cybele to the Greeks; she is found in Egypt in the form of Isis; male divinities are subordinated to her. Supreme idol in faraway regions of heaven and Hades, woman on earth is surrounded by taboos like all sacred beings – she is herself taboo; because of the powers she holds, she is seen as a magician or a sorceress; she is included in prayers, and she can be at times a priestess like the druids among the ancient Celts; in certain cases she participates in the government of the tribe, and at times she even governs on her own. These distant ages have left us no literature. But the great patriarchal periods conserve in their mythology, monuments and traditions the memory of times when women occupied very high positions. From a feminine point of view, the Brahman period is a regression from that of Rig-Veda, and the latter a regression from the primitive stage that preceded it. The pre-Islamic Bedouin women had a much higher status than that accorded them by the Koran. The great figures of Niobe and Medea evoke an era when mothers, considering their children to be their own property, took pride in them. And in the Homeric poems, Andromache and Hecuba have an importance that classic Greece no longer granted to women hidden in the shadows of the gynaeceum.

These facts all lead to the supposition that in primitive times a veritable reign of women existed; this hypothesis, proposed by Bachofen, was adopted by Engels; the passage from matriarchy to patriarchy seems to him to be 'the great historical defeat of the feminine sex'. But in reality this golden age of Woman is only a myth. To say that woman was the *Other* is to say that a relationship of reciprocity between the sexes did not exist: whether Earth, Mother or Goddess, she was never a peer for man; her power asserted itself *beyond* human rule: she was thus *outside* of this rule. Society has always been male; political power has always been in men's hands. 'Political authority, or simply social authority, always belongs to men,' Lévi-Strauss affirms at the close of his study of primitive societies. For men, the counterpart – or the other – who is also the same, with whom reciprocal relationships are established, is always another male individual. The duality that can be seen in one form or another at the heart of society pits one group of men against another; and women are part of the goods men possess and a means of exchange among themselves: the mistake comes from confusing two forms of mutually exclusive alterity. Insofar as woman is considered the absolute Other, that is – whatever magic powers she has – as the inessential, it is precisely impossible to regard her as another subject.* Women have thus never constituted a separate

---

* It will be seen that this distinction has been perpetuated. Periods that regard woman as *Other* are those that refuse most harshly to integrate her into society as a human being. Today she only becomes an *other* peer by losing her mystical aura. Antifeminists have always played on this ambiguity. They readily agree to exalt the woman as Other in order to make her alterity absolute and irreducible, and to refuse her access to the human *Mitsein*.

group that posited itself *for-itself* before a male group; they have never had a direct or autonomous relationship with men. 'The relationship of reciprocity which is the basis of marriage is not established between men and women, but between men by means of women, who are merely the occasion of this relationship,' said Lévi-Strauss.*[1] Woman's concrete condition is not affected by the type of lineage that prevails in the society to which she belongs; whether the regime is patrilineal, matrilineal, bilateral, or undifferentiated (undifferentiation never being precise), she is always under men's guardianship; the only question is if, after marriage, she is still subjected to the authority of her father or her oldest brother – authority that will also extend to her children – or of her husband. In any case: 'The woman is never anything more than the symbol of her lineage. Matrilineal descent is the authority of the woman's father or brother extended to the brother-in-law's village.'[†] She only mediates the law; she does not possess it. In fact, it is the relationship of two masculine groups that is defined by the system of filiation, and not the relation of the two sexes. In practice, woman's concrete condition is not consistently linked to any given type of law. It may happen that in a matrilineal system she has a very high position: but – beware – the presence of a woman chief or a queen at the head of a tribe absolutely does not mean that women are sovereign: the reign of Catherine the Great changed nothing in the fate of Russian peasant women; and they lived no less frequently in a state of abjection. And cases where a woman remains in her clan and her husband makes rapid, even clandestine visits to her are very rare. She almost always goes to live under her husband's roof: this fact is proof enough of male domination. 'Behind the variations in the type of descent,' writes Lévi-Strauss, 'the permanence of patrilocal residence attests to the basic asymmetrical relationship between the sexes which is characteristic of human society.' Since she keeps her children with her, the result is that the territorial organisation of the tribe does not correspond to its totemic organisation: the former is contingent, the latter rigorously constructed; but in practice, the first was the more important because the place where people work and live counts more than their mystical connection. In the more widespread transitional regimes, there are two kinds of rights, one based on religion and the other on the occupation and labour on the land, and they overlap. Though only

---

* Lévi-Strauss, *The Elementary Structures of Kinship*.
† Ibid.

a secular institution, marriage nevertheless has great social importance, and the conjugal family, though stripped of religious signification, is very alive on a human level. Even within groups where great sexual freedom is found, it is considered conventional for a woman who brings a child into the world to be married; alone with an offspring, she cannot constitute an autonomous group; and her brother's religious protection does not suffice; a husband's presence is required. He often has many heavy responsibilities for the children; they do not belong to his clan, but it is nonetheless he who feeds and raises them; between husband and wife, and father and son, bonds of cohabitation, work, common interest and tenderness are formed. Relations between this secular family and the totemic clan are extremely complex, as the diversity of marriage rites attests. In primitive times, a husband buys a wife from a foreign clan, or at least there is an exchange of goods from one clan to another, the first giving over one of its members and the second delivering cattle, fruits, or work in return. But as husbands take charge of wives and their children, it also happens that they receive remuneration from their brides' brothers. The balance between mystical and economic realities is an unstable one. Men often have a closer attachment to their sons than to their nephews; it is as a father that a man will choose to affirm himself when such affirmation becomes possible. And this is why every society tends towards a patriarchal form as its development leads man to gain awareness of himself and to impose his will. But it is important to emphasise that even at times when he was still confused by the mysteries of Life, Nature and Woman, he never relinquished his power; when, terrified by the dangerous magic woman possesses, he posits her as the essential, it is he who posits her, and he who realises himself thereby as the essential in this alienation he grants; in spite of the fecund virtues that infuse her, man remains her master, just as he is master of the fertile earth; she is destined to be subordinated, possessed and exploited, as is also Nature, whose magic fertility she incarnates. The prestige she enjoys in the eyes of men comes from them; they kneel before the Other, they worship the Goddess Mother. But as powerful as she may appear, she is defined through notions created by the male consciousness. All of the idols invented by man, however terrifying he may have made them, are in fact dependent upon him, and this is why he is able to destroy them. In primitive societies, this dependence is not acknowledged and posited, but its existence is implicit, in itself: and it will readily become mediatory as soon as man develops a clearer consciousness of self, as soon as he dares to assert himself and stand in opposition. And in fact, even when man grasps himself as given, passive and subject to the vagaries of rain and sun, he still realises himself as transcendence, as project; already, spirit and will assert themselves within him against life's confusion and contingencies. The totem ancestor, of which woman assumes multiple incarnations, is more or less distinctly a male principle under its animal or tree name; woman perpetuates carnal existence, but her role is only that of nourisher, not of creator; in no domain whatsoever does she create; she maintains the life of the tribe by providing children and bread, nothing more; she lives condemned to immanence; she incarnates only the static aspect of society, closed in on itself. Meanwhile, man continues to monopolise the functions that open this society to nature and to the whole of humanity; the only efforts worthy of him are war, hunting or fishing; he conquers foreign prey and annexes it to the tribe; war, hunting and fishing represent an expansion of existence, his going beyond into the world; the male is still the only incarnation of transcendence. He does not yet have the practical means to totally dominate Woman-Earth, he does not yet dare stand up to her: but already he wants to tear himself away from her. I think the profound reason for the well-known custom of exogamy, so widespread in matrilineal societies, is to be found in this determination. Even though man is unaware of the role he plays in procreation, marriage has great importance for him; this is where he attains adult dignity and receives his share of a piece of the world; through his mother he is bound to the clan, his ancestors, and everything that constitutes his own subsistence; but in all of these secular functions – work or marriage – he aspires to escape this circle and assert transcendence against immanence, to open up a future different from the past where he is rooted; depending on the types of relations recognised in different societies, the banning of incest takes on different forms, but from primitive times to our days it has remained the same: man wishes to possess that which he *is* not; he unites himself to what appears to him to be Other than himself. The wife must not be part of the husband's mana, she must be foreign to him: thus foreign to his clan. Primitive marriage is sometimes founded on abduction, real or symbolic: because violence done to another is the clearest affirmation of another's alterity. Taking his wife by force, the warrior proves he is able to annex the riches of others and burst through the bounds of the destiny assigned to him at birth; purchasing her under various forms – paying tribute, rendering services – has, less dramatically, the same signification.*

Little by little, man mediated his experience, and in his representations, as in his practical existence, the male principle triumphed. Spirit prevailed over Life, transcendence over immanence, technology over magic, and reason over superstition. The devaluation of woman represents a necessary stage in the history of humanity: for she derived her prestige not from her positive value but from man's weakness; she incarnated disturbing natural mysteries: man escapes her grasp when he frees himself from nature. In passing from stone to bronze he is able to conquer the land through his work and conquer himself as well. The farmer is subjected to the vagaries of the soil, of germination and of seasons; he is passive, he beseeches and he waits: this explains why totem spirits peopled the human world; the peasant endured the whims of these forces that took possession of him. On the contrary, the worker fashions a tool according to his own design; he imposes on it the form that fits his project; facing an inert nature that defies him but that he overcomes, he asserts himself as sovereign will; if he quickens his strokes on the anvil, he quickens the completion of the tool, whereas nothing can hasten the ripening of grain; his responsibility develops with what he makes: his movement, adroit or maladroit, makes it or breaks it; careful, skilful, he brings it to a point of perfection he can be proud of: his success depends not on the favour of the gods but on himself; he challenges his fellow workers, he takes pride in his success; and while he still leaves some

---

* In Lévi-Strauss's thesis already cited, there is, in a slightly different form, a confirmation of this idea. What comes out of this study is that the prohibition of incest is in no way the primal factor underlying exogamy; but it reflects the positive desire for exogamy in a negative form. There is no intrinsic reason that it be improper for a woman to have intercourse with men in her clan; but it is socially useful that she be part of the goods by which each clan, instead of closing in on itself, establishes a reciprocal relationship with another clan: 'Exogamy has a value less negative than positive... it prohibits endogamous marriage... certainly not because a biological danger is attached to consanguineous marriage, but because exogamous marriage results in a social benefit.' The group should not for its own private purposes consume women who constitute one of its possessions, but should use them as an instrument of communication; if marriage with a woman of the same clan is forbidden, 'the sole reason is that she is *same* whereas she must (and therefore can) become *other*... the same women that were originally offered can be exchanged in return. All that is necessary on either side is the *sign of otherness*, which is the outcome of a certain position in a structure and not of any innate characteristic.'

place for rituals, applied techniques seem far more important to him; mystical values become secondary, and practical interests take precedence; he is not entirely liberated from the gods, but he distances himself by distancing them from himself; he relegates them to their Olympian heaven and keeps the terrestrial domain for himself; the great Pan begins to fade at the first sound of his hammer, and man's reign begins. He discovers his power. He finds cause and effect in the relationship between his creating arm and the object of his creation: the seed planted germinates or not, while metal always reacts in the same way to fire, to tempering and to mechanical treatment; this world of tools can be framed in clear concepts: rational thinking, logic and mathematics are thus able to emerge. The whole representation of the universe is overturned. Woman's religion is bound to the reign of agriculture, a reign of irreducible duration, contingencies, chance, anticipation and mystery; the reign of *Homo faber* is the reign of time that can be conquered like space, the reign of necessity, project, action and reason. Even when he contends with the earth, he will henceforth contend with it as a worker; he discovers that the soil can be fertilised, that it is good to let it lie fallow, that certain seeds should be treated certain ways: it is he who makes the crops grow; he digs canals, he irrigates or drains the land, he lays out roads, he builds temples: he creates the world anew. The peoples who remained under the heel of the Mother Goddess where matrilineal filiation was perpetuated were also those arrested in a primitive state of civilisation. Woman was venerated only inasmuch as man was a slave to his own fears, a party to his own impotence: it was out of fear and not love that he worshipped her. Before he could accomplish himself, he had to begin by dethroning her.* It is the male principle of creative force, light, intelligence and order that he will henceforth recognise as a sovereign. Standing beside the Mother Goddess emerges a god, a son, or a lover who is still inferior to her, but who looks exactly like her, and who is associated with her. He also incarnates the fertility principle: he is a bull, the Minotaur, or the Nile fertilising the plains of Egypt. He dies in autumn and is reborn in spring after the spouse-mother, invulnerable yet tearful, has devoted her forces to searching for his body and bringing him back to life. Appearing in Crete, this couple can also be found all

---

* Of course, this condition is necessary but not sufficient: there are patrilineal civilisations immobilised in a primitive stage; others, like the Mayas, regressed. There is no absolute hierarchy between societies of maternal right and those of paternal right: but only the latter have evolved technically and ideologically.

along the banks of the Mediterranean: Isis and Horus in Egypt, Astarte and Adonis in Phoenicia, Cybele and Attis in Asia Minor, and Rhea and Zeus in Hellenic Greece. And then the Great Mother was dethroned. In Egypt, where woman's condition is exceptionally favourable, the goddess Nout, incarnating the sky, and Isis, the fertile land, wife of the Nile, Osiris, continue to be extremely important; but it is nonetheless Ra, the sun god, virile light and energy, who is the supreme king. In Babylon, Ishtar is only the wife of Bel-Marduk; and it is he who created things and guaranteed harmony. The god of the Semites is male. When Zeus reigns in heaven, Gaea, Rhea and Cybele have to abdicate: all that is left to Demeter is a still imposing but secondary divinity. The Vedic gods have wives, but these are not worshipped as they are. The Roman Jupiter has no equal.*

Thus, the triumph of patriarchy was neither an accident nor the result of a violent revolution. From the origins of humanity, their biological privilege enabled men to affirm themselves alone as sovereign subjects; they never abdicated this privilege; they alienated part of their existence in Nature and in Woman; but they won it back afterwards; condemned to play the role of the Other, woman was thus condemned to possess no more than precarious power: slave or idol, it was never she who chose her lot. 'Men make gods and women worship them,' said Frazer; it is men who decide if their supreme divinities will be females or males; the place of woman in society is always the one they assign her; at no time has she imposed her own law.

Perhaps, however, if productive work had remained at the level of her strength, woman would have achieved the conquest of nature *with* man; the human species affirmed itself against the gods through male and female individuals; but she could not obtain the benefits of tools for herself. Engels only incompletely explained her decline: it is insufficient to say that the invention of bronze and iron profoundly modified the balance of productive forces and brought about women's inferiority; this

---

* It is interesting to note (according to H. Bégouën, *Journal of Psychology*, 1934) that in the Aurignacian period there were numerous statuettes representing women with overly emphasised sexual attributes: they are noteworthy for their plumpness and the size accorded to their vulvas. Moreover, grossly sketched vulvas on their own were also found in caves. In the Solutrean and Magdalenian epochs, these effigies disappear. In the Aurignacian, masculine statuettes are very rare, and there are never any representations of the male organ. In the Magdalenian epoch, some representations of vulvas are still found, though in small quantities, but a great quantity of phalluses was discovered.

inferiority is not in itself sufficient to account for the oppression she has suffered. What was harmful for her was that, not becoming a labour partner for the worker, she was excluded from the human *Mitsein*: that woman is weak and has a lower productive capacity does not explain this exclusion; rather, it is because she did not participate in his way of working and thinking and because she remained enslaved to the mysteries of life that the male did not recognise in her an equal; by not accepting her, once she kept in his eyes the dimension of *other*, man could only become her oppressor. The male will for expansion and domination transformed feminine incapacity into a curse. Man wanted to exhaust the new possibilities opened up by new technology: he called upon a servile workforce and he reduced his fellow man to slavery. Slave labour being far more efficient than work that woman could supply, she lost the economic role she played within the tribe. And in his relationship with the slave, the master found a far more radical confirmation of his sovereignty than the tempered authority he exercised on woman. Venerated and revered for her fertility, being *other* than man, and sharing the disquieting character of the *other*, woman, in a certain way, kept man dependent on her even while she was dependent on him; the reciprocity of the master–slave relationship existed *in the present* for her and it was how she escaped slavery. As for the slave, he had no taboo to protect him, being nothing but a servile man, not just different, but inferior: the dialectic of the slave–master relationship will take centuries to be actualised; within the organised patriarchal society, the slave is only a beast of burden with a human face: the master exercises tyrannical authority over him; this exalts his pride: and he turns it against the woman. Everything he wins, he wins against her; the more powerful he becomes, the more she declines. In particular, when he acquires ownership of land,* he also claims woman as property. Formerly he was possessed by *the* mana, by *the* earth: now he has *a* soul, *property*; freed from *Woman*, he now lays claim to *a* woman and a posterity of his own. He wants the family labour he uses for the benefit of his fields to be totally *his,* and for this to happen, the workers must belong to him: he subjugates his wife and his children. He must have heirs who will extend his life on earth because he bequeaths them his possessions, and who will give him in turn, beyond the tomb, the necessary honours for the repose of his soul. The cult of the domestic gods is superimposed on the constitution of private property, and the function of heirs is both economic and

* See Part One, Chapter 3.

mystical. Thus, the day agriculture ceases to be an essentially magic operation and becomes creative labour, man finds himself to be a generative force; he lays claim to his children and his crops at the same time.*

There is no ideological revolution more important in the primitive period than the one replacing matrilineal descent with agnation; from that time on, the mother is lowered to the rank of wet nurse or servant, and the father's sovereignty is exalted; he is the one who holds rights and transmits them. Apollo, in Aeschylus's *Eumenides*, proclaims these new truths: 'The mother is no parent of that which is called her child, but only nurse of the new-planted seed that grows. The parent is he who mounts. A stranger she preserves a stranger's seed, if no god interfere.'² It is clear that these affirmations are not the results of scientific discoveries; they are acts of faith. Undoubtedly, the experience of technical cause and effect from which man draws the assurance of his creative powers makes him recognise he is as necessary to procreation as the mother. Idea guided observation; but the latter is restricted to granting the father a role equal to that of the mother: it led to the supposition that, as for nature, the condition for conception was the encounter of sperm and menses; Aristotle's idea that woman is merely matter, and 'the principle of movement which is male in all living beings is better and more divine,' is an idea that expresses a will to power that goes beyond all of what is known. In attributing his posterity exclusively to himself, man frees himself definitively from subjugation by women, and he triumphs over woman in the domination of the world. Doomed to procreation and secondary tasks, stripped of her practical importance and her mystical prestige, woman becomes no more than a servant.

Men represented this triumph as the outcome of a violent struggle. One of the most ancient cosmologies, belonging to the Assyro-Babylonians, tells of their victory in a text that dates from the seventh century but that recounts an even older legend. The Sun and the Sea, Aton and Tiamat, gave birth to the celestial world, the terrestrial world and the great gods; but finding them too turbulent, they decided to destroy them; and Tiamat, the woman-mother, led the struggle against

* In the same way that woman was identified with furrows, the phallus was identified with the plough, and vice versa. In a drawing representing a plough from the Kassite period, there are traces of the symbols of the generative act; afterwards, the phallus-plough identity was frequently reproduced in art forms. The word *lak* in some Austro-Asian languages designates both phallus and plough. An Assyrian prayer addresses a god whose 'plough fertilised the earth'.

the strongest and most fine-looking of her descendants, Bel-Marduk; he, having challenged her in combat, killed her and slashed her body in two after a frightful battle; with one half he made the vault of heaven, and with the other the foundation for the terrestrial world; then he gave order to the universe and created humanity. In the *Eumenides* drama, which illustrated the triumph of patriarchy over maternal right, Orestes also assassinates Clytemnestra. Through these bloody victories, the virile force and the solar forces of order and light win over feminine chaos. By absolving Orestes, the tribunal of the gods proclaims he was the son of Agamemnon before being the son of Clytemnestra. The old maternal right is dead: the audacious male revolt killed it. But we have seen that in reality, the passage to paternal rights took place through gradual transitions. Masculine conquest was a reconquest: man only took possession of that which he already possessed; he put law into harmony with reality. There was neither struggle, nor victory, nor defeat. Nevertheless, these legends have profound meaning. At the moment when man asserts himself as subject and freedom, the idea of the Other becomes mediatory. From this day on, the relationship with the Other is a drama; the existence of the Other is a threat and a danger. The ancient Greek philosophy, which Plato, on this point, does not deny, showed that alterity is the same as negation, thus Evil. To posit the Other is to define Manichaeism. This is why religions and their codes treat woman with such hostility. By the time humankind reaches the stage of writing its mythology and laws, patriarchy is definitively established: it is males who write the codes. It is natural for them to give woman a subordinate situation; one might imagine, however, that they would consider her with the same benevolence as children and animals. But no. Afraid of woman, legislators organise her oppression. Only the harmful aspects of the ambivalent virtues attributed to her are retained: from sacred she becomes unclean. Eve, given to Adam to be his companion, lost humankind; to punish men, the pagan gods invent women, and Pandora, the firstborn of these female creatures, is the one who unleashes all the evil humanity endures. The Other is passivity confronting activity, diversity breaking down unity, matter opposing form, disorder resisting order. Woman is thus doomed to Evil. 'There is a good principle that created order, light and man and a bad principle that created chaos, darkness and woman,' says Pythagoras. The Laws of Manu define her as a vile being to be held in slavery. Leviticus assimilates her to beasts of burden, owned by the patriarch. The laws of Solon confer no rights on her. The Roman Code puts her in guardianship and proclaims her 'imbecility'. Canon law considers her 'the devil's gateway'. The Koran treats her with the most absolute contempt.

And yet Evil needs Good, matter needs the idea and night needs light. Man knows that to satisfy his desires, to perpetuate his existence, woman is indispensable to him; he has to integrate her in society: as long as she submits to the order established by males, she is cleansed of her original stain. This idea is forcefully expressed in the Laws of Manu: 'Whatever be the qualities of the man with whom a woman is united according to the law, such qualities even she assumes, like a river united with the ocean, and she is admitted after death to the same celestial paradise.' The Bible too praises the 'virtuous woman'. Christianity, in spite of its loathing of the flesh, respects the devoted virgin and the chaste and docile wife. Within a religious group, woman can even hold an important religious position: Brahmani in India and Flaminia in Rome are as holy as their husbands; in a couple, the man is dominant, but both male and female principles remain essential to the childbearing function, to life and to the social order.

This very ambivalence of the Other, of the Female, will be reflected in the rest of her history; until our times she will be subordinated to men's will. But this will is ambiguous: by total annexation, woman will be lowered to the rank of a thing; of course, man attempts to cover with his own dignity what he conquers and possesses; in his eyes the Other retains some of her primitive magic; one of the problems he will seek to solve is how to make his wife both a servant and a companion; his attitude will evolve throughout the centuries, and this will also entail an evolution in woman's destiny.*

---

* We will examine this evolution in the Western world. The history of the woman in the East, in India and in China was one of long and immutable slavery. From the Middle Ages to today, we will centre this study on France, where the situation is typical.

CHAPTER 3

Once woman is dethroned by the advent of private property, her fate is linked to it for centuries: in large part, her history is intertwined with the history of inheritance. The fundamental importance of this institution becomes clear if we keep in mind that the owner alienated his existence in property; it was more important to him than life itself; it goes beyond the strict limits of a mortal lifetime, it lives on after the body is gone, an earthly and tangible incarnation of the immortal soul; but this continued survival can occur only if property remains in the owner's hands: it can remain his after death only if it belongs to individuals who are extensions of himself and recognised, who are *his own*. Cultivating paternal lands and worshipping the father's spirit are one and the same obligation for the heir: to assure the survival of ancestors on earth and in the underworld. Man will not, therefore, agree to share his property or his children with woman. He will never really be able to go that far, but at a time when patriarchy is powerful, he strips woman of all her rights to hold and transmit property. It seems logical, in fact, to deny her these rights. If it is accepted that a woman's children do not belong to her, they inevitably have no link with the group the woman comes from. Woman is no longer passed from one clan to another through marriage: she is radically abducted from the group she is born into and annexed to her husband's; he buys her like a head of cattle or a slave, he imposes his domestic divinities on her: and the children she conceives belong to her spouse's family. If she could inherit, she would thus wrongly transmit her paternal family's riches to that of her husband: she is carefully excluded from the succession. But inversely, because she owns nothing, woman is not raised to the dignity of a person; she herself is part of man's patrimony, first her father's and then her husband's. Under a strictly patriarchal regime, a father can condemn to death his male and female children at birth; but in the case of a male child, society most often puts limits on this power: a normally constituted newborn male is allowed to live; whereas the custom of exposure is very wide-spread for girls; there was massive infanticide among Arabs: as soon as they were born, girls were thrown into ditches. Accepting a female child is an act of generosity on the father's part; the woman enters such societies only through a kind of grace bestowed on her, and not legitimately like males. In any case, the stain of birth is far more serious for the mother when a girl is born: among Hebrews, Leviticus demands twice as much cleansing as for a newborn boy. In societies where 'blood money' exists, only a small sum is required when the victim is of the feminine sex or a girl: her value compared with a male's is like a slave's with a free man's. When she is a young girl, the father has total power over her; on her marriage he transmits it entirely to her spouse. Since she is his property like the slave, the beast of burden, or the thing, it is natural for a man to have as many wives as he wishes; only economic reasons put limits on polygamy; the husband can disown his wives at whim, and society barely accords them any guarantees. In return, woman is subjected to rigorous chastity. In spite of the taboos, matriarchal societies allow great freedom of behaviour; prenuptial chastity is rarely demanded; and adultery not judged severely. On the contrary, when woman becomes man's property, he wants a virgin, and he demands total fidelity at the risk of severe penalty; it would be the worst of crimes to risk giving heritage rights to a foreign offspring: this is why the paterfamilias has the right to put a guilty wife to death. As long as private property lasts, conjugal infidelity on the part of a woman is considered a crime of high treason. All codes up to our time have perpetuated inequality in issues concerning adultery, arguing the seriousness of the fault committed by the woman who might bring an illegitimate child into the family. And though the right to take the law into one's own hands has been abolished since Augustus, the Napoleonic Code still holds out the promise of the jury's leniency for a husband who avenges himself. When woman belonged to both a patrilineal clan and a conjugal family, she was able to preserve a good amount of freedom, as the two series of bonds overlapped and even conflicted with each other and as each system served to support her against the other: for example, she could often choose the husband of her fancy, since marriage was only a secular event and had no effect on society's deep structure. But under the patriarchal regime, she was the property of a father who married her off as he saw fit; then attached to her husband's household, she was no more than his thing and the thing of the family (*genos*) in which she was placed.

When family and private patrimony incontestably remain the bases of society, woman also remains totally alienated. This is what has happened in the Muslim world. The structure is feudal in that there has never been a state strong enough to unify and dominate the numerous tribes: no power holds in check that of the patriarch chief. The religion that was created when the Arab people were warriors and conquerors professed the utmost disdain towards women. 'Men are superior to women on account of the qualities with which God has gifted the one above the other, and on account of the outlay they make from their substance for them,' says the Koran; the woman has never held real power or mystic prestige. The Bedouin woman works hard, she ploughs and carries burdens: this is how she sets up a reciprocal bond with her husband; she moves around freely, her face uncovered. The Muslim woman, veiled and shut in, is still today a kind of slave in most levels of society. I recall an underground cave in a troglodyte village in Tunisia where four women were squatting: the old, one-eyed and toothless wife, her face ravaged, was cooking dough on a small brazier surrounded by acrid smoke; two slightly younger but equally disfigured wives were rocking children in their arms; one was breast-feeding; seated before a weaver's loom was a young idol, magnificently dressed in silk, gold and silver, knotting strands of wool. Leaving this gloomy den – realm of immanence, womb and tomb – in the corridor leading up towards the light, I met the male, dressed in white, sparklingly clean, smiling, sunny. He was returning from the market, where he had bantered about world affairs with other men; he would spend a few hours in this retreat of his own, in the heart of this vast universe to which he belonged and from which he was not separated. For the old withered creatures, for the young bride doomed to the same degeneration, there was no other universe but the murky cave from which they would emerge only at night, silent and veiled.

The Jews of biblical times have more or less the same customs as the Arabs. The patriarchs are polygamous and can renounce their wives almost at whim; at the risk of harsh punishment, the young bride has to be delivered to her spouse as a virgin; in cases of adultery, she is stoned; she is confined to domestic labour, as the image of virtuous women demonstrates: 'She seeketh wool and flax . . . she riseth also while it is yet night . . . her candle goeth not off at night . . . she eateth not the bread of idleness.' Even chaste and industrious, she is impure and burdened with taboos; she cannot testify in court. Ecclesiastes treats her with the deepest disgust: 'And I find more bitter than death the woman, whose heart is snares and nets, and her hands as bands . . . one man among a thousand have I found; but a woman among all those have I not found.'[3] When her husband dies, custom and even law require her to marry a brother of the deceased.

This custom called levirate is found among many oriental peoples. In all regimes where woman is under guardianship, one of the problems is what to do with widows. The most radical solution is to sacrifice them on their husbands' tombs. But it is not true that even in India the law imposes such holocausts; the Laws of Manu permit a wife to survive a husband; spectacular suicides have never been more than an aristocratic fashion. It is far more frequent for the widow to be handed over to her husband's heirs. The levirate sometimes takes the form of polyandry; to avoid the ambiguities of widowhood, all the brothers in the family become the husbands of the woman, a custom that serves to preserve the clan against the possible infertility of the husband. According to a text of Caesar's, in Brittany all the men of one family had a certain number of women in common.

This form of radical patriarchy was not established everywhere. In Babylon, Hammurabi's Code recognised certain rights of woman: she receives a share of the paternal inheritance, and when she marries, her father provides her with a dowry. In Persia, polygamy is customary; woman is bound to absolute obedience to the husband her father chooses for her as soon as she is nubile; but she is more respected than among most Oriental peoples; incest is not forbidden, and marriage takes place frequently among sisters and brothers; she is in charge of educating the children up to the age of seven for boys and until marriage for girls. Woman can share in her husband's estate if the son proves himself unworthy; if she is a 'privileged wife', she is entrusted with the guardianship of minor children in the case of her husband's death and with the business management in the absence of an adult son. The rules of marriage clearly point out the importance posterity has for the head of a family. It is likely that there were five forms of marriage:* (1) The woman married with the consent of her parents; she was then called the 'privileged wife'; her children belonged to her husband. (2) When the woman was an only child, her firstborn would be given up to her parents to replace their daughter; then she would become a 'privileged wife'. (3) If a man died unmarried, his family would take a woman from outside, give her a dowry and marry her: she was called an 'adopted wife'; half of her children

* This account is taken from Clement Huart, *La Perse antique et la civilisation iranienne* (*Ancient Persia and Iranian Civilization*).

belonged to the deceased and the other half to the living husband. (4) A widow without children who remarried was called a servant wife: she owed half of the children of her second marriage to her deceased husband. (5) The woman who married without the consent of her parents could not inherit from them until the oldest son, coming of age, would give her to his father as a 'privileged wife'; if her husband died before, she was considered to be a minor and put under guardianship. The status of the adopted wife and the servant wife establishes the right of every man to be survived by descendants who are not necessarily connected by a blood relationship. This confirms what was said above; this relationship was in a way invented by man when he sought to annex for himself – beyond his finite life – immortality in this world and in the underworld.

In Egypt, woman's condition was the most favourable. When Goddess Mothers married, they maintained their standing; social and religious unity resides in the couple; woman is an ally, a complement to man. Her magic is so unthreatening that even the fear of incest is overcome, and no differentiation is made between a sister and a spouse.* She has the same rights as men, the same legal power; she inherits, and she owns property. This uniquely fortunate situation is in no way haphazard: it stems from the fact that in ancient Egypt the land belonged to the king and the higher castes of priests and warriors; for private individuals, landed property was only usufructuary; the land was inalienable, property transmitted by inheritance had little value, and there was no problem about sharing it. Because of this absence of personal patrimony, woman maintained the dignity of a person. She married whom she wanted, and as a widow she could remarry as she wished. The male practised polygamy, but although all of his children were legitimate, he had only one real wife, the only one associated with religion and linked to him legally: the others were mere slaves, deprived of all rights. The chief wife did not change status by marrying: she remained mistress of her possessions and was free to engage in contracts. When the pharaoh Bocchoris established private property, woman's position was too strong to be dislodged; Bocchoris opened the era of contracts, and marriage itself became contractual. There were three types of contract: one dealt with servile marriage; woman became man's thing, but she could specify that he would not have a concubine other than her; nonetheless, the legal spouse was considered equal to man and all their property was held in common; the husband would often agree to pay her a sum of money

---

* In some cases the brother *had to* marry his sister.

in the case of divorce. Later, this custom led to a type of contract remarkably favourable to women; the husband agreed to absolve her of her debt. There were serious punishments for adultery, but divorce was fairly open for the two spouses. The presence of contracts soundly restrained polygamy; women got possession of the wealth and transmitted it to their children, which brought about the creation of a plutocratic class. Ptolemy Philopator decreed that women could no longer alienate their property without marital authorisation, which kept them as eternal minors. But even in times when they had a privileged status, unique in the ancient world, they were not socially equal to men; taking part in religion and government, they could have the role of regent, but the pharaoh was male; priests and warriors were males; woman's role in public life was a secondary one; and in private life, fidelity was required of her without reciprocity.

The customs of the Greeks are very similar to oriental ones; yet they do not practise polygamy. No one knows exactly why. Maintaining a harem always entails heavy costs: only the ostentatious Solomon, the sultans from *The Thousand and One Nights*, kings, chiefs or rich property owners could afford the luxury of a vast seraglio; an ordinary man had to be satisfied with three or four women; a peasant rarely possessed more than two. Besides – except in Egypt where there was no specific landed property – the concern for preserving the patrimony intact led to granting the oldest son special rights on paternal inheritance; from this stemmed a hierarchy among women, the mother of the principal heir invested with dignity far superior to that of his other wives. If the wife herself has property of her own or if she is dowered, she is considered a person by her husband: he is joined to her by both a religious and an exclusive bond. From there on, the custom that only recognises one wife was undoubtedly established: but the reality was that the Greek citizen continued to be comfortably 'polygamous' since he could find the satisfaction of his desires from street prostitutes or gynaeceum servants. 'We have hetarias for spiritual pleasures,' says Demosthenes, 'concubines *(pallakes)* for sensual pleasure, and wives to give us sons.' The *pallakis* replaced the wife in the master's bed if she was ill, indisposed, pregnant or recovering from childbirth; so there was no great difference between a gynaeceum and a harem. In Athens, the wife is shut up in her quarters, held by law under severe constraint and watched over by special magistrates. She spends her whole life as a minor; she is under the control of her guardian: either her father, or her husband, or her husband's heir or, by default, the state, represented by public officials;

here are her masters, and they use her like merchandise, the guardian's control extending over both her person and her property; the guardian can transmit her rights as he wishes: the father gives his daughter up for adoption or in marriage; the husband can repudiate his wife and hand her over to another husband. But Greek law assures woman of a dowry used to support her and that must be restored in full to her if the marriage is dissolved; the law also authorises the woman to file for divorce in certain rare cases; but these are the only guarantees that society grants. Of course, all inheritance is bequeathed to the male children, and the dowry is not considered acquired property but a kind of duty imposed on the guardian. However, thanks to this dowry custom, the widow no longer passes for a hereditary possession in the hands of her husband's heirs: she returns to her family's guardianship.

One of the problems arising from societies based on agnation is the fate of inheritance in the absence of any male descendants. The Greeks had instituted the custom of *epiklerate*: the female heir had to marry her oldest relative in the paternal family *(genos)*; thus the property her father bequeathed to her would be transmitted to children belonging to the same group, and the estate remained the property of the paternal *genos*; the *epikleros* was not a female heir but only a machine to procreate a male heir; this custom placed her entirely at man's mercy as she was automatically handed over to the firstborn of her family's men, who most often turned out to be an old man.

Since the cause of women's oppression is found in the resolve to perpetuate the family and keep the patrimony intact, if she escapes the family, she escapes this total dependence as well; if society rejects the family by denying private property, woman's condition improves considerably. Sparta, where community property prevailed, was the only city-state where the woman was treated almost as the equal of man. Girls were brought up like boys; the wife was not confined to her husband's household; he was only allowed furtive nocturnal visits; and his wife belonged to him so loosely that another man could claim a union with her in the name of eugenics: the very notion of adultery disappears when inheritance disappears; as all the children belonged to the city as a whole, women were not jealously enslaved to a master: or it can be explained inversely, that possessing neither personal wealth nor individual ancestry, the citizen does not possess a woman either. Women underwent the burdens of maternity as men did war: but except for this civic duty, no restraints were put on their freedom.

Along with the free women just discussed and slaves living within

the *genos* – unconditionally owned by the family head – are the prostitutes found in Greece. Primitive people were familiar with hospitality
prostitution, turning over a woman to a guest passing through, which
undoubtedly had mystical explanations; and with sacred prostitution,
intended for the common good by releasing the mysterious forces of
fertility. These customs existed in classical antiquity. Herodotus reports
that in the fifth century BC, every woman in Babylon had to give herself
once in her life to a stranger in the Temple of Mylitta for a coin she
contributed to the temple's coffers; she then returned home to live in
chastity. Religious prostitution has continued to our day among Egyptian
almahs and Indian *bayadères* who make up respectable castes of musicians and dancers. But most often, in Egypt, India and western Asia,
sacred prostitution slipped into legal prostitution, the priestly class finding
this trade profitable. There were venal prostitutes even among the
Hebrews. In Greece, especially along the coast or in the islands where
many foreigners stopped off, temples of 'young girls hospitable to
strangers', as Pindar called them, could be found: the money they earned
was intended for religious establishments, that is, for priests and indirectly for their maintenance. In reality, in a hypocritical way, sailors' and
travellers' sexual needs – in Corinth and other places – were exploited;
and this was already venal prostitution. Solon was the one who turned
this into an institution. He bought Asian slaves and shut them up in
dicterions located in Athens near the temple of Venus, not far from the
port, under the management of *pornotropos* in charge of the financial
administration of the establishment; each girl received wages, and the
net profit went to the state. After that, *kapaileia*, private establishments,
were opened: a red Priapus served as their display sign. Soon, in
addition to slaves, poor Greek women were taken in as residents. The
dicterions were considered so necessary that they were recognised as in-
violable places of asylum. Nonetheless, courtesans were marked with
infamy, they had no social rights, and their children were exempted from
providing for them; they had to wear specific outfits made of multi-
coloured cloth decorated with flower bouquets, and their hair was dyed
with saffron. Besides the women shut up in *dicterions*, there were free
courtesans, who could be placed in three categories: *dicteriads*, much like
today's registered prostitutes; *auletrids*, who were dancers and flute
players, and hetaeras, demimondaines who often came from Corinth
having had official liaisons with high-ranking Greek men and who played
the social role of modern-day 'worldly women'. The first ones were
found among freed women or lower-class Greek girls; exploited by

procurers, they led a pitiful life. The second type succeeded in getting rich thanks to their musical talent: the most famous of all was Lamia, mistress of Ptolemy of Egypt, then of his vanquisher, the king of Macedonia, Demetrius Poliorcetes. As for the last category, many were well known for sharing in the glory of their lovers. Disposing of themselves and their fortunes freely, intelligent, cultivated and artistic, they were treated like persons by the men who were captivated by their charms. And because they escaped from their families, because they lived on the margins of society, they also escaped men: they could seem to be their counterparts, almost their equals. In Aspasia, in Phryne and in Lais, the superiority of the free woman asserted itself over the virtuous mother of a family.

These brilliant exceptions aside, the Greek woman is reduced to semi-slavery; she does not even have the freedom to complain: Aspasia and the more passionate Sappho are barely able to make a few grievances heard. In Homer, there are still remnants of the heroic period when women had some power: still, the warriors roundly send them off to their chambers. The same scorn is found in Hesiod: 'He who confides in a woman confides in a thief.' In the great classical period, woman is resolutely confined to the gynaeceum. 'The best woman is she of whom men speak the least,' said Pericles. Plato, who proposed admitting a council of matrons to the Republic's administration and giving girls a liberal education, is an exception; he provoked Aristophanes' raillery; to a woman who questions him about public affairs, a husband responds, in *Lysistrata*: 'This is none of your business. Shut up, or you'll be beaten . . . go back to your weaving.' Aristotle expresses the common point of view in declaring that woman is woman because of a deficiency, that she must live closed up at home and obey man. 'The slave is entirely deprived of the freedom to deliberate; woman does have it, but she is weak and powerless,' he states. According to Xenophon, a woman and her spouse are complete strangers to each other: 'Are there people you communicate with less than your wife? – There are not many'; all that is required of a woman in *Oeconomicus* is to be an attentive, prudent, economical housewife, busy as a bee, a model of organisation. The modest status to which women are reduced does not keep the Greeks from being deeply misogynous. In the seventh century BC, Archilochus writes biting epigrams against women; Simonides of Amorgos says, 'Women are the greatest evil God ever created: if they sometimes seem useful, they soon change into trouble for their masters.' For Hipponax: 'There are but two days in life when your wife brings you joy: her wedding day and her funeral.' But it is the Ionians who, in Miletus's stories, are the most spiteful: for example, the tale of the matron of Ephesus. Mostly women are attacked for being lazy, shrewish or spendthrift, in fact precisely the absence of the qualities demanded of them. 'There are many monsters on the earth and in the sea, but the greatest is still woman,' wrote Menander. 'Woman is a pain that never goes away.' When the institution of the dowry brought a certain importance to women, it was her arrogance that was deplored; this is one of Aristophanes' – and notably Menander's – familiar themes. 'I married a witch with a dowry. I took her for her fields and her house, and that, O Apollo, is the worst of evils . . . !' 'Damn him who invented marriage and then the second, the third, the fourth and the rest who followed them.' 'If you are poor and you marry a rich woman, you will be reduced to being both a slave and poor.' The Greek woman was too closely controlled to be attacked for her conduct; and it was not the flesh in her that was vilified. It was more the responsibilities and duties of marriage that weighed on men; this leads to the supposition that in spite of her rigorous conditions, and although she had almost no recognised rights, she must have held an important place in the household and enjoyed some authority; doomed to obedience, she could disobey; she could bombard her husband with tantrums, tears, nagging and insults; marriage, meant to enslave woman, was a ball and chain for the husband as well. In the character of Xanthippe are embodied all the grievances of the Greek citizen against the shrewish wife and the adversities of conjugal life.

The conflict between family and state defines the history of the Roman woman. The Etruscans constituted a matrilineal filiation society and it is probable that at the time of the monarchy Rome still practised exogamy linked to a matriarchal regime: the Latin kings did not transmit power through heredity. What is certain is that after Tarquinius's death, patriarchy asserts itself: agricultural property and the private estate – thus the family – become society's nucleus. Woman will be strictly subservient to the patrimony and thus to the family group: laws deprive her of even those guarantees accorded to Greek women; she lives her life in powerlessness and servitude. She is, of course, excluded from public affairs and prohibited from any 'masculine office'; she is a perpetual minor in civil life. She is not directly deprived of her paternal inheritance but, through circuitous means, is kept from using it: she is put under the authority of a guardian. 'Guardianship was established in the interest of the guardians themselves,' said Gaius, 'so that woman – of whom they are the presumptive heirs – could not rob them of their inheritance with a will, nor diminish the inheritance by alienations or debts.' Woman's first guardian is her father; in his absence, paternal male relatives fulfil that function. When the woman marries, she passes 'into the hands' of her husband; there are three types of marriage: the *confarreatio*, where the spouses offer a spelt cake to the Capitoline Jupiter in the presence of the *flamen dialis*; the *coemptio*, a fictitious sale in which the plebeian father 'mancipated' his daughter to her husband; and the *usus*, the result of a cohabitation of one year; all three were with *manu*, meaning that the male spouse replaces the father or his male relatives; his wife is considered one of his daughters, and he thenceforth has complete power over her person and her property. But from the time of the Law of the Twelve Tables, because the Roman woman belonged to both paternal and conjugal clans, conflicts arose, giving rise to her legal emancipation. As a result, the *manu* marriage dispossesses her male agnates. To defend the paternal relatives' interests, *sine manu* marriage comes into being; in this case, the woman's property remains under the guardians' control, and the husband's rights are only over her person; and even this power is shared with the paterfamilias, who keeps his daughter under his absolute authority. The family court is in charge of settling disputes arising between father and husband: such an institution gives the woman recourse from her father to her husband or from her husband to her father; she is not one individual's thing. Moreover, although a gens is very powerful – as the existence of this court proves – independent of public courts, the father, as head of the family, is above all a citizen: his authority is unlimited, he rules absolutely over wife and children; but they are not his property; rather he administers their existence for the public good; the woman, who brings his children into the world and whose domestic duties often extend to agricultural tasks, is very useful to the country and deeply respected. Here is an important fact that recurs throughout history: abstract rights cannot sufficiently define the concrete situation of woman; this situation depends in great part on the economic role she plays; and very often, abstract freedom and concrete powers vary inversely. Legally more enslaved than the Greek woman, the Roman is more deeply integrated in society; at home she sits in the atrium which is the centre of the domicile, rather than being relegated to the gynaeceum; it is she who presides over the slaves' work; she oversees the children's education, and her influence on them often extends to an advanced age; she shares her husband's work and his concerns, she is considered a co-owner of his property; the marriage formula: '*Ubi tu Gaius, ego*

Gaia'[4] is not an empty formula; the matron is called 'domina'; she is mistress of the home, associate in religion, not a slave but man's companion; the tie that unites her to him is so sacred that in five centuries not one divorce is recorded. She is not confined to her quarters: she is present at meals and celebrations, she goes to the theatre; men give her right-of-way on the street, consuls and lictors stand aside for her. Legend accords her an eminent role in history: those of the Sabine women, Lucretia, and Virginia are well known; Coriolanus yields to the supplications of his mother's and wife's pleas; the law of Licinius consecrating the triumph of Roman democracy is said to have been inspired by his wife; Cornelia forges the soul of the Gracchi. 'Everywhere men govern women,' said Cato, 'and we who govern all men are governed by our women.'

Little by little the legal situation of Roman women adapts to their practical situation. During the patrician oligarchy, each paterfamilias is an independent ruler within the Republic; but when state power becomes established, it opposes the concentration of wealth and the arrogance of powerful families. Family courts bow to public justice. And woman acquires ever greater rights. Four powers originally limited her freedom: the father and the husband controlled her person, her guardian and *manus* her property. The state takes authority over the opposition of father and husband to restrict their rights: the state court will now rule over adultery cases, divorce, and so on. In the same way, guardians and *manus* destroy each other. In the interest of the guardian, the *manus* had already been separated from marriage; later, the *manus* becomes an expedient that women use to escape their guardians, either by contracting fictitious marriages or by securing obliging guardians from their father or from the state. Under imperial legislation, guardianship will be entirely abolished. Woman simultaneously gains a positive guarantee of her independence: her father is obliged to provide her with a dowry; and it will not go back to the agnates after the marriage's dissolution, nor does it ever belong to her husband; a woman can at any moment demand restitution by a sudden divorce, which puts man at her mercy. 'In accepting the dowry, he sold his power,' said Plautus. From the end of the Republic on, the mother's right to her children's respect was recognised as equal to the father's; she is granted custody of her children in case of guardianship or of the husband's bad conduct. When she had three children and the deceased had no heirs, a Senate decree, under Hadrian, entitled her to an *ab intestat* succession right for each of them. And under Marcus Aurelius the Roman family's evolution was completed: from 178 on, the mother's children become her heirs, over her male relatives; from then on, the family is based on *coniunctio sanguinis* and the mother is equal to the father; the daughter inherits like her brothers.

Nevertheless, the history of Roman law shows a tendency that contradicts the one just described: rendering the woman independent of the family, the central power takes her back under its guardianship and subjects her to various legal restraints.

In fact, she would assume an unsettling importance if she could be both rich and independent; so what is conceded with one hand is taken away from her with the other. The Oppian law that banned luxury was voted when Hannibal threatened Rome; when the danger passed, women demanded its abrogation; in a famous speech, Cato asked that it be upheld: but a demonstration by matrons assembled in the public square carried the repeal against him. More severe laws were proposed as mores loosened, but without great success: they did little more than give rise to fraud. Only the Velleian Senate decree triumphed, forbidding woman to 'intercede' for others,* depriving her of nearly every legal capacity. It is when woman is probably the most emancipated that the inferiority of her sex is proclaimed, a remarkable example of the male justification process already discussed: when her rights as girl, wife or sister are no longer limited, she is refused equality with men because of her sex; the pretext for persecuting her becomes 'imbecility and fragility of the sex'.

The fact is that matrons did not put their newfound freedom to the best use; but it is also true that they were forbidden to take the best advantage of it. These two contradictory strains – an individualistic strain that tears woman from the family and a state-controlled strain that abuses her as an individual – result in an unbalanced situation for her. She can inherit, she has equal rights with the father concerning the children, she can will her property thanks to the institution of the dowry, she escapes conjugal restraints, she can divorce and remarry as she wishes: but she is emancipated only in a negative way because she is offered no employment for her vital forces. Economic independence remains abstract since it yields no political capacity; therefore, lacking the power to *act*, Roman women *demonstrate*: they cause a ruckus in towns, they besiege the courts, they brew, they foment plots, they lay down prescriptions, they inflame civil wars, they march along the Tiber carrying the statue of the Mother of the Gods, thus introducing Oriental divinities to Rome; in the year 114

* That is, to enter into contracts with another.

the scandal of the vestal virgins breaks out, and their college is then
disbanded. As public life and virtue are out of reach, and when the dissolution of the family renders the former private virtues useless and
outdated, there is no longer any moral code for women. They have two
choices: either to respect the same values as their grandmothers; or to
no longer recognise any. The end of the first century and beginning of
the second see numerous women living as companions and partners of
their spouses, as in the time of the Republic: Plotina shares the glory
and responsibilities of Trajan; Sabina becomes so famous for her good
deeds that statues deify her while she is still alive; under Tiberius, Sextia
refuses to live on after Aemilius Scaurus and Pascea to live on after
Pomponius Labeus; Paulina opens her veins at the same time as Seneca;
Pliny the Younger makes Arria's 'Paete, non dolet' famous; Martial
admires the irreproachable wives and devoted mothers Claudia Rufina,
Virginia and Sulpicia. But numerous women refuse motherhood, and
many women divorce; laws continue to ban adultery: some matrons even
go so far as to register as prostitutes to avoid being constrained in their
debaucheries.* Until then, Latin literature had always respected women:
then satirists went wild against them. They attacked, in fact, not women
in general but mainly contemporary women. Juvenal reproaches their
hedonism and gluttony; he accuses them of aspiring to men's professions: they take an interest in politics, they immerse themselves in court
cases, debate with grammarians and rhetoricians, develop passions for
hunting, chariot racing, fencing and wrestling. But in fact they rival men
mainly because of their own taste for amusement and vice; they lack
sufficient education for higher aims; and besides, no objective is even
proposed to them; action remains forbidden to them. The Roman woman
of the ancient Republic has a place on earth, but she is still chained to
it by lack of abstract rights and economic independence; the Roman
woman of the decline is typical of false emancipation, possessing, in a
world where men are still the only masters, nothing but empty freedom:
she is free 'for nothing'.

---

* Rome, like Greece, officially tolerated prostitution. There were two categories of courtesans: those living closed up in brothels, and others, *bonae meretrices*, freely exercising
their profession. They did not have the right to wear the clothing of matrons; they had
a certain influence on fashion, customs and art, but they never held a position as lofty
as the hetaeras of Athens.

CHAPTER 4

The evolution of the feminine condition was not a continuous process. With the great invasions, all of civilisation is put into question. Roman law itself is under the influence of a new ideology, Christianity; and in the centuries that follow, barbarians impose their laws. The economic, social and political situation is overturned: and women's situation suffers the consequences.

Christian ideology played no little role in women's oppression. Without a doubt, there is a breath of charity in the Gospels that spread to women as well as to lepers; poor people, slaves and women are the ones who adhere most passionately to the new law. In the very early days of Christianity, women who submitted to the yoke of the Church were relatively respected; they testified along with men as martyrs; but they could nonetheless worship only in secondary roles; deaconesses were authorised only to do lay work: caring for the sick or helping the poor. And although marriage is considered an institution demanding mutual fidelity, it seems clear that the wife must be totally subordinate to the husband: through St Paul the fiercely antifeminist Jewish tradition is affirmed. St Paul commands self-effacement and reserve from women; he bases the principle of subordination of women to man on the Old and New Testaments. 'The man is not of the woman; but the woman of the man'; and 'Neither was man created for the woman; but the woman for the man.' And elsewhere: 'For the husband is the head of the wife, even as Christ is the head of the church.' In a religion where the flesh is cursed, the woman becomes the devil's most fearsome temptation. Tertullian writes: 'Woman! You are the devil's gateway. You have convinced the one the devil did not dare to confront directly. It is your fault that God's Son had to die. You should always dress in mourning and rags.' St Ambrose: 'Adam was led to sin by Eve and not Eve by Adam. It is right and just that he whom she led into sin, she shall receive as master.' And St John Chrysostom: 'Of all the wild animals, none can be found as harmful as woman.' When canon law is written in the fourth century, marriage is treated as a concession to human failings, incompatible with Christian perfection. 'Take up the hatchet and cut the roots of the sterile tree of marriage,' writes St Jerome. In the time of Gregory VI, when celibacy was imposed on priests, woman's dangerous character was more harshly asserted: all the Fathers of the Church proclaim her wretchedness. St Thomas will remain true to this tradition, declaring that woman is only an 'occasional' and incomplete being, a sort of failed man. 'Man is the head of woman just as Christ is the head of man,' he writes. 'It is a constant that woman is destined to live under the authority of man and has no authority of her own.' Thus, the only marriage regime canon law recognises is by dowry, rendering woman helpless and powerless. Not only is she prohibited from male functions, but she is also barred from making court depositions, and her testimony holds no weight. The emperors are more or less under the influence of the Church Fathers; Justinian's legislation honours woman as spouse and mother but subjugates her to those functions; her helplessness is not due to her sex but to her situation within the family. Divorce is prohibited and marriage has to be a public event; the mother has the same authority over her children as the father and she has equal rights to their inheritance; if her husband dies, she becomes their legal tutor. The Velleian Senate decree is modified: from that time on she can intercede for the benefit of a third party; but she cannot contract for her husband; her dowry becomes inalienable; it is her children's patrimony and she is forbidden to dispose of it.

In barbarian-occupied territories, these laws are juxtaposed with Germanic traditions. The German customs were unique. They had chiefs only in wartime; in peacetime the family was an autonomous society; it seemed to be midway between matrilineal filiation clans and patriarchal gens; the mother's brother had the same power as the father and the same authority over their niece and daughter as her husband. In a society where all capacity was rooted in brute force, woman was entirely powerless; but the rights that were guaranteed to her by the twofold domestic powers on which she depended were recognised; subjugated, she was nonetheless respected; her husband purchased her, but the price of this purchase constituted a dowry that belonged to her; and besides, her father dowered her; she received her portion of the paternal inheritance and, in the case of parents being murdered, a portion of the fine paid by the murderer. The family was monogamous, adultery being severely punished and marriage respected. The woman still lived under wardship, but she was a close partner of her husband. 'In peace and in war, she shares his lot; she lives with him, she dies with him,' says Tacitus. She went to war with him, brought food to the soldiers and encouraged them by her presence. As a widow, part of her deceased husband's power was transmitted to her. Since her incapacity was rooted in her physical frailty, it was not considered an expression of moral inferiority. Some women were priestesses and prophets, so it could be assumed that their education was superior to men's. Among the objects that legally reverted to women in questions of inheritance were, later, jewellery and books.

This is the tradition that continues into the Middle Ages. The woman is absolutely dependent on her father and husband: during Clovis's time, the *mundium*[5] weighs on her throughout her life; but the Franks rejected Germanic chastity: under the Merovingians and Carolingians polygamy reigns; the woman is married without her consent and can be repudiated by her husband, who holds the right of life or death over her according to his whim. She is treated like a servant. Laws protect her but only inasmuch as she is the man's property and the mother of his children. Calling her a prostitute without having proof is considered an insult liable to a fine fifteen times more than any insult to a man; kidnapping a married woman is equivalent to a free man's murder; taking a married woman's hand or arm is liable to a fine of 15 to 35 sous; abortion is forbidden under threat of a 100-sou fine; murder of a pregnant woman costs four times that of a free man; a woman who has proved herself fertile is worth three times a free man; but she loses all worth when she can no longer be a mother; if she marries a slave, she becomes an outlaw and her parents have the right to kill her. She has no rights as an individual. But while the state is becoming powerful, the shift that had occurred in Rome occurs here as well: the wardship of the disabled, children and women no longer belongs to family law but becomes a public office; starting from Charlemagne, the *mundium* that weighs down the woman belongs to the king; he only intervenes at first in cases in which the woman is deprived of her natural guardians; then, little by little, he confiscates the family powers; but this change does not bring about the Frank woman's emancipation. The *mundium* becomes the guardian's responsibility; his duty is to protect his ward: this protection brings about the same slavery for woman as in the past.

When feudalism emerges out of the convulsions of the early Middle Ages, woman's condition looks very uncertain. What characterises feudal law is the confusion between sovereign and property law, between public and private rights. This explains why woman is both put down and raised

up by this system. She first finds herself denied all private rights because
she lacks political capacity. Until the eleventh century, order is based on
force alone and property on armed power. A fief, legal experts say, is
'property held against military service'; woman cannot hold feudal property because she is incapable of defending it. Her situation changes when
fiefs become hereditary and patrimonial; in Germanic law some aspects
of maternal law survived, as has already been shown: if there were no
male heirs, the daughter could inherit. This leads, around the eleventh
century, to the feudal system's acceptance of female succession. However,
military service is still required of the vassals; and woman's lot does not
improve with her ability to inherit; she still needs a male guardian; the
husband plays that role: he is invested with the title, holds the fief and
has the usufruct of the goods. Like the Greek *epikleros*, woman is the
instrument and not the bearer through which the domain is transmitted;
that does not emancipate her; in a way she is absorbed by the fief, she
is part of the real property. The domain is no longer the family's thing
as it was for Roman gens: it is the lord's property, and the woman also
belongs to the lord. He is the one who chooses a spouse for her; when
she has children, she gives them to him rather than to her husband: they
will be vassals who will defend his property. She is therefore a slave of
the domain and of its master through the 'protection' of a husband who
was imposed on her: few periods of history seem harsher for woman's
lot. An heiress means land and a château: suitors fight over this prey and
the girl is sometimes not even twelve years old when her father or his
lord gives her to some baron as a gift. The more marriages, the more
domains for a man; and thus the more repudiations; the Church hypocritically authorises them; as marriage was forbidden between relatives
up to the seventh degree, and as kinship was defined by spiritual relations such as godmother and godfather as well as by blood relations,
some pretext or other can always be found for an annulment; many
women in the eleventh century were repudiated four or five times. Once
widowed, the woman immediately has to accept a new master. In the
chansons de geste Charlemagne has, all at once, the widows of his barons
who had died in Spain remarry; in *Girard de Vienne*, the Burgundy duchess
goes herself to the king to demand a new spouse. 'My husband has just
died, but what good is mourning? Find me a powerful husband because
I need to defend my land'; many epics show the king or lord dealing
tyrannically with girls and widows. One also sees the husband treating
the woman given to him as a gift without any respect; he abuses and
slaps her, drags her by her hair and beats her; all that Beaumanoir in

Coutumes de Beauvaisis (*Customs of Beauvaisis*) asks is that the husband 'punish his wife reasonably'. This warlike civilisation has only scorn for women. The knight is not interested in women: his horse is a treasure of much higher value to him; in the epics, girls are always the ones to make the first step towards young men; once married, they alone are expected to be faithful; the man dissociates them from his life. 'Cursed be the knight who takes counsel from a lady on when to joust.' And in Renaud de Montauban, there is this diatribe: 'Go back into your painted and golden quarters, sit ye down in the shade, drink, eat, embroider, dye silk, but do not busy yourself with our affairs. Our business is to fight with the sword and steel. Silence!' The woman sometimes shares the males' harsh life. As a girl, she excels in all physical exercises, she rides, hunts, hawks; she barely receives any education and is raised with no regard for modesty: she welcomes the château's guests, takes care of their meals and baths, and she 'pleasures' them to sleep; as a woman, she some-times has to hunt wild animals, undertake long and difficult pilgrimages; when her husband is far away, it is she who defends the seigneury. These ladies of the manor, called viragoes, are admired because they behave exactly like men: they are greedy, treacherous, cruel, and they tyrannise their vassals. History and legend have bequeathed the memory of several of them: the chatelaine Aubie, after having a tower built higher than any donjon, then had the architect's head cut off so her secret would be kept; she chased her husband from his domain: he stole back and killed her. Mabel, Roger de Montgomerie's wife, delighted in reducing her seigneury's nobles to begging: their revenge was to decapitate her. Juliane, bastard daughter of Henry I of England, defended the château of Breteuil against him, luring him into an ambush for which he punished her severely. Such acts remain exceptional, however. Ordinarily, the lady spent her time spin-ning, praying for the dead, waiting for her spouse, and being bored.

It has often been claimed that courtly love, born in the twelfth century in the Mediterranean south of France, brought about an improvement in woman's lot. There are several opposing hypotheses as to its origins: according to some people, 'courtliness' comes from the lord's relations with his young vassals; others link it to Cathar heresies and the cult of the Virgin; still others say that profane love derives from the love of God in general. It is not so sure that courts of love ever existed. What is sure is that faced with Eve the sinner, the Church comes to glorify the Mother of the Redeemer: she has such a large following that in the thirteenth century it can be said that God was made woman; a mysticism of woman thus develops in religion. Moreover, leisure in château life enables the

noble ladies to promote and nurture the luxury of conversation, politeness and poetry; women of letters such as Béatrice de Valentinois, Eleanor
of Aquitaine and her daughter Marie de France, Blanche de Navarre and
many others attract and patronise poets; first in the Midi and then in
the North culture thrives, giving women new prestige. Courtly love was
often described as platonic; Chrétien de Troyes, probably to please his
protector, banishes adultery from his novels: the only guilty love he
depicts is that of Lancelot and Guinevere; but in fact, as the feudal husband
was both a guardian and a tyrant, the wife sought a lover outside of
marriage; courtly love was a compensation for the barbarity of official
customs. 'Love in the modern sense does not exist in antiquity except
outside of official society,' notes Engels: at the very point where antiquity broke off its penchant for sexual love, the Middle Ages took it
up again with adultery. And this is the form that love will take as long
as the institution of marriage lasts.

While courtly love might ease woman's lot, it does not modify it
substantially. Ideologies like religion and poetry do not lead to female
liberation; woman gains a little ground at the end of the feudal age for
other reasons entirely. When the supremacy of royal power is imposed
on feudatories, the lord loses a large part of his rights: his right, in particular, to decide on his vassals' marriages is progressively suppressed; at
the same time, the feudal lord loses the use of his ward's property; the
benefits attached to wardship fall into disuse; and when the service of
the fief is converted to a monetary fee, wardship itself disappears; woman
was unable to perform military service, but she was as capable as a man
of paying the financial obligations; the fief is then little more than a
simple patrimony and there is no longer any reason for the two sexes
not to be placed on an equal footing. In fact, women in Germany,
Switzerland and Italy remain subjected to a perpetual wardship; but
France accepts, in Beaumanoir's words, that 'a girl is worth a man'.
Germanic tradition gave women a defender as a guardian; when she no
longer needs a defender, she goes without a guardian; as a sex, she is no
longer taxed with incapacity. Unmarried or widowed, she has all the
rights of man; property grants her sovereignty: she governs the fief that
she owns, meaning she dispenses justice, signs treaties and decrees laws.
She is even seen playing a military role, commanding troops, taking part
in fighting; before Joan of Arc there were women soldiers and, however
surprising La Pucelle is, she is not shocking.

Nonetheless, so many factors converge to thwart woman's independence that they are never all abolished simultaneously; physical weakness is no longer an issue; but feminine subordination remains useful to society in cases where the woman is married. Thus marital power outlives the feudal regime. The paradox still being perpetuated today is established: the woman most fully integrated into society is the one with the fewest privileges in the society. In civil feudality, marriage has the same features as in military feudality: the husband remains the wife's guardian. When the bourgeoisie is formed, it observes the same laws. In common law as in feudal law, the only emancipation is outside marriage; the daughter and the widow have the same capacities as the man; but by marrying, the woman falls under the husband's guardianship and administration; he can beat her; he watches over her behaviour, relations and correspondence, and disposes of her fortune, not through a contract, but by the very fact of marriage. 'As soon as the marriage is consummated,' Beaumanoir says, 'the possessions of each party are held in common by virtue of the marriage and the man is the guardian of them.' It is in the interest of property that the nobility and the bourgeoisie demand one master to administer it. The wife is not subordinated to the husband because she is judged basically incapable: when nothing else prevents it, woman's full capacities are recognised. From feudality to today, the married woman is deliberately sacrificed to private property. It is important to see that the greater the property owned by the husband, the greater this servitude: the propertied classes are those in which woman's dependence has always been the most concrete; even today, the patriarchal family survives among rich landowners; the more socially and economically powerful man feels, the more he plays the paterfamilias with authority. On the contrary, shared destitution makes the conjugal link reciprocal. Neither feudality nor the Church enfranchised woman. Rather, it was from a position of servitude that the patriarchal family moved to an authentically conjugal one. The serf and his wife owned nothing; they simply had the common use of their house, furniture and utensils: man had no reason to want to become master of woman who owned nothing; but the bonds of work and interest that joined them raised the spouse to the rank of companion. When serfdom is abolished, poverty remains; in small rural communities and among artisans, spouses live on an equal footing; woman is neither a thing nor a servant: those are the luxuries of a rich man; the poor man experiences the reciprocity of the bond that attaches him to his other half; in freely contracted work, woman wins concrete autonomy because she has an economic and social role. The farces and *fabliaux* of the Middle Ages reflect a society of artisans, small merchants and peasants in which the husband's only privilege over his wife is to be able to beat her: but she pits craftiness against force to reestablish equality. However, the rich woman pays for her idleness with submission.

In the Middle Ages, the woman still retained some privileges: she took part in local meetings in the villages, she participated in the primary meetings for the deputies' election to the Estates-General; her husband could exercise his own authority only over movables: his wife's consent was necessary to alienate real estate. The sixteenth century sees the codification of the laws perpetuated throughout the ancien régime; by that time feudal habits and customs had totally disappeared, and nothing protects women from men's claims that they should be chained to the household. The influence of Roman law, so condescending for women, can be perceived here; as in Roman times, the violent diatribes against the stupidity and fragility of the sex were not at the root of the code but are used as justifications; it is after the fact that men find reasons to act as it suits them. 'Among all the bad characteristics that women possess,' one reads in the *Songe du verger*,[6]

> I find that there are nine principal ones: To begin with, a woman hurts herself as a result of her own nature; second, women are by nature extremely stingy; third, they are driven by sudden whims; fourth, they are bad by their own volition; fifth, they are impostors. Women are known to be false and according to civil law a woman may not be accepted as a witness to a will. A woman always does the opposite of what she is commanded to do ... Women accuse themselves willingly and announce their own vituperation and shame. They are crafty and malicious. St Augustine said that 'A woman is a beast who is neither firm nor stable'; she is hateful, to the confusion of her husband; she nourishes wrongdoing and stands at the beginning of all the pleas and tensions; and is the path and road of all iniquity.

Similar texts abound around this time. The interest of this one is that each accusation is meant to justify one of the provisions of the code against women and the inferior situation in which they are kept. Naturally, any 'male office' is forbidden to them; the Velleian decree of the Senate is reinstated, depriving them of all civil capacity; birthright and masculine privilege place them second in line for the paternal inheritance. Unmarried, the daughter remains under the father's guardianship; if he does not marry her off, he generally sends her to a convent. An unwed mother has the right to seek out the father, but such a right merely provides for the costs of lying-in and the infant's food; a married woman becomes subject to the husband's authority: he determines the place of residence, directs the household, repudiates the adulteress wife, shuts her up in a monastery, or later obtains a *lettre de cachet*[7] to send her to the Bastille; no deed is valid without his authorisation; everything the wife brings to the marriage becomes part of the dowry in the Roman meaning of the word; but as marriage is indissoluble, the husband has to die before the wife can recover her property, giving rise to the adage: *Uxor non est proprie socia sed speratur fore.*[8] As she does not manage her capital, although she has rights to it, she does not have the responsibility for it; it does not provide any substance to her action: she has no concrete grasp on the world. Even her children belong to the father rather than to her, as in the time of the *Eumenides*: she 'gives' them to her spouse, whose authority is far greater than hers and who is the real master of her posterity; even Napoleon will use this argument, declaring that just as a pear tree is the property of the owner of the pears, the wife is the property of the man to whom she provides children. The status of the French wife remains as such throughout the ancien régime; little by little jurisprudence will abolish the Velleian decree, but not until the Napoleonic Code does it disappear definitively. The husband is responsible for the wife's debts as well as her behaviour, and she is accountable to him alone; she has almost no direct relations with public authorities or autonomous relations with anyone outside her family. She looks more like a servant in work and motherhood than an associate: objects, values and human beings that she creates are not her own property but her family's, that is, man's, as he is the head. Her situation is far from being more liberal in other countries – it is, on the contrary, less liberal; some maintained guardianship; and in all of them, the married woman's capacities are nonexistent and moral standards strict. All the European codes were drafted on the basis of canon, Roman and Germanic law, all were unfavourable to the woman, and all the countries recognised private property and the family, deferring to the demands of these institutions.

In all these countries, one of the consequences of the 'honest wife's' servitude to the family is prostitution. Hypocritically kept on society's fringes, prostitutes fill a highly important role. Christianity pours scorn on them but accepts them as a necessary evil. 'Getting rid of the prostitutes', said St Augustine, 'will trouble society by dissoluteness.' Later, St Thomas – or at least the theologian that signed his name to Book IV of *De regimine principium* – asserted: 'Remove public women from society and debauchery will disrupt it by disorder of all kinds. Prostitutes are to a city what a cesspool is to a palace: get rid of the cesspool and the palace will become an unsavoury and loathsome place.' In the early Middle Ages, moral licence was such that women of pleasure were hardly necessary; but when the bourgeois family became institutionalised and monogamy rigorous, man obviously had to go outside the home for his pleasure.

In vain did one of Charlemagne's capitularies vigorously forbid it, in vain did St Louis order prostitutes to be chased out of the city in 1254 and brothels to be destroyed in 1269: in the town of Damietta, Joinville tells us, prostitutes' tents were adjacent to the king's. Later, attempts by Charles IX of France and Marie-Thérèse of Austria in the eighteenth century also failed. The organisation of society made prostitution necessary. 'Prostitutes', Schopenhauer would pompously say later, 'are human sacrifices on the altar of monogamy.' And Lecky, a historian of European morality, expressed the same idea: 'Supreme type of vice, prostitutes are the most active guardians of virtue.' Their situation and the Jews' were often rightly compared:* usury and money lending were forbidden by the Church exactly as extra-conjugal sex was; but society can no more do without financial speculators than free love, so these functions fell to the damned castes: they were relegated to ghettos or reserved neighbourhoods. In Paris, loose women worked in pens where they arrived in the morning and left after the curfew had tolled; they lived on special streets and did not have the right to stray, and in most other cities brothels were outside town walls. Like Jews, they had to wear distinctive signs on their clothes. In France the most common one was a specific-coloured aiguillette hung on the shoulder; silk, fur, and honest women's apparel were often prohibited. They were *by law* taxed with infamy, had no recourse whatsoever to the police and the courts, and could be thrown out of their lodgings on a neighbour's simple claim. For most of them, life was difficult and wretched. Some were closed up in public houses. Antoine de Lalaing, a French traveller, left a description of a Spanish establishment in Valencia in the late fifteenth century. 'The place', he said, was

> about the size of a small city, surrounded by walls with only one
> door. And in front of it there were gallows for criminals that might
> be inside; at the door, a man appointed to this task takes the canes

---

* 'Those coming to Sisteron by the Peipin passage, like the Jews, owed a toll of five sols to the ladies of Sainte-Claire' (Bahutaud).

of those wishing to enter and tells them that if they want to hand over their money, and if they have the money, he will give it to the porter. If it is stolen overnight, the porter will not answer for it. In this place there are three or four streets full of small houses, in each of which are prettily and cleanly dressed girls in velvet and satin. There are almost three hundred of them; their houses are well kept and decorated with good linens. The decreed price is four pennies of their money, which is the equivalent of our gros . . . There are taverns and cabarets. It is not easy to recognise these houses by daylight, while at night or in the evening the girls are seated at their doorways, with pretty lamps hanging near them in order to make it easier to see them at leisure. There are two doctors appointed and paid by the town to visit the girls every week in order to discover if they have any disease or intimate illness. If the town is stricken with any sickness, the lords of the place are required to maintain the girls at their expense and the foreigners are sent away to any place they wish to go.*[9]

The author even marvels at such effective policing. Many prostitutes lived freely; some of them earned their living well. As in the period of the courtesans, high gallantry provided more possibilities for feminine individualism than the life of an 'honest woman'.

A condition unique to France is that of the unmarried woman; legal independence is in stark and shocking contrast to the wife's servitude; she is an oddity and so customs hasten to withdraw everything law grants her; she has total civil capacity: but those laws are abstract and empty; she has no economic autonomy, no social dignity, and generally the spinster remains hidden in the shadow of the paternal family or finds others like her behind convent walls: there she knows no other form of freedom but disobedience and sin – just as decadent Roman women were emancipated only by vice. Negativity continues to be women's lot as long as their emancipation remains negative.

In such conditions it is clear how rare it was for a wife to act or merely to make her presence felt: among the working classes, economic oppression cancels out sexual inequality; but it deprives the individual of opportunities; among the nobility and bourgeoisie, the wife is abused because of her sex; she has a parasitic existence; she is poorly educated; she needs exceptional circumstances if she is to envisage and carry out any concrete

* De Reiffenberg, *Dictionary of Conversation*. 'Women and Girls of the Low Life'.

project. Queens and regents have that rare good fortune: their sovereignty exalts them above their sex; French Salic law denies women the right of access to the throne; but they sometimes play a great role beside their husbands or after their deaths: for example, St Clotilda, St Radegunda and Blanche de Castille. Convent life makes woman independent of man: some abbesses wield great power; Héloïse gained fame as an abbess as much as a lover. In the mystical, thus autonomous, relation that binds them to God, feminine souls draw their inspiration and force from a virile soul; and the respect society grants them enables them to undertake difficult projects. Joan of Arc's adventure is something of a miracle: and it is, moreover, a very brief adventure. But St Catherine of Siena's story is meaningful; she creates a great reputation in Siena for charitable activity and for the visions that testify to her intense inner life within a very normal existence; she thus acquires the necessary authority for success generally lacking in women; her influence is invoked to hearten those condemned to death, to bring back to the fold those who are lost, to appease quarrels between families and towns. She is supported by the community that recognises itself in her, which is how she is able to fulfil her pacifying mission, preaching submission to the pope from city to city, carrying on a vast correspondence with bishops and sovereigns, and finally chosen by Florence as ambassador to go and find the pope in Avignon. Queens, by divine right, and saints, by their shining virtues, are assured of support in the society that allows them to be men's equal. Of others, a silent modesty is required. The success of a Christine de Pizan is due to exceptional luck: even so, she had to be widowed and burdened with children for her to decide to earn her living by her pen.

Altogether, men's opinion in the Middle Ages is not favourable to women. Courtly poets did exalt love; many codes of courtly love appear, such as André le Chapelain's poem and the famous *Roman de la Rose*,[10] in which Guillaume de Lorris encourages young men to devote themselves to the service of ladies. But against this troubadour-inspired literature are pitted bourgeois-inspired writings that cruelly attack women: fabliaux, farces and plays criticise women for their laziness, coquetry and lust. Their worst enemies are the clergy. They incriminate marriage. The Church made it a sacrament and yet prohibited it for the Christian elite: this is the source of the contradiction of the *querelle des femmes*.[11] It is denounced with singular vigour in *The Lamentations of Matheolus*, famous in its time, published fifteen years after the first part of the *Roman de la Rose*, and translated into French one hundred years later.

Matthew lost his 'clergy' by taking a wife; he cursed his marriage, cursed women and marriage in general. Why did God create woman if there is this incompatibility between marriage and clergy? Peace cannot exist in marriage: it had to be the devil's work; or else God did not know what he was doing. Matthew hopes that woman will not rise on Judgment Day. But God responds to him that marriage is a purgatory thanks to which heaven is reached; and carried to the heavens in a dream, Matthew sees a legion of husbands welcoming him to the shouts of 'Here, here the true martyr!' Jean de Meung, another cleric, is similarly inspired; he enjoins young men to get out from under the yoke of women; first he attacks love:

> Love is hateful country
> Love is amorous hate.

He attacks marriage that reduces man to slavery, that dooms him to be cuckolded; and he directs a violent diatribe against woman. In return, woman's champions strive to demonstrate her superiority. Here are some of the arguments apologists for the weaker sex drew on until the seventeenth century:

> Mulier perfetur viro scilicet. Materia: quia Adam factus est de limo terrae, Eva de costa Adae. Loco: quia Adam factus est extra paradisum, Eva in paradiso. In conceptione: quia mulier concepit Deum, quid homo non potuit. Apparicione: quia Christus apparuit mulieri post mortem resurrectionem, scilicet Magdalene. Exaltatione: quia mulier exaltata est super chorus angelorum, scilicet beata Maria . . .*

To which their opponents replied that if Christ first appeared to women, it is because he knew they were talkative and he was in a hurry to make his resurrection known.

The quarrel continues throughout the fifteenth century. The author of *Fifteen Joys of Marriage* indulgently describes the misfortunes of poor husbands. Eustache Deschamps writes an interminable poem on the

---

* 'Woman is superior to man, namely: *Materially*: because Adam was made of clay, Eve from one of Adam's ribs. *In terms of place*: because Adam was created outside of paradise, Eve in paradise. *In terms of conception*: because woman conceived God, something man couldn't do. *In terms of appearance*: because Christ after his death appeared to a woman, namely Magdalene. *In terms of glorification*: because a woman was glorified above the choir of angels, namely blessed Mary.'

same theme. It is here that the 'quarrel of the *Roman de la Rose*' begins.
This is the first time a woman takes up her pen to defend her sex:
Christine de Pizan attacks the clerics energetically in *The Epistle to the
God of Love*. The clerics rise up immediately to defend Jean de Meung;
but Gerson, chancellor of the University of Paris, takes Christine's side;
he writes his treatise in French to reach a wide public. Martin le Franc
throws the indigestible *Ladies' Chaperon* – still being read two hundred
years later – on to the battlefield. And Christine intervenes once again.
Her main demand is for women's right to education: 'If the custom were
to put little girls in school and they were normally taught sciences like
the boys, they would learn as perfectly and would understand the
subtleties of all the arts and sciences as they do.'

In truth this dispute concerns women only indirectly. No one dreams
of demanding a social role for them other than what they are assigned.
It is more a question of comparing the life of the cleric to the state of
marriage; it is a masculine problem brought up by the Church's
ambiguous attitude to marriage. Luther settles this conflict by rejecting
the celibacy of priests. Woman's condition is not influenced by this literary
war. While railing against society as it is, the satire of farces and fabliaux
does not claim to change it: it mocks women but does not plot against
them. Courtly poetry glorifies femininity: but such a cult does not in
any way imply the assimilation of the sexes. The *querelle* is a secondary
phenomenon in which society's attitude is reflected but which does not
modify it.

It has already been said that the wife's legal status remained practically
unchanged from the early fifteenth century to the nineteenth century;
but in the privileged classes her concrete condition does change. The
Italian Renaissance is a period of individualism propitious to the
burgeoning of strong personalities, regardless of sex. There were some
women at that time who were powerful sovereigns, like Jean d'Aragon,
Joan of Naples and Isabella d'Este; others were adventurer *condottieri*
who took up arms like men: thus Girolamo Riario's wife fought for
Forli's freedom; Hippolyta Fioramenti commanded the Duke of Milan's
troops and during the siege of Pavia led a company of noblewomen to
the ramparts. To defend their city against Montluc, Sienese women
marshalled three thousand troops commanded by women. Other Italian
women became famous thanks to their culture or talents: for example,
Isotta Nogarola, Veronica Gambara, Gaspara Stampa, Vittoria Colonna
who was Michelangelo's friend, and especially Lucrezia Tornabuoni,

mother of Lorenzo and Giuliano de' Medici, who wrote, among other things, hymns and a life of St John the Baptist and the Virgin. A majority of these distinguished women were courtesans; joining free moral behaviour with freethinking, ensuring their economic autonomy through their profession, many were treated by men with deferential admiration; they protected the arts and were interested in literature and philosophy, and they themselves often wrote or painted: Isabella da Luna, Catarina di San Celso, and Imperia, who was a poet and musician, took up the tradition of Aspasia and Phryne. For many of them, though, freedom still takes the form of licence: the orgies and crimes of these great Italian ladies and courtesans remain legendary.

This licence is also the main freedom found in the following centuries for women whose rank or fortune liberates them from common morality; in general, it remains as strict as in the Middle Ages. As for positive accomplishments, they are possible only for a very few. Queens are always privileged: Catherine de Medici, Elizabeth of England and Isabella the Catholic are great sovereigns. A few great saintly figures are also worshipped. The astonishing destiny of St Teresa of Avila is explained approximately in the same way as St Catherine's: her self-confidence is inspired by her confidence in God; by carrying the virtues connected with her status to the highest, she garners the support of her confessors and the Christian world: she is able to emerge beyond a nun's ordinary condition; she founds and runs monasteries, she travels, takes initiatives, and perseveres with a man's adventurous courage; society does not thwart her; even writing is not effrontery: her confessors order her to do it. She brilliantly shows that a woman can raise herself as high as a man when, by an astonishing chance, a man's possibilities are granted to her.

But in reality such possibilities are very unequal; in the sixteenth century, women are still poorly educated. Anne of Brittany summons many women to the court, where previously only men had been seen; she strives to form a retinue of girls of honour: but she is more interested in their upbringing than in their culture. Among women who a little later distinguish themselves by their minds, intellectual influence and writings, most are noblewomen: the duchess of Retz, Mme de Lignerolle, the Duchess of Rohan and her daughter Anne; the most famous were princesses: Queen Margot and Margaret de Navarre. Pernette du Guillet seems to have been a bourgeois; but Louise Labé is undoubtedly a courtesan: in any case, she felt free to behave unconventionally.

Women in the seventeenth century will continue to distinguish themselves essentially in intellectual spheres; social life and culture are spreading; women play a considerable role in salons; by the very fact they are not involved in the construction of the world, they have the leisure to indulge in conversation, the arts and literature; they are not formally educated, but through discussions, readings and instruction by private preceptors or public lectures, they succeed in acquiring greater knowledge than their husbands: Mlle de Gournay, Mme de Rambouillet, Mlle de Scudéry, Mme de La Fayette and Mme de Sévigné enjoy great reputations in France; and outside France similar renown is associated with the names of Princess Elisabeth, Queen Christine and Mlle de Schurman who corresponded with the whole scholarly world. Thanks to this culture and the ensuing prestige, women manage to encroach on the masculine universe; from literature and amorous casuistry many ambitious women slide towards political intrigue. In 1623 the papal nuncio wrote: 'In France all the major events, all the important plots, most often depend on women.' The princesse de Condé foments the 'women's conspiracy'; Anne of Austria readily takes the advice of the women surrounding her; Richelieu lends an indulgent ear to the duchesse d'Aiguillon; the roles played by Mme de Montbazon, the duchesse de Chevreuse, Mlle de Montpensier, the duchesse de Longueville, Anne de Gonzague and many others in the Fronde are well known. Lastly, Mme de Maintenon is a brilliant example of the influence a skilful woman adviser could wield on state affairs. Organisers, advisers and schemers, women assure themselves of a highly effective role by oblique means: the princesse des Ursins in Spain governs with more authority but her career is brief. Alongside these great noblewomen, a few personalities assert themselves in a world that escapes bourgeois constraints; a hith-erto unknown species appears: the actress. The presence of a woman on stage is noted for the first time in 1545; in 1592 there is still only one; at the beginning of the sixteenth century most of them are actors' wives; they then become more and more independent both onstage and in their private lives. As far as the courtesan is concerned, after being Phryne or Imperia, she finds her highest incarnation in Ninon de Lenclos: from capitalising on her femininity, she surpasses it; from living among men, she takes on virile qualities; her independent moral behaviour disposes her to independent thinking: Ninon de Lenclos brought freedom to the highest point a woman could at that time.

In the eighteenth century, woman's freedom and independence continue to grow. Customs remained strict in principle: girls receive no more than a cursory education; they are married off or sent to a convent without being consulted. The bourgeoisie, the rising class that is being consolidated, imposes a strict morality on the wife. But on the other hand, with the nobility breaking up, the greatest freedom of behaviour is possible for women of the world, and even the *haute bourgeoisie* is contaminated by these examples; neither convent nor conjugal home can contain the woman. Once again, for the majority of women, this freedom remains negative and abstract: they limit themselves to the pursuit of pleasure. But those who are intelligent and ambitious create avenues for action for themselves. Salon life once again blossoms: the roles played by Mme Geoffrin, Mme du Deffand, Mlle de Lespinasse, Mme d'Epinay, and Mme de Tencin are well known; protectors and inspiration, women make up the writer's favourite audience; they are personally interested in literature, philosophy and sciences: like Mme du Châtelet, for example, they have their own physics workshops or chemistry laboratory; they experiment; they dissect; they intervene more actively than ever before in political life: one after the other, Mme de Prie, Mme de Mailly, Mme de Châteauneuf, Mme de Pompadour and Mme du Barry govern Louis XV; there is barely a minister without his Egeria, to such a point that Montesquieu thinks that in France everything is done by women; they constitute, he says, 'a new state within the state'; and Collé writes on the eve of 1789: 'They have so taken over Frenchmen, they have subjugated them so greatly that they think about and feel only for themselves.' Alongside society women there are also actresses and prostitutes who enjoy great fame: Sophie Arnould, Julie Talma and Adrienne Lecouvreur.

Throughout the ancien régime the cultural domain is the most accessible to women who try to assert themselves. Yet none reached the summits of a Dante or a Shakespeare; this can be explained by the general mediocrity of their condition. Culture has never been the privilege of any but the feminine elite, never of the masses; and masculine geniuses often come from the masses; even privileged women encountered obstacles that barred their access to the heights. Nothing stopped the ascent of a St Teresa, a Catherine of Russia, but a thousand circumstances conspired against the woman writer. In her small book, A *Room of One's Own*, Virginia Woolf enjoyed inventing the destiny of Shakespeare's supposed sister; while he learned a little Latin, grammar and logic in school, she was closed up at home in total ignorance; while he poached, ran around in the countryside and slept with local women, she was mending kitchen towels under her parents' watchful eyes; if, like him, she bravely left to seek her fortune in London, she could not become an actress earning her living freely: either she would be brought back to her family and married off by force; or, seduced, abandoned and dishonoured, she would commit suicide out of despair. She could also be imagined as a happy prostitute, a Moll Flanders, as Daniel Defoe portrayed her: but she would never have run a theatre and written plays. In England, Virginia Woolf notes, women writers always engender hostility. Dr Johnson compared them to 'a dog's walking on his hinder legs. It is not done well; but you are surprised to find it done at all.' Artists care about what people think more than anyone else; women narrowly depend on it: it is easy to imagine how much strength it takes for a woman artist simply to dare to carry on regardless; she often succumbs in the fight. At the end of the seventeenth century, Lady Winchilsea, a childless noblewoman, attempts the feat of writing; some passages of her work show she had a sensitive and poetic nature; but she was consumed by hatred, anger and fear:

> Alas! A woman that attempts the pen,
> Such an intruder on the rights of men,
> Such a presumptuous creature is esteemed,
> The fault can by no virtue be redeemed.[12]

Almost all her work is filled with indignation about woman's condition. The Duchess of Newcastle's case is similar; also a noblewoman, she creates a scandal by writing. 'Women live like cockroaches or owls, they die like worms,' she furiously writes. Insulted and ridiculed, she had to shut herself up in her domain; and in spite of a generous temperament and going half-mad, she produced nothing more than wild imaginings. It is not until the eighteenth century that a bourgeois widow, Mrs Aphra Behn,[13] lived by her pen like a man; others followed her example, but even in the nineteenth century they were often obliged to hide; they did not even have a 'room of their own'; that is, they did not enjoy material independence, one of the essential conditions for inner freedom.

As has already been seen, because of the development of social life and its close link to intellectual life, French women's situation is a little more favourable. Nevertheless, people are largely hostile to the blue-stockings. During the Renaissance, noblewomen and intellectuals inspire a movement in favour of their sex; Platonic doctrines imported from Italy spiritualise love and woman. Many well-read men strive to defend her. The Ship of Virtuous Ladies,[14] The Ladies' Chevalier, and so on were published. Erasmus in *The Little Senate* gives the floor to Cornelia who unabashedly details the grievances of her sex. 'Men are tyrants . . . They treat us like toys . . . they make us their launderers and cooks.' Erasmus demands that women be allowed to have an education. Cornelius Agrippa, in a very famous work, *Declamation on the Nobility and Preeminence of the Female Sex*,[15] devotes himself to showing feminine superiority. He takes up the old cabbalistic arguments: Eve means Life and Adam Earth. Created after man, woman is more finished then he. She is born in paradise, he outside. When she falls into the water, she floats; man sinks. She is made from Adam's rib and not from earth. Her monthly cycles cure all illnesses. Eve merely wandered in her ignorance, whereas Adam sinned, which is why God made Himself a man: moreover, after his resurrection He appeared to women. Then Agrippa declares that women are more virtuous than men. He lists 'virtuous women' that the sex can take pride in, which is also a commonplace of these praises. Lastly, he mounts an indictment of male tyranny: 'Acting against divine right and violating natural law with impunity, the tyranny of men has deprived women of the freedom they receive at birth.' Yet she engenders children; she is as intelligent and even subtler than man; it is scandalous that her activities are limited, 'undoubtedly done not by God's order, nor by necessity or reason, but by the force of usage, by education, work and principally by violence and oppression'. He does not, of course, demand sexual equality, but wants woman to be treated with respect. The work was immensely successful; there is also *The Impregnable Fort*,[16] another in praise of woman; and *The Perfect Friend*[17] by Héroët, imbued with Platonic mysticism. In a curious book introducing Saint-Simonian doctrine, Postel announces the coming of a new Eve, the regenerating mother of humankind: he thinks he has even met her; she is dead and she is perhaps reincarnated in him. With more moderation, Marguerite de Valois, in her *Learned and Subtle Discourse*[18] proclaims that there is something divine in woman. But the writer who best served the cause of her sex was Margaret de Navarre, who proposed an ideal of sentimental mysticism and chastity without prudery to counter licentiousness, attempting to reconcile marriage and love for women's honour with happiness. Women's opponents do not, of course, give up. Among others, *Controversies over the Masculine and Feminine Sexes*,[19] in response to Agrippa, puts forward the old medieval arguments. Rabelais has a good time in *The Third Book*[20] satirising marriage in the tradition of Mathieu and Deschamps: however, it is women who lay down the law in the privileged abbey of Thélème. Antifeminism becomes virulent once again in 1617, with the *A Discourse*

of Women, Shewing Their Imperfections Alphabetically,[21] by Jacques Olivier;
the cover pictures an engraving of a woman with a harpy's hands, covered
with the feathers of lust and perched on her feet, because, like a hen,
she is a bad housewife: under every letter of the alphabet is one of her
defects. Once more it was a man of the Church who rekindled the old
quarrel; Mlle de Gournay answered back with *Equality of Men and Women*.[22]
This is followed by a quantity of libertine literature, including *Parnassus
and Satyrical Cabinets*,[23] that attacks women's moral behaviour, while the
holier-than-thous quoting Paul, the Church Fathers and Ecclesiastes drag
them down. Woman provided an inexhaustible theme for the satires of
Mathurin Régnier and his friends. In the other camp, the apologists outdo
themselves in taking up and commenting on Agrippa's arguments. Father
du Boscq in *The Honest Woman*[24] calls for women to be allowed to be
educated. The *Astrée* and a great quantity of courtly literature praise their
merits in rondeaux, sonnets, elegies, and such.

Even the successes women achieved were cause for new attacks; *The
Pretentious Young Ladies* set public opinion against them; and a bit later
The Learned Ladies[25] are applauded. Molière is not, however, woman's
enemy: he vigorously attacks arranged marriages, he demands freedom
for young girls in their love lives and respect and independence for the
wife. On the other hand, Bossuet does not spare them in his sermons.
The first woman, he preaches, is 'only a part of Adam and a kind of
diminutive. Her mind is about the same size.' Boileau's satire against
women is not much more than an exercise in rhetoric but it raises an
outcry: Pradon, Regnard and Perrault counterattack violently. La Bruyère
and Saint-Evremond take the part of women. The period's most determined feminist is Poulain de la Barre who in 1673 publishes a Cartesian-
inspired work, *On the Equality of the Two Sexes*.[26] He thinks that since
men are stronger, they favour their sex and women accept this dependence out of custom. They never had their chances: in either freedom or
education. Thus they cannot be judged by what they did in the past.
Nothing indicates their inferiority to men. Anatomy reveals differences,
but none of them constitutes a privilege for the male. And Poulain de
la Barre concludes with a demand for a solid education for women.
Fontenelle writes the *Conversations on the Plurality of Worlds*[27] for women.
And while Fénelon, following Mme de Maintenon and Abbot Fleury,
puts forward a very limited educational programme, the Jansenist
academic Rollin wants women to undertake serious studies.

The eighteenth century is also divided. In 1744, the author of the
Controversy over Woman's Soul[28] declares that 'woman created uniquely for

man will cease to be at the end of the world because she will cease to be useful for the object for which she had been created, from which follows necessarily that her soul is not immortal.' In a slightly less radical way, Rousseau is the spokesman of the bourgeoisie and dooms woman to her husband and motherhood. 'All the education of women should be relative to men . . . Woman is made to yield to man and to bear his injustices,' he asserts. However, the democratic and individualist ideal of the eighteenth century is favourable to women; for most philosophers they are human beings equal to those of the strong sex. Voltaire denounces the injustice of their lot. Diderot considers their inferiority largely *made* by society. 'Women, I pity you!' he writes. He thinks that 'In all customs the cruelty of civil laws makes common cause with the cruelty of nature against women. They have been treated as idiot beings.' Montesquieu, paradoxically, believes that women should be subordinate to man in the home but that everything predisposes them to political action. 'It is against reason and against nature for women to be mistresses in the house . . . but not for them to govern an empire.' Helvétius shows that woman's inferiority is created by the absurdity of her education; d'Alembert is of the same opinion. Economic feminism timidly makes its appearance through a woman, Mme de Ciray.* But it is Mercier almost alone in his *Tableau de Paris* who rises up against the destitution of women workers and tackles the fundamental question of women's work. Condorcet wants women to enter political life. He considers them man's equals and defends them against classic attacks: 'Women are said . . . not to have their own feeling of justice, that they listen to their feelings more than to their conscience . . . [But] it is not nature, it is education, it is the social existence that causes this difference.' And elsewhere: 'The more women have been enslaved by laws, the more dangerous their empire has been . . . It would lessen if women had less interest in keeping it, if it ceased being for them the sole means of defending themselves and escaping oppression.'

---

* The name Ciray is untraceable. Emilie Du Châtelet and Voltaire lived and worked in the Château de Cirey from 1734 to 1749, giving rise to some speculation about the possibility of a misspelling or an erroneous transcription from the original manuscript of the name Ciray. But there is no conclusive evidence of this.

CHAPTER 5

The Revolution might have been expected to change the fate of woman. It did nothing of the kind. This bourgeois revolution respected bourgeois institutions and values; and it was waged almost exclusively by men. It must be pointed out that during the entire ancien régime working-class women as a sex enjoyed the most independence. A woman had the right to run a business and she possessed all the necessary capacities to exercise her trade autonomously. She shared in production as linen maid, laundress, burnisher, shopgirl, and so on; she worked either at home or in small businesses; her material independence allowed her great freedom of behaviour: a woman of modest means could go out, go to taverns, and control her own body almost like a man; she is her husband's partner and his equal. She is oppressed on an economic and not on a sexual level. In the countryside, the peasant woman plays a considerable role in rural labour; she is treated like a servant; often she does not eat at the same table as her husband and sons; she toils harder and the burdens of maternity add to her fatigue. But as in old farming societies, since she is necessary to man, he respects her for it; their goods, interests and concerns are shared; she enjoys great authority in the home. From within their difficult lives, these women could have asserted themselves as individuals and demanded their rights; but a tradition of timidity and submission weighed on them: the Estates-General *cahiers* record an insignificant number of feminine claims, limited to: 'Men should not engage in trades that are the prerogative of women.' And it is true that women are found alongside their men in demonstrations and riots: they are the ones who go to Versailles to find 'the baker, the baker's wife, and the baker's little boy'.[29] But it is not the people who led the Revolution and reaped its fruits. As for bourgeois women, a few rallied ardently to the cause of freedom: Mme Roland, Lucile Desmoulins and Théroigne de Méricourt; one of them, Charlotte Corday, significantly influenced the outcome when she assassinated Marat. There were a few feminist movements. In 1791, Olympe de Gouges proposed a 'Declaration of the Rights of Woman and the Female Citizen' equivalent to the 'Declaration of the Rights of Man', demanding that all masculine privileges be abolished. In 1790 the same ideas are found in *Poor Javotte's Motion*[30] and in other similar lampoons; but in spite of Condorcet's support, these efforts are abortive and Olympe perishes on the scaffold. In addition to *L'Impatient*, the newspaper she founded, a few other short-lived papers appear. Women's clubs merge for the most part with men's and are taken over by them. On 28 Brumaire 1793, when actress Rose Lacombe, president of the Society of Republican and Revolutionary Women, along with a delegation of women, forces the doors of the Conseil Général, the prosecutor Chaumette pronounces words in the assembly that could be inspired by St Paul and St Thomas: 'Since when are women allowed to renounce their sex and become men? . . . [Nature] has told woman: Be a woman. Childcare, household tasks, sundry motherhood cares, those are your tasks.' Women are banned from entering the Conseil and soon even from the clubs where they had learned their politics. In 1790, the rights of the firstborn and of masculine privilege were eliminated; girls and boys became equals regarding succession; in 1792 divorce law was established, relaxing strict marital ties; but these were feeble conquests. Bourgeois women were too integrated into the family to find concrete grounds for solidarity with each other; they did not constitute a separate caste capable of forcing their demands: on an economic level, they existed as parasites. Thus, while women could have participated in events in spite of their sex, they were prevented by their class, and those from the agitating class were condemned to stand aside because they were women. When economic power falls into the hands of the workers, it will then be possible for the working woman to gain the capacities that the parasitic woman, noble or bourgeois, never obtained.

During the liquidation of the Revolution woman enjoys an anarchic freedom. But when society is reorganised, she is rigidly enslaved again. From the feminist point of view, France was ahead of other countries; but for the unfortunate modern French woman, her status was determined during a military dictatorship; the Napoleonic Code, which sealed her fate for a century, greatly held back her emancipation. Like all military leaders, Napoleon wants to see woman solely as a mother; but, heir to a bourgeois revolution, he does not intend to demolish the social structure by giving the mother priority over the wife: he prohibits the querying of paternity; he sets down harsh conditions for the unwed mother and the illegitimate child. Yet the married woman herself does not find recourse in her dignity as mother; the feudal paradox is perpetuated. Girls and wives are deprived of citizens' rights, prohibiting them from functions such as the practice of law or wardship. But the unmarried woman enjoys her civil role fully while marriage preserves the *mundium*. Woman owes *obedience* to her husband; he can have her confined in cases of adultery and obtain a divorce from her; if he kills the guilty wife when caught in the act, he is excusable in the eyes of the law; the husband, on the other hand, receives an infraction only if he brings a concubine into the home, and this is the only ground that would allow his wife to divorce him. Man decides where they will live, and he has many more rights over the children than the mother; and – except in cases where the woman manages a business – his authorisation is necessary for her contracts. Marital power is rigorously exercised, both over the wife herself as a person, and over her possessions.

Throughout the nineteenth century, the legal system continues to reinforce the code's severity, depriving, among other things, the woman of all rights of alienation. In 1826[31] the Restoration abolishes divorce and the 1848 Constitutional Assembly refuses to reestablish it; it does not reappear until 1884: and then it is still difficult to obtain. The bourgeoisie was never more powerful, yet they recognise the dangers implicit in the Industrial Revolution; they assert themselves with nervous authority. The freedom of ideas inherited from the eighteenth century never makes inroads into family moral principles; these remain as they are defined by the early-nineteenth-century reactionary thinkers Joseph de Maistre and Bonald. They base the value of order on divine will and demand a strictly hierarchical society; the family, the indissoluble social cell, will be the microcosm of society. 'Man is to woman what woman is to the child'; or 'power is to the minister what the minister is to the people,' says Bonald. Thus the husband governs, the wife administers and the children obey. Divorce is, of course, forbidden; and woman is confined to the home. 'Women belong to the family and not to politics, and nature made them for housework and not for public service,' adds Bonald. These hierarchies were respected in the family as described by Le Play in the middle of the century.

In a slightly different way, Auguste Comte also demands a hierarchy of the sexes; between men and women there are 'radical differences, both physical and moral, profoundly separating one from the other, in every species of animal and *especially in the human race*'. Femininity is a kind of 'prolonged childhood' that sets women apart from the 'ideal type of the race'. This biological infantilism expresses an intellectual weakness; the role of this purely affective being is that of spouse and housewife, no match for man: 'neither instruction nor education is suitable for her'. As with Bonald, woman is confined to the family, and within this miniature society the father governs because woman is 'inept in all government even domestic'; she only administers and advises. Her instruction has to be limited. 'Women and the proletariat cannot and must not become originators, nor do they wish to.' And Comte foresees society's evolution as totally eliminating woman's work outside the family. In the second part of his work, Comte, swayed by his love for Clotilde de Vaux, exalts woman to the point of almost making her a divinity, the emanation of the Great Being; in the Temple of Humanity, positivist religion will propose her for the adoration of the people, but only for her morality; man acts while she loves: she is more deeply altruistic than he. But according to the positivist system, she is still no less confined to the family; divorce is still forbidden for her, and it would even be preferable for her widowhood to last for ever; she has no economic or political rights; she is only a wife and an educator.

Balzac expresses the same ideal in more cynical ways: woman's destiny, and her only glory, is to make the hearts of men beat, he writes in *The Physiology of Marriage*.[32] 'Woman is a possession acquired by contract; she is personal property, and the possession of her is as good as security – indeed properly speaking, woman is only man's annexe.' Here he is speaking for the bourgeoisie which intensified its antifeminism in reaction to eighteenth-century licence and threatening progressive ideas. Having brilliantly presented the idea at the beginning of *The Physiology of Marriage* that this loveless institution forcibly leads the wife to adultery, Balzac exhorts husbands to rein wives into total subjugation if they want to avoid the ridicule of dishonour. They must be denied training and culture, forbidden to develop their individuality, forced to wear uncomfortable clothing, and encouraged to follow a debilitating dietary regime. The bourgeoisie follows this programme exactly, confining women to the kitchen and to housework, jealously watching their behaviour; they are enclosed in daily life rituals that hindered all attempts at independence. In return, they are honoured and endowed with the most exquisite respect. 'The married woman is a slave who must be seated on a throne,' says Balzac; of course men must give in to women in all irrelevant circumstances, yielding them first place; women must not carry heavy burdens as in primitive societies; they are readily spared all painful tasks and worries: at the same time this relieves them of all responsibility. It is hoped that, thus duped, seduced by the ease of their condition, they will accept the role of mother and housewife to which they are being confined. And in fact, most bourgeois women capitulate. As their education and their parasitic situation make them dependent on men, they never dare to voice their claims: those who do are hardly heard. It is easier to put people in chains than to remove them if the chains bring prestige, said George Bernard Shaw. The bourgeois woman clings to the chains because she clings to her class privileges. It is drilled into her and she believes that women's liberation would weaken bourgeois society; liberated from the male, she would be condemned to work; while she might regret having her rights to private property subordinated to her husband's, she would deplore even more having this property abolished; she feels no solidarity with working-class women: she feels closer to her husband than to a woman textile worker. She makes his interests her own.

Yet these obstinate examples of resistance cannot stop the march of history; the advent of the machine ruins landed property and brings about working-class emancipation and concomitantly that of woman. All forms of socialism, wresting woman from the family, favour her liberation: Plato, aspiring to a communal regime, promised women a similar autonomy to that enjoyed in Sparta. With the utopian socialism of Saint-Simon, Fourier and Cabet is born the utopia of the 'free woman'. The Saint-Simonian idea of universal association demands the abolition of all slavery: that of the worker and that of the woman; and it is because women like men are human beings that Saint-Simon, and Leroux, Pecqueur and Carnot after him, demand their freedom. Unfortunately, this reasonable theory has no credibility in the Saint-Simonian school. Instead, woman is exalted in the name of femininity, the surest way to disserve her. Under the pretext of considering the couple as the basis of social unity, Père Enfantin tries to introduce a woman into each 'director-couple' called the priest-couple; he awaits a better world from a woman messiah, and the Compagnons de la Femme embark for the East in search of this female saviour. He is influenced by Fourier, who confuses the liberation of woman with the restoration of the flesh; Fourier demands the right of all individuals to follow their passionate attractions; he wants to replace marriage with love; he considers the woman not as a person, but only in her amorous functions. And Cabet promises that Icarian communism will bring about complete equality of the sexes, though he accords women a limited participation in politics. In fact, women hold second place in the Saint-Simonian movement: only Claire Bazard, founder and main support for a brief period of the magazine *La Femme nouvelle* (The New Woman), plays a relatively important role. Many other minor publications appear later, but their claims are timid; they demand education rather than emancipation for women; Carnot, and later Legouvé, is committed to raising the level of education for women. The idea of the woman partner or the woman as a regenerating force persists throughout the nineteenth century in Victor Hugo. But woman's cause is discredited by these doctrines that, instead of assimilating her, oppose her to man, emphasising intuition and sentiment instead of reason. The cause is also discredited by some of its partisans' mistakes. In 1848 women founded clubs and journals; Eugénie Niboyet published *La Voix des femmes* (Women's Voice), a magazine that Cabet worked on. A female delegation went to the city hall to demand 'women's rights' but obtained nothing. In 1849, Jeanne Deroin ran for deputy and her campaign foundered in ridicule. Ridicule also killed the 'Vesuvians' movement and the Bloomerists, who paraded in extravagant costumes. The most intelligent women of the period took no part in these movements: Mme de Staël fought for her own cause rather than her sisters'; George Sand demanded the right for free love but refused to collaborate on *La Voix des femmes*; her claims are primarily sentimental. Flora Tristan believed in the people's redemption through woman; but she is more interested in the emancipation of the working class than that of her own sex. Daniel Stern and Mme de Girardin, however, joined the feminist movement.

On the whole, the reform movement that develops in the nineteenth century seeks justice in equality, and is thus generally favourable to feminism. There is one notable exception: Proudhon. Undoubtedly because of his peasant roots, he reacts violently against Saint-Simonian mysticism; he supports small property owners and at the same time believes in confining woman to the home. 'Housewife or courtesan' is the dilemma he locks her in. Until then, attacks against women had been led by conservatives, bitterly combating socialism as well: *Le Charivari* was one of the inexhaustible sources of jokes; it is Proudhon who breaks the alliance between feminism and socialism; he protests against the socialist women's banquet presided over by Leroux and he fulminates against Jeanne Deroin. In his work, *Justice*,[33] he posits that woman should be dependent on man; he alone counts as a social individual; a couple is not a partnership, which would suppose equality, but a union; woman is inferior to man first because her physical force is only two-thirds that of the male, then because she is intellectually and morally inferior to the same degree: she is worth 2 x 2 x 2 against 3 x 3 x 3 or $\frac{8}{27}$ of the stronger sex. When two women, Mme Adam and Mme d'Héricourt, respond to him – one quite firmly, the other less effusively – Proudhon retorts with *Pornocracy, or Women in Modern Times*.[34] But, like all anti-feminists, he addresses ardent litanies to the 'real woman', slave and mirror to the male; in spite of this devotion, he has to recognise himself that the life he gave his own wife never made her happy: Mme Proudhon's letters are one long lament.

But it is not these theoretical debates that influenced the course of events; they only timidly reflected them. Woman regains the economic importance lost since prehistoric times because she escapes the home and plays a new role in industrial production. The machine makes this upheaval possible because the difference in physical force between male and female workers is cancelled out in a great number of cases. As this abrupt industrial expansion demands a bigger labour market than male workers can provide, women's collaboration is necessary. This is the great nineteenth-century revolution that transforms the lot of woman and opens a new era to her. Marx and Engels understand the full impact this will have on women, promising them a liberation brought about by that of the proletariat. In fact, 'women and workers both have oppression in common,' says Bebel. And both will escape oppression thanks to the importance their productive work will take on through technological development. Engels shows that woman's lot is closely linked to the history of private property; a catastrophe substituted patriarchy for matriarchy and enslaved woman to the patrimony; but the Industrial Revolution is the counterpart of that loss and will lead to feminine emancipation. He writes: 'Woman cannot be emancipated unless she takes part in production on a large social scale and is only incidentally bound to domestic work. And this has become possible only within a large modern industry that not only accepts women's work on a grand scale but formally requires it.'

At the beginning of the nineteenth century, woman was more shamefully exploited than workers of the opposite sex. Domestic labour constituted what the English termed the 'sweating system'; in spite of constant work, the worker did not earn enough to make ends meet. Jules Simon in *The Woman Worker*[35] and even the conservative Leroy-Beaulieu in *Women's Work in the Nineteenth Century*,[36] published in 1873, denounce loathsome abuses; the latter declares that more than 200,000 French workers earn less than 50 centimes a day. It is clear why they hasten to migrate to the factories; in fact, it is not long before nothing is left outside workshops except needlework, laundering and housework, all slave labour paying famine wages; even lacemaking, millinery, and such are taken over by the factories; in return, job offers are massive in the cotton, wool and silk industries; women are mainly used in spinning and weaving mills. Employers often prefer them to men. 'They do better work for less pay.' This cynical formula clearly shows the drama of feminine labour. It is through labour that woman won her dignity as a human being; but it was a singularly difficult and slow conquest. Spinning and weaving are done under lamentable hygienic conditions. 'In Lyon,' writes Blanqui, 'in the trimmings workshops, some women are obliged to work almost hanging in a kind of harness in order to use both their feet and hands.' In 1831, silk workers work in the summer from three o'clock in the morning to eleven at night, or seventeen[37] hours a day, 'in often unhealthy workshops where sunlight never enters', says Norbert Truquin. 'Half of the young girls develop consumption before the end of their apprenticeship. When they complain, they are accused of dissimulating.'*[38] In addition, the male assistants take advantage of the young women workers. 'To get what they wanted they used the most revolting means, hunger and want,' says the anonymous author of *The Truth about the Events of Lyon*.[39] Some of the women work on farms as well as in factories. They are cynically exploited. Marx relates in a footnote of *Das Kapital*: 'Mr E—, manufacturer, let me know that he employed only women on his mechanical weaving looms, and that he gave preference to married women, and among them, women who had a family to care for at home, because they were far more docile and attentive than unmarried women, and had to work until ready to drop from exhaustion to provide indispensable means of subsistence to support their families. This is how', adds Marx, 'the qualities proper to woman are misrepresented to her disadvantage, and all the delicate and moral elements of her nature become means to enslave her and make her suffer.' Summarising *Das Kapital* and commenting on Bebel, G. Derville writes: 'Beast of luxury or beast of burden, such is woman almost exclusively today. Kept by man when she does not work, she is still kept by him when she works herself to death.' The situation of the woman worker was so lamentable that Sismondi and Blanqui called for women to be denied access to workshops. The reason is in part that women did not at first know how to defend themselves and organise unions. Feminine 'associations' date from 1848 and are originally production associations. The movement progressed extremely slowly, as the following figures show:

* N. Truquin, *Memoirs and Adventures of a Proletarian in Times of Revolution*. Cited from E. Dolléans, *History of the Working Class Movement*, vol. I.

in 1905, out of 781,392 union members, 69,405 are women;

in 1908, out of 957,120 union members, 88,906 are women;

in 1912, out of 1,064,413 union members, 92,336 are women.

In 1920, out of 1,580,967 workers, 239,016 are women and unionised female employees, and among 1,083,957 farmworkers, only 36,193 women are unionised; in all, 292,000 women are unionised out of a total of 3,076,585 union workers.[40] A tradition of resignation and submission as well as a lack of solidarity and collective consciousness leaves them disarmed in front of the new possibilities available to them.

The result of this attitude is that women's work was regulated slowly and late. Legislation does not intervene until 1874, and in spite of the campaigns waged under the Empire, only two provisions affect women: one banning minors from night work, requiring a day off on Sundays and holidays, and limiting the work day to twelve hours; as for women over twenty-one, all that is done is to prohibit underground mine and quarry work. The first feminine work charter, dated 2 November 1892, bans night work and limits the work day in factories; it leaves the door open for all kinds of fraud. In 1900 the work day is limited to ten hours; in 1905 a weekly day of rest becomes obligatory; in 1907 the woman worker is granted free disposal of her income; in 1909 maternity leave is granted; in 1911 the 1892 provisions are reinforced; in 1913 laws are passed for rest periods before and after childbirth, and dangerous and excessive work is prohibited. Little by little, social legislation takes shape and health guarantees are set up for women's work; seats are required for salesgirls, long shifts at outdoor display counters are prohibited, and so on. The International Labour Office succeeded in getting international agreements on sanitary conditions for women's work, maternity leave, and such.

A second consequence of the resigned inertia of women workers was the salaries they were forced to accept. Various explanations with multiple factors have been given for the phenomenon of low female salaries. It is insufficient to say that women have fewer needs than men: that is only a subsequent justification. Rather, women, as we have seen, did not know how to defend themselves against exploitation; they had to compete with prisons that dumped products without labour costs on the market; they competed with each other. Besides, in a society based on the marital community, woman seeks emancipation through work: bound to her father's or husband's household, she is most often satisfied just to bring home some extra money; she works outside the family, but for it; and since the working woman does not have to support herself completely, she ends up accepting remuneration far inferior to that which a man demands. With a significant number of women accepting bargain wages, the whole female salary scale is, of course, set up to the advantage of the employer.

In France, according to an 1889–93 survey, for a day of work equal to a man's, a woman worker received only half the male's wages. A 1908 survey showed that the highest hourly rates for women working from home never rose above 20 centimes an hour and dropped as low as 5 centimes: it was impossible for a woman so exploited to live without charity or a protector. In America in 1918, women earned half men's salary. Around this period, for the same amount of coal mined in Germany, a woman earned approximately 25 per cent less than a man. Between 1911 and 1943 women's salaries in France rose a bit more rapidly than men's, but they nonetheless remained clearly inferior.

While employers warmly welcomed women because of the low wages they accepted, this provoked resistance on the part of the male workers. Between the cause of the proletariat and that of women there was no such direct solidarity as Bebel and Engels claimed. The problem was similar to that of the black labour force in the United States. The most oppressed minorities in a society are readily used by the oppressors as a weapon against the class they belong to; thus they at first become enemies, and a deeper consciousness of the situation is necessary so that blacks and whites, women and male workers, form coalitions rather than opposition. It is understandable that male workers at first viewed this cheap competition as an alarming threat and became hostile. It is only when women were integrated into unions that they could defend their own interests and cease endangering those of the working class as a whole.

In spite of all these difficulties, progress in women's work continued. In 1900, in France, 900,000 women worked from home making clothes, leather goods, funeral wreaths, purses, beadwork and Paris souvenirs, but this number diminished considerably. In 1906, 42 per cent of working-age women (between eighteen and sixty) worked in farming, industry, business, banks, insurance, offices and liberal professions. This movement spread to the whole world because of the 1914–18 labour crisis and the world war. The lower middle class and the middle class were determined to follow this movement, and women also invaded the liberal professions. According to one of the last prewar censuses, in France 42 per cent of all women between eighteen and sixty worked; in Finland 37 per cent; in Germany 34.2 per cent; in India 27.7 per cent; in England 26.9 per cent; in the Netherlands 19.2 per cent; and in the United States,

17.7 per cent. But in France and in India the high figures reflect the extent of rural labour. Excluding the peasantry, France had in 1940 approximately 500,000 heads of establishments, one million female employees, two million women workers and 1.5 million women working alone or unemployed women. Among women workers, 650,000 were domestic workers; 1.2 million worked in light industry including 440,000 in textiles, 315,000 in clothing, and 380,000 at home in dressmaking.[41] For commerce, liberal professions and public service, France, England and the USA ranked about the same.

One of the basic problems for women, as has been seen, is reconciling the reproductive role and productive work. The fundamental reason that woman, since the beginning of history, has been consigned to domestic labour and prohibited from taking part in shaping the world is her enslavement to the generative function. In female animals there is a rhythm of heat and seasons that assures the economy of their energies; nature, on the contrary, between puberty and menopause, places no limits on women's gestation. Some civilisations prohibit early marriage; Indian tribes are cited where women are guaranteed a two-year rest period between births; but in general over the centuries, women's fertility has not been regulated. Contraceptives have existed since antiquity,* generally for women's use – potions, suppositories or vaginal tampons – but they remained the secrets of prostitutes and doctors; maybe the secret was available to women of the Roman decadence whose sterility satirists reproached. But the Middle Ages knew nothing of them; no trace is found until the eighteenth century. For many women in these times, life was an uninterrupted series of pregnancies; even women of easy virtue paid for their licentious love lives with frequent births. At certain periods, humanity felt the need to reduce the size of the population; but at the same time, nations worried about becoming weak; in periods of crisis and great poverty, postponing marriage lowered the birthrates. The general rule was to marry young and have as many children as the woman could carry, infant mortality alone reducing the

---

*'The earliest known reference to birth-control methods appears to be an Egyptian papyrus from the second millennium BC, recommending the vaginal application of a bizarre mixture composed of crocodile excrement, honey, natron, and a rubbery substance' (P. Ariès, *Histoire des populations françaises* [*History of French Populations*]). Medieval Persian physicians knew of thirty-one recipes, of which only nine were intended for men. Soranus, in the Hadrian era, explains that at the moment of ejaculation, if the woman does not want a child, she should 'hold her breath, pull back her body a little so that the sperm cannot penetrate the *os uteri*, get up immediately, squat down and make herself sneeze'.

number of living children. Already in the seventeenth century, the abbé de Pure*[42] protests against the 'amorous dropsy' to which women are condemned; and Mme de Sévigné urges her daughter to avoid frequent pregnancies. But it is in the eighteenth century that the Malthusian movement develops in France. First the well-to-do class, then the population in general deem it reasonable to limit the number of children according to parents' resources, and anticonception procedures begin to enter into social practices. In 1778 Moreau, the demographer, writes, 'Rich women are not the only ones who considered the propagation of the species the greatest old-fashioned dupe; these dark secrets, unknown to all animals except man, have already made their way into the countryside; nature is confounded even in the villages.' The practice of coitus interruptus spreads first among the bourgeoisie, then among rural populations and workers; the prophylactic, which already existed as an antivenereal device, becomes a contraceptive device, widespread after the discovery of vulcanisation, towards 1840.[†] In Anglo-Saxon countries, birth control is official and numerous methods have been discovered to dissociate these two formerly inseparable functions: the sexual and the reproductive. Viennese medical research, precisely establishing the mechanism of conception and the conditions favourable to it, has also suggested methods for avoiding it. In France contraception propaganda and the sale of pessaries, vaginal tampons, and such are prohibited; but birth control is no less widespread.

As for abortion, it is nowhere officially authorised by law. Roman law granted no special protection to embryonic life; the *nasciturus* was not considered a human being, but part of the woman's body. '*Partus antequam edatur mulieris portio est vel viscerum.*'[‡] In the era of decadence, abortion seems to have been a normal practice, and even a legislator who wanted to encourage birthrates would never dare to prohibit it. If the woman refused a child against her husband's will, he could have her punished; but her crime was her disobedience. Generally, in Oriental and Graeco-Roman civilisation, abortion was allowed by law.

It was Christianity that overturned moral ideas on this point by endowing the embryo with a soul; so abortion became a crime against the foetus itself. 'Any woman who does what she can so as not to give

---

* In *La Précieuse* (1656).

† 'Around 1930 an American firm sold twenty million prophylactics in one year. Fifteen American factories produced a million and a half of them per day' (P. Ariès, *History*).

‡ 'The infant, before being born, is a part of the woman, a kind of organ.'

birth to as many children as she is capable of is guilty of that many homicides, just as is a woman who tries to injure herself after conception,' says St Augustine. In Byzantium, abortion led only to a temporary relegation; for the barbarians who practised infanticide, it was punishable only if it was carried out by violence, against the mother's will: it was redeemed by paying blood money. But the first councils issued edicts for the severest penalties against this 'homicide', whatever the presumed age of the foetus. Nonetheless, one question arises that has been the object of infinite discussion: at what moment does the soul enter the body? St Thomas and most other writers settled on life beginning towards the fortieth day for males and the eightieth for females; thus was established a distinction between the animated and non-animated foetus. A Middle Ages penitential book declares: 'If a pregnant woman destroys her fruit before forty-five days, she is subject to a penitence of one year. For sixty days, three years. And finally, if the infant is already animated, she should be tried for homicide.' The book, however, adds: 'There is a great difference between a poor woman who destroys her infant for the pain she has to feed it and the one who has no other reason but to hide a crime of fornication.' In 1556, Henri II published a well-known edict on concealing pregnancy; since the death penalty was applied for simple concealment, it followed that the penalty should also apply to abortion manoeuvres; in fact, the edict was aimed at infanticide, but it was used to authorise the death penalty for practitioners and accomplices of abortion. The distinction between the quickened and non-quickened foetus disappeared around the eighteenth century. At the end of the century, Beccaria, a man of considerable influence in France, pleaded in favour of the woman who refuses to have a child. The 1791 Code excuses the woman but punishes her accomplices with 'twenty years of irons'. The idea that abortion is homicide disappeared in the nineteenth century: it is considered rather to be a crime against the state. The Law of 1810 prohibits it absolutely under pain of imprisonment and forced labour for the woman who aborts and her accomplices; but doctors practise abortion whenever it is a question of saving the mother's life. Because the law is so strict, juries at the end of the century stopped applying it and few arrests were made, with four-fifths of the accused acquitted. In 1923 a new law is passed, again with forced labour for the accomplices and the practitioner of the operation, but punishing the woman having the abortion with only prison or a fine; in 1939 a new decree specifically targets the technicians: no reprieve would be granted. In 1941 abortion was decreed a crime against state security. In other countries, it is a misdemeanour punishable by a short prison sentence; in England, it is a crime – a felony – punishable by prison or forced labour. Overall, codes and courts are more lenient with the woman having the abortion than with her accomplices. The Church, however, has never relaxed its severity. The 27 March 1917 code of canon law declares: 'Those who procure abortions, the mother not excepted, incur excommunication *latae sententiae*, once the result has been obtained, reserved to the Ordinary.' No reason can be invoked, even the danger of the mother's death. The Pope again declared recently that between the mother's life and the child's the former must be sacrificed: the fact is, the mother, being baptised, can enter heaven – curiously, hell never enters into these calculations – while the foetus is condemned to perpetual limbo.*

Abortion was officially recognised, but only for a short time, in Germany before Nazism and in the Soviet Union before 1936. But in spite of religion and laws, it has been practised in all countries to a large extent. In France, every year 800,000 to one million abortions are performed – as many as births – and two-thirds of the women are married, many already having one or two children. In spite of the prejudices, resistance and an outdated morality, unregulated fertility has given way to fertility controlled by the state or individuals. Progress in obstetrics has considerably decreased the dangers of childbirth; childbirth pain is disappearing; at this time – March 1949 – legislation has been passed in England requiring the use of certain anaesthetic methods; they are already generally applied in the United States and are beginning to spread in France. With artificial insemination, the evolution that will permit humanity to master the reproductive function comes to completion. These changes have tremendous importance for woman in particular; she can reduce the number of pregnancies and rationally integrate them into her life, instead of being their slave. During the nineteenth century, woman in her turn is freed from nature; she wins control

---

* In volume II, we will return to the discussion of this view. Let it just be said here that Catholics are far from keeping to the letter of St Augustine's doctrine. The confessor whispers to the young fiancée, on the eve of her wedding, that she can do anything with her husband, as long as 'proper' coitus is achieved; positive birth-control practices – including coitus interruptus – are forbidden; but the calendar established by Viennese sexologists can be used, where the act whose only recognised aim is reproduction is carried out on the days conception is impossible for the woman. There are spiritual advisers who even indicate this calendar to their flocks. In fact, there are ample 'Christian mothers' who only have two or three children and have nonetheless not interrupted their conjugal relations after the last delivery.

of her body. Relieved of a great number of reproductive servitudes, she can take on the economic roles open to her, roles that would assure her control over her own person.

The convergence of these two factors – participation in production and freedom from reproductive slavery – explains the evolution of woman's condition. As Engels predicted, her social and political status necessarily had to change. The feminist movement begun in France by Condorcet, in England by Mary Wollstonecraft in *Vindication of the Rights of Woman*, and followed up at the beginning of the century by the Saint-Simonians, never succeeded for lack of a concrete base. But now, women's claims would have ample weight. They would be heard even within the heart of the bourgeoisie. With the rapid development of industrial civil-isation, landed property is falling behind in relation to personal property: the principle of family group unity is losing force. The mobility of capital allows its holder to own and dispose of his wealth without reciprocity instead of being held by it. Through patrimony, woman was substan-tially attached to her husband: with patrimony abolished, they are only juxtaposed, and even children do not constitute as strong a bond as interest. Thus, the individual will assert himself against the group; this evolution is particularly striking in America where modern capitalism has triumphed: divorce is going to flourish, and husbands and wives are no more than provisional associates. In France, where the rural popula-tion is large and where the Napoleonic Code placed the married woman under guardianship, evolution will be slow. In 1884, divorce was restored and a wife could obtain it if the husband committed adultery; nonethe-less, in the penal area, sexual difference was maintained: adultery was an offence only when perpetrated by the wife. The right of guardian-ship, granted with restrictions in 1907, was fully granted only in 1917. In 1912, the right to determine natural paternity was authorised. It was not until 1938 and 1942 that the married woman's status was modified: the duty of obedience was then abrogated, although the father remains the family head; he determines the place of residence, but the wife can oppose his choice if she advances valid arguments; her powers are increasing; but the formula is still confused: 'The married woman has full legal powers. These powers are only limited by the marriage contract and law'; the last part of the article contradicts the first. The equality of spouses has not yet been achieved.

As for political rights, they have not easily been won in France, England or the United States. In 1867, John Stuart Mill pleaded the first case ever officially pronounced before Parliament in favour of the vote for women.

In his writings he imperiously demanded equality of men and women in the family and society: 'The principle which regulates the existing social relations between the two sexes – the legal subordination of one sex to the other – is wrong in itself, and now one of the hindrances to human improvement; and . . . it ought to be replaced by a principle of perfect equality.'[43] After that, English women organised politically under Mrs Fawcett's leadership; French women rallied behind Maria Deraismes, who between 1868 and 1871 dealt with women's issues in a series of public lectures; she joined in the lively controversy against Alexandre Dumas *fils* who advised the husband of an unfaithful wife, 'Kill her.' Léon Richer was the true founder of feminism; in 1869 he launched *Le Droit des Femmes* (*The Rights of Women*) and organised the International Congress of Women's Rights, held in 1878. The question of the right to vote was not yet dealt with; women limited themselves to claiming civil rights; for thirty years the movement remained timid in France and in England. Nonetheless, a woman, Hubertine Auclert, started a suffragette campaign; she created a group called Women's Suffrage and a newspaper, *La Citoyenne*. Many groups were organised under her influence, but they accomplished little. This weakness of feminism stemmed from its internal division; as already pointed out, women as a sex lack solidarity: they are linked to their classes first; bourgeois and proletarian interests do not intersect. Revolutionary feminism adhered to the Saint-Simonian and Marxist tradition; it is noteworthy, moreover, that a certain Louise Michel spoke against feminism because it diverted the energy that should be used entirely for class struggle; with the abolition of capital the lot of woman will be resolved.

The Socialist Congress of 1879 proclaimed the equality of the sexes, and as of that time the feminist–socialist alliance would no longer be denounced, but since women hope for their liberty through the emancipation of workers in general, their attachment to their own cause is secondary. The bourgeoisie, on the contrary, claim new rights within existing society and they refuse to be revolutionary; they want to introduce virtuous reforms into rules of behaviour: elimination of alcohol, pornographic literature and prostitution. In 1892, the Feminist Congress convenes and gives its name to the movement, but nothing comes of it. However, in 1897 a law is passed permitting women to testify in court, but the request of a woman doctor of law to become a member of the bar is denied. In 1898, women are allowed to vote for the Commercial Court, to vote and be eligible for the National Council on Labour and Employment, to be admitted to the National Council for Public Health Services and the Ecole des Beaux-Arts. In 1900, feminists hold a new congress, again without significant results. But in 1901, for the first time, Viviani presents the question of the woman's vote to the French parliament; he proposes limiting suffrage to unmarried and divorced women. The feminist movement gains importance at this time. In 1909 the French Union for Women's Suffrage is formed, headed by Mme Brunschvicg; she organises lectures, meetings, congresses and demonstrations. In 1909, Buisson presents a report on Dussaussoy's bill allowing women to vote in local assemblies. In 1910, Thomas presents a bill in favour of women's suffrage; presented again in 1918, it passes the Chamber in 1919; but it fails to pass the Senate in 1922. The situation is quite complex. Christian feminism joins forces with revolutionary feminism and Mme Brunschvicg's so-called independent feminism: in 1919, Benedict XV declares himself in favour of the women's vote, and Monsignor Baudrillart and Père Sertillanges follow his lead with ardent propaganda; Catholics believe in fact that women in France constitute a conservative and religious element; this is just what the radicals fear: the real reason for their opposition is their fear of the swing votes that women represented. In the Senate, numerous Catholics, the Union Republican group, as well as extreme left parties are for the women's vote: but the majority of the assembly is against it. Until 1932 delaying procedures are used by the majority, which refuses to discuss bills concerning women's suffrage; nevertheless, in 1932, the Chamber having voted the women's voting and eligibility amendment, 319 votes to 1, the Senate opens a debate extending over several sessions: the amendment is voted down. The record in *L'officiel* is of great importance; all the antifeminist arguments developed over half a century are found in the report, which fastidiously lists all the works in which they are mentioned. First of all come these types of gallantry arguments: we love women too much to let them vote; the 'real woman' who accepts the 'housewife or courtesan' dilemma is exalted in true Proudhon fashion; woman would lose her charm by voting; she is on a pedestal and should not step down from it; she has everything to lose and nothing to gain in becoming a voter; she governs men without needing a ballot; and so on. More serious objections concern the family's interest: woman's place is in the home; political discussions would bring about disagreement between spouses. Some admit to moderate antifeminism. Women are different from men. They do not serve in the military. Will prostitutes vote? And others arrogantly affirm male superiority: voting is a duty and not a right; women are not worthy of it. They are less intelligent and educated than men. If women voted, men would become effeminate. Women lacked political education. They would vote according to their husbands' wishes. If they want to be free, they should first free themselves from their dressmakers. Also proposed is that superbly naive argument: there are more women in France than men. In spite of the flimsiness of all these objections, French women would have to wait until 1945 to acquire political power.

New Zealand gave woman full rights in 1893. Australia followed in 1908. But in England and America victory was difficult. Victorian England imperiously isolated woman in her home; Jane Austen wrote in secret; it took great courage or an exceptional destiny to become George Eliot or Emily Brontë; in 1888 an English scholar wrote: 'Women are not only not part of the race, they are not even half of the race but a sub-species destined uniquely for reproduction.' Mrs Fawcett founded a suffragist movement towards the end of the century, but as in France the movement was hesitant. Around 1903, feminist claims took a singular turn. In London, the Pankhurst family created the Women's Social and Political Union, which joined with the Labour Party and embarked on resolutely militant activities. It was the first time in history that women took on a cause as women: this is what gave particular interest to the suffragettes in England and America. For fifteen years, they carried out a policy recalling in some respects a Ghandi-like attitude: refusing violence, they invented more or less ingenious symbolic actions. They marched on the Albert Hall during Liberal Party meetings, carrying banners with the words 'Vote for Women'; they forced their way into Lord Asquith's office, held meetings in Hyde Park or Trafalgar Square, marched in the streets carrying signs and held lectures; during demonstrations they insulted the police or threw stones at them, provoking their arrest; in prison they adopted the hunger strike tactic; they raised money and rallied millions of women and men; they influenced opinion so well that in 1907 two hundred members of Parliament made up a committee for women's suffrage; every year from then on some of them would propose a law in favour of women's suffrage, a law that would be rejected every year with the same arguments. In 1907 the WSPU organised the first march on Parliament with workers covered in shawls, and a few aristocratic women; the police pushed them back; but the following year, as married women were threatened with a ban on work in certain mines, the Lancashire women workers were called by the WSPU to hold a grand meeting. There were new arrests and the imprisoned suffragettes responded with a long hunger strike. Released, they organised new parades: one of the women rode a horse painted with the head of Queen Elizabeth. On 18 July 1910, the day the women's suffrage law went to the

Chamber, a nine-kilometre-long column paraded through London; the law rejected, there were more meetings and new arrests. In 1912, they adopted a more violent tactic: they burned empty houses, slashed pictures, trampled flower beds, threw stones at the police; at the same time, they sent delegation upon delegation to Lloyd George and Sir Edward Grey; they hid in the Albert Hall and noisily disrupted Lloyd George's speeches. The war interrupted their activities. It is difficult to know how much these actions hastened events. The vote was granted to English women first in 1918 in a restricted form, and then in 1928 without restriction: their success was in large part due to the services they had rendered during the war.

The American woman found herself at first more emancipated than the European. Early in the nineteenth century, pioneer women had to share the hard work done by men and they fought by their sides; they were far fewer than men and thus a high value was placed on them. But little by little, their condition came to resemble that of women in the Old World; gallantry towards them was maintained; they kept their cultural privileges and a dominant position within the family; laws granted them a religious and moral role; but the command of society resided in the males' hands. Some women began to claim their political rights around 1830. They undertook a campaign in favour of blacks. As the antislavery congress held in 1840 in London was closed to them, the Quaker Lucretia Mott founded a feminist association. On 18 July 1840,[44] at the Seneca Falls Convention, they drafted a Quaker-inspired declaration, which set the tone for all of American feminism: 'that all men and women are created equal; that they are endowed by their Creator with certain inalienable rights . . . that to secure these rights governments are instituted . . . He [Man] has made her, if married, in the eye of the law, civilly dead . . . He has usurped the prerogative of Jehovah himself, claiming it as his right to assign for her a sphere of action, when that belongs to her conscience and her God.' Three years later, Harriet Beecher Stowe wrote *Uncle Tom's Cabin*, arousing the public in favour of blacks. Emerson and Lincoln supported the feminist movement. When the Civil War broke out, women ardently participated; but in vain they demanded that the amendment giving blacks the right to vote be drafted as follows: 'The right . . . to vote shall not be denied or abridged . . . on account of race, color, *sex*.' Seizing on the ambiguity of one of the articles to the amendment, the great feminist leader Susan B. Anthony voted in Rochester with fourteen comrades; she was fined a hundred dollars. In 1869, she founded what later came to be called the National American

Woman Suffrage Association, and that same year the state of Wyoming gave women the right to vote. But it was only in 1893 that Colorado, then in 1896 Idaho and Utah, followed this example. Progress was slow afterwards. But women succeeded better economically than in Europe. In 1900, 5 million women worked, 1.3 million in industry, 500,000 in business; a large number worked in business, industry and liberal professions. There were lawyers, doctors and 3,373 women pastors. The famous Mary Baker Eddy founded the Christian Science Church. Women formed clubs; in 1900, they totalled about two million members.

Nonetheless, only nine states had given women the vote. In 1913, the suffrage movement was organised on the militant English model. Two women led it: Doris Stevens and a young Quaker, Alice Paul. From Wilson[45] they obtained the right to march with banners and signs; they then organised a campaign of lectures, meetings, marches and manifestations of all sorts. From the nine states where women voted, women voters went with great pomp and circumstance to the Capitol, demanding the feminine vote for the whole nation. In Chicago, the first group of women assembled in a party to liberate their sex; this assembly became the Women's Party. In 1917, suffragettes invented a new tactic: they stationed themselves at the doors of the White House, banners in hand, and often chained to the gates so they could not be driven away. After six months, they were stopped and sent to the Occuquan penitentiary; they went on hunger strike and were finally released. New demonstrations led to the beginning of riots. The government finally consented to naming a House Committee on Woman Suffrage. The executive committee of the Women's Party held a conference in Washington, and an amendment favouring the woman's vote went to the House and was voted on 10 January 1918. The vote still had to go to the Senate. Wilson would not promise to exert enough pressure, so the suffragettes began to demonstrate again. They held a rally at the White House doors. The president decided to address an appeal to the Senate, but the amendment was rejected by two votes. A Republican Congress voted for the amendment in June 1919. The battle for complete equality of the sexes went on for the next ten years. At the sixth International Conference of American States held in Havana in 1928, women obtained the creation of the Inter-American Commission of Women. In 1933, the Montevideo treaties elevated women's status by international convention. Nineteen American republics signed the convention giving women equality in all rights.

Sweden also had a very sizeable feminist movement. Invoking old traditions, Swedish women demanded the right 'to education, work and liberty'. It was largely women writers who led the fight, and it was the moral aspect of the problem that interested them at first; then, grouped in powerful associations, they won over the liberals but ran up against the hostility of the conservatives. Norwegian women in 1907 and Finnish women in 1906 obtained the suffrage that Swedish women would have to wait years to attain.

In Latin and Eastern countries woman was oppressed by customs more than by laws. In Italy, fascism systematically hindered feminism's progress. Seeking the alliance of the Church, which continued to uphold family tradition and a tradition of feminine slavery, fascist Italy held woman in double bondage: to public authority and to her husband. The situation was very different in Germany. In 1790, Hippel, a student, launched the first German feminist manifesto. Sentimental feminism analogous to that of George Sand flourished at the beginning of the nineteenth century. In 1848, the first German woman feminist, Louise Otto, demanded the right for women to assist in the transformation of their country: her feminism was largely nationalistic. She founded the General German Women's Association in 1865. German socialists, along with Bebel, advocated the abolition of the inequality of the sexes. In 1892, Clara Zetkin joined the party's council. Women workers and women socialists grouped together in a federation. German women failed in 1914 to establish a women's national army, but they took an active part in the war. After the German defeat, they obtained the right to vote and participated in political life: Rosa Luxemburg fought next to Liebknecht in the Spartacus group and was assassinated in 1919. The majority of German women chose the party of order; several took seats in the Reichstag. It was thus upon emancipated women that Hitler imposed the new Napoleonic ideal: 'Kinder, Küche, Kirche'. 'Woman's presence dishonours the Reichstag,' he declared. As Nazism was anti-Catholic and antibourgeois, he gave the mother a privileged place; protection granted to unmarried mothers and illegitimate children greatly freed woman from marriage; as in Sparta, she was more dependent on the state than on any individual, giving her both more and less autonomy than a bourgeois woman living under a capitalist regime.

In Soviet Russia the feminist movement made the greatest advances. It began at the end of the nineteenth century among women students of the intelligentsia; they were less attached to their personal cause than to revolutionary action in general; they 'went to the people' and used nihilistic methods against the Okhrana: in 1878 Vera Zasulich shot the police chief Trepov. During the Russo-Japanese War, women replaced men in many areas of work; their consciousness raised, the Russian Union for Women's Rights demanded political equality of the sexes; in the first Duma, a parliamentary women's rights group was created, but it was powerless. Women workers' emancipation would come from the revolution. Already in 1905, they were actively participating in the mass political strikes that broke out in the country, and they mounted the barricades. On 8 March 1917, International Women's Day and a few days before the revolution, they massively demonstrated in the streets of St Petersburg[46] demanding bread, peace and their husbands' return. They took part in the October insurrection; between 1918 and 1920, they played an important economic and even military role in the USSR's fight against the invaders. True to Marxist tradition, Lenin linked women's liberation to that of the workers; he gave them political and economic equality.

Article 122 of the 1936 constitution stipulates: 'In the USSR, woman enjoys the same rights as man in all aspects of economic, official, cultural, public and political life.' And these principles were spelled out by the Communist International. It demands 'social equality of man and woman before the law and in daily life. Radical transformation in conjugal rights and in the family code. Recognition of maternity as a social function. Entrusting society with the care and education of children and adolescents. Organisation of a civil effort against ideology and traditions that make woman a slave.' In the economic area, woman's conquests were stunning. She obtained equal wages with male workers, and she took on a highly active role in production; thereby gaining considerable political and social importance. The brochure recently published by the Association France-USSR reports that in the 1939 general elections there were 457,000 women deputies in the regional, district, town and village soviets; 1,480 in the socialist republics of higher soviets, and 227 seated in the Supreme Soviet of the USSR. Close to 10 million are members of unions. They constitute 40 per cent of the population of USSR workers and employees, and a great number of workers among the Stakhanovites are women. The role of Russian women in the last war is well-known; they provided an enormous labour force even in production branches where masculine professions are dominant: metallurgy and mining, timber rafting and railways and so forth. They distinguished themselves as pilots and parachutists, and they formed partisan armies.

This participation of woman in public life has raised a difficult problem: her role in family life. For a long while, means were sought to free her from her domestic constraints: on 16 November 1942, the plenary assembly of the Comintern proclaimed, 'The revolution is impotent as long as the notion of family and family relations subsists.' Respect for free unions, liberalisation of divorce and legalisation of abortion ensured woman's liberty relative to men; laws for maternity leave, child-care centres, kinder-gartens, and so on lightened the burdens of motherhood. From passionate and contradictory witness reports, it is difficult to discern what woman's concrete situation really was; what is sure is that today the demands of repopulation have given rise to a different family policy: the family has become the elementary social cell and woman is both worker and house-keeper.* Sexual morality is at its strictest; since the law of June 1936, rein-forced by that of 7 June 1941, abortion has been banned and divorce almost suppressed; adultery is condemned by moral standards. Strictly subordinated to the state like all workers, strictly bound to the home, but with access to political life and the dignity that productive work gives, the Russian woman is in a singular situation that would be worth studying in its singularity; circumstances unfortunately prevent me from doing this.

The recent session of the United Nations Commission on the Status of Women demanded that equal rights for both sexes be recognised in all nations, and several motions were passed to make this legal status a concrete reality. It would seem, then, that the match is won. The future can only bring greater and greater assimilation of women in a hitherto masculine society.

★

Several conclusions come to the fore when taking a look at this history as a whole. And first of all this one: women's entire history has been written by men. Just as in America there is no black problem but a white one;[†] just as 'anti-Semitism is not a Jewish problem, it's our problem',[‡47] so the problem of woman has always been a problem of men. Why they had moral prestige at the outset along with physical strength has been discussed; they created the values, customs and religions; never did women attempt to vie for that empire. A few isolated women – Sappho, Christine de Pizan, Mary Wollstonecraft, Olympe de Gouges – protested

---

* Olga Michakova, secretary of the Central Committee of the Communist Youth Organisation, stated in 1944 in an interview: 'Soviet women should try to make them-selves as attractive as nature and good taste permit. After the war, they should dress like women and act feminine ... Girls will be told to act and walk like girls and that is why they will wear skirts that will probably be very tight, making them carry them-selves gracefully.'
† Cf. Myrdal, *An American Dilemma*.
‡ J. P. Sartre, *Anti-Semite and Jew*.

against their harsh destiny; and there were some collective demonstrations: but Roman matrons in league against the Oppian law or Anglo-Saxon suffragettes only managed to wield pressure because men were willing to submit to it. Men always held woman's lot in their hands; and they did not decide on it based on her interest; it is their own projects, fears and needs that counted. When they revered the Mother Goddess, it is because Nature frightened them, and as soon as the bronze tool enabled them to assert themselves against Nature, they instituted patriarchy; henceforth it was the family–state conflict that has defined woman's status; it is the attitude of the Christian before God, the world and his own flesh that is reflected in the condition he assigned to her; what was called the *querelle des femmes* in the Middle Ages was a quarrel between clergy and laity about marriage and celibacy; it is the social regime founded on private property that brought about the married woman's wardship, and it is the technical revolution realised by men that enfranchised today's women. It is an evolution of the masculine ethic that led to the decrease in family size by birth control and partially freed woman from the servitude of motherhood. Feminism itself has never been an autonomous movement: it was partially an instrument in the hands of politicians and partially an epiphenomenon reflecting a deeper social drama. Never did women form a separate caste: and in reality they never sought to play a role in history as a sex. The doctrines that call for the advent of woman as flesh, life, immanence, or the Other are masculine ideologies that do not in any way express feminine claims. For the most part, women resign themselves to their lot without attempting any action; those who did try to change attempted to overcome their singularity and not to confine themselves in it triumphantly. When they intervened in world affairs, it was in concert with men and from a masculine point of view.

This intervention, in general, was secondary and occasional. The women who enjoyed a certain economic autonomy and took part in production were the oppressed classes, and as workers they were even more enslaved than male workers. In the ruling classes woman was a parasite and as such was subjugated to masculine laws: in both cases, it was almost impossible for her to act. Law and custom did not always coincide: and a balance was set up between them so that woman was never concretely free. In the ancient Roman Republic, economic conditions give the matron concrete powers: but she has no legal independence; the same is often true in peasant civilisations and among lower-middle-class tradesmen; mistress-servant inside the home, woman is socially a minor. Inversely, in periods when society fragments, woman becomes freer, but she loses her fief when she ceases to be man's vassal; she has nothing but a negative freedom that is expressed only in licence and dissipation, as, for example, during the Roman decadence, the Renaissance, the eighteenth century, and the Directoire. Either she finds work but is enslaved; or she is enfranchised but can do nothing else with herself. It is worth noting among other points that the married woman had her place in society but without benefiting from any rights, while the single woman, honest girl or prostitute, had all man's capacities; but until this century she was more or less excluded from social life. The opposition between law and custom produced this among other curious paradoxes: free love is not prohibited by law, but adultery is a crime; the girl that 'falls', however, is often dishonoured, while the wife's shocking behaviour is treated indulgently: from the eighteenth century to today many young girls got married so that they could freely have lovers. This ingenious system kept the great mass of women under guardianship: it takes exceptional circumstances for a feminine personality to be able to affirm itself between these two series of constraints, abstract or concrete. Women who have accomplished works comparable to men's are those whom the force of social institutions had exalted beyond any sexual differentiation. Isabella the Catholic, Elizabeth of England and Catherine of Russia were neither male nor female: they were sovereigns. It is remarkable that once socially abolished, their femininity no longer constituted inferiority: there were infinitely more queens with great reigns than kings. Religion undergoes the same transformation: Catherine of Siena and St Teresa are saintly souls, beyond any physiological condition; their lay life and their mystical life, their actions and their writings, rise to heights that few men ever attain. It is legitimate to think that if other women failed to mark the world deeply, it is because they were trapped by their conditions. They were only able to intervene in a negative or indirect way. Judith, Charlotte Corday and Vera Zasulich assassinate; the Frondeuses conspire; during the Revolution and the Commune, women fight alongside men against the established order; intransigent refusal and revolt against a freedom without rights and power are permitted, whereas it is forbidden for a woman to participate in positive construction; at best she will manage to insinuate herself into masculine enterprises by indirect means. Aspasia, Mme de Maintenon and the princesse des Ursins were precious advisers: but someone still had to consent to listen to them. Men tend to exaggerate the scope of this influence when trying to convince woman she has the greater role; but in fact feminine voices are silenced when concrete action begins; they might foment wars, not suggest battle tactics; they oriented politics only inasmuch as politics was limited to intrigue: the real reins of the world have never been in women's hands; they had no role either in technology or in economy, they neither made nor unmade states, they did not discover worlds. They did set off some events: but they were pretexts more than agents. Lucretia's suicide had no more than a symbolic value. Martyrdom remains allowed for the oppressed; during Christian persecutions and in the aftermath of social or national defeats, women played this role of witness; but a martyr has never changed the face of the world. Even feminine demonstrations and initiatives were only worth something if a masculine decision positively prolonged them. The American women united around Harriet Beecher Stowe aroused public opinion to fever pitch against slavery; but the real reasons for the Civil War were not sentimental. The 8 March 1917 'woman's day' might have triggered the Russian Revolution: but it was nonetheless merely a signal. Most feminine heroines are extravagant: adventurers or eccentrics notable less for their actions than for their unique destinies; take Joan of Arc, Mme Roland and Flora Tristan: if they are compared with Richelieu, Danton, or Lenin, it is clear their greatness is mainly subjective; they are exemplary figures more than historical agents. A great man springs from the mass and is carried by circumstances: the mass of women is at the fringes of history, and for each of them, circumstances are an obstacle and not a springboard. To change the face of the world, one has first to be firmly anchored to it; but women firmly rooted in society are those subjugated by it; unless they are designated for action by divine right – and in this case they are shown to be as capable as men – the ambitious woman and the heroine are strange monsters. Only since women have begun to feel at home on this earth has a Rosa Luxemburg or a Mme Curie emerged. They brilliantly demonstrate that it is not women's inferiority that has determined their historical insignificance: it is their historical insignificance that has doomed them to inferiority.*

This fact is striking in the cultural field, the area in which they have

---

* It is worth noting that out of one thousand statues in Paris (not counting the queens that compose the corbel of the Luxembourg and fulfil a purely architectural role) there are only ten raised to women. Three are devoted to Joan of Arc. The others are Mme de Ségur, George Sand, Sarah Bernhardt, Mme Boucicaut and the Baronne de Hirsch, Maria Deraismes and Rosa Bonheur.

been the most successful in asserting themselves. Their lot has been closely linked to literature and the arts; among the ancient Germans, the roles of prophetess and priestess fell to women; because they are marginal to the world, men will look to them when they strive, through culture, to bridge the limits of their universe and reach what is other. Courtly mysticism, humanist curiosity, and the taste for beauty that thrives in the Italian Renaissance, the preciousness of the seventeenth century, and the progressive ideal of the eighteenth century bring about an exaltation of femininity in diverse forms. Woman is thus the main pole of poetry and the substance of works of art; her leisure allows her to devote herself to the pleasures of the mind: inspiration, critic, writer's audience, she emulates the writer; she can often impose a type of sensitivity, an ethic that feeds men's hearts, which is how she intervenes in her own destiny: women's education is mainly a feminine conquest. And yet as important as this collective role played by intellectual women is, their individual contributions are, on the whole, of a lesser order. Woman holds a privileged place in the fields of the mind and art because she is not involved in action; but art and thinking derive their impetus in action. Being on the fringes of the world is not the best place for someone who intends to re-create it: here again, to go beyond the given, one must be deeply rooted in it. Personal accomplishments are almost impossible in human categories collectively kept in an inferior situation. 'Where can one go in skirts?' asked Marie Bashkirtseff. And Stendhal: 'All the geniuses who are born *women* are lost for the public good.' If truth be told, one is not born, but becomes, a genius; and the feminine condition has, until now, rendered this becoming impossible.

Antifeminists draw two contradictory arguments from examining history: (1) women have never created anything grand; (2) woman's situation has never prevented great women personalities from blossoming. There is bad faith in both of these assertions; the successes of some few privileged women neither compensate for nor excuse the systematic degrading of the collective level; and the very fact that these successes are so rare and limited is proof of their unfavourable circumstances. As Christine de Pizan, Poulain de la Barre, Condorcet, John Stuart Mill, and Stendhal stated, women have never been given their chances in any area. This explains why many of them today demand a new status; and once again, their demand is not to be exalted in their femininity: they want transcendence to prevail over immanence in themselves as in all of humanity; they want abstract rights and concrete possibilities to be granted to them, without which freedom is merely mystification.*

This will is being fulfilled. But this is in a period of transition; this world that has always belonged to men is still in their hands; patriarchal civilisation's institutions and values are still, to a great extent, alive. Abstract rights are far from being wholly granted to women: in Switzerland, women still cannot vote; in France, the 1942 law upholds the husband's prerogatives in a weaker form. And abstract rights, as has just been said, have never been sufficient to guarantee woman a concrete hold on the world: there is not yet real equality today between the two sexes.

First, the burdens of marriage are still much heavier for woman than for man. We have seen that the constraints of pregnancy have been limited by the overt or clandestine use of birth control, but the practice is neither universally disseminated nor rigorously applied; as abortion is officially forbidden, many women either jeopardise their health by resorting to unregulated abortion methods or are overwhelmed by the number of their pregnancies. Child care, like housekeeping, is still almost exclusively the woman's burden. In France in particular, the antifeminist tradition is so tenacious that a man would think it demeaning to participate in chores previously reserved for women. The result is that woman has a harder time reconciling her family and work life. In cases where society demands this effort from her, her existence is much more difficult than her spouse's.

Take, for example, the lot of peasant women. In France they make up the majority of the women involved in productive labour, and they are generally married. The single woman most often remains a servant in the father's, brother's or sister's household; she only becomes mistress of a home by accepting a husband's domination; depending on the region, customs and traditions impose various roles on her: the Norman peasant woman presides over the meal, while the Corsican woman does not sit at the same table as the men; but in any case, as she plays one of the most important roles in the domestic economy, she shares the man's responsibilities, his interests and his property; she is respected and it is often she who really governs: her situation is reminiscent of the place she held in ancient agricultural communities. She often has as much moral prestige

* Here too the antifeminists are equivocal. At times, holding abstract liberty to be nothing, they glorify the great concrete role the enslaved woman can play in this world: what more does she want? And other times, they underestimate the fact that negative licence does not open any concrete possibilities and they blame abstractly enfranchised women for not having proven themselves.

as her husband and sometimes even more; but her concrete condition is much harsher. The care of the garden, barnyard, sheepfold and pigpen falls on her alone; she takes part in the heavy work: cleaning the cowshed, spreading the manure, sowing, ploughing, hoeing and hay making; she digs, weeds, harvests, picks grapes and sometimes helps load and unload wagons of straw, hay, wood and sticks, litter and so on. In addition, she prepares the meals and manages the household: washing, mending and such. She assumes the heavy burdens of pregnancies and child care. She rises at dawn, feeds the barnyard and small animals, serves the first meal to the men, takes care of the children and goes out to the fields or the woods or the kitchen garden; she draws water from the well, serves the second meal, washes the dishes, works in the fields again until dinner, and after the last meal she occupies her evening by mending, cleaning, husking the corn and so forth. As she has no time to take care of her health, even during her pregnancies, she loses her shape quickly and is prematurely withered and worn out, sapped by illnesses. She is denied the few occasional compensations man finds in his social life: he goes to the city on Sundays and fair days, meets other men, goes to the café, drinks, plays cards, hunts and fishes. She stays on the farm and has no leisure. Only the rich peasant women helped by servants or dispensed from field work lead a pleasantly balanced life: they are socially honoured and enjoy greater authority in the home without being crushed by labour. But most of the time rural work reduces woman to the condition of a beast of burden.

The woman shopkeeper, the small-business owner, have always been privileged; they are the only ones since the Middle Ages whose civil capacities have been recognised by the code; women grocers, hoteliers, or tobacconists and dairy women have positions equal to man's; single or widowed, they have a legal identity of their own; married, they possess the same autonomy as their husbands. They are fortunate in working and living in the same place, and the work is not generally too consuming.

The situation of the woman worker, employee, secretary or saleswoman working outside the home is totally different. It is much more difficult to reconcile her job with managing the household (errands, preparation of meals, cleaning, and upkeep of her wardrobe take at least three and a half hours of work a day and six on Sunday; this adds a lot of time to factory or office hours). As for the learned professions, even if women lawyers, doctors and teachers manage to have some help in their households, the home and children still entail responsibilities and cares that are a serious handicap for them. In America, ingenious technology has simplified housework; but the appearance and elegance demanded of the working woman impose another constraint on her; and she maintains responsibility for the house and children. In addition, the woman who seeks her independence through work has far fewer possibilities than her masculine competitors. Her salary is inferior to man's in many fields; her job is less specialised and hence doesn't pay as well as that of a skilled worker; and for the same job, the woman is paid less. Because she is new to the world of males, she has fewer chances of success than they. Men and women alike are loath to work under a woman's orders; they always give more confidence to a man; if being a woman is not a defect, it is at least a pecularity. To 'get ahead', it is useful for a woman to make sure she has a man's support. Men are the ones who take the best places, who hold the most important jobs. It must be emphasised that in economic terms men and women constitute two castes.*

What determines women's present situation is the stubborn survival of the most ancient traditions in the new emerging civilisation. Hasty observers are wrong to think woman is not up to the possibilities offered her today or even to see only dangerous temptations in these possibilities. The truth is that her situation is tenuous, which makes it very difficult for her to adapt. Factories, offices and universities are open to women, but marriage is still considered a more honourable career, exempting her from any other participation in collective life. As in primitive civilisations, the amorous act is a service she has the right to be paid for more or less directly. Everywhere but in the USSR,† the modern woman is allowed to use her body as capital. Prostitution is tolerated,‡

---

* In America, great business fortunes often end up in women's hands: younger than their husbands, women outlive and inherit from them; but they are then older and rarely take the initiative of new investments; they act as usufructuaries rather than owners. It is men who *dispose* of the capital. In any case, these rich privileged women make up a small minority. In America more than in Europe, it is almost impossible for a woman to reach a top position as a lawyer or doctor.

† At least according to official doctrine.

‡ In Anglo-Saxon countries prostitution has never been controlled. Until 1900, American and English common law did not deem it a crime unless it was scandalous and disturbed the peace. Since then, there has been more or less repression, applied with varying degrees of harshness and of success in England and America, whose legislation on this point varies a great deal from one state to the other. In France after a long abolitionist campaign, the 13 April 1946 law ordered brothels to be closed and the fight against procurement to be reinforced: 'Considering that the existence of these brothels is incompatible with the essential principles of human dignity and the role granted to woman in modern society . . .' Prostitution nevertheless still continues to be practised. Negative and hypocritical measures are obviously not the way the situation can be modified.

seduction encouraged. And the married woman can legally make her husband support her; in addition, she is cloaked in much greater social dignity than the unmarried woman. Social customs are far from granting her sexual possibilities on a par with those of the single male, in particular, the unwed mother is an object of scandal, as motherhood is more or less forbidden to her. How could the Cinderella myth not retain its validity? Everything still encourages the girl to expect fortune and happiness from a 'Prince Charming' instead of attempting the difficult and uncertain conquest alone. For example, she can hope to attain a higher caste through him, a miracle her whole life's work will not bring her. But such a hope is harmful because it divides her strength and interests;* this split is perhaps the most serious handicap for woman. Parents still raise their daughters for marriage rather than promoting their personal development; and the daughter sees so many advantages that she desires it herself; the result is that she is often less specialised, less solidly trained than her brothers, she is less totally committed to her profession; as such, she is doomed to remain inferior in it; and the vicious circle is knotted: this inferiority reinforces her desire to find a husband. Every benefit always has a burden; but if the burden is too heavy, the benefit is no more than a servitude; for most workers today, work is a thankless task: for woman, the chore is not offset by a concrete conquest of her social dignity, freedom of behaviour and economic autonomy; it is understandable that many women workers and employees see no more than an obligation in the right to work from which marriage would deliver them. However, because she has become conscious of self and can emancipate herself from marriage through work, a woman no longer accepts her subjection docilely. What she would hope for is to reconcile family life and profession, something that does not require exhausting acrobatics. Even then, as long as the temptations of facility remain – from the economic inequality that favours certain individuals and the woman's right to sell herself to one of these privileged people – she needs to expend a greater moral effort than the male to choose the path of independence. It has not been well enough understood that temptation is also an obstacle, and even one of the most dangerous. It is amplified here by a mystification since there will be one winner out of the thousands in the lucky marriage lottery. Today's period invites, even obliges women to work; but it lures

*Cf. Philip Wylie, *Generation of Vipers*.

them with an idyllic and delightful paradise: it raises up the happy few far above those still riveted to this earthly world.

Men's economic privilege, their social value, the prestige of marriage, the usefulness of masculine support – all these encourage women to ardently want to please men. They are on the whole still in a state of serfdom. It follows that woman knows and chooses herself not as she exists for herself but as man defines her. She thus has to be described first as men dream of her since her being-for-men is one of the essential factors of her concrete condition.

Part Three
MYTHS

CHAPTER I

History has shown that men have always held all the concrete powers; from patriarchy's earliest times they have deemed it useful to keep woman in a state of dependence; their codes were set up against her; she was thus concretely established as the Other. This condition served males' economic interests; but it also suited their ontological and moral ambitions. Once the subject attempts to assert himself, the Other, who limits and denies him, is nonetheless necessary for him: he attains himself only through the reality that he is not. That is why man's life is never plenitude and rest, it is lack and movement, it is combat. Facing himself, man encounters Nature; he has a hold on it, he tries to appropriate it for himself. But it cannot satisfy him. Either it realises itself as a purely abstract opposition – it is an obstacle and remains foreign – or it passively submits to man's desire and allows itself to be assimilated by him; he possesses it only in consuming it, that is, in destroying it. In both cases, he remains alone; he is alone when touching a stone, alone when digesting a piece of fruit. The other is present only if the other is himself present to himself: that is, true alterity is a consciousness separated from my own and identical to it. It is the existence of other men that wrests each man from his immanence and enables him to accomplish the truth of his being, to accomplish himself as transcendence, as flight towards the object, as a project. But this foreign freedom, which confirms my freedom, also enters into conflict with it: this is the tragedy of the unhappy consciousness; each consciousness seeks to posit itself alone as sovereign subject. Each one tries to accomplish itself by reducing the other to slavery. But in work and fear the slave experiences himself as essential, and by a dialectical reversal the master appears the inessential one. The conflict can be overcome by the free recognition of each individual in the other, each one positing both itself and the other as object and as subject in a reciprocal movement. But friendship and generosity, which accomplish this recognition of freedoms concretely, are not easy virtues;

they are undoubtedly man's highest accomplishment; this is where he is in his truth: but this truth is a struggle endlessly begun, endlessly abolished; it demands that man surpass himself at each instant. Put into other words, man attains an authentically moral attitude when he renounces *being* in order to assume his existence; through this conversion he also renounces all possession, because possession is a way of searching for being; but the conversion by which he attains true wisdom is never finished, it has to be made ceaselessly, it demands constant effort. So much so that, unable to accomplish himself in solitude, man is ceaselessly in jeopardy in his relations with his peers: his life is a difficult enterprise whose success is never assured.

But he does not like difficulty; he is afraid of danger. He has contradictory aspirations to both life and rest, existence and being; he knows very well that 'a restless spirit' is the ransom for his development, that his distance from the object is the ransom for his being present to himself; but he dreams of restfulness in restlessness and of an opaque plenitude that his consciousness would nevertheless still inhabit. This embodied dream is, precisely, woman; she is the perfect intermediary between nature that is foreign to man and the peer who is too identical to him.[*] She pits neither the hostile silence of nature nor the hard demand of a reciprocal recognition against him; by a unique privilege she is a consciousness and yet it seems possible to possess her in the flesh. Thanks to her, there is a way to escape the inexorable dialectic of the master and the slave that springs from the reciprocity of freedoms.

It has been pointed out that there were not at first free women whom the males then enslaved and that the sexual division has never founded a division into castes. Assimilating the woman to the slave is a mistake; among slaves there were women, but free women have always existed, that is, women invested with religious and social dignity: they accepted man's sovereignty, and he did not feel threatened by a revolt that could transform him in turn into an object. Woman thus emerged as the inessential who never returned to the essential, as the absolute Other, without reciprocity. All the creation myths express this conviction that is precious to the male, for example, the Genesis legend, which, through Christianity, has spanned Western civilisation. Eve was not formed at the same time

* 'Woman is not the useless repetition of man but the enchanted space where the living alliance of man and nature occurs. If she disappeared, men would be alone, foreigners without passports in a glacial world. She is earth itself carried to life's summit, the earth become sensitive and joyful; and without her, for man, earth is mute and dead,' wrote Michel Carrouges in 'Woman's Powers', *Cahiers du Sud*, no. 292 (1948).

as man; she was not made either from a different substance or from the same clay that Adam was modelled from: she was drawn from the first male's flank. Even her birth was not autonomous; God did not spontaneously choose to create her for herself and to be directly worshipped in turn: he destined her for man; he gave her to Adam to save him from loneliness, her spouse is her origin and her finality; she is his complement in the inessential mode. Thus, she appears a privileged prey. She is nature raised to the transparency of consciousness, she is a naturally submissive consciousness. And therein lies the marvellous hope that man has often placed in woman: he hopes to accomplish himself as being through carnally possessing a being while making himself confirmed in his freedom by a docile freedom. No man would consent to being a woman, but all want there to be women. 'Thank God for creating woman.' 'Nature is good because it gave men woman.' In these and other similar phrases, man once more asserts arrogantly and naively that his presence in this world is an inevitable fact and a right, that of woman is a simple accident – but a fortunate one. Appearing as the Other, woman appears at the same time as a plenitude of being by opposition to the nothingness of existence that man experiences in itself; the Other, posited as object in the subject's eyes, is posited as in-itself, thus as being. Woman embodies positively the lack the existent carries in his heart, and man hopes to realise himself by finding himself through her.

But she has not represented for him the only incarnation of the Other, and she has not always had the same importance throughout history. In various periods, she has been eclipsed by other idols. When the city or the state devours the citizen, he is no longer in any position to deal with his personal destiny. Dedicated to the state, the Spartan woman has a higher station than that of other Greek women. But she is not transfigured by any masculine dream. The cult of the chief, be it Napoleon, Mussolini or Hitler, excludes any other. In military dictatorships and totalitarian regimes, woman is no longer a privileged object. It is understandable that woman is divinised in a country that is rich and where the citizens are uncertain about what meaning to give to their lives: this is what is happening in America. In contrast, socialist ideologies, which call for the assimilation of all human beings, reject the notion that any human category be object or idol, now and for the future: in the authentically democratic society that Marx heralded, there is no place for the Other. Few men, however, correspond exactly to the soldier or the militant that they have chosen to be; as long as these men remain individuals, woman retains a singular value in their eyes. I have seen letters written by German soldiers to French prostitutes in which, in spite of Nazism, the tradition of sentimentality proved to be naively alive. Communist writers like Aragon in France and Vittorini in Italy give a front row place in their works to woman as lover and mother. Perhaps the myth of woman will be phased out one day: the more women assert themselves as human beings, the more the marvellous quality of Other dies in them. But today it still exists in the hearts of all men.

Any myth implies a Subject who projects its hopes and fears of a transcendent heaven. Not positing themselves as Subject, women have not created the virile myth that would reflect their projects; they have neither religion nor poetry that belongs to them alone: they still dream through men's dreams. They worship the gods made by males. And males have shaped the great virile figures for their own exaltation: Hercules, Prometheus, Parsifal; in the destiny of these heroes, woman has merely a secondary role. Undoubtedly, there are stylised images of man as he is in his relations with woman: father, seducer, husband, the jealous one, the good son, the bad son; but men are the ones who have established them, and they have not attained the dignity of myth; they are barely more than clichés, while woman is exclusively defined in her relation to man. The asymmetry of the two categories, male and female, can be seen in the unilateral constitution of sexual myths. Woman is sometimes designated as 'sex'; it is she who is the flesh, its delights and its dangers. That for woman it is man who is sexed and carnal is a truth that has never been proclaimed because there is no one to proclaim it. The representation of the world as the world itself is the work of men; they describe it from a point of view that is their own and that they confound with the absolute truth.

It is always difficult to describe a myth; it does not lend itself to being grasped or defined; it haunts consciousnesses without ever being posited opposite them as a fixed object. The object fluctuates so much and is so contradictory that its unity is not at first discerned: Delilah and Judith, Aspasia and Lucretia, Pandora and Athena, woman is both Eve and the Virgin Mary. She is an idol, a servant, source of life, power of darkness; she is the elementary silence of truth, she is artifice, gossip and lies; she is the medicine woman and witch; she is man's prey; she is his downfall, she is everything he is not and wants to have, his negation and his raison d'être.

'To be a woman,' says Kierkegaard, 'is something so strange, so confused and so complicated that no one predicate can express it, and the multiple predicates that might be used contradict each other in such a way that only a woman could put up with it.'*² This comes from being considered not positively, as she is for herself: but negatively, such as she appears to man. Because if there are other *Others* than the woman, she is still always defined as Other. And her ambiguity is that of the very idea of Other: it is that of the human condition as defined in its relation with the Other. It has already been said that the Other is Evil; but as it is necessary for the Good, it reverts to the Good; through the Other I accede to the Whole, but it separates me from the Whole; it is the door to infinity and the measure of my finitude. And this is why woman embodies no set concept; through her the passage from hope to failure, hatred to love, good to bad, bad to good takes place ceaselessly. However she is considered, it is this ambivalence that is the most striking.

Man seeks the Other in woman as Nature and as his peer. But Nature inspires ambivalent feelings in man, as has been seen. He exploits it but it crushes him; he is born from and he dies in it; it is the source of his being and the kingdom he bends to his will; it is a material envelope in which the soul is held prisoner, and it is the supreme reality; it is contingency and Idea, finitude and totality; it is that which opposes Spirit and himself. Both ally and enemy, it appears as the dark chaos from which life springs forth, as this very life, and as the beyond it reaches for: woman embodies nature as Mother, Spouse and Idea; these figures are sometimes confounded and sometimes in opposition, and each has a double face.

Man sinks his roots in Nature; he was engendered, like animals and plants; he is well aware that he exists only inasmuch as he lives. But since the coming of patriarchy, life in man's eyes has taken on a dual aspect: it is consciousness, will, transcendence, it is intellect; and it is matter, passivity, immanence, it is flesh. Aeschylus, Aristotle and Hippocrates proclaimed that on earth as on Mount Olympus it is the male principle that is the true creator: form, number and movement come from him; Demeter makes corn multiply but the origin of corn and its truth are in Zeus; woman's fertility is considered merely a passive virtue. She is earth and man seed, she is water and he is fire. Creation has often been imagined as a marriage of fire and water; hot humidity gives birth to living beings; the Sun is the spouse of the Sea; Sun and Fire are male divinities; and the Sea is one of the most universally widespread maternal

* *Stages on Life's Way.*

symbols. Inert, water submits to the flamboyant rays that fertilise it. Likewise, the still earth, furrowed by the labourer's toil, receives the seeds in its rows. But its role is necessary: it is the soil that nourishes the seed, shelters it and provides its substance. Man thus continued to worship fertility goddesses, even once the Great Mother was dethroned;* he owes his harvests, herds and prosperity to Cybele. He owes her his very life. He exalts water and fire equally. 'Glory to the sea! Glory to its waves encircled by sacred fire! Glory to the wave! Glory to the fire! Glory to the strange adventure,' wrote Goethe in *Faust, Part Two*. He venerated earth: 'The matron Clay', as Blake called it. An Indian prophet advised his disciples not to dig up the earth because 'it is a sin to hurt or cut, to tear our common mother in agricultural works . . . Do I take a knife to drive into my mother's breast? . . . Do I mutilate her flesh so as to reach her bones? . . . How could I dare to cut my mother's hair?' In central India the Baidya also thought that it was a sin to 'rip the breast of their earth mother with the plough'. Inversely, Aeschylus says of Oedipus that he 'dared to sow the sacred furrow where he was formed'. Sophocles spoke of 'paternal furrows' and of the 'labourer, master of a remote field that he visited only once during the sowing'. The beloved in an Egyptian song declares: 'I am the earth!' In Islamic texts, woman is called 'field . . . grapevine'. In one of his hymns, St Francis of Assisi speaks of 'our sister, the earth, our mother, who preserves and cares for us, who produces the most varied fruits with many-coloured flowers and with grass'. Michelet, taking mud baths in Acqui, exclaims: 'Dear common mother! We are one. I come from you, I return to you!' And there are even periods of vitalistic romanticism that affirm the triumph of Life over Spirit: so the earth's and woman's magic fertility appear to be even more marvellous than the male's concerted works; so the man dreams of once again losing himself in maternal darkness to find the true sources of his being. The mother is the root driven into the depths of the cosmos that taps its vital juices; she is the fountain from which springs forth sweet water that is also mother's milk, a warm spring, a mud formed of earth and water, rich in regenerating forces.[†]

* 'Of Gaea sing I, Mother firm of all, the eldest one, who feedeth life on earth, whichever walk on land or swim the seas, or fly,' says a Homeric hymn. Aeschylus also glorifies the earth that 'gives birth to all beings, nourishes them, and then receives the fertilised germ once again.'

[†] 'To the letter the woman is Isis, fertile nature. She is the river and the bed of the river, the root and the rose, the earth and the cherry tree, the vine and the grape' (M. Carrouges, 'Woman's Powers').

But man's revolt against his carnal condition is more general; he considers himself a fallen god: his curse is to have fallen from a luminous and orderly heaven into the chaotic obscurity of the mother's womb. He desires to see himself in this fire, this active and pure breath, and it is woman who imprisons him in the mud of the earth. He would like himself to be as necessary as pure Idea, as One, All, absolute Spirit; and he finds himself enclosed in a limited body, in a place and time he did not choose, to which he was not called, useless, awkward, absurd. His very being is carnal contingence to which he is subjected in his isolation, in his unjustifiable gratuitousness. It also dooms him to death. This quivering gelatine that forms in the womb (the womb, secret and sealed like a tomb) is too reminiscent of the soft viscosity of carrion for him not to turn away from it with a shudder. Wherever life is in the process of being made – germination and fermentation – it provokes disgust because it is being made only when it is being unmade; the viscous glandular embryo opens the cycle that ends in the rotting of death. Horrified by death's gratuitousness, man is horrified at having been engendered; he would like to rescind his animal attachments; because of his birth, murderous Nature has a grip on him. For the primitives, childbirth is surrounded by strict taboos; in particular, the placenta must be carefully burned or thrown into the sea, because whoever might get hold of it would hold the newborn's fate in his hands; this envelope in which the foetus is formed is the sign of its dependence; in annihilating it, the individual is able to detach himself from the living magma and to realise himself as an autonomous being. The stain of childbirth falls back on the mother. Leviticus and all the ancient codes impose purification rites on the new mother; and often in the countryside the postpartum ceremony maintains that tradition. Everyone knows that young boys and girls and men feel a spontaneous embarrassment, one often camouflaged by sneering, at seeing a pregnant woman's stomach or the swollen breasts of the wet nurse. In Dupuytren's museums, the curious contemplate the wax embryos and the preserved foetuses with the morbid interest they would show in a defiled grave. Notwithstanding all the respect that society surrounds it with, the function of gestation inspires spontaneous repulsion. And while the little boy in early childhood remains sensually attached to the mother's flesh, when he grows up, when he is socialised and becomes aware of his individual existence, this flesh frightens him; he wants to ignore it and to see his mother as institution only; if he wants to think of her as pure and chaste, it is less from amorous jealousy than from the refusal to acknowledge her as a body. An adolescent boy becomes embarrassed, blushes if he meets his mother, sisters or women in his family when he is out with his friends: their presence recalls the regions of immanence from which he wants to escape; she reveals the roots that he wants to pull himself away from. The boy's irritation when his mother kisses and caresses him has the same significance; he gives up his family, mother, and mother's breast. He would like to have emerged, like Athena, into the adult world, armed from head to toe, invulnerable.* Being conceived and born is the curse weighing on his destiny, the blemish on his being. And it is the warning of his death. The cult of germination has always been associated with the cult of the dead. Mother Earth engulfs the bones of its children within it. Women – the Parcae and Moirai – weave human destiny; but they also cut the threads. In most folk representations, Death is woman and women mourn the dead because death is their work.†

Thus, Mother Earth has a face of darkness: she is chaos, where everything comes from and must return to one day; she is Nothingness. The many aspects of the world that the day uncovers commingle in the night: night of spirit locked up in the generality and opacity of matter, night of sleep and nothing. At the heart of the sea, it is night: woman is the *Mare tenebrarum* dreaded by ancient navigators; it is night in the bowels of the earth. Man is threatened with being engulfed in this night, the reverse of fertility, and it horrifies him. He aspires to the sky, to light, to sunny heights, to the pure and crystal-clear cold of blue; and underfoot is a moist, hot and dark gulf ready to swallow him; many legends have the hero falling and for ever lost in maternal darkness: a cave, an abyss, hell.

But once again ambivalence is at work here: while germination is always associated with death, death is also associated with fertility. Detested death is like a new birth and so it is blessed. The dead hero, like Osiris is resurrected every springtime, and he is regenerated by a new birth. Man's supreme hope, says Jung, 'is that the dark waters of death become the waters of life, that death and its cold embrace are the mother's lap, just as the sea, while engulfing the sun, re-births in the depths.'‡ The theme of the burial of the sun god within the sea and its

---

* See our study on Montherlant, the epitome of this attitude, a little further on.

† Demeter is the archetype of the *mater dolorosa*. But other goddesses – Ishtar and Artemis – are cruel. Kali is holding a blood-filled skull. 'The heads of your newly killed sons hang from your neck like a necklace . . . Your figure is beautiful like rain clouds, your feet are soiled with blood,' says a Hindu poem.

‡ *Metamorphoses of the Libido and its Symbols.*

dazzling re-emergence is common to many mythologies. And man wants to live but he also hopes for rest, sleep, for nothingness. He does not wish for immortality for himself, and thus he can learn to love death. 'Inorganic matter is the mother's breast,' Nietzsche wrote. 'Being delivered from life means becoming real again, completing oneself. Anyone who understands that would consider returning to unfeeling dust as a holiday.' Chaucer puts this prayer into the mouth of an old man who cannot die:

> 'Thus restless I my wretched way must make
> And on the ground, which is my mother's gate,
> I knock with my staff early, aye, and late
> And cry: "Oh dear mother, let me in!'

Man wants to assert his individual existence and proudly rest on his 'essential difference', but he also wants to break the barriers of the self and commingle with water, earth, night, Nothingness, with the Whole. Woman who condemns man to finitude also enables him to surpass his own limits: that is where the equivocal magic surrounding her comes from.

In all civilisations and still today, she inspires horror in man: the horror of his own carnal contingence that he projects on her. The girl who has not yet gone through puberty does not pose a threat; she is not the object of any taboo and has no sacred characteristics. In many primitive societies her sex even seems innocent: erotic games between boys and girls are allowed in childhood. Woman becomes impure the day she might be able to procreate. In primitive societies the strict taboos concerning girls on the day of their first period have often been described; even in Egypt, where the woman is treated with particular respect, she remains confined during her whole menstrual period.* She is often put on a rooftop or relegated to a shack on the outskirts of the town; she can be neither seen nor touched: what's more, she must not even touch herself with her own hand; for peoples that practise daily flea removal, she is given a stick with which she is able to scratch herself; she must not touch food with her fingers; sometimes she is strictly forbidden to eat; in other cases, her mother

---

* The difference between mystical and mythical beliefs and individuals' lived convictions is apparent in the following fact: Lévi-Strauss points out that 'young Winnebago Indians visit their mistresses and take advantage of the privacy of the prescribed isolation of these women during their menstrual period'.

and sister are permitted to feed her with an instrument; but all objects that come in contact with her during this period must be burned. After this first test, the menstrual taboos are a little less strict, but they remain harsh. In particular, in Leviticus: 'And if a woman have an issue, and her issue in her flesh be blood, she shall be put apart seven days: and whosoever toucheth her shall be unclean until the even. And every thing that she lieth upon in her separation shall be unclean: every thing also that she sitteth upon shall be unclean. And whosoever toucheth her bed shall wash his clothes, and bathe himself in water, and be unclean until the even.' This text is perfectly symmetrical with one concerning gonorrhoea-provoked impurity in man. And the purifying sacrifice is identical in the two cases. Seven days after she has been purified of her flow, two turtledoves or two young pigeons have to be brought to the sacrificer, who offers them to the Eternal. Even in matriarchal societies, the virtues connected to menstruation are ambivalent. On one hand, it brings social activities to a halt, destroys the vital force, withers flowers, causes fruit to fall; but it also has beneficial effects: menses are used in love philtres, in remedies, and in particular in healing cuts and bruises. Still today, when some Indians go off to fight spectral monsters haunting their rivers, they place a fibre wad filled with menstrual blood on the bow of their boat: its emanations are harmful to their supernatural enemies. In some Greek cities, young girls pay homage to the Temple of Astarte by wearing linens stained by their first menstrual blood. But since patriarchy, only harmful powers have been attributed to the bizarre liquor flowing from the feminine sex. Pliny in his *Natural History* says: 'The menstruating woman spoils harvests, devastates gardens, kills seeds, makes fruit fall, kills bees; if she touches the wine, it turns to vinegar; milk sours . . .'

An old English poet expresses the same thought:

> *Oh! Menstruating woman, thou'rt a fiend*
> *From whom all nature should be closely screened!*

These beliefs have been vigorously perpetuated right up to today. In 1878, a member of the British Medical Association wrote in the *British Medical Journal*: 'It is an indisputable fact that meat goes bad when touched by menstruating women.' He said that he personally knew of two cases of hams spoiling in such circumstances. In the refineries of the North at the beginning of this century, women were prohibited by law from going into the factory when they were afflicted by what the Anglo-Saxons call the 'curse' because the sugar turned black. And in Saigon, women are not employed in opium factories: because of their periods, the opium goes bad and becomes bitter. These beliefs survive in many areas of the French countryside. Any cook knows how impossible it is to make mayonnaise if she is indisposed or simply in the presence of another woman who is indisposed. In Anjou, recently, an old gardener who had stocked that year's cider harvest in the cellar wrote to the master of the house: 'Don't let the young women of the household and their female guests go through the cellar on certain days of the month: they would prevent the cider from fermenting.' When the cook heard about this letter, she shrugged her shoulders: 'That never prevented cider from fermenting,' she said, 'it is only bad for bacon fat: it cannot be salted in the presence of an indisposed woman; it would rot.'*

Putting this repulsion in the same category as that provoked by blood is most inadequate: more imbued with the mysterious mana that is both life and death than anything else, blood, of course, is in itself a sacred element. But menstrual blood's baleful powers are more particular. Menstrual blood embodies the essence of femininity, which is why its flow endangers woman herself, whose mana is thus materialised. During the Chaga initiation rites, girls are urged to carefully conceal their menstrual blood. 'Do not show it to your mother, for she would die! Do not show it to your age-mates, for there may be a wicked one among them, who will take away the cloth with which you have cleaned yourself, and you will be barren in your marriage. Do not show it to a bad woman, who will take the cloth to place it in the top of her hut . . . with the result that you cannot bear children. Do not throw the cloth on the path or in the bush. A wicked person might do evil things with it. Bury it in the ground. Protect the blood from the gaze of your father, brothers and sisters. It is a sin to let

*A doctor from the Cher region told me that women in that situation are banned from going into the mushroom beds. The question as to whether there is any basis for these preconceived ideas is still discussed today. Dr Binet's only fact supporting them is an observation by Schink (cited by Vignes). Schink supposedly saw flowers wilt in an indisposed servant's hands; yeast cakes made by this woman supposedly rose only three centimetres instead of the five they usually rose. In any case, these facts are pretty feeble and poorly established when considering the importance and universality of the obviously mystical beliefs they come from.

them see it.'* For the Aleuts, if the father sees his daughter during
her first menstruation, she could go blind or deaf. It is thought that
during this period woman is possessed by a spirit and invested with a
dangerous power. Some primitives believe that the flow is provoked
by snakebite, as woman has suspicious affinities with snakes and lizards;
it is supposed to be similar to crawling animals' venom. Leviticus
compares it to gonorrhoea; the bleeding feminine sex is not only a
wound but a suspicious sore. And Vigny associates the notion of soiling
with illness: 'Woman, sick child and impure twelve times.' The result
of interior alchemic troubles, the periodic haemorrhage woman suffers
from is bizarrely aligned with the moon's cycle: the moon also has
dangerous whims.†* Woman is part of the formidable workings that
order the course of planets and the sun, she is prey to the cosmic
forces that determine the destiny of stars and tides, while men are
subjected to their worrisome radiation. But it is especially striking that
menstrual blood's effects are linked to the ideas of cream going sour,
mayonnaise that does not take, fermentation and decomposition; it is
also claimed that it is apt to cause fragile objects to break; to spring
violin and harp strings; but above all it influences organic substances
that are midway between matter and life; this is less because it is
blood than because it emanates from genital organs; even without
knowing its exact function, people understood it to be linked to the
germination of life: ignorant of the existence of the ovary, the
ancients saw in menstruation the complement of the sperm. In fact,
it is not this blood that makes woman impure, but rather, this
blood is a manifestation of her impurity; it appears when the
woman can be fertile; when it disappears, she becomes sterile again;
it pours forth from this womb where the foetus is made. The horror
of feminine fertility that man experiences is expressed through it.

The strictest taboo of all concerning woman in her impure state is the
prohibition of sexual intercourse with her. Leviticus condemns man to seven
days of impurity if he transgresses this rule. The Laws of Manu are even

---

† Quoted in Lévi-Strauss, *The Elementary Structures of Kinship*.

† The moon is a source of fertility; it is seen as the 'master of women'; it is often
believed that the moon, in the form of a man or a snake, couples with women. The
snake is an epiphany of the moon; it moults and regenerates, it is immortal, it is a
power that distributes fertility and science; it watches over holy sources, the Tree of
Life, the Fountain of Youth, and so on., but it is also the snake that takes immortality
away from man. It is said that it couples with women. Persian and rabbinical traditions
claim that menstruation is due to the first woman's intercourse with the snake.

harsher: 'The wisdom, energy, strength, and vitality of a man coming near a woman stained by menstrual excretions perish definitively.' Priests ordered fifty days of penance for men who had sexual relations during menstruation. Since the feminine principle is then considered as reaching its highest power, it is feared that it would triumph over the male principle in intimate contact. Less specifically, man shies away from finding the mother's feared essence in the woman he possesses; he works at dissociating these two aspects of femininity: that explains why incest is prohibited by exogamy or more modern forms and is a universal law; that explains why man distances himself from woman sexually when she is particularly destined for her reproductive role: during her period, when she is pregnant, or when she is nursing. Not only does the Oedipus complex – whose description, incidentally, has to be revised – not contradict this attitude: on the contrary, it even implies it. Man guards himself against woman to the extent that she is the confused source of the world and disorder become organic.

However, this representation of woman also allows the society that has been separated from the cosmos and the gods to remain in communication with them. She still assures the fertility of the fields for the Bedouins and the Iroquois; in ancient Greece, she heard subterranean voices; she understood the language of the wind and the trees: she was the Pythia, Sibyl and prophetess. The dead and the gods spoke through her mouth. Still today, she has these powers of divination: she is medium, palmist, card reader, clairvoyant, inspired; she hears voices and has visions. When men feel the need to delve into vegetable and animal life – like Antaeus, who touched earth to recoup his strength – they call upon woman. Throughout the Greek and Roman rationalist civilisations, chthonian cults subsisted. They could usually be found on the periphery of official religious life; they even ended up, as in Eleusis, taking the form of mysteries: they had the opposite meaning of sun cults, where man asserted his will for separation and spirituality; but they complemented them; man sought to overcome his solitude by ecstasy: that is the goal of mysteries, orgies and bacchanals. In the world reconquered by males, the male god Dionysus usurped Ishtar's and Astarte's magic and wild virtues; but yet it was women who went wild over his image: the maenads, thyades and bacchantes led men to religious drunkenness and sacred madness. The role of sacred prostitution is similar: both to unleash and to channel the powers of fertility. Even today, popular holidays are exemplified by outbreaks of eroticism; woman is not just an object of pleasure but a means of reaching this *hubris* in which the individual surpasses himself. 'What a being possesses in the deepest part of himself, what is lost and tragic, the "blinding wonder" can no longer be found anywhere but on a bed,' wrote Georges Bataille.

In sexual release, man in his lover's embrace seeks to lose himself in the infinite mystery of the flesh. But it has already been seen that his normal sexuality, on the contrary, dissociates Mother from Wife. He finds the mysterious alchemies of life repugnant, while his own life is nourished and enchanted by the tasty fruits of the earth; he desires to appropriate them for himself; he covets Venus freshly emerging from the waters. Woman first discovers herself in patriarchy as wife since the supreme creator is male. Before being the mother of humankind, Eve is Adam's companion; she was given to man for him to possess and fertilise as he possesses and fertilises the soil; and through her, he makes his kingdom out of all nature. Man does not merely seek in the sexual act subjective and ephemeral pleasure. He wants to conquer, take and possess; to have a woman is to conquer her; he penetrates her as the ploughshare in the furrows; he makes her his as he makes his the earth he is working: he ploughs, he plants, he sows: these images are as old as writing; from antiquity to today a thousand examples can be mentioned: 'Woman is like the field and man like the seeds,' say the Laws of Manu. In an André Masson drawing there is a man, shovel in hand, tilling the garden of a feminine sex organ.* Woman is her husband's prey, his property.

Man's hesitation between fear and desire, between the terror of being possessed by uncontrollable forces and the will to overcome them, is grippingly reflected in the virginity myths. Dreaded or desired or even demanded by the male, virginity is the highest form of the feminine mystery; this aspect is simultaneously the most troubling and the most fascinating. Depending on whether man feels crushed by the powers encircling him or arrogantly believes he is able to make them his, he refuses or demands that his wife be delivered to him as a virgin. In the most primitive societies, where woman's power is exalted, it is fear that dominates; woman has to be deflowered the night before the wedding. Marco Polo asserted that for the Tibetans, 'none of them wanted to take a virgin girl as wife'. A rational explanation has sometimes been given for this refusal: man does not want a wife who has not yet aroused masculine desires. Al-Bakri, the Arab geographer, speaking of the Slavic peoples, notes that 'if a man gets married and

* Rabelais called the male sex organ 'the worker of nature'. The religious and historical origin of the phallus-ploughshare–woman-furrow association has already been pointed out.

finds that his wife is a virgin, he says: "If you were worth something, men would have loved you and one of them would have taken your virginity."' He then chases her out and repudiates her. It is also claimed that some primitives refuse to marry a woman unless she has already given birth, thus proving her fertility. But the real reasons for the very widespread deflowering customs are mystical. Certain peoples imagine the presence of a serpent in the vagina that would bite the spouse during the breaking of the hymen; terrifying virtues are given to virginal blood, linked to menstrual blood and capable of ruining the male's vigour. These images express the idea that the feminine principle is so powerful and threatening because it is intact.* Sometimes the deflowering issue is not raised; for example, Malinowski describes an indigenous population in which, because sexual games are allowed from childhood on, girls are never virgins. Sometimes, the mother, older sister or some other matron systematically deflowers the girl and throughout her childhood widens the vaginal opening. Deflowering can also be carried out by women during puberty using a stick, a bone or a stone and this is not considered a surgical operation. In other tribes, the girl at puberty is subjected to savage initiation rites: men drag her out of the village and deflower her with instruments or by raping her. Giving over virgins to passersby is one of the most common rites; either these strangers are not thought to be sensitive to this mana dangerous only for the tribes' males or it does not matter what evils befall them. Even more often, the priest, medicine man, boss or head of the tribe deflowers the fiancée the night before the wedding; on the Malabar coast, the Brahmans have to carry out this act, apparently without joy, for which they demand high wages. All holy objects are known to be dangerous for the outsider, but consecrated individuals can handle them without risk; that explains why priests and chiefs are able to tame the malefic forces against which the spouse has to protect himself. In Rome all that was left of these customs was a symbolic ceremony: the fiancée was seated on a stone Priapus phallus, with the double aim of increasing her fertility and absorbing the over-powerful and therefore harmful fluids within her. The husband defends himself in yet another way: he himself deflowers the virgin but during ceremonies that render him invulnerable at this critical juncture; for example he does it in front of the whole village

---

* The power in combat attributed to the virgin comes from this: the Valkyries and Joan of Arc, for example.

with a stick or bone. In Samoa, he uses his finger covered in a white cloth and distributes bloodstained shreds to the spectators. There is also the case of the man allowed to deflower his wife normally but he has to wait three days to ejaculate in her so that the generating seed is not soiled by hymenal blood.

In a classic reversal in the area of sacred things, virginal blood in less primitive societies is a propitious symbol. There are still villages in France where the bloody sheet is displayed to parents and friends the morning after the wedding. In the patriarchal regime, man became woman's master; and the same characteristics that are frightening in animals or untamed elements become precious qualities for the owner who knows how to subdue them. Man took the ardour of the wild horse and the violence of lightning and waterfalls as the instruments of his prosperity. Therefore, he wants to annex woman to him with all her riches intact. The order of virtue imposed on the girl certainly obeys rational motives: like chastity for the wife, the fiancée's innocence is necessary to protect the father from incurring any risk of bequeathing his goods to a foreign child. But woman's virginity is demanded more imperiously when man considers the wife as his personal property. First of all, the idea of possession is always impossible to realise positively; the truth is that one never has anything or anyone; one attempts to accomplish it in a negative way; the surest way to assert that a good is mine is to prevent another from using it. And then nothing seems as desirable to man as what has never belonged to any other human: thus conquest is a unique and absolute event. Virgin land has always fascinated explorers; alpinists kill themselves every year attempting to assault an untouched mountain or even trying to open up a new trail; and the curious risk their lives to descend underground to the bottom of unprobed caves. An object that men have already mastered has become a tool; cut off from its natural bonds, it loses its deepest attributes; there is more promise in the wild water of torrents than in that of public fountains. A virgin body has the freshness of secret springs, the morning bloom of a closed corolla, the orient of the pearl the sun has never yet caressed. Cave, temple, sanctuary or secret garden: like the child, man is fascinated by these shadowy and closed places never yet touched by animating consciousness, waiting to be lent a soul: it seems to him that he in fact created what he is the only one to grasp and penetrate. Moreover, every desire pursues the aim of consuming the desired object, entailing its destruction. By breaking the hymen, man possesses the feminine body more intimately than by a penetration that leaves it intact; in this irreversible operation, he unequivocally makes it a passive object, asserting his hold on it. This exactly expresses the meaning in the legend of the knight who hacks his way through thorny bushes to pick a rose never before inhaled; not only does he uncover it, but he breaks its stem, thereby conquering it. The image is so clear that in popular language, 'taking a woman's flower' means destroying her virginity, giving the origin of the word 'de-flowering'.

But virginity only has this sexual attraction when allied with youth; otherwise, its mystery reverts to disquiet. Many men today are sexually repulsed by older virgins; psychological reasons alone do not explain why 'old maids' are regarded as bitter and mean matrons. The curse is in their very flesh, this flesh that is object for no subject, that no desire has made desirable, that has bloomed and wilted without finding a place in the world of men; turned away from her destination, the old maid becomes an eccentric object, as troubling as the incommunicable thinking of a madman. Of a forty-year-old, still beautiful, woman presumed to be a virgin, I heard a man say with great vulgarity: 'It's full of cobwebs in there . . .' It is true that deserted and unused cellars and attics are full of unsavoury mystery; they fill up with ghosts; abandoned by humanity, houses become the dwellings of spirits. If feminine virginity has not been consecrated to a god, it is easily then thought to imply marriage with the devil. Virgins that men have not subjugated, old women who have escaped their power, are more easily looked upon as witches than other women; as woman's destiny is to be doomed to another, if she does not submit to a man's yoke, she is available for the devil's.

Exorcised by deflowering rites or on the contrary purified by her virginity, the wife could thus be desirable prey. Taking her gives the lover all the riches of life he desires to possess. She is all the fauna, all the earthly flora: gazelle, doe, lilies and roses, downy peaches, fragrant raspberries; she is precious stones, mother-of-pearl, agate, pearls, silk, the blue of the sky, the freshness of springs, air, flame, earth and water. All the poets of East and West have metamorphosed woman's body into flowers, fruits and birds. Here again, throughout antiquity, the Middle Ages and the modern period, it would be necessary to quote a thick anthology. The Song of Songs is well known, in which the male loved one says to the female loved one:

Thou hast doves' eyes . . .
thy hair is as a flock of goats . . .
Thy teeth are like a flock of sheep that are even shorn . . .
thy temples are like a piece of a pomegranate . . .
Thy two breasts are like two young roes that are twins . . .
Honey and milk are under thy tongue.

In *Arcanum 17*, André Breton took up this eternal song: 'Melusina at the instant of her second scream: she sprang up off her globeless haunches, her belly is the whole August harvest, her torso bursts into fireworks from her arched back, modelled on a swallow's two wings, her breasts are two ermines caught in their own scream, blinding because they are lit by scorching coals of their howling mouth. And her arms are the soul of streams that sing and float perfumes.'[4]

Man finds shining stars and the moody moon, sunlight, and the darkness of caves on woman; wildflowers from hedgerows and the garden's proud rose are also woman. Nymphs, dryads, mermaids, water sprites and fairies haunt the countryside, the woods, lakes, seas and moors. This animism is profoundly anchored in men. For the sailor, the sea is a dangerous woman, perfidious and difficult to conquer but that he cherishes by dint of taming it. Proud, rebellious, virginal and wicked, the mountain is woman for the mountain climber who wants to take it, even at risk of life. It is often said that these comparisons manifest sexual sublimation; rather, they express an affinity between woman and the elements as primal as sexuality itself. Man expects more from possessing woman than the satisfaction of an instinct; she is the special object through which he subjugates Nature. Other objects can also play this role. Sometimes it is on young boys' bodies that man seeks the sand of beaches, the velvet of nights, the fragrance of honeysuckle. But sexual penetration is not the only way to realise this carnal appropriation of the earth. In his novel *To a God Unknown*, Steinbeck shows a man who chooses a mossy rock as mediator between him and nature; in *The Cat*, Colette describes a young husband who settles his love on his favourite female cat because this gentle wild animal enables him to have a grasp on the sensual universe that his woman companion cannot give. The Other can be embodied in the sea and the mountain just as well as in the woman; they provide man with the same passive and unexpected resistance that allows him to accomplish himself; they are a refusal to conquer, a prey to possess.

If the sea and the mountain are woman, it is because woman is also the sea and the mountain for the lover.*

But not just any woman can play the role of mediator between man and the world; man is not satisfied with finding sexual organs complementary to his own in his partner. She must embody the wondrous blossoming of life while concealing its mysterious disturbances at the same time. First of all, she has to have youth and health, for man cannot be enraptured in his embrace of a living thing unless he forgets that all life is inhabited by death. And he desires still more: that his beloved be beautiful. The ideal of feminine beauty is variable; but some requirements remain constant; one of them is that since woman is destined to be possessed, her body has to provide the inert and passive qualities of an object. Virile beauty is the body's adaptation to active functions such as strength, agility, flexibility, and the manifestation of a transcendence animating a flesh that must never collapse into itself. The only symmetry to be found in the feminine ideal is in Sparta, Fascist Italy and Nazi Germany, societies that destined woman for the state and not for the individual and that considered her exclusively as mother, with no place for eroticism. But when woman is delivered to the male as his property, he claims that her flesh be presented in its pure facticity. Her body is grasped not as the emanation of a subjectivity but as a thing weighted in its immanence; this body must not radiate to the rest of the world, it must not promise anything but itself: its desire has to be stopped. The most naive form of

* The sentence by Samivel, quoted by Bachelard in *Earth and Reveries of Will*, is telling: 'I had ceased, little by little, to regard the mountains crouching in a circle at my feet as foes to vanquish, as female to trample underfoot, or trophies to provide myself and others proof of my own worth.' The mountain / woman ambivalence comes across in the common idea of 'foes to vanquish', and 'proof of my own worth'.

This reciprocity can be seen, for example, in these two poems by Senghor:[5]

> Naked woman, dark woman
> Ripe fruit with firm flesh, dark raptures of black wine,
> Mouth that gives music to my mouth
> Savanna of clear horizons, savanna quivering to the fervent caress
> Of the East Wind . . .

And:

> Oho! Congo, lying on your bed of forests, queen of subdued Africa.
> May the mountain phalluses hold high your pavilion
> For you are woman by my head, by my tongue,
> You are woman by my belly.

this requirement is the Hottentot ideal of the steatopygous Venus, as the buttocks are the part of the body with the fewest nerve endings, where the flesh appears as a given without purpose. The taste of people from the East for fleshy women is similar; they love the absurd luxury of this fatty proliferation that is not enlivened by any project, that has no other meaning than to be there.* Even in civilisations of a more subtle sensibility, where notions of form and harmony come into play, breasts and buttocks were prized objects because of the gratuitousness and contingency of their development. Customs and fashions were often applied to cut the feminine body from its transcendence: the Chinese woman with bound feet could barely walk, the Hollywood star's painted nails deprived her of her hands; high heels, corsets, hoops, farthingales and crinolines were meant less to accentuate the woman's body's curves than to increase the body's powerlessness. Weighted down by fat or on the contrary so diaphanous that any effort is forbidden to it, paralysed by uncomfortable clothes and rites of propriety, the body thus appeared to man as his thing. Makeup and jewels were also used for this petrification of the body and face. The function of dress and ornaments is highly complex; for some primitives, it had a sacred character; but its most usual role was to complete woman's metamorphosis into an idol. An equivocal idol: man wanted her erotic, for her beauty to be part of that of flowers and fruits; but she also had to be smooth, hard, eternal like a stone. The role of dress is both to link the body more closely to and to wrest it away from nature, to give a necessarily set artifice to palpitating life. Woman was turned into plant, panther, diamond or mother-of-pearl by mingling flowers, furs, precious stones, shells and feathers on her body; she perfumed herself so as to smell of roses and lilies: but feathers, silk, pearls and perfumes also worked to hide the animal rawness from its flesh and odour. She painted her mouth and her cheeks to acquire a mask's immobile solidity; her gaze was imprisoned in the thickness of kohl and mascara, it was no longer anything but her eyes' shimmering ornamentation; braided, curled or sculpted, her hair lost its troublesome vegetal mystery. In the embellished woman, Nature was present but

* 'Hottentot women, in whom steatopygia is neither as developed nor as consistent as in Bushman women, think this body type is aesthetically pleasing and starting in childhood massage their daughters' buttocks to develop them. Likewise, the artificial fattening of women, a real stuffing by two means, immobility and abundant ingestion of specific foods, especially milk, is found in various regions of Africa. It is still practised by rich Arab and Jewish city dwellers in Algeria, Tunisia and Morocco' (Luquet, 'Les Vénus des cavernes', *Journal de psychologie*, 1934).

captive, shaped by a human will in accordance with man's desire. Woman was even more desirable when nature was shown off to full advantage and more rigorously subjugated: the sophisticated woman has always been the ideal erotic object. And the taste for a more natural beauty is often a specious form of sophistication. Rémy de Gourmont wanted women's hair to be loose, free as the streams and prairie grass: but it is on Veronica Lake's hair that the waves of water and wheat could be caressed, not on a mop of hair totally left to nature. The younger and healthier a woman is and the more her new and glossy body seems destined for eternal freshness, the less useful is artifice; but the carnal weakness of this prey that man takes and its ominous deterioration always have to be hidden from him. It is also because he fears contingent destiny, because he dreams her immutable and necessary, that man looks for the idea's exactitude on woman's face, body and legs. In primitive people, this idea is the perfection of the popular type: a thick-lipped race with a flat nose forged a thick-lipped Venus with a flat nose; later on, the canons of a more complex aesthetics would be applied to women. But in any case, the more the traits and proportions of a woman seemed contrived, the more she delighted the heart of man because she seemed to escape the metamorphosis of natural things. The result is this strange paradox that by desiring to grasp nature, but transfigured, in woman, man destines her to artifice. She is not only physis but just as much antiphysis; and not only in the civilisation of electric permanents, hair waxing, latex girdles, but also in the country of African lip-disk women, in China and everywhere on earth. Swift denounced this mystification in his famous ode to Celia; he railed against the coquette's paraphernalia, pointing out with disgust her body's animal servitudes; he was doubly wrong to become indignant; because man wants woman at the same time to be animal and plant and that she hide behind a fabricated armature; he loves her emerging from the waves and from a high-fashion house, naked and dressed, naked beneath her clothes, exactly as he finds her in the human universe. The city dweller seeks animality in woman; but for the young peasant doing his military service, the brothel embodies the magic of the city. Woman is field and pasture but also Babylonia.

However, here is the first lie, the first betrayal of woman: of life itself, which, even clothed in the most attractive forms, is still inhabited by the ferments of old age and death. The very use man makes of her destroys her most precious qualities; weighed down by childbirth, she loses her sexual attraction; even sterile, the passage of time is enough to alter her charms. Disabled, ugly or old, woman repels. She is said to be withered, faded, like a plant. Man's decrepitude is obviously also frightful; but normal man does not experience other men as flesh; he has only an abstract solidarity with these autonomous and foreign bodies. It is on woman's body, this body meant for him, that man significantly feels the flesh's deterioration. It is through the male's hostile eyes that Villon's 'once beautiful courtesan' contemplates her body's degradation. Old and ugly women not only are objects without assets but also provoke hatred mixed with fear. They embody the disturbing figure of Mother, while the charms of the Wife have faded away.

But even the Wife was a dangerous prey. Demeter survives in Venus emerging from the waters, fresh foam, the blonde harvest; appropriating woman for himself through the pleasure he derives from her, man awakens in her the suspicious powers of fertility; it is the same organ he penetrates that produces the child. This explains why man in all societies is protected against the feminine sex's threats by so many taboos. There is no reciprocity as woman has nothing to fear from the male; his sex is considered secular, profane. The phallus can be raised to the dignity of a god: there is no element of terror in worshipping it, and in daily life woman does not have to be defended against it mystically; it is simply propitious for her. It also has to be pointed out that in many matriarchies, sexuality is very free; but this is only during woman's childhood, in her early youth, when coitus is not linked to the idea of generation. Malinowski is surprised that young people who sleep together freely in the 'house of the unmarried' show off their love lives so readily; the explanation is that an unmarried daughter is considered unable to bear a child and the sexual act is merely a quiet and ordinary pleasure. On the contrary, once married, her spouse cannot give her any public sign of affection, nor touch her, and any allusion to their intimate relations is sacrilegious; she then has to be part of the formidable essence of mother, and coitus becomes a sacred act. From then on it is surrounded by taboos and precautions. Intercourse is forbidden when cultivating the earth, sowing and planting: in this case fertilising forces necessary for the harvests' prosperity cannot be wasted in inter-individual relations; respect for powers associated with fertility enjoins such relations to be economised. But on most occasions, chastity protects the spouse's virility; it is demanded when man goes off fishing or hunting and above all when he is preparing for war; in the union with woman, the male principle weakens and he has to avoid intercourse whenever he needs the totality of his forces. It has been wondered if the horror man feels for woman comes from that inspired by sexuality in general, or vice versa. We have seen that in Leviticus, in particular, wet dreams are considered a stain even though woman has nothing to do with them. And in our modern societies, masturbation is considered a danger and a sin; many children and young boys who indulge in it suffer terrible anxieties because of it. Society and parents above all make solitary pleasure a vice; but more than one young boy has been spontaneously frightened by his first ejac-ulations: blood or sperm, any flow of one's own substance seems worrying; it is one's life, one's mana, that is running out. However, even if subjectively man can go through erotic experiences where woman is not present, she is objectively involved in his sexuality: as Plato said in the myth of the androgynes, the male organism presupposes the woman's. He discovers woman in discovering his own sex, even if she is not given to him in flesh and blood, nor in image; and inversely, woman is fearsome inasmuch as she embodies sexuality. The immanent and tran-scendent aspects of living experience can never be separated: what I fear or desire is always an avatar of my own existence, but nothing comes to me except through what is not my self. The nonself is involved in wet dreams, in erection, and if not in the precise figure of woman, at least in Nature and Life: the individual feels possessed by a foreign magic. Likewise, his ambivalence towards women is seen in his attitude towards his own sex organ; he is proud, he laughs about it, he is embarrassed by it. The little boy defiantly compares his penis with his friends'; his first erection fills him with pride and frightens him at the same time. The adult man looks upon his sex organ as a symbol of transcendence and power; he is as proud of it as a muscle and at the same time as a magical grace: it is a freedom rich with the whole contingence of the given, a given freely desired; this is the contradictory aspect that enchants him; but he suspects the trap in it; this sex organ by which he claims to assert himself does not obey him; full of unassuaged desires, arising unexpect-edly, sometimes relieving itself in dreams, it manifests a suspicious and capricious vitality. Man claims to make Spirit triumph over Life, activity over passivity; his consciousness keeps nature at a distance, his will shapes it, but in the figure of his sex organ he rediscovers life, nature and passivity in himself. 'The sexual parts are the real centre of the will and the oppo-site pole is the brain,' wrote Schopenhauer. What he called will is attach-ment to life, which is suffering and death, while the brain is thought that separates itself from life while representing it: sexual shame according to him is what we feel about our stupid carnal stubbornness. Even if the pessimism of his theories is rejected, he is right to see the expression of man's duality in the sex–brain opposition. As a subject he posits the

world, and, remaining outside the universe he posits, he makes himself
the lord of it; if he grasps himself as flesh, as sex, he is no longer
autonomous consciousness, transparent freedom: he is engaged in the
world, a limited and perishable object; and it is undoubtedly true that
the generative act goes beyond the body's limits: but he constitutes them
at the very same instant. The penis, father of generations, is symmetrical to the maternal womb; grown from a fattened germ in woman's
womb, man is the bearer of germs himself, and by this seed that gives
life, it is also his own life that is disavowed. 'The birth of children is the
death of parents,' said Hegel. Ejaculation is the promise of death, it
affirms the species over the individual; the existence of the sex organ
and its activity negate the subject's proud singularity. The sex organ is
a focus of scandal because of this contestation of spirit over life. Man
exalts the phallus in that he grasps it as transcendence and activity, as a
means of appropriation of the other; but he is ashamed when he sees
in it only passive flesh through which he is the plaything of Life's obscure
forces. This shame is often disguised as irony. The sex organ of others
draws laughter easily; but because the erection looks like a planned movement and yet is undergone, it often looks ridiculous; and the simple
mention of genital organs provokes glee. Malinowski says that for the
wild people among whom he lived, just mentioning the word for these
'shameful parts' made them laugh uncontrollably; many crude or saucy
jokes are not much more than rudimentary puns on these words. For
some primitive peoples, during the days devoted to weeding out gardens,
women had the right to brutally rape any stranger that dared to come
into the village; attacking him all together, they often left him half-dead:
the tribesmen laughed at this exploit; by this rape, the victim was constituted as passive and dependent flesh; he was possessed by the women
and through them by their husbands, while in normal coitus man wants
to affirm himself as possessor.

But this is where he will experience the ambiguity of his carnal condition most obviously. He takes pride in his sexuality only to the extent
that it is a means of appropriation of the Other: and this dream of
possession only ends in failure. In authentic possession, the other as
such is abolished, it is consumed and destroyed: only the sultan of *The
Thousand and One Nights* has the power to cut off his mistresses' heads
when dawn withdraws them from his bed; woman survives man's
embraces and she is thus able to escape from him; as soon as he opens
his arms, his prey once again becomes foreign to him; here she is new,
intact, completely ready to be possessed by a new lover in just as

ephemeral a way. One of the male's dreams is to 'brand' woman so that she remains his for ever; but even the most arrogant male knows only too well that he will never leave her anything more than memories, and the most passionate images are cold compared with real sensation. A whole literature has denounced this failure. It is made objective in the woman, who is called fickle and treacherous because her body destines her to man in general and not to a particular man. Her betrayal is even more perfidious: it is she who turns the lover into a prey. Only a body can touch another body; the male masters the desired flesh only by becoming flesh himself; Eve is given to Adam for him to accomplish his transcendence in her and she draws him into the night of immanence; the mother forges the obscure wrapping for her son from which he now wants to escape, while the mistress encloses him in this opaque clay through the vertigo of pleasure. He wanted to possess: but here he is, possessed himself. Odour, damp, fatigue, boredom: a whole literature describes this dreary passion of a consciousness become flesh. Desire often contains an element of disgust and returns to disgust when it is assuaged. '*Post coitum homo animal triste.*'[6] 'The flesh is sad.' And yet, man has not even found definitive reassurance in his lover's arms. Soon his desire is reborn; and often it is the desire not only for woman in general but for this specific woman. She wields a singularly troubling power. Because in his own body man does not feel the sexual need except as a general one similar to hunger or thirst without a particular object, the bond that links him to this specific feminine body is therefore forged by the Other. The link is mysterious like the foul and fertile womb of his roots, a sort of passive force: it is magic. The hackneyed vocabulary of serialised novels where the woman is described as an enchantress or a mermaid who fascinates man and bewitches him reflects the oldest and most universal of myths. Woman is devoted to magic. Magic, said Alain, is the spirit lurking in things; an action is magic when it emanates from a passivity instead of being produced by an agent; men have always considered woman precisely as the immanence of the given; if she produces harvests and children, it is not because she wills it; she is not subject, transcendence, or creative power, but an object charged with fluids. In societies where man worships such mysteries, woman, because of these qualities, is associated with religion and venerated as a priestess; but when he struggles to make society triumph over nature, reason over life, will over inert fact, woman is regarded as a sorceress. The difference between the priest and the magician is well known: the former dominates and directs the forces he has mastered in keeping with the gods and laws, for the good of the community, on behalf of all its members, while the magician operates outside society, against the gods and laws, according to his own passions. But woman is not fully integrated into the world of men; as other, she counters them; it is natural for her to use the strengths she possesses, not to spread the hold of transcendence across the community of men and into the future, but, being separate and opposed, to draw males into the solitude of separation, into the darkness of immanence. She is the mermaid whose songs dashed the sailors against the rocks; she is Circe, who turned her lovers into animals, the water sprite that attracted the fisherman to the depths of the pools. The man captivated by her spell loses his will, his project, his future; he is no longer a citizen but flesh, slave to his desires, he is crossed out of the community, enclosed in the instant, thrown passively from torture to pleasure; the perverse magician pits passion against duty, the present against the unity of time, she keeps the traveller far from home, she spreads forgetfulness. In attempting to appropriate the Other, man must remain himself; but with the failure of impossible possession, he tries to become this other with whom he fails to unite; so he alienates himself, he loses himself, he drinks the potion that turns him into a stranger to himself, he falls to the bottom of deadly and roiling waters. The Mother dooms her son to death in giving him life; the woman lover draws her lover into relinquishing life and giving himself up to the supreme sleep. This link between Love and Death was pathetically illuminated in the Tristan legend, but it has a more primary truth. Born of flesh, man accomplishes himself in love as flesh, and flesh is destined to the grave. The alliance between Woman and Death is thus confirmed; the great reaper is the inverted figure of corn-growing fertility. But it is also the frightening wife whose skeleton appears under deceitful and tender flesh.*

What man thus cherishes and detests first in woman, lover as well as mother, is the fixed image of her animal destiny, the life essential to her existence, but that condemns her to finitude and death. From the day of birth, man begins to die: this is the truth that the mother embodies. In procreating, he guarantees the species against himself: this is what he learns in his wife's arms; in arousal and in pleasure, even before engendering, he forgets his singular self. Should he try to differentiate them, he still finds in both one fact alone, that of his carnal condition. He wants to accom-

---

* For example in Prévert's ballet, *Le Rendez-vous* and in Cocteau's *Le Jeune homme et la mort* (*The Young Man and Death*), Death is represented as a beloved young girl.

plish it: he venerates his mother; he desires his mistress. But at the same time, he rebels against them in disgust, in fear.

An important text where we will find a synthesis of almost all these myths is Jean-Richard Bloch's *A Night in Kurdistan*,[7] in which he describes young Saad's embraces of a much older but still beautiful woman during the plundering of a city:

> The night abolished the contours of things and feelings alike. He was no longer clasping a woman to him. He was at last nearing the end of an interminable voyage that had been pursued since the beginning of the world. Little by little he dissolved into an immensity that cradled him round without shape or end. All women were confused into one giant land, folded upon him, suave as desire burning in summer . . .
>
> He, meanwhile, recognised with a fearful admiration the power that is enclosed within woman, the long, stretched, satin thighs, the knees like two ivory hills. When he traced the polished arch of the back, from the waist to the shoulders, he seemed to be feeling the vault that supports the world. But the belly ceaselessly drew him, a tender and elastic ocean, whence all life is born, and whither it returns, asylum of asylums, with its tides, horizons, illimitable surfaces.
>
> Then he was seized with a rage to pierce that delightful envelope, and at last win to the very source of all this beauty. A simultaneous urge wrapped them one within the other. The woman now only lived to be cleaved by the share, to open to him her vitals, to gorge herself with the humours of the beloved. Their ecstasy was murderous. They came together as if with stabbing daggers . . .
>
> He, man, the isolated, the separated, the cut off, was going to gush forth from out of his own substance, he, the first, would come forth from his fleshly prison and at last go free, matter and soul, into the universal matrix. To him was reserved the unheard of happiness of overpassing the limits of the creature, of dissolving into the one exaltation object and subject, question and answer, of annexing to being all that is not being, and of embracing, in an unextinguishable river, the empire of the unattainable . . .
>
> But each coming and going of the bow awoke, in the precious instrument it held at its mercy, vibrations more and more piercing. Suddenly, a last spasm unloosed him from the zenith, and cast him down again to earth, to the mire.

As the woman's desire is not quenched, she imprisons her lover between her legs and he feels in spite of himself his desire returning: she is thus an enemy power who grabs his virility and while possessing her again, he bites her throat so deeply that he kills her. The cycle from mother to woman-lover to death meanders to a complex close.

There are many possible attitudes here for man depending on which aspect of the carnal drama he stresses. If a man does not think life is unique, if he is not concerned with his singular destiny, if he does not fear death, he will joyously accept his animality. For Muslims, woman is reduced to a state of abjection because of the feudal structure of society that does not allow recourse to the state against the family and because of religion, expressing this civilisation's warrior ideal, that has destined man to death and stripped woman of her magic: What would anyone on earth, ready to dive without any hesitation into the voluptuous orgies of the Muhammadan paradise, fear? Man can thus enjoy woman without worrying or having to defend himself against himself or her. *The Thousand and One Nights* looks on her as a source of creamy delights much like fruits, jams, rich desserts and perfumed oils. This sensual benevolence can be found today among many Mediterranean peoples: replete, not seeking immortality, the man from the Midi grasps Nature in its luxurious aspect, relishes women; by tradition he scorns them sufficiently so as not to grasp them as individuals: between the enjoyment of their bodies and that of sand and water there is not much difference for him; he does not experience the horror of the flesh either in them or in himself. In *Conversations in Sicily*, Vittorini recounts, with quiet amazement, having discovered the naked body of woman at the age of seven. Greek and Roman rationalist thought confirms this spontaneous attitude. Greek optimist philosophy went beyond Pythagorean Manichaeism; the inferior is subordinate to the superior and as such is useful to him: these harmonious ideologies show no hostility whatsoever to the flesh. Turned towards the heaven of Ideas or in towards the City or State, the individual thinking himself as nous or as a citizen thinks he has overcome his animal condition: whether he gives himself up to voluptuousness or practises asceticism, a woman firmly integrated into male society is only of secondary importance. It is true that rationalism has never triumphed totally and erotic experience remains ambivalent in these civilisations: rites, mythologies and literature are testimony to that. But femininity's attractions and dangers manifest themselves there only in attenuated form. Christianity is what drapes woman anew with frightening pres-

tige: one of the forms the rending of the unhappy consciousness takes
for man is fear of the other sex. The Christian is separated from himself;
the division of body and soul, of life and spirit, is consumed: original
sin turns the body into the soul's enemy; all carnal links appear bad.*
Man can be saved by being redeemed by Christ and turning towards the
celestial kingdom; but at the beginning, he is no more than rottenness;
his birth dooms him not only to death but to damnation; divine grace
can open heaven to him, but all avatars of his natural existence are
cursed. Evil is an absolute reality; and flesh is sin. Since woman never
stopped being Other, of course, male and female are never reciprocally
considered flesh: the flesh for the Christian male is the enemy Other
and is not distinguished from woman. The temptations of the earth,
sex and the devil are incarnated in her. All the Church Fathers emphasise the fact that she led Adam to sin. Once again, Tertullian has to be
quoted: 'Woman! You are the devil's gateway. You have convinced the
one the devil did not dare to confront directly. It is your fault that God's
Son had to die. You should always dress in mourning and rags.' All
Christian literature endeavours to exacerbate man's disgust for woman.
Tertullian defines her as 'Templum aedificatum super cloacam'.[8] St
Augustine points out in horror the proximity of the sexual and excretory organs: 'Inter faeces et urinam nascimur'.[9] Christianity's repugnance
for the feminine body is such that it consents to doom its God to an
ignominious death but spares him the stain of birth: the Council of
Ephesus in the Eastern Church and the Lateran Council in the West
affirm the virgin birth of Christ. The first Church Fathers – Origen,
Tertullian and Jerome – thought that Mary had given birth in blood and
filth like other women; but the opinions of St Ambrose and St Augustine
prevail. The Virgin's womb remained closed. Since the Middle Ages, the
fact of having a body was considered an ignominy for woman. Science
itself was paralysed for a long time by this disgust. Linnaeus, in his treatise on nature, dismissed the study of woman's genital organs as 'abominable'. Des Laurens, the French doctor, dared to ask how 'this divine
animal full of reason and judgement that is called man can be attracted
by these obscene parts of the woman, tainted by humours and placed

* Until the end of the twelfth century theologians – except St Anselm – thought, according
to St Augustine's doctrine, that original sin was implied in the law of generation itself.
'Concupiscence is a vice . . . human flesh born from it is sinful flesh,' wrote St Augustine.
And St Thomas: 'Since sin, the union of the sexes, when accompanied by concupiscence,
transmits original sin to the child.'

shamefully at the lowest part of the trunk'. Many other influences come into play along with Christian thought; and even this has more than one side; but in the puritan world, for example, hatred of the flesh still obtains; it is expressed in *Light in August*, by Faulkner; the hero's first sexual experiences are highly traumatic. In all literature, a young man's first sexual intercourse is often upsetting to the point of inducing vomiting; and if, in truth, such a reaction is very rare, it is not by chance that it is so often described. In puritan Anglo-Saxon countries in particular, woman stirs up more or less avowed terror in most adolescents and many men. This is quite true in France. Michel Leiris wrote in *L'âge d'homme (Manhood)*: 'I have a tendency to consider the feminine organ as a dirty thing or a wound, not less attractive though for that, but dangerous in itself, as everything that is bloody, viscous, and contaminated.' The idea of venereal maladies expresses these frights; woman is feared not because she gives these illnesses; it is the illnesses that seem abominable because they come from woman: I have been told about young men who thought that too frequent sexual relations caused gonorrhoea. People also readily think that sexual intercourse makes man lose his muscular strength and mental lucidity, consumes his phosphorus and coarsens his sensitivity. The same dangers threaten in masturbation; and for moral reasons society considers it even more harmful than the normal sexual function. Legitimate marriage and the desire to have children guard against the evil spells of eroticism. I have already said that the Other is implied in all sexual acts; and its face is usually woman's. Man experiences his own flesh's passivity the most strongly in front of her. Woman is vampire, ghoul, eater, drinker; her sex organ feeds gluttonously on the male sex organ. Some psychoanalysts have tried to give these imaginings scientific foundations: the pleasure woman derives from coitus is supposed to come from the fact that she symbolically castrates the male and appropriates his sex organ. But it would seem that these theories themselves need to be psychoanalysed and that the doctors who invented them have projected on to them ancestral terrors.*

The source of these terrors is that in the Other, beyond any annexation, alterity remains. In patriarchal societies, woman kept many of the disquieting virtues she held in primitive societies. That explains why she is never left to Nature, why she is surrounded by taboos, purified by rites, and placed under the control of priests; man is taught never to approach her in her original nudity but through ceremonies and sacra-

---

* We demonstrated that the myth of the praying mantis has no biological basis.

ments that wrest her from the earth and flesh and metamorphose her into a human creature: thus the magic she possesses is channelled as lightning has been since the invention of lightning rods and electric power plants. It is even possible to use her in the group's interests: this is another phase of the oscillatory movement defining man's relationship to his female. He loves her because she is his, he fears her because she remains other; but it is as the feared other that he seeks to make her most deeply his: this is what will lead him to raise her to the dignity of a person and to recognise her as his peer.

★

Feminine magic was profoundly domesticated in the patriarchal family. Woman gave society the opportunity to integrate cosmic forces into it. In his work, *Mitra-Varuna,* Dumézil points out that in India as in Rome, masculine power asserts itself in two ways: in Varuna and Romulus, and in the Gandharvas and the Luperci, it is aggression, abduction, disorder and hubris; thus, woman is the being to be ravished and violated; if the ravished Sabine women are sterile, they are whipped with goatskin straps, compensating for violence with more violence. But on the contrary, Mitra, Numa, the Brahmin women and the Flamen wives represent reasonable law and order in the city: so the woman is bound to her husband by a ritualistic marriage, and she collaborates with him to ensure his domination over all female forces of nature; in Rome, the *flamen dialis* resigns from his position if his wife dies. In Egypt as well, Isis, having lost her supreme power as Mother Goddess, remains nonetheless generous, smiling, benevolent and obedient, Osiris's magnificent spouse. But when woman is thus man's partner, his complement, his other half, she is necessarily endowed with a consciousness and a soul; he could not so deeply depend on a being who would not participate in the human essence. It has already been seen that the Laws of Manu promised a legal wife the same paradise as her spouse. The more the male becomes individualised and claims his individuality, the more he will recognise an individual and a freedom in his companion. The Oriental man who is unconcerned with his own destiny is satisfied with a female who is his pleasure object; but Western man's dream, once elevated to consciousness of the singularity of his being, is to be recognised by a foreign and docile freedom. The Greek man cannot find the peer he wants in a woman who was prisoner of the gynaeceum: so he confers his love on male companions whose flesh, like his own, is endowed with a consciousness and a freedom, or else he gives his love to hetaeras whose independence, culture and spirit made them near equals. But when circumstances permit, the wife best satisfies man's demands. The Roman citizen recognises a person in the matron; in Cornelia or in Arria, he possesses his double. Paradoxically, it was Christianity that was to proclaim the equality of man and woman on a certain level. Christianity detests the flesh in her; if she rejects the flesh, she is, like him, a creature of God, redeemed by the Saviour: here she can take her place beside males, among those souls guaranteed celestial happiness. Men and women are God's servants, almost as asexual as the angels, who, together with the help of grace, reject earth's temptations. If she agrees to renounce her animality, woman, from the very fact that she incarnated sin, will also be the most radiant incarnation of the triumph of the elect who have conquered sin.* Of course, the divine Saviour who brings about Redemption is male; but humanity must cooperate in its own salvation, and perversely it will be called upon to manifest its submissive good will in its most humiliated figure. Christ is God; but it is a woman, the Virgin Mother, who reigns over all human creatures. Yet only marginal sects restore the great goddesses' ancient privileges to the woman. The Church expresses and serves a patriarchal civilisation where it is befitting for woman to remain annexed to man. As his docile servant she will also be a blessed saint. Thus the image of the most perfected woman, propitious to men, lies at the heart of the Middle Ages: the face of the Mother of Christ is encircled in glory. She is the inverse figure of the sinner Eve; she crushes the serpent under her foot; she is the mediator of salvation, as Eve was of damnation.

It is as Mother that the woman was held in awe; through motherhood she has to be transfigured and subjugated. Mary's virginity has above all a negative value: she by whom the flesh has been redeemed is not carnal; she has been neither touched nor possessed. Neither was the Asiatic Great Mother assumed to have a husband: she had engendered the world and reigned over it alone; she could be lascivious by impulse, but her greatness as Mother was not diminished by imposed wifely servitudes. Likewise, Mary never experienced the stain connected with sexuality. Related to the woman warrior Minerva, she is an ivory tower, a citadel, an impregnable fortress. Like most Christian saints, the priestesses of antiquity were virgins: the woman devoted to good should be devoted with the splendour of her strength intact; she must conserve the principle of her femininity in its unbroken wholeness. One rejects in Mary her character as

* This explains the privileged place she holds, for example, in Claudel's work (see pp. 245–254).

wife in order to more fully exalt in her the Woman-Mother. But she will be glorified only by accepting the subservient role assigned to her. 'I am the handmaiden of the Lord.' For the first time in the history of humanity, the mother kneels before her son; she freely recognises her inferiority. The supreme masculine victory is consummated in the worship of Mary: it is the rehabilitation of woman by the achievement of her defeat. Ishtar, Astarte and Cybele were cruel, capricious and lustful; they were powerful; the source of death as well as life, in giving birth to men, they made them their slaves. With Christianity, life and death now depended on God alone, so man, born of the maternal breast, escaped it for ever, and the earth gets only his bones; his soul's destiny is played out in regions where the mother's powers are abolished; the sacrament of baptism makes ceremonies that burned or drowned the placenta insignificant. There is no longer any place on earth for magic: God alone is king. Nature is originally bad, but powerless when countered with grace. Motherhood as a natural phenomenon confers no power. If woman wishes to overcome the original stain in herself, her only alternative is to bow before God, whose will subordinates her to man. And by this submission she can assume a new role in masculine mythology. As a vassal she will be honoured, whereas she was beaten and trampled underfoot when she saw herself as dominator or as long as she did not explicitly abdicate. She loses none of her primitive attributes; but their meanings change; from calamitous they become auspicious; black magic turns to white magic. As a servant, woman is entitled to the most splendid apotheosis.

And since she was subjugated as Mother, she will, as Mother first, be cherished and respected. Of the two ancient faces of maternity, modern man recognises only the benevolent one. Limited in time and space, possessing only one body and one finite life, man is but one individual in the middle of a foreign Nature and History. Limited like him, similarly inhabited by the spirit, woman belongs to Nature, she is traversed by the infinite current of Life, she thus appears as the mediator between the individual and the cosmos. When the mother image became reassuring and holy, it is understandable that the man turned to her with love. Lost in nature, he seeks escape, but separated from her, he aspires to return to her. Solidly settled in the family and society, in accord with laws and customs, the mother is the very incarnation of the Good: the nature in which she participates becomes Good; she is no longer the spirit's enemy; and though she remains mysterious, it is a smiling mystery, like Leonardo da Vinci's Madonnas. Man does not wish to be woman, but he longs to wrap himself in everything that is,

including this woman he is not: in worshipping his mother, he tries to
appropriate her riches so foreign to him. To recognise himself as his
mother's son, he recognises the mother in him, integrating femininity
in so far as it is a connection to the earth, to life and to the past. In
Vittorini's *Conversations in Sicily*, that is what the hero goes to find from
his mother: his native land, its scents and its fruits, his childhood, his
ancestors' past, traditions and the roots from which his individual existence separated him. It is this very rootedness that exalts man's pride
in going beyond; he likes to admire himself breaking away from his
mother's arms to leave for adventure, the future, and war; this departure would be less moving if there were no one to try to hold him
back: it would look like an accident, not a hard-won victory. And he
also likes to know that these arms are ready to welcome him back.
After the tension of action, the hero likes to taste the restfulness of
immanence again, by his mother's side: she is refuge, slumber; by her
hand's caress he sinks into the bosom of nature, lets himself be lulled
by the vast flow of life as peacefully as in the womb or in the tomb.
And if tradition has him die calling on his mother, it is because under
the maternal gaze death itself, like birth, is tamed, symmetrical with
birth, indissolubly linked with his whole carnal life. The mother remains
connected to death as in ancient Parcae mythology; it is she who buries
the dead, who mourns. But her role is precisely to integrate death with
life, with society, with the good. And so the cult of 'heroic mothers'
is systematically encouraged: if society persuades mothers to surrender
their sons to death, then it thinks it can claim the right to assassinate
them. Because of the mother's hold on her sons, it is useful for society
to make her part of it: this is why the mother is showered with signs
of respect, why she is endowed with all virtues, why a religion is created
around her from which it is forbidden to stray under severe risk of
sacrilege and blasphemy; she is made the guardian of morality; servant
of man, servant of the powers that be, she fondly guides her children
along fixed paths. The more resolutely optimistic the collectivity and
the more docilely it accepts this loving authority, the more transfigured the mother will be. The American 'Mom' has become the idol
described by Philip Wylie in *Generation of Vipers*, because the official
American ideology is the most stubbornly optimistic. To glorify the
mother is to accept birth, life and death in both their animal and social
forms and to proclaim the harmony of nature and society. Auguste
Comte makes the woman the divinity of future Humanity because he
dreams of achieving this synthesis. But this is also why all rebels assail

the figure of the mother; in holding her up to ridicule, they reject the given claims supposedly imposed on them through the female guardian of morals and laws.*[10]

The aura of respect around the Mother and the taboos that surround her repress the hostile disgust that mingles spontaneously with the carnal tenderness she inspires. However, lurking below the surface, the latent horror of motherhood survives. In particular, it is interesting that in France since the Middle Ages, a secondary myth has been forged, freely expressing this repugnance: that of the Mother-in-Law. From fabliau to vaudeville, there are no taboos on man's ridicule of motherhood in general through his wife's mother. He hates the idea that the woman he loves was conceived: the mother-in-law is the clear image of the decrepitude that she doomed her daughter to by giving her life, and her obesity and her wrinkles forecast the obesity and wrinkles that the future so sadly prefigures for the young bride; at her mother's side she is no longer an individual but an example of a species; she is no longer the desired prey or the cherished companion, because her individual

* One ought to quote Michel Leiris's poem 'The Mother' in its entirety. Here are some typical passages:

The mother in black, mauve, violet – robber of nights – that's the sorceress whose hidden industry brings you into the world, the one who rocks you, coddles you, coffins you, when she doesn't abandon her curled-up body – one last little toy – into your hands, that lay it nicely into the coffin . . .

The mother – blind statue, fate set up in the middle of the inviolate sanctuary – she's nature caressing you, the wind censing you, the whole world that penetrates you, lifts you sky-high (borne on multiple spires) and rots you. . . .

The mother – young or old, beautiful or ugly, merciful or obstinate – it's the caricature, the monster jealous woman, the fallen Prototype – assuming the Idea (a wrinkled Pythia perched on the tripod of her austere capital letter) – is but a parody of quick, light, iridescent thoughts . . .

The mother – hip round or dry, breast atremble or firm – is the decline promised to all women right from the start, the progressive crumbling of the rock that sparkles beneath the menstrual flood, the slow burying – under the sand of the old desert – of the luxuriant caravan heaped with beauty.

The mother – angel of spying death, of the embracing universe, of the love time's wave throws back – she's the shell with its senseless graphics (a sure sign of poison) to toss into the deep pools, generator of circles for the oblivious waters.

The mother – sombre puddle, eternally in mourning for everything and ourselves – she is the misty pestilence that shimmers and bursts, expanding its great bestial shadow (shame of flesh and milk) bubble by bubble, a stiff veil that a bolt of lightning as yet unborn ought to rend . . .

Will it ever occur to any of these innocent bitches to drag themselves barefoot through the centuries as pardon for this crime: having given birth to us?

existence dissolves into universality. Her individuality is mockingly contested by generalities, her spirit's autonomy by her being rooted in the past and in the flesh: this is the derision man objectifies as a grotesque character; but through the rancour of his laughter, he knows that the fate of his wife is the same for all human beings; it is his own. In every country, legends and tales have also personified the cruel side of motherhood in the stepmother. She is the cruel mother who tries to kill Snow White. The ancient Kali with the necklace of severed heads lives on in the mean stepmother – Mme Fichini whipping Sophie throughout Mme de Ségur's books.

Yet behind the sainted Mother crowds the coterie of white witches who provide man with herbal juices and stars' rays: grandmothers, old women with kind eyes, good-hearted servants, sisters of charity, nurses with magical hands, the sort of mistress Verlaine dreamed of:

> Sweet, pensive and dark and surprised at nothing
> And who will at times kiss you on the forehead like a child.

They are ascribed the pure mystery of knotted vines, of fresh water; they dress and heal wounds; their wisdom is life's silent wisdom, they understand without words. In their presence man forgets his pride; he understands the sweetness of yielding and becoming a child, because between him and her there is no struggle for prestige: he could not resent the inhuman virtues of nature; and in their devotion, the wise initiates who care for him recognise they are his servants; he submits to their benevolent powers because he knows that while submitting to them, he remains their master. Sisters, childhood girlfriends, pure girls and all future mothers belong to this blessed troupe. And the wife herself, when her erotic magic fades, is regarded by many men less as a lover than as the mother of their children. Once the mother is sanctified and servile, she can safely be with a woman friend, she being also sanctified and submissive. To redeem the mother is to redeem the flesh, and thus carnal union and the wife.

Deprived of her magic weapons by nuptial rites, economically and socially dependent on her husband, the 'good wife' is man's most precious treasure. She belongs to him so profoundly that she shares the same nature with him: 'Ubi tu Gaius, ego Gaia'; she has his name and his gods and she is his responsibility: he calls her his other half. He takes pride in his wife as in his home, his land, his flocks and his wealth, and sometimes even more; through her he displays his power to the rest of the world: she is his yardstick and his earthly share. For Orientals, a wife should be fat: everyone sees that she is well fed and brings respect to her master.* A Muslim is all the more respected if he possesses a large number of flourishing wives. In bourgeois society, one of woman's assigned roles is *to represent*: her beauty, her charm, her intelligence and her elegance are outward signs of her husband's fortune, as is the body of his car. If he is rich, he covers her with furs and jewels. If he is poorer, he boasts of her moral qualities and her housekeeping talents; most deprived, he feels he owns something earthly if he has a wife to serve him; the hero of *The Taming of the Shrew* summons all his neighbours to show them his authority in taming his wife. A sort of King Candaules resides in all men: he exhibits his wife because he believes she displays his own worth.

But woman does more than flatter man's social vanity; she allows him a more intimate pride; he delights in his domination over her; superimposed on the naturalistic images of the ploughshare cutting furrows are more spiritual symbols concerning the wife as a person; the husband 'forms' his wife not only erotically but also spiritually and intellectually; he educates her, impresses her, puts his imprint on her. One of the daydreams he enjoys is the impregnation of things by his will, shaping their form, penetrating their substance: the woman is par excellence the 'clay in his hands' that passively lets itself be worked and shaped, resistant while yielding, permitting masculine activity to go on. A too-plastic material wears out by its softness; what is precious in woman is that something in her always escapes all embraces; so man is master of a reality that is all the more worthy of being mastered as it surpasses him. She awakens in him a being heretofore ignored whom he recognises with pride as himself; in their safe marital orgies he discovers the splendour of his animality: he is the Male; and woman, correlatively, the female, but this word sometimes takes on the most flattering implications: the female who broods, who nurses, who licks her young, who defends them and who risks her life to save them is an example for humans; with emotion, man demands this patience and devotion from his companion; again it is Nature, but imbued with all of the virtues useful to society, family and the head of the family, virtues he knows how to keep locked in his home. A common desire of children and men is to uncover the secret hidden inside things; but in this, the matter can be deceptive: a doll ripped apart with her stomach outside

* See p. 182.

has no more interiority; the interior of living things is more impenetrable; the female womb is the symbol of immanence, of depth; it delivers its secrets in part as when, for example, pleasure shows on a woman's face, but it also holds them in; man catches life's obscure palpitations in his house without the mystery being destroyed by possession. In the human world, woman transposes the female animal's functions: she maintains life, she reigns over the zones of immanence; she transports the warmth and the intimacy of the womb into the home; she watches over and enlivens the dwelling where the past is kept, where the future is presaged; she engenders the future generation and she nourishes the children already born; thanks to her, the existence that man expends throughout the world by his work and his activity is re-centred by delving into her immanence: when he comes home at night, he is anchored to the earth; the wife assures the days' continuity; whatever risks he faces in the outside world, she guarantees the stability of his meals and sleep; she repairs whatever has been damaged or worn out by activity: she prepares the tired worker's food, she cares for him if he is ill, she mends and washes. And within the conjugal universe that she sets up and perpetuates, she brings in the whole vast world: she lights the fires, puts flowers in vases and domesticates the emanations of sun, water and earth. A bourgeois writer cited by Bebel summarises this ideal in all seriousness as follows: 'Man wants not only someone whose heart beats for him, but whose hand wipes his brow, who radiates peace, order and tranquillity, a silent control over himself and those things he finds when he comes home every day; he wants someone who can spread over everything the indescribable perfume of woman who is the vivifying warmth of home life.'

It is clear how spiritualised the figure of woman became with the birth of Christianity; the beauty, warmth and intimacy that man wishes to grasp through her are no longer tangible qualities; instead of being the summation of the pleasurable quality of things, she becomes their soul; deeper than carnal mystery, her heart holds a secret and pure presence that reflects truth in the world. She is the soul of the house, the family and the home, as well as larger groups: the town, province or nation. Jung observes that cities have always been compared to the Mother because they hold their citizens in their bosoms: this is why Cybele was depicted crowned with towers; for the same reason the term 'mother country' is used and not only because of the nourishing soil; rather, a more subtle reality found its symbol in the woman. In the Old Testament and in the Apocalypse, Jerusalem and Babylon are not only mothers: they are also wives. There are virgin cities and prostitute cities such as Babel and Tyre. France too has been called 'the eldest daughter' of the Church; France and Italy are Latin sisters. Woman's function is not specified, but femininity is, in statues that represent France, Rome and Germany and those on the Place de la Concorde that evoke Strasbourg and Lyon. This assimilation is not only allegoric: it is affectively practised by many men.* Many a traveller would ask woman for the key to the countries he visits: when he holds an Italian or Spanish woman in his arms, he feels he possesses the fragrant essence of Italy or Spain. 'When I come to a new city, the first thing I do is visit a brothel,' said a journalist. If a cinnamon hot chocolate can make Gide discover the whole of Spain, all the more reason kisses from exotic lips will bring to a lover a country with its flora and fauna, its traditions and its culture. Woman is the summation neither of its political institutions nor its economic resources; but she is the incarnation of carnal flesh and mystical mana. From Lamartine's *Graziella* to Loti's novels and Morand's short stories, the foreigner is seen as trying to appropriate the soul of a region through women. Mignon, Sylvie, Mireille, Colomba and Carmen uncover the most intimate truth about Italy, Valois, Provence, Corsica or Andalusia. When the Alsatian Frédérique falls in love with Goethë, the Germans take it as a symbol of Germany's annexation; likewise when Colette Baudoche refuses to marry a German, Barrès sees it as Alsace refusing Germany. He personifies Aigues-Mortes and a whole refined and frivolous civilisation in the sole person of Berenice; she represents the sensibility of the writer himself. Man recognises his own mysterious double in her, she who is the soul of nature, cities and the universe; man's soul is Psyche, a woman.

Psyche has feminine traits in Edgar Allan Poe's 'Ulalume':

---

* It is allegoric in Claudel's shameful recent poem, where Indochina is called 'That yellow girl'; it is affectionate, by contrast, in the verses of the black poet [Guy Tyrolien]:

> Soul of the black country where the elders sleep
> Live and speak
> tonight
> in the uneasy strength along your hollow loins
> Here once, through an alley Titanic,
> Of cypress, I roamed with my Soul –
> Of cypress, with Psyche, my soul . . .
> Thus I pacified Psyche and kissed her . . .
> And I said – 'What is written, sweet sister,
> On the door of this legended tomb?'

Here once, through an alley Titanic,
Of cypress, I roamed with my Soul –
Of cypress, with Psyche, my Soul . . .
Thus I pacified Psyche and kissed her . . .
And I said – "What is written, sweet sister,
On the door of this legended tomb?"

And Mallarmé, at the theatre, in a dialogue with 'a soul, or else our idea' (that is, divinity present in man's spirit) called it 'a most exquisite abnormal lady [*sic*]'.*

Thing of harmony, ME, a dream,
Firm, flexible feminine, whose silences lead
To pure acts! . . .
Thing of mystery, ME . . .[11]

Such is Valéry's way of hailing her. The Christian world substituted less carnal presences for nymphs and fairies; but homes, landscapes, cities and individuals themselves are still haunted by an impalpable femininity.

This truth buried in the night of things also shines in the heavens; perfect immanence, the Soul is at the same time the transcendent, the Idea. Not only cities and nations but also entities and abstract institutions are cloaked in feminine traits: the Church, the Synagogue, the Republic and Humanity are women, as well as Peace, War, Liberty, the Revolution, Victory. Man feminises the ideal that he posits before him as the essential Other, because woman is the tangible figure of alterity; this is why almost all the allegories in language and in iconography are women.[†] Soul and Idea, woman is also the mediator between them: she is the Grace that leads the Christian to God, she is Beatrice guiding Dante to the beyond, Laura beckoning Petrarch to the highest peaks of poetry. She appears in all doctrines assimilating Nature to Spirit as Harmony, Reason and Truth. Gnostic sects made Wisdom a woman, Sophia; they attributed the world's redemption to her, and even its creation. So woman is no longer flesh, she is glorious body; rather than trying to possess her, men venerate her for her untouched splendour;

---

* Jotted down at the theatre.
† Philology is rather mysterious on this question; all linguists recognise that the distribution of concrete words into gender is purely accidental. Yet in French most entities are feminine: beauty and loyalty, for example. And in German, most imported foreign words, *others*, are feminine: die Bar, for example.

the pale dead of Edgar Allan Poe are as fluid as water, wind or memory; for courtly love, for *les précieux*, and in all of the gallant tradition, woman is no longer an animal creature but rather an ethereal being, a breath, a radiance. Thus it is that the feminine Night's opacity is converted into transparence and obscurity into purity, as in Novalis's texts:

> Thou, Night-inspiration, heavenly Slumber, didst come upon me – the region gently upheaved itself; over it hovered my unbound, newborn spirit. The mound became a cloud of dust – and through the cloud I saw the glorified face of my beloved.
>
> Dost thou also take a pleasure in us, dark Night? . . . Precious balm drips from thy hand out of its bundle of poppies. Thou upliftest the heavy-laden wings of the soul. Darkly and inexpressibly are we moved – joy-startled, I see a grave face that, tender and worshipful, inclines toward me, and, amid manifold entangled locks, reveals the youthful loveliness of the Mother . . . More heavenly than those glittering stars we hold the eternal eyes which the Night hath opened within us.

The downward attraction exercised by woman is inverted; she beckons man no longer earthward, but towards heaven.

> *The Eternal Feminine*
> *Leads us upwards,*

proclaimed Goethe at the end of *Faust, Part Two.*

As the Virgin Mary is the most perfected image, the most widely venerated image of the regenerated woman devoted to the Good, it is interesting to see how she appears through literature and iconography. Here are passages from medieval litanies showing how fervent Christians addressed her:

> Most high Virgin, thou art the fertile Dew, the Fountain of Joy, the Channel of mercy, the Well of living waters that cools our passions.
>
> Thou art the Breast from which God nurses orphans.
>
> Thou art the Marrow, the Inside, the Core of all good.
>
> Thou art the guileless Woman whose love never changes.
>
> Thou art the Probatic Pool, the Remedy of lepers, the subtle Physician whose like is found neither in Salerno nor Montpellier.
>
> Thou art the Lady of healing hands, whose fingers so beautiful, so white, so long, restore noses and mouths, give new eyes and

ears. Thou calmest passions, givest life to the paralysed, givest
strength to the weak, risest the dead.

Most of the feminine attributes we have referred to are found in these
invocations. The Virgin is fertility, dew and the source of life; many of the
images show her at the well, the spring or the fountain; the expression
'Fountain of Life' was one of the most common; she was not a creator,
but she nourishes, she brings to the light of day what was hidden in the
earth. She is the deep reality hidden under the appearance of things: the
Core, the Marrow. Through her, passions are tempered; she is what is given
to man to satiate him. Wherever life is threatened, she saves and restores
it: she heals and strengthens. And because life emanates from God, she as
the intermediary between man and life is likewise the intermediary between
humanity and God. 'The devil's gateway,' said Tertullian. But transfigured,
she is heaven's portal; paintings represent her opening the gate or the
window onto paradise or raising a ladder from earth to the heavens. More
straightforward, she becomes an advocate, pleading beside her Son for the
salvation of men: many tableaux of the Last Judgment have her baring her
breast in supplication to Christ in the name of her glorious motherhood.
She protects men's children in the folds of her cloak; her merciful love
follows them through dangers over oceans and battlefields. She moves
Divine Justice in the name of charity: the 'Virgins of the Scales' are seen,
smiling, tilting the balance where souls are weighed to the side of the Good.

This merciful and tender role is one of the most important of all those
granted to woman. Even integrated into society, the woman subtly exceeds
its boundaries because she possesses the insidious generosity of Life. This
distance between the males' intended constructions and nature's contingency seems troubling in some cases; but it becomes beneficial when the
woman, too docile to threaten men's work, limits herself to enriching and
softening their too sharp edges. Male gods represent Destiny; on the
goddesses' side are found arbitrary benevolence and capricious favour. The
Christian God has the rigours of Justice; the Virgin has gentleness and
charity. On earth, men are the defenders of laws, reason and necessity;
woman knows the original contingency of man himself and of the necessity he believes in; from this comes her supple generosity and the mysterious irony that touches her lips. She gives birth in pain, she heals males'
wounds, she nurses the newborn and buries the dead; of man she knows
all that offends his pride and humiliates his will. While inclining before
him and submitting flesh to spirit, she remains on the carnal borders of
the spirit; and she contests the sharpness of hard masculine architecture

by softening the angles; she introduces free luxury and unforeseen grace. Her power over men comes from her tenderly recalling a modest conscious-ness of their authentic condition; it is the secret of her illusionless, painful, ironic and loving wisdom. Even frivolity, whimsy and ignorance are charming virtues in her because they thrive beneath and beyond the world where man chooses to live but where he does not want to feel confined. Confronted with arrested meaning and utilitarian instruments, she upholds the mystery of intact things; she brings the breath of poetry into city streets and ploughed fields. Poetry attempts to capture that which exists above everyday prose: woman is an eminently poetic reality since man projects onto her everything he is not resolved to be. She incarnates the Dream; for man, the dream is the most intimate and the most foreign presence, what he does not want, what he does not do, which he aspires to but cannot attain; the mysterious Other who is profound immanence and far-off transcendence will lend him her traits. Thus it is that Aurélia visits Nerval in a dream and gives him the whole world in a dream. 'She began to grow in a bright ray of light so that little by little the garden took on her form, and the flower beds and the trees became the rosettes and festoons of her dress; while her face and her arms impressed their shape upon the reddened clouds in the sky. I was losing sight of her as she was being transfigured, for she seemed to be vanishing into her own grandeur. "Oh flee not from me!" I cried; "for nature dies with you."'

Being the very substance of man's poetic activities, woman is under-standably his inspiration: the Muses are women. The Muse is the conduit between the creator and the natural springs he draws from. It is through woman's spirit deeply connected to nature that man will explore the depths of silence and the fertile night. The Muse creates nothing on her own; she is a wise sibyl making herself the docile servant of a master. Even in concrete and practical spheres, her counsel will be useful. Man wishes to attain the goals he sets without the help of his peers, and he would find another man's opinion inopportune; but he supposes that the woman speaks to him in the name of other values, in the name of a wisdom that he does not claim to have, more instinctive than his own, more immedi-ately in accord with the real; these are the 'intuitions' that Egeria uses to counsel and guide; he consults her without fear for his self-esteem as he consults the stars. This 'intuition' even enters into business or politics: Aspasia and Mme de Maintenon still have flourishing careers today.*

---

* It goes without saying that they, of course, demonstrate intellectual qualities perfectly identical to those of men.

There is another function that man willingly entrusts to woman: being the purpose behind men's activities and the source of their decisions, she is also the judge of values. She is revealed as a privileged judge. Man dreams of an Other not only to possess her, but also to be validated by her; to be validated by men who are his peers entails constant tension on his part: that is why he wants an outside view conferring absolute value on his life, on his undertakings, on himself. God's gaze is hidden, foreign, disquieting: even in periods of faith, only a few mystics felt its intensity. This divine role often devolved on the woman. Close to the man, dominated by him, she does not posit values that are foreign to him: and yet, as she is other, she remains exterior to the world of men and can thus grasp it objectively. It is she who will denounce the presence or absence of courage, of strength and of beauty, while confirming from the outside their universal value. Men are too busy in their cooperative or combative relations to be an audience for each other: they do not think about each other. Woman is removed from their activities and does not take part in their jousts and combats: her entire situation predestines her to play this role of onlooker. The chevalier jousts in tournaments for his lady; poets seek woman's approval. When Rastignac sets out to conquer Paris, he thinks first of *having* women, less about possessing their bodies than enjoying that reputation that only they are capable of creating for a man. Balzac projected the story of his own youth onto his young heroes: his education began with older mistresses; and the woman played the role of educator not only in *The Lily in the Valley;*[12] she was also assigned this role in [Flaubert's] *Sentimental Education,*[13] in Stendhal's novels and in numerous other coming-of-age novels. It has already been observed that the woman is both physis and anti-physis; she personifies Society as well as Nature; through her the civilisation of a period and its culture is summed up, as can be seen in courtly poetry, in the *Decameron* and in *L'Astrée*; she launches fashions, presides over salons, directs and reflects opinion. Fame and glory are women. 'The crowd is woman,' said Mallarmé. In the company of women the young man is initiated into the 'world', and into this complex reality called 'life'. She is one of the privileged prizes promised to heroes, adventurers and individualists. In ancient times, Perseus saved Andromeda, Orpheus went to rescue Eurydice from Hades and Troy fought to keep the beautiful Helen. Novels of chivalry recount barely any prowess other than delivering captive princesses. What would Prince Charming do if he did not wake up Sleeping Beauty, or lavish gifts on Donkey Skin? The myth of the king marrying a shepherdess flatters the man as much as the woman. The rich man needs to give or else his useless wealth remains an abstract object: he needs someone to give to. The Cinderella myth, indulgently described by Philip Wylie in *Generation of Vipers*, thrives in prosperous countries; it is more powerful in America than anywhere else because men are more embarrassed by their wealth: how would they spend this money for which they work their whole lives if they did not dedicate it to a woman? Orson Welles, among others, personifies the imperialism of this kind of generosity in *Citizen Kane:* Kane chooses to smother an obscure singer with gifts and impose her on the public as a great opera singer all for his own affirmation of power; in France there are plenty of small-time Citizen Kanes. In another film, *The Razor's Edge,* when the hero returns from India having acquired absolute wisdom, the only use he finds for it is to rescue a prostitute. Clearly man wants woman's enslavement when fantasising himself as a benefactor, liberator or redeemer; if Sleeping Beauty is to be awakened, she must be sleeping; to have a captive princess, there must be ogres and dragons. And the greater man's taste for difficult undertakings, the greater his pleasure in granting woman independence. Conquering is more fascinating than rescuing or giving. The average Western male's ideal is a woman who freely submits to his domination, who does not accept his ideas without some discussion, but who yields to his reasoning, who intelligently resists but yields in the end. The tougher his pride, the more he relishes dangerous adventure; it is far better to tame Penthesilea than to marry a consenting Cinderella. The 'warrior' loves danger and play, said Nietzsche. 'For that reason he wants woman as the most dangerous plaything.' The man who loves danger and play is not displeased to see woman change into an Amazon as long as he keeps the hope of subjugating her:* what he demands in his heart of hearts is that this struggle remain a game for him, while for woman it involves her very destiny: therein lies the true victory for man, liberator, or conqueror – that woman freely recognise him as her destiny.

Thus the expression 'to have a woman' conceals a double meaning: the object's functions are not dissociated from those of the judge. The moment woman is viewed as a person, she can only be conquered with her consent; she must be won. Sleeping Beauty's smile fulfils Prince Charming: the captive princesses' tears of happiness and gratitude give

---

* American detective novels – or American-style ones – are a striking example. Peter Cheyney's heroes, for instance, are always grappling with an extremely dangerous woman, unmanageable for anyone but them: after a duel that unfolds all through the novel, she is finally overcome by Campion or Callaghan and falls into his arms.

meaning to the knights' prowess. On the other hand, her gaze is not a masculine, abstract, severe one – it allows itself to be charmed. Thus heroism and poetry are modes of seduction: but in letting herself be seduced, the woman exalts heroism and poetry. She holds an even more essential privilege for the individualist: she appears to him not as the measure of universally recognised values but as the revelation of his particular merits and of his very being. A man is judged by his fellow men by what he does, objectively and according to general standards. But certain of his qualities, and among others his vital qualities, can only interest woman; his virility, charm, seduction, tenderness and cruelty only pertain to her: if he sets a value on these most secret virtues, he has an absolute need of her; through her he will experience the miracle of appearing as an other, an other who is also his deepest self. Malraux admirably expresses what the individualist expects from the woman he loves in one of his texts. Kyo wonders:

'We hear the voices of others with our ears, our own voices with our throats.' Yes. 'One hears his own life, too, with his throat, and those of others? . . . To others, I am what I have done.' To May alone, he was not what he had done; to him alone, she was something altogether different from her biography. The embrace by which love holds beings together against solitude did not bring its relief to man; it brought relief only to the madman, to the incomparable monster, dear above all things, that every being is to himself and that he cherishes in his heart. Since his mother had died, May was the only being for whom he was not Kyo Gisors, but an intimate partner . . . Men are not my kind, they are those who look at me and judge me; my kind are those who love me and do not look at me, who love me in spite of everything, degradation, baseness, treason – me, and not what I have done or shall do – who would love me as long as I would love myself – even to suicide.*[14]

What makes Kyo's attitude human and moving is that it implies reciprocity and that he asks May to love him in his authenticity, not to send back an indulgent reflection of himself. For many men, this demand is diluted: instead of a truthful revelation, they seek a glowing image of admiration and gratitude, deified in the depths of a woman's two eyes. Woman

* *Man's Fate.*

has often been compared to water, in part because it is the mirror where the male Narcissus contemplates himself: he leans towards her, with good or bad faith. But in any case, what he wants from her is to be, outside of him, all that he cannot grasp in himself, because the interiority of the existent is only nothingness, and to reach himself, he must project himself on to an object. Woman is the supreme reward for him since she is his own apotheosis, a foreign form he can possess in the flesh. It is this 'incomparable monster', himself, that he embraces when he holds in his arms this being who sums up the World and onto whom he has imposed his values and his laws. Uniting himself, then, with this other whom he makes his own, he hopes to reach himself. Treasure, prey, game and risk, muse, guide, judge, mediator, mirror, the woman is the Other in which the subject surpasses himself without being limited, who opposes him without negating him; she is the Other who lets herself be annexed to him without ceasing to be the Other. And for this she is so necessary to man's joy and his triumph that if she did not exist, men would have had to invent her.

They did invent her.* But she also exists without their invention. This is why she is the failure of their dream at the same time as its incarnation. There is no image of woman that does not invoke the opposite figure as well: she is Life and Death, Nature and Artifice, Light and Night. Whatever the point of view, the same fluctuation is always found, because the inessential necessarily returns to the essential. In the figures of the Virgin Mother and of Beatrice lie Eve and Circe.

'Through woman', wrote Kierkegaard, 'ideality enters into life and what would man be without her? Many a man has become a genius through a girl, . . . but none has become a genius through the girl he married . . .

'It is only by a negative relation to her that man is rendered productive in his ideal endeavours. Negative relations with woman can make us infinite . . . positive relations with woman make the man finite to a far greater extent.'† This means that woman is necessary as long as she remains an Idea into which man projects his own transcendence; but she is detrimental as objective reality, existing for herself and limited to herself. In refusing to marry his fiancée, Kierkegaard believes he has established the only valid relation with woman. And he is right in the

---

* 'Man created woman – but what out of? Out of a rib of his God, of his ideal' (Nietzsche, *Twilight of the Idols*).
† *In Vino Veritas*.

sense that the myth of woman posited as infinite Other immediately entails its opposite.

Because she is faux Infinite, Ideal without truth, she is revealed as finitude and mediocrity and thus as falsehood. That is how she appears in Laforgue: throughout his work he expresses rancour against a mystification he blames on man as much as woman. Ophelia and Salome are nothing but 'little women'. Hamlet might think: 'Thus would Ophelia have loved me as her "possession" and because I was socially and morally superior to her girlish friends' possessions. And those little remarks about comfort and well-being that slipped out of her at lamp-lighting time!' Woman makes man dream, yet she is concerned with comfort and stews; one speaks to her about her soul but she is only a body. And the lover, believing he is pursuing the Ideal, is the plaything of nature that uses all these mystifications for the ends of reproduction. She represents in reality the everydayness of life; she is foolishness, prudence, mediocrity and ennui. Here is an example of how this is expressed, in a poem entitled 'Our Little Companion':

> . . . I have the talent of every school
> I have souls for all tastes
> Pick the flower of my faces
> Drink my mouth and not my voice
> And do not look for more:
> Not even I can see clearly
> Our loves are not equal
> For me to hold out my hand
> You are merely naive males
> I am the eternal feminine!
> My fate loses itself in the Stars!
> I am the Great Isis!
> No one has lifted my veil
> Dream only of my oases . . .[15]

Man succeeded in enslaving woman, but in doing so, he robbed her of what made possession desirable. Integrated into the family and society, woman's magic fades rather than transfigures itself; reduced to a servant's condition, she is no longer the wild prey incarnating all of nature's treasures. Since the birth of courtly love, it has been a commonplace that marriage kills love. Either too scorned, too respected or too quotidian, the wife is no longer a sex object. Marriage rites were originally intended

to protect man against woman; she becomes his property: but everything we possess in turn possesses us; marriage is a servitude for the
man as well; he is thus caught in the trap laid by nature: to have desired
a lovely girl, the male must spend his whole life feeding a heavy matron,
a dried-out old woman; the delicate jewel intended to embellish his existence becomes an odious burden: Xanthippe is one of those types of
women that men have always referred to with the greatest horror.* But
even when the woman is young, there is mystification in marriage because
trying to socialise eroticism only succeeds in killing it. Eroticism implies
a claim of the instant against time, of the individual against the collectivity; it affirms separation against communication; it rebels against all
regulation; it contains a principle hostile to society. Social customs are
never bent to fit the rigour of institutions and laws: love has forever
asserted itself against them. In its sensual form it addresses young people
and courtesans in Greece and Rome; both carnal and platonic, courtly
love is always directed at another's wife. *Tristan* is the epic of adultery.
The period around 1900 that re-creates the myth of the woman is one
where adultery becomes the theme of all literature. Certain writers, like
Bernstein, in the supreme defence of bourgeois institutions, struggle to
reintegrate eroticism and love into marriage; but there is more truth in
Porto-Riche's *A Loving Wife*,[16] which shows the incompatibility of these
two types of values. Adultery can disappear only with marriage itself.
For the aim of marriage is to immunise man against *his* own wife: but
other women still have a dizzying effect on him; it is to them he will
turn. Women are accomplices. For they rebel against an order that tries
to deprive them of their weapons. So as to tear woman from nature, so
as to subjugate her to man through ceremonies and contracts, she was
elevated to the dignity of a human person; she was granted freedom.
But freedom is precisely what escapes all servitude; and if it is bestowed
on a being originally possessed by malevolent forces, it becomes
dangerous. And all the more so as man stopped at half measures; he
accepted woman into the masculine world only by making her a servant,
in thwarting her transcendence; the freedom she was granted could only
have a negative use; it only manifests itself in refusal. Woman became
free only in becoming captive; she renounces this human privilege to
recover her power as natural object. By day she treacherously plays her
role of docile servant, but by night she changes into a kitten, a doe; she

---

* As we have seen, it was the theme of many lamentations in Greece and during the
Middle Ages.

slips back into a siren's skin, or riding on her broomstick, she makes her satanic rounds. Sometimes she exercises her nocturnal magic on her own husband; but it is wiser to conceal her metamorphoses from her master; she chooses strangers as her prey; they have no rights over her, and she remains for them a plant, wellspring, star or sorceress. So there she is, fated to infidelity: it is the only concrete form her freedom could assume. She is unfaithful over and above her own desires, her thoughts or her consciousness; because she is seen as an object, she is given up to any subjectivity that chooses to take her; it is still not sure that locked in harems, hidden behind veils, she does not arouse desire in some person: to inspire desire in a stranger is already to fail her husband and society. But worse, she is often an accomplice in this fate; it is only through lies and adultery that she can prove that she is nobody's thing, that she refutes male claims on her. This is why man's jealousy is so quick to awaken, and in legends woman can be suspected without reason, condemned on the least suspicion, as were Geneviève de Brabant and Desdemona; even before any suspicion, Griselda is subjected to the worst trials; this tale would be absurd if the woman were not suspected beforehand; there is no case presented against her: it is up to her to prove her innocence. This is also why jealousy can be insatiable; it has already been shown that possession can never be positively realised; even if all others are forbidden to draw from the spring, no one possesses the thirst-quenching spring: the jealous one knows this well. In essence, woman is inconstant, just as water is fluid; and no human force can contradict a natural truth. Throughout all literature, in *The Thousand and One Nights* as in the *Decameron*, woman's ruses triumph over man's prudence. But it is more than simply individualistic will that makes him a jailer: society itself, in the form of father, brother and husband, makes him responsible for the woman's behaviour. Chastity is imposed upon her for economic and religious reasons, every citizen having to be authenticated as the son of his own father. But it is also very important to compel woman to conform exactly to the role society devolves on her. Man's double demand condemns woman to duplicity: he wants the woman to be his own and yet to remain foreign to him; he imagines her as servant and sorceress at the same time. But he admits publicly only to the former desire; the latter is a deceitful demand hidden in the depths of his heart and flesh; it goes against morality and society; it is evil like the Other, like rebel Nature, like the 'bad woman'. Man is not wholly devoted to the Good he constructs and attempts to impose; he maintains a shameful connivance with the Bad. But whenever the Bad imprudently dares to show its face openly, he goes to war against it. In the darkness of night, man invites woman to sin. But in the light of day, he rejects sin and her, the sinner. And women, sinners themselves in the mysteries of the bed, show all the more passion for the public worship of virtue. Just as in primitive society the male sex is secular and woman's is laden with religious and magic qualities, today's modern societies consider man's failings harmless peccadilloes; they are often lightly dismissed; even if he disobeys community laws, the man continues to belong to it; he is merely an *enfant terrible*, not a profound threat to the collective order. If, on the other hand, the woman deviates from society, she returns to Nature and the devil, she triggers uncontrollable and evil forces within the group. Fear has always been mixed with the blame for licentious behaviour. If the husband cannot keep his wife virtuous, he shares her fault; his misfortune is, in society's eyes, a dishonour, and there are civilisations so strict that it is necessary to kill the criminal to dissociate him from her crime. In others, the complaisant husband will be punished by noisy demonstrations or led around naked on a donkey. And the community will take it upon itself to punish the guilty woman in his place: because she offended the group as a whole and not only her husband. These customs were particularly brutal in superstitious and mystical Spain, sensual and terrorised by the flesh. Calderón, Lorca and Valle-Inclán made it the theme of many plays. In Lorca's *La casa de Bernarda Alba* (*The House of Bernard Alba*) the village gossips want to punish the seduced girl by burning her with live coal 'in the place where she sinned'. In Valle-Inclán's *Divine Words*, the adulteress appears as a witch who dances with the devil: her fault discovered, the whole village assembles to tear off her clothes and drown her. Many traditions reported that the sinner was stripped; then she was stoned, as told in the Gospel, and she was buried alive, drowned or burned. The meaning of these tortures is that she was thus returned to Nature after being deprived of her social dignity; by her sin she had released bad natural emanations: the expiation was carried out as a kind of sacred orgy where the women stripped, beat and massacred the guilty one, releasing in turn their mysterious but beneficial fluids since they were acting in accordance with society.

This savage severity fades as superstitions diminish and fear dissipates. But in the countryside, godless and homeless bohemian women are still regarded with suspicion. The woman who freely exercises her charms – adventuress, vamp, *femme fatale* – remains a disquieting type. In Hollywood films the Circe image survives as the bad woman. Women were burned as witches simply because they were beautiful. And in the prudish intimidation of provincial virtues, the old spectre of dissolute women is perpetuated.

These very dangers make woman captivating game for an adventurous man. Disregarding his rights as a husband, refusing to uphold society's laws, he will try to conquer her in single combat. He tries to annex the woman, including her resistance; he pursues in her the same freedom through which she escapes him. In vain. Freedom cannot be carved up: the free woman will often be free at the expense of man. Sleeping Beauty might wake up with displeasure, she might not recognise her Prince Charming in the one who awakens her, she might not smile. This is precisely the case of Citizen Kane, whose protégée is seen to be oppressed and whose generosity is revealed to be a will for power and tyranny; the hero's wife listens to his exploits indifferently, the Muse yawns, listening to the verses of the poet who dreams of her. Out of boredom, the Amazon can refuse combat; and she can also emerge victorious. Roman women of the decadence, and many American women today, impose their whims or their law on men. Where is Cinderella? The man wanted to give and here is the woman taking. No longer a game, it is a question of self-defence. From the moment the woman is free, her only destiny is one she freely creates for herself. So the relation between the two sexes is a relation of struggle. Having become a peer to man, she seems as formidable as when she faced him as foreign Nature. The female nurturer, devoted and patient, turns into an avid and devouring beast. The bad woman also sets her roots in the earth, in Life; but the earth is a grave, and life a bitter combat: so the myth of the industrious honeybee or mother hen is replaced by the devouring insect, the praying mantis, the spider; the woman is no longer the one who nurses her young but the one who eats the male; the egg is no longer the storehouse of abundance but a trap of inert matter drowning the mutilated spermatozoid; the womb, that warm, peaceful and safe haven, becomes the rank octopus, the carnivorous plant, abyss of convulsive darkness; within it lives a serpent who insatiably swallows the male's strength. Such a dialectic turns the erotic object into female black magic, turns the female servant into a traitor, Cinderella into a witch, and changes all women into the enemy: here is the ransom man pays for having posited himself in bad faith as the sole essential.

But this enemy face is not woman's definitive form either. Instead, Manichaeism is introduced within the feminine kind. Pythagoras linked the good principle to man and the bad principle to woman; men have tried to overcome the bad by annexing woman; they have been partially

successful; but just as Christianity, by introducing the ideas of redemption and salvation, gave its full sense to the word 'damnation', in the
same way the bad woman stands out in opposition to the sanctified
woman. In the course of this *querelle des femmes*, which has endured from
the Middle Ages to our times, some men want only to see the blessed
woman they dream of, while others want the cursed woman who belies
their dreams. But in fact, if man can find *everything* in woman, it is
because she has both faces. In a carnal and living way, she represents all
the values and anti-values that give life meaning. Here, clear-cut, we
have the Good and the Bad, in opposition to each other in the guise of
devoted Mother and perfidious Lover; in the old English ballad, 'Lord
Randal, My Son', a young knight dies in his mother's arms, poisoned by
his mistress. Richepin's *The Leech*[17] takes up the same theme, but with
more pathos and bad taste. Angelic Michaela is contrasted with dark
Carmen. The mother, the faithful fiancée and the patient wife provide
healing to the wounds inflicted on men's hearts by vamps and witches.
Between these clearly fixed poles a multitude of ambiguous figures were
yet to be defined, the pitiful, the detestable, sinners, victims, coquettes,
the weak, the angelic, the devilish. A multitude of behaviours and feelings
thereby solicit man and enrich him.

The very complexity of woman enchants him: here is a wonderful
servant who can excite him at little expense. Is she angel or devil?
Uncertainty makes her a sphinx. One of the most famous brothels of
Paris was placed under its aegis. In the grand epoch of Femininity, in
the time of corsets, of Paul Bourget, of Henri Bataille and of the French
cancan, the Sphinx theme is all the rage in comedies, poems and songs:
'Who are you, where do you come from, strange Sphinx?' And dreams
and queries about the feminine mystery continue still. To preserve this
mystery, men have long implored women not to give up their long
dresses, petticoats, veils, long gloves and high boots: whatever accentuates difference in the Other makes them more desirable, since it is
the Other as such that man wants to possess. In his letters, Alain-
Fournier reproaches English women for their boyish handshake: French
women's modest reserve flusters him. Woman must remain secret,
unknown, to be adored as a faraway princess; Fournier seems not to
have been terribly deferential to the women who entered his life, but
it is in a woman, whose main virtue was to seem inaccessible, that he
incarnates all the wonder of childhood, of youth, the nostalgia for a
lost paradise. In Yvonne de Galais he traced a white and gold image.
But men cherish even feminine defects if they create mystery. 'A woman

must have her caprices,' said a man authoritatively to a reasonable woman. Caprices are unpredictable; they lend woman the grace of undulating water; lying embellishes her with glittering reflections; coquetry, even perversity, is her intoxicating perfume. Deceitful, evasive, misunderstood, duplicitous, it is thus that she best lends herself to men's contradictory desires; she is Maya of the innumerable metamorphoses. It is a commonplace to represent the Sphinx as a young woman: virginity is one of the secrets that men – and all the more so if they are libertines – find the most disconcerting; a girl's purity gives hope for all kinds of licence and no one knows what perversities are concealed beneath her innocence; still close to animal and plant, already compliant with social rites, she is neither child nor adult; her timid femininity does not inspire fear, but mild unrest. It is understandable that she is one of the privileged figures of the feminine mystery. But as the 'real young lady' fades, worshipping her has become a bit outdated. On the other hand, the prostitute's character that Gantillon, in his triumphantly successful play, gave to Maya still has a great deal of prestige. She is one of the most flexible of feminine types, one that best allows the great game of vices and virtues. For the timorous puritan, she embodies evil, shame, disease and damnation; she inspires horror and disgust; she belongs to no man, but gives herself to all of them and lives on the trade; therein she regains the fearsome independence of lewd primitive Goddess Mothers and she embodies the Femininity that masculine society has not sanctified, that remains rife with malevolent powers; in the sexual act, the male cannot imagine that he possesses her, he is only given over to demons of the flesh, a humiliation, a stain particularly felt by Anglo-Saxons in whose eyes the flesh is more or less reviled. On the other hand, a man who is not frightened by the flesh will love the prostitute's generous and rudimentary affirmation; in her he will see exalted femininity that no morality has diminished; he will find in her body again those magic virtues that in the past made the woman kin to the stars and the sea: a Henry Miller, sleeping with a prostitute, feels he has dived into the very depths of life, death, the cosmos; he meets God in the moist shadows of the receptive vagina. Because she is on the margins of a hypocritically moral world, a sort of pariah, the 'lost girl' can be regarded as the challenger of all official virtues; her indignity relates her to authentic saints; for the oppressed shall be exalted; Christ looked upon Mary Magdalene with favour; sin opens the gates of heaven more easily than hypocritical virtue. Thus Raskolnikov sacrificed, at Sonya's feet, the arrogant masculine pride that led him to crime; murder exacerbated this will for separation that is in all men: resigned, abandoned by all, a humble prostitute is best suited to receive his vow of abdication.*[18] The words 'lost girl' awaken disturbing echoes; many men dream of losing themselves: it is not so easy, one does not easily attain Evil in a positive form; and even the demoniac is frightened by excessive crimes; the woman enables the celebration of the black masses, where Satan is evoked without exactly being invited; she is on the margin of the masculine world: acts that concern her are really without consequence; yet she is a human being and through her, dark revolts against human laws can be carried out. From Musset to Georges Bataille, visiting 'girls' was hideous and fascinating debauchery. Sade and Sacher-Masoch satisfied their haunting desires; their disciples, and most men who had to satisfy their 'vices', commonly turned to prostitutes. Of all women, they were the ones who were the most subjected to the male, and yet the ones who best escaped him; this is what makes them likely to take on numerous meanings. There is, however, no feminine figure – virgin, mother, wife, sister, servant, lover, fierce virtue, smiling odalisque – capable of encapsulating the inconstant yearnings of men.

It is for psychology – specifically psychoanalysis – to discover why an individual is drawn more particularly to one aspect or another of the multi-faceted Myth and why he incarnates it in any one particular form. But this myth is involved in all complexes, obsessions and psychoses. In particular, many neuroses are rooted in the vertigo of prohibition: and this vertigo can only emerge if taboos have previously been established; external social pressure is not enough to explain its presence; in fact, social prohibitions are not simply conventions; they have – among other significations – an ontological meaning that each individual experiences in his own way. For example, it is interesting to examine the Oedipus complex; it is too often considered as being produced by a struggle

---

* Marcel Schwob poetically renders this myth in the *Book of Monelle*:

> I will speak to you of the Little Women of Pleasure that you may know of the beginning . . . For you see, these little women call out to you . . . they utter a cry of compassion, and they hold your hand in their emaciated hands. They only understand you when you are unhappy; they can cry with you and console you . . . None of them may stay long with you. They would be too sad and too ashamed to remain. When you no longer weep, you have no need of them. They teach you the lesson they have learned from you, then they flee. They come through the cold and the rain to kiss your brow, to brush their lips across your eyes, to drive from you the terror and the sadness that you know . . . You must not think of what they do in the shadows.

between instinctive tendencies and social directives; but it is first of all an interior conflict within the subject himself. The infant's attachment to the mother's breast is first an attachment to Life in its immediate form, in its generality and its immanence; the rejection of weaning is the rejection of the abandonment to which the individual is condemned once he is separated from the Whole; from then on, and as he becomes more individualised and separated, the taste he retains for the mother's flesh now torn from his own can be termed 'sexual'; his sensuality is thus mediated, it has become transcendence towards a foreign object. But the sooner and more decidedly the child assumes itself as subject, the more the carnal bond that challenges his autonomy will become problematic for him. So he shuns his mother's caresses; his mother's authority, the rights she has over him, even her very presence, inspires a kind of shame in him. Particularly he finds it embarrassing and obscene to be aware of her as flesh, and he avoids thinking of her body; in the horror that he feels towards his father or a second husband or a lover, there is less jealousy than scandal; to be reminded that his mother is a carnal being is to be reminded of his own birth, an event he repudiates with all his force; or at least he wishes to give it the majesty of a great cosmic phenomenon; he thinks that Nature, which invests all individuals but belongs to none, should be contained in his mother; he hates her to become prey, not – as it is often presumed – because he wants to possess her himself, but because he wants her to exist above all possession: she must not have the ordinary features of wife or mistress. When in adolescence, however, his sexuality becomes virile, his mother's body begins to disturb him; but it is because he grasps femininity in general in her; and often the desire aroused by the sight of her thigh or her breast disappears as soon as the young boy realises that this flesh is maternal flesh. There are many cases of perversion, since adolescence, being the age of confusion, is the age of perversion where disgust leads to sacrilege, where temptation is born from the forbidden. But it must not be thought that the son naively wishes to sleep with his mother and that exterior prohibitions interfere and oppress him; on the contrary, desire is born because this prohibition is constituted within the heart of the individual himself. This censure is the most normal, the most general reaction. But there again, it does not arise from social regulation masking instinctive desires. Rather, respect is the sublimation of an original disgust; the young man refuses to regard his mother as carnal; he transfigures her, he associates her with one of the pure images of the sacred woman society offers. This is how he helps strengthen the image of the ideal

Mother who will save the next generation. But this image has such force only because it emanates from an individual dialectic. And since every woman is inhabited by the general essence of Woman, thus Mother, it is certain that the attitude to the Mother will have repercussions in his relations with wife and mistress; but less simply than is often imagined. The adolescent who has concretely and sensually desired his mother may have desired woman in general in her: and the fervour of his temperament will be appeased with any woman, no matter who; he is not doomed to incestuous nostalgia.* On the other hand, a young man who has had a tender but platonic respect for his mother may in every case wish for woman to be part of maternal purity.

The importance of sexuality, and therefore ordinarily of woman, in both pathological and normal behaviour is well known. Other objects can also be feminised; because since woman is certainly to a large extent man's invention, he could also invent her in the male body: in homosexuality, sexual division is maintained. But ordinarily Woman is sought in feminine beings. Through her, through the best and the worst of her, man learns happiness, suffering, vice and virtue, lust, renunciation, devotion and tyranny, and learns about himself; she is play and adventure, but also contest; she is the triumph of victory and more bitter, of failure overcome; she is the giddiness of loss, the fascination of damnation, of death. There is a world of significations that exist only through woman; she is the substance of men's actions and feelings, the embodiment of all the values that seek their freedom. It is understandable that even if he were condemned to the cruellest disavowals, man would not want to relinquish a dream containing all other dreams.

Here, then, is why woman has a double and deceptive image: she is everything he craves and everything he does not attain. She is the wise mediator between auspicious Nature and man; and she is the temptation of Nature, untamed against all reason. She is the carnal embodiment of all moral values and their opposites, from good to bad; she is the stuff of action and its obstacle, man's grasp on the world and his failure; as such she is the source of all man's reflection on his existence and all expression he can give of it; however, she works to divert him from himself, to make him sink into silence and death. As his servant and companion, man expects her also to be his public and his judge, to confirm him in his being; but she opposes him with her indifference, even with her mockery and her laughter. He projects onto her what he

* Stendhal is a striking example.

desires and fears, what he loves and what he hates. And if it is difficult to say anything about her, it is because man seeks himself entirely in her and because she is All. But she is All in that which is inessential: she is wholly the *Other*. And as other she is also other than herself, other than what is expected of her. Being all, she is never exactly *this* that she should be; she is everlasting disappointment, the very disappointment of existence that never successfully attains or reconciles itself with the totality of existents.

CHAPTER 2

In order to confirm this analysis of the feminine myth, as it is collectively presented, we will look at the singular and syncretic form it takes
on in certain writers. The attitude to women seems typical in, among
others, Montherlant, D. H. Lawrence, Claudel, Breton and Stendhal.

I
MONTHERLANT OR THE BREAD OF DISGUST

Montherlant belongs to the long male tradition of adopting the arrogant Manichaeism of Pythagoras. Following Nietzsche, he believes that
the Eternal Feminine was exalted only during periods of weakness and
that the hero has to rise up against the Magna Mater. As a specialist in
heroism, he has undertaken the task of dislodging her. Woman is night,
disorder and immanence. 'These convulsive shadows are nothing more
than "the feminine in its pure state",'*[19] he writes about Mme Tolstoy.
The stupidity and baseness of men today, he thinks, give a positive image
of feminine deficiencies: the feminine instinct, feminine intuition, and
women's clairvoyance are spoken about, while their absence of logic,
stubborn ignorance and inability to grasp the real should be denounced;
they are neither good observers nor psychologists; they neither know
how to see things nor understand human beings; their mystery is a trap,
their unfathomable treasures have the depth of nothingness; they have
nothing to give man and can only harm him. For Montherlant the
mother is the first major enemy; in Exile,[20] an early play of his, he depicts
a mother who keeps her son from enlisting; in Les Olympiques, the
teenager who wants to devote himself to sport is barred by his mother's
fearful egotism; in The Bachelors[21] and in The Girls,[22] the mother is vilified. Her crime is to want to keep her son locked up for ever in her
womb's depths; she mutilates him to make him her own and thus to

* Pity for Women.

fill up the sterile vacuum of her being; she is the worst educator; she cuts the child's wings; she pulls him back from the heights he aspires to; she turns him into a moron and diminishes him. These reproaches are not without some basis. But it is clear from the explicit criticisms that Montherlant addresses to woman-mother that what he hates in her is his own birth. He thinks he is God; he wants to be God: because he is male, because he is a 'superior man', because he is Montherlant. A god is not engendered; his body, if he has one, is a will moulded in hard and disciplined muscles, not in flesh mutely inhabited by life and death; this flesh that he repudiates is perishable, contingent and vulnerable and is his mother's fault. 'The only part of Achilles' body that was vulnerable was the part his mother had held.'* Montherlant never wanted to assume the human condition; what he calls his pride is, from the beginning, a panicked flight from the risks contained in a freedom engaged in the world through flesh; he claims to affirm freedom but to refuse engagement; without ties, without roots, he dreams he is a subjectivity majestically withdrawn upon itself; the memory of his carnal origins disturbs this dream and he resorts to a familiar process: instead of prevailing over it, he repudiates it.

For Montherlant, the woman lover is just as harmful as the mother; she prevents man from resurrecting the god in himself; woman's lot, he says, is life in its most immediate form, woman lives on feelings, she wallows in immanence; she has a mania for happiness: she wants to trap man in it; she does not experience the élan of her transcendence, she does not have the sense of grandeur; she loves her lover in his weakness and not in his strength, in his troubles and not in his joys; she would like him defenceless, so unhappy as to try to convince him of his misery regardless of any proof to the contrary. He surpasses and thus escapes her: she means to reduce him to her size to take him over. Because she needs him, she is not self-sufficient; she is a parasite. Through Dominique's eyes, Montherlant portrayed the promenading women of Ranelagh, women 'hanging on their lovers' arms like beings without backbones, like big disguised slugs';†[23] except for sportswomen, women are incomplete beings, doomed to slavery; soft and lacking muscle, they have no grasp on the world; thus they fiercely work to annex a lover or, even better, a husband. Montherlant, to my knowledge, did not use the praying mantis myth, but the content is there: for woman, to love is to

---

* Ibid.
† *The Dream.*

devour; she pretends to give of herself, and she takes. He quotes Mme Tolstoy's cry: 'I live through him, for him; I demand the same thing for myself,' and he denounces the dangers of such a furious love; he finds a terrible truth in Ecclesiastes:[24] A man who wants to hurt you is better than a woman who wants to help you. He invokes Lyautey's experience: 'A man of mine who marries is reduced to half a man.' He deems marriage to be even worse for a 'superior man'; it is a ridiculous conformism to bourgeois values; could you imagine saying: 'Mrs Aeschylus', or 'I'm having dinner at the Dantes''? A great man's prestige is weakened; and even more, marriage shatters the hero's magnificent solitude; he 'needs not to be distracted from his own self'.* I have already said that Montherlant has chosen a freedom *without object*; that is, he prefers an illusion of autonomy to an authentic freedom engaged in the world; it is this availability that he means to use against woman; she is heavy, she is a burden. 'It was a harsh symbol that a man could not walk straight because the woman he loved was on his arm.'† 'I was burning, she puts out the fire. I was walking on water, she takes my arm, I sink.'‡ How does she have so much power since she is only lack, poverty and negativity and her magic is illusory? Montherlant does not explain it. He simply and proudly says that 'the lion rightly fears the mosquito.'§ But the answer is obvious: it is easy to believe one is sovereign when alone, to believe oneself strong when carefully refusing to bear any burden. Montherlant has chosen ease; he claims to worship difficult values: but he seeks to attain them easily. 'The crowns we give ourselves are the only ones worth being worn,' said the king of *Pasiphaé*. How easy. Montherlant overloaded his brow, draping it with purple, but an outsider's look was enough to show that his diadems were papier-mâché and that, like Hans Christian Andersen's emperor, he was naked. Walking on water in a dream was far less tiring than moving forward on earthly land in reality. And this is why Montherlant the lion avoided the feminine mosquito with terror: he is afraid to be tested by the real.◊

---

* *Pity for Women.*
† *The Girls.*
‡ Ibid.
§ Ibid.
◊ Adler considered this process the classic origin of psychoses. The individual, divided between a 'will for power' and an 'inferiority complex', sets up the greatest distance possible between society and himself so as to avoid the test of reality. He knows it would undermine the claims he can maintain only if they are hidden by bad faith.

If Montherlant had really deflated the Eternal Feminine myth, he would have to be congratulated: women can be helped to assume themselves as human beings by denying the Woman. But he did not smash the idol, as has been shown: he converted it into a monster. He too believed in this obscure and irreducible essence: femininity; like Aristotle and St Thomas, he believed it was defined negatively; woman was woman through a lack of virility; that is the destiny any female individual has to undergo without being able to modify it. Whoever claims to escape it places herself on the lowest rung of the human ladder: she does not manage to become man, she gives up being woman; she is merely a pathetic caricature, a sham; that she might be a body and a consciousness does not provide her with any reality: Platonist when it suited him, Montherlant seems to believe that only the Ideas of femininity and virility possessed being; the individual who partakes of neither has only an appearance of existence. He irrevocably condemns these 'vampires' who dare to posit themselves as autonomous subjects, dare to think and act. And he intends to prove through his depiction of Andrée Hacquebaut that any woman endeavouring to make herself a person would be changed into a grimacing marionette. Andrée is, of course, ugly, ungainly, badly dressed, and even dirty, with dubious nails and forearms: the little culture she is granted is enough to kill all her femininity; Costals assures us she is intelligent, but with every page devoted to her, Montherlant convinces us of her stupidity; Costals claims he feels sympathy for her; Montherlant renders her obnoxious. Through this clever equivocation, the idiocy of feminine intelligence is proven, and an original fall perverting all the virile qualities to which women aspire is established.

Montherlant is willing to make an exception for sportswomen; they can acquire a spirit, a soul, thanks to the autonomous exercise of their body; yet it was easy to bring them down from these heights; he delicately moves away from the 1,000-metre winner to whom he devoted an enthusiastic hymn; knowing he could easily seduce her, he wanted to spare her this disgrace. Alban calls her to the top, but Dominique does not remain there; she falls in love with him: 'She who had been all spirit and all soul sweated, gave off body odours, and out of breath, she cleared her throat.'* Alban chases her away, indignant. If a woman kills the flesh in her through the discipline of sports, she can still be

* The Dream.

esteemed; but an autonomous existence moulded in a woman's flesh is a repulsive scandal; feminine flesh is abhorrent the moment a consciousness inhabits it. What is suitable for woman is to be purely flesh. Montherlant approves the Oriental attitude: as an object of pleasure, the weak sex has a place – modest, of course, but worthwhile – on earth; the pleasure it gives man justifies it, and that pleasure alone. The ideal woman is totally stupid and totally subjugated; she is always willing to welcome the man and never ask anything of him. Such was Douce, and Alban likes her when it is convenient: 'Douce, admirably silly and always lusted after the sillier she is . . . useless outside of love and thus firmly but sweetly avoided'.* Such is Rhadidja, the little Arab woman, a quiet beast of love who docilely accepts pleasure and money. This 'feminine beast' met on a Spanish train can thus be imagined: 'She looked so idiotic that I began to desire her.'†25 The author explains: 'What is irritating in women is their claim to reason; if they exaggerate their animality, they border on the superhuman.'‡

However, Montherlant is in no way an Oriental sultan; in the first place, he does not have the sensuality. He is far from delighting in 'feminine beasts' without ulterior motives; they are 'sick, nasty, never really clean';‡‡ Costals admits that young boys' hair smelled stronger and better than women's; Solange sometimes makes him feel sick, her 'cloying, almost disgusting, smell, and this body without muscles, without nerves, like a white slug'.§ He dreams of more worthy embraces, between equals, where gentleness was born of vanquished strength . . . The Oriental relishes woman voluptuously, thereby bringing about carnal reciprocity between lovers: the ardent invocations of the Song of Songs, the tales of *The Thousand and One Nights* and so much other Arab poetry attest to the glory of the beloved; naturally, there are bad women; but there are also delicious ones, and sensual man lets himself go into their arms confidently, without feeling humiliated. But Montherlant's hero is always on the defensive: 'Take without being taken, the only acceptable formula between superior man and woman.'§§ He speaks readily about the moment of desire, an aggressive moment, a virile one; he avoids the moment of pleasure; he might find that he risks discovering he also

* Ibid.
† *The Little Infanta of Castile.*
‡ Ibid.
‡‡ *The Girls.*
§ Ibid.
§§ Ibid.

sweated, panted, 'gave off body odours'; but no, who would dare breathe in his odour, feel his dampness? His defenceless flesh exists for no one, because there is no one opposite him: his is the only consciousness, a pure transparent and sovereign presence; and if pleasure exists for his own consciousness, he does not take it into account: it would have power over him. He speaks complacently of the pleasure he gave, never what he receives: receiving means dependence. 'What I want from a woman is to give her pleasure';* the living warmth of voluptuousness would imply complicity: he accepts none whatsoever; he prefers the haughty solitude of domination. He seeks cerebral, not sensual, satisfactions in women.

And the first of these is an arrogance that aspires to express itself, but without running any risks. Facing the woman, 'we have the same feeling as facing the horse or the bull: the same uncertainty and the same taste *for testing one's strength*.'† Testing it against other men would be risky; they would be involved in the test; they would impose unpredictable rankings, they would return an outside verdict; with a bull or a horse, one remains one's own judge, which is infinitely safer. A woman also, if she is well chosen, remains alone opposite the man. 'I don't love in equality because I seek the child in the woman.' This truism does not explain anything: why does he seek the child and not the equal? Montherlant would be more sincere if he declared that he, Montherlant, does not have any equal; and more precisely that he does not want to have one: his fellow man frightens him. He admires the rigours of the Olympic Games that create hierarchies in which cheating is not possible; but he has not himself learned the lesson; in the rest of his work and life, his heroes, like him, steer clear of all confrontation: they deal with animals, landscapes, children, women-children, and never with equals. In love with the hard clarity of sports, Montherlant accepts as mistresses only those women from whom his fearful pride risks no judgement. He chooses them 'passive and vegetal', infantile, stupid and venal. He systematically avoids granting them a consciousness: if he finds traces of one, he balks, he leaves; there is never question of setting up any intersubjective relationship with woman: she has to be a simple animated object in man's kingdom; she can never be envisaged as subject; her point of view can never be taken into account. Montherlant's hero has a supposedly arrogant morality but it is merely

* Ibid.
† *The Little Infanta of Castile.*

convenient: he is only concerned with his relations with himself. He is attached to woman – or rather he attaches woman – not to take pleasure in her but to take pleasure in himself: as she is absolutely inferior, woman's existence shows up the substantial, the essential and the indestructible superiority of the male; risk-free.

So Douce's foolishness enables Alban to 'reconstruct in some way the sensations of the *ancient demigod* marrying a fabulous Goose'.* At Solange's first touch, Costals changes into a mighty lion: 'They had barely sat down next to each other when he put his hand on the girl's thigh (on top of her dress), then placed it in the middle of her body *as a lion* holds his paw spread out on the piece of meat he has won . . .'† This gesture made daily by so many men in the darkness of cinemas is for Costals the 'primitive gesture of the *Lord*'.‡ If, like him, they had the sense of grandeur, lovers and husbands who kiss their mistresses before taking them would experience these powerful metamorphoses at low cost. 'He vaguely sniffed this woman's face, *like a lion* who, tearing at the meat he held between his paws, stops to lick it.'‡‡ This carnivorous arrogance is not the only pleasure the male gets out of his female; she is his pretext for him to experience his heart freely, spuriously, and always without risk. One night, Costals takes such pleasure in suffering that, sated with the taste of his own pain, he joyfully attacks a chicken leg. Rarely can one indulge in such a whim. But there are other powerful or subtle joys. For example, condescension; Costals condescends to answer some women's letters, and he even sometimes does it with care; to an unimportant, enthusiastic peasant, he writes at the end of a pedantic dissertation, 'I doubt that you can understand me, but that is better than if I *abase* myself to you.'§ He likes sometimes to shape a woman to his image: 'I want you to be like an Arab scarf for me . . . I did not *raise* you up to me for you to be anything else but me.'§§ It amuses him to manufacture some happy memories for Solange. But it is above all when he sleeps with a woman that he drunkenly feels his prodigality. Giver of joy, giver of peace, heat, strength and pleasure: these riches he doles out

* *The Dream.*
† *The Girls.*
‡ Ibid.
‡‡ Ibid·
§ Ibid.
§§ Ibid.

fill him with satisfaction. He owes nothing to his mistresses; to be absolutely sure of that, he often pays them; but even when intercourse is an equal exchange, the woman is obliged to him without reciprocity: she gives nothing, he takes. He thinks nothing of sending Solange to the bathroom the day he deflowers her; even if a woman is dearly cherished, it would be out of the question for a man to go out of his way for her; he is male by divine right, she by divine right is doomed to the douche and bidet. Costals's pride is such a faithful copy of caddishness that it is hard to tell him apart from a boorish travelling salesman.

Woman's first duty is to yield to his generosity's demands; when he imagines Solange does not appreciate his caresses, Costals turns white with rage. He cherishes Rhadidja because her face lights up with joy when he enters her. So he takes pleasure in feeling both like a beast of prey and a magnificent prince. One may be perplexed, however, by where this fever to take and to satisfy comes from if the woman taken and satisfied is just a poor thing, some tasteless flesh faintly palpitating with an ersatz consciousness. How can Costals waste so much time with these futile creatures?

These contradictions show the scope of a pride that is nothing but vanity.

A more subtle delectation belonging to the strong, the generous, the master, is pity for the unfortunate race. Costals from time to time is moved to feel such fraternal gravity, so much sympathy in his heart for the humble, so much 'pity for women'. What can be more touching than the unexpected gentleness of tough beings? He brings back to life this noble postcard image when deigning to consider these sick animals that are women. He even likes to see sportswomen beaten, wounded, exhausted and bruised; as for the others, he wants them as helpless as possible. Their monthly misery disgusts him and yet Costals confides that 'he had always preferred women on those days when he knew them to be affected'.* He even yields to this pity sometimes; he goes so far as to make promises, if not to keep them: he promises to help Andrée, to marry Solange. When pity retreats from his soul, these promises die: doesn't he have the right to change his mind? He makes the rules of the game that he plays with himself as the only partner.

Inferior and pitiful, that is not enough. Montherlant wants woman

---

* Ibid.

to be despicable. He sometimes claims that the conflict of desire and scorn is a pathetic tragedy: 'Oh! To desire what one disdains: what a tragedy! . . . To have to attract and repel in virtually the same gesture, to light and quickly put out as one does with a match, such is the tragedy of our relations with women!'* In truth, the only tragedy is from the match's point of view, that is, a negligible point of view. For the match lighter, careful not to burn his fingers, it is too obvious that this exercise delights him. If his pleasure were not to 'desire what he disdains', he would not systematically refuse to desire what he esteems: Alban would not repel Dominique; he would choose what he desires: after all, what is so despicable about a little Spanish dancer, young, pretty, passionate and simple; is it that she is poor, from a low social class, and without culture? In Montherlant's eyes, these would seem to be defects. But above all he scorns her as a woman, by decree; he says in fact that it is not the feminine mystery that arouses males' dreams but these dreams that create mystery; but he also projects onto the object what his subjectivity demands: it is not because they are despicable that he disdains women but because he wants to disdain them that they seem abject to him. He feels that the lofty heights he is perched on are all the higher as the distance between them and her is great; that explains why his heroes choose such pathetic sweethearts: against Costals, the great writer, he pits an old provincial virgin tortured by sex and boredom, and a little far-right bourgeois, vacuous and calculating; this is measuring a superior individual with humble gauges: the result is that he comes across as very small to the reader through this awkward caution. But that does not matter as Costals thinks himself grand. The humblest weaknesses of woman are sufficient to feed his pride. A passage in *The Girls* is particularly telling. Before sleeping with Costals, Solange is preparing herself for the night. 'She has to go to the toilet, and Costals remembers this mare he had, so proud, so delicate that she neither urinated nor defecated when he was riding her.' Here can be seen the hatred of the flesh (Swift comes to mind: Celia shits), the desire to see woman as a domestic animal, the refusal to grant her any autonomy, even that of urinating; but Costals's annoyance shows above all that he has forgotten he too has a bladder and intestines; likewise, when he is disgusted by a woman bathed in sweat and body odour, he abolishes all his own secretions: he is a pure spirit served by muscles and a sex organ of steel. 'Disdain is nobler than desire,'

---

* *The Little Infanta of Castile.*

Montherlant declares in *At the Fountains of Desire*²⁶ and Alvaro: 'My bread is disgust.'*²⁷ What an alibi scorn is when it wallows in itself! Because one contemplates and judges, one feels totally other than the other that one condemns, and one dismisses the defects one is accused of free of charge. With what headiness has Montherlant exhaled his scorn for human beings throughout his whole life! It is sufficient for him to denounce their foolishness to believe he is intelligent, to denounce their cowardice to believe himself brave. At the beginning of the Occupation, he indulged in an orgy of scorn for his vanquished fellow countrymen: he who is neither French nor vanquished; he is above it all. Incidentally, all things considered, Montherlant, the accuser, did no more than the others to prevent the defeat; he did not even consent to being an officer; but he quickly and furiously resumed his accusations that take him well beyond himself.†²⁸ He affects to be distressed by his disgust so as to feel it is more sincere and to take more delight in it. The truth is that he finds so many advantages in it that he systematically seeks to drag the woman into abjection. He amuses himself by tempting poor girls with money and jewels: he exults when they accept his malicious gifts. He plays a sadistic game with Andrée, for the pleasure not of making her suffer but of seeing her debase herself. He encourages Solange in infanticide; she welcomes this possibility and Costals's senses are aroused: he takes this potential murderess in a ravishment of scorn.

The apologue of the caterpillars provides the key to this attitude: whatever his hidden intention, it is significant in itself.‡ Pissing on caterpillars, Montherlant takes pleasure in sparing some and exterminating others; he takes a laughing pity on those that are determined to live and generally lets them off; he is delighted by this game. Without the caterpillars, the urinary stream would have been just an excretion; it becomes an instrument of life and death; in front of the crawling insect, man relieves himself and experiences God's despotic solitude, without running the risk of reciprocity. Likewise, faced with female animals, the male, from the top of his pedestal, sometimes cruel, sometimes tender, sometimes fair, sometimes unpredictable, gives, takes back, satisfies, pities or gets irritated; he defers to nothing but his own pleasure; he is sovereign, free and unique. But these

---

* *The Master of Santiago.*
† *June Solstice.*
‡ Ibid.

animals must not be anything but animals; they would be chosen on purpose, their weaknesses would be flattered; they would be treated as animals with such determination that they would end up accepting their condition. In similar fashion, the blacks' petty robberies and lies charmed the whites of Louisiana and Georgia, confirming the superiority of their own skin colour; and if one of these Negroes persists in being honest, he is treated even worse. In similar fashion the debasement of man was systematically practised in the concentration camps: the ruling race found proof in this abjection that it was of superhuman essence.

This was no chance meeting. Montherlant is known to have admired Nazi ideology. He loved seeing the swastika and the sun wheel triumph in a celebration of the sun. 'The victory of the sun wheel is not just a victory of the Sun, of paganism. It is the victory of the sun principle, which is that everything changes . . . I see today the triumph of the principle I am imbued with, that I praised, that with a full consciousness I feel governs my life.'* It is also known with what a relevant sense of grandeur he presented these Germans who 'breathe the great style of strength' as an example to the French during the Occupation.[†] The same panicky taste for facility that makes him run when facing his equals brings him to his knees when facing the winners: kneeling to them is his way of identifying with them; so now he is a winner, which is what he always wanted, be it against a bull, caterpillars or women, against life itself and freedom. It must be said that even before the victory, he was flattering the 'totalitarian magicians'.[‡][29] Like them, he has always been a nihilist, he has always hated humanity. 'People aren't even worth being led (and humanity does not have to have done something to you [for you] to detest it to this extent)';[‡‡] like them, he thinks that certain beings – race, nation, or he, Montherlant, himself – are in possession of an absolute privilege that grants them full rights over others. His morality justifies and calls for war and persecution. To judge his attitude regarding women, this ethic we must scrutinise, because after all it is important to know *in the name of what* they are condemned.

Nazi mythology had a historical infrastructure: nihilism expressed German despair; the cult of the hero served positive aims for which millions of soldiers lost their lives. Montherlant's attitude has no

* Ibid.
† Ibid.
‡ *September Equinox.*
‡‡ *At the Fountains of Desire.*

positive counterweight and it expresses nothing but his own existential choice. In fact, this hero chooses fear. There is a claim to sovereignty in every consciousness: but it can only be confirmed by risking
itself; no superiority is ever given since man is nothing when reduced
to his subjectivity; hierarchies can only be established among men's
acts and works; merit must be ceaselessly won: Montherlant knows it
himself. 'One only has rights over what one is willing to risk.' But he
never wants to risk *himself* amid his peers. And because he does not
dare confront humanity, he abolishes it. 'Infuriating obstacle that of
beings,' says the king in *The Dead Queen*.[30] They give the lie to the
complacent 'fairyland' the conceited creates around himself. They have
to be negated. It is noteworthy that *none* of Montherlant's works depicts
a conflict between man and man; coexistence is the great living drama:
he eludes it. His hero always rises up alone facing animals, children,
women, landscapes; he is prey to his own desires (like the queen of
Pasiphaé) or his own demands (like the master of Santiago), but *no
person* is ever beside him. Even Alban in *The Dream* does not have a
friend: when Prinet was alive, he disdained him; he only exalts him
over his dead body. Montherlant's works, like his life, recognise only
one consciousness.

With this, all feeling disappears from this universe; there can be no
intersubjective relation if there is only one subject. Love is derisory; but
it is not in the name of friendship that it is worthy of scorn, because
'friendship lacks guts.'* And all human solidarity is haughtily rejected.
The hero was not engendered; he is not limited by space and time: 'I
do not see any reasonable reason to be interested in exterior things that
are of my time more than any others of any past year.'†[31] Nothing that
happens to others counts for him: 'In truth events never counted for
me. I only liked them for the rays they made in me by going through
me . . . Let them be what they want to be . . .'‡ Action is impossible:
'Having had passion, energy, and boldness and not being able to put
them to any use through lack of faith in anything human!'‡‡ That means
that any *transcendence* is forbidden. Montherlant recognises that. Love
and friendship are twaddle, scorn prevents action; he does not believe
in art for art's sake, and he does not believe in God. All that is left is

* Ibid.
† *The Possession of Oneself.*
‡ *June Solstice.*
‡‡ *At the Fountains of Desire.*

the immanence of pleasure. 'My one ambition is to use my senses better than others,' he writes in 1925.* And again: 'In fact, what do I want? To possess beings that please me in peace and poetry.'† And in 1941: 'But I who accuse, what have I done with these twenty years? They have been a dream filled with my pleasure. I have lived high and wide, drunk on what I love: what a mouth-to-mouth with life!'‡ So be it. But is it not precisely because she wallows in immanence that woman is trodden upon? What higher aims, what great designs does Montherlant set against the mother's or lover's possessive love? He also seeks 'possession'; and as for the 'mouth-to-mouth with life', many women can give that back in kind. He does partake of unusual pleasures: those that can be had from animals, boys and preadolescent girls; he is indignant that a passionate mistress would not dream of putting her twelve-year-old daughter in his bed: this indignation is not very solar. Can he not be aware that women's sensuality is no less tormented than men's? If that were the criterion for ranking the sexes, women would perhaps be first. Montherlant's inconsistencies are truly abominable. In the name of 'alternation' he declares that since nothing is worth anything, everything is equal; he accepts everything, he wants to embrace everything and it pleases him that mothers with children are frightened by his broad-mindedness; but he is the one who demanded an 'inquisition'§ during the Occupation that would censure films and newspapers; American girls' thighs disgust him, the bull's gleaming penis exalts him: to each his own; everyone re-creates his own 'phantasm'; in the name of what values does this great orgiast spit with disgust on the orgies of others? Because they are not his own? So can all morality be reduced to being Montherlant?

He would obviously answer that pleasure is not everything: style matters. Pleasure should be the other side of renunciation; the voluptuary also has to feel he is made of the stuff of heroes and saints. But many women are expert in reconciling their pleasures with the high image they have of themselves. Why should we think that Montherlant's narcissistic dreams are worth more than theirs?

---

* Ibid.

† Ibid.

‡ *June Solstice.*

§ 'We ask for a body that would have discretionary power to stop anything it deems to be harmful to the essence of French human values. Some sort of an inquisition in the name of French human values' (ibid.).

Because, in truth, this is a question of dreams. Because he denies them any objective content, the words Montherlant juggles with – 'grandeur', 'holiness' and 'heroism' – are merely eye-catchers. Montherlant is afraid of risking his own superiority among men; to be intoxicated on this exalting wine, he retreats into the clouds: the Unique is obviously supreme. He closes himself up in a museum of mirages: mirrors reflect his own image infinitely, and he thinks that he can thus populate the earth; but he is no more than a reclusive prisoner of himself. He thinks he is free; but he alienates his liberty in the interests of his ego; he models the Montherlant statue on postcard-imagery standards. Alban repelling Dominique because he sees a fool in the mirror illustrates this enslavement: it is in the eyes of others that one is a fool. The arrogant Alban subjects his heart to this collective consciousness that he despises. Montherlant's liberty is an attitude, not a reality. Without an aim, action is impossible, so he consoles himself with gestures: it is mimicry. Women are convenient partners; they give him his lines, he takes the leading role, he crowns himself with laurels and drapes himself in purple: but everything takes place on his private stage; thrown onto the public square, in real light, under a real sky, the actor no longer sees clearly, cannot stand, staggers, and falls. In a moment of lucidity, Costals cries out: 'Deep down, these "victories" over women are some farce!'* Yes. Montherlant's values and exploits are a sad farce. The noble deeds that intoxicate him are also merely gestures, never undertakings: he is touched by Peregrinus's suicide, Pasiphaé's boldness, and the elegance of the Japanese who shelters his opponent under his umbrella before taking his life in a duel. But he declares that 'the adversary's specificity and the ideas he is supposedly representing are not all that important'.† This declaration had a particular resonance in 1941. Every war is beautiful, he also says, whatever its aims; force is always admirable, whatever it serves. 'Combat without faith is the formula we necessarily end up with to maintain the only acceptable idea of man: one where he is the hero and the sage.'‡ But it is curious that Montherlant's noble indifference regarding all causes inclines him not towards resistance but towards national revolution, that his sovereign freedom chooses submission and that he looks for the secret of heroic wisdom not in the Maquis but in the conquerors. This is not by

---

* *The Girls.*
† *June Solstice.*
‡ Ibid.

chance either. The pseudo-sublime of *The Dead Queen* and *The Master of Santiago* is where these mystifications lead. In these plays that are all the more significant for their ambition, two imperious males sacrifice women guilty of simply being human beings to their hollow pride; they desire love and earthly happiness: as punishment, one loses her life and the other her soul. If once again one asks, what for? the author answers haughtily: for nothing. He does not want the king's reasons for killing Inès to be too imperious: the murder should be a banal political crime. 'Why do I kill her? There is probably a reason, but I cannot see it,' he says. The reason is that the solar principle triumphs over earthly banality; but this principle does not inform any aim: it calls for destruction, nothing more, as has already been seen. As for Alvaro, Montherlant says in a preface that he is interested in certain men of this period in 'their clear-cut faith, their scorn for the outside reality, their taste for destruction, their passion for nothing'. This is the passion to which the master of Santiago sacrifices his daughter. She will be arrayed in the beautiful shimmer of words mystical. Is it not boring to prefer happiness to mysticism? Sacrifices and renunciations have meaning only in the light of an aim, a human aim; and aims that go beyond singular love or personal happiness can only exist in a world that recognises the price of both love and happiness; the 'shopgirl's morality' is more authentic than hollow phantasms because it is rooted in life and reality, where great aspirations can spring forth. Inès de Castro can easily be pictured in Buchenwald, with the king hurrying to the German Embassy for reasons of state. Many shopgirls were worthy of a respect that we would not grant to Montherlant during the Occupation. The empty words he crams himself with are dangerous for their very hollowness: this superhuman mysticism justifies all kinds of temporal devastations. The fact is that in the plays under discussion, this mystique is attested to by two murders, one physical and the other moral; Alvaro does not have far to go to become a grand inquisitor: wild, solitary, unrecognisable; nor the king – misunderstood, rejected – to become a Himmler. They kill women, they kill Jews, they kill effeminate men and 'Jewed' Christians, they kill everything they want or like to kill in the name of these lofty ideas. Only by negations can negative mysticisms be affirmed. True surpassing is a positive step towards the future, towards humanity's future. The false hero, to convince himself he goes far and flies high, always looks back, at his feet; he despises, he accuses, he oppresses, he persecutes, he tortures, he massacres. It is through the evil he does to his neighbour that he measures his superiority over him. Such are Montherlant's summits that he points out with an arrogant finger when he interrupts his 'mouth-to-mouth with life'.

'Like the donkey at an Arab waterwheel, I turn, I turn, blind and endlessly retracing my steps. But I don't bring up freshwater.' There is not much to add to this avowal that Montherlant signed in 1927. Freshwater never sprang forth. Maybe Montherlant should have lit Peregrinus's pyre: that would have been the most logical solution. He preferred to take refuge in his own cult. Instead of giving himself to this world, which he did not know how to nourish, he settled for seeing himself in it; and he organised his life in the interest of this mirage visible to his eyes alone. 'Princes are at ease in all situations, even in defeat,'* he writes; and because he delighted in defeat, he believes he is king. He learns from Nietzsche that 'woman is the hero's amusement' and he thinks that it is enough to get pleasure from women to be anointed hero. The rest is the same. As Costals might say: 'Deep down, what a farce!'

II
D. H. LAWRENCE OR PHALLIC PRIDE

Lawrence is the very antipode of Montherlant. His objective is not to define the special relations of woman and man but to situate them both in the truth of Life. This truth is neither representation nor will: it envelops the animality in which human beings have their roots. Lawrence passionately rejects the antithesis sex versus brain; he has a cosmic optimism radically opposed to Schopenhauer's pessimism, the will to live expressed in the phallus is joy: thought and action must derive their source from this or else it would be an empty concept and a sterile mechanism. The sexual cycle alone is not sufficient, because it falls back into immanence: it is synonymous with death; but better this mutilated reality – sex and death – than an existence cut off from carnal humus. Unlike Antaeus, man needs more than to renew contact with the earth from time to time; his life as a male has to be wholly the expression of his virility, which posits and requires woman in its immediacy; she is thus neither diversion nor prey, she is not an object confronting a subject but a pole necessary for the existence of the pole of the opposite sign. Men who have misunderstood this truth – a Napoleon for example – have missed their destiny as men: they are fail-

* Ibid.

ures. It is by fulfilling his generality as intensely as possible, and not by affirming his singularity, that the individual can save himself: whether male or female, an individual should never seek the triumph of pride or the exaltation of his self in erotic relations; to use one's sex as a tool of one's will is the irreparable error; it is essential to break the barriers of the ego, transcend the very limits of consciousness and renounce all personal sovereignty. Nothing could be more beautiful than that little statue of a woman giving birth: 'A terrible face, void, peaked, abstracted almost into meaninglessness by the weight of sensation beneath.'* This ecstasy is neither sacrifice nor abandon; there is no question of either sex letting itself be swallowed up by the other; neither the man nor the woman should be like a broken fragment of a couple; one's sex is not a wound; each one is a complete being, perfectly polarised; when one is assured in his virility, the other in her femininity, 'each acknowledges the perfection of the polarised sex circuit';† the sexual act is without annexation, without surrender of either partner, the marvellous fulfilment of each other. When Ursula and Birkin finally found each other, they would give each other this star-equilibrium which alone is freedom . . . 'For she was to him what he was to her, the immemorial magnificence of mystic, palpable real otherness.'‡ Attaining each other in the generous wrenching of passion, two lovers together attain the Other, the All. So it is for Paul and Clara in the moment of their love:‡‡ she is for him 'a strong, strange, wild life, that breathed with his in the darkness through this hour. It was so much bigger than themselves, that he was hushed. They had met, and included in their meeting the thrust of the manifold grass stems, the cry of the peewit, the wheel of the stars.' Lady Chatterley and Mellors attain the same cosmic joys: blending into each other, they blend into the trees, the light and the rain. Lawrence develops this doctrine extensively in *A propos of 'Lady Chatterley's Lover'*: 'Marriage is no marriage that is not basically and permanently phallic, and that is not linked up with the sun and the earth, the moon and the fixed stars and the planets, in the rhythm of days, in the rhythm of months, in the rhythm of quarters, of years, of decades and of centuries. Marriage is no marriage that is not a correspondence of blood. For the blood is

* *Women in Love.*
† Ibid.
‡ Ibid.
‡‡ *Sons and Lovers.*

the substance of the soul.' 'The blood of man and the blood of woman
are two eternally different streams, that can never be mingled.' This is
why these two streams encircle the whole of life in their meanderings.
'The phallus is a column of blood, that fills the valley of blood of a
woman. The great river of male blood touches to its depth the great
river of female blood, yet neither breaks its bounds. It is the deepest
of all communions . . . And it is one of the greatest mysteries.' This
communion is a miraculous enrichment; but it requires that claims to
'personality' be abolished. When personalities seek to reach each other
without surrendering themselves, as usually happens in modern civilisation, their attempt is doomed to failure. There is a personal, blank,
cold, nervous, poetic sexuality that dissolves each one's vital stream.
Lovers treat each other like instruments, breeding hate between them:
so it is with Lady Chatterley and Michaelis; they remain locked in their
subjectivity; they can experience a fever analogous to that procured by
alcohol or opium, but it is without object: they fail to discover the
reality of the other; they attain nothing. Lawrence would have
condemned Costals summarily. He depicted Gerald* as one of those
proud and egotistical males; and Gerald is in large part responsible for
this hell he and Gudrun hurl themselves into. Cerebral and wilful, he
delights in the empty assertion of his self and hardens himself against
life: for the pleasure of mastering a spirited mare, he holds her firm
against a fence where a train thunders past, bloodying her rebellious
flanks and intoxicating himself with his power. This will to dominate
debases the woman against whom it is directed; physically weak, she
is thus transformed into a slave. Gerald leans over Pussum: 'Her inchoate
look of a violated slave, whose fulfilment lies in her further and further
violation, made his nerves quiver . . . his was the only will, she was the
passive substance of his will.' Here is pitiful domination; if the woman
is merely a passive substance, the male dominates nothing. He thinks
he is taking, enriching himself: it is a delusion. Gerald embraces Gudrun
tightly in his arms: 'She was the rich lovely substance of his being . . .
So she was passed away and gone in him, and he was perfected.' But
as soon as he leaves her, he finds himself alone and empty; and the
next day, she fails to appear at their rendezvous. If the woman is strong,
the male claim arouses a symmetrical claim in her; fascinated and rebellious, she becomes masochistic and sadistic in turn. Gudrun is greatly
disturbed when she sees Gerald press the frightened mare's flanks

* Women in Love.

between his thighs; but she is also disturbed when Gerald's wet nurse tells her how in the past she used to 'pinch his little bottom'. Masculine arrogance provokes feminine resistance. While Ursula is won over and saved by Birkin's sexual purity, as Lady Chatterley was by the game-keeper, Gerald drags Gudrun into a struggle with no way out. One night, unhappy, shattered by a death, he abandons himself in her arms. 'She was the great bath of life, he worshipped her. Mother and substance of all life she was . . . But the miraculous, soft effluence of her breast suffused over him, over his seared, damaged brain, like a healing lymph, like a soft, soothing flow of life itself, perfect as if he were bathed in the womb again.' That night he senses what communion with woman might be; but it is too late; his happiness is vitiated because Gudrun is not really present; she lets Gerald sleep on her shoulder, but she stays awake, impatient, apart. It is the punishment of the individual who is his own prey: alone he cannot end his solitude; in erecting barriers around his self, he erected those around the *Other*: he will never connect to it. In the end, Gerald dies, killed by Gudrun and by himself.

Thus it would seem at first that neither of the two sexes is privileged. Neither is subject. Woman is neither a prey nor a simple pretext. As Malraux notes,* Lawrence thinks that it is not enough, unlike Hindus, for woman to be merely the occasion for a contact with the infinite, as would be a landscape: that would be another way of making her an object. She is as real as the man; a real communion has to be reached. This is why Lawrence's heroes demand much more from their mistresses than the gift of their bodies: Paul does not want Miriam to give herself to him as a tender sacrifice; Birkin does not want Ursula to limit herself to seeking pleasure in his arms; cold or burning, the woman who remains closed within herself leaves the man to his solitude: he must reject her. Both have to give themselves to each other, body and soul. If this giving is accomplished, they have to remain forever faithful to each other. Lawrence believed in monogamous marriage. There is only a quest for variety if one is interested in the uniqueness of beings: but phallic marriage is founded on generality. When the virility–femininity circuit is established, desire for change is inconceivable: it is a perfect circuit, closed on itself and definitive.

Reciprocal gift, reciprocal fidelity: is it really the reign of mutual recognition? Far from it. Lawrence passionately believes in male supremacy. The very expression 'phallic marriage', the equivalence he

---

* Preface to *L'amant de Lady Chatterly*.

establishes between the sexual and the phallic, is proof enough. Of the two bloodstreams that mysteriously marry, the phallic stream is favoured. 'The phallus is the connecting link between the two rivers, that establishes the two streams in a oneness.' Thus man is not only one of the terms of the couple, but also their relationship; he is their surpassing: 'The bridge to the future is the phallus.' Lawrence wants to substitute the cult of the phallic for that of the Goddess Mother; when he wants to highlight the sexual nature of the cosmos, it is through man's virility rather than woman's womb. He almost never shows a man excited by a woman: but over and over he shows woman secretly overwhelmed by the vibrant, subtle, insinuating appeal of the male; his heroines are beautiful and healthy, but not sensuous, while his heroes are troubled wild animals. It is male animals that embody the troubling and powerful mystery of Life; women are subjugated by their spell: this one is affected by the fox, that one is taken with a stallion, Gudrun feverishly challenges a herd of young oxen; she is overwhelmed by the rebellious vigour of a rabbit. A social privilege is connected to this cosmic one. Because the phallic stream is impetuous and aggressive and bestrides the future – Lawrence does not make himself perfectly clear on this point – it is up to man to 'carry forward the banner of life';* he reaches for goals, he incarnates transcendence; woman is absorbed by her sentiments, she is all interiority; she is doomed to immanence. Not only does man play the active role in sexual life, but it is through him that this life is transcended; he is rooted in the sexual world, but he escapes from it; she remains locked up in it. Thought and action have their roots in the phallus; lacking the phallus, woman has no rights to either: she can play the man's role, and brilliantly at that, but it is a game without truth. 'Woman is really polarised downwards, towards the centre of the earth. Her deep positivity is in the downward flow, the moon-pull. And man is polarised upwards, towards the sun and the day's activity.'† For woman, 'her deepest consciousness is in the loins and the belly'.‡ If she turns upward, the moment comes when everything collapses.' In the domain of action, man must be the initiator, the positive; woman is the positive on the emotional level. Thus Lawrence goes back to the traditional bourgeois conception of Bonald, Auguste Comte and Clément Vautel. Woman must subordinate

---

* *Fantasia of the Unconscious.*
† Ibid.
‡ Ibid.

her existence to that of man. 'She's got to believe in you . . . and in the deep purpose you stand for.'* Then man will owe her tenderness and infinite gratitude. 'Ah, how good it is to come home to your wife when she *believes* in you and submits to your purpose that is beyond her . . . You feel unfathomable gratitude to the woman who loves you.'† Lawrence adds that to merit this devotion, man must be authentically invested with a higher purpose; if his project is but a sham, the couple sinks into insignificant mystification; better still to enclose one's self in the feminine cycle – love and death – like Anna Karenina and Vronsky or Carmen and Don José, than to lie to each other like Pierre and Natasha. But subject to this reserve, Lawrence, like Proudhon and Rousseau, advocates monogamous marriage where woman derives the justification for her existence from her husband. Lawrence was just as vituperative as Montherlant concerning the woman who wants to reverse the roles. She should cease playing at the Magna Mater, claiming to be in possession of the truth of life; dominating and devouring, she mutilates the male, she forces him to fall back into immanence and she leads him astray from his goals. Lawrence was far from disparaging motherhood: on the contrary; he rejoices in being flesh, he accepts his birth, he cherishes his mother; mothers appear in his work as magnif-icent examples of real femininity; they are pure renunciation, absolute generosity, and all their human warmth is devoted to their children; they accept them becoming men, they are proud of it. But the egois-tical lover who tries to bring the man back to his childhood must be feared; she cuts man down in his flight. 'The moon, the planet of women, sways us back.'‡ She speaks incessantly about love: but to love for her is to take, to fill the void she feels in herself; this love is close to hate; so it is that Hermione, who suffers from a horrible deficiency because she has never been able to give herself, wants to annex Birkin; she fails; she tries to kill him and the voluptuous ecstasy she feels in striking him is identical to the egotistic spasm of pleasure.‡‡ Lawrence detests modern women, celluloid and rubber creatures who claim a consciousness. When the woman has become sexually conscious, 'there she is functioning away from her own head and her own conscious-ness of herself and her own automatic self-will'.§ He forbids her to

* Ibid.
† Ibid.
‡ Ibid.
‡‡ *Women in Love*.
§ *Fantasia of the Unconscious*.

have an autonomous sensuality; she is made to give, not to take. Putting words in Mellors's mouth, Lawrence cries out his horror of lesbians. But he also blames the woman who has a detached or aggressive attitude to the male; Paul feels wounded and irritated when Miriam caresses his loins, telling him: 'You are so fine!' Gudrun, like Miriam, is at fault when she feels enchanted with her lover's beauty: this contemplation separates them, as much as the irony of icy women intellectuals who consider the penis pitiful or male gymnastics ridiculous; the intense quest for pleasure is no less blameworthy: there is an acute, solitary pleasure that also separates, and woman should not aim for it. Lawrence sketched many portraits of these independent, dominating women who have missed their feminine vocation. Ursula and Gudrun are of this type. At first Ursula is a dominator. 'Man must render himself up to her. He must be quaffed to the dregs by her.'* She will learn to overcome her will. But Gudrun is stubborn; cerebral, artistic, she fiercely envies men their independence and their potential for activity; she persists in keeping her individuality intact; she wants to live for herself; ironic and possessive, she will remain forever shut up in her subjectivity. The most significant figure is Miriam† because she is the least sophisticated. Gerald is partially responsible for Gudrun's failure; but vis-à-vis Paul, Miriam alone bears the full weight of her ill fate. She also would like to be a man, and she hates men; she does not accept herself in her generality; she wants to 'distinguish herself'; because the great stream of life does not pass through her, she can be like a sorceress or a priestess, but never a bacchante; she is moved by things only when she has re-created them in her soul, giving them a religious value: this fervour itself separates her from life; she is poetic, mystical, maladapted. 'She was not clumsy, and yet none of her movements seemed quite THE movement . . . she put too much strength into the effort.' She seeks interior joys, and reality frightens her; sexuality frightens her; when she sleeps with Paul, her heart stands aside in a kind of horror; she is always consciousness, never life: she is not a companion; she does not consent to meld with her lover; she wants to absorb him into herself. He is irritated by this will; he becomes violently angry when he sees her caressing flowers: she seems to want to tear their hearts out; he insults her: 'You're always begging things to love you . . . as if you were a beggar for love . . . You don't want to love – your eternal

* *Women in Love.*
† *Sons and Lovers.*

and abnormal craving is to be loved. You aren't positive, you are negative. You absorb, absorb, as if you must fill yourself up with love,
because you've got a shortage somewhere.' Sexuality does not exist to
fill a void; it must be the expression of a whole being. What women
call love is their greed before the virile force they want to grab. Paul's
mother lucidly thinks about Miriam: 'She wants to absorb him. She
wants to draw him out and absorb him till there is nothing left of him,
even for himself. He will never be a man on his own feet – she will
suck him up.' The young girl is happy when her friend is ill because
she can take care of him: she attempts to serve him, but it is a way of
imposing her will on him. Because she lives apart from him, she excites
in Paul 'an intensity like madness. Which fascinated him, as drug taking
might.' But she is incapable of bringing him joy and peace; from the
depth of her love, in her secret self 'she hated him because she loved
him and he dominated her'. And Paul distances himself from her. He
seeks his balance with Clara; beautiful, lively, animal, she gives herself
unreservedly; and the lovers reach moments of ecstasy that surpass
them both; but Clara does not understand this revelation. She believes
that she owes this joy to Paul himself, to his uniqueness, and she wants
to appropriate him: she fails to keep him precisely because she wants
him for herself. As soon as love is individualised, it changes into avid
egotism and the miracle of eroticism vanishes.

The woman must renounce personal love: neither Mellors nor Don
Cipriano consents to saying words of love to his mistress. Teresa, the
model wife, becomes indignant when Kate asks her if she loves Don
Ramón.* 'He is my life,' she replies; the gift she concedes to him is something quite different from love. Woman must, like man, abdicate all pride
and all will; if she embodies life for the man, he embodies it for her as
well; Lady Chatterley only finds peace and joy because she recognises
this truth: 'She would give up her own hard, bright female power. She
was weary of it, stiffened with it. She would sink in the new bath of life,
in the depths of her womb and her bowels, that sang the voiceless song
of adoration': so she is called to the rapture of the bacchantes; blindly
obeying her lover, not seeking herself in his arms, she forms with him
a harmonious couple, in tune with the rain, the trees and the spring
flowers. Likewise, Ursula renounces her individuality in Birkin's hands
and they attain a 'star equilibrium'. But it is *The Plumed Serpent* above all
that reflects in its entirety Lawrence's ideal. For Don Cipriano is one of

* *The Plumed Serpent.*

those men who 'carry forward the banner of life'; he has a mission and is entirely given over to it to such an extent that virility in him is surpassed and exalted to the point of divinity: if he anoints himself god, it is not a mystification; every man who is fully man is a god; he thus deserves the absolute devotion of a woman. Imbued with Western prejudices, Kate at first refuses this dependence; she is attached to her personality and her limited existence; but little by little letting herself be penetrated by the great stream of life, she gives her body and soul to Cipriano. It is not a slave's surrender: before deciding to stay with him, she insists that he recognise his need for her; he recognises it, since in fact woman is necessary for man; so she consents to never being anything other than his companion; she adopts his goals, his values, his universe. This submission expresses itself even in eroticism; Lawrence does not want the woman to be tense in the search for pleasure, separated from the male by the spasm that jolts her; he deliberately refuses to bring her to orgasm; Don Cipriano withdraws from Kate when he feels her close to this nervous pleasure; she renounces even this sexual autonomy. 'Her strange seething feminine will and desire subsided in her and swept away, leaving her soft and powerfully potent, like the hot springs of water that gushed up so noiseless, so soft, yet so powerful, with a sort of secret potency.'

We can see why Lawrence's novels are first and foremost 'guide-books for women'. It is infinitely more difficult for the woman than for the man to submit to the cosmic order, because he submits in an autonomous fashion, whereas she needs the mediation of the male. When the Other takes on the form of a foreign consciousness and will, there is real surrender; on the contrary, an autonomous submission strangely resembles a sovereign decision. Lawrence's heroes are either condemned from the start or else from the start they hold the secret of wisdom;* their submission to the cosmos was consummated so long ago and they derive such interior certitude from it that they seem as arrogant as a self-important individualist; there is a god who speaks through their mouths: Lawrence himself. But the woman must bow to their divinity. Even if the man is a phallus and not a brain, the virile individual keeps his privileges; woman is not evil, she is even good: but subordinated. Once again, it is the ideal of the 'real woman' that Lawrence offers us, that is, of the woman who unhesitatingly assents to defining herself as the Other.

* With the exception of Paul in *Sons and Lovers*, who is the most vibrant of all. But that is the only novel that shows us a masculine learning experience.

III

CLAUDEL OR THE HANDMAIDEN OF THE LORD

The originality of Claudel's Catholicism is of such an obstinate optimism that evil itself turns to good.

> *Evil itself*
> *Abides its own share of good which must not be wasted.**32

Adopting the point of view that can only be that of the Creator – since we assume the Creator to be all-powerful, omniscient and benevolent – Claudel subscribes to creation entirely; without hell and sin, there could be no free will, no salvation; when he brought forth the world from nothing, God foresaw the Fall and the Redemption. In the eyes of Jews and Christians, Eve's disobedience had put her daughters in a very bad position: we see how badly the Fathers of the Church have mistreated women. But here, on the contrary, she is justified if one accepts that she has served divine purposes. 'Woman! that service she once by her disobedience rendered to God in the earthly Paradise; that deep agreement reached between her and Him; that flesh she put at the disposal of Redemption by way of the fault!'†33 There is no doubt she is the source of sin, and through her man lost paradise. But man's sins have been redeemed, and this world is blessed anew: 'We have not left the paradise of delight in which God first put us!'‡34

'Every Land is the Promised Land.'‡‡35

Nothing that has come from God's hands, nothing that is given, can be in itself bad: 'We pray to God with the entirety of His work! Nothing He made is in vain, nothing is alien to anything else.'§36 And furthermore there is nothing that is unnecessary. 'All things that He has created commune together, all at one and the same time are necessary each to each.'§§37 Thus it is that woman has her place in the harmony of the universe; but it is not just an ordinary place; there is a 'strange and, in Lucifer's eyes, scandalous passion that binds the Eternal to this momentary flower of Nothingness.'◊

* *Break of Noon.*
† *The Adventures of Sophie.*
‡ *Cantata for Three Voices.*
‡‡ *Conversations in the Loir-et-Cher.*
§ *The Satin Slipper.*
§§ *The Tidings Brought to Mary.*
◊ *The Adventures of Sophie.*

Of course, woman can be destructive: In Lechy*[38] Claudel incarnated the bad woman who drives man to his destruction; in *Break of Noon*, Ysé ruins the life of those trapped by her love. But if there were not this risk of loss, there would not be salvation either. Woman 'is the element of risk He deliberately introduced into the midst of His marvellous construction'.[†] It is good that man should know the temptations of the flesh. 'It is this enemy within us that gives our lives their dramatic element, their poignant salt. If our souls were not so brutally assailed, they would continue to sleep, yet here they leap up . . . This struggle is the apprenticeship of victory.'[‡39] Man is summoned to become aware of his soul not only by the spiritual path but also by that of the flesh. 'And what flesh speaks more forcefully to man than the flesh of a woman?'[‡‡] Whatever wrenches him from sleep, from security, is useful: love in whatever form it presents has the virtue of appearing in 'our small personal worlds, ordered by our conventional reasoning, as a deeply perturbing element'.[§40] Often woman is but a deceptive giver of illusions:

> I am the promise that cannot be kept, and my grace consists of that very thing. I am the sweetness of what is, with the regret for what is not. I am the truth that has the countenance of error, and he who loves me does not bother to disentangle each from each.[§§41]

But there is also usefulness in illusion; this is what the Guardian Angel announces to Donna Prouhèze:

> *Even sin! Sin also serves.*
> *So it was good for him to love me?*
> *It was good for you to teach him desire.*
> *Desire for an illusion? For a shadow that forever escapes him?*
> *Desire is for what is, illusion is for what is not. Desire pursued to the*
> *furthermost point of illusion*
> *Is desire pursued to the furthermost point of what is not?*[◊]

---

* *The Trade.*
[†] *The Adventures of Sophie.*
[‡] *The Black Bird in the Rising Sun.*
[‡‡] *The Satin Slipper.*
[§] *Positions and Propositions.*
[§§] *The City.*
[◊] *The Satin Slipper.*

By God's will, what Prouhèze was for Rodrigo is 'a sword through his heart'.*

But woman in God's hands is not only this blade, this burn; the riches of this world are not meant to be always refused: they are also nourishment; man must take them with him and make them his own. The loved one will embody for him all the recognisable beauty in the universe; she will be a chant of adoration on his lips.

'How lovely you are, Violaine, and how lovely is the world where you are.'†

'Who is she who stands before me, gentler than the breeze, like the moon among the young foliage? . . . Here she is like the fresh honeybee unfolding its newborn wings, like a lanky doe, and like a flower that does not even know it is beautiful.'‡42

'Let me breathe your scent like that of the earth, when it glows and is washed like an altar, and brings forth blue and yellow flowers.

'And let me breathe the summer's aroma that smells of grass and hay, and is like the autumn's fragrance . . .'‡‡

She is the sum of all nature: the rose and the lily, the star, the fruit, the bird, the wind, the moon, the sun, the fountain, 'the peaceful tumult, in noon's light, of a great port'.§ And she is still more: a peer.

'Now, this time for me, that luminous point of night's living sands is something quite different from a star,

'Someone human like me . . .'§§

'You will be alone no more, and I will be in you and with you, with you for ever, the devoted one. Someone yours for ever who will never be absent, your wife.'◊

'Someone to listen to what I say and trust in me.

'A soft-voiced companion who takes us in her arms and attests she is a woman.'◊◊43

Body and soul, in taking her into his heart, man finds his roots in this earth and accomplishes himself.

---

* Ibid.
† *The Tidings Brought to Mary.*
‡ *The Young Violaine.*
‡‡ *The City.*
§ *The Satin Slipper.*
§§ Ibid.
◊ *The City.*
◊◊ *The Hard Crusts.*

'I took this woman, and she is my measure and my earthly allotment.'* She is a burden, and man is not made to be burdened.

'And the foolish man finds himself surprised by this absurd person, this great heavy and cumbersome thing.

'So many dresses, so much hair, what can he do?

'He is no longer able, he no longer wants to be rid of her.'[†]

This burden is also a treasure. 'I am a great treasure,' says Violaine. Reciprocally, woman achieves her earthly destiny by giving herself to man.

'For what is the use of being a woman, unless to be gathered?

'And being this rose, if not to be devoured? And of being born,

'Unless to belong to another and to be the prey of a powerful lion?'[‡]

'What shall we do, who can only be a woman in his arms, and in his heart a cup of wine?'[‡‡]

'But you my soul say: I have not been created in vain and he who is called to gather me is alive!'

'The heart that was waiting for me, ah! what joy for me to fill it.'[§]

Of course this union of man and woman is to be consummated in the presence of God; it is holy and belongs in the eternal; it should be consented to by a deep movement of the will and *cannot* be broken by an individual caprice. 'Love, the consent that two free people grant each other, seemed to God so great a thing that he made it a sacrament. In this as in all other matters the sacrament gives reality to that which was but the heart's supreme desire.'[§§] And further:

'Marriage is not pleasure but the sacrifice of pleasure, it is the study made by two souls who for ever, henceforth, and to end beyond themselves,

'Must be content with one another.'[◊]

It is not only joy that man and woman will bring to each other through this union; each will take possession of the other's being. 'He it was who knew how to find that soul within my soul! . . . He it was who came to me and held out his hand. He was my calling! How can I describe it? He was my origin: it was he by whom and for whom I came into the world.'[◊◊44]

* *The City.*

[†] *Break of Noon.*

[‡] *Cantata for Three Voices.*

[‡‡] Ibid.

[§] Ibid.

[§§] *Positions and Propositions.*

[◊] *The Satin Slipper.*

[◊◊] *Book of Toby and Sara.*

'A whole part of myself which I thought did not exist because I was busy elsewhere and not thinking of it. Ah! My God, it exists, it does exist, terribly.'*[45]

And this being appears as justified, necessary for the one it completes. 'It is in him that you were necessary,' says Prouhèze's Angel. And Rodrigo:

'For what is it to die but to stop being necessary?

'When was she able to do without me? When shall I cease to be for her that without which she could not have been herself?'[†]

'They say that no soul was made except in a life and in a mysterious relationship with other lives.

'But for us it is still more than that. For I exist as I speak; one single thing resonating between two people.

'When we were being fashioned, Orion, I think that a bit of your substance was left over and that I am made of what you lack.'[‡]

In the marvellous necessity of this union, paradise is regained, death conquered:

'At last the being who existed in paradise is here remade of a man and woman.'[‡‡][46]

'We will never manage to do away with death unless it be by one another.

'As purple mixed with orange gives pure red.'[§]

Finally, in the form of another, each one attains the Other, that is God, in his plenitude.

'What we give one another is God in different guises.'[§§]

'Would your desire for heaven have been so great if you had not glimpsed it once in my eyes?'[◊]

'Ah! Stop being a woman and let me at last see on your face the God you are powerless to hide.'[◊◊]

'The love of God calls in us the same faculty as the love of His creatures, it calls on our feeling that we are not complete in ourselves and

* *The Humiliation of the Father.*
† *The Satin Slipper.*
‡ *The Humiliation of the Father.*
‡‡ *Leaves of Saints.*
§ *The Satin Slipper.*
§§ *Leaves of Saints.*
◊ Ibid.
◊◊ *The Satin Slipper.*

that the supreme God in which we are consummated is someone outside ourselves.'*

Thus each finds in the other the meaning of his earthly life and also irrefutable proof of the insufficiency of this life:

'Since I cannot grant him heaven, at least I can tear him from the earth. I alone can give him need in the measure of his desire.'†

'What I was asking from you, and what I wanted to give you, is not compatible with time but with eternity.'‡

Yet woman's and man's roles are not exactly symmetrical. On the social level, man's primacy is evident. Claudel believes in hierarchies and, among others, the family's: the husband is the head. Anne Vercors rules over her home. Don Pelagio sees himself as the gardener entrusted with the care of this delicate plant, Doña Prouhèze; he gives her a mission she does not dream of refusing. The fact alone of being a male confers privilege. 'Who am I, poor girl, to compare myself to the male of my race?' asks Sygne.‡‡47 It is man who labours in the fields, who builds cathedrals, who fights with the sword, explores the world, who acts, who undertakes. God's plans are accomplished on earth through him. Woman is merely an auxiliary. She is the one who stays in place, who waits and who, like Sygne, maintains: 'I am she who remains and who am always there.'

She defends the heritage of Coûfontaine, keeps his accounts in order while he is far away fighting for the cause. The woman brings the relief of hope to the fighter: 'I bring irresistible hope.'§ And that of pity.

'I had pity on him. For where was he to turn, when he sought his mother, but to his own humiliated mother,

'In a spirit of confession and shame.'§§

And Tête d'Or dying murmurs:

'That is the wounded man's courage, the crippled man's support,

'The dying man's company . . .'

Claudel does not hold it against man that woman knows him in his weakest moments; on the contrary: he would find man's arrogance as

* *Positions and Propositions.*
† *The Satin Slipper.*
‡ *The Humiliation of the Father*
‡‡ *The Hostage.*
§ *The City.*
§§ *The Trade.*

displayed in Montherlant and Lawrence sacrilege. It is good that man knows he is carnal and lowly, that he forgets neither his origin nor his death, which is symmetrical to it. Every wife could say the same words as Marthe:

'It is true, it was not I who gave you life.

'But I am here to ask you for life once more. And a man's confusion in the presence of a woman comes from this very question

'Like conscience in the presence of a creditor.'*

And yet this weakness has to yield to force. In marriage, the wife *gives herself* to the husband, who takes care of her: Lâla lies down on the ground before Coeuvre, who places his foot on her. The relation of woman to husband, of daughter to father, of sister to brother, is a relation of vassalage. In George's hands, Sygne takes the vow of the knight to his sovereign.

'You are the lord and I the poor sibyl who keeps the fire.'†

'Let me take an oath like a new knight! O my lord! O my elder, let me swear in your hands

'After the fashion of a nun who makes her profession,

'O male of my race!'‡

Fidelity and loyalty are the greatest of the female vassal's human virtues. Sweet, humble, resigned as a woman, she is, in the name of her race and her lineage, proud and invincible; such is the proud Sygne de Coûfontaine and Tête d'Or's princess, who carries on her shoulder the corpse of her assassinated father, who accepts the misery of a lonely and wild life, the suffering of a crucifixion, and who assists Tête d'Or in his agony before he dies at her side. Conciliator and mediator is thus how woman often appears: she is docile Esther accountable to Mordecai, Judith obeying the priests; she can overcome her weakness, her faint-heartedness and her modesty through loyalty to the cause that is hers since it is that of her masters; she draws strength from her devotion which makes her a precious instrument.

So on the human level she is seen as drawing her greatness from her very subordination. But in God's eyes, she is a perfectly autonomous person. The fact that for man existence surpasses itself while for woman it maintains itself only establishes a difference between them on earth:

* Ibid.
† *The Hostage.*
‡ Ibid.

in any case, transcendence is accomplished not on earth but in God. And woman has just as direct a connection with Him as her companion does; perhaps hers is even more intimate and secret. It is through a man's voice – what is more, a priest's – that God speaks to Sygne; but Violaine hears his voice in the solitude of her heart, and Prouhèze only deals with the Guardian Angel. Claudel's most sublime figures are women: Sygne, Violaine, Prouhèze. This is partly because saintliness for him lies in renunciation. And woman is less involved in human projects; she has less personal will: made to give and not to take, she is closer to perfect devotion. It is through her that the earthly joys that are permissible and good will be surpassed, but their sacrifice is still better. Sygne accomplishes this for a definite reason: to save the Pope. Prouhèze resigns herself to it first because she loves Rodrigo with a forbidden love:

'Would you then have wanted me to put an adulteress into your hands? . . . I would have been only a woman who soon dies on your heart and not that eternal star that you thirst for.'*

But when this love could become legitimate, she makes no attempt to accomplish it in this world. For the Angel whispers to her:

'Prouhèze, my sister, luminous child of God whom I salute,

'Prouhèze whom the angels see and who does not know that he is watching, she it is whom you made so as to give her to him.'†

She is human, she is woman, and she does not resign herself without revolt: 'He will not know how I taste!'‡

But she knows that her true marriage with Rodrigo is only consummated by her denial:

'When will there no longer be any way to escape, when he will be attached to me for ever in an impossible marriage, when he will no longer find a way to wrench himself from the cry of my powerful flesh and that pitiless void, when I will have proved to him his nothingness and the nothingness of myself, when there will no longer be in his nothingness a secret that my secret cannot confirm.

'It is then that I shall give him to God, naked and torn, so that he may be filled in a blast of thunder, it is then that I will have a husband and clasp a god in my arms.'‡‡

Violaine's resolution is more mysterious and gratuitous still; for she

* *The Satin Slipper.*
† Ibid.
‡ Ibid.
‡‡ Ibid.

chose leprosy and blindness when a legitimate bond could have united her to the man she loved and who loved her.

'Jacques, perhaps we loved each other too much for it to be right for us to belong to each other, for it to be good to be each other's.'*

But if women are so singularly devoted to saintly heroism, it is above all because Claudel still grasps them from a masculine perspective. To be certain, each of the sexes embodies the *Other* in the eyes of the complementary sex; but to his man's eyes it is, in spite of everything, the woman who is often regarded as an *absolute other*. There is a mystical surpassing insofar as 'we know that in and of ourselves we are insufficient, hence the power of woman over us, like the power of Grace.'‡ The 'we' here represents only males and not the human species, and faced with their imperfection, woman is the appeal of infinity. In a way, there is a new principle of subordination here: by the communion of saints each individual is an instrument for all others; but woman is more precisely the instrument of salvation for man, without any reciprocity. *The Satin Slipper* is the epic of Rodrigo's salvation. The drama opens with a prayer his brother addresses to God on his behalf; it closes with the death of Rodrigo, whom Prouhèze has brought to saintliness. But, in another sense, the woman thereby gains the fullest autonomy: for her mission is interiorised in her, and in saving the man, or in serving as an example to him, she saves herself in solitude. Pierre de Craon prophesies Violaine's destiny to her, and he receives in his heart the wonderful fruits of her sacrifice; he will exalt her before mankind in the stones of cathedrals. But Violaine accomplished it without help. In Claudel there is a mystique of woman akin to Dante's for Beatrice, to that of the Gnostics, and even to that of the Saint-Simonian tradition which called woman a regenerator. But because men and women are equally God's creatures, he also attributed an autonomous destiny to her. So that for him it is in becoming *other* – I am the Servant of the Lord – that woman realises herself as subject; and it is in her for-itself that she appears as the Other.

There is a passage from *The Adventures of Sophie* that more or less sums up the whole Claudelian concept. God, we read, has entrusted to woman 'this face which, however remote and deformed it may be, is a certain image of His perfection. He has rendered her desirable. He

* *The Young Violaine.*
‡ *The Satin Slipper*

has joined the end and the beginning. He has made her the keeper of His projects and capable of restoring to man that creative slumber in which even she was conceived. She is the foundation of destiny. She is the gift. She is the possibility of possession . . . She is the connection in this affectionate link that ever unites the Creator to His work. She understands Him. She is the soul that sees and acts. She shares with Him in some way the patience and power of creation.'

In a way, it seems that woman could not be more exalted. But deep down Claudel is only expressing in a poetic way a slightly modernised Catholic tradition. We have seen that the earthly vocation of woman does not cancel out any of her supernatural autonomy; on the contrary, in recognising this, the Catholic feels authorised to maintain male prerogatives in this world. If the woman is venerated *in God*, she will be treated like a servant in this world: and further, the more total submission is demanded of her, the more surely will she move forward on the road to her salvation. Her lot, the lot the bourgeoisie has always assigned to her, is to devote herself to her children, her husband, her home, her realm, to country and to church; man gives activity, woman her person; to sanctify this hierarchy in the name of divine will does not modify it in the least, but on the contrary attempts to fix it in the eternal.

IV
BRETON OR POETRY

In spite of the gulf separating Claudel's religious world and Breton's poetic universe, there is an analogy in the role they assign to women: she is an element that perturbs; she wrests man from the sleep of immanence; mouth, key, door, bridge, it is Beatrice initiating Dante into the beyond. 'The love of man for woman, if we think for a moment about the palpable world, continues to fill the sky with gigantic and wild flowers. It is the most awful stumbling block for the mind that always feels the need to believe itself on safe ground.' The love for an other, a woman, leads to the love of the Other. 'It is at the height of elective love for a particular being that the floodgates of love for humanity open wide.' But for Breton the beyond is not a foreign heaven: it is right here; it unveils itself if one knows how to lift the veils of everyday banality; eroticism, for one, dissipates the lure of false knowledge. 'The sexual world, nowadays . . . has not stopped pitting its unbreakable core of night against our will to penetrate the universe.' Colliding with the mystery is the only way of discovering it. Woman is enigma and poses enigmas; the addition of her multiple faces composes 'the unique being in which we are granted the possibility of seeing the last metamorphosis of the Sphinx'; and that is why she is revelation. 'You were the very image of secrecy,' says Breton to a woman he loved. And a little farther: 'That revelation you brought me: before I even knew what it consisted of, I knew it was a revelation.' This means that woman is poetry. She plays that role in Gérard de Nerval as well: but in *Sylvie* and *Aurélia* she has the consistency of a memory or a phantom because the dream, more real than the real, does not exactly coincide with it; the coincidence is perfect for Breton: there is only one world; poetry is objectively present in things, and woman is unequivocally a being of flesh and bones. She can be found wide-awake and not in a half dream, in the middle of an ordinary day on a date like any other day on the calendar – 5 April, 12 April, 4 October, 29 May – in an ordinary setting: a café, a street corner. But she always stands out through some unusual feature. Nadja 'carried her head high, unlike everyone else on the pavement . . . she was curiously made up . . . I had never seen such eyes.' Breton approaches her. 'She smiles, but quite mysteriously and somehow knowingly.'[48] In *Mad Love*: 'This young woman who just entered appeared to be swathed in mist – clothed in fire? . . . And I can certainly say that here, on the twenty-ninth of May 1934, this woman was *scandalously* beautiful.'*[49] The poet immediately admits she has a role to play in his destiny; at times this is a fleeting, secondary role, such as the child with Delilah's eyes in *Communicating Vessels*;[50] even when tiny miracles emerge around her: the same day Breton has a rendezvous with this Delilah, he reads a good review written by a friend called Samson with whom he had not been in touch for a long time. Sometimes wonders occur; the unknown woman of 29 May, Ondine, who had a swimming piece in her music-hall act, was presaged by a pun heard in a restaurant: 'Ondine, one dines'; and her first long date with the poet had been described in great detail in a poem he wrote eleven years earlier. Nadja is the most extraordinary of these sorceresses: she predicts the future and from her lips spring forth words and images her friend has in mind at the very same instant; her dreams and drawings are oracles: 'I am a soul in limbo,' she says; she went forward in life with 'behaviour based as it was on the purest intuition alone and ceaselessly relying on miracle'; around her, objective

---

* Breton's italics.

chance spreads strange events; she is so marvellously liberated from
appearances that she scorns laws and reason: she ends up in an asylum.
She is a 'free genius, something like one of those spirits of the air which
certain magical practices momentarily permit us to entertain but which
we can never overcome'. This prevents her from fulfilling her feminine
role completely. Medium, prophetess, inspiration, she remains too close
to the unreal creatures that visited Nerval; she opens the doors to the
surreal world: but she is unable to give it because she could not give
herself. Woman accomplishes herself and is really transformed in love;
unique, accepting a unique destiny – and not floating rootless through
the universe – so she is the sum of all. The moment her beauty reaches
its highest point is at night when 'she is the perfect mirror in which
everything that has been and everything that is destined to be is suffused
adorably in what is going to be *this time*'. For Breton 'finding the place
and the formula'[51] is one with 'possessing the truth within one soul and
one body'.[52] And this possession is only possible in reciprocal love, carnal
love, of course. 'The portrait of the woman one loves must be not only
an image one smiles at but even more an oracle one questions'; but
oracle only if this very woman is something other than an idea or an
image; she must be the 'keystone of the material world'; for the seer
this is the same world as Poetry and in this world he has to really possess
Beatrice. 'Reciprocal love alone is what conditions total magnetic attraction which nothing can affect, which makes flesh sun and splendid
impression on the flesh, which makes spirit a forever-flowing stream,
inalterable and alive whose water moves once and for all between
marigold and wild thyme.'

This indestructible love can only be unique. It is the paradox of
Breton's attitude that, from *Communicating Vessels* to *Arcanum 17*, he is
determined to promise love both unique and eternal to different women.
But, according to him, it is social circumstances, thwarting the freedom
of his choice, that lead man into erroneous choices; in fact, through
these errors, he is really looking for *one* woman. And if he remembers
the faces he has loved, he 'will discover at the same time in all these
women's faces one face only: the *last* face* loved. How many times,
moreover, have I noticed that under extremely dissimilar appearances
one exceptional trait was developing.' 'How many times, moreover, have
I noticed that under extremely dissimilar appearances one exceptional
trait was developing.' He asks Ondine in *Mad Love:* 'Are you at last this

* Breton's italics.

woman, is it only today you were to come?' But in *Arcanum 17*: 'You know very well that when I first laid eyes on you I recognised you without the slightest hesitation.'[53] In a completed, renewed world, the couple would be indissoluble, through an absolute and reciprocal gift: since the beloved is all, how could there be any room for another? She is also this other; and all the more fully as she is more her self. 'The unusual is inseparable from love. Because you are unique you can't help being for me always another, another you. Across the diversity of these inconceivable flowers over there, it is you over there changing whom I love in a red blouse, naked, in a grey blouse.' And about a different but equally unique woman, Breton wrote: 'Reciprocal love, such as I envisage it, is a system of mirrors which reflects for me, under the thousand angles that the unknown can take for me, the faithful image of the one I love, always more surprising in her divining of my own desire and more gilded with life.'[54]

This unique woman, both carnal and artificial, natural and human, casts the same spell as the equivocal objects loved by the surrealists: she is like the spoon-shoe, the table-magnifying glass, the sugar cube of marble that the poet discovers at the flea market or invents in a dream; she shares in the secret of familiar objects suddenly discovered in their truth; and the secret of plants and stones. She is all things:

> *My love whose hair is woodfire*
> *Her thoughts heat lightning*
> *Her hourglass waist . . .*
> *My love whose sex is*
> *Algae and sweets of yore . . .*
> *My love of savannah eyes*[55]

But she is Beauty, above and beyond every other thing. Beauty for Breton is not an idea one contemplates but a reality that reveals itself – and therefore exists – only through passion; only through woman does beauty exist in the world.

'And it is there – right in the depths of the human crucible, in this paradoxical region where the fusion of two beings who have really chosen each other renders to all things the lost colours of the times of ancient suns, where, however, loneliness rages also, in one of nature's fantasies which, around the Alaskan craters, demands that under the ashes there remain snow – it is there that years ago I asked that we look for a new beauty, a beauty "envisaged exclusively to produce passion."'

'Convulsive beauty will be veiled-erotic, fixed-explosive, magic-circumstantial, or it will not be.'

It is from woman that everything that is derives meaning. 'Love and love alone is precisely what the fusion of essence and existence realises to the highest degree.' It is accomplished for lovers and thus throughout the whole world. 'The recreation, the perpetual recoloration of the world in a single being, such as they are accomplished through love, light up with a thousand rays the advance of the earth ahead.' For all poets – or almost all – woman embodies nature; but for Breton, she not only expresses it: she delivers it. Because nature does not speak in a clear language, its mysteries have to be penetrated in order to grasp its truth, which is the same thing as its beauty: poetry is not simply the reflection of it but rather its key; and woman here cannot be differentiated from poetry. That is why she is the indispensable mediator without whom the whole earth would be silenced: 'Nature is likely to light up and to fade out, to serve and not to serve me, only to the extent that I feel the rise and the fall of the fire of a hearth which is love, the only love, that for a single being... It was only lacking for a great iris of fire to emerge from me to give its value to what exists... I contemplate to the point of dizziness your hands opened above the fire of twigs which we just kindled and which is now raging, your enchanting hands, your transparent hands hovering over the fire of my life.' Every woman loved is a natural wonder for Breton: 'a tiny, unforgettable fern climbing the inside wall of an ancient well.' 'Something so blinding and serious that she could not but bring to mind . . . the great natural physical necessity while at the same time tenderly dreaming of the nonchalance of some tall flowers beginning to blossom.' But inversely: every natural wonder merges with the beloved; he exalts her when he waxes emotional about a grotto, a flower, a mountain. Between the woman who warms his hands on a landing of Teide and Teide itself, all distance is abolished. The poet invokes both in one prayer: 'Wonderful Teide, take my life! Mouth of the heavens and yet mouth of hell, I prefer you thus in your enigma, able to send natural beauty to the skies and to swallow up everything.'

Beauty is even more than beauty; it fuses with 'the deep night of knowledge'; it is truth and eternity, the absolute; woman does not deliver a temporal and contingent aspect of the world, she is the necessary essence of it, not a fixed essence as Plato imagined it but a 'fixed-explosive' one. 'The only treasure I find in myself is the key that opens this limit-less field since I have known you, this field made of the repetition of one plant, taller and taller, swinging in a wider and wider arc and leading

me to death . . . Because one woman and one man, who until the end
of time must be you and me, will drift in their turn without ever turning
back as far as the path goes, in the optical glow, at the edges of life and
of the oblivion of life . . . The greatest hope, I mean the one encompassing all the others, is that this be for all people, and that for all people
this lasts, that the absolute gift of one being to another who cannot exist
without his reciprocity be in the eyes of all the only natural and supernatural bridge spanning life.'

Through the love she inspires and shares, woman is thus the only
possible salvation for each man. In *Arcanum 17*, her mission spreads
and takes shape: she has to save humanity. Breton has always been
part of the Fourier tradition that, demanding rehabilitation of the
flesh, exalts woman as erotic object; it is logical that he should come
to the Saint-Simonian idea of the regenerating woman. In today's
society, the male dominates to such an extent that it is an insult for
someone like Gourmont to say of Rimbaud: 'a girl's temperament'.
However, 'the time has come to value the ideas of woman at the
expense of those of man, whose bankruptcy is coming to pass fairly
tumultuously today.'[56] 'Yes, it is always the lost woman, she who sings
in man's imagination, but after such trials for her and for him, it must
also be the woman retrieved. And first of all, woman has to retrieve
herself; she has to learn to recognise herself through the hells she is
destined to by the more than problematic view that man, in general,
carries of her.'

The role she should fill is above all that of pacifier. 'I've always been
stupefied that she didn't make her voice heard, that she didn't think of
taking every possible advantage, the immense advantage of the two
irresistible and priceless inflexions given to her, one for talking to men
during love, the other that commands all of a child's trust . . . What
clout, what future would this great cry of warning and refusal from
woman have had . . . When will we see a woman simply as woman
perform quite a different *miracle* of extending her arms between those
who are about to grapple to say: You are brothers.' If woman today
looks ill adapted or off balance, it is due to the treatment masculine
tyranny has inflicted on her; but she maintains a miraculous power
because her roots plunge deep into the wellspring of life whose secrets
males have lost. 'Melusina, half reclaimed by panic-stricken life,
Melusina with lower joints of broken stones, aquatic plants or the down
of a nest, she's the one I invoke, she's the only one I can see who could
redeem this savage epoch. She's all of woman and yet woman as she

exists today, woman deprived of her human base, prisoner of her mobile roots, if you will, but also through them in providential communication with nature's elemental forces. Woman deprived of her human base, legend has it, by the impatience and jealousy of man.'

So today one has to be on woman's side; while waiting for her real worth to be restored to her, 'those of us in the arts must pronounce ourselves unequivocally against man and for woman'. 'The child-woman. Systematically art must prepare her advent into the empire of tangible things.' Why child-woman? Breton explains: 'I choose the child-woman not in order to oppose her to other women, but because it seems to me that in her and in her alone exists in a state of absolute transparency the *other* prism of vision.'*

Insofar as woman is merely assimilated to a human being, she will be as unable as male human beings to save the doomed world; it is femininity as such that introduces this *other* element – the truth of life and poetry – into civilisation, and that alone can free humanity.

As Breton's view is exclusively poetic, it is exclusively as poetry and thus as *Other* that woman is envisaged. If one were to ask about her own destiny, the response would be implied in the ideal of reciprocal love: her only vocation is love; this is in no way inferiority, since man's vocation is also love. However, one would like to know whether for her as well, love is the key to the world, the revelation of beauty; will she find this beauty in her lover? Or in her own image? Will she be capable of the poetic activity that makes poetry happen through a sentient being: or will she be limited to approving her male's work? She is poetry itself, in the immediate that is, for man; we are not told whether she is poetry for herself too. Breton does not speak of woman as subject. Nor does he ever evoke the image of the bad woman. In his work as a whole – in spite of a few manifestos and pamphlets in which he vilifies the human herd – he focuses not on categorising the world's superficial resistances but on revealing the secret truth: woman interests him only because she is a privileged 'mouth'. Deeply anchored in nature, very close to the earth, she also appears to be the key to the beyond. One finds in Breton the same esoteric naturalism as in the Gnostics who saw in Sophia the principle of redemption and even of creation, as in Dante choosing Beatrice for guide, or Petrarch illuminated by Laura's love. That is why the being most rooted in nature, the closest to the earth, is also the key to the beyond. Truth, Beauty,

* Breton's italics.

Poetry, she is All: once more all in the figure of the other, All except herself.

V
ENDHAL OR ROMANCING THE REAL

If now, leaving the present period, I return to Stendhal, it is because, leaving behind these carnivals where Woman is disguised as shrew, nymph, morning star or mermaid, I find it reassuring to approach a man who lives among flesh-and-blood women.

Stendhal loved women sensually from childhood; he projected the hopes of his adolescence onto them: he readily imagined himself saving a beautiful stranger and winning her love. Once he was in Paris, what he wanted the most ardently was a 'charming wife; we will adore each other, she will know my soul'. Grown old, he writes the initials of the women he loved the most in the dust. 'I believe that dreaming was what I preferred above all,' he admits. And his dreams are nourished by images of women; his memories of them enliven the countryside. 'The line of rocks when approaching Arbois and coming from Dôle by the main road was, I believe, a touching and clear image for me of Métilde's soul.' Music, painting, architecture, everything he cherished, he cherished it with an unlucky lover's soul; while he is walking around Rome, a woman emerges at every turn of the page; by the regrets, desires, sadnesses and joys women awakened in him, he came to know the nature of his own heart; it is women he wants as judges: he frequents their salons, he wants to shine; he owes them his greatest joys, his greatest pain, they were his main occupation; he prefers their love to any friendship, their friendship to that of men; women inspire his books, women figures populate them; he writes in great part for them. 'I might be lucky enough to be read in 1900 by the souls I love, the Mme Rolands, the Mélanie Guilberts . . .' They were the very substance of his life. Where did this privilege come from?

This tender friend of women – and precisely because he loves them in their truth – does not believe in feminine mystery; there is no essence that defines woman once and for all; the idea of an eternal feminine seems pedantic and ridiculous to him. 'Pedants have been repeating for two thousand years that women have quicker minds and men more solidity; that women have more subtlety in ideas and men more atten-tion span. A Parisian passerby walking around the Versailles gardens once concluded that from everything he saw, the trees are born pruned.'

The differences that one notices between men and women reflect those of their situation. For example, how could women not be more romantic than their lovers? 'A woman at her embroidery frame, insipid work that only involves her hands, dreams of her lover, who, galloping around the countryside with his troop, is put under arrest if he makes one false move.' Likewise, women are accused of lacking common sense. 'Women prefer emotions to reason; this is so simple: as they are not given responsibility for any family affair by virtue of our pedestrian customs, *reason is never useful to them* . . . Let your wife settle your affairs with the farmers on two of your lands, and I wager that the books are better kept than by you.' If so few female geniuses are found in history, it is because society denies them any means of expression. 'All the geniuses who are born *women** are lost for the public good; when chance offers them the means to prove themselves, watch them attain the most difficult skills.' The worst handicap they have to bear is the deadening education they are given; the oppressor always attempts to diminish those he oppresses; man intentionally refuses women their chances. 'We allow their most brilliant qualities and the ones richest in happiness for themselves and for us to remain idle.' At ten years of age, the girl is quicker, subtler than her brother; at twenty, the scamp is a quick-witted adult and the girl 'a big awkward idiot, shy and afraid of a spider'; at fault is the training she has received. Women should be given exactly as much education as boys. Antifeminists object that cultured and intelligent women are monsters: the whole problem comes from the fact that they are still exceptional; if all women had equal access to culture as naturally as men, they would just as naturally take advantage of it. After having been mutilated, they are then subjected to laws against nature: married against their hearts, they are supposed to be faithful, and even divorce is reproached as wild behaviour. A great number of them are destined to idleness when the fact is that there is no happiness without work. This condition scandalises Stendhal and therein he finds the source of all the faults blamed on women. They are neither angels nor demons nor sphinx: but human beings reduced to semi-slavery by idiotic customs.

It is precisely because they are oppressed that the best of them will avoid the faults that tarnish their oppressors; in themselves they are neither inferior nor superior to man: but by a curious reversal, their unfortunate situation works in their favour. It is well known that Stendhal

* Stendhal's emphasis.

hates the spirit of seriousness:[57] money, honours, rank and power are the saddest of idols to him; the immense majority of men alienate themselves in their pursuit; the pedant, the self-important man, the bourgeois and the husband stifle in themselves any spark of life and truth; armed with preconceived ideas and learned feelings, obeying social routines, they are inhabited only by emptiness; a world populated with these creatures without a soul is a desert of boredom. There are unfortunately many women who stagnate in these dismal swamps; they are dolls with 'narrow and Parisian ideas' or else self-righteous hypocrites; Stendhal experiences 'a mortal disgust for decent women and the hypocrisy that is indispensable to them'; they bring to their frivolous occupations the same seriousness that represses their husbands; stupid through education, envious, vain, talkative, mean through idleness, cold, emotionless, pretentious, harmful, they populate Paris and the provinces; they can be seen swarming about behind the noble figure of a Mme de Rênal or a Mme de Chasteller. The one Stendhal depicted with the most bitter care is undoubtedly Mme Grandet, the exact negative of a Mme Roland or a Métilde. Beautiful but expressionless, condescending and without charm, she intimidates by her 'famous virtue' but does not know real modesty, which comes from the soul; full of admiration for self, imbued with her own personage, she only knows how to copy grandeur from the outside; deep down inside she is vulgar and inferior; 'she has no character . . . she bores me,' thinks M. Leuwen. 'Perfectly reasonable, concerned by the success of her projects', she focuses all of her ambition on making her husband a minister; 'her mind was arid'; careful and conformist, she always kept herself from love, she is incapable of a generous movement; when passion sets into this dry soul, it burns without illuminating her.

It is only necessary to reverse this image to discover what Stendhal asks of women: first, not to fall prey to the traps of seriousness; because the supposedly important things are out of their reach, women risk alienating themselves in them less than men; they have a better chance of preserving this natural side, this naïveté, this generosity that Stendhal places higher than any other merit; what he appreciates in them is what we would call today their authenticity: that is the common trait of all the women he loved or invented with love; all are free and true beings. For some, their freedom is strikingly visible: Angela Pietragrua, 'sublime whore, Italian style, à la Lucrezia Borgia', or Mme Azur, 'whore à la du Barry . . . one of the least doll-like French women that I have met', oppose social custom openly. Lamiel laughs at conventions, customs and laws;

Sanseverina throws herself ardently into the intrigue and does not stop at crime. Others rise above the vulgar through the vigour of their minds: like Menta or Mathilde de la Mole, who criticises, denigrates, and scorns the society that surrounds her and wants to stand apart from it. For others, freedom takes a wholly negative form; what is remarkable in Mme de Chasteller is her indifference to everything secondary; subjected to her father's will and even his opinions, she still manages to contest bourgeois values by means of the indifference she is criticised for as childish, and that is the source of her carefree gaiety; Clélia Conti also stands apart by her reserve; balls and other traditional entertainments for girls leave her cold; she always seems distant 'either out of scorn for what surrounds her or out of regret for some missing chimera'; she judges the world, she takes offence at its indignities. Mme de Rênal is the one whose soul's independence is the most deeply hidden; she herself does not know she is not really resigned to her lot; her extreme delicacy and acute sensitivity show her repugnance for her milieu's vulgarity; she is without hypocrisy; she has kept a generous heart, capable of violent emotions, and she has the taste for happiness; the fire that smoulders barely gives off any heat, but only a breath is needed for it to be fully kindled. These women are, simply, *living*; they know the source of real values is not in exterior things but in the heart; that is what makes the charm of the world they inhabit: they chase away boredom merely by being present with their dreams, desires, pleasures, emotions and inventions. Sanseverina, that 'active soul', dreads boredom more than death. Stagnating in boredom 'is preventing one from dying, she said, it is not living'; she is 'always totally involved in something, always active, always gay'. Foolhardy, childish or deep, gay or serious, reckless or secretive, they all refuse the heavy sleep in which humanity sinks. And these women who have been able to preserve their freedom, albeit unfulfilled, will rise up by passion to heroism as soon as they meet an object worthy of them; their force of soul and their energy attest to the fierce purity of total commitment.

But freedom alone would not be sufficient to endow them with so many romantic attractions: a pure freedom inspires esteem but not emotion; what is touching is their effort to accomplish themselves in spite of the obstacles that beleaguer them; it creates even more pathos in women because the struggle is more difficult. The victory over exterior constraints is sufficient to enchant Stendhal; in *Three Italian Chronicles*[58] he cloisters his heroines in remote convents, he locks them up in a jealous spouse's palace: they have to invent a thousand tricks to meet their lovers; secret doors, rope ladders, bloody chests, kidnappings, sequestrations and assassinations, the unleashing of passion and disobedience is served by an ingenuity in which all the mind's resources are displayed; death and the threat of tortures highlight even more the daringness of the deranged souls he depicts. Even in his more mature work, Stendhal remains sympathetic to this external expression of the romantic: it is the manifestation of the one born from the heart; they cannot be distinguished from each other just as a mouth cannot be separated from its smile. Clélia invents love anew by inventing the alphabet that allows her to correspond with Fabrice; Sanseverina is described to us as 'a soul always sincere who never acts with caution, who totally gives herself over to the impression of the moment'; it is when she schemes, when she poisons the prince and floods Parma, that this soul is revealed to us: she is no other than the sublime and mad escapade that she has chosen to live. The ladder that Mathilde de la Mole leans against her window is much more than a prop: her proud recklessness, her penchant for the extraordinary, and her provocative courage take a tangible form. The qualities of these souls would not be revealed were they not surrounded by enemies: prison walls, a lord's will and a family's harshness.

But the most difficult constraints to overcome are those that one finds in oneself: then the adventure of freedom is the most uncertain, the most poignant and the most piquant. Clearly, the more often Stendhal's heroines are prisoners, the greater his sympathy for them. Yes, he enjoys whores – sublime or not – who have once and for all trampled on the conventions; but he cherishes Métilde more tenderly, restrained by her scruples and modesty. Lucien Leuwen is happy when near Mme de Hocquincourt, that liberated person: but it is Mme de Chasteller, chaste, reserved and hesitant, that he loves passionately; Fabrice admires the undivided soul of Sanseverina that stops at nothing; but he prefers Clélia and it is the young girl who wins his heart. And Mme de Rênal, bound by her pride, her prejudices and her ignorance is perhaps the most astonishing of all the women Stendhal created. He readily places his heroines in the provinces, in a confined milieu, under the authority of a husband or a foolish father; it pleases him that they are uneducated and even full of false ideas. Mme de Rênal and Mme de Chasteller are both obstinately legitimist; the former is a timid mind and without experience, the latter is a brilliant intelligence but she underestimates its worth; they are therefore not responsible for their errors, but they are the victims of them as much as of institutions and social customs; and it is from error that romance springs forth, as poetry is born from failure. A lucid mind that decides on its actions in full knowledge is approved or blamed coldly, whereas the courage and ruses of a generous heart seeking its way in the shadows is admired with fear, pity, irony or love. It is because women are mystified that useless and charming qualities such as their modesty, pride and extreme delicacy flourish; in one sense, these are defects: they lead to lies, susceptibilities and anger, but they can be explained by the situation in which women are placed; it leads them to take pride in little things or at least in 'things determined by feeling' because all the 'supposedly important' objects are out of their reach; their modesty results from the dependence they suffer: because it is forbidden to them to show their worth in action, it is their very being that they put in question; it seems to them that the other's consciousness, and particularly that of their lover, reveals them in their truth: they are afraid, they try to escape it; in their evasions, their hesitations, their revolts, and even their lies an authentic concern for worth is expressed; that is what makes them respectable; but it is expressed awkwardly, even with bad faith, and that makes them touching and even discreetly comic. When freedom is hoist by its own petard and cheats on itself, it is at the most deeply human and so in Stendhal's eyes at its most endearing. Stendhal's women are imbued with pathos when their hearts pose unexpected problems for them: no outside law, recipe, reasoning or example can then guide them; they have to decide alone: this abandon is the extreme moment of freedom. Clélia is brought up with liberal ideas, she is lucid and reasonable: but learned opinions, whether right or wrong, are of no help in a moral conflict; Mme de Rênal loves Julien in spite of his morality, Clélia saves Fabrice in spite of herself: in both cases there is the same surpassing of all accepted values. This daring is what exalts Stendhal; but it is even more moving because it barely dares to declare itself: it is all the more natural, spontaneous and authentic. In Mme de Rênal, boldness is hidden by innocence: because she does not know love, she does not recognise it and yields to it without resistance; one could say that having lived in darkness, she is defenceless against the violent light of passion; she welcomes it, blinded, even against God, against hell; when this fire goes out, she falls back in the shadows that husbands and priests govern; she does not trust her own judgement, but the evidence overwhelms her; as soon as she sees Julien again, she once more unburdens her soul to him; her remorse and the letter her confessor wrests from her show the distance this ardent and sincere soul had to span to tear herself away from the prison society enclosed her in and accede to the heaven of happiness. The conflict is more conscious for Clélia; she hesitates between her loyalty to her father and pity inspired by love; she is searching for a rationale; the triumph of the values in which Stendhal believes are all the more striking to him in that this triumph is experienced as a defeat by the victims of a hypocritical civilisation; and he delights in seeing them use ruses and bad faith to make the truth of passion and happiness prevail against the lies in which they believe: Clélia, promising the Madonna to no longer *see* Fabrice, and accepting his kisses and his embraces for two years, providing she closes her eyes, is both laughable and heartbreaking. Stendhal considers Mme de Chasteller's hesitations and Mathilde de la Mole's inconsistencies with the same tender irony; so many detours, changes of mind, scruples, victories and hidden defeats in order to reach simple and legitimate ends is for him the most delightful of comedies; there is drollery in these dramas because the actress is both judge and party, because she is her own dupe, and because she burdens herself with complicated paths where a decree would suffice for the Gordian knot to be cut; but they nonetheless show the most respectable concern that could torture a noble soul: she wants to remain worthy of her own esteem; she places her own approbation higher than that of others and thus she realises herself as an absolute. These solitary debates without reverberation have more gravity than a ministerial crisis; when she wonders if she is going to respond to Lucien Leuwen's love or not, Mme de Chasteller decides for herself and the world: can one have confidence in others? Can one trust one's own heart? What is the value of love and human vows? Is it mad or generous to believe and to love? These questions challenge the very meaning of life, that of each and every one. The so-called important man is futile, in fact, because he accepts ready-made justifications of his life, while a passionate and deep woman revises established values at each instant; she knows the constant tension of an unassisted freedom; thus she feels herself in constant danger: she can win or lose everything in a second. It is this risk, accepted with apprehension, that gives her story the colour of a heroic adventure. And the stakes are the highest that can be: the very meaning of this existence of which everyone has a share, his only part. Mina de Vanghel's escapade can seem absurd in one sense; but she brings to it a whole ethic. 'Was her life a false calculation? Her happiness lasted eight months. She had too ardent a soul to settle for the real life.' Mathilde de la Mole is less sincere than Clélia or Mme de Chasteller; she orders her acts on the idea she has of herself rather than on the evidence of love and happiness: is it more arrogant, grander to keep oneself than to lose oneself, to humiliate oneself before one's beloved than to resist him? She is alone with her doubts, and she risks this self-esteem that is more important to her than life itself. It is the ardent quest for the real reasons to live through the shadows of ignorance, prejudice and mystifications, in the wavering and feverish light of passion, it is the infinite risk of happiness or death, of grandeur or shame that gives romantic glory to these women's destinies.

The woman is of course unaware of the seduction she radiates; self-contemplation and playacting are always inauthentic attitudes; by the mere fact of comparing herself to Mme Roland, Mme Grandet proves she does not resemble her; if Mathilde de la Mole continues to be endearing, it is because she gets confused in her playacting and is often prey to her heart just when she thinks she governs it; she moves us insofar as she is not ruled by her will. But the purest of heroines lack consciousness of themselves. Mme de Rênal is unaware of her grace just as Mme de Chasteller is of her intelligence. It is one of the deep joys of the lover with whom the author and the reader identify: he is the witness through whom these secret riches are revealed; the vivacity Mme Rênal deploys out of everyone's sight, the 'bright wit, changing and deep', unknown to Mme de Chasteller's milieu, he alone admires them; and even if others appreciate Sanseverina's wit, he is the one who penetrates the deepest into her soul. Faced with the woman, the man tastes the pleasure of contemplation; she intoxicates him like a landscape or a painting; she sings in his heart and lights up the sky. This revelation reveals him to himself: one cannot understand women's delicacy, their sensibilities and their ardour without developing a delicate, sensitive and ardent soul oneself; female feelings create a world of nuances and requirements whose discovery enriches the lover: when with Mme de Rênal, Julien becomes someone other than the ambitious man he had decided to be; he chooses himself anew. If the man has only a superficial desire for the woman, he will find seducing her amusing. But it is real love that will transfigure his life. 'Love à la Werther opens the soul . . . to feeling and pleasure in the *beautiful* in whatever form it takes, even in a hair shirt. It makes happiness attainable even without wealth . . .' 'It is a new aim in life to which everything is connected and that changes the appearance of everything. Love-as-passion throws in man's eyes all of nature with its sublime aspects as if it were a novelty invented yesterday.' Love shatters daily routine, chases away boredom, the boredom in which Stendhal sees such a deep evil because it is the absence of all the reasons for living or dying; the lover has an aim and that is enough for each day to become an adventure: what a pleasure for Stendhal to spend three days hidden in Menta's cellar! Rope ladders and bloody chests represent this taste for the extraordinary in his novels. Love, that is woman, reveals the real ends of existence: beauty, happiness, the freshness of feelings and of the world. It tears man's soul out and thus gives him possession of it; the lover experiences the same tension, the same risks, as his mistress and feels himself more authentically than during a planned career. When Julien hesitates at the base of the ladder Mathilde has set up, he puts his whole destiny into question: in that very moment, he demonstrates his true worth. It is through women, under their influence, in reaction to their behaviour, that Julien, Fabrice and Lucien learn about the world and themselves. Test, reward, judge or friend, the woman in Stendhal is really what Hegel was once tempted to make of her: that other consciousness that, in reciprocal recognition, gives to the other subject the same truth it receives from it. The happy couple that recognises each other in love defies the universe and time; it is sufficient in itself, it realises the absolute.

But this supposes that woman is not pure alterity: she is subject herself. Stendhal never describes his heroines as a function of his heroes: he provides them with their own destinies. He undertook something rarer and that no other novelist, I think, has ever done: he projected himself into a female character. He does not examine Lamiel as Marivaux does Marianne, or Richardson does Clarissa Harlowe: he shares her destiny as he had shared that of Julien. Precisely because of that, the character of Lamiel is singularly significant, if somewhat theoretical. Stendhal sets up all imaginable obstacles around the girl: she is a peasant, poor, ignorant, and brought up harshly by people imbued with every prejudice; but she eliminates from her path all the moral barriers the day she understands the scope of these little words: 'it's stupid.' Her mind's freedom enables her to take responsibility for all the movements of her curiosity, her ambition, her gaiety; faced with such a resolute heart, material obstacles cannot fail to decrease; her only problem will be to carve out a destiny worthy of her in a mediocre world. That destiny accomplishes itself in crime and death: but that is also Julien's lot. There is no place for great souls in society as it is: men and women are in the same boat.

It is remarkable that Stendhal is both so profoundly romantic and so decidedly feminist; feminists are usually rational minds that adopt a universal point of view in all things; but it is not only in the name of freedom in general but also in the name of individual happiness that Stendhal calls for women's emancipation. Love, he thinks, will have nothing to lose; on the contrary, it will be all the truer that woman, as the equal of man, will be able to understand him more completely. Undoubtedly, some of the qualities one enjoys in woman will disappear: but their value comes from the freedom that is expressed in them and that will show in other guises; and the romantic will not fade out of this world. Two separate beings, placed in different situations, confronting each other in their freedom and seeking the justification of existence through each other, will always live an adventure full of risks and promises. Stendhal trusts the truth; as soon as one flees it, one dies a living death; but where it shines, so shine beauty, happiness, love, and a joy that carries in it its own justification. That is why he rejects the false poetry of myths as much as the mystifications of seriousness. Human reality is sufficient for him. Woman, according to him, is simply a human being: dreams could not invent anything more intoxicating.

VI

These examples show that the great collective myths are reflected in each singular writer: woman appears to us as *flesh*; male flesh is engendered by the maternal womb and re-created in the woman lover's embrace: thus, woman is akin to *nature,* she embodies it: animal, little vale of blood, rose in bloom, siren, curve of a hill, she gives humus, sap, tangible beauty and the world's soul to man; she can hold the keys to *poetry*; she can be *mediator* between this world and the beyond: grace or Pythia, star or witch, she opens the door to the supernatural, the surreal; she is destined to *immanence*; and through her passivity she doles out peace and harmony: but should she refuse this role, she becomes praying mantis or ogress. In any case, she appears as the *privileged Other* through whom the subject accomplishes himself: one of the measures of man, his balance, his salvation, his adventure and his happiness.

But these myths are orchestrated differently for each individual. The *Other* is singularly defined according to the singular way the *One* chooses to posit himself. All men assert themselves as freedom and transcendence: but they do not all give the same meaning to these words. For

Montherlant transcendence is a state: he is the transcendent, he soars in the sky of heroes; the woman crouches on the ground, under his feet; he enjoys measuring the distance separating him from her; from time to time, he raises her to him, takes and then rejects her; never does he lower himself towards her sphere of viscous darkness. Lawrence situates transcendence in the phallus; the phallus is life and power only thanks to woman; immanence is thus good and necessary; the false hero who deigns not to touch the earth, far from being a demigod, fails to be a man; woman is not despicable, she is deep wealth, hot spring; but she must renounce all personal transcendence and settle for nourishing that of her male. Claudel demands the same devotion: woman is also for him the one who maintains life, while man prolongs the vital momentum by his activity; but for the Catholic everything that occurs on earth is steeped in vain immanence: the only transcendent is God; in God's eyes the active man and the woman who serves him are exactly equal; each one has to surpass his earthly condition: salvation in any case is an autonomous undertaking. For Breton sexual hierarchy is inverted; action and conscious thought in which the male situates his transcendence are for him a banal mystification that engenders war, stupidity, bureaucracy and negation of the human; it is immanence, the pure opaque presence of the real, that is the truth; true transcendence would be accomplished by the return to immanence. His attitude is the exact opposite of Montherlant's: the latter likes war because women are banished from it, Breton venerates woman because she brings peace; one confuses mind and subjectivity, he rejects the given universe; the other thinks the mind is objectively present in the heart of the world; woman compromises Montherlant because she shatters his solitude; she is, for Breton, revelation because she wrests him from subjectivity. As for Stendhal, we saw that woman barely takes on a mythical value for him: he considers her as also being a transcendence; for this humanist, it is in their reciprocal relations that freedoms are accomplished; and it is sufficient that the *Other* is simply another for life to have, according to him, a little spice; he does not seek a stellar equilibrium, he does not nourish himself with the bread of disgust; he does not expect miracles; he does not wish to concern himself with the cosmos or poetry but with freedoms.

That is, he also experiences himself as a translucent freedom. The others – and this is one of the most important points – posit themselves as transcendences but feel they are prisoners of an opaque presence in their own hearts: they project onto woman this 'unbreakable core of night'. In Montherlant there is an Adlerian complex where heavy bad faith is born: these pretensions and fears are what he incarnates in woman; the disgust he feels for her is what he fears to feel for himself; he intends to trample in her the ever possible proof of his own insufficiency; he asks scorn to save him; woman is the ditch in which he throws all the monsters that inhabit him.* Lawrence's life shows us that he suffered from an analogous complex but more purely sexual: woman in his work has the value of a compensatory myth; through her is found an exalted virility of which the writer was not very sure; when he describes Kate at Don Cipriano's feet, he believes he has won a male triumph over Frieda; nor does he accept that his female companion challenges him: if she contested his aims, he would probably lose confidence in them; her role is to reassure him. He asks for peace, rest and faith from her, just as Montherlant asks for the certitude of his superiority: they demand what they lack. Self-confidence is not lacking in Claudel: if he is shy, it is only the secret of God. Thus, there is no trace of the battle of the sexes. Man bravely takes on the weight of woman: she is the possibility of temptation or of salvation. For Breton it seems that man is only true through the mystery that inhabits him; it pleases him that Nadja sees that star he is going towards and that is like 'a heartless flower'; his dreams, intuitions and the spontaneous unfolding of his inner language: it is in these activities that are out of the control of will and reason that he recognises himself: woman is the tangible figure of this veiled presence infinitely more essential than her conscious personality.

As for Stendhal, he quietly coincides with himself; but he needs woman as she does him so that his dispersed existence is gathered in the unity of a figure and a destiny; it is as for-another that the human being reaches being; but another still has to lend him his consciousness: other men are too indifferent to their peers; only the woman in love opens her heart to her lover and shelters it in its entirety. Except for Claudel, who finds a perfect witness in God, all the writers we have considered expect, in Malraux's words, woman to cherish in them this 'incomparable monster' known to themselves alone. In collaboration or combat, men come up against each other in their generality. Montherlant, for his peers, is a writer, Lawrence a doctrinaire, Breton

* Stendhal judged in advance the cruelties with which Montherlant amuses himself: 'In indifference, what should be done? Love-taste, but without the horrors. The horrors always come from a little soul that needs reassurance of its own merits.'

a leader of a school, Stendhal a diplomat or a man of wit; it is women who reveal in one a magnificent and cruel prince, in another a disturbing animal, in still another a god or a sun or a being 'black and cold . . . like a man struck by lightning, lying at the feet of the Sphinx',* and in the other, a seducer, a charmer, a lover.

For each of them, the ideal woman will be she who embodies the most exactly the *Other* able to reveal him to himself. Montherlant, the solar spirit, looks for pure animality in her; Lawrence, the phallic, demands that she sum up the female sex in its generality; Claudel defines her as a soul sister; Breton cherishes Melusina rooted in nature, he puts his hopes in the child-woman; Stendhal wants his mistress intelligent, cultivated, free of spirit and morals: an equal. But the only earthly destiny reserved to the woman equal, child-woman, soul sister, woman-sex and female animal is always man. Regardless of the ego looking for itself through her, it can only attain itself if she consents to be his crucible. In any case, what is demanded of her is self-forgetting and love. Montherlant consents to be moved by the woman who enables him to measure his virile power; Lawrence addresses an ardent hymn to the woman who renounces herself for him; Claudel exalts the vassal, servant and devoted woman who submits herself to God by submitting herself to the male; Breton puts his hopes in woman for humanity's salvation because she is capable of the most total love for her child and her lover; and even in Stendhal the heroines are more moving than the masculine heroes because they give themselves over to their passion with a more ardent violence; they help man to accomplish his destiny as Prouhèze contributes to Rodrigo's salvation; in Stendhal's novels, women often save their lovers from ruin, prison or death. Feminine devotion is demanded as a duty by Montherlant and Lawrence; less arrogant, Claudel, Breton and Stendhal admire it as a generous choice; they desire it without claiming to deserve it; but – except for the astonishing *Lamiel* – all their works show they expect from woman this altruism that Comte admired in and imposed on her, and which, according to him, also constituted both a flagrant inferiority and an equivocal superiority.

We could find many more examples: they would always lead to the same conclusions. In defining woman, each writer defines his general ethic and the singular idea he has of himself: it is also in her that he often registers the distance between his view of the world and his

* *Nadja.*

egotistical dreams. The absence or insignificance of the female element in a body of work in general is itself symptomatic; it has an extreme importance when it sums up in its totality all the aspects of the Other, as it does for Lawrence; it remains important if woman is grasped simply as another but the writer is interested in her life's individual adventure, which is Stendhal's case; it loses importance in a period like ours in which each individual's particular problems are of secondary import. However, woman as other still plays a role inasmuch as even to transcend himself, each man still needs to take consciousness of himself.

CHAPTER 3

The myth of woman plays a significant role in literature; but what is its importance in everyday life? To what extent does it affect individual social customs and behaviour? To reply to this question, it will be necessary to specify the relation of this myth to reality.

There are different kinds of myths. This one, sublimating an immutable aspect of the human condition, that is, the 'division' of humanity into two categories of individuals, is a static myth; it projects into a Platonic heaven a reality grasped through experience or conceptualised from experience; for fact, value, significance, notion and empirical law, it substitutes a transcendent Idea, timeless, immutable and necessary. This idea escapes all contention because it is situated beyond the given; it is endowed with an absolute truth. Thus, to the dispersed, contingent and multiple existence of *women*, mythic thinking opposes the Eternal Feminine, unique and fixed; if the definition given is contradicted by the behaviour of real flesh-and-blood women, it is women who are wrong: it is said not that Femininity is an entity but that women are not feminine. Experiential denials cannot do anything against myth. Though in a way, its source is in experience. It is thus true that woman is other than man, and this alterity is concretely felt in desire, embrace and love; but the real relation is one of reciprocity; as such, it gives rise to authentic dramas: through eroticism, love, friendship and their alternatives of disappointment, hatred and rivalry, the relation is a struggle of consciousnesses, each of which wants to be essential, it is the recognition of freedoms that confirm each other, it is the undefined passage from enmity to complicity. To posit the Woman is to posit the absolute Other, without reciprocity, refusing, against experience, that she could be a subject, a peer.

In concrete reality, women manifest themselves in many different ways; but each of the myths built around woman tries to summarise her as a whole; each is supposed to be unique; the consequence of this is a multiplicity of incompatible myths, and men are perplexed before the strange inconsistencies of the idea of Femininity; as every woman enters into many of these archetypes, each of which claims to incarnate its Truth alone, men also find the same old confusion before their companions as did the Sophists, who had difficulty understanding how a person could be light and dark at the same time. The transition to the absolute shows up in social representations: relations are quickly fixed in classes and roles in types, just as, for the childlike mentality, relations are fixed in things. For example, patriarchal society, focused on preserving the patrimony, necessarily implies, in addition to individuals who hold and transmit goods, the existence of men and women who wrest them from their owners and circulate them; men – adventurers, crooks, thieves, speculators – are generally repudiated by the group; women using their sexual attraction can lure young people and even family men into dissipating their patrimony, all within the law; they appropriate men's fortunes or seize their inheritance; this role being considered bad, women who play it are called 'bad women'. But in other families – those of their fathers, brothers, husbands or lovers – they can in fact seem like guardian angels; the courtesan who swindles rich financiers is a patroness of painters and writers. The ambiguity of personalities like Aspasia and Mme de Pompadour is easy to understand as a concrete experience. But if woman is posited as the Praying Mantis, the Mandrake or the Demon, then the mind reels to discover in her the Muse, the Goddess Mother and Beatrice as well.

As group representation and social types are generally defined by pairs of opposite terms, ambivalence will appear to be an intrinsic property of the Eternal Feminine. The saintly mother has its correlation in the cruel stepmother, the angelic young girl has the perverse virgin: so Mother will be said sometimes to equal Life and sometimes Death, and every virgin is either a pure spirit or flesh possessed by the devil.

It is obviously not reality that dictates to society or individuals their choices between the two opposing principles of unification; in every period, in every case, society and individual decide according to their needs. Very often they project the values and institutions to which they adhere onto the myth they adopt. Thus paternalism that calls for woman to stay at home defines her as sentiment, interiority and immanence; in fact, every existent is simultaneously immanence and transcendence; when he is offered no goal, or is prevented from reaching any goal, or denied the victory of it, his transcendence falls uselessly into the past, that is, it falls into immanence; this is the lot assigned to women in patriarchy; but this is in no way a vocation, any more than slavery is the slave's vocation. The development of this mythology is all too clear in Auguste Comte. To identify Woman with Altruism is to guarantee man absolute rights to her devotion; it is to impose on women a categorical must-be.

The myth must not be confused with the grasp of a signification; signification is immanent in the object; it is revealed to consciousness in a living experience, whereas the myth is a transcendent Idea that escapes any act of consciousness. When Michel Leiris in *Manhood*[59] describes his vision of female organs, he provides significations and does not develop a myth. Wonder at the feminine body or disgust for menstrual blood are apprehensions of a concrete reality. There is nothing mythical in the experience of discovering the voluptuous qualities of feminine flesh, and expressing these qualities by comparisons with flowers or pebbles does not turn them into myth. But to say that Woman is Flesh, to say that Flesh is Night and Death, or that she is the splendour of the cosmos, is to leave terrestrial truth behind and spin off into an empty sky. After all, man is also flesh for woman; and woman is other than a carnal object; and for each person and in each experience the flesh takes on singular significations. It is likewise perfectly true that woman – like man – is a being rooted in nature; she is more enslaved to the species than the male is, her animality is more manifest; but in her as in him, the given is taken on by existence; she also belongs to the human realm. Assimilating her with Nature is simply a prejudice.

Few myths have been more advantageous to the ruling master caste than this one: it justifies all its privileges and even authorises taking advantage of them. Men do not have to care about alleviating the suffering and burdens that are physiologically women's lot since they are 'intended by Nature'; they take this as a pretext to increase the misery of the woman's condition – for example by denying woman the right to sexual pleasure, or making her work like a beast of burden.*

Of all these myths, none is more anchored in masculine hearts than the feminine 'mystery'. It has numerous advantages. And first it allows an easy explanation for anything that is inexplicable; the man who does not 'understand' a woman is happy to replace his subjective deficiency

---

* Cf. Balzac, *Physiology of Marriage*: 'Do not trouble yourself in any way about her mumurings, her cries, her pains; nature has made her for your use, made her to bear all: the children, the worries, the blows, and the sorrows of man. But do not accuse us of harshness. In the codes of all the so-called civilised nations, man has written the laws which rule the destiny of woman beneath this blood inscription: *Vae Victis!* Woe to the vanquished.'

with an objective resistance; instead of admitting his ignorance, he recognises the presence of a mystery exterior to himself: here is an excuse that flatters his laziness and vanity at the same time. An infatuated heart thus avoids many disappointments: if the loved one's behaviour is capricious, her remarks stupid, the mystery serves as an excuse. And thanks to the mystery, this negative relation that seemed to Kierkegaard infinitely preferable to positive possession is perpetuated; faced with a living enigma, man remains alone: alone with his dreams, hopes, fears, love, vanity; this subjective game that can range from vice to mystical ecstasy is for many a more attractive experience than an authentic relation with a human being. Upon what bases does such a profitable illusion rest?

Surely, in a way, woman is mysterious, 'mysterious like everyone', according to Maeterlinck. Each one is subject only for himself; each one can grasp only his own self in his immanence; from this point of view, the other is always mystery. In men's view, the opacity of the for-itself is more flagrant in the feminine other; they are unable to penetrate her unique experience by any effect of sympathy; they are condemned to ignorance about the quality of woman's sexual pleasure, the discomforts of menstruation and the pains of childbirth. The truth is that mystery is reciprocal: as another, and as a masculine other, there is also a presence closed on itself and impenetrable to woman in the heart of every man; she is without knowledge of male eroticism. But according to a universal rule already mentioned, the categories in which men think the world are constituted from *their point of view as absolutes*: they fail to understand reciprocity here as everywhere. As she is mystery for man, woman is regarded as mystery in herself.

It is true that her situation especially disposes her to be seen in this image. Her physiological destiny is very complex; she herself endures it as a foreign story; her body is not for her a clear expression of herself; she feels alienated from it; the link that for every individual joins physiological to psychic life – in other words, the relation between the facticity of an individual and the freedom that assumes it – is the most difficult enigma brought about by the human condition: for woman, this enigma is posed in the most disturbing way.

But what is called mystery is not the subjective solitude of consciousness, or the secret of organic life. The word's true meaning is found at the level of communication: it cannot be reduced to pure silence, to obscurity, to absence; it implies an emerging presence that fails to appear. To say that woman is mystery is to say not that she is silent but that her language is not heard; she is there, but hidden beneath veils; she exists beyond these uncertain appearances. Who is she? An angel, a demon, an inspiration, an actress? One supposes that either there are answers impossible to uncover, or that none is adequate because a fundamental ambiguity affects the feminine being; in her heart she is indefinable for herself: a sphinx.

The fact is, deciding *who* she *is* would be quite awkward for her; the question has no answer; but it is not that the hidden truth is too fluctuating to be circumscribed: in this area there is no truth. An existent *is* nothing other than what he does; the possible does not exceed the real, essence does not precede existence: in his pure subjectivity, the human being *is nothing*. He is measured by his acts. It can be said that a peasant woman is a good or bad worker, that an actress has or does not have talent: but if a woman is considered in her immanent presence, absolutely nothing can be said about that, she is outside of the realm of qualification. Now, in amorous or conjugal relations and in all relations where woman is the vassal, the Other, she is grasped in her immanence. It is striking that the woman friend, colleague or associate is without mystery; on the other hand, if the vassal is male and if, in front of an older and richer man or woman, a young man, for example, appears as the inessential object, he also is surrounded in mystery. And this uncovers for us an infrastructure of feminine mystery that is economic. A sentiment cannot *be* something, either. 'In the domain of feeling, what is real is indistinguishable from what is imaginary,' writes Gide. 'And it is sufficient to imagine one loves, in order to love, so it is sufficient to say to oneself that when one loves one imagines one loves, in order to love a little less.' There is no discriminating between the imaginary and the real except through behaviour. As man holds a privileged place in this world, he is the one who is able actively to display his love; very often he keeps the woman, or at least he helps her out; in marrying her, he gives her social status; he gives her gifts; his economic and social independence permits his endeavours and innovations: separated from Mme de Villeparisis, M. de Norpois takes twenty-four-hour trips to be with her; very often he is busy and she is idle: he *gives* her the time he spends with her; she takes it: with pleasure, passion or simply for entertainment? Does she accept these benefits out of love or out of one interest? Does she love husband or marriage? Of course, even the proof man gives is ambiguous: is such a gift given out of love or pity? But while normally woman finds numerous advantages in commerce with man, commerce with woman is profitable to man only inasmuch as he loves her. Thus, the degree of his attachment to her can be roughly estimated by his general attitude, while woman barely has the means to sound out her own heart; according to her moods she will take different points of view about her own feelings, and as long as she submits to them passively, no one interpretation will be truer than another. In the very rare cases where it is she who holds the economic and social privileges, the mystery is reversed: this proves that it is not linked to *this* sex rather than to the other, but to a situation. For many women, the roads to transcendence are blocked: because they *do* nothing, they do not make themselves *be* anything; they wonder indefinitely what they *could have* become, which leads them to wonder what they *are*: it is a useless questioning; if man fails to find that secret essence, it is simply because it does not exist. Kept at the margins of the world, woman cannot be defined objectively through this world and her mystery conceals nothing but emptiness.

Furthermore, like all oppressed people, woman deliberately dissimulates her objective image; slave, servant, indigent, all those who depend upon a master's whims have learned to present him with an immutable smile or an enigmatic impassivity; they carefully hide their real sentiments and behaviour. Woman is also taught from adolescence to lie to men, to outsmart, to sidestep them. She approaches them with artificial expressions; she is prudent, hypocritical, playacting.

But feminine Mystery as recognised by mythical thinking is a more profound reality. In fact, it is immediately implied in the mythology of the absolute Other. If one grants that the inessential consciousness is also a transparent subjectivity, capable of carrying out the cogito, one grants that it is truly sovereign and reverts to the essential; for all reciprocity to seem impossible, it is necessary that the Other be another for itself, that its very subjectivity be affected by alterity; this consciousness, which would be alienated as consciousness, in its pure immanent presence, would obviously be a Mystery; it would be a Mystery in itself because it would be it for itself; it would be absolute Mystery. It is thus that, beyond the secrecy their dissimulation creates, there is a mystery of the Black, of the Yellow, insofar as they are considered absolutely as the inessential Other. It must be noted that the American citizen who deeply confounds the average European is nonetheless not considered 'mysterious': one more modestly claims not to understand him; likewise, woman does not always 'understand' man, but there is no masculine mystery; the fact is that rich America and the male are on the side of the Master, and Mystery belongs to the slave.

Of course, one can only dream about the positive reality of the Mystery in the twilight of bad faith; like certain marginal hallucinations, it dissolves once one tries to pin it down. Literature always fails to depict 'mysterious' women; they can only appear at the beginning of a novel as strange and enigmatic; but unless the story remains unfinished, they give up their secret in the end and become consistent and translucent characters. The heroes in Peter Cheyney's books, for example, never cease to be amazed by women's unpredictable caprices; one can never guess how they will behave, they confound all calculations; in truth, as soon as the workings of their actions are exposed to the reader, they are seen as very simple mechanisms: this one is a spy or that one a thief; however clever the intrigue, there is always a key, and it could not be otherwise, even if the author had all the talent, all the imagination possible. Mystery is never more than a mirage; it vanishes as soon as one tries to approach it.

Thus we see that myths are explained in large part by the use man makes of them. The myth of the woman is a luxury. It can appear only if man escapes the imperious influence of his needs; the more relations are lived concretely, the less idealised they are. The fellah in ancient Egypt, the bedouin peasant, the medieval artisan and the worker of today, in their work needs and their poverty, have relations with the particular woman who is their companion that are too basic for them to embellish her with an auspicious or fatal aura. Eras and social classes that had the leisure to daydream were the ones who created the black-and-white statues of femininity. But luxury also has its usefulness; these dreams were imperiously guided by interest. Yes, most myths have their roots in man's spontaneous attitude to his own existence and the world that invests it: but the move to surpass experience towards the transcendent Idea was deliberately effected by patriarchal society for the end of self-justification; through myths, this society imposed its laws and customs on individuals in an imagistic and sensible way; it is in a mythical form that the group imperative insinuated itself into each consciousness. By way of religions, traditions, language, tales, songs and film, myths penetrate even into the existence of those most harshly subjected to material realities. Everyone can draw on myth to sublimate their own modest experiences: betrayed by a woman he loves, one man calls her a slut; another is obsessed by his own virile impotence: this woman is a praying mantis; yet another takes pleasure in his wife's company: here we have Harmony, Repose, Mother Earth. The taste for eternity at bargain prices and for a handy, pocket-sized absolute, seen in most men, is satisfied by myths. The least emotion, a small disagreement, become the reflection of a timeless Idea; this illusion comfortably flatters one's vanity.

The myth is one of those traps of false objectivity into which the spirit of seriousness falls headlong. It is once again a matter of replacing lived experience and the free judgements of experience it requires by a static idol. The myth of Woman substitutes for an authentic relationship with an autonomous existent the immobile contemplation of a mirage. 'Mirage! Mirage! Kill them since we cannot seize them; or else reassure them, instruct them, help them give up their taste for jewellery, make them real equal companions, our intimate friends, associates in the here and now, dress them differently, cut their hair, tell them everything,' cried Laforgue. Man would have nothing to lose, quite the contrary, if he stopped disguising woman as a symbol. Dreams, when collective and controlled – clichés – are so poor and monotonous compared to living reality: for the real dreamer, for the poet, living reality is a far more generous resource than a worn-out fantasy. The times when women were the most sincerely cherished were not courtly feudal ones, nor the gallant nineteenth century; they were the times – the eighteenth century, for example – when men regarded women as their peers; this is when women looked truly romantic: only read *Dangerous Liaisons*,[60] *The Red and the Black*[61] or *A Farewell to Arms* to realise this. Laclos' heroines like Stendhal's and Hemingway's are without mystery: and they are no less engaging for it. To recognise a human being in a woman is not to impoverish man's experience: that experience would lose none of its diversity, its richness or its intensity if it was taken on in its inter-subjectivity; to reject myths is not to destroy all dramatic relations between the sexes, it is not to deny the significations authentically revealed to man through feminine reality; it is not to eliminate poetry, love, adventure, happiness and dreams: it is only to ask that behaviour, feelings and passion be grounded in truth.*

'Woman is lost. Where are the women? Today's women are not women'; we have seen what these mysterious slogans mean. In the eyes of men – and of the legions of women who see through these eyes – it is not enough to have a woman's body or to take on the female function as lover and mother to be a 'real woman'; it is possible for the subject to claim autonomy through sexuality and maternity; the 'real woman' is one who accepts herself as Other. The duplicitous attitude

---

* Laforgue goes on to say about woman: 'As she has been left in slavery, idleness, without arms other than her sex, she has overdeveloped it and has become the Feminine . . . we have permitted her to overdevelop; she is on the earth for us . . . Well, that is all wrong . . . we have played doll with the woman until now. This has gone on too long!'

of men today creates a painful split for women; men accept, for the most part, that woman be a peer, an equal; and yet they continue to oblige her to remain the inessential; for her, these two destinies are not reconcilable; she hesitates between them without being exactly suited to either, and that is the source of her lack of balance. For man, there is no hiatus between public and private life: the more he asserts his grasp on the world through action and work, the more virile he looks; human and vital characteristics are merged in him; but women's own successes are in contradiction with her femininity since the 'real woman' is required to make herself object, to be the Other. It is very possible that on this point even men's sensibility and sexuality are changing. A new aesthetic has already been born. Although the fashion for flat chests and narrow hips – the boyish woman – only lasted a short while, the opulent ideal of past centuries has nevertheless not returned. The feminine body is expected to be flesh, but discreetly so; it must be slim and not burdened with fat; toned, supple, robust, it has to suggest transcendence; it is preferred tanned, having been bared to a universal sun like a worker's torso, not white like a hothouse plant. Woman's clothes, in becoming more practical, have not made her look asexual: on the contrary, short skirts have shown off her legs and thighs more than before. There is no reason for work to deprive her of her erotic appeal. To see woman as both a social person and carnal prey can be disturbing: in a recent series of drawings by Peynet,* there is a young fiancé deserting his fiancée because he was seduced by the pretty mayoress about to celebrate the marriage; that a woman could hold a 'man's office' and still be desirable has long been a subject of more or less dirty jokes; little by little, scandal and irony have lost their bite and a new form of eroticism seems to be coming about: perhaps it will produce new myths.

What is certain is that today it is very difficult for women to assume both their status of autonomous individual and their feminine destiny; here is the source of the awkwardness and discomfort that sometimes leads them to be considered 'a lost sex'. And without doubt it is more comfortable to endure blind bondage than to work for one's liberation; the dead, too, are better suited to the earth than the living. In any case, turning back is no more possible than desirable. What must be hoped is that men will assume, without reserve, the situation being created; only then can women experience it without being torn. Then will Laforgue's wish be fulfilled: 'O, young women, when will you be our

* November 1948.

brothers, our closest brothers without ulterior motives of exploitation? When will we give to each other a true handshake?' Then 'Melusina, no longer under the burden of the fate unleashed on her by man alone, Melusina rescued,' will find 'her human base'.* Then will she fully be a human being, 'when woman's infinite servitude is broken, when she lives for herself and by herself, man – abominable until now –giving her her freedom'.†

---

* Breton, *Arcanum 17.*
† Rimbaud, *Lettre à Demeny,* 15 May 1871.

II
LIVED EXPERIENCE

What a curse to be a woman! And yet the very worst curse when one is a woman is, in fact, not to understand that it is one.

Kierkegaard

Half victim, half accomplice, like everyone.

J. P. Sartre

Introduction

Women of today are overthrowing the myth of femininity; they are
beginning to affirm their independence concretely; but their success in
living their human condition completely does not come easily. As they
are brought up by women, in the heart of a feminine world, their normal
destiny is marriage, which still subordinates them to man from a practical point of view; virile prestige is far from being eradicated: it still
stands on solid economic and social bases. It is thus necessary to study
woman's traditional destiny carefully. What I will try to describe is how
woman is taught to assume her condition, how she experiences this,
what universe she finds herself enclosed in and what escape mechanisms
are permitted her. Only then can we understand what problems women
– heirs to a weighty past, striving to forge a new future – are faced with.
When I use the words 'woman' or 'feminine' I obviously refer to no
archetype, to no immutable essence; 'in the present state of education
and customs' must be understood to follow most of my affirmations.
There is no question of expressing eternal truths here, but of describing
the common ground from which all singular feminine existence stems.

Part One

FORMATIVE YEARS

CHAPTER I

Childhood

One is not born, but rather becomes, woman. No biological, psychical or economic destiny defines the figure that the human female takes on in society; it is civilisation as a whole that elaborates this intermediary product between the male and the eunuch that is called feminine. Only the mediation of another can constitute an individual as an *Other*. Inasmuch as he exists for himself, the child would not grasp himself as sexually differentiated. For girls and boys, the body is first the radiation of a subjectivity, the instrument that brings about the comprehension of the world: they apprehend the universe through their eyes and hands, and not through their sexual parts. The drama of birth and weaning takes place in the same way for infants of both sexes; they have the same interests and pleasures; sucking is the first source of their most pleasurable sensations; they then go through an anal phase in which they get their greatest satisfactions from excretory functions common to both; their genital development is similar; they explore their bodies with the same curiosity and the same indifference; they derive the same uncertain pleasure from the clitoris and the penis; insofar as their sensibility already needs an object, it turns towards the mother: it is the soft, smooth, supple feminine flesh that arouses sexual desires and these desires are prehensile; the girl like the boy kisses, touches and caresses her mother in an aggressive manner; they feel the same jealousy at the birth of a new child; they show it with the same behaviour: anger, sulking, urinary problems; they have recourse to the same coquetry to gain the love of adults. Up to twelve, the girl is just as sturdy as her brothers; she shows the same intellectual aptitudes; she is not barred from competing with them in any area. If well before puberty and sometimes even starting from early childhood she already appears sexually specified, it is not because mysterious instincts immediately destine her to passivity, coquetry or motherhood but because the intervention of others in the infant's life is almost originary, and her vocation is imperiously breathed into her from the first years of her life.

The world is first present to the newborn only in the form of immanent sensations; he is still immersed within the Whole as he was when
he was living in the darkness of a womb; whether raised on the breast
or on a bottle, he is invested with the warmth of maternal flesh. Little
by little he learns to perceive objects as distinct from himself: he separates himself from them; at the same time, more or less suddenly, he
is removed from the nourishing body; sometimes he reacts to this separation with a violent fit;* in any case, when it is consummated – around
six months – he begins to manifest the desire to seduce others by
mimicking, which then turns into a real display. Of course, this attitude is not defined by a reflective choice; but it is not necessary to
think a situation to *exist* it. In an immediate way the newborn lives the
primeval drama of every existent – that is, the drama of one's relation
to the Other. Man experiences his abandonment in anguish. Fleeing
his freedom and subjectivity, he would like to lose himself within the
Whole: here is the origin of his cosmic and pantheistic reveries, of his
desire for oblivion, sleep, ecstasy and death. He never manages to
abolish his separated self: at the least he wishes to achieve the solidity
of the in-itself, to be petrified in thing; it is uniquely when he is fixed
by the gaze of others that he appears to himself as a being. It is in this
vein that the child's behaviour has to be interpreted: in a bodily form
he discovers finitude, solitude and abandonment in an alien world; he
tries to compensate for this catastrophe by alienating his existence in
an image whose reality and value will be established by others. It would
seem that from the time he recognises his reflection in a mirror – a
time that coincides with weaning – he begins to affirm his identity:†
his self merges with this reflection in such a way that it is formed only
by alienating itself. Whether the mirror as such plays a more or less
considerable role, what is sure is that the child at about six months of
age begins to understand his parents' miming and to grasp himself
under their gaze as an object. He is already an autonomous subject
transcending himself towards the world: but it is only in an alienated
form that he will encounter himself.

* Judith Gautier says in her accounts of her memories that she cried and wasted away
so terribly when she was pulled away from her wet nurse that she had to be reunited
with her. She was weaned much later.
† This is Dr Lacan's theory in *Family Complexes in the Formation of the Individual*. This
fundamental fact would explain that during its development 'the self keeps the ambiguous
form of spectacle'.

When the child grows up, he fights against his original abandonment in two ways. He tries to deny the separation: he crushes himself in his mother's arms, he seeks her loving warmth, he wants her caresses. And he tries to win the approbation of others in order to justify himself. Adults are to him as gods: they have the power to confer being on him. He experiences the magic of the gaze that metamorphoses him now into a delicious little angel and now into a monster. These two modes of defence are not mutually exclusive: on the contrary, they complete and infuse each other. When seduction is successful, the feeling of justification finds physical confirmation in the kisses and caresses received: it is the same contented passivity that the child experiences in his mother's lap and under her benevolent eyes. During the first three or four years of life, there is no difference between girls' and boys' attitudes; they all try to perpetuate the happy state preceding weaning; both boys and girls show the same behaviour of seduction and display. Boys are just as desirous as their sisters to please, to be smiled at, to be admired.

It is more satisfying to deny brutal separation than to overcome it, more radical to be lost in the heart of the Whole than to be petrified by the consciousness of others: carnal fusion creates a deeper alienation than any abdication under the gaze of another. Seduction and display represent a more complex and less easy stage than the simple abandonment in maternal arms. The magic of the adult gaze is capricious; the child pretends to be invisible, his parents play the game, grope around for him, they laugh and then suddenly they declare: 'You are bothersome, you are not invisible at all.' A child's phrase amuses, then he repeats it: this time, they shrug their shoulders. In this world as unsure and unpredictable as Kafka's universe, one stumbles at every step.[*2] That is why so many children are afraid of growing up; they desperately want their parents to continue taking them on their laps, taking them into

* In *The Blue Orange*, Yassu Gauclère says about her father: 'His good mood seemed as fearsome as his impatiences because nothing explained to me what could bring it about . . . As uncertain of the changes in his mood as I would have been of a god's whims, I revered him with anxiety . . . I threw out my words as I might have played heads or tails, wondering how they would be received.' And further on, she tells the following anecdote: 'For example, one day, after being scolded, I began my litany: old table, floor brush, stove, large bowl, milk bottle, casserole, and so on. My mother heard me and burst out laughing . . . A few days later, I tried to use my litany to soften my grandmother who once again had scolded me: I should have known better this time. Instead of making her laugh, I made her angrier and got an extra punishment. I told myself that adults' behaviour was truly incomprehensible.'

their bed: through physical frustration they experience ever more cruelly that abandonment of which the human being never becomes aware without anguish.

It is here that little girls first appear privileged. A second weaning, less brutal and slower than the first one, withdraws the mother's body from the child's embraces; but little by little boys are the ones who are denied kisses and caresses; the little girl continues to be doted upon, she is allowed to hide behind her mother's skirts, her father takes her on his knees and pats her hair; she is dressed in dresses as lovely as kisses, her tears and whims are treated indulgently, her hair is done carefully, her expressions and affectations amuse: physical contact and complaisant looks protect her against the anxiety of solitude. For the little boy, on the other hand, even affectations are forbidden; his attempts at seduction, his games irritate. 'A man doesn't ask for kisses . . . A man doesn't look at himself in the mirror . . . A man doesn't cry,' he is told. He has to be 'a little man'; he obtains adults' approbation by freeing himself from them. He will please by not seeming to seek to please.

Many boys, frightened by the harsh independence they are condemned to, thus desire to be girls; in times when they were first dressed as girls, they cried when they had to give dresses up for long trousers and had to have their curls cut. Some obstinately would choose femininity, which is one of the ways of gravitating towards homosexuality: 'I wanted passionately to be a girl, and I was unconscious of the grandeur of being a man to the point of trying to urinate sitting down,' Maurice Sachs*[3] recounts. However, if the boy at first seems less favoured than his sisters, it is because there are greater designs for him. The requirements he is subjected to immediately imply a higher estimation. In his memoirs, Maurras recounts that he was jealous of a younger son his mother and grandmother doted upon: his father took him by the hand and out of the room: 'We are men; let's leave these women,' he told him. The child is persuaded that more is demanded of boys because of their superiority; the pride of his virility is breathed into him in order to encourage him in this difficult path; this abstract notion takes on a concrete form for him: it is embodied in the penis; he does not experience pride spontaneously in his little indolent sex organ; but he feels it through the attitude of those around him. Mothers and wet nurses perpetuate the tradition that assimilates phallus and maleness; whether they recognise

* Witches' Sabbath.

its prestige in amorous gratitude or in submission, or whether they gain revenge by seeing it in the baby in a reduced form, they treat the child's penis with a singular deference. Rabelais[4] reports on Garguanta's* wet nurses' games and words; history has recorded those of Louis XIII's wet nurses. Less daring women, however, give a friendly name to the little boy's sex organ, they speak to him about it as of a little person who is both himself and other than himself; they make of it, according to the words already cited, 'an *alter ego* usually craftier, more intelligent and more clever than the individual'.[†] Anatomically, the penis is totally apt to play this role; considered apart from the body, it looks like a little natural plaything, a kind of doll. The child is esteemed by esteeming his double. A father told me that one of his sons at the age of three was still urinating sitting down; surrounded by sisters and girl cousins, he was a shy and sad child; one day his father took him with him to the toilet and said: 'I will show you how men do it.' From then on, the child, proud to be urinating standing up, scorned the girls 'who urinated through a hole'; his scorn came originally not from the fact that they were lacking an organ but that they had not like him been singled out and initiated by the father. So, far from the penis being discovered as an immediate privilege from which the boy would draw a feeling of superiority, its value seems, on the contrary, like a compensation – invented by adults and fervently accepted by the child – for the hardships of the last weaning: in that way he is protected against regret that he is no longer a breast-feeding baby or a girl. From then on, he will embody his transcendence and his arrogant sovereignty in his sex.[‡]

The girl's lot is very different. Mothers and wet nurses have neither reverence nor tenderness for her genital parts; they do not focus atten-tion on this secret organ of which only the outside envelope can be seen and that cannot be taken hold of; in one sense, she does not have a sex. She does not experience this absence as a lack; her body is evidently a plenitude for her; but she finds herself in the world differently from the

---

* 'And already beginning to exercise his codpiece, which each and every day his nurses would adorn with lovely bouquets, fine ribbons, beautiful flowers, pretty tufts, and they spent their time bringing it back and forth between their hands like a cylinder of salve, then they laughed their heads off when it raised its ears, as if they liked the game. One would call it my little spigot, another my ninepin, another my coral branch, another my stopper, my cork, my gimlet, my ramrod, my awl, my pendant.'
† Cited by A. Bàlint, *The Psychoanalysis of the Nursery.*
‡ See Vol. I, Chapter 2.

boy; and a group of factors can transform this difference into inferiority in her eyes.

Few questions are as much discussed by psychoanalysts as the famous 'female castration complex'. Most accept today that penis envy mani- fests itself in very different ways depending on the individual case.* First, many girls are ignorant of male anatomy until an advanced age. The child accepts naturally that there are men and women as there are a sun and a moon: he believes in essences contained in words and his curiosity is at first not analytical. For many others, this little piece of flesh hanging between boys' legs is insignificant or even derisory; it is a particularity like that of clothes and hair style; often the female child discovers it at a younger brother's birth, and 'when the little girl is very young,' says Helene Deutsch,[6] 'she is not impressed by her younger brother's penis'; she cites the example of an eighteen-month-old girl who remained absolutely indifferent to the discovery of the penis and did not give it any value until much later, in connection with her personal preoccupa- tions. The penis can even be considered an anomaly: it is a growth, a vague hanging thing like nodules, teats and warts; it can inspire disgust. Lastly, the fact is that there are many cases of the little girl being inter- ested in a brother's or a friend's penis; but that does not mean she experiences a specifically sexual jealousy and even less that she feels deeply moved by the absence of this organ; she desires to appropriate it for herself as she desires to appropriate any object; but this desire may remain superficial.

It is certain that the excretory function and particularly the urinary one interest children passionately: wetting the bed is often a protest against the parents' marked preference for another child. There are coun- tries where men urinate sitting down and there are women who urinate standing up: this is the way among many women peasants; but in contem- porary Western society, custom generally has it that they squat, while the standing position is reserved to males. This is the most striking sexual difference for the little girl. To urinate she has to squat down, remove some clothes and above all hide, a shameful and uncomfortable servitude.

---

* Besides Freud's and Adler's works, there is today an abundant literature on the subject. Abraham was the first one to put forward the idea that the girl considered her sex a wound resulting from a mutilation. Karen Horney, Ernest Jones, Jeanne Lampl de Groot, H. Deutsch and A. Bálint studied the question from a psychoanalytical point of view. Saussure tries to reconcile psychoanalysis with Piaget's and Lucquet's ideas. See also Pollack, *Children's Ideas on Sex Differences*.

Shame increases in the frequent cases in which she suffers from involuntary urinary emissions, when bursting out laughing, for example;
control is worse than for boys. For them, the urinary function is like a
free game with the attraction of all games in which freedom is exercised; the penis can be handled, through it one can act, which is one of
the child's deep interests. A little girl seeing a boy urinate declared admir-
ingly: 'How practical!'* The stream can be aimed at will, the urine directed
far away: the boy draws a feeling of omnipotence from it. Freud spoke
of 'the burning ambition of early diuretics'; Stekel discussed this formula
sensibly, but it is true that, as Karen Horney says, 'fantasies of omnipotence, especially of a sadistic character, are as a matter of fact more
easily associated with the jet of urine passed by the male';† there are
many such fantasies in children and they survive in some men.‡ Abraham
speaks of 'the great pleasure women experience watering the garden
with a hose'; I think, in agreement with Sartre's and Bachelard's theories,‡‡ that it is not necessarily the assimilation of the hose with the penis
that is the source of pleasure;§ every stream of water seems like a miracle,
a defiance of gravity: directing or governing it means carrying off a little
victory over natural laws; in any case, for the little boy there is a daily
amusement that is impossible for his sisters. He is also able to establish
many relations with things through the urinary stream, especially in the
countryside: water, earth, moss, snow. There are little girls who lie on
their backs and try to practise urinating 'in the air' or who try to urinate
standing up in order to have these experiences. According to Karen
Horney, they also envy the opportunity to exhibit which the boy is
granted. 'A sick woman suddenly exclaimed, after seeing a man urinating
in the street: "If I might ask a gift of Povidence, it would be to be able
to just for once to urinate like a man,"' Karen Horney reports. It seems
to girls that the boy, having the right to touch his penis, can use it as a
plaything, while their organs are taboo. That these factors make the
possession of a male sex organ desirable for many of them is a fact
confirmed by many studies and confidences gathered by psychiatrists.
Havelock Ellis§§ ⁷ quotes the words of a patient he calls Zenia: 'The noise

* Cited by A. Bálint.
† 'On the Genesis of the Castration Complex in Women', *International Journal of
Psychoanalysis*, 1923–24.
‡ Montherlant ('The Caterpillars', *June Solstice*).
‡‡ See Vol. I, Part One, Chapter 2.
§ It is clear, though, in some cases.
§§ Cf. Havelock Ellis, *Ondinism*.
  14. Cf. Ellis [discussion of "undinism" in *Studies in the Psychology of Sex*. – TRANS.].

of a jet of water, especially coming out of a long hose, has always been very stimulating for me, recalling the noise of the stream of urine observed in childhood in my brother and even in other people.' Another woman, Mme R. S., recounts that as a child she absolutely loved holding a little friend's penis in her hands; one day she was given a hose: 'It seemed delicious to hold that as if I was holding a penis.' She emphasised that the penis had no sexual meaning for her; she only knew its urinary usage. The most interesting case, that of Florrie, is reported by Havelock Ellis*[8] and analysed by Stekel later on. Here is a detailed account from it:

> The woman concerned is very intelligent, artistic, active, biologically normal, and not homosexual. She says that the urinary function played a great role in her childhood; she played urinary games with her brothers, and they wet their hands without feeling disgust. 'My earliest ideas of the superiority of the male were connected with urination. I felt aggrieved with nature because I lacked so useful and ornamental an organ. No teapot without a spout felt so forlorn. It required no one to instil into me the theory of male predominance and superiority. Constant proof was before me.' She took great pleasure in urinating in the country. 'Nothing could come up to the entrancing sound as the stream descended on crackling leaves in the depth of a wood and she watched its absorption. Most of all she was fascinated by the idea of doing it into water' [as are many little boys]. There is a quantity of childish and vulgar imagery showing little boys urinating in ponds and brooks. Florrie complains that the style of her knickers prevented her from trying various desired experiments, but often during country walks she would hold back as long as she could and then suddenly relieve herself standing. 'I can distinctly remember the strange and delicious sensation of this forbidden delight, and also my puzzled feeling that it came standing.' In her opinion, the style of children's clothing has great importance for feminine psychology in general. 'It was not only a source of annoyance to me that I had to unfasten my drawers and then squat down for fear of wetting them in front, but the flap at the back, which must be removed to uncover the posterior parts during the act, accounts for my early impression that in girls this function is connected with those parts. The first distinction in sex that impressed me – the one great difference in sex – was that boys

---

* H. Ellis, *Studies in the Psychology of Sex*, Vol. fl¾¾¾.

urinated standing and that girls had to sit down . . . The fact that my earliest feelings of shyness were more associated with the back than the front may have thus originated.' All these impressions were of great importance in Florrie's case because her father often whipped her until the blood came and also a governess had once spanked her to make her urinate; she was obsessed by masochistic dreams and fancies in which she saw herself whipped by a school mistress under the eyes of all and having to urinate against her will, 'an idea that gives one a curious sense of gratification'. At the age of fifteen it happened that under urgent need she urinated standing in a deserted street. 'In trying to analyse my sensations I think the most prominent lay in the shame that came from standing, and the consequently greater distance the stream had to descend. It seemed to make the affair important and conspicuous, even though clothing hid it. In the ordinary attitude there is a kind of privacy. As a small child, too, the stream had not far to go, but at the age of fifteen I was tall and it seemed to give one a glow of shame to think of this stream falling unchecked such a distance. (I am sure that the ladies who fled in horror from the urinette at Portsmouth* thought it most indecent for a woman to stand, legs apart, and to pull up her clothes and make a stream which descended unabashed all that way.)' She renewed this experience at twenty and frequently there-after. She felt a mixture of shame and pleasure at the idea that she might be surprised and that she would be incapable of stopping. 'The stream seemed to be drawn from me without my consent, and *yet with even more pleasure than if I were doing it freely.*† This curious feeling – that it is being drawn away by some unseen power which is determined that one shall do it – is an entirely feminine pleasure and a subtle charm . . . There is a fierce charm in the torrent that binds one to its will by a mighty force.' Later Florrie developed a flagellatory eroticism always combined with urinary obsessions.

This case is very interesting because it throws light on several elements of the child's experience. But of course there are particular circumstances

---

* In an allusion to an episode she related previously: at Portsmouth a modern urinette for ladies was opened which called for the standing position; all the clients were seen to depart hastily as soon as they entered.
† Florrie's italics.

that confer such a great importance upon them. For normally raised little girls, the boy's urinary privilege is too secondary a thing to engender a feeling of inferiority directly. Psychoanalysts following Freud who think that the mere discovery of the penis would be sufficient to produce a trauma seriously misunderstand the child's mentality; it is much less rational than they seem to think, it does not establish clear-cut categories and is not bothered by contradictions. When the little girl seeing a penis declares: 'I had one too' or 'I'll have one too', or even 'I have one too', this is not a defence in bad faith; presence and absence are not mutually exclusive; the child – as his drawings prove – believes much less in what he *sees* with his eyes than in the signifying *types* that he has determined once and for all: he often draws without looking and in any case he finds in his perceptions only what he puts there. Saussure,*[9] who emphasises this point, quotes this very important observation of Luquet: 'Once a line is considered wrong, it is as if inexistent, *the child literally no longer sees it*, hypnotised in a way by the new line that replaces it, nor does he take into account lines that can be accidentally found on his paper.' Male anatomy constitutes a strong form that is often imposed on the little girl; and *literally she no longer sees* her own body. Saussure brings up the example of a four-year-old girl who, trying to urinate like a boy between the bars of a fence, said she wanted 'a little long thing that runs'. She affirmed at the same time that she had a penis and that she did not have one, which goes along with the thinking by 'participation' that Piaget described in children. The little girl takes it for granted that all children are born with a penis but that the parents then cut some of them off to make girls; this idea satisfies the artificialism of the child who glorifies his parents and 'conceives of them as the cause of everything he possesses', says Piaget; he does not see punishment in castration right away. For it to become a frustration, the little girl has to be unhappy with her situation for some reason; as Deutsch justly points out, an exterior event like the sight of a penis could not lead to an internal development. 'The sight of the male organ can have a traumatic effect,' she says, 'but only if a chain of prior experiences that would create that effect had preceded it.' If the little girl feels powerless to satisfy her desires of masturbation or exhibition, if her parents repress her onanism, if she feels less loved or less valued than her brothers, then she will project her dissatisfaction onto the male organ. 'The little girl's discovery of the anatomical difference with the boy confirms a previously felt need;

* 'Genetic Psychology and Psychoanalysis', *Revue française de psychanalyse*, 1933.

it is her rationalization, so to speak.'* And Adler also insisted on the fact that it is the validation by the parents and others that gives the boy prestige, and that the penis becomes the explanation and symbol in the little girl's eyes. Her brother is considered superior; he himself takes pride in his maleness; so she envies him and feels frustrated. Sometimes she resents her mother and less often her father; either she accuses herself of being mutilated or she consoles herself by thinking that the penis is hidden in her body and that one day it will come out.

It is sure that the absence of a penis will play an important role in the little girl's destiny, even if she does not really envy those who possess one. The great privilege that the boy gets from it is that as he is bestowed with an organ that can be seen and held, he can at least partially alienate himself in it. He projects the mystery of his body and its dangers outside himself, which permits him to keep them at a distance: of course, he feels endangered through his penis, he fears castration, but this fear is easier to dominate than the pervasive overall fear the girl feels concerning her 'insides', a fear that will often be perpetuated throughout her whole life as a woman. She has a deep concern about everything happening inside her; from the start, she is far more opaque to herself and more profoundly inhabited by the worrying mystery of life than the male. Because he recognises himself in an alter ego, the little boy can boldly assume his subjectivity; the very object in which he alienates himself becomes a symbol of autonomy, transcendence and power: he measures the size of his penis; he compares his urinary stream with that of his friends; later, erection and ejaculation will be sources of satisfaction and challenge. But a little girl cannot incarnate herself in any part of her own body. As compensation, and to fill the role of alter ego for her, she is handed a foreign object: a doll. Note that the bandage wrapped on an injured finger is also called a *poupée* ('doll' in French): a finger dressed and separate from the others is looked on with amusement and a kind of pride with which the child initiates the process of its alienation. But it is a figurine with a human face – or a corn husk or even a piece of wood – that will most satisfyingly replace this double, this natural toy, this penis.

The great difference is that, on one hand, the doll represents the whole body and, on the other hand, it is a passive thing. As such, the little girl will be encouraged to alienate herself in her person as a whole and to

* H. Deutsch, *The Psychology of Women*. She also cites the authority of K. Abraham and J. H. W. van Ophuijsen.

consider it as an inert given. While the boy seeks himself in his penis as an autonomous subject, the little girl pampers her doll and dresses her as she dreams of being dressed and pampered; inversely, she thinks of herself as a marvellous doll.* Through compliments and admonishments, through images and words, she discovers the meaning of the words 'pretty' and 'ugly'; she soon knows that to please she has to be 'pretty as a picture'; she tries to resemble an image, she disguises herself, she looks at herself in the mirror, she compares herself to princesses and fairies from tales. Marie Bashkirtseff[10] gives a striking example of this infantile coquetry. It is certainly not by chance that, weaned late – she was three and a half – she fervently felt the need at the age of four or five to be admired and to exist for others: the shock must have been violent in a more mature child and she had to struggle even harder to overcome the inflicted separation. 'At five years old,' she writes in her diary, 'I would dress in Mummy's lace, with flowers in my hair and I would go and dance in the living room. I was Petipa, the great dancer, and the whole house was there to *look at me*.'

This narcissism appears so precociously for the little girl and will play so fundamental a part in her life that it is readily considered as emanating from a mysterious feminine instinct. But we have just seen that in reality it is not an anatomical destiny that dictates her attitude. The difference that distinguishes her from boys is a fact that she could assume in many ways. Having a penis is certainly a privilege, but one whose value naturally diminishes when the child loses interest in his excretory functions and becomes socialised: if he retains interest in it past the age of eight or nine years, it is because the penis has become the symbol of a socially valorised virility. The fact is that the influence of education and society is enormous here. All children try to compensate for the separation of weaning by seductive and attention-seeking behaviour; the boy is forced to go beyond this stage, he is saved from his narcissism by turning his attention to his penis, whereas the girl is reinforced in this tendency to make herself object, which is common to all children. The doll helps her, but it does not have a determining role; the boy can also treasure a teddy bear or a rag doll on whom he can project himself; it is in their life's overall form that each factor – penis, doll – takes on its importance.

---

* The analogy between the woman and the doll remains until the adult age; in French, a woman is vulgarly called a doll; in English, a dressed-up woman is said to be 'dolled up'.

Thus, the passivity that essentially characterises the 'feminine' woman is a trait that develops in her from her earliest years. But it is false to claim that therein lies a biological given; in fact, it is a destiny imposed on her by her teachers and by society. The great advantage for the boy is that his way of existing for others leads him to posit himself for himself. He carries out the apprenticeship of his existence as free movement towards the world; he rivals other boys in toughness and independence; he looks down on girls. Climbing trees, fighting with his companions, confronting them in violent games, he grasps his body as a means to dominate nature and as a fighting tool; he is proud of his muscles, as he is of his sex organ; through games, sports, fights, challenges and exploits, he finds a balanced use of his strength; at the same time, he learns the severe lessons of violence; he learns to take blows, to deride pain, to hold back tears from the earliest age. He undertakes, he invents, he dares. Granted, he also experiences himself as if 'for others'; he tests his own virility, and consequently, trouble ensues with adults and friends. But what is very important is that there is no fundamental opposition between this objective figure that is his and his will for self-affirmation in concrete projects. It is by doing that he makes himself be, in one single movement. On the contrary, for the woman there is, from the start, a conflict between her autonomous existence and her 'being-other'; she is taught that to please, she must try to please, must make herself object; she must therefore renounce her autonomy. She is treated like a living doll and freedom is denied her; thus a vicious circle is closed; for the less she exercises her freedom to understand, grasp and discover the world around her, the less she will find its resources, and the less she will dare to affirm herself as subject; if she were encouraged, she could show the same vibrant exuberance, the same curiosity, the same spirit of initiative, and the same intrepidness as the boy. Sometimes this does happen when she is given a male upbringing; she is thus spared many problems.* Interestingly, this is the kind of education that a father habitually gives his daughter; women brought up by a man escape many of the defects of femininity. But customs oppose treating girls exactly like boys. I knew a village where girls of three and four years old were persecuted because their father made them wear trousers: 'Are they girls or boys?' And the other children tried to find out; the result was their pleading to wear dresses. Unless she leads a very solitary life, even if parents allow her to

---

* At least in her early childhood. In today's society, adolescent conflicts could, on the contrary, be exacerbated.

have boyish manners, the girl's companions, her friends and her teachers will be shocked. There will always be aunts, grandmothers and girl cousins to counterbalance the father's influence. Normally, his role regarding his daughters is secondary. One of the woman's curses – as Michelet has justly pointed out – is that in her childhood she is left in the hands of women. The boy is also brought up by his mother in the beginning; but she respects his maleness and he escapes from her relatively quickly,* whereas the mother wants to integrate the girl into the feminine world.

We will see later how complex the relation is between the mother and the daughter: for the mother, the daughter is both her double and an other, the mother cherishes her and at the same time is hostile to her; she imposes her own destiny on her child: it is a way to proudly claim her own femininity and also to take revenge on it. The same process is found with pederasts, gamblers, drug addicts, and all those who are flattered to belong to a certain community, and are also humili-ated by it: they try through ardent proselytism to win over converts. Thus, women given the care of a little girl are bent on transforming her into women like themselves with zeal and arrogance mixed with resentment. And even a generous mother who sincerely wants the best for her child will, as a rule, think it wiser to make a 'true woman' of her, as that is the way she will be best accepted by society. So she is given other little girls as friends, she is entrusted to female teachers, she lives among matrons as in the days of the gynaeceum, books and games are chosen for her that introduce her to her destiny, her ears are filled with the treasures of feminine wisdom, feminine virtues are presented to her, she is taught cooking, sewing and housework as well as how to dress, how to take care of her personal appearance, charm and modesty; she is dressed in uncomfortable and fancy clothes that she has to take care of, her hair is done in complicated styles, posture is imposed on her: stand up straight, don't walk like a duck; to be graceful she has to repress spontaneous movements, she is told not to look like a tomboy, strenuous exercise is banned, she is forbidden to fight; in short, she is committed to becoming, like her elders, a servant and an idol. Today, thanks to feminism's breakthroughs, it is becoming more and more normal to encourage her to pursue her education, to devote herself to sports; but she is more easily excused for not succeeding; success is made more difficult for her as another kind of

---

* There are, of course, many exceptions: but the mother's role in bringing up a boy cannot be studied here.

accomplishment is demanded of her: she must at least *also* be a woman, she must not *lose* her femininity.

In her early years she resigns herself to this lot without much difficulty. The child inhabits the level of play and dream, he plays at being, he plays at doing; doing and being are not clearly distinguishable when it is a question of imaginary accomplishments. The little girl can compensate for boys' superiority of the moment by those promises inherent in her woman's destiny, which she already achieves in her play. Because she still only knows her childhood universe, her mother seems endowed with more authority than her father; she imagines the world as a sort of matriarchy; she imitates her mother, she identifies with her; often she even inverses the roles: 'When I am big and you are little . . . ,' she often says. The doll is not only her double: it is also her child, functions that are not mutually exclusive insofar as the real child is also an alter ego for the mother; when she scolds, punishes and then consoles her doll, she is defending herself against her mother, and she assumes a mother's dignity: she sums up both elements of the couple as she entrusts herself to her doll, educates her, asserts her sovereign authority over her and sometimes even tears off her arms, beats her, tortures her; that is to say, through her she accomplishes the experience of subjective affirmation and alienation. Often the mother is associated with this imaginary life: in playing with the doll and the mother, the child plays both the father and the mother, a couple where the man is excluded. No 'maternal instinct', innate and mysterious, lies therein either. The little girl observes that child care falls to the mother, that is what she is taught; stories told, books read, all her little experience confirms it; she is encouraged to feel delight for these future riches, she is given dolls so she will already feel the tangible aspect of those riches. Her 'vocation' is determined imperiously. Because her lot seems to be the child, and also because she is more interested in her 'insides' than the boy, the little girl is particularly curious about the mystery of procreation; she quickly ceases to believe that babies are born in cabbages or delivered by the stork; especially in cases where the mother gives her brothers or sisters, she soon learns that babies are formed in their mother's body. Besides, parents today make less of a mystery of it than before; she is generally more amazed than frightened because the phenomenon seems like magic to her; she does not yet grasp all of the physiological implications. First of all, she is unaware of the father's role and supposes that the woman gets pregnant by eating certain foods, a legendary theme (queens in fairy tales give birth to a little girl or a handsome boy after eating this fruit, that fish) and one that later leads some women to link the idea of gestation and the digestive system. Together these problems and these discoveries absorb a great part of the little girl's interests and feed her imagination. I will cite a typical example from Jung,* which bears remarkable analogies with that of little Hans, analysed by Freud around the same time:

When Anna was about three years old she began to question her parents about where babies come from; Anna had heard that children are 'little angels'. She first seemed to think that when people die, they go to heaven and are reincarnated as babies. At age four she had a little brother; she hadn't seemed to notice her mother's pregnancy but when she saw her the day after the birth, she looked at her 'with something like a mixture of embarrassment and suspicion' and finally asked her, 'Aren't you going to die now?' She was sent to her grandmother's for some time; when she came back, a nurse had arrived and was installed near the bed; she at first hated her but then she amused herself playing nurse; she was jealous of her brother: she sniggered, made up stories, disobeyed and threatened to go back to her grandmother's; she often accused her mother of not telling the truth, because she suspected her of lying about the infant's birth; feeling obscurely that there was a difference between 'having' a child as a nurse and having one as a mother, she asked her mother: 'shall I be a different woman from you?' She got into the habit of yelling for her parents during the night; and as the earthquake of Messina was much talked about she made it the pretext of her anxieties; she constantly asked questions about it. One day, she asked outright: 'Why is Sophie younger than I? Where was Freddie before? Was he in heaven and what was he doing there?' Her mother decided she ought to explain that the little brother grew inside her stomach like plants in the earth. Anna was enchanted with this idea. Then she asked: 'But did he come all by himself?' 'Yes.' 'But he can't walk yet!' 'He crawled out.' 'Did he come out here (pointing to her chest), or did he come out of your mouth?' Without waiting for an answer, she said she knew it was the stork that had brought it; but in the evening she suddenly said: 'My brother is in Italy;† he has a house made of cloth and glass and it doesn't fall down'; and she was no longer interested in

---

* Jung, 'Psychic Conflicts of a Child'.
† This was a made-up older brother who played a big role in her games.

the earthquake or asked to see photos of the eruption. She spoke again of the stork to her dolls but without much conviction. Soon however, she had new curiosities. Seeing her father in bed: 'Why are you in bed? Have you got a plant in your inside too?' She had a dream; she dreamed of Noah's Ark: 'And underneath, there was a lid which opened and all the little animals fell out'; in fact, her Noah's Ark opened by the roof. At this time, she again had night-mares: one could guess that she was wondering about the father's role. A pregnant woman having visited her mother, the next day her mother saw Anna put a doll under her skirts and take it out slowly, saying: 'Look, the baby is coming out, now it is all out.' Some time later, eating an orange, she said: 'I'll swallow it all down into my stomach, and then I shall get a baby.' One morning, her father was in the bathroom, she jumped on his bed, lay flat on her face, and flailed with her legs, crying out, 'Look, is that what Papa does?' For five months she seemed to forget her preoccupations and then she began to mistrust her father: she thought he wanted to drown her, etc. One day she was happily sowing seeds in the earth with the gardener, and she asked her father: 'How did the eyes grow into the head? And the hair?' The father explained that they were already there from the beginning and grew with the head. Then, she asked: 'But how did Fritz get into Mama? Who stuck him in? And who stuck you into your mama? Where did he come out?' Her father said, smiling, 'What do you think?' So she pointed to his sexual organs: 'Did he come out from there?' 'Well, yes.' 'But how did he get into Mama? Did someone sow the seed?' So the father explained that it is the father who gives the seed. She seemed totally satisfied and the next day she teased her mother: 'Papa told me that Fritz was a little angel and was brought down from heaven by the stork.' She was much calmer than before; she had, though, a dream in which she saw gardeners urinating, her father among them; she also dreamed, after seeing the gardener plane a drawer, that he was planing her genitals; she was obviously preoccupied with knowing the father's exact role. It seems that, almost completely enlightened at the age of five, she did not experience any other disturbance.[11]

This story is characteristic, although very often the little girl is less precisely inquisitive about the role played by the father, or the parents are much more evasive on this point. Many little girls hide cushions under their pinafores to play at being pregnant, or else they walk around with their doll in the folds of their skirts and let it fall into the cradle, or they give it their breast. Boys, like girls, admire the mystery of motherhood; all children have an 'in depth' imagination that makes them sense secret riches inside things; they are all sensitive to the miracle of 'nesting', dolls that contain other, smaller dolls, boxes containing other boxes, vignettes identically reproduced in reduced form; they are all enchanted when a bud is unfolded before their eyes, when they are shown a chick in its shell or the surprise of 'Japanese flowers' in a bowl of water. One little boy, upon opening an Easter egg full of little sugar eggs, exclaimed with delight: 'Oh! A mummy!' Having a child emerge from a woman's stomach is beautiful, like a magic trick. The mother seems endowed with wonderful fairy powers. Many boys bemoan that such a privilege is denied them; if, later, they take eggs from nests, stamp on young plants, if they destroy life around them with a kind of rage, it is out of revenge at not being able to hatch life, while the little girl is enchanted with the thought of creating it one day.

In addition to this hope made concrete by playing with dolls, a housewife's life also provides the little girl with possibilities of affirming herself. A great part of housework can be accomplished by a very young child; a boy is usually exempted from it; but his sister is allowed, even asked, to sweep, dust, peel vegetables, wash a newborn, watch the stew. In particular, the older sister often participates in maternal chores; either for convenience or because of hostility and sadism, the mother unloads many of her functions onto her; she is then prematurely integrated into the universe of the serious; feeling her importance will help her assume her femininity; but she is deprived of the happy gratuitousness, the carefree childhood; a woman before her time, she understands too soon what limits this specificity imposes on a human being; she enters adolescence as an adult, which gives her story a unique character. The overburdened child can prematurely be a slave, condemned to a joyless existence. But, if no more than an effort equal to her is demanded, she experiences the pride of feeling efficient like a grown person and is delighted to feel solidarity with adults. This solidarity is possible for the child because there is not much distance between the child and the housewife. A man specialised in his profession is separated from the infant stage by years of training; paternal activities are profoundly mysterious for the little boy; the man he will be later is barely sketched in him. On the contrary, the mother's activities are accessible to the little girl. 'She's already a little woman,' say her parents, and often she is considered more precocious than the boy: in fact, if she is closer to the adult stage, it is because this stage traditionally remains more infantile for the majority of women. The fact is that she feels precocious, she is flattered to play the role of 'little mother' to the younger ones; she easily becomes important, she speaks reason, she gives orders, she takes on superior airs with her brothers, who are still closed in the baby circle, she talks to her mother on an equal footing.

In spite of these compensations, she does not accept her assigned destiny without regret; growing up, she envies boys their virility. Sometimes parents and grandparents poorly hide the fact that they would have preferred a male offspring to a female; or else they show more affection to the brother than to the sister: research shows that the majority of parents wish to have sons rather than daughters. Boys are spoken to with more seriousness and more esteem, and more rights are granted them; they themselves treat girls with contempt, they play among themselves and exclude girls from their group, they insult them: they call them names like 'piss pots', thus evoking girls' secret childhood humiliations. In France, in coeducational schools, the boys' caste deliberately oppresses and persecutes the girls'. But girls are reprimanded if they want to compete or fight with them. They doubly envy singularly boyish activities: they have a spontaneous desire to affirm their power over the world and they protest against the inferior situation they are condemned to. They suffer in being forbidden to climb trees, ladders and roofs, among other activities. Adler observes that the notions of high and low have great importance, the idea of spatial elevation implying a spiritual superiority, as can be seen in numerous heroic myths; to attain a peak or a summit is to emerge beyond the given world as sovereign subject; between boys, it is frequently a pretext for challenge. The little girl, to whom exploits are forbidden and who sits under a tree or by a cliff and sees the triumphant boys above her, feels herself, body and soul, inferior. And the same is true if she is left *behind* in a race or a jumping competition, or if she is thrown *to the ground* in a fight or simply pushed to the side.

The more the child matures, the more his universe expands and masculine superiority asserts itself. Very often, identification with the mother no longer seems a satisfactory solution. If the little girl at first accepts her feminine vocation, it is not that she means to abdicate: on the contrary, it is to rule; she wants to be a matron because matrons' society seems privileged to her; but when her acquaintances, studies, amusements and reading material tear her away from the maternal circle, she realises that it is not women but men who are the masters of the world.

It is this revelation – far more than the discovery of the penis – that imperiously modifies her consciousness of herself.

She first discovers the hierarchy of the sexes in the family experience; little by little she understands that the father's authority is not the one felt most in daily life, but it is the sovereign one; it has all the more impact for not being wasted on trifling matters; even though the mother reigns over the household, she is clever enough to put the father's will first; at important moments, she makes demands, rewards and punishes in his name. The father's life is surrounded by mysterious prestige: the hours he spends in the home, the room where he works, the objects around him, his occupations, his habits, have a sacred character. It is he who feeds the family, is the one in charge and the head. Usually he works outside the home and it is through him that the household communicates with the rest of the world: he is the embodiment of this adventurous, immense, difficult and marvellous world; he is transcendence, he is God.* This is what the child feels physically in the power of his arms that lift her, in the strength of his body that she huddles against. The mother loses her place of honour to him just as Isis once did to Ra and the earth to the sun. But for the child, her situation is deeply altered: she was intended one day to become a woman like her all-powerful mother – she will never be the sovereign father; the bond that attached her to her mother was an active emulation; from her father she can only passively expect esteem. The boy grasps paternal superiority through a feeling of rivalry, whereas the girl endures it with impotent admiration. I have already stated that what Freud called the 'Electra complex' is not, as he maintains, a sexual desire; it is a deep abdication of the subject who consents to be object in submission and adoration. If the father shows tenderness for his daughter, she feels her existence magnificently justified; she is endowed with all the merits that others have to acquire the hard way; she is fulfilled and deified. It may be that she nostalgically searches for this plenitude and peace her whole life. If she is refused love, she can feel guilty and condemned for ever; or else she can seek self-esteem elsewhere and become indifferent – even hostile – to her father. Besides, the father is not the only one to hold the keys to the world: all men normally share virile prestige; there is no reason to consider them father 'substitutes'. It is implicitly as men

---

* 'His generous person inspired in me a great love and an extreme fear,' says Mme de Noailles, speaking of her father. 'First of all, he astounded me. The first man astounds a little girl. I well understood that everything depended on him.'

that grandfathers, older brothers, uncles, girlfriends' fathers, friends of the family, professors, priests or doctors fascinate a little girl. The emotional consideration that adult women show the Man would be enough to perch him on a pedestal.*

Everything helps to confirm this hierarchy in the little girl's eyes. Her historical and literary culture, the songs and legends she is raised on, are an exaltation of the man. Men made Greece, the Roman Empire, France and all countries, they discovered the earth and invented the tools to develop it, they governed it, peopled it with statues, paintings and books. Children's literature, mythology, tales and stories reflect the myths created by men's pride and desires: the little girl discovers the world and reads her destiny through the eyes of men. Male superiority is overwhelming: Perseus, Hercules, David, Achilles, Lancelot, du Guesclin, Bayard, Napoleon – so many men for one Joan of Arc; and behind her stands the great male figure of St Michael the archangel! Nothing is more boring than books retracing the lives of famous women: they are very pale figures next to those of the great men; and most are immersed in the shadows of some male hero. Eve was not created for herself but as Adam's companion and drawn from his side; in the Bible few women are noteworthy for their actions: Ruth merely found herself a husband. Esther gained the Jews' grace by kneeling before Ahasuerus, and even then she was only a docile instrument in Mordecai's hands; Judith was bolder but she too obeyed the priests and her exploit has a dubious after-taste: it could not be compared to the pure and shining triumph of young David. Mythology's goddesses are frivolous or capricious and they all tremble before Jupiter; while Prometheus magnificently steals the fire from the sky, Pandora opens the box of catastrophes. There are a few sorceresses, some old women who wield formidable power in stories. Among them is 'The Garden of Paradise' by Andersen, in which the figure of the mother of the winds recalls that of the primitive Great

---

* It is worth noting that the cult of the father is most prevalent with the oldest child: the man is more involved in his first paternal experience; it is often he who consoles his daughter, as he consoles his son, when the mother is occupied with newborns, and the daughter becomes ardently attached to him. On the contrary, the younger child never has her father to herself; she is ordinarily jealous both of him and her older sister; she attaches herself to that same sister whom the devoted father invests with great pres-tige, or she turns to her mother, or she revolts against her family and looks for relief somewhere else. In large families, the youngest girl child finds other ways to have a special place. Of course, many circumstances can motivate the father to have special preferences. But almost all of the cases I know confirm this observation on the contrasting attitudes of the oldest and the youngest sisters.

Goddess: her four enormous sons fearfully obey her; she beats and encloses them in bags when they behave badly. But they are not attractive characters. More seductive are the fairies, mermaids and nymphs who escape male domination; but their existence is dubious and barely individualised; they are involved in the human world without having their own destiny: the day Andersen's little mermaid becomes a woman, she experiences the yoke of love and suffering that is her lot. In contemporary accounts as in ancient legends, the man is the privileged hero. Mme de Ségur's books are a curious exception: they describe a matriarchal society where the husband plays a ridiculous character when he is not absent; but usually the image of the father is, as in the real world, surrounded by glory. It is under the aegis of the father sanctified by his absence that the feminine dramas of *Little Women* take place. In adventure stories it is boys who go around the world, travel as sailors on boats, subsist on breadfruit in the jungle. All important events happen because of men. Reality confirms these novels and legends. If the little girl reads the newspapers, if she listens to adult conversation, she notices that today, as in the past, men lead the world. The heads of state, generals, explorers, musicians and painters she admires are men; it is men who make her heart beat with enthusiasm.

That prestige is reflected in the supernatural world. Generally, as a result of the role religion plays in women's lives, the little girl, more dominated by the mother than the boy, is also more subjected to religious influences. And in Western religions, God the Father is a man, an old man endowed with a specifically virile attribute, a luxuriant white beard.* For Christians, Christ is even more concretely a man of flesh and blood with a long blond beard. Angels have no sex, according to theologians; but they have masculine names and are shown as handsome young men. God's emissaries on earth – the Pope, the bishop whose ring is kissed, the priest who says Mass, the preacher, the person one kneels before in the secrecy of the confessional – these are men. For a pious little girl, relations with the eternal Father are analogous to those she maintains with her earthly father; as they take place on an imaginary level, she experiences an even more total surrender. The

---

* 'Moreover, I was no longer suffering from my inability to *see* God, because I had recently managed to imagine him in the form of my dead grandfather; this image in truth was rather human; but I had quickly glorified it by separating my grandfather's head from his bust and mentally putting it on a sky blue background where white clouds made him a collar,' Yassu Gauclère says in *The Blue Orange*.

Catholic religion, among others, exercises on her the most troubling of influences.* The Virgin welcomes the angel's words on her knees. 'I am the *handmaiden* of the Lord,' she answers. Mary Magdalene is prostrate at Christ's feet and she washes them with her long womanly hair. Women saints declare their love to a radiant Christ on their knees. On his knees, surrounded by the odour of incense, the child gives himself up to God's and the angels' gaze: a man's gaze. There are many analogies between erotic and mystical language as spoken by women; for example, St Thérèse writes of the child Jesus:

Oh, my beloved, by your love I accept not to see on earth the sweetness of your gaze, not to feel the inexpressible kiss from your mouth but I beg of you to embrace me with your love . . .

> *My beloved, of your first smile*
> *Let me soon glimpse the sweetness.*
> *Ah! Leave me in my burning deliriousness,*
> *Yes, let me hide myself in your heart!*

I want to be mesmerised by your divine gaze; I want to become prey to your love. One day, I have hope, you will melt on me carrying me to love's hearth; you will put me into this burning chasm to make me become, once and for all, the lucky victim.

But it must not be concluded from this that these effusions are always sexual; rather, when female sexuality develops, it is penetrated with the religious feeling that woman has devoted to man since childhood. It is true that the little girl experiences a thrill in the confessional and even at the foot of the altar close to what she will later feel in her lover's arms: woman's love is one of the forms of experience in which a consciousness makes itself an object for a being that transcends it; and these are also the passive delights that the young pious girl tastes in the shadows of the church.

Prostrate, her face buried in her hands, she experiences the miracle of renunciation: on her knees she climbs to heaven; her abandon in God's

---

* There is no doubt that women are infinitely more passive, given to man, servile and humiliated in Catholic countries, Italy, Spain and France, than in the Protestant Scandinavian and Anglo-Saxon ones. And this comes in great part from their own attitude: the cult of the Virgin, confession, and so on invites them to masochism.

arms assures her an assumption lined with clouds and angels. She models her earthly future on this marvellous experience. The child can also discover it in other ways: everything encourages her to abandon herself in dreams to the arms of men to be transported to a sky of glory. She learns that to be happy she has to be loved; to be loved, she has to await love. Woman is Sleeping Beauty, Donkey Skin, Cinderella, Snow White, the one who receives and endures. In songs and tales, the young man sets off to seek the woman; he fights against dragons, he combats giants; she is locked up in a tower, a palace, a garden, a cave, chained to a rock, captive, put to sleep: she is waiting. *One day my prince will come . . . Some day he'll come along, the man I love* . . . the popular refrains breathe dreams of patience and hope in her. The supreme necessity for woman is to charm a masculine heart; this is the recompense all heroines aspire to, even if they are intrepid, adventuresome; and only their beauty is asked of them in most cases. It is thus understandable that attention to her physical appearance can become a real obsession for the little girl; princesses or shepherds, one must always be pretty to conquer love and happiness; ugliness is cruelly associated with meanness and when one sees the misfortunes that befall ugly girls, one does not know if it is their crimes or their disgrace that destiny punishes. Young beauties promised a glorious future often start out in the role of victim; the stories of Genevieve de Brabant or of Griselda are not as innocent as it would seem; love and suffering are intertwined in a troubling way; woman is assured of the most delicious triumphs when falling to the bottom of abjection; whether it be a question of God or a man, the little girl learns that by consenting to the most serious renunciations, she will become all-powerful: she takes pleasure in a masochism that promises her supreme conquests. St Blandine, white and bloody in the paws of lions, Snow White lying as if dead in a glass coffin, Sleeping Beauty, Atala fainting, a whole cohort of tender heroines beaten, passive, wounded, on their knees, humiliated, teach their younger sisters the fascinating prestige of martyred, abandoned and resigned beauty. It is not surprising that, while her brother plays at the hero, the little girl plays so easily at the martyr: the pagans throw her to the lions, Bluebeard drags her by her hair, the king, her husband, exiles her to the depth of the forests; she resigns herself, she suffers, she dies and her brow is haloed with glory. 'While still a little girl, I wanted to draw men's attention, trouble them, be saved by them, die in their arms,' Mme de Noailles writes. A remarkable example of these masochistic musings is found in *The Black Sail*[12] by Marie Le Hardouin.

At seven, from I don't know which rib, I made my first man. He was tall, thin, very young, dressed in a suit of black satin with long sleeves touching the ground. His beautiful blond hair cascaded in heavy curls onto his shoulders . . . I called him Edmond . . . Then a day came when I gave him two brothers . . . These three brothers, Edmond, Charles and Cedric, all three dressed in black satin, all three blond and slim, procured for me strange blessings. Their feet shod in silk were so beautiful and their hands so fragile that I felt all sorts of movements in my soul . . . I became their sister Marguerite . . . I loved to represent myself as subjected to the whims of my brothers and totally at their mercy. I dreamed that my oldest brother, Edmond, had the right of life and death over me. I never had permission to raise my eyes to his face. He had me whipped under the slightest pretext. When he addressed himself to me, I was so overwhelmed by fear and respect that I found nothing else to answer him and mumbled constantly, 'Yes, my lordship', 'No, my lordship' and I savoured the strange delight of feeling like an idiot . . . When the suffering he imposed on me was too great, I murmured, 'Thank you, my lordship,' and there came a moment when, almost faltering from suffering, I placed, so as not to shout, my lips on his hand, while, some movement finally breaking my heart, I reached one of these states in which one desires to die from too much happiness.

At an early age, the little girl already dreams she has reached the age of love; at nine or ten, she loves to make herself up, she pads her blouse, she disguises herself as a lady. She does not, however, look for any erotic experience with little boys: if she does go with them into the corner to play 'doctor', it is only out of sexual curiosity. But the partner of her amorous dreaming is an adult, either purely imaginary or based on real individuals: in the latter case, the child is satisfied to love him from afar. In Colette Audry's memoirs*[13] there is a very good example of a child's dreaming; she recounts that she discovered love at five years of age:

This naturally had nothing to do with the little sexual pleasures of childhood, the satisfaction I felt, for example, straddling a certain chair in the dining room or caressing myself before falling asleep . . .

*In the Eyes of Memory.

The only common characteristic between the feeling and the
pleasure is that I carefully hid them both from those around me . . .
My love for this young man consisted of thinking of him before
falling asleep and imagining marvellous stories . . . In Privas, I
was in love with all the department heads of my father's office . . .
I was never very deeply hurt by their departure, because they were
barely more than a pretext for my amorous musings . . . In the
evening in bed I got my revenge for too much youth and shyness.
I prepared everything very carefully, I did not have any trouble
making him present to me, but it was a question of transforming
myself, me, so that I could see myself from the interior because I
became her, and stopped being I. First, I was pretty and eighteen
years old. A tin of sweets helped me a lot: a long tin of rectangular
and flat sweets that depicted two girls surrounded by doves. I was
the dark, curly-headed one, dressed in a long muslin dress. A ten-year
absence had separated us. He returned scarcely aged and the sight
of this marvellous creature overwhelmed him. She seemed to barely
remember him, she was unaffected, indifferent and witty. I
composed truly brilliant conversations for this first meeting. They
were followed by misunderstandings, a whole difficult conquest,
cruel hours of discouragement and jealousy for him. Finally, pushed
to the limit, he admitted his love. She listened to him in silence and
just at the moment he thought all was lost, she told him she had
never stopped loving him and they embraced a little. The scene
normally took place on a park bench, in the evening. I saw the two
forms close together, I heard the murmur of voices, I felt at the
same time the warm body contact. But then everything came
loose . . . never did I broach marriage* . . . The next day I thought
of it a little while washing. I don't know why the soapy face I was
looking at in the mirror delighted me (the rest of the time I didn't
find myself beautiful) and filled me with hope. I would have considered for hours this misty, tilted face that seemed to be waiting for
me from afar on the road to the future. But I had to hurry; once
I dried my face, everything was over, and I got back my banal child's
face, which no longer interested me.

---

* Unlike Le Hardouin's masochistic imagination, Audry's is sadistic. She wants the
beloved to be wounded, in danger, for her to save him heroically, not without humiliating him. This is a personal note, characteristic of a woman who will never accept
passivity and will attempt to conquer her autonomy as a human being.

Games and dreams orient the girl towards passivity; but she is a human being before becoming a woman; and she already knows that accepting herself as woman means resigning and mutilating herself; while renunciation might be tempting, mutilation is abhorrent. Man and Love are still far away in the mist of the future; in the present, the little girl seeks activity, autonomy, like her brothers. The burden of freedom is not heavy for children because it does not involve responsibility; they know they are safe in the shelter of adults: they are not tempted to flee from themselves. The girl's spontaneous zest for life, her taste for games, laughter and adventure, make her consider the maternal circle narrow and stultifying. She wants to escape her mother's authority, an authority that is wielded in a more routine and intimate manner than the one that boys have to accept. Rare are the cases in which she is as understanding and discreet as in this Sido that Colette painted with love. Not to mention the almost pathological cases – there are many*[14] – where the mother is a kind of executioner, satisfying her domineering and sadistic instincts on the child; her daughter is the privileged object opposite whom she attempts to affirm herself as sovereign subject; this attempt makes the child balk in revolt. Colette Audry described this rebellion of a normal girl against a normal mother:

> I wouldn't have known how to answer the truth, however innocent it was, because I never felt innocent in front of Mama. She was the essential adult and I resented her for it as long as I was not yet cured. There was deep inside me a kind of tumultuous and fierce sore that I was sure of always finding raw . . . I didn't think she was too strict; nor that she hadn't the right. I thought: no, no, no with all my strength. I didn't even blame her for her authority or for her orders or arbitrary defences but for *wanting to subjugate me*. She said it sometimes: when she didn't say it, her eyes and voice did. Or else she told ladies that children are much more docile after a punishment. These words stuck in my throat, unforgettable: I couldn't vomit them; I couldn't swallow them. This anger was my guilt in front of her and also my shame in front of me (because in reality she frightened me, and all I had on my side in the form of retaliation were a few violent words or acts of insolence) but also my glory, nevertheless: as long as the sore was there, and living the silent madness that made me only repeat: 'subjugate, docile, punishment, humiliation', I wouldn't be subjugated.

* Cf. V. Leduc, *In the Prison of Her Skin*; S. de Tervagne, *Maternal Hatred*; H. Bazin, *Viper in the Fist*.

Rebellion is even more violent in the frequent cases when the mother has lost her prestige. She appears as the one who waits, endures, complains, cries and makes scenes: and in daily reality this thankless role does not lead to any apotheosis; victim, she is scorned; shrew, she is detested; her destiny appears to be the prototype of bland *repetition*: with her, life only repeats itself stupidly without going anywhere; blocked in her housewifely role, she stops the expansion of her existence, she is obstacle and negation. Her daughter wants *not* to take after her. She dedicates a cult to women who have escaped feminine servitude: actresses, writers and professors; she gives herself enthusiastically to sports and to studies, she climbs trees, tears her clothes, tries to compete with boys. Very often she has a best friend in whom she confides; it is an exclusive friendship like a love affair that usually includes sharing sexual secrets: the little girls exchange information they have succeeded in getting and talk about it. Often there is a triangle, one of the girls falling in love with her girlfriend's brother: thus Sonia in *War and Peace* is in love with her best friend Natasha's brother. In any case, this friendship is shrouded in mystery, and in general at this period the child loves to have secrets; she makes a secret of the most insignificant thing: thus does she react against the secrecies that thwart her curiosity; it is also a way of giving herself importance; she tries by all means to acquire it; she tries to be part of adults' lives, she makes up stories about them that she only half believes and in which she plays a major role. With her friends, she feigns returning boys' scorn with scorn; they form a closed group, they sneer and mock them. But in fact, she is flattered when they treat her as an equal; she seeks their approbation. She would like to belong to the privileged caste. The same movement that in primitive hordes subjects woman to male supremacy is manifested in each new 'arrival' by a refusal of her lot: in her, transcendence condemns the absurdity of immanence. She is annoyed at being oppressed by rules of decency, bothered by her clothes, enslaved to cleaning tasks, held back in all her enthusiasms; on this point there have been many studies that have almost all given the same result:* all the boys – like Plato in the past – say they would have hated to be girls; almost all the girls are sorry not to be boys. According to Havelock Ellis's statistics, one boy out of a hundred wanted to be a

---

* There is an exception, for example, in a Swiss school where boys and girls participating in the same coeducation, in privileged conditions of comfort and freedom, all declared themselves satisfied; but such circumstances are exceptional. Obviously, the girls *could be* as happy as the boys, but in present society the fact is that they are not.

girl; more than 75 per cent of the girls would have preferred to change sex. According to a study by Karl Pipal (cited by Baudouin in his work on *The Mind of the Child*),[15] out of twenty boys of twelve to fourteen years of age, eighteen said they would rather be anything in the whole world than a girl; out of twenty-two girls, ten wished to be boys and gave the following reasons: 'Boys are better: they do not have to suffer like women . . . My mother would love me more . . . A boy does more interesting work . . . A boy has more aptitude for school . . . I would have fun frightening girls . . . I would not fear boys any more . . . They are freer . . . Boys' games are more fun . . . They are not held back by their clothes.' This last observation is recurrent: almost all the girls complain of being bothered by their clothes, of not being free in their movements, of having to watch their skirts or light-coloured outfits that get dirty so easily. At about ten or twelve years of age, most little girls are really tomboys, that is, children who lack the licence to be boys. Not only do they suffer from it as a privation and an injustice but the regime they are condemned to is unhealthy. The exuberance of life is prohibited to them, their stunted vigour turns into nervousness; their goody-goody occupations do not exhaust their brimming energy; they are bored: out of boredom and to compensate for the inferiority from which they suffer, they indulge in morose and romantic daydreams; they begin to have a taste for these facile escapes and lose the sense of reality; they succumb to their emotions with a confused exaltation; since they cannot act, they talk, readily mixing up serious words with totally meaningless ones; abandoned, 'misunderstood', they go looking for consolation in narcissistic sentiments: they look on themselves as heroines in novels, admire themselves and complain; it is natural for them to become keen on their appearance and to playact: these defects will grow during puberty. Their malaise expresses itself in impatience, tantrums, tears; they indulge in tears – an indulgence many women keep later – largely because they love to play the victim: it is both a protest against the harshness of their destiny and a way of endearing themselves to others. 'Little girls love to cry so much that I have known them to cry in front of a mirror in order to double the pleasure,' says Monseigneur Dupanloup. Most of their dramas concern relations with their family; they try to break their bonds with their mothers: either they are hostile to them or they continue to feel a profound need for protection; they would like to monopolise their fathers' love for themselves; they are jealous, touchy, demanding. They often make up stories; they imagine they are adopted, that their parents are not really theirs; they attribute a secret life to them; they dream about their sexual relations; they love to imagine that their father is misunderstood, unhappy, that he is not finding in his wife the ideal companion that his daughter would be for him; or, on the contrary, that the mother rightly finds him rough and brutal, that she is appalled by any physical relations with him. Fantasies, acting out, childish tragedies, false enthusiasms, strange things: the reason must be sought not in a mysterious feminine soul but in the child's situation.

It is a strange experience for an individual recognising himself as subject, autonomy and transcendence, as an absolute, to discover inferiority – as a given essence – in his self: it is a strange experience for one who posits himself for himself as One to be revealed to himself as alterity. That is what happens to the little girl when, learning about the world, she grasps herself as a woman in it. The sphere she belongs to is closed everywhere, limited, dominated by the male universe: as high as she climbs, as far as she dares go, there will always be a ceiling over her head, walls that block her path. Man's gods are in such a faraway heaven that in truth, for him, there are no gods: the little girl lives among gods with a human face.

This is not a unique situation. American blacks, partially integrated into a civilisation that nevertheless considers them as an inferior caste, live it; what Bigger Thomas experiences with so much bitterness at the dawn of his life is this definitive inferiority, this cursed alterity inscribed in the colour of his skin: he watches planes pass and knows that because he is black the sky is out of bounds for him.* Because she is woman, the girl knows that the sea and the poles, a thousand adventures, a thousand joys, are forbidden to her: she is born on the wrong side. The great difference is that the blacks endure their lot in revolt – no privilege compensates for its severity – while for the woman her complicity is invited. Earlier I recalled that in addition to the authentic claim of the subject who claims sovereign freedom, there is an inauthentic desire for renunciation and escape in the existent;† these are the delights of passivity that parents and educators, books and myths, women and men dangle before the little girl's eyes; in early childhood she is already taught to taste them; temptation becomes more and more insidious; and she yields to it even more fatally as the thrust of her transcendence comes up against harsher and harsher resistance. But in accepting her passivity, she also accepts without resistance enduring a destiny that is going to be imposed on her

* Richard Wright, *Native Son*.
† See Vol. I, Introduction.

from the exterior, and this fatality frightens her. Whether ambitious, scatterbrained or shy, the young boy leaps towards an open future; he will be a sailor or an engineer, he will stay in the fields or will leave for the city, he will see the world, he will become rich; he feels free faced with a future where unexpected opportunities await him. The girl will be wife, mother, grandmother; she will take care of her house exactly as her mother does, she will take care of her children as she was taken care of: she is twelve years old and her story is already written in the heavens; she will discover it day after day without shaping it; she is curious but frightened when she thinks about this life whose every step is planned in advance and towards which each day irrevocably moves her.

This is why the little girl, even more so than her brothers, is preoccupied with sexual mysteries; of course boys are interested as well, just as passionately; but in their future, their role of husband and father is not what concerns them the most; marriage and motherhood put in question the little girl's whole destiny; and as soon as she begins to perceive their secrets, her body seems odiously threatened to her. The magic of motherhood has faded: whether she has been informed early or not, she knows, in a more or less coherent manner, that a baby does not appear by chance in the mother's belly and does not come out at the wave of a magic wand; she questions herself anxiously. Often it seems not extraordinary at all but rather horrible that a parasitic body should proliferate inside her body; the idea of this monstrous swelling frightens her. And how will the baby get out? Even if she was never told about the cries and suffering of childbirth, she has overheard things, she has read the words in the Bible: 'In sorrow thou shalt bring forth children'; she has the presentiment of tortures she cannot even imagine; she invents strange operations around her navel; she is no less reassured if she supposes that the foetus will be expelled by her anus: little girls have been seen to have nervous constipation attacks when they thought they had discovered the birthing process. Accurate explanations will not bring much relief: images of swelling, tearing and haemorrhaging will haunt her. The more imaginative she is, the more sensitive the little girl will be to these visions; but no girl could look at them without shuddering. Colette relates how her mother found her in a faint after reading Zola's description of a birth:

[The author depicted the birth] with a rough-and-ready, crude wealth of detail, an anatomical precision, and a lingering over colours, postures and cries, in which I recognised none of the tranquil, knowing experience on which I as a country girl could draw. I felt credulous, startled and vulnerable in my nascent femininity . . . Other words, right in front of my eyes, depicted flesh splitting open, excrement and sullied blood . . . The lawn rose to welcome me . . . like one of those little hares that poachers sometimes brought, freshly killed, into the kitchen.[16]

The reassurance offered by grown-ups leaves the child worried; growing up she learns not to trust the word of adults; often it is on the very mysteries of her conception that she has caught them in lies; and she also knows that they consider the most frightening things normal; if she has ever experienced a violent physical shock – tonsils removed, tooth pulled, whitlow lanced – she will project the remembered anxiety onto childbirth.

The physical nature of pregnancy and childbirth suggests as well that 'something physical' takes place between the spouses. The often-encountered word 'blood' in expressions like 'same-blood children', 'pure blood', 'mixed blood' sometimes orients the childish imagination; it is supposed that marriage is accompanied by some solemn transfusion. But more often the 'physical thing' seems to be linked to the urinary and excremental systems; in particular, children think that the man urinates into the woman. This sexual operation is thought of as *dirty*. This is what overwhelms the child for whom 'dirty' things have been rife with the strictest taboos: how then can it be that they are integrated into adults' lives? The child is first of all protected from scandal by the very absurdity he discovers: he finds there is no sense to what he hears around him, what he reads, what he writes; everything seems unreal to him. In Carson McCullers's charming book *The Member of the Wedding,* the young heroine surprises two neighbours in bed nude; the very anomaly of the story keeps her from giving it too much importance.

It was a summer Sunday and the hall door of the Marlowes' room was open. She could see only a portion of the room, part of the dresser and only the footpiece of the bed with Mrs Marlowe's corset on it. But there was a sound in the quiet room she could not place, and when she stepped over the threshold she was startled by a sight that, after a single glance, sent her running to the kitchen, crying: Mr Marlowe is having a fit! Berenice had hurried through the hall, but when she looked into the front room, she merely bunched her lips and banged the door . . . Frankie had tried to question Berenice and find out what was the matter. But Berenice had only said that they were common people and added that with a certain party in the house they ought at least to know enough to shut a door. Though Frankie knew she was the certain party, still she did not understand. What kind of a fit was it? she asked. But Berenice would only answer: Baby, just a common fit. And Frankie knew from the voice's tones that there was more to it than she was told. Later she only remembered the Marlowes as common people . . .[17]

When children are warned against strangers, when a sexual incident is described to them, it is often explained in terms of sickness, maniacs or madmen; it is a convenient explanation; the little girl fondled by her neighbour at the cinema or the girl who sees a man expose himself thinks that she is dealing with a crazy man; of course, encountering madness is unpleasant: an epileptic attack, hysteria or a violent quarrel upsets the adult world order, and the child who witnesses it feels in danger; but after all, just as there are homeless, beggars and injured people with hideous sores in harmonious society, there can also be some abnormal ones without its base disintegrating. It is when parents, friends and teachers are suspected of celebrating black masses that the child really becomes afraid.

When I was first told about sexual relations between man and woman, I declared that such things were impossible since my parents would have had to do likewise, and I thought too highly of them to believe it. I said that it was much too disgusting for me ever to do it. Unfortunately I was to be disabused shortly after when I heard what my parents were doing . . . that was a fearful moment; I hid my face under the bedcovers, stopped my ears and wished I were a thousand miles from there.*[18]

How to go from the image of dressed and dignified people, these people who teach decency, reserve and reason, to that of naked beasts confronting each other? Here is a contradiction that shakes their pedestal, darkens the sky. Often the child stubbornly refuses the odious revelation: 'My parents don't do that,' he declares. Or he tries to give coitus a decent image: 'When you want a child,' said a little girl, 'you go to the doctor; you undress, you cover your eyes, because you mustn't watch; the doctor ties the parents together and helps them so that it works right'; she had changed the act of love into a surgical operation, rather unpleasant at that, but as

* Cited by Dr W. Liepmann, *Youth and Sexuality*.

honourable as going to the dentist. But despite denial and escape, embarrassment and doubt creep into the child's heart; a phenomenon as painful as weaning occurs: it is no longer separating the child from the maternal flesh, but the protective universe that surrounds him falls apart; he finds himself without a roof over his head, abandoned, absolutely alone before a future as dark as night. What adds to the little girl's anxiety is that she cannot discern the exact shape of the equivocal curse that weighs on her. The information she gets is inconsistent, books are contradictory; even technical explanations do not dissipate the heavy shadow; a hundred questions arise: is the sexual act painful? Or delicious? How long does it last? Five minutes or all night? Sometimes you read that a woman became a mother with one embrace, and sometimes you remain sterile after hours of sexual activity. Do people 'do that' every day? Or rarely? The child tries to learn more by reading the Bible, consulting dictionaries, asking friends, and he gropes in darkness and disgust. An interesting document on this point is the study made by Dr Liepmann; here are a few responses given to him by young girls about their sexual initiation:

> I continued to stray among my nebulous and twisted ideas. No one broached the subject, neither my mother nor my schoolteacher; no book treated the subject fully. Little by little a sort of perilous and ugly mystery was woven around the act, which at first had seemed so natural to me. The older girls of twelve used crude jokes to bridge the gap between themselves and our classmates. All that was still so vague and disgusting; we argued about where the baby was formed, if perhaps the thing only took place once for the man since marriage was the occasion for so much fuss. My period at fifteen was another new surprise. It was my turn to be caught up, in a way, in the round.

> Sexual initiation! An expression never to be mentioned in our parents' house! . . . I searched in books, but I agonised and wore myself out looking for the road to follow . . . I went to a boys' school: for my schoolteacher the question did not even seem to exist . . . Horlam's work, *Little Boy and Little Girl*,[19] finally brought me the truth. My tense state and unbearable overexcitement disappeared, although I was very unhappy and took a long time to recognise and understand that eroticism and sexuality alone constitute real love.

> Stages of my initiation: (1) First questions and a few vague notions (totally unsatisfactory). From three and a half to eleven years old . . .

No answers to the questions I had in the following years. When I was seven, right there feeding my rabbit, I suddenly saw little naked ones underneath her . . . My mother told me that in animals and people little ones grow in their mother's belly and come out through the loins. This birth through the loins seemed unreasonable to me . . . a nursemaid told me about pregnancy, birth and menstruation . . . Finally, my father replied to my last question about his true function with obscure stories about pollen and pistil. (2) Some attempts at personal experimentation (eleven to thirteen years old). I dug out an encyclopaedia and a medical book . . . It was only theoretical information in strange gigantic words. (3) Testing of acquired knowledge (thirteen to twenty): *(a)* in daily life, *(b)* in scientific works.

At eight, I often played with a boy my age. One day we broached the subject. I already knew, because my mother had already told me, that a woman has many eggs inside her . . . and that a child was born from one of these eggs whenever the mother strongly desired it . . . Giving this same answer to my friend, I received this reply: 'You are completely stupid! When our butcher and his wife want a baby, they go to bed and do dirty things.' I was indignant . . . We had then (around twelve and a half) a maid who told me all sorts of scandalous tales. I never said a word to Mama, as I was ashamed; but I asked her if sitting on a man's knees could give you a baby. She explained everything as best she could.

At school I learned where babies emerged, and I had the feeling that it was something horrible. But how did they come into the world? We both formed a rather monstrous idea about the thing, especially since one winter morning on the way to school together in the darkness we met a certain man who showed us his sexual parts and asked us, 'Don't they seem good enough to eat?' Our disgust was inconceivable and we were literally nauseated. Until I was twenty-one, I thought babies were born through the navel.

A little girl took me aside and asked me: 'Do you know where babies come from?' Finally she decided to speak out: 'Goodness! How foolish you are! Kids come out of women's stomachs, and for them to be born, women have to do completely disgusting things with men!' Then she went into details about how disgusting. But I had become totally transformed, absolutely unable to believe that

such things could be possible. We slept in the same room as our
parents . . . One night later I heard take place what I had thought
was impossible, and, yes, I was ashamed, I was ashamed of my
parents. All of this made of me another being. I went through
horrible moral suffering. I considered myself a deeply depraved
creature because I was now aware of these things.

It should be said that even coherent instruction would not resolve the
problem; in spite of the best will of parents and teachers, the sexual experience could not be put into words and concepts; it could only be understood by living it; all analysis, however serious, will have a comic side and
will fail to deliver the truth. When, from the poetic loves of flowers to
the nuptials of fish, by way of the chick, the cat or the kid, one reaches
the human species, the mystery of conception can be theoretically eluci-
dated: that of voluptuousness and sexual love remains total. How would
one explain the pleasure of a caress or a kiss to a dispassionate child?
Kisses are given and received in a family way, sometimes even on the lips:
why do these mucus exchanges in certain encounters provoke dizziness?
It is like describing colours to the blind. As long as there is no intuition
of the excitement and desire that give the sexual function its meaning
and unity, the different elements seem shocking and monstrous. In particular, the little girl is revolted when she understands that she is virgin and
sealed, and that to change into a woman a man's sex must penetrate her.
Since exhibitionism is a widespread perversion, many little girls have seen
the penis in an erection; in any case, they have observed the sexual organs
of animals, and it is unfortunate that the horse's so often draws their
attention; one imagines that they would be frightened by it. Fear of childbirth, fear of the male sex organ, fear of the 'crises' that threaten married
couples, disgust for dirty practices, derision for actions devoid of signification, all of this often leads a young girl to declare: 'I will never marry.'*

---

* 'Filled with repugnance, I implored God to grant me a religious vocation that would
allow me to escape the laws of maternity. And after having long reflected on the repugnant mysteries that I hid in spite of myself, reinforced by such repulsion as by a divine
sign, I concluded: chastity is certainly my vocation,' writes Yassu Gauclère in *The Blue
Orange*. Among others, the idea of perforation horrified her. 'Here, then, is what makes
the wedding night so terrible! This discovery overwhelmed me, adding the physical terror
of this operation that I imagined to be extremely painful to the disgust I previously felt.
My terror would have been all the worse if I had supposed that birth came about through
the same channel; but having known for a long time that children were born from their
mother's belly, I believed that they were detached by segmentation.'

Therein lies the surest defence against pain, folly and obscenity. It is useless to try to explain that when the day comes, neither deflowering nor childbirth would seem so terrible, that millions of women resign themselves to it and are none the worse for it. When a child fears an outside occurrence, he is relieved of the fear, but not by predicting that, later, he will accept it naturally: it is himself he fears meeting in the far-off future, alienated and lost. The metamorphosis of the caterpillar, through chrysalis and into butterfly, brings about a deep uneasiness: is it still the same caterpillar after this long sleep? Does she recognise herself beneath these brilliant wings? I knew little girls who were plunged into an alarming reverie at the sight of a chrysalis.

And yet the metamorphosis takes place. The little girl herself does not understand the meaning, but she realises that in her relations with the world and her own body something is changing subtly: she is sensitive to contacts, tastes and odours that previously left her indifferent; baroque images pass through her head; she barely recognises herself in mirrors; she feels 'funny', things seem 'funny'; such is the case of little Emily described by Richard Hughes in *A High Wind in Jamaica*:[20]

> Emily, for coolness, sat up to her chin in water and hundreds of infant fish were tickling with their inquisitive mouths every inch of her body, a sort of expressionless light kissing. Anyhow she had lately come to hate being touched – but this was abominable. At last, when she could stand it no longer, she clambered out and dressed.

Even Margaret Kennedy's serene Tessa feels this strange disturbance:

> Suddenly she had become intensely miserable. She stared down into the darkness of the hall, cut in two by the moonlight which streamed in through the open door. She could not bear it. She jumped up with a little cry of exasperation. 'Oh!' she exclaimed. 'How I hate it all!' . . . She ran out to hide herself in the mountains, frightened and furious, pursued by a desolate foreboding which seemed to fill the quiet house. As she stumbled up towards the pass she kept murmuring to herself: 'I wish I could die! I wish I were dead!'
>
> She knew that she did not mean this; she was not in the least anxious to die. But the violence of such a statement seemed to satisfy her . . .[21]

This disturbing moment is described at length in Carson McCullers's previously mentioned book, *The Member of the Wedding*.

This was the summer when Frankie was sick and tired of being Frankie. She hated herself, and had become a loafer and a big no-good who hung around the summer kitchen: dirty and greedy and mean and sad. Besides being too mean to live, she was criminal . . . Then the spring of that year had been a long queer season. Things began to change . . . There was something about the green trees and the flowers of April that made Frankie sad. She did not know why she was sad, but because of this peculiar sadness, she began to realise that she ought to leave the town . . . She ought to leave the town and go to some place far away. For the late spring, that year, was lazy and too sweet. The long afternoons flowered and lasted and the green sweetness sickened her . . . Many things made Frankie suddenly wish to cry. Very early in the morning she would sometimes go out into the yard and stand for a long time looking at the sunrise sky. And it was as though a question came into her heart, and the sky did not answer. Things she had never noticed much before began to hurt her: home lights watched from the evening sidewalks, an unknown voice from an alley. She would stare at the lights and listen to the voice, and something inside her stiffened and waited. But the lights would darken, the voice fall silent, and though she waited, that was all. She was afraid of these things that made her suddenly wonder who she was, and what she was going to be in the world, and why she was standing at that minute, seeing a light, or listening, or staring up into the sky: alone. She was afraid, and there was a queer tightness in her chest . . .

  She went around town, and the things she saw and heard seemed to be left somehow unfinished, and there was the tightness in her that would not break. She would hurry to do something, but what she did was always wrong . . . After the long twilights of this season, when Frankie had walked around the sidewalks of the town, a jazz sadness quivered her nerves and her heart stiffened and almost stopped.

What is happening in this troubled period is that the child's body is becoming a woman's body and being made flesh. Except in the case of glandular deficiency where the subject remains fixed in the infantile stage, the puberty crisis begins around the age of twelve or thirteen.* This crisis begins much earlier for girls than for boys and it brings about far greater changes. The little girl approaches it with worry and displeasure. As her breasts and body hair develop, a feeling is born that sometimes changes into pride, but begins as shame; suddenly the child displays modesty, she refuses to show herself nude, even to her sisters or her mother, she inspects herself with surprise mixed with horror and she observes with anxiety the swelling of this hard core, somewhat painful, appearing under nipples that until recently were as inoffensive as a navel. She is worried to discover a vulnerable spot in herself: undoubtedly this pain is slight compared to a burn or a toothache; but in an accident or illness, pain was always abnormal, while the youthful breast is normally the centre of who knows what indefinable resentment. Something is happening, something that is not an illness, but that involves the very law of existence and is yet struggle and suffering. Of course, from birth to puberty the little girl grew up, but she never felt growth; day after day, her body was present like an exact finished thing; now she is 'developing': the very word horrifies her; vital phenomena are only reassuring when they have found a balance and taken on the stable aspect of a fresh flower, a lustrous animal; but in the blossoming of her breasts, the little girl feels the ambiguity of the word 'living'. She is neither gold nor diamond, but a strange matter, moving and uncertain, inside of which impure chemistries develop. She is used to a free-flowing head of hair that falls like a silken skein; but this new growth under her arms, beneath her belly, metamorphoses her into an animal or alga. Whether she is more or less prepared for it, she foresees in these changes a finality that rips her from her self; thus hurled into a vital cycle that goes beyond the moment of her own existence, she senses a dependence that dooms her to man, child and tomb. In themselves, her breasts seem to be a useless and indiscreet proliferation. Arms, legs, skin, muscles, and even the round buttocks she sits on, all have had until now a clear usefulness; only the sex organ defined as urinary was a bit dubious, though secret and invisible to others. Her breasts show through her sweater or blouse, and this body that the little girl identified with self appears to her as flesh; it is an object that others look at and see. 'For two years I wore capes to hide my chest, I was so ashamed of it,' a woman told me. And another: 'I still remember the strange confusion I felt when a friend of my age, but more developed than I was, stooped to pick up a ball, I noticed by the

---

* These purely physiological processes have already been described in Vol. I, Chapter 1. [In Part One, 'Destiny'.]

opening in her blouse two already heavy breasts: this body so similar to mine, on which my body would be modelled, made me blush for myself.' 'At thirteen, I walked around bare-legged, in a short dress,' another woman told me. 'A man, sniggering, made a comment about my fat calves. The next day, my mother made me wear stockings and lengthen my skirt, but I will never forget the shock I suddenly felt in seeing myself *seen*.' The little girl feels that her body is escaping her, that it is no longer the clear expression of her individuality; it becomes foreign to her; and at the same moment, she is grasped by others as a thing: on the street, eyes follow her, her body is subject to comments; she would like to become invisible; she is afraid of becoming flesh and afraid to show her flesh.

This disgust is expressed in many young girls by the desire to lose weight: they do not want to eat any more; if they are forced, they vomit; they watch their weight incessantly. Others become pathologically shy; entering a room or going out on the street becomes a torture. From these experiences, psychoses sometimes develop. A typical example is Nadia, the patient from *Obsessions and Psychasthenia* (*Les obsessions et la psychasthénie*), described by Pierre Janet[22]:

> Nadia, a girl from a wealthy and remarkably intelligent family, was stylish, artistic, and above all an excellent musician; but from infancy she was obstinate and irritable . . . 'She demanded excessive affection from everyone, her parents, sisters and servants, but she was so demanding and dominating that she soon alienated people; horribly susceptible, when her cousins used mockery to try to change her character, she acquired a sense of shame fixed on her body.' Then, too, her need for affection made her wish to remain a child, to remain a little girl to be petted, one whose every whim is indulged, and in short made her fear growing up . . . A precocious puberty worsened her troubles, mixing fears of modesty with fears of growing up: 'Since men like plump women, I want to remain extremely thin.' Pubic hair and growing breasts added to her fears. From the age of eleven, as she wore short skirts, it seemed to her that everyone eyed her; she was given long skirts and was then ashamed of her feet, her hips, etc. The appearance of menstruation drove her half mad; believing that she was the only one in the world having the monstrosity of pubic hair, she laboured up to the age of twenty 'to rid herself of this savage decoration by depilation'. The development of breasts exacerbated these obsessions because she had always had a horror of obesity; she did not detest

it in others; but for herself she considered it a defect. 'I don't care about being pretty, but I would be too *ashamed* if I became bloated, that would horrify me; if by bad luck I became fat, I wouldn't dare let anyone see me.' So she tried every means, all kinds of prayers and conjurations, to prevent normal growth: she swore to repeat prayers five or ten times, to hop five times on one foot. 'If I touch one piano note four times in the same piece, I accept growing and not being loved by anyone.' Finally she decided not to eat. 'I did not want to get fat, nor to grow up, nor resemble a woman because I always wanted to remain a little girl.' She solemnly promised to accept no food at all; when she yielded to her mother's pleas to take some food and broke her vow, she knelt for hours writing out vows and tearing them up. Her mother died when she was eighteen, and she then imposed a strict regime on herself: two clear bouillon soups, an egg yolk, a spoonful of vinegar, a cup of tea with the juice of a whole lemon, was all she would take in a day. Hunger devoured her. 'Sometimes I spent hours thinking of food, I was so hungry: I swallowed my saliva, gnawed on my handkerchief and rolled on the floor from wanting to eat.' But she resisted temptations. She was pretty, but believed that her face was puffy and covered with pimples; if her doctor stated that he did not see them, she said he didn't understand anything, that he couldn't see the pimples between the skin and the flesh. She left her family in the end and hid in a small apartment, seeing only a guardian and the doctor; she never went out; she accepted her father's visit, but only with difficulty; he brought about a serious relapse by telling her that she looked well; she dreaded having a fat face, healthy complexion, big muscles. She lived most of the time in darkness, so intolerable it was for her to be seen or even *visible*.

Very often the parents' attitude contributes to inculcating shame in the little girl for her physical appearance. A woman's testimony:*

I suffered from a very keen sense of physical inferiority, which was accentuated by continual nagging at home . . . Mother, in her excessive pride, wanted me to appear at my best, and she always found many faults which required 'covering up' to point out to the dressmaker; for instance, drooping shoulders! Heavy hips! Too flat in

* Wilhelm Stekel, *Frigidity in Woman*.

the back! Bust too prominent! Having had a swollen neck for years, it was not possible for me to have an open neck. And so on. I was particularly worried on account of the appearance of my feet . . . and I was nagged on account of my gait . . . There was some truth in every criticism . . . but sometimes I was so embarrassed, particularly during my 'backfisch' stage, that at times I was at a loss to know how to move about. If I met someone, my first thought was: 'If I could only hide my feet!'

This shame makes the girl act awkwardly, blush at the drop of a hat; this blushing increases her timidity and itself becomes the object of a phobia. Stekel recounts among others a woman who 'as a young girl blushed so pathologically and violently that for a year she wore bandages around her face with the excuse of toothaches'.*

Sometimes, in prepuberty preceding the arrival of her period, the girl does not yet feel disgust for her body; she is proud of becoming a woman, she eagerly awaits her maturing breasts, she pads her blouse with handkerchiefs and brags around her older sisters; she does not yet grasp the meaning of the phenomena taking place in her. Her first period exposes this meaning and feelings of shame appear. If they existed already, they are confirmed and magnified from this moment on. All the accounts agree: whether or not the child has been warned, the event always appears repugnant and humiliating. The mother very often neglected to warn her; it has been noted[†] that mothers explain the mysteries of pregnancy, childbirth and even sexual relations to their daughters more easily than that of menstruation; they themselves hate this feminine servitude, a hatred that reflects men's old mystical terrors and one that they transmit to their offspring. When the girl finds suspicious stains on her underwear, she thinks she has diarrhoea, a fatal haemorrhage, a venereal disease. According to a survey that Havelock Ellis cited in 1896, out of 125 American high school students 36 at the time of their first period knew absolutely nothing on the question, 39 had vague ideas; that is, more than half of the girls were unaware. And according to Helene Deutsch, things had not changed much by 1946. Ellis cites the case of a young girl who threw herself into the Seine in Saint-Ouen because she thought she had an 'unknown disease'. Stekel, in *Letters to a Mother*,[23]

---

* Ibid.
† Cf. the works of Daly and Chadwick, cited by H. Deutsch, in *The Psychology of Women*, 1946.

tells the story of a little girl who tried to commit suicide, seeing in the menstrual flow the sign of and punishment for the impurities that sullied her soul. It is natural for the young girl to be afraid: it seems to her that her life is seeping out of her. According to Klein and the English psycho-analytic school, blood is for the young girl the manifestation of a wound of the internal organs. Even if cautious advice saves her from excessive anxiety, she is ashamed, she feels dirty: she rushes to the sink, she tries to wash or hide her dirtied underwear. There is a typical account of the experience in Colette Audry's book, *In the Eyes of Memory*:[24]

At the heart of this exaltation, the brutal and finished drama. One evening while getting undressed, I thought I was sick; it did not frighten me and I kept myself from saying anything in the hope that it would disappear the next day . . . Four weeks later, the illness occurred again, but more violently. I was quietly going to throw my knickers into the hamper behind the bathroom door. It was so hot that the diamond-shaped tiles of the hallway were warm under my naked feet. When I then got into bed, Mamma opened my bedroom door: she came to explain things to me. I am unable to remember the effect her words had on me at that time but while she was whispering, Kaki poked her head in. The sight of this round and curious face drove me crazy. I screamed at her to get out of there and she disappeared in fright. I begged Mama to go and beat her because she hadn't knocked before entering. My mother's calmness, her knowing and quietly happy air, were all it took to make me lose my head. When she left, I dug myself in for a stormy night.

Two memories all of a sudden come back: a few months earlier, coming back from a walk with Kaki, Mama and I had met the old doctor from Privas, built like a logger with a full white beard. 'Your daughter is growing up, madam,' he said while looking at me; and I hated him right then and there without understanding anything. A little later, coming back from Paris, Mama put away some new little towels in the chest of drawers. 'What is that?' Kaki asked. Mamma had this natural air of adults who reveal one part of the truth while omitting the other three: 'It's for Colette soon.' Speechless, unable to utter one question, I hated my mother.

That whole night I tossed and turned in my bed. It was not possible. I was going to wake up. Mama was mistaken, it would go away and not come back again . . . The next day, secretly changed and stained, I had to confront the others. I looked at my sister with hatred because she did not yet know, because all of a sudden she found herself, unknown to her, endowed with an overwhelming superiority over me. Then I began to hate men, who would never experience this, and who knew. And then I also hated women who accepted it so calmly. I was sure that if they had been warned of what was happening to me, they would all be overjoyed. 'So it's your turn now,' they would have thought. That one too, I said to myself when I saw one. And this one too. I was had by the world. I had trouble walking and didn't dare run. The earth, the sun-hot greenery, even the food, seemed to give off a suspicious smell . . . The crisis passed and I began to hope against hope that it would not come back again. One month later, I had to face the facts and accept the evil definitively, in a heavy stupor this time. There was now in my memory a 'before'. All the rest of my existence would no longer be anything but an 'after'.

Things happen in a similar way for most little girls. Many of them are horrified at the idea of sharing their secret with those around them. A friend told me that, motherless, she lived between her father and a primary school teacher and spent three months in fear and shame, hiding her stained underwear before it was discovered that she had begun menstruating. Even peasant women who might be expected to be hardened by their knowledge of the harshest sides of animal life are horrified by this malediction, which in the countryside is still taboo: I knew a young woman farmer who washed her underwear in secret in the frozen brook, putting her soaking garment directly back on her naked skin to hide her unspeakable secret. I could cite a hundred similar facts. Even admitting this astonishing misfortune offers no relief. Undoubtedly, the mother who slapped her daughter brutally, saying: 'Stupid! You're much too young,' is exceptional. But this is not only about being in a bad mood; most mothers fail to give the child the necessary explanations and so she is full of anxiety before this new state brought about by the first menstruation crisis: she wonders if the future does not hold other painful surprises for her; or else she imagines that from now on she could become pregnant by the simple presence or contact with a man, and she feels real terror of males. Even if she is spared these anxieties by intelligent explanations, she is not so easily granted peace of mind. Prior to this, the girl could, with a little bad faith, still think herself an asexual being, she could just not think herself; she even dreams of waking up one morning changed into a man; these days, mothers and aunts flatter and whisper to each other: 'She's a big girl now'; the brotherhood of matrons has won: she belongs to them. Here she takes her place on the women's side without recourse. Sometimes, she is proud of it; she thinks she has now become an adult and an upheaval will occur in her existence. As Thyde Monnier recounts:[25]

> Some of us had become 'big girls' during vacation; others would while at school, and then, one after the other in the toilets in the courtyard, where they were sitting on their 'thrones' like queens receiving their subjects, we would go and 'see the blood'.*

But the girl is soon disappointed because she sees that she has not gained any privilege and that life follows its normal course. The only novelty is the disgusting event repeated monthly; there are children that cry for hours when they learn they are condemned to this destiny; what adds to their revolt is that this shameful defect is known by men as well: what they would like is that the humiliating feminine condition at least be shrouded in mystery for them. But no, father, brothers, cousins, men know and even joke about it sometimes. This is when the shame of her too carnal body is born or exacerbated. And once the first surprise has passed, the monthly unpleasantness does not fade away at all: each time, the girl finds the same disgust when faced by this unappetising and stagnant odour that comes from herself – a smell of swamps and wilted violets – this less red and more suspicious blood than that flowing from children's cuts and scratches. Day and night she has to think of changing her protection, watching her underwear, her sheets, and solving a thousand little practical and repugnant problems; in thrifty families sanitary napkins are washed each month and take their place among the piles of handkerchiefs; this waste coming out of oneself has to be delivered to those handling the laundry: the laundress, servant, mother or older sister. The types of bandages pharmacies sell in boxes named after flowers, Camellia or Edelweiss, are thrown out after use; but while travelling, on vacation or on a trip it is not so easy to get rid of them, the toilet bowl being specifically prohibited. The young heroine of the *Psychoanalytical Journal*† described her horror of the sanitary napkin; she did not even consent to undress in front of

* Me.
† Translated by Clara Malraux.

her sister except in the dark during these times. This bothersome, annoying object can come loose during violent exercise; it is a worse humiliation than losing one's knickers in the middle of the street: this horrid possibility sometimes brings about fits of psychasthenia. By a kind of ill will of nature, indisposition and pain often do not begin until the initial bleeding – often hardly noticed – has passed; young girls are often irregular: they might be surprised during a walk, in the street, at friends'; they risk – like Mme de Chevreuse* – dirtying their clothes or their seat; such a possibility makes one live in constant anxiety. The greater the young girl's feeling of revulsion towards this feminine defect, the greater her obligation to pay careful attention to it so as not to expose herself to the awful humiliation of an accident or a little word of warning.

Here is the series of answers that Dr Liepmann obtained during his study of juvenile sexuality:†

At sixteen years of age, when I was indisposed for the first time, I was very frightened in seeing it one morning. In truth, I knew it was going to happen, but I was so ashamed of it that I remained in bed for a whole half day and had one answer to all questions: I cannot get up.

I was speechless in astonishment when, not yet twelve, I was indisposed for the first time. I was struck by horror, and as my mother limited herself to telling me drily that this would happen every month, I considered it as something disgusting and refused to accept that this did not also happen to men.

This adventure made my mother decide to initiate me, without forgetting menstruation at the same time. I then had my second disappointment because as soon as I was indisposed, I ran joyfully to my mother, who was still sleeping, and I woke her up, shouting, 'Mother, I have it!' 'And that is why you woke me up?' she managed to say in response. In spite of everything, I considered this thing as a real upheaval in my existence.

---

* Disguised as a man during the Fronde, Mme de Chevreuse, after a long excursion on horseback, was unmasked because of bloodstains seen on the saddle.
† Dr W. Liepmann, *Youth and Sexuality*.

And so I felt the most intense horror when I was indisposed for the first time seeing that the bleeding did not stop after a few minutes. Nevertheless, I did not whisper a word to anyone, not to my mother either. I had just reached the age of fifteen. In addition I suffered very little. Only one time was I taken with such terrifying pain that I fainted and stayed on the floor in my room for almost three hours. But I still did not say anything to anyone.

When for the first time this indisposition occurred, I was about thirteen. My school friends and I had already talked about it and I was proud to finally become one of the big girls. With great importance I explained to the gym teacher that it was impossible today for me to take part in the lesson because I was indisposed.

It was not my mother who initiated me. It was not until the age of nineteen that she had her period, and for fear of being scolded for dirtying her underwear, she buried it in a field.

I reached the age of eighteen and I then had my period for the first time.* I was totally unprepared for what was happening . . . At night, I had violent bleeding accompanied by heavy diarrhoea and I could not rest for one second. In the morning, my heart racing, I ran to my mother and weeping constantly asked her advice. But I only obtained this harsh reprimand: 'You should have been aware of it sooner and not have dirtied the sheets and bed.' That was all as far as explanation was concerned. Naturally, I tried very hard to know what crime I might have committed, and I suffered terrible anguish.

I already knew what it was. I was waiting for it impatiently because I was hoping my mother would reveal to me how children were made. The celebrated day arrived, but my mother remained silent. Nevertheless, I was joyous. 'From now on,' I said to myself, 'you can make children: you are a lady.'

This crisis takes place at a still tender age; the boy only reaches adolescence at about fifteen or sixteen; the girl changes into a woman at thirteen or fourteen. But the essential difference in their experience does not stem from there; nor does it lie in the physiological manifestations

* She was a girl from a very poor Berlin family.

that give it its awful shock in the case of the girl: puberty has a radically different meaning for the two sexes because it does not announce
the same future to them.

Granted, boys too at puberty feel their body as an embarrassing presence, but because they have been proud of their virility from childhood,
it is towards that virility that they proudly transcend the moment of
their development; they proudly exhibit the hair growing between their
legs and that makes men of them; more than ever, their sex is an object
of comparison and challenge. Becoming adults is an intimidating metamorphosis: many adolescents react with anxiety to a demanding freedom;
but they accede to the dignified status of male with joy. On the contrary,
to become a grown-up, the girl must confine herself within the limits
that her femininity imposes on her. The boy admires undefined promises in the growing hair: she remains confused before the 'brutal and
finished drama' that limits her destiny. Just as the penis gets its privileged value from the social context, the social context makes menstruation a malediction. One symbolises virility and the other femininity: it
is because femininity means alterity and inferiority that its revelation is
met with shame. The girl's life has always appeared to her to be determined by this impalpable essence to which the absence of the penis has
not managed to give a positive image: it is this essence that is revealed
in the red flow that escapes from between her thighs. If she has already
assumed her condition, she welcomes the event with joy: 'Now you are
a lady.' If she has always refused it, the bloody verdict strikes her like
lightning; most often, she hesitates: the menstrual stain inclines her
towards disgust and fear. 'So this is what these words mean: being a
woman!' The fate that until now has weighed on her ambivalently and
from the outside is lodged in her belly; there is no escape; she feels
trapped. In a sexually egalitarian society, she would envisage menstruation only as her unique way of acceding to an adult life; the human
body has many other more repugnant servitudes in men and women:
they make the best of them because as they are common to all they do
not represent a flaw for anyone; menstrual periods inspire horror in
adolescent girls because they thrust them into an inferior and damaged
category. This feeling of degradation will weigh on her heavily. She would
retain the pride of her bleeding body if she did not lose her self-respect
as a human being. And if she succeeds in preserving her self-respect, she
will feel the humiliation of her flesh much less vividly: the girl who
opens paths of transcendence in sports, social, intellectual and mystical
activities will not see a mutilation in her specificity, and she will over-

come it easily. If the young girl often develops psychoses in this period, it is because she feels defenceless in front of a deaf fate that condemns her to unimaginable trials; her femininity signifies illness, suffering and death in her eyes and she is transfixed by this destiny.

One example that vividly illustrates these anxieties is that of the patient called Molly described by Helene Deutsch.

Molly was fourteen when she began to suffer from psychic disorders; she was the fourth child in a family of five siblings. Her father is described as extremely strict and narrow-minded. He criticised the appearance and behaviour of his children at every meal. The mother was worried and unhappy; and every so often the parents were not on speaking terms; one brother ran away from home. The patient was a gifted youngster, a good tap dancer; but she was shy, took the family troubles seriously, and was afraid of boys. Her older sister got married against her mother's wishes and Molly was very interested in her pregnancy: she had a difficult delivery and forceps were necessary and she heard that women often die in childbirth. She took care of the baby for two months; when the sister left the house, there was a terrible scene and the mother fainted. Molly fainted too. She had seen classmates faint in class and her thoughts were much concerned with death and fainting. When she got her period, she told her mother with an embarrassed air: 'That thing is here.' She went with her sister to buy some menstrual pads; on meeting a man in the street, she hung her head. In general she acted 'disgusted with herself'. She never had pain during her periods, but tried to hide them from her mother, even when the latter saw stains on the sheets. She told her sister: 'Anything might happen to me now. I might have a baby.' When told, 'You have to live with a man for that to happen', she replied: 'Well, I am living with two men – my father and your husband.'

The father did not permit his daughters to go out . . . because one heard stories of rape: these fears helped to give Molly the idea of men being redoubtable creatures. From her first menstruation her anxiety about becoming pregnant and dying in childbirth became so severe that after a time she refused to leave her room, and now she sometimes stays in bed all day; if she has to go out of the house, she has an attack and faints. She is afraid of cars and taxis and she cannot sleep, she fears that someone is trying to enter the house at night, she screams and cries. She has eating spells; sometimes she eats too much to keep herself from fainting; she is also afraid when she feels closed in. She cannot go to school any more or lead a normal life.

A similar story not linked to the crisis of menstruation but which shows the girl's anxiety about her insides is Nancy's.*

Toward the age of thirteen the little girl was on intimate terms with her older sister, and she had been proud to be in her confidence when the sister was secretly engaged and then married: to share the secret of a grown-up was to be accepted among the adults. She lived for a time with her sister; but when the latter told her that she was going 'to buy' a baby, Nancy got jealous of her brother-in-law and of the coming child: to be treated again as a child to whom one made little mysteries of things was unbearable. She began to experience internal troubles and wanted to be operated on for appendicitis. The operation was a success, but during her stay at the hospital Nancy lived in a state of severe agitation; she made violent scenes with a nurse she disliked; she tried to seduce the doctor, making dates with him, being provocative and demanding throughout her crises to be treated as a woman. She accused herself of being to blame for the death of a little brother some years before. And in particular she felt sure that they had not removed her appendix or had left a part of it inside her; her claim that she had swallowed a penny was probably intended to make sure an X-ray would be taken.

This desire for an operation – and in particular for the removal of the appendix – is often seen at this age; girls thus express their fear of rape, pregnancy or having a baby. They feel in their womb obscure perils and hope that the surgeon will save them from this unknown and threatening danger.

It is not only the arrival of her period that signals to the girl her destiny as a woman. Other dubious phenomena occur in her. Until then her eroticism was clitoral. It is difficult to know if solitary sexual practices are less widespread in girls than in boys; the girl indulges in them in her first two years, and perhaps even in the first months of her life; it seems that she stops at about two before taking them up again later;

* Cited also by H. Deutsch, *The Psychology of Women* (1946).

because of his anatomical makeup, this stem planted in the male flesh asks to be touched more than a secret mucous membrane: but the chances of rubbing – the child climbing on gym apparatus or on trees or onto a bicycle – of contact with clothes, or in a game or even initiation by friends, older friends or adults, frequently make the girl discover sensations she tries to renew. In any case, pleasure, when reached, is an autonomous sensation: it has the lightness and innocence of all childish amusements.* As a child, she hardly established a relation between these intimate delights and her destiny as a woman; her sexual relations with boys, if there were any, were essentially based on curiosity. And all of a sudden she experiences emotional confusion in which she does not recognise herself. Sensitivity of the erogenous zones is developing and they are so numerous in the woman that her whole body can be considered erogenous: this is what comes across from familial caresses, innocent kisses, the casual touching of a dressmaker, a doctor, a hairdresser, or a friendly hand on her hair or neck; she learns and often deliberately seeks a deeper excitement in her relations of play and fighting with boys or girls: thus Gilberte fighting on the Champs-Elysées with Proust; in the arms of her dancing partners, under her mother's naive eyes, she experiences a strange lassitude. And then, even a well-protected young woman is exposed to more specific experiences; in conventional circles regrettable incidents are hushed up by common agreement; but it often happens that some of the caresses of friends of the household, uncles, cousins, not to mention grandfathers and fathers, are much less inoffensive than the mother thinks; a professor, a priest, a doctor was bold, indiscreet. Such experiences are found in *In the Prison of Her Skin* by Violette Leduc, in *Maternal Hatred* by Simone de Tervagne and in *The Blue Orange* by Yassu Gauclère. Stekel thinks that grandfathers in particular are often very dangerous.

I was fifteen. The night before the funeral, my grandfather came to sleep at our house. The next day, my mother was already up, he asked me if he could get into bed with me to play; I got up immediately without answering him . . . I began to be afraid of men, a woman recounted.

Another girl recalled receiving a serious shock at eight or ten

* Except, of course, in numerous cases where the direct or indirect intervention of the parents, or religious scruples, make a sin of it. Little girls have sometimes been subjected to abominable persecutions, under the pretext of saving them from 'bad habits'.

years of age when her grandfather, an old man of sixty, had groped her genitals. He had taken her on his lap while sliding his finger into her vagina. The child had felt an immense anxiety but yet did not dare talk about it. Since that time she has been very afraid of everything sexual.*

Such incidents are usually endured in silence for the little girl because of the shame they cause. Moreover, if she does reveal them to her parents, their reaction is often to reprimand her. 'Don't say such stupid things . . . you've got an evil mind.' She is also silent about bizarre activities of some strangers. A little girl told Dr Liepmann:

We had rented a room from the shoemaker in the basement. Often when our landlord was alone, he came to get me, took me in his arms and kissed me for a long time all the while wiggling back and forth. His kiss wasn't superficial besides, since he stuck his tongue into my mouth. I detested him because of his ways. But I never whispered a word, as I was very fearful.†

In addition to enterprising companions and perverse girlfriends, there is this knee in the cinema pressed against the girl's, this hand at night in the train, sliding along her leg, these boys who sniggered when she passed, these men who followed her in the street, these embraces, these furtive touches. She does not really understand the meaning of these adventures. In the fifteen-year-old head, there is often a strange confusion because theoretical knowledge and concrete experiences do not match. She has already felt all the burnings of excitement and desire, but she imagines – like Clara d'Ellébeuse invented by Francis Jammes – that a male kiss is enough to make her a mother; she has a clear idea of the genital anatomy but when her dancing partner embraces her, she thinks the agitation she feels is a migraine. It is certain that girls are better informed today than in the past. However, some psychiatrists affirm that there is more than one adolescent girl who does not know that sexual organs have a use other than urinary.‡ In any case, girls do not draw much connection between their sexual agitation and the existence of their genital organs, since there is no sign as precise as the male erection indicating this correlation. There is such a gap between

* *Frigidity in Woman.*
† Liepmann, *Youth and Sexuality.*
‡ Cf. H. Deutsch, *The Psychology of Women,* 1946.

their romantic musings concerning man and love and the crudeness of certain facts that are revealed to them that they do not create any link between them. Thyde Monnier* relates that she had made the pledge with a few girlfriends to see how a man was made and to tell it to the others:

> Having entered my father's room on purpose without knocking, I described it: 'It looks like a leg of lamb, that is, it is like a rolling pin and then there is a round thing.' It was difficult to explain. I drew it. I even did it three times and each one took hers away hidden in her blouse and from time to time she burst out laughing while looking at it and then went all dreamy . . . How could innocent girls like us set up a connection between these objects and sentimental songs, pretty little romantic stories where love as a whole – respect, shyness, sighs and kissing of the hand – is sublimated to the point of making a eunuch?

Nevertheless, through reading, conversations, theatre and words she has overheard, the girl gives meaning to the disturbances of her flesh; she becomes appeal and desire. In her fevers, shivers, dampness and uncertain states, her body takes on a new and unsettling dimension. The young man is proud of his sexual propensities because he assumes his virility joyfully; sexual desire is aggressive and prehensile for him; there is an affirmation of his subjectivity and transcendence in it; he boasts of it to his friends; his sex organ is for him a disturbance he takes pride in; the drive that sends him towards the female is of the same nature as that which throws him towards the world, and so he recognises himself in it. On the contrary, the girl's sexual life has always been hidden; when her eroticism is transformed and invades her whole flesh, the mystery becomes agonising: she undergoes the disturbance as a shameful illness; it is not active: it is a state, and even in imagination she cannot get rid of it by any autonomous decision; she does not dream of taking, pressing, violating: she is wait and appeal; she feels dependent; she feels herself at risk in her alienated flesh.

Her diffuse hope and her dream of happy passivity clearly reveal her body as an object destined for another; she seeks to know sexual experience only in its immanence; it is the contact of the hand, mouth or another flesh that she desires; the image of her partner is left in the

* Me.

shadows or she drowns it in an idealised haze; however, she cannot prevent his presence from haunting her. Her terrors and juvenile revulsions regarding man have assumed a more equivocal character than before and because of that they are more agonising. Before, they stemmed from a profound divorce between the child's organism and her future as an adult; now they come from this very complexity that the girl feels in her flesh. She understands that she is destined for possession because she wants it: and she revolts against her desires. She at once wishes for and fears the shameful passivity of the consenting prey. She is overwhelmed with confusion at the idea of baring herself before a man; but she also senses that she will then be given over to his gaze without recourse. The hand that takes and that touches has an even more imperious presence than do eyes: it is more frightening. But the most obvious and detestable symbol of physical possession is penetration by the male's sex organ. The girl hates the idea that this body she identifies with may be perforated as one perforates leather, that it can be torn as one tears a piece of fabric. But the girl refuses more than the wound and the accompanying pain; she refuses that these be *inflicted*. 'The idea of being *pierced* by a man is horrible,' a girl told me one day. It is not fear of the virile member that engenders horror of the man, but this fear is the confirmation and symbol; the idea of penetration acquires its obscene and humiliating meaning within a more generalised form, of which it is in turn an essential element.

The girl's anxiety shows itself in nightmares that torment her and fantasies that haunt her: just when she feels an insidious complaisance in herself, the idea of rape becomes obsessive in many cases. It manifests itself in dreams and behaviour in the form of many more or less obvious symbols. The girl explores her room before going to bed for fear of finding some robber with shady intentions; she thinks she hears thieves in the house; an aggressor comes in through the window armed with a knife and he stabs her. In a more or less acute way, men inspire terror in her. She begins to feel a certain disgust for her father; she can no longer stand the smell of his tobacco, she detests going into the bathroom after him; even if she continues to cherish him, this physical revulsion is frequent; it takes on an intensified form if the child was already hostile to her father, as often happens in the youngest children. A dream often encountered by psychiatrists in their young female patients is that they imagine being raped by a man in front of an older woman and with her consent. It is clear that they are symbolically asking their mother for permission to give in to their desires. That is because one of the most detestable constraints weighing on them is that of hypocrisy.

The girl is dedicated to 'purity', to innocence, at precisely the moment she discovers in and around her the mysterious disturbances of life and sex. She has to be white like an ermine, transparent like crystal, she is dressed in vaporous organdie, her room is decorated with candy-coloured hangings, people lower their voice when she approaches, she is prohibited from seeing indecent books; yet there is not one child on earth who does not relish 'abominable' images and desires. She tries to hide them from her best friend, even from herself; she only wants to live or to think by the rules; her self-defiance gives her a devious, unhappy and sickly look; and later, nothing will be harder than combating these inhibitions. But in spite of all these repressions, she feels oppressed by the weight of unspeakable faults. Her metamorphosis into a woman takes place not only in shame but in remorse for suffering that shame.

We understand that the awkward age is a period of painful distress for the girl. She does not want to remain a child. But the adult world seems frightening or boring to her. Colette Audry says:

So I wanted to grow up but never did I seriously dream of leading the life I saw adults lead . . . And thus the desire to grow up without ever assuming an adult state, without ever feeling solidarity with parents, mistresses of the house, housewives, or heads of family, was forming in me.

She would like to free herself from her mother's yoke; but she also has an ardent need for her protection. The faults that weigh on her consciousness – solitary sexual practices, dubious friendships, improper books – make this refuge necessary. The following letter, written to a girlfriend by a fifteen-year-old girl, is typical:*

Mother wants me to wear a long dress at the big dance party at W.'s – my first long dress. She is surprised that I do not want to. I begged her to let me wear my short pink dress for the last time . . . I am so afraid. This long dress makes me feel as if Mummy were going on a long trip and I did not know when she would return. Isn't that silly? And sometimes she looks at me as though I were still a little girl. Ah, if she knew! She would tie my hands to the bed and despise me.

* Quoted by H. Deutsch, *Psychology of Women.*

Stekel's book, *Frigidity in Woman*, is a remarkable document on female childhood. In it a Viennese *süsse Mädel*[26] wrote a detailed confession at about the age of twenty-one. It is a concrete synthesis of all the moments we have studied separately.

'At the age of five I chose for my playmate Richard, a boy of six or seven . . . For a long time I had wanted to know how one can tell whether a child is a girl or a boy. I was told: by the earrings . . . or by the nose. This seemed to satisfy me, though I had a feeling that they were keeping something from me. Suddenly Richard expressed a desire to urinate . . . Then the thought came to me of lending him my chamber pot . . . When I saw his organ, which was something entirely new to me, I went into highest raptures: "What have you there? My, isn't that nice! I'd like to have something like that, too." Whereupon I took hold of the membrum and held it enthusiastically . . . My great-aunt's cough awoke us . . . and from that day on our doings and games were carefully watched.'

At nine she played 'marriage' and 'doctor' with two other boys of eight and ten; they touched her parts and one day one of the boys touched her with his organ, saying that her parents had done just the same thing when they got married. 'This aroused my indig-nation: "Oh, no! They never did such a nasty thing!"' She kept up these games for a long time in a strong sexual friendship with the two boys. One day her aunt caught her and there was a frightful scene with threats to put her in the reformatory. She was prevented from seeing Arthur, whom she preferred, and she suffered a good deal from it; her work went badly, her writing was deformed, and she became cross-eyed. She started another intimacy with Walter and Franz. 'Walter became the goal of all thoughts and feeling. I permitted him very submissively to reach under my dress while I sat or stood in front of him at the table, pretending to be busy with a writing exercise; whenever my mother . . . opened the door, he withdrew his hand on the instant; I, of course, was busy writing . . . In the course of time, we also behaved as husband and wife; but I never allowed him to stay long; whenever he thought he was inside me, I tore myself away saying that somebody was coming . . . I did not reflect that this was "sinful" . . .

'My childhood boy friendships were now over. All I had left were girl friends. I attached myself to Emmy, a highly refined, well-educated girl. One Christmas we exchanged gilded heart-shaped lockets with our initials engraved on them – we were, I believe, about twelve years of age at the time – and we looked upon this as a token of "engagement"; we swore eternal faithfulness "until death do us part". I owe to Emmy a goodly part of my training. She taught me also a few things regarding sexual matters. As far back as during my fifth grade at school I began seriously to doubt the veracity of the stork story. I thought that children developed within the body and that the abdomen must be cut open before a child can be brought out. She filled me with particular horror of self-abuse. In school the Gospels contributed a share towards opening our eyes with regard to certain sexual matters. For instance, when Mary came to Elizabeth, the child is said to have "leaped in her womb"; and we read other similarly remarkable Bible passages. We underscored these words; and when this was discovered the whole class barely escaped a "black mark" in deportment. My girl friend told me also about the "ninth month reminder" to which there is a reference in Schiller's *The Robbers* [*Die Räuber*]. . . Emmy's father moved from our locality and I was again alone. We corresponded, using for the purpose a cryptic alphabet which we had devised between ourselves; but I was lonesome and finally I attached myself to Hedl, a Jewish girl. Once Emmy caught me leaving school in Hedl's company; she created a scene on account of her jealousy . . . I kept up my friendship with Hedl until I entered the commercial school. We became close friends. We both dreamed of becoming sisters-in-law sometimes, because I was fond of one of her brothers. He was a student. Whenever he spoke to me I became so confused that I gave him an irrelevant answer. At dusk we sat in the music room, huddled together on the little divan, and often tears rolled down my cheek for no particular reason as he played the piano.

'Before I befriended Hedl, I went to school for a number of weeks with a certain girl, Ella, the daughter of poor people. Once she caught her parents in a "tête-à-tête". The creaking of the bed had awakened her . . . She came and told me that her father had crawled on top of her mother, and that the mother had cried out terribly; and then the father said to her mother: "Go quickly and wash so that nothing will happen!" After this I was angry at her father and avoided him on the street, while for her mother I felt the greatest sympathy. (He must have hurt her terribly if she cried out so!)

'Again with another girl I discussed the possible length of the male membrum; I had heard that it was 12 to 15 cm long. During the fancy-work period (at school) we took the tape-measure and indicated the stated length on our stomachs, naturally reaching to the navel. This horrified us; if we should ever marry we would be literally impaled.'

She saw a male dog excited by the proximity of a female, and felt strange stirrings inside herself. 'If I saw a horse urinate in the street, my eyes were always glued to the wet spot in the road; I believe the length of time (urinating) is what always impressed me.' She watched flies in copulation and in the country domesticated animals doing the same.

'At twelve I suffered a severe attack of tonsillitis. A friendly physician was called in. He seated himself on my bed and presently he stuck his hand under the covers, almost touching me on the genitalia. I exclaimed: "Don't be so rude!" My mother hurried in; the doctor was much embarrassed. He declared I was a horrid monkey, saying he merely wanted to pinch me on the calf. I was compelled to ask his forgiveness . . . When I finally began to menstruate and my father came across the blood-stained cloths on one occasion, there was a terrible scene. How did it happen that he, so clean a man, had to live among such dirty females? . . . I felt the injustice of being put in the wrong on account of my menstruation.' At fifteen she communicated with another girl in shorthand 'so that no one else could decipher our missives. There was much to report about conquests. She copied for me a vast number of verses from the walls of lavatories; I took particular notice of one. It seemed to me that love, which ranged so high in my fantasy, was being dragged in the mud by it. The verse read: "What is love's highest aim? Four buttocks on a stem." I decided I would never get into that situation; a man who loves a young girl would be unable to ask such a thing of her.

'At fifteen and a half I had a new brother. I was tremendously jealous, for I had always been the only child in the family. My friend reminded me to observe "how the baby boy was constructed", but with the best intentions I was unable to give her the desired information . . . I could not look there. At about this time another girl described to me a bridal night scene . . . I think that then I made up my mind to marry after all, for I was very curious; only the "panting like a horse", as mentioned in the description, offended my aesthetic sense . . . Which one of us girls would not have gladly

married then to undress before the beloved and be carried to bed
in his arms? It seemed so thrilling!'

It will perhaps be said – even though this is a normal and not a
pathological case – that this child was exceptionally 'perverse'; she was
only less watched over than others. If the curiosities and desires of
'well-bred' girls do not manifest themselves in acts, they nonetheless
exist in the form of fantasies and games. I once knew a very pious and
disconcertingly innocent girl – who became an accomplished woman,
devoted to maternity and religion – who one evening confided all trembling to an older woman: 'How marvellous it must be to get undressed
in front of a man! Let's suppose you are my husband'; and she began
to undress, all trembling with emotion. No upbringing can prevent the
girl from becoming aware of her body and dreaming of her destiny;
the most one can do is to impose strict repression that will then weigh
on her for her whole sexual life. What would be desirable is that she
be taught, on the contrary, to accept herself without excuses and
without shame.

One understands now the drama that rends the adolescent girl at
puberty: she cannot become 'a grown-up' without accepting her femininity; she already knew her sex condemned her to a mutilated and frozen
existence; she now discovers it in the form of an impure illness and an
obscure crime. Her inferiority was at first understood as a privation: the
absence of a penis was converted to a stain and fault. She makes her
way towards the future wounded, shamed, worried and guilty.

CHAPTER 2

The Girl

Throughout her childhood, the little girl was bullied and mutilated; but she nonetheless grasped herself as an autonomous individual; in her relations with her family and friends, in her studies and games, she saw herself in the present as a transcendence: her future passivity was something she only imagined. Once she enters puberty, the future not only moves closer: it settles into her body; it becomes the most concrete reality. It retains the fateful quality it always had; while the adolescent boy is actively routed towards adulthood, the girl looks forward to the opening of this new and unforeseeable period where the plot is already hatched and towards which time is drawing her. As she is already detached from her childhood past, the present is for her only a transition; she sees no valid ends in it, only occupations. In a more or less disguised way, her youth is consumed by waiting. She is waiting for Man.

Surely the adolescent boy also dreams of woman, he desires her; but she will never be more than one element in his life: she does not encapsulate his destiny; from childhood, the little girl, whether wishing to realise herself as woman or overcome the limits of her femininity, has awaited the male for accomplishment and escape; he has the dazzling face of Perseus or St George; he is the liberator; he is also rich and powerful, he holds the keys to happiness, he is Prince Charming. She anticipates that in his caress she will feel carried away by the great current of life as when she rested in her mother's bosom; subjected to his gentle authority, she will find the same security as in her father's arms: the magic of embraces and gazes will petrify her back into an idol. She has always been convinced of male superiority; this male prestige is not a childish mirage; it has economic and social foundations; men are, without any question, the masters of the world; everything convinces the adolescent girl that it is in her interest to be their vassal; her parents prod her on; the father is proud of his daughter's success, the mother sees the promise of a prosperous future, friends envy and admire the one among them who gets the most masculine admiration; in American colleges, the student's status is based on the number of dates she has. Marriage is not only an honourable and less strenuous career than many others; it alone enables woman to attain her complete social dignity and also to realise herself sexually as lover and mother. This is the role her entourage thus envisages for her future, as she envisages it herself. Everyone unanimously agrees that catching a husband – or a protector in some cases – is for her the most important of undertakings. In her eyes, man embodies the Other, as she does for man; but for her this *Other* appears in the essential mode and she grasps herself as the inessential opposite him. She will free herself from her parents' home, from her mother's hold; she will open up her future not by an active conquest but by passively and docilely delivering herself into the hands of a new master.

It has often been declared that if she resigns herself to this surrender, it is because physically and morally she has become inferior to boys and incapable of competing with them: forsaking hopeless competition, she entrusts the assurance of her happiness to a member of the superior caste. In fact, her humility does not stem from a given inferiority: on the contrary, her humility engenders all her failings; its source is in the adolescent girl's past, in the society around her, and precisely in this future that is proposed to her.

True, puberty transforms the girl's body. It is more fragile than before; female organs are vulnerable, their functioning delicate; strange and uncomfortable, breasts are a burden; they remind her of their presence during strenuous exercise, they quiver, they ache. From here on, woman's muscle force, endurance and suppleness are inferior to man's. Hormonal imbalances create nervous and vasomotor instability. Menstrual periods are painful: headaches, stiffness and abdominal cramps make normal activities painful and even impossible; added to these discomforts are psychic problems; nervous and irritable, the woman frequently undergoes a state of semi-alienation each month; central control of the nervous and sympathetic systems is no longer assured; circulation problems and some auto-intoxications turn the body into a screen between the woman and the world, a burning fog that weighs on her, stifling her and separating her: experienced through this suffering and passive flesh, the entire universe is a burden too heavy to bear. Oppressed and submerged, she becomes a stranger to herself because she is a stranger to the rest of the world. Syntheses disintegrate, instants are no longer connected, others are recognised but only abstractly; and if reasoning and logic do remain intact, as in melancholic delirium, they are subordinated to passions that surge out of organic disorder. These facts are extremely important; but the way the woman becomes conscious of them gives them their weight.

At about thirteen, boys serve a veritable apprenticeship in violence, developing their aggressiveness, their will for power and taste for competition; it is exactly at this moment that the little girl renounces rough games. Some sports remain accessible to her, but sport that is specialisation, submission to artificial rules, does not offer the equivalent of a spontaneous and habitual recourse to force; it is marginal to life; it does not teach about the world and about one's self as intimately as does an unruly fight or an impulsive rock climb. The sportswoman never feels the conqueror's pride of the boy who pins down his comrade. In fact, in many countries, most girls have no athletic training; like fights, climbing is forbidden to them, they only submit to their bodies passively; far more clearly than in their early years, they must forgo *emerging* beyond the given world, affirming themselves *above* the rest of humanity: they are banned from exploring, daring, pushing back the limits of the possible. In particular, the attitude of defiance, so important for boys, is unknown to them; true, women compare themselves with each other, but defiance is something other than these passive confrontations: two freedoms confront each other as having a hold on the world whose limits they intend to push; climbing higher than a friend or getting the better in arm wrestling is affirming one's sovereignty over the world. These conquering actions are not permitted to the girl, and violence in particular is not permitted to her. Undoubtedly, in the adult world brute force plays no great role in normal times; but it nonetheless haunts the world; much of masculine behaviour arises in a setting of potential violence: on every street corner skirmishes are waiting to happen; in most cases they are aborted; but it is enough for the man to feel in his fists his will for self-affirmation for him to feel confirmed in his sovereignty. The male has recourse to his fists and fighting when he encounters any affront or attempt to reduce him to an object: he does not let himself be transcended by others; he finds himself again in the heart of his subjectivity. Violence is the authentic test of every person's attachment to himself, his passions and his own will; to radically reject it is to reject all objective truth, it is to isolate one's self in an abstract subjectivity; an anger or a revolt that does not exert itself in muscles remains imaginary. It is a terrible frustration not to be able to imprint the movements of one's heart on the face of the earth. In the South of the United States, it is strictly impossible for a black person to use violence against whites; this rule is the key to the mysterious 'black soul'; the way the black experiences himself in the white world, his behaviour in adjusting to it, the compensations he seeks, his whole way of feeling and acting, are explained on the basis of the passivity to which he is condemned. During the Occupation, the French who had decided not to let themselves resort to violent gestures against the occupants even in cases of provocation (whether out of egotistical prudence or because they had overriding duties) felt their situation in the world profoundly overturned: depending upon the whims of others, they could be changed into objects, their subjectivity no longer had the means to express itself concretely, it was merely a secondary phenomenon. In the same way, for the adolescent boy who is allowed to manifest himself imperiously, the universe has a totally different face from what it has for the adolescent girl whose feelings are deprived of immediate effectiveness; the former ceaselessly calls the world into question, he can at every instance revolt against the given and thus has the impression of actively conforming it when he accepts it; the latter only submits to it; the world is defined without her and its face is immutable. This lack of physical power expresses itself as a more general timidity: she does not believe in a force she has not felt in her body, she does not dare to be enterprising, to revolt, to invent; doomed to docility, to resignation, she can only accept a place that society has already made for her. She accepts the order of things as a given. A woman told me that all through her youth, she denied her physical weakness with fierce bad faith; to accept it would have been to lose her taste and courage to undertake anything, even in intellectual or political fields. I knew a girl, brought up as a tomboy and exceptionally vigorous, who thought she was as strong as a man; though she was very pretty, though she had painful periods every month, she was completely unconscious of her femininity; she had a boy's toughness, exuberance of life and initiative; she had a boy's boldness: on the street she would not hesitate to jump into a fistfight if she saw a child or a woman harassed. One or two bad experiences revealed to her that brute force is on the male's side. When she became aware of her weakness, a great part of her assurance crumbled; this was the beginning of an evolution that led her to feminise herself, to realise herself as passivity, to accept dependence. To lose confidence in one's body is to lose confidence in one's self. One needs only to see the importance that young men give to their muscles to understand that every subject grasps his body as his objective expression.

The young man's erotic drives only go to confirm the pride that he obtains from his body: he discovers in it the sign of transcendence and its power. The girl can succeed in accepting her desires: but most often they retain a shameful nature. Her whole body is experienced as embarrassment. The defiance she felt as a child regarding her 'insides' contributes to giving the menstrual crisis the dubious nature that renders it loathsome. The psychic attitude evoked by menstrual servitude constitutes a heavy handicap. The threat that weighs on the girl during certain periods can seem so intolerable for her that she will give up expeditions and pleasures out of fear of her disgrace becoming known. The horror that this inspires has repercussions on her organism and increases her disorders and pains. It has been seen that one of the characteristics of female physiology is the tight link between endocrinal secretions and the nervous system: there is reciprocal action; a woman's body – and specifically the girl's – is a 'hysterical' body in the sense that there is, so to speak, no distance between psychic life and its physiological realisation. The turmoil brought about by the girl's discovery of the problems of puberty exacerbates them. Because her body is suspect to her, she scrutinises it with anxiety and sees it as sick: it is sick. It has been seen that indeed this body is fragile and real organic disorders arise; but gynaecologists concur that nine-tenths of their patients have imaginary illnesses; that is, either their illnesses have no physiological reality or the organic disorder itself stems from a psychic attitude. To a great extent, the anguish of being a woman eats away at the female body.

It is clear that if woman's biological situation constitutes a handicap for her, it is because of the perspective from which it is grasped. Nervous frailty and vasomotor instability, when they do not become pathological, do not keep her from any profession: among males themselves, there is a great diversity of temperament. A one- or two-day indisposition per month, even painful, is not an obstacle either; in fact, many women accommodate themselves to it, particularly women for whom the monthly 'curse' could be most bothersome: athletes, travellers and women who do strenuous work. Most professions demand no more energy than women can provide. And in sports, the goal is not to succeed independently of physical aptitudes: it is the accomplishment of perfection proper to each organism; the lightweight champion is as worthy as the heavyweight; a female ski champion is no less a champion than the male who is more rapid than she: they belong to two different categories. It is precisely athletes who, positively concerned with their own accomplishments, feel the least handicapped in comparison to men. But nonetheless her physical weakness does not allow the woman to learn the lessons of violence: if it were possible to assert herself in her body and be part of the world in some other way, this deficiency would be easily compensated. If she could swim, scale rocks, pilot a plane, battle the elements, take risks and venture out, she would not feel the timidity towards the world that I spoke about. It is within the whole context of a situation that leaves her few outlets that these singularities take on their importance, and not immediately but by confirming the inferiority complex that was developed in her by her childhood.

It is this complex as well that will weigh on her intellectual accomplishments. It has often been noted that from puberty, the girl loses ground in intellectual and artistic fields. There are many reasons for this. One of the most common is that the adolescent girl does not receive the same encouragement accorded to her brothers; on the contrary, she is expected to be a *woman as well* and she must add to her professional work the duties that femininity implies. The headmistress of a professional school made these comments on the subject:

> The girl suddenly becomes a being who earns her living by working. She has new desires that have nothing to do with the family. It very often happens that she must make quite a considerable effort . . . she gets home at night exhausted, her head stuffed with the day's events . . . How will she be received? Her mother sends her right out to do an errand. There are home chores left unfinished to do, and she still has to take care of her own clothes. It is impossible to disconnect from the personal thoughts that continue to preoccupy her. She feels unhappy and compares her situation to that of her brother, who has no duties at home, and she revolts.*[27]

Housework or everyday chores that the mother does not hesitate to impose on the girl student or trainee completely exhaust her. During the war I saw my students in Sèvres worn out by family tasks added on top of their schoolwork: one developed Pott's disease, the other meningitis. Mothers – we will see – are blindly hostile to freeing their daughters and, more or less deliberately, work at bullying them even more; for the adolescent boy, his effort to become a man is respected and he is already granted great freedom. The girl is required to stay home; her outside activities are watched over: she is never encouraged to organise her own fun and pleasure. It is rare to see women organise a long hike on their

---

* Cited by Liepmann, *Youth and Sexuality.*

own, a walking or biking trip, or take part in games such as billiards and bowling. Beyond a lack of initiative that comes from their education, customs make their independence difficult. If they wander the streets, they are stared at, accosted. I know some girls, far from shy, who get no enjoyment strolling through Paris alone because, incessantly bothered, they are incessantly on their guard: all their pleasure is ruined. If girl students run through the streets in happy groups as boys do, they attract attention; striding along, singing, talking and laughing loudly or eating an apple are provocations, and they will be insulted or followed or approached. Light-heartedness immediately becomes a lack of decorum. This self-control imposed on the woman becomes second nature for 'the well-bred girl' and kills spontaneity; lively exuberance is crushed. The result is tension and boredom. This boredom is contagious: girls tire of each other quickly; being in the same prison does not create solidarity among them, and this is one of the reasons the company of boys becomes so necessary. This inability to be self-sufficient brings on a shyness that extends over their whole lives and even marks their work. They think that brilliant triumphs are reserved for men; they do not dare aim too high. It has already been observed that fifteen-year-old girls, comparing themselves to boys, declare, 'Boys are better.' This conviction is debilitating. It encourages laziness and mediocrity. A girl – who had no particular deference for the stronger sex – reproached a man for his cowardice; when she was told that she herself was a coward, she complacently declared: 'Oh! It's not the same thing for a woman.'

The fundamental reason for this defeatism is that the adolescent girl does not consider herself responsible for her future; she judges it useless to demand much of herself since her lot in the end will not depend on her. Far from destining herself to man because she thinks she is inferior to him, it is because she is destined for him that, in accepting the idea of her inferiority, she constitutes it.

In fact, she will gain value in the eyes of males not by increasing her human worth but by modelling herself on their dreams. When she is inexperienced, she is not always aware of this. She sometimes acts as aggressively as boys; she tries to conquer them with a brusque authority, a proud frankness: this attitude is almost surely doomed to failure. From the most servile to the haughtiest, girls all learn that to please, they must give in to them. Their mothers urge them not to treat boys like companions, not to make advances to them, to assume a passive role. If they want to flirt or initiate a friendship, they should carefully avoid giving the impression they are taking the initiative; men do not like tomboys, nor bluestockings, nor thinking women; too much audacity, culture, intelligence or character frightens them. In most novels, as George Eliot observes, it is the dumb, blonde heroine who outshines the virile brunette; and in *The Mill on the Floss,* Maggie tries in vain to reverse the roles; in the end she dies and it is blonde Lucy who marries Stephen. In *The Last of the Mohicans,* vapid Alice wins the hero's heart and not valiant Clara; in *Little Women* kindly Jo is only a childhood friend for Laurie; he vows his love to curly-haired and insipid Amy. To be feminine is to show oneself as weak, futile, passive and docile. The girl is supposed not only to primp and dress herself up but also to repress her spontaneity and substitute for it the grace and charm she has been taught by her elder sisters. Any self-assertion will take away from her femininity and her seductiveness. A young man's venture into existence is relatively easy, as his vocations of human being and male are not contradictory; his childhood already predicted this happy fate. It is in accomplishing himself as independence and freedom that he acquires his social value and, concurrently, his manly prestige: the ambitious man, like Rastignac, targets money, glory and women all at once; one of the stereotypes that stimulates him is that of the powerful and famous man adored by women. For the girl, on the contrary, there is a divorce between her properly human condition and her feminine vocation. This is why adolescence is such a difficult and decisive moment for woman. Until then she was an autonomous individual: she now has to renounce her sovereignty. Not only is she torn like her brothers, and more acutely, between past and future, but in addition a conflict breaks out between her originary claim to be subject, activity and freedom, on the one hand and, on the other, her erotic tendencies and the social pressure to assume herself as a passive object. She spontaneously grasps herself as the essential: how will she decide to become the inessential? If I can accomplish myself only as the *Other*, how will I renounce my *Self*? Such is the agonising dilemma the woman-to-be must struggle with. Wavering from desire to disgust, from hope to fear, rebuffing what she invites, she is still suspended between the moment of childish independence and that of feminine submission: this is the incertitude that, as she grows out of the awkward age, gives her the bitter taste of unripe fruit.

The girl reacts to her situation differently depending on her earlier choices. The 'little woman', the matron-to-be, can easily resign herself to her metamorphosis; but she may also have drawn a taste for authority from her condition as 'little woman' that lets her rebel against the masculine yoke: she is ready to establish a matriarchy, not to become an erotic object and servant. This will often be the case of those older sisters who took on important responsibilities at a young age. The 'tomboy', upon becoming a woman, often feels a burning disappointment that can drive her directly to homosexuality; but what she was looking for in independence and intensity was to possess the world: she may not want to renounce the power of her femininity, the experiences of maternity, a whole part of her destiny. Generally, with some resistance, the girl consents to her femininity: already at the stage of childish coquetry, in front of her father, in her erotic fantasies, she understood the charm of passivity; she discovers the power in it; vanity is soon mixed with the shame that her flesh inspires. That hand that moves her, that glance that excites her, they are an appeal, an invitation; her body seems endowed with magic virtues; it is a treasure, a weapon; she is proud of it. Her coquetry, which often has disappeared during her years of childhood autonomy, is revived. She tries makeup, hairstyles; instead of hiding her breasts, she massages them to make them bigger, she studies her smile in the mirror. The link is so tight between arousal and seduction that in all cases where erotic sensibility lies dormant, no desire to please is observed in the subject. Experiments have shown that patients suffering from a thyroid deficiency, and thus apathetic and sullen, can be transformed by an injection of glandular extracts: they begin to smile; they become gay and simpering. Psychologists imbued with materialistic metaphysics have boldly declared flirtatiousness an 'instinct' secreted by the thyroid gland; but this obscure explanation is no more valid here than for early childhood. The fact is that in all cases of organic deficiency – lymphatism, anaemia, and such – the body is endured as a burden; foreign, hostile, it neither hopes for nor promises anything; when it recovers its equilibrium and vitality, the subject at once recognises it as his and through it he transcends towards others.

For the girl, erotic transcendence consists in making herself prey in order to make a catch. She becomes an object; and she grasps herself as object; she is surprised to discover this new aspect of her being: it seems to her that she has been doubled; instead of coinciding exactly with her self, here she is existing *outside* of her self. Thus in Rosamond Lehmann's *Invitation to the Waltz*, Olivia discovers an unknown face in the mirror: it is she-object suddenly rising up opposite herself; she experiences a quickly fading but upsetting emotion:

> Nowadays a peculiar emotion accompanied the moment of looking into the mirror: fitfully, rarely a stranger might emerge: a new self.

It had happened two or three times already . . . She looked in the glass and saw herself . . . Well, what was it? . . . But this was something else. This was a mysterious face; both dark and glowing; hair tumbling down, pushed back and upwards, as if in currents of fierce energy. Was it the frock that did it? Her body seemed to assemble itself harmoniously within it, to become centralised, to expand, both static and fluid; alive. It was the portrait of a young girl in pink. All the room's reflected objects seemed to frame, to present her, whispering: Here are You . . .[28]

What astonishes Olivia are the promises she thinks she reads in this image in which she recognises her childish dreams and which is herself; but the girl also cherishes in her carnal presence this body that fascinates her as if it were someone else's. She caresses herself, she embraces the curve of her shoulder, the bend of her elbow, she contemplates her bosom, her legs; solitary pleasure becomes a pretext for reverie, in it she seeks a tender self-possession. For the boy adolescent, there is an opposition between love of one's self and the erotic movement that thrusts him towards the object to be possessed: his narcissism generally disappears at the moment of sexual maturity. Instead of the woman being a passive object for the lover as for herself, there is a primitive blurring in her eroticism. In one complex step, she aims for her body's glorification through the homage of men for whom this body is intended; and it would be a simplification to say that she wants to be beautiful in order to charm, or that she seeks to charm to assure herself that she is beautiful: in the solitude of her room, in salons where she tries to attract the gaze of others, she does not separate man's desire from the love of her own self. This confusion is manifest in Marie Bashkirtseff.[29] It has already been seen that late weaning disposed her more deeply than any other child to wanting to be gazed at and valorised by others; from the age of five until the end of adolescence, she devotes all her love to her image; she madly admires her hands, her face, her grace, and she writes: 'I am my own heroine.' She wants to become an opera singer to be *gazed at* by a dazzled public so as to *look back* with a proud gaze; but this 'autism' expresses itself through romantic dreams; from the age of twelve, she is in love: she wants to be loved, and the adoration that she seeks to inspire only confirms that which she devotes to herself. She dreams that the Duke of H., with whom she is in love without having ever spoken to him, prostrates himself at her feet: 'You will be dazzled by my splendour and you will love me . . . You are worthy only of such a woman as I intend to be.' The same ambivalence is found in Natasha in *War and Peace*:[30]

> 'Even mama doesn't understand. It's astonishing how intelligent I am and how . . . sweet she is,' she went on, speaking of herself in the third person and imagining that it was some very intelligent man saying it about her, the most intelligent and best of men . . . 'There's everything in her, everything,' this man went on, 'she's extraordinarily intelligent, sweet, and then, too, pretty, extraordinarily pretty, nimble – she swims, she's an excellent horsewoman, and the voice! One may say, an astonishing voice!' . . .
>
> That morning she returned again to her favorite state of love and admiration for herself. 'How lovely that Natasha is!' she said of herself again in the words of some collective male third person. 'Pretty, a good voice, young, and doesn't bother anybody, only leave her in peace.'

Katherine Mansfield (in 'Prelude') has also described, in the character of Beryl, a case in which narcissism and the romantic desire for a woman's destiny are closely intermingled:

> In the dining-room, by the flicker of a wood fire, Beryl sat on a hassock playing the guitar . . . She played and sang half to herself, for she was watching herself playing and singing. The firelight gleamed on her shoes, on the ruddy belly of the guitar, and on her white fingers . . .
>
> 'If I were outside the window and looked in and saw myself I really would be rather struck,' thought she. Still more softly she played the accompaniment – not singing now but listening . . .
>
> '. . . The first time that I ever saw you, little girl – oh, you had no idea that you were not alone – you were sitting with your little feet upon a hassock, playing the guitar. God, I can never forget . . .' Beryl flung up her head and began to sing again:
>
> *Even the moon is aweary . . .*
>
> But there came a loud bang at the door. The servant girl's crimson face popped through . . . But no, she could not stand that fool of a girl. She ran into the dark drawing-room and began walking up and down . . . Oh, she was restless, restless. There was a mirror over the

mantel. She leaned her arms along and looked at her pale shadow in it. How beautiful she looked, but there was nobody to see, nobody . . .

Beryl smiled, and really her smile *was* so adorable that she smiled again.[31]

This cult of the self is not only expressed by the girl as the adoration of her physical person; she wishes to possess and praise her entire self. This is the purpose of these diaries into which she freely pours her whole soul: Marie Bashkirtseff's is famous and it is a model of the genre. The girl speaks to her notebook the way she used to speak to her dolls, as a friend, a confidante, and addresses it as if it were a person. Recorded in its pages is a truth hidden from parents, friends and teachers, and which enraptures the author when she is all alone. A twelve-year-old girl, who kept a diary until she was twenty, wrote the inscription:

> *I am the little notebook*
> *Nice, pretty and discreet*
> *Tell me all your secrets*
> *I am the little notebook.**[32]

Others announce: 'To be read after my death' or 'To be burned when I die'. The little girl's sense of secrecy that developed at prepuberty only grows in importance. She closes herself up in fierce solitude: she refuses to reveal to those around her the hidden self that she considers to be her real self and that is in fact an imaginary character: she plays at being a dancer like Tolstoy's Natasha, or a saint like Marie Lenéru, or simply that singular wonder that is herself. There is still an enormous difference between this heroine and the objective face that her parents and friends recognise in her. She is also convinced that she is misunderstood: her relationship with herself becomes even more passionate: she becomes intoxicated with her isolation, feels different, superior, exceptional: she promises that the future will take revenge on the mediocrity of her present life. From this narrow and petty existence she escapes by dreams. She has always loved to dream: she gives herself up to this penchant more than ever; she uses poetic clichés to mask a universe that intimidates her, she sanctifies the male sex with moonlight, rose-coloured clouds, velvet nights; she turns her body into a marble, jasper or mother-of-pearl temple; she tells herself foolish fairy tales. She sinks so often

---

* Cited by Debesse in *The Adolescent Identity Crisis*.

into such nonsense because she has no grasp on the world; if she had to *act*, she would be forced to see clearly, whereas she can *wait* in the fog. The young man dreams as well: he dreams especially of adventures where he plays an active role. The girl prefers wonderment to adventure; she spreads a vague magic light on things and people. The idea of magic is that of a passive force; because she is doomed to passivity and yet wants power, the adolescent girl must believe in magic: her body's magic that will bring men under her yoke, the magic of destiny in general that will fulfil her without her having *to do* anything. As for the real world, she tries to forget it.

'In school I sometimes escape, I know not how, the subject being explained and fly away to dreamland . . .' writes a young girl.*[33] 'I am thus so absorbed in delightful chimeras that I completely lose the notion of reality. I am nailed to my bench and, when I awake, I am amazed to find myself within four walls.'

'I like to daydream much more than doing my verses,' writes another, 'to dream up nice, nonsensical stories or make up fairy tales when looking at mountains in the starlight. This is much more lovely because it is *more vague* and leaves the impression of repose, of refreshment.'

Daydreaming can take on a morbid form and invade the whole existence, as in the following case:†[34]

Marie B. . . . an intelligent and dreamy child, entering puberty at fourteen, had a psychic crisis with delusions of grandeur. 'She suddenly announces to her parents that she is the queen of Spain, assumes haughty airs, wraps herself in a curtain, laughs, sings, commands and orders.' For two years, this state is repeated during her periods, then for eight years she leads a normal life but is dreamy, loves luxury and often says bitterly, 'I'm an employee's daughter.' Toward twenty-three she grows apathetic, hateful of her surroundings and manifests ambitious ideas; she gets worse to the point of being interned in Sainte-Anne asylum, where she spends eight months; she returns to her family, where, for three years she remains in bed,

* Cited by Marguerite Evard, *The Adolescent Girl*.
† From Borel and Robin, *Morbid Reveries*. Cited by Minkowski in *Schizophrenia*.

'disagreeable, mean, violent, capricious, unoccupied and a burden
to all those around her'. She is taken back to Sainte-Anne for good
and does not come out again. She remains in bed, interested in
nothing. At certain periods – seeming to correspond to menstrual
periods – she gets up, drapes herself in her bedcovers, strikes
theatrical attitudes, poses, smiles at doctors or looks at them ironically . . . Her comments often express a certain eroticism and her
regal attitude expresses megalomaniac concepts. She sinks further
and further into her dreamworld, where smiles of satisfaction appear
on her face; she is careless of her appearance and even dirties her
bed. 'She adorns herself with bizarre ornaments, shirtless, often
naked, with a tinfoil diadem on her head and string or ribbon
bracelets on her arms, her wrists, her shoulders, her ankles. Similar
rings adorn her fingers.' Yet at times she makes lucid comments on
her condition. 'I recall the crisis I had before. I knew deep down
that it was not real. I was like a child who plays with dolls and who
knows that her doll is not alive but wants to convince herself . . . I
fixed my hair; I draped myself. I was having fun and then little by
little, as if in spite of myself, I became bewitched; it was like a dream
I was living . . . I was like an actress who would play a role. I was
in an imaginary world. I lived several lives at a time and *in each life,
I was the principal player* . . . Ah! I had so many different lives; once
I married a handsome American who wore golden glasses . . . We
had a grand hotel and a room for each of us. What parties I gave! . . .
I lived in the days of cavemen . . . I was wild in those days. I couldn't
count how many men I slept with. Here people are a little backward. They don't understand why I go naked with a gold bracelet
on my thigh. I used to have friends that I liked a lot. We had parties
at my house. There were flowers, perfume, ermine fur. My friends
gave me art objects, statues, cars . . . When I get into my sheets
naked, it reminds me of old times. *I admired myself in mirrors,* as an
artist . . . In my bewitched state, I was anything I wanted. I was even
foolish. I took morphine, cocaine. I had lovers . . . They came to my
house at night. They came two at a time. They brought hairdressers
and we looked at postcards.' She was also the mistress of two of
her doctors. She says she had a three-year-old daughter. She has
another six-year-old, very rich, who travels. Their father is a very
chic man. 'There are ten other similar stories. Every one is a feigned
existence that she lives in her imagination.'

Clearly this morbid daydreaming was essentially to satiate the girl's narcissism, as she feels that her life was inadequate and is afraid to confront the reality of her existence. Marie B. merely carried to the extreme a compensation process common to many adolescents.

Nonetheless, this self-provided solitary cult is not enough for the girl. To fulfil herself, she needs to exist in another consciousness. She often turns to her friends for help. When she was younger, her best girlfriend provided support for her to escape the maternal circle, to explore the world and in particular the sexual world; now her friend is both an object wrenching her to the limits of her self and a witness who restores that self to her. Some girls exhibit their nudity to each other, they compare their breasts: an example would be the scene in *Girls in Uniform*[35] that shows the daring games of boarding-school girls; they exchange random or particular caresses. As Colette recounts in *Claudine at School*[36] and Rosamond Lehmann less frankly in *Dusty Answer*,[37] nearly all girls have lesbian tendencies; these tendencies are barely distinguishable from narcissistic delights: in the other, it is the sweetness of her own skin, the form of her own curves that each of them covets; and vice versa, implicit in her self-adoration is the cult of femininity in general. Sexually, man is subject; men are thus normally separated by the desire that drives them towards an object different from themselves; but woman is an absolute object of desire; this is why 'special friendships' flourish in lycées, schools, boarding schools and workshops; some are purely spiritual and others deeply carnal. In the first case, it is mainly a matter of friends opening their hearts to each other, exchanging confidences; the most passionate proof of confidence is to show one's intimate diary to the chosen one; short of sexual embraces, friends exchange extreme signs of tenderness and often give to each other, in indirect ways, a physical token of their feelings: thus Natasha burns her arm with a red-hot ruler to prove her love for Sonia; mostly they call each other thousands of affectionate names and exchange ardent letters. Here is an example of a letter written by Emily Dickinson, a young New England Puritan, to a beloved female friend:

> I think of you all day, and dreamed of you last night . . . I was walking with you in the most wonderful garden, and helping you pick roses, and although we gathered with all our might, the basket was never full. And so all day I pray I may walk with you, and gather roses again, and as night draws on, it pleases me, and I count

impatiently the hours 'tween me and the darkness, and the dream
of you and the roses, and the basket never full . . .

In his work on the adolescent girl's soul,[38] Mendousse cites a great
number of similar letters:

My Dear Suzanne . . . I would have liked to copy here a few verses
from Song of Songs: how beautiful you are, my friend, how beautiful you are! Like the mystical bride, you were like the rose of
Sharon, the lily of the valley, and like her, you have been for me
more than an ordinary girl; you have been a symbol, the symbol
of all things beautiful and lofty . . . and because of this, pure
Suzanne, I love you with a pure and unselfish love that hints of the
religious.

Another confesses less lofty emotions in her diary:

I was there, my waist encircled by this little white hand, my hand
resting on her round shoulder, my arm on her bare, warm arm,
pressed against the softness of her breast, with her lovely mouth
before me, parted on her dainty teeth . . . I trembled and felt my
face burning.*

In her book *The Adolescent Girl*, Mme Evard also collected a great
number of these intimate effusions:

To my beloved fairy, my dearest darling. My lovely fairy. Oh! Tell
me that you still love me, tell me that for you I am still the devoted
friend. I am sad, I love you so, oh my L. . . . and I cannot speak to
you, tell you enough of my affection for you; there are no words
to describe my love. *Idolise* is a poor way to say what I feel; sometimes it seems that my heart will burst. To be loved by you is too
beautiful, I cannot believe it. *Oh my dear*, tell, will you love me
longer still?

It is easy to slip from these exalted affections into guilty juvenile
crushes; sometimes one of the two girlfriends dominates and exercises her power sadistically over the other; but often, they are reciprocal

* Cited by Mendousse, *The Adolescent Girl's Soul*.

loves without humiliation or struggle; the pleasure given and received remains as innocent as it was at the time when each one loved alone, without being doubled in a couple. But this very innocence is bland; when the adolescent girl decides to enter into life and becomes the Other, she hopes to rekindle the magic of the paternal gaze to her advantage; she demands the love and caresses of a divinity. She will turn to a woman less foreign and less fearsome than the male, but one who will possess male prestige: a woman who has a profession, who earns her living, who has a certain social base, will easily be as fascinating as a man: we know how many 'flames' are lit in school-girls' hearts for professors and tutors. In *Regiment of Women*,[39] Clemence Dane uses a chaste style to describe ardently burning passions. Sometimes the girl confides her great passion to her best friend; they even share it, adding spice to their experience. A schoolgirl writes to her best friend:

> I'm in bed with a cold, and can think only of Mlle X. . . . I never loved a teacher to this point. I already loved her a lot in my first year, but now it is real love. I think that I'm more passionate than you. I imagine kissing her; I half faint and thrill at the idea of seeing her when school begins.*

More often, she even dares admit her feeling to her idol herself:

> Dear Mademoiselle, I am in an indescribable state over you. When I do not see you, I would give the world to meet you; I think of you every moment. If I spot you, my eyes fill up with tears, I want to hide; I am so small, so ignorant in front of you. When you chat with me, I am embarrassed, moved, I seem to hear the sweet voice of a fairy and the humming of loving things, impossible to trans-late; I watch your slightest moves; I lose track of the conversation and mumble something stupid: you must admit, dear Mademoiselle, that this is all mixed up. I do see one thing clearly, that I love you from the depths of my soul.†

The headmistress of a professional school recounts:

* Cited by Marguerite Evard, *The Adolescent Girl*.
† Ibid.

I recall that, in my own youth, we fought over one of our young professors' lunch papers and paid up to twenty pfennigs to have it. Her used metro tickets were also objects of our collectors' rage.

Since she must play a masculine role, it is preferable for the loved woman not to be married; marriage does not always discourage the young admirer, but it interferes; she detests the idea that the object of her adoration could be under the control of a spouse or a lover. Her passions often unfold in secret, or at least on a purely platonic level; but the passage to a concrete eroticism is much easier here than if the loved object is masculine; even if she has had difficult experiences with friends her age, the feminine body does not frighten the girl; with her sisters or her mother, she has often experienced an intimacy where tenderness was subtly penetrated with sensuality, and when she is with the loved one she admires, slipping from tenderness to pleasure will take place just as subtly. When Dorothea Wieck kisses Herta Thiele on the lips in *Girls in Uniform*, this kiss is both maternal and sexual. Between women there is a complicity that disarms modesty; the excitement one arouses in the other is generally without violence; homosexual embraces involve neither defloration nor penetration: they satisfy infantile clitoral eroticism without demanding new and disquieting metamorphoses. The girl can realise her vocation as passive object without feeling deeply alienated. This is what Renée Vivien expresses in her verses, where she describes the relation of 'damned women' and their lovers:

> *Our bodies to theirs are a kindred mirror . . .*
> *Our lunar kisses have a pallid softness,*
> *Our fingers do not ruffle the down on a cheek,*
> *And we are able, when the sash becomes untied,*
> *To be at the same time lovers and sisters.*[40]

And in these verses:

> *For we love gracefulness and delicacy,*
> *And my possession does not bruise your breasts . . .*
> *My mouth would not know how to bite your mouth roughly.*

> *My mouth will not bitterly bite your mouth.*[41]

* *At the Sweet Hour of Hand in Hand.*
† *Sea Wakes.*

Through the poetic impropriety of the words 'breasts' and 'mouth', she clearly promises her friend not to brutalise her. And it is in part out of fear of violence and of rape that the adolescent girl often gives her first love to an older girl rather than to a man. The masculine woman reincarnates for her both the father and the mother: from the father she has authority and transcendence, she is the source and standard of values, she rises beyond the given world, she is divine; but she remains woman: whether she was too abruptly weaned from her mother's caresses or if, on the contrary, her mother pampered her too long, the adolescent girl, like her brothers, dreams of the warmth of the breast; in this flesh similar to hers she loses herself again in that immediate fusion with life that weaning destroyed; and through this foreign enveloping gaze, she overcomes the separation that individualises her. Of course, all human relationships entail conflicts; all love entails jealousies. But many of the difficulties that arise between the virgin and her first male love are smoothed away here. The homosexual experience can take the shape of a true love; it can bring to the girl so happy a balance that she will want to continue it, repeat it, and will keep a nostalgic memory of it; it can awaken or give rise to a lesbian vocation.* But most often, it will only represent a stage: its very facility condemns it. In the love that she declares to a woman older than herself, the girl covets her own future: she is identifying with an idol; unless this idol is exceptionally superior, she loses her aura quickly; when she begins to assert herself, the younger one judges and compares: the other, who was chosen precisely because she was close and unintimidating, is not *other* enough to impose herself for very long; the male gods are more firmly in place because their heaven is more distant. Her curiosity and her sensuality incite the girl to desire more aggressive embraces. Very often, she has envisaged, from the start, a homosexual adventure just as a transition, an initiation, a temporary situation; she acts out jealousy, anger, pride, joy and pain with the more or less admitted idea that she is imitating, without great risk, the adventures of which she dreams but that she does not yet dare, nor has had the occasion, to live. She is destined for man, she knows it, and she wants a normal and complete woman's destiny.

Man dazzles yet frightens her. To reconcile the contradictory feelings she has about him, she will dissociate in him the male that frightens her from the shining divinity whom she piously adores. Abrupt, awkward with her masculine acquaintances, she idolises distant Prince Charmings:

* See Chapter 4 of this volume.

movie actors whose pictures she pastes over her bed, heroes, living or
dead but inaccessible, an unknown glimpsed by chance and whom she
knows she will never meet again. Such loves raise no problems. Very
often she approaches a socially prestigious or intellectual man who is
physically unexciting: for example, an old slightly ridiculous professor;
these older men emerge from a world beyond the world where the
adolescent girl is enclosed, and she can secretly devote herself to them,
consecrate herself to them as one consecrates oneself to God: such a
gift is in no way humiliating, it is freely given since the desire is not
carnal. The romantic woman in love freely accepts that the chosen one
be unassuming, ugly, a little foolish: she then feels all the more secure.
She pretends to deplore the obstacles that separate her from him; but
in reality she has chosen him precisely because no real rapport between
them is possible. Thus she can make of love an abstract and purely
subjective experience, unthreatening to her integrity; her heart beats,
she feels the pain of absence, the pangs of presence, vexation, hope,
bitterness, enthusiasm, but not authentically; no part of her is engaged.
It is amusing to observe that the idol chosen is all the more dazzling the
more distant it is: it is convenient for the everyday piano teacher to be
ridiculous and ugly; but if one falls in love with a stranger who moves
in inaccessible spheres, it is preferable that he be handsome and masculine. The important thing is that, in one way or another, the sexual issue
not be raised. These make-believe loves prolong and confirm the narcissistic attitude where eroticism appears only in its immanence, without
real presence of the Other. Finding a pretext that permits her to elude
concrete experiences, the adolescent girl often develops an intense imaginary life. She chooses to confuse her fantasies with reality. Among other
examples, Helene Deutsch*[42] describes a particularly significant one: a
pretty and seductive girl, who could have easily been courted, refused
all relations with young people around her; but at the age of thirteen,
in her secret heart, she had chosen to idolise a rather ugly seventeen-
year-old boy who had never spoken to her. She got hold of a picture of
him, wrote a dedication to herself on it, and for three years kept a diary
recounting her imaginary experiences: they exchanged kisses and
passionate embraces; there were sometimes crying scenes where she left
with her eyes all red and swollen; then they were reconciled, and she
sent herself flowers, and so on. When a move separated her from him,
she wrote him letters she never sent him but that she answered herself.

* The Psychology of Women.

This story was most obviously a defence against real experiences that she feared.

This case is almost pathological. But it illustrates a normal process by magnifying it. Marie Bashkirtseff gives a gripping example of an imaginary sentimental existence. The Duke of H., with whom she claims to be in love, is someone to whom she has never spoken. What she really desires is to exalt herself; but being a woman, and especially in the period and class she belongs to, she had no chance of achieving success through an independent existence. At eighteen years of age, she lucidly notes: 'I write to C. that I would like to be a man. I know that I could be someone; but where can one go in skirts? Marriage is women's only career; men have thirty-six chances, women have but one, zero, like in the bank.' She thus needs a man's love; but to be able to confer a sovereign value on her, he must himself be a sovereign consciousness. 'Never will a man beneath my position be able to please me,' she writes. 'A rich and independent man carries pride and a certain comfortable air with him. Self-assurance has a certain triumphant aura. I love H.'s capricious air, conceited and cruel: something of Nero in him.' And further: 'This annihilation of the woman before the superiority of the loved man must be the greatest thrill of self-love that the superior woman can experience.' Thus narcissism leads to masochism: this liaison has already been seen in the child who dreams of Bluebeard, of Griselda, of the martyred saints. The self is constituted as for others, by others: the more powerful others are, the more riches and power the self has; captivating its master, it envelops in itself the virtues possessed by him; loved by Nero, Marie Bashkirtseff *would be* Nero; to annihilate oneself before others is to realise others at once in oneself and for oneself; in reality this dream of nothingness is an arrogant will to be. In fact, Bashkirtseff never met a man superb enough to alienate herself through him. It is one thing to kneel before a far-off god shaped by one's self and another thing to give one's self over to a flesh-and-blood man. Many girls long persist in stubbornly following their dream throughout the real world: they seek a male who seems superior to all others in his position, his merits, his intelligence; they want him to be older than themselves, already having carved out a place for himself in the world, enjoying authority and prestige; fortune and fame fascinate them: the chosen one appears as the absolute Subject who by his love will convey to them his splendour and his indispensability. His superiority idealises the love that the girl brings to him: it is not only because he is a male that she wants to give herself to him, it is because he is *this* elite being. 'I would like giants and all I find is men,' a friend once said to me. In the name of these high standards, the girl disdains too-ordinary suitors and eludes the problem of sexuality. In her dreams and without risk, she cherishes an image of herself that enchants her as an image, though she has no intention of conforming to it. Thus, Maria Le Hardouin explains that she gets pleasure from seeing herself as a victim, ever devoted to a man, when she is really authoritarian.*43

> Out of a kind of modesty, I could never in reality express my nature's hidden tendencies that I lived so deeply in my dreams. As I learned to know myself, I am in fact authoritarian, violent and deeply incapable of flexibility.
>
> Always obeying a need to suppress myself, I sometimes imagined that I was an admirable woman, living only by duty, madly in love with a man whose every wish I endeavoured to anticipate. We struggled within an ugly world of needs. He killed himself working and came home at night pale and undone. I lost my sight mending his clothes next to a lightless window. In a narrow smoky kitchen, I cooked some miserable meals. Sickness ceaselessly threatened our only child with death. Yet a sweet, crucified smile was always on my lips and my eyes always showed that unbearable expression of silent courage that in reality I could never stand without disgust.

Beyond these narcissistic gratifications, some girls do concretely find the need for a guide, a master. From the time they escape their parents' hold, they find themselves encumbered by an autonomy that they are not used to; they only know how to make negative use of it; they fall into caprice and extravagance; they want to give up their freedom. The story of the young and capricious girl, rebellious and spoiled, who is tamed by the love of a sensible man, is a standard of cheap literature and cinema: it is a cliché that flatters both men and women. It is the story, among others, told by Mme de Ségur in *Such an Adorable Child!*44 As a child, Gisèle, disappointed by her overly indulgent father, becomes attached to a severe old aunt; as a girl, she comes under the influence of an irritable young man, Julien, who judges her harshly, humiliates her and tries to reform her; she marries a rich, characterless duke with whom she is extremely unhappy, and when, as a widow, she accepts the demanding love of her mentor, she finally finds joy and wisdom. In Louisa

---

* *The Black Sail.*

May Alcott's *Good Wives*, independent Jo begins to fall in love with her future husband because he seriously reproaches her for an imprudent act; he also scolds her, and she rushes to excuse herself and submit to him. In spite of the edgy pride of American women, Hollywood films have hundreds of times presented *enfants terribles* tamed by the healthy brutality of a lover or husband: a couple of slaps, even a good spanking, seem to be a good means of seduction. But in reality, the passage from ideal love to sexual love is not so simple. Many women carefully avoid approaching the object of their passion through more or less admitted fear of disappointment. If the hero, the giant or the demigod responds to the love he inspires and transforms it into a real-life experience, the girl panics; her idol becomes a male she shies away from, disgusted. There are flirtatious adolescents who do everything in their power to seduce a seemingly 'interesting' or 'fascinating' man, but paradoxically they recoil if he manifests too vivid an emotion in return; he was attractive because he seemed inaccessible: in love, he becomes commonplace. 'He's just a man like the others.' The young woman blames him for her disgrace; she uses this pretext to refuse physical contacts that shock her virgin sensibilities. If the girl gives in to her 'Ideal one', she remains unmoved in his arms and 'it happens', says Stekel,*[45] 'that obsessed girls commit suicide after such scenes where the whole construction of amorous imagination collapses because the Ideal one is seen in the form of a "brutal animal".' The taste for the impossible often leads the girl to fall in love with a man when he begins to court one of her friends, and very often she chooses a married man. She is readily fascinated by a Don Juan; she dreams of submitting and attaching herself to this seducer that no woman has ever held on to, and she kindles the hope of reforming him: but in fact, she knows she will fail in her undertaking and this is the reason for her choice. Some girls end up for ever incapable of knowing real and complete love. They will search all their lives for an ideal impossible to reach.

But there is a conflict between the girl's narcissism and the experiences for which her sexuality destines her. The woman only accepts herself as the inessential on the condition of finding herself the essential once again by abdicating. In making herself object, suddenly she has become an idol in which she proudly recognises herself; but she refuses the implacable dialectic that makes her return to the inessential. She wants to be a fascinating treasure, not a thing to be taken. She loves to

* *Frigidity in Woman.*

seem like a marvellous fetish, charged with magic emanations, not to see herself as flesh that lets herself be seen, touched, bruised: thus man prizes the woman prey, but flees the ogress Demeter.

Proud to capture masculine interest and to arouse admiration, woman is revolted by being captured in return. With puberty she learned shame: and shame is mixed with her coquetry and vanity, men's gazes flatter and hurt her at the same time; she would only like to be seen to the extent that she shows herself: eyes are always too penetrating. Hence the inconsistency disconcerting to men: she displays her décolletage and her legs, but she blushes and becomes vexed when someone looks at her. She enjoys provoking the male, but if she sees she has aroused his desire, she backs off in disgust: masculine desire is an offence as much as a tribute; in so far as she feels responsible for her charm, as she feels she is using it freely, she is enchanted with her victories: but while her features, her forms, her flesh are given and endured, she wants to keep them from this foreign and indiscreet freedom that covets them. Here is the deep meaning of this primal modesty, which interferes in a disconcerting way with the boldest coquetry. A little girl can be surprisingly audacious because she does not realise that her initiatives reveal her in her passivity: as soon as she sees this, she becomes indignant and angry. Nothing is more ambiguous than a look; it exists at a distance, and that distance makes it seem respectable: but insidiously it takes hold of the perceived image. The unripe woman struggles with these traps. She begins to let herself go, but just as quickly she tenses up and kills the desire in herself. In her as yet uncertain body, the caress is felt at times as an unpleasant tickling, at times as a delicate pleasure; a kiss moves her first, and then abruptly makes her laugh; she follows each surrender with a revolt; she lets herself be kissed, but then she wipes her mouth noticeably; she is smiling and caring, then suddenly ironic and hostile; she makes promises and deliberately forgets them. In such a way, Mathilde de La Mole is seduced by Julien's beauty and rare qualities, desirous to reach an exceptional destiny through her love, but fiercely refusing the domination of her own senses and that of a foreign consciousness; she goes from servility to arrogance, from supplication to scorn; she demands an immediate payback for everything she gives. Such is also Monique whose profile is drawn by Marcel Arland, who confuses excitement with sin, for whom love is a shameful abdication, whose blood is hot but who detests this ardour and who, while bridling, submits to it.

The 'unripe fruit' defends herself against man by exhibiting a childish and perverse nature. This is often how the girl has been described:

half-wild, half-dutiful. Colette, for one, depicted her in *Claudine at School* and also in *Green Wheat*[46] in the guise of the seductive Vinca. She maintains an interest in the world around her, over which she reigns sovereign; but she is also curious and feels a sensual and romantic desire for man. Vinca gets scratched by brambles, fishes for prawns and climbs trees and yet she quivers when her friend Phil touches her hand; she knows the agitation of the body becoming flesh, the first revelation of woman as woman; aroused, she begins to want to be pretty: at times she does her hair, she uses makeup, dresses in gauzy organdie, she takes pleasure in appearing attractive and seductive; she also wants to exist *for herself* and not only *for others*, at other times, she throws on old formless dresses, unbecoming trousers; there is a whole part of her that criticises seduction and considers it as giving in: so she purposely lets herself be seen with ink-stained fingers, messy hair, dirty. This rebelliousness gives her a clumsiness she resents: she is annoyed by it, blushes, becomes even more awkward and is horrified by these aborted attempts at seduction. At this point, the girl no longer wants to be a child, but she does not accept becoming an adult, and she blames herself for her childishness and then for her female resignation. She is in a state of constant denial.

This is the characteristic trait of the girl and gives the key to most of her behaviour; she does not accept the destiny nature and society assign to her; and yet, she does not actively repudiate it: she is too divided internally to enter into combat with the world; she confines herself to escaping reality or to contesting it symbolically. Each of her desires is matched by an anxiety: she is eager to take possession of her future, but she fears breaking with her past; she would like 'to have' a man, she balks at being his prey. And behind each fear hides a desire: rape is abhorrent to her but she aspires to passivity. Thus she is doomed to bad faith and all its ruses; she is predisposed to all sorts of negative obsessions that express the ambivalence of desire and anxiety.

One of the most common forms of adolescent contestation is giggling. High school girls and shopgirls burst into laughter while recounting love or risqué stories, while talking about their flirtations, meeting men, or seeing lovers kiss; I have known schoolgirls going to lovers' lane in the Luxembourg Gardens just to laugh; and others going to the Turkish baths to make fun of the fat women with sagging stomachs and hanging breasts they saw there; scoffing at the female body, ridiculing men, laughing at love, are ways of disavowing sexuality: this laughter that defies adults is a way of overcoming one's own embarrassment; one plays with images and words to kill the dangerous magic of them: for example, I saw twelve-year-old students burst out laughing when they saw a Latin text with the word *femur*. If in addition the girl lets herself be kissed and petted, she will get her revenge in laughing outright at her partner or with friends. I remember in a train compartment one night two girls being fondled one after the other by a travelling salesman overjoyed with his good luck: between each session they laughed hysterically, reverting to the behaviour of the awkward age in a mixture of sexuality and shame. Girls giggle and they also resort to language to help them: some use words whose coarseness would make their brothers blush; half ignorant, they are even less shocked by those expressions that do not evoke very precise images; the aim, of course, is to prevent these images from taking shape, at least to defuse them; the dirty stories high school girls tell each other are less to satisfy sexual instincts than to deny sexuality: they only want to consider the humorous side, like a mechanical or almost surgical operation. But like laughter, the use of obscene language is not only a protest: it is also a defiance of adults, a sort of sacrilege, a deliberately perverse kind of behaviour. Rebuffing nature and society, the girl nettles and challenges them by many oddities. She often has food manias: she eats pencil lead, sealing wax, bits of wood, live prawns, she swallows dozens of aspirins at a time, or she even ingests flies or spiders; I knew a girl – very obedient otherwise – who made horrible mixtures of coffee and white wine that she forced herself to swallow; other times she ate sugar soaked in vinegar; I saw another chewing determinedly into a white worm found in lettuce. All children endeavour to experience the world with their eyes, their hands and more intimately their mouths and stomachs: but at the awkward age, the girl takes particular pleasure in exploring what is indigestible and repugnant. Very often, she is attracted by what is 'disgusting'. One of them, quite pretty and attractive when she wanted to be and carefully dressed, proved really fascinated by everything that seemed 'dirty' to her: she touched insects, looked at dirty sanitary napkins, sucked the blood of her cuts. Playing with dirty things is obviously a way of overcoming disgust; this feeling becomes much more important at puberty: the girl is disgusted by her too-carnal body, by menstrual blood, by adults' sexual practices, by the male she is destined for; she denies it by indulging herself specifically in the familiarity of everything that disgusts her. 'Since I have to bleed each month, I prove that my blood does not scare me by drinking that of my cuts. Since I will have to submit myself to a revolting test, why not eat a white worm?' This attitude is affirmed more clearly in self-mutilation, so frequent at this age. The girl gashes her thigh with a razor, burns herself with cigarettes, cuts and scratches herself; so as not to go to a boring garden party, a girl during my youth cut her foot with an axe and had to spend six weeks in bed. These sadomasochistic practices are both an anticipation of the sexual experience and a revolt against it; girls have to undergo these tests, hardening themselves to all possible ordeals and rendering them harmless, including the wedding night. When she puts a slug on her chest, when she swallows a bottle of aspirin, when she wounds herself, the girl is defying her future lover: you will never inflict on me anything more horrible than I inflict on myself. These are morose and haughty initiations in sexual adventure. Destined to be a passive prey, she claims her freedom right up to submitting to pain and disgust. When she inflicts the cut of the knife, the burning of a coal on herself, she is protesting against the penetration that deflowers her: she protests by nullifying it. Masochistic, since she welcomes the pain caused by her behaviour, she is above all sadistic: as autonomous subject, she beats, scorns and tortures this dependent flesh, this flesh condemned to submission that she detests but from which she does not want to separate herself. Because, in all these situations, she does not choose authentically to reject her destiny. Sadomasochistic crazes imply a fundamental bad faith: if the girl indulges in them, it means she accepts, through her rejections, her future as woman; she would not mutilate her flesh with hatred if first she did not recognise herself as flesh. Even her violent outbursts arise from a situation of resignation. When a boy revolts against his father or against the world, he engages in effective violence; he picks a quarrel with a friend, he fights, he affirms himself as subject with his fists: he imposes himself on the world, he goes beyond it. But affirming herself, imposing herself, are forbidden to the adolescent girl, and that is what fills her heart with revolt: she hopes neither to change the world nor to emerge from it; she knows or at least believes, and perhaps even wishes, herself tied up: she can only destroy; there is despair in her rage; during a frustrating evening, she breaks glasses, windows, vases: it is not to overcome her lot; it is only a symbolic protest. The girl rebels against her future enslavement through her present powerlessness; and her vain outbursts, far from freeing her from her bonds, often merely restrict her even more. Violence against herself or the universe around her always has a negative character: it is more spectacular than effective. The boy who climbs rocks or fights with his friends regards physical pain, the injuries and the bumps, as an insignificant consequence of the positive activities he indulges in; he neither seeks nor flees them for themselves (except if an inferiority complex puts him in a situation similar to women's). The girl watches herself suffer: she seeks in her own heart the taste of violence and revolt rather than being concerned with their results. Her perversity stems from the fact that she remains stuck in the childish universe from which she cannot or does not really want to escape; she struggles in her cage rather than seeking to get out of it; her attitudes are negative, reflexive and symbolic. This perversity can take disturbing forms. Many young virgins are kleptomaniacs; kleptomania is a very ambiguous 'sexual sublimation'; the desire to transgress laws, to violate a taboo, the giddiness of the dangerous and forbidden act are certainly essential in the girl thief: but there is a double face. Taking objects without having the right is affirming one's autonomy arrogantly, it is putting oneself forward as subject facing the things stolen and the society that condemns stealing, and it is rejecting the established order as well as defying its guardians; but this defiance also has a masochistic side; the thief is fascinated by the risk she runs, by the abyss she will be thrown into if she is caught; it is the danger of being caught that gives such a voluptuous attraction to the act of taking; thus looked at with blame, or with a hand placed on her shoulder in shame, she can realise herself as object totally and without recourse. Taking without being taken in the anguish of becoming prey is the dangerous game of adolescent feminine sexuality. All perverse or illegal conduct found in girls has the same meaning. Some specialise in sending anonymous letters, others find pleasure in mystifying those around them: one fourteen-year-old persuaded a whole village that a house was haunted by spirits. They simultaneously enjoy the clandestine exercise of their power, disobedience, defiance of society, and the risk of being exposed; this is such an important element of their pleasure that they often unmask themselves, and they even sometimes accuse themselves of faults or crimes they have not committed. It is not surprising that the refusal to become object leads to constituting oneself as object: this process is common to all negative obsessions. It is in a single movement that in a hysterical paralysis the ill person fears paralysis, desires it and brings it on: he is cured from it only by no longer thinking about it; likewise with psychasthenic tics. The depth of the girl's bad faith is what links her to these types of neuroses: manias, tics, conspiracies, perversities; many neurotic symptoms are found in her due to this ambivalence of desire and anxiety that has been pointed out. It is quite common, for example, for her to 'run away'; she goes away at random, she wanders far from her father's house and two or three days later she comes back by herself. It is not a real departure or a real act of rupture with the family; it is mere playacting and the girl is often totally disconcerted if it is suggested that she leave her circle definitively: she wants to leave while not wanting to at the same time. Running away is sometimes linked to fantasies of prostitution: the girl dreams she is a prostitute, she plays this role more or less timidly; she wears excessive makeup, she leans out the window and winks at passersby; in some cases, she leaves the house and carries the drama so far that it becomes confused with reality. Such conduct often expresses a disgust with sexual desire, a feeling of guilt: since I have these thoughts, these appetites, I am no better than a prostitute, I am one, thinks a girl. Sometimes, she attempts to free herself: let's get it over with, let's go to the limit, she says to herself; she wants to prove to herself that sexuality is of little importance by giving herself to the first one. At the same time, such an attitude is often a manifestation of hostility to the mother, either that the girl is horrified by her austere virtue or that she suspects her mother of being, herself, of easy morality; or she holds a grudge against her father who has shown himself too indifferent. In any case, in this obsession – as in the fantasies of pregnancy about which we have already spoken and that are often associated with it – there is the meeting of this inextricable confusion of revolt and complicity, characterised by psychasthenic dizziness. It is noteworthy that in all these behaviours the girl does not seek to go beyond the natural and social order, she does not attempt to push back the limits of the possible or to effectuate a transmutation of values; she settles for manifesting her revolt within an established world where boundaries and laws are preserved; this is the often-defined 'devilish' attitude, implying a basic deception: the good is recognised so that it can be trampled upon, the rule is set so that it can be violated, the sacred is respected so that it is possible to perpetrate the sacrileges. The girl's attitude is defined essentially by the fact that in the agonising shadows of bad faith, she refuses the world and her own destiny at the same time as she accepts them.

However, she does not confine herself to contesting negatively the situation imposed on her; she also tries to compensate for its insufficiencies. Although the future frightens her, the present dissatisfies her; she hesitates to become woman; she frets at still being only a child; she has already left her past; she is not yet committed to a new life. She is occupied but she does not *do* anything; because she does not do anything, she *has* nothing, she *is nothing*. She tries to fill this void by playacting and mystifications. She is criticised for being devious, a liar, and troublesome. The truth is she is doomed to secrets and lies. At sixteen, a woman has already gone through disturbing experiences: puberty, menstrual periods, awakening of sexuality, first arousals, first passions, fears, disgust and ambiguous experiences: she has hidden all these things in her heart; she has learned to guard her secrets preciously. The mere fact of having to hide her sanitary napkins and of concealing her periods inclines her to lies. In the short story 'Old Mortality', Katherine Anne Porter recounts that young American women from the South, around 1900, made themselves ill by swallowing mixtures of salt and lemon to stop their periods when going to balls: they were afraid that the young men would recognise their state by the bags under their eyes, by contact with their hands, by a smell perhaps, and this idea upset them. It is difficult to play the idol, the fairy or the remote princess when one feels a bloody piece of material between one's legs and more generally, when one knows the primal misery of being a body. Modesty, a spontaneous refusal to let oneself be grasped as flesh, comes close to hypocrisy. But above all, the adolescent girl is condemned to the lie of pretending to be object, and a prestigious one, while she experiences herself as an uncertain, dispersed existence, knowing her failings. Makeup, false curls, corsets, padded bras, are lies; the face itself becomes a mask: spontaneous expressions are produced artfully, a wondrous passivity is imitated; there is nothing more surprising than suddenly discovering in the exercise of one's feminine functions a physiognomy with which one is familiar; its transcendence denies itself and imitates immanence; one's eyes no longer perceive, they reflect; one's body no longer lives: it waits; every gesture and smile becomes an appeal; disarmed, available, the girl is nothing but a flower offered, a fruit to be picked. Man encourages her in these lures by demanding to be lured: then he gets irritated, he accuses. But for the guileless girl, he has nothing but indifference and even hostility. He is seduced only by the one who sets traps for him; offered, she is still she who stalks her prey; her passivity takes the form of an undertaking, she makes her weakness a tool of her strength; since she is forbidden to attack outright, she is reduced to manoeuvres and calculations; and it is in her interest to appear freely given; therefore, she will be criticised for being perfidious and treacherous, and she is. But it is true that she is obliged to offer man the myth of her submission because he insists on dominating. And can one demand that she stifle her most essential claims? Her complaisance can only be perverted right from the outset. Besides, she cheats not only out of concerted, deliberate ruse. Because all roads are barred to her, because she cannot *do*, because she must *be*, a curse weighs on her. As a child, she played at being a dancer or a saint; later, she plays at being herself; what is really the truth? In the area in which she has been shut up, this is a word without sense. Truth is reality unveiled, and unveiling occurs through acts: but she does not act. The romances she tells herself about herself – and that she also often tells others – seem better ways of expressing the possibilities she feels in herself than the plain account of her daily life. She is unable to take stock of herself: so she consoles herself by playacting; she embodies a character she seeks to give importance to; she tries to stand out by extravagant behaviour because she does not have the right to distinguish herself in specific activities. She knows she is without responsibilities, insignificant in this world of men: she makes trouble because she has nothing else important to do. Giraudoux's Electra is a woman who makes trouble, because it is up to Orestes alone to accomplish a real murder with a real sword. Like the child, the girl wears herself out in scenes and rages, she makes herself ill, she manifests signs of hysteria to try to attract attention and be someone who *counts*. She interferes in the destiny of others so that she can count; she uses any weapon she can; she tells secrets, she invents others, she betrays, she calumniates; she needs tragedy around her to feel alive since she finds no support in her own life. She is unpredictable for the same reason; the fantasies we form and the images by which we are lulled are contradictory: only action unifies the diversity of time. The girl does not have a real will but has desires, and she jumps from one to the other at random. What makes her flightiness sometimes dangerous is that at every moment, committing herself in dream only, she commits herself wholly. She puts herself on a level of intransigence and perfection; she has a taste for the definitive and absolute: if she cannot control the future, she wants to attain the eternal. 'I will never give up. I want everything always. I need to prefer my life in order to accept it,' writes Marie Lenéru. So echoes Anouilh's Antigone: 'I want everything, immediately.' This childish impe-rialism can only be found in an individual who dreams his destiny: dreams abolish time and obstacles, they need to be exaggerated to compensate for the small amount of reality; whoever has authentic projects knows a finitude that is the gauge of one's concrete power. The girl wants to receive *everything* because there is *nothing* that depends on her. That is where her character of *enfant terrible* comes from, faced with adults and man in particular. She does not accept the limitations an individual's insertion in the real world imposes; she defies him to go beyond them. Thus Hilda* expects Solness to give her a kingdom: as she is not the one who has to conquer it, she wants it without limits; she demands

* See Ibsen, *The Master Builder*.

that he build the highest tower ever built and that he 'climb as high as he builds': he hesitates to climb, because he is afraid of heights; she who remains on the ground and looks on denies contingency and human weakness; she does not accept that reality imposes a limit on her dreams of grandeur. Adults always seem mean and cautious to the girl who stops at nothing because she has nothing to lose; imagining herself taking the boldest risks, she dares them to match her in reality. Unable to put herself to the test, she invests herself with the most astonishing qualities without fear of being contradicted.

However, her uncertainty also stems from this lack of control; she dreams she is infinite; she is nevertheless alienated in the character she offers for the admiration of others; it depends on these foreign consciousnesses: this double she identifies with herself but to whose presence she passively submits is dangerous for her. This explains why she is touchy and vain. The slightest criticism or gibe destabilises her. Her worth does not derive from her own effort but from a fickle approbation. This is not defined by individual activities but by general reputation; it seems to be quantitatively measurable; the price of merchandise decreases when it becomes too common: thus the girl is only rare, exceptional, remarkable or extraordinary if no other one is. Her female companions are rivals or enemies; she tries to denigrate, to deny them; she is jealous and hostile.

It is clear that all the faults for which the adolescent girl is reproached merely express her situation. It is a painful condition to know one is passive and dependent at the age of hope and ambition, at the age where the will to live and to take a place in the world intensifies; woman learns at this conquering age that no conquest is allowed her, that she must disavow herself, that her future depends on men's good offices. New social and sexual aspirations are awakened but they are condemned to remain unsatisfied; all her vital or spiritual impulses are immediately barred. It is understandable that she should have trouble establishing her balance. Her erratic mood, her tears and her nervous crises are less the result of a physiological fragility than the sign of her deep maladjustment.

However, this situation that the girl flees by a thousand inauthentic paths is also one that she sometimes assumes authentically. Her shortcomings make her irritating: but her unique virtues sometimes make her astonishing. Both have the same origin. From her rejection of the world, from her unsettled waiting, and from her nothingness, she can create a springboard for herself and emerge then in her solitude and her freedom.

The girl is secretive, tormented, in the throes of difficult conflicts. This complexity enriches her; her interior life develops more deeply than her brothers'; she is more attentive to her heart's desires that thus become more subtle, more varied; she has more psychological sense than boys turned towards external goals. She is able to give weight to these revolts that oppose her to the world. She avoids the traps of seriousness and conformism. The concerted lies of her circle meet with her irony and clear-sightedness. She tests her situation's ambiguity on a daily basis: beyond sterile protest, she can have the courage to throw into question established optimism, preconceived values, and hypocritical and re-assuring morality. Such is Maggie, the moving example given in *The Mill on the Floss*, in which George Eliot embodied the doubts and courageous rebellions of her youth against Victorian England; the heroes – particularly Tom, Maggie's brother – stubbornly affirm conventional wisdom, immobilising morality in formal rules: Maggie tries to reintroduce a breath of life, she overturns them, she goes to the limits of her solitude and emerges as a pure freedom beyond the fossilised male universe.

The adolescent girl barely finds anything but a negative use of this freedom. But her openness can engender a precious faculty of recep-tivity; she will prove to be devoted, attentive, understanding and loving. Rosamond Lehmann's heroines are marked by this docile generosity. In *Invitation to the Waltz*, Olivia, still shy and gauche, and barely interested in her appearance, is seen scrutinising this world she will enter tomorrow with excited curiosity. She listens with all her heart to her succession of dancers, she endeavours to answer them according to their wishes, she is their echo, she vibrates, she accepts everything that is offered. Judy, the heroine of *Dusty Answer*, has the same endearing quality. She has not relinquished childhood joys; she likes to bathe naked at night in the park river; she loves nature, books, beauty and life; she does not cultivate a narcissistic cult; without lies, without egotism, she does not look for an exaltation of self through men: her love is a gift. She bestows it on any being who seduces her, man or woman, Jennifer or Roddy. She gives herself without losing herself: she leads an independent student life; she has her own world, her own projects. But what distinguishes her from a boy is her attitude of expectation, her tender docility. In a subtle way, she is, in spite of everything, destined to the Other: the Other has a marvellous dimension in her eyes to the point that she is in love with all the young men of the neighbouring family, their house, their sister and their universe, all at the same time; it is not as a friend, it is as Other that Jennifer fascinates her. And she charms Roddy and his cousins by her capacity to yield to them, to shape herself to their desires; she is patience, sweetness, acceptance and silent suffering.

Different but also captivating in the way she welcomes into her heart those she cherishes, Tessa, in Margaret Kennedy's *The Constant Nymph*, is simultaneously spontaneous, wild and giving. She refuses to abdicate anything of herself: finery, makeup, disguises, hypocrisy, acquired charms, caution and female submission are repugnant to her; she desires to be loved but not behind a mask; she yields to Lewis's moods, but without servility; she understands him, she vibrates in unison with him; but if they ever argue, Lewis knows that caresses will not subdue her: while authoritarian and vain Florence lets herself be conquered by kisses, Tessa succeeds in the extraordinary accomplishment of remaining free in her love, allowing her to love without either hostility or pride. Her nature has all the lures of artifice; to please, she never degrades herself, never lowers herself or locks herself in as object. Surrounded by artists who have committed their whole existence to musical creation, she does not feel this devouring demon within her; she wholly endeavours to love, understand and help them: she does it effortlessly, out of a tender and spontaneous generosity, which is why she remains perfectly autonomous even in the instances in which she forgets herself in favour of others. Thanks to this pure authenticity, she is spared the conflicts of adolescence; she can suffer from the world's harshness, she is not divided within herself; she is harmonious both as a carefree child and as a very wise woman. The sensitive and generous girl, receptive and ardent, is very ready to become a great lover.

When not encountering love, she may encounter poetry. Because she does not act, she watches, she feels, she records; she responds deeply to a colour or a smile; because her destiny is scattered outside her, in cities already built, on mature men's faces, she touches and tastes both passionately and more gratuitously than the young man. As she is poorly integrated into the human universe, and has trouble adapting to it, she is, like the child, able to see it; instead of being interested only in her grasp of things, she focuses on their meaning; she perceives particular profiles, unexpected metamorphoses. She rarely feels a creative urge and all too often she lacks the techniques that would allow her to express herself; but in conversations, letters, literary essays and rough drafts, she does show an original sensibility. The girl throws herself passionately into things, because she is not yet mutilated in her transcendence; and the fact that she does not accomplish anything, that she is nothing, will make her drive even more fervent: empty and unlimited, what she will seek to reach from within her nothingness is All. That is why she will devote a special love to Nature: more than the adolescent boy, she worships it. Untamed and inhuman, Nature encompasses most obviously the totality of what is. The adolescent girl has not yet annexed any part of the universe: thanks to this impoverishment, the whole universe is her kingdom; when she takes possession of it, she also proudly takes possession of herself. Colette often recounted these youthful orgies:*

> For even then I so loved the dawn that my mother granted it to me as a reward. She used to agree to wake me at half-past three and off I would go, an empty basket on each arm, towards the kitchen-gardens that sheltered in the narrow bend of the river, in search of strawberries, blackcurrants, and hairy gooseberries.
>
> At half-past three everything slumbered still in a primal blue, blurred and dewy, and as I went down the sandy road the mist, grounded by its own weight, bathed first my legs, then my well-built little body, reaching at last my mouth and ears, and finally to that most sensitive part of all, my nostrils . . . It was on that road and at that hour that I first became aware of my own self, experienced an inexpressible state of grace, and felt one with the first breath of air that stirred, the first bird, and the sun so newly born that it still looked not quite round . . . I came back when the bell rang for the first Mass. But not before I had eaten my fill, not before I had described a great circle in the woods, like a dog out hunting on its own, and tasted the water of the two hidden springs which I worshipped.[47]

Mary Webb describes in *The House in Dormer Forest* the intense joys a girl can know in communion with a familiar landscape:

> When the atmosphere of the house became too thunderous and Amber's nerves were strained to breaking-point, she crept away to the upper woods . . . It seemed to her that while Dormer lived by law, the forest lived by impulse. Through a gradual awakening to natural beauty, she reached a perception of beauty peculiar to herself. She began to perceive analogies. Nature became for her, not a fortuitous assemblage of pretty things, but a harmony, a poem

---

* *Sido.*

solemn and austere . . . Beauty breathed there, light shone there
that was not of the flower or the star. A tremor, mysterious and
thrilling, seemed to run with the light . . . through the whispering
forest . . . So her going out into the green world had in it something of a religious rite . . . On a still morning . . . she went up to
the Birds' Orchard. She often did this before the day of petty
irritation began . . . she found some comfort in the absurd inconsequence of the bird people . . . she came at last to the upper wood,
and was instantly at grips with beauty. There was for her literally
something of wrestling, of the mood which says: 'I will not let thee
go until thou bless me' . . . Leaning against a wild pear tree, she
was aware, by her inward hearing, of the tidal wave of sap that
rose so full and strong that she could almost imagine it roaring like
the sea. Then a tremor of wind shook the flowering tree-tops, and
she awoke again to the senses, to the strangeness of these utter-
ances of the leaves . . . Every petal, every leaf, seemed to be conning
some memory of profundities whence it had come. Every curving
flower seemed full of echoes too majestic for its fragility . . . A breath
of scented air came from the hilltops and stole among the branches.
That which had form, and knew the mortality which is in form,
trembled before that which passed, formless and immortal . . .
Because of it the place became no mere congregation of trees, but
a thing fierce as stellar space . . . For it possesses itself forever in a
vitality withheld, immutable. It was this that drew Amber with
breathless curiosity into the secret haunts of nature. It was this that
struck her now into a kind of ecstasy . . . [48]

Women as different as Emily Brontë and Anna de Noailles experienced
similar fervour in their youth – and it continued throughout their lives.

The texts I have cited convincingly show the comfort the adolescent
girl finds in fields and woods. In the paternal house reign mother, laws,
custom and routine, and she wants to wrest herself from this past; she
wants to become a sovereign subject in her own turn: but socially she
only accedes to her adult life by becoming woman; she pays for her liberation with an abdication; but in the midst of plants and animals she is a
human being; a subject, a freedom, she is freed both from her family
and from males. She finds an image of the solitude of her soul in the
secrecy of forests and the tangible figure of transcendence in the vast
horizons of the plains; she is herself this limitless land, this summit
jutting towards the sky; she can follow, she will follow, these roads that

leave for an unknown future; sitting on the hilltop she dominates the riches of the world spread out at her feet, given to her; through the water's palpitations, the shimmering of the light, she anticipates the joys, tears and ecstasies that she does not yet know; the adventures of her own heart are confusedly promised her by ripples on the pond and patches of sun. Smells and colours speak a mysterious language but one word stands out with triumphant clarity: 'life'. Existence is not only an abstract destiny inscribed in town hall registers; it is future and carnal richness. Having a body no longer seems like a shameful failing; in these desires that the adolescent girl repudiates under the maternal gaze, she recognises the sap mounting in the trees; she is no longer cursed, she proudly claims her kinship with leaves and flowers; she rumples a corolla and she knows that a living prey will fill her empty hands one day. Flesh is no longer filth: it is joy and beauty. Merged with sky and heath, the girl is this vague breath that stirs up and kindles the universe, and she is every sprig of heather; an individual rooted in the soil and infinite consciousness, she is both spirit and life; her presence is imperious and triumphant like that of the earth itself.

Beyond Nature she sometimes seeks an even more remote and stunning reality; she is willing to lose herself in mystical ecstasies; in periods of faith many young female souls demanded that God fill the emptiness of their being; the vocations of Catherine of Siena and Teresa of Avila were revealed to them at a young age.* Joan of Arc was a girl. In other periods, humanity appears the supreme end; so the mystical impulse flows into defined projects; but it is also a youthful desire for the absolute that gave birth to the flame that nourished the lives of Mme Roland or Rosa Luxemburg. From her subjugation, her impoverishment, and the depths of her refusal, the girl can extract the most daring courage. She finds poetry; she finds heroism too. One of the ways of assuming the fact that she is poorly integrated into society is to go beyond its restricting horizons.

The richness and strength of their nature and fortunate circumstances have enabled some women to continue in their adult lives their passionate projects from adolescence. But these are exceptions. George Eliot had Maggie Tulliver and Margaret Kennedy had Tessa die for good reason. It was a bitter destiny that the Brontë sisters had. The girl is touching because she rises up against the world, weak and alone; but the world is too powerful; she persists in refusing it, she is broken. Belle de Zuylen,

* We will return to the specific characteristics of the feminine mystic.

who overwhelmed all of Europe with her mind's originality and caustic power, frightened all her suitors: her refusal to make concessions condemned her to long years of celibacy that weighed on her since she declared that the expression 'virgin and martyr' was a pleonasm. This stubbornness is rare. In the immense majority of cases, the girl is aware that the fight is much too unequal, and she ends up yielding. 'You will all die at fifteen,' writes Diderot to Sophie Volland. When the fight has only been – as happens most often – a symbolic revolt, defeat is certain. Demanding in dreams, full of hope but passive, the girl makes adults smile with pity; they doom her to resignation. And in fact, the rebellious and eccentric girl that we left is found two years later, calmer, ready to consent to her woman's life. This is the future Colette predicted for Vinca; this is how the heroines of Mauriac's early novels appear. The adolescent crisis is a type of 'work' similar to what Dr Lagache calls 'the work of mourning'. The girl buries her childhood slowly – this autonomous and imperious individual she has been – and she enters adult existence submissively.

Of course, it is not possible to establish defined categories based on age alone. Some women remain infantile their whole lives; the behaviours we have described are sometimes perpetuated to an advanced age. Nevertheless, on the whole, there is a big difference between the girlish fifteen-year-old and an older girl. The latter is adapted to reality; she scarcely advances on the imaginary level; she is less divided within herself than before. At about eighteen, Marie Bashkirtseff writes:

The more I advance in age towards the end of my youth, the more I am covered with indifference. Little agitates me and everything used to agitate me.

Irène Reweliotty comments:

To be accepted by men you have to think and act like them; if you don't they treat you like a black sheep and solitude becomes your lot. And I, now, I'm fed up with solitude and I want people not only around me but with me . . . Living now and no longer existing and waiting and dreaming and telling yourself everything within yourself, your mouth shut and your body motionless.

And further along:

> With so much flattery, wooing, and such, I become terribly ambi-
> tious. This is no longer the trembling, marvellous happiness of the
> fifteen-year-old. It is a kind of cold and hard intoxication to take
> my revenge on life, to climb. I flirt; I play at loving. I do not love . . .
> I gain in intelligence, in sangfroid, in ordinary lucidity. I lose my
> heart. It was as if it cracked . . . In two months, I left childhood
> behind.

Approximately the same sound comes from these secrets of a nineteen-
year-old girl:*

> In the old days Oh! What a conflict against a mentality that seemed
> incompatible with this century and the appeals of this century itself!
> I now have a peaceful feeling. Each new big idea that enters me,
> instead of provoking a painful upheaval, a destruction, and an inces-
> sant reconstruction, adapts marvellously to what is already in me . . .
> Now I go seamlessly from theoretical thinking to daily life without
> attempting continuity.

The girl – unless she is particularly graceless – accepts her femininity
in the end; and she is often happy to enjoy gratuitously the pleasures
and triumphs she gets from settling definitively into her destiny; as she
is not yet bound to any duty, irresponsible, available, for her the present
seems neither empty nor disappointing since it is just one step; dressing
and flirting still have the lightness of a game and her dreams of the
future disguise their futility. This is how Virginia Woolf describes the
impressions of a young coquette during a party:

> I feel myself shining in the dark. Silk is on my knee. My silk legs
> rub smoothly together. The stones of a necklace lie cold on my
> throat . . . I am arrayed, I am prepared . . . My hair is swept in one
> curve. My lips are precisely red. I am ready now to join men and
> women on the stairs, my peers. I pass them, exposed to their gaze,
> as they are to mine . . . I now begin to unfurl, in this scent, in this
> radiance, as a fern when its curled leaves unfurl . . . I feel a thou-
> sand capacities spring up in me. I am arch, gay, languid, melancholy

* Cited by Debesse in *Adolescent Identity Crisis*.

by turns; I am rooted, but I flow. All gold, flowing that way, I say
to this one, 'Come' . . . He approaches. He makes towards me.
This is the most exciting moment I have ever known. I flutter. I
ripple . . . Are we not lovely sitting together here, I in my satin;
he in black and white? My peers may look at me now. I look
straight back at you, men and women. I am one of you. This is
my world . . . The door opens. The door goes on opening. Now
I think, next time it opens the whole of my life will be changed . . .
The door opens. Come, I say to this one, rippling gold from head
to heels. 'Come,' and he comes towards me.*[49]

But the more the girl matures, the more maternal authority weighs
on her. If she leads a housekeeper's life at home, she suffers from being
only an assistant, she would like to devote her work to her own home,
to her own children. Often the rivalry with her mother worsens: in particular, the older daughter is irritated if younger brothers and sisters are
born; she feels her mother 'has done her time' and it is up to her now
to bear children, to reign. If she works outside the house, she suffers
when she returns home from still being treated as a simple member of
the family and not as an autonomous individual.

Less romantic than before, she begins to think much more of marriage
than love. She no longer embellishes her future spouse with a prestigious halo: what she wishes for is to have a stable position in this world
and to begin to lead her life as a woman. This is how Virginia Woolf
describes the imaginings of a rich country girl:

For soon in the hot midday when the bees hum round the holly-
hocks my lover will come. He will stand under the cedar tree. To
his one word I shall answer my one word. What has formed in me
I shall give him. I shall have children; I shall have maids in aprons;
men with pitchforks; a kitchen where they bring the ailing lambs
to warm in baskets, where the hams hang and the onions glisten.
I shall be like my mother, silent in a blue apron locking up the
cupboards.

A similar dream dwells in poor Prue Sarn:†

---

* *The Waves.*
† Mary Webb, *Precious Bane.*

It seemed such a terrible thing never to marry. All girls got married . . . And when girls got married, they had a cottage, and a lamp, maybe, to light when their man came home, or if it was only candles it was all one, for they could put them in the window, and he'd think 'There's my missus now, lit the candles!' And then one day Mrs Beguildy would be making a cot of rushes for 'em, and one day there'd be a babe in it, grand and solemn, and bidding letters sent round for the christening, and the neighbours coming round the babe's mother like bees round the queen. Often when things went wrong, I'd say to myself, 'N'er mind, Prue Sarn! There'll come a day when you'll be queen in your own skep.'[50]

For most older girls, whether they have a laborious or frivolous life, whether they be confined to the paternal household or partially get away from it, the conquest of a husband – or at the least a serious lover – turns into a more and more pressing enterprise. This concern is often harmful for feminine friendships. The 'best friend' loses her privileged place. The girl sees rivals more than partners in her companions. I knew one such girl, intelligent and talented but who had chosen to think herself a 'faraway princess': this is how she described herself in poems and literary essays; she sincerely admitted she did not remain attached to her childhood friends: if they were ugly and stupid, she did not like them; if seductive, she feared them. The impatient wait for a man, often involving manoeuvres, ruses and humiliations, blocks the girl's horizon; she becomes egotistical and hard. And if Prince Charming takes his time appearing, disgust and bitterness set in.

The girl's character and behaviour express her situation: if it changes, the adolescent girl's attitude also changes. Today, it is becoming possible for her to take her future in her hands, instead of putting it in those of the man. If she is absorbed by studies, sports, a professional training, or a social and political activity, she frees herself of the male obsession; she is less preoccupied by love and sexual conflicts. However, she has a harder time than the young man in accomplishing herself as an autonomous individual. I have said that neither her family nor customs assist her attempts. Besides, even if she chooses independence, she still makes a place in her life for the man, for love. She will often be afraid of missing her destiny as a woman if she gives herself over entirely to any undertaking. She does not admit this feeling to herself: but it is there, it distorts all her best efforts, it sets up limits. In any case, the woman who works wants to reconcile her success with purely feminine successes; that not only requires devoting considerable time to her appearance and beauty but also, what is more serious, implies that her vital interests are divided. Outside of his regular studies, the male student amuses himself by freely exercising his mind and from there emerge his best discoveries; the woman's daydreams are oriented in a different direction: she will think of her physical appearance, of man, of love, she will give the bare minimum to her studies, to her career, whereas in these areas nothing is as necessary as the superfluous. It is not a question of mental weakness, of a lack of concentration, but of a split in her interests that do not coincide well. A vicious circle is knotted here: people are often surprised to see how easily a woman gives up music, studies, or a job as soon as she has found a husband; this is because she had committed too little of herself to her projects to derive benefit from their accomplishment. Everything converges to hold back her personal ambition while enormous social pressure encourages her to find a social position and justification in marriage. It is natural that she should not seek to create her place in this world by and for herself or that she should seek it timidly. As long as perfect economic equality is not realised in society and as long as customs allow the woman to profit as wife and mistress from the privileges held by certain men, the dream of passive success will be maintained in her and will hold back her own accomplishments.

However the girl approaches her existence as an adult, her apprenticeship is not yet over. By small increments or bluntly, she has to undergo her sexual initiation. There are girls who refuse. If sexually difficult incidents marked their childhood, if an awkward upbringing has gradually rooted a horror of sexuality in them, they carry over their adolescent repugnance of men. There are also circumstances that cause some women to have an extended virginity in spite of themselves. But in most cases, the girl accomplishes her sexual destiny at a more or less advanced age. How she braves it is obviously closely linked to her whole past. But this is also a novel experience that presents itself in unforeseen circumstances and to which she freely reacts. This is the new stage we must now consider.

CHAPTER 3

Sexual Initiation

In a sense, woman's sexual initiation, like man's, begins in infancy. There is a theoretical and practical initiation period that follows continuously from the oral, anal and genital phases up to adulthood. But the young girl's erotic experiences are not a simple extension of her previous sexual activities; they are very often unexpected and brutal; they always constitute a new occurrence that creates a rupture with the past. While she is going through them, all the problems the girl faces are concentrated in an urgent and acute form. In some cases, the crisis is easily resolved; there are tragic situations where the crisis can only be resolved through suicide or madness. In any case, the way woman reacts to the experiences strongly affects her destiny. All psychiatrists agree on the extreme importance her erotic beginnings have for her: their repercussions will be felt for the rest of her life.

The situation is profoundly different here for man and woman from the biological, social and psychological points of view. For man, the passage from childhood sexuality to maturity is relatively simple: erotic pleasure is objectified; now, instead of being realised in his immanent presence, this erotic pleasure is intended for a transcendent being. The erection is the expression of this need; with penis, hands, mouth, with his whole body, the man reaches out to his partner, but he remains at the heart of this activity, as the subject generally does before the objects he perceives and the instruments he manipulates; he projects himself towards the other without losing his autonomy; feminine flesh is a prey for him and he seizes in woman the attributes his sensuality requires of any object; of course he does not succeed in appropriating them: at least he holds them; the embrace and the kiss imply a partial failure: but this very failure is a stimulant and a joy. The act of love finds its unity in its natural culmination: orgasm. Coitus has a specific physiological aim; in ejaculation the male releases burdensome secretions; after orgasm, the male feels complete relief regularly accompanied by pleasure. And, of

course, pleasure is not the only aim; it is often followed by disappointment: the need has disappeared rather than having been satisfied. In any
case, a definite act is consummated and the man's body remains intact:
the service he has rendered to the species becomes one with his own
pleasure. Woman's eroticism is far more complex and reflects the
complexity of her situation. It has been seen* that instead of integrating
forces of the species into her individual life, the female is prey to the
species, whose interests diverge from her own ends; this antinomy reaches
its height in woman; one of its manifestations is the opposition of two
organs: the clitoris and the vagina. At the infant stage, the former is the
centre of feminine eroticism: some psychiatrists uphold the existence of
vaginal sensitivity in little girls, but this is a very inaccurate opinion; at
any rate, it would have only secondary importance. The clitoral system
does not change with adulthood† and woman preserves this erotic
autonomy her whole life; like the male orgasm, the clitoral spasm is a
kind of detumescence that occurs quasi-mechanically; but it is only indirectly linked to normal coitus, it plays no role whatsoever in procreation.
The woman is penetrated and impregnated through the vagina; it
becomes an erotic centre uniquely through the intervention of the male,
and this always constitutes a kind of rape. In the past, a woman was
snatched from her childhood universe and thrown into her life as a wife
by a real or simulated rape; this was an act of violence that changed the
girl into a woman: it is also referred to as 'ravishing' a girl's virginity, or
'taking' her flower. This deflowering is not the harmonious outcome of
a continuous development; it is an abrupt rupture with the past, the
beginning of a new cycle. Pleasure is then reached by contractions of
the inside surface of the vagina; do these contractions result in a precise
and definitive orgasm? This point is still being debated. The anatomical
data are vague. 'There is a great deal of anatomic and clinical evidence
that most of the interior of the vagina is without nerves,' states, among
other things, the Kinsey Report. 'A considerable amount of surgery may
be performed inside the vagina without need for anesthetics. Nerves
have been demonstrated inside the vagina only in an area in the anter-
ior wall, proximate to the base of the clitoris.' However, in addition to
the stimulation of this innervated zone, 'the female may be conscious
of the intrusion of an object into the vagina, particularly if vaginal
muscles are tightened; but the satisfaction so obtained is probably related

* Vol. I, Chapter 1.
† Unless excision is practised, which is the rule in some primitive cultures.

more to muscle tonus than it is to erotic nerve stimulation.'[51] Yet, it is beyond doubt that vaginal pleasure exists; and even vaginal masturbation – for adult women – seems to be more widespread than Kinsey says.* But what is certain is that the vaginal reaction is very complex and can be qualified as psychophysiological because it not only concerns the entire nervous system but also depends on the whole situation lived by the subject: it requires profound consent of the individual as a whole; to establish itself, the new erotic cycle launched by the first coitus demands a kind of 'preparation' of the nervous system, the elaboration of a totally new form that has to include the clitoral system as well; it takes a long time to be put in place, and sometimes it never succeeds in being created. It is striking that woman has the choice between two cycles, one of which perpetuates youthful independence, while the other destines her to man and children. The normal sexual act effectively makes woman dependent on the male and the species. It is he – as for most animals – who has the aggressive role, and she who submits to his embrace. Ordinarily she can be taken at any time by man, while he can take her only when he is in the state of erection; feminine refusal can be overcome except in the case of a rejection as profound as vaginismus, sealing woman more securely than the hymen; still vaginismus leaves the male the means to relieve himself on a body that his muscular force permits him to reduce to his mercy. Since she is object, her inertia does not profoundly alter her natural role: to the extent that many men are not interested in whether the woman who shares their bed wants coitus or only submits to it. One can even go to bed with a dead woman. Coitus cannot take place without male consent, and male satisfaction is its natural end result. Fertilisation can occur without the woman deriving any pleasure. On the other hand, fertilisation is far from representing the completion of the sexual process for her; by contrast, it is at this moment

---

* 'The use of an artificial penis in solitary sexual gratification may be traced down from classic times, and doubtless prevailed in the very earliest human civilization . . . in more recent years the following are a few of the objects found in the vagina or bladder whence they could only be removed by surgical interference: Pencils, sticks of sealing-wax, cotton-reels, hair-pins (and in Italy very commonly the bone-pins used in the hair), bodkins, knitting-needles, crochet-needles, needle-cases, compasses, glass stoppers, candles, corks, tumblers, forks, tooth-picks, toothbrushes, pomade-pots (in a case recorded by Schroeder with a cockchafer inside, a makeshift substitute for the Japanese rin-no-tama), while in one recent English case a full-sized hen's egg was removed from the vagina of a middle-aged married woman . . . the large objects, naturally, are found chiefly in the vagina, and in the married woman' (Havelock Ellis, Studies in the Psychology of Sex, Volume I).

that the service demanded of her by the species begins: it takes place slowly and painfully in pregnancy, birth and breast-feeding.

Man's 'anatomical destiny' is profoundly different from woman's. Their moral and social situations are no less different. Patriarchal civilisation condemned woman to chastity; the right of man to relieve his sexual desires is more or less openly recognised, whereas woman is confined within marriage: for her the act of the flesh, if not sanctified by the code, by a sacrament, is a fault, a fall, a defeat, a weakness; she is obliged to defend her virtue, her honour; if she 'gives in' or if she 'falls', she arouses disdain, whereas even the blame inflicted on her vanquisher brings him admiration. From primitive civilisations to our times, the bed has always been accepted as a 'service' for a woman for which the male thanks her with gifts or guarantees her keep: but to serve is to give herself up to a master; there is no reciprocity at all in this relationship. The marriage structure, like the existence of prostitutes, proves it: the woman *gives herself*; the man remunerates her and takes her. Nothing forbids the male to act the master, to take inferior creatures: ancillary loves have always been tolerated, whereas the bourgeois woman who gives herself to a chauffeur or a gardener is socially degraded. Fiercely racist American men in the South have always been permitted by custom to sleep with black women, before the Civil War as today, and they exploit this right with a lordly arrogance; a white woman who had relations with a black man in the time of slavery would have been put to death, and today she would be lynched. To say he slept with a woman, a man says he 'possessed' her, that he 'had' her; on the contrary, 'to have' someone is sometimes vulgarly expressed as 'to fuck someone'; the Greeks called a woman who did not have sexual relations with the male *Parthenos adamatos*, an untaken virgin; the Romans called Messalina *invicta* because none of her lovers gave her satisfaction. So for the male lover, the love act is conquest and victory. While, in another man, the erection often seems like a ridiculous parody of voluntary action, each one nonetheless considers it in his own case with a certain pride. Males' erotic vocabulary is inspired by military vocabulary: the lover has the ardour of a soldier, his sexual organ stiffens like a bow, when he ejaculates, he 'discharges', it is a machine gun, a cannon; he speaks of attack, assault, of victory. In his arousal there is a certain flavour of the heroic. 'The generative act, consisting in the occupation of one being by another,' writes Benda,*[52] 'imposes, on the one hand, the idea of a conqueror, on

* *Uriel's Report.*

the other of something conquered. Thus when they refer to their most civilised love relationships, they talk of conquest, attack, assault, siege and defence, defeat, and capitulation, clearly copying the idea of love from that of war. This act, involving the pollution of one being by another, imposes a certain pride on the polluter and some humiliation on the polluted, even when she is consenting.' This last phrase introduces a new myth: that man inflicts a stain on woman. In fact, sperm is not excrement; one speaks of 'nocturnal pollution' because the sperm does not serve its natural purpose; while coffee can stain a light-coloured dress, it is not said to be waste that defiles the stomach. Other men maintain, by contrast, that woman is impure because it is she who is 'soiled by discharges' and that she pollutes the male. In any case, being the one who pollutes confers a dubious superiority. In fact, man's privileged situation comes from the integration of his biologically aggressive role into his social function of chief and master; it is through this function that physiological differences take on all their full meaning. Because man is sovereign in this world, he claims the violence of his desires as a sign of his sovereignty; it is said of a man endowed with great erotic capacities that he is strong and powerful: epithets that describe him as an activity and a transcendence; on the contrary, woman being only an object is considered *hot* or *cold*; that is, she will never manifest any qualities other than passive ones.

So the climate in which feminine sexuality awakens is nothing like the one surrounding the adolescent boy. Besides, when woman faces the male for the first time, her erotic attitude is very complex. It is not true, as has been held at times, that the virgin does not know desire and that the male awakens her sensuality; this legend once again betrays the male's taste for domination, never wanting his companion to be autonomous, even in the desire that she has for him; in fact, for man as well, desire is often aroused through contact with woman, and, on the contrary, most girls feverishly long for caresses before a hand ever touches them. Isadora Duncan in *My Life*[53] says,

> My hips, which had been like a boy's, took on another undulation, and through my whole being I felt one great surging, longing, unmistakable urge, so that I could no longer sleep at night but tossed and turned in feverish, painful unrest.

In a long confession of her life to Stekel, a young woman recounts:

I began vigorously to flirt. I had to have 'my nerves tickler [sic].' I was a passionate dancer, and while dancing I always shut my eyes the better to enjoy it . . . During dancing, I was somewhat exhibition-istic; my sensuality seemed to overcome my feeling of shame. During the first year, I danced with avidity and great enjoyment. I slept many hours, masturbated daily, often keeping it up for an hour . . . I mastur-bated often until I was covered with sweat, too fatigued to continue, I fell asleep . . . I was burning and I would have taken anyone who would relieve me. I wasn't looking for a person, just a man.*54

The issue here is rather that virginal agitation is not expressed as a precise need: the virgin does not know exactly what she wants. Aggressive childhood eroticism still survives in her; her first impulses were prehensile and she still has the desire to embrace, to possess; she wants the prey that she covets to be endowed with the qualities which through taste, smell and touch have been shown to her as values; for sexuality is not an isolated domain, it extends the dreams and joys of sensuality; children and adolescents of both sexes like what is smooth, creamy, satiny, soft, elastic: that which yields to pressure without collapsing or decomposing and slips under the gaze or the fingers; like man, woman is charmed by the warm softness of sand dunes, so often compared to breasts, or the light touch of silk, of the fluffy softness of an eiderdown, the velvet feeling of a flower or fruit; and the young girl especially cherishes the pale colours of pastels, froths of tulle and muslin. She has no taste for rough fabrics, gravel, rocks, bitter flavours, acrid odours; like her brothers, it was her mother's flesh that she first caressed and cherished; in her narcissism, in her diffuse or precise homosexual experiences, she posited herself as a subject and she sought the posses-sion of a female body. When she faces the male, she has, in the palms of her hands and on her lips, the desire to actively caress a prey. But man, with his hard muscles, his scratchy and often hairy skin, his crude odour and his coarse features, does not seem desirable to her, and he even stirs her repulsion. Renée Vivien expresses it this way:

> I am a woman, I have no right to beauty
> They have condemned me to the ugliness of men . . .
> They have forbidden me your hair, your eyes
> Because your hair is long and scented with odours55

* Frigidity in Woman.

If the prehensile, possessive tendency exists in woman more strongly, her orientation, like that of Renée Vivien, will be towards homosexuality. Or she will become attached only to males she can treat like women: thus the heroine of Rachilde's *Monsieur Vénus* buys herself a young lover whom she enjoys caressing passionately, but will not let herself be deflowered by him. There are women who love to caress young boys of thirteen or fourteen years old or even children, and who reject grown men. But we have seen that passive sexuality has also been developed since childhood in the majority of women: the woman loves to be hugged and caressed, and especially from puberty she wishes to be flesh in the arms of a man; the role of subject is normally his; she knows it; 'A man does not need to be handsome,' she has been told over and over; she should not look for the inert qualities of an object in him but for strength and virile force. She thus becomes divided within herself: she wants a strong embrace that will turn her into a trembling thing; but brutality and force are also hostile obstacles that wound her. Her sensuality is located both in her skin and in her hand: and their exigencies are in opposition to each other. Whenever possible, she chooses a compromise; she gives herself to a man who is virile but young and seductive enough to be an object of desire; she will be able to find all the traits she desires in a handsome adolescent; in the Song of Songs, there is a symmetry between the delights of the wife and those of the husband; she grasps in him what he seeks in her: earthly fauna and flora, precious stones, streams, stars. But she does not have the means to *take* these treasures; her anatomy condemns her to remaining awkward and impotent, like a eunuch: the desire for possession is thwarted for lack of an organ to incarnate it. And man refuses the passive role. Often, besides, circumstances lead the young girl to become the prey of a male whose caresses move her, but whom she has no pleasure to look at or caress in return. Not enough has been said not only about the fear of masculine aggressiveness but also about a deep feeling of frustration at the disgust that is mixed with her desires: sexual satisfaction must be achieved against the spontaneous thrust of her sensuality, while for the man the joy of touching and seeing merges with the sexual experience as such.

Even the elements of passive eroticism are ambiguous. Nothing is murkier than *contact*. Many men who triturate all sorts of material in their hands without disgust hate it when grass or animals touch them; women's flesh can tremble pleasantly or bristle at the touch of silk or velvet: I recall a childhood friend who had gooseflesh simply at the sight of a peach; the transition is easy from agitation to titillation, from irritation to pleasure; arms enlacing a body can be a refuge and protection, but they also imprison and suffocate. For the virgin, this ambiguity is perpetuated because of her paradoxical situation: the organ that will bring about her metamorphosis is sealed. Her flesh's uncertain and burning longing spreads through her whole body except in the very place where coitus should occur. No organ permits the virgin to satisfy her active eroticism; and she does not have the lived experience of he who dooms her to passivity.

However, this passivity is not pure inertia. For the woman to be aroused, positive phenomena must be produced in her organism: stimulation in erogenous zones, swelling of certain erectile tissue, secretions, temperature rise, pulse and breathing acceleration. Desire and sexual pleasure demand a vital expenditure for her as for the male; receptive, the female need is in one sense active and is manifested in an increase of nervous and muscular energy. Apathetic and languid women are always cold; there is a question as to whether constitutional frigidity exists, and surely psychic factors play a preponderant role in the erotic capacities of woman; but it is certain that physiological insufficiencies and a depleted vitality are manifested in part by sexual indifference. If, on the other hand, vital energy is spent in voluntary activities – sports, for example – it is not invested in sex. Scandinavians are healthy, strong and cold. 'Fiery' women are those who combine their languor with 'fire', like Italian or Spanish women, that is to say, women whose ardent vitality flows from their flesh. To *make* oneself object, to *make* oneself passive, is very different from *being* a passive object: a woman in love is neither asleep nor a corpse; there is a surge in her that ceaselessly falls and rises: it is this surge that creates the spell that perpetuates desire. But the balance between ardour and abandon is easy to destroy. Male desire is tension; it can invade a body where nerves and muscles are taut: positions and movements that demand a voluntary participation of the organism do not work against it, and instead often serve it. On the contrary, every voluntary effort keeps female flesh from being 'taken'; this is why the woman spontaneously* refuses forms of coitus that demand work and tension from her; too many and too abrupt changes in position, the demands of consciously directed activities – actions or words – break the spell. The violence of uncontrolled tendencies can

* We will see further on that there can be psychological reasons that modify her immediate attitude.

bring about tightening, contraction or tension: some women scratch or bite, their bodies arching, infused with an unaccustomed force; but these phenomena are only produced when a certain paroxysm is attained, and it is attained only if first the absence of all inhibition – physical as well as moral – permits a concentration of all living energy into the sexual act. This means that it is not enough for the young girl to *let it happen*; if she is docile, languid or removed, she satisfies neither her partner nor herself. She must participate actively in an adventure that neither her virgin body nor her consciousness – laden with taboos, prohibitions, prejudices and exigencies – desire positively.

In the conditions we have just described, it is understandable that woman's erotic beginnings are not easy. Quite frequently, incidents that occur in childhood and youth provoke deep resistance in her, as has been seen; sometimes it is insurmountable; most often, the girl tries to overcome it, but violent conflicts build up in her. Her strict education, the fear of sinning and feelings of guilt toward her mother all create powerful blocks. Virginity is valued so highly in many circles that to lose it outside marriage seems a veritable disaster. The girl who surrenders by coercion or by surprise thinks she dishonours herself. The 'wedding night', which delivers the virgin to a man whom she has ordinarily not even chosen, and which attempts to condense into a few hours – or instants – the entire sexual initiation, is not a simple experience. In general, any 'passage' is distressing because of its definitive and irreversible character: becoming a woman is breaking with the past, without recourse; but this particular passage is more dramatic than any other; it creates not only a hiatus between yesterday and tomorrow; it tears the girl from the imaginary world where a great part of her existence took place and hurls her into the real world. By analogy with a bullfight, Michel Leiris calls the nuptial bed 'a moment of truth'; for the virgin, this expression takes on its fullest and most fearsome meaning. During the engagement, dating or courtship period, however basic it may have been, she continued to live in her familiar universe of ceremony and dreams; the suitor spoke a romantic, or at least courteous, language; it was still possible to make believe. And suddenly there she is, gazed upon by real eyes, handled by real hands: it is the implacable reality of this gazing and grasping that terrifies her.

Both anatomy and customs confer the role of initiator on the man. Without doubt, for the young male virgin, his first mistress also provides his initiation; but he possesses an erotic autonomy clearly manifested in the erection; his mistress only delivers to him the object in its reality that he already desires: a woman's body. The girl needs a man to make her discover her own body: her dependence is much greater. From his very first experiences, man is ordinarily active and decisive, whether he pays his partner or courts and solicits her. By contrast, in most cases, the young girl *is* courted and solicited; even if it is she who first flirts with the man, he is the one who takes their relationship in hand; he is often older and more experienced, and it is accepted that he has the responsibility for this adventure that is new for her; his desire is more aggressive and imperious. Lover or husband, he is the one who leads her to the bed, where her only choice is to let go of herself and obey. Even if she had accepted this authority in her mind, she is panic-stricken the moment she must concretely submit to it. She first of all fears this gaze that engulfs her. Her modesty may have been taught her, but it has deep roots; men and women all know the shame of their flesh; in its pure, immobile presence, its unjustified immanence, the flesh exists in the gaze of another as the absurd contingence of facticity and yet flesh is *oneself*: we want to prevent it from existing for others; we want to deny it. There are men who say they cannot stand to be naked in front of a woman, except in the state of erection; through the erection, the flesh becomes activity, force, the penis is no longer an inert object but, like the hand or the face, the imperious expression of a subjectivity. This is one reason why modesty paralyses young men much less than young women; their aggressive role exposes them less to being gazed at; and if they are, they do not fear being judged because it is not inert qualities that their mistresses demand of them: it is rather their amorous potency and their skill at giving pleasure that will give rise to complexes; at least they can defend themselves and try to win their match. Woman does not have the option of transforming her flesh into will: when she stops hiding it, she gives it up without defences; even if she longs for caresses, she recoils from the idea of being seen and felt; all the more so as her breasts and buttocks are particularly fleshy; many adult women cannot bear to be seen from the rear even when they are dressed; imagine the resistance a naive girl in love has to overcome to consent to showing herself. A Phryne undoubtedly does not fear being gazed at; she bares herself, on the contrary, superbly. Her beauty clothes her. But even if she is the equal of Phryne, a young girl never feels it with certainty; she cannot have arrogant pride in her body as long as male approval has not confirmed her young vanity. And this is just what frightens her; the lover is even more terrifying than a gaze: he is a judge; he is going to reveal her to herself in her truth; even passionately taken with her own image, every young girl doubts herself at the moment of the masculine verdict; this is why she demands darkness, she hides in the sheets; when she admired herself in the mirror, she was only dreaming: she was dreaming through man's eyes; now the eyes are really there; impossible to cheat; impossible to fight: a mysterious freedom decides, and this decision is final. In the real ordeal of the erotic experience, the obsessions of child-hood and adolescence will finally fade or be confirmed for ever; many young girls suffer from muscular calves, breasts that are too little or too big, narrow hips, a wart; or else they fear some secret malformation. Stekel writes,*

> Every young girl carries in her all sorts of ridiculous fears that she barely dares to admit to herself. One would not believe how many young girls suffer from the obsession of being physically abnormal and torment themselves secretly because they cannot be sure of being normally constructed. One young girl, for example, believed that her 'lower opening' was not in the right place. She thought that sexual intercourse took place through the navel. She was unhappy because her navel was closed and she could not stick her finger in it. Another thought she was a hermaphrodite. And another thought she was crippled and would never be able to have sexual relations.

Even if they are unfamiliar with these obsessions, they are terrified by the idea that certain regions of their bodies that did not exist for them or for anyone, that absolutely did not exist, will suddenly be seen. Will this unknown figure that the young girl must assume as her own provoke disgust? Indifference? Irony? She can only submit to male judgement: the die is cast. This is why man's attitude will have such deep resonance. His ardour and tenderness can give woman a confidence in herself that will stand up to every rejection: until she is eighty years old, she will believe she is this flower, this exotic bird that made man's desire bloom one night. On the contrary, if the lover or husband is clumsy, he will arouse an infer-iority complex in her that is sometimes compounded by long-lasting neuroses; and she will hold a grudge that will be expressed in a stubborn frigidity. Stekel describes striking examples:

* *Frigidity in Woman.*

A woman of 36 years of age suffers from such back pain across 'the small of her back' for the past 14 years. These pains are so unbearable that she is forced to stay in bed for weeks . . . she felt the great pains for the first time during her wedding night. On that occasion, during the defloration, which caused her considerable pain, her husband exclaimed: 'You have deceived me! You are not a virgin!' Her pains in the back represent the fixation of this painful episode. Her illness is her vengeance on the man. The various cures have cost him considerable money for her innumerable treatments . . . This woman was anaesthetic during her wedding night and she remained in this condition throughout her marital experience . . . The wedding night was for her a terrible mental shock that has influenced her whole life.

A woman consults me for various nervous troubles and particularly on account of her complete sexual frigidity . . . During her wedding night, her husband, after uncovering her, exclaimed: 'Oh, how stubby and thick your limbs are!' Then he tried to carry out intercourse. She felt only pain and remained wholly frigid . . . She knows very well that the slightest remark he made about her during the wedding night was responsible for her sexual frigidity.

Another frigid woman says that 'during her wedding night, her husband deeply insulted her' seeing her get undressed, he allegedly said: 'My God, how thin you are!' Then he nevertheless decided to caress her. For her this moment was unforgettable and horrible. What brutality!

Mme. Z. W. is also completely frigid. The great traumatism of her wedding night was that her husband supposedly said after the first intercourse: 'You have a big hole, you tricked me.'

The gaze is danger; hands are another threat. Woman does not usually have access to the universe of violence; she has never gone through the ordeal the young man overcame in childhood and adolescent fights: to be a thing of flesh on which others have a hold; and now that she is grasped, she is swept away in a body-to-body clasp where man is the stronger; she is no longer free to dream, to withdraw, to manoeuvre: she is given over to the male; he disposes of her. These wrestling-like embraces terrorise her, she who has never wrestled. She had let herself go to the caresses of a fiancé, a fellow student, a colleague, a civilised and courteous man: but he has assumed an unfamiliar, selfish and stubborn attitude; she no longer has recourse against this stranger. It is not

uncommon that the young girl's first experience is a real rape and that
man's behaviour is odiously brutal; particularly in the countryside, where
customs are harsh, it often happens that a young peasant woman, half-
consenting, half-outraged, in shame and fright, loses her virginity at the
bottom of some ditch. What is in any case extremely frequent in all societies and classes is that the virgin is rushed by an egotistical lover seeking
his own pleasure quickly, or by a husband convinced of his conjugal
rights who takes his wife's resistance as an insult, to the point of becoming
furious if the defloration is difficult.

In any case, however deferential and courteous a man might be, the
first penetration is always a violation. While she desires caresses on her
lips and breasts and perhaps yearns for a familiar or anticipated orgasm,
here is a male sex organ tearing the girl and introducing itself into regions
where it was not invited. The painful surprise of a swooning virgin –
who thinks she has finally reached the accomplishment of her voluptuous dreams and who feels in the secret of her sex an unexpected pain
– in a husband's or lover's arms has often been described; the dreams
faint away, the excitement dissipates, and love takes on the appearance
of a surgical operation.

In the confessions gathered by Dr Liepmann,* there is the following
typical account. It concerns a very sexually unaware girl from a modest
background.

'I often imagined that one could have a child just by the exchange
of a kiss. During my eighteenth year, I made the acquaintance of
a man with whom I really fell madly in love.' She often went out
with him and during their conversations he explained to her that
when a young girl loves a man, she must give herself to him because
men cannot live without sexual relations and that as long as they
cannot afford to get married, they have to have relations with young
girls. She resisted. One day, he organised an excursion so that they
could spend the night together. She wrote him a letter to repeat
that 'it would harm her too much'. The morning of the arranged
day, she gave him the letter but he put it in his pocket without
reading it and took her to the hotel; he dominated her morally, she
loved him, she followed him. 'I was as if hypnotised. As we were
going along, I begged him to spare me . . . How I arrived at the
hotel, I do not know at all. The only memory that remained is that

* Published in French under the title *Jeunesse et sexualité* [*Youth and Sexuality*].

my whole body trembled violently. My companion tried to calm me; but he succeeded only after much resistance. I was no longer mistress of my will and in spite of myself I let myself go. When I found myself later in the street, it seemed to me that everything had only been a dream I had just awakened from.' She refused to repeat the experience and for nine years did not have sexual relations with any other man. She then met one who asked her to marry him and she agreed.

In this case, the defloration was a kind of rape. But even if it is consensual, it can be painful. Look at the fevers that tormented young Isadora Duncan. She met an admirably handsome actor with whom she fell in love at first sight and who courted her ardently.*

I myself felt ill and dizzy, while an irresistible longing to press him closer and closer surged in me, until, losing all control and falling into a fury, he carried me into the room. Frightened but ecstatic, the realisation was made clear to me. I confess my first impressions were a horrible fright, but a great pity for what he seemed to be suffering prevented me from running away from what was at first sheer torture . . . [The next day], what had been for me only a painful experience began again amid my martyr's sobs and cries.[56]

She was soon to know the paradise she lyrically described, first with this lover and then with others.

However, in actual experience, as previously in one's virginal imagination, it is not pain that plays the greatest role: the fact of penetration counts far more. In intercourse the man introduces only an exterior organ: woman is affected in her deepest interior. Undoubtedly, there are many young men who tread with anguish in the secret darkness of woman; their childhood terrors resurface at the threshold of caves and graves and so does their fright in front of jaws, scythes and wolf traps: they imagine that their swollen penis will be caught in the mucous sheath; the woman, once penetrated, does not have this feeling of danger; but she does feel carnally alienated. The property owner affirms his rights over his lands, the housewife over her house by proclaiming 'no trespassing'; because of their frustrated transcendence, women, in

* My Life.

particular, jealously defend their privacy: their room, their wardrobe and their chests are sacred. Colette tells of an old prostitute who told her one day: 'In my room, Madame, no man has ever set foot; for what I have to do with men, Paris is quite big enough.' If not her body, at least she possessed a plot of land where entry was prohibited. The young girl, though, possesses little of her own except her body: it is her most precious treasure; the man who enters her *takes* it from her; the familiar word is confirmed by her lived experience. She experiences concretely the humiliation she had felt: she is dominated, subjugated, conquered. Like almost all females, she is *under* the man during intercourse.* Adler emphasised the feeling of inferiority resulting from this. Right from infancy, the notions of superior and inferior are extremely important; climbing trees is a prestigious act; heaven is above the earth; hell is underneath; to fall or to descend is to degrade oneself and to climb is to exalt oneself; in wrestling, victory belongs to the one who pins his opponent down, whereas the woman lies on the bed in a position of defeat; it is even worse if the man straddles her like an animal subjugated by reins and a bit. In any case, she feels passive: she *is* caressed, penetrated, she undergoes intercourse, whereas the man spends himself actively. It is true that the male sex organ is not a striated muscle commanded by will; it is neither ploughshare nor sword but merely flesh; but it is a voluntary movement that man imprints on her; he goes, he comes, stops, resumes while the woman receives him submissively; it is the man – especially when the woman is a novice – who chooses the amorous positions, who decides the length and frequency of intercourse. She feels herself to be an instrument: all the freedom is in the other. This is what is poetically expressed by saying that woman is comparable to a violin and man to the bow that makes her vibrate. 'In love,' says Balzac,† 'leaving the soul out of consideration, woman is a lyre which only yields up its secrets to the man who can play upon it skillfully.'[57] He *takes* his pleasure with her; he *gives* her pleasure; the words themselves do not imply reciprocity. Woman is imbued with collective images of the glorious aura of masculine sexual

---

* The position can undoubtedly be reversed. But in the first experiences, it is extremely rare for the man not to practise the so-called normal coitus.

† *Physiology of Marriage*. In *Bréviaire de l'amour expérimental* (*A Ritual for Married Lovers*), Jules Guyot also says of the husband: 'He is the minstrel who produces harmony or cacophony with his hand and bow. From this point of view woman is really a many-stringed instrument producing harmonious or discordant sounds depending on how she is tuned.'

excitement that make feminine arousal a shameful abdication: her intimate experience confirms this asymmetry. It must not be forgotten that boy and girl adolescents experience their bodies differently: the former tranquilly takes his body for granted and proudly takes charge of his desires; for the latter, in spite of her narcissism, it is a strange and disturbing burden. Man's sex organ is neat and simple, like a finger; it can be innocently exhibited, and boys often show it off to their friends proudly and defiantly; the feminine sex organ is mysterious to the woman herself, hidden, tormented, mucous and humid; it bleeds each month, it is sometimes soiled with bodily fluids, it has a secret and dangerous life. It is largely because woman does not recognise herself in it that she does not recognise her own desires. They are expressed in a shameful manner. While the man has a 'hard-on', the woman 'gets wet'; there are in the very word infantile memories of the wet bed, of the guilty and involuntary desire to urinate; man has the same disgust for his nocturnal unconscious wet dreams; projecting a liquid, urine or sperm, is not humiliating: it is an active operation; but there is humiliation if the liquid escapes passively since the body then is no longer an organism, muscles, sphincters and nerves, commanded by the brain and expressing the conscious subject, but a vase, a receptacle made of inert matter and the plaything of mechanical caprices. If the flesh oozes – like an old wall or a dead body – it does not seem to be emitting liquid but deliquescing: a decomposition process that horrifies. Feminine heat is the flaccid palpitation of a shellfish; where man has impetuousness, woman merely has impatience; her desire can become ardent without ceasing to be passive; the man dives on his prey like the eagle and the hawk; she, like a carnivorous plant, waits for and watches the swamp where insects and children bog down; she is sucking, suction, sniffer, she is pitch and glue, immobile appeal, insinuating and viscous: at least this is the way she indefinably feels. Thus, there is not only resistance against the male who attempts to subjugate her but also internal conflict. Superimposed on the taboos and inhibitions that arise from her education and society are disgust and refusals that stem from the erotic experience itself: they all reinforce each other to such an extent that often after the first coitus the woman is more in revolt against her sexual destiny than before.

Lastly, there is another factor that often gives man a hostile look and changes the sexual act into a grave danger: the danger of a child. An illegitimate child in most civilisations is such a social and economic handicap for the unmarried woman that one sees young girls committing

suicide when they know they are pregnant and unwed mothers cutting
the throats of their newborns; such a risk constitutes a quite powerful
sexual brake, making many young girls observe the prenuptial chastity
prescribed by customs. When the brake is insufficient, the young girl,
while yielding to the lover, is horrified by the terrible danger he possesses
in his loins. Stekel cites, among others, a young girl who for the entire
duration of intercourse shouted: 'Don't let anything happen! Don't let
anything happen!' Even in marriage, the woman often does not want
a child, her health is not good enough, or a child would be too great a
burden on the young household. Whether he is lover or husband, if she
does not have absolute confidence in her partner, her eroticism will be
paralysed by caution. Either she will anxiously watch the man's behaviour, or else, once intercourse is over, she will run to the bathroom to
chase the living germ from her belly, put there in spite of herself. This
hygienic operation brutally contradicts the sensual magic of the caresses;
she undergoes an absolute separation of the bodies that were merged
in one single joy; thus the male sperm becomes a harmful germ, a
soiling; she cleans herself as one cleans a dirty vase, while the man
reclines on his bed in his superb wholeness. A young divorcee told me
how horrified she was when – after a dubiously pleasurable wedding
night – she had to shut herself in the bathroom and her husband noncha-
lantly lit a cigarette: it seems that the ruin of the couple was decided
at that instant. The repugnance of the douche, the beaker and the bidet
is one of the frequent causes of feminine frigidity. The existence of
surer and more convenient contraceptive devices is helping woman's
sexual freedom a great deal; in a country like America where these practices are widespread, the number of young girls still virgins at marriage
is much lower than in France; such practices make for far greater abandon
during the love act. But there again, the young woman has to overcome
her repugnance before treating her body as a thing: she can no more
resign herself to being 'corked' to satisfy a man's desires than she can
to being 'pierced' by him. Whether she has her uterus sealed or introduces some sperm-killing tampon, a woman who is conscious of the
ambiguities of the body and sex will be bridled by cold premeditation:
besides, many men consider the use of condoms repugnant. It is sexual
behaviour as a whole that justifies its various moments: conduct that
when analysed would seem repugnant seems natural when bodies are
transfigured by the erotic virtues they possess; but inversely, when bodies
and behaviours are decomposed into separate elements and deprived of
meaning, these elements become disgusting and obscene. The surgical

and dirty perception that penetration had in the eyes of the child returns if it is not carried out with the arousal, desire and pleasure a woman in love will joyfully experience as union and fusion with the beloved: this is what happens with the concerted use of prophylactics. In any case, these precautions are not at the disposal of all women; many young girls do not know of any defence against the threats of pregnancy and they feel great anguish that their lot depends on the good will of the man they give themselves up to.

It is understandable that an ordeal experienced through so much resistance, fraught with such weighty implications, often creates serious traumas. A latent precocious dementia has often been revealed by the first experience. Stekel gives several examples:

> Mlle M. G. . . . suddenly developed an acute delirium in her 19th year. I found her storming in her room, shouting repeatedly: 'I won't! No! I won't!' She tore off her clothes and wanted to flee into the street naked . . . she had to be taken to the psychiatric clinic. There her delirium gradually abated and she passed into a catatonic state . . . This girl . . . was a clerk in an office, in love with the head clerk in the company . . . She had gone to the country with a girl friend . . . and a couple of young men who worked in the same office . . . she went to her room with one of the men [who] promised not to touch her and that 'it was merely a prank'. He roused her to slight tenderness for three nights without touching her virginity . . . She apparently remained 'as cold as a dog's muzzle' and declared that it was disgraceful. For a few fleeting minutes her mind seemed confused and she exclaimed: 'Alfred, Alfred.' (Alfred was the head clerk's first name.) She was reproaching herself for what she had done (What would mother say about this if she knew?). Once she returned home, she took to her bed, complaining of a migraine.

> Mlle L. X.[58] . . . very depressed . . . She cried often and could not sleep; she had begun to have hallucinations and failed to recognise her environment. She had jumped to the windows and tried to throw herself out . . . She was taken to the sanitarium. I found this twenty-three-year-old girl sitting up in bed; she paid no attention to me when I entered . . . Her face depicted abject fear and horror; her limbs were crossed and they twitched vigorously. She was shouting. 'No! No! No! You villain! Men such as you ought to be locked up! It hurts! Oh!' Then there followed some unintelligible

mumbling. Suddenly her whole facial expression changed. Her eyes lit up, her lips pursed in the manner of kissing someone, her limbs ceased twitching and she gave forth outcries which suggested delight and rapture and love . . . Finally the attack ended in a subdued but persistent weeping . . . The patient kept pushing down her nightgown as if it were a dress, at the same time continually repeating the exclamation, 'Don't!' It was known that a married colleague had often come to see her when she was ill, that she was first happy about it, but that later on she had had hallucinations and attempted suicide.[59] She got better but keeps all men at a distance and has rejected an earnest marriage offer.

In other cases the illness triggered is less serious. Here is an example where regret for lost virginity plays the main role in the problems following the first coitus:

A young twenty-three-year-old girl suffers from various phobias. The illness began at Franzensbad out of fear of catching a pregnancy by a kiss or a contact in a toilet . . . Perhaps a man had left some sperm in the water after masturbation; she insisted that the bathtub be cleaned three times in her presence and did not dare to move her bowels in the normal position. Some time afterwards she developed a phobia of tearing her hymen, she did not dare to dance, jump, cross a fence or even walk except with very little steps; if she saw a post, she feared being deflowered by a clumsy movement and went around it, trembling all the way. Another of her phobias in a train or in the middle of a crowd was that a man could introduce his member from behind, deflower her and provoke a pregnancy . . . During the last phase of the illness, she feared finding pins in her bed or on her shirt that could enter her vagina. Each evening the sick girl stayed naked in the middle of her room while her unfortunate mother was forced to go through a difficult examination of the bedclothes . . . She had always affirmed her love for her fiancé. An examination revealed that she was no longer a virgin and was putting off marriage because she feared her fiancé's disastrous observations. She admitted to him that she had been seduced by a tenor, married him and was cured.*

---

* Stekel, *Frigidity in Woman.*

In another case, remorse – uncompensated by voluptuous satisfaction – provoked psychic troubles:

Mlle. H. B., twenty years old, after a trip to Italy with a girl friend, went into a serious depression. She refused to leave her room and did not utter one word. She was taken to a nursing home, where her situation got worse. She heard voices that were insulting her, everyone made fun of her, etc. She was brought back to her parents' where she stayed in a corner without moving. She asked the doctor: 'Why didn't I come before the crime was committed?' She was dead. Everything was killed, destroyed. She was dirty. She could not sing one note, bridges with the world were burnt . . . The fiancé admitted having followed her to Rome where she gave herself to him after resisting a long time; she had crying fits . . . She admitted never having pleasure with her fiancé. She was cured when she found a lover who satisfied her and married her.

The 'sweet Viennese girl' whose childish confessions I summarised also gave a detailed and gripping account of her first adult experiences. It will be noticed that – in spite of the very advanced nature of her previous adventures – her 'initiation' still has an absolutely new character.

'At sixteen, I began working in an office. At seventeen and a half, I had my first holiday; it was a great period for me. I was courted on all sides . . . I was in love with a young office colleague . . . We went to the park. It was 15 April 1909. He made me sit next to him on a bench. He kissed me, begging me: open your lips; but I closed them convulsively. Then he began to unbutton my jacket. I would have let him when I remembered that I did not have any breasts; I gave up the voluptuous sensation I would have had if he had touched me . . . On 7 April a married colleague invited me to go to an exhibition with him. We drank wine at dinner. I lost some of my reserve and began telling him some ambiguous jokes. In spite of my begging, he hailed a cab, pushed me into it and hardly had the horses started than he kissed me. He became more and more intimate, he pushed his hand farther and farther; I defended myself with all my strength and I do not remember if he got his way. The next day I went to the office rather flustered. He showed me his hands covered with the scratches I had given him . . . He asked me to come see him more often . . . I yielded, not very comfortable but still full of curiosity . . . As soon as he came near my sex I pulled away and returned to my place; but once, more clever than I, he overcame me and probably put his finger into my vagina. I cried with pain. It was June 1909 and I left on vacation. I took a trip with my girl friend. Two tourists arrived. They invited us to accompany them. My companion wanted to kiss my friend, she punched him. He came towards, grabbed me from behind, bent me to him, and kissed me. I did not resist . . . He invited me to come with him. I gave him my hand and we went into the middle of the forest. He kissed me . . . he kissed my sex, to my great indignation. I said to him: "How can you do such a disgusting thing?" He put his penis in my hand . . . I caressed it . . . all of a sudden he pulled away my hand and threw a handkerchief over it to keep me from seeing what was happening . . . Two days later we went to Liesing. All of a sudden in a deserted field he took off his coat and put it on the grass . . . he threw me down in such a way that one of his legs was placed between mine. I still did not think how serious the situation was. I begged him to kill me rather than deprive me of "my most beautiful finery". He became very rough, swore at me and threatened me with the police. He covered my mouth with his hand and introduced his penis. I thought my last hour had arrived. I had the feeling my stomach was turning. When he was finally finished, I began to be able to put up with him. He had to pick me up because I was still stretched out. He covered my eyes and face with kisses. I did not see or hear anything. If he had not held me back, I would have fallen blindly in front of the traffic . . . We were alone in a second-class compartment; he opened his trousers again to come towards me. I screamed and ran quickly through the whole train until the last running board . . . Finally he left me with a vulgar and strident laugh that I will never forget, calling me a stupid goose who does not know what is good. He let me return to Vienna alone. I went quickly to the bathroom because I had felt something warm running along my thigh. Frightened, I saw traces of blood. How could I hide this at home? I went to bed as early as possible and cried for hours. I still felt the pressure on my stomach caused by the pushing of his penis. My strange attitude and lack of appetite told my mother something had happened. I admitted everything to her. She did not see anything so terrible in it . . . My colleague did what he could to console me. He took advantage of dark evenings to take walks with me in the park and caress me under my skirts. I let him; but as soon as I felt my vagina become wet I pulled myself away because I was terribly ashamed.'

She goes to a hotel with him sometimes but without sleeping with him. She makes the acquaintance of a very rich young man that she would like to marry. She sleeps with him but without feeling anything and with disgust. She resumes her relations with her colleague but she misses the other one and begins to be cross-eyed and to lose weight. She is sent to a sanatorium where she almost sleeps with a young Russian, but she chases him from her bed at the last minute. She begins affairs with a doctor and an officer but without consenting to complete sexual relations. Then she became mortally ill and decided to go to a doctor. After her treatment she consented to give herself to a man who loved her and then married her. In marriage her frigidity disappeared.

In these few examples chosen from many similar ones, the partner's brutality or at least the abruptness of the event is the determining factor in the traumatism or disgust. The best situation for sexual initiation is one in which the girl learns to overcome her modesty, to get to know her partner, and to enjoy his caresses without violence or surprise, without fixed rules or a precise time frame. In this respect, the freedom of behaviour appreciated by young American girls and more and more by French girls today can only be endorsed: they slip almost without noticing from necking and petting to complete sexual relations. The less tabooed it is, the smoother the initiation, and the freer the girl feels with her partner and the more the domination aspect of the male fades; if her lover is also young, a novice, shy, and an equal, the girl's defences are not as strong; but her metamorphosis into a woman will also be less of a transformation. In *Green Wheat*,[60] Colette's Vinca, the day after a rather brutal defloration, displays surprising placidity to her friend Phil: she did not feel 'possessed', on the contrary, she took pride in freeing herself of her virginity; she did not feel an overwhelming mental turmoil; in truth, Phil is wrong to be surprised as his girlfriend did not really know the male. Claudine was less unaffected after a turn on the dance floor in Renaud's arms. I was told of a French high school student still stuck in the 'green fruit' stage, who, having spent a night with a male school-friend, ran to a girlfriend's the next morning to announce: 'I slept with C. . . . it was a lot of fun.' An American high school teacher told me his students stopped being virgins long before becoming women; their partners respect them too much to offend their modesty; the boys themselves are too young and too prudish to awaken any demon in the girls. There are girls who throw themselves into many erotic experiences in order to escape sexual anxiety; they hope to rid themselves of their curiosity and obsessions, but their acts often have a theoretical cast, rendering such behaviour as unreal as the fantasies through which others anticipate the future. Giving oneself out of defiance, fear or puritan rationalism is not achieving an authentic erotic experience: one merely reaches a pseudo-experience without danger and without much flavour; the sexual act is not accompanied by either anguish or shame, because arousal remains superficial and pleasure has not permeated the flesh. These deflowered virgins are still young girls; and it is likely that the day they find themselves in the grip of a sensual and imperious man, they will put up virginal resistance to him. Meanwhile, they remain in a kind of awkward age; caresses tickle them, kisses sometimes make them laugh: they look on physical love as a game and if they are not in the mood to have fun, the lover's demands quickly seem importunate and abusive; they hold on to the disgusts, phobias and prudishness of the adolescent girl. If they never go beyond this stage – which is, according to American males, the case with many American girls – they spend their life in a state of semi-frigidity. Real sexual maturity for the woman who consents to becoming flesh can only occur in arousal and pleasure.

But it must not be thought that all difficulties subside in women with a passionate temperament. On the contrary, they sometimes worsen. Feminine arousal can reach an intensity unknown by man. Male desire is violent but localised, and he comes out of it – except perhaps in the instant of ejaculation – conscious of himself; woman, by contrast, undergoes a real alienation; for many, this metamorphosis is the most voluptuous and definitive moment of love; but it also has a magical and frightening side. The woman he is holding in his arms appears so absent from herself, so much in the throes of turmoil, that the man may feel afraid of her. The upheaval she feels is a far more radical transmutation than the male's aggressive frenzy. This fever frees her from shame; but when she awakes, it in turn makes her feel ashamed and horrified; for her to accept it happily – or even proudly – she has at least to be sexually and sensually fulfilled; she can admit to her desires if she has gloriously satisfied them: if not, she repudiates them angrily.

Here we reach the crucial problem of feminine eroticism: at the beginning of her erotic life, woman's abdication is not rewarded by a wild and confident sensual pleasure. She would readily sacrifice modesty and pride if it meant opening up the gates of paradise. But it has been seen that defloration is not a successful accomplishment of youthful eroticism; it is on the contrary an unusual phenomenon; vaginal pleasure is not attained immediately; according to Stekel's statistics – confirmed by many sexologists and psychologists – barely 4 per cent of women experience pleasure at the first coitus; 50 per cent do not reach vaginal pleasure for weeks, months, or even years. Psychic factors play an essential role in this. Woman's body is singularly 'hysterical' in that there is often no distance between conscious facts and their organic expression; her moral inhibitions prevent the emergence of pleasure; as they are not counterbalanced by anything, they are often perpetuated and form a more and more powerful barrier. In many cases, a vicious circle is created: the lover's first clumsiness – a word, an awkward gesture, or an arrogant smile – will resonate throughout the whole honeymoon or even married life; disappointed by not experiencing pleasure immediately, the young woman feels a resentment that badly prepares her for a happier experience. It is true that if the man cannot give her normal satisfaction, he can always give her clitoral pleasure that, in spite of moralising legends, can provide her with relaxation and contentment. But many women reject it because it seems to be *inflicted* even more than vaginal pleasure; because if women suffer from the egotism of men concerned only with their own satisfaction, they are also offended by too obvious a determination to give them pleasure. 'Making the other come,' says Stekel, 'means dominating him; giving oneself to someone is abdicating one's will.' Woman will accept pleasure more easily if it seems to flow naturally from man's own pleasure, as happens in normal and successful coitus. 'Women submit themselves joyously as soon as they understand that the partner does not *want* to subjugate them,' continues Stekel; inversely, if they feel this desire, they resist. Many shy away from being caressed by the hand because it is an instrument that does not participate in the pleasure it gives, it is activity and not flesh; and if sex itself does not come across as flesh penetrated with desire but as a cleverly used tool, woman will feel the same repulsion. Besides, anything else will seem to confirm the woman's failure to experience a normal woman's feelings. Stekel notes, after many, many observations, that all the desire of so-called frigid women aims at the norm. 'They want to reach orgasm like a normal woman; no other process satisfies them morally.'

Man's attitude is thus of extreme importance. If his desire is violent and brutal, his partner feels changed into a mere thing in his arms; but if he is too self-controlled, too detached, he does not constitute himself as flesh; he asks woman to make herself object without her being able to have a hold on him in return. In both cases, her pride rebels; to reconcile her metamorphosis into a carnal object with the demands of her subjectivity, she must make him her prey as she makes herself his. This is often why the woman obstinately remains frigid. If the lover lacks seductive techniques, if he is cold, negligent or clumsy, he fails to awaken her sexuality or he leaves her unsatisfied; but if he is virile and skilful, he can provoke reactions of rejection; woman fears his domination: some can find pleasure only with timid, inept, or even almost impotent men, ones who do not scare them away. It is easy for a man to awaken hostility and resentment in his mistress. Resentment is the most common source of feminine frigidity; in bed, the woman makes the male pay for all the affronts she considers she has been subjected to by an insulting coldness; her attitude is often one of an aggressive inferiority complex: since you do not love me, since I have flaws preventing me from being liked and since I am despicable, I will not surrender to love, desire and pleasure either. This is how she exacts vengeance both on him and on herself if he has humiliated her by his negligence, if he has aroused her jealousy, if he has declared himself too slowly, if he has made her his mistress whereas she desired marriage; the complaint can appear suddenly and set off this reaction even during a relationship that began happily. The man who caused this hostility can rarely succeed in undoing it: a persuasive testimony of love or appreciation may, however, sometimes modify the situation. It also happens that women who are defiant or stiff in their lovers' arms can be transformed by a ring on their finger: happy, flattered, their conscience at peace, they let all their defences fall. But a newcomer, respectful, in love and delicate can best transform the disenchanted woman into a happy mistress or wife; if he frees her from her inferiority complex she will give herself to him ardently.

Stekel's work *Frigidity in Woman* essentially focuses on demonstrating the role of psychic factors in feminine frigidity. The following examples clearly show that it is often an act of resentment of the husband or lover:

> Mlle G. S. . . . had given herself to a man while waiting for him to marry her, while insisting on the fact 'that she did not care about marriage', that she did not want 'to be attached'. She played the free woman. In truth, she was a slave to morality like her whole family. But her lover believed her and never spoke of marriage. Her stubbornness increased more and more until she became apathetic.

When he finally did ask her to marry him, she took her revenge by admitting her numbness and no longer wanting to hear anything about a union. She no longer wanted to be happy. She had waited too long . . . She was consumed by jealousy and waited anxiously for the day he proposed so she could refuse it proudly. Then she wanted to commit suicide just to punish her lover in style.

A very jealous woman who until then had found pleasure with her husband imagines that her husband is cheating on her while she was ill. Coming home, she decides to be cold to her husband. She would never be aroused by him again because he did not appreciate her and used her only when in need. Since her return she has been frigid. At first she used little tricks not to be aroused. She pictured to herself that her husband was flirting with her girl friend. But soon orgasm was replaced by pain.

A young seventeen-year-old had an affair with a man and derived intense pleasure from it. Pregnant at nineteen, she asked her lover to marry her; he was ambivalent and advised her to get an abortion, which she refused to do. Three weeks later, he declared he was ready to marry her and she became his wife. But she never forgave those three tormented weeks and became frigid. Later on, a talk with her husband overcame her frigidity.

Mme N. M . . . learns that two days after the wedding, her husband went to see a former mistress. The orgasm she had had previously disappeared forever. She was obsessed by the thought that she no longer pleased her husband whom she thought she had disappointed; that is the cause of frigidity for her.

Even when a woman overcomes her resistance and eventually experiences vaginal pleasure, not all her problems are eliminated: the rhythm of her sexuality and that of the male do not coincide. She is much slower to reach orgasm than the man. The Kinsey Report states:

For perhaps three-quarters of all males, orgasm is reached within two minutes after the initiation of the sexual relation . . . Considering the many upper level females who are so adversely conditioned to sexual situations that they may require ten to fifteen minutes of the most careful stimulation to bring them to climax, and considering the fair number of females who never come to climax in their whole lives, it is, of course, demanding that the male be quite abnormal in his ability to prolong sexual activity without ejaculation if he is required to match the female partner.

It is said that in India the husband, while fulfilling his conjugal duties, smokes his pipe to distract himself from his own pleasure and to make his wife's last; in the West, it is more the number of 'times' that a Casanova boasts of; and his supreme pride is to have a woman beg for mercy: according to erotic tradition, this is not often a successful feat; men often complain of their partners' exacting demands: she is a wild uterus, an ogre, insatiable; she is never assuaged. Montaigne demonstrates this point of view in the third book of his *Essays*:[61]

They are incomparably more capable and ardent than we in the acts of love – and that priest of antiquity so testified, who had been once a man and then a woman . . . and besides, we have learned from their own mouth the proof that was once given in different centuries by an emperor and an empress of Rome, master workmen and famous in this task: he indeed deflowered in one night ten captive Sarmatian virgins; but she actually in one night was good for twenty-five encounters, changing company according to her need and liking,

> *Adhuc ardens rigidae tentigine vulvo*
> *Et lassata viris, necdum satiata recessite**[62]

We know about the dispute that occurred in Catalonia from a woman complaining of the over-assiduous efforts of her husband: not so much, in my opinion, that she was bothered by them (for I believe in miracles only in matters of faith) . . . There intervened that notable sentence of the Queen of Aragon, by which, after mature deliberation with her council, this good queen . . . ordained as the legitimate and necessary limit the number of six a day, relinquishing and giving up much of the need and desire of her sex, in order, she said, to establish an easy and consequently permanent and immutable formula.

---

* Juvenal.

It is true that sexual pleasure for woman is not at all the same as for man. I have already said that it is not known exactly if vaginal pleasure ever results in a definite orgasm: feminine confidences on this point are rare and even when they try to be precise, they remain extremely vague; reactions seem to vary greatly according to the subject. What is certain is that coitus for man has a precise biological end: ejaculation. And certainly many other very complex intentions are involved in aiming at this end; but once obtained, it is seen as an achievement, and if not as the satisfaction of desire, at least as its suppression. On the other hand, the aim for woman is uncertain in the beginning and more psychic than physiological; she desires arousal and sexual pleasure in general, but her body does not project any clear conclusion of the love act: and thus for her coitus is never fully completed: it does not include any finality. Male pleasure soars; when it reaches a certain threshold it fulfils itself and dies abruptly in the orgasm; the structure of the sexual act is finite and discontinuous. Feminine pleasure radiates through the whole body; it is not always centred in the genital system; vaginal contractions then even more than a true orgasm constitute a system of undulations that rhythmically arise, subside, re-form, reach for some instants a paroxysm, then blur and dissolve without ever completely dying. Because no fixed goal is assigned to it, pleasure aims at infinity: nervous or cardiac fatigue or psychic satiety often limit the woman's erotic possibilities rather than precise satisfaction; even fully fulfilled, even exhausted, she is never totally relieved: *Lassata necdum satiata*, according to Juvenal.

Man commits a grave error when he attempts to impose his own rhythm on his partner and when he is determined to give her an orgasm: often he only manages to destroy the form of pleasure she was experiencing in her own way.* This form is malleable enough to give itself a conclusion: spasms localised in the vagina, in the whole genital system or coming from the whole body can constitute a resolution; for certain women, they are produced fairly regularly and with sufficient violence to be likened to an orgasm; but a woman lover can also find a conclusion in the masculine orgasm that calms and satisfies her. And it is also possible that in a gradual and gentle way, the erotic phase dissolves calmly. Success requires not a mathematical synchronisation of pleasure, what-

---

* Lawrence clearly saw the opposition of these two erotic forms. But it is arbitrary to declare as he does that the woman *must* not experience orgasm. It might be an error to try to provoke it at all costs, but it is also an error to reject it in all cases, as Don Cipriano does in *The Plumed Serpent*.

ever many meticulous but simplistic men believe, but the establishment of a complex erotic form. Many think that 'making a woman come' is a question of time and technique, therefore of violence; they disregard the extent to which woman's sexuality is conditioned by the situation as a whole. Sexual pleasure for her, we have said, is a kind of spell; it demands total abandon; if words or gestures contest the magic of caresses, the spell vanishes. This is one of the reasons that the woman often closes her eyes: physiologically there is a reflex that compensates for the dilation of the pupil; but even in the dark she still lowers her eyelids; she wants to do away with the setting, the singularity of the moment, herself and her lover; she wants to lose herself within the carnal night as indistinct as the maternal breast. And even more particularly, she wants to abolish this separation that sets the male in front of her; she wants to merge with him. We have said already that she desires to remain a subject while making herself an object. More deeply alienated than man, as her whole body is desire and arousal, she remains a subject only through union with her partner; receiving and giving have to merge for both of them; if the man just takes without giving or if he gives pleasure without taking, she feels used; as soon as she realises herself as Other, she is the inessential other; she has to invalidate alterity. Thus the moment of the separation of bodies is almost always painful for her. Man, after coitus, whether he feels sad or joyous, duped by nature or conqueror of woman, whatever the case, he repudiates the flesh; he becomes a whole body; he wants to sleep, take a bath, smoke a cigarette, get a breath of fresh air. She would like to prolong the bodily contact until the spell that made her flesh dissipates completely; separation is a painful wrenching like a new weaning; she resents the lover who pulls away from her too abruptly. But what wounds her even more are the words that contest the fusion in which she believed for a moment. The 'wife of Gilles', whose story Madeleine Bourdouxhe told, pulls back when her husband asks her: 'Did you come?' She puts her hand on his mouth; many women hate this word because it reduces the pleasure to an immanent and separated sensation. 'Is it enough? Do you want more? Was it good?' The very fact of asking the question points out the separation and changes the love act into a mechanical operation assumed and controlled by the male. And this is precisely the reason he asks it. Much more than fusion and reciprocity, he seeks domination; when the unity of the couple is undone, he becomes the sole subject: a great deal of love or generosity is necessary to give up this privilege; he likes the woman to feel humiliated, possessed in spite of herself; he always wants to take her a little more than she gives herself. Woman would be spared many difficulties were man not to trail behind him so many complexes making him consider the love act a battle: then it would be possible for her not to consider the bed as an arena.

However, along with narcissism and pride, one observes in the girl a desire to be dominated. According to some psychoanalysts, masochism is a characteristic of women, by means of which they can adapt to their erotic destiny. But the notion of masochism is very confused and has to be considered attentively.

Freudian psychoanalysts distinguish three forms of masochism: one is the link between pain and sexual pleasure, another is the feminine acceptance of erotic dependence, and the last resides in a mechanism of self-punishment. Woman is masochistic because pleasure and pain in her are linked through defloration and birth, and because she consents to her passive role.

It must first be pointed out that attributing erotic value to pain does not in any way constitute behaviour of passive submission. Pain often serves to raise the tonus of the individual who experiences it, to awaken a sensitivity numbed by the very violence of arousal and pleasure; it is a sharp light bursting out in the carnal night, it removes the lover from the limbo where he is swooning so that he might once more be thrown into it. Pain is normally part of erotic frenzy; bodies that delight in being bodies for their reciprocal joy seek to find each other, unite with each other, and confront each other in every possible way. There is a wrenching from oneself in eroticism, a transport, an ecstasy: suffering also destroys the limits of the self, it is a going beyond and a paroxysm; pain has always played a big role in orgies; and it is well known that the exquisite and the painful converge: a caress can become torture, torment gives pleasure. Embracing easily leads to biting, pinching, scratching; such behaviour is not generally sadistic; it expresses a desire to merge and not to destroy; and the subject that submits to it does not seek to disavow and humiliate himself but to unite; besides, it is far from being specifically masculine. In fact, pain has a masochistic meaning only when it is grasped and desired as the manifestation of enslavement. As for the pain of defloration, it is specifically not accompanied by pleasure; and all women fear the suffering of giving birth and they are happy that modern methods free them from it. Pain has neither more nor less place in their sexuality than in that of man.

Feminine docility is, moreover, a very equivocal notion. We have seen that most of the time the young girl accepts in her *imagination* the domination of a demigod, a hero, a male, but it is still only a narcissistic game. She is in no way disposed to submit to the carnal expression of this authority in reality. By contrast, she often refuses to give herself to a man she admires and respects, giving herself to an ordinary man instead. It is an error to seek the key to concrete behaviour in fantasy, because fantasies are created and cherished as fantasies. The little girl who dreams of rape with a mixture of horror and complicity does not *desire* to be raped and the event, if it occurred, would be a loathsome catastrophe. We have already seen in Marie Le Hardouin a typical example of this dissociation. She writes:

> But there remained an area on the path of abolition that I only entered with pinched nostrils and a beating heart. This was the path that beyond amorous sensuality led me to sensuality itself . . . there was no deceitful infamy that I did not commit in dreams. I suffered from the need to affirm myself in every possible way.*[63]

The case of Marie Bashkirtseff should also be recalled:

> All my life I have tried to place myself *voluntarily* under some kind of *illusory domination*, but all the people I tried were so ordinary in comparison with me that all I felt for them was disgust.

Moreover, it is true that the woman's sexual role is largely passive; but to live this passive situation in its immediacy is no more masochistic than the male's normal aggressiveness is sadistic; woman can transcend caresses, arousal and penetration towards achieving her own pleasure, thus maintaining the affirmation of her subjectivity; she can also seek union with the lover and give herself to him, which signifies a surpassing of herself and not an abdication. Masochism exists when the individual chooses to constitute himself as a pure thing through the consciousness of the other, to represent oneself to oneself as a thing, to play at being a thing. 'Masochism is an attempt not to fascinate the other by my objectivity but to make myself be fascinated by my objectivity for others.'†[64] Sade's Juliette or the young virgin from *Philosophy in the Boudoir*,[65] who both give themselves to the male in all possible ways, but for their own pleasure, are not in any way masochists. Lady Chatterley and Kate, in the total

---

* *The Black Sail.*
† J. P. Sartre, *Being and Nothingness.*

abandon they consent to, are not masochists. To speak of masochism, one has to posit the *self* and this alienated double has to be considered as founded on the other's freedom.

In this sense, true masochism can be found in some women. The girl is susceptible to it since she is easily narcissistic and narcissism consists in alienating one's self in one's ego. If she experienced arousal and violent desire right from the beginning of her erotic initiation, she would live her experiences authentically and stop projecting them towards this ideal pole that she calls self; but in frigidity, the self continues to affirm itself; making it the thing of a male seems then like a fault. But 'masochism, like sadism, is an assumption of guilt. I am guilty due to the very fact that I am an object.'[66] This idea of Sartre's fits in with the Freudian notion of self-punishment. The young girl considers herself guilty of delivering her self to another and she punishes herself for it by willingly increasing humiliation and subjugation; we have seen that virgins defied their future lovers and punished themselves for their future submission by inflicting various tortures on themselves. When the lover is real and present, they persist in this attitude. Frigidity itself can be seen as a punishment that woman imposes as much on herself as on her partner: wounded in her vanity, she resents him and herself, and she does not permit herself pleasure. In masochism, she will wildly enslave herself to the male, she will tell him words of adoration, she will wish to be humiliated, beaten; she will alienate herself more and more deeply out of fury for having agreed to the alienation. This is quite obviously Mathilde de La Mole's behaviour, for example; she regrets having given herself to Julien; which is why she sometimes falls at his feet, bends over backwards to indulge each of his whims, sacrifices her hair; but at the same time, she is in revolt against him as much as against herself; one imagines that she is icy in his arms. The fake abandon of the masochistic woman creates new barriers that keep her from pleasure; and at the same time, she is taking vengeance against herself for this inability to experience pleasure. The vicious circle from frigidity to masochism can establish itself for ever, bringing sadistic behaviour along with it as compensation. Becoming erotically mature can also deliver woman from her frigidity and her narcissism, and assuming her sexual passivity, she lives it immediately instead of playing the role. Because the paradox of masochism is that the subject reaffirms itself constantly even in its attempt to abdicate itself, it is in the gratuitous gift, in the spontaneous movement towards the other, that he succeeds in forgetting himself. It is thus true that woman will be more prone than man to masochistic temptation; her erotic situation as passive object commits her to playing passivity; this game is the self-punishment to which her narcissistic revolts and consequent frigidity lead her; the fact is that many women and in particular young girls are masochists. Colette, speaking of her first amorous experiences, confides to us in *My Apprenticeship:*

> Ridden by youth and ignorance, I had known intoxication – a guilty rapture, an atrocious, impure, adolescent impulse. There are many scarcely nubile girls who dream of becoming the show, the play-thing, the licentious masterpiece of some middle-aged man. It is an ugly dream that is punished by its fulfilment, a morbid thing, akin to the neuroses of puberty, the habit of eating chalk and coal, of drinking mouthwash, of reading dirty books and sticking pins into the palm of the hand.[67]

This perfectly expresses the fact that masochism is part of juvenile perver-sions, that it is not an authentic solution of the conflict created by woman's sexual destiny, but a way of escaping it by wallowing in it. In no way does it represent the normal and happy blossoming of feminine eroticism.

This blossoming supposes that – in love, tenderness and sensuality – woman succeeds in overcoming her passivity and establishing a relation-ship of reciprocity with her partner. The asymmetry of male and female eroticism creates insoluble problems as long as there is a battle of the sexes; they can easily be settled when a woman feels both desire and respect in a man; if he covets her in her flesh while recognising her freedom, she recovers her essentialness at the moment she becomes object, she remains free in the submission to which she consents. Thus, the lovers can experience shared pleasure each in their own way; each partner feels pleasure as being his own while at the same time having its source in the other. The words 'receive' and 'give' exchange mean-ings, joy is gratitude, pleasure is tenderness. In a concrete and sexual form the reciprocal recognition of the self and the other is accomplished in the keenest consciousness of the other and the self. Some women say they feel the masculine sex organ in themselves as a part of their own body; some men think they *are* the woman they penetrate; these expres-sions are obviously inaccurate; the dimension of the *other* remains; but the fact is that alterity no longer has a hostile character; this conscious-ness of the union of the bodies in their separation is what makes the sexual act moving; it is all the more overwhelming that the two beings

who together passionately negate and affirm their limits are fellow creatures and yet are different. This difference that all too often isolates them
becomes the source of their marvelling when they join together; woman
recognises the virile passion in man's force as the reverse of the fever
that burns within her, and this is the power she wields over him; this
sex organ swollen with life belongs to her just as her smile belongs to
the man who gives her pleasure. All the treasures of virility and femininity reflecting off and reappropriating each other make a moving and
ecstatic unity. What is necessary for such harmony is not technical refinements but rather, on the basis of an immediate erotic attraction, a reciprocal generosity of body and soul.

This generosity is often hampered in man by his vanity and in woman
by her timidity; if she does not overcome her inhibitions, she will not
be able to make it thrive. This is why full sexual blossoming in woman
arrives rather late: she reaches her erotic peak at about thirty-five.
Unfortunately, if she is married, her husband is too used to her frigidity;
she can still seduce new lovers, but she is beginning to fade: time is
running out. At the very moment they cease to be desirable, many women
finally decide to assume their desires.

The conditions under which woman's sexual life unfolds depend not
only on these facts but also on her whole social and economic situation.
It would be too vague to attempt to study this further without this
context. But several generally valid conclusions emerge from our examination. The erotic experience is one that most poignantly reveals to
human beings their ambiguous condition; they experience it as flesh and
as spirit, as the other and as subject. Woman experiences this conflict at
its most dramatic because she assumes herself first as object and does
not immediately find a confident autonomy in pleasure; she has to recon-
quer her dignity as transcendent and free subject while assuming her
carnal condition: this is a delicate and risky enterprise that often fails.
But the very difficulty of her situation protects her from the mystifications by which the male lets himself be duped; he is easily deceived by
the fallacious privileges that his aggressive role and satisfied solitude of
orgasm imply; he hesitates to recognise himself fully as flesh. Woman
has a more authentic experience of herself.

Even if woman accommodates herself more or less exactly to her
passive role, she is still frustrated as an active individual. She does not
envy man his organ of possession: she envies in him his prey. It is a curious
paradox that man lives in a sensual world of sweetness, tenderness, softness – a feminine world – while woman moves in the hard and harsh

male universe; her hands still long for the embrace of smooth skin and soft flesh: adolescent boy, woman, flowers, furs, child; a whole part of herself remains available and wishes to possess a treasure similar to the one she gives the male. This explains why there subsists in many women, in a more or less latent form, a tendency towards homosexuality. For a set of complex reasons, there are those for whom this tendency asserts itself with particular authority. Not all women agree to give their sexual problems the one classic solution officially accepted by society. Thus must we envisage those who choose forbidden paths.

CHAPTER 4

The Lesbian

People are always ready to see the lesbian as wearing a felt hat, her hair short and a necktie; her mannishness is seen as an abnormality indicating a hormonal imbalance. Nothing could be more erroneous than this confusion of the homosexual and the virago. There are many homosexual women among odalisques, courtesans and the most deliberately 'feminine' women; by contrast, a great number of 'masculine' women are heterosexual. Sexologists and psychiatrists confirm what ordinary observation suggests: the immense majority of 'cursed women' are constituted exactly like other women. Their sexuality is not determined by anatomical 'destiny'.

There are certainly cases where physiological givens create particular situations. There is no rigorous biological distinction between the two sexes; an identical soma is modified by hormonal activity whose orientation is genotypically defined, but can be diverted in the course of the foetus's development; this results in individuals halfway between male and female. Some men take on a feminine appearance because of late development of their male organs, and sometimes girls as well – athletic ones in particular – change into boys. Helene Deutsch tells of a young girl who ardently courted a married woman, wanted to run off and live with her: she realised one day that she was in fact a man, so she was able to marry her beloved and have children. But it must not be concluded that every homosexual woman is a 'hidden man' in false guise. The hermaphrodite who has elements of two genital systems often has a female sexuality: I knew of one, exiled by the Nazis from Vienna, who greatly regretted her inability to appeal to either heterosexuals or homosexuals as she loved only men. Under the influence of male hormones, 'viriloid' women present masculine secondary sexual characteristics; in infantile women, female hormones are deficient and their development remains incomplete. These particularities can more or less directly trigger a lesbian orientation. A person with a vigorous, aggressive and exuberant vitality wishes to exert himself actively and usually rejects passivity; an unattractive and malformed woman may try to compensate for her inferiority by acquiring virile attributes; if her erogenous sensitivity is undeveloped, she does not desire masculine caresses. But anatomy and hormones never define anything but a situation and do not posit the object towards which the situation will be transcended. Deutsch also cites the case of a wounded Polish legionnaire she treated during World War I, who was, in fact, a young girl with marked viriloid characteristics; she had joined the army as a nurse, then succeeded in wearing the uniform; she nevertheless fell in love with a soldier – whom she later married – which caused her to be regarded as a male homosexual. Her masculine behaviour did not contradict a feminine type of eroticism. Man himself does not exclusively desire woman; the fact that the male homosexual body can be perfectly virile implies that a woman's virility does not necessarily destine her to homosexuality.

Even in woman physiologically normal themselves, it has sometimes been asserted that there is a distinction between 'clitoral' and 'vaginal' women, the former being destined to sapphic love; but it has been seen that all childhood eroticism is clitoral; whether it remains fixed at this stage or is transformed has nothing to do with anatomical facts; nor is it true, as has often been maintained, that infant masturbation explains the ulterior primacy of the clitoral system: a child's masturbation is recognised today by sexologists as an absolutely normal and generally widespread phenomenon. The development of feminine eroticism is – we have seen – a psychological situation in which physiological factors are included, but which depends on the subject's overall attitude to existence. Marañón considered sexuality to be 'one-way', and that man attains a completed form of it, while for woman, it remains 'halfway'; only the lesbian could possess a libido as rich as a male's and would thus be a 'superior' feminine type. In fact, feminine sexuality has its own structure, and the idea of a hierarchy in male and female libidos is absurd; the choice of sexual object in no way depends on the amount of energy woman might have.

Psychoanalysts have had the great merit of seeing a psychic phenomenon and not an organic one in inversion; to them, nonetheless, it still seems determined by external circumstances. But in fact they have not studied it very much. According to Freud, female erotic maturation requires the passage from the clitoral to the vaginal stage, symmetrical with the change transferring the love the little girl felt first for her mother to her father; various factors may hinder this development; the woman is not resigned to castration, hides the absence of the penis from herself, or remains fixated on her mother, for whom she seeks substitutes. For Adler, this fixation is not a passively endured accident: it is desired by the subject who, in her will for power, deliberately denies her mutilation and seeks to identify with the man whose domination she refuses. Whether from infantile fixation or masculine protest, homosexuality would appear in any case as unfinished development. In truth, the lesbian is no more a 'failed' woman than a 'superior' woman. The individual's history is not an inevitable progression: at every step, the past is grasped anew by a new choice, and the 'normality' of the choice confers no privileged value on it: it must be judged by its authenticity. Homosexuality can be a way for woman to flee her condition or a way to assume it. Psychoanalysts' great error, through moralising conformity, is that they never envisage it as anything but an inauthentic attitude.

Woman is an existent who is asked to make herself object; as subject she has an aggressive sensuality that does not find satisfaction in the masculine body: from this are born the conflicts her eroticism must overcome. The system is considered normal that, delivering her as prey to a male, restores her sovereignty by putting a baby in her arms: but this 'naturalism' is determined by a more or less well understood social interest. Even heterosexuality permits other solutions. Homosexuality for woman is one attempt among others to reconcile her autonomy with the passivity of her flesh. And if nature is invoked, it could be said that every woman is naturally homosexual. The lesbian is characterised simply by her refusal of the male and her preference for feminine flesh; but every adolescent female fears penetration and masculine domination, and she feels a certain repulsion for the man's body; on the contrary, the feminine body is for her, as for man, an object of desire. As I have already said: men posit themselves as subjects and at the same time they posit themselves as separate; to consider the other as a thing to take is to attack the virile ideal in the other and thus jointly in one's self as well; by contrast, the woman who regards herself as object sees herself and her fellow creatures as prey. The homosexual man inspires hostility from male and female heterosexuals as they both demand that man be a dominating subject;* by contrast, both sexes spontaneously view lesbians with

---

* A heterosexual woman can easily have a friendship with certain homosexual men, because she finds security and amusement in these asexual relations. But on the whole, she feels hostile towards these men who in themselves or in others degrade the sovereign male into a passive thing.

indulgence. 'I swear,' says the comte de Tilly, 'it is a rivalry that in no way bothers me; on the contrary, I find it amusing and I am immoral enough to laugh at it.' Colette attributed this same amused indifference to Renaud faced with the couple Claudine and Rézi.* A man is more irritated by an active and autonomous heterosexual woman than by a non-aggressive homosexual one; only the former challenges masculine prerogatives; sapphic loves in no way contradict the traditional model of the division of the sexes: in most cases, they are an assumption of femininity and not a rejection of it. We have seen that they often appear in the adolescent girl as an ersatz form of heterosexual relations she has not yet had the opportunity or the audacity to experience: it is a stage, an apprenticeship, and the one who most ardently engages in such loves may tomorrow be the most ardent of wives, lovers and mothers. What must be explained in the female homosexual is thus not the positive aspect of her choice but the negative side: she is not characterised by her preference for women but by the exclusiveness of this preference.

According to Jones and Hesnard, lesbians mostly fall into two categories: 'masculine lesbians', who 'try to act like men', and 'feminine' ones, who 'are afraid of men'. It is a fact that one can, on the whole, observe two tendencies in homosexual women; some refuse passivity, while others choose to lose themselves passively in feminine arms; but these two attitudes react upon each other reciprocally; relations to the chosen object and to the rejected one are explained by each other reciprocally. For numerous reasons, as we shall see, the distinction given seems quite arbitrary.

To define the lesbian as 'virile' because of her desire to 'imitate man' is to doom her to inauthenticity. I have already said how psychoanalysts create ambiguities by accepting masculine-feminine categories as currently defined by society. Thus, man today represents the positive and the neuter – that is, the male and the human being – while woman represents the negative, the female. Every time she behaves like a human being, she is declared to be identifying with the male. Her sports, her political and intellectual activities, and her desire for other women are interpreted as 'masculine protest'; there is a refusal to take into account the values towards which she is transcending, which inevitably leads to the belief that she is making the inauthentic choice of a subjective attitude. The great misunderstanding upon which this system of interpretation rests is to hold that it is *natural* for the human female to make a *feminine* woman

---

* It is noteworthy that English law punishes homosexuality in men while not considering it a crime for women.

of herself: being a heterosexual or even a mother is not enough to realise this ideal; the 'real woman' is an artificial product that civilisation produces the way eunuchs were produced in the past; these supposed 'instincts' of coquetry or docility are inculcated in her just as phallic pride is for man; he does not always accept his virile vocation; she has good reasons to accept even less docilely the vocation assigned to her. The notions of inferiority complex and masculinity complex remind me of the anecdote that Denis de Rougement recounts in *The Devil's Share*:[68] a woman imagined that birds were attacking her when she went walking in the country; after several months of psychoanalytical treatment that failed to cure her of her obsession, the doctor accompanied her to the clinic garden and realised that *the birds were attacking her*. Woman feels undermined because in fact the restrictions of femininity undermine her. She spontaneously chooses to be a complete individual, a subject and a freedom before whom the world and future open: if this choice amounts to the choice of virility, it does so to the extent that femininity today means mutilation. Homosexuals' confessions collected by Havelock Ellis and Stekel – platonic in the first case and openly declared in the second – clearly show that feminine *specificity* is what outrages the two subjects.

Ever since I can remember anything at all I could never think of myself as a girl and I was in perpetual trouble, with this as the real reason. When I was 5 or 6 years old I began to say to myself that, whatever anyone said, if I was not a boy at any rate I was not a girl . . . I regarded the conformation of my body as a mysterious accident . . . When I could only crawl my absorbing interest was hammers and carpet-nails. Before I could walk I begged to be put on horses' backs . . . By the time I was 7 it seemed to me that everything I liked was called wrong for a girl . . . I was not at all a happy little child and often cried and was made irritable; I was so confused by the talk about boys and girls . . . Every half-holiday I went out with the boys from my brothers' school . . . When I was about 11 my parents got more mortified at my behaviour and perpetually threatened me with boarding school . . . My going was finally announced to me as a punishment to me for being what I was . . . In whatever direction my thoughts ran I always surveyed them from the point of view of a boy . . . A consideration of social matters led me to feel very sorry for women, whom I regarded as made by a deliberate process of manufacture into the fools I thought they were, and by the same process that I myself was being made one.

I felt more and more that men were to be envied and women pitied.
I lay stress on this for it started in me a deliberate interest in women
as women, I began to feel protective and kindly toward women.

As for Stekel's transvestite:

Until her sixth year, in spite of assertions of those around her, she
thought she was a boy, dressed like a girl for reasons unknown to
her ... At 6, she told herself, 'I'll be a lieutenant, and if God wills
it, a marshal.' She often dreamed of mounting a horse and riding
out of town at the head of an army. Though very intelligent, she
was miserable to be transferred from an ordinary school to a
lycée ... *she was afraid of becoming effeminate.*

This revolt by no means implies a sapphic predestination; most little
girls feel the same indignation and despair when they learn that the accidental conformation of their bodies condemns their tastes and aspirations; Colette Audry*[69] angrily discovered at the age of twelve that she
could never become a sailor; the future woman naturally feels indignant
about the limitations her sex imposes on her. The question is not why
she rejects them: the real problem is rather to understand why she accepts
them. Her conformism comes from her docility and timidity; but this
resignation will easily turn to revolt if society's compensations are judged
inadequate. This is what will happen in cases where the adolescent girl
feels unattractive as a woman: anatomical configurations become particularly important when this happens; if she is, or believes she is, ugly or
has a bad figure, woman rejects a feminine destiny for which she feels
ill adapted; but it would be wrong to say that she acquires a mannish
attitude to compensate for a lack of femininity: rather, the opportunities offered to the adolescent girl in exchange for the masculine advantages
she is asked to sacrifice seem too meagre to her. All little girls envy boys'
practical clothes; it is their reflection in the mirror and the promises of
things to come that make their furbelows little by little all the more
precious; if the mirror harshly reflects an ordinary face, if it offers no
promise, then lace and ribbons are an embarrassing, even ridiculous,
livery, and the 'tomboy' obstinately wishes to remain a boy.

Even if she has a good figure and is pretty, the woman who is involved
in her own projects or who claims her freedom in general refuses to

* *In the Eyes of Memory.*

abdicate in favour of another human being; she recognises herself in her acts, not in her immanent presence: male desire reducing her to the limits of her body shocks her as much as it shocks a young boy; she feels the same disgust for her submissive female companions as the virile man feels for the passive homosexual. She adopts a masculine attitude in part to repudiate any involvement with them; she disguises her clothes, her looks and her language, she forms a couple with a female friend where she assumes the male role: this playacting is in fact a 'masculine protest'; but it is a secondary phenomenon; what is spontaneous is the conquering and sovereign subject's shame at the idea of changing into a carnal prey. Many women athletes are homosexual; they do not perceive this body that is muscle, movement, extension and momentum as passive flesh; it does not magically beckon caresses, it is a hold on the world, not a thing of the world: the gap between the body for-itself and the body for-others seems in this case to be unbreachable. Analogous resistance is found in women of action, 'brainy' types for whom even carnal submission is impossible. Were equality of the sexes concretely realised, this obstacle would be in large part eradicated; but man is still imbued with his own sense of superiority, which is a disturbing conviction for the woman who does not share it. It should be noted, however, that the most wilful and domineering women seldom hesitate to confront the male: the woman considered 'virile' is often clearly heterosexual. She does not want to renounce her claims as a human being; but she has no intention of mutilating her femininity either; she chooses to enter the masculine world, even to annex it for herself. Her robust sensuality has no fear of male roughness; she has fewer defences to overcome than the timid virgin in finding joy in a man's body. A rude and animal nature will not feel the humiliation of coitus; an intellectual with an intrepid mind will challenge it; sure of herself and in a fighting mood, a woman will gladly engage in a duel she is sure to win. George Sand had a predilection for young and 'feminine' men; but Mme de Staël looked for youth and beauty only in her later life: dominating men by her sharp mind and proudly accepting their admiration, she could hardly have felt a prey in their arms. A sovereign such as Catherine the Great could even allow herself masochistic ecstasies: she alone remained the master in these games. Isabelle Eberhardt, who dressed as a man and traversed the Sahara on horseback, felt no less diminished when she gave herself to some vigorous sharpshooter. The woman who refuses to be the man's vassal is far from always fleeing him; rather she tries to make him the instrument of her pleasure. In certain favourable circumstances – mainly dependent on her partner – the very notion of competition will disappear and she will enjoy experiencing her woman's condition just as man experiences his.

But this arrangement between her active personality and her role as passive female is nevertheless more difficult for her than for man; rather than wear themselves out in this effort, many women will give up trying. There are numerous lesbians among women artists and writers. It is not because their sexual specificity is the source of creative energy or a manifestation of the existence of this superior energy; it is rather that being absorbed in serious work, they do not intend to waste their time playing the woman's role or struggling against men. Not admitting male superiority, they do not wish to pretend to accept it or tire themselves contesting it; they seek release, peace and diversion in sexual pleasure: they could spend their time more profitably without a partner who acts like an adversary; and so they free themselves from the chains attached to femininity. Of course, the nature of her heterosexual experiences will often lead the 'virile' woman to choose between assuming or repudiating her sex. Masculine disdain confirms the feeling of unattractiveness in an ugly woman; a lover's arrogance will wound a proud woman. All the motives for frigidity we have envisaged are found here: resentment, spite, fear of pregnancy, abortion trauma, and so on. They become all the weightier the more woman defies man.

However, homosexuality is not always an entirely satisfactory solution for a domineering woman; since she seeks to affirm herself, it vexes her not to fully realise her feminine possibilities; heterosexual relations seem to her at once an impoverishment and an enrichment; in repudiating the limitations implied by her sex, she may limit herself in another way. Just as the frigid woman desires pleasure even while rejecting it, the lesbian would often like to be a normal and complete woman, while at the same time not wanting it. This hesitation is evident in the case of the transvestite studied by Stekel.

We have seen that she was only comfortable with boys and did not want to 'become effeminate'. At sixteen years of age, she formed her first relations with young girls; she had a profound contempt for them, which gave her eroticism a sadistic quality; she ardently, but platonically, courted a friend she respected: she felt disgust for those she possessed. She threw herself fiercely into difficult studies. Disappointed by her first serious Sapphic love affair, she frenetically indulged in purely sensual experiences and began to drink.

At seventeen, she met the young man she married: but she thought
of him as her wife; she dressed in a masculine way, and she continued
to drink and study. At first she only had vaginismus and intercourse
never produced an orgasm. She considered her position 'humiliating'; she was always the one to take the aggressive and active role.
She left her husband even while being 'madly in love with him' and
took up relations with women again. She met a male artist to whom
she gave herself, but still without an orgasm. Her life was divided
into clearly defined periods; for a while she wrote, worked creatively
and felt completely male; she episodically and sadistically slept with
women during these periods. Then she would have a female period.
She underwent analysis because she wanted to reach orgasm.

The lesbian would easily be able to consent to the loss of her femininity if in doing so she gained triumphant masculinity. But no. She obviously remains deprived of the virile organ; she can deflower her girl-friend
with her hand or use an artificial penis to imitate possession; but she is
still a eunuch. She may suffer acutely from this. Because she is incomplete
as a woman, impotent as a man, her malaise sometimes manifests itself
in psychoses. A patient told Roland Dalbiez,[*][70] 'It would be better if I had
a thing to penetrate with.' Another wished that her breasts were rigid.
The lesbian will often try to compensate for her virile inferiority by arrogance or exhibitionism, which in fact reveals inner imbalance. Sometimes,
also, she will succeed in establishing with other women a type of relation
completely analogous to those a 'feminine' man or an adolescent still
unsure of his virility might have with them. A striking case of such a
destiny is that of Sandor reported by Krafft-Ebing. She used this means
to attain a perfect balance destroyed only by the intervention of society:

Sarolta came of a titled Hungarian family known for its eccentric-
ities. Her father had her reared as a boy, calling her Sandor; she
rode horseback, hunted and so on. She was under such influences
until, at thirteen, she was placed in an institution. A little later she
fell in love with an English girl, pretending to be a boy, and ran
away with her. At home again, she resumed the name Sandor and
wore boys' clothing, while being carefully educated. She went on
long trips with her father, always in male attire; she was addicted
to sports, drank, and visited brothels. She felt particularly drawn

---

* *Psychoanalytical Method and the Doctrine of Freud.*

toward actresses and other such detached women, preferably not too young but 'feminine in nature'. 'It delighted me,' she related, 'if the passion of a lady was disclosed under a poetic veil. All immodesty in a woman was disgusting to me. I had an indescribable aversion to female attire – indeed, for everything feminine. But only insofar as it concerned me; for, on the other hand, I was all enthusiasm for the beautiful Sex.' She had numerous affairs with women and spent a good deal of money on them. At the same time, she was a valued contributor to two important journals.

She lived for three years in 'marriage' with a woman ten years older than herself, from whom she broke away only with great difficulty. She was able to inspire violent passions. Falling in love with a young teacher, she was married to her in an elaborate ceremony, the girl and her family believing her to be a man; her father-in-law on one occasion noticed what seemed to be an erection (probably a priapus); she shaved as a matter of form, but servants in the hotel room suspected the truth from seeing blood on her bedclothes and from spying through the keyhole.

Thus unmasked, Sandor was put in prison and later acquitted, after thorough investigation. She was greatly saddened by her enforced separation from her beloved Marie, to whom she wrote long and impassioned letters from her cell.

The examination showed that her conformation was not wholly feminine: her pelvis was small and she had no waist. Her breasts were developed, her sexual parts quite feminine but not maturely formed. Her menstruation appeared late, at seventeen, and she felt a profound horror of the function. She was equally horrified at the thought of sexual relations with the male; her sense of modesty was developed only in regard to women and to the point that she would feel less shyness in going to bed with a man than with a woman. It was very embarrassing for her to be treated as a woman, and she was truly in anguish at having to wear feminine clothes. She felt that she was 'drawn as by a magnetic force toward women of twenty-four to thirty'. She found sexual satisfaction exclusively in caressing her loved one, never in being caressed. At times she made use of a stocking stuffed with oakum as a priapus. She detested men. She was very sensitive to the moral esteem of others, and she had much literary talent, wide culture, and a colossal memory.[71]

Sandor was not psychoanalysed but several salient points emerge just from the presentation of the facts. It seems that most spontaneously and 'without a masculine protest', she always thought of herself as a man, thanks to the way she was brought up and her body's constitution; the way her father included her in his trips and his life obviously had a decisive influence on her; her virility was so confirmed that she did not show the slightest ambivalence towards women: she loved them like a man, without feeling compromised by them; she loved them in a purely dominating and active way, without accepting reciprocity. However, it is striking that she 'detested men' and that she particularly cherished older women. This suggests that Sandor had a *masculine* Oedipus complex vis-à-vis her mother; she perpetuated the infantile attitude of the very young girl who, forming a couple with her mother, nourished the hope of one day protecting and dominating her. Very often the maternal tenderness a child has been deprived of haunts her whole adult life: raised by her father, Sandor must have dreamed of a loving and treasured mother, whom she sought afterwards in other women; this explains her deep jealousy of other men, linked to her respect and 'poetic' love for 'isolated' and older women who were endowed in her eyes with a sacred quality. Her attitude was exactly that of Rousseau with Mme de Warens and the young Benjamin Constant concerning Mme de Charrière: sensitive, 'feminine' adolescent boys also turn to maternal mistresses. This type of lesbian is found in more or less pronounced forms, one who has never identified with her mother – because she either admired or detested her too much – but who, refusing to be a woman, desires the softness of feminine protection around her. From the bosom of this warm womb she can emerge into the world with boyish daring; she acts like a man but as a man she has a fragility that makes her desire the love of an older mistress; the couple will reproduce the classic heterosexual couple: matron and adolescent boy.

Psychoanalysts have clearly noted the importance of the relationship a homosexual woman had earlier with her mother. There are two cases where the adolescent girl has difficulty escaping her influence: if she has been overly protected by an anxious mother; or if she was mistreated by a 'bad mother' who inculcated a deep feeling of guilt in her. In the first case, their relations often bordered on homosexuality: they slept together, caressed or kissed each other's breasts; the young girl will seek this same pleasure in new arms. In the second case, she will feel an ardent need of a 'good mother' who protects her against her own mother, who removes the curse she feels weighing on her. One of the stories Havelock Ellis recounts concerns a subject who detested her mother throughout her childhood; she describes the love she felt at sixteen for an older woman:

> I felt like an orphan child who had suddenly acquired a mother, and through her I began to feel less antagonistic to grown people and to feel . . . respect [for them] . . . My love for her was perfectly pure, and I thought of hers as simply maternal . . . I liked her to touch me and she sometimes held me in her arms or let me sit on her lap. At bedtime she used to come and say good-night and kiss me upon the mouth.[72]

If the older woman is willing, the younger one will joyfully abandon herself to more ardent embraces. She will usually assume the passive role because she desires to be dominated, protected, rocked and caressed like a child. Whether these relations remain platonic or become carnal, they often have the characteristics of a truly passionate love. However, the very fact that they appear as a classic stage in the adolescent girl's development means that they cannot suffice to explain a determined choice of homosexuality. The young girl seeks in it both a liberation and a security she can also find in masculine arms. Once the period of amorous enthusiasm has passed, the younger one often experiences the ambivalent feeling for her older partner she felt towards her mother; she falls under her influence while at the same time wishing to extricate herself from it; if the other persists in holding her back, she will remain her 'prisoner'* for a time; but either in violent scenes or amicably, she will manage to escape; having succeeded in expunging her adolescence, she feels ready to face a normal woman's life. For her lesbian vocation to affirm itself she either has to reject her femininity – like Sandor – or her femininity has to flourish more happily in feminine arms. Thus, fixation on the mother is clearly not enough to explain homosexuality. And it can be chosen for completely different reasons. A woman may discover or sense through complete or tentative experiences that she will not derive pleasure from heterosexual relations, that only another woman is able to satisfy her: in particular, for the woman who worships her femininity, the sapphic embrace turns out to be the most satisfying.

It is very important to emphasise this: the refusal to make oneself an object is not always what leads a woman to homosexuality; most lesbians, on the contrary, seek to claim the treasures of their femininity. Consenting

---

* As in Dorothy Baker's novel, *Trio*, which is, moreover, very superficial.

to metamorphose oneself into a passive thing does not mean renouncing all claims to subjectivity: the woman thereby hopes to realise herself as the in-itself; but she will then seek to grasp herself in her alterity. Alone, she does not succeed in separating herself in reality; she might caress her breasts but she does not know how they would seem to a foreign hand, nor how they would come to life under the foreign hand; a man can reveal to her the existence *for itself* of her flesh, but not what it is *for an other.* It is only when her fingers caress a woman's body whose fingers in turn caress her body that the miracle of the mirror takes place. Between man and woman love is an act; each one torn from self becomes other: what delights the woman in love is that the passive listlessness of her flesh is reflected in the man's ardour; but the narcissistic woman is clearly baffled by the charms of the erect sex organ. Between women, love is contemplation; caresses are meant less to appropriate the other than to re-create oneself slowly through her; separation is eliminated, there is neither fight nor victory nor defeat; each one is both subject and object, sovereign and slave in exact reciprocity; this duality is complicity. 'The close resemblance,' says Colette,*[73] 'validates even sensual pleasure. The woman friend basks in the certitude of caressing a body whose secrets she knows and whose own body tells her what she prefers.' And Renée Vivien:

> Our heart is alike in our woman's breast,[74]
> Dearest! Our body is identically formed.
> The same heavy fate was laid on our soul
> I translate your smile and the shadow on your face.
> My softness is equal to your immense softness,
> At times it even seems we are of the same race
> I love in you my child, my friend and my sister.†[75]

   This uncoupling can occur in a maternal form; the mother who recognises and alienates herself in her daughter often has a sexual attachment to her; the desire to protect and rock in her arms a soft object made of flesh is shared with the lesbian. Colette emphasises this analogy, writing in *Tender Shoot:*[76] 'You will give me pleasure, bent over me, your eyes full of maternal concern, you who seek, through your passionate woman friend, the child you never had.'

* *The Pure and the Impure.*
† *Sortilèges.*

And Renée Vivien expresses the same feeling:

> *Come, I shall carry you off like a child who is sick,*
> *Like a child who is plaintive and fearful and sick.*
> *Within my firm arms I clasp your slight body,*
> *You shall see that I know how to heal and protect,*
> *And my arms are strong, the better to protect you.**[77]

And again:

> *I love you to be weak and calm in my arms . . .*
> *Like a warm cradle where you will take your rest.*[78]

In all love – sexual or maternal – there is both greed and generosity, the desire to possess the other and to give the other everything; but when both women are narcissists, caressing an extension of themselves or their reflection in the child or the lover, the mother and the lesbian are notably similar.

However, narcissism does not always lead to homosexuality either, as Marie Bashkirtseff's example shows; there is not the slightest trace of affection for women in her writings; intellectual rather than sensual, extremely vain, she dreams from childhood of being validated by man: nothing interests her unless it contributes to her glory. A woman who idolises only herself and who strives for abstract success is incapable of a warm complicity with other women; for her, they are only rivals and enemies.

In truth, there is never only one determining factor; it is always a question of a choice made from a complex whole, contingent on a free decision; no sexual destiny governs an individual's life: on the contrary, his eroticism expresses his general attitude to existence.

Circumstances, however, also have an important part in this choice. Today, the two sexes still live mostly separated: in boarding schools and in girls' schools the passage from intimacy to sexuality is quick; there are far fewer lesbians in circles where girl and boy camaraderie encourages heterosexual experiences. Many women who work among women in workshops and offices and who have little opportunity to be around men will form amorous friendships with women: it will be materially and morally practical to join their lives. The absence or failure of heterosexual relations will destine them to inversion. It is difficult to determine

* *At the Sweet Hour of Hand in Hand.*

the boundary between resignation and predilection: a woman can devote herself to women because a man has disappointed her, but sometimes he disappoints her because she was looking for a woman in him. For all these reasons, it is wrong to establish a radical distinction between heterosexual and homosexual. Once the indecisive time of adolescence has passed, the normal male no longer allows himself homosexual peccadilloes; but the normal woman often returns to the loves – platonic or not – that enchanted her youth. Disappointed by men, she will seek in feminine arms the male lover who betrayed her; in *The Vagabond*, Colette wrote about this consoling role that forbidden sexual pleasures often play in the lives of women: some of them can spend their whole existence consoling each other. Even a woman fulfilled by male embraces might not refuse calmer sexual pleasures. Passive and sensual, a woman friend's caresses will not shock her since all she has to do is let herself go, let herself be fulfilled. Active and ardent, she will seem 'androgynous', not because of a mysterious combination of hormones, but simply because aggressiveness and the taste for possession are looked on as virile attributes; Claudine in love with Renaud still covets Rézi's charms; as fully woman as she is, she still continues to desire to take and caress. Of course, these 'perverse' desires are carefully repressed in 'nice women'; they nonetheless manifest themselves as pure but passionate friendships or in the guise of maternal tenderness; sometimes they are suddenly revealed during a psychosis or a menopausal crisis.

So it is all the more useless to try to place lesbians in two definitive categories. Because social role-playing is sometimes superimposed on their real relations – taking pleasure in imitating a bisexual couple – they themselves suggest the division into 'virile' and 'feminine'. But the fact that one wears an austere suit and the other a flowing dress must not create an illusion. Looking more closely, one can ascertain – except in special cases – that their sexuality is ambiguous. A woman who becomes lesbian because she rejects male domination often experiences the joy of recognising the same proud Amazon in another; not long ago many guilty loves flourished among the women students of Sèvres who lived together far from men; they were proud to belong to a feminine elite and wanted to remain autonomous subjects; this complexity that united them against the privileged caste enabled each one to admire in a friend this prestigious being she cherished in herself; embracing each other, each one was both man and woman and was enchanted with the other's androgynous virtues. Inversely, a woman who wants to enjoy the pleasures of her femininity in feminine arms also knows the pride of obeying

no master. Renée Vivien ardently loved feminine beauty and she wanted
to be beautiful; she took great care of her appearance, she was proud
of her long hair; but she also liked to feel free and intact; in her poems
she expresses scorn for those women who through marriage consent to
become serfs of a male. Her taste for hard liquor and her sometimes
obscene language manifested her desire for virility. The truth is that for
most couples caresses are reciprocal. Thus it follows that the roles are
distributed in very uncertain ways: the most infantile woman can play
an adolescent boy towards a protective matron, or a mistress leaning on
her lover's arm. They can love each other as equals. Because her partners are counterparts, all combinations, transpositions, exchanges and
scenarios are possible. Relations balance each other out depending on
the psychological tendencies of each woman friend and on the situation
as a whole. If there is one who helps or keeps the other, she assumes
the male's functions: tyrannical protector, exploited dupe, respected lord
or even sometimes a pimp; a moral, social and intellectual superiority
will often confer authority on her; however, the one more loved will
enjoy the privileges that the more loving one's passionate attachment
invests her with. Like that of a man and a woman, the association of
two women can take many different forms; it is based on feeling, interest
or habit; it is conjugal or romantic; it has room for sadism, masochism,
generosity, faithfulness, devotion, caprice, egotism and betrayal; there
are prostitutes as well as great lovers among lesbians.

There are, however, certain circumstances that give these relations
particular characteristics. They are not established by an institution or
customs, nor regulated by conventions: they are lived more sincerely
because of this. Men and women – even husband and wife – more or
less play roles with each other, and woman, on whom the male always
imposes some kind of directive, does so even more: exemplary virtue,
charm, coquetry, childishness or austerity; never in the presence of the
husband and the lover does she feel fully herself; she does not show off
to a woman friend, she has nothing to feign, they are too similar not to
show themselves as they are. This similarity gives rise to the most
complete intimacy. Eroticism often has only a very small part in these
unions; sexual pleasure has a less striking character, less dizzying than
between man and woman, it does not lead to such overwhelming metamorphoses; but when male and female lovers have separated into their
individual flesh, they become strangers again; and even the male body
is repulsive to the woman; and the man sometimes feels a kind of bland
distaste for the woman's body; between women, carnal tenderness is

more equal, continuous, they are not transported in frenetic ecstasy but they never fall into hostile indifference; seeing and touching each other are calm pleasures discreetly prolonging those of the bed. Sarah Ponsonby's union with her beloved lasted for almost fifty years without a cloud: they seem to have been able to create a peaceful Eden on the fringes of the world. But sincerity also has a price. Because they show themselves freely, without caring either to hide or control themselves, women incite each other to incredible violence. Man and woman intimidate each other because they are different: he feels pity and apprehension towards her; he strives to treat her courteously, indulgently and circumspectly; she respects him and somewhat fears him, she tries to control herself in front of him; each one tries to spare the mysterious other whose feelings and reactions are hard to discern. Women among themselves are pitiless; they foil, provoke, chase, attack and lead each other on to the limits of abjection. Masculine calm – be it indifference or self-control – is a barrier feminine emotions come up against: but between two women friends, there is escalation of tears and convulsions; their patience in endlessly going over criticisms and explanations is insatiable. Demands, recriminations, jealousy, tyranny – all these plagues of conjugal life pour out in heightened form. If such love is often stormy, it is also usually more threatened than heterosexual love. It is criticised by the society into which it cannot always integrate. A woman who assumes the masculine attitude – by her character, situation and the force of her passion – will regret not giving her woman friend a normal and respectable life, not being able to marry her, leading her along unusual paths: these are the feelings Radclyffe Hall attributes to her heroine in *The Well of Loneliness*;[79] this remorse is conveyed by a morbid anxiety and an even greater torturous jealousy. The more passive or less infatuated woman will suffer from society's censure; she will think herself degraded, perverted, frustrated, she will resent the one who has imposed this lot on her. It might be that one of the two women desires a child; either she sadly resigns herself to her childlessness or both adopt a child or the one who desires motherhood asks a man for his services; the child is sometimes a link, sometimes also a new source of friction.

What gives women enclosed in homosexuality a masculine character is not their erotic life, which, on the contrary, confines them to a feminine universe: it is all the responsibilities they have to assume because they do without men. Their situation is the opposite of that of the courtesan who sometimes has a male mind by dint of living among males – like Ninon de Lenclos – but who depends on them. The particular

atmosphere around lesbians stems from the contrast between the gynaeceum character of their private life and the masculine independence of
their public existence. They behave like men in a world without men.
A woman alone always seems a little unusual; it is not true that men
respect women: they respect each other through their women – wives,
mistresses, 'kept' women; when masculine protection no longer extends
over her, woman is disarmed before a superior caste that is aggressive,
sneering or hostile. As an 'erotic perversion', feminine homosexuality
elicits smiles; but inasmuch as it implies a way of life, it provokes scorn
or scandal. If there is an affectation in lesbians' attitudes, it is because
they have no way of living their situation naturally: natural implies that
one does not reflect on self, that one acts without representing one's
acts to oneself; but people's behaviour constantly makes the lesbian
conscious of herself. She can only follow her path with calm indifference if she is older or secure in her social prestige.

It is difficult to determine, for example, if it is by taste or by defence
mechanism that she so often dresses in a masculine way. It certainly
comes in large part from a spontaneous choice. Nothing is less *natural*
than dressing like a woman; no doubt masculine clothes are also artificial, but they are more comfortable and simple and made to favour action
rather than impede it; George Sand and Isabelle Eberhardt wore men's
suits; Thyde Monnier in her last book*[80] spoke of her predilection for
wearing trousers; all active women like flat shoes and sturdy clothes.
The meaning of feminine attire is clear: it is a question of decoration,
and decorating oneself is offering oneself; heterosexual feminists were
formerly as intransigent as lesbians on this point: they refused to make
themselves merchandise on display, they wore suits and felt hats; fancy
low-cut dresses seemed to them the symbol of the social order they were
fighting. Today they have succeeded in mastering reality and the symbolic
has less importance in their eyes. But it remains for the lesbian insofar
as she must still assert her claim. It might also be – if physical particularities have motivated her vocation – that austere clothes suit her better.
It must be added that one of the roles clothing plays is to gratify woman's
tactile sensuality; but the lesbian disdains the consolations of velvet and
silk: like Sandor she will appreciate them on her woman friend, or her
friend's body may even replace them. This is why a lesbian often likes
hard liquor, smokes strong tobacco, uses rough language and imposes
rigorous exercise on herself: erotically, she shares in feminine softness;

* *Me.*

by contrast, she likes an intense environment. This aspect can make her enjoy men's company. But a new factor enters here: the often ambiguous relationship she has with them. A woman who is very sure of her masculinity will want only men as friends and associates: this assurance is rarely seen except in a woman who shares interests with men, who – in business, action or art – works and succeeds like a man. When Gertrude Stein entertained, she only talked with the men and left to Alice Toklas the job of talking with their women companions.* It is towards women that the very masculine homosexual woman will have an ambivalent attitude: she scorns them but she has an inferiority complex in relation to them both as a woman and as a man; she fears being perceived by them as a tomboy, an incomplete man, which leads her either to display a haughty superiority or to manifest – like Stekel's transvestite – a sadistic aggressiveness towards them. But this case is rather rare. We have seen that most lesbians partially reject men. For them as well as for the frigid woman, there is disgust, resentment, shyness or pride; they do not really feel similar to men; to their feminine resentment is added a masculine inferiority complex; they are rivals, better armed to seduce, possess and keep their prey; they detest their power over women, they detest the 'soiling' to which they subject women. They also take exception to seeing men hold social privileges and to feeling that men are stronger than they: it is a crushing humiliation not to be able to fight with a rival, to know he can knock you down with one blow. This complex hostility is one of the reasons some homosexual women declare themselves as homosexuals; they see only other homosexual women; they group together to show they do not need men either socially or sexually. From there one easily slides into useless boastfulness and all the playacting of inauthenticity. The lesbian first plays at being a man; then being lesbian itself becomes a game; a transvestite goes from disguise to livery; and the woman under the pretext of freeing herself from man's oppression makes herself the slave of her personage; she did not want to confine herself in a woman's situation, but she imprisons herself in that of the lesbian. Nothing gives a worse impression of small-mindedness and mutilation than these clans of liberated women. It must be added that many women only declare themselves homosexual out of self-interest: they adopt equivocal appearances with exaggerated consciousness, hoping to catch men

---

* A heterosexual woman who believes – or wants to persuade herself – that she transcends the difference of the sexes by her own worth will often have the same attitude; for example, Mme de Staël.

who like 'perverts'. These show-off zealots – who are obviously those one notices most – contribute to throwing discredit on what public opinion considers a vice and a pose.

In truth, homosexuality is no more a deliberate perversion than a fatal curse.* It is an attitude that is *chosen in situation*; it is both motivated and freely adopted. None of the factors the subject accepts in this choice – physiological facts, psychological history or social circumstances – is determining, although all contribute to explaining it. It is one way among others for woman to solve the problems posed by her condition in general and by her erotic situation in particular. Like all human behaviour, this will involve playacting, imbalance, failure or lies, or, on the other hand, it will be the source of fruitful experiences, depending on whether it is lived in bad faith, laziness and inauthenticity or in lucidity, generosity and freedom.

---

* *The Well of Loneliness* presents a heroine marked by a psychophysiological inevitability. But the documentary value of this novel is very insubstantial in spite of its reputation.

Part Two
SITUATION

CHAPTER 5

The Married Woman

The destiny that society traditionally offers women is marriage. Even today, most women are, were, or plan to be married, or they suffer from not being so. Marriage is the reference by which the single woman is defined, whether she is frustrated by, disgusted at, or even indifferent to this institution. Thus we must continue this study by analysing marriage.

The economic evolution of woman's condition is in the process of upsetting the institution of marriage: it is becoming a union freely entered into by two autonomous individuals; the commitments of the two parties are personal and reciprocal; adultery is a breach of contract for both parties; either of them can obtain a divorce on the same grounds. Woman is no longer limited to the reproductive function: it has lost, in large part, its character of natural servitude and has come to be regarded as a freely assumed responsibility;* and it is considered productive work since, in many cases, maternity leave necessitated by pregnancy must be paid to the mother by the state or the employer. For a few years in the USSR, marriage was a contract between individuals based on complete freedom of the spouses; today it seems to be a duty the state imposes on them both. Which of these tendencies prevails in tomorrow's world depends on the general structure of society: but in any case, masculine guardianship is becoming extinct. Yet, from a feminist point of view, the period we are living through is still a period of transition. Only a part of the female population participates in production, and those same women belong to a society where ancient structures and values still survive. Modern marriage can be understood only in light of the past it perpetuates.

Marriage has always been presented in radically different ways for men and for women. The two sexes are necessary for each other, but this necessity has never fostered reciprocity; women have never constituted

* See Vol. I.

a caste establishing exchanges and contracts on an equal footing with men. Man is a socially autonomous and complete individual; he is regarded above all as a producer and his existence is justified by the work he provides for the group; we have already seen* the reasons why the reproductive and domestic role to which woman is confined has not guaranteed her an equal dignity. Of course, the male needs her; with some primitive peoples, a bachelor, unable to support himself alone, may become a sort of pariah; in agricultural societies, a woman partner-worker is indispensable to the peasant; and for most men, it is advantageous to unload some of the chores onto a woman; the man himself wishes to have a stable sexual life, he desires posterity, and society requires him to contribute to its perpetuation. But man does not address his appeal to woman herself: it is men's society that allows each of its members to accomplish himself as husband and father; woman, integrated as slave or vassal into the family group dominated by fathers and brothers, has always been given in marriage to males by other males. In primitive times, the clan, the paternal gens, treats her almost like a thing: she is part of payments to which two groups mutually consent; her condition was not deeply modified when marriage evolved† into a contractual form; dowered or receiving her share of an inheritance, woman becomes a civil person: but a dowry or an inheritance still enslaves her to her family; for a long period, the contracts were signed between father-in-law and son-in-law, not between husband and wife; in those times, only the widow bene-fited from an economic independence.‡ A girl's free choice was always highly restricted; and celibacy – except in rare cases where it bears a sacred connotation – ranked her as a parasite and pariah; marriage was her only means of survival and the only justification of her existence. It was doubly imposed on her: she must give children to the commu-nity; but rare are the cases where – as in Sparta and to some extent under the Nazi regime – the state takes her under its guardianship and asks only that she be a mother. Even civilisations that ignore the father's generative role demand that she be under the protection of a husband; and she also has the function of satisfying the male's sexual needs and caring for the home. The charge society imposes on her is considered as a *service* rendered to the husband: and he owes his wife gifts or a marriage

---

* See Vol. I.

† This evolution took place in a discontinuous manner. It was repeated in Egypt, Rome and in modern civilisation; see Vol. I.

‡ Hence the special character of the young widow in erotic literature.

dowry and agrees to support her; using him as an intermediary, the community acquits itself of its responsibilities to the woman. The rights the wife acquires by fulfilling her duties have their counterpart in the obligations the male submits to. He cannot break the conjugal bond at whim; repudiation and divorce can only be granted by public authority, and then sometimes the husband owes a monetary compensation: the practice even becomes abusive in Bocchoris's Egypt, as it is today with alimony in the United States. Polygamy was always more or less tolerated: a man can have slaves, *pallakès*, concubines, mistresses and prostitutes in his bed; but he is required to respect certain privileges of his legitimate wife. If she thinks she is maltreated or wronged, she has the option – more or less concretely guaranteed – to return to her family and to obtain a separation or divorce in her own right. Thus for both parties marriage is a charge and a benefit at the same time; but their situations are not symmetrical; for girls, marriage is the only way to be integrated into the group, and if they are 'rejects', they are social waste. This is why mothers have always at all costs tried to marry them off. Among the bourgeoisie of the last century, girls were barely consulted. They were offered to possible suitors through 'interviews' set up in advance. Zola describes this custom in *Pot-Bouille*.[1]

'A failure, it's a failure,' said Mme Josserand, falling into her chair.

'Ah!' M. Josserand simply said.

'But you don't seem to understand,' continued Mme Josserand in a shrill voice. 'I'm telling you that here's another marriage gone down the river, and it's the fourth to fall through!

'Listen,' went on Mme Josserand, advancing toward her daughter. 'How did you spoil *this* marriage too?'

Bertha realised that her turn had come.

'I don't know, Mamma,' she murmured.

'An assistant department head,' continued her mother, 'not yet thirty, a superb future. Every month it brings you money: solid, that's all that counts . . . You did something stupid, as you did with the others?'

'I swear I didn't, Mamma.'

'When you were dancing, you slipped into the small parlour.'

Bertha was unnerved: 'Yes, Mamma . . . and as soon as we were alone, he wanted to do disgraceful things, he kissed me and grabbed me like this. So I got scared and pushed him against the furniture!'

Her mother interrupted her: 'Pushed him against the furniture! Ah, you foolish girl, pushed him against the furniture!'

'But, Mamma, he was holding on to me.'

'And what? He was holding on to you . . . how bad is that! Putting you idiots in boarding school! What do they teach you there, tell me! . . . For a kiss behind a door! Should you really even tell us about this, us, your parents? And you push people against furniture and you ruin your chances of getting married!'

Assuming a pontificating air, she continued:

'It's over, I give up, you are just stupid, my dear . . . Since you have no fortune, just understand that you have to catch men some other way. By being pleasant, gazing tenderly, forgetting your hand, allowing little indulgences without seeming to; in short, you have to fish a husband . . . And what bothers me is that she is not too bad when she wants,' continued Mme Josserand. 'Come now, dry your eyes, look at me as if I were a gentleman courting you. You see, you drop your fan so that when the gentleman picks it up he'll touch your fingers . . . And don't be stiff, let your waist bend. Men don't like boards. And above all, don't be a simpleton if they go too far. A man who goes too far is caught, my dear.'

The clock in the parlour rang two o'clock; and in the excitement of the long evening, fired by her desire for an immediate marriage, the mother let herself think aloud, twisting and turning her daughter like a paper doll. The girl, docile and dispirited, gave in, but her heart was heavy and fear and shame wrung her breast.

This shows the girl becoming absolutely passive; she is *married, given* in marriage by her parents. Boys *marry*, they *take* a wife. In marriage they seek an expansion, a confirmation of their existence but not the very right to exist; it is a charge they assume freely. So they can question its advantages and disadvantages just as the Greek and medieval satirists did; for them it is simply a way of life, not a destiny. They are just as free to prefer a celibate's solitude or to marry late or not at all.

In marrying, the woman receives a piece of the world as property; legal guaranties protect her from man's caprices; but she becomes his vassal. He is economically the head of the community, and he thus embodies it in society's eyes. She takes his name; she joins his religion, integrates into his class, his world; she belongs to his family, she becomes his other 'half'. She follows him where his work calls him: where he works essentially determines where they live; she breaks with her past more or less brutally, she is annexed to her husband's universe; she gives him her person: she owes him her virginity and strict fidelity. She loses part of the legal rights of the unmarried woman. Roman law placed the woman in the hands of her husband *loco filiae*; at the beginning of the nineteenth century, Bonald declared that the woman is to her husband what the child is to the mother; until the 1942 law, French law demanded a wife's obedience to her husband; law and customs still confer great authority on him: it is suggested by her very situation within the conjugal society. Since he is the producer, it is he who goes beyond family interest to the interest of society and who opens a future to her by cooperating in the construction of the collective future: it is he who embodies transcendence. Woman is destined to maintain the species and care for the home, which is to say, to immanence.* In truth, all human existence is transcendence and immanence at the same time; to go beyond itself, it must maintain itself; to thrust itself towards the future, it must integrate the past into itself; and while relating to others, it must confirm itself in itself. These two moments are implied in every living movement: for *man,* marriage provides the perfect synthesis of them; in his work and political life, he finds change and progress, he experiences his dispersion through time and the universe; and when he tires of this wandering, he establishes a home, he settles down, he anchors himself in the world; in the evening he restores himself in the house, where his wife cares for the furniture and children and safeguards the past she keeps in store. But the wife has no other task save the one of maintaining and caring for life in its pure and identical generality; she perpetuates the immutable species, she assures the even rhythm of the days and the permanence of the home she guards with locked doors; she is given no direct grasp on the future, nor on the universe; she goes beyond herself towards the group only through her husband as mouthpiece.

Marriage today still retains this traditional form. And, first of all, it is imposed far more imperiously on the girl than on the young man. There are still many social strata where she is offered no other perspective; for peasants, an unmarried woman is a pariah; she remains the servant of her father, her brothers and her brother-in-law; moving to the city is

* Cf. Vol. I. This thesis is found in St Paul, the Church Fathers, Rousseau, Proudhon, Auguste Comte, D. H. Lawrence, and others.

virtually impossible for her; marriage chains her to a man and makes her mistress of a home. In some bourgeois classes, a girl is still left incapable of earning a living; she can only vegetate as a parasite in her father's home or accept some lowly position in a stranger's home. Even when she is more emancipated, the economic advantage held by males forces her to prefer marriage over a career: she will look for a husband whose situation is superior to her own, a husband she hopes will 'get ahead' faster and further than she could. It is still accepted that the love act is a *service* she renders to the man; he *takes* his pleasure and he owes compensation in return. The woman's body is an object to be purchased; for her it represents capital she has the right to exploit. Sometimes she brings a dowry to her husband; she often agrees to provide some domestic work: she will keep the house, raise the children. In any case, she has the right to let herself be supported, and traditional morality even exhorts it. It is understandable that she is tempted by this easy solution, especially as women's professions are so unrewarding and badly paid; marriage is a more beneficial career than many others. Mores still make sexual enfranchisement for a single woman difficult; in France a wife's adultery was a crime until recent times, while no law forbade a woman free love; however, if she wanted to take a lover, she had to be married first. Many strictly controlled young bourgeois girls still marry 'to be free'. A good number of American women have won their sexual freedom; but their experiences are like those of the young primitive people described by Malinowski in 'The Bachelors' House'[2] – girls who engage in pleasures without consequences; they are expected to marry, and only then will they be fully considered adults. A woman alone, in America even more than in France, is a socially incomplete being, even if she earns her living; she needs a ring on her finger to achieve the total dignity of a person and her full rights. Motherhood in particular is respected only in the married woman; the unwed mother remains an object of scandal, and a child is a severe handicap for her. For all these reasons, many Old and New World adolescent girls, when interviewed about their future projects, respond today just as they did in former times: 'I want to get married.' No young man, however, considers marriage as his fundamental project. Economic success is what will bring him to respectable adulthood: it may involve marriage – particularly for the peasant – but it may also exclude it. Modern life's conditions – less stable, more uncertain than in the past – make marriage's responsibilities particularly heavy for the young man; the benefits, on the other hand, have decreased since he can easily live on his own and sexual satisfaction is generally available.

Without doubt, marriage brings material conveniences ('Eating home is better than eating out') and erotic ones ('This way we have a brothel at home'), and it frees the person from loneliness, it establishes him in space and time by providing him with a home and children; it is a definitive accomplishment of his existence. In spite of this, overall there is still less masculine demand than feminine supply. The father does not so much give his daughter as get rid of her; the girl seeking a husband does not respond to a masculine call: she provokes it.

Arranged marriages have not disappeared; there is still a right-minded bourgeoisie perpetuating them. In France, near Napoleon's tomb, at the Opera, at balls, on the beach or at a tea, the young hopeful with every hair in place, in a new dress, shyly exhibits her physical grace and modest conversation; her parents nag her: 'You've already cost me enough in meeting people; make up your mind. The next time it's your sister's turn.' The unhappy candidate knows her chances diminish the older she gets; there are not many suitors: she has no more freedom of choice than the young bedouin girl exchanged for a flock of sheep. As Colette says,[*3] 'A young girl without a fortune or a trade, who is dependent on her brothers for everything, has only one choice: shut up, be grateful for her good luck, and thank God!'

In a less crude way, high society permits young people to meet under mothers' watchful eyes. Somewhat more liberated, girls go out more, attend university, take jobs that give them the chance to meet men. Between 1945 and 1947, Claire Leplae conducted a survey on the Belgian bourgeoisie, about the problem of matrimonial choice.[†4] The author conducted interviews; I will cite some questions she asked and the responses given:

Q: *Are arranged marriages common?*
A: There are no more arranged marriages (51%).
   Arranged marriages are very rare, 1% at most (16%).
   1 to 3% of marriages are arranged (28%).
   5 to 10% of marriages are arranged (5%).

The people interviewed point out that arranged marriages, frequent before 1945, have almost disappeared. Nonetheless, 'specific interests,

* *Claudine's House.*
† Cf. Claire Leplae, *The Engagement.*

poor relations, self-interest, not much family, shyness, age and the desire to make a good match are motives for some arranged marriages'. These marriages are often conducted by priests; sometimes the girl marries by correspondence. 'They describe themselves in writing, and it is put on a special sheet with a number. This sheet is sent to all persons described. It includes, for example, two hundred female and an equal number of male candidates. They also write their own profiles. They can all freely choose a correspondent to whom they write through the agency.'

Q: *How did young people meet their fiancées or fiancés over the past ten years?*
A: Social events (48%).
   School or clubs (22%).
   Personal acquaintances, travel (30%).

Everyone agrees that 'marriages between childhood friends are very rare. Love is found in unexpected places.'

Q: *Is money a primary factor in the choice of a spouse?*
A: 30% of marriages are based on money (48%).
   50% of marriages are based on money (35%).
   70% of marriages are based on money (17%).

Q: *Are parents anxious to marry their daughters?*
A: Parents are anxious to marry their daughters (58%).
   Parents are eager to marry their daughters (24%).
   Parents wish to keep their daughters at home (18%).

Q: *Are girls anxious to marry?*
A: Girls are anxious to marry (36%).
   Girls are eager to marry (38%).
   Girls prefer not to marry than to have a bad marriage (26%).

'Girls besiege boys. Girls marry the first boy to come along simply to get married. They all hope to marry and work at doing so. A girl is humiliated if she is not sought after: to escape this, she will often marry her first prospect. Girls marry to get married. Girls marry to be married. Girls settle down because marriage assures them more freedom.' Almost all the interviews concur on this point.

Q: *Are girls more active than boys in seeking marriage?*

A: Girls declare their intentions to boys and ask them to marry them (43%).

Girls are more active than boys in seeking marriage (43%).

Girls are discreet (14%).

Here again the response is nearly unanimous: it is the girls who usually take the initiative in pursuing marriage. 'Girls realise they are not equipped to get along on their own; not knowing how they can work to make a living, they seek a lifeline in marriage. Girls make declarations, throw themselves at boys. They are frightening! Girls use all their resources to get married . . . it's the woman who pursues the man,' and so forth.

No such document exists in France; but as the situation of the bourgeoisie is similar in France and Belgium, the conclusions would probably be comparable; 'arranged' marriages have always been more numerous in France than in any other country, and the famous 'Green Ribbon Club',[5] whose members have parties for the purpose of bringing people of both sexes together, is still flourishing; matrimonial announcements take up columns in many newspapers.

In France, as in America, mothers, older sisters and women's magazines cynically teach girls the art of 'catching' a husband like flypaper catching flies; this is 'fishing' and 'hunting', demanding great skill: do not aim too high or too low; be realistic, not romantic; mix coquetry with modesty; do not ask for too much or too little. Young men mistrust women who 'want to get married'. A young Belgian man* declares, 'There is nothing more unpleasant for a man than to feel himself pursued, to realise that a woman wants to get her hooks into him.' They try to avoid their traps. A girl's choice is often very limited: it would be truly free only if she felt free enough not to marry. Her decision is usually accompanied by calculation, distaste and resignation rather than enthusiasm. 'If the young man who proposes to her is more or less suitable (background, health, career), she accepts him without loving him. She will accept him without passion even if there are "buts".'

At the same as she desires it, however, a girl is often apprehensive of marriage. It represents a more considerable benefit for her than for the man, which is why she desires it more fervently; but it demands weighty sacrifices as well; in particular, it implies a more brutal rupture with the past. We have seen that many adolescent girls are anguished by the idea

* Ibid.

of leaving the paternal home: when the event draws near, this anxiety is heightened. This is the moment when many neuroses develop; the same thing is true for young men who are frightened by the new responsibilities they are assuming, but such neuroses are much more widespread in girls for the reasons we have already seen and they become even more serious in this crisis. I will cite only one example, taken from Stekel.[6] He treated a girl from a good family who manifested several neurotic symptoms.

When Stekel meets her, she is suffering from vomiting, takes morphine every night, has fits of temper, refuses to wash, eats in bed, refuses to leave her room. She is engaged to be married and affirms that she loves her fiancé. She admits to Stekel that she gave herself to him. Later she says that she derived no pleasure from it: the memory of his kisses was even repugnant to her and they are the cause of her vomiting. It is discovered that, in fact, she succumbed to him to punish her mother, who she felt never loved her enough; as a child, she spied on her parents at night because she was afraid they might give her a brother or sister; she adored her mother. 'And now she had to get married, leave [her parents'] home, abandon her parents' bedroom? It was impossible.' She lets herself grow fat, scratches and hurts her hands, deteriorates, falls ill, tries to offend her fiancé in all ways. The doctor heals her, but she pleads with her mother to give up this idea of marriage: 'She wanted to stay home, to remain a child for ever.' Her mother insists that she marry. A week before the wedding day, she is found in her bed, dead; she shot herself with a revolver.

In other cases, the girl wilfully falls into a protracted illness; she becomes desperate because her state keeps her from marrying the man 'she adores'; in fact, she makes herself ill to avoid marrying him and finds her balance only by breaking her engagement. Sometimes the fear of marriage originates in former erotic experiences that have left their mark on her; in particular, she might dread that her loss of virginity will be discovered. But frequently the idea of submitting to a male stranger is unbearable because of her ardent feelings for her father and mother or a sister, or her attachment to her family home in general. And many of those who decide to marry because it is what they should do, because of the pressure on them, because they know it is the only reasonable solution, because they want a normal existence of wife and mother, nonetheless keep a secret and obstinate resistance in their deepest hearts, making the early days of their married lives difficult and even keeping themselves from ever finding a happy balance.

Marriages, then, are generally not based on love. 'The husband is, so to speak, never more than a substitute for the loved man, and not that man himself,' said Freud. This dissociation is not accidental. It is implicit in the very nature of the institution. The economic and sexual union of man and woman is a matter of transcending towards the collective interest and not of individual happiness. In patriarchal regimes, a fiancé chosen by parents had often never seen his future wife's face before the wedding day – and this still happens today with some Muslims. There would be no question of founding a lifelong enterprise, considered in its social aspect, on sentimental or erotic caprice. Montaigne says:

> In this sober contract the appetites are not so wanton; they are dull and more blunted. Love hates people to be attached to each other except by himself, and takes a laggard part in relations that are set up and maintained under another title, as marriage is. Connections and means have, with reason, as much weight in it as graces and beauty, or more. We do not marry for ourselves, whatever we say; we marry just as much or more for our posterity, for our family.[7]

Because it is the man who 'takes' the woman – and especially when there is a good supply of women – he has rather more possibilities for choosing. But since the sexual act is considered to be a *service* imposed on the woman and upon which are founded the advantages conceded to her, it is logical to ignore her own preferences. Marriage is intended to defend her against man's freedom: but as there is neither love nor individuality without freedom, she must renounce the love of a particular individual to ensure the protection of a male for life. I heard a mother of a family teach her daughters that 'love is a vulgar sentiment reserved for men and unknown to women of good standing'. In a naïve form, this was the very doctrine Hegel professed in *Phenomenology of the Spirit*:[8]

> The relationships of mother and wife, however, are those of particular individuals, partly in the form of something natural pertaining to desire, partly in the form of something negative which sees in those relationships only something evanescent and also, again, the particular individual is for that very reason a contingent element which can be replaced by another individual. In the ethical household, it is not a question of *this* particular husband, *this* particular child, but simply of husband and children generally; the relationships of the woman

are based, not on feeling, but on the universal. The difference between the ethical life of the woman and that of the man consists just in this, that in her vocation as an individual and in her pleasure, her interest is centred on the universal and remains alien to the particularity of desire; whereas in the husband these two sides are separated; and since he possesses as a citizen the self-conscious power of universality, he thereby acquires the right of desire and, at the same time, preserves his freedom in regard to it. Since, then, in this relationship of the wife there is an admixture of particularity, her ethical life is not pure; but in so far as it *is* ethical, the particularity is a matter of indifference, and the wife is without the moment of knowing herself as *this* particular self in the other partner.

This points out that for a woman it is not at all a question of establishing individual relations with a chosen husband, but rather of justifying the exercise of her feminine functions in their generality; she should have sexual pleasure only in a generic form and not an individualised one; this results in two essential consequences that touch upon her erotic destiny. First, she has no right to sexual activity outside marriage; for both spouses, sexual congress becoming an institution, desire and pleasure are superseded by the interest of society; but man, as worker and citizen transcending towards the universal, can savour contingent pleasures prior to marriage and outside of married life: in any case, he finds satisfaction in other ways; but in a world where woman is essentially defined as female, she must be justified wholly as a female. Second, it has been seen that the connection between the general and the particular is biologically different for the male and the female: in accomplishing his specific task as husband and reproducer, the male unfailingly finds his sexual pleasure;* on the contrary, very often for the woman, there is a dissociation between the reproductive function and sexual pleasure. This is so to the extent that in claiming to give ethical dignity to her erotic life, marriage, in fact, means to suppress it.

Woman's sexual frustration has been deliberately accepted by men; it has been seen that men rely on an optimistic naturalism to tolerate her frustrations: it is her lot; the biblical curse confirms men's convenient

---

* Of course, the adage 'A hole is always a hole' is vulgarly humorous; man does seek something other than brute pleasure; nonetheless, the success of certain 'slaughter-houses' is enough to prove a man can find some satisfaction with the first available woman.

opinion. Pregnancy's pains – the heavy ransom inflicted on the woman in exchange for a brief and uncertain pleasure – are often the object of various jokes. 'Five minutes of pleasure: nine months of pain . . . It goes in more easily than it comes out.' This contrast often makes them laugh. It is part of this sadistic philosophy: many men relish feminine misery and are repulsed by the idea of reducing it.* One can understand, then, that males have no scruples about denying their companion sexual happiness; and it even seems advantageous to them to deny woman the temptations of desire along with the autonomy of pleasure.[†]

This is what Montaigne expresses with a charming cynicism:

And so it is a kind of incest to employ in this venerable and sacred alliance the efforts and extravagances of amorous license, as it seems to me I have said elsewhere. A man, says Aristotle, should touch his wife prudently and soberly, lest if he caresses her too lasciviously the pleasure should transport her outside the bounds of reason . . . I see no marriages that sooner are troubled and fail than those that progress by means of beauty and amorous desires. It needs more

---

* There are some, for example, who support the idea that painful childbirth is necessary to awaken the maternal instinct: those who deliver under anaesthesia have been known to abandon their fawns. Such alleged facts are at best vague; and a woman is in no way a doe. The truth is that some males are shocked that the burdens of womanhood might be lightened.

† Still, in our times, woman's claim to pleasure incites male anger; a striking document on this subject is Dr Grémillon's treatise, 'The Truth about the Genital Orgasm of the Woman' (La vérité sur l'orgasme vénérien de la femme). The preface informs us that the author, a World War I hero who saved the lives of fifty-five German prisoners, is a man of the highest moral standing. Taking serious issue with Stekel in Frigidity in Woman, he declares, 'The normal and fertile woman does not have a genital orgasm. Many are the mothers (and the best of them) who have never experienced these wondrous spasms . . . the most latent erogenous zones are not natural but artificial. They are delighted to have them, but they are stigmas of decadence . . . Tell all that to a man seeking pleasure and he does not care. He wants his depraved partner to have a genital orgasm, and she will have it. If it does not exist, it will be made to exist. Modern woman wants a man to make her vibrate. To her we answer: Madam, we don't have the time and hygiene forbids it! . . . The creator of erogenous zones works against himself: he creates insatiable women. The female ghoul can tirelessly exhaust innumerable husbands . . . the "zoned" one becomes a new woman with a new spirit, sometimes a terrible woman capable of crime . . . there would be no neuroses, no psychoses if we understood that the "two-backed beast" is an act as indifferent as eating, urinating, defecating or sleeping.'

solid and stable foundations, and we need to go at it circumspectly; this ebullient ardor is no good for it. . . . A good marriage, if such there be, rejects the company and conditions of love.[9]

He also says:

Even the pleasures they get in making love to their wives are condemned, unless moderation is observed; and . . . it is possible to err through licentiousness and debauchery, just as in an illicit affair. Those shameless excesses that our first heat suggests to us in this sport are not only indecently but detrimentally practiced on our wives. Let them at least learn shamelessness from another hand. They are always aroused enough for our need . . . Marriage is a religious and holy bond. That is why the pleasure we derive from it should be a restrained pleasure, serious, and mixed with some austerity; it should be a somewhat discreet and conscientious voluptuousness.

In fact, if the husband awakens feminine sensuality, he awakens it in its general form, since he was not singularly chosen by her; he is preparing his wife to seek pleasure in other arms; 'to love one's wife too well,' says Montaigne, is to 'shit in your hat and then put it on your head'. He admits in good faith that masculine prudence puts the woman in a thankless situation:

Women are not wrong at all when they reject the rules of life that have been introduced into the world, inasmuch as it is the men who have made these without them. There is naturally strife and wrangling between them and us . . . we treat them inconsiderately in the following way. We have discovered . . . that they are incomparably more capable and ardent than we in the acts of love . . . we have gone and given women continence as their particular share, and upon utmost and extreme penalties . . . We, on the contrary, want them to be healthy, vigorous, plump, well-nourished, and chaste at the same time: that is to say, both hot and cold. For marriage, which we say has the function of keeping them from burning, brings them but little cooling off, according to our ways.

Proudhon is less scrupulous: according to him, separating love from marriage conforms to justice:

Love must be buried in justice . . . all love conversations, even between people who are engaged, even between husband and wife, are unsuitable, destructive of domestic respect, of the love of work and of the practice of one's social duty . . . (once the function of love has been fulfilled) . . . we have to discard it like the shepherd who removes the rennet once the milk has coagulated.

Yet, during the nineteenth century, conceptions of the bourgeoisie changed somewhat; it ardently strove to defend and maintain marriage; and besides, the progress of individualism made it impossible to stifle feminine claims; Saint-Simon, Fourier, George Sand and all the Romantics had too intensely proclaimed the right to love. The problem arose of integrating into marriage those individual feelings that had previously and carelessly been excluded. It was thus that the ambiguous notion of conjugal love was invented, miraculous fruit of the traditional marriage of convenience. Balzac expresses the ideas of the conservative bourgeoisie in all their inconsequence. He recognises that the principle of marriage has nothing to do with love; but he finds it repugnant to assimilate a respectable institution with a simple business deal where the woman is treated like a thing; and he ends up with the disconcerting inconsistencies in *The Physiology of Marriage*,[10] where we read:

Marriage can be considered politically, civilly, or morally, as a law, a contract, or an institution . . .

Thus marriage ought to be an object of general respect. Society has only considered it under these three heads – they dominate the marriage question.

Most men who get married have only in view reproduction, propriety, or what is due to the child; yet neither reproduction, propriety, nor the child constitute happiness. 'Crescite et multiplicamini' [increase and multiply] does not imply love. To ask a girl whom one has seen fourteen times in a fortnight for her love on behalf of the law, the king and justice, is an absurdity only worthy of the fore-ordained!

This is as clear as Hegelian theory. But Balzac continues without any transition:

Love is the union of desire and tenderness, and happiness in marriage comes from a perfect understanding between two souls.

And from this it follows that to be happy a man is obliged to bind himself by certain rules of honour and delicacy. After having enjoyed the privilege of the social laws which consecrate desire, he should obey the secret laws of nature which bring to birth the affections. If his happiness depends on being loved, he himself must love sincerely; nothing can withstand true passion.

But to be passionate is always to desire.

Can one always desire one's wife?

Yes.

After that, Balzac exposes the science of marriage. But one quickly sees that for the husband it is not a question of being loved but of not being deceived: he will not hesitate to inflict a debilitating regime on his wife, to keep her uncultured, and to stultify her solely to safeguard his honour. Is this still about love? If one wants to find a meaning in these murky and incoherent ideas, it seems man has the right to choose a wife through whom he can satisfy his needs in their generality, a generality that is the guarantee of his faithfulness: then it is up to him to waken his wife's love by applying certain recipes. But is he really *in love* if he marries for his property or for his posterity? And if he is not, how can his passion be irresistible enough to bring about a reciprocal passion? And does Balzac really not know that an unshared love, on the contrary, annoys and disgusts? His bad faith is clearly visible in *Letters of Two Brides*,[11] an epistolary novel with a message. Louise de Chaulieu believes that marriage is based on love: in a fit of passion, she kills her first husband; she dies from the jealous fixation she feels for her second. Renée de l'Estorade sacrifices her feelings to reason: but the joys of motherhood mostly compensate her and she builds a stable happiness. One wonders first what curse – except the author's own decree – deprives the amorous Louise of the motherhood she desires: love has never prevented conception; and one also thinks that to accept her husband's embraces joyfully, Renée had to accept this 'hypocrisy' Stendhal hated in 'honest women'. Balzac describes the wedding night in these words:

'The animal that we call a husband,' to quote your words, disappeared, and one balmy evening I discovered in his stead a lover, whose words thrilled me and on whose arm I leant with pleasure beyond words . . . I felt a fluttering of curiosity in my heart . . . [Know that] nothing was lacking either of satisfaction for the most fastidious sentiment, or of that unexpectedness which brings, in a sense, its own sanction. Every witchery of imagination, of passion, of reluctance overcome, of the ideal passing into reality, played its part.

This beautiful miracle must not have occurred too often, since, several letters later, we find Renée in tears: 'Formerly I was a person, now I am a chattel'; and she consoles herself after her nights 'of conjugal love' by reading Bonald. But one would nevertheless like to know what recipe was used for the husband to change into an enchanter, during the most difficult moment of feminine initiation; those Balzac gives in *The Physiology of Marriage* are succinct: 'Never begin marriage by rape,' – or vague: 'The genius of the husband lies in deftly handling the various shades of pleasure, in developing them, and endowing them with a new style, an original expression.' He quickly goes on to say, moreover, that 'between two people who do not love one another, this genius is wanton'; then, precisely, Renée does not love Louis; and as he is depicted, where does this 'genius' come from? In truth, Balzac has cynically skirted the problem. He underestimates the fact that there are no neutral feelings and that in the absence of love, constraints, together with boredom, engender tender friendship less easily than resentment, impatience and hostility. He is more sincere in *The Lily in the Valley*[12] and the destiny of the unfortunate Mme de Mortsauf seems to be far less instructive.

Reconciling marriage and love is such a feat that at the very least divine intervention is necessary; this is the solution Kierkegaard adopts after complicated detours. He likes to denounce the paradox of marriage:

Indeed, what a passing strange device is marriage! And what makes it all the stranger is that it could be a step taken without thought. And yet no step is more decisive . . . And such an important step as marriage ought to be taken without reflection!*

This is the difficulty: love and falling in love are spontaneous, marriage is a decision; yet falling in love should be awakened by marriage or by decision: wanting to marry; this means that what is the most spontaneous must at the same time be the freest decision, and what is, because of the spontaneity, so inexplicable that

* *In Vino Veritas.*

it must be attributed to a divinity, must at the same time take place because of reflection and such exhausting reflection that a decision results from it. Besides, these things must not follow each other, the decision must not come sneaking up behind; everything must occur simultaneously, the two things have to come together at the moment of dénouement.*[13]

This underlines that loving is not marrying and it is quite difficult to understand how love can become duty. But paradoxes do not faze Kierkegaard: his whole essay on marriage is an attempt to elucidate this mystery. It is true, he agrees: 'Reflection is the angel of death for spontaneity . . . If it were true that reflection must take precedence over falling in love, there would never be marriage.' But 'decision is a new spontaneity obtained through reflection, experienced in a purely ideal way, a spontaneity that precisely corresponds to that of falling in love. Decision is a religious view of life constructed upon ethical presuppositions, and must, so to speak, pave the way for falling in love and securing it against any danger, exterior or interior.' This is why 'a husband, a real husband, is himself a miracle! . . . Being able to keep the pleasure of love while existence focuses all the power of seriousness on him and his beloved!'

As for the wife, reason is not her lot, she is without 'reflection'; so 'she goes from the immediacy of love to the immediacy of the religious'. Expressed in simple language, this doctrine means a man in love chooses marriage by an act of faith in God that guarantees him the accord of both feelings and duty; and the woman wishes to marry as soon as she is in love. I knew an old Catholic woman who, most naively, believed in a 'sacramental falling in love'; she asserted that at the moment the couple pronounce the definitive 'I do' at the altar, they feel their hearts burst into flame. Kierkegaard does admit there must previously be an 'inclination', but that it be thought to last a whole lifetime is no less miraculous.

However, in France, late nineteenth-century novelists and playwrights, less confident in the value of the holy vows, try to ensure conjugal happiness by more human means; more boldly than Balzac, they envisage the possibility of integrating eroticism with legitimate love. Porto-Riche affirms, in the play A Loving Wife,[14] the incompatibility of sexual love and home life: the husband, worn out by his wife's

---

* 'Some Reflections on Marriage'.

ardour, seeks peace with his more temperate mistress. But at Paul Hervieu's instigation, 'love' between spouses is a legal duty. Marcel Prévost preaches to the young husband that he must treat his wife like a mistress, alluding to conjugal pleasures in a discreetly libidinous way. Bernstein is the playwright of legitimate love: the husband is put forward as a wise and generous being next to the amoral, lying, sensual, fickle and mean wife; and he is also understood to be a virile and expert lover. Much romantic defence of marriage comes out in reaction to novels of adultery. Even Colette yields to this moralising wave in *The Innocent Libertine*,[15] when, after describing the cynical experiences of a clumsily deflowered young bride, she has her experience sexual pleasure in her husband's arms. Likewise, Martin Maurice, in a somewhat controversial book, brings the young woman, after a brief incursion into the bed of an experienced lover, to that of her husband, who benefits from her experience. For other reasons and in a different way, Americans today, who are both respectful of the institution of marriage and individualistic, endeavour to integrate sexuality into marriage. Many books on initiation into married life come out every year aimed at teaching couples to adapt to each other, and in particular teaching man how to create harmony with his wife. Psychoanalysts and doctors play the role of 'marriage counsellors'; it is accepted that the wife too has the right to pleasure and that the man must know the right techniques to provide her with it. But we have seen that sexual success is not merely a technical question. The young man, even if he has memorised twenty textbooks such as *What Every Husband Should Know, The Secret of Conjugal Happiness* and *Love without Fear*,[16] is still not sure he will know how to make his new wife love him. She reacts to the psychological situation as a whole. And traditional marriage is far from creating the most propitious conditions for the awakening and blossoming of feminine eroticism.

In the past, in matriarchal communities, virginity was not demanded of the new wife, and for mystical reasons she was normally supposed to be deflowered before the wedding. In some French regions, these ancient prerogatives can still be observed; prenuptial chastity is not required of girls; and even girls who have 'sinned' or unmarried mothers sometimes find a husband more easily than others. Moreover, in circles that accept woman's liberation, girls are granted the same sexual freedom as boys. However, paternalistic ethics imperiously demand that the bride be delivered to her husband as a virgin; he wants to be sure she does not carry within her a foreign germ; he wants the entire and exclusive property of this flesh he makes his own;* virginity has taken on a moral, religious and mystical value, and this value is still widely recognised today. In France, there are regions where friends of the husband stay outside the door of the bridal suite, laughing and singing until the husband comes out triumphantly showing them the bloodstained sheet; or else the parents display it in the morning to the neighbours.† The custom of the 'wedding night' is still widespread, albeit in a less brutal form. It is no coincidence that it has spawned a whole body of ribald literature: the separation of the social and the animal necessarily produces obscenity. A humanist morality demands that all living experience have a human meaning, that it be invested with freedom; in an authentically moral erotic life, there is the free assumption of desire and pleasure, or at least a deeply felt fight to regain freedom within sexuality: but this is only possible if a *singular* recognition of the other is accomplished in love or in desire. When sexuality is no longer redeemed by the individual, but God or society claims to justify it, the relationship of the two partners is no more than a bestial one. It is understandable that right-thinking matrons spurn adventures of the flesh: they have reduced them to the level of scatological functions. This is also why one hears so many sniggers at wedding parties. There is an obscene paradox in the super-imposing of a pompous ceremony on a brutally real animal function. The wedding presents its universal and abstract meaning: a man and a woman are united publicly according to symbolic rites; but in the secrecy of the bed it is concrete and singular individuals who confront each other face to face and all gazes turn away from their embraces. Colette, attending a peasant wedding at the age of thirteen, was terribly conster-nated when a girlfriend took her to see the wedding chamber:

> The young couple's bedroom . . . Under its curtains of Adrianople red, the tall, narrow bed, the bed stuffed with down and crammed with goose-down pillows, the bed that is to be the final scene of this wedding day all steaming with sweat, incense, the breath of cattle, the aroma of different sauces . . . Shortly the young couple will be arriving here. I hadn't thought of that. They will dive into that deep mound of feathers . . . They will embark on that obscure struggle

---

* See Vol. I, 'Myths'.

† 'Today, in certain regions of the United States, first-generation immigrants still send the bloody sheet back to the family in Europe as proof of the consummation of the marriage,' says the Kinsey Report.

about which my mother's bold and direct language and the life of
animals have taught me both too much and too little . . . And
then? . . . I'm afraid of that bedroom, afraid of that bed which I
hadn't thought of.*[17]

In her childish distress, the girl felt the contrast between the pomp
of the family feast and the animal mystery of the enclosed double
bed. Marriage's comic and lewd side is scarcely found in civilisations
that do not individualise woman: in the East, in Greece, in Rome; the
animal function appears there in as generalised a form as do the social
rites; but today in the West, men and women are grasped as individuals and wedding guests snigger because it is this particular man and
this particular woman who, in an altogether individual experience, are
going to consummate the act that we disguise in rites, speeches and
flowers. It is true that there is also a macabre contrast between the
pomp of great funerals and the rot of the tomb. But the dead person
does not awaken when he is put into the ground, while the bride is
terribly surprised when she discovers the singularity and contingence
of the *real* experience to which the mayor's tricoloured sash and church
organ pledged her. It is not only in vaudeville that one sees young
women returning in tears to their mothers on their wedding night:
psychiatric books are full of this type of account; several have been
told to me directly: they concern girls, too well brought up, without
any sexual education and whose sudden discovery of eroticism overwhelmed them. Last century, Mme Adam thought it was her duty to
marry a man who had kissed her on the mouth because she believed
that was the completed form of sexual union. More recently, Stekel
writes about a young bride: 'When during the honeymoon, her husband
deflowered her, she thought he was of unsound mind and did not dare
say a word for fear of dealing with an insane person.'†[18] It even happens
that the girl is so innocent she marries a woman invert and lives with
her pseudo-husband for a long time without doubting that she is
dealing with a man.

If on your marriage day, returning home, you set your wife in a
well to soak for the night, she will be dumbfounded. No comfort
to her now that she has always had a vague uneasiness . . .

* *Claudine's House.*
† *Conditions of Nervous Anxiety and Their Treatment.*

'Well now!' she will say, 'so that's what marriage is. That's why they keep it all so secret. I've let myself be taken in.'

But being annoyed, she will say nothing. That is why you will be able to dip her for long periods and often, without causing any scandal in the neighbourhood.

This fragment of a poem by Michaux,* called 'Bridal Night',[19] accurately conveys the situation. Today, many girls are better informed; but their consent remains abstract; and their defloration has the characteristics of a rape. 'There are certainly more rapes committed in marriage than outside of marriage,' says Havelock Ellis. In his work, *Monatsschrift für Geburtshülfe*, 1889, Vol. IX, Neugebauer found more than 150 cases of injuries inflicted on women by the penis during coitus; the causes were brutality, drunkenness, false position, and a disproportion of the organs. In England, Havelock Ellis reports, a woman asked six intelligent, married, middle-class women about their reactions on their wedding night: for all of them intercourse was a shock; two of them had been ignorant of everything; the others thought they knew but were no less psychically wounded. Adler also emphasised the psychic importance of the act of defloration.

> The first moment man acquires his full rights often decides his whole life. The inexperienced and over-aroused husband can sow the germ of feminine insensitivity and through his continual clumsiness and brutality transform it into permanent desensitisation.

Many examples of these unfortunate initiations were given in the previous chapter. Here is another case reported by Stekel:

> Mme H. N. . . ., raised very prudishly, trembled at the idea of her wedding night. Her husband undressed her almost violently without allowing her to get into bed. He undressed, asking her to look at him nude and to admire his penis. She hid her face in her hands. And so he exclaimed: 'Why didn't you stay at home, you halfwit!' Then he threw her on the bed and brutally deflowered her. Naturally, she remained frigid for ever.

---

* In *Night Moves*.

We have, thus far, seen all the resistance the virgin has to overcome to accomplish her sexual destiny: her initiation demands 'labour', both physiological and psychic. It is stupid and barbaric to want to put it all into one night; it is absurd to transform an operation as difficult as the first coitus into a duty. The woman is all the more terrorised by the fact that the strange operation she is subjected to is sacred, and that society, religion, family and friends delivered her solemnly to the husband as to a master; and in addition, that the act seems to engage her whole future, because marriage still has a definitive character. This is when she feels truly revealed in the absolute: this man to whom she is pledged to the end of time embodies all of Man in her eyes; and he is revealed to her, too, as a figure she has not heretofore known, which is of immense importance since he will be her lifelong companion. However, the man himself is anguished by the duty weighing on him; he has his own difficulties and his own complexes that make him shy and clumsy or on the contrary brutal; many men are impotent on their wedding night because of the very solemnity of marriage. Janet writes in *Obsessions and Psychasthenia*:[20]

> Who has not known these young grooms ashamed of their bad fortune in not succeeding in accomplishing the conjugal act and who are plagued by it with an obsession of shame and despair? We witnessed a very curious tragi-comic scene last year when a furious father-in-law dragged his humble and resigned son-in-law to Salpêtrière: the father-in-law demanded a medical attestation enabling him to ask for a divorce. The poor boy explained that in the past he had been potent, but since his wedding a feeling of awkwardness and shame had made everything impossible.

Too much impetuousness frightens the virgin, too much respect humiliates her; women forever hate the man who has taken his pleasure at the expense of their suffering; but they feel an eternal resentment against the one who seems to disdain them,* and often against the one who has not attempted to deflower them the first night or who was unable to do it. Helene Deutsch points out† that some timid or clumsy husbands ask the doctor to deflower their wife surgically on the pretext that she is not normally constituted; the reason is not usually valid. Women, she

---

* See Stekel's observations quoted in the previous chapter.
† *Psychology of Women.*

says, harbour scorn and resentment for the husband unable to penetrate them normally. One of Freud's* observations shows that the husband's impotence can traumatise the woman:

> One patient would run from one room to another in which there was a table in the middle. She put on the tablecloth in a certain way, rang for the maid who was supposed to go towards the table and then sent her away ... When she tried to explain this obsession, she recalled that this cloth had a bad stain and that she arranged it each time so that the stain should jump out at the maid ... The whole thing was a reproduction of the wedding night in which the husband had not shown himself as virile. He ran from his room to hers a thousand times to try again. Being ashamed in front of the maid who had to make the beds, he poured some red ink on the sheet to make her think there was blood.

The 'wedding night' transforms the erotic experience into an ordeal that neither partner is able to surmount, too involved with personal problems to think generously of each other; it is invested with a solemnity that makes it formidable; and it is not surprising that it often dooms the woman to frigidity forever. The difficult problem facing the husband is this: if he 'titillates his wife too lasciviously', she might be scandalised or outraged; it seems this fear paralyses American husbands, among others, especially in college-educated couples, says the Kinsey Report, because wives, more conscious of themselves, are more deeply inhibited. But if he 'respects' her, he fails to waken her sensuality. This dilemma is created by the ambiguity of the feminine attitude: the young woman both wants and rejects pleasure; she demands a delicateness from which she suffers. Unless he is exceptionally lucky, the husband will necessarily appear as either clumsy or a libertine. It is thus not surprising that 'conjugal duties' are often only a repugnant chore for the wife. According to Diderot,†

> Submission to a master she dislikes is a torture to her. I have seen a virtuous wife shiver with horror at her husband's approach. I have seen her plunge into a bath and never think herself properly cleansed from the soilure of her duty. This sort of repugnance is almost

* We summarise it following Stekel in *Frigidity in Woman*.
† 'On Women'.

unknown with us. Our organ is more indulgent. Many women die without having experienced the extreme of pleasure. This sensation which I am willing to consider a passing attack of epilepsy is rare with them, but never fails to come when we call for it. The sovereign happiness escapes them in the arms of the man they adore. We experience it with an easy woman we dislike. Less mistresses of their *sensations* than we are, their reward is less prompt and certain. A hundred times their expectation is deceived.[21]

Many women, indeed, become mothers and grandmothers without ever having experienced pleasure or even arousal; they try to get out of their soilure of duty by getting medical certificates or using other pretexts. The Kinsey Report says that, in America, many wives 'report that they consider their coital frequencies already too high and wish that their husbands did not desire intercourse so often. A very few wives wish for more frequent coitus.' We have seen, though, that woman's erotic possibilities are almost indefinite. This contradiction points up the fact that marriage, claiming to regulate feminine eroticism, kills it.

In *Thérèse Desqueyroux*, Mauriac described the reactions of a young 'reasonably married' woman to marriage in general and conjugal duties in particular:

Perhaps she was seeking less a dominion or a possession out of this marriage than a refuge. What finally pushed her into it, after all – wasn't it a kind of panic? A practical girl, a child housewife, she was in a hurry to take up her station in life, to find her definitive place; she wanted assurance against some peril that she could not name. She was never so rational and determined as she had been during the engagement period; she embedded herself in the family bloc, 'she settled down,' she entered into an order of life. She saved herself . . .

The suffocating wedding day in the narrow Saint-Clair church, where the women's cackling drowned out the wheezing harmonium, and the body odor overpowered the incense – this was the day when Thérèse realised she was lost. She had entered the cage like a sleepwalker and, as the heavy door groaned shut, the miserable child in her reawakened. Nothing had changed, but she had the sensation that she would never again be able to be alone. In the thick of a family, she would smolder, like a hidden fire that leaps up on to a branch, lights up a pine tree, then another, then step by step creates a whole forest of torches . . .

On the evening of that half-peasant, half-bourgeois wedding day, groups of the guests crowded around their car, forcing it to slow down; the girls' dresses fluttered in the crowd . . . Thérèse, thinking of the night that was coming, murmured, 'It was horrible . . .' but then caught herself and said, 'no – not so horrible.' On their trip to the Italian lakes, had she suffered so much? No – she played the game; don't lie . . . Thérèse knew how to bend her body to these charades, and she took a bitter pleasure in the accomplishment. This unknown world of sensual pleasure into which the man forced her – her imagination helped her conceive that there was a real pleasure there for her too, a possible happiness – but what happiness? As when, before a country scene pouring with rain, we imagine to ourselves what it looks like in the sunshine – thus it was that Thérèse looked upon sensuality.

Bernard, the boy with the vacant stare, . . . what an easy dupe! He was as sunk in his pleasure as those sweet little pigs you can watch through the fence, snorting with happiness in their trough ('and I was the trough,' thought Thérèse) . . . Where had he learned it, this ability to classify everything relating to the flesh, to distinguish the honorable caress from that of the sadist? Never a moment's hesitation . . .

'Poor Bernard! He's no worse than others. But desire transforms the one who approaches us into a monster, a different being. . . . I played dead, as if the slightest movement on my part could make this madman, this epileptic, strangle me.'[22]

Here is a blunter account. Stekel obtained this confession from which I quote the passage about married life. It concerns a twenty-eight-year-old woman, brought up in a refined and cultivated home:

I was a happy fiancée; I finally had the feeling I was safe, all at once I was the focus of attention. I was spoiled, my fiancé admired me, all this was new for me . . . our kisses (my fiancé had never attempted any other caresses) had aroused me to such a point that I could not wait for the wedding day . . . The morning of the wedding I was in such a state of excitement that my camisole was soaking with sweat: Just the idea that I was finally going to know the stranger I had so desired. I had the infantile image that the man was supposed to urinate in the woman's vagina . . . In our room, there was already a little disappointment when my husband asked me if he should move away. I asked him to do that because I was really ashamed in front of him. The undressing scene had played such a role in my imagination. He came back, very embarrassed, when I was in bed. Later on, he admitted that my appearance had intimidated him: I was the incarnation of radiant and eager youth. Barely had he undressed than he shut out the light. Barely kissing me, he immediately tried to take me. I was frightened and asked him to let me alone. I wanted to be very far from him. I was horrified at this attempt without prior caresses. I found him brutal and often criticised him for it later. It was not brutality but very great clumsiness and a lack of sensitivity. All the attempts that night were in vain. I began to be very unhappy, I was ashamed of my stupidity, I thought I was at fault and badly formed . . . Finally, I settled for his kisses. Ten days later he succeeded in deflowering me, I had felt nothing. It was a major disappointment! Then I felt a little joy during coitus but success was very disturbing, my husband labouring hard to reach his goal . . . In Prague in my brother-in-law's bachelor apartment I imagined my brother-in-law's feelings learning I had slept in his bed. That is when I had my first orgasm, making me very happy. My husband made love with me every day during the first weeks. I was still reaching orgasm but I was not satisfied because it was too short and I was excited to the point of crying . . . After two births . . . coitus became less and less satisfying. It rarely led to orgasm, my husband always reaching it before me; I followed each session anxiously (how long is it going to continue?). If he was satisfied leaving me at halfway, I hated him. Sometimes, I imagined my cousin during coitus or the doctor who had delivered me. My husband tried to excite me with his finger . . . I was very aroused but, at the same time, I found this means shameful and abnormal and experienced no pleasure . . . During the whole time of our marriage, he never caressed even one part of my body. One day he told me that he did not dare do anything with me . . . He never saw me naked because we always kept on our night-clothes, he performed coitus only at night.

This very sensual woman was perfectly happy in the arms of a lover later on.

Engagements are specifically meant to create gradations in the young girl's initiation; but mores often impose extreme chastity on the engaged couple. When the virgin 'knows' her future husband during this period, her situation is not very different from that of the young bride; she yields only because her engagement already seems to her as definitive as marriage and the first coitus has the characteristics of a test; once she has given herself – even if she is not pregnant, which would keep her in chains – it is very rare for her to assert herself again.

The difficulties of the first experiences are easily overcome if love or desire generates total consent from the two partners; physical love draws its strength and dignity from the joy lovers give each other and take in the reciprocal consciousness of their freedom; thus there are no degrading practices since, for both of them, their practices are not submitted to but generously desired. But the principle of marriage is obscene because it transforms an exchange that should be founded on a spontaneous impulse into rights and duties; it gives bodies an instrumental, thus degrading, side by dooming them to grasp themselves in their generality; the husband is often frozen by the idea that he is accomplishing a duty, and the wife is ashamed to feel delivered to someone who exercises a right over her. Of course, relations can become individualised at the beginning of married life; sexual apprenticeship is sometimes accomplished in slow gradations; as of the first night, a happy physical attraction can be discovered between the spouses. Marriage facilitates the wife's abandon by suppressing the notion of sin still so often attached to the flesh; regular and frequent cohabitation engenders carnal intimacy that is favourable to sexual maturity: there are wives fully satisfied in their first years of marriage. It is to be noted that they remain grateful to their husbands, which makes it possible to pardon them later for the wrongs they might be responsible for. 'Women who cannot get out of an unhappy home life have always been satisfied by their husbands,' says Stekel. It remains that the girl runs a terrible risk in promising to sleep exclusively and for her whole life with a man she does not know sexually, whereas her erotic destiny essentially depends on her partner's personality: this is the paradox Léon Blum rightfully denounced in his work, *Marriage*.

To claim that a union founded on convention has much chance of engendering love is hypocritical; to ask two spouses bound by practical, social and moral ties to satisfy each other sexually for their whole lives is pure absurdity. Yet advocates of marriages of reason have no trouble showing that marriages of love do not have much more chance of assuring the spouses' happiness. In the first place, ideal love, which is often what the girl knows, does not always dispose her to sexual love; her platonic adorations, her daydreaming, and the passions into which she projects her infantile or juvenile obsessions are not meant to resist the tests of daily life nor to last for a long time. Even if there is a sincere and violent erotic attraction between her and her fiancé, that is not a solid basis on which to construct the enterprise of a life. Colette writes:*

> But voluptuous pleasure is not the only thing. In the limitless desert of love it holds a very small place, so flaming that at first one sees nothing else . . . All about this flickering hearth there lies the unknown, there lies danger . . . After we have risen from a short embrace, or even from a long night, we shall have to begin to live at close quarters to each other, and in dependence on each other.[23]

Moreover, even in cases where carnal love exists before marriage or awakens at the beginning of the marriage, it is very rare for it to last many long years. Certainly fidelity is necessary for sexual love, since the two lovers' desire encompasses their singularity; they do not want it contested by outside experiences, they want to be irreplaceable for each other; but this fidelity has meaning only as long as it is spontaneous; and spontaneously, erotic magic dissolves rather quickly. The miracle is that it gives to each of the lovers, in the instant and in their carnal presence, a being whose existence is an unlimited transcendence: and *possession* of this being is undoubtedly impossible, but at least each of them is reached in a privileged and poignant way. But when individuals no longer want to reach each other because of hostility, disgust or indifference between them, erotic attraction disappears; and it dies almost as surely in esteem and friendship: two human beings who come together in the very movement of their transcendence through the world and their common projects no longer need carnal union; and further, because this union has lost its meaning, they are repelled by it. The word 'incest' that Montaigne pronounces is very significant. Eroticism is a movement towards the *Other,* and this is its essential character; but within the couple, spouses become, for each other, the *Same*; no exchange is possible between them anymore, no giving, no conquest. If they remain lovers, it is often in embarrassment: they feel the sexual act is no longer an intersubjective experience where each one goes beyond himself, but rather a kind of mutual masturbation. That they consider each other a necessary tool for the satisfaction of their needs is a fact conjugal politeness disguises but

* *The Vagabond.*

which bursts out when this politeness is rejected, for example in observations reported by Dr Lagache in his work *The Nature and Forms of
Jealousy*:[24] the wife regards the male member as a certain source of
pleasure that belongs to her, and she guards it in as miserly a way as the
preserves she stores in the cupboard: if the man gives some away to a
woman neighbour, there will be no more for her; she looks at his underwear to see if he has not wasted the precious semen. In *The Bold Chronicle
of a Strange Marriage*,[25] Jouhandeau notes this 'daily censure practised by
the legitimate wife who scrutinises your shirt and your sleep to discover
the sign of ignominy'. For his part, the man satisfies his desires on her
without asking her opinion.

This brutal satisfaction of need is, in fact, not enough to satisfy human
sexuality. That is why there is often an aftertaste of vice in these seemingly most legitimate embraces. The woman often helps herself along
with erotic imaginings. Stekel cites a twenty-five-year-old woman who
'could reach a slight orgasm with her husband by imagining that a
strong, older man is taking her by force, so she cannot defend herself'.
She sees herself as being raped, beaten, and her husband is not himself
but an Other. He indulges in the same dream: in his wife's body he
possesses the legs of a dancer seen in a music hall, the breasts of this
pin-up whose photo he has dwelled on, a memory, an image; or else
he imagines his wife desired, possessed or raped, which is a way to give
her back her lost alterity. 'Marriage,' says Stekel, 'creates gross transpositions and inversions, refined actors, scenarios played out between the
two partners who risk destroying the limits between appearance and
reality.' Pushed to the limit, real vices appear. The husband becomes a
voyeur: he needs to see his wife, or know she is sleeping with a lover
to feel a little of her magic again; or he sadistically strives to provoke
her to refuse him, so her consciousness and freedom show through,
assuring it is really a human being he is possessing. Inversely, masochistic
behaviour can develop in the wife who seeks to bring out in the man
the master and tyrant he is not; I knew an extremely pious woman,
brought up in a convent, who was authoritarian and dominating during
the day and who, at night, begged her husband to whip her, which,
though horrified, he consented to do. In marriage, vice itself takes on
an organised and cold aspect, a sombre aspect that makes it the saddest
of possible choices.

The truth is that physical love can be treated neither as an absolute
end in itself nor as a simple means; it cannot justify an existence: but
it can receive no outside justification. It means it must play an episodic

and autonomous role in all human life. This means it must above all be free.

Love, then, is not what bourgeois optimism promises the young bride: the ideal held up to her is happiness, that is, a peaceful equilibrium within immanence and repetition. At certain prosperous and secure times, this ideal was that of the whole bourgeoisie and specifically of landed property owners; their aim was not the conquest of the future and the world but the peaceful conservation of the past, the status quo. A gilded mediocrity with neither passion nor ambition, days leading nowhere, repeating themselves indefinitely, a life that slips towards death without looking for answers, this is what the author of 'Sonnet to Happiness' prescribes; this pseudo-wisdom loosely inspired by Epicurus and Zenon has lost currency today: to conserve and repeat the world as it is seems neither desirable nor possible. The male's vocation is action; he needs to produce, fight, create, progress, go beyond himself towards the totality of the universe and the infinity of the future; but traditional marriage does not invite woman to transcend herself with him; it confines her in immanence. She has no choice but to build a stable life where the present, prolonging the past, escapes the threats of tomorrow, that is, precisely to create a happiness. In the place of love, she will feel for her husband a tender and respectful sentiment called conjugal love; within the walls of her home she will be in charge of managing, she will enclose the world; she will perpetuate the human species into the future. Yet no existent ever renounces his transcendence, especially when he stubbornly disavows it. The bourgeois of yesterday thought that by conserving the established order, displaying its virtue by his prosperity, he was serving God, his country, a regime, a civilisation: to be happy was to fulfil his function as man. For woman as well, the harmonious home life has to be transcended towards other ends: it is man who will act as intermediary between woman's individuality and the universe; it is he who will imbue her contingent facticity with human worth. Finding in his wife the force to undertake, to act, to fight, he justifies her: she has only to put her existence in his hands, and he will give it its meaning. This presupposes humble renunciation on her end; but she is rewarded because guided and protected by male force, she will escape original abandonment; she will become necessary. Queen of her hive, tranquilly resting on herself within her domain, but carried by man's mediation through the universe and limitless time, wife, mother and mistress of the house, woman finds in marriage both the force to live and life's meaning. We must see how this ideal is expressed in reality.

The home has always been the material realisation of the ideal of happiness, be it a cottage or a château; it embodies permanence and separation. Inside its walls, the family constitutes an isolated cell and affirms its identity beyond the passage of generations; the past, preserved in the form of furniture and ancestral portraits, prefigures a risk-free future; in the garden, seasons mark their reassuring cycle with edible vegetables; every year the same spring adorned with the same flowers promises the summer's immutable return and autumn's fruits, identical to those of every autumn: neither time nor space escapes into infinity, but instead quietly go round and round. In every civilisation founded on landed property, an abundant literature sings of the poetry and virtues of the home; in Henry Bordeaux's novel precisely entitled *The Home*,[26] the home encapsulates all the bourgeois values: faithfulness to the past, patience, economy, caution, love of family, of native soil, and so forth; the home's champions are often women, since it is their task to assure the happiness of the familial group; as in the days when the *domina* sat in the atrium, their role is to be 'mistress of the house'. Today the home has lost its patriarchal splendour; for most men, it is simply a place to live, no longer overrun by memories of deceased generations and no longer imprisoning the centuries to come. But woman still tries to give her 'interior' the meaning and value a true home possessed. In *Cannery Row*, Steinbeck describes a woman hobo determined to decorate with rugs and curtains the old abandoned jalopy she lives in with her husband: he objects in vain that not having windows makes curtains useless.

This concern is specifically feminine. A normal man considers objects around him as instruments; he arranges them according to the purpose for which they are intended; his 'order' – where woman will often only see disorder – is to have his cigarettes, his papers and his tools within reach. Artists – sculptors and painters, among others – whose work it is to recreate the world through material, are completely insensitive to the surroundings in which they live. Rilke writes about Rodin:

When I first came to Rodin . . . I knew that his house was nothing to him, a paltry little necessity perhaps, a roof for time of rain and sleep; and that it was no care to him and no weight upon his solitude and composure. Deep in himself he bore the darkness, shelter, and peace of a house, and he himself had become sky above it, and wood around it, and distance and great stream always flowing by.[27]

But to find a home in oneself, one must first have realised oneself in works or acts. Man has only a middling interest in his domestic interior because he has access to the entire universe and because he can affirm himself in his projects. Woman, instead, is locked into the conjugal community: she has to change this prison into a kingdom. Her attitude to her home is dictated by this same dialectic that generally defines her condition: she takes by becoming prey, she liberates herself by abdicating; by renouncing the world, she means to conquer a world.

She regrets closing the doors of her home behind herself; as a girl, the whole world was her kingdom; the forests belonged to her. Now she is confined to a restricted space; Nature is reduced to the size of a geranium pot; walls block out the horizon. One of Virginia Woolf's heroines murmurs:

> Whether it is summer, whether it is winter, I no longer know by the moor grass and the heath flower; only by the steam on the window-pane, or the frost on the window-pane . . . I, who used to walk through beech woods noting the jay's feather turning blue as it falls, past the shepherd and the tramp, . . . go from room to room with a duster.*[28]

But she is going to make every attempt to refuse this limitation. She encloses faraway countries and past times within her four walls in the form of more or less expensive earthly flora and fauna; she encloses her husband, who personifies human society for her, and the child who gives her the whole future in a portable form. The home becomes the centre of the world and even its own one truth; as Bachelard appropriately notes, it is 'a sort of counter- or exclusionary universe';[29] refuge, retreat, grotto, womb, it protects against outside dangers: it is this confused exteriority that becomes unreal. Especially at evening time, when the shutters are closed, woman feels like a queen; the light shed at noon by the universal sun disturbs her; at night she is no longer dispossessed because she does away with that which she does not possess; from under the lampshade she sees a light that is her own and that illuminates her abode alone: nothing else exists. Another text by Virginia Woolf shows us reality concentrated in the house, while the outside space collapses.

* The Waves.

The night was now shut off by panes of glass, which, far from giving any accurate view of the outside world, rippled it so strangely that here, inside the room, seemed to be order and dry land; there, outside, a reflection in which things wavered and vanished, waterily.[30]

Thanks to the velvets, silks and china with which she surrounds herself, woman can in part assuage this grasping sensuality that her erotic life cannot usually satisfy; she will also find in this decor an expression of her personality; it is she who has chosen, made and 'hunted down' furniture and knick-knacks, who has aesthetically arranged them in a way where symmetry is important; they reflect her individuality while bearing social witness to her standard of living. Her home is thus her earthly lot, the expression of her social worth and her intimate truth. Because she *does* nothing, she avidly seeks herself in what she *has*.

It is through housework that the wife comes to make her 'nest' her own; this is why, even if she has 'help', she insists on doing things herself; at least by watching over, controlling and criticising, she endeavours to make her servants' results her own. By administrating her home, she achieves her social justification; her job is also to oversee the food, clothing and care of the familial society in general. Thus she too realises herself as an activity. But, as we will see, it is an activity that brings her no escape from her immanence and allows her no individual affirmation of herself.

The poetry of housework has been highly praised. It is true that housework makes the woman grapple with matter, and she finds an intimacy in objects that is the revelation of being and that consequently enriches her. In *Marie*, Madeleine Bourdouxhe describes her heroine's pleasure in spreading the cleaning paste on her stove. In her fingertips she feels the freedom and power that the brilliant image from scrubbed cast iron reflects back to her:

When she comes up from the cellar, she enjoys the weight of the full coal-buckets, even though they seem heavier with every step. She has always felt affection for simple things that have their own particular smell, their own particular roughness, and she's always known how to handle them. Without fear or hesitation her hands plunge into dead fires or into soapy water, they rub the rust off a piece of metal and grease it, spread polish, and after a meal, sweep the scraps from a table in one great circular movement. It's a perfect harmony, a mutual understanding between the palms of her hands and the objects they touch.[31]

Numerous women writers have lovingly spoken of freshly ironed linens, of the whitening agents of soapy water, of white sheets, of shining copper. When the housewife cleans and polishes furniture, 'dreams of saturating penetration nourish the gentle patience of the hand striving to bring out the beauty of the wood with wax', says Bachelard. Once the job is finished, the housewife experiences the joy of contemplation. But for the precious qualities to show themselves – the polish of a table, the shine of a chandelier, the icy whiteness and starch of the laundry – a negative action must first be applied; all foul causes must be expelled. There, writes Bachelard, is the essential reverie to which the housewife surrenders: the dream of active cleanliness, that is, cleanliness conquering dirt. He describes it this way:

> It would seem that in imagination the struggle for tidiness requires provocation. The imagination needs to work itself up into a cunning rage. With a nasty grin and dirty greasy rag one smears the copper faucet with a thick paste of scouring powder. Bitterness and hostility build up in the worker's heart. Why does the chore have to be so foul? But the moment for the dry cloth arrives and, along with it, a lighter-hearted malice, vigorous and talkative: faucet, you'll soon be like a mirror; kettle, you'll soon be like a sun! In the end, when the copper shines and laughs with the churlishness of an amiable fellow, peace is made. The housewife contemplates her gleaming victories.*[32]

Ponge has evoked the struggle, in the heart of the laundrywoman, between uncleanliness and purity:†

> Whoever has not lived for at least one winter in the company of a wash boiler[33] knows nothing of a certain order of highly touching qualities and emotions.
> It is necessary – wincing – to have heaved it, brimful with soiled fabrics, off the ground and carried it over to the stove – where one

---

*Gaston Bachelard, *Earth and Reveries of Repose.*
†Ponge, 'The Wash Boiler', in *Sheaf.*

must then drag it in a particular way so as to sit it right on top of the burner.

Beneath it one needs to have stirred up the fire, to set the boiler in motion gradually, touched its warm or burning sides often; next listened to the deep internal hum, from that point onwards to have lifted the lid several times to check the tension of the spurts and the regularity of the wettings.

Finally, it is necessary to have embraced it once again, boiling hot, so as to set it back down on the ground . . .

The wash boiler is so conceived that, filled with a heap of disgusting rags, the inner emotion, the boiling indignation it feels, conducted towards the higher part of its being, rains back down on this heap of disgusting rags that turns its stomach – and this virtually endlessly – and that the outcome is a purification . . .

True, the linens, when the boiler received them, had already been soaked free of the worst of their filth.

Nonetheless it has an idea or a feeling of the diffuse dirtiness of things inside it, which by dint of emotion, seethings and exertions, it manages to get the best of – to remove the spots from the fabrics: so that these, rinsed in a catastrophe of cool water, will appear white to an extreme . . .

And here in effect the miracle takes place:

Thousands of white flags are all at once deployed – which mark, not a capitulation, but a victory – and are perhaps not merely the sign of the bodily cleanness of this place's inhabitants.[34]

These dialectics can give housework the charm of a game: the little girl readily enjoys shining the silver, polishing doorknobs. But for a woman to find positive satisfaction, she must devote her efforts to an interior she can be proud of; if not, she will never know the pleasure of contemplation, the only pleasure that can repay her efforts. An American reporter,* who lived several months among American Southern 'poor whites', has described the pathetic destiny of one of these women, over-whelmed with burdens, who laboured in vain to make a hovel livable. She lived with her husband and seven children in a wooden shack, the walls covered with soot, crawling with cockroaches; she had tried to 'make the house pretty'; in the main room, the fireplace covered with bluish plaster, a table and a few pictures hanging on the wall suggested

* James Agee, *Let Us Now Praise Famous Men.*

a sort of altar. But the hovel remained a hovel, and Mrs G. said with tears in her eyes, 'Oh, I hate this house. It seems there is nothing that can be done to make it pretty!' Legions of women have in common only endlessly recurrent fatigue in a battle that never leads to victory. Even in the most privileged cases, this victory is never final. Few tasks are more similar to the torment of Sisyphus than those of the housewife; day after day, one must wash dishes, dust furniture, mend clothes that will be dirty, dusty and torn again. The housewife wears herself out running on the spot; she does nothing; she only perpetuates the present; she never gains the sense that she is conquering a positive Good, but struggles indefinitely against Evil. It is a struggle that begins again every day. We know the story of the valet who despondently refused to polish his master's boots. 'What's the point?' he asked. 'You have to begin again the next day.' Many still unresigned girls share this discouragement. I recall an essay of a sixteen-year-old student that opened with words like these: 'Today is housecleaning day. I hear the noise of the vacuum Mama walks through the living room. I would like to run away. I swear when I grow up, there will never be a housecleaning day in my house.' The child thinks of the future as an indefinite ascent towards some unidentified summit. Suddenly in the kitchen, where her mother is washing dishes, the little girl realises that over the years, every afternoon at the same time, these hands have plunged into greasy water and wiped the china with a rough dish towel. And until death they will be subjected to these rites. Eat, sleep, clean . . . the years no longer reach towards the sky, they spread out identical and grey as a horizontal tablecloth; every day looks like the previous one; the present is eternal, useless and hopeless. In the short story 'Dust',*[35] Colette Audry subtly describes the sad futility of an activity that stubbornly resists time:

> The next day while cleaning the sofa with a horsehair brush, she picked up something that she first took for an old morsel of cotton or a big feather. But it was only a dust ball like those that form on high wardrobes that you forget to dust or behind furniture between the wall and the wood. She remained pensive before this curious substance. So here they were living in these rooms for eight or ten weeks and already, in spite of Juliette's vigilance, a dust ball had had the time to take form, to grow, crouching in a shadow like those grey beasts that frightened her when she was small. A fine

* *Playing a Losing Game.*

ash of dust proclaims negligence, the beginning of carelessness, it's the impalpable sediment from the air we breathe, clothes that flutter, from the wind coming through open windows; but this tuft already represented a second stage of dust, triumphant dust, a thickening that takes shape and from sediment becomes waste. It was almost pretty to look at, transparent and light like bramble puffs, but more drab.

. . . The dust had beaten out all the world's vacuum power. It had taken over the world and the vacuum cleaner was no more than a witness object destined to show everything the human race was capable of ruining in work, matter and ingenuity in struggling against all-powerful dirt. It was waste made instrument . . .

It was their life together that was the cause of everything, their little meals that left skin peelings, dust from both of them that mingled everywhere . . . Every couple secretes these little bits of litter that must be destroyed to make space for new ones . . . What a life one spends – and to be able to go out with a fresh little shirt, attractive to passersby, so your engineer husband looks good in his life. Mantras replayed in Marguerite's head: take care of the wooden floors . . . for the care of brass, use . . . she was in charge of the care of two ordinary beings for the rest of their days.

Washing, ironing, sweeping, routing out tufts of dust in the dark places behind the wardrobe, this is holding away death but also refusing life: for in one movement time is created and destroyed; the housewife only grasps the negative aspect of it. Hers is the attitude of a Manichaean. The essence of Manichaeism is not only to recognise two principles, one good and one evil: it is also to posit that good is attained by the abolition of evil and not by a positive movement; in this sense, Christianity is hardly Manichaean in spite of the existence of the devil, because it is in devoting oneself to God that one best fights the devil and not in trying to conquer him. All doctrines of transcendence and freedom subordinate the defeat of evil to progress towards good. But the wife is not called to build a better world; the house, the bedroom, the dirty laundry, the wooden floors, are fixed things: she can do no more than rout out indefinitely the foul causes that creep in; she attacks the dust, stains, mud and filth; she fights sin, she fights with Satan. But it is a sad destiny to have to repel an enemy without respite instead of being turned towards positive aims; the housewife often submits to it in rage. Bachelard uses the word 'malice' for it; psychoanalysts have written about it. For them, housekeeping mania is a form of sadomasochism; it is characteristic of mania and vice to make freedom want what it does not want; because the maniacal housewife detests having negativity, dirt and evil as her lot, she furiously pursues dust, accepting a condition that revolts her. She attacks life itself through the rubbish left from any living growth. Whenever a living being enters her sphere, her eye shines with a wicked fire. 'Wipe your feet; don't mess up everything; don't touch that.' She would like to stop everyone from breathing: the least breath is a threat. Every movement threatens her with more thankless work: a child's somersault is a tear to sew up. Seeing life as a promise of decomposition demanding more endless work, she loses her joie de vivre; her eyes sharpen, her face looks preoccupied and serious, always on guard; she protects herself through prudence and avarice. She closes the windows because sun would bring in insects, germs and dust; besides, the sun eats away at the silk wall coverings; the antique armchairs are hidden under loose covers and embalmed in mothballs: light would fade them. She does not even care to let her visitors see these treasures: admiration sullies. This defiance turns to bitterness and causes hostility to everything that lives. In the provinces, some bourgeois women have been known to put on white gloves to make sure no invisible dust remains on the furniture: these were the kind of women the Papin sisters murdered several years ago; their hatred of dirt was inseparable from their hatred of their servants, of the world and of each other.

Few women choose such a gloomy vice when they are young. Those who generously love life are protected from it. Colette tells us about Sido:

> The fact is that, though she was active and always on the go, she was not a sedulous housewife. She was clean and tidy, fastidious even but without a trace of that solitary, maniacal spirit that counts napkins, lumps of sugar, and full bottles. With a flannel in her hands, and one eye on the servant dawdling over her window-cleaning and smiling at the man next door, she would utter nervous exclamations like impatient cries for freedom.
>
> 'When I take a lot of time and trouble wiping my Chinese cups,' she would say, 'I can actually feel myself getting older.'
>
> But she always persevered loyally until the job was finished. Then off she would go, down the two steps that led into the garden, and at once her resentment and her nervous exasperation subsided.[36]

It is in this nervousness and resentment that frigid or frustrated women, old maids, desperate housewives, and those condemned by their husbands to a solitary and empty existence are satisfied. I knew, among others, an elderly woman who woke up every morning at five o'clock to inspect her wardrobes and begin rearranging them; it seems that at twenty she was gay and coquettish; closed up in her isolated estate, with a husband who neglected her and a single child, she took to arranging as others take to drink. For Élise in *The Bold Chronicle of a Strange Marriage*, the taste for housework stems from the exasperated desire to rule the universe, from a living exuberance and from a will for domination, which, for lack of an outlet, leads nowhere; it is also a challenge to time, the universe, life, men and everything that exists:

> Since dinner from nine o'clock onwards, she has been doing the washing. It is midnight. I had been dozing, but her fortitude annoys me because it insults my rest by making it look like laziness.
>
> *Élise*: 'If you want things to be clean, you shouldn't be afraid of getting your hands dirty first.'
>
> And the house will soon be so spotless that we shall hardly dare live in it. There are divans, but you are expected to lie down beside them on the parquet floor. The cushions are too clean. You are afraid to soil or crumple them by putting your head or your feet on them, and every time I step on a carpet, I am followed with a carpet sweeper to remove the marks that I've made.
>
> In the evening:
> 'It's done.'
>
> What is the point of her moving every object and every piece of furniture and going over all the floors, the walls, and the ceilings from the time she gets up till the time she goes to bed?
>
> For the moment, it is the housewife who is uppermost in her. Once she has dusted the insides of her cupboards, she dusts the geraniums on the windowsills.
>
> *His mother*: Élise always keeps so busy she does not notice she is alive.[37]

Housework in fact allows the woman an indefinite escape far from herself. Chardonne rightly remarks:

Here is a meticulous and disordered task, with neither stops nor limits. In the home, a woman certain to please quickly reaches her breaking point, a state of distraction and mental void that effaces her . . .'[38]

This escape, this sadomasochism in which woman persists against both objects and self, is often precisely sexual. 'The kind of housecleaning that calls for bodily gymnastics amounts to a bordello for women,' says Violette Leduc.*[39] It is striking that the taste for cleanliness is of utmost importance in Holland, where women are cold, and in puritanical civil-isations that juxtapose the joys of the flesh with an ideal of order and purity. If the Mediterranean Midi lives in joyous filth, it is not only because water is scarce there: love of the flesh and its animality is conducive to tolerating human odour, squalor and even vermin.

Preparing meals is more positive work and often more enjoyable than cleaning. First of all, it involves going to the market, which is for many housewives the best time of the day. The loneliness of the household weighs on the woman just as routine tasks leave her head empty. She is happy when, in Midi towns, she can sew, wash and peel vegetables while chatting on her doorstep; fetching water from the river is a grand adven-ture for half-cloistered Muslim women: I saw a little village in Kabyle where the women tore down the fountain an official had built on the plaza; going down every morning to the wadi flowing at the foot of the hill was their only distraction. All the time they are doing their marketing, waiting in queues, in shops, on street corners, they talk about things that affirm their 'homemaking worth' from which each one draws the sense of her own importance; they feel part of a community that – for an instant – is opposed to the society of men as the essential to the inessen-tial. But above all, making a purchase is a profound pleasure: it is a discovery, almost an invention. Gide observes in his *Journals* that the Muslims, unfamiliar with games of chance, have replaced them with the discovery of hidden treasures; this is the poetry and adventure of mercan-tile civilisations. The housewife is oblivious to the gratuitousness of games: but a good firm cabbage and a ripe Camembert are treasures that must be subtly discovered in spite of the cunning shopkeeper;

* *The Starved Woman.*

between seller and buyer, relations of dealing and ruse are established: for her, winning means getting the best goods for the lowest price; concern for a restricted budget is not enough to explain the extreme importance given to being economical: winning the game is what counts. When she suspiciously inspects the stalls, the housewife is queen; the world, with its riches and traps, is at her feet, for her taking. She tastes a fleeting triumph when she empties her shopping basket on the table. She puts her canned food and nonperishables in the larder, guarding her against the future, and she contemplates with satisfaction the raw vegetables and meats she is about to submit to her power.

Gas and electricity have killed the magic of fire; but in the countryside, many women still know the joys of kindling live flames from inert wood. With the fire lit, the woman changes into a sorceress. With a simple flip of the hand – beating the eggs or kneading the dough – or by the magic of fire, she effects transmutations of substances; matter becomes food. Colette, again, describes the enchantment of this alchemy:

> All is mystery, magic, spell, all that takes place between the time the casserole, kettle, stewpot and their contents are put on the fire and the moment of sweet anxiety, of voluptuous expectation, when the dish is brought steaming to the table and its headdress removed.

Among other things, she lovingly depicts the metamorphoses that take place in the secret of hot ashes:

> Wood ash does a flavoursome job of cooking whatever it is given to cook. The apple, the pear nestling among the ashes, come out wrinkled and smoke-tanned but soft under the skin like a mole's belly, and however *bonne femme* the apple cooked in the stove might be, it is a far cry from this jam enclosed in its original robe, thick with flavour, and – if you go about it right – has oozed but a single tear of honey . . . a tall three-legged cauldron held sifted ash that never saw the fire. But stuffed with potatoes lying side by side without touching, its black claws planted in the embers, the cauldron laid tubers for us white as snow, burning hot, flaky.[40]

Women writers have particularly celebrated the poetry of making preserves: it is a grand undertaking, marrying pure solid sugar and the soft pulp of fruit in a copper preserving pan; foaming, viscous, boiling, the substance being made is dangerous: it is a bubbling lava the house-wife proudly captures and pours into jars. When she covers them with parchment paper and inscribes the date of her victory, it is a triumph over time itself: she has captured the passage of time in the snare of sugar, she has put life in jars. Cooking is more than penetrating and revealing the intimacy of substances. It reshapes and re-creates them. In working the dough she experiences her power. 'The hand as well as the eye has its reveries and poetry,' says Bachelard.*[41] And he speaks of this 'suppleness that fills one's hands, rebounding endlessly from matter to hand and from hand to matter'. The hand of the cook who kneads is a 'gratified hand' and cooking lends the dough a new value still. 'Cooking is thus a great material transformation from whiteness to golden brown, from dough to crust':† women can find a special satisfaction in a successful cake or a flaky pastry because not everyone can do it: it takes a gift. 'Nothing is more complicated than the art of pastry,' writes Michelet. 'Nothing proceeds less according to rule, or is less dependent on educa-tion. One must be *born* with it. It is wholly a gift of the mother.'[42]

Here again, it is clear that the little girl passionately enjoys imitating her female elders: with chalk and grass she plays at make-believe; she is happier still when she has a real little oven to play with, or when her mother lets her come into the kitchen and roll out the pastry with her palms or cut the hot burning caramel. But this is like housework: repe-tition soon dispels these pleasures. For Indians who get their nourishment essentially from tortillas, the women spend half their days kneading, cooking, reheating and kneading again identical tortillas, under every roof, identical throughout the centuries: they are hardly sensitive to the magic of the oven. It is not possible to transform marketing into a treasure hunt every day, nor to delight in a shiny water tap. Women and men writers can lyrically exalt these triumphs because they never or rarely do housework. Done every day, this work becomes monotonous and mechan-ical; it is laden with waiting: waiting for the water to boil, for the roast to be cooked just right, for the laundry to dry; even if different tasks are well organised, there are long moments of passivity and emptiness; most of the time, they are accomplished in boredom; between present life and the life of tomorrow, they are but an inessential intermediary. If the indi-vidual who executes them is himself a producer or creator, they are inte-grated into his existence as naturally as body functions; this is why everyday

* Gaston Bachelard, *Earth and Reveries of Will.*
† Ibid.

chores seem less dismal when performed by men; they represent for them only a negative and contingent moment they hurry to escape. But what makes the lot of the wife-servant ungratifying is the division of labour that dooms her wholly to the general and inessential; home and food are useful for life but do not confer any meaning on it: the housekeeper's immediate goals are only means, not real ends, and they reflect no more than anonymous projects. It is understandable that to give meaning to her work, she endeavours to give it her individuality and to attach an absolute value to the results obtained; she has her rituals, her superstitions, she has her ways of setting the table, arranging the living room, mending, cooking a dish; she persuades herself that in her place, no one could make such a good roast, or do the polishing as well; if her husband or daughter wants to help her or tries to do without her, she grabs the needle or the broom. 'You don't know how to sew a button.' Dorothy Parker* described with a pitying irony the dismay of a young woman convinced she should bring a personal note to the arrangement of her house, but not knowing how:

Mrs Ernest Weldon wandered about the orderly living-room, giving it some of those little feminine touches. She was not especially good as a touch-giver. The idea was pretty, and appealing to her. Before she was married, she had dreamed of herself as moving softly about her new dwelling, deftly moving a vase here or straightening a flower there, and thus transforming it from a house to a home. Even now, after seven years of marriage, she liked to picture herself in the gracious act.

But, though she conscientiously made a try at it every night as soon as the rose-shaded lamps were lit, she was always a bit bewildered as to how one went about performing those tiny miracles that make all the difference in the world to a room . . . Touch-giving was a wife's job. And Mrs Weldon was not one to shirk the business she had entered.

With an almost pitiable air of uncertainty, she strayed over to the mantel, lifted a small Japanese vase, and stood with it in her hand, gazing helplessly around the room . . .

Then she stepped back, and surveyed her innovations. It was amazing how little difference they made to the room.[43]

* 'Too Bad!'

The wife wastes a great deal of time and effort searching for originality or her individual perfection; this gives her work the characteristic of a 'meticulous and disordered task, with neither stops nor limits', as Chardonne points out, which makes it so difficult to measure the burden that household cares really mean. According to a recent report (published in 1947 by the newspaper *Combat*, written by C. Hébert), married women devote about three hours and forty-five minutes to housework (cleaning, food shopping, and so on) each working day, and eight hours on the day of rest, that is thirty hours a week, which corresponds to three-quarters of the working week of a woman worker or employee; this is enormous if it is added to a paid job; it is not much if the wife has nothing else to do (especially as woman workers and employees lose time travelling that has no equivalent here). Caring for children, if there are many, considerably adds to the wife's fatigue: a poor mother depletes her strength every one of her hectic days. By contrast, bourgeois women who have help are almost idle; and the ransom of this leisure is boredom. Because they are bored, many complicate and endlessly multiply their duties so that they become more stressful than a skilled job. A woman friend who had gone through nervous breakdowns told me that when she was in good health she took care of her house almost without thinking of it, leaving her time for much more challenging occupations; when neurasthenia prevented her from giving herself to other jobs, she allowed herself to be swallowed up by household cares, devoting whole days to them without managing to finish.

The saddest thing is that this work does not even result in a lasting creation. Woman is tempted – all the more as she is so attentive to it – to consider her work as an end in itself. Contemplating the cake she takes out of the oven, she sighs: what a pity to eat it! What a pity husband and children drag their muddy feet on the waxed floor. As soon as things are used, they are dirtied or destroyed: she is tempted, as we have already seen, to withdraw them from being used; she keeps the jam until mould invades it; she locks the living room doors. But time cannot be stopped; supplies attract rats; worms start their work. Covers, curtains and clothes are eaten by moths: the world is not a dream carved in stone, it is made of a suspicious-looking substance threatened by decomposition; edible stuff is as questionable as Dalí's meat monsters: it seemed inert and inorganic but hidden larvae have metamorphosed it into corpses. The housewife who alienates herself in things depends, like things, on the whole world: linens turn grey, the roast burns, china breaks; these are absolute disasters because when things disappear, they disappear irremediably. It is impossible to obtain permanence and security through them. Wars with their looting and bombs threaten wardrobes and the home.

Thus, the product of housework has to be consumed; constant renunciation is demanded of the wife whose work is finished only with its destruction. For her to consent to it without regret, these small holocausts must spark some joy or pleasure somewhere. But as housework is spent in maintaining the status quo, the husband – when he comes home – notices disorder and negligence but takes order and neatness for granted. He attaches more positive importance to a well-prepared meal. The triumphant moment of the cook is when she places a successful dish on the table: husband and children welcome it warmly, not only with words but also by consuming it joyously. Culinary alchemy continues with the food becoming chyle and blood. Taking care of a body is of more concrete interest, is more vital than taking care of a parquet floor; the cook's effort transcends towards the future in an obvious way. However, while it is less futile to depend on an outside freedom than to alienate oneself in things, it is no less dangerous. It is only in the guests' mouths that the cook's work finds its truth; she needs their approval; she demands that they appreciate her dishes, that they take more; she is irritated if they are no longer hungry: to the point that one does not know if the fried potatoes are destined for the husband or the husband for the fried potatoes. This ambiguity is found in the housewife's whole attitude: she keeps the house for her husband; but she also insists on his devoting all the money he earns to buying furniture or a refrigerator. She wants to make him happy: but she approves of his activities only if they fit into the framework of the happiness she has constructed.

There have been periods when these claims were generally satisfied: periods when happiness was also the man's ideal, when he was primarily attached to his house and family and when the children themselves chose to define themselves by family, their traditions and their past. Then she who ruled the home, who presided over the table, was recognised as sovereign; she still plays this glorious role as wife in relation to some landowners, or some rich farmers who occasionally still perpetuate the patriarchal civilisation. But on the whole, marriage today is the survival of obsolete customs with the wife's situation much more thankless than before since she still has the same duties while these no longer confer the same rights; she has the same chores without the rewards or honour from doing them. Today, man marries to anchor himself in immanence but not to confine himself in it; he wants a home but also to remain free to escape from it; he settles down but he often remains a vagabond in his heart; he does not scorn happiness but he does not make it an end in itself; repetition bores him; he seeks novelty, risk, resistance to overcome, camaraderie, friendships that wrest him from the solitude of the couple. Children even more than husbands want to go beyond the home's limits: their life is elsewhere, in front of them; the child always desires what is other. The wife tries to constitute a universe of permanence and continuity: husband and children want to go beyond the situation she creates and which for them is only a given. Thus, if she is loath to admit the precariousness of the activities to which her whole life is devoted, she is led to impose her services by force: from mother and housewife she becomes cruel mother and shrew.

So the wife's work within the home does not grant her autonomy; it is not directly useful to the group, it does not open on to the future, it does not produce anything. It becomes meaningful and dignified only if it is integrated into existences that go beyond themselves, towards the society in production or action: far from enfranchising the matron, it makes her dependent on her husband and children; she justifies her existence through them: she is no more than an inessential mediation in their lives. That the civil code erased 'obedience' from her duties changes nothing in her situation; her situation is not based on what the couple wants but on the very structure of the conjugal community. The wife is not allowed to *do* any positive work and consequently to have herself known as a complete person. Regardless of how well she is respected, she is subjugated, secondary, parasitic. The heavy curse weighing on her is that the very meaning of her existence is not in her hands. This is the reason the successes and failures of her conjugal life have much more importance for her than for the man: he is a citizen, a producer before being a husband; she is above all, and often exclusively, a wife; her work does not extract her from her condition; it is from her condition, on the contrary, that her work derives its price or not. Loving, generously devoted, she will carry out her tasks joyously; these chores will seem insipid to her if she accomplishes them with resentment. They will never play more than an inessential role in her destiny; in the misadventures of conjugal life they will be of no help. We thus have to see how this condition is concretely lived, one that is essentially defined by bed 'service' and housework 'service' in which the wife finds her dignity only in accepting her vassalage.

It is a crisis that pushes the girl from childhood to adolescence; an even more acute crisis thrusts her into adult life. The anxieties inherent in all passages from one condition to another are superimposed on those that a somewhat brusque sexual initiation provokes in a woman. Nietzsche writes:

And then to be hurled, as by a gruesome lightning bolt, into reality and knowledge, by marriage . . . To catch love and shame in a contradiction and to be forced to experience at the same time delight, surrender, duty, pity, terror, and who knows what else, in the face of the unexpected neighbourliness of God and beast! . . . Thus a psychic knot has been tied that may have no equal.[44]

The excitement that surrounded the traditional 'honeymoon' was meant in part to hide this confusion: thrown outside her everyday world for a few weeks, all connections with society being temporarily broken, the young woman was no longer situated in space, in time, in reality.* But sooner or later she has to take her place there again; and she finds herself in her new home, but never without apprehension. Her ties with her father's home are much stronger than her ties with the young man's. Tearing oneself away from one's family is a definitive weaning: this is when she experiences the anguish of abandon and the giddiness of freedom. The break is more or less painful, depending on the case; if she has already broken the ties connecting her to her father, brothers and sisters, and above all her mother, she can leave painlessly; if, still dominated by them, she can practically remain in their protection, she will be less affected by her change in condition; but ordinarily, even if she wanted to escape from the paternal household, she feels disconcerted when she is separated from the little society in which she was integrated, cut off from her past, her child's universe with its familiar principles and unquestioned values. Only an ardent and full erotic life could make her bathe again in the peace of immanence; but usually she is at first more upset than fulfilled; that sexual initiation is more or less successful simply adds to her confusion. The day after her wedding finds many of the same reactions she had on her first menstruation: she often experiences disgust at this supreme revelation of her femininity, horror at the idea that this experience will be renewed. She also feels the bitter disappointment of the day after; once she began menstruating, the girl sadly realised she was not an adult; deflowered, now the young woman is an adult and the last step is taken: and now what? This worrying disappointment is moreover linked as much to marriage itself as it is to defloration: a woman who had already 'known' her fiancé, or who had 'known' other men but for whom marriage represents the full accession to adult life will often

* Fin-de-siècle literature often has defloration take place in the sleeping car, which is a way of placing it 'nowhere'.

have the same reaction. Living the beginning of an enterprise is exalting; but nothing is more depressing than discovering a destiny over which one no longer has a hold. From this definitive, immutable background, freedom emerges with the most intolerable gratuitousness. Previously the girl, sheltered by her parents' authority, made use of her freedom in revolt and hope; she used it to refuse and go beyond a condition in which she nevertheless found security; her own transcendence toward marriage took place from within the warmth of the family; now she *is* married, there is no *other* future in front of her. The doors of home are closed around her: of all the earth, this will be her portion. She knows exactly what tasks lie ahead of her: the same as her mother's. Day after day, the same rites will be repeated. As a girl her hands were empty: in hope, in dreams, she possessed everything. Now she has acquired a share of the world and she thinks in anguish: there is nothing more than this, forever. Forever this husband, this home. She has nothing more to expect, nothing more to want. However, she is afraid of her new responsibilities. Even if her husband is older and has authority, the fact that she has sexual relations with him removes some of his prestige: he cannot replace a father, and even less a mother, and he cannot give her her freedom. In the solitude of the new home, tied to a man who is more or less a stranger, no longer child but wife and destined to become mother in turn, she feels numb; definitively removed from her mother's breast, lost in the middle of a world to which no aim calls her, abandoned in an icy present, she discovers the boredom and blandness of pure facticity. This is the distress so stunningly expressed in the young Countess Tolstoy's diary;[45] she enthusiastically gave her hand to the great writer she admired; after the passionate embraces she submitted to on the wooden balcony at Yasnaya Polyana, she found herself disgusted by carnal love, far from her family, cut off from her past, at the side of a man to whom she had been engaged for one week, someone who was seventeen years her senior, with a totally foreign past and interests; everything seems empty, icy to her; her life is no more than an eternal sleep. Her diary account of the first years of her marriage must be quoted.

On 23 September 1862, Sophia gets married and leaves her family in the evening:

A difficult and painful feeling gripped my throat and held me tight. I then felt that the time had come to leave forever my family and all those I loved deeply and with whom I had always lived . . . The farewells began and were ghastly . . . Now the last minutes.

I had intentionally reserved the farewells to my mother till the end . . . When I pulled myself from her embrace and without turning around I went to take my place in the car, she uttered a heart-rending cry I have never forgotten all my life. Autumn rain did not cease to fall . . . Huddled in my corner, overwhelmed with fatigue and sorrow, I let my tears flow. Leon Nikolaivitch seemed very surprised, even discontent . . . When we left the city, I felt in the depths a sentiment of fear . . . The darkness oppressed me. We barely said anything to each other until the first stop, Birioulev, if I am not mistaken. I remember that Leon Nikolaivitch was very tender and attentive to my every need. At Birioulev, we were given the rooms said to be for the tsar, big rooms with furniture uphol-stered in red rep that was not very welcoming. We were brought the samovar. Cuddled up in a corner of the couch, I kept silent as a condemned person. 'Well!', said Leon Nikolaivitch to me, 'if you did the honors.' I obeyed and served the tea. I was upset and could not free myself from a kind of fear. I did not dare address Leon Nikolaivitch in the familiar form and avoided calling him by his name. For a long time I continued to use the formal form.

Twenty-four hours later, they arrive at Yasnaya Polyana. She resumes her diary again on 8 October. She feels anxious. She suffers from the fact that her husband has a past:

I always dreamt of the man I would love as a completely whole, new, *pure*, person . . . in these childish dreams, which I still find hard to give up . . . When he kisses me I am always thinking, 'I am not the first woman he has loved.'

The following day she notes:

I feel downcast all the same. I had such a depressing dream last night, and it is weighing on me, although I do not remember it in detail. I thought of Maman today and grew dreadfully sad . . . I seem to be asleep all the time and unable to wake up . . . Something is weighing on me. I keep thinking that at any moment I might die. It is so strange to be thinking such things now that I have a husband. I can hear him in there sleeping. I am frightened of being on my own. He will not let me go into his room, which makes me very sad. All physical things disgust him.

October 11: I am terribly, terribly sad, and withdrawing further and further into myself. My husband is ill and out of sorts and doesn't love me. I expected this, yet I could never have imagined it would be so terrible. Why do people always think I am so happy? What no one seems to realise is that I cannot create happiness, either for him or for myself. Before when I was feeling miserable I would ask myself, 'What is the use of living when you make others unhappy and yourself wretched?' This thought keeps recurring to me now, and I am terrified. He grows colder and colder every day, while I, on the contrary, love him more and more ... I keep thinking of my own family and how happy my life was with them; now, my God, it breaks my heart to think that nobody loves me. Darling Mother, Tanya – what wonderful people they were, why did I ever leave them? ... it gnaws at my conscience ... Lyovochka is a wonderful man ... Now I have lost everything I once possessed, all my energy for work, life and household tasks has been wasted. Now I want only to sit in silence all day, doing nothing but think bitter thoughts. I wanted to do some work, but could not; ... I long to play the piano but it is so awkward in this place ... He suggested today that I stay at home while he went off to Nikolskoe. I should have agreed and set him free from my presence, but I simply could not ... Poor man, he is always looking for something to divert him and take him away from me. What is the point of living?

November 13: It is true, I cannot find anything to occupy me. He is fortunate because he is talented and clever. I am neither ... It is not difficult to find work, there is plenty to do, but first you have to enjoy such petty household tasks as breeding hens, tinkling on the piano, reading a lot of fourth-rate books and precious good ones, and pickling cucumbers. I am asleep now, since nothing brings me any excitement or joy – neither the trip to Moscow nor the thought of the baby. I wish I could take some remedy to refresh me and wake me up ...

It is terrible to be alone. I am not used to it. There was so much life and love at home, and it's so lifeless here without him. He is almost always on his own ... He ... finds pleasure not in the company of those close to him, as I do, but in his work ... he never had a family.

November 23: . . . Of course I am idle at present, but I am not so by nature; I simply have not discovered anything I could do . . . Sometimes I long to break free of his rather oppressive influence and stop worrying about him, but I cannot. I find his influence oppressive because I have begun thinking his thoughts and seeing with his eyes, trying to become like him, and losing myself. And I have changed too, which makes it even harder for me.

April 1: I have a very great misfortune: I have no inner resources to draw on . . . Lyova has his work and the estate to think about while I have nothing . . . What am I good for? I would like to *do* more, something *real*. At this wonderful time of year, I always used to long for things, aspire to things, dream about God knows what. But I no longer need anything, no longer have those foolish aspirations, for I know instinctively that I have all I need now and there is nothing left to strive for . . . Everything seems stupid now and I get irritable.

April 20:[46] . . . Lyova ignores me more and more. The physical side of love is very important for him. This is terrible, for me it is quite the opposite.

It is clear, during these first six months, that the young woman is suffering from her separation from her family, from solitude, and from the definitive turn her destiny has taken; she detests her physical relations with her husband and she is bored. This is the same ennui Colette's mother feels to the point of tears after the first marriage her brothers imposed on her.*

So she left the cosy Belgian house, the cellar-kitchen that smelled of gas, warm bread and coffee; she left her piano, her violin, the big Salvator Rosa she had inherited from her father, the tobacco jar and the fine long-stemmed clay pipes, the coke braziers, the books that lay open and the crumpled newspapers, and as a new bride entered the house with its flight of steps, isolated by the harsh winter of the forest lands all around . . . Here she found, to her surprise, a white and gold living room on the ground floor, but a first floor with barely even rough-cast walls, as abandoned as a loft . . .

---

* *Claudine's House.*

the bedrooms were icy-cold and prompted no thoughts of either love or sweet sleep ... Sido, who longed for friends and an innocent and cheerful social life, found on her estate only servants, cunning farmers ... She filled the big house with flowers, had the dark kitchen whitewashed, oversaw in person the preparation of the Flemish dishes, kneaded cakes with raisins and looked forward to having her first child. The savage would smile at her between two outings and then set off once more ... When she had exhausted her tasty recipes, her patience and her furniture polish, Sido – who had grown thin with loneliness – started to cry ...[47]

In *Letters to Françoise, Married*[48] Marcel Prévost describes the young woman's dismay upon her return from her honeymoon.

She thinks of her mother's apartment with its Napoleon III and MacMahon furniture, its plush velvet, its wardrobes in black plum wood, everything she judged so old-fashioned, so ridiculous ... In one instant all of that is evoked in her memory as a real haven, a true *nest*, the nest where she was watched over with disinterested tenderness, sheltered from all storms and danger. This apartment with its new-carpet smell, its unadorned windows, the chairs in disarray, its whole air of improvisation and haste, no; it is not a nest. It is only the place of the nest that has to be built ... she suddenly felt horribly sad, as if she had been abandoned in a desert.

This distress is what often causes long depressions and various psychoses in the young woman. In particular, in the guise of different psychasthenic obsessions, she feels the giddiness of her empty freedom; she develops, for example, fantasies of prostitution we have already seen in girls. Pierre Janet* cites the case of a young bride who could not stand being alone in her apartment because she was tempted to go to the window and wink at passersby. Others remain abulic faced with a universe that 'no longer seems real', peopled only with ghosts and painted cardboard sets. There are those who try to refuse their adulthood, who will obstinately persist in refusing it their whole life, like another patient† whom Janet designates with the initials Qi:[49]

* *Obsessions and Psychasthenia.*
† Ibid.

Qi, a thirty-six-year-old woman, is obsessed by the idea that she is
a little ten- to twelve-year-old girl; especially when she is alone, she
lets herself jump, laugh, dance; she lets her hair down, lets it loose
on her shoulders, sometimes cuts it in places. She would like to
lose herself completely in this dream of being a child: It is so unfortunate that she cannot play hide-and-seek, play tricks . . . in front
of everyone . . . 'I would like people to think I am nice, I am afraid
of being the ugly duckling, I would like to be liked, talked to,
petted, to be constantly told that I am loved as one loves little children . . . A child is loved for his mischievousness, for his good little
heart, for his kindness and what is asked of him in return? To love
you, nothing more. That is what is good, but I cannot say that to
my husband, he would not understand me. Look, I would so much
like to be a little girl, have a father or a mother who would take
me on their lap, caress my hair . . . but no, I am Madame, a mother;
I have to keep the home, be serious, think on my own, oh, what
a life!'

Marriage is often a crisis for man as well: the proof is that many
masculine psychoses develop during the engagement period or the early
period of conjugal life. Less attached to his family than his sisters are,
the young man belongs to some group: a special school, a university, a
guild, a team, something that protects him from loneliness; he leaves it
behind to begin his real existence as an adult; he is apprehensive of his
future solitude and it is often to exorcise it that he gets married. But he
is fooled by the illusion maintained by the whole community that depicts
the couple as a 'conjugal *society*'. Except in the brief fire of a passionate
affair, two individuals cannot form a world that protects each of them
against the world: this is what they both feel the day after the wedding.
The wife, soon familiar, subjugated, does not obstruct her husband's
freedom: she is a burden, not an alibi; she does not free him from the
weight of his responsibilities but on the contrary she exacerbates them.
The difference of the sexes often means differences in age, education
and situation that do not bring about any real understanding: familiar,
the spouses are still strangers. Previously, there was often a real chasm
between them: the girl, raised in a state of ignorance and innocence,
had no 'past', while her fiancé had 'lived'; it was up to him to initiate
her into the reality of life. Some males feel flattered by this delicate role;
more lucid, they warily measure the distance that separates them from
their future companion. In her novel, *The Age of Innocence*,[50] Edith

Wharton describes the scruples of a young American of 1870 concerning the woman destined for him:

> With a new sense of awe he looked at the frank forehead, serious eyes and gay innocent mouth of the young creature whose soul's custodian he was to be. That terrifying product of the social system he belonged to and believed in, the young girl who knew nothing and expected everything, looked back at him like a stranger . . . What could he and she really know of each other, since it was his duty, as a 'decent' fellow, to conceal his past from her, and hers, as a marriage-able girl, to have no past to conceal? . . . The young girl who was the centre of this elaborate system of mystification remained the more inscrutable for her very frankness and assurance. She was frank, poor darling, because she had nothing to conceal, assured because she knew of nothing to be on her guard against; and with no better prepara-tion than this, she was to be plunged overnight into what people evasively called 'the facts of life' . . . But when he had gone the brief round of her he returned discouraged by the thought that all this frankness and innocence were only an artificial product . . . so cunningly manufactured by a conspiracy of mothers and aunts and grandmothers and long-dead ancestresses, because it was supposed to be what he wanted, what he had a right to, in order that he might exercise his lordly pleasure in smashing it like an image made of snow.

Today, the gap is not as wide because the girl is a less artificial being; she is better informed, better armed for life. But she is often much younger than her husband. The importance of this point has not been emphasised enough; the consequences of an unequal maturity are often taken as differences of sex; in many cases the wife is a child not because she is a woman but because she is in fact very young. The seriousness of her husband and his friends overwhelms her. Sophia Tolstoy wrote about one year after her wedding day:

> He is old and self-absorbed, whereas I feel young and long to do something wild. I'd like to turn somersaults instead of going to bed. But with whom?
> Old age hovers over me; everything here is old. I try to suppress all youthful feelings, for they would seem odd and out of place in this somber environment.[51]

As for the husband, he sees a 'baby' in his wife; for him she is not the companion he expected, and he makes her feel it; she is humiliated by it. No doubt she likes finding a guide when she leaves her father's home, but she also wants to be seen as a 'grown-up'; she wants to remain a child, she wants to become a woman; her older spouse can never treat her in a way that totally satisfies her.

Even if their age difference is slight, the fact remains that the young woman and young man have generally been brought up very differently; she is the product of a feminine universe where she was inculcated with feminine sagacity and respect for feminine values, whereas he is imbued with the male ethic. It is often very difficult for them to understand each other and conflicts soon arise.

Because marriage usually subordinates the wife to the husband, the intensity of the problem of conjugal relations rests mainly on her. The paradox of marriage is that it brings into play an erotic function as well as a social one: this ambivalence is reflected in the figure the husband presents to the young wife. He is a demigod endowed with virile prestige and destined to replace her father: protector, overseer, tutor, guide; the wife has to thrive in his shadow; he is the holder of values, the guarantor of truth, the ethical justification of the couple. But he is also a male with whom she must share an experience often shameful, bizarre, disgusting, or upsetting, and in any case, contingent; he invites his wife to wallow with him in bestiality while directing her with a strong hand towards the ideal.

> One night in Paris – where they had come on their return journey – Bernard made a show of walking out of a nightclub, shocked at the revue: 'To think that foreign visitors will see that! What shame! And that's how they'll judge us . . .' Thérèse could only marvel that this so chaste man was the same one who would be making her submit, in less than an hour, to his patient inventions in the dark.*[52]

There are many hybrid forms between mentor and beast. Sometimes man is at once father and lover; the sexual act becomes a sacred orgy and the loving wife finds ultimate salvation in the arms of her husband, redeemed by total abdication. This love-passion within married life is very rare. And at times the wife will love her husband platonically but will be unable to abandon herself in the arms of a man she respects too

* Mauriac, *Thérèse Desqueyroux.*

much. Such is this woman whose case Stekel reports. 'Mme D. S., a great artist's widow, is now forty years old. Although she adored her husband, she was completely frigid with him.' On the contrary, she may experience pleasure with him that she suffers as a common disgrace, killing all respect and esteem she has for him. Besides, an erotic failure relegates her husband to the ranks of a brute: hated in his flesh, he will be reviled in spirit; inversely, we have seen how scorn, antipathy and rancour doomed the wife to frigidity. What often happens is that the husband remains a respected superior being after the sexual experience, excused of his animalistic weaknesses; it seems that this was the case, among others, of Adèle Hugo. Or else he is a pleasant partner, without prestige. Katherine Mansfield described one of the forms this ambivalence can take in her short story, 'Prelude':

> For she really was fond of him; she loved and admired and respected him tremendously. Oh, better than anyone else in the world. She knew him through and through. He was the soul of truth and decency, and for all his practical experience he was awfully simple, easily pleased and easily hurt . . . If only he wouldn't jump at her so, and bark so loudly, and watch her with such eager, loving eyes. He was too strong for her; she had always hated things that rushed at her, from a child. There were times when he was frightening – really frightening – when she just had not screamed at the top of her voice: 'You are killing me.' And at those times she had longed to say the most coarse, hateful things . . . Yes, yes, it was true . . . For all her love and respect and admiration she hated him. It had never been so plain to her as it was at this moment. There were all her feelings for him, sharp and defined, one as true as the other. And there was this other, this hatred, just as real as the rest. She could have done her feelings up in little packets and given them to Stanley. She longed to hand him that last one, for a surprise. She could see his eyes as he opened that.[53]

The young wife rarely admits her feelings to herself with such sincerity. To love her husband and to be happy is a duty to herself and society; this is what her family expects of her; or if her parents were against the marriage, she wants to prove how wrong they were. She usually begins her conjugal life in bad faith; she easily persuades herself that she feels great love for her husband; and this passion takes on a more manic, possessive and jealous form the less sexually satisfied she is; to console herself for this disappointment that she refuses at first to admit, she has an insatiable need for her husband's presence. Stekel cites numerous examples of these pathological attachments:

> A woman remained frigid for the first years of her marriage, due to childhood fixations. She then developed a hypertrophic love as is frequently found in women who cannot bear to see that their husbands are indifferent to them. She lived only for her husband, and thought only of him. She lost all will. He had to plan her day every morning, tell her what to buy, etc. She carried out everything conscientiously. If he did not tell her what to do, she stayed in her room doing nothing and worried about him. She could not let him go anywhere without accompanying him. She could not stay alone, and she liked to hold his hand . . . She was unhappy and cried for hours, trembling for her husband and if there were no reasons to tremble, she created them.
>
> My second case concerned a woman closed up in her room as if it were a prison for fear of going out alone. I found her holding her husband's hands, pleading with him to stay near her . . . Married for seven years, he was never able to have relations with his wife.

Sophia Tolstoy's case was similar; it comes out clearly in the passage I have cited and all throughout her diaries that as soon as she was married, she realised she did not love her husband. Sexual relations with him disgusted her; she reproached him for his past, found him old and boring, had nothing but hostility for his ideas; and it seems that, greedy and brutal in bed, he neglected her and treated her harshly. To her hopeless cries, her confessions of ennui, sadness and indifference were nevertheless added Sophia's protestations of passionate love; she wanted her beloved husband near her always; as soon as he was away from her, she was tortured with jealousy. She writes:

> January 11, 1863: My jealousy is a congenital illness, or it may be because in loving him I have nothing else to love; I have given myself so completely to him that my only happiness is with him and from him . . .

> January 15, 1863:[54] I have been feeling [out of sorts and] angry that he should love everything and everyone, when I want him to love only me . . . The moment I think fondly of something or someone

I tell myself no, I love only Lyovochka. But I absolutely *must* learn to love something else as he loves his *work* . . . but I hate being alone without him . . . My need to be near him grows stronger every day.

October 17, 1863: I feel I don't understand him properly, that's why I am always jealously following him . . .

July 31, 1868: It makes me laugh to read my diary. What a lot of contradictions – as though I were the unhappiest of women! . . . Could any marriage be more happy and harmonious than ours? I have been married six years now, but I love him more and more . . . I still love him with the same passionate, poetic, fevered, jealous love, and his composure occasionally irritates me.

September 16, 1876:[55] I avidly search his diaries for any reference to love, and am so tormented by jealousy that I can no longer see anything clearly. I am afraid of my resentment of Lyovochka for leaving me . . . I choke back the tears, or hide away several times a day and weep with anxiety. I have a fever every day and a chill at night . . . 'What is he punishing me for?' I keep asking myself? 'Why, for loving him so much.'

These pages convey the feeling of a vain effort to compensate for the absence of a real love with moral and 'poetic' exaltation; demands, anxieties, jealousy, are expressions of the emptiness in her heart. A great deal of morbid jealousy develops in such conditions; in an indirect way, jealousy conveys a dissatisfaction that woman objectifies by inventing a rival; never feeling fulfilment with her husband, she rationalises in some way her disappointment by imagining him deceiving her.

Very often, the wife persists in her pretence through morality, hypocrisy, pride or timidity. 'Often, an aversion for the dear husband will go unnoticed for a whole life: it is called melancholia or some other name,' says Chardonne.* But the hostility is no less felt even though it is not named. It is expressed with more or less violence in the young wife's effort to refuse her husband's domination. After the honeymoon and the period of confusion that often follows, she tries to win back her autonomy. This is not an easy undertaking. The fact that her husband is often older than she is, that he possesses in any case masculine prestige

* *Eva.*

and that he is the 'head of the family' according to the law means he
bears moral and social superiority; very often he also possesses – or at
least appears to – an intellectual superiority. He has the advantage of
culture or at least professional training over his wife; since adolescence,
he has been interested in world affairs: they are his affairs; he knows a
little law, he follows politics, he belongs to a party, a union, clubs; worker
and citizen, his thinking is connected to action; he knows that one cannot
cheat reality: that is, the average man has the technique of reasoning,
the taste for facts and experience, a certain critical sense; here is what
many girls lack; even if they have read, listened to lectures, touched upon
the fine arts, their knowledge amassed here and there does not constitute culture; it is not because of an intellectual defect that they have not
learned to reason: it is because they have not had to practise it; for them
thinking is more of a game than an instrument; lacking intellectual
training, even intelligent, sensitive and sincere women do not know how
to present their opinions and draw conclusions from them. That is why
a husband – even if far more mediocre – will easily take the lead over
them; he knows how to prove himself right, even if he is wrong. Logic
in masculine hands is often violence. Chardonne explained this kind of
sly oppression well in *Epithalamium*. Older, more cultivated and educated
than Berthe, Albert uses this pretext to deny any value to opinions of
his wife that he does not share; he untiringly *proves* he is right; for her
part she becomes adamant and refuses to accept that there is any
substance in her husband's reasoning: he persists in his ideas, and that
is the end of it. Thus a serious misunderstanding deepens between them.
He does not try to understand feelings or deep-rooted reactions she
cannot justify; she does not understand what lives behind her husband's
pedantic and overwhelming logic. He even goes so far as to become irritated by the ignorance she never hid from him, and challenges her with
questions about astronomy; he is flattered, nonetheless, to tell her what
to read, to find in her a listener he can easily dominate. In a struggle
where her intellectual shortcomings condemn her to losing every time,
the young wife has no defence other than silence, or tears or violence:

> Her head spinning, as if overcome by blows, Berthe could no longer
> think when she heard that erratic and strident voice, and Albert
> continued to envelop her in an imperious drone to confuse her, to
> injure her in the distress of her humiliated spirit . . . she was
> defeated, disarmed before the asperities of an inconceivable argu-
> mentation, and to release herself from this unjust power, she cried:

Leave me alone! These words seemed too weak to her; she saw a crystal flask on her dressing table, and all at once threw the bottle at Albert . . .

Sometimes a wife will fight back. But often, with good or bad will, like Nora in *A Doll's House*,*[56] she lets her husband think for her; it is he who will be the couple's consciousness. Through timidity, awkwardness or laziness, she leaves it up to the man to formulate their common opinions on all general and abstract subjects. An intelligent woman, cultivated and independent but who, for fifteen years, had admired a husband she deemed superior, told me how, after his death, she was obliged, to her dismay, to have her own convictions and behaviour: she is still trying to guess what he would have thought and decided in each situation. The husband is generally comfortable in this role of mentor and chief.† In the evening after a difficult day dealing with his equals and obeying his superiors, he likes to feel absolutely superior and dispense incontestable truths.‡ Happy to find in his wife a double who shores up his self-confidence, he tells her about the day's events, tells her how he wins over his adversaries; he comments on the daily paper and the political

* 'When I was at home with papa, he told me his opinion about everything, and so I had the same opinions; and if I differed from him I concealed the fact, because he would not have liked it . . . I mean that I was simply transferred from papa's hands into yours. You arranged everything according to your own taste, and so I got the same tastes as yours – or else I pretended to, I am really not quite sure which – I think sometimes the one and sometimes the other . . . You and papa have committed a great sin against me. It is your fault that I have made nothing of my life.'

† Helmer says to Nora: 'But do you suppose you are any the less dear to me, because you don't understand how to act on your own responsibility? No, no; only lean on me; I will advise you and direct you. I should not be a man if this womanly helplessness did not just give you a double attractiveness in my eyes . . . Be at rest, and feel secure; I have broad wings to shelter you under . . . There is something so indescribably sweet and satisfying, to a man, in the knowledge that he has forgiven his wife . . . she has in a way become both wife and child to him. So you shall be for me after this, my little scared, helpless darling. Have no anxiety about anything, Nora; only be frank and open with me, and I will serve as will and conscience both to you.'

‡ Cf. Lawrence, *Fantasia of the Unconscious*: 'You'll have to fight to make a woman believe in you as a real man, a real pioneer. No man is a man unless to his woman he is a pioneer. You'll have to fight still harder to make her yield her goal to yours . . . ah, then, how wonderful it is! How wonderful it is to come back to her, at evening, as she sits half in fear and waits! How good it is to come home to her! . . . How rich you feel, tired, with all the burden of the day in your veins, turning home! . . . And you feel an unfathomable gratitude to the woman who loves you and believes in your purpose . . .'

news, he gladly reads aloud to his wife so that even her connection with culture should not be her own. To increase his authority, he likes to exaggerate feminine incapacity; she accepts this subordinate role with more or less docility. We have seen the surprised pleasure of women who, sincerely regretting their husbands' absence, discover in themselves at such times unsuspected possibilities; they run businesses, bring up children, decide and administer without help. They suffer when their husbands return and doom them again to incompetence.

Marriage incites man to a capricious imperialism: the temptation to dominate is the most universal and the most irresistible there is; to turn over a child to his mother or to turn over a wife to her husband is to cultivate tyranny in the world; it is often not enough for the husband to be supported and admired, to give counsel and guidance; he gives orders, he plays the sovereign; all the resentments accumulated in his childhood, throughout his life, accumulated daily among other men whose existence vexes and wounds him, he unloads at home by unleashing his authority over his wife; he acts out violence, power, intransigence; he issues orders in a severe tone, or he yells and hammers the table: this drama is a daily reality for the wife. He is so convinced of his rights that his wife's least show of autonomy seems a rebellion to him; he would keep her from breathing without his consent. She, nonetheless, rebels. Even if she started out recognising masculine prestige, her dazzlement is soon dissipated; one day the child recognises his father is but a contingent individual; the wife soon discovers she is not before the grand Suzerain, the Chief, the Master, but a man; she sees no reason to be subjugated to him; in her eyes, he merely represents unjust and unrewarding duty. Sometimes she submits with a masochistic pleasure: she takes on the role of victim and her resignation is only a long and silent reproach; but she often fights openly against her master as well, and begins tyrannising him back.

Man is being naive when he imagines he will easily make his wife bend to his wishes and 'shape' her as he pleases. 'A wife is what her husband makes her,' says Balzac; but he says the opposite a few pages further on. In the area of abstraction and logic, the wife often resigns herself to accepting male authority; but when it is a question of ideas and habits she really clings to, she opposes him with covert tenacity. The influence of her childhood and youth is deeper for her than for the man, as she remains more closely confined in her own personal history. She usually does not lose what she acquires during these periods. The husband will impose a political opinion on his wife, but he will not change her religious convictions, nor will he shake her superstitions: this is what Jean Barois saw, he who imagined having a real influence on the devout little ninny who shared his life. Overcome, he says: 'A little girl's brain, conserved in the shadows of a provincial town: all the assertions of ignorant stupidity: this can't be cleaned up.' In spite of opinions she has learned and principles she reels off like a parrot, the wife retains her own vision of the world. This resistance can render her incapable of understanding a husband smarter than herself; or, on the contrary, she will rise above masculine seriousness like the heroines in Stendhal or Ibsen. Sometimes, out of hostility towards the man – either because he has sexually disappointed her or, on the contrary, because he dominates her and she wants revenge – she will clutch on to values that are not his; she relies on the authority of her mother, father, brother, or some masculine personality who seems 'superior' to her, a confessor or a sister to prove him wrong. Or rather than opposing him with anything positive, she continues to contradict him systematically, attack him, insult him; she strives to instil in him an inferiority complex. Of course, if she has the necessary capacity, she will delight in outshining her husband, imposing her advice, opinions, directives; she will seize all moral authority. In cases where it is impossible to contest her husband's intellectual superiority, she will try to take her revenge on a sexual level. Or she will refuse him, as Halévy tells us about Mme Michelet:[57]

> She wanted to dominate everywhere; in bed because she had to do that and at the worktable. It was the table she aimed for and Michelet defended it at first while she defended the bed. For several months, the couple was chaste. Finally Michelet got the bed and Athénaïs Mialaret soon after had the table: she was born a woman of letters and it was her true place . . .

Either she stiffens in his arms and inflicts the insult of her frigidity on him; or she shows herself to be capricious and coquettish, imposing on him the attitude of suppliant; she flirts, she makes him jealous, she is unfaithful to him: in one way or another, she tries to humiliate him in his virility. While caution prevents her from pushing him too far, at least she preciously keeps in her heart the secret of her haughty coldness; she confides sometimes to her diary, more readily to her friends: many married women find it amusing to share 'tricks' they use to feign pleasure they claim not to feel; and they laugh wildly at the vain naïveté of their dupes; these confidences are perhaps another form of playacting: between frigidity and wilful frigidity, the boundaries are uncertain. In any case, they consider themselves to be unfeeling and satisfy their resentment this way. There are women – ones likened to the praying mantis – who want to triumph night and day: they are cold in embrace, contemptuous in conversations, and tyrannical in their behaviour. This is how – according to Mabel Dodge's testimony – Frieda behaved with Lawrence. Unable to deny his intellectual superiority, she attempted to impose her own vision of the world on him where only sexual values counted.[58]

> He must see life through her and she had to see life from the sex center. She endorsed or repudiated experience from that angle.

One day she declared to Mabel Dodge:

> 'He has to get it all from me. Unless I am there, he feels nothing. Nothing. And he gets his books from me,' she continued, boastfully. 'Nobody knows that. Why, I have done pages of his books for him.'

Nonetheless, she bitterly and ceaselessly needs to prove this need he has for her; she demands he take care of her without respite: if he does not do it spontaneously, she corners him:

> I discovered that Frieda would not let things slide. I mean between them. Their relationship was never allowed to become slack. When . . . they were going along smoothly . . . not noticing each other much, when the thing between them tended to slip into unconsciousness and *rest*, Frieda would burst a bombshell at him. She *never* let him forget her. What in the first days must have been the splendor of fresh and complete experience had become, when I knew them, the attack and the defense between enemies. . . . Frieda would sting him in a tender place . . . At the end of an evening when he had not particularly noticed her, she would begin insulting him.

Married life had become for them a series of scenes repeated over and over in which neither of them would give in, turning the least quarrel into a titanic duel between Man and Woman.

In a very different way, the same untamed will to dominate is found in Jouhandeau's Élise,* driving her to undermine her husband as much as possible:[59]

> *Élise*: Right from the start, around me, I undermine everything. Afterwards, I don't have anything to worry about. I don't only have to deal with monkeys or monsters.
>
> When she wakes up she calls me:
>
> —My ugly one.
>
> It is a policy.
>
> She wants to humiliate me.
>
> She went about making me give up all my illusions about myself, one after the other, with such outright pleasure. She has never missed the chance to tell me that I am this or that miserable thing, in front of my astonished friends or our embarrassed servants. So I finally ended up believing her . . . To despise me, she never misses an occasion to make me feel that my work interests her less than any of her own improvements.
>
> It is she who dried up the source of my thoughts by patiently, slowly and purposefully discouraging me, methodically humiliating me, making me renounce my pride, in spite of myself, by chipping away with a precise, imperturbable, implacable logic.
>
> —In the end, you earn less than a worker, she threw out at me one day in front of the polisher . . .
>
> She wants to belittle me to seem superior or at least equal, and this disdain keeps her in her high place over me . . . She only has esteem for me insofar as what I do serves her as a stepping-stone or piece of merchandise.

To posit themselves before the male as essential subjects, Frieda and Élise make use of a tactic men have often denounced: they try to deny them their transcendence. Men readily suppose that woman entertains dreams of castration against them; in fact, her attitude is ambiguous: she desires to humiliate the masculine sex rather than suppress it. Far more exact, she wishes to damage man in his projects, his future. She is triumphant when her husband or child is ill, tired, reduced to a bodily presence. They then appear to be no more than an object among others in the house over which she reigns; she treats them with a housewife's skill; she bandages them like she glues together a broken dish, she

---

* *The Bold Chronicle of a Strange Marriage* and *New Marriage Chronicles.*

cleans them as one cleans a pot; nothing resists her angelic hands, friends of peelings and dishwater. In speaking about Frieda, Lawrence told Mabel Dodge, 'You cannot imagine what it is to feel the hand of that woman on you if you are sick . . . The heavy, German hand of the flesh . . .' Consciously, the woman imposes her hand with all its weight to make the man feel he also is no more than a being of flesh. This attitude cannot be pushed further than it is with Jouhandeau's Élise:

> I remember, for example, Tchang Tsen lice in the beginning of our marriage . . . I really only became intimate with a woman thanks to it, the day Élise took me naked on her lap to shave me like a sheep, lighting me up with a candle she moved around my body down to my secret parts. Oh, her close inspection of my armpits, my chest, my navel, the skin of my testicles taut like a drum between her fingers, her prolonged pauses along my thighs, between my feet and the passage of the razor around my asshole: the final drop into the basket a tuft of blond hair where the lice were hiding, and that she burned, giving me over in one fell swoop, delivering me at the same time from the lice and their den, to a new naked-ness and to the desert of isolation.

Woman loves man to be passive flesh and not a body that expresses subjectivity. She affirms life against existence, values of the flesh against values of the spirit; she readily adopts Pascal's humorous attitude to male enterprises; she thinks as well, 'All man's miseries derive from not being able to sit quiet in a room alone'; she would gladly keep him shut up at home; all activity that does not directly benefit family life provokes her hostility; Bernard Palissy's wife is indignant when he burns the furniture to invent a new enamel without which the world had done very well until then; Mme Racine makes her husband take an interest in her red currants and refuses to read his tragedies. Jouhandeau is often peeved in the *The Bold Chronicles of a Strange Marriage* because Élise stubbornly considers his literary work merely a source of mat-erial profit.

> I said to her: My latest story was published this morning. She replied (without in any way wishing to be cynical and merely because it is the only thing that matters to her): That means we shall have at least three hundred francs extra this month.

It happens that these conflicts worsen and then provoke a rupture. But generally the woman wants to 'hold on to' her husband as well as to refuse his domination. She struggles against him to defend her autonomy, and she fights against the rest of the world to conserve the 'situation' that dooms her to dependence. This double game is difficult to play, which explains in part the worried and nervous state in which multitudes of women spend their lives. Stekel gives a very significant example:

Mme Z. T., who never had an orgasm, is married to a very cultivated man. But she cannot bear his superiority and she began to want to be his equal by studying his speciality. As it was too difficult, she gave up her studies as soon as they were engaged.

The very famous man had many students chasing after him. She decides not to partake in this ridiculous cult. In her marriage she was insensitive from the start and she remained that way. She attained an orgasm only through masturbation when her husband had finished, satisfied, and she would tell him about it. She refused his attempts to excite her by his caresses . . . Soon she began to ridicule him and undermine her husband's work. She could not 'understand these ninnies who pursued him, she who knew the behind-the-scenes of the great man's private life'. In their daily quarrels, expressions arose such as: 'You can't put anything over on me with your scribbling!' Or: 'You think you can do what you want with me because you're a little writer.' The husband spent more and more time with his students, she surrounded herself with young men. She continued this way for years until her husband fell in love with another woman. She always stood for his little liaisons, she even made friends of his abandoned 'poor idiots' . . . But then she changed her attitude and gave in, without orgasm, to the first adolescent who came along. She admitted to her husband that she had cheated on him, which he accepted without a problem. They could peacefully separate . . . She refused the divorce. There followed a long explanation and reconciliation. She broke down in tears and experienced her first intense orgasm.

It is clear that in her struggle against her husband she never intended to leave him.

There is an art to 'catching a husband': 'keeping' him is a profession. It takes a great deal of skill. A prudent sister said to a cranky young wife: 'Be careful, making scenes with Marcel will make you lose your *situation*.'

The stakes are the highest: material and moral security, a home of one's own, wifely dignity, a more or less successful substitute for love and happiness. The wife quickly learns that her erotic attraction is the weakest of her weapons; it disappears with familiarity; and there are, alas, other desirable women in the world; so she still works at being seductive and pleasing: she is often torn between the pride that inclines her to frigidity and the notion that her sensual ardour will flatter and keep her husband. She also counts on the force of habit, on the charm he finds in a pleasant home, his taste for good food, his affection for his children; she tries to 'make him proud' by her way of entertaining, dressing and exercising authority over him with her advice and her influence; as much as she can, she will make herself indispensable, either by her social success or by her work. But, above all, a whole tradition teaches wives the art of 'how to catch a man'; one must discover and flatter his weaknesses, cunningly use flattery and disdain, docility and resistance, vigilance and indulgence. This last blend is especially subtle. One must not give a husband too much or too little freedom. If she is too indulgent, the wife finds her husband escaping her; the money and passion he spends on other women are her loss; she runs the risk of having a mistress get enough power over him to seek a divorce or at least take first place in his life. Yet, if she forbids him all adventure, if she overwhelms him by her close scrutiny, her scenes, her demands, she can seriously turn him against her. It is a question of knowing how to 'make concessions' advisedly; if the husband puts 'a few dents in the contract', she will close her eyes; but at other moments, she must open them wide; in particular the married woman mistrusts girls who would be only too happy to take over her 'position'. To tear her husband from a worrying rival, she will take him on a trip, she will try to distract him; if necessary – following Mme de Pompadour's model – she will seek out another, less dangerous rival; if nothing succeeds, she will resort to crying, nervous fits, suicide attempts, and such; but too many scenes and recriminations will chase her husband from the house; the wife will make herself unbearable just when she most needs to seduce; if she wants to win her hand, she will skilfully combine touching tears and heroic smiles, blackmail and coquetry. Dissimulate, trick, hate and fear in silence, bet on the vanity and weakness of a man, learn how to foil him, play him, manipulate him, it is all quite a sad science. The wife's great excuse is that she is forced to involve her whole self in marriage: she has no profession, no skills, no personal relations, even her name is not her own; she is nothing but her husband's 'other half'. If he abandons her, she will most often find no help, either within or outside of herself. It is easy to cast a stone at Sophia Tolstoy, as A. de Monzie and Montherlant do: but if she had refused the hypocrisy of conjugal life, where could she have gone? What destiny awaited her? True, she seems to have been a contemptible shrew: but could one ask her to love her tyrant and bless her enslavement? For there to be loyalty and friendship between spouses, the *sine qua non* is that both must be free vis-à-vis each other and concretely equal. As long as man alone possesses economic autonomy and holds – by law and custom – privileges conferred on him by his masculinity, it is natural that he should so often appear a tyrant, inciting woman to revolt and duplicity.

No one dreams of denying the tragedies and nastiness of married life: but advocates of marriage defend the idea that spouses' conflicts arise out of the bad faith of individuals and not out of the institution's. Tolstoy, among others, describes the ideal couple in the epilogue to *War and Peace*:[60] Pierre and Natasha. She was a coquettish and romantic girl; when married she astounds those who knew her by giving up her interest in her appearance, society and pastimes and devoting herself exclusively to her husband and children; she becomes the very epitome of a matron:

> In her face there was not, as formerly, that ceaselessly burning fire of animation that had constituted her charm. Now one often saw only her face and body, while her soul was not seen at all. One saw only a strong, beautiful, and fruitful female.

She demands from Pierre a love as exclusive as the one she swears to him; she is jealous of him; he gives up going out, all his old friends, and devotes himself entirely to his family as well.

> Pierre's subjection consisted in his . . . not daring to go to clubs or dinners . . . not daring to leave for long periods of time except on business, in which his wife also included his intellectual pursuits, of which she understood nothing, but to which she ascribed great importance.

Pierre is 'under the slipper of his wife', but in return:

> At home Natasha put herself on the footing of her husband's slave . . . The entire household was governed only by the imaginary orders of the husband, that is, by Pierre's wishes, which Natasha tried to guess.

When Pierre goes far away from her, Natasha impatiently greets him upon his return because she suffers from his absence; but a wonderful harmony reigns over the couple; they understand each other with barely a few words. Between her children, her home, her loved and respected husband, she savours nearly untainted happiness.

This idyllic tableau merits closer scrutiny. Natasha and Pierre are united, says Tolstoy, like soul and body; but when the soul leaves the body, only one dies; what would happen if Pierre should cease to love Natasha? Lawrence, too, rejects the hypothesis of masculine inconstancy: Don Ramón will always love the little Indian girl Teresa, who gave him her soul. Yet one of the most ardent zealots of unique, absolute, eternal love, André Breton, is forced to admit that at least in present circumstances this love can mistake its object: error or inconstancy, it is the same abandonment for the woman. Pierre, robust and sensual, will be physically attracted to other women; Natasha is jealous; soon the relationship will sour; either he will leave her, which will ruin her life, or he will lie and resent her, which will spoil his life, or they will live with compromises and half measures, which will make them both unhappy. One might object that Natasha will at least have her children: but children are a source of joy only within a well-balanced structure, where the husband is one of its peaks; for the neglected, jealous wife they become a thankless burden. Tolstoy admires Natasha's blind devotion to Pierre's ideas; but another man, Lawrence, who also demands blind devotion from women, mocks Pierre and Natasha; so in the opinion of other men, a man can be a clay idol and not a real god; in worshipping him, one loses one's life instead of saving it; how is one to know? Masculine claims compete with each other, authority no longer plays a part: the wife must judge and criticise, she cannot be but a feeble echo. Moreover, it is degrading to her to impose principles and values on her that she does not believe in with her own free will; what she might share of her husband's thinking, she can only share through her own independent judgement; she should not have to accept or refuse what is foreign to her; she cannot borrow her own reasons for existing from another.

The most radical condemnation of the Pierre-Natasha myth comes from the Leon-Sophia couple. Sophia feels repulsion for her husband, she finds him 'tedious'; he cheats on her with all the surrounding peasants, she is jealous and bored; she is frustrated by her multiple pregnancies and her children do not fill the emptiness in her heart or her days; home for her is an arid desert; for him it is hell. And it ends up with an old hysterical woman lying half-naked in the humid night of the forest, with this old hounded man fleeing, renouncing finally the 'union' of a whole life.

Of course, Tolstoy's case is exceptional; there are many marriages that 'work well', that is, where the spouses reach a compromise; they live next to each other without antagonising each other, without lying to each other too much. But there is a curse they rarely escape: boredom. Whether the husband succeeds in making his wife an echo of himself, or whether each one entrenches himself in his universe, they have nothing else to share with each other after a few months or years. The couple is a community whose members have lost their autonomy without escaping their solitude; they are statically assimilated to each other instead of sustaining a dynamic and lively relation together; this is why they can give nothing to each other, exchange nothing on a spiritual or erotic level. In one of her best short stories, 'Too Bad!', Dorothy Parker sums up the sad saga of many conjugal lives; it is night and Mr Weldon comes home:

Mrs Weldon opened the door at his ring.

'Well!' she said, cheerily.

They smiled brightly at each other.

'Hel-lo,' he said. 'Well! You home?'

They kissed, slightly. She watched with polite interest while he hung up his hat and coat, removed the evening papers from his pocket, and handed one to her.

'Bring the papers?' she said, taking it . . .

'Well, what have you been doing with yourself today?' he inquired.

She had been expecting the question. She had planned before he came in, how she would tell him all the little events of her day . . . But now, . . . it seemed to her a long, dull story . . .

'Oh, nothing,' she said, with a gay little laugh. 'Did you have a nice day?'

'Why—' he began . . . But his interest waned, even as he started to speak. Besides, she was engrossed in breaking off a loose thread from the wool fringe of one of the pillows beside her.

'Oh, pretty fair,' he said . . .

She could talk well enough to other people . . .

Ernest, too, seemed to be talkative enough when he was with others . . .

She tried to remember what they used to talk about before they

were married, when they were engaged. It seemed to her that they
never had had much to say to each other. But she hadn't worried
about it then . . . Then, besides, there had been always kissing and
things, to take up your mind . . . And you can't depend on kisses
and all the rest of it to while away the evenings, after seven years.

You'd think that you would get used to it, in seven years, would
realise that that was the way it was, and let it go at that. You don't,
though. A thing like that gets on your nerves. It isn't one of those
cozy, companionable silences that people occasionally fall into
together. It makes you feel as if you must do something about it,
as if you weren't performing your duty. You have the feeling a
hostess has when her party is going badly . . .

Ernest would read industriously, and along toward the middle
of the paper, he would start yawning aloud. Something happened
inside Mrs Weldon when he did this. She would murmur that she
had to speak to Delia, and hurry to the kitchen. She would stay
there rather a long time, looking vaguely into jars and inquiring
half-heartedly about laundry lists, and when she returned, he would
have gone in to get ready for bed.

In a year, three hundred of their evenings were like this. Seven
times three hundred is more than two thousand.[61]

It is sometimes claimed this very silence is the sign of an intimacy
deeper than any word; and obviously no one dreams of denying that
conjugal life creates intimacy: this is true of all family relations, even
those that include hatreds, jealousies and resentments. Jouhandeau
strongly emphasises the difference between this intimacy and a real
human fraternity, writing:

Élise is my wife and it is probable that none of my friends, none
of the members of my family, not a single one of my own limbs
is more intimate with me than she; but however close to me is the
place that she has made for herself and that I have made for her
in my own most private universe; however deeply rooted she has
become in the inextricable web of my body and soul (and there
lies the whole mystery and the whole drama of our indissoluble
union), the unknown person, whoever he may be, who happens to
pass in the street at this particular moment and whom I can barely
see from my window is less of a stranger to me than she is.[62]

He says elsewhere:

> We discover that we are the victims of poisoning, but that we have
> grown used to it. How can we give it up without giving up
> ourselves?

Still more:

> When I think of her, I feel that married love has nothing to do
> with sympathy, with sensuality, with passion, with friendship, or
> with love. It alone is adequate to itself and cannot be reduced to
> one or other of these different feelings, it has its own nature, its
> particular essence, and its unique mode which depends on the
> couple that it brings together.

Advocates of conjugal love* readily admit it is not love, which is precisely
what makes it marvellous. For in recent years the bourgeoisie has invented
an epic style: routine takes on the allure of adventure, faithfulness that
of sublime madness, boredom becomes wisdom and family hatreds are
the deepest form of love. In truth, that two individuals hate each other
without, however, being able to do without each other is not at all the
truest, the most moving of all human relations, it is one of the most
pitiful. The ideal would be, on the contrary, that each human being,
perfectly self-sufficient, be attached to another by the free consent of their
love alone. Tolstoy admires the fact that the link between Natasha and
Pierre is something 'indefinable, but firm, solid, as was the union of his
own soul with his body'. If one accepts the dualist hypothesis, the body
represents only a pure facticity for the soul; so in the conjugal union,
each one would have for the other the inevitable weight of contingent
fact; one would have to assume and love the other as an absurd and
unchosen presence as the necessary condition for and very matter of existence. There is a deliberate confusion between these two words – 'assuming' and 'loving' – and the mystification stems from this: one does not
love what one assumes. One assumes one's body, past, and present situation: but love is a movement towards an other, towards an existence

---

* There can be love within marriage; but then one does not speak of 'conjugal love';
when these words are uttered, it means that love is missing; likewise, when one says of
a man that he is 'very communist', one means that he is not a communist; 'a great gentleman' is a man who does not belong to the simple category of gentlemen, and so on.

separated from one's own, towards a finality, a future; the way to assume or take on a load or a tyranny is not to love it but to revolt. A human relation has no value if it is lived in the immediacy; children's relations with their parents, for example, only have value when they are reflected in a consciousness; one cannot admire conjugal relations that degenerate into the immediate in which the spouses squander their freedom. One claims to respect this complex mixture of attachment, resentment, hatred, rules, resignation, laziness and hypocrisy called conjugal love only because it serves as an alibi. But what is true of friendship is true of physical love: for friendship to be authentic, it must first be free. Freedom does not mean whim: a feeling is a commitment that goes beyond the instant; but it is up to the individual alone to compare his general will to his personal behaviour so as either to uphold his decision or, on the contrary, to break it; feeling is free when it does not depend on any outside command, when it is lived in sincerity without fear. The message of 'conjugal love' is an invitation, by contrast, to all kinds of repression and lies. And above all it keeps the husband and wife from genuinely knowing each other. Daily intimacy creates neither understanding nor sympathy. The husband respects his wife too much to be interested in the meta-morphoses of her psychological life: that would mean recognising in her a secret autonomy that could prove to be bothersome, dangerous; does she really get pleasure in bed? Does she really love her husband? Is she really happy to obey him? He prefers not to question himself; these questions even seem shocking to him. He married a 'good woman'; by nature she is virtuous, devoted, faithful, pure and happy, and she thinks what she should think. A sick man, after thanking his friends, his family and his nurses, says to his young wife who, for six months, had not left his bedside: 'I do not have to thank you, you merely did your duty.' He gives her no credit for any of her good qualities: they are guaranteed by society, they are implied by the very institution of marriage; he does not notice that his wife does not come out of a book by Bonald, that she is an individual of flesh and blood; he takes for granted her faithfulness to the orders she imposes on herself: he takes no account of the fact that she might have temptations to overcome, that she might succumb to them, that in any case, her patience, her chastity and her decency might be difficult conquests; he ignores even more completely her dreams, her fantasies, her nostalgia, and the emotional climate in which she spends her days. Thus Chardonne shows us in *Eva* a husband who has for years kept a journal of his conjugal life: he speaks of his wife with delicate nuances; but only of his wife as he sees her, as she is for him without

ever giving her dimensions as a free individual: he is stunned when he
suddenly learns she does not love him, that she is leaving him. One often
speaks of the naive and loyal man's disillusionment in the face of feminine perfidy: the husbands in Bernstein are scandalised to discover that
the women in their lives are fickle, mean or adulterous; they take it with
a virile courage but the author does not fail to make them seem generous
and strong: they seem more like boors to us, without sensitivity and
goodwill; man criticises women for their duplicity but he must be very
complacent to let himself be duped with so much constancy. Woman is
doomed to immorality because morality for her consists in embodying
an inhuman entity: the strong woman, the admirable mother, the virtuous
woman, and so on. As soon as she thinks, dreams, sleeps, desires and
aspires without orders, she betrays the masculine ideal. This is why so
many women do not let themselves 'be themselves' except in their
husbands' absence. Likewise, the woman does not know her husband:
she thinks she perceives his true face because she grasps it in its daily
contingency: but the man is first what he *does* in the world among other
men. Refusing to understand the movement of his transcendence is dena-
turing it. 'One marries a poet,' says Élise, 'and when one is his wife, the
first thing she notices is he forgets to flush the toilet.'* He nevertheless
remains a poet and the wife who is not interested in his works knows
him less than a remote reader. It is often not the wife's fault that this
complicity is forbidden to her: she cannot share her husband's affairs,
she lacks the experience and the necessary culture to 'follow' him: she
fails to join him in the projects that are far more essential for him than
the monotonous repetition of everyday life. In certain privileged cases
the wife can succeed in becoming a real companion for her husband:
she discusses his plans, gives him advice, participates in his work. But
she is deluding herself if she thinks she can accomplish work of her own
like that: he alone remains the active and responsible freedom. To find
joy in serving him, she must love him; if not she will experience only
vexation because she will feel frustrated by the fruit of her efforts. Men
– faithful to the advice given by Balzac to treat the wife as a slave while
persuading her she is queen – exaggerate to the utmost the importance
of the influence women wield; deep down, they know well they are
lying. Georgette Leblanc was duped by this mystification when she
demanded of Maeterlinck that he write their two names on the book
they had, or so she thought, written together; in the preface to the

* Jouhandeau, *The Bold Chronicle of a Strange Marriage.*

singer's *Souvenirs*, Grasset bluntly explains that any man is ready to hail the woman who shares his life as an associate and an inspiration but that he nevertheless still regards his work as belonging to him alone; rightfully. In any action, any work, what counts is the moment of choice and decision. The wife generally plays the role of the crystal ball clairvoyants use: another would do just as well. And the proof is that often the man welcomes another adviser, another collaborator, with the same confidence. Sophia Tolstoy copied her husband's manuscripts and put them in order: he later gave the job to one of his daughters; she understood that even her zeal had not made her indispensable. Only autonomous work can assure the wife an authentic autonomy.*

Conjugal life takes different forms depending on the case. But for many wives, the day begins approximately in the same way. The husband leaves his wife hurriedly in the morning: she is happy to hear the door close after him; she likes to find herself free, without duties, sovereign in her home. The children in turn leave for school: she will stay alone all day; the baby squirming in his crib or playing in his playpen is not company. She spends more or less time getting dressed, doing the housework; if she has a maid, she gives her instructions, lingers a little in the kitchen while chatting; or else she will stroll in the market, exchanging comments on the cost of living with her neighbours or shopkeepers. If her husband and children come home for lunch, she cannot take advantage of their presence very much; she has too much to do to get the meal ready, serve and clean up; most often, they do not come back for lunch. In any case, she has a long, empty afternoon in front of her. She takes her youngest children to the public park and knits or sews while keeping an eye on them; or, sitting at the window at home, she does her mending; her hands work, her mind is not occupied; she ruminates over her worries; she makes plans; she daydreams, she is bored; none of her occupations suffices in itself; her thoughts are directed towards her husband and her children who will wear these shirts, who will eat the meal she is preparing; she lives for them alone; and are they at all grateful to her? Little by little her boredom changes into impatience, she begins to wait for their return anxiously. The children come back

---

* There is sometimes a *real* collaboration between a man and a woman, in which the two are equally autonomous: in the Joliot-Curie couple, for example. But then the wife who is as skilled as the husband goes out of her wifely role; their relation is no longer of a conjugal order. There are also wives who use the man to achieve personal aims; they escape the condition of the married woman.

from school, she kisses them, questions them; but they have homework to do, they want to have fun together, they escape, they are not a distraction. And then they have bad grades, they have lost a scarf, they are noisy, messy, they fight with each other: she almost always has to scold them. Their presence annoys the mother more than it soothes her. She waits for her husband more and more urgently. What is he doing? Why is he not home already? He has worked, seen the world, chatted with people, he has not thought of her; she starts ruminating nervously that she is stupid to sacrifice her youth to him; he is not grateful to her. The husband making his way towards the house where his wife is closed up feels vaguely guilty; early in the marriage, he would bring a bunch of flowers, a little gift, as an offering; but this ritual soon loses any meaning; now he arrives empty-handed, and he is even less in a hurry when he anticipates the usual greeting. Indeed, the wife often takes revenge with a scene of boredom, of the daily wait; this is how she wards off the disappointment of a presence that does not satisfy the expectation of her waiting. Even if she does not express her grievances, her husband too is disappointed. He has not had a good time at his office, he is tired; he has a contradictory desire for stimulation and for rest. His wife's too familiar face does not free him from himself; he feels she would like to share his worries with him, that she also expects distraction and relaxation from him: her presence weighs on him without satisfying him, he does not find real abandon with her. Nor do the children bring entertainment or peace; during the meal and the evening there is a vague bad mood; reading, listening to the radio, chatting idly, each one, under the cover of intimacy, will remain alone. Yet the wife wonders with an anxious hope – or a no less anxious apprehension – if tonight – finally! again! – something will happen. She goes to sleep disappointed, irritated or relieved; she will be happy to hear the door slam shut tomorrow. The lot of wives is even harsher if they are poor and overburdened with chores; it lightens when they have both leisure and distractions. But this pattern – boredom, waiting and disappointment – is found in many cases.

There are some escapes* available to the wife; but in practice they are not available to all. The chains of marriage are heavy, particularly in the provinces; a wife has to find a way of coming to grips with a situation she cannot escape. Some, as we have seen, are puffed up with importance and become tyrannical matrons and shrews. Others take refuge in

* See Chapter 7.

the role of the victim, they make themselves their husbands' and children's pathetic slaves and find a masochistic joy in it. Others perpetuate the narcissistic behaviour we have described in relation to the young girl: they also suffer from not realising themselves in any undertaking, and, being able to do nothing, they are nothing; undefined, they feel undetermined and consider themselves misunderstood; they worship melancholy; they take refuge in dreams, playacting, illnesses, fads, scenes; they create problems around them or close themselves up in an imaginary world; the 'smiling Mme Beudet' that Amiel depicted is one of these. Shut up in provincial monotony with a boorish husband, with no chance to act or to love, she is devoured by the feeling of her life's emptiness and uselessness; she tries to find compensation in romantic musings, in the flowers she surrounds herself with, in her clothes, her person: her husband interferes even with these games. She ends up trying to kill him. The symbolic behaviour into which the wife escapes can bring about perversions, and these obsessions can lead to crime. There are conjugal crimes dictated less by interest than by pure hatred. Thus, Mauriac shows us Thérèse Desqueyroux trying to poison her husband as Mme Lafarge did previously. A forty-year-old woman who had endured an odious husband for twenty years was recently acquitted for having coldly strangled her husband with the help of her elder son. There had been no other way for her to free herself from an intolerable situation.

For a wife who wants to live her situation in lucidity, in authenticity, her only resort is often to stoic pride. Because she is totally dependent, she can only have a deeply interior and therefore abstract freedom; she refuses ready-made principles and values, she judges, she questions, and thus escapes conjugal slavery; but her haughty reserve and her acceptance of the saying 'Suffer and be still' constitute no more than a negative attitude. Confined in denial, in cynicism, she lacks a positive use of her strength; as long as she is passionate and living, she finds ways to use it: she helps others, she consoles, protects, gives, she has many interests; but she suffers from not finding any truly demanding job, from not devoting her activity to an end. Often eaten away by loneliness and sterility, she ends up by giving up, destroying herself. Mme de Charrière provides us with a notable example of such a destiny. In the sympathetic book* he devotes to her, Geoffrey Scott depicts her with 'a frond of flame; a frond of frost'. But it is not her reason that put out this flame of life which Hermenches said could 'warm the heart of a Laplander', it is

---

* Geoffrey Scott, *The Portrait of Zélide*.

marriage that slowly assassinates the brilliant Belle de Zuylen; she resigned herself and called it reason: either heroism or genius would have been necessary to invent a different outcome. That her lofty and rare qualities were not sufficient to save her is one of the most stunning condemnations of the conjugal institution found in history.

Brilliant, cultivated, intelligent and ardent, Mlle de Zuylen astonished Europe; she frightened away suitors; she rejected more than twelve of them, but others, perhaps more acceptable, backed off. Hermenches was the only man who interested her, but it was out of the question to make him her husband: she carried on a twelve-year correspondence with him; but this friendship and her studies no longer satisfied her. 'Virgin and martyr' was a pleonasm, she said; and the constraints of Zuylen's life were unbearable; she wanted to become a woman, a free being. At thirty, she married M. de Charrière; she liked the 'honesty of heart' she found in him, his 'sense of justice', and she first decided to make him 'the most tenderly loved husband in the world'. Later, Benjamin Constant recounts that 'she had tormented him greatly to impress upon him reactions equal to hers'; she did not manage to overcome his methodical impassivity; shut up in Colombier with this honest and dull husband, a senile father-in-law, two dull sisters-in-law, Mme de Charrière began to be bored; the narrow-mindedness of Neufchâtel provincial society displeased her; she killed her days in washing the household linen and playing 'Comet' in the evening. A young man briefly crossed her life and left her lonelier than before. 'Taking ennui as muse', she wrote four novels on the customs of Neufchâtel, and the circle of her friends grew narrower. In one of her works, she described the long sadness of a marriage between a lively and sensitive woman and a good but ponderous and cold man: conjugal life seemed to her like a chain of misunderstandings, disappointments, petty resentments. It was clear she herself was unhappy; she fell ill, recovered, returned to the long accompanied solitude that was her life. 'It is clear that the routine of the life at Colombier and the negative, unresisting smoothness of her husband's temperament were like a perpetual pause which no activity of Mme de Charrière's could fill,' writes her biographer. And then appears Benjamin Constant, who passionately occupied her for eight years. When, too proud to wrest him from Mme de Staël, she gave him up, her pride hardened. She wrote to him one day: 'The stay at Colombier was abhorrent to me and I never went back there without despair. I decided not to leave it any more and made it bearable for myself.' She closed herself up there and did not leave her garden for fifteen years; this is how she applied the stoic precept: seek to conquer one's heart rather than fortune. As a prisoner, she could only find freedom by choosing her prison. 'She accepted M. de Charrière at her side as she accepted the Alps,' says Scott. But she was too lucid not to understand that this resignation was, after all, only deception; she became so withdrawn, so hard, she was thought to be so despairing that she was frightening. She had opened her house to the immigrants who were pouring into Neufchâtel; she protected them, helped them, guided them; she wrote elegant and disillusioned works that Huber, a poor German philosopher, translated; she lavished advice on a circle of young women and taught Locke to her favourite one, Henriette; she loved to play the role of divine protection for the peasants of the area; avoiding Neufchâtel society more and more carefully, she preciously limited her life; she 'sought only to create routine, and to endure it. Even her infinite acts of kindness had something frightening about them, in the chill of her self-control . . . She seemed to those around her like one moving in an empty room.'* On rare occasions – a visit, for example – the flame of life awakened. But 'the years passed aridly. Ageing side by side live M. and Mme de Charrière, a whole universe apart; and often a visitor would turn from the house with relief, and hearing the gate clang behind him, would feel that he was leaving a shut tomb . . . The clock ticked; M. de Charrière sat below, alone, poring over his mathematics. Rhythmically, from the barn outside, came the sound of the threshers, it throbbed, and it ceased. Life went on, though it was threshed out . . . A life of small things, desperately compelled to fill every crevice of the day: to this Zélide, who hated littleness, had come.'

One might say M. de Charrière's life was no livelier than his wife's: at least he had chosen it; and it seems it suited his mediocrity. If one imagines a man endowed with the exceptional qualities of Belle de Zuylen, he surely would not be consumed in Colombier's arid solitude. He would have carved out a place for himself in the world where he would undertake things, fight, act and live. How many wives swallowed up in marriage have been, in Stendhal's words, 'lost to humanity'! It is said that marriage diminishes man: it is often true; but it almost always destroys woman. Marcel Prévost, advocate of marriage, admits it himself:

How many times have I met after a few months or years of marriage a young woman I had known as a girl and been struck by the ordinariness of her character, the meaninglessness of her life.

* Ibid.

Sophia Tolstoy uses almost the same words six months after her marriage:

> My life is so mundane, and my death. But he has such a rich internal
> life, talent and immortality. (23 December 1863)[63]

A few months earlier, she had uttered another complaint:

> . . . You simply cannot be happy just sitting there sewing or playing
> the piano alone, completely *alone*, and gradually realizing, or rather
> becoming convinced that even though your husband may not love
> you, you are stuck there forever and there you must sit. (9 May
> 1863)

Twelve years later, she writes these words that many women today
subscribe to:

> . . . day after day, month after month, year after year – nothing ever
> changes. I wake up in the morning and just lie there wondering
> who will get me up, who is waiting for me. The cook is bound to
> come in, then the nurse, . . . so then I get up, . . . and sit silently
> darning holes, and then it's time for the children's grammar and
> piano lessons. Then in the evening more darning, with Auntie and
> Lyovochka playing endless . . . games of patience. (22 October 1875)[64]

Mme Proudhon's complaint resonates with the same sound. 'You have
your ideas,' she said to her husband. 'And I, when you are at work, when
the children are in school, I have nothing.'

In the first years the wife often lulls herself with illusions, she tries
to admire her husband unconditionally, to love him unreservedly, to feel
she is indispensable to him and her children; and then her true feelings
emerge; she sees her husband can get along without her, that her children are made to break away from her: they are always more or less
thankless. The home no longer protects her from her empty freedom;
she finds herself alone, abandoned, a subject, and she finds nothing to
do with herself. Affections and habits can still be of great help, but not
salvation. All sincere women writers have noted this melancholy that
inhabits the heart of 'thirty-year-old women'; this is a characteristic
common to the heroines of Katherine Mansfield, Dorothy Parker
and Virginia Woolf. Cécile Sauvage who sang so gaily of marriage and
children at the beginning of her life, later expresses a subtle distress. It

is noteworthy that the number of single women who commit suicide, compared with married women, shows that the latter are solidly protected from revulsion against life between twenty and thirty years of age (especially between twenty-five and thirty) but not in the following years. 'As for marriage,' writes Halbwachs,* 'it protects provincial as well as Parisian women until thirty years of age but not after.'[65]

The drama of marriage is not that it does not guarantee the wife the promised happiness – there is no guarantee of happiness – it is that it mutilates her; it dooms her to repetition and routine. The first twenty years of a woman's life are extraordinarily rich; she experiences menstruation, sexuality, marriage and motherhood; she discovers the world and her destiny. She is mistress of a home at twenty, linked from then on to one man, a child in her arms, now her life is finished forever. Real activity, real work are the privilege of man: her only occupations are sometimes exhausting but never fulfil her. Renunciation and devotion have been extolled; but it often seems highly futile to devote herself to 'the upkeep of any two beings until the end of their lives'. It is all very grand to forget oneself, but one must know for whom and for what. Worst of all is that her devotion itself is exasperating; in her husband's eyes, it changes into a tyranny from which he tries to escape; and yet it is he who imposes his presence on woman as her supreme, one justification; by marrying her he obliges her to give herself to him completely; he does not accept the reciprocal obligation, which is to accept this gift. Sophia Tolstoy's words: 'I live through him and for him, I demand the same thing for me', are certainly revolting; but Tolstoy demanded she only live for him and through him, an attitude reciprocity alone can justify. It is the husband's duplicity that dooms the wife to a misfortune of which he later complains to be the victim. Just as he wants her both hot and cold in bed, he claims her totally given and yet weightless; he asks her to fix him to earth and to let him be free, to ensure the daily monotonous repetition and not to bother him, always to be present and never nag him; he wants her entirely for himself and not to belong to him; to live in a couple and to remain alone. Thus, as soon as he marries her, he mystifies her. She spends her life measuring the extent of this betrayal. What D. H. Lawrence says about sexual love is generally valid: the union of two human beings is doomed to failure if it requires an effort for each of them to complete each other, which supposes a primal mutilation;

---

* *The Causes of Suicide.* The comment applies to France and Switzerland but not to Hungary or Oldenburg.

marriage must combine two autonomous existences, not be a withdrawal, an annexation, an escape, a remedy. This is what Nora* understands when she decides that before being able to be a wife and mother, she has to be a person. The couple should not consider itself as a community, a closed cell: instead, the individual as individual has to be integrated into a society in which he can thrive without assistance; he will then be able to create links in pure generosity with another individual equally adapted to the group, links founded on the recognition of two freedoms.

This balanced couple is not a utopia; such couples exist sometimes even within marriage, more often outside of it; some are united by a great sexual love that leaves them free in their friendships and occupations; others are linked by a friendship that does not hamper their sexual freedom; more rarely there are still others who are both lovers and friends but without seeking in each other their exclusive reason for living. Many nuances are possible in the relations of a man and a woman: in companionship, pleasure, confidence, tenderness, complicity and love, they can be for each other the most fruitful source of joy, richness and strength offered to a human being. It is not the individuals who are responsible for the failure of marriage: it is – unlike what Bonald, Comte and Tolstoy claim – the institution that is perverted at its base. Declaring that a man and a woman who do not even choose each other *must* meet each other's needs in all respects, at once, for their whole life, is a monstrosity that necessarily gives rise to hypocrisy, hostility and unhappiness.

The traditional form of marriage is changing: but it still constitutes an oppression that both spouses feel in different ways. Considering the abstract rights they enjoy, they are almost equals; they choose each other more freely than before, they can separate much more easily, especially in America, where divorce is commonplace; there is less difference in age and culture between the spouses than previously; the husband more easily acknowledges the autonomy his wife claims; they might even share housework equally; they have the same leisure interests: camping, bicycling, swimming, and so on. She does not spend her days waiting for her spouse's return: she practises sports, she belongs to associations and clubs, she has outside occupations, sometimes she even has a little job that brings her some money. Many young couples give the impression of perfect equality. But as long as the man has economic responsibility for the couple, it is just an illusion. He is the one who determines the conjugal domicile according to the demands of his job: she *follows* him

* Ibsen, *A Doll's House.*

from the provinces to Paris, from Paris to the provinces, the colonies, abroad; the standard of living is fixed according to his income; the rhythm of the days, the weeks and the year is organised on the basis of his occupations; relations and friendships most often depend on his profession. Being more positively integrated than his wife into society, he leads the couple in intellectual, political and moral areas. Divorce is only an abstract possibility for the wife, if she does not have the means to earn her own living: while alimony in America is a heavy burden for the husband, in France the lot of the wife and mother abandoned with a derisory pension is scandalous. But the deep inequality stems from the fact that the husband finds concrete accomplishment in work or action while for the wife in her role as wife, freedom has only a negative form: the situation of American girls, among others, recalls that of the emancipated girls of the Roman decadence. We saw that they had the choice between two types of behaviour: some perpetuated the style of life and the virtues of their grandmothers; others spent their time in futile activity; likewise, many American women remain 'housewives' in conformity with the traditional model; the others mostly whittle away their energy and time. In France, even if the husband has all the goodwill in the world, the burdens of the home do not weigh on him anymore once the young wife is a mother.

It is a commonplace to say that in modern households, and especially in the United States, the wife has reduced the husband to slavery. The fact is not new. Since the Greeks, males have complained of Xanthippe's tyranny; what is true is that the wife intervenes in areas that previously were forbidden to her; I know, for example, of students' wives who contribute to the success of their man with frenetic determination; they organise their schedules, their diet, they watch over their work; they cut out all distractions, and almost keep them under lock and key. It is also true that man is more defenceless than previously against this despotism; he recognises his wife's abstract rights and he understands that she can concretise them only through him: it is at his own expense that he will compensate for the powerlessness and the sterility the wife is condemned to; to realise an apparent equality in their association, he has to give her more because he possesses more. But precisely because she receives, takes and demands, she is the poorer. The dialectic of the master and slave has its most concrete application here: in oppressing, one becomes oppressed. Males are in chains by their very sovereignty; it is because they alone earn money that the wife demands cheques, because men alone practise a profession that the wife demands that they succeed, because they alone embody transcendence that the wife wants to steal it from them by taking over their projects and successes. And inversely, the tyranny wielded by the woman only manifests her dependence: she knows the success of the couple, its future, its happiness, and its justification, reside in the hands of the other; if she bitterly seeks to subjugate him to her will, it is because she is alienated in him. She makes a weapon of her weakness; but the fact is she is weak. Conjugal slavery is ordinary and irritating for the husband; but it is deeper for the wife; the wife who keeps her husband near her for hours out of boredom irritates him and weighs on him; but in the end, he can do without her more easily than she him; if he leaves her, it is she whose life will be ruined. The big difference is that for the wife, dependence is interiorised; she *is* a slave even when she conducts herself with apparent freedom, while the husband is essentially autonomous and enchained from the outside. If he has the impression he is the victim, it is because the burdens he bears are more obvious: the wife feeds on him like a parasite; but a parasite is not a triumphant master. In reality, just as biologically males and females are never victims of each other but all together of the species, the spouses together submit to the oppression of an institution they have not created. If it is said *men* oppress *women*, the husband reacts indignantly; he feels oppressed: he is; but in fact, it is the masculine code, the society developed by males and in their interest, that has defined the feminine condition in a form that is now for both sexes a source of distress.

The situation has to be changed in their common interest by prohibiting marriage as a 'career' for the woman. Men who declare themselves anti-feminist with the excuse that 'women are already annoying enough as it is' are not very logical: it is precisely because marriage makes them 'praying mantises', 'bloodsuckers' and 'poison' that marriage has to be changed and, as a consequence, the feminine condition in general. Woman weighs so heavily on man because she is forbidden to rely on herself; he will free himself by freeing her, that is, by giving her something *to do* in this world.

There are young women who are already trying to win this positive freedom; but seldom do they persevere in their studies or their jobs for long: they know the interests of their work will most often be sacrificed to their husband's career; their salary will only 'help out' at home; they hesitate to commit themselves to undertakings that do not pull them away from conjugal enslavement. Those who do have a serious profession will not draw the same social advantages as men: lawyers' wives, for example, are entitled to a pension on their husbands' death; women lawyers are prohibited from paying a corresponding pension to their husbands in case of death. This shows that the woman who works cannot keep the couple at the same level as the man. There are women who find real independence in their profession; but many discover that work 'outside' only represents another source of fatigue within the framework of marriage. Moreover and most often, the birth of a child forces them to confine themselves to their role of matron; it is still very difficult to reconcile work and motherhood.

According to tradition, it is the child who should assure the wife a concrete autonomy that dispenses her from devoting herself to any other aim. If she is not a complete individual as a wife, she becomes it as a mother: the child is her joy and justification. She reaches sexual and social self-realisation through him; it is thus through him that the institution of marriage has meaning and reaches its aim. Let us examine this ultimate step in woman's development.

CHAPTER 6

The Mother

It is through motherhood that woman fully achieves her physiological destiny; that is her 'natural' vocation, since her whole organism is directed towards the perpetuation of the species. But we have already shown that human society is never left to nature. And in particular, for about a century, the reproductive function has no longer been controlled by biological chance alone but by design.* Some countries have officially adopted specific methods of birth control; in Catholic countries, it takes place clandestinely: either man practises coitus interruptus, or woman rids her body of the sperm after the sexual act. This is often a source of conflict or resentment between lovers or married partners; the man gets irritated at having to check his pleasure; the woman detests the chore of douching; he begrudges her too-fertile womb; she dreads these living germs he risks leaving in her. And for both of them there is consternation when, in spite of precautions, she finds herself 'caught'. This happens frequently in countries where contraceptive methods are rudimentary. Then anti-physis takes a particularly acute form: abortion. As it is even banned in countries that authorise birth control, there are many fewer occasions to have recourse to it. But in France, many women are forced to have this operation, which haunts the love lives of most of them.

There are few subjects on which bourgeois society exhibits more hypocrisy: abortion is a repugnant crime to which it is indecent to make an allusion. For an author to describe the joys and suffering of a woman giving birth is perfectly fine; if he talks about a woman who has had an abortion, he is accused of wallowing in filth and describing humanity in an abject light: meanwhile, in France every year there are as many abortions as births. It is such a widespread phenomenon that it has to

* See Vol. I, Part Two, 'History', Chapter 5, where a historical account of the question of birth control and abortion can be found.

be considered one of the risks normally involved in the feminine condition. The law persists, however, in making it a misdemeanour: it demands that this delicate operation be executed clandestinely. Nothing is more absurd than the arguments used against legislating abortion. It is claimed to be a dangerous operation. But honest doctors recognise, along with Dr Magnus Hirschfeld, that 'abortion performed by a competent specialist, in a clinic and with proper preventative measures, does not involve the serious dangers penal law asserts.' It is, on the contrary, its present form that makes it a serious risk for women. The incompetence of 'back-alley' abortionists and their operating conditions cause many accidents, some of them fatal. Forced motherhood results in bringing miserable children into the world, children whose parents cannot feed them, who become victims of public assistance or 'martyr children'. It must be pointed out that the same society so determined to defend the rights of the foetus shows no interest in children after they are born; instead of trying to reform this scandalous institution called public assistance, society prosecutes abortionists; those responsible for delivering orphans to torturers are left free; society closes its eyes to the horrible tyranny practised in 'reform schools' or in the private homes of child abusers; and while it refuses to accept that the foetus belongs to the mother carrying it, it nevertheless agrees that the child is his parents' thing; this very week, a surgeon committed suicide because he was convicted of performing abortions and a father who had beaten his son nearly to death has been condemned to three months of prison *with a suspended sentence*. Recently a father let his son die of whooping cough by not providing medical care; a mother refused to call a doctor for her daughter in the name of unconditional submission to God's will: in the cemetery, other children threw stones at her; but when some journalists showed their indignation, a group of right-thinking people protested that children belong to their parents, that outside control would be unacceptable. Today there are 'a million children in danger', says the newspaper *Ce Soir;* and *France-Soir* writes that: 'Five hundred thousand children are *reported* to be in physical or moral danger.' In North Africa, the Arab woman has no recourse to abortion: out of ten children she gives birth to, seven or eight die, and no one is disturbed because painful and absurd childbirth has killed maternal sentiments. If this is morality, then what kind of morality is it? It must be added that the men who most respect embryonic life are the same ones who do not hesitate to send adults to death in war.

The practical reasons invoked against legal abortion are completely unfounded; as with moral reasons, they are reduced to the old Catholic argument: the foetus has a soul and the gates to paradise are closed to it without baptism. It is worth noting that the Church authorises the killing of adult men in war, or when it is a question of the death penalty; but it stands on intransigent humanitarianism for the foetus. It is not redeemed by baptism: but in the times of the holy wars against the infidel, the infidels were not baptised either and massacre was still strongly encouraged. Victims of the Inquisition were undoubtedly not all in a state of grace, nor are criminals who are guillotined and soldiers killed on the battlefield. In all these cases, the Church leaves it to the grace of God; it accepts that man is only an instrument in His hands and that the soul's salvation depends on the Church and God. Why, then, keep God from welcoming the embryonic soul into His heaven? If a council authorised it, he would not protest against the pious massacre of the Indians any more than in the good old days. The truth is that this is a conflict with a stubborn old tradition that has nothing to do with morality. The masculine sadism I have already discussed also has to be taken into account. The book Dr Roy dedicated to Pétain in 1943 is a striking example; it is a monument of bad faith. In a paternalistic way it underlines the dangers of abortion; but nothing seems more hygienic to him than a Caesarean. He wants abortion to be considered a crime and not a misdemeanour; and he wishes to have it banned even in its therapeutic form, that is, when the mother's life or health are in danger: it is immoral to choose between one life and another, he declares, and bolstered by this argument, he advises sacrificing the mother. He declares that the foetus does not belong to the mother, that it is an autonomous being. But when these same 'right-thinking' doctors exalt motherhood, they affirm that the foetus is part of the mother's body, that it is not a parasite nourished at the mother's expense. This fervour on the part of some men to reject everything that might liberate women shows how alive antifeminism still is.

Besides, the law that dooms young women to death, sterility and illness is totally powerless to ensure an increase of births. A point of agreement for both partisans and enemies of legal abortion is the total failure of repression. According to Professors Doléris, Balthazard and Lacassagne, there were 500,000 abortions a year around 1933; a statistic (cited by Dr Roy) established in 1938 estimated the number at a million. In 1941, Dr Aubertin from Bordeaux hesitated between 800,000 and a million. This last figure seems closest to the truth. In a March 1948 article in *Combat*, Dr Desplas wrote:

Abortion has entered into our customs . . . Repression has practically failed . . . In the Seine district, in 1943, 1,300 investigations found 750 charged and of them, 360 women were arrested, 513 condemned to a minimum of one to five years in prison, which is low compared to the 15,000 presumed abortions in the district. There are 10,000 reported cases in the territory.

He adds:

So-called criminal abortion is as familiar to all social classes as the contraceptive policies accepted by our hypocritical society. Two-thirds of abortions are performed on married women . . . it can be roughly estimated that there are as many abortions as births in France.

Due to the fact that the operation is often carried out in disastrous conditions, many abortions end in these women's deaths.

Two bodies of women who had abortions arrive per week at the medical-legal institute in Paris; many abortions result in permanent illnesses.

It is sometimes said that abortion is a 'class crime' and this is very often true. Contraceptive practices are more prevalent in the bourgeoisie; the existence of bathrooms makes their use easier than for workers or farmers deprived of running water; young girls in the bourgeoisie are more careful than others; a child is less of a burden in these households: poverty, insufficient housing and the necessity for the wife to work outside the home are among the most common reasons for abortions. It seems that most often couples decide to limit births after two children; an ugly woman can have an abortion just as can this magnificent mother rocking her two blond angels in her arms: she is the same woman. In a document published in *Les Temps Modernes* in October 1945, under the title, 'Common Ward', Mme Geneviève Serreau describes a hospital room where she had to go once, and where many of the patients had just undergone curettages: fifteen out of eighteen had had miscarriages, half of which were induced. Number 9 was the wife of a market porter; she had had ten children in two marriages, of which only three were still living, and she had seven miscarriages, five of which were induced; she regularly used the 'coat hanger' technique that she complaisantly displayed, as well as pills whose names she shared with her companions. Number 16, sixteen years old and married, had had affairs and contracted salpingitis as the result of an abortion. Number 7, thirty-five, explained: 'I've been married twenty years. I never loved him: for twenty years I behaved properly. Three months ago I took a lover. One time, in a hotel room. I got pregnant . . . So what else could I do? I had it taken out. No one knows anything, not my husband, not . . . him. Now it's over; I'll never go through it again. I've suffered too much . . . I'm not speaking about the curettage . . . No, no, it's something else: it's . . . it's self-respect, you see.' Number 14 had had five children in five years; at forty she looked like an old woman. All of them had an air of resignation that comes from despair: 'Women are made to suffer,' they said sadly.

The seriousness of this ordeal varies a great deal depending on the circumstances. The conventionally married woman or one comfortably provided for, supported by a man, having money and relations, is better off: first, she finds ways to have a 'therapeutic' abortion much more easily; if necessary, she has the means to pay for a trip to Switzerland, where abortion is liberally tolerated; gynaecology today is such that it is a benign operation when performed by a specialist with all hygienic guarantees and, if necessary, anaesthetic resources; failing official approval, she can find unofficial help that is just as safe: she has the right addresses, she has enough money to pay for conscientious care, without waiting until her pregnancy is advanced; she will be treated respectfully; some of these privileged people even maintain that this little accident can be beneficial to one's health and improve the complexion. On the other hand, there is little distress more pathetic than that of an isolated and penniless girl who sees herself ensnared in a 'crime' to erase a 'fault' that people around her consider unpardonable: in France this is the case of approximately 300,000 women employees, secretaries, students, workers and peasants; illegitimate motherhood is still so terrible a stain that many prefer suicide or infanticide to being an unmarried mother: proof that no punishment will ever stop them from 'getting rid of the infant'. A typical case heard thousands of times is one related by Dr Liepmann.* It concerns a young Berlin woman, the natural child of a shoemaker and a maid:

I became friendly with a neighbour's son ten years older than myself . . . His caresses were so new to me that, well, I let myself go.

* *Youth and Sexuality.*

However, in no way was it a question of love. But he continued to teach me a lot of things, giving me books to read on women; and finally I gave him the gift of my virginity. When, two months later, I accepted a situation as a teacher in a nursery school in Speuze, I was pregnant. I didn't see my period for two more months. My seducer wrote to me that I absolutely had to make my period come back by drinking gasoline and eating black soap. I can no longer now describe the torments I went through . . . I had to see this misery through to the end on my own. The fear of having a child made me do the awful thing. This is how I learned to hate men.

The school pastor, having learned the story from a letter gone astray, gave her a long sermon and she left the young man; she was called a black sheep.

That was how I ended up doing eighteen months in a reformatory.

Afterwards she became a children's maid in a professor's home and stayed for four years.

At that period, I came to know a judge. I was happy to have a real man to love. I gave him all my love. Our relations were such that at twenty-four years old, I gave birth to a healthy boy. Today that child is ten. I have not seen the father for nine and a half years . . . as I found the sum of two thousand five hundred marks insufficient, and as he refused to give the child his name and denied paternity, everything was over between us. No other man has aroused my desire since.

It is often the seducer himself who convinces the woman that she should rid herself of the child. Either he has already abandoned her when she learns she is pregnant, or she altruistically wants to hide her disgrace from him, or else she finds no support from him. Sometimes it is not without regret that she refuses to have the child; either because she does not decide to abort early enough, or because she does not know where to go to do it, or because she does not have the money to hand and she has wasted her time trying ineffective drugs, she is in the third, fourth, fifth month of her pregnancy when she tries to eliminate it; the miscarriage will be infinitely more dangerous, more painful, more

compromising than in the course of the first weeks. The woman knows
this; in anguish and fear, she tries to find a way out. In the countryside,
using a catheter is hardly known; the peasant woman who has 'sinned'
accidentally lets herself fall off an attic ladder, throws herself from the
top of a staircase, often hurts herself with no result; it also happens that
a small strangled corpse is found in the bushes, in a ditch, or in an
outhouse. In towns, women help each other out. But it is not always
easy to get hold of a backstreet abortionist, and still less easy to get the
money demanded; the pregnant woman requests help from a friend or
she may perform the operation herself; these cut-price women surgeons
are often incompetent; it does not take long to perforate oneself with a
coat hanger or knitting needle; a doctor told me that an ignorant woman,
trying to inject vinegar into her uterus, injected it into her bladder instead,
provoking unspeakable pain. Brutally begun and poorly treated, the
miscarriage, often more painful than an ordinary delivery, is accompanied by nervous disorders that can verge on epileptic fits, sometimes
provoke serious internal illnesses, and bring on fatal haemorrhaging. In
Gribiche, Colette recounts the harsh agony of a little music-hall dancer
abandoned to the ignorant hands of her mother; a standard remedy, she
says, is to drink a concentrated soap solution and then to run for a quarter
of an hour: with such treatments, it is often by killing the mother that
one gets rid of the child. I was told about a secretary who stayed in her
room for four days, lying in her blood, without eating or drinking,
because she did not dare call anyone. It is difficult to imagine abandonment more frightful than the kind where the threat of death converges
with that of crime and shame. The ordeal is less harsh in the case of
poor but married women who act in accord with their husbands and
without being tormented by useless scruples: a social worker told me
that in 'poor neighbourhoods' women share advice, borrow and lend
instruments, and help each other out as simply as if they were removing
corns. But they undergo severe physical suffering; hospitals are obliged
to accept a woman whose miscarriage has already commenced; but she
is sadistically *punished* by being refused sedatives during labour and during
the final curettage procedure. As seen in reports by Serreau, for example,
these persecutions do not even shock women all too used to suffering:
but they are sensitive to the humiliations heaped on them. The fact that
the operation they undergo is a clandestine and criminal one multiplies
the dangers and makes it abject and anguishing. Pain, sickness and death
seem like chastisement: we know what distance separates suffering
from torture, accident from punishment; with the risks she assumes, the

woman feels guilty, and it is this interpretation of pain and blame that is particularly distressful.

This moral aspect of the drama is more or less intensely felt depending on the circumstances. For very 'liberated' women, thanks to their finan-cial resources, their social situation, the free milieu they belong to, or for those who have learned through poverty and misery to disdain bour-geois morality, the question hardly arises: there is a difficult moment to go through, but it must be gone through, and that is all. But many women are intimidated by a morality that maintains its prestige in their eyes, even though their behaviour cannot conform to it; inwardly, they respect the law they are breaking, and they suffer from committing a crime; they suffer even more for having to find accomplices. In the first place, they undergo the humiliation of begging: they beg for an address, a doctor's care, a midwife; they risk being haughtily snubbed; or they expose themselves to a degrading connivance. To deliberately invite another to commit a crime is a situation that most men never know and that the woman experiences with a mixture of fear and shame. This intervention she demands is one she often rejects in her own heart. She is divided inside herself. It might be that her spontaneous desire is to keep this child whose birth she is preventing; even if she does not posi-tively want this motherhood, she feels ill at ease with the ambiguity of the act she is about to perform. For even if abortion is not murder, it cannot be assimilated to a simple contraceptive practice; an event has taken place that is an absolute commencement and whose development is being halted. Some women are haunted by the memory of this child who did not come to be. Helene Deutsch* cites the case of a psychologi-cally normal married woman who, having twice lost third-month foetuses due to her physical condition, made them little tombs that she treated with great piety even after the birth of many other children. If the miscar-riage was induced, this is all the more reason to feel she has committed a sin. The childhood remorse that follows the jealous desire for the death of a newborn little brother is revived, and the woman blames herself for really killing a child. This feeling of guilt can be expressed in patho-logical melancholies. In addition to women who think they tried to kill a living thing, there are many who feel they have mutilated a part of themselves; from here stems a resentment against the man who accepted or solicited this mutilation. Deutsch, once again, cites the case of a young girl who, deeply infatuated with her lover, herself insisted on eliminating

* *The Psychology of Women.*

a child who would have been an obstacle to their happiness; leaving the hospital, she refused to see the man she loved from then on. Even if such a definitive rupture is rare, it is, on the contrary, common for a woman to become frigid, either with all men or with the one who made her pregnant.

Men tend to take abortion lightly; they consider it one of those numerous accidents to which the malignity of nature has destined women: they do not grasp the values involved in it. The woman repudiates feminine values, her values, at the moment the male ethic is contested in the most radical way. Her whole moral future is shaken by it. Indeed, from childhood woman is repeatedly told she is made to bear children, and the praises of motherhood are sung; the disadvantages of her condition – periods, illness, and such – the boredom of household tasks, all this is justified by this marvellous privilege she holds, that of bringing children into the world. And in an instant, the man, to keep his freedom and not to handicap his future, in the interest of his job, asks the woman to renounce her female triumph. The child is no longer a priceless treasure: giving birth is no longer a sacred function: this proliferation becomes contingent and inopportune, and it is again one of femininity's defects. The monthly labour of menstruation becomes a blessing by comparison: now the return of the red flow that once plunged the girl into horror is anxiously awaited; it was in promising her the joys of childbearing that she had been consoled. Even consenting to and wanting an abortion, woman feels her femininity sacrificed: she will from now on definitively see in her sex a malediction, a kind of infirmity, a danger. Taking this denial to its extreme, some women become homosexual after the trauma of abortion. Yet when man asks woman to sacrifice her bodily possibilities for the success of his male destiny, he is denouncing the hypocrisy of the male moral code at the same time. Men universally forbid abortion; but they accept it individually as a convenient solution; they can contradict themselves with dizzying cynicism; but woman feels the contradictions in her wounded flesh; she is generally too shy to deliberately revolt against masculine bad faith; while seeing herself as a victim of an injustice that decrees her to be a criminal in spite of herself, she still feels dirtied and humiliated; it is she who embodies man's fault in a concrete and immediate form, in herself; he commits the fault, but unloads it onto her; he just says words in a pleading, threatening, reasonable or furious tone: he forgets them quickly; it is she who translates these phrases into pain and blood. Sometimes he says nothing, he just walks away; but his silence and avoidance are a far more obvious indictment of the whole moral code instituted by men. What is called 'immorality' in women, a favourite theme with misogynists, should surprise no one; how could women not feel inwardly defiant against the arrogant principles men publicly advocate and secretly denounce? Women learn to believe men no longer when they exalt women or when they exalt men; the one sure thing is the manipulated and bleeding womb, those shreds of red life, that absence of a child. With her first abortion, the woman begins to 'understand'. For many women, the world will never be the same. And yet, for lack of access to contraceptives, abortion is the only way out today in France for women who do not want to bring into the world children condemned to death and misery. Stekel* said it correctly: 'Prohibition of abortion is an immoral law, since it must be forcibly broken every day, every hour.'

Birth control and legal abortion would allow women to control their pregnancies freely. In fact, what decides woman's fecundity is in part a considered desire and in part chance. As long as artificial insemination is not widely practised, a woman might desire to become pregnant but be unable to – because either she does not have relations with men, or her husband is sterile, or she is unable to conceive. And, on the other hand, she is often forced to give birth against her will. Pregnancy and motherhood are experienced in very different ways depending on whether they take place in revolt, resignation, satisfaction or enthusiasm. One must keep in mind that the decisions and feelings the young mother expresses do not always correspond to her deep desires. An unwed mother can be overwhelmed in material terms by the burden suddenly imposed on her, be openly distressed by it, and yet find in the child the satisfaction of secretly harboured dreams; inversely, a young married woman who joyfully and proudly welcomes her pregnancy can fear it in silence, hate it with obsessions, fantasies and infantile memories that she herself refuses to recognise. This is one of the reasons why women are so secretive on this subject. Their silence comes in part from liking to surround an experience that is theirs alone in mystery; but they are also disconcerted by the contradictions and conflicts of which they themselves are the centre. 'The preoccupations of pregnancy are a dream that is forgotten as entirely as the dream of birth pains,'† one woman said. These are complex

* *Frigidity in Woman.*
† N. Hale.

truths that come to the fore in women and that they endeavour to bury in oblivion.

We have seen that in childhood and adolescence woman goes through several phases in connection with motherhood. When she is a little girl, it is a miracle and a game: she sees in the doll and she feels in the future child an object to possess and dominate. As an adolescent girl, on the contrary, she sees in it a threat to the integrity of her precious person. Either she rejects it violently, like Colette Audry's heroine who confides to us:

> Each little child playing in the sand, I loathed him for coming out of a woman . . . I loathed the adults too for lording it over the children, purging them, spanking them, dressing them, shaming them in all ways: women with their soft bodies always ready to bud out with new little ones, men who looked at all this pulp of their women and children belonging to them with a satisfied and independent air. My body was mine alone, I only liked it brown, encrusted with sea salt, scratched by the rushes. It had to stay hard and sealed.*[66]

Or else she fears it at the same time as she wishes it, which leads to pregnancy fantasies and all kinds of anxieties. Some girls enjoy exercising maternal authority but are not at all disposed to assume the responsibilities fully. Such is the case of Lydia cited by Helene Deutsch who, at sixteen, placed as a maid with foreigners, took the most extraordinarily devoted care of the children entrusted to her: it was a prolongation of her childish dreams in which she formed a couple with her mother to raise a child; suddenly she began to neglect her service, to be indifferent to the children, to go out, flirt; the time of games was finished and she was beginning to pay attention to her real life, where desire for motherhood did not hold a great place. Some women have the desire to dominate children their whole lives but they are horrified by the biological labour of parturition: they become midwives, nurses, grammar school teachers; they are devoted aunts, but they refuse to have children. Others too, without being disgusted by maternity, are too absorbed by their love lives or careers to make a place for it in their existence. Or they are afraid of the burden a child would mean for them or their husbands.

Often a woman deliberately ensures her sterility either by refusing all

---

* 'The Child', in *Playing a Losing Game.*

sexual relations or by birth-control practices; but there are also cases where she does not admit her fear of the infant and where conception is prevented by a psychic defence mechanism; functional problems of nervous origin occur that can be detected in a medical examination. Dr Arthus* cites a striking example, among others:

> Mme H. . . . had been poorly prepared for her life as a woman by her mother; who had always warned her of the worst catastrophes if she became pregnant . . . When Mme H. . . . was married she thought she was pregnant the following month; she realised her error; then once more after three months; new mistake. A year later she went to a gynaecologist, who did not see any cause of infertility in her or her husband. Three years later, she saw another one who told her: 'You will get pregnant when you talk less.' After five years of marriage, Mme H. . . . and her husband had accepted that they would not have a child. A baby was born after six years of marriage.

The acceptance or refusal of conception is influenced by the same factors as pregnancy in general. The subject's infantile dreams and her adolescent anxieties are revived during pregnancy; it is experienced in different ways depending on the woman's relations with her mother, her husband, and herself.

Becoming a mother in turn, woman somehow takes the place of the one who gave birth to her: this means total emancipation for her. If she sincerely desires her pregnancy, it will be of utmost importance for her to carry it out without assistance; still dominated and consenting to it, she will put herself on the contrary in her mother's hands: the newborn will seem like a brother or sister to her rather than her own offspring; if at the same time she wants and does not dare to liberate herself, she fears that the child, instead of saving her, will make her fall back under the yoke: this anguish can cause miscarriages; Deutsch cites the case of a young woman who, having to accompany her husband on a trip and leaving the child with her mother, gave birth to a stillborn child; she wondered why she had not mourned it more because she had ardently desired it; but she would have hated giving it over to her mother, who would have dominated her through this child. Guilt feelings towards one's mother are common, as was seen, in the adolescent girl; if they

* *Marriage (Le Mariage).*

are still strong, the wife imagines that a curse weighs on her offspring or on herself: the child, she thinks, will kill her upon coming into the world or he will die in birth. This anguish that they will not carry their pregnancy to term – so frequent in young women – is often provoked by remorse. This example reported in Deutsch shows how the relation- ship to the mother can have a negative importance.

> Mrs Smith was the youngest in a family with many other children, one boy and several girls. After this boy had disappointed the ambi- tious hopes of the parents, they wanted to have another son, but instead my patient was born. Her mother never concealed her disappointment over this fact . . . the patient was saved from trau- matic reactions to this attitude by two compensations – her father's deep and tender love for her, and the maternal affection of one of her sisters . . . As a little girl she had reacted to her mother's rejec- tions with conscious hatred . . . Up to her pregnancy she had been able to disregard her mother problem; but this method no longer worked when she herself was about to become a mother . . . she gave birth one month before term to a stillborn child. Soon she was again pregnant; and her joy was now even more mixed with fear of loss than during her first pregnancy. By this time she had come into close relation with a former friend of hers who was also pregnant . . . The friend had a mother who was the opposite of her own . . . full to the brim with maternal warmth. She spread her motherly wings both over her own loving daughter and Mrs Smith. [But] her friend had conceived a whole month before her; thus during the last month she would be left to her own fate . . . to the surprise of everyone concerned, her friend did not have her child at the expected time . . . and gave birth to a boy overdue by a whole month on the very day that Mrs Smith expected her own delivery.* The two friends now consciously adjusted themselves to each other in regard to their next pregnancies and conceived in the same month. This second time, Mrs Smith had no fears or doubts. But during the third month of her pregnancy her friend told her that her husband had been offered a position in another town and that the family would probably move there. That very day Mrs Smith started on a miscarriage. This woman could not

* H. Deutsch affirms that she verified the fact that the child was really born ten months after conception.

manage to have a second child . . . After her friend had failed her she could no longer chase away the shadow of the mother she had rejected.

The woman's relationship with her child's father is no less important. An already mature and independent woman can desire a child belonging wholly to herself: I knew one whose eyes lit up at the sight of a handsome male, not out of sensual desire, but because she judged his stud-like capacities; there are maternal Amazons who enthusiastically welcome the miracle of artificial insemination. Even if the child's father shares their life, they deny him any right over their offspring; they try – like Paul's mother in *Sons and Lovers* – to form a closed couple with their child. But in most cases, a woman needs masculine support to accept her new responsibilities; she will only devote herself joyously to a newborn if a man devotes himself to her.

The more infantile and shy she is, the more she needs this. Deutsch thus recounts the story of a young woman who at fifteen years of age married a sixteen-year-old boy who had got her pregnant. As a little girl, she had always loved babies and helped her mother take care of her brothers and sisters. But once she herself became a mother of two children, she panicked. She demanded that her husband constantly stay with her; he had to take a job that allowed him to remain home for long periods. She lived in a state of constant anxiety, exaggerating her children's fights, giving excessive importance to the slightest incidents of their days. Many young mothers demand so much help from their husbands that they drive them away by overburdening them with their problems. Deutsch cites other curious cases, like this one:

A young married woman thought she was pregnant and was extremely happy about it; separated from her husband by a trip, she had a very brief adventure that she accepted specifically because, delighted by her pregnancy, nothing else seemed to be of consequence; back with her husband, she learned later on that in truth, she had been mistaken about the conception date: it dated from his trip. When the child was born, she suddenly wondered if he was her husband's son or her fleeting lover's; she became incapable of feeling anything for the desired child; anguished and unhappy, she resorted to a psychiatrist and was not interested in the baby until she decided to consider her husband as the newborn's father.[67]

The woman who feels affection for her husband will often tailor her feelings to his: she will welcome pregnancy and motherhood with joy or misery depending on whether he is proud or put upon. Sometimes a child is desired to strengthen a relationship or a marriage, and the mother's attachment depends on the success or failure of her plans. If she feels hostility towards the husband, the situation is quite different: she can fiercely devote herself to the child, denying the father possession, or on the other hand, hate the offspring of the detested man. Mme H. N., whose wedding night we recounted as reported by Stekel, immediately became pregnant and she detested the little girl conceived in the horror of this brutal initiation her whole life. In Sophia Tolstoy's *Diaries* too, the ambivalence of her feelings for her husband is reflected in her first pregnancy. She writes:

I am in an unbearable state, physically and mentally. Physically I am always ill with something, mentally there is this awful emptiness and boredom, like a dreadful depression. As far as Lyova is concerned I do not exist . . . I can do nothing to make him happy, because I am pregnant.

The only pleasure she feels in this state is masochistic: it is probably the failure of her sexual relations that gives her an infantile need for self-punishment.

I have been ill since yesterday. I am afraid I may miscarry, yet I even take pleasure from the pain in my stomach. It is like when I did something naughty as a child, and Maman would always forgive me but I could never forgive myself, and would pinch and prick my hand. The pain would become unbearable but I would take intense pleasure in enduring it . . . I shall enjoy my new baby and also enjoy physical pleasures again – how disgusting . . . Everything here seems so depressing. Even the clock sounds melancholy when it strikes the hour; . . . everything is dead. But if Lyova . . . !

But pregnancy is above all a drama playing itself out in the woman between her and herself. She experiences it both as an enrichment and a mutilation; the foetus is part of her body and it is a parasite exploiting her; she possesses it and she is possessed by it; it encapsulates the whole future and in carrying it, she feels as vast as the world; but this very richness annihilates her, she has the impression of not being anything else. A new existence is going to manifest itself and justify her own existence, she is proud of it; but she also feels like the plaything of obscure forces, she is tossed about, assaulted. What is unique about the pregnant woman is that at the very moment her body transcends itself, it is grasped as immanent: it withdraws into itself in nausea and discomfort; it no longer exists for itself alone and then becomes bigger than it has ever been. The transcendence of an artisan or a man of action is driven by a subjectivity, but for the future mother the opposition between subject and object disappears; she and this child who swells in her form an ambivalent couple that life submerges; snared by nature, she is plant and animal, a collection of colloids, an incubator, an egg; she frightens children who are concerned with their own bodies and provokes sniggers from young men because she is a human being, consciousness and freedom, who has become a passive instrument of life. Life is usually just a condition of existence; in gestation it is creation; but it is a strange creation that takes place in contingency and facticity. For some women the joys of pregnancy and nursing are so strong they want to repeat them indefinitely; as soon as the baby is weaned, they feel frustrated. These 'breeders' rather than mothers eagerly seek the possibility of alienating their liberty to the benefit of their flesh: their existence appears to them to be tranquilly justified by the passive fertility of their body. If flesh is pure inertia, it cannot embody transcendence, even in a degraded form; it is idleness and ennui, but as soon as it burgeons, it becomes progenitor, source, flower, it goes beyond itself, it is movement towards the future while being a thickened presence at the same time. The separation woman suffered from in the past during her weaning is compensated for; it is submerged again in the current of life, reintegrated into the whole, a link in the endless chain of generations, flesh that exists for and through another flesh. When she feels the child in her heavy belly or when she presses it against her swollen breasts, the mother accomplishes the fusion she sought in the arms of the male, and that is refused as soon as it is granted. She is no longer an object subjugated by a subject; nor is she any longer a subject anguished by her freedom, she is this ambivalent reality: life. Her body is finally her own since it is the child's that belongs to her. Society recognises this possession in her and endows it with a sacred character. She can display her breast that was previously an erotic object, it is a source of life: to such an extent that pious paintings show the Virgin Mary uncovering her breast and begging her Son to save humanity. Alienated in her body and her social dignity, the mother has the pacifying illusion of feeling she is a being *in itself*, a ready-made *value*.

But this is only an illusion. Because she does not really make the child: it is made in her; her flesh only engenders flesh: she is incapable of founding an existence that will have to found itself; creations that spring from freedom posit the object as a value and endow it with a necessity: in the maternal breast, the child is unjustified, it is still only a gratuitous proliferation, a raw fact whose contingency is symmetrical with that of death. The mother can have *her* reasons for wanting *a* child, but she cannot give to *this* other – who tomorrow is going to be – his own raisons d'être; she engenders him in the generality of his body, not in the specificity of his existence. This is what Colette Audry's heroine understands when she says:

> I never thought he could give meaning to my life . . . His being had grown in me and I had to go through with it to term, what-ever happened, without being able to hasten things, even if I had to die from it. Then he was there, born from me; so he was like the work I might have done in my life . . . but after all he was not.*

In one sense the mystery of incarnation is repeated in each woman; every child who is born is a god who becomes man: he could not realise himself as consciousness and freedom if he did not come into the world; the mother lends herself to this mystery, but she does not control it; the supreme truth of this being taking shape in her womb escapes her. This is the ambivalence she expresses in two contradictory fantasies: all mothers have the idea that their child will be a hero; they thus express their wonderment at the idea of giving birth to a consciousness and a liberty; but they also fear giving birth to a cripple, a monster, because they know the awful contingency of flesh, and this embryo who inhabits them is merely flesh. There are cases where one of these myths wins out: but often the woman wavers between them. She is also susceptible to another ambivalence. Trapped in the great cycle of the species, she affirms life against time and death: she is thus promised to immortality; but she also experiences in her flesh the reality of Hegel's words: 'The birth of children is the death of parents.' The child, he also says, is for the parents 'the being for itself of their love that falls outside of them';

* 'The Child', in *Playing a Losing Game*.

and inversely, he will obtain his being for himself 'in separating from the source, a separation in which this source dries up'. Going beyond self for woman is also the prefiguration of her death. She manifests this truth in the fear she feels when imagining the birth: she fears losing her own life in it.

As the meaning of pregnancy is thus ambiguous, it is natural for the woman's attitude to be ambivalent as well: it changes moreover with the various stages of the foetus's evolution. It has to be noted first that at the beginning of the process the child is not present; he has only an imaginary existence; the mother can dream of this little individual who will be born in a few months, be busy preparing his cradle and layette: she grasps concretely only the organic and worrisome phenomena of which she is the seat. Some priests of Life and Fecundity mystically claim that woman knows the man has just made her a mother by the quality of the pleasure she experiences: this is one of the myths to be put into the trash heap. She never has a decisive intuition of the event: she deduces it from uncertain signs. Her periods stop, she thickens, her breasts become heavy and hurt, she has dizzy spells and is nauseous; sometimes she thinks she is simply ill and it is the doctor who informs her. Then she knows her body has been given a destination that transcends it; day after day a polyp born of her flesh and foreign to it is going to fatten in her; she is the prey of the species that will impose its mysterious laws on her, and generally this alienation frightens her: her fright manifests itself in vomiting. It is partially provoked by modifications in the gastric secretions then produced; but if this reaction, unknown in other female mammals, becomes more serious, it is for psychic reasons; it expresses the acute character of the conflict between species and individual in the human female.* Even if the woman deeply desires the child, her body revolts at first when it has to deliver. In *Conditions of Nervous Anxiety and Their Treatment*, Stekel asserts that the pregnant woman's vomiting always expresses a certain rejection of the child; and if the child is greeted with hostility – often for unavowed reasons – gastric troubles are exacerbated.

'Psychoanalysis has taught us that psychogenic intensification of the oral pregnancy symptom of vomiting takes place only when the oral expulsion tendencies are accompanied by unconscious and sometimes even manifest emotions of hostility to pregnancy or to the foetus,' says Deutsch. She adds, 'the psychologic content in pregnancy vomiting was

* See Vol. I, Chapter I.

exactly the same as that in the hysterical vomiting of young girls that is induced by an unconscious pregnancy fantasy and not by a real condition'.* In both cases, the old idea that children have of fertilisation through the mouth comes back to life. For infantile women in particular, pregnancy is, as in the past, assimilated to an illness of the digestive apparatus. Deutsch cites a woman patient who anxiously studied her vomit to see if there were not fragments of the foetus; but she *knew*, she said, that this obsession was absurd. Bulimia, lack of appetite and feeling sick signal the same hesitation between the desire to conserve and the desire to destroy the embryo. I knew a young woman who suffered from both excessive vomiting and fierce constipation; she told me that one day she had the impression both of trying to reject the foetus and of striving to keep it, corresponding exactly to her avowed desires. Dr Arthus† cites the following example, which I have summarised:

> Mme T. . . . presents serious pregnancy problems with irrepressible vomiting . . . The situation is so worrisome that an abortion is being considered . . . The young woman is disconsolate . . . The brief analysis that can be practised shows [that]: Mme T. subconsciously identifies with one of her former boarding-school friends who had played a great role in her emotional life and who died during her first pregnancy. As soon as this cause could be uncovered, the symptoms improved; vomiting continued somewhat for two weeks but does not present any more danger.

Constipation, diarrhoea and expulsion tendencies always express the same mixture of desire and anguish; the result is sometimes a miscarriage: almost all spontaneous miscarriages have a psychic origin. The more importance woman gives these malaises and the more she coddles herself, the more intense they are. In particular, pregnant women's famous 'cravings' are indulgently nurtured infantile obsessions: they are always focused on food, and have to do with the old idea of fertilisation by food; feeling distressed in her body, woman expresses, as often happens

---

* I was specifically told about the case of a man who for the first months of his wife's pregnancy – a wife he did not even love very much – presented the exact symptoms of nausea, dizziness and vomiting seen in pregnant women. They obviously express unconscious conflicts in a hysterical form.

† *Marriage.*

in psychasthenies, this feeling of strangeness through a desire that fascinates her. There is moreover a 'culture', a tradition, of these cravings as there once was a culture of hysteria; woman expects to have these cravings, she waits for them, she invents them for herself. I was told of a teenage mother who had such a frenetic craving for spinach that she ran to the market to buy it and jumped up and down in impatience watching it cook: she was thus expressing the anxiety of her solitude; knowing she could only count on herself, she was in a feverish rush to satisfy her desires. The duchesse d'Abrantès described very amusingly in her *Memoirs*[68] a case where the craving is imperiously suggested by the woman's circle of friends. She complains of having been surrounded by too much solicitude during her pregnancy:

> These cares and kind attentions increased the discomfort, nausea, nervousness and thousands of sufferings that almost always accompany first pregnancies. I found it so . . . It was my mother who started it one day when I was having dinner at her house . . . 'Good heavens,' she cried suddenly, putting down her fork and looking at me with dismay. 'Good heavens! I forgot to ask what you especially *craved*.'
>
> 'But there is nothing in particular,' I replied.
>
> 'You have no special craving,' exclaimed my mother, 'nothing! But that is unheard of. You must be wrong. You haven't noticed. I'll speak to your mother-in-law about it.'
>
> And so there were my two mothers in consultation. And there was Junot, afraid I would bear him a child with a wild boar's head . . . asking me every morning: 'Laura, what do you crave?' My sister-in-law came back from Versailles and added her voice to the choir of questions, saying that she had seen innumerable people disfigured because of unsatisfied longings . . . I finally got frightened myself . . . I tried to think of what would please me most and couldn't think of a thing. Then, one day, it occurred to me when I was eating pineapple lozenges that a pineapple had to be a very excellent thing . . . Once I persuaded myself that I had a *longing* for a pineapple I felt at first a very lively desire, increased when Corcelet declared that . . . they were not in season. Ah, then I felt that mad desire which makes you feel that you will die if it is not satisfied.

Junot, after many attempts, finally received a pineapple from Mme Bonaparte. The duchess of Abrantès welcomed it joyously and spent the night feeling and touching it as the doctor had ordered her not to eat it until morning, when Junot finally served it to her.

> I pushed the plate away. 'But – I don't know what is the matter with me. I can't eat pineapple.' He put my nose into the cursed plate, which made it clear that I could not eat pineapple. They not only had to take it away but also to open the windows and perfume my room in order to remove the least traces of an odour that had become hateful to me in an instant. The strangest part of it is that since then I have never been able to eat pineapple without practically forcing myself.

Women who are too coddled or who coddle themselves too much are the ones who present the most morbid phenomena. Those that go through the ordeal of pregnancy the most easily are, on the one hand, matrons totally devoted to their function as breeders, and on the other hand, mannish women who are not fascinated by the adventures of their bodies and who do everything they can to triumph over them with ease: Mme de Staël went through pregnancy as easily as a conversation.

As the pregnancy proceeds, the relation between mother and foetus changes. It is solidly settled in the maternal womb, the two organisms adapt to each other and there are biological exchanges between them allowing the woman to regain her balance. She no longer feels possessed by the species: she herself possesses the fruit of her womb. The first months she was an ordinary woman, and diminished by the secret labour taking place in her; later she is obviously a mother and her malfunctions are the reverse of her glory. The increasing weakness she suffers from becomes an excuse. Many women then find a marvellous peace in their pregnancy: they feel justified; they always liked to observe themselves, to spy on their bodies; because of their sense of social duty, they did not dare to focus on their body with too much self-indulgence: now they have the right to; everything they do for their own well-being they also do for the child. They are not required to work or make an effort; they no longer have to pay attention to the rest of the world; the dreams of the future they cherish have meaning for the present moment; they only have to enjoy the moment: they are on vacation. The reason for their existence is there, in their womb, and gives them a perfect impression of plenitude. 'It is like a stove in winter that is always lit, that is there for you alone, entirely subject to your will. It is also like a constantly gushing cold shower in the summer, refreshing you. It is there,' says a woman quoted by Helene Deutsch. Fulfilled, woman also experiences the satisfaction of feeling 'interesting', which has been, since her adolescence, her deepest desire; as a wife, she suffered from her dependence on man; at present she is no longer sex object or servant, but she embodies the species, she is the promise of life, of eternity; her friends and family respect her; even her caprices become sacred: this is what encourages her, as we have seen, to invent 'cravings'. 'Pregnancy permits woman to rationalise performances which otherwise would appear absurd,' says Helene Deutsch. Justified by the presence within her of another, she finally fully enjoys being herself.

Colette wrote about this phase of her pregnancy in *The Evening Star*:[69]

Insidiously, unhurriedly, I was invaded by the beatitude of the woman great with child. I was no longer the prey of any malaise, any unhappiness. Euphoria, purring – what scientific or familiar name can one give to this saving grace? It must certainly have filled me to overflowing, for I haven't forgotten it . . . One grows weary of suppressing what one has never said – such as the state of pride, of banal magnificence which I savoured in ripening my fruit . . . Every evening I said a small farewell to one of the good periods of my life. I was well aware that I should regret it. But the cheerfulness, the purring, the euphoria submerged everything, and I was governed by the calm animality, the unconcern, with which I was charged by my increasing weight and the muffled call of the being I was forming.

Sixth, seventh month . . . the first strawberries, the first roses . . . Can I call pregnancy anything but a long holiday? One forgets the anguish of the term, one doesn't forget a unique long holiday; I've forgotten none of it. I particularly recall that sleep used to overwhelm me at capricious hours, and that I would be seized, as in my childhood, by the desire to sleep on the ground, on the grass, on warm straw. Unique 'craving', healthy craving . . .

Towards the end I had the air of a rat that drags a stolen egg. Uncomfortable in myself, I would be too tired to go to bed . . . Even then, the weight and the tiredness did not interrupt my long holiday. I was borne on a shield of privilege and solicitude.

This happy pregnancy was called by one of Colette's friends 'a man's pregnancy'. And she seemed to be the epitome of these women who valiantly support their state because they are not absorbed in it. She continued her work as a writer at the same time. 'The child showed signs of coming first and I screwed on the top of my pen.'

Other women are more weighed down; they mull indefinitely over their new importance. With just a little encouragement they adopt masculine myths: they juxtapose the lucidity of the mind to the fertile night of Life, clear consciousness to the mysteries of interiority, sterile freedom to the weight of this womb there in its enormous facticity; the future mother smells of humus and earth, spring and root; when she dozes, her sleep is that of chaos where worlds ferment. There are those more forgetful of self who are especially enchanted with the treasure of life growing in them. This is the joy Cécile Sauvage expresses in her poems in *The Soul in Bud:*[70]

> *You belong to me as dawn to the plain*
> *Around you my life is a warm fleece*
> *Where your chilly limbs grow in secret.*

And further on:

> *Oh you whom I fearfully cuddle in fleecy cotton*
> *Little soul in bud attached to my flower*
> *With a piece of my heart I fashion your heart*
> *Oh my cottony fruit, little moist mouth.*[71]

And in a letter to her husband:

It's funny, it seems to me I am watching the formation of a tiny planet and that I am kneading its frail globe. I have never been so close to life. I have never so felt I am sister of the earth with all vegetation and sap. My feet walk on the earth as on a living beast. I dream of the day full of flutes, of awakened bees, of dew because here he is bucking and stirring in me. If you knew what springtime freshness and what youth this soul in bud puts in my heart. And to think this is Pierrot's infant soul and that in the night of my being it is elaborating two big eyes of infinity like his.

In contrast are women who are very flirtatious, who grasp themselves essentially as erotic objects, who love themselves in the beauty of their bodies, and who suffer from seeing themselves deformed, ungainly, incapable of arousing desire. Pregnancy does not at all appear to them as a celebration or an enrichment, but as a diminishing of their self.

In *My Life* by Isadora Duncan one can read, among other observations:[72]

> The child asserted itself now, more and more. It was strange to see my beautiful marble body softened and broken and stretched and deformed . . . As I walked beside the sea, I sometimes felt an excess of strength and prowess, and I thought this creature would be mine, mine alone, but on other days . . . I felt myself some poor animal in a mighty trap . . . With alternate hope and despair, I often thought of the pilgrimage of my childhood, my youth, my wanderings . . . my discoveries in Art, and they were as a misty, far-away prologue, leading up to this – the before-birth of a child. What any peasant woman could have! . . . I began to be assailed with all sorts of fears. In vain I told myself that every woman had children . . . It was all in the course of life, etc. I was, nevertheless, conscious of fear. Of what? Certainly not of death, nor even of pain – some unknown fear, of what I did not know . . . More and more my lovely body bulged under my astonished gaze . . . Where was my lovely, youthful naiad form? Where my ambition? My fame? Often, in spite of myself, I felt very miserable and defeated. This game with the giant Life was too much. But then I thought of the child to come, and all such painful thoughts ceased . . . Helpless, cruel hours of waiting in the night . . . With what a price we pay for the glory of motherhood.

In the last stage of pregnancy begins the separation between mother and child. Women experience his first movement differently, his kick knocking at the doors of the world, knocking against the wall of the womb that encloses him away from the world. Some women welcome and marvel at this signal announcing the presence of an autonomous life; others think of themselves with repugnance as the receptacle of a foreign individual. Once again, the union of foetus and maternal body is disturbed: the uterus descends, the woman has a feeling of pressure, tension, respiratory trouble. She is possessed this time not by the indistinct species but by this child who is going to be born; until then, he was just an image, a hope; he becomes heavily present. His reality creates new problems. Every passage is anguishing: the birth appears particularly frightening. When the woman comes close to term, all the infantile terrors come back to life; if, from a feeling of guilt, she thinks she is cursed by her mother, she persuades herself she is going to die or that the child will die. In *War and Peace*, Tolstoy painted in the character of Lise one of these infantile women who see a death sentence in birth: and she does die.

Depending on the case, the birth takes many different forms: the mother wants both to keep in her womb the treasure of her flesh that is a precious piece of her self and to get rid of an intruder; she wants finally to hold her dream in her hands but she is afraid of new responsibilities this materialisation will create: either desire can win, but she is often divided. Often, also, she does not come to the anguishing ordeal with a determined heart: she intends to prove to herself and to her family – her mother, her husband – that she is capable of surmounting it without help; but at the same time she resents the world, life and her family for the suffering inflicted on her and in protest she adopts a passive attitude. Independent women – matrons or masculine women – attach great importance to playing an active role in the period preceding and even during the birth; very infantile women let themselves passively go to the midwife, to their mother; some take pride in not crying out; others refuse to follow any recommendations. On the whole, it can be said that in this crisis they express their deepest attitude to the world in general, and to their motherhood in particular: they are stoic, resigned, demanding, imperious, revolted, inert, tense . . . These psychological dispositions have an enormous influence on the length and difficulty of the birth (which also, of course, depends on purely organic factors). What is significant is that normally woman – like some domesticated female animals – needs help to accomplish the function to which nature destines her; there are peasants in rough conditions and shamed young unmarried mothers who give birth alone: but their solitude often brings about the death of the child or for the mother incurable illnesses. At the very moment woman completes the realisation of her feminine destiny, she is still dependent: which also proves that in the human species nature can never be separated from artifice. With respect to nature, the conflict between the interest of the feminine person and that of the species is so acute it often brings about the death of either the mother or the child: human interventions by doctors and surgeons have considerably reduced – and even almost eliminated – the accidents that were previously so frequent. Anaesthetic methods are in the process of giving the lie to the biblical affirmation 'In sorrow thou shalt bring forth children'; they are commonly used in America and are beginning to spread to France; in March 1949, a decree has just made them compulsory in England.*

It is difficult to know exactly what suffering these methods save women from. The fact that delivery sometimes lasts more than twenty-four hours and sometimes is completed in two or three hours prevents any generalisation. For some women, childbirth is martyrdom. Such is the case of Isadora Duncan: she lived through her pregnancy in anxiety, and psychic resistance undoubtedly aggravated the pains of childbirth even more. She writes:

> Talk about the Spanish Inquisition! No woman who has borne a child would have to fear it. It must have been a milk sport in comparison. Relentless, cruel, knowing no release, no pity, this terrible, unseen genie had me in his grip, and was, in continued spasms, tearing my bones and my sinews apart. They say such suffering is soon forgotten. All I have to reply is that I have only to shut my eyes and I hear again my shrieks and groans as they were then.

On the other hand, some women think it is a relatively easy ordeal to bear. A small number experience sensual pleasure in it.

One woman writes:[†]

> I am so strongly sexed that even childbirth means to me a sexual act . . . I had a very pretty 'madame' for a nurse. She bathed me and gave me my vaginal douches. This was enough for me – it kept me in such a high state of sexual agitation that I trembled.

---

* I have already said that some antifeminists, in the name of nature and the Bible, were indignant at the attempt to eliminate the suffering of childbirth; it is supposed to be one of the sources of the maternal 'instinct'. Helene Deutsch seems tempted by this opinion; she writes that when the mother has not felt the labour of childbirth, she does not profoundly recognise the child as her own at the moment she is presented with him; however, she agrees that the same feeling of emptiness and strangeness is encountered in women who have given birth and suffered; and she maintains all through her book that maternal love is a feeling, a conscious attitude, and not an instinct; that it is not necessarily linked to pregnancy; according to her, a woman can maternally love an adopted child or one her husband has had from a first marriage, and so on. This contradiction obviously comes from the fact that she has destined woman to masochism and her thesis demands she grant a high value to feminine suffering.

† Stekel recorded this subject's confession, which I have partially summarised.

Some women say they felt creative power during childbirth; they truly accomplished a voluntary and productive piece of work; many others feel passive, a suffering and tortured instrument.

The mother's first relations with the newborn vary as well. Some women suffer from this emptiness they now feel in their bodies: it seems to them that someone has stolen their treasure. Cécile Sauvage writes:

> I am the hive without speech
> Whose swarm has flown into the air
> No longer do I bring back the beakful
> Of my blood to your frail body
> My being is a closed-up house
> From which they have removed a body,

And more:

> No longer are you mine alone. Your head
> Already reflects other skies.

And also:

> He is born, I have lost my young beloved
> Now that he is born, I am alone, I feel
> Terrifying within me the void of my blood . . .[73]

Yet, at the same time, there is a wondrous curiosity in every young mother. It is a strange miracle to see, to hold a living being formed in and coming out of one's self. But what part has the mother really had in the extraordinary event that brings a new existence into the world? She does not know. The being would not exist without her and yet he escapes her. There is a surprising sadness in seeing him outside, cut off from herself. And there is almost always a disappointment. The woman would like to feel him *hers* as surely as her own hand: but everything he feels is closed up inside him, he is opaque, impenetrable, apart; she does not even recognise him, since she does not know him; she lived her pregnancy without him: she has no common past with this little stranger; she expected to be familiar right away; but no, he is a newcomer and she is stupefied by the indifference with which she receives him. In her pregnancy reveries he was an image, he was infinite and the mother mentally played out her future motherhood; now he is a tiny, finite individual, he is really there, contingent, fragile, demanding. The joy that he is finally here, quite real, is mingled with the regret that this is all he is.

After the initial separation, many young mothers regain an intimate animal relationship with their children through nursing; this is a more stressful fatigue than that of pregnancy, but it allows the nursing mother to prolong the 'vacation' state of peace and plenitude she relished in pregnancy. Colette Audry* says of one of her heroines:

> When the baby was suckling, there was really nothing else to do, and it could last for hours; she did not even think of what would come after. She could only wait for him to release her breast like a big bee.

But there are women who cannot nurse, and in whom the surprising indifference of the first hours continues until they regain concrete bonds with the child. This was the case, among others, with Colette, who was not able to nurse her daughter and who describes her first maternal feelings with her customary sincerity:[†74]

> The outcome is the contemplation of a new person who has entered the house without coming in from outside . . . Did I devote enough love to my contemplation? I should not like to say so. True, I had the capacity – I still have – for wonder. I exercised it on that assembly of marvels which is the newborn. Her nails, resembling in their transparency the convex scale of the pink shrimp – the soles of her feet, which have reached us without touching the ground . . . The light plumage of her lashes, lowered over her cheek, interposed between the scenes of earth and the bluish dream of her eye . . . The small sex, a barely incised almond, a bivalve precisely closed, lip to lip. . . . But the meticulous admiration I devoted to my daughter – I did not call it, I did not feel it as love. I waited . . . I did not derive from these scenes, so long awaited in my life, the vigilance and emulation of besotted mothers. When, then, would be vouchsafed to me the sign that was to mark my second, more difficult, violation? I had to accept that an accumulation of warnings, of furtive, jealous outbursts, of false premonitions – and even of real ones – the pride in managing an existence of which I was

* *Playing a Losing Game.*
† *Evening Star.*

the humble creditor, the somewhat perfidious awareness of giving the other love a lesson in modesty, would eventually change me into an ordinary mother. Yet I only regained my equanimity when intelligible speech blossomed on those ravishing lips, when recognition, malice and even tenderness turned a run-of-the-mill baby into a little girl, and a little girl into my daughter!

There are also many mothers who are terrified of their new responsibilities. During pregnancy, they had only to abandon themselves to their flesh; no initiative was demanded of them. Now in front of them is a person who has rights to them. Some women happily caress their babies while they are still in the hospital, still gay and carefree, but upon returning home, they start to regard them as burdens. Even nursing brings them no joy, and, on the contrary, they worry about ruining their breasts; they resent feeling their cracked breasts, their painful glands; the baby's mouth hurts them: he seems to be sucking their strength, life and happiness from them. He inflicts a harsh servitude on them, and he is no longer part of his mother: he is like a tyrant; she feels hostility for this little individual who threatens her flesh, her freedom, her whole self.

Many other factors are involved. The woman's relations with her mother are still of great importance. Helene Deutsch cites the case of a young nursing mother whose milk dried up whenever her mother came to see her; she often solicits help, but is jealous of the care someone else gives to the baby and feels depressed about this. Her relations with the infant's father and the feelings he himself fosters also have a strong influence. A whole set of economic and sentimental considerations define the infant as a burden, a shackle, or a liberation, a jewel, a form of security. There are cases where hostility becomes outright hatred resulting in extreme neglect or bad treatment. Most often the mother, conscious of her duties, combats this hostility; she feels remorse that gives rise to anxieties prolonging the apprehensions of pregnancy. All psychoanalysts agree that mothers who are obsessed about harming their children, or who imagine horrible accidents, feel an enmity towards them they force themselves to repress. What is nonetheless remarkable and distinguishes this relationship from all other human relationships is that in the beginning the child himself does not play a part: his smiles, his babbling, have no meaning other than the one his mother gives them; it depends on her, not him, whether he seems charming, unique, bothersome, ordinary or obnoxious. This is why cold, unsatisfied, melancholic women who expect a child to be a companion, or to provide warmth and excitement that draw them out of themselves, are always deeply disappointed. Like the 'passage' into puberty, sexual initiation, and marriage, motherhood generates morose disappointment for subjects who are waiting for an external event to renew and justify their lives. This is the sentiment found in Sophia Tolstoy. She writes:

> 'These past nine months have been practically the worst in my life,' to say nothing of the tenth.[75]

She tries in vain to express a conventional joy: we are struck by her sadness and fear of responsibilities.

> It is all over, the baby has been born and my ordeal is at last at an end. I have risen from my bed and am gradually entering into life again, but with a constant feeling of fear and dread about my baby and especially my husband. Something within me seems to have collapsed, and I sense that whatever it is it will always be there to torment me; it is probably the fear of not doing my duty towards *my family* . . . I have become insincere, for I am frightened by the womb's vulgar love for its offspring, and frightened by my somewhat unnatural love for my husband . . . I sometimes comfort myself with the thought that most people see this love of one's husband and children as a virtue . . . But how strong these maternal feelings are! . . . He is Lyovochka's child, that's why I love him.

But we know very well that she only exhibits so much love for her husband because she does not love him; this antipathy marks the child conceived in embraces that disgusted her.

Katherine Mansfield describes the hesitation of a young mother who loves her husband but is repulsed by his caresses. For her children she feels tenderness and at the same time has an impression of emptiness she sadly interprets as complete indifference. Linda, resting in the garden next to her newborn, thinks about her husband, Stanley.*

> Well, she was married to him. And what was more she loved him. Not the Stanley whom everyone saw, not the everyday one; but a timid, sensitive, innocent Stanley who knelt down every night to say

---

*'At the Bay'.

his prayers ... But the trouble was ... she saw her Stanley so seldom. There were glimpses, moments, breathing spaces of calm, but all the rest of the time it was like living in a house that couldn't be cured of the habit of catching on fire, on a ship that got wrecked every day. And it was always Stanley who was in the thick of the danger. Her whole time was spent in rescuing him, and restoring him, and calming him down, and listening to his story. And what was left of her time was spent in the dread of having children ... It was all very well to say it was the common lot of women to bear children. It wasn't true. She, for one, could prove that wrong. She was broken, made weak, her courage was gone, through child-bearing. And what made it doubly hard to bear was, she did not love her children. It was useless pretending ... No, it was as though a cold breath had chilled her through and through on each of those awful journeys; she had no warmth left to give them. As to the boy – well, thank Heaven, mother had taken him; he was mother's, or Beryl's, or anybody's who wanted him. She had hardly held him in her arms. She was so indifferent about him that as he lay there ... Linda glanced down ... There was something so quaint, so unexpected about that smile that Linda smiled herself. But she checked herself and said to the boy coldly, 'I don't like babies.' 'Don't like babies?' The boy couldn't believe her. 'Don't like me?' He waved his arms foolishly at his mother. Linda dropped off her chair on to the grass. 'Why do you keep on smiling?' she said severely. 'If you knew what I was thinking about, you wouldn't' ... Linda was so astonished at the confidence of this little creature ... Ah no, be sincere. That was not what she felt; it was something far different, it was something so new, so ... The tears danced in her eyes; she breathed in a small whisper to the boy, 'Hallo, my funny!'

These examples all prove that there is no such thing as maternal 'instinct': the word does not in any case apply to the human species. The mother's attitude is defined by her total situation and by the way she accepts it. It is, as we have seen, extremely variable.

But the fact is that if circumstances are not positively unfavourable, the mother will find herself enriched by a child. 'It was like a response to the reality of her own existence ... through him she had a grasp on all things and on herself to begin with,' wrote Colette Audry about a young mother.

And she has another character say these words:

He was heavy in my arms, and on my breast, like the heaviest thing in the world, to the limit of my strength. He buried me in silence and darkness. All at once he had put the weight of the world on my shoulders. That was indeed why I wanted him. I was too light myself. Alone, I was too light.

While some women are 'breeders' rather than mothers and lose interest in their child as soon as it is weaned, or as soon as it is born, and only desire another pregnancy, many others by contrast feel that it is the separation itself that gives them the child; it is no longer an indistinct part of themselves but a piece of the world; it no longer secretly haunts the body, but can be seen, touched; after the melancholy of delivery, Cécile Sauvage expresses the joy of possessive motherhood:

> *Here you are my little lover*
> *On your mother's big bed*
> *I can kiss you, hold you,*
> *Feel the weight of your fine future;*
> *Good day my little statue*
> *Of blood, of joy and naked flesh,*
> *My little double, my excitement . . .*

It has been said again and again that woman happily finds an equivalent of the penis in the infant: this is completely wrong. In fact, the adult man no longer sees his penis as a wonderful toy: his organ is valued in relation to the desirable objects it allows him to possess; by the same token, the adult woman envies the male for the prey he acquires, not the instrument of this acquisition; the infant satisfies this aggressive eroticism that the male embrace does not fulfil: the infant is homologous to this mistress that she is for the male and that he is not for her; of course there is no exact correspondence; every relation is unique; but the mother finds in the child – like the lover in the beloved – a carnal plenitude, not in surrender but in domination; she grasps in the child what man seeks in woman: an other, both nature and consciousness, who is her prey, her *double*. He embodies all of nature. Audry's heroine tells us she found in her child:

The skin that was for my fingers to touch, that fulfilled the promise
of all little kittens, all flowers . . .

His skin has that sweetness, that warm elasticity that, as a little girl,
the woman coveted in her mother's flesh and, later, everywhere in the
world. He is plant and animal, he holds rains and rivers in his eyes, the
azure of the sky and the sea, his fingernails are coral, his hair a silky
growth, he is a living doll, a bird, a kitten; my flower, my pearl, my
chick, my lamb . . . His mother murmurs words almost of a lover and
uses, like a lover, the possessive adjective; she uses the same words of
appropriation: caresses, kisses; she hugs the infant to her body, she
envelops him in the warmth of her arms, of her bed. At times these
relations have a clearly sexual cast. Thus in the confession collected by
Stekel I have already cited, we read:

> I nursed my baby but I took no particular joy in doing so because
> he did not thrive well. We were both losing ground. The act of
> nursing seemed something sexual to me. I was always ashamed
> of it . . . it was for me a majestic experience to feel the warm
> little body snuggling up to me . . . The touch of his little hands
> thrilled me . . . My whole love went out to him . . . The child
> would cling to me and did not leave my side. It was troublesome
> to try to keep him away from me . . . When he saw me in bed
> he crawled up at once – he was two years of age at the time –
> and tried to lie on top of me. At the same time his little hands
> wandered over my breasts and tried to reach down. I found this
> very pleasurable; it was not easy for me to send the child away.
> Frequently I fought against the temptation of playing with his
> genitals.

Motherhood takes on a new aspect when the child grows older; at
first he is only a 'standard baby', existing in his generality: little by little
he becomes individualised. Very dominating or very carnal women grow
cold towards him; it is then that some others – like Colette – begin to
take an interest in him. The mother's relation to the child becomes more
and more complex: he is a double and at times she is tempted to alienate
herself completely in him, but he is an autonomous subject, and therefore rebellious; today he is warmly real, but in the far-off future he is
an adolescent, an imaginary adult; he is her wealth, a treasure: but he
is also a responsibility, a tyrant. The joy the mother can find in him is

a joy of generosity; she must take pleasure in serving, giving, creating
happiness, such as the mother depicted by Colette Audry:

> Thus, he had a happy storybook infancy, but his infancy was to
> storybook infancy as real roses were to postcard roses. And this
> happiness of his came out of me like the milk with which I nour-
> ished him.

Like the woman in love, the mother is delighted to feel needed; she
is justified by the demands she responds to; but what makes maternal
love difficult and great is that it implies no reciprocity; the woman is not
before a man, a hero, a demigod, but a little stammering consciousness,
lost in a fragile and contingent body; the infant possesses no value, and
he can bestow none; the woman remains alone before him; she expects
no compensation in exchange for her gifts, she justifies them with her
own freedom. This generosity deserves the praise that men forever bestow
on her; but mystification begins when the religion of Motherhood
proclaims that all mothers are exemplary. For maternal devotion can be
experienced in perfect authenticity; but in fact, this is rarely the case.
Ordinarily, maternity is a strange compromise of narcissism, altruism,
dream, sincerity, bad faith, devotion and cynicism.

The great risk our mores present for the infant is that the mother to
whom he is tied and bound is almost always an unfulfilled woman: sexually she is frigid or unsatisfied; socially she feels inferior to man; she has
no hold on the world or the future; she will try to compensate for her
frustrations through the child; when one recognises how the present
situation of woman makes her full development difficult, how many
desires, revolts, pretensions and claims she secretly harbours, one is frightened that helpless little children are given over to her. Just as when she
both pampered and tortured her dolls, her behaviour is symbolic: but
these symbols become bitter reality for the child. A mother who beats
her child does not only beat the child, and in a way she does not beat
him at all: she is taking her vengeance on man, on the world, or on
herself; but it is the child who receives the blows. Mouloudji expresses
this painful misunderstanding in *Enrico*: Enrico well understands it is not
he whom his mother beats so wildly; and waking from her delirium, she
sobs with remorse and tenderness; he does not hold it against her, but
he is no less disfigured by her blows. And the mother described in Violette
Leduc's *In the Prison of Her Skin*, in lashing out against her daughter is
in fact taking revenge on the seducer who abandoned her, on life that

humiliated and defeated her. This cruel aspect of motherhood has always been known; but with hypocritical prudishness, the idea of the 'bad mother' has been defused by inventing the cruel stepmother; the father's second wife torments the child of the deceased 'good mother'. Indeed, Mme Fichini is a mother figure, the exact counterpart of the edifying Mme de Fleurville described by Mme de Ségur. Since Jules Renard's *Carrot Top*,[76] there have been more and more accusations: *Enrico, In the Prison of Her Skin*, Simone de Tervagne's *Maternal Hatred*,[77] Hervé Bazin's *Viper in the Fist*.[78] While the types sketched in these novels are somewhat exaggerated, the majority of women suppress their spontaneous impulses out of morality and decency; but these impulses flare up in scenes, slaps, anger fits, insults, punishments, and so on. In addition to frankly sadistic women, there are many who are especially capricious; what delights them is to dominate; when the baby is tiny, he is a toy: if it is a boy, they shamelessly play with his penis; if it is a girl, they treat her like a doll; later they only want a little slave who will blindly obey them: vain, they show the child off like a trained pet; jealous and exclusive, they set him apart from the rest of the world. Also, the woman often continues to expect gratitude for the care she gives the child: she shapes an imaginary being through him who will recognise her with gratitude for being an admirable mother and one in whom she recognises herself. When Cornelia, proudly showing her children, said, 'These are my jewels,' she gave an ill-fated example to posterity; too many mothers live in the hope of one day repeating this arrogant gesture; and they do not hesitate to sacrifice the little flesh-and-blood individual whose contingent and indecisive existence does not fulfil them. They force him to resemble their husbands, or on the contrary, not to resemble them, or to reincarnate a father, a mother or a venerated ancestor; they model him on someone prestigious: a German socialist deeply admired Lily Braun, recounts Helene Deutsch; the famous activist had a brilliant son who died young; her imitator was determined to treat her own son like a future genius and as a result he became a bandit. Harmful to the child, this ill-adapted tyranny is always a source of disappointment for the mother. Deutsch cites another striking example, of an Italian woman whose case history she followed for several years.

> Mrs Mazzetti . . . had a number of small children . . . who caused her difficulties, all of them, one after the other. Personal contact with Mrs Mazzetti soon revealed that although she sought help it was difficult to influence her . . . Her entire bearing . . . was

consistently used only in face of the outside world, but . . . in relations with her family, she gave way to uncontrolled emotional
outbursts . . . we learned that coming from a poor, uncultured
milieu, she had always had the urge to become something 'better'.
She always attended night schools and would perhaps have achieved
something in harmony with her aspirations if she had not met her
husband. He . . . exerted an irresistible sexual attraction upon her.
At the age of sixteen she had sexual relations with him, soon became
pregnant, and found herself compelled to marry him . . . She continually tried to raise herself again . . . she went to night school, etc.
The man was a first class workman . . . Mrs Mazzetti evidently had
emphasised her superiority to him in a very aggressive way, which
drove this simple man to . . . alcoholism. He tried to devaluate his
wife's superiority by . . . making her repeatedly pregnant . . . After
her separation from her husband she turned all her emotions to
the children, and began to treat them as she had treated her
husband . . . As long as the children were small she appeared to be
attaining her goal. They were very ambitious, successful in school,
etc. When Louise, the oldest child, approached the age of sixteen,
her mother seems to have fallen into a state of anxiety that was
based upon her own past experiences. This anxiety was expressed
in heightened watchfulness and strictness, to which Louise reacted
with protests, and had an illegitimate child . . . The children
emotionally clung to their father and were against their mother
who tried to impose her moral standards on them . . . She could
never be kind to more than one of her older children at a time,
and always indulged her negative, aggressive emotions at the
expense of the others. Since the children thus alternated as objects
of her love, the child who had just been loved, was driven to rage,
jealousy and revenge . . . one daughter after another became promiscuous, they brought syphilis and illegitimate children into the home,
the little boys began to steal, and Mrs Mazzetti could not understand that ideal demands instead of tender harmony pushed them
in that direction.

This authoritarian upbringing and capricious sadism I spoke of are often
mixed together; to justify her anger, the mother uses the pretext
of wanting to 'shape' the child; and inversely, failure in her endeavour
exacerbates her hostility.

Masochistic devotion is another quite common attitude, and no less harmful for the child; some mothers make themselves slaves of their offspring to compensate for the emptiness in their hearts and to punish themselves for the hostility they do not want to admit; they endlessly cultivate a morbid anxiety, they cannot bear to let their child do anything on his own; they give up all pleasure, all personal life, enabling them to assume the role of victim; and from these sacrifices they derive the right to deny the child all independence; this renunciation is easily reconciled with a tyrannical will to domination; the *mater dolorosa* turns her suffering into a weapon she uses sadistically; her displays of resignation spur guilt feelings in the child, which he will often carry through his whole life: they are more harmful than aggressive displays. Tossed about, baffled, the child finds no defence mechanism: sometimes blows, sometimes tears, show him to be a criminal. The mother's main excuse is that the child is far from bringing her that satisfying self-accomplishment she was promised since childhood: she takes out on him the mystification of which she was a victim and that the child innocently exposes. She did what she wanted with her dolls; when she helped care for her sister's or a friend's baby, it was without responsibility. But now society, her husband, her mother and her own pride hold her responsible for this little foreign life as if it were her own composition: the husband in particular is irri-tated by the child's faults just as he is by a spoiled dinner or his wife's improper behaviour; his abstract demands often weigh heavily on the mother's relation to the child; an independent woman – thanks to her solitude, her carefree state or her authority in the household – will be much more serene than those carrying the weight of dominating demands in making her child obey. For the great difficulty is to contain within a fixed framework a mysterious existence like that of animals, turbulent and disorderly, like the forces of nature, but human nonetheless; one cannot train a child in silence like training a dog, nor persuade him with adult words: he plays on this ambiguity, pitting words against the animality of sobs and tantrums, and constraints against the insolence of language. Of course, the problem thus posed is challenging and, when she has time for it, the mother enjoys being an educator: peacefully settled in a park, the baby is still as good an excuse as he was when he nestled in her stomach; often still more or less infantile herself, she delights in being silly with him, reviving games, words, interests and joys of days gone by. But when she is washing, cooking, nursing another infant, shopping, entertaining callers, and mainly when she is taking care of her husband, the child is no more than a bothersome, harassing presence; she does not have the leisure time to 'train' him; she must first keep him from making trouble; he demolishes, tears, dirties, he is a constant danger to objects and to himself; he fidgets, he screams, he talks, he makes noise: he lives for himself; and this life disturbs his parents' life. Their interest and his do not converge: therein lies the drama. Forever burdened by him, parents inflict sacrifices on him for reasons he does not understand: they sacrifice him for their tranquillity and his own future. It is natural for him to rebel. He does not understand the explanations his mother tries to give him: she cannot penetrate his consciousness; his dreams, his phobias, his obsessions and his desires shape an opaque world: the mother can only gropingly control a being who sees these abstract laws as absurd violence from the outside. As the child grows older, this lack of comprehension remains: he enters a world of interests and values from which his mother is excluded; he often scorns her for it. The boy in particular, proud of his masculine prerogatives, laughs off a woman's orders: she insists on him doing his homework, but she cannot solve his problems, translate his Latin text; she cannot 'keep up' with him. The mother is sometimes driven to tears over this task whose difficulty the husband rarely appreciates: raising an individual with whom one does not communicate but who is nonetheless a human being; interfering in a foreign freedom that defines and affirms itself only by rebelling against you.

The situation differs, depending on whether the child is a boy or a girl; and while boys are more 'difficult', the mother generally gets along better with them. Because of the prestige woman attributes to men, and also the privileges they hold concretely, many women wish for a son. 'It's marvellous to bring a man into the world,' they say; as has been seen, they dream of giving birth to a 'hero', and the hero is obviously of the male sex. The son will be a chief, a leader of men, a soldier, a creator; he will impose his will on the face of the earth and his mother will share in his immortality; the houses she did not build, the countries she did not explore, the books she did not read, he will give to her. Through him she will possess the world: but on condition that she possesses her son. This is the source of her paradoxical attitude. Freud believes that the mother–son relationship contains the least ambivalence; but in fact in motherhood, as in marriage and love, woman has an ambiguous attitude to masculine transcendence; if her conjugal or love life has made her hostile to men, she will find satisfaction in dominating the male reduced to his infantile figure; she will treat the arrogantly pretentious sex organ with an ironic familiarity: at times she will frighten the child by announcing she will cut it off if he does not behave. Even if she is humble and more peaceful and respects the future hero in her son, she does what she can to reduce him to his immanent reality in order to ensure that he is really hers: just as she treats her husband like a child, she treats her child like a baby. It is too rational, too simple, to think she wishes to castrate her son; her dream is more contradictory: she wants him to be infinite and yet fit in the palm of her hand, dominating the whole world and kneeling before her. She encourages him to be soft, greedy, selfish, shy, sedentary, she forbids sports and friends and she makes him unsure of himself because she wants to have him for herself; but she is disappointed if he does not at the same time become an adventurer, a champion, a genius she can be proud of. There is no doubt that her influence is often harmful – as Montherlant maintains and as Mauriac demonstrates in *Génitrix*.[79] Luckily, boys can fairly easily escape this hold; customs and society encourage them to. And the mother herself is resigned to it: she knows very well that the struggle against man is unfair. She consoles herself by acting the *mater dolorosa* or by pondering the pride of having given birth to one of her conquerors.

The little girl is more wholly under the control of her mother; her claims on her daughter are greater. Their relations assume a much more dramatic character. The mother does not greet a daughter as a member of the chosen caste: she seeks a double in her. She projects on to her all the ambiguity of her relationship with her self; and when the alterity of this alter ego affirms itself, she feels betrayed. The conflicts we have discussed become all the more intensified between mother and daughter.

There are women who are satisfied enough with their lives to want to reincarnate themselves in a daughter, or at least welcome her without disappointment; they would like to give their child the same chances they had, as well as those they did not have: they will give her a happy youth. Colette traced the portrait of one of those well-balanced and generous mothers; Sido cherishes her daughter in her freedom; she fulfils her without ever making demands in return because her joy comes from her own heart. It can happen that in devoting herself to this double in whom she recognises and transcends herself, the mother ends up totally alienating herself in her; she renounces herself, her only care is for her child's happiness; she will even be egotistical and hard towards the rest of the world; she runs the danger of becoming annoying to the one she adores, as did Mme de Sévigné for Mme de Grignan; the disgruntled daughter will try to rid herself of such tyrannical devotion; often she is unsuccessful and she lives her whole life as a child, frightened of responsibilities because she has been too 'sheltered'. But it is especially a certain masochistic form of motherhood that risks weighing heavily on the young daughter. Some women feel their femininity as an absolute curse: they wish for or accept a daughter with the bitter pleasure of finding another victim; and at the same time they feel guilt at having brought her into the world; their remorse and the pity they feel for themselves through their daughter are manifested in endless anxieties; they will never take a step away from the child; they will sleep in the same bed for fifteen or twenty years; the little girl will be destroyed by the fire of this disquieting passion.

Most women both claim and detest their feminine condition; they experience it in resentment. The disgust they feel for their sex could incite them to give their daughters a virile education: they are rarely generous enough to do so. Irritated at having given birth to a female, the mother accepts her with this ambiguous curse: 'You will be a woman.' She hopes to redeem her inferiority by turning this person she considers a double into a superior being; and she also has a tendency to inflict on her the defect she has had to bear. At times she tries to impose exactly her own destiny on her child: 'What was good enough for me is good enough for you; this is the way I was brought up, so you will share my lot.' And at times, by contrast, she fiercely forbids her to resemble her: she wants her own experience to be useful, it is a way to get even. The courtesan will send her daughter to a convent, the ignorant woman will give her an education. In *In the Prison of Her Skin*, the mother who sees the hated consequence of a youthful error in her daughter tells her with fury:

> Try to understand. If such a thing happened to you, I would disown you. I did not know a thing. Sin! A vague idea, sin! If a man calls you, don't go. Go on your way. Don't turn back. Do you hear me? You've been warned, this must not happen to you, and if it happened, I would have no pity, I would leave you in the gutter.[80]

We have seen that Mrs Mazzetti, because she wanted to spare her daughter from her own error, precipitated it. Stekel recounts a complex case of 'maternal hatred' of a daughter:

> I know a mother who disliked at birth her fourth daughter, a quiet charming girl . . . She claimed that this child had inherited, in concentrated measure, all her father's unpleasant traits . . . The child was born to her during the year when this exalted, dreamy woman had fallen passionately in love with another man, a poet, who was

courting her . . . during her husband's embraces she permitted her mind to dwell on the poet, hoping that the child would thus become endowed with her beloved's traits – as in Goethe's *Elective Affinities*. However, the child looked so much like its father, from the moment of its birth, that its paternity was obvious . . . She saw in the child a reflection of herself – a reflection of the dreamy, tender, yielding, sensual side of herself. She despised these qualities, scorned them in herself. She would have preferred to have been strong, unyielding, vigorous, prudish and energetic. Thus she hated herself even more than she hated her husband through her hatred of the child.[81]

It is when the girl grows up that real conflicts arise; we have seen that she wishes to affirm her autonomy from her mother: this is, in her mother's eyes, a mark of detestable ingratitude; she obstinately tries to 'tame' this determination that is lurking; she cannot accept that her double becomes *an other*. The pleasure man savours in women – feeling absolutely superior – is something a woman experiences only towards her children, and her daughters in particular; she feels frustration if she renounces these privileges and her authority. Whether she is a passionate or a hostile mother, her child's independence ruins her hopes. She is doubly jealous: of the world that takes her daughter, and of her daughter who, in conquering part of the world, robs her of it. This jealousy first involves the father–daughter relationship; sometimes the mother uses the child to keep her husband home: if this fails, she is vexed, but if her manoeuvre succeeds, she is sure to revive her infantile complex in an inverted form: she becomes irritated by her daughter as she was once by her own mother; she sulks, she feels abandoned and misunderstood. A French woman, married to a foreigner who loved his daughters very much, angrily said one day: 'I've had enough of living with these "wogs"!' Often the eldest daughter, the father's favourite, is the target of the mother's persecution. The mother heaps the worst chores on her, demands a seriousness beyond her age: since she is a rival, she will be treated as an adult; she too will learn that 'life is not a storybook romance, everything is not rosy, you can't do whatever you please, you're not on earth to have fun.' Very often, the mother strikes the child for no reason, simply 'to teach her a lesson'; she wants to show her she is still in charge: for what vexes her the most is that she does not have any real superiority to set against a girl of eleven or twelve; the latter can already perform household tasks perfectly well, she is 'a little woman'; she even has a liveliness, curiosity and lucidity that, in many regards, makes her

superior to adult women. The mother likes to rule over her feminine
universe without competition; she wants to be unique, irreplaceable; and
yet here her young assistant reduces her to the pure generality of her
function. She scolds her daughter sternly if, after being away for two
days, she finds her household in disorder; but she goes into fits of anger
if it so happens that family life continued along well without her. She
cannot accept that her daughter will really become her double, a substitute of herself. Yet it is still more intolerable that she should boldly assert
herself as an other. She systematically detests the girlfriends in whom
her daughter seeks succour against family oppression, friends who 'spur
her on'; she criticises them, prevents her daughter from seeing them too
often or even uses the pretext of their 'bad influence' to radically forbid
her to be with them. All influence that is not her own is bad; she has
a particular animosity towards women of her own age – teachers,
girlfriends' mothers – towards whom her daughter turns her affection:
she declares these sentiments absurd or unhealthy. At times, gaiety, silliness or children's games and laughter are enough to exasperate her; she
more readily accepts this of boys; they are exercising their male privilege, as is natural, and she has long given up this impossible competition. But why should this other woman enjoy advantages that she has
been refused? Imprisoned in the snares of seriousness, she envies all
occupations and amusements that wrench her daughter from the
boredom of the household; this escape makes a sham of all the values
to which she has sacrificed herself. The older the child gets, the more
this bitterness eats at the mother's heart; every year brings the mother
closer to her decline; from year to year the youthful body develops and
flourishes; this future opening up to her daughter seems to be stolen
from the mother; this is why some mothers become irritated when their
daughters first get their period: they begrudge their consecration from
now on as newly-become women. This new woman is offered still-indef-
inite possibilities in contrast to the repetition and routine that are the
lot of the older woman: these chances are what the mother envies and
detests; not able to take them herself, she tries to diminish or suppress
them: she keeps her daughter home, watches over her, tyrannises her,
dresses her like a frump on purpose, refuses her all pastimes, goes into
rages if the adolescent puts on makeup, if she 'goes out'; she turns all
her own rage towards life against this young life who is embarking on
a new future; she tries to humiliate the girl, she ridicules her ventures,
she bullies her. Open war is often declared between them, and it is usually
the younger woman who wins as time is on her side; but victory has a

guilty taste: her mother's attitude gives rise to both revolt and remorse; her mother's presence alone makes her the guilty one: we have seen how this sentiment can seriously affect her future. Willy-nilly, the mother accepts her defeat in the end; when her daughter becomes an adult, they reestablish a more or less distressed friendship. But one of them will forever be disappointed and frustrated; the other will often be haunted by a curse.

We will return later to the older woman's relations with her adult children: but it is clear that for their first twenty years they occupy a most important place in the mother's life. A dangerous misconception about two currently accepted preconceived ideas strongly emerges from the descriptions we have made. The first is that motherhood is enough in all cases to fulfil a woman: this is not at all true. Many are the mothers who are unhappy, bitter and unsatisfied. The example of Sophia Tolstoy, who gave birth more than twelve times, is significant; she never stops repeating, all through her diary, that everything seems useless and empty in the world and in herself. Children bring a kind of masochistic peace for her. 'With the children, I do not feel young anymore. I am calm and happy.' Renouncing her youth, her beauty and her personal life brings her some calm; she feels old, justified. 'The feeling of being indispensable to them is my greatest happiness.' They are weapons enabling her to reject her husband's superiority. 'My only resources, my only weapons to establish equality between us, are the children, energy, joy, health . . .' But they are absolutely not enough to give meaning to an existence worn down by boredom. On 25 January 1875, after a moment of exaltation, she writes:

> I too want and can do everything.* But as soon as this feeling goes away, I realise that I don't want and can't do anything, except care for my babies, eat, drink, sleep, love my husband and my children, which should really be happiness but which makes me sad and like yesterday makes me want to cry.

And eleven years later:

> I devote myself energetically to my children's upbringing and education and have an ardent desire to do it well. But my God! How impatient and irascible I am, how I yell! . . . This eternal fighting with the children is so sad.

* S. Tolstoy's emphasis.

The mother's relation with her children is defined within the overall context of her life; it depends on her relations with her husband, her past, her occupations, herself; it is a fatal and absurd error to claim to see a child as a panacea. This is also Helene Deutsch's conclusion in the work I have often cited, where she studies phenomena of motherhood on the basis of her experience in psychiatry. She ranks this function highly; she believes woman accomplishes herself totally through it: but under the condition that it is freely assumed and sincerely desired; the young woman must be in a psychological, moral and material situation that allows her to bear the responsibility; if not, the consequences will be disastrous. In particular, it is criminal to advise having a child as a remedy for melancholia or neuroses; it causes unhappiness for mother and child. Only a balanced, healthy woman, conscious of her responsibilities, is capable of becoming a 'good mother'.

I have said that the curse weighing on marriage is that individuals too often join together in their weakness and not in their strength, that each one asks of the other rather than finding pleasure in giving. It is an even more deceptive lure to dream of attaining through a child a plenitude, warmth and value one is incapable of creating oneself; it can bring joy only to the woman capable of disinterestedly wanting the happiness of another, to the woman who seeks to transcend her own existence without any reward for her. To be sure, a child is an undertaking one can validly aspire to; but like any other undertaking, it does not represent a justification in itself; and it must be desired for itself, not for hypothetical benefits. Stekel quite rightly says:

> Children are not substitutes for one's disappointed love; they are not substitutes for one's thwarted ideal in life, children are not mere material to fill out an empty existence. Children are a responsibility and an opportunity. Children are the loftiest blossoms upon the tree of untrammeled love . . . They are neither playthings, nor tools for the fulfillment of parental needs or ungratified ambitions. Children are obligations; they should be brought up so as to become happy human beings.

Such an obligation is not at all *natural*: nature could never dictate a moral choice; this implies an engagement. To have a child is to take on a commitment; if the mother shrinks from it, she commits an offence against human existence, against a freedom; but no one can impose it on her. The relation of parents to children, like that of spouses, must be freely chosen. And it is not even true that the child is a privileged accomplishment for a woman; it is often said that a woman is coquettish, or amorous, or lesbian, or ambitious as a result of 'being childless'; her sexual life, her goals and the values she pursues are deemed to be substitutes for the child. In fact, from the beginning there is indetermination: one can just as well say that lacking love, an occupation, or the power to satisfy her homosexual tendencies, a woman wants to have a child. A social and artificial morality hides behind this pseudo-naturalism. That the child is the ultimate end for woman is an affirmation worthy of an advertising slogan.

The second preconceived idea immediately following the first is that the child is sure to find happiness in his mother's arms. There is no such thing as an 'unnatural mother', since maternal love has nothing natural about it: but precisely because of that, there are bad mothers. And one of the great truths that psychoanalysis has proclaimed is the danger 'normal' parents constitute for a child. The complexes, obsessions and neuroses adults suffer from have their roots in their family past; parents who have their own conflicts, quarrels and dramas are the least desirable company for children. Deeply marked by the paternal household, they approach their own children through complexes and frustrations: and this chain of misery perpetuates itself indefinitely. In particular, maternal sadomasochism creates guilt feelings for the daughter that will express themselves in sadomasochistic behaviour towards her own children, without end. There is extravagant bad faith in the conflation of contempt for women and respect shown for mothers. It is a criminal paradox to deny women all public activity, to close masculine careers to them, to proclaim them incapable in all domains, and to nonetheless entrust to them the most delicate and most serious of all undertakings: the formation of a human being. There are many women who, out of custom and tradition, are still refused education, culture, responsibilities and activities that are the privileges of men, and in whose arms, nevertheless, babies are placed without scruple, as in earlier life they were consoled for their inferiority to boys with dolls; they are deprived of living their lives; as compensation, they are allowed to play with flesh-and-blood toys. A woman would have to be perfectly happy or a saint to resist the temptation of abusing her rights. Montesquieu was perhaps right when he said it would be better to entrust women with the government of the state than with a family; for as soon as she is given the opportunity, woman is as reasonable and efficient as man: it is in abstract thought, in concerted action that she most easily rises above her sex; it is far more difficult in this day and age to free herself from her feminine past, to find an emotional balance that nothing in her situation favours. Man is also much more balanced and rational in his work than at home; he calculates with mathematical precision: he 'lets himself go' with his wife, becoming illogical, a liar, capricious; likewise, she 'lets herself go' with her child. And this self-indulgence is more dangerous because she can better defend herself against her husband than the child can defend himself against her. It would obviously be better for the child if his mother were a complete person and not a mutilated one, a woman who finds in her work and her relations with the group a self-accomplishment she could not attain through his tyranny; and it would be preferable also for the child to be left infinitely less to his parents than he is now, that his studies and amusements take place with other children under the control of adults whose links with him are only impersonal and dispassionate.

Even in cases where the child is a treasure within a happy or at least balanced life, he cannot be the full extent of his mother's horizons. He does not wrest her from her immanence; she shapes his flesh, she supports him, she cares for him: she can do no more than create a situation that solely the child's freedom can transcend; when she invests in his future, it is again by proxy that she transcends herself through the universe and time; that is, once again she dooms herself to dependency. Not only his ingratitude but the failure of her son will refute all of her hopes: as in marriage or love, she puts the care of justifying her life in the hands of another, whereas the only authentic behaviour is to assume it freely herself. Woman's inferiority, as we have seen, originally came from the fact that she was restricted to repeating life, while man invented reasons for living, in his eyes more essential than the pure facticity of existence; confining woman to motherhood is the perpetuation of this situation. But today she demands participation in the movement by which humanity ceaselessly tries to find justification by surpassing itself; she can only consent to give life if life has meaning; she cannot try to be a mother without playing a role in economic, political or social life. It is not the same thing to produce cannon fodder, slaves, victims, as to give birth to free men. In a properly organised society where the child would in great part be taken charge of by the group, where the mother would be cared for and helped, motherhood would absolutely not be incompatible with women's work. On the contrary, a woman who works – farmer, chemist or writer – has the easiest pregnancy because she is not centred on her own person; it is the woman who has the richest personal life who will give the most to her child and who will ask for the least, she who acquires real human values through effort and struggle will be the most fit to bring up children. If too often today a woman has a hard time reconciling the interests of her children with a profession that demands long hours away from home and all her strength, it is because, on the one hand, woman's work is still too often a kind of slavery; on the other hand, no effort has been made to assure children's health, care and education outside the home. This is social neglect: but it is a sophism to justify it by pretending that a law was written in heaven or in the bowels of the earth that requires that the mother and child belong to each other exclusively; this mutual belonging in reality only constitutes a double and harmful oppression.

It is a mystification to maintain that woman becomes man's equal through motherhood. Psychoanalysts have tried hard to prove that the child provides the equivalent of the penis for her: but enviable as this attribute may be, no one believes that possessing one can justify an existence or that such possession can be a supreme end in itself. There has been an enormous amount of talk about the sacred rights of women, but being a mother is not how women gained the right to vote; the unwed mother is still scorned; it is only in marriage that the mother is glorified – in other words, as long as she is subordinate to the husband. As long as he is the economic head of the family, even though it is she who cares for the children, they depend far more on him than on her. This is why, as has been seen, the mother's relationship with her children is deeply influenced by the one she maintains with her husband.

So conjugal relations, homemaking and motherhood form a whole in which all the parts are determinant; tenderly united to her husband, the wife can cheerfully carry out the duties of the home; happy with her children, she will be understanding of her husband. But this harmony is not easy to attain, for the different functions assigned to the wife conflict with each other. Women's magazines amply advise the housewife on the art of maintaining her sexual attraction while doing the dishes, of remaining elegant throughout pregnancy, of reconciling flirtation, motherhood and economy; but if she conscientiously follows their advice, she will soon be overwhelmed and disfigured by care; it is very difficult to remain desirable with chapped hands and a body deformed by pregnancies; this is why a woman in love often feels resentment of the children who ruin her seduction and deprive her of her husband's caresses; if she is, by contrast, deeply maternal, she is jealous of the man who also claims the children as his. But then, the perfect homemaker, as has been seen, contradicts the movement of life: the child is the enemy of waxed floors. Maternal love is often lost in the reprimands and outbursts that underlie the concern for a well-kept home. It is not surprising that the woman torn between these contradictions often spends her day in a state of nervousness and bitterness; she always loses on some level, and her gains are precarious, they do not count as any sure success. She can never save herself by her work alone; it keeps her occupied, but does not constitute her justification: her justification rests on outside freedoms. The wife shut up in her home cannot establish her existence on her own; she does not have the means to affirm herself in her singularity: and this singularity is consequently not acknowledged. For Arabs or Indians, and in many rural populations, a wife is only a female servant appreciated according to the work she provides, and who is replaced without regret if she disappears. In modern civilisation, she is more or less individualised in her husband's eyes; but unless she completely renounces her self, swallowed up like Natasha in a passionate and tyrannical devotion to her family, she suffers from being reduced to pure generality. She is *the* mistress of the house, the wife, the unique and indistinct mother; Natasha delights in this supreme self-effacement, and in rejecting all confrontation, she negates others. But the modern Western woman, by contrast, wants to be noticed by others as *this* mistress of the house, *this* wife, *this* mother, *this* woman. Herein lies the satisfaction she will seek in her social life.

CHAPTER 7

Social Life

The family is not a closed community: notwithstanding its separateness, it establishes relations with other social units; the home is not only an 'interior' in which the couple is confined; it is also the expression of its living standard, its wealth, its tastes: it must be exhibited for others to see. It is essentially the woman who will organise this social life. The man is connected to the community as producer and citizen, by ties of an organic solidarity based on the division of labour; the couple is a social person, defined by the family, class, milieu and race to which it belongs, attached by ties of mechanical solidarity to groups socially similar to themselves; the woman is the one most likely to embody this most purely: the husband's professional relations often do not reflect his social level, while the wife, who does not have the obligations brought about by work, can limit herself to the company of her peers; besides, she has the leisure, through her 'visits' and 'receptions', to promote these relations, useless in practice, and that, of course, matter only in categories of people wanting to hold their rank in the social hierarchy, that is, who consider themselves superior to certain others. She delights in showing off her home and even herself, which her husband and children do not see because they have a vested interest in them. Her social duty, which is to 'represent', will become part of the pleasure she has in showing herself to others.

First, she has to represent herself; at home, going about her occupations, she merely dresses: to go out, to entertain, she 'dresses up'. Dressing has a twofold significance: it is meant to show the woman's social standing (her standard of living, her wealth, the social class she belongs to) but at the same time it concretises feminine narcissism; it is her uniform and her attire; the woman who suffers from not *doing* anything thinks she is expressing her *being* through her dress. Beauty treatments and dressing are kinds of work that allow her to appropriate her person as she appropriates her home through housework; she thus believes that she is choosing and re-creating her own self. And social customs encourage her to alienate herself in her image. Like his body, a man's clothes must convey his transcendence and not attract attention;* for him neither elegance nor beauty constitutes him as object; thus he does not usually consider his appearance as a reflection of his being. By contrast, society even requires woman to make herself an erotic object. The goal of the fashion to which she is in thrall is not to reveal her as an autonomous individual but, on the contrary, to cut her from her transcendence so as to offer her as a prey to male desires: fashion does not serve to fulfil her projects but on the contrary to thwart them. A skirt is less convenient than trousers and high-heeled shoes impede walking; the least practical dresses and high heels, the most fragile hats and stockings, are the most elegant; whether the outfit disguises, deforms or moulds the body, in any case, it delivers it to view. This explains why dressing is an enchanting game for the little girl who wants to look at herself; later on her child's autonomy rises up against the constraints of light-coloured muslin and patent-leather shoes; at the awkward age she is torn between the desire and the refusal to show herself off; once she has accepted her vocation as sex object, she enjoys adorning herself.

As we have said,† by adorning herself, woman is akin to nature, while attesting to nature's need for artifice; she becomes flower and jewel for man and for herself as well. Before giving him rippling water or the soft warmth of furs, she takes them for herself. More intimately than her knick-knacks, rugs, cushions and bouquets, she prizes feathers, pearls, brocade and silks that she mingles with her flesh; their shimmer and their gentle contact compensate for the harshness of the erotic universe that is her lot: the more her sensuality is unsatiated, the more importance she gives to it. If many lesbians dress in a masculine way, it is not only out of imitation of males and defiance of society: they do not need the caresses of velvet and satin because they grasp such passive qualities‡ on a feminine body. The woman given to the harsh masculine embrace – even if she savours it and even more if she gets no pleasure from it – can embrace no carnal prey other than her own body: she

* See Vol. I. Homosexuals are an exception as they specifically grasp themselves as sexual objects; dandies also, who must be studied separately. Today, in particular, the 'zoot-suitism' of the American blacks who dress in light-coloured, noticeable suits is explained with very complex reasons.
† See Vol. I, Part Three, 'Myths', Chapter 1.
‡ Sandor, whose case Krafft-Ebing detailed, adored well-dressed women but did not 'dress up'.

perfumes it to change it into a flower, and the shine of the diamonds she puts around her neck is no different from that of her skin; in order to possess them, she identifies with all the riches of the world. She covets not only sensual treasures but sometimes also sentimental values and ideals. This jewel is a souvenir, that one is a symbol. Some women make themselves bouquets, aviaries; others are museums and still others hieroglyphs. Georgette Leblanc tells us in her memoirs, evoking her youth:

> I was always dressed like a painting. I walked around in Van Eyck, in an allegory of Rubens or in the Virgin of Memling. I still see myself crossing a street in Brussels one winter day in a dress of amethyst velvet embellished with old silver binding taken from some tunic. Dragging insouciantly my long train behind me, I was conscientiously sweeping the pavement. My folly of yellow fur framed my blond hair but the most unusual thing was the diamond placed on the frontlet on my forehead. Why all this? Simply because it pleased me and so I thought I was living outside of all convention. The more I was laughed at as I went by, the more extravagant my burlesque inventions. I would have been ashamed to change anything in my appearance just because I was being mocked. That would have seemed to me to be a degrading capitulation . . . At home it was something else again. The angels of Gozzoli, Fra Angelico, Burne Jones and Watts were my models. I was always attired in azure and aurora; my flowing dresses spread out in manifold trains around me.

The best examples of this magical appropriation of the universe are found in mental institutions. A woman who does not control her love for precious objects and symbols forgets her own appearance and risks dressing outlandishly. The very little girl thus sees in dressing a disguise that changes her into a fairy, a queen, a flower; she thinks she is beautiful as soon as she is laden with garlands and ribbons because she identifies with these flashy clothes; charmed by the colour of a piece of material, the naive young girl does not notice the wan complexion it gives her; one also finds this excessive bad taste in women artists or intellectuals more fascinated by the outside world than conscious of their own appearance: infatuated by these old materials and antique jewels, they delight in conjuring up China or the Middle Ages and give the mirror no more than a cursory or passing glance. It is sometimes surprising to see the strange getups elderly women like: tiaras, lace, bright dresses, and extravagant necklaces unfortunately draw attention to their ravaged features. Now that they have given up seduction, clothes often become once again a gratuitous game for them as in their childhood. An elegant woman by contrast can seek sensual or aesthetic pleasures in her clothes if need be, but she must reconcile them in harmony with her image: the colour of her dress will flatter her complexion, the cut will emphasise or improve her figure; arrayed, she complaisantly cherishes her adorned self and not the objects that adorn her.

Dressing is not only adornment: it expresses, as we have said, woman's social situation. Only the prostitute whose function is exclusively that of a sex object displays herself exclusively in this light; in the past it was her saffron hair and the flowers that dotted her dress; today it is her high heels, skimpy satin, harsh makeup and heavy perfume that are the signature of her profession. Any other woman is criticised for dressing 'like a strumpet'. Her erotic qualities are integrated into social life and can only appear in this toned-down form. But it must be emphasised that decency does not mean dressing with strict modesty. A woman who teases male desire too blatantly is considered vulgar; but a woman who is seen to repudiate this is disreputable as well: she is seen as wanting to look like a man: she's a lesbian; or to single herself out: she's an eccentric; refusing her role as object, she defies society: she's an anarchist. If she simply does not want to be noticed, she must still conserve her femininity. Custom dictates the compromise between exhibitionism and modesty; sometimes it is the neckline and sometimes the ankle that the 'virtuous woman' must hide; sometimes the young girl has the right to highlight her charms so as to attract suitors, while the married woman gives up all adornment: such is the usage in many peasant civilisations; sometimes young girls have to dress in flowing clothes of baby colours and modest cut, while their elders are allowed tight-fitting dresses, heavy material, rich hues and daring cuts; on a sixteen-year-old, black stands out because the rule at that age is not to wear it.* One must, of course, conform to these laws; but in any case, and even in the most austere circles, woman's sexual attributes will be emphasised: the pastor's wife curls her hair, wears some makeup, is discreetly fashion-conscious, indicating through the attention to her physical charm that she accepts her female role. This integration of eroticism into social life is particularly obvious

* In a film set last century – and rather a stupid one – Bette Davis created a scandal by wearing a red dress to the ball whereas white was de rigueur until marriage. Her act was considered a rebellion against the established order.

in the 'evening gown'. To mark a social gathering, that is, luxury and waste, these dresses must be costly and delicate, they must be as uncomfortable as possible; skirts are long and so wide or so complicated that they impede walking; under the jewels, ruffles, sequins, flowers, feathers and false hair, woman is changed into a flesh-doll; even this flesh is exposed; just as flowers bloom gratuitously, the woman displays her shoulders, back, bosom; except in orgies, the man must not indicate that he covets her: he only has the right to looks and the embraces of the dance; but he can take delight in being the king of a world of such tender treasures. From one man to another, the festivity takes on the appearance of a potlatch; each of them gives the vision of this body that is his property to all the others as a gift. In her evening dress, the woman is disguised as woman for all the males' pleasure and the pride of her owner.

This social significance of the toilette allows woman to express her attitude to society by the way she dresses; subject to the established order, she confers on herself a discreet and tasteful personality; many nuances are possible: she will make herself fragile, childlike, mysterious, candid, austere, gay, poised, a little daring, self-effacing, as she chooses. Or, on the contrary, she will affirm her rejection of conventions by her originality. It is striking that in many novels the 'liberated' woman distinguishes herself by an audacity in dressing that emphasises her character as sex object, and thus of dependence: so in Edith Wharton's *The Age of Innocence*, the young divorced woman with an adventuresome past and a bold heart is first presented with a plunging décolletage; the whiff of scandal she provokes becomes the tangible reflection of her scorn for conformity. Thus the girl will enjoy dressing as a woman, the older woman as a little girl, the courtesan as a sophisticated woman of the world and the woman of the world as a vamp. Even if every woman dresses according to her status, there is still play in it. Artifice like art is situated in the imagination. Not only do girdle, bra, hair dyes and makeup disguise body and face; but as soon as she is 'dressed up', the least sophisticated woman is not concerned with perception: she is like a painting, a statue, like an actor on stage, an analogon through which is suggested an absent subject who is her character but is not she. It is this confusion with an unreal object – necessary, perfect like a hero in a novel, like a portrait or a bust – that flatters her; she strives to alienate herself in it and so to appear frozen, justified to herself.

Page by page we see Marie Bashkirtseff in *Intimate Writings*[82] endlessly remaking her image. She does not spare us any of her dresses:

for each new outfit, she believes she is an other and she adores herself anew.

> I took one of Mama's great shawls, I made a slit for my head and I sewed up the two sides. This shawl that falls in classic folds gives me an oriental, biblical, strange look.
>
> I go to the Laferrières' and in just three hours Caroline makes me a dress in which I look as if I'm enveloped in a cloud. This is a piece of English crepe that she drapes over me, making me thin, elegant, and long.
>
> Enveloped in a warm wool dress hanging in harmonious folds, a character out of Lefebvre who knows so well how to draw these lithe and young bodies in modest fabrics.

This refrain is repeated day after day: 'I was charming in black ... In grey, I was charming ... I was in white, charming.'

Mme de Noailles, who also accorded much importance to her dress, speaks sadly in her *Memoirs* of the crisis of a failed dress:

> I loved the vividness of the colours, their daring contrast, a dress seemed like a landscape, the beginning of adventure. Just as I was putting on the dress made by unsure hands, I suffered from all the defects I saw.

If the toilette has so much importance for many women, it is because they are under the illusion that it provides them both with the world and their own self. A German novel, *The Artificial Silk Girl*,* tells the story of a poor girl's passion for a vair coat; sensually she loved the caressing warmth of it, the furry tenderness; in precious skins it is her transfigured self she cherishes; she finally possesses the beauty of the world she had never embraced and the radiant destiny that had never been hers.

> And then I saw a coat hanging from a hook, a fur so soft, so smooth, so tender, so grey, so shy: I felt like kissing it I loved it so much. It looked like consolation and All Saints' Day and total safety, like the sky. It was genuine vair. Silently, I took off my raincoat and put on the vair. This fur was like a diamond on my skin that loved it and

---

* By Irmgard Keun.

what one loves, one doesn't give it back once one has it. Inside, a Moroccan crepe lining, pure silk, with hand embroidery. The coat enveloped me and spoke more than I to Hubert's heart . . . I am so elegant in this fur. It is like the rare man who would make me precious through his love for me. This coat wants me and I want it: we have each other.

As woman is an object, it is obvious that how she is adorned and dressed affects her intrinsic value. It is not pure frivolousness for her to attach so much importance to silk stockings, gloves and a hat: keeping her rank is an imperious obligation. In America, a great part of the working woman's budget is devoted to beauty care and clothes; in France, this expense is lighter; nevertheless, a woman is all the more respected if she 'presents well'; the more she needs to find work, the more useful it is to look well-off: elegance is a weapon, a sign, a banner of respect, a letter of recommendation.

It is a servitude; the values it confers have a price; they sometimes have such a high price that a detective catches a socialite or an actress shoplifting perfumes, silk stockings or underwear. Many women prostitute themselves or 'get help' in order to keep themselves well dressed; it is their clothes that determine their need for money. Being well dressed also requires time and care; it is a chore that is sometimes a source of positive joy: in this area there is also the 'discovery of hidden treasures', trades, ruses, arrangements and invention; a clever woman can even be creative. Showroom days – especially the sales – are frenetic adventures. A new dress is a celebration in itself. Makeup and hair are substitutes for a work of art. Today, more than before,* woman knows the joys of shaping her body by sports, gymnastics, swimming, massage and diets; she decides on her weight, her figure and her complexion; modern beauty treatments allow her to combine beauty and activity: she has the right to toned muscles, she refuses to put on weight; in physical culture, she affirms herself as subject; this gives her a kind of liberation from her contingent flesh; but this liberation easily lapses back into dependence. The Hollywood star triumphs over nature: but she finds herself a passive object in the producer's hands.

Next to these victories in which woman rightly takes delight, taking

---

* According to recent studies, however, it seems that women's gymnasiums in France are almost empty; it was especially between 1920 and 1940 that French women indulged in physical culture. Household problems weigh too heavy on them at this time.

care of one's appearance implies – like household tasks – a fight against time, because her body too is an object eroded by time. Colette Audry describes this fight, comparable to the one the housewife engages against dust.*

> Already it was no longer the compact flesh of youth; along her arms and thighs the pattern of her muscles showed through a layer of fat and slightly flabby skin. Upset, she once again changed her schedule: her day would begin with half an hour of gymnastics and in the evening, before getting into bed, a quarter of an hour of massage. She took to reading medical books and fashion magazines, to watching her waistline. She prepared fruit juices, took a laxative from time to time and did the dishes with rubber gloves. Her two concerns – rejuvenating her body and refurbishing her home – finally became one so that one day she would reach a kind of steadiness, a kind of dead centre . . . the world would be as if stopped, suspended outside of ageing and decay . . . At the swimming pool, she now took serious lessons to improve her style and the beauty magazines kept her breathless with infinitely renewed recipes. Ginger Rogers confides to us: 'I brush my hair 100 strokes every morning, it takes exactly two and a half minutes and I have silky hair . . .' How to get thinner ankles: stand on your toes every day, thirty times in a row, without putting your heels down, this exercise only takes a minute; what is a minute in a day? Another time it is an oil bath for nails, lemon paste for hands, crushed strawberries on cheeks.

Routine, here again, turns beauty care and wardrobe maintenance into chores. The horror of degradation that all living change involves in some cold or frustrated women arouses a horror of life itself: they seek to preserve themselves as others preserve furniture or jam; this negative stubbornness makes them enemies of their own existence and hostile to others: good meals damage their figures, wine spoils their complexions, smiling too much gives you wrinkles, the sun hurts the skin, rest makes you lethargic, work wears you out, love gives you circles under your eyes, kisses make your cheeks red, caresses deform your breasts, embraces shrivel the flesh, pregnancies disfigure your face and body; you know how young mothers angrily push away the child marvelling at

---

* *Playing a Losing Game.*

their ball gown. 'Don't touch me, your hands are all sticky, you're going to get me dirty'; the appearance-conscious rejects her husband's or lover's ardour with the same rebuffs. Just as one covers furniture with loose covers, she would like to withdraw from men, the world, time. But none of these precautions prevents the appearance of grey hair and crow's-feet. Starting from youth, woman knows this destiny is inevitable. And, regardless of her vigilance, she is a victim of accidents: a drop of wine falls on her dress, a cigarette burns it; and so the creature of luxury and parties who smilingly struts about the living room disappears: she turns into the serious and hard housewife; suddenly one discovers that her toilette was not a bouquet of flowers, fireworks, a gratuitous and perishable splendour destined to generously light up an instant: it is an asset, capital, an investment, it demands sacrifices; its loss is an irreparable disaster. Stains, holes, dresses that are failures and ruined perms are far more serious catastrophes than a burnt roast or a broken vase: because the coquettish woman is not only alienated in things, she wants to be a thing and without an intermediary she feels insecure in the world. The relations she maintains with her dressmaker and milliner, her impatience, her demands are manifestations of her seriousness and insecurity. A successful dress creates in her the character of her dreams; but in a soiled, ruined outfit, she feels demeaned.

Marie Bashkirtseff writes: 'My mood, my manners, the expression on my face, everything depended on my dress.' And then: 'Either you have to go around naked, or you have to dress according to your body, taste and character. When they are not right, I feel gauche, common and therefore humiliated. What happens to the mood and mind? They think about clothes and so one becomes stupid, boring and one does not know what to do with oneself.'

Many women prefer to miss a party than go badly dressed, even if they are not going to be noticed.

However, although some women affirm: 'I dress for myself only,' we have seen that even in narcissism the gaze of the other is involved. Only in asylums do the fashion-conscious stubbornly keep their faith in absent gazes; normally, they demand witnesses. After ten years of marriage, Sophia Tolstoy writes:

> I want people to admire me and say how pretty I am, and I want
> Lyova to see and hear them too . . . I hate people who tell me I am
> beautiful. I never believed them . . . what would be the point of it?
> My darling little Petya loves his old nanny just as much as he would

love a great beauty . . . I am having my hair curled today, and have been happily imagining how nice it will look, even though nobody will see me and it is quite unnecessary. I adore ribbons, and I would like a new leather belt – and now I have written this I feel like crying . . .[83]

Husbands do not perform this role well. Here again the husband's demands are duplicitous. If his wife is too attractive, he becomes jealous; but every husband is more or less King Candaules; he wants his wife to make him proud; for her to be elegant, pretty or at least 'presentable'; if not, he will humorously tell her these words of Pére Ubu: 'You are quite ugly today! Is it because we are expecting company?' In marriage, as we have seen, erotic and social values are not very compatible; such antagonism is reflected in this situation. The wife who accentuates her sexual attraction is considered vulgar in her husband's eyes; he criticises this boldness that would seduce him in an unknown woman and this criticism kills all desire for her; if his wife dresses decently, he approves but coldly: he does not find her attractive and vaguely reproaches her for it. Because of that, he rarely looks at her on his own account: he inspects her through the eyes of others. 'What will they say about her?' He does not see clearly because he projects his spousal point of view onto others. Nothing is more irritating for a woman than to see him appreciate in another the dresses or way of dressing he criticises in her. Naturally, of course, he is too close to her to see her; her face is immutable for him; nor does he notice her outfits or hairstyle. Even a husband in love or an infatuated lover is often indifferent to a woman's clothes. If they love her ardently in her nudity, the most attractive adornments merely disguise her; and they will cherish her whether badly dressed, tired or dazzling. If they no longer love her, the most flattering dresses will be of no avail. Clothes can be an instrument of conquest but not a weapon of defence; their art is to create mirages, they offer the viewer an imaginary object: in the erotic embrace and in daily relations mirages fade; conjugal feelings like physical love exist in the realm of reality. Women do not dress for the loved man. Dorothy Parker, in one of her short stories,*[84] describes a young woman who, waiting impatiently for her husband, who is on leave, decides to make herself beautiful to welcome him:

* 'The Lovely Eva'.

She bought a new dress; black – he liked black dresses – simple –
he liked plain dresses – and so expensive that she would not think
of its price . . .

'Do you . . . like my dress?'

'Oh yes,' he said. 'I always liked that dress on you.'

It was as if she turned to wood. 'This dress,' she said, enun-
ciating with insulting distinctness, 'is brand new. I have never had
it on before in my life. In case you are interested, I bought it especially for this occasion.'

'I'm sorry, honey,' he said. 'Oh, sure, now I see it's not the other
one at all. I think it's great. I like you in black.'

'At moments like this,' she said, 'I almost wish I were in it for
another reason.'

It is often said that women dress to arouse jealousy in other women:
this jealousy is really a clear sign of success; but this is not its only aim.
Through envious or admiring approbation, woman seeks an absolute
affirmation of her beauty, her elegance, her taste: of herself. She dresses
to display herself; she displays herself to make herself be. She thus submits
herself to a painful dependence; the housewife's devotion is useful even
if it is not recognised; the effort of the fashion-conscious woman is in
vain unless consciousness is involved. She is looking for a definitive valorisation of herself; it is this attempt at the absolute that makes her quest
so exhausting; criticised by only one voice – this hat *is* not beautiful –
she is flattered by a compliment but a contradiction demolishes her; and
as the absolute only manifests itself in an indefinite series of appearances, she will never have entirely won; this is why the fashion-conscious
woman is sensitive; it is also why some pretty and much-admired women
can be sadly convinced they are neither beautiful nor elegant, that this
supreme approbation of an unknown judge is exactly what is missing:
they are aiming for an in-itself that is unrealisable. Rare are the gorgeous
stylish women who embody in themselves the laws of elegance, whom
no one can fault because they are the ones who define success or failure;
as long as their reign endures, they can think of themselves as an exemplary success. What is unfortunate is that this success serves nothing and
no one.

Clothes immediately imply going out and receptions, and besides,
that is their original intent. The woman parades her new outfit from
place to place and invites other women to see her reign over her 'interior'. In certain particularly important situations, the husband accompanies

her on her 'calls'; but most often she fulfils her 'social obligations' while he is at work. The implacable ennui weighing on these gatherings has been described hundreds of times. It comes from the fact that these women gathered there by 'social obligations' have nothing to say to each other. There is no common interest linking the lawyer's wife to the doctor's – and none between Dr Dupont's and Dr Durand's. It is bad taste in a general conversation to talk of one's children's pranks or problems with the help. What is left is discussion of the weather, the latest novel, and a few general ideas borrowed from their husbands. This custom of 'calling' is tending to disappear; but the chore of the 'call' in various forms survives in France. American women often replace conversation with bridge, which is an advantage only for women who enjoy this game.

However, social life has more attractive forms than carrying out this idle duty of etiquette. Entertaining is not just welcoming others into one's own home; it is changing one's home into an enchanted domain; the social event is both festivity and potlatch. The mistress of the house displays her treasures: silver, table linen, crystal; she dresses the house with flowers: ephemeral and useless, flowers exemplify the gratuitousness of occasions that mean expenses and luxury; blooming in vases, doomed to a rapid death, flowers are ceremonial bonfires, incense and myrrh, libation, sacrifice. The table is laden with fine food, precious wines; it means satisfying the guests' needs, it is a question of inventing gracious gifts that anticipate their desires; the meal becomes a mysterious ceremony. Virginia Woolf emphasises this aspect in this passage from *Mrs Dalloway*:[85]

And so there began a soundless and exquisite passing to and fro through swing doors of aproned, white-capped maids, handmaidens not of necessity but adepts in a mystery or grand deception practised by hostesses in Mayfair from one-thirty to two, when, with a wave of the hand, the traffic ceases, and there rises instead this profound illusion in the first place about the food – how it is not paid for; and then that the table spreads itself voluntarily with glass and silver, little mats, saucers of red fruit; films of brown cream mask turbot; in casseroles severed chickens swim; coloured, un-domestic, the fire burns; and with the wine and the coffee (not paid for) rise jocund visions before musing eyes; gently speculative eyes; eyes to whom life appears musical, mysterious.

The woman who presides over these mysteries is proud to feel she is the creator of a perfect moment, the dispenser of happiness and gaiety. She is the one bringing the guests together, she is the one making the event take place, she is the gratuitous source of joy and harmony.

This is exactly what Mrs Dalloway feels:

> But suppose Peter said to her, 'Yes, yes, but your parties – what's the sense of your parties?' all she could say was (and nobody could be expected to understand): They're an offering; . . . Here was So-and-so in South Kensington; someone up in Bayswater; and somebody else, say, in Mayfair. And she felt quite continuously a sense of their existence; and she felt what a waste; and she felt what a pity; and she felt if only they could be brought together; so she did it. And it was an offering; to combine, to create; but to whom? . . . An offering for the sake of offering, perhaps. Anyhow, it was her gift. Nothing else had she of the slightest importance . . . anybody could do it; yet this anybody she did a little admire, couldn't help feeling that she had, anyhow, made this happen.

If there is pure generosity in this homage to others, the party is really a party. But social routine quickly changes the potlatch into an institution, the gift into an obligation and the party hardens into a rite. All the while savouring the 'dinner out', the invited woman ponders having to return the invitation: she sometimes complains of having been entertained too well. 'The Xs . . . wanted to impress us,' she says bitterly to her husband. I have been told that during the last war in a little Portuguese city, tea parties had become the most costly of potlatches: at each gathering the mistress of the house had to serve more varied cakes and in greater number than the previous one; this burden became so heavy that one day all the women decided together not to serve anything anymore with the tea. The party loses its generous and magnificent character in such circumstances; it is one more chore; the accessories that make up a party are only a source of worry: you have to check the crystal and the tablecloth, measure the champagne and petits fours; a broken cup, the silk upholstering of a burned armchair are a disaster; tomorrow you have to clean, put away, put in order: the woman dreads this extra work. She feels this multiple dependence that defines the housewife's destiny: she is dependent on the soufflé, the roast, the butcher, the cook, the extra help; she is dependent on the husband who frowns every time something goes wrong; she is dependent on the guests who judge the furniture and wine and who decide if the evening has been a success or not. Only generous or self-confident women will go through this ordeal with a light heart. A triumph can give them a heady satisfaction. But in this respect many resemble Mrs Dalloway, about whom Woolf tells us: Although she loved these triumphs . . . and their brilliance and the excitement they brought, she also felt the hollowness, the sham. The woman can only take pleasure in it if she does not attach too much importance to it; if she does she will be tormented by a perpetually unsatisfied vanity. Besides, few women are wealthy enough to find their life's occupation in 'socialising'. Those who devote themselves to it entirely usually try not only to make a cult of it but also to go beyond this social life towards other aims: genuine salons have a literary or political side. These women try to influence men and to play a personal role. They escape from the condition of the married woman. She is not usually fulfilled by the pleasures and ephemeral triumphs rarely bestowed on her and that often mean as much fatigue as distraction. Social life demands that woman 'represent', that she show off, but does not create between her and others real communication. It does not wrest her from her solitude.

'It is painful to think,' writes Michelet, 'that woman, the relative being who can only live in a couple, is more often alone than man. He finds social life everywhere, makes new contacts. As for her, she is nothing without her family. And the family weighs her down; all weight is on her.' And, in fact, the woman kept confined, isolated, does not have the joys of a comradeship that involves pursuing aims together; her work does not occupy her mind, her education did not give her either the taste or the habit of independence, and yet she spends her days in solitude; we have seen that this is one of the miseries Sophia Tolstoy complained of. Her marriage often took her away from her father's home and the friends of her youth. In My Apprenticeships, Colette[86] described the uprooting of a bride transported from her province to Paris; only the long correspondence she exchanged with her mother provided any relief; but letters are no substitute for presence and she cannot admit her disappointments to Sido. Often, there is no longer any real closeness between the young woman and her family: neither her mother nor her sisters are her friends. Nowadays, due to a housing crisis, many young couples live with their families or in-laws; but this enforced presence is far from ever providing real companionship for the young woman.

The feminine friendships she is able to keep or make are precious for a woman; they are very different from relations men have; men relate to each other as individuals through their ideas, their own personal projects;

women, confined within the generality of their destiny as women, are united by a kind of immanent complicity. And what they seek first of all from each other is the affirmation of their common universe. They do not discuss opinions: they exchange confidences and recipes; they join together to create a kind of counter-universe whose values outweigh male values; when they meet, they find the strength to shake off their chains; they negate male sexual domination by confiding their frigidity to each other and cynically deriding the appetites or the clumsiness of their males; they also contest with irony the moral and intellectual superiority of their husbands and men in general. They compare their experiences: pregnancies, deliveries, children's illnesses, their own illnesses and housework become the essential events of human history. Their work is not technical: in transmitting recipes for cooking or housework, they give them the dignity of a secret science founded in oral traditions. Sometimes they examine moral problems together. Letters to the editor in women's magazines are a good example of these exchanges; we can hardly imagine a Lonely Hearts column reserved for men; they meet in *the* world which is *their* world, whereas women must define, measure and explore their own space; mostly they share beauty tips cooking or knitting recipes, and they ask each other for advice; real anxieties can sometimes be perceived in women's tendency to talk and show off. The woman knows the male code is not hers, that man even expects she will not observe it since he pushes her to abortion, adultery, misdeeds, betrayal, and lies he officially condemns; she then asks other women to help her to define a sort of 'parallel law', a specifically feminine moral code. It is not only out of malevolence that women comment on and criticise the conduct of their girlfriends so much: to judge them and to lead their own lives, they need much more moral invention than men.

What makes these relationships valuable is their truthfulness. When confronting man, woman is always on stage; she lies when pretending to accept herself as the inessential other, she lies when she presents to him an imaginary personage through impersonations, clothes and catch-phrases; this act demands constant tension; every woman thinks more or less, 'I am not myself' around her husband or her lover; the male world is hard, there are sharp angles, voices are too loud, lights are too bright, contacts brusque. When with other women, the wife is backstage; she sharpens her weapons, she does not enter combat; she plans her clothes, devises makeup, prepares her ruses: she lies around in slippers and robe in the wings before going on stage; she likes this lukewarm, soft, relaxed atmosphere. Colette describes the moments she spends with her girlfriend Marco like this: 'Brief confidences, the amusements of two women shut away from the world, hours that were now like those in a sewing room, now like the idle ones of convalescence.'*[87]

She enjoys playing the adviser to the older woman:

As we sat under the balcony awning on those hot afternoons, Marco mended her underclothes. She sewed badly, but conscientiously, and I flattered my vanity by giving her pieces of advice, such as: 'You're using too coarse a thread for fine needles . . . You shouldn't put blue baby ribbon in chemises, pink is much prettier in lingerie and up against the skin.' It was not long before I gave her others, concerning her face powder, the colour of her lipstick, a hard line she pencilled around the edge of her beautifully shaped eyelids. 'D'you think so? D'you think so?' she would say. My youthful authority was adamant. I took the comb, I made a charming little gap in her tight, sponge-like fringe, I proved expert at softly shadowing her eyes and putting a faint pink glow high up on her cheekbones, near her temples.

A bit further on, she shows us Marco anxiously preparing to face a young man she wants to win over:

She was about to wipe her wet eyes but I stopped her.

'Let me do it, Marco.'

With my two thumbs, I raised her upper eyelids so that the two tears about to fall should be reabsorbed and not smudge the mascara on her lashes by wetting them.

'There! Wait, I haven't finished.'

I retouched all her features. Her mouth was trembling a little. She submitted patiently, sighing as if I were dressing a wound. To complete everything, I filled the puff in her handbag with a rosier shade of powder. Neither of us uttered a word meanwhile.

'Whatever happens,' I told her, 'don't cry. At all costs, don't let yourself give way to tears' . . .

She pressed her hand to her forehead, under her fringe.

'I *ought* to have bought that black dress last Saturday – the one I saw in the secondhand shop . . . Tell me, could you possibly lend me some very fine stockings? I've left it too late now to . . .'

* *The Kepi.*

'Yes, yes, of course.'

'Thank you. Don't you think a flower to brighten up my dress? No, *not* a flower on the bodice. Is it true that iris is a scent that's gone out of fashion? I'm sure I had heaps of other things to ask you . . . heaps of things.'

And in still another of her books, *Le toutounier*, Colette evoked this other side of women's life. Three sisters, unhappy or troubled in their loves, gather every night around the old sofa from their childhood; there they relax, pondering the worries of the day, preparing tomorrow's battles, tasting the ephemeral pleasures of a reparative rest, a good sleep, a warm bath, a crying session, they barely speak but each one creates a nesting space for the others; and everything taking place with them is real.

For some women, this frivolous and warm intimacy is more precious than the serious pomp of their relations with men. It is in another woman that the narcissist, as in the days of her adolescence, sees a favourite double; it is through her attentive and competent eyes that she can admire her well-cut dress, her elegant interior. Over and above marriage, the best friend remains her favourite witness: she can still continue to be a desirable and desired object. In almost every young girl, as we have seen, there are homosexual tendencies; the often awkward embraces of her husband do not efface these tendencies; this is the source of the sensual softness woman feels for her counterparts and that has no equal in ordinary men. Sensual attachment between two women friends can be sublimated into exalted sentimentality or expressed in diffuse or real caresses. Their embraces can also be no more than a distracting pastime – such is the case for harem women whose principal concern is to kill time – or they can become of primary importance.

It is nonetheless rare for feminine complicity to reach true friendship; women feel more spontaneous solidarity with each other than men do, but from within this solidarity they do not transcend towards each other: together they are turned towards the masculine world whose values each hopes to monopolise for herself. Their relations are not built on their singularity, but are lived immediately in their generality: and from there, the element of hostility comes into play. Natasha,* who cherished the women in her family because they could witness the births of her babies, nevertheless felt jealous of them: every one of them could embody *the*

* Tolstoy, *War and Peace.*

woman in Pierre's eyes. Women's mutual understanding lies in the fact
that they identify with each other: but then each one competes with her
companion. A housewife has a more intimate relationship with her maid
than a man – unless he is homosexual – has with his valet or chauffeur;
they tell each other secrets, and sometimes they are accomplices; but
there are also hostile rivalries between them, because while freeing herself
from the actual work, the mistress of the house wants to assume the
responsibility and credit for the work she assigns; she wants to think of
herself as irreplaceable, indispensable. 'Everything goes wrong as soon
as I'm not there.' She harasses her maid in order to find fault with her;
if she does her job too well, the mistress cannot be proud of feeling
unique. Likewise, she systematically becomes irritated with teachers,
governesses, nurses and children's maids who care for her offspring, with
parents and friends who help her out; she gives the excuse that they do
not respect 'her will', that they do not carry out 'her ideas'; the truth is
that she has neither particular will nor ideas; what irritates her, on the
contrary, is that others carry out her functions exactly as she would. This
is one of the main sources of family and domestic discussions that poison
the life of the home: the less able she is to show her own merits, the
fiercer she is in wanting to be sovereign. But where women especially
see each other as enemies is in the area of seduction and love; I have
pointed out this rivalry in girls: it often continues throughout life. We
have seen how they seek absolute validation in the ideal of the fashionable
woman or the socialite; she suffers from not being surrounded by glory;
she cannot bear to perceive the slightest halo around someone else's head;
she steals all the credit others receive; and what is an absolute if not unique?
A woman who truly loves is satisfied to be glorified in one heart, she will
not envy her friends' superficial success; but she feels threatened in her
very love. The fact is that the theme of the woman betrayed by her best
friend is not only a literary cliché; the closer two women are as friends,
the more their duality becomes dangerous. The confidante is invited to see
through the eyes of the woman in love, to feel with her heart, with her
flesh: she is attracted by the lover, fascinated by the man who seduces her
friend; she feels protected enough by her loyalty to let her feelings go; she
does not like playing an inessential role: soon she is ready to surrender, to
offer herself. Many women prudently avoid their 'intimate girlfriends' as
soon as they fall in love. This ambivalence keeps women from relying on
their mutual feelings. The shadow of the male always weighs heavily on
them. Even when not mentioning him, the verse of Saint-John Perse applies:

'And the sun is not named, but its presence is among us.'

Together women take revenge on him, set traps for him, malign him, insult him: but they wait for him. As long as they stagnate in the gynae-ceum, they bask in contingency, in blandness, in boredom; this limbo has retained some of the warmth of the mother's breast: but it is still limbo. Woman is content to linger there on condition that she will soon be able to emerge from it. She is thus content enough in the dampness of her bathroom imagining she will later make her entrance into the luminous salon. Women are comrades for each other in captivity, they help each other endure their prison, even prepare their escape: but their liberator will come from the masculine world.

For most women, this world keeps its glow after marriage; only the husband loses his prestige; the wife discovers that his pure manly essence tarnishes: but man still remains the truth of the universe, the supreme authority, the wonderful, adventure, master, gaze, prey, pleasure, salvation; he still embodies transcendence, he is the answer to all questions. And the most loyal wife never consents to give him up completely and close herself in a dismal tête-à-tête with a contingent individual. Her childhood left her in absolute need of a guide; when the husband fails to fulfil this role, she turns to another man. Sometimes her father, a brother, an uncle, a relative or an old friend has kept his former prestige: so she will lean on him. There are two categories of men whose professions destine them to become confidants and mentors: priests and doctors. The first have that great advantage of not having to be paid for these consultations; the confessional renders them defenceless in the face of the babbling of the pious; they avoid 'sacristy pests' and 'holy Marys' as best they can; but their duty is to lead their flock on the moral path, a most urgent duty as women gain social and political importance and the Church endeavours to make instru-ments of them. The 'spiritual guide' dictates his political opinions to his penitent and influences her vote; and many husbands are irritated by his interference in their conjugal life: it is he who defines what they do in the privacy of the bedroom as licit or illicit; he is concerned in the education of the children; he advises the woman on her conduct with her husband; she who always hailed man as a god kneels with pleasure before the male who is the earthly substitute for God. The doctor is better protected as he requires payment; and he can close his door to clients who are too indis-creet; but he is the target of more specific, more stubborn aims; three-quarters of the men harassed by nymphomaniacs are doctors; to undress in front of a man is a great exhibitionistic pleasure for many women.

Stekel says: I know some women who find satisfaction only in an examination by a doctor they like. In particular, there are among spinsters many rich women who see their doctor for 'a very careful' examination because of minor discharges or a banal problem. Others suffer from a cancer phobia or infections from toilets and these phobias provide them with the pretext to have an examination.

He cites two cases among others:

A spinster, B. V. . . ., 43 years old and rich, goes to see a doctor once a month, after her period, demanding a very careful examination because she believed that something was wrong. She changes doctors every month and plays the same game each time. The doctor asks her to undress and lie down on the table or couch. She refuses, saying that she is too modest, that she cannot do such a thing, that it is against nature! The doctor forces her or gently persuades her, and she finally undresses, explaining she is a virgin and he should not hurt her. He promises to give her a rectal exam. Her orgasm often comes as soon as the doctor examines her; it is repeated, intensified, during the rectal exam. She always uses a false name and pays right away . . . She admits to having entertained the hope of being raped by a doctor.

Mrs L. M. . . ., 38 years old, married, tells me she is completely unfeeling when with her husband. She comes to be analysed. After two sessions only, she admits to having a lover. But he cannot make her reach orgasm. She could only have one by being examined by a gynaecologist (her father was a gynaecologist!). Every two or three sessions or so, she had the urge to go to the doctor and have an examination. From time to time, she requested a treatment and those were the happiest times. The last time, a gynaecologist massaged her at length because of a supposed fallen womb. Each massage brought about several orgasms. She explains her passion for these examinations by the first touch that had caused the first orgasm of her life . . .[88]

The woman easily imagines that the man to whom she has exhibited herself is impressed by her physical charm or her soul's beauty, and she thus is persuaded, in pathological cases, that she is loved by a priest or doctor. Even if she is normal, she has the impression that a subtle bond exists between them; she basks in respectful obedience to him; in addition, she sometimes finds in him a source of security that helps her accept her life.

There are women, nonetheless, who are not content to prop up their existence with moral authority; they also need romantic exaltation in their lives. If they do not want to cheat on or leave their husbands, they will seek recourse in the same tactic as a girl who fears flesh-and-blood males: they give themselves over to imaginary passions. Stekel gives several examples of this.*

A decent married woman of the better social class suffers from 'nervous anxiety' and is predisposed to depressions. One evening during the performance at the opera she falls in love with the tenor. His singing suffuses her with a strange warmth. She becomes the singer's fanatic admirer. Thenceforth she does not miss a single performance in which he appears. She obtains his photograph, she dreams of him, and once she sent him an imposing bouquet of roses with the inscription: 'From a grateful unknown admirer!' She even goes so far as to write him a letter . . . This letter she also signs, 'From an unknown admirer!' but she keeps at a distance. An occasion unexpectedly arises, making it possible for her to meet this singer at a social gathering. She decides very promptly that she will not go. She does not care to become personally acquainted with him. She does not require closer contact. She is happy to be able to love so warmly and still remain a faithful wife!

I became acquainted with a woman obsessed with the most remarkable Kainz, a famous actor from Vienna. She had a special Kainz room, embellished with numerous portraits of the famous artist. There was a Kainz library in one corner. Here there was to be found everything in the shape of his books, pamphlets and clippings which she could gather bearing on her hero. She had also gathered in this library a collection of theatre programs, including, of course, Kainz festivals and premières. A particularly precious possession was the portrait of the great artist bearing his autograph. This woman wore mourning for a whole year after the artist's death. She took long journeys to attend lectures on Kainz . . . This Kainz cult served to preserve the woman's physical chastity, it protected her against all temptation, leaving no room for any other erotic thoughts.

* Stekel, *Frigidity in Woman.*

We recall what tears Rudolph Valentino's death brought forth. Married women and young girls alike worship cinema heroes. Women often evoke their images when engaged in solitary pleasures, or they call up such fantasies in conjugal lovemaking; these images also often revive some childhood memory in the figure of a grandfather, a brother, a teacher, and so on.

Nevertheless, there are also men of flesh and blood in women's circles; whether she is sexually fulfilled, frigid or frustrated – except in the rare case of a complete, absolute, and exclusive love – the woman places great value on their approbation. Her husband's too mundane gaze no longer nurtures her image; she needs eyes still full of mystery to discover her as mystery; she needs a sovereign consciousness before her to receive her confidences, to revive the faded photographs, to bring to life that dimple in the corner of her mouth, the fluttering eyelashes that are hers alone; she is only desirable, lovable, if she is desired, loved. While she more or less makes the best of her marriage, she looks to other men mainly to satisfy her vanity: she invites them to share in her cult; she seduces, she pleases, happy to dream about forbidden loves, to think: If I wanted to . . .; she prefers to charm many admirers than to attach herself deeply to any one; more ardent, less shy than a young girl, her coquetry needs males to confirm her in the consciousness of her worth and power; she is often all the bolder as, anchored in her home and having succeeded in conquering one man, she leads him on without great expectations and without great risks.

It happens that after a longer or shorter period of fidelity, the woman no longer confines herself to these flirtations or coquetries. Often, she decides to deceive her husband out of resentment. Adler maintains that woman's infidelity always stems from revenge; this is going too far; but the fact is that she often yields less to a lover's seduction than to a desire to defy her husband: 'He is not the only man in the world – I can attract others – I am not his slave, he thinks he is clever but he can be duped.' It may happen that the derided husband retains his primordial importance for the wife; just as the girl will sometimes take a lover to rebel against her mother or protest against her parents, disobey them, affirm herself, so a woman whose very resentment attaches her to her husband seeks a confidant in her lover, an observer who considers her a victim, an accomplice who helps her humiliate her husband; she talks to him endlessly about her husband under the pretext of subjecting him to his scorn; and if the lover does not play his role well, she moodily turns from him either to go back to her husband or to find another consoler.

But, very often, it is less resentment than disappointment that drives her into the arms of a lover; she does not find love in marriage; she resigns herself with difficulty to never knowing the sensual pleasures and joys whose expectations charmed her youth. Marriage, by frustrating women's erotic satisfaction, denies them the freedom and individuality of their feelings, drives them to adultery by way of a necessary and ironic dialectic.

Montaigne says:

We train them from childhood to the ways of love. Their grace, their dressing up, their knowledge, their language, all their instruction, has only this end in view. Their governesses imprint in them nothing else but the idea of love, if only by continually depicting it to them in order to disgust them with it.[89]

Thus it is folly to try to bridle women's desire which is so burning and natural.

And Engels declares:

With monogamous marriage, two constant social types, unknown hitherto, make their appearance on the scene – the wife's attendant lover and the cuckold husband . . . Together with monogamous marriage and hetaerism, adultery became an unavoidable social institution – denounced, severely penalised, but impossible to suppress.[90]

If conjugal sex has excited the wife's curiosity without satisfying her senses, like in Colette's *Innocent Libertine*,[91] she tries to complete her education in the beds of strangers. If she has no singular attachment to her husband, but he has succeeded in awakening her sexuality, she will want to taste the pleasures she has discovered through him with others.

Some moralists have been outraged by the preference shown to the lover, and I have pointed out the efforts of bourgeois literature to rehabilitate the figure of the husband; but it is absurd to defend him by showing that often in the eyes of society – that is to say, other men – he is better than his rival: what is important here is what he represents for the wife. So there are two traits that make him detestable. First of all, it is he who assumes the thankless role of initiator; the contradictory demands of the virgin who dreams of being both violated and respected almost surely condemn him to failure; she remains for ever frigid in his arms; with her lover she experiences neither the torment of defloration nor the initial humiliation of modesty overcome; she is spared the trauma of surprise: she knows more or less what to expect; more honest, less vulnerable, less naive than on her wedding night, she does not confuse ideal love and physical hunger, sentiment and sexual excitement: when she takes a lover, it is a lover she wants. This lucidity is an aspect of the freedom of her choice. For here lies the other defect weighing on her husband: he was usually imposed and not chosen. Either she accepted him in resignation, or she was given over to him by her family; in any case, even if she married him for love, she makes him her master by marrying him; their relations have become a duty and he often takes on the figure of tyrant. Her choice of lover is doubtless limited by circumstances, but there is an element of freedom in this relationship; to marry is an obligation, to take a lover is a luxury; it is because he has solicited her that the woman yields to him: she is sure, if not of his love, at least of his desire; it is not for the purpose of obeying laws that he acts upon his desire. He also has this advantage: that his seduction and prestige are not tarnished by the frictions of everyday life; he remains removed, an other. Thus the woman has the impression of getting out of herself in their meetings, of finding new riches: she feels other. This is above all what some women seek in a liaison: to be involved, surprised, rescued from themselves by the other. A rupture leaves them with a desperate empty feeling. Janet*[92] cites several cases of this melancholia that show us bluntly what the woman looks for and finds in her lover:

A thirty-nine-year-old woman, heartbroken at having been abandoned by a writer with whom she worked for five years, writes to Janet: 'He had such a rich life and was so tyrannical that all I could do was take care of him, and I could not think of anything else . . .'

Another woman, thirty-one, fell ill after breaking with a lover she adored. 'I wanted to be an inkwell on his desk to see him, hear him,' she writes. And she explains: 'Alone, I am bored, my husband brings me no intellectual stimulation, he knows nothing, he teaches me nothing, he does not *surprise* me . . . , he has nothing but common sense, it crushes me.' But by contrast, she writes about her lover: 'He is an *astonishing* man, I never saw in him a moment of confusion, emotion, gaiety, carelessness, always in control,

* See *Obsessions and Psychasthenia*.

mocking, cold enough to make you die of shame. In addition, an impudence, sang-froid, a sharp mind, a lively intelligence that made my head spin . . .'

There are women who savour this feeling of plenitude and joyful excitement only in the first moments of a liaison; if a lover does not give them instant pleasure – and this frequently happens the first time as the partners are intimidated and ill adapted to each other – they feel resentment and disgust towards him; these 'Messalinas' have multiple affairs and leave one lover after another. But it also happens that a woman, enlightened by the failure of her marriage, is attracted this time by a man who suits her well, and a lasting relation is created between them. Often he will appeal to her because he is of a radically different type from her husband. This is without a doubt the contrast that Sainte-Beuve, who seduced Adèle, provides with Victor Hugo. Stekel cites the following case:

> Mrs P. H. has been married for the past eight years to a man who is a member of an athletic club. She visits the gynaecologic clinic on account of a slight inflammation of the ovaries. There she complains that her husband gives her no peace . . . She perceives only pain and does not know the meaning of gratification. The man is rough and violent . . . Finally he takes a sweetheart . . . [This does not trouble her in the least.] She is happy . . . she wants a divorce and calls on an attorney. In his office she meets a clerk who is the exact opposite of her husband. The clerk is humble, delicate, weak, but he is also loving and tender. They become closely acquainted and he begins to court her. He writes her tender letters. His petty attentions flatter and please her . . . They find that they have similar intellectual interests . . . With his first kiss her anaesthesia vanishes . . . This man's relatively weak *potentia* has roused the keenest orgasm in the woman. After the divorce they married; now they live very happily together . . . He is also able to rouse this woman's orgasm with kisses and other caresses. This was the same woman whose frigidity in the embrace of a highly potent man drove her to take a lover!

Not all affairs have fairy-tale endings. It happens that just as the young girl dreams of a liberator who will wrest her from under her father's roof, the wife awaits the lover who will save her from the conjugal yoke: an often-told story is that of the ardent lover who cools off and flees when his mistress starts talking about marriage; she is often hurt by his reluctance, and from then on, their relations become distorted by resentment and hostility. If a relationship becomes a stable one, it often takes on a familiar conjugal character in the end; all the vices of marriage – boredom, jealousy, prudence, deception – can be found in it. And the woman dreams of another man who will rescue her from this routine.

Adultery, furthermore, has very different characteristics according to customs and circumstances. In our civilisation of enduring patriarchal traditions, marital infidelity is still more serious for the woman than the man. Montaigne says:

> Iniquitous appraisal of vices! . . . But we create and weigh vices not according to nature but according to our interest, whereby they assume so many unequal shapes. The severity of our decrees makes women's addiction to this vice more exacerbated and vicious than its nature calls for, and involves it in consequences that are worse than their cause.

We have seen the primary reasons for this severity: women's adultery risks introducing the child of a stranger into a family, dispossessing legitimate heirs; the husband is master, the wife his property. Social changes and the practice of birth control have taken much of the force out of these motives. But the will to keep woman in a state of dependency perpetuates the proscriptions that still surround her. She often interiorises them; she closes her eyes to the conjugal escapades that her religion, morality and her 'virtue' do not permit her to envisage with reciprocity. The control imposed by her social environment – in particular in 'small towns' in the Old as well as the New World – is far more severe for her than for her husband: he goes out more, he travels, and his dalliances are more indulgently tolerated; she risks losing her reputation and her situation as a married woman. The ruses women use to thwart this scrutiny have often been described; I know a small Portuguese town of ancient severity where young women only go out in the company of a mother-in-law or sister-in-law; but the hairdresser rents out rooms above his shop; between hair being set and combed out, lovers steal a furtive embrace. In large cities, women have far fewer wardens: but the old custom of 'afternoon dalliances' was hardly more conducive to the happy fulfilment of illicit feelings. Furtive and clandestine, adultery does not create human and free relationships; the lies it entails rob conjugal relations of what is left of their dignity.

In many circles today, women have partially gained sexual freedom. But it is still a difficult problem for them to reconcile their conjugal life with sexual satisfaction. As marriage generally does not mean physical love, it would seem reasonable to clearly differentiate one from the other. A man can admittedly make an excellent husband and still be inconstant: his sexual caprices do not in fact keep him from carrying out the enterprise of a friendly communal life with his wife; this amity will be all the purer, less ambivalent if it does not represent a shackle. One might allow that it could be the same for the wife; she often wishes to share in her husband's existence, create a home with him for their children, and still experience other embraces. It is the compromises of prudence and hypocrisy that make adultery degrading; a pact of freedom and sincerity would abolish one of the defects of marriages. It must be recognised, however, that *today* the irritating formula that inspired *Francillon* by Dumas, fils – 'It is not the same thing for women' – retains a certain truth. There is nothing *natural* about the difference. It is claimed that woman needs sexual activity less than man: nothing is less sure. Repressed women make shrewish wives, sadistic mothers, fanatical housekeepers, unhappy and dangerous creatures; in any case, even if her desires were more infrequent, there is no reason to consider it superfluous for her to satisfy them. The difference stems from the overall erotic situation of man and woman as defined by tradition and today's society. For woman, the love act is still considered a *service* woman renders to man, thus giving him the status of master; we have seen that he can always *take* an inferior woman, but she degrades herself if she *gives herself* to a male who is not her equal; her consent, in any case, is of the same nature as a surrender, a fall. A woman often graciously accepts her husband having other women: she is even flattered; Adèle Hugo apparently saw her fiery husband take his ardours to other beds without regret; some women even copy Mme de Pompadour and act as procurers.* By contrast, in lovemaking, the woman is changed into object, into prey; it seems to the husband that she is possessed by a foreign mana, that she ceases to belong to him, she is stolen from him. And the fact is that in bed the woman often feels, wants to be and, consequently, is dominated; the fact also is that because of virile prestige, she tends to approve, to imitate the male who, having possessed her, embodies in her eyes all men. The husband is irritated, not without reason, to hear in his wife's familiar

---

* I am speaking here of marriage. We will see that the attitude of the couple is reversed in a love affair.

mouth the echo of a stranger's thinking: it seems to him in a way that it is he who is possessed, violated. If Mme de Charrière broke with the young Benjamin Constant – who played the feminine role between two virile women – it was because she could not bear to feel him marked by the hated influence of Mme de Staël. As long as the woman acts like a slave and the reflection of the man to whom she 'gives herself', she must recognise the fact that her infidelities wrest her from her husband more radically than do his reciprocal infidelities.

If she does preserve her integrity, she may nonetheless fear that her husband will be compromised in her lover's consciousness. Even a woman is quick to imagine that in sleeping with a man – if only once, in haste, on a sofa – she has gained a certain superiority over the legitimate spouse; a man who believes he possesses a mistress thinks, with even more reason, that he has trumped her husband. This is why the woman is careful to choose her lover from a lower social class in Bataille's *Tenderness* or Kessel's *Belle de Nuit*;[93] she seeks sexual satisfaction from him, but she does not want to give him an advantage over her respected husband. In *Man's Fate*,[94] Malraux shows us a couple where man and woman make a pact for reciprocal freedom: yet when May tells Kyo she has slept with a friend, he grieves over the fact that this man thinks he 'had' her; he chose to respect her independence because he knows very well that one never *has* anyone; but the complaisant ideas held by another man hurt and humiliate him through May. Society confuses the free woman and the loose woman; the lover himself may not recognise the freedom from which he profits; he would rather believe his mistress has yielded, let herself go, that he has conquered her, seduced her. A proud woman might personally come to terms with her partner's vanity; but it would be detestable for her that her esteemed husband should stand such arrogance. For as long as this equality is not universally recognised and concretely realised, it is very difficult for a woman to act as an equal to a man.

In any case, adultery, friendships and social life are but diversions within married life; they can help its constraints to be endured, but they do not break them. They are only artificial escapes that in no way authentically allow the woman to take her destiny into her own hands.

CHAPTER 8

Prostitutes and Hetaeras

Marriage, as we have seen,* has an immediate corollary in prostitution. 'Hetaerism', says Morgan, 'follows mankind in civilization as a dark shadow upon the family.' Man, out of prudence, destines his wife to chastity but he does not derive satisfaction from the regime he imposes on her.

Montaigne says:

> The kings of Persia used to invite their wives to join them at their feasts; but when the wine began to heat them in good earnest and they had to give completely free rein to sensuality, they sent them back to their private rooms, so as not to make them participants in their immoderate appetites, and sent for other women in their place, to whom they did not have this obligation of respect.[95]

Sewers are necessary to guarantee the sanitation of palaces, said the Church Fathers. And Mandeville, in a very popular book, said: 'It is obvious that some women must be sacrificed to save others and to prevent an even more abject filth.' One of the arguments of American slaveholders and defenders of slavery is that, released from slavish drudgery, Southern whites could establish the most democratic and refined relations with each other; likewise, the existence of a caste of 'lost women' makes it possible to treat 'the virtuous woman' with the most chivalric respect. The prostitute is a scapegoat; man unloads his turpitude onto her and he repudiates her. Whether a legal status puts her under police surveillance or she works clandestinely, she is in any case treated as a pariah.

From the economic point of view, her situation is symmetrical to the married woman's. 'Between those who sell themselves through prostitution and those who sell themselves through marriage, the only difference

* Vol. I, Part Two.

resides in the price and length of the contract,' says Marro.*[96] For both, the sexual act is a service; the latter is engaged for life by one man; the former has several clients who pay her per item. One male against all the others protects the former; the latter is defended by all against the exclusive tyranny of each one. In any case, the advantages they derive from giving their bodies are limited by competition; the husband knows he could have had another wife: the accomplishment of his 'conjugal duties' is not a favour; it is the execution of a contract. In prostitution, masculine desire can be satisfied on any body as it is specific and not individual. Wives or courtesans do not succeed in exploiting man unless they wield a singular power over him. The main difference between them is that the legitimate woman, oppressed as a married woman, is respected as a human person; this respect begins seriously to bring a halt to oppression. However, the prostitute does not have the rights of a person; she is the sum of all types of feminine slavery at once.

It is naive to wonder what motives drive a woman to prostitution; Lombroso's theory that assimilated prostitutes with criminals and that saw them both as degenerates is no longer accepted; it is possible, as the statistics show, that in general prostitutes have a slightly below-average mental level and that some are clearly retarded: women with fewer mental faculties readily choose jobs that do not demand of them any specialisation; but most are normal and some very intelligent. No hereditary fate, no physiological defect, weighs on them. In reality, as soon as a profession opens in a world where misery and unemployment are rife, there are people to enter it; as long as there are police and prostitution, there will be policemen and prostitutes. Especially because these professions are, on average, more lucrative than many others. It is very hypocritical to be surprised by the supply masculine demand creates; this is a rudimentary and universal economic process. 'Of all the causes of prostitution,' wrote Parent-Duchâtelet in his study of 1857,[97] 'none is more active than the lack of work and the misery that is the inevitable consequence of inadequate salaries.' Right-thinking moralists respond sneeringly that the pitiful accounts of prostitutes are just stories for the naive client. It is true that in many cases a prostitute could earn her living in a different way: that the living she has chosen does not seem the worst to her does not prove she has this vice in her blood; rather, it condemns a society where this profession is still one that seems the least repellent to many women. One asks, why did she choose it? The question should be: Why

* 'Puberty'.

should she not choose it? It has been noted that, among other things, many 'girls' were once servants; this is what Parent-Duchâtelet established for all countries, what Lily Braun noted in Germany and Ryckère in Belgium. About 50 per cent of prostitutes were first servants. One look at 'maids' rooms' is enough to explain this fact. Exploited, enslaved, treated as an object rather than as a person, the maid or chambermaid cannot look forward to any improvement of her lot; sometimes she has to submit to the whims of the master of the house: from domestic slavery and sexual subordination to the master, she slides into a slavery that could not be more degrading and that she dreams will be better. In addition, women in domestic service are very often uprooted; it is estimated that 80 per cent of Parisian prostitutes come from the provinces or the countryside. Proximity to one's family and concern for one's reputation are thought to prevent a woman from turning to a generally discredited profession; but if she is lost in a big city, no longer integrated into society, the abstract idea of 'morality' does not provide any obstacle. While the bourgeoisie invests the sexual act – and above all virginity – with daunting taboos, the working class and peasantry treat it with indifference. Numerous studies agree on this point: many girls let themselves be deflowered by the first comer and then find it natural to give themselves to anyone who comes along. In a study of one hundred prostitutes, Dr Bizard recorded the following facts: one had been deflowered at eleven, two at twelve, two at thirteen, six at fourteen, seven at fifteen, twenty-one at sixteen, nineteen at seventeen, seventeen at eighteen, six at nineteen; the others, after twenty-one. There were thus 5 per cent who had been raped before puberty. More than half said they gave themselves out of love; the others consented out of ignorance. The first seducer is often young. Usually it is someone from the workshop, an office colleague, a childhood friend; then come soldiers, foremen, valets and students; Dr Bizard's list also included two lawyers, an architect, a doctor and a pharmacist. It is rather rare, as legend has it, for the employer himself to play this initiating role: but often it is his son or nephew or one of his friends. Commenge, in his study, also reports on forty-five girls from twelve to seventeen who were deflowered by strangers whom they never saw again; they had consented with indifference, and without experiencing pleasure. Dr Bizard recorded the following, more detailed cases, among others:

Mlle G. de Bordeaux, leaving the convent at eighteen, is persuaded, out of curiosity and without thinking of any danger, to follow a stranger from the fair into his caravan where she is deflowered.

Without thinking, a thirteen-year-old child gives herself to a man she has met in the street, whom she does not know and whom she will never see again.

M. . . . tells us explicitly that she was deflowered at seventeen by a young man she did not know . . . she let it happen out of total ignorance.

R. . . . , deflowered at seventeen and a half by a young man she had never seen whom she had met by chance at the doctor's, where she had gone to get the doctor for her sick sister; he brought her back by car so that she could get home more quickly, but in fact he left her in the middle of the street after getting what he wanted from her.

B. . . . deflowered at fifteen and a half 'without thinking about what she was doing', in our client's words, by a young man she never saw again; nine months later, she gave birth to a healthy boy.

S. . . . , deflowered at fourteen by a young man who drew her to his house under the pretext that he wanted her to meet his sister. The young man in reality did not have a sister, but he had syphilis and contaminated the girl.

R. . . . deflowered at eighteen in an old trench from the front by a married cousin with whom she was visiting the battlefields; he got her pregnant and made her leave her family.

C. . . . at seventeen, deflowered on the beach one summer evening by a young man whom she had just met at the hotel and at 100 metres from their two mothers, who were talking about trifles. Contaminated with gonorrhoea.

L. . . . deflowered at thirteen by her uncle while listening to the radio at the same time as her aunt, who liked to go to bed early, was sleeping quietly in the next room.[98]

We can be sure that these girls who gave in passively nevertheless suffered the trauma of defloration; one would like to know what psychological influence this brutal experience had on their future; but 'girls' are not psychoanalysed, they are inarticulate in describing themselves and take refuge behind clichés. For some, the facility of giving themselves to the first comer can be explained by the existence of prostitution fantasies about which we have spoken: out of family resentment, horror of their budding sexuality, the desire to act grown-up, some young girls imitate prostitutes; they use harsh makeup, see boys, act flirtatiously and provocatively; they who are still infantile, asexual and cold think they can play with fire with impunity; one day a man takes them at their word and they slip from dreams to acts.

'When a door has been broken open, it is then hard to keep it closed,' said one fourteen-year-old prostitute.* However, the girl rarely decides to be a streetwalker immediately following her defloration. In some cases, she remains attached to her first lover and continues to live with him; she takes an 'honest' job; when the lover abandons her, another consoles her; since she no longer belongs to one man, she decides she can give herself to all; sometimes it is the lover – the first, the second – who suggests this means of earning money. There are also many girls who are prostituted by their parents: in some families, like the famous American family, the Jukes, all the women are doomed to this job. Among young female vagabonds, there are also many girls abandoned by their families who begin by begging and slip from there to the streets. In 1857, out of 5,000 prostitutes, Parent-Duchâtelet found that 1,441 were influenced by poverty, 1,425 seduced and abandoned, 1,255 abandoned and left penniless by their parents. Contemporary studies suggest approximately the same conclusions. Illness often leads to prostitution as the woman has become unable to hold down a real job or has lost her place; it destroys her precarious budget, it forces the woman to come up with new resources quickly. So it is with the birth of a child. More than half the women of Saint-Lazare had at least one child; many raised from three to six children; Dr Bizard points out one who brought fourteen into the world of whom eight were still living when he knew her. Few of them, he says, abandon their children; and sometimes the unwed mother becomes a prostitute in order to feed the child. He cites this case among others:

> Deflowered in the provinces, at nineteen, by a sixty-year-old director while she was still living at home, she had to leave her family, as she was pregnant, and she gave birth to a healthy girl that she brought up well. After nursing, she went to Paris, found a job as a nanny and began to carouse at the age of twenty-nine. She has been a prostitute for thirty-three years. Weak and exhausted, she is now asking to be hospitalised in Saint-Lazare.

It is well known that there is an increase of prostitution in wars and the crises of their aftermath.

* Cited by Marro, 'Puberty'.

The author of *The Life of a Prostitute*, published in part in *Les Temps Modernes*,* tells of her beginnings:

I got married at sixteen to a man thirteen years older than I. I did it to get out of my parents' house. My husband only thought of making me have kids. 'Like that, you'll stay at home, you won't go out,' he said. He wouldn't let me wear makeup, didn't want to take me to the movies. I had to stand my mother-in-law who came to the house every day and always took the side of her bastardly son. My first child was a boy, Jacques; fourteen months later, I gave birth to another, Pierre . . . As I was very bored, I took courses in nursing, which I liked a lot . . . I got work at a hospital on the outskirts of Paris, working with women. A nurse who was just a girl taught me things I hadn't known about before. Sleeping with my husband was mostly a chore. As for men, I didn't have a fling with anyone for six months. Then one day, a real tough guy, a cad but good-looking, came into my own room. He convinced me I could change my life, that I could go with him to Paris, that I wouldn't work any more . . . He knew how to fool me . . . I decided to go off with him . . . I was really happy for a month . . . One day he brought along a well-dressed, chic woman, saying: 'So here, this one does all right for herself.' At the beginning, I didn't go along with it. I even found a job as a nurse in a local hospital to show him that I didn't want to walk the streets, but I couldn't carry on for long. He would say: 'You don't love me. When you love a man, you work for him.' I cried. At the hospital, I was sad. Finally, I was persuaded to go to the hairdresser's . . . I began to turn tricks! Julot followed me to see if I was doing well and to be able to warn me if the cops were on to me . . .

In some ways, this story is the classic one of the girl doomed to the street by a pimp. This role might also be played by the husband. And sometimes, by a woman as well. L. Faivre made a study in 1931 of 510 young prostitutes;[†99] he found that 284 of them lived alone, 132 with a male friend, and 94 with a female friend with whom they usually had homosexual ties. He cites (with their spelling) extracts of the following letters:

---

* She had this story published in secret under the pseudonym Marie-Thérèse; I will refer to her by this name.
† *Young Vagabond Prostitutes in Prison.*

Suzanne, seventeen. I gave myself to prostitution, especially with women prostitutes. One of them who kept me for a long time was very jealous, and so I left that street.

Andrée, fifteen and a half. I left my parents to live with a friend I met at a dance, I understood right away that she wanted to love me like a man, I stayed with her four months, then . . .

Jeanne, fourteen. My poor sweet papa's name was X . . . he died in the hospital from war wounds in 1922. My mother got married again. I was going to school to get my primary school diploma, then having got it, I went to study sewing . . . then as I earned very little, the fights with my stepfather began . . . I had to be placed as a maid at Mme X's, on X street . . . I was alone with a girl who was probably twenty-five for about ten days; I noticed a very big change in her. Then one day, just like a boy, she admitted her great love. I hesitated, then afraid of being let go, I finally gave in; I understood then certain things . . . I worked, then finding myself without a job, I had to go to the Bois where I continued with women. I met a very generous lady, and so forth.[100]

Quite often, the woman only envisages prostitution as a temporary way of increasing her resources. But the way in which she then finds herself enslaved to it has been described many times. While cases of the 'white slave trade', where she is dragged into the spiral by violence, false promises, mystifications, and so on, are relatively rare, what happens more often is that she is kept in this career against her will. The capital necessary to get her started is provided by a pimp or a madam who acquires rights over her, who gets most of her profits and from whom she is not able to free herself. Marie-Thérèse carried on a real fight for several years before succeeding.

I finally understood that Julot[101] didn't want anything but my dough and I thought that far from him, I could save a bit of money . . . At home in the beginning, I was shy, I didn't dare go up to clients and tell them 'come on up'. The wife of one of Julot's buddies watched me closely and even counted my tricks . . . So Julot writes to me that I should give my money every evening to the madam, 'Like that, nobody will steal it from you.' When I wanted to buy a dress, the hotel manager told me that Julot had forbidden her to give my dough ... I decided to get out of this trick house as fast as I could. When the boss lady found out I wanted to leave, she didn't give me the tampon* before the visit like the other times and I was stopped and put into the hospital ... I had to return to the brothel to earn some money for my trip ... but I only stayed in the house for four weeks ... I worked a few days in Barbès like before but I was too furious at Julot to stay in Paris: we fought, he beat me, once he almost threw me out of the window ... I made an arrangement with a go-between to go to the provinces. When I realised he knew Julot, I didn't show up at the rendezvous. The agent's two broads met me on rue Belhomme and gave me a thrashing ... The next day, I packed my bags and left alone for the isle of T ... Three weeks later I was fed up with the brothel, I wrote to the doctor to mark me as going out when he came for the visit ... Julot saw me on Boulevard de Magenta and beat me ... My face was scarred after the thrashing on Boulevard de Magenta. I was fed up with Julot. So I signed a contract to go to Germany ...

Literature has popularised the character of the fancy man. He plays a protective role in the girl's life. He advances her money to buy outfits, then he defends her against the competition of other women and the police – sometimes he himself is a policeman – and against the clients. They would like to be able to consume without paying; there are those who would readily satisfy their sadism on a woman. In Madrid a few years ago Fascist and gilded youth amused themselves by throwing prostitutes into the river on cold nights; in France students having fun sometimes brought women into the countryside and abandoned them, entirely naked, at night; in order to get her money and avoid bad treatment, the prostitute needs a man. He also provides her with moral support: 'You work less well alone, you don't have your heart in it, you let yourself go,' some say. She often feels love for him; she takes on this job or justifies it out of love; in this milieu, man's superiority over woman is enormous: this distance favours love-religion, which explains some prostitutes' passionate abnegation. They see in their male's violence the sign of his virility and submit to him even more docilely. They experience jealousy and torment with him, but also the joys of the woman in love. But sometimes they feel only hostility and resentment for him: it is

---

* 'A tampon to anaesthetise the gono was given to prostitutes before the doctor's visit so that he only found a woman to be sick if the madam wanted to get rid of her.'

out of fear, because he has a hold over them, that they remain under his thumb, as we just saw in the case of Marie-Thérèse. So sometimes they console themselves with a 'fling' with one of their clients. Marie-Thérèse writes:

> All the women have flings, me too, in addition to their Julot. He was a very handsome sailor. Even though he was a good lover, he didn't turn me on but we felt a lot of friendship for each other. Often he came up with me without making love, just to talk; he told me I should get out of this, that my place wasn't here.

They also find consolation with women. Many prostitutes are homosexual. We saw that there was often a homosexual adventure at the beginning of their careers and that many continued to live with a woman. According to Anna Rueling, about 20 per cent of prostitutes in Germany are homosexual. Faivre points out that in prison young women prisoners correspond with each other with pornographic and passionate letters that they sign 'United for life'. These letters are similar to those schoolgirls write to each other, feeding the 'flames' in their hearts; these girls are less aware, shyer; the prisoners carry their feelings to the limit, in both their words and their actions. We can see in the life of Marie-Thérèse – who was launched into lovemaking by a woman – what special role the female 'pal' plays in comparison to the despised male client or the authoritarian pimp:

> Julot brought around a girl, a poor drudge who didn't even have a pair of shoes to wear. At the flea market they buy what she needed and then she comes to work with me. She was sweet and in addition she liked women, so we got along well. She reminded me of everything I learned with the nurse. We had a lot of fun and instead of working we went to the movies. I was happy to have her with us.

One can see that the girlfriend plays approximately the same role that the best friend plays for the virtuous woman surrounded by women: she is the companion in pleasure, she is the one with whom she has free, gratuitous relations, that can thus be chosen; tired of men, disgusted by them or wishing for a diversion, the prostitute will often seek relief and pleasure in the arms of another woman. In any case, the complicity I spoke of and that immediately unites women exists more strongly in this case than in any other. Because their relations with half of humanity are commercial, because the whole of society treats them as pariahs, there is great solidarity among prostitutes; they might be rivals, jealous of each other, insult each other, fight with each other; but they have a great need of each other to form a 'counter-universe' in which they regain their human dignity; the friend is the confidante and the privileged witness; she is the one who approves of the dress and hairdo meant to seduce the man, but which are ends in themselves in other women's envious or admiring gazes.

As for the prostitute's relations with her clients, opinions vary and cases undoubtedly vary. It is often emphasised that she reserves kissing on the lips, the expression of real tenderness, for her true love, and she makes no connection between amorous embraces and professional ones. Men's views are dubious because their vanity incites them to let themselves be duped by simulated orgasm. It must be said that the circumstances are very different when it is a question of a 'mass turnover', often physically exhausting, a quick trick, or regular relations with a familiar client. Marie-Thérèse generally did her job indifferently, but she mentions some nights of delights; she had 'crushes' and says that all her friends did too; a woman might refuse to be paid by a client she liked, and sometimes, if he is in a difficult situation, she offers to help him. In general, however, the woman works 'cold'. Some only feel indifference tinged with scorn for their clientele. 'Oh! What saps men are! Women can put anything they want into men's heads!' writes Marie-Thérèse. But many feel a disgusted resentment of men; they are sickened, for one thing, by their perversions, either because they go to the brothel to satisfy the perversions they do not dare to admit to their wives or mistresses, or because being at a brothel incites them to invent perversions; many men demand 'fantasies' from the woman. Marie-Thérèse complained in particular that the French have an insatiable imagination. The sick women treated by Dr Bizard confided in him that 'all men are more or less perverted'. One of my female friends spoke at great length at the Beaujon hospital with a young, very intelligent prostitute who started off as a servant and who lived with a pimp she adored. 'All men are perverted,' she said, 'except mine. That's why I love him. If I ever discover he's a pervert, I'll leave him. The first time the client doesn't always dare, he seems normal; but when he comes back, he begins to want things . . . You say your husband isn't a pervert: you'll see. They all are.' Because of these perversions she detested them. Another of my female friends, in 1943 in Fresnes, became intimate with a prostitute. She emphasised that 90 per cent of her clients were perverts and about 50 per cent were self-hating pederasts. Those who showed too much imagination terrified her. A German officer asked her to walk about the room naked with flowers in her arms while he imitated the flight of a bird; in spite of her courtesy and generosity, she ran away every time she caught sight of him. Marie-Thérèse hated 'fantasy' even though it had a much higher rate than simple coitus, and was often less demanding for the woman. These three women were particularly intelligent and sensitive. They certainly understood that as soon as they were no longer protected by the routine of the job, as soon as man stopped being a client in general and became individualised, they were prey to consciousness, to a capricious freedom: it was no longer just a simple business transaction. Some prostitutes, though, specialise in 'fantasy' because it brings in more money. In their hostility to the client there is often class resentment. Helene Deutsch speaks at great length about the story of Anna, a pretty blonde prostitute, childlike, generally very gentle, but who had fierce fits of anger against some men. She was from a working-class family; her father drank, her mother was sickly: this unhappy household gave her such a horrible idea of family life that she rejected all proposals to marry, even though throughout her career she had many opportunities. The young men of the neighbourhood debauched her; she liked her job well enough; but when, ill with tuberculosis, she was sent to the hospital, she developed a fierce hatred of doctors; 'respectable' men were abhorrent to her; she could not stand gentility, her doctor's solicitude. 'Don't we know better than anyone that these men easily drop their masks of gentility, self-control, and behave like brutes?' she said. Other than that, she was mentally perfectly well balanced. She pretended to have a child that she left with a wet nurse, but otherwise she did not lie. She died of tuberculosis. Another young prostitute, Julia, who gave herself to every boy she met from the age of fifteen, only liked poor and weak men; she was gentle and nice with them; she considered the others 'wicked beasts who deserved harsh treatment'. (She had an obvious complex that manifested an unsatisfied maternal vocation: she had fits as soon as 'mother', 'child' or similar-sounding words were uttered.)

Most prostitutes are morally adapted to their condition; that does not mean they are hereditarily or congenitally immoral, but they rightly feel integrated into a society that demands their services. They know well that the edifying lecture of the policeman who puts them through an inspection is pure verbiage, and the lofty principles their clients pronounce outside the brothel do little to intimidate them. Marie-Thérèse explains to the baker woman with whom she lives in Berlin:

Myself, I like everyone. When it's a question of dough, madame . . . Yes, because sleeping with a man for free, for nothing, says the same thing about you, that one's a whore; if you get paid, they call you a whore, yes, but a smart one; because when you ask a man for money, you can be sure that he'll tell you right off: 'Oh! I didn't know you did that kind of work,' or 'Do you have a man?' There you are. Paid or not, for me it's the same thing. 'Ah, yes!' she answers. 'You're right.' Because, I tell her, you're going to stand in line for a half hour to have a ticket for shoes. Myself, for a half hour, I'll turn a trick. I get the shoes without paying, and on the contrary, if I do my thing right, I'm paid as well. So you see, I'm right.

It is not their moral and psychological situation that makes prostitutes' existence miserable. It is their material condition that is deplorable for the most part. Exploited by their pimps and hotel keepers, they have no security, and three-quarters of them are penniless. After five years in the trade, around 75 per cent of them have syphilis, says Dr Bizard, who has treated thousands; among others, inexperienced minors are frighteningly susceptible to contamination; close to 25 per cent must be operated on for complications resulting from gonorrhoea. One in twenty has tuberculosis, 60 per cent become alcoholics or drug addicts; 40 per cent die before forty. It must be added that, in spite of precautions, they do become pregnant from time to time, and they are generally operated on in bad conditions. Common prostitution is a hard job where the sexually and economically oppressed woman – subjected to the arbitrariness of the police, humiliating medical checkups, the whims of her clients, and the prospect of germs, sickness and misery – is really reduced to the level of a thing.*

There are many degrees between the common prostitute and the grand hetaera. The main difference is that the former trades in her pure generality, so that competition keeps her at a miserable level of living, while the latter tries to be recognised in her singularity: if she succeeds, she can aspire to a lofty future. Beauty, charm and sex appeal are necessary for this, but they are not sufficient: the woman must be considered

---

* Obviously, it is not through negative and hypocritical measures that this situation can be changed. For prostitution to disappear, two conditions are necessary: a decent job must be guaranteed to all women; customs must not place any obstacles to free love. Prostitution will be suppressed only by suppressing the needs to which it responds.

distinguished. Her value will often be revealed through a man's desire: but she will be 'launched' only when the man declares her price to the eyes of the world. In the last century, it was the town house, carriage and pair, and pearls that proved the influence of the cocotte on her protector and that raised her to the rank of demimondaine; her worth was confirmed as long as men continued to ruin themselves for her. Social and economic changes abolished the Blanche d'Antigny types. There is no longer a demimonde in which a reputation can be established. An ambitious woman has to try to attain fame in other ways. The most recent incarnation of the hetaera is the movie star. Flanked by her husband or serious male friend – rigorously required by Hollywood – she is no less related to Phryne, Imperia or Casque d'Or. She delivers Woman to the dreams of men who give her fortune and glory in exchange.

There has always been a vague connection between prostitution and art, because beauty and sexuality are ambiguously associated with each other. In fact, it is not Beauty that arouses desire: but the Platonic theory of love suggests hypocritical justifications for lust. Phryne baring her breast offers Areopagus the contemplation of a pure idea. Exhibiting an unveiled body becomes an art show; American burlesque has turned undressing into a stage show. 'Nudity is chaste,' proclaim those old gentlemen who collect obscene photographs in the name of 'artistic nudes'. In the brothel, the moment of choice begins as a display; if choosing is more complicated, *'tableaux vivants'* and 'artistic poses' are offered to the client. The prostitute who wishes to acquire a singular distinction does not limit herself to showing her flesh passively; she tries to have her own talents. Greek flute-playing women charmed men with their music and dances. The Ouled Nails performing belly dances and Spanish women dancing and singing in the Barrio Chino are simply offering themselves in a refined manner to enthusiasts. Nana goes on stage to find herself a 'protector'. Some music halls, like some concert cafés before them, are simply brothels. All occupations where a woman displays herself can be used for amatory purposes. Of course there are showgirls, taxi dancers, nude dancers, escorts, pin-ups, models, singers and actresses who do not let their sexual lives interfere with their occupations; the more skill and invention involved in their work, the more it can be taken as a goal in itself; but a woman who 'goes onstage' to earn a living is often tempted to use her charms for more intimate commercial ends. Inversely, the courtesan wishes to have an occupation that will serve as her alibi. Rare are those like Colette's Léa who, addressed by a friend as 'Dear artist', would respond: 'Artist? My lovers are truly most indiscreet.' We have said that her reputation confers a market value on her: the stage or screen where she makes a 'name' for herself will become her capital.

Cinderella does not always dream of Prince Charming: husband or lover, she fears he may change into a tyrant; she prefers to dream of her own smiling face on a movie theatre marquee. But it is more often thanks to her masculine 'protection' that she will attain her goal; and it is men – husbands, lovers, suitors – who confirm her triumph by letting her share their fortune or their fame. It is this need to *please* another or a crowd that connects the movie star to the hetaera. They play a similar role in society: I will use the word hetaera to designate women who use not only their bodies but also their entire person as exploitable capital. Their attitude is very different from that of a creator who, transcending himself in a work, goes beyond the given and appeals to a freedom in others to whom he opens up the future; the hetaera does not uncover the world, she opens no road to human transcendence:* on the contrary, she seeks to take possession of it for her profit; offering herself for the approval of her admirers, she does not disavow this passive femininity that dooms her to man: she endows it with a magic power that allows her to take males into the trap of her presence, and to feed herself on them; she engulfs them with herself in immanence.

In this way, woman succeeds in acquiring a certain independence. Giving herself to many men, she belongs to none definitively; the money she accumulates, the name she 'launches' as one launches a product, assure her economic autonomy. The freest women in Ancient Greece were neither matrons nor common prostitutes but hetaeras. Renaissance courtesans and Japanese geishas enjoy an infinitely greater freedom than their contemporaries. In France, the woman who seems to be the most virile and independent is perhaps Ninon de Lenclos. Paradoxically, those women who exploit their femininity to the extreme create a situation for themselves nearly equal to that of a man; moving from this sex that delivers them to men as objects, they become subjects. They not only earn their living like men but they live in nearly exclusively masculine company; free in their mores and speech, they can rise to the rarest intellectual freedom – like Ninon de Lenclos. The most distinguished among

---

* It may happen that she is *also* an artist and seeking to please, she invents and creates. She can either combine these two functions or go beyond the amatory level and class herself in the category of actress, opera singer, dancer, and so on, which will be discussed later.

them are often surrounded with artists and writers who find 'virtuous women' boring. Masculine myths find their most seductive incarnation in the hetaera; more than any other woman, she is flesh and conscious-ness, idol, inspiration, muse; painters and sculptors want her as their model; she will nourish poets' dreams; it is in her that the intellectual will explore the treasures of feminine 'intuition'; she is more readily intelligent than the matron, because she is less set in hypocrisy. Women who are extremely talented will not readily settle for the role of Egeria; they will feel the need to show autonomously the value that the admir-ation of others confers on them; they will try to transform their passive virtues into activities. Emerging in the world as sovereign subjects, they write poems, prose; they paint and compose music. Thus Imperia became famous among Italian courtesans. A woman might also use man as an instrument, so as to practise through him masculine functions: the 'favourite royal mistresses' participated in the government of the world through their powerful lovers.*

This liberation can be conveyed on the erotic level as well. Woman might find compensation for the feminine inferiority complex in the money and services she extorts from man; money has a purifying role; it abolishes the war of the sexes. If many nonprofessional women insist on extracting cheques and gifts from their lovers – making the man pay – and paying him, as we will see further on, it is not out of cupidity alone: it is to change him into an instrument. In that way, the woman defends herself from becoming one herself; perhaps he believes he 'has' her, but this sexual possession is illusory; it is she who *has* him on the far more solid economic ground. Her self-esteem is satisfied. She can abandon herself to her lover's embraces; she is not yielding to a foreign will; pleasure will not be 'inflicted' on her, it will become rather a supple-mentary benefit; she will not be 'taken' because she is paid.

Nevertheless, the courtesan has the reputation of being frigid. It is useful for her to know how to govern her heart and her sexual appetite: sentimental or sensual, she risks being under the influence of a man who will exploit or dominate her or make her suffer. Among the sexual acts she accepts, there are many – especially early in her career – that humil-iate her; her revolt against male arrogance is expressed by her frigidity. Hetaeras, like matrons, freely confide 'tricks' to each other that enable

---

* Just as some women use marriage to serve their own ends, others use their lovers as means for attaining a political or economic aim. They go beyond the hetaera's situa-tion as others go beyond the matron's.

them to 'fake' their work. This contempt, this disgust for men clearly shows they are not at all sure they have won the game of exploiter-exploited. And in fact, in the great majority of cases, dependence is still their lot.

No man is their definitive master. But they have the most urgent need of man. The courtesan loses all her means of existence if he ceases to desire her: the novice knows that her whole future is in his hands; deprived of masculine support, even the movie star sees her prestige fade: abandoned by Orson Welles, Rita Hayworth wandered over Europe like a sickly orphan until she found Ali Khan. The most beautiful woman is never sure of tomorrow because her weapons are magic, and magic is capricious; she is bound to her protector – husband or lover – nearly as tightly as a 'virtuous' wife is bound to her husband. She not only owes him bed service but also is subjected to his presence, conversation, friends and especially his vanity's demands. By paying for his steady's high heels and satin skirts, the pimp makes an investment that will bring a return; by offering his girlfriend pearls and furs, the industrialist or the producer displays his wealth and power through her: whether the woman is a means for earning money or a pretext for spending it, it is the same servitude. The gifts showered on her are chains. And are these clothes and jewels she wears really hers? The man sometimes reclaims them after they break up, as Sacha Guitry once did with elegance. To 'keep' her protector without renouncing her pleasures, the woman uses ruses, manoeuvres, lies and hypocrisy that dishonour conjugal life; even if she only feigns servility, this game is itself servile. Beautiful and famous, she can choose another if the master of the moment becomes odious. But beauty is a worry, a fragile treasure; the hetaera is totally dependent on her body, which time pitilessly degrades; the fight against ageing is most dramatic for her. If she is endowed with great prestige, she will be able to survive the ruin of her face and figure. But caring for this renown, her surest asset, subjects her to the hardest of tyrannies: that of public opinion. We know that Hollywood stars fall into slavery. Their bodies are no longer their own; the producer decides on their hair colour, weight, figure and type; teeth are pulled out to change the shape of a cheek. Diets, exercise, fittings and makeup are daily chores. Going out and flirting are part of 'personal appearances'; private life is just a moment in their public life. In France there is no written contract, but a careful and clever woman knows what 'promotion' demands of her. The star who refuses to give in to these demands will face a brutal or slow but ineluctable decline. The prostitute who only gives her body is perhaps less of a slave than the woman whose occupation it is to entertain. A woman who has 'arrived' through a real profession and whose talent is recognised – actress, opera singer, dancer – escapes the hetaera's condition; she can experience true independence; but most spend their entire lives in danger; they must seduce the public and men over and over without respite.

Very often the kept woman interiorises her dependence; subjected to public opinion, she accepts its values; she admires the 'fashionable world' and adopts its customs; she wants to be regarded according to bourgeois standards. She is a parasite of the rich bourgeoisie and she adheres to its ideas; she is 'right thinking'; in former times she would readily send her daughters to a convent school and as she got older, she even went to Mass and openly converted. She is on the conservatives' side. She is too proud to have made her place in this world to want to change. The struggle she wages to 'arrive' does not dispose her to feelings of brotherhood and human solidarity; she paid for her success with too much slavish compliance to sincerely wish for universal freedom. Zola highlights this trait in Nana:[102]

> As for books and plays, Nana had very definite opinions: she wanted tender and noble works, things to make her dream and elevate her soul . . . she was riled up against the republicans. What on earth did those dirty people who never washed want? Weren't people happy, didn't the emperor do everything he could for the people? A pretty bit of filth, the people! She knew them, she could talk about them: No, you see, their republic would be a great misfortune for everyone. Oh, may God preserve the emperor as long as possible!

In times of war, no one displays a more aggressive patriotism than high-level prostitutes; they hope to rise to the level of duchess through the noble sentiments they affect. Commonplaces, clichés, prejudices and conventional feelings form the basis of their public conversations, and they have often lost all sincerity deep in their hearts. Between lies and hyperbole, language is destroyed. The hetaera's whole life is a show: her words, her gestures, are intended not to express her thoughts but to produce an effect. She plays a comedy of love for her protector: at times she plays it for herself. She plays comedies of respectability and prestige for the public: she ends up believing herself to be a paragon of virtue and a sacred idol. Stubborn bad faith governs her inner life and permits her studied lies to seem true. There are moments of spontaneity in her life: she does experience love; she has 'flings' and 'infatuations'; sometimes she is even 'mad about' someone. But the one who spends too much time on caprices, feelings or pleasure will soon lose her 'position'. Generally, she composes her fantasies with the prudence of an adulterous wife; she hides from her producer and the public; thus, she cannot give too much of herself to her 'true loves'; they can only be a distraction, a respite. Besides, she is usually too obsessed with her own success to be able to lose herself in a real love affair. As for other women, it often happens that the hetaera loves them sensually; as an enemy of men who impose their domination on her, she will find sensual relaxation as well as revenge in the arms of a woman friend: so it was with Nana and her dear Satin. Just as she wishes to play an active role in the world to put her freedom to positive use, she likes to possess other beings: very young men whom she enjoys 'helping', or young women she will willingly support and, in any case, for whom she will be a virile personage. Whether she is homosexual or not, she will have the complex relations I have discussed with women in general: she needs them as judges and witnesses, as confidantes and accomplices, to create this 'counter-universe' that every woman oppressed by man must have. But feminine rivalry reaches its paroxysm here. The prostitute who trades on her generality has competition; but if there is enough work for everyone, they feel solidarity, even with their disputes. The hetaera who seeks to 'distinguish' herself is a priori hostile to the one who, like her, lusts for a privileged place. This is where the well-known theme of feminine 'cattiness' proves true.

The greatest misfortune for the hetaera is that not only is her independence the deceptive reverse side of a thousand dependencies, but this very freedom is negative. An actress like Rachel, a dancer like Isadora Duncan, even if they are aided by men, have occupations that are demanding and justify them; they attain concrete freedom from the work they choose and love. But for the great majority of them, their art, their occupations are only a means; they are not involved in real projects. Cinema in particular, which subjects the star to the director, allows her no invention, no progress, in creative activity. *Others* exploit what she *is*; she does not create a new object. Still it is quite rare to become a star. In 'amorous adventures', properly speaking, no road opens onto transcendence. Here again, ennui accompanies the confinement of woman in immanence. Zola shows this with Nana:

However, in the midst of all this luxury, and surrounded by her courtiers, Nana was bored to tears. She had men for every minute of the night, and money all over the house, even among the brushes and combs in the drawers of her dressing-table. But all this had ceased to satisfy her; and she was conscious of a void in her existence, a gap which made her yawn. Her life dragged on without occupation, each day bringing back the same monotonous hours. The next day did not exist: she lived like a bird, sure of having enough to eat, and ready to perch on the first branch she came to. This certainty of being fed caused her to stretch out in languid ease all day, lulled to sleep in conventional idleness and submission as if she were the prisoner of her own profession. Never going out except in her carriage, she began to lose the use of her legs. She reverted to her childish habits, kissing Bijou from morning to night and killing time with stupid pleasures, as she waited for some man or other.[103]

American literature abounds with this opaque ennui that stifles Hollywood and chokes the traveller as soon as he arrives there: actors and extras are as bored as the women whose condition they share. Even in France, official events are often burdensome. The protector who rules the starlet's life is an older man whose friends are his age: their preoccupations are foreign to the young woman, their conversations weary her; there is a chasm far deeper than in bourgeois marriages between the twenty-year-old novice and the forty-five-year-old banker who spend their days and nights side by side.

The Moloch to whom the hetaera sacrifices pleasure, love and freedom is her career. The matron's ideal is static happiness that envelops her relations with her husband and children. Her 'career' stretches across time, but it is nonetheless an immanent object that is summed up in a name. The name gets bigger on billboards and on people's lips as the steps mounted up the social ladder get higher. According to her temperament, the woman administers her enterprise prudently or boldly. One woman will find satisfaction in housekeeping, folding laundry in her closet, the other in the headiness of adventure. Sometimes the woman limits herself to perpetually balancing a perpetually threatened situation that sometimes breaks down; or sometimes she endlessly builds – like a Tower of Babel aiming in vain for the sky – her renown. Some of them, mixing amorous commerce with other activities, are true adventurers: they are spies, like Mata Hari, or secret agents; they generally are not the ones who initiate the projects, they are rather instruments in men's hands. But overall, the hetaera's attitude is similar to that of the adventurer; like him, she is often halfway between the *serious* and the *adventure* as such; she seeks ready-made values – money and glory – but she attaches as much value to winning them as to possessing them; and finally, the supreme value in her eyes is subjective success. She, too, justifies this individualism by a more or less systematic nihilism, but experienced with all the more conviction as she is hostile to men and sees enemies in other women. If she is intelligent enough to feel the need for moral justification, she will invoke a more or less well assimilated Nietzscheism; she will affirm the right of the elite being over the vulgar. Her person belongs to her like a treasure whose mere existence is a gift: so much so that in being dedicated to herself, she will claim to serve the group. The destiny of the woman devoted to man is haunted by love: she who exploits the male fulfils herself in the cult of self-adoration. If she attaches such a price to her glory, it is not only for economic interest: she seeks there the apotheosis of her narcissism.

CHAPTER 9

From Maturity to Old Age

The history of woman – because she is still trapped in her female functions – depends much more than man's on her physiological destiny; and the arc of this destiny is more erratic, more discontinuous, than the masculine one. Every period of woman's life is fixed and monotonous: but the passages from one stage to another are dangerously abrupt; they reveal themselves in far more decisive crises than those of the male: puberty, sexual initiation, menopause. While the male grows older continuously, the woman is brusquely stripped of her femininity; still young, she loses sexual attraction and fertility, from which, in society's and her own eyes, she derives the justification of her existence and her chances of happiness: bereft of all future, she has approximately half of her adult life still to live.

The 'dangerous age' is characterised by certain organic troubles,* but the symbolic value they embody gives them their importance. The crisis is felt much less acutely by women who have not essentially staked everything on their femininity; those who work hard – in their home or outside – are relieved when their menstrual servitude ends; peasants and workers' wives who are constantly threatened with new pregnancies are happy when, finally, that risk no longer exists. In this situation as in many others, women's disorders come less from the body itself than from their anxious consciousness of it. The moral drama usually begins before the onset of the physiological phenomena and it does not end until long after they have been eliminated.

Well before the definitive mutilation, woman is haunted by the horror of ageing. The mature man is engaged in more important enterprises than those of love; his sexual ardour is less pressing than in his youth; and as he is not expected to have the passive qualities of an object, the alteration of his face and body do not spoil his possibilities of seduction.

* See Vol. I, Chapter i.

By contrast, woman reaches her full sexual blossoming at about thirty-five, having finally overcome all her inhibitions: this is when her desires are the most intense and when she wants to satisfy them the most ardently; she has counted on her sexual attributes far more than man has; to keep her husband, to be assured of protection and to succeed in most jobs she holds, she has to please; she has not been allowed a hold on the world except through man's mediation: what will become of her when she no longer has a hold on him? This is what she anxiously wonders while she witnesses, powerless, the degradation of this object of flesh with which she is one; she fights; but dyes, peeling and plastic surgery can never do more than prolong her dying youth. At least she can play tricks with the mirror. But when the inevitable, irreversible process starts, which is going to destroy in her the whole edifice constructed during puberty, she feels touched by the very inevitability of death.

One might think that the woman who experiences the greatest distress is the one who has been the most passionately enraptured by her beauty and youth; but no; the narcissist is too attentive to her person not to have envisaged the ineluctable moment and not to have worked out an alternative position; she will certainly suffer from her mutilation: but at least she will not be caught short and will adapt rather quickly. The woman who has forgotten, devoted and sacrificed herself will be disrupted much more by the sudden revelation. 'I had only one life to live; this was my lot, so here I am!' To the surprise of her family and friends, a radical change takes place in her: expelled from her shelter, torn away from her projects, she brusquely finds herself, without resources, face-to-face with herself. Beyond this barrier she has unexpectedly struck, she has the feeling that she will do no more than survive; her body will be without promise; the dreams and desires she has not realised will for ever remain unaccomplished; she will look back on the past from this new perspective; the time has come to draw the line, to take stock. And she is horrified by the narrow strictures inflicted on her life. Faced with this, her brief and disappointing story, she behaves like an adolescent girl on the threshold of a still inaccessible future: she denies her finitude; to the poverty of her existence she contrasts the nebulous treasures of her personality. Because as a woman she endured her destiny more or less passively, she feels that her chances were taken from her, that she was duped, that she slid from youth to maturity without being aware of it. She discovers that her husband, her milieu and her occupations were not worthy of her; she feels misunderstood. She withdraws from the surroundings to which she esteems herself superior; she shuts herself up with the secret she carries in her heart and which is the mysterious key to her unfortunate lot; she tries to see the possibilities she has not exhausted. She begins to keep a diary; if she has understanding confidantes, she pours out her heart in endless conversations; and she ruminates on her regrets, her grievances, all day and all night. Just as the girl dreams of what her future *will be*, she recalls what her past *could have been*; she remembers the missed occasions and constructs beautiful retrospective romances. Helene Deutsch cites the case of a woman who had broken off an unhappy marriage very early on and who had then spent long serene years with a second husband: at forty-five, she painfully began to miss her first husband and to sink into melancholy. The cares of childhood and puberty come back to life, the woman constantly mulls over the story of her youth, and forgotten feelings for her parents, brothers and sisters and childhood friends come alive once again. Sometimes she indulges in dreamy and passive moroseness. But more often she is jolted into saving her wasted existence. She displays, exhibits and praises the merits of this personality she has just discovered in contrast with the pettiness of her destiny. Matured by experience, she believes she is finally able to prove her worth; she would like to have another chance. And first in a pathetic effort, she tries to stop time. A maternal woman is sure she can still have a child: she passionately seeks to create life once more. A sensual woman strives to conquer a new lover. The coquette is more than ever determined to please. They all declare they have never felt so young. They want to persuade others that the passage of time has not really touched them; they begin to 'dress young', they act childishly. The ageing woman well knows that if she has ceased being a sexual object, it is not only because her flesh no longer provides man with fresh treasures: it is also that her past and her experience make a person of her whether she likes it or not; she has fought, loved, wanted, suffered and taken pleasure for herself: this autonomy is intimidating; she tries to disavow it; she exaggerates her femininity, she adorns herself, wears perfume, she becomes totally charming, gracious, pure immanence; she admires her male interlocutor with a naive eye and childish intonations; she ostentatiously brings up her memories of girlhood; instead of speaking, she chirps, she claps her hands, bursts out laughing. She plays this game with a kind of sincerity. This newfound interest in herself and her desire to wrench herself from old routines and start over again give her the impression of a new beginning.

In fact, it is not really a question of a new start; she discovers no goals in the world towards which she could project herself in a free and effective movement. Her agitation is more eccentric, incoherent and useless because it only serves as symbolic compensation for past errors and failures. Among other things and before it is too late, the woman will try to realise all her childhood and adolescent desires: this one goes back to the piano, that one begins to sculpt, to write, to travel; she takes up skiing, foreign languages. She welcomes everything she had refused until then – again before it is too late. She admits her repugnance for a husband she had previously tolerated and she becomes frigid in his arms; or by contrast, she abandons herself to the passions she repressed; she overwhelms the husband with her demands; she goes back to practising masturbation, which she had given up since childhood. Her homosexual tendencies – that are latent in almost all women – come out. The subject often carries them over to her daughter; but sometimes unusual feelings arise for a woman friend. In his work, *Sex, Life and Faith*, Rom Landau tells the following story, confided to him by the person herself:

> Mrs X., a woman in the late forties, married for over twenty-five years, mother of three grown-up children, occupied a prominent position in . . . the social and charitable activities of the town in which she lived. Mrs X. met a woman in London some ten years her junior who, like herself, was a leading social worker. The two . . . became friends. Miss Y. invited Mrs X. to stay as her guest during her next visit to London, and Mrs X. . . . . accepted. During the second evening of her visit – Mrs X. assured me repeatedly that she had not the least idea how it happened – she suddenly found herself passionately embracing her hostess, and subsequently she spent the whole night with her . . . she was terrified . . . and left London the same day . . . Never in her life had she read or heard anything about homosexuality and had had no idea that 'such things' existed . . . she could do nothing to stifle her ever-growing feelings for Miss Y. . . . For the first time in her life she found [her husband's] caresses unwelcome, even his routine kiss . . . Finally, she decided to revisit Miss Y. and 'clear up' the situation . . . she only found herself more deeply involved in it; . . . to be with her filled her with a delight that she had never experienced before . . . she was troubled by a profound sin-consciousness, and was anxious to discover whether there was a 'scientific explanation' of her state and any moral justification for it.[104]

In this case, the subject gave in to a spontaneous drive and was herself deeply disconcerted by it. But often the woman deliberately seeks to live the romances she has not experienced and that soon she will no longer be able to experience. She leaves her home, both because it seems unworthy of her and because she desires solitude as well as the chance to seek adventure. If she finds it, she throws herself into it greedily. Thus, in this story by Stekel:

> Mme B. Z. was forty years old, had three children and twenty years of married life behind her when she began to think she was misunderstood, that she had wasted her life; she took up various new activities among which was going skiing in the mountains; there she met a thirty-year-old man and became his mistress; but soon after, he fell in love with Mme B. Z.'s daughter . . . she agreed to their marriage so as to keep her lover near her; there was an unacknowledged but very strong homosexual love between mother and daughter, which partially explains this decision. Nevertheless, the situation soon became intolerable, the lover sometimes leaving the mother's bed during the night to be with the daughter. Mme B. Z. . . . attempted suicide. It was then – she was forty-six – that she was treated by Stekel. She decided to break it off and while her daughter gave up her marriage plans Mme B. Z. . . . then became an exemplary wife and fell into piousness.

A woman influenced by a tradition of decency and honesty does not always follow through with action. But her dreams are peopled with erotic fantasies that she calls up during waking hours as well; she manifests an exalted and sensual tenderness to her children; she cultivates incestuous obsessions with her son; she secretly falls in love with one young man after another; like an adolescent girl, she is haunted by ideas of rape; she also feels the attraction of prostitution; the ambivalence of her desires and fears produces an anxiety that sometimes leads to neuroses: she scandalises her family and friends by bizarre behaviour that in fact merely expresses her imaginary life.

The boundary between the imaginary and the real is even less distinct in this troubled period than during puberty. One of the most salient characteristics in the ageing woman is the feeling of depersonalisation that makes her lose all objective landmarks. People in good health who have come close to death also say they have felt a curious impression of doubling; when one feels oneself to be consciousness, activity and freedom, the passive object affected by fate seems necessarily like another: *I* am not the one run over by a car; *I* am not the old woman the mirror shows me. The woman who 'never felt so young' and who never saw herself so old is not able to reconcile these two aspects of herself; time passes and diminishes her in dreams. So reality fades and becomes less important: likewise, she can no longer tell herself apart from the illusion. The woman relies on interior proof rather than on this strange world where time proceeds in reverse, where her double no longer resembles her, where events have betrayed her. She is thus inclined to ecstasies, visions and deliriums. And since love is even more than ever her essential preoccupation, it is understandable that she lets herself go to the illusion that she is loved. Nine out of ten erotomaniacs are women; and they are almost all between forty and fifty years old.

However, not everyone is able to cross over the wall of reality so boldly. Deprived of all human love, even in their dreams, many women seek relief in God; the flirt, the lover and the dissolute become pious around menopause. The vague ideas of destiny, secrecy and misunderstood personality of woman in her autumn years find a rational unity in religion. The devotee considers her wasted life as a test sent by the Lord; in her unhappiness, her soul has drawn exceptional advantages from misfortune, making her worthy of being visited by the grace of God; she will readily believe that heaven sends her illuminations or even – like Mme Krüdener – that it imperiously entrusts her with a mission. As she has more or less lost the sense of reality during this crisis, the woman is open to any suggestion: any spiritual guide is in a strong position to wield power over her soul. She will also enthusiastically accept more questionable authorities; she is an obvious prey for religious sects, spirits, prophets, faith healers and any charlatan. Not only has she lost all critical sense by losing contact with the given world, but she is also desperate for a definitive truth: she has to have the remedy, the formula, the key, that will suddenly save her by saving the universe. She scorns more than ever a logic that obviously could not possibly apply to her own case; the only arguments that seem convincing to her are those that are particularly destined for her: revelations, inspirations, messages, signs or even miracles begin to appear around her. Her discoveries sometimes draw her into paths of action: she throws herself into schemes, undertakings and adventures whose idea is whispered to her by some adviser or inner voices. Sometimes, she simply deems herself the holder of the truth and absolute wisdom. Whether she is active or contemplative, her attitude is accompanied by feverish exaltation. The crisis of menopause brutally cuts feminine life into two: it is this discontinuity that gives woman the illusion of a 'new life'; it is an *other* time opening before her: she approaches it with the fervour of a convert; she is converted to love, life, God, art and humanity: she loses and magnifies herself in these entities. She is dead and resuscitated, she views the earth with a gaze that has pierced the secrets of the beyond and she thinks she is flying towards uncharted heights.

Yet the earth does not change; the summits remain out of reach; the messages received – even in blinding clarity – are hard to decipher; the inner lights go out; what remains before the mirror is a woman one day older than yesterday. Doleful hours of depression follow moments of fervour. The body determines this rhythm since a reduction in hormonal secretions is offset by a hyperactive hypophysis; but it is above all the psychological state that orders this alternation. For the agitation, illusions and fervour are merely a defence against the inevitability of what has been. Once again, anxiety grabs the throat of the one whose life is already finished even though death is not imminent. Instead of fighting against despair, she often chooses to intoxicate herself with it. She rehashes grievances, regrets and recriminations; she imagines that her neighbours and family are engaging in dark machinations; if she has a sister or woman friend of her age who is associated with her life, they may construct persecution fantasies together. But above all she becomes morbidly jealous of her husband: she is jealous of his friends, his sisters, his job; and rightly or wrongly, she accuses some rival of being responsible for all her problems. Cases of pathological jealousy mostly occur between fifty and fifty-five years of age.

The problems of menopause will last – sometimes until death – if the woman does not decide to let herself grow old; if she does not have any resources other than the use of her charms, she will fight tooth and nail to maintain them; she will also fight with rage if her sex drives remain alive. This is not unusual. Princess Metternich was asked at what age a woman stops being tormented by the flesh: 'I don't know,' she said, 'I'm only sixty-five.' Marriage, which Montaigne thought provided 'little relief' for woman, becomes a more and more inadequate solution as a woman gets older; she often pays for the resistance and coldness of her youth in maturity; when she finally begins to experience the fevers of desire, her husband has been resigned to her indifference for a long time: he has found a solution for himself. Stripped of her attraction by habit and time, the wife seldom has the opportunity to awaken the conjugal flame. Vexed, determined to 'live her life', she will have fewer scruples than before – if she ever had any – in taking lovers; but there again they have to let themselves be taken: it is a manhunt. She deploys a thousand ruses: feigning to offer herself, she imposes herself; she uses charm, friendship and gratitude as traps. It is not only out of a desire for fresh flesh that she goes after young men: they are the only ones from whom she can hope for this disinterested tenderness the adolescent male can sometimes feel for a maternal mistress; she has become aggressive and domineering: Léa is fulfilled by Chéri's docility as well as by his beauty. Once she reached her forties, Mme de Staël chose pages whom she overwhelmed with her prestige; and a shy man, a novice, is also easier to capture. When seduction and intrigue really prove useless, there is still one resource: paying. The tale of the little knife, popular in the Middle Ages, illustrates these insatiable ogresses' fate: a young woman, as thanks for her favours, asked each of her lovers for a little knife, which she kept in a cupboard; the day came when the cupboard was full: but it was then that the lovers began to demand from her a little knife after each night of love; the cupboard was soon emptied; all the little knives had been returned: others had to be bought. Some women take a cynical view of the situation: they have had their moment, now it is their turn to 'return the little knives'. Money in their eyes can even play the opposite – but equally purifying – role of the one it plays for the courtesan: it changes the male into an instrument and provides woman with the erotic freedom that her young pride used to deny her. But more romantic than lucid, the mistress-benefactress often attempts to buy a mirage of tenderness, admiration and respect; she even persuades herself that she gives for the pleasure of giving, without being asked: here too a young man is the perfect choice because a woman can pride herself on maternal generosity towards him; and then there is a little of this 'mystery' the man also asks of the woman he 'helps' so that this crude deal is thus camouflaged as enigma. But it is rare for this bad faith to be moderate for long; the battle of the sexes changes into a duel between exploiter and exploited where woman, disappointed and ridiculed, risks suffering cruel defeats. If she is prudent, she will resign herself to 'disarming', without waiting too long, even if all her passions are not yet spent.

From the day woman agrees to grow old, her situation changes. Until then, she was still young, determined to fight against an evil that mysteriously made her ugly and deformed her; now she becomes a different being, asexual but complete: an elderly woman. It may be thought that the change-of-life crisis is then finished. But one must not conclude that it will be easy to live from then on. When she has given up the fight against the inevitability of time, another combat opens: she has to keep a place on earth.

Woman frees herself from her chains in her autumn and winter years; she uses the pretext of her age to escape burdensome chores; she knows her husband too well to let herself still be intimidated by him, she avoids his embraces, she carves out – in friendship, indifference or hostility – a real life of her own alongside him; if he declines more quickly than she, she takes the lead in the couple. She can also allow herself to disdain fashion and public opinion; she refuses social obligations, diets and beauty treatment: like Léa, whom Chéri finds liberated from dressmakers, corset-makers and hairdressers, and happily settled down indulging herself in food. As for her children, they are old enough not to need her, they get married, they leave home. Relieved of her duties, she finally discovers her freedom. Unfortunately, every woman's history repeats the fact we have observed throughout the history of woman: she discovers this freedom when she can find nothing more to do with it. This repetition has nothing coincidental about it: patriarchal society has made all feminine functions servile; woman escapes slavery only when she loses all productivity. At fifty, she is in full possession of her strength, she feels rich in experience; this is the age when man rises to the highest positions, the most important jobs: and as for her, she is forced into retirement. She has only been taught to devote herself and there is no one who requires her devotion any more. Useless, unjustified, she contemplates these long years without promise she still has to live and murmurs: 'No one needs me!'

She does not resign herself right away. Sometimes, out of despair, she clings to her husband; she overwhelms him more imperiously than ever with her ministrations; but the routine of conjugal life has been too well established; either she has known for a long time that her husband does not need her, or he does not seem precious enough to her to justify her any longer. Assuring the maintenance of their shared life is as contingent a task as watching over herself alone. She turns to her children with hope: for them the die is not yet cast; the world, the future is open to them; she would like to dive into it after them. The woman who has had the chance of giving birth at an advanced age finds herself privileged: she is still a young mother when the others are becoming grandparents. But in general, between forty and fifty, the mother sees her little ones become adults. It is at the very instant they are escaping her that she passionately attempts to live through them.

Her attitude is different depending on whether she is counting on being saved by a son or a daughter; she usually puts her strongest hope in her son. Here he finally comes to her from the far past, the man whose marvellous appearance she waited to see coming over the horizon; from the first scream of the newborn she has waited for this day when he will hand out all the treasures the father was never able to satisfy her with. During that time, she has doled out slaps and purges but she has forgotten them; he whom she carried in her womb was already one of these demigods who govern the world and women's destiny: now he will recognise her in the glory of her motherhood. He will defend her against her spouse's supremacy, avenge her for the lovers she has had and those she has not had; he will be her liberator, her saviour. She will behave like the seductive and ostentatious girl waiting for Prince Charming; when she is walking beside him, elegant and still charming, she thinks she looks like his 'older sister'; she is delighted if – taking after the heroes of American films – he teases and jostles her, laughing and respectful: with proud humility she recognises the virile superiority of the one she carried in her womb. To what extent can these feelings be considered incestuous? It is sure that when she thinks of herself complaisantly on her son's arm, the expression 'older sister' prudishly expresses ambivalent fantasies; when she sleeps, when she does not control herself, her musings sometimes carry her very far; but I have already said that dreams and fantasies are far from always expressing the hidden desire of a real act: they are often sufficient, they are the completion of a desire that only requires an imaginary satisfaction. When the mother plays in a more or less veiled way at seeing her son as a lover, it is just a game. Real eroticism usually has little place in this couple. But it is a couple; it is from the depths of her femininity that the mother hails in her son the sovereign man; she puts herself in his hands with as much fervour as a lover, and in exchange for this gift, she counts on being raised to the right hand of the god. To gain this assumption, the woman in love appeals to the lover's freedom: she generously assumes a risk; her anxious demands are the ransom. The mother reckons she has acquired holy rights by the simple fact of giving birth; she does not expect her son to see himself in her in order for her to consider him her creation, her property; she is less demanding than the woman lover because she is of a more tranquil bad faith; having made a being of flesh, she makes an existence her own: she appropriates its acts, accomplishments and merits. In exalting her fruit, she is carrying her own person to the heights.

Living by proxy is always a precarious expedient. Things may not turn out as one wished. It often happens that a son is no more than a good-for-nothing, a hooligan, a failure, a lost cause, an empty promise, ungrateful. The mother has her own ideas about the hero her son is supposed to embody. Nothing is rarer than a mother who authentically respects the human person her child is, who recognises his freedom even in his failures, who assumes with him the risks implied by any engagement. One more often encounters mothers who emulate that over-glorified Spartan woman who cavalierly condemns her son to glory or death; on earth, the son has to justify his mother's existence by taking hold of values she herself respects for their mutual advantage. The mother demands that the child-god's projects conform to her own ideal and that their success be assured. Every woman wants to give birth to a hero, a genius; but all mothers of heroes and geniuses began by proclaiming they were breaking their mothers' hearts. It is in reaction to his mother that man most often wins the trophies she dreamed of displaying for herself and that she does not recognise even when he lays them at her feet. Though she may approve in principle of her son's undertakings, she is torn by a contradiction similar to one that tortures the woman in love. To justify his life – and his mother's – the son must surpass her towards his ends; and to attain them, he is led to risk his health and put himself in danger: but he contests the value of the gift she gave him when he places certain goals above the pure fact of living. She is shocked by this; she reigns sovereign over man only if this flesh she has engendered is for him the supreme good: he does not have the right to destroy this work she has produced through suffering. 'You'll tire yourself out, you'll make yourself ill, you'll be sorry,' she drones in his ears. Yet she knows very well that to live is not enough, or else procreation itself would be superfluous; she is the first to be irritated if her offspring is a loafer, a coward. She is never at rest. When he goes to war, she wants him home alive but decorated. In his career, she wishes him to 'make it' but trembles when he overworks. Whatever he does, she always worries that she will stand by powerless in the unfolding of a story that is hers but over which she has no control: she fears he will make the wrong decision, that he will not succeed, that if he succeeds, he will ruin his health. Even if she has confidence in him, differences of age and sex keep a real complicity from being established between

her son and her; she is not informed about his work; no collaboration
is demanded of her.

This is why the mother remains unsatisfied, even if she admires her
son with inordinate pride. Believing that she has not only engendered
a being of flesh but also founded an absolutely necessary existence, she
feels retrospectively justified; but having rights is not an occupation:
to fill her days she needs to perpetuate her beneficent activity; she
wants to feel indispensable to her god; the mystification of devotion
in this case is denounced in the most brutal manner: his wife will strip
her of her functions. The hostility she feels to this stranger who 'steals'
her child has often been described. The mother has raised the contingent facticity of parturition to the height of divine mystery: she refuses
to accept that a human decision can have more weight. In her eyes,
values are preestablished, they proceed from nature, from the past:
she does not understand the value of a freely made engagement. Her
son owes her his life; what does he owe this woman he did not know
until yesterday? It is through some evil spell that she convinced him of
the existence of a bond that until now did not *exist*; she is devious,
calculating and dangerous. The mother impatiently waits for the imposture to be revealed; encouraged by the old myth of the good mother
with healing hands who binds the wounds inflicted on him by the bad
wife, she watches her son's face for signs of unhappiness: she finds
them, even if he denies it; she feels sorry for him even when he
complains of nothing; she spies on her daughter-in-law, she criticises
her, she counters all her innovations with the past and the customs
that condemn the intruder's very presence. Each woman understands
the beloved's happiness in her own way: the wife wants to see in him
a man through whom she will control the world; the mother tries to
keep him by taking him back to his childhood; to the projects of the
young wife who expects her husband to *become* rich or important, the
mother counters with the laws of his unchanging essence: he *is* fragile,
he must not tire himself. The conflict between the past and the future
is exacerbated when it is the newcomer's turn to get pregnant. 'The
birth of children is the death of parents'; here this truth is at its cruellest:
the mother who had hoped to live on through her son understands he
has condemned her to death. She gave life: life will continue without
her; she is no longer *the* Mother: simply a link; she falls from the heaven
of timeless idols; she is no more than a finished, outdated individual.
It is then that in pathological cases her hatred intensifies to the point
where she has a neurosis or is driven to commit a crime; it was when

her daughter-in-law's pregnancy was announced that Mme Lefebvre, who had long hated her, decided to kill her.*

Normally, the grandmother overcomes her hostility; sometimes she obstinately sees the newborn as her son's alone, and she loves it tyrannically; but generally the young mother and her own mother claim it for their own; the jealous grandmother cultivates an ambiguous affection for the baby, where hostility hides in the guise of concern.

The mother's attitude to her grown daughter is very ambivalent: she seeks a god in her son; in her daughter, she finds a double. The 'double' is an ambiguous personage; it assassinates the one from which it emanates, as can be seen in the tales of Poe, in *The Picture of Dorian Gray* and in the story told by Marcel Schwob. Thus the girl condemns her mother to death by becoming a woman; and yet, she permits her to survive. The mother's behaviour depends on whether she grasps her child's healthy development as a promise of ruin or of resurrection.

Many mothers become rigid in hostility; they do not accept being supplanted by the ingrate who owes them her life; we have often pointed out the coquette's jealousy of the fresh adolescent who denounces her artifices: a woman who has detested a rival in any woman will hate the rival even in her child; she sends her away, hides her, or finds ways to deprive her of opportunities. A woman who took pride in being the Wife and the Mother in an exemplary and unique way will refuse no less fiercely to give up her throne; she continues to affirm that her daughter is merely a child, and she considers her undertakings to be childish games; she is too young to marry, too delicate to give birth; if she insists on wanting a husband, a home and children, they will never be more than look-alikes; the mother tirelessly criticises, derides or prophesies misfortune. If she can, she condemns her daughter to eternal childhood; if not, she tries to ruin this adult life the daughter is trying to lead on her own.

---

* In August 1925, a sixty-year-old bourgeois woman from the North, Mme Lefebvre, who lived with her husband and her children, killed her daughter-in-law, six months pregnant, during a car trip while her son was driving. Condemned to death and then pardoned, she spent the rest of her life in a reformatory where she showed no remorse; she believed God approved of her when she killed her daughter-in-law 'as one kills a weed, a bad seed, as one kills a savage beast'. The only savagery she gave as proof was that the young woman one day said to her: 'You have me now, so you now have to take me into account.' It was when she suspected her daughter-in-law's pregnancy that she bought a revolver, supposedly to defend herself against robbers. After her menopause, she was desperately attached to her maternity: for twelve years she had suffered from malaises that manifested themselves symbolically in an imaginary pregnancy.

We have seen that she often succeeds: many young women remain sterile, have miscarriages, prove incapable of nursing and raising their children or running their homes because of this evil influence. Their conjugal life becomes impossible. Unhappy and isolated, they will find refuge in the sovereign arms of their mothers. If they resist her, a perpetual conflict will pit them against each other; the frustrated mother largely transfers onto her son-in-law the irritation her insolent daughter's independence provokes in her.

The mother who passionately identifies with her daughter is no less tyrannical; what she wants, having acquired mature experience, is to relive her youth: thus will she save her past while saving herself from it; she herself will choose a son-in-law who conforms to the perfect husband she never had; flirtatious and tender, she will easily imagine somewhere in her heart that it is she he is marrying; through her daughter, she will satisfy her old desires for wealth, success and glory; such women, who ardently 'push' their children along the paths of seduction, cinema or theatre, have often been described; under the pretext of watching over them, they take over their lives: I have been told about some who go so far as to take the girl's suitor to bed with them. But it is rare for the girl to put up with this guardianship indefinitely; the day she finds a husband or a serious protector, she will rebel. The mother-in-law who had begun by cherishing her son-in-law then becomes hostile to him; she moans about human ingratitude, takes the role of victim herself; she becomes in her turn an enemy mother. Foreseeing these disappointments, many women feign indifference when they see their children grow up: but they take little joy from it. A mother must have a rare mixture of generosity and detachment to find enrichment in her children's lives without becoming a tyrant or turning them into her tormentors.

The grandmother's feelings towards her grandchildren are an extension of those she has for her daughter: she often transfers her hostility onto them. It is not only out of fear of public opinion that so many women force their seduced daughter to have an abortion, to abandon the child, to do away with it: they are only too happy to keep her from motherhood; they obstinately wish to keep the privilege for themselves. They readily advise even a legitimate mother to provoke a miscarriage, not to breast-feed the child, or to rid herself of it. They themselves will deny the existence of this impudent little being by their indifference; or else they will spend their time endlessly scolding the child, punishing him, even mistreating him. By contrast, the mother who identifies with her daughter often welcomes the children more avidly than the young woman does; the daughter is disconcerted by the arrival of the little stranger; the grandmother recognises him: she goes back twenty years in time, she becomes the young woman giving birth again; all the joys of possession and domination her children long ago ceased to give her are returned to her, all the desires of motherhood she had renounced with menopause are miraculously fulfilled; she is the real mother, she takes charge of the baby with authority, and if the baby is given over to her, she will passionately devote herself to him. Unfortunately for her, the young woman is keen to hold on to her rights: the grandmother is authorised only to play the role of assistant that her elders formerly played with her; she feels dethroned; and besides, she has to share this with her son-in-law's mother, of whom she is naturally jealous. Resentment often distorts the spontaneous love she felt at first for the child. The anxiety often observed in grandmothers expresses the ambivalence of their feelings: they cherish the baby insofar as it belongs to them, they are hostile to the little stranger that he is to them, they are ashamed of this enmity. Yet if the grandmother maintains her warm affection for her grandchildren while giving up the idea of entirely possessing them, she can play the privileged role of guardian angel in their lives: recognising neither rights nor responsibilities, she loves them out of pure generosity; she does not entertain narcissistic dreams through them, she asks nothing of them, she does not sacrifice their future in which she will not be present: what she loves are the little flesh-and-blood beings who are there today in their contingency and their gratuitousness; she is not an educator; she does not represent abstract justice or law. This is where the conflicts that at times set her in opposition to the parents will sometimes arise.

It may be that the woman has no descendants or is not interested in posterity; lacking natural bonds with children or grandchildren, she sometimes tries to create them artificially with counterparts. She offers maternal tenderness to young people; whether or not her affection remains platonic, it is not necessarily hypocrisy that makes her declare that she loves her young protégé 'like a son': the mother's feelings, inversely, are love feelings. It is true that Mme de Warens's competitors take pleasure in generously satisfying, helping and shaping a man: they want to be the source, the necessary condition and the foundation of an existence that has passed them by; they become mothers and find their identity in their lovers far more in this role than in the role of mistress. Very often also the maternal woman adopts girls: here again their relations take more or less sexual forms; but whether platonic or carnal, what she seeks in her protégées is her own double, miraculously rejuvenated. The actress, the dancer, the singer become teachers – they form pupils – and the intellectual woman – such as Mme de Charrière, alone in Colombier – indoctrinates disciples; the devotee gathers spiritual daughters around her; the seductress becomes a madam. It is never pure self-interest that brings such ardent zeal to their proselytising: they are passionately seeking to reincarnate themselves. Their tyrannical generosity gives rise to more or less the same conflicts as between mothers and daughters united by blood. It is also possible to adopt grandchildren: great-aunts and godmothers gladly play a role similar to that of grandmothers. But in any case, it is rare for a woman to find in posterity – natural or selected – a justification of her declining life: she fails to make the enterprise of these young existences her own. Either she persists in the effort to appropriate it, consumed in the struggles and dramas that leave her disappointed and broken; or she resigns herself to a modest participation. This is the most common case. The aged mother and grandmother repress their dominating desires, they conceal their resentments; they are satisfied with whatever their children choose to give them. But then they get little help from them. They remain available facing the desert of the future, prey to solitude, regret and ennui.

Here we touch upon the older woman's tragedy: she realises she is useless; all through her life, the bourgeois woman often has to resolve the derisory problem: how to kill time? For once the children are raised and the husband has become successful, or at least settled, days drag on. 'Women's handiwork' was invented to mask this horrible idleness; hands embroider, knit, they are busy hands and they move; it is not a question here of real work because the object produced is not the goal; it has little importance and it is often a problem to know what to do with it: one gets rid of it by giving it to a friend or a charitable organisation or by cluttering mantelpieces or coffee tables; neither is it a game that reveals the pure joy of existence in its gratuitousness; and it is hardly a diversion because the mind is vacant: it is an absurd distraction, as Pascal described it; with needle or hook, woman sadly weaves the very nothingness of her days. Watercolours, music or reading have the very same role; the unoccupied woman does not try to extend her grasp on the world in giving herself over to such activities, but only to relieve boredom; an activity that does not open up the future slides into the vanity of immanence; the idle woman begins a book, then puts it down, opens the piano, closes it, returns to her embroidery, yawns and ends up on the telephone. In fact, she is more likely to seek relief in social life; she goes out, makes visits, and – like Mrs Dalloway – attaches enormous importance to her parties; she goes to every wedding, every funeral; no longer having any existence of her own, she feeds on the company of others; she goes from being a coquette to a gossip: she watches, she comments; she compensates for her inaction by dispensing criticism and advice to those around her. She gives her experienced advice even to those around her who do not seek it. If she has the means, she holds a salon; in this way she hopes to appropriate undertakings and successes that are not hers; Mme du Deffand's and Mme Verdurin's despotism over their subjects is well known. To be a centre of attraction, a crossroads, an inspiration, or to create an 'atmosphere' is in itself an ersatz activity. There are other more direct ways to intervene in the course of the world; in France, there are 'charities' and a few 'clubs', but it is particularly true in America that women group together in clubs where they play bridge, hand out literary prizes, or reflect on social improvement. What characterises most of these organisations on the two continents is that they are in themselves their own reason for existence: the aims they claim to pursue serve only as a pretext. Things happen exactly as in Kafka's fable:* no one is concerned about building the Tower of Babel; a vast city is built around its ideal place, consuming all its resources for administration, growth and resolving internal dissensions. So charity women spend most of their time organising their organisation; they elect a board, discuss its statutes, dispute among themselves and struggle to keep their prestige over rival associations: no one must steal *their* poor, *their* sick, *their* wounded, *their* orphans; they would rather leave them to die than yield them to their neighbours. And they are far from wanting a regime that, in doing away with injustice and abuse, would make their dedication useless; they bless the wars and famines that transform them into benefactresses of humanity. It is clear that in their eyes the knitted hats and parcels are not intended for soldiers and the hungry: instead the soldiers and hungry are made expressly to receive knitted goods and parcels.

In spite of everything, some of these groups attain positive results. In the United States, the influence of venerated 'Moms' is strong; this is explained by the leisure time their parasitic existence leaves them: and this is why it is harmful. 'Knowing nothing about medicine, art, science, religion, law, health, sanitation . . .' says Philip Wylie,† speaking of the American Mom, 'she seldom has any special interest in *what*, exactly, she is doing as a member of any of these endless organizations,

---

* 'The City Coat of Arms'.
† *Generation of Vipers.*

so long as it is *something*.' Their effort is not integrated into a coherent and constructive plan, it does not aim at objective ends: imperiously, it tends only to show their tastes and prejudices or to serve their interests. They play a considerable role in the domain of culture, for example: it is they who buy the most books; but they read as one plays the game of solitaire; literature takes its meaning and dignity when it is addressed to individuals committed to projects, when it helps them surpass themselves towards greater horizons; it must be integrated into the movement of human transcendence; instead, woman devalues books and works of art by swallowing them into her immanence; a painting becomes a knick-knack, music an old song, a novel a reverie as useless as crocheted antimacassars. It is American women who are responsible for the degradation of best sellers: these books are only intended to please, and worse to please idle women who need escape. As for their activities in general, Philip Wylie defines them like this:

> They frighten politicians into sniveling servility and they terrify pastors; they bother bank presidents and they pulverise school boards. Mom has many such organizations, the real purpose of which is to compel an abject compliance of her environs to her personal desires . . . she drives out of the town and the state, if possible, all young harlots . . . she causes bus lines to run where they are convenient for her rather than for workers . . . throws prodigious fairs and parties for charity and gives the proceeds . . . to the janitor to buy the committee some beer for its headache on the morning after . . . The clubs afford mom an infinite opportunity for nosing into other people's business.

There is much truth in this aggressive satire. Not being specialised in politics or economics or any technical discipline, old women have no concrete hold on society; they are unaware of the problems action poses; they are incapable of elaborating a constructive programme. Their morality is abstract and formal, like Kant's imperatives; they issue prohibitions instead of trying to discover the paths of progress; they do not positively try to create new situations; they attack what already exists in order to do away with the evil in it; this explains why they are always forming coalitions against something – against alcohol, prostitution or pornography – they do not understand that a purely negative effort is doomed to be unsuccessful, as evidenced by the failure of prohibition in America or the law in France voted by Marthe Richard. As long as woman remains a parasite, she cannot effectively participate in the building of a better world.

It does happen that in spite of everything, some women entirely committed to a cause truly have an impact; these women are not merely seeking to keep themselves busy, they have ends in view; autonomous producers, they escape from the parasitic category we are considering here: but this conversion is rare. In their private or public activities, most women do not aim for a goal that can be reached but for a way to keep busy: and no occupation is meaningful if it is only a pastime. Many of them suffer from this; with a life already behind them, they feel the same distress as adolescent boys whose lives have not yet opened up; nothing is calling them, around them both is a desert; faced with any action, they murmur: What's the use? But the adolescent boy is drawn, willingly or not, into a man's existence that reveals responsibilities, goals and values; he is thrown into the world, he takes a stand, he becomes committed. If it is suggested to the older woman that she begin to move towards the future, she responds sadly: it's too late. It is not that her time is limited from here on: a woman is made to retire very early; but she lacks the drive, confidence, hope and anger that would allow her to discover new goals in her own life. She takes refuge in the routine that has always been her lot; she makes repetition her system, she throws herself into household obsessions; she becomes more deeply religious; she becomes rigidly stoic, like Mme de Charrière. She becomes brittle, indifferent, egotistical.

The old woman often finds serenity towards the end of her life when she has given up the fight, when death's approach frees her from anxiety about the future. Her husband was often older than she, she witnesses his decline with silent complacency: it is her revenge; if he dies first, she cheerfully bears the mourning; it has often been observed that men are far more overwhelmed by being widowed late in life: they profit more from marriage than women do, and particularly in their old age, because then the universe is concentrated within the limits of the home; the present does not spill over into the future: it is their wife who assures their monotonous rhythm and reigns over them; when he loses his public functions, man becomes totally useless; woman continues at least to run the home; she is necessary to her husband, whereas he is only a nuisance. Women are proud of their independence, they finally begin to view the world through their own eyes; they realise they have been duped and mystified their whole lives; now lucid and wary, they often attain a delicious cynicism. In particular, the woman who 'has lived' has a knowledge of men that no man shares: for she has seen not their public image but the contin-gent individual that every one of them lets show in the absence of their counterparts; she also knows women, who only show themselves in their spontaneity to other women: she knows what happens behind the scenes. But even if her experience allows her to denounce mystifications and lies, it is not enough to reveal the truth to her. Whether she is amused or bitter, the old woman's wisdom still remains completely negative: it is contestation, accusation, refusal; it is sterile. In her thoughts as in her acts, the highest form of freedom a woman-parasite can have is stoic defi-ance or sceptical irony. At no time in her life does she succeed in being both effective and independent.

CHAPTER 10

Woman's Situation and Character

We can now understand why, from Ancient Greece to today, there are so many common features in the indictments against woman; her condition has remained the same throughout superficial changes, and this condition defines what is called the woman's 'character': she 'wallows in immanence', she is argumentative, she is cautious and petty, she does not have the sense either of truth or of accuracy, she lacks morality, she is vulgarly self-serving, selfish, she is a liar and an actress. There is some truth in all these affirmations. But the types of behaviour denounced are not dictated to woman by her hormones or predestined in her brain's compartments: they are suggested in negative form by her situation. We will attempt to take a synthetic point of view of her situation, necessarily leading to some repetition, but making it possible to grasp the Eternal Feminine in her economic, social and historical conditioning as a whole.

The 'feminine world' is sometimes contrasted with the masculine universe, but it must be reiterated that women have never formed an autonomous and closed society; they are integrated into the group governed by males, where they occupy a subordinate position; they are united by a mechanical solidarity only insofar as they are similar: they do not share that organic solidarity upon which any unified community is founded; they have always endeavoured – in the period of the Eleusinian mysteries just like today in clubs, salons and recreation rooms – to band together to assert a 'counter-universe', but it is still within the masculine universe that they frame it. And this is where the paradox of their situation comes in: they belong both to the male world and to a sphere in which this world is challenged; enclosed in this sphere, involved in the male world, they cannot peacefully establish themselves anywhere. Their docility is always accompanied by refusal, their refusal by acceptance; this is similar to the girl's attitude; but it is more difficult to maintain because it is no longer simply a question of the adult woman dreaming her life through symbols, but of living it.

The woman herself recognises that the universe as a whole is masculine; it is men who have shaped it, ruled it and who still today dominate it; as for her, she does not consider herself responsible for it; it is understood that she is inferior and dependent; she has not learned the lessons of violence, she has never emerged as a subject in front of other members of the group; enclosed in her flesh, in her home, she grasps herself as passive opposite to these human-faced gods who set goals and standards. In this sense there is truth in the saying that condemns her to remaining 'an eternal child'; it has also been said of workers, black slaves, and colonised natives that they were 'big children' as long as they were not threatening; that meant they had to accept without argument the truths and laws that other men gave them. Woman's lot is obedience and respect. She has no grasp, even in thought, on this reality that involves her. It is an opaque presence in her eyes. That means she has not learned the technology that would enable her to dominate matter; as for her, she is not fighting with matter but with life, and life cannot be mastered by tools: one can only submit to its secret laws. The world does not appear to the woman as a 'set of tools' halfway between her will and her goals, as Heidegger defines it: on the contrary, it is a stubborn, indomitable resistance; it is dominated by fate and run through with mysterious caprices. No mathematics can make an equation out of this mystery of a spot of blood that changes into a human being in the mother's womb, no machine can rush it or slow it down; she experiences the resistance of a duration that the most ingenious machines fail to divide or multiply; she experiences it in her flesh that is subjected to the rhythm of the moon, and that the years first ripen and then corrode. Daily cooking teaches her patience and passivity; it is alchemy; one must obey fire, water, 'wait for the sugar to melt', the dough to rise and also the clothes to dry, the fruit to ripen. Housework comes close to a technical activity; but it is too rudimentary, too monotonous to convince the woman of the laws of mechanical causality. Besides, even in this area, things are capricious; there is material that 'revives' and material that does not 'revive' in the wash, spots that come out and others that persist, objects that break on their own, dust that grows like plants. Woman's mentality perpetuates that of agricultural civilisations that worship the earth's magical qualities: she believes in magic. Her passive eroticism reveals her desire not as will and aggression but as an attraction similar to that which makes the dowser's pendulum quiver; the mere presence of her flesh makes the male sex swell and rise; why should hidden water not make the dowser's wand jump? She feels surrounded by waves, radiation, fluid; she believes in telepathy, astrology, divination, Mesmer's *baquet*, theosophy, table turning, mind readers and healers; she introduces primitive superstitions into religion – candles, ex votos, and such – she embodies ancient spirits of nature in the saints – this one protects travellers, that one women who have just given birth, another one finds lost objects – and of course no marvel surprises her. Her attitude will be that of conjuration and prayer; to obtain a certain result, she will follow certain time-tested rites. It is easy to understand why she is ruled by routine; time has no dimension of novelty for her, it is not a creative spring; because she is doomed to repetition, she does not see in the future anything but a duplication of the past; if one knows the word and the recipe, duration is allied with the powers of fecundity: but this too obeys the rhythm of months and seasons; the cycle of each pregnancy, of each flowering, reproduces the preceding one identically; in this circular movement, time's sole becoming is slow degradation: it eats at furniture and clothes just as it disfigures the face; fertile powers are destroyed little by little by the flight of years. So the woman does not trust this force driven to destroy.

Not only is she unaware of what real action is, that is able to change the face of the world, but she is lost in the middle of this world as in the heart of an immense and confused mass. She does not know how to use masculine logic well. Stendhal noted that she handles it as skilfully as man if she has to. But it is an instrument she does not often have the occasion to use. A syllogism is not useful in making mayonnaise or calming a child's tears; masculine reasoning is not relevant to the reality she experiences. And in the man's world, since she does not *do* anything, her thinking, as it does not flow into any project, is no different from a dream; she does not have the sense of truth, because she lacks efficacy; she struggles only by means of images and words: that is why she accepts the most contradictory assertions without a problem; she does not care about clarifying the mysteries of a sphere, which in any case is beyond her scope; she settles for horribly vague knowledge when it concerns her: she confuses parties, opinions, places, people and events; there is a strange jumble in her head. But after all, seeing clearly is not her business: she was taught to accept masculine authority; she thus forgoes criticising, examining and judging for herself. She leaves it to the superior caste. This is why the masculine world seems to be a transcendent reality, an absolute to her. 'Men make gods,' says Frazer, 'and women worship them.' Men cannot kneel with total conviction in front of idols they themselves have created but when women come across these imposing statues on their path they cannot imagine any hand making them and they meekly bow down before them.*[105] They specifically like Law and Order to be embodied in a chief. In all Olympus, there is one sovereign god; the prestigious virile essence must be gathered in one archetype of which father, husband and lovers are merely vague reflections. It is somewhat humorous to say that their worship of this great totem is sexual; what is true is that women fully realise their infantile dream of abdication and prostration. In France, the generals Boulanger, Pétain and de Gaulle[†] have always had the support of women; one remembers the purple prose of *L'Humanité*'s women journalists when writing about Tito and his beautiful uniform. The general the dictator – eagle eye, prominent chin – is the celestial father the serious universe demands, the absolute guarantor of all values. The respect women grant to heroes and to the masculine world's laws stems from their powerlessness and ignorance; they acknowledge these laws not through judgement but through an act of faith: faith draws its fanatical power from the fact that it is not knowledge: it is blind, passionate, stubborn and stupid; what it puts forward is done unconditionally, against reason, against history, against all refutation. This stubborn reverence can take two forms depending on circumstances: sometimes it is the content of the law and sometimes the empty form alone that the woman passionately abides by. If she belongs to the privileged elite that profits from the given social order, she wants it unshakeable and she is seen as intransigent. The man knows he can reconstruct other institutions, another ethics, another code; grasping himself as transcendence, he also envisages history as a becoming; even the most conservative knows that some change is inevitable and that he has to adapt his action and thinking to it; as the woman does not participate in history, she does not understand its necessities; she mistrusts the future and wants to stop time. If the idols her father, brothers and husband propose are knocked down, she cannot imagine any way of repopulating the heavens; she is determined to defend them. Among the Southerners during the Civil War, no one was as

---

* Cf. J.-P. Sartre, *Dirty Hands*: 'HOEDERER: They need props, you understand, they are given ready-made ideas, then they believe in them as they do in God. We're the ones who make these ideas and we know how they are cooked up; we are never quite sure of being right.'

† 'On the general's passage, the public was made up mostly of women and children' (*Les Journaux*, about the September 1948 tour in Savoy).

　'The men applauded the general's speech, but the women stood out by their enthusiasm. Some were literally in ecstasy, singling out almost every word and clapping and shouting with a fervour that made their faces turn poppy-red' (*Aux Écoutes*, 11 April 1947).

passionately in favour of slavery as the women; in England during the Boer war, and in France against the Commune, it was the women who were the most enraged; they seek to compensate for their inaction by the force of the feelings they display; in victory they are as wild as hyenas against the beaten enemy; in defeat, they bitterly refuse any arrangement; as their ideas are only attitudes, they do not mind defending the most outdated causes: they can be legitimists in 1914, tsarists in 1949. Sometimes the man smilingly encourages them: it pleases him to see his measured opinions reflected in a fanatical form; but sometimes he is also bothered by the stupid and stubborn way his own ideas are transformed.

It is only in strongly integrated civilisations and classes that the woman looks so intransigent. Generally, as her faith is blind, she respects the laws simply because they are laws; the laws may change, but they keep their prestige; in the eyes of women, power creates law since the laws they recognise in men come from their power; that is why they are the first to throw themselves at the victors' feet when a group collapses. In general, they accept what is. One of their typical features is resignation. When the ashes of Pompeii's statues were dug out, it was observed that the men were caught in movements of revolt, defying the sky or trying to flee, while the women were bent, withdrawn into themselves, turning their faces towards the earth. They know they are powerless against things: volcanoes, policemen, employers or men. 'Women are made to suffer,' they say. 'That's life; nothing can be done about it.' This resignation engenders the patience often admired in women. They withstand physical suffering much better than men; they are capable of stoic courage when circumstances demand it: without the aggressive daring of the male, many women are distinguished by the calm tenacity of their passive resistance; they deal with crises, misery and misfortune more energetically than their husbands; respectful of duration that no haste can conquer, they do not measure their time; when they apply their calm stubbornness to any undertaking, they are sometimes brilliantly successful. 'Whatever woman wants',[106] says the proverb. In a generous woman, resignation looks like indulgence: she accepts everything, she condemns no one because she thinks that neither people nor things can be different from what they are. A proud woman can make a lofty virtue of it, like Mme de Charrière, rigid in her stoicism. But she also engenders a sterile prudence; women always try to keep, to fix, to arrange rather than to destroy and reconstruct anew; they prefer compromises and exchanges to revolutions. In the nineteenth century, they constituted one of the biggest obstacles to the effort of women workers' emancipation: for every

Flora Tristan or Louise Michel, how many utterly timid housewives begged their husbands not to take any risk! They were afraid not only of strikes, unemployment and misery; they also feared that the revolt was a mistake. Submission for submission, it is understandable that they prefer routine to adventure: they eke out for themselves a more meagre happiness at home than on the streets. Their lot is one with that of perishable things: they would lose everything in losing them. Only a free subject, asserting himself beyond time, can foil destruction; this supreme recourse is forbidden to the woman. It is mainly because she has never experienced the powers of liberty that she does not believe in liberation: the world to her seems governed by an obscure destiny against which it is presumptuous to react. These dangerous paths that she is compelled to follow are ones she herself has not traced: it is understandable that she does not take them enthusiastically.*[107] When the future is open to her, she no longer hangs on to the past. When women are concretely called to action, when they identify with the designated aims, they are as strong and brave as men.†

Many of the faults for which they are reproached – mediocrity, meanness, shyness, pettiness, laziness, frivolity and servility – simply express the fact that the horizon is blocked for them. Woman, it is said, is sensual, she wallows in immanence; but first she was enclosed in it. The slave imprisoned in the harem does not feel any morbid passion for rose jelly and perfumed baths: she has to kill time somehow; inasmuch as the woman is stifling in a dismal gynaeceum – brothel or bourgeois home – she will also take refuge in comfort and well-being; moreover, if she avidly pursues sexual pleasure, it is often because she is frustrated; sexually unsatisfied, destined to male brutality, 'condemned to masculine ugliness', she consoles herself with creamy sauces, heady wines, velvets, the caresses of water, sun, a woman friend or a young lover. If

---

* Cf. Gide, *Journals*: 'Creusa or Lot's wife: one tarries and the other looks back, which is a worse way of tarrying . . . There is no greater cry of passion than this:

> *And Phaedra having braved the Labyrinth with you*
> *Would have been found with you or lost with you.*

But passion blinds her; after a few steps, to tell the truth, she would have sat down, or else would have wanted to go back – or even would have made him carry her.'
† This is how the attitude of the proletarian women has changed over the century; during the recent strikes in the mines of the North, for example, they showed as much passion and energy as men, demonstrating and fighting side by side.

she appears to man as such a 'physical' being, it is because her condition incites her to attach a great deal of importance to her animality. Carnality does not cry out any more strongly in her than in the male: but she watches out for its slightest signs and amplifies it; sexual pleasure, like the wrenching of suffering, is the devastating triumph of immediacy; the violence of the instant negates the future and the universe: outside of the carnal blaze, what is there is nothing; during this brief apotheosis, she is no longer mutilated or frustrated. But once again, she attaches such importance to these triumphs of immanence because it is her only lot. Her frivolity has the same cause as her 'sordid materialism'; she gives importance to little things because she lacks access to big ones: moreover the futilities that fill her days are often of great seriousness; she owes her charm and her opportunities to her toilette and beauty. She often seems lazy, indolent; but the occupations that are offered her are as useless as the pure flowing of time; if she is talkative or a scribbler, it is to while away her time: she substitutes words for impossible acts. The fact is that when a woman is engaged in an undertaking worthy of a human being, she knows how to be as active, effective and silent, as ascetic, as a man. She is accused of being servile; she is always willing, it is said, to lie at her master's feet and to kiss the hand that has beaten her. It is true that she generally lacks real self-regard; advice to the 'lovelorn', to betrayed wives and abandoned lovers is inspired by a spirit of abject submission; the woman exhausts herself in arrogant scenes and in the end gathers up the crumbs the male is willing to throw her. But what can a woman – for whom the man is both the only means and the only reason for living – do without masculine help? She has no choice but to endure all humiliations; a slave cannot understand the meaning of 'human dignity'; for him it is enough if he manages to survive. Finally, if she is 'down to earth', a homebody, simply useful, it is because she has no choice but to devote her existence to preparing food and cleaning nappies: she cannot draw the meaning of grandeur from this. She must ensure the monotonous repetition of life in its contingency and facticity: it is natural for her to repeat herself, to begin again, without ever inventing, to feel that time seems to be going around in circles without going anywhere; she is busy without ever *doing* anything: so she is alienated in what she *has;* this dependence on things, a consequence of the dependence in which she is held by men, explains her cautious management, her avarice. Her life is not directed towards goals: she is absorbed in producing or maintaining things that are never more than means – food, clothes, lodging – these are inessential intermediaries between animal life and free existence; the only value that is attached to inessential means is usefulness; the housewife lives at the level of utility, and she takes credit for herself only when she is useful to her family. But no existent is able to satisfy itself with an inessential role: he quickly makes ends out of means – as can be observed in politicians, among others – and in his eyes the value of the means becomes an absolute value. Thus utility reigns higher than truth, beauty and freedom in the housewife's heaven; and this is the point of view from which she envisages the whole universe; and this is why she adopts the Aristotelian morality of the golden mean, of mediocrity. How could one find daring, ardour, detachment and grandeur in her? These qualities appear only where a freedom throws itself across an open future, emerging beyond any given. A woman is shut up in a kitchen or a boudoir and one is surprised her horizon is limited; her wings are cut and then she is blamed for not knowing how to fly. Let a future be open to her and she will no longer be obliged to settle in the present.

The same foolishness is seen when, closed up in the limits of her self or her home, she is criticised for her narcissism and egotism with their corollaries: vanity, touchiness, meanness, and so forth. All possibility of concrete communication with others is removed from her; in her experience she does not recognise either the appeal or the advantages of solidarity, since, separated, she is entirely devoted to her own family; she cannot be expected therefore to go beyond herself towards the general interest. She obstinately confines herself in the only familiar area where she has the power to grasp things and where she finds a precarious sovereignty.

Although she might close the doors and cover the windows, the woman does not find absolute security in her home; this masculine universe that she respects from afar without daring to venture into it involves her; and because she is unable to grasp it through technology, sound logic or coherent knowledge, she feels like a child and a primitive surrounded with dangerous mysteries. She projects her magic conception of reality: the flow of things seems inevitable to her and yet anything can happen; she has difficulty differentiating the possible and the impossible, she is ready to believe anyone; she welcomes and spreads rumours, she sets off panics; even in calm periods she lives in worry; at night half-asleep, the inert body is frightened by the nightmare images reality acquires: so for the woman condemned to passivity, the opaque future is haunted by phantoms of war, revolution, famine and misery; not being able to act, she worries. When her husband and son embark on a job, when they are passionately involved in an event, they take their own risks: their

projects and the orders they follow show them a sure way even in darkness; but the woman struggles in the blurry night; she 'worries' because
she does not do anything; in imagination all possibilities are equally real:
the train may derail, the operation may be unsuccessful, the affair may fail;
what she vainly tries to ward off in her long, despondent ruminations
is the spectre of her own powerlessness.

Worry expresses her mistrust of the given world; if it seems threatening, ready to sink into obscure catastrophes, it is because she does not
feel happy in it. Most often, she is not resigned to being resigned; she
knows what she is going through, she goes through it in spite of herself:
she is woman without being asked; she does not dare revolt; she submits
against her will; her attitude is a constant recrimination. Everyone who
receives women's confidences – doctors, priests, social workers – knows
that complaint is the commonest mode of expression; together, women
friends groan individually about their own ills and all together about the
injustice of their lot, the world and men in general. A free individual
takes the blame for his failures on himself, he takes responsibility for
them: but what happens to the woman comes from others, it is others
who are responsible for her misfortune. Her furious despair rejects all
remedies; suggesting solutions to a woman determined to complain does
not help: no solution seems acceptable. She wants to live her situation
exactly as she lives it: in impotent anger. If a change is suggested to her,
she throws her arms up: 'That's all I need!' She knows that her malaise
is deeper than the pretexts she gives for it, and that one expedient is not
enough to get rid of it; she takes it out on the whole world because it
was put together without her, and against her; since adolescence, since
childhood, she has protested against her condition; she was promised
compensations, she was assured that if she abdicated her opportunities
into the hands of the man, they would be returned to her a hundred-
fold and she considers herself duped; she accuses the whole masculine
universe; resentment is the other side of dependence: when one gives
everything, one never receives enough in return. But she also needs to
respect the male universe; if she contested it entirely, she would feel in
danger, and without a roof over her head: she adopts the Manichaean
attitude also suggested to her by her experience as a housewife. The individual who acts accepts responsibility for good and evil just like the
others, he knows that it is up to him to define ends, to see that they
triumph; in action he experiences the ambiguity of all solutions; justice
and injustice, gains and losses, are inextricably intermingled. But whoever
is passive puts himself on the sidelines and refuses to pose, even in

thought, ethical problems: good *must* be realised and if it is not, there is wrongdoing for which the guilty must be punished. Like the child, the woman imagines good and evil in simple storybook images; Manichaeism reassures the mind by eliminating the anguish of choice; deciding between one scourge and a lesser one, between a benefit today and a greater benefit tomorrow, having to define by oneself what is defeat and what is victory: this means taking terrible risks; for the Manichaean, the wheat is clearly distinguishable from the chaff, and the chaff has to be eliminated; dust condemns itself and cleanliness is the absolute absence of filth; cleaning means getting rid of waste and mud. Thus the woman thinks that 'everything is the Jews' fault' or the Masons' or the Bolsheviks' or the government's; she is always *against* someone or something; women were even more violently anti-Dreyfusard than men; they do not always know what the evil principle is; but what they expect from a 'good government' is that it get rid of it as one gets rid of dust from the house. For fervent Gaullists, de Gaulle is the king sweeper; they imagine him, dust mops and rags in hand, scrubbing and polishing to make a 'clean' France.

But these hopes are always placed in an uncertain future; meanwhile evil continues to eat away at good; and as woman does not have Jews, Masons and Bolsheviks to hand, she seeks someone against whom she can rise up concretely: the husband is the perfect victim. He embodies the masculine universe, it is through him that the male society took the woman in hand and duped her; he bears the weight of the world and if things go wrong, it is his fault. When he comes home in the evening, she complains to him about the children, the suppliers, the housework, the cost of living, her rheumatism and the weather: and she wants him to feel guilty. She often harbours specific complaints about him; but he is particularly guilty of being a man; he might well have illnesses and problems too – 'It just isn't the same thing' – he is privy to a privilege she constantly resents as an injustice. It is noteworthy that the hostility she feels for the husband or the lover binds her to him instead of moving her away from him; a man who begins to detest wife or mistress tries to get away from her: but she wants to have the man she hates nearby to make him pay. Choosing to recriminate is choosing not to get rid of one's misfortunes but to wallow in them; her supreme consolation is to set herself up as martyr. Life and men have conquered her: she will make a victory of this very defeat. Thus, as she did in childhood, she quickly gives way to the frenzy of tears and scenes.

It is surely because her life takes place against a background of powerless revolt that the woman cries so easily; she undoubtedly has less physiological control of her nervous and sympathetic systems than the man; her education taught her to let herself go: orders and instruction play a great role here since, although Diderot and Benjamin Constant shed rivers of tears, men stopped crying when custom forbade it for them. But the woman is still inclined to be defeatist vis-à-vis the world because she has never frankly assumed it. The man accepts the world; even misfortune will not change his attitude, he will cope with it, he will 'not let it get him down', while a little setback is enough for the woman to rediscover the universe's hostility and the injustice of her lot; so she throws herself into her safest refuge: herself; this moist trace on her cheeks, this burning in her eyes, are the tangible presence of her suffering soul; gentle on one's skin, barely salty on one's tongue, tears are also a tender and bitter caress; the face burns under a stream of mild water; tears are both complaint and consolation, fever and soothing coolness. They are also a supreme alibi; sudden as a storm, coming out in fits, a cyclone, shower, deluge, they metamorphose the woman into a complaining fountain, a stormy sky; her eyes can no longer see, mist blurs them: they are no longer even a gaze, they melt in rain; blinded, the woman returns to the passivity of natural things. She must be vanquished: she is lost in her defeat; she sinks, she drowns, she escapes man who contemplates her, powerless as if before a cataract. He judges this way of behaving as unfair: but she thinks that the battle has been unfair from the beginning because no effective weapon has been put into her hands. She resorts once again to magical conjuration. And the fact that these sobs exasperate the male provides her with one more reason to indulge herself in them.

If tears are not sufficient to express her revolt, she will carry on in such incoherent violence that it will disconcert the man even more. In some circles, the man might strike his wife with actual blows; in others, because he is the stronger and his fist an effective instrument, he will forgo all violence. But the woman, like the child, indulges in symbolic outbursts: she might throw herself on the man, scratch him; these are only gestures. But above all, through nervous fits in her body she attempts to express the refusals she cannot carry out concretely. It is not only for physiological reasons that she is subject to convulsive manifestations: a convulsion is an interiorisation of an energy that, thrown into the world, fails to grasp any object; it is a useless expenditure of all the powers of negation caused by the situation. The mother rarely has crying fits in front of her young children because she can beat or punish them: it is in front of her older son, her husband or her lover on whom she has no hold that the woman gives vent to furious hopelessness. Sophia Tolstoy's hysterical scenes are significant; it is true that she made the big mistake of never trying to understand her husband and in her diary she does not seem generous, sensitive or sincere, she is far from coming across as an endearing person; but whether she was right or wrong does not change the horror of her situation at all: she never did anything in her whole life but submit to the conjugal embraces, pregnancies, solitude and mode of life that her husband imposed on her while receiving constant recriminations; when new decisions of Tolstoy's worsened the conflict, she found herself weaponless against the enemy's will, which she rejected with all her powerless will; she threw herself into rejection scenes – fake suicides, false escapes, false illnesses – unpleasant to her family and friends, exhausting for herself: it is hard to see any other solution available to her since she had no positive reason to silence her feelings of revolt and no effective way of expressing them.

There is only one solution available to the woman when rejection runs its course: suicide. But it would seem that she resorts to it less than the man. The statistics are very ambiguous:[*108] if one considers successful suicides, there are many more men than women who put an end to their lives; but suicide attempts are more frequent in women. This may be because they settle more often for playacting: they *play* at suicide more often than man but they *want* it more rarely. It is also in part because such brutal means are repugnant to them: they almost never use knives or firearms. They drown themselves more readily, like Ophelia, showing woman's affinity for water, passive and full of darkness, where it seems that life might be able to dissolve passively. On the whole, this is the ambiguity I already mentioned: the woman does not sincerely seek to take leave of what she detests. She plays at rupture but in the end remains with the man who makes her suffer; she pretends to leave the life that mistreats her but it is relatively rare for her to kill herself. She does not favour definitive solutions: she protests against man, against life, against her condition, but she does not escape from it.

There is much feminine behaviour that has to be interpreted as protest. We have seen that the woman often cheats on her husband by defiance and not for pleasure; she will be absentminded and a spendthrift on purpose because he is methodical and careful. Misogynists who accuse woman of 'always being late' think she lacks 'the sense of exactitude'.

* See Halbwachs, *The Causes of Suicide.*

In truth, we have seen how docilely she adapts to the demands of time. Being late is deliberate. Some flirtatious women think that this is the way to excite the desire of the man, who will thus attach more importance to their presence; but above all, in keeping a man waiting for a few minutes, the woman protests against this long wait that is her own life. In one sense, her whole existence is a waiting since she is enclosed in the limbo of immanence and contingency and her justification is always in someone else's hands: she is waiting for a tribute, men's approval, she is waiting for love, she is waiting for gratitude and her husband's or lover's praise; she expects to gain from them her reasons to exist, her worth and her very being. She awaits her subsistence from them; whether she has her own chequebook or receives the money her husband allocates to her every week or month, he has to have been paid, obtained the raise for her to pay the grocer or buy a new dress. She awaits men's presence: her economic dependence puts her at their disposal; she is only one element of masculine life, whereas the man is her whole life; the husband has occupations outside the home, the woman endures his absence every day; it is the lover – even if passionate – who decides on the separation and meetings according to his obligations. In bed, she awaits the male's desire, she awaits – sometimes anxiously – her own pleasure. The only thing she can do is to be late for the date the lover set up; or not to be ready at the time the husband fixed; this is the way she asserts the importance of her own occupations, she claims her independence, she becomes the essential subject for a moment while the other passively submits to her will. But this is meagre revenge; no matter how determined she might be to make men stew, she will never compensate for the infinite hours she has spent being subjected to and watching out and hoping for the male's goodwill.

In general, while more or less acknowledging men's supremacy and accepting their authority, worshipping their idols, she will contest their reign tooth and nail; hence the famous 'contrariness' for which she is so often criticised; as she does not possess an autonomous domain, she cannot put forward truths or positive values different from those that males assert; she can only negate them. Her negation is more or less systematic depending on her particular balance of respect and resentment. But the fact is, she knows all the fault lines of the masculine system and she hastens to denounce them.

Women do not have a hold on the world of men because their experience does not teach them to deal with logic and technology: conversely, the power of male instruments disappears at the borders of the feminine domain. There is a whole region of human experience that the male deliberately chooses to ignore because he fails to *think* it: this experience, the woman *lives* it. The engineer, so precise when making his plans, behaves like a demigod at home: one word and his meal is served, his shirts starched, his children silenced: procreating is an act that is as quick as Moses's magic rod; he sees nothing surprising in these miracles. The notion of miracle differs from the idea of magic: from within a rationally determined world a miracle posits the radical discontinuity of an event without cause against which any thinking shatters, whereas magic phenomena are united by secret forces of which a docile consciousness can embrace the continuous becoming – without understanding it. The newborn is miraculous for the demigod father, magic for the mother who has undergone the ripening in her womb. Man's experience is intelligible but full of holes; that of the wife is, in its own limits, obscure but complete. This opacity weighs her down; the male is light in his relations with her: he has the lightness of dictators, generals, judges, bureaucrats, codes and abstract principles. This is undoubtedly what this housewife meant when, shrugging her shoulders, she murmured: 'Men, they don't think!' Women also say: 'Men, they don't know; they don't know life.' As a contrast to the myth of the praying mantis, they juxtapose the symbol of the frivolous and importunate bumblebee.

It is understandable why, from this perspective, woman objects to masculine logic. Not only does it have no bearing on her experience, but she also knows that in men's hands reason becomes an insidious form of violence; their peremptory affirmations are intended to mystify her. They want to confine her in a dilemma: either you agree or you don't; she has to agree in the name of the whole system of accepted principles: in refusing to agree, she rejects the whole system; she cannot allow herself such a dramatic move; she does not have the means to create another society: yet she does not agree with this one. Halfway between revolt and slavery, she unwillingly resigns herself to masculine authority. He continuously uses force to make her shoulder the consequences of her reluctant submission. He pursues the chimera of a freely enslaved companion: he wants her to yield to him as yielding to the proof of a theorem; but she knows he himself has chosen the postulates on which his vigorous deductions are hung; as long as she avoids questioning them, he will easily silence her; nevertheless, he will not convince her, because she senses their arbitrariness. Thus will he accuse her, with stubborn irritation, of being illogical: she refuses to play the game because she knows the dice are loaded.

The woman does not positively think that the truth is *other* than what men claim: rather, she holds that there *is* no truth. It is not only life's becoming that makes her suspicious of the principle of identity, nor the magic phenomena surrounding her that ruin the notion of causality: it is at the heart of the masculine world itself, it is in her as belonging to this world, that she grasps the ambiguity of all principles, of all values, of all that exists. She knows that when it comes to her, masculine morality is a vast mystification. The man pompously drums his code of virtue and honour into her; but secretly he invites her to disobey it: he even counts on this disobedience; the whole lovely façade he hides behind would collapse without it.

The man readily uses the pretext of the Hegelian idea that the male citizen acquires his ethical dignity by transcending himself towards the universal: as a singular individual, he has the right to desire and pleasure. His relations with woman thus lie in a contingent region where morality no longer applies, where conduct is inconsequential. His relations with other men are based on certain values; he is a freedom confronting other freedoms according to laws universally recognised by all; but with woman – she was invented for this reason – he ceases to assume his existence, he abandons himself to the mirage of the in-itself, he situates himself on an inauthentic plane; he is tyrannical, sadistic, violent or puerile, masochistic or querulous; he tries to satisfy his obsessions, his manias; he 'relaxes', he 'lets go' in the name of rights he has acquired in his public life. His wife is often surprised – like Thérèse Desqueyroux – by the contrast between the lofty tone of his remarks, of his public conduct and 'his patient inventions in the dark'.[109] He preaches population growth: but he is clever at not having more children than are convenient for him. He praises chaste and faithful wives: but he invites his neighbour's wife to commit adultery. We have seen the hypocrisy of men decreeing abortion to be criminal when every year in France a million women are put by men into the situation where they have to abort; very often the husband or lover imposes this solution on them; and often these men tacitly assume that it will be used if necessary. They openly count on the woman to consent to making herself guilty of a crime: her 'immorality' is necessary for the harmony of moral society, respected by men. The most flagrant example of this duplicity is man's attitude to prostitution: it is his demand that creates the offer; I have spoken of the disgusted scepticism with which prostitutes view respectable gentlemen who condemn vice in general but show great indulgence for their personal foibles; they consider girls who make a living with their bodies perverse and debauched, and not the men who use them. An anecdote illustrates this state of mind: at the end of the last century, the police discovered two little girls of twelve or thirteen in a bordello; a trial was held where they testified; they spoke of their clients who were important gentlemen; one of them opened her mouth to give a name. The judge abruptly stopped her: *Do not sully the name of an honest man!* A gentleman decorated with the Legion of Honour remains an honest man while deflowering a little girl; he has his weaknesses, but who does not? However, the little girl who has no access to the ethical region of the universal – who is neither judge nor general nor a great French man, nothing but a little girl – gambles her moral value in the contingent region of sexuality: she is perverted, corrupted, depraved and good only for the reformatory. In many cases, the man can commit acts with woman's complicity that degrade her without tarnishing his lofty image. She does not understand these subtleties very well; what she does understand is that the man's actions do not conform to the principles he professes and that he asks her to disobey them; he does not want what he says he wants: she therefore does not give him what she pretends to give him. She will be a chaste and faithful wife: and in secret she will give in to her desires; she will be an admirable mother: but she will carefully practise birth control and she will have an abortion if she must. Officially the man renounces her, those are the rules of the game; but he is clandestinely grateful to one for her 'easy virtue', to another for her sterility. The woman has the role of those secret agents who are left to the firing squad if they are caught, and who are covered with rewards if they succeed; it is for her to shoulder all of males' immorality: it is not only the prostitute; it is all the women who serve as the gutter to the luminous and clean palaces where respectable people live. When one speaks to these women of dignity, honour, loyalty and of all the lofty virile virtues, one should not be surprised if they refuse to 'go along'. They particularly snigger when virtuous males reproach them for being calculating, actresses, liars:* they know well that no other way is open to them. The man also is 'calculating' about money and success: but he has the means to acquire them through his work: the woman has been assigned the role of parasite: all parasites are necessarily exploiters; she needs the male to

---

* 'All these women with this little delicate and touch-me-not air accumulated by a whole past of slavery, with no other means of salvation and livelihood than this unintentional seductive air biding its time' (Jules Laforgue).

acquire human dignity, to eat, to feel pleasure, to procreate; she uses the service of sex to ensure her benefits; and since she is trapped in this function, she is entirely an instrument of exploitation. As for falsehoods, except in the case of prostitution, there is no fair arrangement between her and her protector. Man even requires her to playact: he wants her to be the *Other;* but every existent, as desperately as he may disavow himself, remains a subject; he wants her to be object: she *makes* herself object; at the moment she makes herself being, she is exercising a free activity; this is her original treason; the most docile, the most passive woman is still consciousness; and it is sometimes enough to make him feel duped by her for the male to glimpse that in giving herself to him she is watching and judging him; she should be no more than an offered thing, a prey. Nonetheless, he also demands that she surrender this thing to him freely: in bed he asks her to feel pleasure; at home, she must sincerely recognise his superiority and his strengths; at the very moment she obeys, she must also feign independence, even though she actively plays the role of passivity at other moments. She lies to keep her man and ensure her daily bread – scenes and tears, uncontrollable transports of love, hysterics – and she lies as well to escape the tyranny she accepts out of self-interest. He encourages playacting as it feeds his imperialism and vanity: she uses her powers of dissimulation against him; revenge is thus doubly delicious: for in deceiving him, she satisfies her own particular desires and she savours the pleasure of mocking him. The wife and the courtesan lie in feigning transports they do not feel; afterwards with their lovers or girlfriends, they make fun of the naive vanity of their dupe: 'Not only do they "botch it", but they want us to wear ourselves out moaning with pleasure,' they say resentfully. These conversations resemble those of servants who criticise their 'bosses' in the servants' kitchen. The woman has the same faults because she is a victim of the same paternalistic oppression; she has the same cynicism because she sees the man from head to toe as a valet sees his master. But it is clear that none of these traits manifests a perverted essence or perverted original will; they reflect a situation. 'There is duplicity wherever there is a coercive regime,' says Fourier. 'Prohibition and contraband are inseparable in love as in business.' And men know so well that the woman's faults show her condition that, careful to maintain the hierarchy of the sexes, they encourage these very traits in their companion that allow them to scorn her. Doubtless the husband or lover is irritated by the faults of the particular woman he lives with; yet, extolling the charms of femininity in general, he considers it to be inseparable from its flaws.

If the woman is not perfidious, futile, cowardly or indolent, she loses her seduction. In *A Doll's House,* Helmer explains how just, strong, understanding and indulgent man feels when he pardons his weak wife for her puerile faults. Thus Bernstein's husbands are moved – with the author's complicity – by the thieving, cruel, adulterous wife; bowing indulgently to her, they prove their virile wisdom. American racists and French colonialists wish the black man to be thieving, indolent and lying: he proves his indignity, putting the oppressors in the right; if he insists on being honest and loyal, he is regarded as quarrelsome. Woman's faults are amplified all the more to the extent that she will not try to combat them but, on the contrary, will make an ornament of them.

Rejecting logical principles and moral imperatives, sceptical about the laws of nature, woman lacks a sense of the universal; the world seems to her a confused collection of individual cases; this is why she more readily accepts a neighbour's gossip than a scientific explanation; she doubtless respects the printed book, but this respect skims along the written pages without grasping the content; by contrast, the anecdote told by an unknown person waiting in a queue or in a drawing room instantly takes on overwhelming authority; in her domain, everything is magic; outside, everything is mystery; she is ignorant of the criterion for credibility; only immediate experience convinces her: her own experience or another's, as long as it is forcefully affirmed. As for herself, she feels she is a special case because she is isolated in her home and has no active contact with other women; she always expects destiny and men to make an exception in her favour; she believes in whatever insights come her way far more than in reasoning that is valid for everyone; she readily admits that they have been sent by God or by some obscure world spirit; in relation to misfortunes or accidents, she calmly thinks, 'That can't happen to me,' or else she imagines, 'I'll be the exception': she enjoys special favours; the shopkeeper will give her a discount, the policeman will let her go to the head of the queue; she has been taught to overestimate the value of her smile, but no one told her that all women smiled. It is not that she thinks herself more special than her neighbour: it is that she does not make comparisons; for the same reason experience rarely proves her wrong: she suffers one failure, then another, but she does not add them up.

This is why women do not succeed in building a solid 'counter-universe' where they can defy males; they sporadically rant against men in general, they tell stories about the bedroom or childbirth, they exchange horoscopes and beauty secrets. But to truly build this 'world of grievances' that their resentment calls for, they lack conviction; their attitude to man is too ambivalent. Indeed, he is a child, a contingent and vulnerable body, an innocent, an unwanted drone, a mean tyrant, an egotist, a vain man: and he is also the liberating hero, the divinity who sets the standards. His desire is a gross appetite, his embraces a degrading chore: yet his ardour and virile force are also a demiurgic energy. When a woman ecstatically utters, 'This is a man!' she is evoking both the sexual vigour and the social effectiveness of the male she admires: in both are expressed the same creative sovereignty; she does not think he can be a great artist, a grand businessman, a general or a chief without being a great lover: his social success is always a sexual attraction; inversely, she is ready to recognise genius in the man who satisfies her. She is, in fact, turning to a masculine myth here. The phallus for Lawrence and many others is both living energy and human transcendence. Thus in the pleasures of the bed, woman can see a communion with the spirit of the world. Worshipping man as in a mystical cult, she loses and finds herself in his glory. The contradiction is easily perceived here due to the different types of individual who are virile. Some – whose contingence she encounters in everyday life – are the incarnation of human misery; in others, man's grandeur is exalted. But the woman even accepts that these two figures be fused into one. 'If I become famous,' wrote a girl in love with a man she considered superior, 'R . . . will surely marry me because it will flatter his vanity; his chest will swell with me on his arm.' Yet she admired him madly. The same individual, in the eyes of the woman, may very well be stingy, mean, vain, foolish and a god; after all, gods have their weaknesses. One feels a demanding severity – the opposite of authentic esteem – for an individual who is loved in his freedom and humanity; whereas a woman kneeling before her male can very well pride herself on 'knowing how to deal with him', or 'handle him', and she complaisantly flatters his 'weaknesses' without his losing prestige; this is the proof that she does not feel friendship for his individual person as expressed in his real acts; blindly she bows to the general essence her idol is part of: virility is a sacred aura, a given fixed value, which is affirmed despite the weaknesses of the individual who bears it; this individual does not count; by contrast, the woman, jealous of his privilege, is delighted to exercise sly superiority over him.

The same ambiguity of woman's feelings for man is found in her general attitude concerning her self and the world; the domain in which she is enclosed is invested by the masculine universe; but it is haunted by obscure forces of which men themselves are the playthings; if she allies herself with these magical virtues, she will, in her turn, acquire power. Society subjugates Nature; but Nature dominates it; the Spirit affirms itself over Life; but it dies if life no longer supports it. Woman uses this ambivalence to assign more truth to a garden than a city, to an illness than an idea, to a birth than a revolution; she tries to reestablish this reign of the earth, of the Mother, imagined by Bachofen, to be able to find herself as the essential facing the inessential. But as she herself is an existent that a transcendence inhabits, she will be able to valorise this region where she is confined only by transfiguring it: she lends it a transcendent dimension. Man lives in a coherent universe that is a thought reality. Woman struggles with a magic reality that does not allow thinking: she escapes through thoughts lacking real content. Instead of assuming her existence, she contemplates in the heavens the pure Idea of her destiny; instead of acting, she erects her statue in her imagination; instead of reasoning, she dreams. From here comes the fact that while being so 'physical', she is also so artificial, while being so terrestrial, she can be so ethereal. Her life is spent scrubbing pots and pans and it is a marvellous romance; vassal to man, she believes she is his idol; debased in her flesh, she exalts Love. Because she is condemned to know only life's contingent facticity, she becomes priestess of the Ideal.

This ambivalence is marked by the way woman deals with her body. It is a burden: weakened by the species, bleeding every month, passively propagating, for her it is not the pure instrument of her grasp on the world but rather an opaque presence; it is not certain that it will give her pleasure and it creates pains that tear her apart; it contains threats: she feels danger in her 'insides'. Her body is 'hysterical' because of the close connection between endocrine secretions and nervous and sympathetic systems commanding muscles and viscera; it expresses reactions the woman refuses to accept: in sobs, convulsions and vomiting, her body escapes her, it betrays her; it is her most intimate reality, but it is a shameful reality that she keeps hidden. And yet it is her marvellous double; she contemplates it in the mirror with amazement; it is the promise of happiness, a work of art, a living statue; she shapes it, adorns it, displays it. When she smiles into the mirror she forgets her carnal contingence; in love's embrace, in motherhood, her image disappears. But often, dreaming about herself, she is surprised to be both that heroine and that flesh.

Nature symmetrically provides her with a double face: it supplies the stew and incites mystical effusions. In becoming a housewife and mother, woman gave up her free getaways into fields and woods, she preferred the calm cultivation of the kitchen garden, she tamed flowers and put them in vases: yet she is still exalted by moonlights and sunsets. In the terrestrial fauna and flora, she sees food and ornamentation before all; yet a sap flows that is generosity and magic. Life is not only immanence and repetition: it is also a dazzling face of light; in flowering meadows, it is revealed as Beauty. In tune with nature by the fertility of her womb, woman also feels swept by the breath that animates her and is spirit. And insofar as she is unsatisfied and feels like the uncompleted and unlimited girl, her soul will then rush forward on endlessly unwinding roads towards limitless horizons. Slave to her husband, children and home, she finds it intoxicating to be alone, sovereign on the hillside; she is no longer spouse, mother, housewife, but a human being; she contemplates the passive world: and she recalls that she is a whole consciousness, an irreducible freedom. In front of the mystery of water and the mountain summit's thrust, male supremacy is abolished; walking through the heather, dipping her hand in the river, she lives not for others but for herself. The woman who maintained her independence through all her servitudes will ardently love her own freedom in Nature. The others will find in it only the pretext for refined raptures and they will hesitate at twilight between the fear of catching a cold and a swooning soul.

This double belonging to the carnal world and to a 'poetic' world defines the metaphysics and wisdom to which the woman more or less explicitly adheres. She tries to combine life and transcendence; this is to say she rejects Cartesianism and all doctrines connected to it; she is comfortable in a naturalism similar to that of the Stoics or Neoplatonists of the sixteenth century: it is not surprising that women, Margaret of Navarre being the first of them, should be attached to such a philosophy, at once so material and so spiritual. Socially Manichaean, the woman has a deep need to be ontologically optimistic: the moralities of action do not suit her, since it is forbidden for her to act; she submits to the given: so the given must be Good; but a Good recognised by reason like that of Spinoza or by calculation like that of Leibniz cannot touch her. She requires a good that is a living Harmony and within which she situates herself by the mere fact of living. The notion of harmony is one of the keys of the feminine universe: it implies perfection in immobility, the immediate justification of each element as part of the whole and her passive participation in the totality. In a harmonious world, woman thus attains what man will seek in action: she has purchase on the world, she is necessary to it, she cooperates in the triumph of Good. Moments women consider as revelations are those where they discover they are in harmony with a reality based on peace with one's self. These are the moments of luminous happiness that Virginia Woolf – in *Mrs Dalloway*, in *To the Lighthouse* – that Katherine Mansfield, all through her work, grant to their heroines as a supreme recompense. The joy that is a surge of freedom is reserved for the man; what the woman knows is an impression of smiling plenitude.* One understands that simple ataraxia, in her eyes, can be of utmost importance, as she normally lives in the tension of denial, recrimination and demands; one could never reproach her for savouring a beautiful afternoon or the sweetness of an evening. But it is a delusion to try to find here the true definition of the hidden soul of the world. Good *is* not; the world is not harmony and no individual has a necessary place in it.

There is a justification, a supreme compensation that society has always been bent on dispensing to woman: religion. There must be religion for women as for the people, for exactly the same reasons: when a sex or a class is condemned to immanence, the mirage of transcendence must be offered to it. It is to man's total advantage to have God endorse the codes he creates: and specifically because he exercises sovereign authority over the woman, it is only right that this authority be conferred on him by the sovereign being. Among others, for Jews, Muslims and Christians, man is the master by divine right: fear of God will stifle the slightest inclination of revolt in the oppressed. Their credulity can be counted on. Woman adopts an attitude of respect and faith before the masculine universe: God in His heaven seems barely farther from her than a government minister, and the mystery of Genesis matches that of an electrical power station. But more important, if she throws herself so willingly into religion, it is because religion fills a profound need. In modern civilisation where freedom plays an important role – even for the woman – religion becomes less of an instrument of constraint than of mystification. The woman is less often asked to accept her inferiority in the name of God than to believe, thanks to Him,

---

* Out of reams of texts, I will cite Mabel Dodge's lines where the passage to a global vision of the world is not explicit but is clearly suggested: 'It was a still, autumn day, all yellow and crimson. Frieda and I, in a lapse of antagonism, sat on the ground together, with the red apples piled all around us. We were warmed and scented by the sun and the rich earth – and the apples were living tokens of plenitude and peace and rich living; the rich, natural flow of the earth, like the sappy blood in our veins, made us feel gay, indomitable and fruitful like orchards. We were united for a moment, Frieda and I, in a mutual assurance of self-sufficiency, made certain, as women are sometimes, of our completeness by the sheer force of our bountiful health.'

that she is equal to the male lord; even the temptation to revolt is avoided by pretending to overcome injustice. The woman is no longer robbed of her transcendence, since she will dedicate her immanence to God; souls' merits are judged only in heaven and not according to their terrestrial accomplishments; here below, as Dostoevsky would have said, they are never more than occupations: shining shoes or building a bridge is the same vanity; over and above social discriminations, equality of the sexes is reestablished. This is why the little girl and the adolescent girl throw themselves into devotion with an infinitely greater fervour than their brothers; God's gaze that transcends his transcendence humiliates the boy: he will for ever remain a child under this powerful guardianship, it is a more radical castration than that with which he feels his father's existence threatens him. But the 'eternal girl child' finds her salvation in this gaze that metamorphoses her into a sister of the angels; it cancels out the privilege of the penis. A sincere faith helps the girl avoid all inferiority complexes: she is neither male nor female, but God's creature. This is why we find a virile steadfastness in the great female saints: St Bridget and St Catherine of Siena arrogantly tried to rule the world; they recognised no male authority: Catherine even directed her directors very severely; Joan of Arc and St Teresa followed their own paths with an intrepidness surpassed by no man. The Church sees to it that God never authorises women to escape from male guardianship; it has put these powerful weapons in masculine hands only: refusal of absolution and excommunication; for her obstinate visions, Joan of Arc was burned at the stake. Nevertheless, even subjected by God's will to men's laws, the woman finds a solid recourse against them through Him. Masculine logic is refuted by mysteries; males' pride becomes a sin, their agitation is not only absurd but culpable: why remodel this world created by God Himself? The passivity to which woman is doomed is sanctified. Reciting her rosary by the fire, she knows she is closer to heaven than her husband, who is out at political meetings. There is no need to *do* anything to save her soul, it is enough to *live* without disobeying. The synthesis of life and spirit is completed: the mother not only engenders body but also gives God a soul; this is higher work than penetrating the secrets of the atom. With the complicity of the heavenly Father, woman can make a claim to the glory of her femininity against man.

Not only does God thus reestablish the dignity of the feminine sex in general, but every woman will find special support in the celestial absence; as a human person, she carries little weight; but as soon as she acts in the name of divine inspiration, her desires become sacred. Mme Guyon says that, concerning a nun's illness, she learned 'what it meant to command by the Word and obey by the same Word'; thus the devotee camouflages her authority in humble obedience; raising her children, governing a convent or organising a charity, she is but a docile tool in supernatural hands; one cannot disobey her without offending God Himself. To be sure, men do not disdain this support either; but it loses its force when they encounter other men who make equal claim to it: the conflict finishes by being solved on a human level. Woman invokes divine will to justify her authority absolutely in the eyes of those who are naturally subordinated to her, and to justify it in her own eyes. If this cooperation is useful for her, it is because she is above all concerned with her relations with herself – even when those relations interest others; it is only in these totally interior debates that the Supreme Silence can have the force of law. In truth, woman uses the pretext of religion to satisfy her desires. Frigid, masochistic or sadistic, she sanctifies herself by renouncing the flesh, playing the victim, stifling every living impulse around her; mutilating and annihilating herself, she rises in the ranks of the chosen; when she martyrs husband and children by depriving them of all terrestrial happiness, she is preparing them for a choice place in paradise; 'to punish herself for having sinned', Margaret of Cortona's pious biographers recount, she maltreated the child of her sin; she fed him only after feeding all the beggars she passed; we have seen that hatred of the unwanted child is common: it is a godsend to be able to express it in a virtuous rage. On her side, a woman whose morals are loose conveniently makes an arrangement with God; the certainty of being purified from sin by absolution tomorrow often helps the pious woman conquer her scruples now. Whether she has chosen asceticism or sensuality, pride or humility, the concern she has for her salvation encourages her to give in to this pleasure that she prefers over all others: taking care of self; she listens to her heart beat, she watches every quiver of her flesh, justified by the presence of grace within herself, like the pregnant woman with her fruit. Not only does she examine herself with tender vigilance, but she reports to her confessor; in days gone by, she could savour the headiness of public confessions. We are told that Margaret of Cortona, to punish herself for an act of vanity, climbed onto her terrace and began to cry out like a woman in labour: 'Wake up, people of Cortona, wake up and bring candles and lanterns and come out to hear the sinner!' She enumerated all her sins, proclaiming her misery to the stars. By this noisy humility, she satisfied this need for exhibitionism, found in so many examples of narcissistic women. For the woman, religion authorises self-indulgence; it gives her the guide, father, lover, titular divinity she nostalgically needs; it feeds her reveries; it fills her empty hours. But especially, it confirms the world order; it justifies resignation by bringing hope for a better future in an asexual heaven. This is why today women are still a powerful asset in the hands of the Church; it is why the Church is so hostile to any measure that might facilitate their emancipation. Women must have religion; there must be women, 'real women', to perpetuate religion.

It is clear that woman's whole 'character' – her convictions, values, wisdom, morality, tastes and behaviour – is explained by her situation. The fact that she is denied transcendence usually prohibits her from having access to the loftiest human attitudes – heroism, revolt, detachment, invention and creation – but they are not so common even in men. There are many men who are, like woman, confined within the domain of the intermediary, of inessential means; the worker escapes from it through political action, expressing a revolutionary will; but men from what we precisely call the 'middle' class settle in this sphere deliberately; destined like the woman to the repetition of daily tasks, alienated in ready-made values, respecting public opinion and only seeking vague comforts on earth, the employee, the shopkeeper and the bureaucrat hold no superiority over their women companions; cooking, washing, running her home, raising her children, the woman shows more initiative and independence than the man enslaved to orders; he must obey his superiors every day, wear a removable collar and affirm his social rank; she can lie about in a housecoat in her apartment, sing, laugh with her women neighbours; she acts as she pleases, takes small risks and efficiently tries to attain a few results. She lives much less according to convention and appearances than does her husband. The bureaucratic world described by Kafka – among others – this universe of ceremonies, absurd gestures, meaningless behaviour is essentially masculine; she has greater purchase on reality; when he lines up his figures, or converts sardine boxes into money, he grasps nothing but abstracts; the child content in his cradle, clean laundry, the roast are more tangible things; yet, just because she feels their contingence – and consequently her own contingence – in the concrete pursuit of these objectives, it often happens that she does not alienate herself in them: she remains available. Man's undertakings are both projects and escapes: he lets himself be overwhelmed by his career, his personage; he is readily self-important, serious; contesting masculine logic and morality, woman does not fall into these traps: that is what Stendhal appreciated so strongly in her; she does not resort to pride to elude the ambiguity of her condition; she does not hide behind the mask of human dignity; she reveals her undisciplined thoughts, her emotions, her spontaneous reactions with more sincerity. This is why her conversation is far less boring than her husband's whenever she speaks in her own name and not as her seigneur's loyal half; he recites so-called general ideas, meaning words and formulas found in the columns of his newspaper or in specialist works; she brings experience, limited but concrete. The famous 'feminine sensitivity' is part myth, part theatre; but the fact remains that woman is more attentive than man to herself and the world. Sexually, she lives in a crude masculine climate: she compensates by appreciating 'pretty things', which can lead to sentimentality, but also to refinement; because her sphere is limited, the objects she touches are precious to her: by not binding them in concepts or projects, she displays their splendour; her desire for escape is expressed in her taste for festiveness: she enjoys the gratuitousness of a bouquet of flowers, a cake, a well-laid table, she is pleased to transform the emptiness of her idle hours into a generous offering; loving laughter, songs, adornment and knickknacks, she is also ready to welcome everything that palpitates around her: the spectacle of the street, of the sky; an invitation or an excursion offer her new horizons; the man often refuses to participate in these pleasures; when he comes home, joyous voices become silent and the women in the family assume the bored and proper air expected of them. From the depths of solitude, of separation, the woman finds the sense of the singularity of her life: she has a more intimate experience than the man of the past, death, of time passing; she is concerned with the adventures of her heart, her flesh, her mind because she knows that on earth she has but one lot; and also, because she is passive, she bears the reality that submerges her in a more passionate manner, with more pathos than the individual absorbed by an ambition or job; she has the leisure and the tendency to abandon herself to her emotions, study her feelings and draw conclusions from them. When her imagination is not lost in vain dreams, she becomes full of sympathy: she tries to understand the other in his uniqueness and re-create him in herself; regarding her husband, her lover, she is capable of true identification: she makes his projects and his cares her own in a way he could not imitate. She watches anxiously over the whole world; it seems to be an enigma to her: each being, every object, can be a reply; she questions avidly. When she grows older, her disenchanted expectation is converted into irony and an often piquant cynicism; she refuses masculine mystifications, she sees the contingent, absurd, gratuitous reverse side of the imposing structure built by males. Her dependence prohibits detachment for her; but she draws real generosity from her imposed devotion; she forgets herself in favour of her husband, her lover, her child, she ceases to think of herself, she is pure offering, gift. Being poorly adapted to men's society, she is often forced to invent her own conduct; she is less able to settle for ready-made patterns and clichés; if she is of good will, her apprehensions are closer to authenticity than is her husband's self-confidence.

But she will only have these advantages over her husband if she rejects the mystifications he offers her. In the upper classes, women are willing accomplices to their masters because they stand to profit from the benefits they are guaranteed. We have seen that women of the high bourgeoisie and aristocracy have always defended their class interests more stubbornly than their husbands: they do not hesitate to radically sacrifice their autonomy as human beings; they stifle all thinking, all critical judgement, all spontaneity; they parrot conventional wisdom, they identify with the ideal imposed on them by the male code; in their hearts, and even on their faces, all sincerity is dead. The housewife regains independence in her work, in caring for the children: she draws a limited but concrete experience from it: a woman who is 'waited on' no longer has any grasp on the world; she lives in dreams and abstraction, in a void. She is unaware of the reach of the ideas she professes; the words she rattles off have lost all meaning in her mouth; the banker, the businessman and even at times the general take risks, accepting exhaustion and problems; they purchase their privileges in an unfair market, but at least they pay for them themselves; for all they receive, their wives give nothing, do nothing in return; and they even more righteously believe in their imprescriptible rights with a blind faith. Their vain arrogance, their radical incapability, their stubborn ignorance, turn them into the most useless beings, the most idiotic that the human species has ever produced.

It is thus as absurd to speak of 'the woman' in general as of 'the eternal man'. And we can see why all comparisons where we try to decide if the woman is superior, inferior or equal to the man are pointless: their situations are profoundly different. If these same situations are compared, it is obvious that the man's is infinitely preferable, that is to say he has far more concrete opportunities to project his freedom in the world; the inevitable result is that masculine realisations outweigh by far those of women: for women, it is practically forbidden to *do* anything. But to compare the use that, within their limits, men and women make of their freedom is a priori meaningless, precisely because they use it freely. In various forms, the traps of bad faith and the mystifications of seriousness are lying in wait for both of them; freedom is entire in each. However, because of the fact that in woman this freedom remains abstract and empty, it cannot authentically assume itself except in revolt: this is the only way open to those who have no chance to build anything; they must refuse the limits of their situation and seek to open paths to the future; resignation is only a surrender and an evasion; for woman there is no other way out than to work for her liberation.

This liberation can only be collective, and it demands above all that the economic evolution of the feminine condition be accomplished. There have been and there still are many women who do seek to attain individual salvation on their own. They try to justify their existence within their own immanence, that is, to achieve transcendence through immanence. It is this ultimate effort – sometimes ridiculous, often pathetic – of the imprisoned woman to convert her prison into a heaven of glory, her servitude into sovereign freedom, that we find in the narcissist, the woman in love and the mystic.

Part Three
JUSTIFICATIONS

CHAPTER II

The Narcissist

It has sometimes been asserted that narcissism is the fundamental attitude of all women;* but overextending this notion destroys it as La Rochefoucauld destroyed the notion of egotism. In fact, narcissism is a well-defined process of alienation: the self is posited as an absolute end and the subject escapes itself in it. There are many other – authentic or inauthentic – attitudes found in woman: we have already studied some of them. What is true is that circumstances invite woman more than man to turn towards self and to dedicate her love to herself.

All love demands the duality of a subject and an object. Woman is led to narcissism by two convergent paths. As subject, she is frustrated; as a little girl, she was deprived of this alter ego that the penis is for the boy; later on, her aggressive sexuality remained unsatisfied. Of far greater importance is that she is forbidden virile activities. She is busy but she does not *do* anything; in her functions as wife, mother and housewife, she is not recognised in her singularity. Man's truth is in the houses he builds, the forests he clears, the patients he cures: not being able to accomplish herself in projects and aims, woman attempts to grasp herself in the immanence of her person. Parodying Sieyès's words, Marie Bashkirtseff wrote: 'Who am I? Nothing. What would I like to be? All.' It is because they are nothing that many women fiercely limit their interests to their self alone, that their self becomes hypertrophied so as to be confounded with All. 'I am my own heroine,' continues Marie Bashkirtseff. A man who acts necessarily confronts himself. Inefficient and separated, woman can neither situate nor assess herself; she gives herself sovereign importance because no important object is accessible to her.

If she can put *herself* forward in her own desires, it is because since childhood she has seen herself as an object. Her education has encouraged her to alienate herself wholly in her body, puberty having revealed

* Cf. Helene Deutsch, *The Psychology of Women.*

this body as passive and desirable; it is a thing she can touch, that satin or velvet arouses, and that she can contemplate with a lover's gaze. In solitary pleasure, it may happen that the woman splits into a male subject and a female object; Dalbiez*¹ studied the case of Irène, who said to herself, 'I'm going to love myself', or more passionately, 'I'm going to possess myself', or in a paroxysm: 'I'm going to fecundate myself.' Marie Bashkirtseff is also both subject and object when she writes, 'It's really a pity that no one sees my arms and torso, all this freshness and youth.'

In truth, it is not possible to be *for self* positively Other and grasp oneself as object in the light of consciousness. Doubling is only dreamed. For the child, it is the doll that materialises this dream; she recognises herself in it more concretely than in her own body because there is separation between the two. Mme de Noailles expresses this need to be two so as to establish a tender dialogue between self and self in, among other works, *The Book of My Life*.²

> I loved dolls, I endowed their immobility with the life of my own existence; I could not have slept under the warmth of a cover if they were not also wrapped in wool and feathers . . . I dreamt of truly savouring pure solitude as two . . . This need to persist intact, to be twice myself, I felt it avidly as a little child . . . Oh! How I wanted in the tragic instants where my dreamy sweetness was the plaything of hurtful tears to have another little Anna next to me who would throw her arms around my neck, who would console me, understand me . . . during my life I met her in my heart and I held her tight: she helped me not in the form of hoped-for consolation but in the form of courage.

The adolescent girl leaves her dolls dormant. But throughout her life, woman will be vigorously encouraged to leave and come back to herself by the magic of the mirror. Otto Rank brought to light the mirror-double relation in myths and dreams. It is above all in woman that the reflection allows itself to be assimilated to the self. Male beauty is a sign of transcendence, that of woman has the passivity of immanence: the latter alone is made to arrest man's gaze and can thus be caught in

---

* *Psychoanalytical Method and the Doctrine of Freud.* In her childhood, Irène liked to urinate like boys; she often sees herself in her dreams in undine form, which confirms Havelock Ellis's ideas on the relation between narcissism and what he calls 'undinism'; that is, a certain urinary eroticism.

the immobile trap of the mirror's silvering; man who feels and wants himself to be activity and subjectivity does not recognise himself in his immobile image; it does not appeal to him since the man's body does not appear to him as an object of desire; while the woman, knowing she is and making herself object, really believes she is seeing *herself* in the mirror: passive and given, the reflection is a thing like herself; and as she covets feminine flesh, her flesh, she enlivens the inert qualities she sees with her admiration and desire. Mme de Noailles, who knew about this, confides to us:

> I was less vain about the gifts of the mind, so vigorous in me that I did not doubt them, than about the image reflected by a frequently consulted mirror . . . Only physical pleasure satisfies the soul fully.

The words 'physical pleasure' are vague and inadequate here. What satisfies the soul is that, while the mind will have to prove its worth, the contemplated face is here, today, given and indubitable. The whole future is concentrated in this rectangle of light and its frame makes a universe; outside these narrow limits, things are no more than disorganised chaos; the world is reduced to this piece of glass where one image shines: the One and Only. Every woman drowned in her reflection reigns over space and time, alone, sovereign; she has total rights over men, fortune, glory and sensual pleasure. Marie Bashkirtseff was so intoxicated by her beauty that she wanted to fix it in indestructible marble; it is herself she would have thus destined to immortality:

> Coming home I get undressed, I am naked and am struck by the beauty of my body as if I had never seen it. A statue has to be made of me, but how? Without getting married, it is almost impossible. And I have to, I would only get ugly, spoiled . . . I have to take a husband, if only to have my statue made.

Cécile Sorel, preparing for an amorous rendezvous, depicts herself like this:

> I am in front of my mirror. I would like to be more beautiful. I fight with my lion's mane. Sparks fly from my comb. My head is a sun in the middle of my tresses set like golden rays.

I also recall a young woman I saw one morning in the restroom of a café; she was holding a rose and she looked a little drunk; she brought her lips to the mirror as if to drink her image and she was murmuring while smiling: 'Adorable, I find myself adorable.' Both priestess and idol, the narcissist crowned with glory hovers in the heart of eternity and on the other side of the clouds kneeling creatures worship her: she is God contemplating Himself. 'I love myself, I am my God!' said Mme Mejerowsky. To become God is to realise the impossible synthesis of the in-itself and for-itself: the moments an individual thinks he has succeeded are special times of joy, exaltation and plenitude. One day in an attic, Roussel, at nineteen, felt the aura of glory around his head: he never got over it. The girl who saw beauty, desire, love and happiness deep in her mirror, endowed with her own features – animated, so she thinks, by her own consciousness – will try her whole life to use the promises of this blinding revelation. 'It is you I love,' confides Marie Bashkirtseff to her reflection one day. Another day she writes: 'I love myself so much, I make myself so happy that I was as if crazy at dinner.' Even if the woman is not of irreproachable beauty, she will see her soul's unique riches appear on her face and that will be enough to make her drunk. In the novel where she portrayed herself as Valérie, Mme Krüdener describes herself like this:

> She has something special that I have never yet seen in any woman. One can be as graceful, much more beautiful, and be far from her. She is perhaps not admired, but she has something ideal and charming that makes one pay attention. Seeing her so delicate, so svelte that she is a thought . . .

It should not be surprising that those less advantaged might sometimes experience the ecstasy of the mirror: they are moved by the mere fact of being a thing of flesh, which is there; like man, all they need is the pure generosity of young feminine flesh; and since they grasp themselves as a singular subject, with a little bad faith they will also endow their generic qualities with an individual charm; they will discover some gracious, rare or amusing feature in their face or body; they will think they are beautiful just because they feel they are women.

Moreover, the mirror is not the only instrument of doubling, although it is the favoured one. Each person can try to create a twin brother in his inner dialogue. Alone most of the day, fed up with household tasks, woman has the leisure to shape her own figure in dreams. As a young girl, she dreamed of the future; trapped in an uncertain present, she tells her story to herself; she retouches it so as to introduce an aesthetic order, transforming her contingent life into a destiny well before her death.

We know, for example, how attached women are to their childhood memories; women's literature makes it clear; in general, childhood takes a secondary place in men's autobiographies; women, on the other hand, often go no further than recounting their early years; these are the favourite subjects of their novels and stories. A woman who confides in a woman friend or a lover almost always begins her stories with these words: 'When I was a little girl . . .' They are nostalgic for this period when they felt their father's beneficent and imposing hand on their head while tasting the joys of independence; protected and justified by adults, they were autonomous individuals with a free future opening before them: now, however, they are poorly protected by marriage and love and have become servants or objects, imprisoned in the present. They reigned over the world, conquering it day after day: and now they are separated from the universe, doomed to immanence and repetition. They feel dispossessed. But what they suffer from the most is being swallowed up in generality: a wife, mother, housewife, or one woman among millions of others; as a child, by contrast, the woman lived her condition in an individual way; she was unaware of the analogies between her apprenticeship to the world and that of her friends; through her parents, teachers and friends, she was recognised in her individuality, she thought herself incomparable to any other woman, unique, promised to unique possibilities. She returns emotionally to this younger sister whose freedom, demands and sovereignty she abdicated and whom she more or less betrayed. The woman she has become misses this human being she was; she tries to find this dead child in her deepest self. The words 'little girl' move her; but 'What a funny little girl' do even more, words that revive her lost originality.

She is not satisfied with marvelling from afar at this precious childhood: she tries to revive it in her. She tries to convince herself that her tastes, ideas and feelings have kept their exceptional freshness. Perplexed, quizzical and playing with her necklace or twisting her ring, she murmurs: 'That's funny . . . That's just how I am . . . You know? Water fascinates me . . . Oh! I adore the countryside.' Each preference seems like an eccentricity, each opinion a challenge to the world. Dorothy Parker captured this widespread true-to-life characteristic:

> She liked to think of herself as one for whom flowers would thrive, who must always have blossoms about her, if she would be truly

happy . . . She told people, in little bursts of confidence, that she loved flowers. There was something almost apologetic in her way of uttering her tender avowal, as if she would beg her listeners not to consider her too bizarre in her taste. It seemed rather as though she expected the hearer to fall back, startled, at her words, crying, 'Not really! Well, what *are* we coming to?' She had other little confessions of affection . . . always with a little hesitation, as if understandably delicate about baring her heart, she told her love for color, the country, a good time, a really interesting play, nice materials, well-made clothes, and sunshine. But it was her fondness for flowers that she acknowledged oftenest. She seemed to feel that this, even more than her other predilections, set her apart from the general.[3]

The woman eagerly tries to confirm these analyses in her behaviour; she chooses a colour: 'Green is really my colour'; she has a favourite flower, perfume, musician, superstitions and fetishes that she treats with respect; she does not have to be beautiful to express her personality in her outfits and home. The character she portrays is more or less coherent and original according to her intelligence, obstinacy and depth of alien-ation. Some women just randomly put together a few sparse and mismatched traits; others systematically create a figure whose role they consistently play: it has already been said that women have trouble differ-entiating this game from the truth. Around this heroine, life goes on like a sad or marvellous novel, always somewhat strange. Sometimes it is a novel already written. I do not know how many girls have told me they see themselves in Judy of *Dust*.[4] I remember an old, very ugly lady who used to say: 'Read *The Lily in the Valley*:[5] it's my story'; as a child I used to contemplate this wilted lily for hours. Others, more vaguely, murmur: 'My life is a novel.' A good or bad star hovers over them. 'Things like this only happen to me,' they say. Rotten luck dogs them or good luck smiles on them: in any case they have a destiny. Cécile Sorel writes with the naïveté that characterises her *Mémoires*: 'This is how I made my debut in the world. My first friends were genius and beauty.' And in *The Book of My Life*, a fabulous narcissistic monument, Mme de Noailles writes:

The governesses disappeared one day: chance took their place. It mistreated the creature both powerful and weak as much as it had satisfied it, it kept it from shipwrecks where it was like a combative Ophelia, saving her flowers and whose voice ever rises. It asked the creature to hope that this final promise be kept: the Greeks use death.

This other example of narcissistic literature must be cited:

From the sturdy little girl I was with delicate but rounded arms and legs and healthy cheeks, I acquired a more frail physique, more evanescent that made me a pathetic adolescent, in spite of the source of life that can spring forth from my desert, my famine, and my brief and mysterious deaths as strangely as Moses's rock. I will not boast of my courage as I have the right to. It is part of my strengths, my luck. I could describe it as one says: I have green eyes, black hair, a small and powerful hand.

And these lines too:

Today I can recognise that, bolstered by my soul and its harmonious powers, I have lived to the sound of my voice.

Without beauty, brilliance or happiness, woman will choose the character of a victim; she will obstinately embody the *mater dolorosa*, the misunderstood wife, she will be 'the unhappiest woman in the world'. This is the case of this melancholic woman Stekel describes:*

Each time around Christmas, Mrs H. W. appears at my office, pale-faced, clad in somber black and complains of her fate. She relates a sad story while tears stream down her face. A thwarted existence, an unfortunate marriage! . . . The first time I was moved to tears and would have almost wept with her . . . Two[6] years has since flown . . . but she is still at the threshold of her hopes, still bewailing her misspent life . . . her face begins to show the early signs of the disintegration brought on by age. She thus has an additional reason for bemoaning her fate . . . 'What has become of me! I was once so beautiful and so much admired' . . . Her complaints are cumulative; she stresses her despair. Her friends . . . are well familiar with her sad plight . . . She makes herself a nuisance to everybody with her perpetual complaints . . . this in turn again furnishes her the opportunity to feel herself lonely, abandoned, not understood . . .

* *Frigidity in Woman.*

This woman found her satisfaction in the *tragic role*. The thought
that she was the unhappiest woman on earth intoxicated her . . .
All attempts to awaken her interest in the active current life ended
in failure.

A trait shared by young Mrs Weldon, stunning Anna de Noailles,
Stekel's unfortunate patient and the multitude of women marked by
an exceptional destiny is that they feel misunderstood; their family
and friends do not recognise – or inadequately recognise – their singularity; they transform this ignorance, this indifference of others, into
the positive idea that they hold a secret inside them. The fact is that
many have silently buried childhood and youthful memories that had
a great importance for them; they know their official biography is not
to be confused with their real history. But above all, because she has
not realised herself in her life, the heroine cherished by the narcissist
is merely an imaginary character; her unity does not come from the
concrete world: it is a hidden principle, a kind of 'strength', 'virtue'
as obscure as phlogistonism; the woman believes in its presence but
if she wanted to show it to others she would be as bothered as the
psychasthenic determined to confess to intangible crimes. In both cases,
the 'secret' is reduced to the empty conviction of possessing in one's
deepest self a key to decipher and justify feelings and behaviour. It is
their abulia and inertia that give this illusion to psychasthenics; and
it is because of her inability to express herself in daily action that
woman believes an inexpressible mystery inhabits her: the famous
myth of the eternal feminine encourages her in this and is thus, in
turn, confirmed.

Enriched by these misunderstood treasures, whether she be under a
lucky or an unlucky star, woman, in her own eyes, adopts the tragic
hero's need to be governed by destiny. Her whole life is transfigured into
a sacred drama. In her solemnly chosen dress emerges both a priestess
clothed in holy garb and an idol attired by faithful hands, offered for the
adoration of devotees. Her home becomes her temple of worship. Marie
Bashkirtseff gives as much care to the decoration she places around her
as to her dresses:

Near the desk, an old-style armchair, so that upon entering, I need
make only a small movement in the chair to find myself facing
the people . . . near the pedantic-looking desk with books in the
background, in between, paintings and plants, legs and feet visible

instead of being cut in two as before by this black wood. Hanging above the divan are two mandolins and the guitar. Put a blond and white girl with fine small blue-veined hands in the middle of this.

When she parades in salons, when she abandons herself on the arm of a lover, the woman accomplishes her mission: she is Venus dispensing the treasures of her beauty to the world. It is not she herself, it is Beauty that Cécile Sorel defended when she broke the glass covering Bib's caricature of her; one can see in her *Mémoires* that she invited mortals to the cult of Art at each moment of her life. Likewise Isadora Duncan, as she depicts herself in *My Life*:

After a performance, in my tunic, with my hair crowned with roses, I was so lovely. Why should not this loveliness be enjoyed? . . . A man who labours all day with his brain . . . why should he not be taken in those beautiful arms and find comfort for his pain and a few hours of beauty and forgetfulness?

The narcissist's generosity is profitable to her: better than in mirrors it is in others' admiring eyes that she sees her double haloed in glory. Without a complaisant audience, she opens her heart to a confessor, doctor or psychoanalyst; she will consult chiromancers, mediums. 'It's not that I believe in it,' said an aspiring starlet, 'but I love it so much when I'm spoken about!' She talks about herself to her women friends; more avidly than in anything else, she seeks a witness in the lover. The woman in love quickly forgets herself; but many women are incapable of real love, precisely because they never forget themselves. They prefer the wider stage to the privacy of the bedroom. Thus the importance of society life for them: they need gazes to contemplate them, ears to listen to them; they need the widest possible audience for their personage. Describing her room once more, Marie Bashkirtseff reveals: 'Like this, *I am on stage* when someone enters and finds me writing.' And further on: 'I decided to buy myself a *considerable mise en scène*. I am going to build a more beautiful townhouse and grander workshops than Sarah's.'

And Mme de Noailles writes:

I loved and love the agora . . . And so I have often reassured my friends who apologised for the many guests they feared I would be importuned by with this sincere admission: I don't like *to play to empty seats.*

Dressing up and conversation largely satisfy this feminine taste for display. But an ambitious narcissist wants to exhibit herself in a more recherché and varied way. In particular, making her life a play offered to public applause, she will take delight in really staging herself. In *Corinne*, Mme de Staël recounts at length how she charmed Italian crowds by reciting poems that she accompanied on a harp. At Coppet, one of her favourite pastimes was to declaim tragic roles; playing Phaedra, she would readily make ardent declarations to young lovers whom she dressed up as Hippolytus. Mme Krüdener specialised in the dance of the shawl that she describes in *Valérie*.

> Valérie required a dark blue muslin shawl, she took her hair away from her forehead; she put the shawl on her head; it went down along her temples and shoulders; her forehead appeared in an antique manner, her hair disappeared, her eyelids lowered, her usual smile faded little by little: her head bent, her shawl fell softly on her crossed arms, on her bust, and this blue piece of clothing and this pure and gentle figure seem to have been drawn by Correggio to express tranquil resignation; and when her eyes looked up, and her lips dared a smile, one could say that one was seeing, as Shakespeare described it, Patience on a monument smiling at Grief.
>
> One has to see Valérie. She is simultaneously timid, noble and profoundly sensitive and she troubles, leads, moves, draws tears and makes the heart beat as it beats when dominated by a great ascendant; it is she who possesses this charming grace that cannot be taught but that nature secretly reveals to some superior beings.

If circumstances allow it, nothing will give the narcissist deeper satisfaction than devoting herself publicly to the theatre. 'The theatre,' says Georgette Leblanc, 'provided me what I had sought in it: a reason for exaltation. Today, it is for me the *caricature of action*, something indispensable for excessive temperaments.' The expression she uses is striking: if she cannot take action, the woman invents substitutes for action; the theatre represents a privileged subsitute for some women. The actress can have very different aims. For some, acting is a means of earning one's living, a simple profession; for others, it is access to fame that will be exploited for amorous aims; for still others, the triumph of their narcissism; the greatest – Rachel, Eleonora Duse – are authentic artists who transcend themselves in the role they create; the ham, by contrast, cares not for what she accomplishes but for the glory that will cascade over her; she seeks above all to put herself in the limelight. The stubborn narcissist will be as limited in art as in love because she does not know how to give herself.

This failing will be seriously felt in all her activities. She will be tempted by all roads leading to glory; but she will never unreservedly take any. Painting, sculpture and literature are disciplines requiring strict training and demanding solitary work; many women try such work but quickly abandon it if they are not driven by a positive desire to create; and many of those who persevere never do more than 'play' at working. Marie Bashkirtseff, so avid for glory, spent hours in front of her easel; but she loved herself too much to seriously love to paint. She admits it herself after years of bitterness. 'Yes, I don't take the trouble to paint, I watched myself today, I *cheat*.' When a woman succeeds, like Mme de Staël or Mme de Noailles, in building a body of work, it is because she is not exclusively absorbed by self-worship: but one of the burdens that weighs on many women writers is a self-indulgence that hurts their sincerity, limits and diminishes them.

Many women imbued with a feeling of superiority, however, are not able to show it to the world; their ambition will thus be to use a man whom they convince of their worth as their means of intervention; they do not aim for specific values through free projects; they want to attach ready-made values to their egos; they will thus turn – by becoming muses, inspiration and stimulation – to those who hold influence and glory in the hope of being identified with them. A striking example is Mabel Dodge in her relations with Lawrence:

> I wanted to seduce his spirit so that I could make him carry out certain things . . . It was his soul I needed for my purpose, his soul, his will, his creative imagination, and his lighted vision. The only way to obtain the ascendancy over these essential tools was by way of the blood . . . I was always trying to get things done: I didn't often even try to do anything myself. I seemed to want to use all my power upon delegates to carry out the work. This way – *perhaps a compensation for that desolate and barren feeling of having nothing to do!* – I achieved a sense of fruitfulness and activity vicariously.[7]

And further on:

> I wanted Lawrence to understand things for me. To take *my* expe-
> rience, *my* material, through *my* Taos, and to formulate it all into
> a magnificent creation.

In a similar way, Georgette Leblanc wanted to be 'food and flame' for
Maeterlinck; but she also wanted to see her name inscribed in the poet's
book. This is not, here, a question of ambitious women having chosen
personal aims and using men to reach them – as did Mme de Staël and
the princesse des Ursins – but rather of women animated by a wholly
subjective desire for *importance*, with no objective aim, trying to appropriate for themselves the transcendence of another. They do not always
succeed – far from it – but they are skilful in hiding their failure and in
persuading themselves that they are endowed with irresistible seduction.
Knowing they are lovable, desirable and admirable, they feel certain of
being loved, desired and admired. Bélise is wholly narcissistic. Even the
innocent Brett, devoted to Lawrence, invents for herself a little personage
she endows with weighty seduction:

> I raise my eyes and see that you are looking at me with your mischie-
> vous fawn-like air, a provocative gleam in your eyes, Pan. I stare
> back at you with a solemn and dignified air until the gleam goes
> out of your face.

These illusions can give rise to real derangement; Clérambault had
good reason to consider erotomania 'a kind of professional derangement'; to feel like a woman is to feel like a desirable object, to believe
oneself desired and loved. It is significant that nine out of ten patients
with 'illusions of being loved' are women. They are clearly seeking in
their imaginary lover the apotheosis of their narcissism. They want him
to be endowed with unconditional distinction: priest, doctor, lawyer,
superior man; and the unquestionable truth his behaviour reveals is that
his ideal mistress is superior to all other women, that she possesses irresistible and sovereign virtues.

Erotomania can be part of various psychoses; but its content is always
the same. The subject is illuminated and glorified by the love of an
admirable man who was suddenly fascinated by her charms – though
she expected nothing from him – and displays his feelings in a circuitous
but imperious way; this relation at times remains ideal and at other times

assumes a sexual form; but what characterises it essentially is that the powerful and glorious demigod loves more than he is loved and he displays his passion in bizarre and ambiguous behaviour. Among the great number of cases reported by psychiatrists, here is a typical one adapted from Ferdière.* It concerns a forty-eight-year-old woman, Marie-Yvonne, who makes the following confession:

This is about Mr. Achille, Esq., former deputy and under-secretary of state, member of the bar and the Conseil de l'Ordre. I have known him since 12 May 1920; the evening before, I tried to meet him at the courts; from afar I had noticed his strong stature, but I did not know who he was; it sent chills up my spine . . . Yes, there is an affair of feeling between us, a reciprocal feeling: our eyes, our gazes met. From the moment I saw him, I had a liking for him; it is the same for him . . . In any case, he declared his feeling first: it was early in 1922; he received me in his home, always alone; one day he even sent his son out . . . One day . . . he got up and came towards me, carrying on with his conversation. I understood right away that it was a sentimental surge . . . His words made me understand. By various kindnesses he made me understand we had reciprocal feelings. Another time, once again in his office, he approached me saying: 'It is you, it is you alone and no one else, Madam, you understand clearly.' I was so taken aback that I did not know what to answer; I simply said, 'Thank you, sir!' Then another time he accompanied me from his office to the street; he even got rid of a man who was with him, he gave him twenty sous on the staircase and told him: 'Leave me, my boy, you see I am with Madam!' All of that was to accompany me and be alone with me. He always shook my hands tightly. During his first court pleading, he made a comment to let me know he was a bachelor.

He sent a singer to my courtyard to demonstrate his love to me . . . He watched my windows; I could sing you his romance . . . He had a town band march by my door. I was foolish. I should have responded to his advances. I gave M. Achille the cold shoulder . . . he thus thought I was rejecting him and he took action; he should have spoken out openly; he took revenge on me. M. Achille thought that I had feelings for B. . . . and he was jealous . . . He made me suffer by putting a magic spell on my photograph; at

* *Erotomania (L'érotomanie).*

least that is what I discovered this year through studies in books and dictionaries. He worked enough on this photo: it all comes from that.

This delusion easily changes, in fact, into a persecution complex. And this process is found even in normal cases. The narcissist cannot accept that others are not passionately interested in her; if she has the clear proof she is not adored, she immediately supposes she is hated. She attributes all criticism to jealousy or spite. Her failures are the result of dark machinations: and thus they confirm her in the idea of her importance. She easily slips into megalomania or the opposite, persecution delirium: as centre of her universe and aware of no other universe except her own, she becomes the absolute centre of the world.

But narcissist drama plays itself out at the expense of real life; an imaginary personage solicits the admiration of an imaginary public; a woman tormented by her ego loses all hold on the concrete world, she does not care about establishing any real relationship with others; Mme de Staël would not have declaimed *Phaedra* so wholeheartedly if she had foreseen the mockeries her 'admirers' noted that night in their notebooks; but the narcissist refuses to accept she can be seen other than as she shows herself: this is what explains why, so busy contemplating herself, she totally fails to judge herself, and she falls so easily into ridiculousness. She no longer listens, she talks, and when she talks, she recites her lines. Marie Bashkirtseff writes: 'It amuses me. I don't speak with him, I *act* and, feeling I am in front of a receptive audience, I am excellent at childlike and fanciful intonations and attitudes.'

She looks at herself too much to see anything; she understands in others only what she recognises about them; whatever she cannot assimilate to her own case, to her own story, remains foreign to her. She likes to expand her experiences: she wants to experience the headiness and torments of being in love, the pure joys of motherhood, friendship, solitude, tears and laughter; but because she can never give herself, her sentiments and emotions are fabricated. Isadora Duncan undoubtedly cried real tears on the death of her children. But when she cast their ashes into the sea with a great theatrical gesture, she was merely being an actress; and one cannot read this passage where she evokes her sorrow in *My Life* without embarrassment:

I feel the warmth of my own body. I look down on my bare legs
– stretching them out. The softness of my breasts, my arms that

are never still but continually waving about in soft undulations, and I realise that for twelve years I have been weary, this breast has harboured a never-ending ache, these hands before me have been marked with sorrow, and when I am alone these eyes are seldom dry.

In the worship of self, the adolescent girl can muster the courage to face the disturbing future; but it is a stage she must go beyond quickly: if not, the future closes up. The woman in love who encloses her lover in the couple's immanence dooms him to death with herself: the narcissist, alienating herself in her imaginary double, destroys herself. Her memories become fixed, her behaviour stereotyped, she dwells on the same words, repeats gestures that have lost all meaning: this is what gives the impression of poverty found in 'secret diaries' or 'feminine autobiographies'; so occupied in flattering herself, the woman who does nothing becomes nothing and flatters a nothing.

Her misfortune is that, in spite of all her bad faith, she is aware of this nothingness. There cannot be a real relationship between an individual and his double because this double does not exist. The woman narcissist suffers a radical failure. She cannot grasp herself as a totality, as plenitude; she cannot maintain the illusion of being in itself – for itself. Her solitude, like that of every human being, is felt as contingence and abandonment. And this is why – unless there is a conversion – she is condemned to hide relentlessly from herself in crowds, noise, and others. It would be a grave error to believe that in choosing herself as the supreme end she escapes dependence: on the contrary, she dooms herself to the most severe slavery; she does not make the most of her freedom, she makes herself an endangered object in the world and in foreign consciousnesses. Not only are her body and face vulnerable flesh worn by time, but from a practical point of view it is a costly enterprise to adorn the idol, to put her on a pedestal, to erect a temple to her: we have seen that to preserve her form in immortal marble, Marie Bashkirtseff had to consent to marry for money. Masculine fortunes paid for the gold, incense and myrrh that Isadora Duncan and Cécile Sorel laid at the foot of their thrones. As it is man who incarnates destiny for woman, women usually gauge their success by the number and quality of men subjected to their power. But reciprocity comes into play again here; the 'praying mantis', attempting to make the male her instrument, does not free herself from him like this, because to catch him, she must please him. The American woman, trying to be an idol, makes herself the slave of her admirers, does not dress, live or breathe other than through the man and for him. In fact, the narcissist is as dependent as the hetaera. If she escapes an individual man's domination, it is by accepting the tyranny of public opinion. This link that rivets her to others does not imply reciprocity; if she sought recognition by others' freedom while also recognising that freedom as an end through activity, she would cease to be narcissistic. The paradox of her attitude is that she demands to be valued by a world to which she denies all value, since she alone counts in her own eyes. Outside approbation is an inhuman, mysterious and capricious force that must be tapped magically. In spite of her superficial arrogance, the narcissistic woman knows she is threatened; it is why she is uneasy, susceptible, irritable and constantly suspicious; her vanity is never satisfied; the older she grows, the more anxiously she seeks praise and success, the more she suspects plots around her; lost and obsessed, she sinks into the darkness of bad faith and often ends up by building a paranoid delirium around herself. The words 'Whosoever shall save his life will lose it' apply specifically to her.

CHAPTER 12

The Woman in Love

The word 'love' has not at all the same meaning for both sexes and this is a source of the grave misunderstandings that separate them. Byron rightly said that love is merely an occupation in the life of the man, while it is life itself for the woman. The same idea is expressed by Nietzsche in *The Gay Science*: the same word 'love', he says, means, in fact, two different things for the man and for the woman:

> What woman means by love is clear enough: total devotion (not mere surrender) with soul and body, without any consideration or reserve . . . In this absence of conditions her love is a faith; woman has no other *faith*.* Man, when he loves a woman, *wants*† precisely this love from her and is thus himself as far as can be from the presupposition of feminine love. Supposing, however, that there should also be men to whom the desire for total devotion is not alien; well, then they simply are not men.⁸

Men might be passionate lovers at certain moments of their existence, but there is not one who could be defined as 'a man in love'; in their most violent passions, they never abandon themselves completely; even if they fall on their knees before their mistresses, they still wish to possess them, annex them; at the heart of their lives, they remain sovereign subjects; the woman they love is merely one value among others; they want to integrate her into their existence, not submerge their entire existence in her. By contrast, love for the woman is a total abdication for the benefit of a master.

Cécile Sauvage writes: 'When the woman loves, she must forget her

---

* Nietzsche's emphasis.
† Also Nietzsche's emphasis.

own personality. This is a law of nature. A woman does not exist without a master. Without a master, she is a scattered bouquet.'

In reality, this has nothing to do with a law of nature. It is the difference in their situations that is reflected in the conceptions man and woman have of love. The individual who is a subject, who is himself, endeavours to extend his grasp on the world if he has the generous inclination for transcendence: he is ambitious, he acts. But an inessential being cannot discover the absolute in the heart of his subjectivity; a being doomed to immanence could not realise himself in his acts. Closed off in the sphere of the relative, destined for the male from her earliest childhood, used to seeing him as a sovereign, with whom equality is not permitted, the woman who has not suppressed her claim to be human will dream of surpassing her being towards one of those superior beings, of becoming one, of fusing with the sovereign subject; there is no other way out for her than losing herself body and soul in the one designated to her as the absolute, as the essential. Since she is, in any case, condemned to dependence, she would rather serve a god than obey tyrants – parents, husband, protector; she chooses to want her enslavement so ardently that it will seem to her to be the expression of her freedom; she will try to overcome her situation as inessential object by radically assuming it; through her flesh, her feelings and her behaviour, she will exalt as sovereign the one she loves, she will posit him as value and supreme reality: she will efface herself before him. Love becomes a religion for her.

We have seen that the adolescent girl at first wishes to identify with males; once she renounces this, she then seeks to participate in their virility by being loved by one of them; it is not the individuality of one man or another that seduces her; she is in love with man in general. 'And you, the men I will love, how I await you,' writes Irène Reweliotty. 'How I rejoice in soon knowing you. You, especially, the first one.' Of course, the man must belong to the same class and the same race as her own: the privilege of sex works only within this framework; for him to be a demigod, he must obviously be a human being first; for the daughter of a colonial officer, the native is not a man; if the young girl gives herself to an 'inferior', she is trying to degrade herself because she does not think she is worthy of love. Normally, she looks for the man who represents male superiority; she is rapidly led to discover that many individuals of the chosen sex are sadly contingent and mundane; but first she is favourably disposed towards them; they have less to prove their value than to keep from grossly disavowing it: this explains many often lamentable errors; the naive young girl is taken in by virility. According to the circumstances, male worth will appear to her as physical force, elegance, wealth, culture, intelligence, authority, social situation or a military uniform: but what she always hopes for is that her lover will be the summation of the essence of man. Familiarity often is enough to destroy his prestige; it breaks down with the first kiss, or in everyday contact, or on the wedding night. Love at a distance is nonetheless merely a fantasy, not a real experience. When it is carnally consummated, desire for love becomes passionate love. Inversely, love can arise from making love, the sexually dominated woman exalting the man who first seemed insignificant to her. But it often happens that the woman is unable to transform any of the men she knows into a god. Love holds less place in feminine life than is often believed. Husband, children, home, pleasures, social life, vanity, sexuality and career are far more important. Almost all women have dreamed of the 'great love': they have had imitations, they have come close to it; it has come to them in incomplete, bruised, trifling, imperfect and false forms; but very few have really dedicated their existence to it. The great women lovers are often those who did not waste their emotions on juvenile crushes; they first accepted the traditional feminine destiny: husband, home, children; or they lived in difficult solitude; or they counted on some venture that more or less failed; when they glimpse the chance to save their disappointing life by dedicating it to an elite being, they desperately give themselves up to this hope. Mlle Aïssé, Juliette Drouet and Mme d'Agoult were nearly thirty when they began their love lives, Julie de Lespinasse was close to forty; no goal was available to them, they were unprepared to undertake any venture that seemed worthwhile to them, love was their only way out.

Even if they are allowed independence, this road is still the one that seems the most attractive to most women; it is agonising to take responsibility for one's life endeavour; the adolescent boy too readily turns to older women, seeking a guide, a tutor, a mother in them; but his education, customs and the inner constraints he faces prevent him from definitively accepting the easy solution of abdication; he views such loves merely as a phase. It is man's luck – in adulthood as in childhood – to be made to take the most arduous roads but the surest ones; woman's misfortune is that she is surrounded by nearly irresistible temptations; everything incites her to take the easy way out: instead of being encouraged to fight on her own account, she is told that she can let herself get by and she will reach enchanted paradises; when she realises she was fooled by a mirage, it is too late; she has been worn out in this adventure.

Psychoanalysts like to claim that the woman seeks her father's image in her lover; but it is because he is man, not father, that he dazzles the child, and every man shares this magic; the woman wishes not to reincarnate one individual in another but to bring back to life a situation: one she knew as a little girl, sheltered by adults; she was an integral part of her family home life, she felt the peace of quasi-passivity; love will bring her mother as well as her father back to her, and her childhood as well; what she wishes is to find a roof over her head, walls that hide her from her abandonment within the world, laws that protect her from her freedom. This childish dream haunts many feminine loves; the woman is happy when her lover calls her 'my little girl, my dear child'; men know the words well: 'You look like a little girl' are among the words that most surely touch the hearts of women: we have seen how many of them have suffered becoming adults; many persist in 'acting like a child', and indefinitely prolonging their childhood in their attitude and dress. To become a child again in the arms of a man brings them great satisfaction. It is the theme of this popular tune:

> *I feel so small in your arms*
> *So small, o my love . . .*

a theme tirelessly repeated in lovers' conversations and correspondence. 'Baby, my baby,' murmurs the lover and the woman calls herself, 'little one, your little one'. Irène Reweliotty writes: 'When, then, will he come, the one who will be able to dominate me?' And thinking she had met him: 'I love feeling you a man and better than me.'

A psychasthenic woman studied by Janet* illustrates this attitude in the most striking way:

As far back as I can recall, all the foolish acts or all the good deeds I have done stem from the same cause, an aspiration to the perfect and ideal love where I can give myself entirely, confide all my being to another being, God, man or woman, so superior to me that I would no longer think of leading my life or watching over myself. To find someone who would love me enough to take the trouble to make me live, someone whom I would blindly and confidently obey, sure that he would keep me from all failure and would put me on the right track, very gently and with much love, towards

---

* *Obsessions and Psychasthenia.*

perfection. How I envy the ideal love of Mary Magdalene and Jesus: to be the ardent disciple of an adored and worthy master; to live and die for one's idol, believe in him without any possible shadow of doubt, to hold at last the final victory of the Angel over the beast, to be held in his enveloping arms, so small, so pressed in his protection and so much his that I no longer exist.[9]

Many examples have already proven to us that this dream of annihilation is in fact an avid will to be. In all religions, the adoration of God is part of the devotee's desire for his own salvation; by giving herself up entirely to the idol, the woman hopes he will give her possession both of herself and of the universe contained in him. In most cases, it is first the justification, the exaltation of her ego, she asks of her lover. Many women do not abandon themselves to love unless they are loved in return: and the love they are shown is sometimes enough to make them fall in love. The young girl has dreamed of herself as seen through the man's eyes: it is in man's eyes that the woman believes she has at last found herself.

Cécile Sauvage writes:

Walking beside you, moving my tiny little feet that you loved, feeling them so slender in their high felt-topped shoes, made me love all the love you surrounded them with. The slightest movements of my hands in my muff, of my arms, of my face, the inflections of my voice, filled me with happiness . . .[10]

The woman feels endowed with a sure and high value; at last she has the right to cherish herself through the love she inspires. She is exhilarated at finding a witness in her lover. This is what Colette's 'Vagabond' admits:

I must confess that, in allowing this man to return tomorrow, I was giving way to my desire to keep, not an admirer, not a friend, but an eager spectator of my life and my person. 'One has to get terribly old,' said Margot to me one day, 'before one can give up the vanity of living in the presence of someone else.'[11]

In one of her letters to Middleton Murry, Katherine Mansfield recounts that she has just bought a ravishing mauve corset; she quickly adds: 'What a pity there is no one to *see* it!' Nothing is more discouraging than to feel that one is the flower, the perfume, the treasure that no desire seeks: what good is an asset that does not enrich me and that no one wants as a gift? Love is the revealer that shows up in positive and clear traits the dull negative image as empty as a blank print; the woman's face, the curves of her body, her childhood memories, her dried tears, her dresses, her habits, her universe, everything she is, everything that belongs to her escapes contingence and becomes necessary: she is a marvellous gift at the foot of her god's altar.

> Before his hands were laid gently on her shoulders, before his eyes took their fill of hers, she had been a plain dull woman in a plain dull world. He kissed her, and she stood in the rose-light of immortality.*[12]

Thus, men endowed with social prestige and good at flattering feminine vanity will arouse passion even if they have no physical charm. Because of their lofty situation, they incarnate Law and Truth: their consciousness discloses an uncontested reality. The woman they praise feels transformed into a priceless treasure. According to Isadora Duncan,[†] D'Annunzio's success came from this.

> When D'Annunzio loves a woman, he lifts her spirit from this earth to the divine regions where Beatrice moves and shines. In turn he transforms each woman to a part of the divine essence, he carries her aloft until she believes herself really with Beatrice . . . he flung over each favourite in turn a shining veil. She rose above the heads of ordinary mortals and walked surrounded by a strange radiance. But when the caprice of the poet ended, this veil vanished, the radiance was eclipsed, and the woman turned again to common clay . . . To hear oneself praised with that magic peculiar to D'Annunzio is, I imagine, something like the experience of Eve when she heard the voice of the serpent in Paradise. D'Annunzio can make any woman feel that she is the centre of the universe.[13]

Only in love can woman harmoniously reconcile her eroticism and her narcissism; we have already seen an opposition between these two systems that makes the woman's adaptation to her sexual destiny very difficult.

* Mary Webb, *The House in Dormer Forest*.
† Isadora Duncan, *My Life*.

Making herself carnal object and prey contradicts her self-adoration: it seems to her that lovemaking disfigures and defiles her body or degrades her soul. Some women, therefore, choose frigidity, thinking they can thus preserve the integrity of their ego. Others dissociate animal sensuality and lofty sentiments. A very characteristic case is Mme D. S.'s, reported by Stekel and which I have already cited concerning marriage:

> Frigid, and married to a respected man, after his death, there came into her life a young man . . . he, too, was an artist and a wonderful musician . . . She became his mistress. Her love was and is to this day so great that she feels happy only in his presence. Her whole life is wrapped in her Lothar. In spite of her great love for him she has remained cool in his arms. Another man, too, crossed her path. He was a forester, a powerful, rough individual who, on finding himself alone with her one day, took possession of her without saying a word. She was so consternated that she didn't object. In his embrace she experienced the keenest orgasm. 'In his arms,' she states, 'I have regained my health for the past months. It is like a wild intoxication, but followed by an indescribable disgust when I think of my Lothar. Paul I hate; Lothar I love. Nevertheless, Paul is the one who gratifies me. Everything about Lothar holds me to him; but it seems I must act like a harlot in order to feel. As a lady I can never respond.' [She refuses to marry Paul but continues to sleep with him; in those moments][14] she becomes like a person transformed and the raw words which escape her lips she would never be guilty of using on any other occasion.

Stekel adds that 'for many women, the descent into animality is the condition for orgasm'. They see an abasement in physical love impossible to reconcile with feelings of esteem and affection. For others, by contrast, it is by the man's esteem, tenderness and admiration that this abasement can be abolished. They only consent to give themselves to a man if they believe they are deeply loved by him; a woman has to be very cynical, indifferent or proud to consider physical relations as an exchange of pleasures in which each partner equally gets something out of it. The man revolts as much as – and perhaps more than – the woman against anyone who wants to exploit* him sexually; but she is the one

* See, among others, *Lady Chatterley's Lover*. Through Mellors, Lawrence expresses his horror of women who make him a tool of pleasure.

who generally has the impression that her partner is using her as an instrument. Only exalted admiration can make up for the humiliation of an act she considers a defeat. We have seen that the love act requires a woman's profound alienation; she is awash in the indolence of passivity; eyes closed, anonymous, lost, she feels transported by waves, caught up in torment, buried in the night: night of flesh, of the womb, of the tomb; reduced to nothing, she reaches the Whole, her self effaced. But when the man separates himself from her, she finds herself thrown back to earth, on a bed, in the light; she has a name and a face again: she is a conquered person, a prey, an object. This is when love becomes necessary to her. Just as after being weaned the child seeks the reassuring gaze of his parents, it is in the eyes of the lover who contemplates her that the woman whose flesh has been painfully detached has to feel reunited with the Whole. She is rarely completely satisfied; even if she experienced the relief of pleasure, she is not entirely freed of the carnal spell, her arousal becomes feeling; in providing her with sensuality, the man attaches her to him and does not liberate her. He, though, no longer feels desire for her: she only forgives him for this momentary indifference if he has vowed timeless and absolute feeling to her. Then the immanence of the instant is transcended; the burning memories are no longer a regret but a treasure; as it dies down, the sensuality becomes hope and promise; sexual pleasure is justified; the woman can gloriously assume her sexuality because she transcends it; arousal, pleasure and desire are no longer a state but a gift; her body is no longer an object: it is a song, a flame. Thus she can abandon herself passionately to the magic of eroticism; night becomes light; the woman in love can open her eyes, look at the man who loves her and whose gaze glorifies her; through him nothingness becomes plenitude of being and being is transfigured into value; she no longer sinks into a sea of darkness, she is transported on wings, exalted to the sky. Abandon becomes holy ecstasy. When she *receives* the loved man, the woman is inhabited, visited like the Virgin by the Holy Spirit, like the believer by the wafer; this explains the obscene analogy between holy hymns and ribald songs: it is not that mystical love always has a sexual side; but the sexuality of the woman in love takes on a mystical tone. 'My God, my beloved, my master', the same words spill from the lips of the kneeling saint and the woman in love lying on the bed; the saint offers her flesh to Christ's arrows, she holds out her hands to receive the stigmata, she implores the burning of divine Love; the woman in love also offers and waits: darts, stinger and arrows are embodied in the male sex. In both of them there is the same dream, the infantile, mystical, love dream: to exist sovereignly by effacing oneself within the other.

It has sometimes been claimed* that this desire for effacement leads to masochism. But as I have noted concerning eroticism, one can only speak of masochism if I try 'to cause myself to be fascinated by my objectivity-for-others',†15 that is if the consciousness of the subject turns back to the ego to grasp it in its humiliated situation. But the woman in love is not only a narcissist alienated in her self: she also experiences a passionate desire to go beyond her own limits and become infinite, thanks to the intervention of another who has access to infinite reality. She abandons herself first to love to save *herself*; but the paradox of idol-atrous love is that in order to save herself she ends up totally disavowing *herself*. Her feeling takes on a mystical dimension; she no longer asks God to admire her or approve her; she wants to melt into him, forget herself in his arms. 'I would have liked to be a love saint,' writes Mme d'Agoult. 'I envied the martyr in such moments of exaltation and ascetic furore.' What comes through in these words is the desire for a radical destruction of the self, abolishing the frontiers that separate her from her beloved: it is not masochism but a dream of ecstatic union. The same dream inspires these words of Georgette Leblanc: 'At that time, had I been asked what I most wanted in the world, without any hesita-tion I would have said: to be food and flame for his spirit.'

To achieve this union, the woman first wants to serve; she will feel necessary in responding to her lover's demands; she will be integrated into his existence, she will be a part of his value, she will be justified; even mystics like to believe, according to Angelus Silesius, that God needs man, otherwise the gift they make of themselves would be in vain. The more demands the man makes, the more fulfilled the woman feels. Although the seclusion Hugo imposed on Juliette Drouet weighed on the young woman, one feels she is happy to obey him: staying seated close to the fire is doing something for the master's happiness. She passion-ately tries to be positively useful to him. She prepares special dishes for him, creates a home for him: your little 'nest for two', she said sweetly; she takes care of his clothes.

She writes to him: 'I want you to stain and tear all your clothes as much as possible and that I alone should mend and clean them and nobody else.'

* It is, among others, H. Deutsch's theory in *The Psychology of Women*.
† Cf. Sartre, *Being and Nothingness*.

For him she reads newspapers, cuts out articles, organises letters and notes, copies manuscripts. She is upset when the poet entrusts part of this work to his daughter Léopoldine. Similar characteristics are found in all women in love. If need be she tyrannises herself in the lover's name; everything she is, everything she has, every second of her life must be devoted to him and thus find their raison d'être; she does not want to possess anything except in him; what would make her unhappy is that he demand nothing of her, and so an attentive lover invents demands. She first sought in love a confirmation of what she was, her past, her personage; but she also commits her future: to justify it she destines it to the one who possesses all values; she thus gives up her transcendence: she subordinates it to that of the essential other whose vassal and slave she makes herself. It is to find herself, to save herself that she began by losing herself in him: the fact is that little by little she loses herself; all reality is in the other. Love that was originally defined as a narcissistic apotheosis is accomplished in the bitter joys of a devotion that often leads to self-mutilation. At the outset of a consuming passion, the woman becomes prettier, more elegant than before. 'When Adèle does my hair, I look at my forehead because you love it', writes Mme d'Agoult. This face, this body, this room, this me, she has found a raison d'être for them, she cherishes them through the mediation of this beloved man who loves her. But later, she gives up all coquetry; if the lover so desires, she changes this face that had once been more precious than love itself; she loses interest in it; she makes what she is and what she has the fief of her lord; what he disdains, she disavows; she would like to devote to him each beat of her heart, each drop of blood, the marrow of her bones; this is what a dream of martyrdom expresses: to exaggerate the gift of self to the point of torture, of death, to be the ground the beloved treads on, to be nothing but that which responds to his call. She vigorously eliminates everything the beloved finds useless. If this gift she makes of self is totally accepted, there is no masochism: few traces of it are seen in Juliette Drouet. In her excessive adoration she sometimes knelt before the poet's portrait and asked him to excuse the mistakes she might have committed; she did not angrily turn against herself. But the slide from generous enthusiasm to masochistic rage is easy. The woman in love who finds herself before her lover in the same situation as the child before his parents also recovers the feeling of guilt she experienced around them; she does not choose to revolt against him as long as she loves him: she revolts against her self. If he loves her less than she desires, if she fails to interest him, to make him happy, to be sufficient to him, all her

narcissism turns into disgust, humiliation and self-hatred that push her
to self-punishment. During a longer or shorter crisis, sometimes for a
whole life, she will be a willing victim; she will go out of her way to
harm this self that has not been able to satisfy the lover. Then her attitude is specifically masochistic. But cases where the woman in love seeks
her own suffering so as to get revenge on herself and those where she
seeks confirmation of the man's freedom and power must not be confused.
It is a commonplace – and seems to be a reality – that the prostitute is
proud to be beaten by her man: but it is not the idea of her battered and
enslaved person that exalts her, it is the strength, authority and sovereignty of the male on whom she depends; she also likes to see him
mistreat another male, she often pushes him into dangerous competi-
tions: she wants her master to hold the values recognised in the milieu
to which she belongs. The woman who gladly submits to masculine
caprices also admires the proof of a sovereign freedom in the tyranny
that is wielded over her. One must be careful to note that, if for some
reason the lover's prestige is ruined, his blows and demands become
odious to her: they are only worth something if they manifest the beloved's
divinity. In that case, it is intoxicatingly joyous to feel oneself the prey of
a foreign freedom: for any existent the most surprising adventure is to
find oneself sustained by the diverse and imperious will of another; one
is tired of inhabiting the same skin all the time; blind obedience is the
only chance of radical change that a human being might experience. So
here is the woman slave, queen, flower, doe, stained-glass window,
doormat, servant, courtesan, muse, companion, mother, sister or child
depending on the lover's fleeting dreams, the lover's imperious orders:
she complies with delight with these metamorphoses as long as she does
not recognise that she still has the same taste of submission on her lips.
In love as well as in eroticism, it appears that masochism is one of the
paths the unsatisfied woman takes, disappointed by the other and by
herself; but this is not the natural slope of a happy resignation. Masochism
perpetuates the presence of the self as a hurt, fallen figure; love aims at
the forgetting of self in favour of the essential subject.

The supreme aim of human love, like mystical love, is identification
with the loved one. The measure of values and the truth of the world
are in his own consciousness; that is why serving him is still not enough.
The woman tries to see with his eyes; she reads the books he reads,
prefers the paintings and music he prefers, she is only interested in the
landscapes she sees with him, in the ideas that come from him; she
adopts his friends, his enemies and his opinions; when she questions

herself, she endeavours to hear the answer he gives; she wants the air he has already breathed in her lungs; the fruit and flowers she has not received from his hands have neither fragrance nor taste; even her hodological space is upset: the centre of the world is no longer where she is but where the beloved is; all roads leave from and lead to his house. She uses his words, she repeats his gestures, adopts his manias and tics. 'I *am* Heathcliff,' says Catherine in *Wuthering Heights*; this is the cry of all women in love; she is another incarnation of the beloved, his reflection, his double: she is *he*. She lets her own world founder in contingence: she lives in his universe.

The supreme happiness of the woman in love is to be recognised by the beloved as part of him; when he says 'we', she is associated and identified with him, she shares his prestige and reigns with him over the rest of the world; she does not tire of saying – even if it is excessive – this delicious 'we'. Necessary to a being who is absolute necessity, who projects himself in the world towards necessary goals and who reconstitutes the world as necessity, the woman in love experiences in her resignation the magnificent possession of the absolute. It is this certitude that gives her such great joys; she feels exalted at the right hand of the god; what does it matter that she is always in second place as long as it is *her* place, forever, in a marvellously ordered world? As long as she loves, as she is loved and necessary for the beloved, she feels completely justified: she savours peace and happiness. Such was perhaps Mlle Aïssé's lot at Knight d'Aydie's side before religious scruples troubled her soul, of Juliette Drouet's in Hugo's shadow.

But this glorious felicity is seldom stable. No man is God. The relations the mystic has with the divine absence depend on his fervour alone: but the deified man – who is not God – is present. That is where the torments of the woman in love stem from. Her most ordinary destiny can be summarised in Julie de Lespinasse's famous words: 'At every instant of my life, my friend, I love you, I suffer and I await you.' Of course for men too suffering is linked to love; but their heartbreaks either do not last long or are not all consuming; Benjamin Constant wanted to die for Juliette Récamier: in one year, he was cured. Stendhal missed Métilde for years, but it was a regret that enriched his life more than destroying it. In accepting herself as the inessential and as total dependence, the woman creates a hell for herself; all women in love see themselves in Andersen's Little Mermaid, who, having exchanged her fish tail for a woman's legs out of love, walked on needles and burning coals. It is not true that the beloved man is unconditionally necessary and that she is not necessary to him; it is not up to him to justify the woman who worships him, and he does not let himself be possessed by her.

An authentic love should take on the other's contingence, that is, his lacks, limitations and originary gratuitousness; it would claim to be not a salvation but an inter-human relation. Idolatrous love confers an absolute value on the loved one: this is the first lie strikingly apparent to all outsiders: 'He doesn't deserve so much love,' people whisper around the woman in love; posterity smiles pityingly when evoking the pale figure of Count Guibert. It is a heartrending disappointment for the woman to discover her idol's weaknesses and mediocrity. Colette – in The Vagabond and Mes apprentissager (My Apprenticeships) – often alludes to this bitter agony; this disillusion is even crueller than the child's at seeing paternal prestige crumble, because the woman herself chose the one to whom she made a gift of her whole being. Even if the chosen one is worthy of the deepest attachment, his truth is earthbound: it is not he whom the woman kneeling before a supreme being loves; she is duped by that spirit of seriousness which refuses to put values 'in parentheses', not recognising that they stem from human existence; her bad faith erects barriers between her and the one she worships. She flatters him, she bows down before him, but she is not a friend for him since she does not realise he is in danger in the world, that his projects and finalities are as fragile as he himself is; considering him the Law and Truth, she misunderstands his freedom, which is hesitation and anguish. This refusal to apply a human measure to the lover explains many feminine paradoxes. The woman demands a favour from the lover, he grants it: he is generous, rich, magnificent, he is royal, he is divine; if he refuses, he is suddenly stingy, mean and cruel, he is a devilish being or bestial. One might be tempted to counter: If a 'yes' is understood as a superb extravagance, why should one be surprised by a 'no'? If the no manifests such an abject egotism, why admire the yes so much? Between the superhuman and the inhuman is there not room for the human?

A fallen god, then, is not a man: it is an imposture; the lover has no alternative other than to prove he is really the king one adulates or to denounce himself as a usurper. When he is no longer worshipped, he has to be trampled on. In the name of this halo with which the woman in love adorns her beloved, she forbids him all weakness; she is disappointed and irritated if he does not conform to this image she put in his place; if he is tired, confused, if he is hungry or thirsty when he should not be, if he makes a mistake, if he contradicts himself, she decrees he is 'not himself' and she reproaches him for this. Likewise, she will go so far as to reproach him for all the initiatives she does not appreciate; she judges her judge, and in order for him to deserve to remain her master, she refuses him his freedom. Her adoration is sometimes better served by his absence than his presence; there are women, as we have seen, who devote themselves to dead or inaccessible heroes so that they never have to compare them with flesh-and-blood beings; the latter inevitably fail to live up to their dreams. Hence the disillusioned sayings: 'You shouldn't believe in Prince Charming. Men are just poor things.' They would not seem like dwarfs if they were not required to be giants.

This is one of the curses weighing on the passionate woman: her generosity is immediately converted into demands. Being alienated in another, she also wants to salvage herself: she has to annex this other who holds her being. She gives herself to him entirely: but he has to be totally available to receive this gift honourably. She dedicates all her moments to him: he has to be present at every moment; she only wants to live through him: but she wants to live; he has to devote himself to making her live.

Mme d'Agoult writes to Liszt: 'I love you sometimes stupidly and at such times I do not understand that I could not, would not be able to and should not be for you the same absorbing thought as you are for me.' She tries to curtail her spontaneous wish: to be everything for him. There is the same appeal in Mlle de Lespinasse's complaint:

> My God! If you only knew what the days are like, what life is like without the interest and pleasure of seeing you! My friend, dissipation, occupation and movement satisfy you; and I, my happiness is you, it is only you; I would not want to live if I could not see you and love you every minute of my life.

At first, the woman in love is delighted to satisfy her lover's desire; then – like the legendary fireman who out of love for his job lights fires everywhere – she works at awakening this desire so as to have to satisfy it; if she does not succeed, she feels humiliated, useless to such an extent that the lover will feign passion he does not feel. In making herself a slave, she has found the surest means of subjugating him. This is another lie of love that many men – Lawrence, Montherlant – have resentfully denounced: he takes himself for a gift when he is a tyranny. In *Adolphe*, Benjamin Constant fiercely painted the chains the overly generous passion of a woman entwines around the man. 'She did not count her sacrifices because she was busy making me accept them,' he says cruelly about

Ellénore. Acceptance is thus a commitment that ties the lover up, without his even having the benefit of appearing to be the one who gives; the woman demands that he graciously welcome the loads she burdens him with. And her tyranny is insatiable. The man in love is authoritarian: but when he has obtained what he wanted, he is satisfied; but there are no limits to the demanding devotion of the woman. A lover who has confidence in his mistress shows no displeasure at her absences or if she is occupied when away from him: sure that she belongs to him, he prefers to possess a freedom more than a thing. By contrast, the absence of the lover is always torture for the woman: he is a gaze, a judge, as soon as he looks at something other than her, he frustrates her; everything he sees, he steals from her; far from him, she is dispossessed both of herself and of the world; even seated at her side, reading, writing, he abandons her, he betrays her. She hates his sleep. Baudelaire is touched by the sleeping woman: 'Your beautiful eyes are weary, poor lover.' Proust delights in watching Albertine* sleep; male jealousy is thus simply the desire for exclusive possession; the woman beloved, when sleep gives her back the disarming candour of childhood, belongs to no one: for the man, this certitude suffices. But the god, the master, must not abandon himself to the repose of immanence; it is with a hostile look that the woman contemplates this destroyed transcendence; she detests his animal inertia, this body that no longer exists *for her* but *in itself*, abandoned to a contingence whose ransom is her own contingence. Violette Leduc forcefully expressed this feeling:

> I hate sleepers. I lean over them with bad intent. Their submission exasperates me. I hate their unconscious serenity, their false anaesthesia, their studiously blind face, their reasonable drunkenness, their incompetent earnestness . . . I hovered, I waited for a long time for the pink bubble that would come out of my sleeper's mouth. I only wanted a bubble of presence from him. I didn't get it . . . I saw that his night eyelids were eyelids of death . . . I took refuge in his eyelids' gaiety when this man was impossible. Sleep is hard when it wants to be. He walked off with everything. I hate my sleeper who can create peace for himself with an unconsciousness that is alien to me. I hate his sweet forehead . . . He is deep down inside himself busy with his rest. He

---

* That Albertine is an Albert does not change anything; Proust's attitude here is in any case the masculine attitude.

is recapitulating who knows what . . . We had left posthaste. We wanted to leave the earth by using our personality. We had taken off, climbed up, watched out, waited, hummed, arrived, whined, won and lost together. It was a serious school for playing hooky. We had uncovered a new kind of nothingness. Now you're sleeping. Your effacement is not honest . . . If my sleeper moves, my hand touches, in spite of itself, the seed. It is the barn with fifty sacks of grain that is stifling, despotic. The scrotum of a sleeping man fell on my hand . . . I have the little bags of seed. I have in my hand the fields that will be ploughed, the orchards that will be pruned, the force of the waters that will be transformed, the four boards that will be nailed, the tarpaulins that will be lifted. I have in my hand the fruit, flowers and chosen animals. I have in my hand the lancet, the clippers, the probe, the revolver, the forceps and all that does not fill my hand. The seed of the sleeping world is only the dangling extra of the soul's prolongation . . .

You, when you sleep, I hate you.*[16]

The god must not sleep, or he becomes clay and flesh; he must not cease to be present, or his creature founders in nothingness. For woman, man's sleep is avarice and betrayal. At times the lover wakes his mistress: it is to make love to her; she wakes him simply to keep him from sleeping, to keep him nearby, thinking only of her, there, closed up in the room, in the bed, in her arms – like God in the tabernacle – this is what the woman desires: she is a gaoler.

And yet, she does not really consent to have the man be nothing else but her prisoner. Here is one of the painful paradoxes of love: captive, the god sheds his divinity. The woman preserves her transcendence by handing it over to him: but he must bring it to the whole world. If two lovers disappear into the absolute of passion together, all freedom deteriorates into immanence; only death can provide a solution: this is one of the meanings of the Tristan and Isolde myth. Two lovers who are exclusively destined for each other are already dead: they die of boredom. Marcel Arland in *Foreign Lands*[17] described this slow agony of a love that devours itself. The woman understands this danger. Except for cases of jealous frenzy, she herself demands that man be project and action: he has to accomplish exploits to remain a hero. The chevalier who embarks

* *I Hate Sleepers.*

on new feats of prowess offends his lady; but she scorns him if he stays seated at her feet. This is the torture of impossible love; woman wants to *have* man all to herself, but she demands that he go beyond all the givens he could possibly possess; one does not *have* a freedom; she wants to lock up *here* an existent who is, in Heidegger's words, a 'being from afar', she knows full well that this effort is futile. 'My friend, I love you as one should love, with excess, madness, rapture and despair,' writes Julie de Lespinasse. Idolatrous love, if lucid, can only be hopeless. For the woman in love who asks her lover to be a hero, giant, demigod, demands not to be everything for him, whereas she can find happiness only if she contains him entirely within herself.

Nietzsche says:*[18]

A woman's passion in its unconditional renunciation of rights of her own presupposes precisely that . . . there is no equal pathos, no equal will to renunciation; for if both partners felt impelled by love to renounce themselves, we should then get – I do not know what; perhaps an empty space? Woman wants to be taken . . . she wants someone who *takes*, who does not give himself or give himself away; on the contrary, he is supposed to become richer in 'himself' . . . Woman gives herself away, man acquires more.

In any case, the woman will be able to find her joy in this enrichment she brings to her loved one; she is not All for him: but she will try to believe herself indispensable; there are no degrees in necessity. If he cannot 'get along without her', she considers herself the foundation of his precious existence, and she derives her own worth from that. Her joy is to serve him: but he must gratefully recognise this service; giving becomes demand according to the customary dialectic of devotion.† And a woman of scrupulous mind asks herself: is it really *me* he needs? The man cherishes her, desires her with singular tenderness and desire: but would he not have just as singular feelings for another? Many women in love let themselves be deluded; they want to ignore the fact that the general is enveloped in the particular, and the man facilitates this illusion because he shares it at first; there is often in his desire a passion that seems to defy time; at the moment he desires this woman, he desires her with passion, he wants only her: and certainly, the moment is an

---

* *The Gay Science.*
† I have tried to show this in *Pyrrhus et Cinéas.*

absolute, but a momentary absolute. Duped, the woman passes into the eternal. Deified by the embrace of the master, she believes she has always been divine and destined for the god: she alone. But male desire is as fleeting as it is imperious; once satisfied, it dies rather quickly, while it is most often after love that the woman becomes his prisoner. This is the theme of a whole type of shallow literature and songs. 'A young man was passing by, a girl was singing . . . A young man was singing, a girl was crying.' And even if the man is seriously attached to the woman, it still does not mean that she is necessary to him. Yet this is what she demands: her abdication only saves her if it reinstates her empire; one cannot escape the play of reciprocity. So she must suffer or lie to herself. Most often she clutches first at the lie. She imagines the man's love as the exact counterpart of the love she bears him; with bad faith, she takes desire for love, an erection for desire, love for religion. She forces the man to lie to her. Do you love me? As much as yesterday? Will you always love me? She cleverly asks the questions just when there is not enough time to give nuanced and sincere answers or when circumstances prevent them; imperiously she asks her questions during lovemaking, at the moment of convalescence, when sobbing, or on a railway station platform; she makes trophies of the answers she extorts; and in the absence of responses, she interprets the silences; every genuine woman in love is more or less paranoid. I remember a woman friend who, when faced with the long silence from a far-off lover, declared, 'When one wants to break up, one writes to announce it'; then upon receiving an unambiguous letter: 'When one really wants to break up, one doesn't write.' It is often very difficult to decide where pathological delirium begins when hearing such confidences. Described by the panicking woman in love, the man's behaviour always seems extravagant: he's neurotic, sadistic, repressed, a masochist, a devil, unstable, cowardly or all of these together; he defies the most subtle psychological explanations. 'X. . . . adores me, he's wildly jealous, he wants me to wear a mask when I go out; but he's such a strange being and so suspicious of love that he keeps me in the hallway and doesn't invite me in when I ring his bell.' Or: 'Z. . . . adored me. But he was too proud to ask me to go to Lyon where he lives: I went there, I moved in with him. After eight days, without an argument, he threw me out. I saw him twice afterwards. The third time I called him and he hung up in the middle of the conversation. He's a neurotic.' These mysterious stories become clearer when the man explains: 'I absolutely did not love her,' or 'I liked her well enough, but I could not have lived one month with her.' Bad faith in excess leads to the mental asylum: one of the constants of erotomania is that the lover's behaviour seems enigmatic and paradoxical; from this slant, the patient's delirium always succeeds in breaking down the resistance of reality. A normal woman sometimes finally realises the truth, recognising that she is no longer loved. But as long as her back is not to the wall, she always cheats a little. Even in reciprocal love, there is a fundamental difference between the lovers' feelings that she tries to hide. The man must of course be capable of justifying himself without her since she hopes to be justified through him. If he is necessary to her, it is because she is fleeing her freedom: but if he assumes the freedom without which he would be neither a hero nor simply man, nothing and no one will be necessary for him. The dependence woman accepts comes from her weakness: how could she find a reciprocal dependence in the man she loves in his strength?

A passionately demanding soul cannot find tranquillity in love, because she sets her sights on a contradictory aim. Torn and tormented, she risks being a burden to the one for whom she dreamed of being a slave; she becomes importunate and obnoxious for want of feeling indispensable. Here is a common tragedy. Wiser and less intransigent, the woman in love resigns herself. She is not all, she is not necessary: it is enough for her to be useful; another can easily take her place: she is satisfied to be the one who is there. She recognises her servitude without asking for reciprocity. She can thus enjoy modest happiness; but even in these limits, it will not be cloudless. Far more painfully than the wife, the woman in love waits. If the wife herself is exclusively a woman in love, the responsibilities of the home, motherhood, her occupations and her pleasures will have little value in her eyes: it is the presence of her husband that lifts her out of the limbo of ennui. 'When you are not there, it seems not even worthwhile to greet the day; everything that happens to me seems lifeless, I am no more than a little empty dress thrown on a chair,' writes Cécile Sauvage early in her marriage.* And we have seen that, very often, it is outside marriage that passionate love arises and blooms. One of the most remarkable examples of a life entirely devoted to love is Juliette Drouet's: it is an endless wait. 'I must always come back to the same starting point, meaning eternally waiting for you,' she writes to Victor Hugo. 'I wait for you like a squirrel in a cage.' 'My God! How sad it is for someone with my nature to wait from one end of life to

* The case is different if the wife has found her autonomy in the marriage; in such a case, love between the two spouses can be a free exchange of two self-sufficient beings.

another.' 'What a day! I thought it would never end waiting for you and now I feel it went too quickly since I did not see you.' 'I find the day eternal.' 'I wait for you because after all I would rather wait than believe you are not coming at all.' It is true that Hugo, after having made her break off from her rich protector, Prince Demidoff, confined Juliette to a small apartment and forbade her to go out alone for twelve years, to prevent her from seeing her former friends. But even when her lot – she called herself 'your poor cloistered victim' – had improved, she still continued to have no other reason to live than her lover and not to see him very much. 'I love you, my dearest Victor,' she wrote in 1841, 'but my heart is sad and full of bitterness; I see you so little, so little, and the little I see you, you belong to me so little that all these littles make a whole of sadness that fills my heart and mind.' She dreams of reconciling independence and love. 'I would like to be both independent and slave, independent through a state that nourishes me and slave only to my love.' But having totally failed in her career as an actress, she had to resign herself to being no more than a lover 'from one end of life to the other'. Despite her efforts to be of service to her idol, the hours were too empty: the 17,000 letters she wrote to Hugo at the rate of three to four hundred every year are proof of this. Between visits from the master, she could only kill time. The worst horror of woman's condition in a harem is that her days are deserts of boredom: when the male is not using this object that she is for him, she is absolutely nothing. The situation of the woman in love is analogous: she only wants to be this loved woman and nothing else has value in her eyes. For her to exist, then, her lover must be by her side, taken care of by her; she awaits his return, his desire, his waking; and as soon as he leaves her, she starts again to wait for him. Such is the curse that weighs on the heroines of *Back Street*[*19] and *The Weather in the Streets*,[†20] priestesses and victims of pure love. It is the harsh punishment inflicted on those who have not taken their destiny in their own hands.

Waiting can be a joy; for the woman who watches for her loved one, knowing he is hurrying to her, that he loves her, the wait is a dazzling promise. But over and above the confident intoxication of love that changes absence itself into presence, the torment of worry gets confused with the emptiness of absence: the man might never return. I knew a woman who greeted her lover with surprise each time they met: 'I

---

* Fanny Hurst, *Back Street*.
† Rosamond Lehmann, *The Weather in the Streets*.

thought you would never return,' she would say. And if he asked her why: 'Because you *could* never return; when I wait, I always have the impression that I will never see you again.' Above all, he may cease to love her: he may love another woman. The vehemence with which she tries to fool herself by saying 'He loves me madly, he can love no one but me' does not exclude the torture of jealousy. It is characteristic of bad faith that it allows passionate and contradictory affirmations. Thus the madman who stubbornly takes himself for Napoleon does not mind admitting he is also a barber. The woman rarely consents to ask herself does he really love me? but asks herself a hundred times: Does he love another? She does not accept that her lover's fervour could have dimmed little by little, nor that he gives less value to love than she does: she immediately invents rivals. She considers love both a free feeling and a magic spell; and she assumes that 'her' male continues to love her in his freedom while being 'snared' or 'tricked' by some clever schemer. The man grasps the woman as being assimilated to him, in her immanence; here is why he easily plays the Boubouroche; he cannot imagine that she too could be someone who slips away from him; jealousy for him is ordinarily just a passing crisis, like love itself: the crisis may be violent and even murderous, but rarely does it last long in him. Jealousy for him mainly appears derivative: when things go badly for him or when he feels threatened by life, he feels derided by his wife.*[21] By contrast, a woman loving a man in his alterity and transcendence feels in danger at every moment. There is no great distance between betrayal by absence and infidelity. As soon as she feels unloved, she becomes jealous: given her demands, it is always more or less true; her reproaches and her griev-ances, whatever their pretexts, are converted into jealous scenes: this is how she will express her impatience, the ennui of waiting, the bitter feeling of her dependence, the regret of having only a mutilated exis-tence. Her whole destiny is at stake in every glance her lover casts at another woman since she has alienated her entire being in him. And she becomes irritated if for one instant her lover turns his eyes to another woman; if he reminds her that she has just been dwelling on a stranger for a long time, she firmly answers: 'It's not the same thing.' She is right. A man looked at by a woman receives nothing: giving begins only at the moment when the feminine flesh becomes prey. But the coveted woman is immediately metamorphosed into a desirable and desired

* This comes to the fore, for example, in Lagache's work *The Nature and Forms of Jealousy*.

object; and the neglected woman in love 'returns to ordinary clay'. Thus she is always on the lookout. What is he doing? At whom is he looking? To whom is he talking? What one smile gave her, another smile can take back from her; an instant is enough to hurl her from 'the pearly light of immortality' to everyday dusk. She has received everything from love; she can lose everything by losing it. Vague or definite, unfounded or justified, jealousy is frightening torture for the woman because it is a radical contestation of love: if the betrayal is certain, it is necessary to either renounce making a religion of love or renounce that love; it is such a radical upheaval that one can understand how the woman in love, both doubting and deceived, can be obsessed by the desire and fear of discovering the mortal truth.

Being both arrogant and anxious, the woman is often constantly jealous but wrongly so: Juliette Drouet had pangs of suspicion towards all the women who came near Hugo, only forgetting to fear Léonie Biard, who was his mistress for eight years. When unsure, every woman is a rival and a danger. Love kills friendship insofar as the woman in love encloses herself in the universe of the loved man; jealousy exasperates her solitude, thus constricting her dependence even more. But she finds there recourse against boredom; keeping a husband is work; keeping a lover is a kind of vocation. The woman who, lost in happy adoration, neglected her personal appearance begins to worry about it again the moment she senses a threat. Dressing, caring for her home or social appearances become moments of combat. Fighting is stimulating activity; as long as she is fairly certain to win, the woman warrior finds a poignant pleasure in it. But the tormented fear of defeat transforms the generously consented gift into a humiliating servitude. The man attacks in defence. Even a proud woman is forced to be gentle and passive; manoeuvres, prudence, trickery, smiles, charm and docility are her best weapons. I still see this young woman whose bell I unexpectedly rang; I had just left her two hours before, badly made up, sloppily dressed, her eyes dull; but now she was waiting for *him*; when she saw me, she put on her ordinary face again, but for an instant I had the time to see her, prepared for him, her face contracted in fear and hypocrisy, ready for any suffering behind her breezy smile; her hair was carefully coiffed, special makeup brightened her cheeks and lips, and she was dressed up in a sparkling white lace blouse. Party clothes, fighting clothes. The masseuse, beauty consultant and 'aesthetician' know how tragically serious their women clients are about treatments that seem useless; new seductions have to be invented for the lover, she has to become that woman he wishes to

meet and possess. But all effort is in vain: she will not resurrect in herself
that image of the Other that first attracted him, that might attract him
to another. There is the same duplicitous and impossible imperative in
the lover as in the husband; he wants his mistress absolutely his and yet
another; he wants her to be the answer to his dreams and still be different
from anything his imagination could invent, a response to his expectations and an unexpected surprise. This contradiction tears the woman
apart and dooms her to failure. She tries to model herself on her lover's
desire; many women who bloomed at the beginning of a love affair that
reinforced their narcissism become frightening in their maniacal servility
when they feel less loved; obsessed and diminished, they irritate their
lover; giving herself blindly to him, the woman loses that dimension of
freedom that made her fascinating at first. He was looking for his own
reflection in her: but if he finds it too faithful, he becomes bored. One
of the misfortunes of the woman in love is that her love itself disfigures
her, demolishes her; she is no more than this slave, this servant, this too-
docile mirror, this too-faithful echo. When she realises it, her distress
reduces her worth even more; she ends up losing all attraction with her
tears, demands and scenes. An existent is what he does; to be, she has
to put her trust in a foreign consciousness and give up doing anything.
'I only know how to love,' writes Julie de Lespinasse. *I Who Am Only
Love*:[22] this title of a novel* is the motto of the woman in love; she is
only love and when love is deprived of its object, she is nothing.

Often she understands her mistake; and so she tries to reaffirm her
freedom, to find her alterity; she becomes flirtatious. Desired by other
men, she interests her blasé lover again: such is the hackneyed theme of
many awful novels, absence is sometimes enough to bring back her prestige; Albertine seems insipid when she is present and docile; from afar
she becomes mysterious again and the jealous Proust appreciates her
again. But these manoeuvres are delicate; if the man sees through them,
they only serve to reveal to him how ridiculous his slave's servitude is.
And even their success can be dangerous: because she is his the lover
disdains his mistress, but he is attached to her because she is his; is it
disdain or is it attachment that an infidelity will kill? It may be that,
vexed, the man turns away from the indifferent one: he wants her free,
yes; but he wants her given. She knows this risk: it paralyses her flirtatiousness. It is almost impossible for a woman in love to play this game
skilfully; she is too afraid to be caught in her own trap. And insofar as

* By Dominique Rolin.

she still reveres her lover, she is loath to dupe him: how can he remain a god in her eyes? If she wins the match, she destroys her idol; if she loses it, she loses herself. There is no salvation.

A cautious woman in love – but these words clash – tries to convert the lover's passion into tenderness, friendship, habit; or she tries to attach him with solid ties: a child or marriage; this desire of marriage haunts many liaisons: it is one of security; the clever mistress takes advantage of the generosity of young love to take out insurance on the future: but when she gives herself over to these speculations, she no longer deserves the name of woman in love. For she madly dreams of securing the lover's freedom for ever, but not of destroying it. And this is why, except in the rare case where free commitment lasts a whole life, love-religion leads to catastrophe. With Mora, Mlle de Lespinasse was lucky enough to tire of him first: she tired of him because she had met Guibert, who in return promptly tired of her. The love between Mme d'Agoult and Liszt died of this implacable dialectic: the passion, vitality and ambition that made Liszt so easy to love destined him to other loves. The Portuguese nun could only be abandoned. The fire that made d'Annunzio so captivating* had a price: his infidelity. A rupture can deeply mark a man: but in the end, he has his life as man to live. The abandoned woman is nothing, has nothing. If she is asked 'How did you live before?' she cannot even remember. She let fall into ashes the world that was hers to adopt a new land from which she is brutally expelled; she gave up all the values she believed in, broke off her friendships; she finds herself without a roof over her head and the desert all around her. How could she begin a new life when outside her lover there is nothing? She takes refuge in delirious imaginings as in former times in the convent; or if she is too reason-able, there is nothing left but to die: very quickly, like Mlle de Lespinasse, or little by little; the agony can last a long time. When a woman has been devoted to a man body and soul for ten or twenty years, when he has remained firmly on the pedestal where she put him, being aban-doned is a crushing catastrophe. 'What can I do,' asks this forty-year-old woman, 'what can I do if Jacques no longer loves me?' She dressed, fixed her hair and made herself up meticulously; but her hardened face, already undone, could barely arouse a new love; and she herself, after twenty years spent in the shadow of a man, could she ever love another? There are many years still to live at forty. I still see that other woman who kept her beautiful eyes and noble features in spite of a face swollen with

* According to Isadora Duncan.

suffering and who let her tears flow down her cheeks in public, blind and deaf, without even realising it. Now the god is telling another the words invented for her; dethroned queen, she no longer knows if she ever reigned over a true kingdom. If the woman is still young, she has the chance of healing; a new love will heal her; sometimes she will give herself to it with somewhat more reserve, realising that what is not unique cannot be absolute; but often she will be crushed even more violently than the first time because she will have to redeem herself for her past defeat. The failure of absolute love is a productive ordeal only if the woman is capable of taking herself in hand again; separated from Abélard, Héloïse was not a wreck, because, directing an abbey, she constructed an autonomous existence. Colette's heroines have too much pride and too many resources to let themselves be broken by an amorous disillusion; Renée Néré is saved by her work. And Sido tells her daughter that she was not too worried about her emotional destiny because she knew that Colette was much more than a woman in love. But there are few crimes that bring worse punishment than this generous mistake: to put one's self entirely in another's hands.

Authentic love must be founded on reciprocal recognition of two freedoms; each lover would then experience himself as himself and as the other; neither would abdicate his transcendence, they would not mutilate themselves; together they would both reveal values and ends in the world. For each of them, love would be the revelation of self through the gift of self and the enrichment of the universe. In his work *The Discovery of Self*, Georges Gusdorf summarises precisely what *man* demands of love:

> Love reveals us to ourselves by making us come out of ourselves. We affirm ourselves by contact with that which is foreign and complementary to us. Love as a form of understanding discovers new heavens and new earths even in the very landscape where we have always lived. Here is the great secret: the world is other, *I myself am other*. And I am no longer alone in knowing it. Even better: someone taught me this. Woman therefore plays an indispensable and capital role in the consciousness man has of himself.[23]

This accounts for the importance the young man gives to love's apprenticeship;* we have seen how Stendhal and Malraux marvel at the miracle

---

* See Vol. I.

that 'I myself am another.' But Gusdorf is wrong to write: 'and *in the same way* man represents for the woman an indispensable intermediary of herself to herself', because today her situation is not *the same*; man is revealed in the guise of another, but he remains himself and his new face is integrated into the whole of his personality. It would only be the same for woman if she also existed essentially for-herself; this would imply that she possessed an economic independence, that she projected herself towards her own ends and surpassed herself without intermediary towards the group. Thus equal loves are possible, such as the one Malraux describes between Kyo and May. It can even happen that the woman plays the virile and dominating role like Mme de Warens with Rousseau, Léa with Chéri. But in most cases, the woman knows herself only as other: her for-others merges with her very being; love is not for her an intermediary between self and self, because she does not find herself in her subjective existence; she remains engulfed in this loving woman that man has not only revealed but also created; her salvation depends on this despotic freedom that formed her and can destroy her in an instant. She spends her life trembling in fear of the one who holds her destiny in his hands without completely realising it and without completely wanting it; she is in danger in an other, an anguished and powerless witness of her own destiny. Tyrant and executioner in spite of himself, this other wears the face of the enemy in spite of her and himself: instead of the sought-after union, the woman in love experiences the bitterest of solitudes; instead of complicity, struggle and often hate. Love, for the woman, is a supreme attempt to overcome the dependence to which she is condemned by assuming it; but even consented to, dependence can only be lived in fear and servility.

Men have rivalled each other proclaiming that love is a woman's supreme accomplishment. 'A woman who loves like a woman becomes *a more perfect woman*,'[24] says Nietzsche; and Balzac: 'In the higher order, man's life is glory, woman's is love. Woman is equal to man only in making her life a perpetual offering, as his is perpetual action.' But there again is a cruel mystification since what she offers, he cares not at all to accept. Man does not need the unconditional devotion he demands, nor the idolatrous love that flatters his vanity; he only accepts them on the condition that he does not satisfy the demands these attitudes reciprocally imply. He preaches to the woman about giving: and her gifts exasperate him; she finds herself disconcerted by her useless gifts, disconcerted by her vain existence. The day when it will be possible for the woman to love in her strength and not in her weakness, not to escape from herself but to find herself, not out of resignation but to affirm herself, love will become for her as for man the source of life and not a mortal danger. For the time being, love epitomises in its most moving form the curse that weighs on woman trapped in the feminine universe, the mutilated woman, incapable of being self-sufficient. Innumerable martyrs to love attest to the injustice of a destiny that offers them as ultimate salvation a sterile hell.

CHAPTER 13

The Mystic

Love has been assigned to woman as her supreme vocation, and when she addresses it to a man, she is seeking God in him: if circumstances deny her human love, if she is disappointed or demanding, she will choose to worship the divinity in God himself. It is true that there are also men who have burned with this flame; but they are rare and their fervour has been of a highly refined intellectual form. Women, though, who abandon themselves to the delights of celestial marriages are legion: and they experience them in a strangely affective way. Women are accustomed to living on their knees; normally, they expect their salvation to descend from heaven, where males reign; men too are enveloped in clouds: their majesty is revealed from beyond the veils of their bodily presence. The Beloved is always more or less absent; he communicates with her, his worshipper, in ambiguous signs; she only knows his heart by an act of faith; and the more superior to her he seems, the more impenetrable his behaviour seems to her. We have seen that in erotomania this faith resisted all refutations. A woman does not need to see or touch to feel the Presence at her side. Whether it be a doctor, a priest or God, she will find the same incontestable proof; she will welcome as a slave the waves of a love that falls from on high into her heart. Human love and divine love melt into one not because the latter is a sublimation of the former but because the former is also a movement towards a transcendent, towards the absolute. In any case, the woman in love has to save her contingent existence by uniting with the Whole incarnated in a sovereign Person.

This ambiguity is flagrant in many cases – pathological or normal – where the lover is deified, where God has human traits. I will only cite this one reported by Ferdière in his work on erotomania.[25] It is the patient who is speaking:

In 1923, I corresponded with a journalist from *La Presse*; every day I read his articles about morality. I read between the lines; it seemed to me that he was answering me, giving me advice; I wrote him love letters; I wrote to him a lot . . . In 1924, it suddenly came to me: it seemed to me that God was looking for a woman, that he was going to come and speak to me; I had the impression he had given me a mission, chosen me to found a temple; I believed myself to be the centre of a big complex where doctors would take care of women . . . It was then that . . . I was transferred to the Clermont mental institution . . . There were young doctors who wanted to change the world: in my cabin, I felt their kisses on my fingers, I felt their sex organs in my hands; once, they told me: 'You are not sensitive, but sensual; turn over'; I turned over and I felt them in me: it was very pleasant . . . The head doctor, Dr D. . . ., was like a god; I really felt there was something when he came near my bed; he looked at me as if to say: I am all yours. He really loved me: one day, he looked at me insistently in a truly extraordinary way . . . his green eyes became blue as the sky; they widened intensely in an incredible way . . . he saw the effect that produced all the while speaking to another woman patient and he smiled . . . and I thus remained fixated, fixated on Dr D. . . . one nail does not replace another and in spite of all my lovers (I have had fifteen or sixteen), I could not separate myself from him; that's why he's guilty . . . For more than twelve years, I have been having mental conversations with him . . . when I wanted to forget him, he reappeared . . . he was sometimes a bit mocking . . . 'You see, I frighten you,' he said again, 'you can love others, but you always will come back to me . . .' I often wrote him letters, even making appointments I would keep. Last year, I went to see him; he was remote; there was no warmth; I felt so silly and I left . . . People tell me he married another woman, but he will always love me . . . he is my husband and yet the act has never taken place, the act that would make the fusion . . . 'Abandon everything,' he sometimes says, 'with me you will always rise upwards, you will not be like a being of the earth.' You see: each time I look for God, I find a man; now I don't know what religion I should turn to.

This is a pathological case. But there is this inextricable confusion in many devotees between man and God. In particular, the confessor occupies an ambiguous place between heaven and earth. He listens with carnal ears to the penitent who bares her soul, but it is a supernatural light that shines in the gaze with which he enfolds her; he is a divine man, he is God in the appearance of a man. Mme Guyon describes her meeting with Father La Combe in these terms: 'It seemed to me that an effect of grace came from him to me by the most intimate soul and returned from me to him so that he felt the same thing.' The priest's intercession pulled her out of the drought she had been suffering from for years and inflamed her soul once again with ardour. She lived by his side during her entire great mystical period. And she admits: 'There was nothing but one whole unity, so that *I could no longer tell him apart from God.*' It would be too simple to say she was really in love with a man and she feigned to love God: she also loved this man because he was something other than himself in her eyes. Like Ferdière's patient, what she was groping for was the supreme source of values. That is what every mystic is aiming for. The male intermediary is sometimes useful for her to launch herself toward heaven's desert; but he is not indispensable. Having difficulty separating reality from play, the act from magical behaviour, the object from imagination, woman is singularly likely to presentify through her body an absence. What is much less humorous is confusing mysticism with erotomania, as has sometimes been done: the erotomaniac feels glorified by the love of a sovereign being; he is the one who takes the initiative in the love relationship, he loves more passionately than he is loved; he makes his feelings known by clear but secret signs; he is jealous and irritated by the chosen woman's lack of fervour: he does not hesitate then to punish her; he almost never manifests himself in a carnal and concrete form. All these characteristics are found in mystics; in particular, God cherishes for all eternity the soul He inflames with His love, He shed His blood for her, He prepares splendid apotheoses for her; the only thing she can do is abandon herself to His flames without resistance.

It is accepted today that erotomania takes a sometimes platonic and sometimes sexual form. Likewise, the body has a greater or lesser role in the feelings the mystic devotes to God. Her effusions are modelled on those that earthly lovers experience. While Angela de Foligno contemplates an image of Christ holding St Francis in his arms, he tells her: 'This is how I will hold you tight and much more than can be seen by the body's eyes . . . I will never leave you if you love me.' Mme Guyon writes: 'Love gave me no respite. I said to him: Oh my love, enough, leave me.' 'I want the love that thrills my soul with ineffable tremors, the love that makes me swoon . . .' 'Oh my God! If You made the most

sensual of women feel what I feel, they would soon quit their false pleasures to partake of such true riches.' St Teresa's vision is well known:

> In [an angel's] hands I saw a great golden spear . . . This he plunged
> into my heart several times so that it penetrated my entrails. When
> he pulled it out I felt that he took them with it, and left me utterly
> consumed by the great love of God. The pain was so severe that
> it made me utter several moans. What I am certain of is that the
> pain penetrates the depths of my entrails and it seems to me that
> they are torn when my spiritual spouse withdraws the arrow he
> uses to enter them.

It is sometimes piously claimed that the poverty of language makes
it necessary for the mystic to borrow this erotic vocabulary; but she also
has only one body and she borrows from earthly love not only words
but also physical attitudes; she has the same behaviour when offering
herself to God as offering herself to a man. This, however, does not at
all diminish the validity of her feelings. When Angela of Foligno becomes
'pale and dry' or then 'full and flushed', according to the rhythm of her
heart, when she breaks down in deluges of tears,* when she comes back
to earth, it is hardly possible to consider these phenomena as purely
'spiritual'; but to explain them by her excessive 'emotivity' alone is to
invoke the poppy's 'sleep-inducing virtue'; the body is never the *cause* of
subjective experiences since it is the subject himself in his objective form:
the subject experiences his attitudes in the unity of his existence. Both
adversaries and admirers of mystics think that giving a sexual content
to St Teresa's ecstasies is to reduce her to the rank of a hysteric. But
what diminishes the hysterical subject is not the fact that his body actively
expresses his obsessions: it is that he is obsessed, that his freedom is
subjugated and annulled; the mastery a fakir acquires over his body does
not make him its slave; bodily gestures can be part of the expression of
a freedom. St Teresa's texts are not at all ambiguous and they justify
Bernini's statue showing us the swooning saint in thrall to a stunning
sensuality; it would be no less false to interpret her emotions as simple
'sexual sublimation'; there is not first an unavowed sexual desire that
takes the form of divine love; the woman in love herself is not first the
prey of a desire without object that then fixes itself on an individual; it

---

* 'Tears burned her cheeks to such an extent that she had to apply cold water,' says
one of her biographers.

is the presence of the lover that arouses an excitement in her immediately intended to him; thus, in one movement, St Teresa seeks to unite with God and experiences this union in her body; she is not slave to her nerves and hormones: rather, she should be admired for the intensity of a faith that penetrates to the most intimate regions of her flesh. In truth, as St Teresa herself understood, the value of a mystical experience is measured not by how it has been subjectively experienced but by its objective scope. The phenomena of ecstasy are approximately the same for St Teresa and Marie Alacoque: the interest of their message is very different. St Teresa situates the dramatic problem of the relationship between the individual and the transcendent Being in a highly intellectual way; she lived an experience as a woman whose meaning extends beyond any sexual specification; it has to be classified along with that of St John of the Cross. But it is a striking exception. What her minor sisters provide is an essentially feminine vision of the world and of salvation; it is not transcendence they are aiming for: it is the redemption of their femininity.*

The woman first seeks in divine love what the woman asks for in man's love: the apotheosis of her narcissism; this sovereign gaze fixed on her attentively and lovingly is a miraculous chance for her. Throughout her life as a girl and young woman, Mme Guyon had always been tormented by the desire to be loved and admired. A modern Protestant mystic, Mlle Vé, writes: 'Nothing makes me unhappier than having no one interested in me in a special and sympathetic way, in what is taking place in me.' Mme Krüdener imagined that God was constantly occupied with her, to such an extent that, says Sainte-Beuve, 'in the most decisive moments with her lover she moaned: "My God how happy I am! I ask You to forgive my extreme happiness!"' One can understand the intoxication that permeates the heart of the narcissist when all of heaven becomes her mirror; her deified image is infinite like God Himself, it will never disappear; and at the same time she feels in her burning, palpitating and love-drowned breast her soul created, redeemed and cherished by the adoring Father; it is her double, it is she herself she is embracing, infinitely magnified by God's mediation. These texts of St Angela of Foligno are particularly significant. This is how Jesus speaks to her:

---

* For Catherine of Siena, theological preoccupations nevertheless remain very important. She also is of a rather virile type.

My daughter, sweeter to me than I am to you, my temple, my delight. My daughter, my beloved, *love me because you are very much loved by me;* much more than you could love me. Your whole life, your eating, drinking, your sleeping, and all that you do are pleasing to me. I will do great things in you in the sight of the nations. Through you, I shall be known and my name will be praised by many nations. My daughter and my sweet spouse, I love you so much more than any other woman.

And again:

My daughter, sweeter to me than I am to you, . . . my delight, the heart of God almighty is now upon your heart . . . God almighty has deposited much love in you, more than any woman of this city. He takes delight in you.

And once more:

Such is the love I have for you that I am totally unable to remember your faults and my eyes no longer see them. In you I have deposited a great treasure.

The chosen woman cannot fail to respond passionately to such ardent declarations falling from such a lofty place. She tries to connect with the lover using the usual technique of the woman in love: annihilation. 'I have only one concern, which is to love, to forget myself, and to annihilate myself,' writes Marie Alacoque. Ecstasy bodily mimics this abolition of self; the subject no longer sees or feels, he forgets his body, disavows it. The blinding and sovereign Presence is indirectly indicated by the intensity of this abandon, by the hopeless acceptance of passivity. Mme Guyon's quietism erected this passivity into a system: as for her, she spent a great deal of her time in a kind of catalepsy; she slept wide awake.

Most women mystics are not satisfied with abandoning themselves passively to God: they actively apply themselves to self-annihilation by the destruction of their flesh. Of course, asceticism was also practised by monks and brothers. But woman's relentlessness in violating her flesh has specific characteristics. We have seen how ambiguous the woman's attitude to her body is: it is through humiliation and suffering that she metamorphoses it into glory. Given over to a lover as a thing of pleasure, she becomes a temple, an idol; torn by the pain of childbirth, she creates heroes. The mystic will torture her flesh to have the right to claim it; reducing it to abjection, she exalts it as the instrument of her salvation. This accounts for the strange excesses of some women saints. St Angela of Foligno recounts her delectation in drinking the water in which she had just washed the lepers' hands and feet:

> This concoction filled us with such sweetness that joy followed us and brought it home with us. Never had I drunk with such delight. A piece of scaly skin from one of the lepers' wounds had stuck in my throat. Rather than spitting it out, I tried very hard to swallow it and I succeeded. It seemed to me that I had just received communion. Never will I be able to express the delights that flooded over me.

It is known that Marie Alacoque cleaned a sick person's vomit with her tongue; she describes in her autobiography her happiness when she had filled her mouth with the excrement of a man with diarrhoea; Jesus rewarded her by keeping her lips glued to his Sacred Heart for three hours. Devotion has a carnal coloration in countries of ardent sensuality like Italy and Spain: in a village in Abruzzo, even today women tear their tongues by licking the rocks on the ground along the stations of the cross. In all these practices they are only imitating the Redeemer, who saved flesh by the abasement of his own flesh: women show their sensitivity to this great mystery in a much more concrete way than males.

God appears to woman more readily in the figure of the husband; sometimes He reveals Himself in His glory, dazzlingly white and beautiful, and dominating; He clothes her in a wedding dress, He crowns her, takes her by the hand and promises her a celestial apotheosis. But most often He is a being of flesh: the wedding ring Jesus had given to St Catherine and that she wore, invisible, on her finger, was this 'ring of flesh' that circumcision had cut off. Above all, He is a mistreated and bloody body: it is in the contemplation of the Crucified that she drowns herself the most fervently; she identifies with the Virgin Mary holding the corpse of her Son in her arms, or with Magdalene standing at the foot of the cross and being sprinkled with the Beloved's blood. Thus does she satisfy her sadomasochistic fantasies. In the humiliation of God, she admires Man's fall: inert, passive, covered with sores, the crucified is the inverted image of the white and red martyr offered to wild beasts, to the knife, to males, and with whom the little girl has so often identified: she is thrown into confusion seeing that Man, Man-God, has assumed His role. It is she who is placed on the wood, promised the splendour of the Resurrection. It is she: she proves it; her forehead bleeds under the crown of thorns; her hands, her feet, her side are transpierced by an invisible iron. Out of the 321 people with stigmata recognised by the Catholic Church, only forty-seven are men; the others – including Helen of Hungary, Joan of the Cross, G. van Oosten, Osanna of Mantua, and Clare of Montefalco – are women, who are, on average, past the age of menopause. Catherine Emmerich, the most famous, was marked prematurely. At the age of twenty-four, having desired the sufferings of the crown of thorns, she saw coming towards her a dazzling young man who pushed this crown onto her head. The next day, her temples and forehead swelled and blood began to flow. Four years later, in ecstasy, she saw Christ with rays pointed like fine blades coming from his wounds, and drops of blood then sprang from the saint's hands, feet and side. She sweated blood, she spat blood. Still today, every good Friday, Therese Neumann turns a face dripping with Christ's blood towards her visitors. The mysterious alchemy that changes flesh into glory ends in the stigmata since, in the form of a bloody pain, they are the presence of divine love itself. It is quite understandable why women particularly are attached to the metamorphosis of the red flow into pure golden flame. They have a horror of this blood that runs out of the side of the King of men. St Catherine of Siena speaks of it in almost all her letters. Angela of Foligno lost herself in the contemplation of the heart of Jesus and the gaping wound in His side. Catherine Emmerich put on a red shirt so as to resemble Jesus when He was like 'a cloth soaked in blood'; she saw all things 'through Jesus's blood'. We have seen in which circumstances Marie Alacoque quenched her thirst for three hours from the Sacred Heart of Jesus. It was she who offered the enormous red clot surrounded by flamboyant darts of love to the adoration of the faithful. That is the emblem symbolising the great feminine dream: from blood to glory through love.

Ecstasies, visions and dialogues with God, this interior experience is sufficient for some women. Others feel the need to communicate it to the world through acts. The connection between action and contemplation takes two very different forms. There are women of action like St Catherine, St Teresa and Joan of Arc who are well aware of the goals they set themselves and who lucidly invent the means to reach them: their revelations merely give an objective form to their certainties; they encourage them to take the paths they have carefully planned. There are women narcissists like Mme Guyon and Mme Krüdener who, at the limit of silent fervour, feel suddenly 'in an apostolic state'.* They are not very precise concerning their tasks; and – like patronesses seeking excitement – they do not care too much what they do as long as it is *something*. Thus after displaying herself as ambassador and novelist, Mme Krüdener interiorised the conception she had of her own worth: it was not to see definite ideas triumph but to see herself confirmed in her role as God's inspired one that she took the destiny of Alexander I in hand. If a little beauty and intelligence are often enough for a woman to feel endowed with a holy character, it is even more so when she knows she is God's chosen; she feels filled with a mission: she preaches dubious doctrines, she eagerly founds sects, and this allows her to effectuate, through the members of the group she inspires, a thrilling multiplication of her personality.

Mystical fervour, like love and even narcissism, can be integrated into active and independent lives. But in themselves these attempts at individual salvation can only result in failures; either the woman establishes a relation with an unreal: her double or God; or she creates an unreal relation with a real being; in any case, she has no grasp on the world; she does not escape her subjectivity; her freedom remains mystified; there is only one way of accomplishing it authentically: it is to project it by a positive action into human society.

* Mme Guyon.

Part Four

TOWARDS LIBERATION

CHAPTER 14

The Independent Woman

French law no longer includes obedience among a wife's duties, and every woman citizen has become a voter; these civic liberties remain abstract if there is no corresponding economic autonomy; the kept woman – wife or mistress – is not freed from the male just because she has a ballot paper in her hands; while today's customs impose fewer constraints on her than in the past, such negative licences have not fundamentally changed her situation; she remains a vassal, imprisoned in her condition. It is through work that woman has been able, to a large extent, to close the gap separating her from the male; work alone can guarantee her concrete freedom. The system based on her dependence collapses as soon as she ceases to be a parasite; there is no longer need for a masculine mediator between her and the universe. The curse on the woman vassal is that she is not allowed to do anything; so she stubbornly pursues the impossible quest for being through narcissism, love or religion; when she is productive and active, she regains her transcendence; she affirms herself concretely as subject in her projects; she senses her responsibility relative to the goals she pursues and to the money and rights she appropriates. Many women are conscious of these advantages, even those with the lowest-level jobs. I heard a cleaning woman as she was washing a hotel lobby floor say, 'I never asked anyone for anything. I made it on my own.' She was as proud of being self-sufficient as a Rockefeller. However, one must not think that the simple juxtaposition of the right to vote and a job amounts to total liberation; work today is not freedom. Only in a socialist world would the woman who has one be sure of the other. Today, the majority of workers are exploited. Moreover, social structures have not been deeply modified by the changes in women's condition. This world has always belonged to men and still retains the form they have imprinted on it. It is important not to lose sight of these facts that make the question of women's work complex. An important and self-righteous woman recently carried out a study on women workers at a Renault factory: she asserts that they would rather to stay at home than work in a factory. Without a doubt, they are economically independent only within an economically oppressed class; and besides, tasks carried out in a factory do not free them from household chores.* If they had been able to choose between forty hours of weekly work in a factory *or* at home, they would undoubtedly have responded quite differently; and they might even accept both jobs eagerly if, as women workers, they would become part of a world that would be their world, that they would proudly and happily participate in building. In today's work, without even mentioning women who work on the land,† most working women do not escape the traditional feminine world; neither society nor their husbands give them the help needed to become, in concrete terms, the equals of men. Only those women with political convictions, active in trade unions, who are confident in the future, can give an ethical meaning to the thankless daily labour; but as women deprived of leisure time and inheriting a tradition of submissiveness, it is understandable that women are just beginning to develop their political and social awareness. It is understandable that since they do not receive the moral and social benefits they could legitimately expect in exchange for their work, they simply resign themselves to its constraints. It is also understandable that a shopgirl, an office worker or a secretary should not want to give up the advantages of having a male to lean on. I have already said that it is an almost irresistible temptation for a young woman to be part of a privileged caste when she can do so simply by surrendering her body; she is doomed to have love affairs because her wages are minimal for the very high standard of living society demands of her; if she settles for what she earns, she will be no more than a pariah: without decent living accommodation or clothes, all amusement and even love will be refused her. Virtuous people preach asceticism to her; in fact, her diet is often as austere as a Carmelite's; but not everyone can have God as a lover: she needs to please men to succeed in her life as a woman. So she will accept help: her employer cynically counts on this when he pays her a pittance. Sometimes this help will enable her to improve her situation and achieve real independence; but sometimes she will give up her job to become a kept woman. She often does both: she frees herself from

* I said in Vol. I, Part Two, 'History', chapter 5, how burdensome these are for the woman who works outside the home.
† Whose condition we examined, ibid.

her lover through work, and she escapes work thanks to her lover; but then she experiences the double servitude of a job and masculine protection. For the married woman, her salary usually only means extra income; for the 'woman who is helped' it is the man's protection that seems inessential; but neither woman buys total independence through her own efforts.

However, there are quite a lot of privileged women today who have gained economic and social autonomy in their professions. They are the ones who are at issue when the question of women's possibilities and their future is raised. While they are still only a minority, it is particularly interesting to study their situation closely; they are the subject of continuing debate between feminists and antifeminists. The latter maintain that today's emancipated women do not accomplish anything important, and that besides they have trouble finding their inner balance. The former exaggerate the emancipated women's achievements and are blind to their frustrations. In fact, there is no reason to assume that they are on the wrong track; and yet it is obvious that they are not comfortably settled in their new condition: they have come only halfway as yet. Even the woman who has emancipated herself economically from man is still not in a moral, social or psychological situation identical to his. Her commitment to and focus on her profession depend on the context of her life as a whole. And, when she starts her adult life, she does not have the same past as a boy; society does not see her with the same eyes; she has a different perspective on the universe. Being a woman poses unique problems to an autonomous human being today.

The advantage man enjoys and which manifests itself from childhood onwards is that his vocation as a human being in no way contradicts his destiny as a male. The fact that the phallus is assimilated with transcendence means that man's social and spiritual successes endow him with virile prestige. He is not divided. However, for a woman to accomplish her femininity she is required to be object and prey; that is, she must renounce her claims as a sovereign subject. This is the conflict that singularly characterises the situation of the emancipated woman. She refuses to confine herself to her role as female because she does not want to mutilate herself; but it would also be a mutilation to repudiate her sex. Man is a sexed human being; woman is a complete individual, and equal to the male, only if she too is a sexed human being. Renouncing her femininity means renouncing part of her humanity. Misogynists have often reproached intellectual women for 'letting themselves go'; but they also preach to them: if you want to be our equals, stop wearing makeup and polishing your nails. This advice is absurd. Precisely because the idea of femininity is artificially defined by customs and fashion, it is imposed on every woman from the outside; it may evolve so that its fashion standards come closer to those of men: on the beach, women now wear trousers. That does not change the core of the problem: the individual is not free to shape the idea of femininity at will. By not conforming, a woman devalues herself sexually and consequently socially because society has incorporated sexual values. Rejecting feminine attributes does not mean acquiring virile ones; even a transvestite cannot turn herself into a man: she is a transvestite. We have seen that homosexuality also constitutes a specification: neutrality is impossible. There is no negative attitude that does not imply a positive counterpart. The adolescent girl often thinks she can simply scorn convention; but by doing so, she is making a statement; she is creating a new situation involving consequences she will have to assume. Whenever one ignores an established convention, one becomes a rebel. A flamboyantly dressed woman is lying when she ingenuously claims she is simply dressing to suit herself, and that is all: she knows perfectly well that suiting herself is an absurdity. Inversely, if she does not want to look eccentric, she follows the rules. Choosing defiance is a risky tactic unless it is a positively effective action; more time and energy are spent than saved. A woman who has no desire to shock, no intention to devalue herself socially, has to live her woman's condition as a woman: very often her professional success even requires it. But while conformity is quite natural for a man – custom being based on his needs as an autonomous and active individual – the woman who is herself also subject and activity has to fit into a world that has doomed her to passivity. This servitude is even greater since women confined to the feminine sphere have magnified its importance: they have made dressing and housekeeping difficult arts. The man barely has to care about his clothes; they are comfortable, adapted to his active life, and need not be original; they are hardly part of his personality; what's more, no one expects him to take care of them himself: some woman, volunteer or paid, delivers him from this chore. The woman, on the other hand, knows that when people look at her, they do not distinguish her from her appearance: she is judged, respected or desired in relation to how she looks. Her clothes were originally meant to doom her to impotence, and they still remain fragile: stockings run; heels wear down; light-coloured blouses and dresses get dirty; pleats unpleat; but she must still repair most of these accidents herself; her peers will never volunteer to help her out, and she will have second thoughts about straining her budget for work she *can* do herself: perms, hairdos, makeup and new dresses are already expensive enough. Secretary or student, when she goes home at night, there is always a stocking to mend, a blouse to wash, a skirt to iron. The woman who earns a good living will spare herself these chores; but she will be held to a higher standard of elegance, she will waste time on shopping and dress fittings, and such. Tradition also demands that the woman, even unmarried, pay attention to her home; a government official sent to a new city thinks nothing of living in a hotel; his woman colleague will try to 'set up house'; she has to keep it spotless because her negligence will not be excused whereas a man's will be overlooked. However, public opinion is not the only concern that makes her devote so much time and care to her looks and home. She wants to feel like a real woman for her own personal satisfaction. She only succeeds in accepting herself from the perspective of both the present and the past by combining the life she has made for herself with the destiny prepared for her by her mother, her childhood games and her adolescent fantasies. She has cultivated narcissistic dreams; she continues to pit the cult of her image against the phallic pride of the male; she wants to show off, to charm. Her mother and other older women have fostered her nesting instinct: a home of her own was the earliest form of her dream of independence; she would not think of discarding it, even when she finds freedom in other ways. And not yet feeling secure in the male universe, she still needs a retreat, a symbol of that interior refuge she has been used to finding in herself. Following docilely in the feminine tradition, she will wax her floors or do her own cooking instead of going to a restaurant like her male colleague. She wants to live both like a man and like a woman; her workload and her fatigue are multiplied as a result.

If she intends to remain fully woman, it also means she intends to approach the opposite sex with the maximum of odds on her side. It is in the area of sex that the most difficult problems will arise. To be a complete individual, equal to man, woman has to have access to the male world as man does to the female one, access to the *other*; but the demands of the *other* are not symmetrical in the two cases. Once acquired, the seemingly immanent virtues of fame and fortune can enhance the woman's sexual attraction; but being an autonomous activity contradicts her femininity: she knows this. The independent woman – and especially the intellectual who thinks through her situation – will suffer from an inferiority complex as a female; she does not have as much free time for beauty care as a flirt, whose only preoccupation is to seduce; while she might follow all the experts' advice, she will never be more than an amateur in the elegance department; feminine charm demands that transcendence deteriorating into immanence no longer be anything more than a subtle carnal throb; she must be a spontaneously offered prey: the intellectual woman knows she is offering herself, she knows she is a consciousness, a subject; one cannot wilfully kill one's gaze and change one's eyes into empty pools; a body that reaches out to the world cannot be thwarted and metamorphosed into a statue animated by hidden vibrations. The more the intellectual woman fears failure, the more zealously she will try; but this conscious zeal remains an activity and falls short of its goal. She makes mistakes like those blamed on menopause: she tries to deny her intelligence as an ageing woman tries to deny her age; she dresses like a girl, she overdoes the flowers, the frills and the loud materials; she carries childish and wide-eyed mimicry too far. She romps, skips, prattles, acts overly casual, scatterbrained and impulsive. But she looks like those actors who, failing to feel the emotion that would relax certain muscles, purposely contract antagonistic ones instead, lowering their eyelids or the corners of their mouths instead of letting them drop; thus the intelligent woman, wishing to appear uninhibited, stiffens instead. She senses this, and it irritates her; suddenly an unintended piercing spark of intelligence passes over her totally naive face; her lips full of promise become pursed. If she has trouble pleasing men, it is because she is not like her little slave sisters, a pure will to please; her desire to seduce may be strong, but it has not penetrated into the marrow of her bones; as soon as she feels awkward, she gets fed up with her servility; she tries to take her revenge by playing the game with masculine weapons: she talks instead of listening, she flaunts clever ideas, unusual feelings; she contradicts her interlocutor instead of going along with him, she tries to outdo him. Mme de Staël cleverly mixed both methods with stunning triumphs: she was almost always irresistible. But defiance, so frequent, for example, among American women, irritates men more than it wins them over; it is men, however, who provoke it by their own defiance; if men were content to love a peer instead of a slave – as indeed some men do who are without either arrogance or an inferiority complex – then women would be far less obsessed with their femininity; they would become more natural and simple and would easily rediscover themselves as women, which, after all, they are.

The fact is that men are beginning to come to terms with the new condition of women; no longer feeling condemned a priori, women feel more at ease; today the working woman does not neglect her femininity, nor does she lose her sexual attraction. This success – already a step towards equality – remains, nonetheless, incomplete; it is still much harder for a woman than for a man to have the type of relationship she would like with the other sex. Many obstacles stand in the way of her sex and love life. And the vassal woman is no better off: sexually and emotionally, most wives and mistresses are radically frustrated. These difficulties are more obvious for the independent woman because she has chosen not resignation but combat. All living problems find a silent solution in death; so a woman who works at living is more torn than one who buries her will and desires; but she will not accept being offered this as an example. She will consider herself at a disadvantage only when she compares herself with man.

A woman who works hard, who has responsibilities and who knows how harsh the struggle is against the world's obstacles needs – like the male – not only to satisfy her physical desires but also to experience the relaxation and diversion provided by enjoyable sexual adventures. Now there are still some environments where it is not concretely recognised that she should have this freedom; if she avails herself of it, she risks compromising her reputation and career; at the least, a burdensome hypocrisy is demanded of her. The more she has succeeded in making her mark socially, the more willingly will people close their eyes; but she is severely scrutinised, especially in the provinces. Even in the most favourable circumstances – when fear of public opinion is not an issue – her situation is not the same in this area as the man's. Differences stem from both tradition and the problems posed by the particular nature of feminine sexuality.

The man can easily engage in casual sex that at least calms his physical needs and is good for his morale. There have been women – a small number – who have demanded the opening of bordellos for women; in a novel entitled *Number 17*,[1] a woman proposed creating houses where women could go and find 'sexual relief' with a sort of 'taxi-boy'.* It seems that such an establishment once existed in San Francisco; it was frequented only by the girls from the bordellos, amused by the idea of paying instead of being paid: their pimps had them closed. Besides the fact that this solution is utopian and undesirable, it would also probably have little success: we have seen that woman does not attain 'relief' as mechanically as man;

---

* The author – whose name I have forgotten, but it is unimportant – explains at length how they could be trained to satisfy any client, what kind of life should be imposed on them, and so forth.

most women would hardly consider this solution favourable to sexual abandon. In any case, the fact is that this recourse is not open to them today. The solution of women picking up a partner for a night or an hour – assuming that the woman, endowed with a strong temperament and having overcome all her inhibitions, can consider it without disgust – is far more dangerous for her than for the male. The risk of venereal disease is more serious for her in that it is up to him to take precautions to avoid contamination; and, however prudent she may be, she is never completely covered against the threat of becoming pregnant. But the difference in physical strength is also very significant, especially in relations between strangers – relations that take place on a physical level. A man has little to fear from the woman he takes home; a little vigilance is enough. It is not the same for the woman who lets a man into her house. I have been told of two young women, newly arrived in Paris and avid to 'see life', who, after doing the town, invited two seductive Montmartre pimps to a late supper: in the morning they found themselves robbed, brutalised and threatened with blackmail. A worse case is that of a divorced woman of about forty who worked hard all day to feed her three grown children and elderly parents. Still beautiful and attractive, she had absolutely no leisure time to have a social life, to flirt or to make any of the usual efforts necessary for seduction, which in any case would have bored her. Yet she had strong physical desires; and she felt that, like a man, she had the right to satisfy them. Some evenings she went out to roam the streets and managed to pick up a man. But one night, after an hour or two spent in a thicket in the Bois de Boulogne, her lover refused to let her leave: he wanted her name, her address, to see her again, to live with her; when she refused, he beat her violently and only left her when she was wounded and terrorised. As for taking on a lover by supporting him or helping him out, as men often take on a mistress, it is possible only for wealthy women. There are some for whom this deal works: by paying the male, they make an instrument of him, permitting them to use him with disdainful abandon. But women must usually be older to dissociate eroticism from sentiment so crudely, because in feminine adolescence this connection is, as we have seen, so deep. There are also many men who never accept this division between flesh and consciousness. For even more reasons, the majority of women will refuse to consider it. Besides, there is an element of deception they are more aware of than men: the paying client is an instrument as well, used by the partner as a livelihood. Virile arrogance hides the ambiguities of the erotic drama from the male: he sponta-neously lies to himself; the woman is more easily humiliated, more susceptible, and also more lucid; she will succeed in blinding herself only at the price of a more cunning bad faith. Even supposing she has the means, she will not find it generally satisfying to buy a man.

For most women – and also for some men – it is a question not only of satisfying their desires but of maintaining their dignity as human beings while satisfying them. When the male gets sexual satisfaction from the woman, or when he satisfies her, he posits himself as the unique subject: imperious victor, generous donor, or both. She wants to affirm reciprocally that she submits her partner to her pleasure and covers him with her gifts. Thus when she convinces the man of her worth, either by the benefits she promises him or by relying on his courtesy or by skilfully arousing his desire in its pure generality, she easily persuades herself that she is satisfying him. Thanks to this beneficial conviction, she can solicit him without feeling humiliated since she claims she is acting out of generosity. Thus in *Green Wheat*,[2] the 'woman in white' who lusts for Phil's caresses archly tells him: 'I only like beggars and the hungry.' In fact, she is cleverly angling for him to act imploringly. So, says Colette, 'she rushed toward the narrow and dark kingdom where her pride could believe that a moan is a confession of distress and where the aggressive beggars of her sort drink the illusion of generosity.' Mme de Warens exemplifies these women who choose their lovers young, unhappy or of a lower social class to make their appetite look like generosity. But there are also fearless women who take on the challenge of the most robust males and who are delighted to have satisfied them even though they may have succumbed only out of politeness or fear.

On the other hand, while the woman who traps the man likes to imagine herself giving, the woman who gives herself wants it understood that she takes. 'As for me, I am a woman who takes,' a young woman journalist told me one day. The truth in these cases is that, except for rape, no one really takes the other; but the woman is lying doubly to herself. For the fact is that man does often seduce by his passion and aggressiveness, thereby actively gaining his partner's consent. Except in special cases – like Mme de Staël, to whom I have already referred – it is otherwise for the woman: she can do little else than offer herself; for most males are fiercely jealous of their role; they want to awaken a personal sexual response in the woman, not to be selected to satisfy her need in its generality: chosen, they feel exploited.* 'A woman who is not

---

* This feeling corresponds to the one we have pointed out in the girl. Only she resigns herself to her destiny in the end.

afraid of men frightens them,' a young man told me. And I have often heard adults declare: 'I am horrified by a woman who takes the initiative.' If the woman proposes herself too boldly, the man flees: he insists on conquering. The woman can thus take only when she is prey: she must become a passive thing, a promise of submission. If she succeeds, she will think she has willingly performed this magic conjuration; she will see herself become subject again. But she runs the risk of being turned into a fixed and useless object by the male's disdain. This is why she is so deeply humiliated if he rejects her advances. The man also sometimes gets angry when he feels he has been taken in; nonetheless, he has only failed in an enterprise, nothing more. The woman, on the other hand, has consented to make herself flesh through her sexual arousal, anticipation and promise; she could only win by losing: she remains lost. One must be particularly blind or exceptionally lucid to choose such a defeat. And even when seduction succeeds, victory remains ambiguous; thus, according to public opinion, it is the man who conquers, who *has* the woman. It does not accept that she can, like the man, assume her desires: she is their prey. It is understood that the male has integrated the forces of the species into his individuality, whereas the woman is the slave of the species.* She is represented alternately as pure passivity: she is a 'slut; open for business'; ready and willing, she is a utensil; she limply gives in to the spell of arousal, she is fascinated by the male who picks her like a fruit. Or else she is seen as an alienated activity: there is a devil raging in her womb, a serpent lurks in her vagina, craving to devour male sperm. In any case, it is out of the question to think of her as simply free. In France especially, the free woman and the easy woman are stubbornly confused, as the idea of easy implies an absence of resistance and control, a lack, the very negation of freedom. Women authors try to combat this prejudice: for example, in *Portrait of Grisela*,[3] Clara Malraux emphasises that her heroine does not let herself be drawn in, but accomplishes an act for which she accepts full responsibility. In America, a freedom is recognised in woman's sexual activity, which is very favourable to her. But in France, men's disdain for women who 'sleep around', the very men who profit from their favours, paralyses many women. They fear the remonstrances they would incite, the remarks they would provoke.

---

* We have seen in Vol. I, Chapter 1 that there is a certain truth in this opinion. But it is precisely not at the moment of desire that this asymmetry appears: it is in procreation. In desire man and woman assume their natural function identically.

Even if the woman scorns anonymous rumours, she has concrete difficulties in her relations with her partner, for public opinion is embodied in him. Very often, he considers the bed the terrain for asserting his aggressive superiority. He wants to take and not receive, not exchange but ravish. He seeks to possess the woman beyond that which she gives him; he demands that her consent be a defeat, and that the words she murmurs be avowals that he extracts from her; if she admits her pleasure, she is acknowledging her submission. When Claudine defies Renaud by her promptness in submitting to him, he anticipates her: he rushes to rape her when she was going to offer herself; he forces her to keep her eyes open to contemplate his triumph in their torment. Thus, in *Man's Fate*,[4] the overbearing Ferral insists on switching on the lamp Valérie wants to put out. Proud and demanding, the woman faces the male as an adversary; she is far less well armed in this battle than he; first of all, he has physical force and it is easier for him to impose his desires; we have also noted that tension and activity correspond to his eroticism, whereas the woman who refuses passivity breaks the spell that brings her sexual satisfaction; if she mimics domination in her attitudes and movements, she fails to reach a climax: most women who surrender to their pride become frigid. Rare are those lovers who allow their mistresses to satisfy their dominating or sadistic tendencies; and even rarer still are those women who derive full erotic satisfaction from this male docility.

There is a road that seems much less thorny for the woman, that of masochism. When one works, struggles and takes responsibilities and risks during the day, it is relaxing to abandon oneself at night to vigorous caprices. In love or naive, the woman in fact is often happy to annihilate herself for the benefit of a tyrannical will. But she still has to feel truly dominated. It is not easy for a woman who lives daily among men to believe in the unconditional supremacy of males. I have been told about the case of a not really masochistic but very 'feminine' woman, that is, one who deeply appreciated the pleasure of abdication in masculine arms; from the age of seventeen, she had had several husbands and numerous lovers, all of whom gave her great satisfaction; having successfully carried out a difficult project where she managed men, she complained of having become frigid: her once-blissful submission became impossible for her because she had become used to dominating males and because their prestige had vanished. When the woman begins to doubt men's superiority, their claims can only diminish her esteem for them. In bed, at moments where the man feels he is most fiercely male, the very fact of his miming virility makes him look infantile to knowing eyes: he is merely warding off the old castration complex, the shadow of his father, or some other fantasy. It is not always out of pride that the mistress refuses to give in to her lover's caprices: she wants to interact with an adult who is living a real moment of his life, not a little boy fooling himself. The masochistic woman is particularly disappointed: a maternal, exasperated or indulgent complaisance is not the abdication she dreams of. Either she herself will also have to make do with meaningless games, pretending to be dominated and subjugated, or she will run after men considered 'superior' in the hope of coming across a master, or else she will become frigid.

We have seen that it is possible to escape the temptations of sadism and masochism when both partners recognise each other as equals; as soon as there is a little modesty and some generosity between men and women, ideas of victory and defeat are abolished: the act of love becomes a free exchange. But, paradoxically, it is harder for woman than for man to recognise an individual of the opposite sex as her equal. Precisely because the male caste enjoys superiority, man can hold many individual women in affectionate esteem: a woman is easy to love; she has, first of all, the privilege of introducing her lover to a world different from his own and one that he is pleased to explore at her side; she fascinates, she amuses, at least for a little while; and then, because her situation is limited and subordinate, all her qualities seem like conquests while her errors are excusable. Stendhal admires Mme de Rênal and Mme de Chasteller in spite of their detestable prejudices; the man does not hold a woman responsible for not being very intelligent, clear-sighted or courageous: she is a victim, he thinks – often rightly – of her situation; he dreams of what she could have been, of what she will perhaps be: she can be given credit, one can grant her a great deal because she *is* nothing definite in particular; this lack is what will cause the lover to grow tired of her quickly: but it is the source of her mystery, the charm that seduces him and inclines him to feel superficial tenderness for her. It is far less easy to show friendship for a man: for he is what he made himself be, without help; he must be loved in his presence and his reality, not in his promises and uncertain possibilities; he is responsible for his behaviour, his ideas; he has no excuse. There is fraternity with him only if his acts, goals and opinions are approved; Julien can love a legitimist; a Lamiel could not cherish a man whose ideas she detests. Even ready to compromise, the woman has trouble adopting a tolerant attitude. For the man does not offer her a green paradise of childhood, she meets him in this world that is common to both of them: he brings only himself. Closed in on himself, defined, decided, he does not inspire dreams; when he speaks, one must listen; he takes himself seriously: if he does not prove interesting, he becomes bothersome, his presence weighs heavily. Only very young men allow themselves to appear adorned by the marvellous; one can seek mystery and promise in them, find excuses for them, take them lightly: this is one of the reasons mature women find them so seductive. But they themselves prefer young women in most cases. The thirty-year-old woman has no choice but to turn to adult males. And she will undoubtedly meet some who deserve both her esteem and her friendship; but she will be lucky if they do not then display arrogance. The problem she has when looking for an affair or an adventure involving her heart as well as her body is meeting a man she can consider her equal, without his seeing himself as superior.

One might say that in general women do not make such a fuss; they seize the occasion without much questioning, and then they make do with their pride and sensuality. That is true. But it is also true that they bury in the secret of their hearts many disappointments, humiliations, regrets and grievances whose equivalents are unknown – on the whole – to men. The man will almost surely get the benefit of pleasure from a more or less unsuccessful affair; the woman might well not profit from it at all; even if indifferent, she politely lends herself to lovemaking when the decisive moment arrives. The lover might prove to be impotent, and she will suffer from having compromised herself in a ludicrous escapade; if she does not reach arousal, then she feels 'had', deceived; if she is satisfied, she will want to hold on to her lover for a longer time. She is rarely completely sincere when she claims to envisage nothing more than a short-term adventure just for pleasure, because pleasure, far from freeing her, binds her; separation, even a so-called friendly one, wounds her. It is far more rare to hear a woman talk good-naturedly about a former lover than a man about his mistresses.

The nature of her eroticism and the difficulties of a free sexual life push the woman towards monogamy. Nonetheless, a liaison or marriage is far less easily reconciled with a career for her than for the man. The lover or husband may ask her to give up her career: she hesitates, like Colette's Vagabond, who ardently wishes to have a man's warmth at her side but who dreads the conjugal shackles; if she gives in, she is once again a vassal; if she refuses, she condemns herself to a withering solitude. Today, the man generally accepts the idea that his partner should continue working; novels by Colette Yver that show young women cornered into sacrificing their professions to maintain peace at home are somewhat outdated; living together is an enrichment for two free beings, who find a guarantee of their own independence in the partner's occupations; the self-sufficient wife frees her husband from the conjugal slavery that was the price of her own. If the man is scrupulously well intentioned, lovers and spouses can attain perfect equality in undemanding generosity.* Sometimes the man himself plays the role of devoted servant; thus did Lewes create for George Eliot the favourable atmosphere the wife usually creates around the lord-husband. But most of the time, it is still the woman who pays the price for harmony at home. It seems natural to the man that she run the house and oversee the care and raising of the children alone. The woman herself believes that her personal life does not dispense her from the duties she assumed in marrying; she does not want her husband to be deprived of the advantages he would have had in marrying a 'real woman': she wants to be elegant, a good housekeeper and devoted mother as wives traditionally are. It is a task that easily becomes overwhelming. She assumes it out of both consideration for her partner and fidelity to herself: for she insists, as we have seen, on fulfilling every aspect of her destiny as woman. She will be a double for her husband at the same time as being herself; she will take charge of his worries, she will participate in his successes just as much as taking care of her own lot, and sometimes even more so. Taught to respect male superiority, she may still believe that man takes first place; and sometimes she fears that claiming it would ruin her family; split between the desire to affirm herself and self-effacement, she is divided and torn.

There is nonetheless one advantage woman can gain from her very inferiority: since from the start she has fewer chances than man, she does not feel a priori guilty towards him; it is not up to her to compensate for social injustice, and she is not called upon to do so. A man of goodwill feels it his duty to 'help' women because he is more favoured than they are; he will let himself be caught up in scruples or pity, and he risks being the prey of 'clinging' or 'devouring' women because they are at a disadvantage. The woman who achieves a virile independence has the great privilege of dealing sexually with autonomous and active individuals who – generally – will not play a parasite's role in her life, who will not bind her by their weaknesses and the demands of their needs. But women who know how to create a free relation with their partners are

* Clara and Robert Schumann's life seems to have had this kind of success for a certain time.

in truth rare; they themselves forge the chains with which men do not wish to burden them: they adopt towards their partner the attitude of the woman in love. For twenty years of waiting, dreaming and hoping, the young girl has embraced the myth of the liberating hero and saviour: independence won through work is not enough to abolish her desire for a glorious abdication. She would have had to be brought up exactly like a boy* to be able to comfortably overcome adolescent narcissism: but in her adult life she perpetuates this cult of self towards which her whole youth has predisposed her; she uses the merits of her professional success to enrich her image; she needs a gaze from above to reveal and consecrate her worth. Even if she is severe on men whom she judges daily, she reveres Man nonetheless and if she encounters him, she is ready to fall on her knees. To be justified by a god is easier than to be justified by her own effort; the world encourages her to believe in the possibility of a *given* salvation: she chooses to believe in it. At times she entirely renounces her autonomy, she is no more than a woman in love; more often she tries conciliation; but adoring love, the love of abdication, is devastating: it takes up all thoughts, all instants, it is obsessive, tyrannical. If she encounters a professional disappointment, the woman passionately seeks refuge in love: her failures find expression in scenes and demands at the lover's expense. But her heartbreaks in no way have the effect of increasing her professional zeal: generally she becomes irritated, on the contrary, by the kind of life that keeps her from the royal road of the great love. A woman who worked ten years ago for a political magazine run by women told me that in the office people talked rarely about politics but incessantly about love: one would complain that she was loved only for her body, ignoring her fine intelligence; another would whine that she was only appreciated for her mind and no one ever appreciated her physical charms. Here again, for the woman to be in love like a man – that is to say, without putting her very *being* into question, freely – she would have to think herself his equal, and be his equal concretely: she would have to commit herself with the same decisiveness to her enterprises, which, as we will see, is still not common.

There is one female function that is still almost impossible to undertake in complete freedom, and that is motherhood; in England and in America, the woman can at least refuse it at will, thanks to the practice of birth control; we have seen that in France she is often compelled to

---

* That is, not only with the same methods, but in the same climate, which today is impossible in spite of all the efforts of educators.

have painful and costly abortions; she often finds herself burdened with a child she did not want, ruining her professional life. If this burden is a heavy one, it is because, inversely, social norms do not allow the woman to procreate as she pleases: the unwed mother causes scandal and for the child an illegitimate birth is a stain; it is rare for a woman to become a mother without accepting the chains of marriage or lowering herself. If the idea of artificial insemination interests women so much, it is not because they wish to avoid male lovemaking: it is because they hope that voluntary motherhood will finally be accepted by society. It must be added that given the lack of well-organised day nurseries and kindergartens, even one child is enough to entirely paralyse a woman's activity; she can continue to work only by abandoning the child to her parents, friends or servants. She has to choose between sterility, often experienced as a painful frustration, and burdens hardly compatible with a career.

Thus the independent woman today is divided between her professional interests and the concerns of her sexual vocation; she has trouble finding her balance; if she does, it is at the price of concessions, sacrifices and juggling that keep her in constant tension. More than in physiological facts, it is here that one must seek the reason for the nervousness and frailty often observed in her. It is difficult to decide how much woman's physical makeup in itself represents a handicap. The obstacle created by menstruation, for example, has often been examined. Women known for their work or activities seem to attach little importance to it: is this because they owe their success to the fact that their monthly problems are so mild? One may ask if it is not on the contrary the choice of an active and ambitious life that confers this privilege on them: the attention women pay to their ailments exacerbates them; athletic women and women of action suffer less than the others because they pass over their sufferings. It is clear that menstrual pain does have organic causes, and I have seen the most energetic women spend twenty-four hours in bed every month in the throes of pitiless tortures; but their enterprises were never hindered by them. I am convinced that most ailments and illnesses that weigh women down have psychic causes: this is in fact what gynaecologists have told me. Women are constantly overwhelmed by the psychological tension I have spoken about, because of all the tasks they take on and the contradictions they struggle against; this does not mean that their ills are imaginary: they are as real and devouring as the situation they convey. But a situation does not depend on the body, it is rather the body that depends on it. So woman's health will not detract from her work when the working woman has the place she deserves in society; on the contrary, work will strongly reinforce her physical balance by keeping her from being endlessly preoccupied with it.

When we judge the professional accomplishments of women and try to speculate on their future on that basis, we must not lose sight of all these facts. The woman embarks on a career in the context of a highly problematic situation, subjugated still by the burdens traditionally implied by her femininity. Objective circumstances are no more favourable to her either. It is always hard to be a newcomer trying to make one's way in a hostile society, or at least a mistrustful one. Richard Wright showed in *Black Boy* how blocked from the start the ambitions of a young American black man are and what struggle he has to endure merely to raise himself to the level where whites begin to have problems; the blacks who came to France from Africa also have – within themselves as well as from outside – difficulties similar to those encountered by women.

The woman first finds herself in a state of inferiority during her period of apprenticeship: I have already pointed this out in relation to the period of girlhood, but it must be dealt with in more detail. During her studies and in the early decisive years of her career, it is rare for the woman to be able to make full use of her possibilities: many will later be handicapped by a bad start. In fact, the conflicts I have discussed will reach their greatest intensity between the ages of eighteen and thirty: and this is when their professional future is determined. Whether the woman lives with her family or is married, her friends and family will rarely respect her efforts as they respect a man's; they will impose duties and chores on her, and curtail her freedom; she herself is still profoundly marked by her upbringing, respectful of the values the older women around her represent, haunted by childhood and adolescent dreams; she has difficulty reconciling the inheritance of her past with the interest of her future. Sometimes she rejects her femininity, she hesitates between chastity, homosexuality or a provocative virago attitude, she dresses badly or like a man: she wastes a lot of time and energy in defiance, scenes and anger. More often she wants, on the contrary, to assert her femininity: she dresses up, goes out and flirts, she is in love, wavering between masochism and aggressiveness. In all cases, she questions herself, is agitated and scattered. By the very fact that she is in thrall to outside preoccupations, she does not commit herself entirely to her enterprise; thus she profits from it less, and is more tempted to give it up. What is extremely demoralising for the woman trying to be self-sufficient is the existence of other women of her class, having from the start the same situation and chances, and who live as parasites; the man might resent privileged people: but he feels solidarity with his class; on the whole, those who begin on an equal footing with equal chances arrive at approximately the same standard of living, while women in similar situations have greatly differing fortunes because of man's mediation; the woman friend who is married or comfortably kept is a temptation for the woman who has to ensure her success alone; she feels she is arbitrarily condemning herself to the most difficult paths: at each obstacle she wonders if it would not be better to choose a different way. 'When I think I have to get everything from my brain!' a young, poor student told me indignantly. The man obeys an imperious necessity: the woman must constantly renew her decision; she goes forward, not with her eye fixed on a goal directly in front of her, but letting her attention wander all around her; thus her progress is timid and uncertain. And moreover – as I have already said – it seems to her that the farther she advances, the more she renounces her other chances; in becoming a bluestocking, a cerebral woman, she will either displease men in general or humiliate her husband or lover by being too dazzling a success. Not only will she apply herself all the more to appearing elegant and frivolous, but she will also hold herself back. The hope of one day being free from looking after herself and the fear of having to give up this hope by coping with this anxiety come together to prevent her from devoting herself single-mindedly to her studies and career.

Inasmuch as the woman wants to be woman, her independent status produces an inferiority complex; inversely, her femininity leads her to doubt her professional opportunities. This is a most important point. A study showed that fourteen-year-old girls believed: 'Boys are better; they find it easier to work.' The girl is convinced that she has limited capacities. Because parents and teachers accept that the girl's level is lower than the boy's, students readily accept it too; and in truth, in spite of the fact that the curricula are identical, girls' intellectual growth in secondary schools is given less importance. With few exceptions, the students in a female philosophy class overall have a markedly lower achievement level than a class of boys: many female students do not intend to continue their studies, they work superficially and others suffer from a lack of competitiveness. As long as the exams are fairly easy, their inadequacy will not be noticed too much; but when serious competitive exams are in question, the female student will become aware of her weaknesses; she will attribute them to the unjust curse of femaleness and not to the mediocrity of her education; resigning herself to this inequality, she exacerbates it; she persuades herself that her chances of success are related to her patience and assiduity; she decides to use her strength sparingly: this is a bad calculation. Above all, in studies and professions requiring a degree of inventiveness, originality and some small discoveries, a utilitarian attitude is disastrous; conversations, reading outside the syllabus, or a walk that allows the mind to wander freely can be far more profitable even for the translation of a Greek text than the dreary compilation of complex syntaxes. Crushed by respect for those in authority and the weight of erudition, her vision blocked by blinkers, the overly conscientious female student kills her critical sense and even her intelligence. Her methodical determination gives rise to tension and ennui: in classes where female secondary school students prepare for the Sèvres examination, there is a stifling atmosphere that discourages even slightly spirited individuality. Having created her own jail, the female examination candidate wants nothing more than to escape from it; as soon as she closes her books, she thinks about any other subject. She does not experience those rich moments where study and amusement merge, where adventures of the mind acquire living warmth. Overwhelmed by the thanklessness of her chores, she feels less and less able to carry them out. I remember a female student doing the *agrégation* who said, at the time when there was a coed competitive exam in philosophy: 'Boys can succeed in one or two years; we need at least four.' Another – who was recommended a book on Kant, a writer on the curriculum – commented: 'This book is too difficult: It's for Normalians!'[5] She seemed to think that women could take easier exams; beaten before even trying, she was in effect giving all chances of success to the men.

Because of this defeatist attitude, the woman easily settles for a mediocre success; she does not dare to aim higher. Starting out in her job with a superficial education, she very quickly curtails her ambitions. She often considers the very fact of earning her own living a great enough feat; like so many others, she could have entrusted her future to a man; to continue to want her independence she needs to take pride in her effort but it exhausts her. It seems to her she has done enough just in choosing to do something. 'That's not so bad for a woman,' she thinks. A woman in an unusual profession said: 'If I were a man, I would feel obliged to be in the top rank; but I am the only woman in France holding such a position: that's enough for me.' There is prudence in her modesty. In trying to go further, the woman is afraid of failing miserably. She is bothered, and rightly so, by the idea that no one has confidence in her. In general, the superior caste is hostile to the parvenus of the inferior caste: whites will not go to see a black doctor, nor men a woman doctor; but individuals from the lower caste, imbued with the feeling of their generic inferiority and often full of resentment of someone who has prevailed over destiny, will also prefer to turn to the masters; in particular, most women, steeped in the adoration of the male, avidly seek him in the doctor, lawyer, office manager. Neither men nor women like working under a woman's orders. Even if her superiors appreciate her, they will always be somewhat condescending; to be a woman is, if not a defect, at least a peculiarity. The woman must ceaselessly earn a confidence not initially granted to her: at the outset she is suspect; she has to prove herself. If she is any good, she will, people say. But worth is not a given essence: it is the result of a favourable development. Feeling a negative judgement weighing on one rarely helps one to overcome it. The initial inferiority complex most usually leads to the defensive reaction of an exaggerated affectation of authority. Most women doctors, for example, have too much or too little. If they are natural, they are not intimidating because their life as a whole disposes them more to seduce than to command; the patient who likes to be dominated will be disappointed by advice simply given; conscious of this, the woman doctor uses a low voice, a decisive tone, but then she does not have the cheerful simplicity that is so seductive in the confident doctor. The man is used to being imposing; his clients believe in his competence; he can let himself go: he is sure to impress. The woman does not inspire the same feeling of security; she stiffens, exaggerates, overdoes it. In business, in the office, she is scrupulous, a stickler and easily aggressive. Just as she is in her studies, she lacks confidence, inspiration and daring. In an effort to succeed she becomes tense. Her behaviour is a series of provocations and abstract self-affirmations. The greatest failure a lack of self-assurance brings about is that the subject cannot forget himself. He does not generously aim for a goal: he tries to prove he is worth what is demanded of him. Throwing oneself boldly towards goals risks setbacks: but one also attains unexpected results; prudence necessarily leads to mediocrity. It is rare to see in the woman a taste for adventure, gratuitous experience or disinterested curiosity; she seeks 'to build a career' the way others construct a happy life; she remains dominated, invested by the male universe, she lacks the audacity to break through the ceiling, she does not passionately lose herself in her projects; she still considers her life an immanent enterprise: she aims not for an object, but through an object for her subjective success. This is a very striking attitude in, among others, American women; it pleases them to have a job and to prove to themselves they are able to carry it out properly: but they do not become passionate about the *content* of their tasks. Likewise, the woman has a tendency to attach too much importance to minor failures and modest successes; she either gets discouraged or she swells with vanity; when success is expected, it is welcomed with simplicity; but it becomes an intoxicating triumph if one doubted obtaining it; that is the excuse of women who get carried away with their own importance and who ostentatiously display their least accomplishments. They constantly look back to see how far they have come: this curbs their drive. They can have honourable careers with such methods, but will not accomplish great things. It should be said that many men too are only able to build mediocre careers. It is only in relation to the best of them that the woman – with very rare exceptions – seems to us still to be bringing up the rear. The reasons I have given sufficiently explain this and do not in any way compromise the future. To do great things, today's woman needs above all forgetfulness of self: but to forget oneself one must first be solidly sure that one has already found oneself. Newly arrived in the world of men, barely supported by them, the woman is still much too busy looking for herself.

There is one category of women to whom these remarks do not apply because their careers, far from harming the affirmation of their femininity, reinforce it; through artistic expression they seek to go beyond the very given they constitute: actresses, dancers and singers. For three centuries they have almost been the only ones to possess concrete independence in society, and today they still hold a privileged place in it. In the past, actresses were cursed by the Church: this excessive severity allowed them great freedom of behaviour; they are often involved in seduction, and like courtesans they spend much of their days in the company of men: but as they earn their living themselves, finding the meaning of their existence in their work, they escape men's yoke. Their great advantage is that their professional successes contribute – as for males – to their sexual worth; by realising themselves as human beings, they accomplish themselves as women: they are not torn between contradictory aspirations; on the contrary, they find in their jobs a justification for their narcissism: clothes, beauty care and charm are part of their professional duties; a woman infatuated with her image finds great satisfaction in *doing* something simply by exhibiting what she *is*; and this exhibition requires sufficient amounts of both artifice and study if it is to be, in Georgette Leblanc's words, a substitute for action. A great actress will aim even higher: she will go beyond the given in the way she expresses it, she will really be an artist, a creator who gives meaning to her life by lending meaning to the world.

But these rare advantages also conceal traps: instead of integrating her narcissistic indulgence and the sexual freedom she enjoys into her artistic life, the actress often falls into self-worship or seduction; I have already spoken of these pseudo-artists who seek only 'to make a name for themselves' in the cinema or theatre by representing capital to exploit in a man's arms; the comfort of masculine support is very tempting compared with the risks of a career and the harshness any real work involves. The desire for a feminine destiny – a husband, a home, children – and the spell of love are not always easily reconcilable with the desire to succeed. But above all, the admiration she feels for herself limits the actress's talent in many cases; she deludes herself as to the value of her mere presence to the extent that serious work seems useless to her; more than anything else, she prefers to place herself in the limelight and sacrifices the character she is interpreting to ham acting; she, like others, does not have the generosity to forget herself, which keeps her from going beyond herself: rare are the Rachels or the Duses who overcome this risk and who make of their person the instrument of their art instead of seeing in art a servant of their self. In her private life, though, the ham will exaggerate all her narcissistic defects: she will appear vain, touchy and a phoney; she will treat the whole world as a stage.

Today the expressive arts are not the only ones open to women: many try their hand at creative activities. Woman's situation encourages her to seek salvation in literature and in art. Living on the margin of the masculine world, she does not grasp it in its universal guise but through a particular vision; for her it is not a group of implements and concepts but a source of feelings and emotions; she is interested in the qualities of things inasmuch as they are gratuitous and secret; taking on a negative attitude, one of refusal, she does not lose herself in the real: she protests against it, with words; she looks for the image of her soul in nature, she abandons herself to her reveries, she wants to reach her *being*: she is doomed to failure; she can only recover it in the realm of imagination. So as not to allow an inner life that does not *serve* any purpose to sink into nothingness, so as to assert herself against the given that she endures in revolt, so as to create a world other than the one in which she cannot succeed in reaching herself, she needs *to express herself*. Thus it is well known that she is talkative and a scribbler; she pours out her feelings in conversations, letters and diaries. If she is at all ambitious, she will be writing her memoirs, transposing her biography into a novel, breathing her feelings into poems. She enjoys vast leisure time that favours these activities.

But the very circumstances that orient the woman towards creation also constitute obstacles she will often be unable to overcome. When she decides to paint or write just to fill the emptiness of her days, paintings and essays will be treated as 'ladies' work'; she will devote little time or care to them and they will be worth about as much. To compensate for the flaws in her existence, often the woman at menopause feverishly takes up the brush or pen: it is late; without serious training, she will never be more than an amateur. But even if she begins quite young, she rarely envisages art as serious work; used to idleness, never having experienced in her life the austere necessity of a discipline, she will not be capable of a steady and persevering effort, she will not compel herself to acquire a solid technique; she balks at the thankless and solitary trials and errors of work that is never exhibited, that has to be destroyed and done over again a hundred times; and as from childhood she was taught to cheat in order to please, she hopes to get by with a few ruses. This is what Marie Bashkirtseff admits. 'Yes, I don't take the trouble to paint. I watched myself today, *I cheat*.' The woman easily *plays* at working but she does not work; believing in the magic virtues of passivity, she confuses conjurations and acts, symbolic gestures and effective behaviour; she disguises herself as a Beaux-Arts student, she arms herself with her arsenal of brushes; planted in front of her easel, her gaze wanders from the blank canvas to her mirror; but the bouquet of flowers, the bowl of apples, do not appear on their own on the canvas. Seated at her desk, musing over vague stories, the woman acquires a peaceful alibi in imagining she is a writer: but she must at some point make signs on the blank page; they have to have a meaning in the eyes of others. So the trickery is exposed. To please one needs only to create mirages: but a work of art is not a mirage, it is a solid object; to construct it, one must know one's craft. It is not only thanks to her gifts or personality that Colette became a great writer; her pen was often her livelihood and she demanded of it the careful work that a good artisan demands of his tool; from *Claudine* to *Break of Day*,[6] the amateur became professional: the progress brilliantly shows the advantages of a strict apprenticeship. Most women, though, do not understand the problems that their desire for communication poses: and this is what largely explains their laziness. They have always considered themselves as givens; they believe their worth comes from an inner grace and they do not imagine that value can be acquired;

to seduce, they know only how to display themselves: their charm works or does not work, they have no grasp on its success or failure; they suppose that, in a similar way, to express oneself, one needs only show what one is; instead of constituting their work by a thoughtful effort, they put their confidence in spontaneity; writing or smiling is all one to them: they try their luck, success will come or will not. Sure of themselves, they reckon that the book or painting will be successful without effort; timid, they are discouraged by the least criticism; they do not know that error can open the road to progress, they take it for an irreparable catastrophe, like a malformation. This is why they often over-react, which is harmful to themselves: they become irritated and discouraged when recognising their errors rather than drawing valuable lessons from them. Unfortunately, spontaneity is not as simple as it appears: the paradox of the commonplace – as Paulhan explains in *The Flowers of Tarbes*[7] – is that it is nothing more than the immediate translation of the subjective impression. Thus, when the woman produces the image she creates without taking others into account, she thinks she is most unusual, but she is merely reinventing a banal cliché; if she is told, she is surprised and vexed and throws down her pen; she is not aware that the public reads with its own eyes and its own mind and that a brand-new epithet can awaken in it many old memories; of course, it is a precious gift to be able to dig down into oneself and bring up vibrant impressions to the surface of language; one admires Colette for a spontaneity not found in any male writer; but – although these two terms seem to contradict each other – hers is a thoughtful spontaneity: she refuses some of its contributions and accepts others as she sees fit; the amateur, rather than seizing words as an interindividual relation, an appeal to the other, sees in them the direct revelation of her feelings; editing or crossing out for her means repudiating a part of self; she does not want to sacrifice anything both because she delights in what she *is* and because she hopes not to become other. Her sterile vanity comes from the fact that she cherishes herself without daring to construct herself.

Thus, very few of the legions of women who attempt to dabble in literature and art persevere; those who overcome this first obstacle very often remain divided between their narcissism and an inferiority complex. Not being able to forget oneself is a failure that will weigh on them more heavily than in any other career; if their essential goal is an abstract self-affirmation, the formal satisfaction of success, they will not abandon themselves to the contemplation of the world: they will be incapable of creating it anew. Marie Bashkirtseff decided to paint because she wanted to become famous; the obsession with glory comes between her and reality; she does not really like to paint: art is merely a means; it is not her ambitious and empty dreams that will reveal to her the meaning of a colour or face. Instead of giving herself generously to the work she undertakes, the woman all too often considers it a simple ornament of her life; books and paintings are only an inessential intermediary allowing her to exhibit this essential reality publicly: her own person. Thus it is her person that is the main – sometimes only – subject that interests her: Mme Vigée-Lebrun does not tire of putting her smiling maternity on her canvases. Even if she speaks of general themes, the woman writer will still speak of herself: one cannot read such and such theatre reviews without being informed of the size and corpulence of their author, the colour of her hair and the peculiarities of her personality. Of course, the self is not always detestable. Few books are as fascinating as certain confessions: but they have to be sincere and the author has to have something to confess. Instead of enriching the woman, her narcissism impoverishes her; involved in nothing but self-contemplation, she eliminates herself; even the love she bestows on herself becomes stereotyped: she does not discover in her writings her authentic experience but an imaginary idol constructed from clichés. She cannot be criticised for projecting herself in her novels as Benjamin Constant and Stendhal did: but unfortunately she sees her story too often as a silly fairy tale; the young girl hides the brutal and frightening reality from herself with good doses of fantasising: it is a pity that once she is an adult, she still buries the world, its characters, and herself in the fogginess of poetry. When the truth emerges from this travesty, there are sometimes charming successes, but next to *Dusty Answer*[8] or *The Constant Nymph*,[9] how many bland and dull escapist novels there are!

It is natural for women to try to escape this world where they often feel unrecognised and misunderstood; what is regrettable is that they do not dare the bold flights of a Gérard de Nerval or a Poe. Many reasons excuse woman's timidity. Her great concern is to please; and as a woman she is often already afraid of displeasing just because she writes: the term 'bluestocking', albeit a bit overused, still has a disagreeable connotation; she lacks the courage to displease even more as a writer. The writer who is original, as long as he is not dead, is always scandalous; what is new disturbs and antagonises; women are still astonished and flattered to be accepted into the world of thinking and art, a masculine world: the woman watches her manners; she does not dare to irritate, explore, explode; she thinks she has to excuse her literary pretensions by her modesty and good taste; she relies on the proven values of conformism; she introduces just the personal note that is expected of her into her literature: she points out that she is a woman with some well chosen affectations, simpering and preciosities; so she will excel at producing 'bestsellers' but she cannot be counted on to blaze new trails. Women do not lack originality in their behaviour and feelings: there are some so singular that they have to be locked up; on the whole, many of them are more baroque and eccentric than the men whose strictures they reject. But they put their bizarre genius into their lives, conversation and correspondence; if they try to write, they feel crushed by the universe of culture because it is a universe of men: they just babble. Inversely, the woman who chooses to reason, to express herself using masculine techniques, will do her best to stifle an originality she distrusts; like a female student, she will be assiduous and pedantic; she will imitate rigour and virile vigour. She may become an excellent theoretician and acquire a solid talent; but she will make herself repudiate everything in her that is 'different'. There are women who are mad and there are women of talent: none of them has this madness in talent called genius.

This reasonable modesty is what has above all defined the limits of feminine talent until now. Many women have eluded – and they increasingly elude – the traps of narcissism and faux wonderment; but no woman has ever thrown prudence to the wind to try to *emerge* beyond the given world. In the first place, there are, of course, many who accept society just as it is; they are par excellence the champions of the bourgeoisie since they represent the most conservative element of this threatened class; with well-chosen adjectives, they evoke the refinements of a civilisation 'of quality'; they extol the bourgeois ideal of happiness and disguise their class interests under the banner of poetry; they orchestrate the mystification intended to persuade women to 'remain women'; old houses, parks and kitchen gardens, picturesque grandparents, mischievous children, laundry, jams and jellies, family gatherings, clothes, salons, balls, suffering but exemplary wives, the beauty of devotion and sacrifice, small disappointments and great joys of conjugal love, dreams of youth, mature resignation – women novelists from England, France, America, Canada and Scandinavia have exploited these themes to the utmost; they have attained glory and wealth but have not enriched our vision of the world. Far more interesting are the women insurgents who have indicted this unjust society; protest literature can give rise to strong and sincere works; George Eliot drew from her revolt a detailed and dramatic vision of Victorian England; however, as Virginia Woolf shows,

Jane Austen, the Brontë sisters and George Eliot had to spend so much negative energy freeing themselves from external constraints that they arrived out of breath at the point where the major masculine writers were starting out; they have little strength left to benefit from their victory and break all the ties that bind them: for example, they lack the irony, the nonchalance, of a Stendhal or his calm sincerity. Nor have they had the wealth of experience of a Dostoevsky, a Tolstoy: it is why the great book *Middlemarch* does not equal *War and Peace*; *Wuthering Heights*, in spite of its stature, does not have the scope of *The Brothers Karamazov*. Today, women already have less trouble asserting themselves; but they have not totally overcome the age-old specification that confines them in their femininity. Lucidity, for example, is a conquest they are justly proud of but with which they are a little too quickly satisfied. The fact is that the traditional woman is a mystified consciousness and an instrument of mystification; she tries to conceal her dependence from herself, which is a way of consenting to it; to denounce this dependence is already a liberation; cynicism is a defence against humiliation and shame: it is the first stage of assuming responsibility. In trying to be lucid, women writers render the greatest service to the cause of women; but – without generally realising it – they remain too attached to serving this cause to adopt, in front of the whole world, the disinterested attitude that opens up wider horizons. When they pull away the veils of illusion and lies, they think they have done enough: nonetheless, this negative daring still leaves us with an enigma; for truth itself is ambiguity, depth, mystery: after its presence is acknowledged, it must be thought, re-created. It is all well and good not to be duped: but this is where it all begins; the woman exhausts her courage in dissipating mirages and she stops in fear at the threshold of reality. This is why, for example, there are sincere and endearing women's autobiographies: but none can compare with *Confessions* or *Memoirs of an Egotist*.[10] We women are still too preoccupied with seeing clearly to try to penetrate other shadows beyond that clarity.

'Women never go beyond the pretext,' a writer told me. This is true enough. Still amazed at having had permission to explore the world, they take its inventory without trying to discover its meaning. Where they sometimes excel is in the observation of facts: they make remarkable reporters; no male journalist has outdone Andrée Viollis's eyewitness reports on Indochina and India. They know how to describe atmosphere and people, to show the subtle relations between them, and let us share in the secret workings of their souls: Willa Cather, Edith Wharton,

Dorothy Parker and Katherine Mansfield have sharply and sensitively brought to life individuals, climates and civilisations. They have rarely succeeded in creating as convincing a masculine hero as Heathcliff: they grasp little more than the male in man; but they often describe their own interior lives, experiences and universe very well; attached to the secret side of objects, fascinated by the uniqueness of their own sensations, they convey their fresh experience through the use of savoury adjectives and sensual images; their vocabulary is usually more noticeable than their syntax because they are interested in things more than their relations; they do not aim for abstract elegance; instead, their words speak to the senses. One area they have most lovingly explored is Nature; for the girl or the woman who has not completely abdicated, nature represents what woman represents for man: herself and her negation, a kingdom and a place of exile; she is all in the guise of the other. The woman writer will most intimately reveal her experience and dreams in speaking of moors or kitchen gardens. There are many who enclose the miracles of sap and seasons in pots, vases and flower beds; others, without imprisoning plants and animals, nonetheless try to appropriate them by the attentive love they dispense to them: so it is with Colette and Katherine Mansfield; very rare are those who approach nature in its inhuman freedom, who try to decipher its foreign meanings and lose themselves in order to unite with this other presence: hardly any women venture down these roads Rousseau invented, except for Emily Brontë, Virginia Woolf and sometimes Mary Webb. And to an even greater extent we can count on the fingers of one hand the women who have traversed the given in search of its secret dimension: Emily Brontë explored death, Virginia Woolf life, and Katherine Mansfield sometimes – not very often – daily contingence and suffering. No woman ever wrote *The Trial, Moby-Dick, Ulysses*, or *The Seven Pillars of Wisdom*. Women do not challenge the human condition because they have barely begun to be able to assume it entirely. This explains why their works generally lack metaphysical resonance and black humour as well; they do not set the world apart, they do not question it, they do not denounce its contradictions: they take it seriously. The fact is that most men have the same limitations as well; it is when she is compared with the few rare artists who deserve to be called 'great' that woman comes out as mediocre. Destiny is not what limits her: it is easy to understand why it has not been possible for her to reach the highest summits, and why it will perhaps not be possible for some time.

Art, literature and philosophy are attempts to found the world anew on a human freedom: that of the creator; to foster such an aim, one must first unequivocally posit oneself as a freedom. The restrictions that education and custom impose on woman limit her grasp of the universe; when the struggle to claim a place in this world gets too rough, there can be no question of tearing oneself away from it; one must first emerge within it in sovereign solitude if one wants to try to grasp it anew: what woman primarily lacks is learning from the practice of abandonment and transcendence, in anguish and pride. Marie Bashkirtseff writes:

> What I want is the freedom to walk around alone, come and go, sit on park benches in the Tuileries Gardens. Without this freedom you cannot become a true artist. You think you can profit from what you see when you are being accompanied or when you must wait for your car, your nursemaid, your family to go to the Louvre! . . . This is the freedom that is missing and without which one cannot seriously become something. *Thinking is imprisoned by this stupid and incessant constraint . . . That is all it takes to clip one's wings.* This is one of the reasons there are no women artists.

Indeed, for one to become a creator, it is not enough to be cultivated, that is, to make going to shows and meeting people part of one's life; culture must be apprehended through the free movement of a transcendence; the spirit with all its riches must project itself in an empty sky that is its to fill; but if a thousand fine bonds tie it to the earth, its surge is broken. The girl today can certainly go out alone, stroll in the Tuileries; but I have already said how hostile the street is: eyes everywhere, hands waiting; if she wanders absentmindedly, her thoughts elsewhere, if she lights a cigarette in a café, if she goes to the cinema alone, an unpleasant incident can quickly occur; she must inspire respect by the way she dresses and behaves: this concern rivets her to the ground and to self. 'Her wings are clipped.' At eighteen, T. E. Lawrence went on a grand tour through France by bicycle; a young girl would never be permitted to take on such an adventure: still less would it be possible for her to take off on foot for a half-desert and dangerous country as Lawrence did. Yet, such experiences have an inestimable impact: this is how an individual in the headiness of freedom and discovery learns to look at the entire world as his fief. The woman is already naturally deprived of the lessons of violence: I have said how physical weakness disposes her to passivity; when a boy settles a fight with punches, he feels he can rely on himself in his own interest; at least the girl should be allowed to compensate by sports, adventure and the pride of obstacles overcome. But no. She may feel alone *within* the world: she never stands up *in front* of it, unique and sovereign. Everything encourages her to be invested and dominated by foreign existences: and particularly in love, she disavows rather than asserts herself. Misfortune and distress are often learning experiences in this sense: it was isolation that enabled Emily Brontë to write a powerful and unbridled book; in the face of nature, death and destiny, she relied on no one's help but her own. Rosa Luxemburg was ugly; she was never tempted to wallow in the cult of her image, to make herself object, prey and trap: from her youth she was wholly mind and freedom. Even then, it is rare for a woman to fully assume the agonising tête-à-tête with the given world. The constraints that surround her and the whole tradition that weighs on her keep her from feeling responsible for the universe: this is the profound reason for her mediocrity.

Men we call great are those who – in one way or another – take the weight of the world on their shoulders; they have done more or less well, they have succeeded in re-creating it or they have failed; but they took on this enormous burden in the first place. This is what no woman has ever done, what no woman has ever been *able* to do. It takes belonging to the privileged caste to view the universe as one's own, to consider oneself as guilty of its faults and take pride in its progress; those alone who are at the controls have the opportunity to justify it by changing, thinking and revealing it; only they can identify with it and try to leave their imprint on it. Until now it has only been possible for Man to be incarnated in the man, not the woman. Moreover, individuals who appear exceptional to us, the ones we honour with the name of genius, are those who tried to work out the fate of all humanity in their particular lives. No woman has thought herself authorised to do that. How could van Gogh have been born woman? A woman would not have been sent on mission to Borinage, she would not have felt men's misery as her own crime, she would not have sought redemption; so she would never have painted van Gogh's sunflowers. And this is without taking into account that the painter's kind of life – the solitude in Arles, going to cafés, whorehouses, everything that fed into van Gogh's art by feeding his sensibility – would have been prohibited to her. A woman could never have become Kafka: in her doubts and anxieties, she would never have recognised the anguish of Man driven from paradise. St Teresa is one of the only women to have lived the human condition for herself, in total abandonment: we have seen why. Placing herself beyond earthly hierarchies, she, like St John of the Cross, felt no reassuring sky over her head. For both of them it was the same night, the same flashes of light, in each the same nothingness, in God the same plenitude. When finally it is possible for every human being to place his pride above sexual differences in the difficult glory of his free existence, only then will woman be able to make her history, her problems, her doubts and her hopes those of humanity; only then will she be able to attempt to discover in her life and her works all of reality and not only her own person. As long as she still has to fight to become a human being, she cannot be a creator.

Once again, to explain her limits, we must refer to her situation and not to a mysterious essence: the future remains wide open. The idea that woman has no 'creative genius' has been defended ad nauseam; Mme Marthe Borély, a noted antifeminist of former times, defends this thesis, among others: but it looks as if she tried to make her books the living proof of incoherence and feminine silliness, and so they contradict themselves. Besides, the idea of a given creative 'instinct' must be rejected like that of the 'eternal feminine' and put away in the attic of entities. Some misogynists affirm a bit more concretely that because women are neurotic, they will never create anything of value: but these same people often declare that genius is a neurosis. In any case, the example of Proust shows clearly enough that psychophysiological imbalance does not mean powerlessness or mediocrity. As for the argument drawn from history, we have just seen what we should think of it; the historical past cannot be considered as defining an eternal truth; it merely translates a situation that is showing itself to be historical precisely in that it is in the process of changing. How could women ever have had genius when all possibility of accomplishing a work of genius – or just a work – was refused them? Old Europe formerly heaped its contempt on barbarian Americans for possessing neither artists nor writers: 'Let us live before asking us to justify our existence,' Jefferson wrote, in essence. Blacks give the same answers to racists who reproach them for not having produced a Whitman or Melville. Neither can the French proletariat invoke a name like Racine or Mallarmé. The free woman is just being born; when she conquers herself, she will perhaps justify Rimbaud's prophecy: 'Poets will be. When woman's infinite servitude is broken, when she lives for herself and by herself, man – abominable until now – giving her her freedom, she too will be a poet! Woman will find the unknown! Will her worlds of ideas differ from ours? She will find strange, unfathomable, repugnant, delicious things, we will take them, we will understand them.'* Her 'worlds of ideas' are not necessarily different from men's, because she will free herself by assimilating them; to know how singular she will remain and how important these singularities will continue to be, one would have to make some foolhardy predictions. What is beyond doubt is that until now women's possibilities have been stifled and lost to humanity, and in her and everyone's interest it is high time she be left to take her own chances.

* Rimbaud to Paul Demeny, 15 May 1871.

Conclusion

'No, woman is not our brother; through negligence and corruption, we have made her a being apart, unknown, having no weapon but her sex, which is not only perpetual war but in addition an unfair weapon – adoring or hating, but not a frank companion or a being with *esprit de corps* and freemasonry – of the eternal little slave's defiances.'

Many men would still subscribe to these words of Jules Laforgue; many think that there will always be Sturm und Drang between the two sexes and that fraternity will never be possible for them. The fact is that neither men nor women are satisfied with each other today. But the question is whether it is an original curse that condemns them to tear each other apart or whether the conflicts that pit them against each other express a transitory moment in human history.

We have seen that in spite of legends, no physiological destiny imposes eternal hostility on the Male and Female as such; even the notorious praying mantis devours her male only for lack of other food and for the good of the species: in the animal kingdom, from the top of the ladder to the bottom, all individuals are subordinated to the species. Moreover, humanity is something other than a species: it is an historical becoming; it is defined by the way it assumes natural facticity. Indeed, even with the greatest bad faith in the world, it is impossible to detect a rivalry between the male and the female human that is specifically physiological. And so their hostility is located on that ground that is intermediate between biology and psychology, namely, psychoanalysis. Woman, it is said, envies man's penis and desires to castrate him, but the infantile desire for the penis only has importance in the adult woman's life if she experiences her femininity as a mutilation; and it is only to the extent that the penis embodies all the privileges of virility that she wishes to appropriate the male organ for herself. It is generally agreed that her dream of castration has a symbolic significance: she wishes, so it is thought, to deprive the male of his transcendence. Her wish, as we have seen, is much more ambiguous: she wishes, in a contradictory way, *to have* this transcendence, which presupposes that she both respects and denies it, and that she intends both to throw herself into it and to keep it within herself. This means that the drama does not unfold on a sexual level; sexuality, moreover, has never seemed to us to define a destiny or to provide in itself the key to human behaviour, but to express the totality of a situation it helps define. The battle of the sexes is not immediately implied by the anatomy of man and woman. In fact, when it is mentioned, it is taken for granted that in the timeless heaven of Ideas a battle rages between these uncertain essences: the Eternal Feminine and the Eternal Masculine; and it is not noticed that this titanic combat assumes two totally different forms on earth, corresponding to different historical moments.

The woman confined to immanence tries to keep man in this prison as well; thus the prison will merge with the world and she will no longer suffer from being shut up in it: the mother, the wife, the lover are the gaolers; society codified by men decrees that woman is inferior: she can only abolish this inferiority by destroying male superiority. She does her utmost to mutilate, to dominate man, she contradicts him, she denies his truth and values. But in doing that, she is only defending herself; neither immutable essence nor flawed choice has doomed her to immanence and inferiority. They were imposed on her. All oppression creates a state of war. This particular case is no exception. The existent considered as inessential cannot fail to attempt to reestablish his sovereignty.

Today, the combat is taking another form; instead of wanting to put man in prison, woman is trying to escape from it; she no longer seeks to drag him into the realms of immanence but to emerge into the light of transcendence. And the male attitude here creates a new conflict: the man petulantly 'dumps' the woman. He is pleased to remain the sovereign subject, the absolute superior, the essential being; he refuses to consider his companion concretely as an equal; she responds to his defiance by an aggressive attitude. It is no longer a war between individuals imprisoned in their respective spheres: a caste claiming its rights lays siege but is held in check by the privileged caste. Two transcendences confront each other; instead of mutually recognising each other, each freedom wants to dominate the other.

This difference in attitude is manifest on the sexual as well as the spiritual level; the 'feminine' woman, by becoming a passive prey, tries to reduce the male to carnal passivity as well; she works at entrapping him, at imprisoning him, by the desire she arouses, docilely making herself a thing; the 'emancipated' woman, on the contrary, wants to be active and prehensile and refuses the passivity the man attempts to impose on her. Likewise, Élise[1] and her followers do not accord any value to virile activities; they place flesh above spirit, contingence above freedom, conventional wisdom above creative daring. But the 'modern' woman accepts masculine values: she prides herself on thinking, acting, working and creating on the same basis as males; instead of trying to belittle them, she declares herself their equal.

This claim is legitimate insofar as it is expressed in concrete ways; and it is men's insolence that is then reprehensible. But in their defence it must be said that women themselves tend to confuse the issue. A Mabel Dodge attempted to enslave Lawrence by her feminine wiles in order to then dominate him spiritually; to show by their successes that they equal a man, many women strive to secure masculine support through sex; they play both sides, demanding both old-fashioned respect and modern esteem, relying on their old magic and their fledgling rights; it is understandable that the irritated man should go on the defensive, but he too is duplicitous when he demands that the woman play the game loyally whereas he, in his hostility and distrust, refuses to grant her indispensable trump cards. In reality, the struggle between them cannot be clear-cut, since woman's very being is opacity; she does not stand in front of man as a subject but as an object paradoxically endowed with subjectivity; she assumes herself as both *self* and *other*, which is a contradiction with disconcerting consequences. When she makes a weapon of both her weakness and her strength, it is not a deliberate calculation: she is spontaneously seeking her salvation in the path imposed on her, that of passivity, at the same time as she is actively demanding her sovereignty; and this process is undoubtedly not 'fair play', but it is dictated by the ambiguous situation assigned to her. Man, though, when he treats her like a freedom, is indignant that she is still a trap for him; while he flatters and satisfies her in her role as his prey, he gets annoyed at her claims to autonomy; whatever he does, he feels duped and she feels wronged.

The conflict will last as long as men and women do not recognise each other as peers, that is, as long as femininity is perpetuated as such; which of them is the most determined to maintain it? The woman who frees herself from it nevertheless wants to conserve its prerogatives; and the man then demands that she assume its limitations. 'It is easier to accuse one sex than to excuse the other,' says Montaigne. Meting out blame and approbation is useless. In fact, the vicious circle is so difficult to break here because each sex is victim both of the other and of itself; between two adversaries confronting each other in their pure freedom, an agreement could easily be found, especially as this war does not benefit anyone; but the complexity of this whole business comes from the fact that each camp is its enemy's accomplice; the woman pursues a dream of resignation, the man a dream of alienation; inauthenticity does not pay: each one blames the other for the unhappiness brought on himself by taking the easy way out; what the man and the woman hate in each other is the striking failure of their own bad faith or their own cowardice.

We have seen why men originally enslaved women; the devaluation of femininity was a necessary step in human development; but this step could have brought about a collaboration between the two sexes; oppression is explained by the tendency of the existent to flee from himself by alienating himself in the other that he oppresses for that purpose; this tendency can be found in each individual man today: and the vast majority give in to it; a husband looks for himself in his wife, a lover in his mistress, in the guise of a stone statue; he seeks in her the myth of his virility, sovereignty, his unmediated reality. 'My husband never goes to the movies,' says the woman, and the dubious masculine pronouncement is engraved in the marble of eternity. But he himself is a slave to his double: what effort to build up an image in which he is always in danger! After all, it is founded on the capricious freedom of women: it must constantly be made favourable; man is consumed by the concern to appear male, important, superior; he playacts so that others will playact with him; he is also aggressive and nervous; he feels hostility for women because he is afraid of them, and he is afraid of them because he is afraid of the character with whom he is assimilated. What time and energy he wastes in getting rid of, idealising and transposing complexes, in speaking about women, seducing and fearing them! He would be liberated with their liberation. But that is exactly what he fears. And he persists in the mystifications meant to maintain woman in her chains.

That she is mystified is something of which many men are conscious. 'What a curse to be a woman! And yet the very worst curse when one is a woman is, in fact, not to understand that it is one,' says Kierkegaard.* Attempts have been made to disguise this misfortune for a long time.

---

* *In Vino Veritas*. He also says: 'Gallantry is essentially woman's due; and the fact that she unconsciously accepts it may be explained by the solicitude of nature for the weak and the disadvantaged, those who feel more than recompensed by an illusion. But this illusion is precisely fatal . . . Is it not an even worse mockery to feel freed from misery – thanks to one's imagination, to be the dupe of imagination? Woman certainly is far from being *verwahrlost* [abandoned]; but inasmuch as she never can free herself from the illusion with which nature consoles her, she is.'

Guardianship, for example, was eliminated: the woman was given 'protectors' and if they were endowed with the rights of the old guardians, it was in her best interest. Forbidding her to work and keeping her at home is intended to defend her against herself and ensure her happiness. We have seen the poetic veils used to hide the monotonous burdens she bears: housework and maternity; in exchange for her freedom she was given fallacious treasures of 'femininity' as a gift. Balzac described this manoeuvre very well in advising a man to treat her as a slave while persuading her she is a queen. Less cynical, many men endeavour to convince themselves she is truly privileged. There are American sociologists seriously teaching today the theory of 'low-class gain', that is, the 'advantages of the lower castes'. In France as well it has often been proclaimed – albeit less scientifically – that workers are indeed lucky not to be obliged to 'present well', and, even more so tramps who could dress in rags and sleep on the streets, pleasures that were forbidden to the conte de Beaumont and those poor Wendel gentlemen. Like the filthy carefree souls cheerfully scratching their vermin, like the joyful Negroes laughing while being lashed, and like these gay Arabs of Sousse with a smile on their lips, burying their children who starved to death, the woman enjoys this incomparable privilege: irresponsibility. Without difficulties, without responsibility, without cares, she obviously has 'the best part'. What is troubling is that by a stubborn perversity – undoubtedly linked to original sin – across centuries and countries, the people who have the best part always shout to their benefactors: It's too much! I'll settle for yours! But the magnanimous capitalists, the generous colonialists, the superb males persist: Keep the best part, keep it!

The fact is that men encounter more complicity in their woman companions than the oppressor usually finds in the oppressed; and in bad faith they use it as a pretext to declare that woman *wanted* the destiny they imposed on her. We have seen that in reality her whole education conspires to bar her from paths of revolt and adventure; all of society – beginning with her respected parents – lies to her in extolling the high value of love, devotion and the gift of self and in concealing the fact that neither lover, husband nor children will be disposed to bear the burdensome responsibility of it. She cheerfully accepts these lies because they invite her to take the easy slope: and that is the worst of the crimes committed against her; from her childhood and throughout her life, she is spoiled, she is corrupted by the fact that this resignation, tempting to any existent anxious about her freedom, is meant to be her vocation; if one encourages a child to be lazy by entertaining him all day, without giving him the occasion to study, without showing him its value, no one will say when he reaches the age of man that he chose to be incapable and ignorant; this is how the woman is raised, without ever being taught the necessity of assuming her own existence; she readily lets herself count on the protection, love, help and guidance of others; she lets herself be fascinated by the hope of being able to realise her being without *doing* anything. She is wrong to yield to this temptation; but the man is ill advised to reproach her for it since it is he himself who tempted her. When a conflict breaks out between them, each one will blame the other for the situation; she will blame him for creating it: no one taught me to reason, to earn my living . . . He will blame her for accepting it: you know nothing, you are incompetent . . . Each sex thinks it can justify itself by taking the offensive: but the wrongs of one do not absolve the other.

The innumerable conflicts that set men and women against each other stem from the fact that neither sex assumes all the consequences of this situation that one proposes and the other undergoes: this problematic notion of 'equality in inequality' that one uses to hide his despotism and the other her cowardice does not withstand the test of experience: in their exchanges, woman counts on the abstract equality she was guaranteed, and man the concrete inequality he observes. From there ensues the endless debate on the ambiguity of the words 'give' and 'take' in all relationships: she complains of giving everything; he protests that she takes everything from him. The woman has to understand that an exchange – a basic law of political economy – is negotiated according to the value the proposed merchandise has for the buyer and not for the seller: she was duped by being persuaded she was priceless; in reality she is merely a distraction, a pleasure, company, an inessential article for the man; for her he is the meaning, the justification of her existence; the two objects exchanged are thus not of the same quality; this inequality will be particularly noticeable because the time they spend together – and that fallaciously seems to be the same time – does not have the same value for both partners; during the evening the lover spends with his mistress, he might be doing something useful for his career, seeing friends, cultivating relations, entertaining himself; for a man normally integrated into his society, time is a positive asset: money, reputation, pleasure. By contrast, for the idle and bored woman time is a burden she aspires to get rid of; she considers it a benefit to succeed in killing time: the man's presence is pure profit; in many cases, what interests man the most in a relationship is the sexual gain he draws from it: he can, at worst, settle for spending just enough time with his mistress to perform the sex act, but what she herself wants – with rare exceptions – is to 'dispose of' all this excess time she has on her hands: and – like the shopkeeper who will not sell his potatoes if one does not 'take' his turnips – she only gives her body if the lover 'takes' hours of conversation and outings into the bargain. Balance can be established if the cost of the whole matter does not seem too high to the man: that depends, of course, on how intense is his desire and how important to him the occupations he sacrifices; but if the woman demands – offers – too much time, she becomes completely importunate, like the river that overflows its banks, and the man will choose to have nothing rather than to have too much. So she moderates her demands; but very often a balance is found at the price of a twofold tension: she believes that the man *has* her at a bargain price; he thinks he is paying too much. Of course this explanation is somewhat humorous; but – except in cases of jealous and exclusive passion where the man wants the woman in her entirety – this conflict, in tenderness, desire, even love, is always present; the man always has 'something else to do' with his time, whereas she is trying to get rid of hers; and he does not consider the hours she devotes to him as a gift but as a burden. Generally, he consents to tolerate it because he knows he is on the privileged side, he has a 'guilty conscience'; and if he has any goodwill, he tries to compensate for the unequal conditions with generosity; however, he gives himself credit for being compassionate and at the first clash he treats the woman as ungrateful, he gets irritated: I am too generous. She feels she is acting like a beggar while she is convinced of the high value of her gifts, and this humiliates her. This explains the cruelty of which the woman often shows herself capable; she feels 'self-righteous' because she has the bad role; she does not feel any obligation to accommodate the privileged caste, she thinks only of defending herself; she will even be very happy if she has the opportunity to display her resentment to the lover who has not been able to satisfy her: since he does not give enough, she will take everything back with fierce pleasure. Then the wounded man discovers the total price of the relationship whose every minute he disdained: he agrees to all the promises, even if it means he will again consider himself exploited when he has to honour them; he accuses his mistress of blackmailing him: she blames him for his stinginess; both consider themselves frustrated. Here too it is useless to allocate excuses and criticism: justice can never be created within injustice. It is impossible for a colonial administrator to conduct himself well with the indigenous population, or a general with his soldiers; the only solution is to be neither colonialist nor military leader; but a man cannot prevent himself from being a man.

So here he is, thus guilty in spite of himself and oppressed by this fault that he has not committed himself; likewise she is a victim and a shrew in spite of herself; sometimes he revolts, he chooses cruelty, but then he makes himself an accomplice of injustice, and the fault really becomes his; sometimes he allows himself to be destroyed, devoured, by his protesting victim: but then he feels duped; often he settles for a compromise that both diminishes him and puts him ill at ease. A man of goodwill will be more torn by the situation than the woman herself: in one sense, one is always better off being on the side of the defeated; but if she is also of goodwill, unable to be self-sufficient, unwilling to crush the man with the weight of her destiny, she struggles with herself in an inextricable confusion. One meets so many of these cases in daily life for which there are no satisfactory solutions because they are defined by unsatisfactory conditions: a man who sees himself as obligated to maintain a woman he no longer loves materially and morally feels he is a victim; but if he abandoned without resources the one who has committed her whole life to him, she would be a victim in an equally unjust manner. The wrong does not come from individual perversity – and bad faith arises when each person attacks the other – it comes from a situation in the face of which all individual behaviour is powerless. Women are 'clingy', they are a burden and they suffer from it; their lot is that of a parasite that sucks the life from a foreign organism; were they endowed with an autonomous organism, were they able to fight against the world and wrest their subsistence from it, their dependence would be abolished: the man's also. Both would undoubtedly be much better off for it.

A world where men and women would be equal is easy to imagine because it is exactly the one the Soviet revolution *promised*: women raised and educated exactly like men would work under the same conditions* and for the same salaries; erotic freedom would be accepted by custom, but the sexual act would no longer be considered a remunerable 'service'; women would be *obliged* to provide another livelihood for themselves; marriage would be based on a free engagement that the spouses could break when they wanted to; motherhood would be freely chosen – that is, birth control and abortion would be allowed – and in return all mothers and their children would be given the same rights; maternity

---

* That some arduous professions are prohibited to them does not contradict this idea: even men are seeking professional training more and more; their physical and intellectual capacities limit their choices; in any case, what is demanded is that no boundaries of sex or caste be drawn.

leave would be paid for by the society that would have responsibility for the children, which does not mean that they would be *taken* from their parents but that they would not be *abandoned* to them.

But is it enough to change laws, institutions, customs, public opinion and the whole social context for men and women to really become peers? 'Women will always be women,' say the sceptics; other seers prophesy that in shedding their femininity, they will not succeed in changing into men and will become monsters. This would mean that today's woman is nature's creation; it must be repeated again that within the human collectivity nothing is natural, and woman, among others, is a product developed by civilisation; the intervention of others in her destiny is originary: if this process were driven in another way, it would produce a very different result. Woman is defined neither by her hormones nor by mysterious instincts but by the way she grasps, through foreign consciousnesses, her body and her relation to the world; the abyss that separates adolescent girls from adolescent boys was purposely dug out from early infancy; later, it would be impossible to keep woman from being what she *was made*, and she will always trail this past behind her; if the weight of this past is accurately measured, it is obvious that her destiny is not fixed in eternity. One must certainly not think that modifying her economic situation is enough to transform woman: this factor has been and remains the primordial factor of her development, but until it brings about the moral, social and cultural consequences it heralds and requires, the new woman cannot appear; as of now, these consequences have been realised nowhere: in the USSR no more than in France or the United States; and this is why today's woman is torn between the past and the present; most often, she appears as a 'real woman' disguised as a man, and she feels as awkward in her woman's body as in her masculine garb. She has to shed her old skin and cut her own clothes. She will only be able to do this if there is a collective change. No one teacher can today shape a 'female human being' that would be an exact homologue to the 'male human being': if raised like a boy, the girl feels she is an exception and that subjects her to a new kind of specification. Stendhal understood this, saying: 'The forest must be planted all at once.' But if we suppose, by contrast, a society where sexual equality is concretely realised, this equality would newly assert itself in each individual.

If, from the earliest age, the little girl were raised with the same demands and honours, the same severity and freedom, as her brothers, taking part in the same studies and games, promised the same future, surrounded by women and men who are unambiguously equal to her, the meanings of the 'castration complex' and the 'Oedipus complex' would be profoundly modified. The mother would enjoy the same lasting prestige as the father if she assumed equal material and moral responsibility for the couple; the child would feel an androgynous world around her and not a masculine world; were she more affectively attracted to her father – which is not even certain – her love for him would be nuanced by a will to emulate him and not a feeling of weakness: she would not turn to passivity; if she were allowed to prove her worth in work and sports, actively rivalling boys, the absence of a penis – compensated for by the promise of a child – would not suffice to cause an 'inferiority complex'; correlatively, the boy would not have a natural 'superiority complex' if it were not instilled in him and if he held women in the same esteem as men.* The little girl would not seek sterile compensations in narcissism and dreams, she would not take herself as given, she would be interested in what she does, she would throw herself into her pursuits. I have said how much easier puberty would be if she surpassed it, like the boy, towards a free adult future; menstruation horrifies her only because it signifies a brutal descent into femininity; she would also assume her youthful eroticism more peacefully if she did not feel a frightening disgust for the rest of her destiny; a coherent sexual education would greatly help her to surmount this crisis. And thanks to coeducation, the august mystery of Man would have no occasion to arise: it would be killed by everyday familiarity and open competition. Objections to this system always imply respect for sexual taboos; but it is useless to try to inhibit curiosity and pleasure in children; this only results in creating repression, obsessions and neuroses; exalted sentimentality, homosexual fervour and the platonic passions of adolescent girls along with the whole procession of nonsense and dissipation are far more harmful than a few childish games and actual experiences. What would really be profitable for the girl is that, not seeking in the male a demigod – but only a pal, a friend, a partner – she not be diverted from assuming her own existence; eroticism and love would be a free surpassing and not a resignation; she could experience them in a relationship of equal to equal. Of course, there is no question of writing off all the difficulties a child must overcome to become an adult; the most intelligent, tolerant education could not free her from having her own experi-

---

* I know a little boy of eight who lives with a mother, aunt and grandmother, all three independent and active, and a grandfather who is half-senile. He has a crushing inferiority complex in relation to the female sex, though his mother tries to combat it. In his lycée he scorns his friends and professors because they are poor males.

ences at her own expense; what one would want is that obstacles should not accumulate gratuitously on her path. It is already an improvement that 'depraved' little girls are no longer cauterised with red-hot irons; psychoanalysis has enlightened parents somewhat; yet the conditions in which woman's sexual education and initiation take place today are so deplorable that none of the objections to the idea of a radical change are valid. It is not a question of abolishing the contingencies and miseries of the human condition in her but of giving her the means to go beyond them.

Woman is the victim of no mysterious fate; the singularities that make her different derive their importance from the meaning applied to them; they can be overcome as soon as they are grasped from new perspectives; we have seen that in her erotic experience, the woman feels – and often detests – male domination: it must not be concluded that her ovaries condemn her to living on her knees eternally. Virile aggressiveness is a lordly privilege only within a system where everything conspires to affirm masculine sovereignty; and woman *feels* so deeply passive in the love act only because she already *thinks* herself that way. Many modern women who claim their dignity as human beings still grasp their sexual lives by referring back to a tradition of slavery: so it seems humiliating to them to lie under the man and be penetrated by him, and they tense up into frigidity; but if reality were different, the meaning sexual gestures and postures symbolically express would be different as well: a woman who pays, who dominates her lover, can for example feel proud of her superb inertia and think that she is enslaving the male who is actively exerting himself; and today there are already many sexually balanced couples for whom notions of victory and defeat yield to an idea of exchange. In fact, man is, like woman, a flesh, thus a passivity, the plaything of his hormones and the species, uneasy prey to his desire; and she, like him, in the heart of carnal fever, is consent, voluntary gift and activity; each of them lives the strange ambiguity of existence made body in his or her own way. In these combats where they believe they are tackling each other, they are fighting their own self, projecting onto their partner the part of themselves they repudiate; instead of living the ambiguity of their condition, each one tries to make the other accept the abjection of this condition and reserves the honour of it for one's self. If, however, both assumed it with lucid modesty, as the correlate of authentic pride, they would recognise each other as peers and live the erotic drama in harmony. The fact of being a human being is infinitely more important than all the singularities that distinguish human beings; it is never the given that confers superiority: 'virtue', as the Ancients called it, is defined at the level of 'what depends on us'. The same drama of flesh and spirit, and of fini- tude and transcendence, plays itself out in both sexes; both are eaten away by time, stalked by death, they have the same essential need of the other; and they can take the same glory from their freedom; if they knew how to savour it, they would no longer be tempted to contend for false privileges; and fraternity could then be born between them.

People will say that all these considerations are merely utopian because to 'remake woman', society would have had to have already made her *really* man's equal; conservatives have never missed the chance to denounce this vicious circle in all analogous circumstances: yet history does not go round in circles. Without a doubt, if a caste is maintained in an inferior position, it remains inferior: but freedom can break the circle; let blacks vote and they become worthy of the vote; give woman responsibilities and she knows how to assume them; the fact is, one would not think of expecting gratuitous generosity from oppressors; but the revolt of the oppressed at times and changes in the privileged caste at other times create new situations; and this is how men, in their own interest, have been led to partially emancipate women: women need only pursue their rise and the success they obtain encourages them; it seems most certain that they will sooner or later attain perfect economic and social equality, which will bring about an inner metamorphosis.

In any case, some will object that if such a world is possible, it is not desirable. When woman is 'the same' as her male, life will lose 'its spice'. This argument is not new either: those who have an interest in perpet- uating the present always shed tears for the marvellous past about to disappear without casting a smile on the young future. It is true that by doing away with slave markets, we destroyed those great plantations lined with azaleas and camellias, we dismantled the whole delicate Southern civilisation; old lace was put away in the attics of time along with the pure timbres of the Sistine castrati, and there is a certain 'femi- nine charm' that risks turning to dust as well. I grant that only a barbarian would not appreciate rare flowers, lace, the crystal-clear voice of a eunuch or feminine charm. When shown in her splendour, the 'charming woman' is a far more exalting object than 'the idiotic paintings, over-doors, décors, circus backdrops, sideboards or popular illuminations' that maddened Rimbaud; adorned with the most modern of artifices, worked on with the newest techniques, she comes from the remotest ages, from Thebes, Minos, Chichén Itzá; and she is also the totem planted in the heart of the African jungle; she is a helicopter and she is a bird; and here is the greatest wonder: beneath her painted hair, the rustling of leaves becomes a thought and words escape from her breasts. Men reach out their eager hands to the marvel; but as soon as they grasp it, it vanishes; the wife and the mistress speak like everyone else, with their mouths: their words are worth exactly what they are worth; their breasts as well. Does such a fleeting miracle – and one so rare – justify perpetuating a situation that is so damaging for both sexes? The beauty of flowers and women's charms can be appreciated for what they are worth; if these treasures are paid for with blood or misery, one must be willing to sacrifice them.

The fact is that this sacrifice appears particularly heavy to men; few of them really wish in their hearts to see women accomplish themselves; those who scorn woman do not see what they would have to gain, and those who cherish her see too well what they have to lose; and it is true that present-day developments not only threaten feminine charm: in deciding to live for herself, woman will abdicate the functions as double and mediator that provide her with her privileged place within the masculine universe; for the man caught between the silence of nature and the demanding presence of other freedoms, a being who is both his peer and a passive thing appears as a great treasure; he may well perceive his companion in a mythical form, but the experiences of which she is the source or pretext are no less real: and there are hardly more precious, intimate or urgent ones; it cannot be denied that feminine dependence, inferiority and misfortune give women their unique character; assuredly, women's autonomy, even if it spares men a good number of problems, will also deny them many conveniences; assuredly, there are certain ways of living the sexual adventure that will be lost in the world of tomorrow: but this does not mean that love, happiness, poetry and dreams will be banished from it. Let us beware lest our lack of imagination impoverish the future; the future is only an abstraction for us; each of us secretly laments the absence in it of what was; but tomorrow's humankind will live the future in its flesh and in its freedom; that future will be its present and humankind will in turn prefer it; new carnal and affective relations of which we cannot conceive will be born between the sexes: friend-ships, rivalries, complicities, chaste or sexual companionships that past centuries would not have dreamed of are already appearing. For example, nothing seems more questionable to me than a catchphrase that dooms the new world to uniformity and then to boredom. I do not see an absence of boredom in this world of ours nor that freedom has ever created uniformity. First of all, certain differences between man and woman will always exist; her eroticism, and thus her sexual world, possessing a singular form, cannot fail to engender in her a sensuality, a singular sensitivity: her relation to her body, to the male body and to the child will never be the same as those man has with his body, with the female body and with the child; those who talk so much about 'equality in difference' would be hard put not to grant me that there are differences in equality. Besides, it is institutions that create monotony: young and pretty, slaves of the harem are all the same in the sultan's arms; Christianity gave eroticism its flavour of sin and legend by endowing the human female with a soul; restoring woman's singular sovereignty will not remove the emotional value from amorous embraces. It is absurd to contend that orgies, vice, ecstasy and passion would become impossible if man and woman were concretely peers; the contradictions opposing flesh to spirit, instant to time, the vertigo of immanence to the appeal of transcendence, the absolute of pleasure to the nothingness of oblivion will never disappear; tension, suffering, joy and the failure and triumph of existence will always be materialised in sexuality. To emancipate woman is to refuse to enclose her in the relations she sustains with man, but not to deny them; while she posits herself for herself, she will nonetheless continue to exist for him *as well*: recognising each other as subject, each will remain an *other* for the other; reciprocity in their relations will not do away with the miracles that the division of human beings into two separate categories engenders: desire, possession, love, dreams, adventure; and the words that move us: 'to give', 'to conquer', and 'to unite' will keep their meaning; on the contrary, it is when the slavery of half of humanity is abolished and with it the whole hypocritical system it implies that the 'division' of humanity will reveal its authentic meaning and the human couple will discover its true form.

'The direct, natural, and necessary relation of person to person is the *relation of man to woman*,' said Marx.* From the character of this relationship follows how much man as *a species-being*, as man, has come to be himself and to comprehend himself; the relation of man to woman is the most natural relation of human being to human being. It therefore reveals the extent to which man's *natural* behaviour has become *human*, or the extent to which the *human* essence in him has become a *natural* essence – the extent to which his *human nature* has come to be *natural* to him.[2]

This could not be better said. Within the given world, it is up to man to make the reign of freedom triumph; to carry off this supreme victory, men and women must, among other things and above and beyond their natural differentiations, unequivocally affirm their brotherhood.

* *Philosophical Works*, Vol. VI. Marx's italics.

Notes

These translators' notes do not in any way constitute an annotated version of *The Second Sex*. They provide the translated versions of books and works to which Beauvoir makes reference and which we used in our translation. Where published translations do not exist, we give the title of the work in French only. When a translation into English exists, we have provided both French and English titles and bibliographic information for the title in English. Despite our best efforts, we were not able to find all of them. In addition we have noted a few discrepancies between the original text and our research.

Vol I: Introduction
1. Julien Benda, *Le rapport d'Uriel*.
2. Emmanuel Levinas, *Le Temps et l'autre. Time and the Other*, trans. Richard Cohen, Duquesne University Press, 1987.
3. Claude Lévi-Strauss, *Les structures élémentaires de la parenté. The Elementary Structures of Kinship*, trans. James Harle Bell, Rodney Needham and John Richard von Sturmer, Beacon Press, 1969.
4. *Mitsein* can be translated as 'being with'. The French term *réalité humaine* has been erroneously used to translate Heidegger's *Dasein*.
5. '*L'égalité dans la différence*' in the French text. Literal translation: 'different but equal'.

Vol I: Part One
Chapter 1 Biological Data
1. G. W. F. Hegel, *The Philosophy of Nature*, trans. J. N. Findlay and A. V. Miller, Oxford University Press, 1979.
2. Maurice Merleau-Ponty, *Phénomenologie de la perception. Phenomenology of Perception*, trans. Colin Smith, Routledge, 2005.
3. Jean-Paul Sartre, *L'Etre et le Néant. Being and Nothingness*, trans. Hazel Barnes, Citadel Press, 2001.

4. Paul Ancel, 'Histogenèse et structure de la glande hermaphrodite d'Helix pomatia (Linn.)', in *Archives de Biologie*, tome XIX, 1903.
5. Alfred Fouillée, *Tempérament et caractère selon les individus, les sexes et les races*.
6. *Bonellia viridis* is a sandworm that has no sex chromosomes.

Chapter 2 The Psychoanalytical Point of View

7. Roland Dalbiez, *La méthode psychanalytique et la doctrine freudienne. Psychoanalytical Method and the Doctrine of Freud*, Longmans, Green, & Co., 1941.
8. Sigmund Freud, *Moses and Monotheism*, trans. Katherine Jones, Knopf, 1939.
9. Charles Baudouin, *L'âme enfantine et la psychanalyse*.
10. Alice Bálint, *The Psychoanalysis of the Nursery*, Routledge and Kegan Paul, 1953.
11. Wilhelm Stekel, *Frigidity in Woman*, trans. James S. Van Teslaar, Liveright Publishing Corporation, 1943. *Frigidity in Woman* was published in French translation by Gallimard in 1937.
12. Sir James Donaldson, *Woman, Her Position and Influence in Ancient Greece and Rome, and Among the Early Christians*, Elibron Classics, 1906.

Chapter 3 The Point of View of Historical Materialism

13. Friedrich Engels, *The Origin of the Family, Private Property and the State*, trans. Alick West and Dona Torr, Marxist-Leninist Library, 1942.
14. Gaston Bachelard, *La Terre et les rêveries de la volonté. Earth and Reveries of Will*, trans. Kenneth Haltman, Dallas Institute of Humanities and Culture, 2002.

Vol I: Part Two, History
Chapter 2

1. Lévi-Strauss, *Les structures élémentaires de la parenté. The Elementary Structures of Kinship*.
2. Aeschylus, *Eumenides*, trans. Richard Lattimore, University of Chicago Press, 1969.

Chapter 3

3. King James Bible (Authorised Version).
4. '*Ubi tu Gaius, ego Gaia*': 'Where you are Gaius, I am Gaia.'

Chapter 4

5. *Mundium*: almost total legal guardianship over women by father and husband.

6. *Songe du verger*: treatise of political doctrine, written first in Latin (1370) and then in French (1378). Title usually kept in French.

7. *Lettre de cachet*: letter with a seal. It carries an official seal, usually signed by the king of France, authorising the imprisonment without trial of a named person.

8. *Uxor non est proprie socia sed speratur fore*: the wife is not exactly a partner, but it is hoped she will become one.

9. *Dictionnaire de la conversation*, 'Femmes et filles de folles vie'. Translation of Old French by Gabrielle Spiegel.

10. The title *Roman de la Rose* is usually kept in French.

11. *Querelle des femmes*: a literary quarrel traced to Christine de Pizan's objection to the portrayal of women in the *Roman de la Rose*, voiced in her *Epître au dieu d'amour (Epistle to the God of Love)*, 1399, a debate that helped nurture literary production throughout the early modern period.

12. The original is from Lady Winchilsea's poem 'The Introduction'. Beauvoir shortened and paraphrased the quote when she translated it.

13. Discrepancy: In fact Mrs Aphra Behn, dramatist and novelist, lived from 1640 to 1689.

14. *La Nef des dames vertueuses, Le Chevalier des dames* and *Le Petit Sénat*.

15. *Déclamation de la noblesse et de l'excellence du sexe féminin. Declamation on the Nobility and Preeminence of the Female Sex*, ed. and trans. Albert Rabil, Jr; repr. University of Chicago Press, 1996.

16. *Le fort inexpugnable*.

17. *La parfaite amye*.

18. *Docte et subtil discours*.

19. *Les controverses des sexes masculin et féminin*.

20. Rabelais, *Tiers livre*.

21. *Alphabet de l'imperfection et malice des femmes*.

22. *Egalité des hommes et des femmes*.

23. *Parnasse et cabinets satyriques*. This title might be a confusion and combination of *Le cabinet satyrique* (1618) and *Le parnasse des poètes sartyriques* (1622).

24. *L'honneste femme*.

25. Molière, *Les précieuses ridicules* and *Les femmes savants*.

26. *De l'égalité des deux sexes*.

27. *Entretiens sur la pluralité des mondes.*
28. *Controverse sur l'âme de la femme.*

Chapter 5

29. The 'baker, the baker's wife and the baker's little boy' refer to King Louis XVI, the queen and the dauphin, forced by the starving people to leave Versailles for Paris, October 1789.
30. *Motion de la pauvre Javotte.*
31. Divorce was in fact abolished in 1816.
32. Balzac, Honoré de, *La Physiologie du mariage. The Physiology of Marriage.* trans. Sharon Maras, Johns Hopkins University Press, 1997.
33. Proudhon, Pierre-Joseph, *La Justice.*
34. Proudhon, *La pornocratie, ou Les femmes dans les temps modernes.*
35. *L'ouvrière.*
36. *Le travail des femmes au XIXe siècle.*
37. Beauvoir's calculations. 3 a.m. to 11 p.m adds up to twenty hours.
38. *Mémoires et aventures d'un prolétaire.* Cited from E. Dolléans, *Histoire du mouvement ouvrier,* vol. I.
39. *La verité sur les événements de Lyon.*
40. Discrepancy in Beauvoir's calculations. The totals are 2,664,924 unionised workers, and 275,209 women.
41. Discrepancy in Beauvoir's calculations. The totals are 1.850 million.
42. *La Précieuse, l'abbé de Pure.* Usually kept in French. Literally 'the precious woman', i.e. sophisticated, refined.
43. From John Stuart Mill, 'The Subjection of Women', reprinted in *Philosophy of Women,* ed. Mary Briody Mahowald.
44. The convention actually took place 19–20 July, 1848.
45. President Woodrow Wilson.
46. The name of the city was Petrograd from 1914–24.
47. Jean-Paul Sartre, *Réflexions sur la question juive. Anti-Semite and Jew,* trans. George J. Becker, Schocken, 1948.

Vol I: Part Three, Myths
Chapter 1

1. Michel Carrouges, 'Les pouvoirs de la femme' (Chapter 1), *Cahiers du Sud,* no. 292 (1948).
2. Søren Kierkegaard, *Stages on Life's Way,* trans. H. V. Hong, Princeton University Press, 1989.
3. Carl Jung, *Metamorphoses of the Libido and its Symbols,* in *Collected Works of C. G. Jung,* trans. R. F. C. Hull, Princeton University Press, 1967.

4. André Breton, *Arcanum 17*, trans. Zach Rogow, Green Integer, 2004.

5. Leopold Sédar Senghor, *Oeuvres Poetiques Completes. The Collected Poetry*, trans. Melvin Dixon, University of Virginia Press, 1991.

6. Most likely: '*Post coitum omne animal triste.*' All animals are sad after sex.

7. Jean-Richard Bloch, *La Nuit kurde. A Night in Kurdistan*, trans. Stephen Haden Guest, Victor Gollancz Ltd, 1930.

8. 'A temple built over a sewer.'

9. 'We are born between shit and piss.'

10. Michel Leiris, *La mère. 'The Mother'*, trans. Beverley Bie Brahic.

11. Paul Valéry. Poem translated by James Lawler.

12. Honoré de Balzac, *Le lys dans la vallée. The Lily in the Valley*, trans. Lucienne Hill, Carroll & Graf Publishers, Inc., 1997.

13. Gustave Flaubert, *L'education sentimentale. Sentimental Education*, trans. Robert Baldick, Penguin, 1964.

14. André Malraux, *La condition humaine. Man's Fate*, trans. Haakon M. Chevalier, The Modern Library, 1934.

15. '*Notre petite campagne*'. No source for this poem is provided by Simone de Beauvoir.

16. Georges de Porto-Riche, *Amoureuse*, 1891.

17. *La Glu*, a play by Jean Richepin, 1883.

18. Schwob, Marcel, *Le Livre de Monelle. The Book of Monelle*, trans. William Brown-Maloney, Bobbs-Merrill Company, 1929.

Chapter 2
Montherlant or the Bread of Disgust

19. Henry de Montherlant, *Pitié pour les femmes. Pity for Women*, Knopf, 1937.

20. Montherlant, *L'exil*.

21. Montherlant, *Les Célibataires. The Bachelors*, trans. Terence Kilmartin, Greenwood Press, 1977.

22. Montherlant, *Les Jeunes Filles. The Girls*, trans. Terence Kilmartin, Harper & Row, 1968.

23. Montherlant, *Le Songe. The Dream*, trans. Terence Kilmartin, Macmillan, 1963.

24. Quotation from Ecclesiastes not found.

25. Montherlant, *La Petite Infante de Castille. The Little Infanta of Castile*, French & European Pubns, 1973.

26. *Aux Fontaines du désir*.

27. *Le Maitre de Santiago. The Master of Santiago*, trans. Jonathan Griffen, Knopf, 1951.

28. *Le solstice de juin.*
29. *L'equinoxe de septembre.*
30. *La reine morte.*
31. *La possession de soi-même.*

Claudel or the Handmaiden of the Lord

32. *Partage de midi*, trans. Wallace Fowlie. All other Claudel translations are by James Lawler.
33. *Les aventures de Sophie.*
34. *La cantate à trois voix.*
35. *Conversations dans le Loir-et-Cher.*
36. *Le soulier de satin.*
37. *L'annonce faite à Marie.*
38. *L'échange.*
39. *L'oiseau noir dans le soleil levant.*
40. *Positions et propositions.*
41. *La ville.*
42. *La jeune fille Violaine.*
43. *Le pain dur.*
44. *Livre de Tobie et de Sara.*
45. *Le père humilié.*
46. *Feuilles de saints.*
47. *L'otage.*

Breton or Poetry

48. *Nadja*, trans. Richard Howard, Grove Press, 1994.
49. *L'amour fou. Mad Love*, trans. Mary Ann Caws, University of Nebraska Press, 1988.
50. *Les vases communicants. Communicating Vessels*, trans. Mary Ann Caws and Geoffrey Harris, University of Nebraska Press, 1990.
51. Arthur Rimbaud, 'Vagabonds' in *Illuminations:* trans. Helen Rootham, New Directions, 1943.
52. Arthur Rimbaud, 'Adieu (Farewell) in *Une saison en enfer, A Season in Hell*, Part III: trans. Delmore Schwartz, New Directions, 1939.
53. Breton, *Arcanum 17*.
54. *Poems of André Breton: A Bilingual Anthology*, trans. Mary Ann Caws, University of Texas Press, 1982.
55. Ibid.
56. Ibid.

Stendhal or Romancing the Real

57. 'L'esprit de sérieux': conventional thinking.
58. *Chroniques italiennes.*

Chapter 3

59. *L'âge d'homme.*
60. Choderlos de Laclos, *Les liaisons dangereuses. Dangerous Liaisons*, trans. P. W. K. Stone, Penguin, 1961.
61. Stendhal, *Le rouge et le noir. The Red and the Black*, trans. Roger Gard, Penguin, 2002.

Vol. II: Part One
Chapter 1 Childhood

1. Jacques Lacan, *Les complexes familiaux dans la formation de l'individu.*
2. Yassu Gauclère, *L'orange bleue.*
3. Maurice Sachs, *Le Sabbat. Witches' Sabbath*, trans. Richard Howard, Jonathan Cape, 1965.
4. François Rabelais, *The Complete Works*, trans. Donald M. Frame, University of California Press, 1991.
5. Bàlint, *The Psychoanalysis of the Nursery.*
6. Helene Deutsch, *The Psychology of Women*, Bantam, 1973.
7. Havelock Ellis, *Ondinism*, Random House.
8. Havelock Ellis, *Studies in the Psychology of Sex*, vol. XIII, The Minerva Group Inc., 2001.
9. Raymond de Saussure, 'Psycholgie génétique et psychanalyse'. 'Psychogenesis and Psychoanalysis'.
10. Marie Bashkirtseff, *Mon Journal. I am the Most Interesting Book of All.*
11. Carl Jung, *The Development of Personality*, 'Psychic Conflicts of a Child', trans. R. F. C. Hull, Princeton University Press, 1970.
12. Marie Le Hardouin, *La voile noire.*
13. Colette Audry, *Aux yeux du souvenir.*
14. Violette Leduc, *L'asphyxie*; S. de Tervagne, *La haine maternelle*; H. Bazin, *Vipère au poing*, trans. W. J. Strachan, Prentice Hall, 1951.
15. Charles Baudouin, *l'âme enfantine.*
16. Colette, *La maison de Claudine, Claudine's House*, trans. Andrew Brown, Hesperus Press, 2006.
17. Carson McCullers, *The Member of the Wedding*, Penguin Classics, 1962.
18. Wilhelm Liepmann, *Jeunesse et sexualité.*
19. Horlam, *Garçonnet et fillette.*

20. Richard Hughes, *A High Wind in Jamaica*, Harper & Brothers, 1925.
21. Margaret Kennedy, *The Constant Nymph*, Doubleday, Page, 1925.
22. Stekel, *Frigidity in Woman*.
23. Wilhelm Stekel, *Lettres à une mère*.
24. Colette Audry, *Aux yeux du souvenir*.
25. Thyde Monnier, *Moi*, du Rocher, Monaco, 1949.
26. 'Sweet girl'.

Chapter 2 The Girl

27. Wilhelm Liepmann, *Jeunesse et sexualité*.
28. Rosamond Lehmann, *Invitation to the Waltz*, Virago, 2006.
29. Marie Bashkirtseff, *I Am the Most Interesting Book of All*.
30. Leo Tolstoy, *War and Peace*, trans. Richard Pevear and Larissa Volokhonsky, Knopf, 2008.
31. Katherine Mansfield, 'Prelude', in *The Short Stories of Katherine Mansfield*, Knopf, 1937.
32. Maurice Debesse, *La crise d'originalité juvénile*. This is cited by de Beauvoir as *La Crise d'originalité de l'adolescent*.
33. Marguerite Evard, *L'adolescente*.
34. From Borel and Robin, *Les reveries morbides*. Cited by Minkowski in *La schizophrénie*. Borel and Robin wrote *Les rêveurs éveillés* (Daydreamers). Minkowski wrote an article, 'De la rêverie morbide au délire d'influence' (From Morbid Reverie to Delusions of Grandeur).
35. *Mädchen in Uniform* (German film), 1931.
36. Colette, *Claudine à l'école. Claudine at School*, trans. Antonia White, Farrar, Straus & Giroux, 2001.
37. Rosamond Lehmann, *Dusty Answer*, Virago Press, 2008.
38. P. Mendousse, *L'âme de l'adolescente*.
39. Clemence Dane, *Regiment of Women*, Virago Press, 1995.
40. Renée Vivien, 'Psappha revit', in *A l'heure des mains jointes*, trans. Gillian Spraggs.
41. Renée Vivien, 'Pareilles', in *Sillages*, trans. Gillian Spraggs.
42. Deutsch, *The Psychology of Women*.
43. Le Hardouin, *La voile noire*.
44. Mme de Ségur, *Quel amour d'enfant!*
45. Stekel, *Frigidity in Woman*.
46. Colette, *Le blé en herbe. Green Wheat*, trans. Zach Rogow, Sarabande Books, 2004.
47. Colette, *Sido*, trans. Una Vicenzo Troubridge and Enid McLeod, Farrar, Straus & Giroux, 2002.

48. Mary Webb, *The House in Dormer Forest*, Kessinger Publishing, 1945.

49. Virginia Woolf, *The Waves*, Hogarth Press, 1931.

50. Mary Webb, *Precious Bane*, E. P. Dutton, New York, 1926.

Chapter 3 Sexual Initiation

51. The Kinsey Reports are two books on human sexual behaviour: *Sexual Behavior in the Human Male*, 1948, and *Sexual Behavior in the Human Female*, 1953, by Alfred Kinsey, Wardell Pomeroy and others.

52. Benda, *Le rapport d'Uriel*.

53. Isadora Duncan, *My Life*, Boni & Liveright, 1955.

54. Stekel, *Frigidity in Woman*.

55. Renée Vivien, *At the Sweet Hour of Hand in Hand*, trans. Gillian Spraggs.

56. Duncan, *My Life*. Discrepancy between Isadora Duncan's words: 'The next day we remained in the country, Romeo frequently hushing my cries and drying my tears. I felt as if I were crippled', and those of Simone de Beauvoir in the text.

57. www.gutenberg.org.

58. Stekel, *Frigidity in Woman*. Discrepancy in initials: 'K. L.' in the English translation of Stekel's German text.

59. Ibid. Not in the English translation of Stekel's German text.

60. Colette, *Le blé en herbe. Green Wheat*.

61. Michel de Montaigne, *The Complete Essays of Montaigne*, trans. Donald M. Frame, Stanford University Press, 1965.

62. Juvenal: 'Her secret parts burning are tense with lust,/And, tired by men, but far from sated, she withdrew.'

63. Marie Le Hardouin, *La voile noire*.

64. Jean-Paul Sartre, *L'Etre et le Néant. Being and Nothingness*.

65. Marquis de Sade, *La Philosophie dans le boudoir. Philosophy in the Boudoir*, trans. Joachim Neugroschel, Penguin, 2006.

66. Jean-Paul Sartre, *L'Etre et le Néant. Being and Nothingness*.

67. Colette, *Mes apprentissages. My Apprenticeships & Music-Hall Sidelights*, trans. Helen Beauclerk, Penguin Books, 1967.

Chapter 4 The Lesbian

68. Denis de Rougement, *La part du diable. The Devil's Share*, trans. Haakon Chevalier, Pantheon Books, 1944.

69. Colette, *Aux yeux du souvenir*.

70. Roland Dalbiez, *La méthode psychanalytique et la doctrine freudienne. Psychoanalytical Method and the Doctrine of Freud*.

71. Richard von Krafft-Ebing, *Psychopathia Sexualis*, Rebman, Kessinger Publishing, 1906.
72. Havelock Ellis, *Studies in the Psychology of Sex*, Vol. 2, *Sexual Inversion*, The Minerva Group, Inc., 2001.
73. Colette, *Ces plaisirs. The Pure and the Impure*, trans. Herma Briffault, New York Review of Books, 2001.
74. Discrepancy between Renée Vivien's poem quoted by Beauvoir and Vivien's published version, both translated by Gillian Spraggs.
75. Cited incorrectly by Beauvoir as *Sortilèges*, which is non-existent; poem from translation of *Sillages* (*Sea Wakes*), 1908.
76. Colette, *Les vrilles de la vigne. Tender Shoot*, trans. Antonia White, Farrar, Straus & Giroux, 1975.
77. From *At the Sweet Hour of Hand in Hand*.
78. Discrepancy between Vivien's poem quoted by Beauvoir and Vivien's published version, both translated by Gillian Spraggs; from 'Je t'aime d'être faible' (I love you to be weak), in *At the Sweet Hour of Hand in Hand*.
79. Radclyffe Hall, *The Well of Loneliness*, Wordsworth Editions, 2005.
80. Thyde Monnier, *Moi*.

Vol. II: Part Two
Chapter 5 The Married Woman

1. Emile Zola, *Pot-Bouille*, Everyman/Orion, London, 1999.
2. Bronislaw Malinowski, 'The Bachelors' House', in *The Sexual Life of Savages in North-Western Melanesia*, Liveright, 1929.
3. Colette, *La maison de Claudine. Claudine's House*.
4. Claire Leplae, *Les fiancailles*.
5. Our translation of '*Club des lisières vertes*', source unknown.
6. Stekel, *Frigidity in Woman*.
7. Michel de Montaigne, *The Complete Essays of Montaigne*, trans. Donald M. Frame.
8. G. W. F. Hegel, *Phenomenology of the Spirit*, trans. A. V. Miller, Oxford University Press, 1977.
9. All Montaigne quotes are from *Complete Essays*.
10. Balzac, *Physiologie du mariage. The Physiology of Marriage*.
11. Honoré de Balzac, *Mémoires de jeune Mariés. Letters of Two Brides*, trans. R. S. Scott, Hard Press, 2006.
12. Balzac, *Le lys dans la vallée. The Lily in the Valley*.
13. Søren Kierkegaard, 'Some Reflections on Marriage', in *Stages on Life's Way*.
14. Georges de Porto-Riche, *Amoureuse*, 1891.

15. Colette, *L'ingénue libertine. The Innocent Libertine*, trans. Antonia White, Farrar Straus & Giroux, 1978.
16. *Ce que tout mari doit savoir, Le secret du bonheur conjugal* and *L'amour sans peur.*
17. Colette, *La maison de Claudine. Claudine's House.*
18. Wilhelm Stekel, *Conditions of Nervous Anxiety and Their Treatment*, Liveright Publishing Corporation, 1950.
19. Henri Michaux, 'Nuit de noces'. 'Bridal Night', in 'La nuit remue' – See *Selected Writings*, A New Directions Book, 1968.
20. Pierre Janet, *Les obsessions et la psychasthénie*, 1903.
21. Denis Diderot, *Sur les femmes. On Women*, trans. Francis Birrell, Routledge, 1927.
22. François Mauriac, *Thérèse Desqueyroux*, trans. Raymond MacKenzie, Rowman & Littlefield Publishers Inc., 2005.
23. Colette, *La vagabonde. The Vagabond*, trans. Enid McLeod, Farrar, Straus & Giroux, 1955.
24. *Nature et formes de la jalousie.* Beauvoir's title is mistaken. Lagache's work on jealousy is called *La Jalousie amoureuse (Jealousy in Love).*
25. Marcel Jouhandeau, *Chroniques maritales. Marcel and Elise, The Bold Chronicle of a Strange Marriage*, trans. Martin Turnell, Pantheon Books, 1953.
26. Henry Bordeaux, *La maison.*
27. Rilke to Lou Andreas-Salomé, 8 August 1903.
28. Virginia Woolf, *The Waves*, Hogarth Press, 1931.
29. Gaston Bachelard, *La terre et les rêveries du repos. Earth and Reveries of Repose*, trans. Kenneth Haltman.
30. Virginia Woolf, *To the Lighthouse*, in *The Selected Works of Virginia Woolf*, Wordsworth Editions, 2005.
31. Madeleine Bourdouxhe, *A la recherche de Marie. Marie*, trans. Faith Evans, Bloomsbury, 1997.
32. Bachelard, *La terre et les rêveries du repos. Earth and Reveries of Repose.*
33. In French 'wash boiler', or *lessiveuse*, is feminine, and where English uses the pronoun 'it', French uses *elle*, that is, 'she'. Playing on this ambiguity throughout his text, Ponge gives the wash boiler a feminine identity and presence.
34. Francis Ponge, 'The Wash Boiler' from *Liasse (Sheaf)*; passage translated by Beverley Bie Brahic.
35. Colette, 'La poussière' in *On joue perdant.* 'Dust' in *Playing a Losing Game.*
36. Colette, *Sido.*

37. Jouhandeau, *Chroniques maritales. The Bold Chronicle of a Strange Marriage.*

38. Jacques Chardonne, *L'épithalame.* Epithalamium.

39. Violette Leduc, *L'affamée.*

40. Passage translated by Nina de Voogd Fuller.

41. Bachelard, *La terre et les rêveries de la volonté. Earth and Reveries of Will.*

42. Jules Michelet, *La Montagne. The Mountain,* from *Complete Works,* trans. W. H. Davenport Adams, T. Nelson & Sons, 1872.

43. Dorothy Parker, 'Too Bad!', in *The Portable Dorothy Parker,* Penguin Books, 1944.

44. Friedrich Nietzsche, *The Gay Science,* trans. Walter Kaufmann, Vintage, 1974.

45. *The Diaries of Sophia Tolstoy,* trans. Cathy Porter, Random House, 1985.

46. Ibid. Discrepancy between the French and English translations. In the English text the date is given as April 29.

47. Colette, *La maison de Claudine. Claudine's House.*

48. Marcel Prévost, *Lettres à Françoise mariée.*

49. Janet, *Obsessions.*

50. Edith Wharton, *The Age of Innocence,* Random House, 1999.

51. *Diaries of Sophia Tolstoy,* 19 December 1863.

52. Mauriac, *Thérèse Desqueyroux.*

53. 'Prelude', in *The Short Stories of Katherine Mansfield,* Knopf, 1937.

54. *Diaries of Sophia Tolstoy.* Discrepancy between French and English translations. The date is given as January 17 in the English translation of *The Diaries.*

55. Ibid. In the English translation the date given is September 17.

56. Henrik Ibsen, *A Doll's House,* in *Four Major Plays,* trans. James McFarlane and Jens Arup, Oxford University Press, 1981.

57. Daniel Halévy, *Jules Michelet,* Hachette, 1928 and 1947.

58. Mabel Dodge Luhan, *Lorenzo in Taos,* Knopf, 1932.

59. Jouhandeau, *Nouvelles Chroniques maritales. The Bold Chronicle of a Strange Marriage.*

60. Leo Tolstoy, *War and Peace.*

61. Dorothy Parker, 'Too Bad!'.

62. Jouhandeau, *Nouvelles Chroniques maritales. The Bold Chronicle of a Strange Marriage.*

63. *Diaries of Sophia Tolstoy.* The date is given as November 13 1863 in the English translation.

64. Ibid. The date is given in the English text as October 12 1863.

65. Maurice Halbwachs, *Les causes du suicide. The Causes of Suicide*, trans. Harold Goldblatt, Free Press, 1978.

Chapter 6 The Mother

66. Colette, 'L'enfant', in *Playing a Losing Game*.
67. Helene Deutsch, *The Psychology of Women*.
68. Duchesse d'Abrantès, *Mémoires. Memoirs*, J & J Harper, 1832.
69. Colette, *L'étoile vesper. The Evening Star*, in *Recollections*, trans. David Le Vay, Collier Books, 1973.
70. Cecile Sauvage, *L'âme en bourgeon*.
71. Translated by Beverley Bie Brahic.
72. Isadora Duncan, *My Life*, Liveright Publishing Corporation, 1955.
73. Translated by Beverley Bie Brahic.
74. Colette, *L'étoile vesper. The Evening Star*.
75. *Diaries of Sophia Tolstoy*. Beauvoir attributes this quote to Sophia, but it is in fact Leo's.
76. Jules Renard, *Poil de carotte. Carrot Top*, trans. Ralph Manheim, Farrar, Straus & Giroux, 1975.
77. Simone de Tervagne, *La haine maternelle*.
78. Hervé Bazin, *Vipère au poing. Viper in the Fist*, trans. W. J. Strachan, Prentice Hall, 1951.
79. François Mauriac, *Génétrix. A Kiss for the Leper/Genitrix*, trans. Gerard Hopkins, Eyre & Spottiswoode, 1953.
80. Violette Leduc, *In the Prison of Her Skin*.
81. Stekel, *Conditions of Nervous Anxiety and Their Treatment*.

Chapter 7 Social Life

82. Marie Bashkirtseff, *Ecrits intimes*.
83. *The Diaries of Sophia Tolstoy*.
84. Dorothy Parker, 'The Lovely Leave'. Beauvoir mistakenly calls this short story 'The Lovely Eva'.
85. Virginia Woolf, *Mrs Dalloway*, Penguin Books, 1967.
86. Colette, *Mes apprentissages. My Apprenticeships & Music-Hall Sidelights*.
87. Colette, *Le képi. The Kepi*, trans. Antonia White, Secker & Warburg, 1984.
88. Stekel, *Frigidity in Woman*.
89. Montaigne, *Complete Essays*: 'On Some Verses of Virgil'.
90. Engels, *The Origin of the Family*.
91. Colette, *L'ingenue libertine. The Innocent Libertine*.
92. Janet, *Les obsessions et la psychasthénie*.

93. Joseph Kessel; the real title is *Belle de Jour*.
94. André Malraux, *La condition humaine*. *Man's Fate*, trans. Haakon M. Chevalier, The Modern Library, 1934.

Chapter 8 Prostitutes and Hetaeras

95. Montaigne, *Complete Essays*.
96. A. Marro, 'The Psychology of Puberty', *British Journal of Psychiatry* (1910).
97. A.J.B. Parent-Duchâtelet, 'De la prostitution dans la ville de Paris' ('Prostitution in the City of Paris'), Brussels: Société Encyclographique des Sciences Médicales, 1838.
98. Dr Léon Bizard, *Souvenirs d'un médecin . . . des prisons de Paris* (*Memoirs of a Doctor of Paris Prisons*), 1925.
99. Dr Louis Faivre, *Les jeunes prostituées vagabondes en prison*, Librairie Le François, 1931. Medical thesis.
100. In the French text of these passages there are grammar and spelling errors that we have not reproduced in English.
101. Pet name for a prostitute's pimp.
102. From internet: bookaddicts.wordpress.com/
103. Ibid.

Chapter 9 From Maturity to Old Age

104. Rom Landau, *Sex, Life and Faith*, Faber & Faber, 1946.

Chapter 10 Woman's Situation and Character

105. Jean-Paul Sartre, 'Les mains sales'. 'Dirty Hands', in *Three Plays*, trans. Lionel Abel, Knopf, 1949.
106. French proverb: 'What woman wants, God wants.'
107. André Gide, *Les journaux d'André Gide*. *The Journals of André Gide*, trans. Justin O'Brien, Penguin Modern Classics, 1967.
108. Halbwachs, *The Causes of Suicide*.
109. Mauriac, *Thérèse Desqueyroux*.

Vol. II: Part Three
Chapter 11 The Narcissist

1. Dalbiez, *La méthode psychanalytique et la doctrine freudienne. Psychoanalytical Method and the Doctrine of Freud*.
2. Mme de Noailles, *Le livre de ma vie*.
3. Dorothy Parker, 'Too Bad!'
4. Colette Audry, *La poussière*.

5. Balzac, *Le lys dans la vallée*. *The Lily in the Valley*.

6. 'Ten years' in the English translation of Stekel's *Frigidity in Woman*.

7. Mabel Dodge Luhan, *Lorenzo in Taos*, Simone de Beauvoir's italics.

Chapter 12 The Woman in Love

8. Nietzsche, *Le Gai Savoir*. *The Gay Science*.

9. Pierre Janet, *Les obsessions et la psychasthénie*.

10. Translated by Beverley Bie Brahic.

11. Colette, *La vagabonde*. *The Vagabond*.

12. Mary Webb, *The House in Dormer Forest*, Kessinger Publishing, 1945.

13. Isadora Duncan, *My Life*.

14. Comment inserted by Beauvoir and not part of the English translation.

15. Jean-Paul Sartre, *L'etre et le Néant*. *Being and Nothingness*.

16. Violette Leduc, *Je hais les dormeurs*.

17. Marcel Arland, *Terres étrangères*.

18. Nietzsche, *Le Gai Savoir*. *The Gay Science*.

19. Fanny Hurst, *Back Street*, Grosset, 1931.

20. Rosamond Lehmann, *Intempéries*. *The Weather in the Streets*, Virago Press, 1981.

21. The correct title of Lagache's work on jealousy is *La jalousie amoureuse* (*Jealousy in Love*).

22. Dominique Rolin, *Moi qui ne suis qu'amour*.

23. Georges Gusdorf, *La découverte de soi*. Simone de Beauvoir gives the title of his work as *La connaissance de soi*.

24. Nietzsche, *Le Gai Savoir*. *The Gay Science*.

Chapter 13 The Mystic

25. Gaston Ferdière, *L'erotomanie*. *Erotomania*.

Vol. II: Part Four
Chapter 14 The Independent Woman

1. *Le numéro 17*.

2. Colette, *Le blé en herbe*. *Green Wheat*.

3. Clara Malraux, *Portrait de Grisélidis*.

4. André Malraux, *La condition humaine*. *Man's Fate*.

5. 'Normalians' are students or graduates from the Ecole Normale Supérieure, prestigious school of higher education in France.

6. Colette, *La naissance du jour*. *Break of Day*, trans. Enid McLeod, Limited Editions Club, 1983.

7. Paulhan, *Les fleurs de Tarbes*.
8. *'Poussières'* in the French: Beauvoir does not specify the author, but this is probably a reference to Rosamond Lehmann's *Dusty Answer*.
9. Margaret Kennedy, *The Constant Nymph*.
10. Stendhal, *Souvenirs d'égotisme. Memoirs of an Egotist*, trans. David Ellis, Horizon Press, 1975.

Conclusion

1. Marcel Jouhandeau, *Chroniques maritales. Marcel and Elise, The Bold Chronicle of a Strange Marriage*.
2. Marx and Engels, *Collected Works*, Vol. VI.

Selected Sources

The works listed below are the published English translations that the translators consulted for Simone de Beauvoir's French quotes, as well as the English-language books and publications themselves, for example, when she paraphrases an author. But the works are also included here as 'selected sources'.

Abrantès, Laure Junot: *Memoires of the Duchess d'Abrantès (Madame Junot)*. J&J Harper 1882.

Aeschylus: *Eumenides*. Translated by Richard Lattimore. University of Chicago Press 1969.

Angela of Foligno: *Complete Works*, Paulist Press 1993.

Bachelard, Gaston: *Earth and Reveries of Repose*. Translated by Kenneth Haltman. Unpublished.

Bachelard, Gaston: *Earth and Reveries of Will*. Translated by Kenneth Haltman. Dallas Institute of Humanities and Culture 2002.

Bálint, Alice: *The Psychoanalysis of the Nursery*. Routledge and Kegan Paul 1953.

Balzac, Honoré de: *Letters of Two Brides*. Translated by R. S. Scott. Hard Press 2006.

Balzac, Honoré de: *The Lily in the Valley*. Translated by Lucienne Hill. Carroll & Graf 1997.

Balzac, Honoré de: *The Physiology of Marriage*. Translated by Sharon Marcus, Johns Hopkins University Press 1997.

Bashkirtseff, Marie: *I Am the Most Interesting Book of All: The Diary of Marie Bashkirtseff*. Translated by Phyllis Howard Kernberger and Katherine Kernberger. Chronicle Books 1997.

Bazin, Hervé: *Viper in the Fist*. Translated by W. J. Strachan. Prentice Hall 1951.

Bloch, Jean-Richard: *A Night in Kurdistan*. Translated by Stephen Haden Guest. Victor Gollancz 1930.

Bourdouxhe, Madeleine: *Marie*. Translated by Faith Evans. Bloomsbury 1997.

Breton, André: *Arcanum 17.* Translated by Zach Rogow. Green Integer 2004.

Breton, André: *Communicating Vessels.* Translated by Mary Ann Caws and Geoffrey Harris. Nebraska University Press 1990.

Breton, André: *Mad Love.* Translated by Mary Ann Caws. Bison Books 1988.

Breton, André: *Nadja.* Translated by Richard Howard. Grove Press 1994.

Breton, André: *Poems of André Breton: A Bilingual Anthology.* Translated by Mary Ann Caws, University of Texas Press 1982.

Colette: *Break of Day.* Translated by Enid McLeod. Limited Editions Club 1983.

Colette: *Claudine at School.* Translated by Antonia White. Farrar, Straus & Giroux 2001.

Colette: *Claudine's House.* Translated by Andrew Brown. Hesperus Press 2006.

Colette: *The Evening Star,* in *Recollections.* Translated by David Le Vay. Bobbs-Merrill 1973.

Colette: *Green Wheat.* Translated by Zach Rogow. Sarabande Books 2004.

Colette: *The Innocent Libertine.* Translated by Antonia White. Farrar, Straus & Giroux 1978.

Colette: *The Kepi.* Translated by Antonia White. Secker and Warburg 1984.

Colette: *My Apprenticeships & Music-Hall Sidelights.* Translated by Helen Beauclerk. Penguin 1967.

Colette: *The Pure and the Impure.* Translated by Herma Briffault. New York Review of Books 2000.

Colette: *Sido.* Translated by Una Vicenzo Troubridge and Enid McLeod. Farrar, Straus & Giroux 2002.

Colette: *The Tender Shoot.* Translated by Antonia White. Farrar Straus & Giroux 1975.

Colette: *The Vagabond.* Translated by Enid McLeod. Farrar, Straus & Giroux 1955.

Dalbiez, Roland: *Psychoanalytical Method and the Doctrine of Freud.* Longmans, Green & Co. 1941.

Deutsch, Helene: *The Psychology of Women.* Bantam Books 1973.

Diderot, Denis: 'On Women in Dialogues'. Translated by Francis Birrell. Routledge 1927.

Duncan, Isadora: *My Life.* Boni & Liveright 1955.

Ellis, Havelock: *Studies in the Psychology of Sex: Sexual Inversion.* The Minerva Group, Inc. 2001.

Engels, Friedrich: *The Origin of the Family, Private Property and the State.* Translated by Alick West and Dona Torr. Marxist-Leninist Library 1942.

Flaubert, Gustave: *Sentimental Education.* Translated by Robert Baldich. Penguin Books 1964.

Freud, Sigmund: *Moses and Monotheism*. Translated by Katherine Jones. Knopf 1939.

Gide, André: *The Coiners*. Translated by Dorothy Bussy. Cassell 1950.

Gide, André: *The Journals of André Gide*. Translated by Justin O'Brien. Penguin Modern Classics 1967.

Halbwachs, Maurice: *The Causes of Suicide*. Translated by Harold Goldblatt. Free Press 1978.

Halévy, Daniel: *Jules Michelet*. Hachette 1928 and 1947.

Hall, Radclyffe: *The Well of Loneliness*. Wordsworth Editions 2005.

Hegel, G. W. F.: *Phenomenology of Spirit*. Translated by A. V. Miller. Oxford University Press 1977.

Hegel, G. W. F.: *The Philosophy of Nature*. Translated by J. N. Findlay and A. V. Miller. Oxford University Press 1979.

Huart, Clément: *Ancient Persia and Iranian Civilization*. Knopf 1927.

Hughes, Richard: *High Wind in Jamaica*. Harper & Brothers 1929.

Hurst, Fanny: *Back Street*. Grosset 1931.

Ibsen, Henrik: *A Doll's House*, in *Eleven Plays of Henrik Ibsen*. Modern Library 1935.

Jouhandeau, Marcel: *Marcel and Elise, The Bold Chronicle of a Strange Marriage*. Translated by Martin Turnell. Pantheon Books 1953.

Jung, Carl: *The Development of Personality*. Translated by R. F. C. Hull. Bollingen Series, Princeton University Press 1970.

Jung, Carl: *Metamorphoses of the Libido and its Symbols*, in *Collected Works of C. G. Jung*. Translated by R. F. C. Hull. Princeton University Press 1967.

Kennedy, Margaret: *The Constant Nymph*. William Heinemann 1924.

Kierkegaard, Søren: *Stages on Life's Way*. Translated by H. V. and E. H. Hong. Princeton University Press 2009.

Krafft-Ebing, Richard von: *Psychopathia Sexualis*. Rebman Kessinger 1906.

Landau, Rom: *Sex, Life and Faith*. Faber and Faber 1946.

Lawrence, D. H.: *Fantasia of the Unconscious*. Dover Publications 2006.

Lawrence, D. H.: *Lady Chatterley's Lover*. Modern Library 2003.

Lawrence, D. H.: *Sons and Lovers*. Modern Library 1999.

Lawrence, D. H.: *The Plumed Serpent*. Vintage 1992.

Lehmann, Rosamond: *Dusty Answer*. Virago Press 2008.

Lehmann, Rosamond: *Invitation to the Waltz*. Virago 2006.

Lehmann, Rosamond: *The Weather in the Streets*. Virago 1981.

Levinas, Emmanuel: *Time and the Other*. Translated by Richard Cohen. Duquesne University Press 1987.

Lévi-Strauss, Claude: *The Elementary Structures of Kinship*. Translated by

James Harle Bell, Rodney Needham and John Richard von Sturmer. Beacon Press 1969.

Luhan, Mabel Dodge: *Lorenzo in Taos*. Knopf 1932.

Malinowski, Bronislaw: 'The Bachelors' House', from *The Sexual Life of Savages in North-Western Melanesia*. Liveright 1929.

Malraux, André: *Man's Fate*. Translated by Haakon M. Chevalier. The Modern Library 1934.

Mansfield, Katherine: 'Prelude', in *The Short Stories of Katherine Mansfield*. Knopf 1937.

Marx, Karl & Friedrich Engels: *Collected Works*, Vol. VI. From Internet site www.marxists.org/archive/marx/works/1844/manuscripts/comm.htm.

Mauriac, François: *A Kiss for the Leper/Genitrix*. Translated by Gerard Hopkins. Eyre and Spottiswoode 1950.

Mauriac, François: *Thérèse Desqueyroux*. Translated by Raymond MacKenzie. Rowman & Littlefield Publishers 2005.

McCullers, Carson: *The Member of the Wedding*. Penguin Classics 1962.

Merleau-Ponty, Maurice: *Phenomenology of Perception*. Translated by Colin Smith. Routledge 2005.

Michaux, Henri: 'Bridal Night', in *Selected Writings*. New Directions 1968.

Michelet, Jules: *The Mountain*. Translated by W. H. Davenport Adams. T. Nelson and Sons 1872.

Mill, John Stuart: 'The Subjection of Women' as reprinted in *Philosopy of Women* edited by Mary Briody Mahowald. Hackett 1994.

Montaigne, Michel de: *The Complete Essays of Montaigne*. Translated by Donald M. Frame. Stanford University Press 1965.

Montherlant, Henry de: *The Bachelors*. Translated by Terence Kilmartin. Greenwood 1977.

Montherlant, Henry de: *The Dream*. Translated by Terence Kilmartin. Macmillan 1963.

Montherlant, Henry de: *The Girls*. Translated by Terence Kilmartin. Harper & Row 1968.

Montherlant, Henry de: *The Master of Santiago*. Translated by Jonathan Griffin. Knopf 1951.

Montherlant, Henry de: *La Petite Infante de Castille*. French & European Publications 1973.

Montherlant, Henry de: *Pity For Women*. Knopf 1937.

Nietzsche, Friedrich: *The Gay Science*. Translated by Walter Kaufmann. Vintage 1974.

Nietzsche, Friedrich: *Thus Spoke Zarathustra*. Translated by R. J. Hollingdale. Penguin Classics 1961.

Parker, Dorothy: 'Too Bad!' and 'The Lovely Leave', in *The Portable Dorothy Parker*. Penguin Books 1944.

Rabelais, François: *The Complete Works*. Translated by Donald M. Frame. University of California Press 1991.

Rimbaud, Arthur: *Illuminations*. Translated by Helen Rootham. New Directions 1943.

Rimbaud, Arthur: *A Season in Hell*. Translated by Delmore Schwartz. New Directions 1939.

Rougement, Denis de: *The Devil's Share*. Translated by Haakon M. Chevalier. Pantheon Books 1944.

Sachs, Maurice: *Witches' Sabbath*. Translated by Richard Howard. Jonathan Cape 1965.

Sade, Marquis de: *Philosophy in the Boudoir*. Translated by Joachim Neugroschel. Penguin Classics 2006.

Sartre, Jean-Paul: *Anti-Semite and Jew*. Translated by George J. Becker. Schocken 1948.

Sartre, Jean-Paul: *Being and Nothingness*. Translated by Hazel Barnes. Citadel Press 2001.

Sartre, Jean-Paul: *Dirty Hands*, in *Three Plays*. Translated by Lionel Abel. Knopf 1949.

Scott, Geoffrey: *The Portrait of Zélide*. Turtle Point Press 1997.

Senghor, Leopold Sédar: *The Collected Poetry*. Translated by Melvin Dixon. University of Virginia Press 1998.

Stekel, Wilhelm: *Conditions of Nervous Anxiety and Their Treatment*. Liveright 1950.

Stekel, Wilhelm: *Frigidity in Woman*. Translated by James S. Van Teslaar. Liveright 1943.

Stendhal: *Memoirs of an Egotist*. Translated by David Ellis. Horizon Press 1975.

Stendhal: *The Red and the Black*. Translated by Roger Gard. Penguin Classics 2002.

Stendhal: *Three Italian Chronicles*. Translated by C. K. Scott-Moncrieff. New Directions 1991.

Tolstoy, Leo: *War and Peace*. Translated by Richard Pevear and Larissa Volokhonsky. Knopf 2008.

Tolstoy, Sophia: *The Diaries of Sophia Tolstoy*. Translated by Cathy Porter. Random House 1985.

Webb, Mary: *The House in Dormer Forest*. Jonathan Cape 1928.

Webb, Mary: *Precious Bane*. E.P. Dutton 1926.

Wharton, Edith: *The Age of Innocence*. Random House 1999.

Woolf, Virginia: *Mrs. Dalloway*. Penguin Books 1967.

Woolf, Virginia: *To the Lighthouse*, in *The Selected Works of Virginia Woolf*. Wordsworth Editions 2005.

Woolf, Virginia: *The Waves*. Hogarth Press 1931.

Zola, Emile: *Nana*. Unpublished translation by Constance Borde and Sheila Malovany-Chevallier.

Zola, Emile: *Pot-Bouille*. Everyman 1999.

Index

Contents

List of Contributors

Irene Conn *RGN, DN, PWT, Dip N, Cert Ed, DNT, BA, M Ed*, Lecturer in Nursing, University of Ulster, Jordanstown and Coleraine.

David Dickson *BA (Hons), Dip Ed, MA, PhD, AFBPsS, C Psychol*, Head of Social Skills Training Centre, School of Behavioural and Communication Sciences, University of Ulster, Jordanstown.

Pippa Gough *RGN, RM, HV, PGCEA, MSc*, Professional Officer, Health Visiting and Community Nursing, United Kingdom Central Council for Nursing, Midwifery and Health Visiting, London.

Aine Haughey *BA (Hons), SRN, Cert Oncological N, DN Cert, Cert Care of Dying Patient & Family, Ad Dip Ed, RNT, M Ed*, Lecturer, Nursing Group, School of Social and Health Sciences, University of Ulster, Jordanstown.

Eileen James *BA (Hons) Social Studies (Hull), MSc Health Administration (Hull), Ad Dip Ed (Ulster), SRN, OND, NDN*, Principal Lecturer in Community Studies, Canterbury Christ Church College, Canterbury.

Alan Kay *RNMH, Cert CPN, BA (Hons), RNT*, Lecturer in Nursing and Community Health, Glasgow Caledonian University, Glasgow.

Ann Long *BSc (Hons) Psychology, MSc Counselling, RGN, RMN, HV, Dip N (London), RNT, HVT*, Lecturer in Nursing, Senior Course Tutor in Mental Health Nursing, University of Ulster, Jordanstown.

Ann Lowis *M Ed, RGN, OHNC, Dip N (London), Teaching Cert*, Director of Nursing, Robert Gordon University, Aberdeen.

Carolyn Mason *BA, RGN, RHV, PhD, RNT*, Lecturer/Assistant Director of Nursing (Joint Appointment), The Queens University of Belfast/Eastern Health and Social Services Board, Belfast.

Lindsay Prior *BSc (Sociology), MA, PhD, BSc*, Senior Lecturer in Sociology, University of Ulster, Jordanstown.

Anna Sidey *RSCN, RGN, DN Cert*, Vice Chair of Paediatric Community Nurses Forum, RCN, Member of Editorial Board of Paediatric Nursing, Member of ENB Working Party for *'The Nursing of Children'*, Paediatric Community Nurse Specialist, Rockingham Forest NHS Trust, Kettering.

Tony Thompson *RMN, RNMH, DN (London), Cert Ed, B Ed (Hons), RNT, MA*, College Coordinator, Mid Trent College of Nursing and Midwifery, Queen's Medical Centre, Nottingham.

Foreword

We live in a climate of unprecedented social, political and cultural change. Nowhere is this change felt more keenly than in the NHS, which has had to radically rethink its total philosophy and accommodate the needs and demands of an ever more enlightened public. Changing disease patterns, major technological advances, demographic change and the need to provide health care in settings close to where people live and work rather than in institutions have all had their impact on health professionals. Nurses, especially community health care nurses, have not escaped unscathed. More than any other group, community health care nurses must be attuned to the social/ economic climate in which they practise and the societal changes and issues that affect their clients. They must adapt their practice to take account of up-to-date research findings as well as contribute to the body of new nursing and health care knowledge. Their practice must always be open to scrutiny and kept under constant review.

Accountability for the efficient and effective use of scarce resources, both human and financial, should be clear. Yet, good collaborative working across professional and organizational boundaries, minimizing duplication, is vital if patients and clients are to benefit fully from these improved practices.

If community health care nurses, whatever their specialism, are to work to their true potential alongside their patients and their clients within their respective communities or work places, they must acknowledge professional accountability for their practice, and receive appropriate ongoing professional development, education and opportunities to learn and work in teams with a range of professional colleagues. They will also need space to create good networks with statutory and voluntary bodies as well as excellent managerial and professional support and facilitation.

Community Health Care Nursing is an excellent and timely publication tackling all of the above. It straddles both the conceptual and practical aspects of the health care system. It leaves few stones unturned for new community health care practice and is an excellent textbook for those embarking on a career in the community health care nursing field. It is a useful source book for those wishing to have a detailed knowledge of the new world of primary and community care and for those wishing to glean information about discrete areas of specialist practice.

Ainna Fawcett-Henesy
Director – Nurse Practitioner Unit, NHS Executive
Formerly Head of Primary Care for the
NHS Executive London Implementation Group

Preface

During the past decade the future of community health care nursing has been established as the focus for investment for health gain for the population and its constituent neighbourhoods. Government investment in the design of a new infrastructure to support 'care in the community' initiatives has further strengthened the need for the nursing and health visiting professions to review the standard, kind and content of the education and practice base of community health care nursing. One further challenge has been the entry of pre-qualifying and post-qualifying nurse education into the higher education sector with its demand for further rigour in quality control and academic compliance. This text acknowledges the changing face of community health care nursing in the UK and firmly places its academic base within a scientific framework that is underpinned and influenced by contemporary changes in social and economic policy.

There is no doubt that the pace of change involved in designing and developing a new culture of community health care nursing has required a radical and sometimes traumatic revision of personal attitudes and customized care and managerial practices. In their place we are now witnessing the advent and creation of new structures, processes and service systems, many of which have been developed and implemented by nurses working in the many constituent parts of the family of 'community health care nursing'.

This book considers some of the main issues to be addressed in the design and introduction of the 'new' profession of community health care nursing. Its roots are firmly established in the evolutionary nature of professional development and recognize the innovative, adaptable and flexible nature of the practitioners themselves. Consequently, the book contains examples of these changes and traces their origins and potential contribution to the implementation of community care. Lessons have been learnt from experimentation and research design and from experiential learning, and in so doing there will be, inevitably, some overlap between individual contributions and the solutions they propose for the delivery of effective community nursing care.

It is suggested that there is no one solution or 'blue-print' for local service design for any client group. The nature of our communities is as varied as the sub-cultural influences that shape them. No standard model has been prescribed and wherever possible contributors have deliberately avoided the inclusion of specific solutions. However, the book presents many ideas, examples and suggestions for the introduction and implementation of sound infrastructures for community health nursing delivery which may be adapted to suit local conditions and requirements.

Within any attempt to describe the basis for comprehensive service design and implementation there will always be a temptation to capitalize on the experiences of others who have pioneered excellence in local services. This, in essence, is the business of community health care nursing. Contributors to this text have certainly been selected for their own knowledge, experience and excellence in curriculum and service design, but they also share their commitment for excellence in service delivery. Many who have realized the introduction of excellence in their localities will recognize common elements as they read this book that relate to their own experience, and this is of course the intention.

It is our contention that the realization of excellence in the design and delivery of community health care nursing services relies upon the principle that both service users and their nurses require (and deserve) mutual recognition as key stake holders in the development and implementation of future policy imperatives that aim to shape and influence the nature of our neighbourhood nursing services. Some may challenge the 'realism' of our suggestions and recommendations, but there is one statement that cannot be challenged – they are all feasible – and evidence exists to suggest that further investment in the community nursing workforce will result in effective health gain and maintenance for our population.

David Sines (Editor)

Part 1

The Context and Scientific Principles of Community Health Care Nursing

Chapter 1

Community Health Care Nursing

1.1 The philosophy and practice of service provision

In 1990 the government published the NHS and Community Care Act which presented the strategic framework for the provision of all health and social care services in the UK. The Act unites the principles through which care is delivered between Health and Social Service agencies and encourages statutory agencies to form positive partnerships with consumers, their representatives and with the voluntary and independent sectors to provide a positive choice in the provision of services. The Act was the result of three White Papers aimed at improving the way in which the NHS and local authorities provide services and support networks. The White Papers in question were *Working for Patients* (DOH, 1989b), *Caring for People* (DOH, 1989a) and *People First* (DHSS NI, 1990).

In each of these White Papers emphasis was placed on the importance of developing partnerships between consumers, their representatives and statutory agencies with the aim of promoting an open economy in care provision. As a result a new philosophy of care has emerged based on the principle that care should be shared with consumers and that, wherever possible, care should be provided as close to the person's home as possible.

The enactment of this policy has now reduced patient/client dependency on in-patient or long-stay residential care in favour of seeking the development of a range of options based on local need which will be flexible enough to meet the demands of service provision required by local people in their neighbourhoods.

The NHS, through its Management Executive, now requires all health authorities to secure significant improvements in the way in which services are delivered to the population, emphasizing the promotion of positive health and the promotion of high quality care in the community. In order to provide these services health authorities must demonstrate that they provide

3

a range of services to their clients and families as equal participants whenever decisions that will affect their life are involved. Such principles now underpin the NHS philosophy and form the basis of the government's *Patient's Charter* (DOH, 1992b).

One other issue – a major one for community practitioners – was the government's issue of a mandate for the creation of NHS Trusts and GP Fundholding practices. In the 1990 Act NHS Trusts and Fundholding practices were empowered to apply for independence within a centrally monitored NHS (monitored by the NHS Management Executive). The primary responsibility of these emergent agencies is to provide effective health care to a locally defined population and to ensure that they do so in accordance with user wishes. This role and function requires that each NHS Trust and Fundholding practice gathers intelligence data or information to advise on the actual health care needs of the local population. In partnership with central government targets for health care delivery (which reflect national trends on health care) will be set by NHS health authority and NHS Management Executive commissioners of health care, and these must be reflected in local contract setting exercises with local providers (DOH, 1989b *Working for Patients*; DOH 1994a).

The 'Purchaser' is also required to seek actively new or potential providers to deliver its health services and does so through engaging in local negotiation with statutory and nonstatutory providers (for example voluntary agencies and private providers). In order to ensure equity in purchasing and provision of services the health authorities compile detailed specifications of their requirements which are presented to all potential providers who are, in turn, invited to submit proposals or bids for each specific service contract. Successful providers must demonstrate both cost-effectiveness and efficiency in their delivery of care and must comply with each contract placed with them.

Purchasers and providers must also determine the roles they are going to play with local authority social service departments in providing their contributions to a range of comprehensive service developments for clients. The NHS and Community Care Act (1990) also demands that planning agreements should be reached between health and social service departments which clearly identify which services will be provided by each agency and which identify the processes to be adopted in assessing the needs of individuals in their care. (As a rule of thumb it has been suggested that client care should be assessed on the basis of whether the client's needs fit into one or both of two distinct categories: health and/or social care.)

Both health authorities and local authorities are required to set contracts with their own agencies and with other organizations which specify the way in which health and social care will be provided for their local population. Essentially, this will mean that health authorities will become the purchasers of care rather than directly providing care themselves. Similar changes are taking place within local authorities and although the statutory agencies may choose to place contracts within their own providers, they will be closely monitored, reviewed and inspected by both the local authority and the health authority in accordance with the expectations of service contracts.

The 1990 Act has also encouraged the NHS to adopt a community based focus for the provision of all its work within the next decade and the reliance on in-patient services will consequently change as resources are diverted to locally based services.

These changes will have particular relevance for inner-city areas throughout the UK where attention has been paid to reviewing the distribution of acute sector beds and related in-patient services. London has been the focus for this review following the publication of a government-sponsored report (The Tomlinson Report) into the capital's health service provision (DOH, 1993). The report recommended that there should be a systematic transfer of resources from the acute sector to primary and community health services, and that this would necessitate the closure of a significant number of in-patient beds in acute hospitals. Similar reviews followed throughout UK cities, precipitating a major refocusing of the context of health care delivery.

Thus it is expected that resources will be concentrated in local communities through the provision of skilled, peripatetic support from a range of professionals who will include doctors, community health care nurses, clinical psychologists, physiotherapists, speech therapists and occupational therapists (supported by an efficient, but reduced acute sector, in-patient service). These specialists will in turn complement the work of local primary health care teams which will continue to provide the first point of contact for clients and their families. Such teams are made up of general practitioners, district nurses, health visitors (or public health nurses) and general practice nurses who work in collaboration with social workers from the local social work office (additional members of the team also include community mental health and learning disability nurses, community children's nurses and school nurses).

1.2 The community context for care

Since the publication of the Alma Ata Declaration (WHO, 1978), the UK government has produced a number of action plans and targets (e.g. *The Health of the Nation*, DOH, 1992a) to ensure that the provision of primary health care becomes a priority in respect of the commissioning of health care services.

A range of initiatives surrounding public health, the reduced reliance on the in-patient sector and the development of community care have resulted in an acceleration of activity in primary health care practice. Specialist areas for community health care nursing practice have been identified as:

- General practice nursing;
- Occupational health care nursing;
- Community children's nursing;
- Community mental health nursing;
- Public health nursing (health visiting);
- School nursing;
- District nursing;
- Community mental handicap nursing.

Consequently the provision of nursing care in the community is dependent on acquisition and development of competence in different care environments. The philosophy of care operates in a client-controlled environment demanding responsive, proactive skills, such as health surveillance, risk analysis, communication skills and social action which are needed to meet the expectations and needs of consumers (UKCC, 1994).

The following factors have influenced the pattern of communality care in the UK.

(1) In the Declaration of Alma Ata, WHO (1978) stated that its aim of 'health for all' by the year 2000 should be realized through the introduction of a range of targets for the promotion of health (and the prevention of ill-health) for the population. The government has adopted this aim within resource constraints as part of a Eurostrategy and as a consequence students must be provided with opportunities throughout the course of their educational programme to acquire competence as 'knowledgeable specialist practitioners' in the community.

(2) The NHS and Community Care Act (1990) and its associated White Papers emphasize the importance of caring for people in the community which will be accompanied by reduced dependency on secondary health care service provision. The White Paper *People First*, (DHSS NI, 1990) noted that '... nurses working in the community are ideally placed to respond quickly to the needs of individuals and families'. Changes in child care legislation will also place new demands on nurses (The Children Act, 1989).

(3) The growth of consumerism and nonstatutory sector care in the mixed economy of service provision suggests a demand for more equal relationships with clients/patients and health care professionals. There is also a growing expectation that individuals will assume responsibility for their own health and lifestyles.

(4) Changes in social policy have also placed increasing continuing care responsibilities on informal carers in the home. Demographic changes

and economic demands are changing the nature of the family's caring role which may be influenced by the number of women entering the labour market. Similarly the projected increase in the number of elderly persons requiring community care has also demanded additional nursing resources.

(5) Rapid technological and pharmacological developments, nurse pre-scribing, the emergence of new patterns of disease and disability and the emergence of 'new' diseases, such as HIV infection, indicate a need for nurses who are flexible and able to respond to change.

(6) The development of primary health care teams has also provided an impetus for change. The importance of interprofessional teamwork and interagency co-operation is emphasized. Community nursing teams have a major contribution to make in the assessment of individual and community health needs and priorities for their local communities. Nurses must therefore be prepared to identify, communicate, influence and evaluate the development of community care plans to ensure the provision of access to a range of support services for clients and their families.

(7) The introduction of GP Fundholding within the UK will influence the purchase and provision of a range of differentiated community health care nursing services. Skill-mix reviews and increased attention on the provision of cost-effective packages of care will influence the deployment profile of community health care nurses in the future who must be able to compete within the context of an 'open economy' of care provision.

(8) International perspectives on the provision of community care will also demand the preparation of a more responsive and informed nurse in the future.

These influences have affected (and in many cases confirmed) the status of community health care nurses as 'lynchpins' within the context of a multi-disciplinary team of specialist health care practitioners. Their work has also been directed by the advent of consumerism which has placed new demands for new competences amongst the workforce, with an emphasis on therapeutic skills and care management (this concept will be discussed later in Chapter 6).

Specialist community health care nurses must be able to respond to the health needs, health gain requirements and expressed demands of their clients so as to:

■ stimulate a healthy lifestyle and self-care;
■ further educate families, informal carers, the community and other care workers;
■ solve or assist in the solution of both individual and community health problems;

- direct their own as well as community efforts for health promotion and for the prevention of diseases, unnecessary suffering, disability and death;
- work in, and with, interprofessional teams, and participate in the development and leadership of such teams;
- participate in the enhancement and delivery of primary health care in a multidisciplinary care context.

1.3 The changing focus of care in the community

In 1994 the four chief nursing officers for the UK published a report (DOH, 1994b) outlining the challenges confronting the nursing and midwifery professions by the year 2010. Commonly known as the Heathrow Report, it confirmed that technological, demographic and organizational changes will have a major influence on the pattern of health care delivery in the twenty first century.

Societal change moulds the institutions that are created to respond to the needs of the population. Demands change over time and in so doing socio-demographic factors drive the process of change which in turn requires the NHS to adapt its operational base. Examples of such changes relate to the needs of an increasingly ageing population, a reduction in the number of available informal carers, advances in scientific knowledge and technological innovation and a heightened awareness of ethical challenges (such as genetics, embryology and euthanasia). Changes in government policy and ideology also shape the health care agenda and the reduced reliance upon the long-stay hospital for mental health and learning disability care provide clear examples of the need for the refocusing of care in the community (DOH, 1994c).

The impact of change, pushed by a growing demand for flexible, high quality services provided within local communities, will inevitably remould the NHS of the future. Resources have already been shifted to the community (although at a pace that is all too often criticized as being grossly inadequate to meet client need) and commissioners and providers are now required to demonstrate that the care they purchase and deliver is effective and responsive to consumer need.

The Heathrow Report (DOH, 1994b) identifies a scenario for the year 2010 that is characterized by the development of highly focused community services that will respond to the needs of local practice populations. In this model much of the activity currently carried out by the district general hospitals could be transferred to local care units. Such units could undertake minor and invasive surgery, routine diagnostic testing, cases requiring observation and most outpatient activity. Centralised hospital facilities would continue to deal with severely ill people and major surgery. Care for older people and those with mental health needs or learning disabilities would also be undertaken (almost exclusively) in community care settings.

Movement towards this vision for the future may be measured against a series of benchmarks. By the year 2002:

- Health promotion targets on smoking, physical exercise and weight are met.
- For each local community there will be arrangements for pooling NHS and local authority funds to provide local access to:
  - minor surgery
  - a minor accident service
  - certain specified diagnostic services
  - therapy services
  - social work assistance.
- All mental illness and mental handicap hospitals that were open in 1985 will be closed.
- Everyone over 85 will have a key worker.
- Referrals from GPs to specialist medical services will be reduced by 20%.
- 15% of births will take place outside hospitals.
- 40% of outpatient consultations with specialist medical staff will occur in locations other than a district general hospital (DGH).
- 80% of surgical interventions will be by minimal access.
- 60% of surgery will be day case.
- Hospital acute beds in DGHs will be reduced by at least 40%.' (DOH, 1994b)

There is little doubt that these benchmarks provide the nursing profession with a range of major challenges that must be addressed if the balance of care is to shift according to government policy to the community. One specific question must relate to the future education and training that will be required to equip practitioners with the necessary skills, knowledge and value base to enable them to function effectively in the community. In reality, there is also likely to be a reallocation of tasks between nurses and others, including informal carers and other professionals. Nurses must therefore be prepared to develop and change, drawing upon the very best of their past experience and becoming increasingly reliant upon the production of research evidence to inform their future practice.

In March 1993 the DOH published a document entitled *New World, New Opportunities* (DOH, 1993b) which has paved the way for many of the principles outlined in the Heathrow Report (DOH, 1994b). The New World document placed primary health care nursing at the forefront of a 'health service revolution'. With increasing recognition of the importance of public health and health promotion, the authors produced the following cardinal principles:

'Primary health care is highly professional and intensely personal. People are entitled to expect:

- safe, effective, clinical practice;
- accessible and appropriate local services;
- access to 'named' professional practitioners, including 'named nurses';
- services that can overcome barriers of language, discrimination and deprivation;
- 24-hour cover;
- confidentiality at all times;
- continuity, with a minimum number of individuals involved;
- a range of treatment choices and options to meet their health needs;
- value for money;
- clarity of provision without confusion over who does what;
- the ability to be involved in decision making about their care and to be informed about the range of choices available to them;
- services that work well together and with other agencies.' (DOH, 1993b)

The general practice population was envisaged as the locus for care in both the Heathrow and New World reports. Both recognized the potential role that community health care nursing can undertake to fulfil the cardinal principles referred to above and both acknowledged the need to share care in partnership with clients, their families and other carers within the context of interprofessional teamwork.

The New World report identified a series of 'keys to progress' for policy makers, managers in purchasing and providing agencies, and health professionals, pointing out that, as key players in the NHS, all have an influence on the development of primary health care nursing.

The New World report states that the best way to meet the health needs of the local population is to focus primary health care services within the very heart of naturally occurring communities and neighbourhoods. In so doing (using the general practice population as the focus and locus for care) opportunities for the further improvement of multidisciplinary teamwork and improved communication systems with clients (and others) would be provided.

The general practice setting provides an excellent focus for the collection of data relating to local health care needs and allows for a full picture of a locality's health to be profiled and developed.

1.4 The scope of community health care nursing education and practice

Current government policy provides considerable opportunities for the development of a free market within which nurses (often in partnership with social workers and other support staff) will be able to provide services which are responsive to clients' identified needs. As agency boundaries break down between the hospital and the community (and professional skills transcend previously defended frontiers), service users will have freer access to skills of nurses. In the future, access to nursing skills will be negotiated through care management or contractual processes; this should make nursing skills more easily accessible to the general practice population. Nurses' understanding (often acquired from many years of experience and proven competence in the delivery of care to their clients) has placed them in an ideal position in the newly created open health care market to respond more flexibly to locally identified health related needs.

As the scope of primary health care widens (as evidenced in government reports (DOH, 1994b)), opportunities for appropriately skilled and experienced community health care nurses will come to be recognized by GPs and by other health and social care professionals. Nurses will need to respond to the challenge of articulating their skills and marketing their contribution effectively to both their clients/patients and to commissioners of health care services.

Effective care delivery requires that nurses co-ordinate and plan their care effectively with their clients and with other professionals. Their managers also need to understand the contribution that community health care nurses can make to their agenda:

'This calls for partnership between health care professionals themselves and between them and health service managers, all based on interprofessional respect. It calls for partnership with other statutory and voluntary agencies. And it calls for partnership with the people they all serve, based on open, honest relationships with them – relationships in which the people, and not only the professionals, are active partners in the pursuit of personal and family health and in action for the health of the community.' (DOH, 1993b)

New practice developments must emerge to fulfil patient and provider agency expectations as increasingly complex care packages are transferred from the hospital sector to the primary health care team. In order to ensure that nurses provide effective care to their clients nurses must ensure that they are effectively supervised in all areas of their practice and 'keep in touch' with the aims and objectives of their clients and senior managers. There are many ways of achieving this objective and perhaps the most successful has been the provision of clinical supervision and positive feedback from line managers. Clinical supervision has been introduced in various forms by the UKCC for all its nurses with the aim of providing staff with a framework within which to receive positive feedback on their performance and to share their own perceptions of how effective they consider their contribution to client care to be (Kohner, 1994).

The main professional challenges confronting community health care nurses may be summarized as the need to:

- maintain and develop specialist competence;
- expand knowledge and skills and act upon research evidence;
- recognize and accept personal accountability for nursing actions;
- pursue continuing education;
- market their skills to an increasingly diverse range of health care commissioners;
- engage in effective clinical supervision;
- constantly evaluate their performance.

Every nurse has a personal responsibility to maintain knowledge of the competence needed to practise in their speciality (UKCC, 1992a, *The Code of Professional Conduct*). In so doing nurses must abide by the tenets included in the *Scope of Professional Practice* (UKCC, 1992b) and must adhere to the UKCC's principles for adjusting their scope of clinical practice.

The UKCC (1994) affirms that 'nurses, midwives and health visitors practise in an environment which is subject to constant change – in relation to the organizations of services, and boundaries and delivery of care and technological advances in treatment and care'. In March 1994 the UKCC published the profession's response to this challenge of change and presented the nursing professions with a new agenda for education and practice development.

The publication of the *Post Registration Education and Practice* (PREP) framework (UKCC, 1994) described standards for all practitioners engaged in care delivery with the aim of enhancing their professional accountability, skills, knowledge and competence for practice.

New educational standards were published in this document for community health care nursing which focused upon the emergence of a new 'unified discipline'. Core skills were prescribed for all nurses and health visitors practising in the community as well as specialist skills required for discrete application to clients of a particular age or nature. Public health nursing (health visiting) and occupational health nursing were further identified as specialist areas for preparation for community health care nursing practice.

The UKCC recognized that the unified discipline of community health care nursing draws on the strengths of current practice in order to meet a diversity of health care needs within noninstitutional settings. The four principles adopted for the community focus within PREP were:

(1) The need to build upon the contributions of current community nursing skill, whilst providing a vision for the future of community nursing.
(2) The provision of a logical and cost-effective approach to education.
(3) Removal of unnecessary barriers to practice and overlaps in preparation

to enable nursing to continue to adapt and make an effective contribution to the care and health of communities.

(4) Recognition of the need to prepare practitioners for work in the community following the completion of Project 2000 courses.

The UKCC (1994) report establishes community health nursing at specialist practice level and all new courses presented for validation after September 1995 will have their programmes accredited at first degree level. Full- and part-time modes of study may be pursued and flexible learning will be encouraged within the new programmes.

The common core element of the course will consist of no fewer than two-thirds of the total programme and will demand the acquisition of clinical nursing practice, care and programme management, clinical practice leadership and clinical practice development.

Clinical nursing practice

This part of the programme aims to offer a range of opportunities to specialist nursing practitioners to enhance their knowledge and skills to meet the specialist clinical needs of their clients. The acquisition of competence to undertake the responsibilities required for the prescribing of medicines is also included (RCN, 1994).

Care and programme management

This component relates to the individual client, the family and the community/environment of care. Co-ordination of care between community and hospital settings forms a core focus. Health promotion, disease prevention, risk taking analysis and diagnosis also feature as key areas for competence development.

Clinical practice leadership

Community health care nurses will be expected to lead and deliver services to consumers sensitively in response to their actual needs and to support and supervise nurses in professional practice. Other skills include teaching, student supervision, assessment and resource management. These competences form the nucleus of this section of the curriculum.

Clinical practice development

This part of the programme is designed to prepare community health care nurses to set, monitor and evaluate care standards and the effectiveness of their nursing actions. Practitioners will be expected to acquire in-depth knowledge of clinical practice developments in their own specialist and related fields. New innovative methods of care delivery will also be encouraged and active participation in research projects will be an expected learning outcome (see Appendix 1.1).

All new courses will have a 50% supervised practice component. Eight specialist groups for discrete practice have been approved:

- GP nursing;
- occupational health care nursing;
- community children's nursing;
- community mental health nursing;
- public health nursing (health visiting);
- school nursing;
- district nursing;
- community mental handicap nursing.

The framework for professional education and practice in the community complements the policy agenda outlined earlier in Chapter 1.

In addition, as for all nurses, community health care nurses will be expected to engage in a systematic audit and appraisal of their performance. To assist them in this process information technology will also provide practitioners with a range of tools with which to plan and evaluate care delivery. Such systems will assist staff in identifying service deficiencies and making bids for additional resources (both manpower and physical) as individual care management contracts are placed with each agency and make demands for staff skills and services.

Computerized care planning systems are in the process of being introduced in hospital- and community-based services and by 1997 a new computerized thesaurus of nursing terms will be implemented (Casey, 1993) within the UK to assist in this process. Clearly, then, community health care nurses will become increasingly involved in the evaluation and management of local resources aimed at the provision of a high quality service which provides choice and value for money for consumers and for their employers.

The provision of information to all service users and their carers will encourage active participation and is a requirement of *The Patient's Charter* (DOH, 1992b). This may be seen as the first step in a process that aims to develop a partnership between users and service providers with the aim of monitoring the effectiveness and quality of service. This requires that responsibility for services is shared with service users and that arrangements for service monitoring and evaluation are jointly negotiated.

Above all services must be open to constructive criticism and an independent inspection should provide clear statements of intent against which the quality of their service can be evaluated.

The information provided may be in different forms:

(1) activity data relating to the amount of service provided;
(2) evidence of the effectiveness of service delivery (measured, for example, by consumer feedback, audit reports and practitioner comments);
(3) resource management information or data;
(4) statements relating to service deficiencies;
(5) public audit reports provided by community health councils;
(6) published surveys of service performance;
(7) reports from local purchaser visits to provider sites;
(8) annual reports relating to contract compliance;
(9) results of internal inspections undertaken by provider agencies.

Health authorities, and their provider agencies, are also subjected to formal audit procedures implemented by the government Audit Commission. This independent body provides objective information relating to an organization's performance and measures service efficiency and effectiveness. Specific attention is also provided in respect of the extent to which each agency provides 'value for money' to its customers.

While all providers are required to inspect the quality of their own services, the NHS and Community Care Act (1990) also makes provision for the independent inspection of residential care homes and nursing homes. Responsibility for these functions is delegated to the Monitoring and Inspection Units of Local Authorities in England, Scotland and Wales (and to the Health and Personal Social Service Boards in Northern Ireland). Announced and unannounced visits are made by inspectors to all registered care and nursing homes and a thorough audit of service quality is undertaken. The views of service users are reflected in the resultant reports and managers/proprietors are required to act upon the published findings of these inspection visits.

Finally, in this section, the importance of public health is emphasized. Public health can be defined as 'the science and art of preventing disease, prolonging life and promoting health through organized efforts of society' (DOH, 1994d).

Protecting, promoting and improving public health is a government responsibility. Community health care nurses have a key role to play in this process by:

■ monitoring and profiling the health of their community/practice area;
■ ensuring that public health issues are identified and reported to managers and commissioners;
■ monitoring the health outcomes of their interventions;
■ improving the effectiveness of their activities;

- developing local health strategies and building healthy alliances necessary to implement these;
- developing and maintaining partnerships with clients, informal carers, other community members, and other professionals;
- collaborating with local authorities and other agencies to monitor and control health-related issues considered to be hazardous to the well-being of the community;
- informing the public about public health issues; engaging in health promotion programmes;
- ensuring that community members have access to appropriate public health advice.

1.5 International influences on the health care agenda

The organization of health care delivery and nursing activity in the UK is also influenced by a number of international agreements and agendas that are negotiated within the World Health Organization and within the European Community.

For example, the Public Health chapter of the EC Treaty of the EU (The Maastricht Treaty) requires all European countries to contribute to the promotion of health awareness and health protection by encouraging the design and implementation of local health initiatives and community health programmes. Such activities are directed towards action that prevents the incidence of major diseases, including drug dependence, by promoting research into their causes and means of transmission, as well as health information and education.

Within the EC epidemiological investigations are also conducted to assess the 'State of the Community's Health' and specific health promotion targets have been negotiated and implemented for all member States for achievement by the year 2000.

European influences also regulate the movement of nurses between member States, and systems and directives have been agreed to enable European countries to ascribe mutual recognition to their prequalifying systems of nurse education. These systems have been designed to facilitate mutual harmonization and recognition between countries in the EC and provide a shared framework for the preparation of nurse specialists throughout the region.

Within the wider context, the World Health Organization also sets targets for health gain and health promotion. For example, in 1987 (WHO, 1987), targets were published with the aim of improving the quality of health care delivery and surveillance for all world citizens. These targets have assisted in shaping the health care agenda in the UK and have facilitated the introduction of common standards for primary health services throughout the world. Other policy matters relate to the design of global health and nursing strategies based on the following principles:

- *Equity* thus reducing the existence of inequalities between countries and within countries.
- *Health promotion* providing for the development of personal self-reliance and the acquisition of a positive sense of health.
- *Participation* requiring the active participation of world citizens in informing themselves (and others) about health matters.
- *Multi-sectoral co-operation* promoting international agreements on health targets, policies and strategies.
- *Primary health care* focusing attention on the importance of primary care delivery as the health care system closest to where clients live and work.
- *International co-operation* recognizing that health problems cross international frontiers, e.g. pollution.

The Standing Committee of Nurses of the EU reaffirmed their support for the promotion of an active role for community health care nursing in public health following the publication of the Maastricht Treaty (Standing Committee of Nurses of the EU, 1994). In that document the Committee stated that:

'Nurses are one of the most appropriate groups to speak with authority in the field of public health. Many nurses work in communities and with families, often with people who are well. This gives nurses unique insight into how social and environmental factors influence the health and well-being of people in society and enables them to identify, at a very early stage, health care issues that could eventfully be of significance to the European Union.'

1.6 Conclusion

This chapter has considered the rapidly changing context within which the unified discipline of community health care nursing operates. It has outlined the challenges that face health care providers and commissioners and has demonstrated the nursing profession's commitment to furthering the role and function of the community health care nurse within the public health agenda.

The move to the community will challenge traditional boundaries and working practices for all staff and previous allegiance to undisciplinary patterns of working will require redefinition as new opportunities develop within a new mixed economy of care provision.

Such developments offer exciting opportunities for nurses and their clients/patients and provide the basis for infinite experiment in the design and implementation of new patterns of care delivery.

Therefore, the context within which health care is delivered in the UK influences the strategic and operational objectives that determine its standards and applications. The ideology or philosophy adopted by the State determines the nature of our health and social care systems and directs the structures and processes that we employ to meet the needs of our citizens.

During the past ten years the UK has witnessed a re-examination of personal and public values, thus reinforcing the need for clients to assume personal responsibility for their own social and health care needs. The reduction in dependency upon in-patient beds in our hospitals has assisted in the transfer of care to the community and to our naturally occurring neighbourhood support systems. Care in the community will become an increasing feature of our health care philosophy and, in partnership with a rationalized (and smaller) acute sector, will provide the context for our health care system for the foreseeable future.

The emergence of NHS Trusts and GP Fundholders further reinforces the government's commitment to introducing new competitive measures into the public sector, whilst ensuring that central control over expenditure is strengthened through the NHS Management Executive in each of the four UK countries.

The importance of leadership in community health care nursing must be acknowledged and responsive systems put in place to facilitate the emergence of innovative practice in local practice settings. Nurses must also continue to advocate for their clients, families and communities and engage in raising health-related issues for inclusion in local and government policy agendas. Above all they must demonstrate confidence and competence to assess risks and to practise safely in accordance with their professional code of practice.

As professionals, community health care nurses also have a primary responsibility to aim to remove any barriers that militate against ease of access for the population to health care services. Similarly they should initiate and engage in community-focused action programmes to tackle discrimination (in accordance with government policy (DSS, 1994)).

This chapter has also noted the influences that health care economics and international policy initiatives have had on the current health care agenda.

The chief nursing officers in the Heathrow Report (DOH, 1994b) examined the challenges that face the nursing profession in the years ahead. They identified the need for a strategy to co-ordinate the many practice, leadership, managerial, educational and ethical issues that will inevitably shape the nursing agenda in the years to come. The following quotation from their report provides a pertinent conclusion to this chapter:

'The changes offer great opportunities – which must be carefully weighed. The results should be a strategy that embodies a concept for the future, is reflected in training and development at all levels, and produces caring, positive nurses who can face a turbulent and uncertain future with confidence in themselves and their values.'

This book has been designed to examine many of the key issues raised in this introductory chapter.

1.7 References

Casey, A. (1993) The clinical thesaurus: nursing terms project. *IMG News*, **16**(3), 1–3.

The Children Act (1989). HMSO, London.

DHSS NI (1990) *People First: Community Care in Northern Ireland*. HMSO, Belfast.

DOH (1989a) *Caring for people – community care in the next decade and beyond*. Cm 849. HMSO, London.

DOH (1989b) *Working for Patients*. Cm 555. HMSO, London.

DOH (1992a) *The Health of the Nation*. HMSO, London.

DOH (1992b) *The Patient's Charter*. HMSO, London.

DOH (1993a) *Making London Better*. (Chair: Sir Bernard Tomlinson.) HMSO, London.

DOH (1993b) *New World, New Opportunities – Nursing in Primary Health Care*. NHS Management Executive, London.

DOH (1994a) *Managing the New NHS: Functions and Responsibilities in the New NHS*. NHS Management Executive, London.

DOH (1994b) *The Challenges for Nursing and Midwifery in the 21st Century – The Heathrow Report*. HMSO, London.

DOH (1994c) *Working in Partnership – A Collaborative Approach to Care – Report of the Mental Health Nursing Review Team*. HMSO, London.

DOH (1994d) *Public Health in England – Roles and Responsibilities of the Department of Health and the NHS*. NHS Management Executive, London.

DSS (1989) *General Practice in the Health and Personal Social Services – The 1990 Contract*. HMSO, Belfast.

DSS (1994) *A Consultation on Government Measures to Tackle Discrimination Against Disabled People – A Report published by The Disability Unit on Behalf of the Minister for Disabled People*. The Disability Unit, London.

European Parliament Committee on the Environment, Public Health and Consumer Protection (1993) *Draft Report on Public Health Policy After Maastricht*. PE 205.804 Or. EN. European Parliament, Brussels.

Kohner, N. (1994) *Clinical Supervision in Practice*. King's Fund Centre, London.

NHS and Community Care Act (1990). HMSO, London.

RCN (1994) *Nurse Prescribing – RCN Community Health Briefing*. RCN, London.

Standing Committee of Nurses of the EU (1994) *Public Health After Maastricht*. European Parliament, Brussels.

WHO (1978) *Internal Conference on Primary Health Care*. Alma Ata, Geneva.

WHO (1987) *Health for all*. Declaration of WHO Conference on Primary Health Care. Alma Ata. WHO, Geneva.

UKCC (1992a) *The Code of Professional Conduct*. UKCC, London.

UKCC (1992b) *The Scope of Professional Practice*. UKCC, London.

UKCC (1994) *The Future of Professional Practice – the Council's Standards for Education and Practice Following Registration*. UKCC, London.

Appendix 1.1
Standards for Specialist Community Nursing Education and Practice

Reproduced from the UKCC (1994) document *The Future of Professional Practice – The Council's Standards for Education and Practice Following Registration*, pp. 11–15 inc.

Common core learning outcomes

20　The nurse should achieve the following common core outcomes derived as appropriate from a specific area of specialist nursing practice:

Clinical nursing practice

20.1　assess the health and health-related needs of patients, clients, their families and other carers and identify and initiate appropriate steps for effective care for individuals, groups and communities;

20.2　plan, provide and evaluate skilled nursing care in differing environments with varied resources. Specialist community nurses must be able to adapt to working in people's homes and also small institutions, health centres, surgeries, schools and places of work;

20.3　support informal carers in a partnership for the giving of care. The majority of care in the community is given by informal carers. They need guidance, support and resources to carry out tasks so that there is continuity of care for the patient;

20.4　assess and manage care needs in a range of settings. These are complex activities which call for informed judgement to distinguish between health and social needs and the distinction is often a fine, but critical, one;

20.5　provide counselling and psychological support for individuals and their carers;

20.6 facilitate learning in relation to identified health needs for patients, clients and their carers;

20.7 prescribe from a nursing formulary, where the legislation permits;

20.8 act independently within a multi-disciplinary multi-agency context;

20.9 support and empower patients, clients and their carers to influence and use available services, information and skills to the full and to participate in decisions concerning their care;

Care and programme management

20.10 advise on the range of services available to assist with care. The services may be at local, regional and national levels. Knowledge of these services will need to be kept up-to-date and advice given to people on how to access and use them;

20.11 recognise ethical and legal issues which have implications for nursing practice and take appropriate action;

20.12 identify the social, political and economic factors which influence patient/client care and impact on health;

20.13 stimulate an awareness of health and care needs at both an individual and structural level. Activities will include work with individuals, families, groups and communities and will relate to those who are well, ill, dying, handicapped or disabled. Those who are able should be assisted to recognise their own health needs in order to decide on action appropriate to their own lifestyle. Those who are not able will require skilled and sensitive help;

20.14 identify and select from a range of health and social agencies, those which will assist and improve the care of individuals, groups and communities;

20.15 search out and identify evolving health care needs and situations hazardous to health and take appropriate action. This is a continuous activity and involves being pro-active, it must not be dependent on waiting for people to request care;

20.16 initiate and contribute to strategies designed to promote and improve health and prevent disease in individuals, groups and communities;

20.17 empower people to take appropriate action to influence health policies. Individuals, families and groups must have a say in how they live their lies and must know about the services they need to help them to do so;

20.18 provide accurate and rigorously collated health data to employing authorities and purchasers through health profiles in order to inform health policies and the provision of health care;

Clinical practice leadership

20.19 act as a source of expert advice in clinical nursing practice to the primary health care team and others;

20.20 lead and clinically direct the professional team to ensure the implementation and monitoring of quality assured standards of care by effective and efficient management of finite resources;

20.21 identify individual potential in registered nurses and specialist practitioners, through effective appraisal systems. As a clinical expert advise on educational opportunities that will facilitate the development and support of their specialist knowledge and skills to ensure they develop their clinical practice;

20.22 ensure effective learning experiences and opportunity to achieve learning outcomes for students through preceptorship, mentorship, counselling, clinical supervision and provision of an educational environment;

Clinical practice development

20.23 initiate and lead practice developments to enhance the nursing contribution and quality of care;

20.24 identify, apply and disseminate research findings relating to specialist nursing practice;

20.25 undertake forms of audit review and appropriate quality assurance activities;

20.26 create an environment in which clinical practice development is fostered, evaluated and disseminated and

20.27 explore and implement strategies for staff appraisal, quality assurance and quality audit. Determine criteria against which they should be judged, how success might be measured and who should measure success.

Content

21 The content of the programme of education should be applied to an area of specialist practice as appropriate:

21.1 health promotion, education and health need identification;

21.2 biological, behavioural, sociological and environmental studies;

21.3 development of the individual;

21.4 nature and causation of disease and/or conditions and their physical, emotional and social consequences;

21.5 advanced pharmacology studies and nurse prescribing from a nursing formulary, where the legislation permits;

21.6 diagnostic, therapeutic, resuscitative and technological procedures and techniques;

21.7 ethics of professional practice and relevant legislation;
21.8 care and case management;
21.9 problem solving and decision making;
21.10 intervention techniques for abuse and violence;
21.11 negotiation and person-effectiveness skills;
21.12 counselling, supportive, communicative and related therapeutic techniques;
21.13 quality assurance – evaluation of standards and outcomes of nursing, health and care interventions;
21.14 leadership, management and resource management skills;
21.15 health economics and policy;
21.16 community development skills;
21.17 research approaches, methodology and techniques and application to practice;
21.18 appreciation of information technology and its application to practice;
21.19 approaches to education and teaching skills and
21.20 clinical supervision of practice, peer review and peer assessment techniques.

Chapter 2

Social Policy

From the first acknowledgement of the need for central direction for health and welfare in 1848 to the establishment of the NHS in 1946, the words *change*, *choice* and *conflict* probably describe this period best.

According to Titmuss (1963) 'Welfare can serve different masters, a multitude of sins can be committed in its appealing name'. Is he right? An examination of the aims of the Elizabethan Poor Law (1602), the era of Social Imperialism (1900–15) and finally, legislation for a new NHS (1944–46) are just three responses that would prove Titmuss to have been more than accurate.

Between 1906 and 1948 there were periods of unrest, abroad and at home, that pushed the frontiers of social policy forwards. Great Britain survived two world wars, the great depression, the general strike and various changes of government. Each of these left a legacy, good and bad, that had to be lived with later. The use of social policy in these changes has been seen by some as a method of gaining ascendency for the prevailing government's ideologies and by others as a means of social control.

2.1 Defining social policy

Social policy is the end result of defining social problems. In very simplistic terms a deficit is recognized, a solution postulated and a response developed. Prevailing ideology has always dictated the policy response. For example, following the defeat of the Empire at the hands of the South African Boers (1899) central government was concerned about maintaining Great Britain's economic and political superiority overseas. This imperialistic stance was combined with a recognition that in order to secure an effective presence overseas Great Britain required a sufficiently healthy base upon which to draw. The recommendations of the Report of the Interdepartmental Committee on Physical Deterioration (MOH, 1902) highlighted the fact that

24

other sections of the population – children in particular – also required attention. The question for social policy analysts is twofold.

(1) Was the philosophy behind the recognition of the need for social improvements based on a desire to improve the condition of recruits to the army in order to maintain overseas supremacy? Or
(2) Was there a desire and a concerted effort to improve the welfare of the population generally and in particular, the future citizens?

In effect, both were desired. Without a healthy base there was little chance of Britain's maintaining success as a definitive world power – in military terms at least. To achieve this some efforts had to be made to improve the health and stability of the population that would provide that base. This confluence of ideals gave rise to a period of 'welfare' which has been given the label Social Imperialism.

A similar question could be asked of the changes brought about by two world wars, both of which had significant effects on the social, political and economic environments that ensued. The social consequences of the 1914–18 conflict were by and large ignored in the period of reconstruction that followed. The Second World War (1939–45) is seen by some historians to have been almost cataclysmic in its effects on the social structure of society (Saville & Briggs, 1971; Bruce, 1968; Donnison, 1975).

The use of the term 'social' does not, however, invest those responses with an inherently beneficial quality and perhaps most importantly it cannot be seen as 'value free'. Social policy is a ubiquitous yet imprecise term covering everything from education to crime and penal policy to housing to health and welfare. The most that can be said is that the end result of social policy is underpinned by the prevailing ideological beliefs and values of central government who achieve that position by the will (i.e. the vote) of the people. As Titmuss (1983) puts it:

> 'Social policy is basically about *choices* between conflicting political objectives and goals and how they are formulated; what constitutes the good society or that part of a good society which culturally distinguishes between the needs and aspirations of social man in contradiction to the needs and aspirations of economic man.'

Those choices are made by central government on behalf of society balancing levels of social provision with their economic and political ideology.

2.2 Social values and beliefs

George and Wilding (1976) have attempted to define social policy according to the philosophical basis from which it springs. They refrain from attaching party labels to the ideological divisions which they describe – divisions that explain the values and beliefs which give rise to policy styles and responses.

The social values that people hold affect how they feel about political ideals. At one end of the spectrum those who hold choice as important must also value freedom and liberty – the freedom to choose one course of action over another without attempts by others to curtail that freedom. Total non-conformity is not an option but if there is no outside interference people will respond to their fullest potential, participate in social processes and adjust their behaviour to meet agreed conventions. These beliefs sit well with those who have faith in market forces and see substantial intervention by government as socially disruptive and having the potential to waste resources.

At the other end of the spectrum are those who feel that there can be no freedom without recognizing that man is a social being who is influenced by fellow human beings. It follows from this ideal of fraternity that each should contribute according to individual capabilities and be rewarded by society according to individual needs. This Marxian dialectic sees government playing a strong role in the social and economic aspects of society. The role of social policy is important in reducing tension between competing groups, promoting social cohesion and ensuring stability within the social system.

Between these two extremes are those who espouse the centralist values of the Marxists tempered with an intellectual pragmatism. In their terms for society to function efficiently and fairly some allowance must be made for social regulation and control but these decisions should be made according to the merits of the case for intervention. Social policy should be concerned with maintaining a framework that allows individuals to achieve their fullest potential but be supported if their efforts do not produce the optimum condition.

The temptation to see those divisions as mutually exclusive encourages a compartmentalism that denies the development of modern social policy. The current ideology has been termed the Age of Consensus, i.e. a merging of the ideologies of both ends of the spectrum giving rise to a belief in the middle ground.

Within the UK social policy is aimed at meeting the needs of society as a whole; policies are intended to take a broad brush approach with safety net provision for the more vulnerable. This universality of provision, however, has to be achieved within specific economic parameters which, in theory, are dictated by the wealth-producing capabilities of the country. This universality also suggests that each member of society has contributed according to his or her own potential and therefore should receive the fruits of their labour according to their needs.

2.3 Pluralism, social problems and society

Within the pluralist society the State is seen as impartial, providing the structures to facilitate social legislation without dictating individual social values. Pluralist societies accept more than one ultimate principle, i.e. others are free to express their views though the legitimacy of those views is not always recognized. In this sort of environment social problems can be roughly divided into deviance and social disorganization.

Deviance can be nonconformist behaviour which can be dealt with to a degree by accommodating this as a measure of freedom or it can be seen as aberrant behaviour which requires a realignment to the 'norm'. Social disorganization indicates a breakdown in the social system which interferes with the normal socialization processes causing an imbalance of competing demands and ultimately anarchy.

Using these two categorizations it is possible to assess the cause of some of the problems. For example, in health care better housing facilities are correlated with improved levels of health and well-being (DOH, 1980; Whitehead, 1990). These inequalities can be the result of social disorganization where the stronger demands result in better environmental surroundings. On the other hand, poor lifestyles, ignoring medical advice, etc., are characteristics relating to individual behaviour and can be seen as deviant behaviour.

The response to each approach or classification of problems will be different: disorganization requires active resource allocation or re-allocation whereas deviance often relies on victim blaming and allows for passive or negative responses. In both of these categorizations there are social costs, i.e. no policy can be totally equitable, it must inevitably be utilitarian in its approach – the greatest good for the greatest number.

Social costs are also related to social change and the values and beliefs that mould responses to that change. Modern technology has improved production systems but it has also brought smoke and chemical pollution; mobility has improved dramatically as the motor industry has improved, but it has also increased road traffic and brought about an increased need for bigger and better motorways. New therapeutic regimes and medical advances have improved life expectancy at all ages but there is the possibility that they also create a dependency on the state that requires a social policy response. Policy must be redefined into operational responses which means defining such concepts as need, education, poverty, etc. None of these areas is a totally twentieth century phenomenon; all have been met before and depending on the prevailing beliefs, values and social system a response has been made.

The UK as a pluralist society has experienced a continuum of values and beliefs which in turn has given society a varying climate of provision in health and welfare, education, penal policy, housing and so on. Importantly, these provisions have had to be financed from variety of sources and it is this economic underbelly that has often dictated the overt social policy response (Fig. 2.1).

These provisions have focused mainly on the 'formal' organizations of government of which social welfare is one. Formal organizations have the

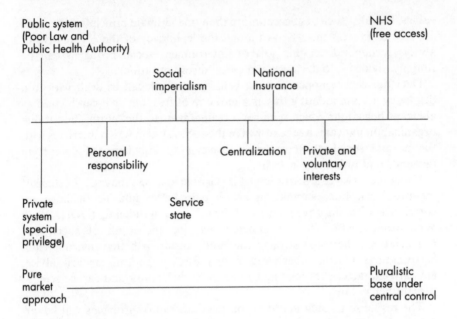

Fig. 2.1 The provision continuum.

explicit purpose of achieving specific goals, a status structure and rules to shape the behaviour of the organization. What began essentially as public initiatives (e.g. the Poor Law, Sanitation and Nuisance Acts, Public Health infirmaries, educational systems, etc.) are now the observable aspects of the welfare state – 'social' services. As each social policy response has been translated into social action there has been constant debating over the structure, function and funding of the resulting frameworks for provision of services.

The present debate over the structure, organization, delivery and cost of health services reflects this continuing concern over the ownership of services and the search for a service provision that combines maximum effectiveness with cost efficiency. Equally significant is the debate over who should benefit from them.

2.4 Nationalization or rationalization?

It took almost 100 years to establish an NHS, the Beveridge Report (MOH, 1942) perhaps being seen as the final catalyst for change. The report highlighted what Beveridge saw as 'five giant evils' – want, idleness, disease, squalor and ignorance. Acceptance of the 'spirit' of Beveridge was later translated into solutions more acceptable within the then social and political framework than some of Beveridge's more radical recommendations (Bruce, 1968).

The evil of disease was attacked by the rationalization of existing private and public health 'services'. The private sector had been experiencing financial difficulties for some time, their major source of funding coming from philanthropic gestures and support from the King Edward Hospital Fund. The fund was running out of money and the voluntary and private institutions felt the lack of support quite keenly. Coincidentally, the public sector hospitals had been expanding rapidly as a result of changes in the Poor Law and its eventual abolition in 1929.

The experiences of a 'centralized' medical service – the Emergency Medical Service – throughout two world wars had shown the possibility of the provision of a centrally funded network for health and medical services. The growth in technology and skills during the Second World War, the increased expectations of the population at large and the will of the people never to return to the dark prewar recession fuelled social consciousness. This atmosphere of social change in which Beveridge produced his report in 1942 explains the enthusiasm with which it was received.

The new NHS was a tripartite structure, paid for from rates, taxes and contributions and, importantly, free at the point of consumption. The original assumption upon which the NHS was based was that of a gradually reducing pool of illness as the services developed. In fact, the NHS was a victim of its own success: as many of the old infectious diseases and major killers of the day were conquered, skills and technology increased and with this the ability to diagnose and treat 'newer' disease.

Medicine turned its attention to research and development bringing more modern techniques into use; the inevitable result was an NHS that could absorb any amount of resources, financial and physical, that could be made available. This fact became clear with an investigation into the organization and management of the NHS just four years after its inception. The Guillebaud Report (MOH, 1952) was expected to expose an NHS which was profligate with resources in the extreme. In fact, the report eulogized the success of the NHS and even recommended that it be given more money and a significant increase in the numbers of beds available.

The NHS settled into a sort of limbo: services seemed to develop at random, planning for their provision was haphazard and the distribution of resources inequitable. Concern over the costs of the NHS and containing them within so-called acceptable economic parameters was to be a recurring theme over the next 40 years. The politicization of health and welfare services had begun.

2.5 'Big is beautiful' – the 1960s

The NHS of 1948 was never considered to be the best way of organizing health care; prevailing political considerations and relationships with those involved at the time dictated the main characteristics of the service. The 1960s and early 1970s saw a change in the political beliefs about the merits of administrative change and what form that should take. The underlying assumptions appeared to be that the problems that faced a variety of services, particularly in the field of communication and co-ordination, could be solved by upgrading these services into larger administrative units. The purpose was to engender within units a corporate identity that would bring about decisions made by a team rather than separate individuals.

The NHS itself was at variance organizationally with some of its participants who had already improved their own administrative structure. The hospital nurses had achieved a breakthrough in the old style of matriarchal management, epitomized by the position of the hospital matron, in the implementation of the Salmon Report (MOH, 1966). Similarly, hospital doctors' administrative participation was reviewed in the 'Cogwheel' Reports (MOH 1967, 1972, 1974). In the community the Mayston Report (DOH, 1969) dealt with nurses, midwives and health visitors and the social services had been addressed by the Seebohm Report (DHSS, 1969). The trend was towards a *systems* theory of management which carried the assumption that changing the structure of an organization would effect a change in the behaviour of those participating. This restructuring would clear relationships and give points at which participants would be clearly accountable to an appropriate level of authority.

This administrative philosophy has tended to overshadow other considerations that were contributing towards an overall re-assessment of the style and delivery of public services across the board. The focus on administrative mechanisms was meant to provide a vehicle that would mean totally integrated and comprehensively planned services that incorporated social as well as health considerations.

In reality, resources were being stretched, patterns of disease were changing, medical knowledge and expertise were increasing, social categorizations were being re-assessed. All of these strands were converging and coalescing into a philosophy of care that could only be applied within a unified network of services that would 'offer solid advantages to the individual and family' (NHS, 1968).

The original tripartite structure of the NHS was seen as increasingly hampering medical care rather than assisting it. The growth of the NHS and services outside hospitals meant that scarce resources were being stretched and inefficiently allocated. Two criticisms were levelled at the NHS; the first was that the service was inefficient managerially and the second was that it was spending beyond its means. The solution was the same for both problems – reorganize the structure into a unified service. Reorganization would not increase the amount of resources available but it would, hopefully, release those resources that had been compartmentalized by the 1948 NHS Act. It would also open up management of the service to scrutiny by the public, the government and participating professions. The NHS had been dubbed the 'ill-health' service by the Royal Commission on the NHS (MOH, 1979) and to survive it needed to achieve economic probity and managerial competence. The concept of serial re-organization had begun.

2.6 The new lexicon of health

From the early 1970s until the present day almost every aspect of the NHS has been put under the microscope and in political and economic terms found wanting. The ideas generated by the 1974 reorganization of accountability, cost-effectiveness, co-operation and collaboration have been remodelled into those of value for money and the right to purchase care. The result of this has been to encourage what is seen by some to be a mixed economy of welfare and by others as the privatization of health and welfare.

Since 1973 the NHS has been subject to major scrutiny with a variety of reports, consultative documents and White Papers dealing with expanding community care, re-aligning responsibilities, developing GP Fundholding and budgets. In addition, there were reports on primary health care services, nurses working in the community, dentist, pharmaceutical and chiropody services all culminating in two of the most radical blueprints for service development to date – *Working for Patients* (DOH, 1989a) and *People First* (DHSS NI, 1990). The market economy, pluralist provision, value for money and accountability are among numerous terms that are part of a new lexicon of health that has gathered momentum over the last three decades (Fig. 2.2). For just over half of that period one ideology has dominated the political environment within which the NHS has existed: that of the Conservative government that came to power in 1979, led by the then prime minister Margaret Thatcher.

2.7 Selling off the family silver

The Thatcherite policies of the 1980s developed the concept of privatization to its maximum potential. Many of the services that had been part of the public domain were launched onto the sea of free enterprise, beginning with the privatization of British Telecom and leading to that of British Rail. These actions were applauded in the early years of the government's period of office but gradually concerns surfaced about the apparent totality of the privatization policy. Misgivings reached a crescendo in the late 1980s when even the Conservative elder statesman, ex-prime minister Harold Macmillan, counselled against such radical and wholesale privatization policies, likening them to 'selling off the family silver'.

The rationale behind such privatization was that these public services

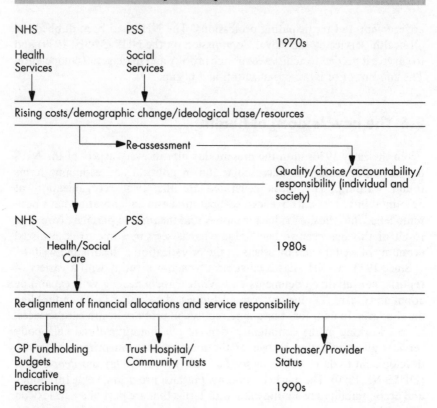

Fig. 2.2 Three decades of change.

could only be successful (i.e. profitable) if they were given the opportunity to develop without central interference. The Conservative government believed in a mixture of provision, decentralization, contractual accountability and consumer participation. For the NHS this meant voluntary and statutory agencies working in tandem with social services, encouraging a growing private sector to become partners in care and what was to be their avowed aim: raising the voice and the consciousness of the consumers of health care in order to prompt a system that was more responsive to consumer needs.

In order to achieve these aims the government produced a virtual cornucopia of reports and documents which described the structures that would be required, the major functions of these structures and, most importantly, how they would be supported financially. The policies of the new government were based on a return to a free market economy, a belief in the sovereignty of the consumer, an implicit trust in the goodness of the Christian work ethic and a return to individual responsibility for personal and material growth – beliefs which had their origins during the latter half of the nineteenth century. This rebirth of the social construction of wealth, health and welfare could only be realized with a radical reorganization of the major public services, of which the NHS and Personal Social Services were only two.

2.8 The political paperchase begins

On their arrival in government the Conservatives issued a consultative document from Conservative Central Office indicating their intentions for the NHS (MOH, 1979). This document carried the aspirations of a government determined to reduce costs in care, improve accountability for the allocation, distribution and utilization of services and to do these things within a revamped and more streamlined framework.

Patients First (DOH, 1974) claimed to point the way to a better service that was 'more responsive to patient needs'. It was not, however, based on the individuals' and families' needs but on the managerial structure of the service, dealing '... only with the structure and management of the service...' The document was in fact over-concerned with the hospital sector and neglected relationships within the NHS and between the NHS and other agencies. The basic thinking behind the document was that the tenet of managerialism had not failed the NHS but that the NHS (i.e. its personnel) had failed managerialism. This conclusion fitted in quite nicely with the premise that the NHS was inefficient rather than under-resourced. If management could be improved then decisions about the allocation of scarce resources would result in cost-effective care and value for money for both the consumer and the taxpayer.

2.9 The importance of care in the community

Through the 1970s there had been a thrust towards increasing the role of the community in the service scenario: more care should be given *in the community* and preferably by the families of those needing that care. The rationale for this, amongst other things, was the cost of high technology within the acute sector becoming prohibitive, the apparent blocking of beds by less than acute patients, keeping patients in hospital for periods that were too long and not using day surgery effectively or consistently.

Community care was part of the original Act in 1946 but the first real move to the community idea could probably be dated by the 1959 Mental Health Act. The Act called for more patients to be discharged into the community via halfway housing, bed and breakfast accommodation and then eventually into their own homes, either with their families or alone. The aim was to close down some of the larger mental institutions in favour of more humane environments. There has not been a great deal of evidence to show that this Act was effective but it did encourage further consideration of community care as a reasonable and cheap alternative to expensive hospital provision.

Primary health care based on the team approach was given substance by the BMA report on primary health care teams (BMA, 1974). This was the BMA's contribution to the team concept debate (Norell, 1973). It reflected the growing move towards group practices, the development of health centres and the increasing practice of attaching community nurses to general practice surgeries (Godber, 1967). It also provided a framework within which community care could be increased and improved. This team approach, however, required resources that were not available in any quantity. The thrust into the community was based on the naive assumption that if the acute sector could reduce the fiscal drag on its resources by discharging more people back into the community and therefore into the care of relatives or friends then the cost of care would necessarily be cheaper.

The Royal Commission on the NHS (MOH, 1979) (The Merrison Report) had pointed out the fallaciousness of assuming that the capacity of the community was limitless, citing numerous deficiencies apparent in respect of services as evidence. The Commission made 58 recommendations on patient services, the majority of which were concerned with community health services. Three years earlier the document *Priorities for Health* (DOH, 1976) had set out the successes that the NHS had achieved and what future goals the service should strive towards. These were mainly concerned with personal and individual responsibility in partnership with an increasingly improving NHS.

The functioning of the community was assessed by the report *Access to Primary Health Care* (DOH, 1981), an enquiry carried out for all UK health departments. In essence it only looked at physical access to GPs, dental, chiropody and pharmacy services. It found that almost 90% of those surveyed had easy access to their GP's surgery and 70% lived within one mile of a pharmacy. Figures on health centres, use of large general practices and size of GP lists were examined to determine the distribution pattern of services and what could be done to improve supply, preferably without increasing the cost. For example, the report found that 15% of their sample went to the pharmacist for advice rather than going to a doctor or nurse or a casualty department – a practice that could be encouraged with minimal cost to the NHS. Subsequent moves from institutional to community care all carried this same rationale for transfer.

2.10 The 'new' NHS

The government's belief in market forces and the power of private enterprise encouraged it to seek a 'business' view of the NHS. Between 1980 and 1990 a variety of reports were completed on major aspects of the organization and management of the NHS. The availability of primary care services (DOH,

1981), information on data collection, management of the NHS acute sector (DOH, 1983), nursing in the community (DOH, 1986a), the delivery and efficiency of community services (SSC, 1986–7), Reform of Social Security (DOH, 1986b), management of community services (DOH, 1986c), the feasibility of devolving responsibilities for the planning and purchasing of care to the professionals involved (DOH, 1989a) and finally, the reform of community care (DOH, 1989b), all produced a thrust into the community that implied the more efficient use of existing resources rather than increasing them.

The reports were largely concerned with more effective and efficient management structures. Some only implied that the structures and the professionals within them were not producing the most cost-effective services. Rather than focus on the professionals they were more concerned with the structures within which they worked. Others were more explicit and stated positively that they were not concerned with patients but with management and administration. All of them had the needs of the consumer apparently as the main beneficiary of their deliberations either by improving access and delivery at the grass roots level or as a side effect of streamlining managerial frameworks.

2.11 Consumer sovereignty or informed choice?

The notion of consumer sovereignty is at the heart of a free market economy. In theory it should dictate the supply of goods and services based on demand. The market will respond to demand by increasing supply and vice versa.

Within the commercial market this theory works reasonably well, given the variety of influences that can encourage the consumer to seek one product over another. Production will always respond to what the market can bear and consumers have the opportunity to 'shop around' until they find the good or service that they require and are willing to pay for. Consumers use their knowledge of the goods and services on offer and make their selection based on that knowledge. They buy their goods and services with certain guarantees that give them the right to recompense should the good or service be lacking in some respect or should it have been 'sold' to them for a purpose which it could not fulfil. An example might be the purchase of a computer that fails to work once you get it home. It can be returned to the shop and replaced, it can be returned to the manufacturer for repair or you can get a refund on the grounds that it did not fulfil its description as a working computer. Despite all these options, however, there are still loopholes that could negate most or all your rights to recompense.

There is a common stricture, *caveat emptor* – buyer beware – that urges consumers to be aware of what they purchase which in turn means being aware of their rights on purchase and their rights to compensation *before* they buy. The purchasing of health care within the new NHS does not, however, apply to the individual consumer. Consumers do not have the sovereignty that a market economy implies. Since 1948 the NHS has relied on a similar phrase to *caveat emptor* and that is *credat emptor* – buyer believe in us.

The mechanism for access has been most often via a GP who acts as the 'gatekeeper' to resources and source of referral to further services. The medical profession generally has the key role to play in deciding who should get what, where, when and how within the NHS. They have been given this imputed authority by society by virtue of their training, demonstrated expertise and acceptance of the moral and ethical issues of clinical responsibility. In other words the consumer has delegated that role to the doctor and trusts, or even assumes, that he/she will apply their knowledge and expertise for the good of all. They will accept decisions made by the doctor on the basis of clinical discretion being exercised appropriately by medical and other health professionals. The professionals must, in turn, respond to consumer needs as and when they arise.

This is in fact the crux of the NHS reforms; *People First* (DHSS NI, 1990) actually stipulates that 'the new arrangements should begin with the actual needs and wishes of the clients and their carers . . .'. However, they must do so within certain financial and physical resource parameters with both health and social services working together 'with both engaged in trying to achieve the best value for money' (*Caring for People*, (DOH 1989b)). In effect, the reforms apparently endorse a needs-led approach which has the potential to plunder central coffers if left unchecked. To obviate this the NHS must pursue a policy of establishing priorities based on value for money, or as Øvretveit (1992) puts it:

'. . . meeting the needs of those who need the service most, at the lowest cost to the organization, within limits and directives set by higher authorities and services.'

The 'new' consumerism in this environment immediately reverts to the old belief of *credat emptor*. If the consumer does not have unhampered access to the full market for health care then effectively their sovereignty is negated. Patients do not choose their doctors on the basis of their abilities, knowledge and skills in medicine. The choice is more often than not a geographical accident rather than a conscious decision. Within this environment they cannot choose one course of action over another, one service over another, one GP over another and so on. They lack both consumer sovereignty and informed choice. In effect, the consumer of health care is in an invidious position, having need of a service without knowing its full range and availability and usually at a time when the question of selectivity and value for money in paying for that service is never further from their mind.

2.12 The competitive market

Competition has been introduced into health care in order to rationalize the cost of providing comprehensive services free at the point of delivery. The NHS reforms have an economic base which relies on assessing priorities for care and the use of explicit measurements in terms of costs and outcomes. At the heart of the reforms a distinction is made between the provider of health care and the purchaser of health care. The purchaser and provider roles may be separated out financially but in practice they are two roles which can apply to one body, institution or individual.

This was certainly the case prior to the reforms where the NHS was virtually the sole purchaser/provider of all health services. In effect the NHS was what was termed a monopsony – a monolithic structure that was both the purchaser and provider of health care and therefore without effective competitors. The small private sector which existed did not have any commercial relationship with the NHS for all practical purposes and could not therefore constitute a co-trader within the health care framework. The reforms were meant to dismantle the monopsony status of the NHS, open up the market for care to other providers and as a result introduce competition for the provision of services. In turn this would, as Culyer (1990) says, separate:

> '... the purchaser provider functions ... so that prices, volumes and quality of services are explicit and providers be made more accountable.'

The reforms focused on the provision of acute services, GP services and community services. In the acute sector the White Paper, *Working for Patients* (DOH, 1989a) was concerned with specifying 'core' services, measurement of process and audit of activity and cost. It introduced the concept of hospital and community trusts, the purchaser/provider role and the contracting out of services. Trust status allowed hospitals to become self-governing, control their own expenditure and develop income generating activities which they could then use to enhance their own functioning as they saw fit.

For GP services the concept of fundholding was the central theme. The general practice could opt to be given a budget which would cover a variety of purchasing costs for services to be delivered, the provision of physical resources, staff costs, training costs, etc. To be eligible to become a fundholder a practice had to have a particular base number of patients on their lists and agree to be monitored and measured against specific performance criteria. Within community services the major focus was to be on provision for the elderly, the mentally ill and those with a learning disability. Services were subject to audit; individual provision was according to assessed social or health need and provided as a co-ordinated and collaborative response between health and social services.

For all three sectors the purchaser/provider role was of paramount importance. It allowed the existence of an internal market which gave participants the option of choosing one service over another, one GP over another, one hospital over another, one consultant over another and so on. All these choices would be based on the assessment and availability of the kind, quality and content of service to be purchased, and the commensurate cost.

It also opened up the market to free enterprise in that individuals or groups could provide a service within the private or voluntary sector that could be competitively priced against state provision. At the macro level this gave the private and voluntary sectors access to the market in terms of such global provision as private hospitals, day centres, nursing agencies. It also gave the individual entrepreneur the opportunity to develop and sell services on a much smaller scale. A good example of this was the provision of bathing services for the immobile or the elderly for which the customer paid on a one-off basis as and when they requested the service. The provision of the same service by the local health authority was not so flexible and the grade of staff involved in its delivery made this an expensive activity.

Within this environment the NHS must produce competitively priced services which will be purchased not only by other members of the NHS but also by private enterprise and individuals. The market is open to all and only constrained by its delivery of the end product and how that end product is both received and perceived in terms of quality, fit and cost. Or is it? The idea of total freedom in purchase and provision only applies to those who do purchase and provide and not to the consumer who continues to rely for the most part on the recommendations of health personnel.

In order to prevent economic anarchy the government has applied numerous controls on the services to be offered. Providers are subject to a whole panoply of regulatory mechanisms designed in theory to protect the consumer from abuse, damage and danger. For the consumer the government has published a Patient's Charter (DOH, 1992a) which sets out consumer rights and targets and what to expect from providers and what to do if the service they require does not come up to expectations.

Despite these mechanisms there are still problems which arise almost directly as a result of the reforms. If a consumer is unable, for example, to have access to private care because they cannot afford it then they are still able to take advantage of a 'free' service via the NHS. That service, however, might not be available within their area. Given the contractual basis of referral they may find themselves waiting an inordinate length of time before access to that service is available. Referral to institutional and other health and social services may depend on whether or not the consumer's GP is a fundholder and therefore in a position to negotiate such access via the contracting process.

Concern has been expressed in the media, by individuals and non-fundholding GPs that given the budgetary limits those who are chronically ill or elderly might be too much of a drain on the new GP budgets and therefore refused a place on a GP's list or even asked to move to another practice. Indeed, non-fundholding GPs have pointed out that they are having to wait to get their patients admitted for elective surgery, investigations, etc., because the beds and consultants are contracted to fundholders via block contracts for specific services. Criticism has gone so far as to intimate that a two-tier service has supervened – the fast track to services being reserved for those who are part of a fundholding practice. In addition, should the GP fund-holder overspend his budget then the shortfall is topped up, intimating a reduction in the resources available overall. In this instance the non-fund-holding GP is further constrained by a lack of resources available to support basic and general services.

NHS authorities are equally constrained by their budgets in the amount of a particular service they can offer. Priorities have to be decided on the basis of cost versus demonstrated need. The most expensive element of a community budget, for example, is the provision of nursing services. The substitution of fully trained community nurses by unqualified health care assistants has been the line of least resistance taken to date by many authorities. The right of the consumers to an expected level of expertise and skill becomes almost irrelevant when they have no control over the personnel caring for them.

On the plus side, the freedom to purchase has allowed many innovative and entrepreneurial schemes to arise. The consumer does at least have an avenue of complaint and the expansion of opportunity for referral has reduced waiting lists measurably. The opening up of the health and social care market has increased the supply of nursing and residential care and the quality and quantity of service provision is open to scrutiny and action where they are less then acceptable. Service users and those involved in the purchase and provision of health care now appear to appreciate the real cost of service provision. Part of the strategy to increase accountability, quality control, consumer satisfaction, efficiency and cost-effectiveness has indeed been successful. Whether the idea of open competition has been as successful is a moot point which still needs discussion.

2.13 Equity and access

People First (DHSS NI 1990) sets out the future relationships for professionals working in the community. This relationship was to be based on the assumption that the majority of needs expressed could be seen as requiring a social response rather than a health one. The division was important because it would dictate the professional group most appropriate to meet those needs. For example, if a client was assessed as requiring residential care then the lead agency would be social services. If that same client was to be kept at home but required assistance and support with activities of living the response could be a health service one. This is a simplistic example that ignores the gradations of need that might be expressed but it serves to demonstrate the grey area that the social/health care divide did not address.

The lead agency for community care was designated as the social service department which would be the lone assessor and gatekeeper of all *new* clients to community care. The overall requirement for the success of this assessment and referral procedure was the need to secure the co-operation and collaboration of the agencies involved, from the actions of the field-workers to the formulation of community care plans. The latter would include a total assessment of local needs against which resources would be allocated within the process of care management. The public were less than aware of the changes taking place, the reasons perhaps lying at the feet of the accepted public image of the major service providers. The professionals involved, however, were more concerned, or possibly insecure, as to how these changes would influence the scope of their professional jurisdiction in the future.

The combination of *People First* (DHSS NI, 1990) and *Working for Patients* (DOH, 1989a) has produced a number of questions which relate to the equity and quality of service provision. Neither of these issues is yet fully evaluated though the political rhetoric suggests that the NHS reforms have improved service quality overall.

The advent of trust status where hospitals and community services can 'opt out' of central control, generating their own funds by marketing their services, the introduction of GP fundholding, budgets and indicative pre-scribing have all had a knock-on effect on the ways in which services are delivered and experienced by patients. In some cases the breadth and quality of services have shown a significant improvement in such things as service availability, reduction in waiting lists, increased consumer satisfaction and recognition of the importance of costs in delivering care. Critics would argue that when accountancy becomes the main tool of decision-making then equity and access to a wide range of services is necessarily negated.

In reality, those at the 'business' end of delivering care have embraced the responsibility of budget holding as a means of re-stating professional accountability. On the other hand, it has raised questions of resource allo-cation that rest on the professional becoming the arbiter of legitimate need – legitimate, in this case, indicating whether one resource can be used over another based on the principle of professional judgement rather than upon actuality of client needs.

2.14 The future – planning for care

The political paperchase culminated in the NHS and Community Care Act 1990 which incorporated virtually all the preceding White Papers' recommendations. Its considered aim was to rationalize and clarify the future of the NHS and its community services. Planning was of prime importance and both the acute and community services were expected to be prepared to respond flexibly and sensitively to the needs of patients and their carers. It was intended that they should do this by planning for, and examining a range of options which would meet both client needs and service capabilities.

Within the acute sector the NHS and Community Care Act placed a major responsibility on NHS general management systems and within the community on the social service departments who would liaise with other organizations to produce community care plans which were responsive to 'assessed' need. These new responsibilities have encouraged both management and professional groups to reassess their individual roles in care delivery and reiterate the need for mutuality in decision-making which will fulfil the original premise of the NHS – a comprehensive service free at the point of consumption. Alongside this planning imperative are the plans for the nation's health embodied in documents such as *The Health of the Nation* (DOH, 1992b) and *New World, New Opportunities* (DOH, 1993). Together, these documents embody the Government's hopes for the future and both provide many challenges for nursing actions and practice.

The question that has to be asked is whether or not these initiatives present a firm commitment which will be backed by the necessary finances and political support to achieve their aims, or whether they are to be regarded as purely a summary of the 'spirit' of the Government's aims to improve care.

2.15 References

BMA (1974) *The Organisation of Primary Medical Care*. Planning Report, 4, BMA, London.

Bruce, M. (1968) *The Coming of the Welfare State*. Macmillan, London.

Culyer, A., Maynard, A. & Posnet, J. (1990) *Competition in Health Care: Reforming the NHS*. Macmillan, London.

DHSS (1969) *Report of the Committee on Local Authority and Allied Personal Social Services* (Chair: H. Seebohm) Cm 3093. HMSO, London.

DHSS NI (1990) *People First: Community Care in Northern Ireland*. HMSO, Belfast.

DOH (1968) *The Administrative Structure of the Medical and Related Services in England and Wales*. HMSO, London.

DOH (1969) *Report of the Working Party on the Management Structure in the Local Authority Nursing Services* (Chair: Mayston). HMSO, London.

DOH (1974) *Patients First*. Consultative Paper on the Structure and Management of the NHS in England and Wales. HMSO, London.

DOH (1976) *Priorities for Health*. HMSO, London.

DOH (1980) *Inequalities in Health*. Report of a Research Working Group (Chair: Sir Douglas Black). HMSO, London.

DOH (1981) *Access to Primary Health Care*. HMSO, London.

DOH (1983) *Agenda for Discussion*. Report to the Secretaries of State for Health, Wales, Northern Ireland and Scotland (Chair: Sir Roy Griffiths). HMSO, London.

DOH (1986a) *Neighbourhood Nursing – a focus for care*. Report of the Community Nursing Review Team (Chair: Julia Cumberlege). HMSO, London.

DOH (1986b) *Reform of Social Security*. HMSO, London.

DOH (1986c) *Community Care: Agenda for Action*. Report to the Secretary of State for Social Services (Chair: Sir Roy Griffiths). HMSO, London.

DOH (1989a) *Working for Patients*. Cm 555. HMSO, London.

DOH (1989b) *Caring for People: Community Care in the Next Decade and Beyond*. Cm 849. HMSO, London.

DOH (1992a) *The Patient's Charter*. HMSO, London.

DOH (1992b) *The Health of the Nation: Working together for better health*. HMSO, London.

DOH (1993) *New World, New Opportunities – Nursing in Primary health care*. NHSME, London.

Donnison, D. (1975) *Social Policy Re-visited: the Development of Social Services at Local Level*. Allen & Unwin, London.

George, P. & Wilding, P. (1976) *Ideology in Social Welfare*. Routledge, Kegan-Paul, London.

Godber, Sir George (1967) *Report of the Joint Working Party on the Organisation of Medical Personnel*. HMSO, London.

MOH (1904) *Report of the Interdepartmental Committee on Physical Deterioration* (1902). HMSO, London.

MOH (1942) *Report on Social and Allied Services*. Cm 6404. (Chair: Sir William Beveridge). HMSO, London.

MOH (1952) *Report of the Committee of Enquiry into the Cost of the NHS*. Presented to Parliament by the Ministry of Health and Secretary of State for Scotland (Chair: C.W. Guillebaud). Cm 9663. HMSO, London.

MOH (1966) Report of the Committee on Senior Nursing Staff Structure (Chair: B. Salmon). HMSO, London.

MOH (1967; 1972; 1974). *Report of the Joint Working Party on the Organisation of Medical Work in Hospitals*. HMSO, London.

MOH (1979) *Royal Commission on the NHS* (Chair: Sir Alec Merrison). Cm 5615. HMSO, London.

NHS and Community Care Act (1990). HMSO, London.

NHS/DHSS (1982–4) *Reports of the Steering Group on Health Services Information* (Chair: Dame Edith Korner). HMSO, London.

Norell, J.S. & Ballint, E. (eds) (1973) *Six minutes for the patient interaction in general practice consultation*. Mind & Medicine Monographs, Tavistock, London.

Øvretveit, P. (1992) *Health Service Quality: An Introduction to Quality Methods for Health Services*. Blackwell Science, Oxford.

Royal Commission on the NHS (Chair: Sir Alec Merrison). Cm 5615. HMSO, London.

SSC (1986–7) *Primary Health Care*. Report from the Social Services Committee. HMSO, London.

Saville, J. & Briggs, A. (eds) (1971) *Essays in Labour History*. Macmillan, London.

Titmuss, R. (1963) *Essays on the Welfare State* (2nd edn). Allen & Unwin, London.

Whitehead, M. (1987) *The Health Care Divide: Inequalities in Health in the 1980s*. Health Education Council, London.

Chapter 3

Primary Health Care in the Community

The last four decades have shown changes in attitudes towards institutionalization, growing concern over financial support for all health and welfare services, the emergence of the concept of value for money and an apparent obsession with reorganization and renewal. They have coalesced, bringing a shift of emphasis from the acute sector to the idea of community care as a cost-effective and complementary method of delivering a service.

The naive belief in the idea of the community as a 'cheap' alternative to institutional care has been addressed in Chapter 2 and will not be revisited here. Nevertheless, the political and professional ambience emergent during the 1990s was seen as ripe for the introduction of a more comprehensive system of care in the community than had previously existed. The context of primary health care will be addressed in this chapter.

3.1 The same but different?

It is important to note from the outset that the terms 'community care' and 'primary care' are often used interchangeably. This can cause some confusion when making the distinction between health service and social service responses within the community and the apparently modern concept of delineating the appropriate locus for care. In effect, the differences are few and levels of primary care can be easily translated into those applying to social care, which allows for both professional foci to be accommodated individually and collaboratively.

Theoretically, primary health care had been structured on three levels, i.e. primary, secondary and tertiary, though in practice the boundaries between each level are often blurred and overlapping.

- *Primary care*. This was aimed at promotional and preventative measures whereby the focus was on maintaining health and well-being, screening for possible disease and developing preventative programmes such as immunization and vaccination.

■ *Secondary care.* At this level measures could be both curative and preventative, i.e. towards the amelioration of existing conditions and combatting deterioration.

■ *Tertiary care.* At the third and final level existing disease is evident and the major aim was containment and maintenance of the status quo – care at this level was palliative rather than curative.

It takes very little imagination and professional familiarity with other disciplines to translate these levels into a personal social service perspective. Essentially, social work, nursing and medicine have the same focus, i.e. the patient or client. The difference is in the problems that might present and the solutions that may be most appropriate.

Nevertheless, the development of primary care has been almost subsumed under the title 'community' as a descriptive label for all services delivered outside of the hospital ward environment. In effect, the idea of making institutions centrifugal rather than centripetal had been around since the Dawson Report in 1919 which outlined a system of care using health centres as the focus for primary care. The role of social services in the community has been separate from that of health services simply by historical accident and the initial development of the tripartite structure of the NHS in 1948. The result has been to consider 'primary' services as essentially concerned with health care and in particular medical care.

It is important, however, to make the distinction in the context of community nursing which, again by an accident of history, has been linked traditionally with home nursing and in particular, primary medical care services. The background to primary health care begins therefore with the general development of community care.

3.2 Community care – the poor relation

Though part of the 1948 NHS act, responsibility for the 'community' and general practice was consigned to local authorities and executive councils. The rationalization of services in 1948 created a tripartite structure that did little to integrate preventative and curative services. The dichotomy between acute and community care was never meant to be resolved by the 1948 Act and the physical divisions within the structure encouraged territorial and isolationist responses. The training of staff solidified these attitudes and relationships so that the professions were divided not only amongst themselves but divorced, physically and psychologically, from each other.

Access to specialist treatment was essentially cut off and only accepted via referral from the GP. In this way the practice of referral gained a status that raised it from an administrative necessity to a cardinal virtue. The specialist practitioner was sectioned off from the public and awarded a standing that was to affect the recruitment to general practice. A general hypothesis over the nature of specialist and general practice stated that specialists would make mistakes because they did not know enough about people and GPs would make mistakes because they did not know enough about medicine (Forsythe, 1966). This effectively underlined the lowly status of the GP during the first decades of the new NHS.

The changes in attitude since owe more to improving medical techniques and advancing technology than to an appreciation of the role of the GP as the first point of contact for the patient. Nevertheless, the improvement in standards of living and use of new drugs, like the antibiotics and sulphonamides, meant increasingly that the GP was expected to provide a wider and wider range of care.

3.3 Defining the 'community'

Mechanic (1976) points out that '... health and health care has to be understood within the larger context of human strivings and adjustments to life situations...'. The changing demands for health care have almost overtaken the provision of services to meet those life situations. Indeed, community care within the UK has not always been in the vanguard of service delivery and the rhetoric of community care has been more evident than the actual reality.

The reorganizations of the NHS from 1973 onwards have had as one of their main features attempts to realign the relationships between the acute sector and the community (DHSS, 1976). The major difficulty has been actually to define what is meant by the term 'the community' and how its resources can be organized most effectively and efficiently. In addition, the roles and relationships of professionals working in the community have retained a compartmentalism which has the potential to fragment any unified approach to community provision.

It would be easy to say that care in the community is based on a service infrastructure which provides an holistic response to all kinds of needs, encompassing physical, psychological, social and environmental aspects of daily life. This does not, however, define what the community actually *is* but rather what the *function* of the community might be. The Oxford English Dictionary defines the word 'community' as 'joint ownership as in goods; identity of character; fellowship; organized political, social or municipal body; body of people living in the same locality...'. This might be closer to defining what the community means in both a physical and professional sense. The professionals in the community experience the fellowship of a body of people which influences them in their working and possibly their private lives. There is an identity of character in the professional sense – all professionals, whether within institutions or the wider community, have a mutual aim that is a characteristic of the job – they are there to serve the patient/client and meet their needs.

Everyone has a social right of access to all that health authorities can supply – they have joint ownership of NHS services. Accordingly, the professional has the responsibility of decision-making in meeting needs, how the needs can be met most effectively and what physical resources are necessary to meet these needs – they are part of the organized political, social and municipal body. The professional may be regarded as the patient's representative within the community and advocate within the health system.

Even with this interpretation the tangibility of the community concept is lacking and trying to define the term 'community' becomes an exercise in semantics. Just as 'good health' is a subjective judgement of health status so 'the community' is a philosophical label intimating a concrete structure that facilitates the existence of levels of social and health care services. Health status is a measurable entity but the term 'good health' is not; similarly 'the community' is a nebulous, if commonly held, view of the environment within which those services which have been given the generic title of social and health care services are organized and delivered.

3.4 Community care in practice

Most recently, the White Paper *Caring for People: Community Care in the Next Decade and Beyond* (DOH, 1989c) has reiterated the rights of the individual to receive care in the community. This document, however, is more concerned with administrative aspects of community care:

> 'It complements the proposals in ... *Working for Patients* (Cm 555) for the management of the hospital and family practitioner services. Taken together the two White Papers set out how the government believes health and social care should develop....' (para 1.2)

Only two of the six key objectives of the document are directly concerned with meeting the expressed needs of patients and their carers. Nevertheless, the emphasis on the community as an appropriate arena for care is assured even if the provision of the necessary services is subject to physical and financial limitations. It was in effect the changes brought about by *Working for Patients* (DOH, 1989b) and *Caring for People* (DOH, 1989c) which set the seal on the future of collaboration, co-operation and communication in community health and social care. *Caring for People* was explicit in its intention to produce a change in the delivery of care:

'... clarifying roles and responsibilities, bringing together the relevant sources of finance, delegating responsibility for decision-making to the local level wherever possible, improving accountability and providing the right incentives.' (para 1.7)

That clarification relied on the co-operation of all the professional personnel involved in care provision and planning and urged them to consider and accept the common purpose at the interface of care, to meet and work with each other and to recognize their own professional limitations and the multifactorial nature of social and health problems: 'There is no room in community care for a narrow view of individuals' needs, nor of ways of meeting them' (para 2.20).

The reality of community care was complex and covered social as well as health needs, and indeed, *Caring for People* saw the division between social and health care as essentially two separate strands that would overlap on occasions. Each client had to be assessed individually and an appropriate package of care designed to meet those particular needs. Such a realignment of responsibilities required the reassessment of the focus of community care and within that determining the differences between health and social care.

In 1986, Sir Roy Griffiths was asked by the Secretary of State for Social Services to review the use made of public funds in the delivery of community care. His report, *Agenda for Action* (DOH, 1986c), recognized the different contributions of both arms of community care, i.e. health and personal social services, and proposed that the social service agencies should become the lead agency for identifying and planning to meet community care needs.

Despite the tenor of the document in delineating responsibility for social and health care, the role of primary health care services was referred to in only one paragraph. This trend was continued in the above-mentioned White Paper, *Caring for People* (DOH, 1989c), which essentially took the 'spirit' of the recommendations of the Griffiths Report (DOH, 1986c) by utilizing the major themes to underpin the government's own philosophy of community care. Again, the lack of reference to primary health care was apparent though on this occasion three paragraphs were devoted to the role of the GP and primary care. In essence, primary health and medical services appear to have been left to develop in the absence of strategic intent alongside the various changes that have been inaugurated for the rest of the community. The reality is, however, that primary care, it seems, will be both a part of, and complementary to, the rest of the administratively based health and social services.

3.5 The development of primary health care

Essentially, the primary health care concept stems from a communal ideology which recognizes that the weaker sections of society can be aided and assisted by those in better positions – either materially or educationally. This is not a new concept; the Lazar Houses in earlier centuries were religious communes which provided institutional and community care (Abel-Smith, 1964). Similarly, the 'Bare Foot Doctors' of China were the result of Mao Zedong's criticism of the health ministry prior to the Cultural Revolution (Chang, 1992). The barefoot doctors aimed to serve the people – the aim was a communal one, different in format but similar in focus to that of the Western world where the community is the raison d'être, and vehicle for, primary health care.

The first cohesive approach to defining primary health care was developed by the BMA following the production of a planning paper outlining a framework for primary health care for developing countries (BMA, 1974). This blueprint for care has been generally accepted and since 1974 most organizational approaches have followed the principles outlined in the original framework outlined by the BMA. In the same year the Office of Health Economics (OHE, 1974) produced a paper which examined the work of primary medical care and stated:

'There is a general recognition that primary medical care is the setting in which most expansion in the future reorganized health service should take place.'

Alongside these developments there was also a universal thrust towards expanding primary health care epitomized by the World Health Organization's declaration at Alma Ata, Kazakstan which is now known as *Health for all 2000* (WHO, 1978). Though aimed mainly at developing countries, the philosophy behind the Alma Ata Declaration was designed to lend itself to universal application and to encourage developed countries to be cognizant also of the needs of their populations and the importance of preventative and promotional health initiatives. The Declaration asserted the fundamental right of individuals to 'complete physical, mental and social well-being and not merely the absence of disease or infirmity' (WHO, 1978).

Within the EC efforts have also been made to harmonize each individual country's responses, both in the development of responsive community services and in the utilization of professionally qualified staff. The strategy for primary health care is now a significant tool in illness prevention and health promotion and of course, as part of the ongoing battle for the amelioration, where possible, of existing diseases and disabilities.

The major foci for primary health care can therefore be summarized as promoting good health, preventing ill-health, supporting informal carers and providing direct care in the community to those who do not require institutional care. It is not simply a medical or nursing service but one which includes all professionals working in the community within the total health and personal social services. Above all primary care recognizes this complexity and the stresses involved in caring for a sick or elderly relative or friend at home.

3.6 The framework for primary health care

The emergence of health centres in the early 1960s gave the implementation of primary health care a specific base from which services could be developed (DHSS NI, 1972). The health centre gave a common physical base which allowed for a multidisciplinary approach to primary health care. It was seen to be important that the environment of the health centre should promote interdisciplinary collaboration and co-operation. This was meant to engender the sort of service that would not only produce operational advantages but improve both the availability and environmental context for service delivery to patients.

Despite the aim of the health centre programme there was also the question of considering the role and contribution of individual professionals involved in the provision of care. They were expected to demonstrate a mutual appreciation of the holistic approach to health care and the social implications of illness, disease and deviations from the 'norm'. Once these issues were defined a framework was considered to be in place to ensure that the most appropriate service, or services, to meet needs which had been recognized as many and varied (DOH, 1969; DOH, 1986; SSC, 1986–7; DOH, 1989c) would be in place in the community.

Again, central government's assumption that structural change would also alter the relationships interprofessionally was somewhat naive and misguided. For example, in 1982 the Office of Population Census and Surveys (OPCS) carried out a survey for the DHSS on nurses working in the community. This survey showed that community nurses did not see themselves as part of a team unless it was specifically defined in terms of general practice. The survey also examined how nurses communicated between themselves and with general practitioners. The results indicated a hierarchy of appreciation of the nurse's role by the GP that was based on what the latter considered the legitimacy of their qualification. For example, health visitors had specific case conference periods with the GP whereas the district nurse was expected to speak with the GP between patient appointments. The integration of social and health service personnel had not been the subject of specific research into collaboration and co-operation up to this point and given the internecine rivalry existing in community nursing it was unlikely that any more positive results would have been forthcoming.

In order to carry out individual professional responsibilities and also to achieve the sort of collaboration and co-operation that is required by the most recent legislation there must be some vehicle for implementation which allows for such mutuality of purpose. In addition, there is one point at which the majority of requests for services will occur and that is most often referral from the first line or primary health services. The major vehicle for the delivery of primary health and social care is the primary health care team (PHCT), which is recognized as the first point of contact for the public requiring a response from the NHS.

3.7 The structure of the primary health care team (PHCT)

The stratified layers of care which comprise primary health care also reflect the organizational framework within which PHCTs operate. A variety of labels have been attached to this organizational structure and most references to primary health care see this functioning at the first or primary level without acknowledging the importance of the wider teams required at the secondary and tertiary levels (Fig. 3.1). However, the BMA did recognize the necessity for this multiprofessional approach depending on the circumstances, noting that '... the composition of the primary health care team will vary, being dependent upon demographic, and socio-economic, as well as health factors' (BMA, 1974).

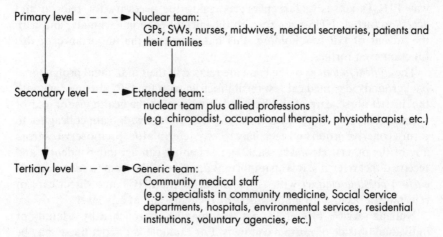

Fig. 3.1 Relationship between primary health care and functional primary health care teams.

The importance of delineating levels becomes apparent when the functioning of the teams is taken into account. Though clinical responsibilities can be allocated to each level there is no hard and fast rule that stipulates a definitive role and function, and each level can act with reference to communal responsibilities and within broad guidelines. The focus on the first level of primary care services is often seen to be a distinct role for the primary health care team and the extended and generic team relegated to a bureau-cratic and institutional response in service delivery. Given this caveat the remainder of this chapter will follow custom and practice by focusing on the first level of primary health care and its attendant team. The reader is urged, however, to be aware of the breadth of responsibilities which rest on the shoulders of professionals at all levels of care and the interrelationship of those levels in the delivery of comprehensive community health and welfare services.

3.8 The role and function of the PHCT

The parameters of care for PHCTs are many and varied; most importantly they are the first point of contact with health services and therefore control further consultations with specialist practitioners. In the 1986 Agenda for Discussion (DOH, 1983) it was noted that 97% of the population were registered with 29 000 GPs who provided 225 million consultations per year at a cost of £1.2 billion (1985 figures). The potential for referral from this number of consultations is enormous not only for institutional care or treatment or investigations but also to other members of the PHCT. In this way PHCTs act as 'gatekeepers', assessing the necessity for referral and access to further NHS resources. In the current economic climate, and with the advent of GP fundholding, this has increased the importance of this function even further.

The *clinical functions* of the team are related to their individual professional backgrounds, e.g. medical responsibilities lie with the GP, nursing care with the district nurse, care of children and families with the health visitor and/or social worker, etc. Each member of the team works with team colleagues to form a cohesive group and each may receive referrals for specific services from any of the others. However, each team member can act independently and receive direct referrals. It is an important function of the team to *encourage the earliest possible contact* with any member of the PHCT and direct care or referral can occur with all members of the team and at any level.

Nursing services often find that they may be approached by a family or individual outside of normal channels. For example, a district nurse may be visiting one household and a concerned neighbour may direct the nurse to another house in the same street. The district nurse can make initial contact and following assessment refer as necessary. The visibility of district nurses within the community makes this a fairly common response and anecdotal evidence suggests that in small communities the nurse is so well known that such referrals can often occur outside working hours. In addition to the PHCT's clinical responsibilities each team member carries a significant *pastoral role*.

The total response to patients, clients and families demands more than just physical maintenance and the team responds to each care episode holistically. For the GP, for example, this means recognizing that a surgery consultation includes opportunities for the patient to explore the metaphysical symptoms of their illness. Based on the premise that each individual presents with a unique collection of characteristics and that for every action there is a reaction, the team member responds according to the specific physical and psychosocial signs and symptoms being displayed at the time. The response will differ according to the professional orientation of the individual team member involved in the consultation. The social worker, for example, may find that the crux of a problem with an overstressed mother who is showing potential for physical abuse of her children is the lack of nursery school places for her younger children. On the other hand the district nurse visiting an elderly relative in the same household might see periodic respite care as a solution to relieving the burden on the mother and allowing her more time with her children. For both groups of professionals the response is one of examining the wider implications of the environment of care and selecting a course of action that benefits as many household members as possible.

The pastoral role of the team is to support the family as a unit. Targeting the family specifically intimates that the intangible benefits will also promote the well-being of the community as a whole. This pastoral role also has definite repercussions for the organization of the PHCT and in particular, the management of individual professional caseloads. For example, the use of an appointment system within the general practice means allowing sufficient time for each appointment and anticipating that one consultation may take more time than theoretically allocated. Similarly, the health visitor may find a situation within a home that requires that the opportunity be given for the mother to express her feelings, problems, etc., in greater depth than in previous visits. Time management combined with empathy and flexibility are important considerations in carrying out this role.

Health promotion is a significant component of the PHCT role and function; it has always been of primary importance and since the early 1970s has been a central responsibility of all of the PHCT members. Government publications such as *Promoting Better Health* (DOH, 1989a) have recognized that the first line of defence is at the primary care level, and the role of the PHCT in this is paramount. Consequently health promotion is both a specific responsibility and part of the ongoing care provided by the team. Increased importance of the concepts of health promotion and illness prevention have been detailed most recently in *The Health of the Nation* (DOH, 1992) which notes that the NHS reforms (1989): '... established that the prime role of health authorities is an explicit responsibility for the health of their residents'. Chapter 9 of the document deals specifically with the translation of targets for the nation's health to the local level and in particular, the role of the family health service authorities, GP Fundholders and primary health care services. This was followed up by a handbook *The Health of the Nation: Working Together for Better Health* (DOH, 1993a), outlining strategies for healthy alliances and the benefits for all those involved. The PHCT represents a concrete framework within which these health promotion activities can be operationalized and in particular, accommodates the range of personnel required for provision of effective health and social care.

The PHCT also has a major function in *research and data collection*. The records of each professional may be utilized for planning and resource allocation; for example, the Royal College of General Practitioners has, since 1969, collected practice data from 300 practices in England and Wales on a weekly basis covering the frequency of infectious disease and monthly returns on noninfectious diseases. Similarly, local registers may be kept to track the prevalence of particular problems; for example, a register of congenital defects has been in operation since the problems first experienced with the use of the drug Thalidomide. Some cities have set up coronary health disease registers; and nationally, since 1962, a register for the follow-up of malignant disease, allowing longer term observation, has been in operation. The importance attributed to nursing and health visiting records has increased as they have become recognized as legal documents which may be produced when investigating complaints or in a court of law.

Other sources of social and health data include the notifiable disease list, social security statistics, hospital in-patient enquiry and activity analysis. All of these assist in the production of the information necessary to provide a comprehensive service both nationally and for primary health care services based on informed local intelligence/data sources.

3.9 The location of teams

Though the prime location for the PHCT might appear to be the health centre there are other bases within which the teams can operate efficiently. The health centre certainly carries the advantage of enabling daily contact between members, the possibility of improving communication and collaboration and speedier referrals between team members. Reference has already been made to the communication difficulties which may be experienced both by nursing staff intraprofessionally and interprofessionally between nurses and GPs; similar problems can occur between other members of the team such as social workers. A common base, therefore, may not necessarily produce the sorts of working relationships that are almost a prerequisite to effective PHCTs and teamwork. Nevertheless, the collaborative focus of the PHCT can, and does, exist without a common base.

There are many different locations for PHCTs where distinct professional groups are physically separated but nonetheless work collaboratively. Many community nurses are based within geographical areas following the model of neighbourhood nursing proposed by Cumberlege (DOH, 1986a). Members of the team can also be based at their own service centres such as social service departments or community nursing centres; some nurses may be group attached and working from GP surgeries and so on.

3.10 Working in collaboration

Whatever the physical location of the team, the members must be in a position to communicate effectively and efficiently. This means that the environment must facilitate communication and the relationships between individual team members should be such that interprofessional rivalry and territorialism does not become an option.

There are a variety of ways in which communication and co-operation can be facilitated. Regular team meetings can be established at which general as well as specific items can be raised. This was always regarded as an integral part of the work of some general practices who saw the holistic approach to care as paramount. The personal experience of the author, as a district nurse, was that these meetings were important to the professionals involved in terms of support and advice but also in the development of professional collegiality.

Case conferencing has assumed an even greater importance in the new environment of the NHS and especially within primary health care; for example, as required by the Children Act 1989. In the past the practice of conferencing has been a core component of social work practice, bringing in appropriate personnel when necessary. Health visitors have been involved for many years with conferences relating to children and families, and more recently district nurses have become equally important in the information exchange process. This latter development owes much to the recent NHS reforms, in particular the requirement to develop individual care packages for clients (NHS and Community Care Act, 1990).

Health and social service professionals have not always enjoyed the closest of working relationships from an organizational viewpoint but at the grass roots level individual community professionals have always been able to draw on an informal network. This was at times the only means of securing access to particular arms of the service, sometimes resulting in a less than satisfactory response to expressed needs (Skeet, 1970).

The introduction of liaison personnel between members of the PHCT and the acute sector has improved both the transfer of information and of patients/clients into and out of hospital and residential institutions. The role has increased in importance as the concept of discharge planning has developed.

The NHS reforms aiming to reduce costs in patient services, have had a significant impact on the community care. As hospitals have aimed for shorter stays in hospital, thereby increasing their bed utilization, so the community teams have received more patients requiring a wider range of care provision. Discharge planning has become a prime requisite in ensuring that there are 'services that respond flexibly and sensitively to the needs of individuals and their carers' (DOH, 1989c). Approximately 90% of care takes place in the community, of which 95% is undertaken by informal carers. Without the full support of health and social services these informal carers can find themselves under exceptional stress and unable to cope physically; sometimes the pressure they are experiencing causes them to fall ill themselves, and it can also bring financial insecurity. Occasionally it encourages physical abuse of their relatives. In order to obviate these unintentional end results community care must be structured carefully, comprehensively and effectively.

3.11 Prerequisites for success

Funding and physical resources

Opinions will differ as to what makes any health care activity a success but most will agree that for the PHCT concept to promote teamwork and comprehensive care provision there must be adequate financial and physical resources. According to *Caring for People* (DOH, 1989c) expenditure on core community care increased by 68% between 1979 and 1988. Community health service expenditure increased by 35% and personal social services achieved a 37% growth rate. Their concern was not the growth rate of the services but in the practical responses of community care which they felt 'contained a built-in bias towards residential and nursing home care, rather than services for people at home' (DOH, 1989c).

Within Northern Ireland the health and personal social services have been administered within one structure since 1973. In addition, Northern Ireland has more health centres per head of population than the rest of the UK. Taken together these arrangements have allowed a mutuality of purpose to focus on providing the most comprehensive health and social care response for the individuals and/or client groups. Physical resources are not restricted to the 'bricks and mortar' of the health centre or to the activities that take place therein. They also include the professional and ancillary staff required to deliver a comprehensive service.

Staffing

Most recently the reorganization of the health and welfare services has resulted in an increase in the number of untrained staff providing care, albeit under the supervision of qualified professionals. this has caused some concern, particularly within the nursing profession which has been the subject of a variety of skill mix reviews both nationally and locally.

The specific contribution of the nursing profession in achieving the targets set out in *Health of the Nation* (DOH, 1991; 1992) and the alliances document is detailed in *Targeting Practice – The Contribution of Nurses, Midwives and Health Visitors* (DOH, 1993b). Without adequate skilled staff these targets become almost a paper exercise and the development of healthy alliances between professionals and the public seems like the pursuit of the impossible dream. There is a need for the provision of flexible staffing ratios in all areas of expertise within primary health and social care that does not reduce either the choices to be made by the patient/client or the quality of service provision at grass roots level.

Concept validity

The Roy Report (DOH, 1990) set out five managerial models which were in common usage across the UK detailing the philosophy behind each model and the pros and cons for employing such managerial and organizational strategy. They emphasize the view that choice in the selection and development of organizational strategies was a matter for *local* decisions and refrained from supporting one strategy over another.

The concept of PHCTs has been termed 'The search for the holy grail' (James, 1991). The constant organizational and administrative changes that have taken place over the last decade or so have produced a variety of methods of delivering health care services within which the PHCT has become one such method rather than the central theme of community care as the Roy Report (DOH, 1990) has demonstrated. The voluntary sector, for example, in providing a further support network and services that cannot, or will not, be provided by central government has been given enhanced status within the NHS and Community Care Act (1990). Similarly, encouragement has been given to the private sector to provide complementary and alternative avenues of care in both the acute and community care sectors and GP Fundholding via the contracting process offers opportunities for further diversification.

It has been noted earlier that the primary health care sector has been given a minimal role in government deliberations aimed at devising its pluralistic policy on health and social service organization. The absence of a strategic policy for the corporate status of primary health care services may result in the fragmentation and potential disappearance of the PHCT.

Despite the factors outlined above there is much to be gained from a concerted effort to ensure that the organization of primary health care continues within the context of multidisciplinary professional teams.

3.12 Advantages of PHCTs

The planning and management role of the PHCTs was underlined by *Promoting Better Health* (DOH, 1989a), a declaration of the government's philosophy on improving primary health care. This document placed the onus on the then family practitioner committees (now the family and health service authorities (FHSAs)) to make services responsive to needs and ensure the widest range of choice; monitor and improve the quality of care; and set clear priorities for care, ensuring value for money and special attention to health promotion and illness prevention.

The PHCT, in conjunction with the FHSAs, has the ability and potential to meet all of these responsibilities within a realistic financial and physical framework. It can accommodate a need for care which could be quantitatively increased and qualitatively superior in effect to other forms of care provision. Monitoring quality and ensuring quality control can lead to the optimal use of scarce resources and encourage greater co-ordination in health promotion activities.

Success can be indicated by lower morbidity, prevalence and incidence rates in disease. The social environment of care can be greatly enhanced by the generation of greater understanding of different professional roles and responsibility within the PHCT and a recognition of different spheres of expertise. Peer influence and informal learning networks within the team will enhance the development of corporate status and increase job satisfaction for the team members. Above all the PHCT can generate better quality services, producing efficient and effective care and treatment for individuals, families and population groups.

3.13 Some thoughts for the future

Despite its existence as a specific structure, the PHCT concept is still in its infancy. The major problem which has dogged the structure since its inception has been the lack of a suitable model job specification. This has arisen partly as a result of the number of professional groups involved, each with a different method of working and each with a different perception of its role in the delivery of care to the patient or client. PHCTs have also suffered from the structure of the NHS which was created by the coming together of disparate entities in 1948. These were further reorganized in 1973/4 and, most recently, radically reassessed and remodelled along business lines in accordance with the NHS and Community Care Act (1990). The orientation of the PHCT has altered as one administrative change has superseded another.

It remains accepted, however, that the primary health services have the potential both to bring the preventative and curative services together and play an important part in the State's support service network. The role of primary health care and the PHCT does not imply but facilitates a reconstruction of the link between consultant and GP. It encourages institutions to relate their functions to the community they serve and shifts the emphasis from institutionalized activity to a community concept of health care. Importantly, it provides a vehicle and a medium for health promotion and illness prevention and identifies the epidemiological data that must underpin such programmes.

For the personnel involved the concept of teamwork is fostered and professional interaction can become a reality whilst negating the danger of overspecialization by providing appropriate training and education for all team members. Perhaps most importantly, the concept of primary health care places responsibility back in the community with the people it aims to serve. *The Health of the Nation: Working Together for Better Health* (DOH, 1993a) sums up the challenge in this way:

'... living longer brings new problems – modern threats to health such as coronary heart disease, cancers or accidents. While there remains an important role for central and local government and the statutory and voluntary services in tackling the causes – whatever they might be – at the same time there is emphasis on how individual people can themselves contribute to better health, and how they can be supported in this by all who help to shape their lives and working or living environments.'

The starting point has to be assurance that health care should be delivered within the context of local living or working environments and placing services at a point to meet, respond to and overcome these new and emergent problems. The concept of primary health care and the primary health care team have the potential to support both individuals and the health care system in the development of comprehensively planned services which are effective and efficient in meeting the needs of the local populations they serve.

3.14 References

Abel-Smith, B. (1964) *The Hospitals 1800–1848: A Study in Social Administration in England and Wales.* Heinemann, London.

BMA (1974) *The Organisation of Primary Medical Care.* Planning Report No. 4, BMA, London.

Chang, L. (1992) *Wild Swans.* Chapman & Hall, London.

DHSS NI (1972) *Health and Personal Social Services (NI) Order.* HMSO, Belfast.

DHSS (1973) *Consultative Paper on the Structure and Management of Health and Personal Social Services in Northern Ireland.* HMSO, Belfast.

DHSS (1976) *Report on the Committee on Child Care Health Services; Fit for the Future.* HMSO, London.

DHSS (1991) *Health and Personal Social Services (NI) Order.* HMSO, Belfast.

DOH (1969) *Report of the Committee on Local Authority and Allied Personal Social Services* (Chair: H. Seebohm). Cm 3093. HMSO, London.

DOH (1983) *Agenda for Discussion.* Report to the Secretaries of State for Health, Wales, Northern Ireland and Scotland (Chair: Sir Roy Griffiths). HMSO, London.

DOH (1986a) *Neighbourhood Nursing – a Focus for Care.* Report of the Community Nursing Review Team (Chair: Julia Cumberlege). HMSO, London.

DOH (1986b) *Mix and Match: A Review of Nursing Skill Mix.* HMSO, London.

DOH (1986c) *Community Care: An Agenda for Action* (The Griffiths Report). HMSO, London.

DOH (1989a) *Promoting Better Health: The Government's Programme for Improving Primary Health Care.* Cm 2459. HMSO, London.

DOH (1989b) *Working for Patients.* Cm 555. HMSO, London.

DOH (1989c) *Caring for People: Community Care in the Next Decade and Beyond.* Cm 849. HMSO, London.

DOH (1990) (The Roy Report). HMSO, London.

DOH (1991) *The Health of the Nation: A Consultative document for health in England.* HMSO, London.

DOH (1992) *The Health of the Nation: A Strategy for England.* Cm 1986. HMSO, London.

DOH (1993a) *The Health of the Nation: Working Together for Better Health.* HMSO, London.

DOH (1993b) *The Health of the Nation: Targeting Practice – The Contribution of Nurses, Midwives and Health Visitors.* Report of a steering group of NHSME. HMSO, London.

Forsythe, D. (1966) *Doctors and State Medicine.* Pitmans Medical, London.

James, E. (1991) Future Uncertain. *Primary Health Care,* 1(3).

Mechanic, D. (1978) *Medical Sociology.* Macmillan, London.

MOH (1944) *A National Health Service.* Cm 6502. HMSO, London.

MOH (1919) Consultative Council on Medical and Allied Services. *Interim Report on the Future Provision of Medical and Allied Services* (Chair: Lord Dawson). HMSO, London.

OHE (1974) *The Work of Primary Medical Care.* Office of Health Economics, London.

OPCS (1982) A survey carried out on behalf of the DHSS in England and Wales. HMSO, London.

Skeet, M. (1970) *Home from home.* Dan Mason Research Committee, London.

SSC (1986–7) *Primary Health Care*. Report from the Social Services Committee. HMSO, London.
WHO (1978) *Health for All*. Declaration of WHO Conference on Primary Health Care, Alma Ata. WHO, Geneva.

Chapter 4

Communication and Interpersonal Skills

There is an ever-increasing recognition and explicit acknowledgement of the fundamental relationship between communication and health care. The importance of effective communication between the community health care nurse and those with whom he or she deals is widely accepted (Cronin-Stubbs, 1983; Raymond, 1983; Llewelyn & Trent, 1987; Long & McGreevy, 1993; Trojan & Yonge, 1993). As far as care delivery is concerned, the processes of initially engaging with recipients of the service; establishing, maintaining and indeed terminating facilitative relationships; accurately assessing needs; negotiating realistic goals; effecting an appropriate intervention and evaluating outcome – all depend, for their individual success and hence the overall quality of care provision, on the scope and effectiveness of communication achieved (Faulkner, 1992). Approached from the recipient's perspective, the community health care nurse can only gain 'entry to a patient's experience, which is unique and peculiar to him ... by what the patient tells her either verbally or by other behaviour...' (Baly *et al.*, 1987).

On a broader front, Ruben (1990) makes the point that the relationship between communication and health goes much beyond practitioner–client interaction. Communication is the means by which health practitioners receive training, organize and co-ordinate services, conduct research and disseminate findings. Indeed, it is through communication that societies ultimately define and formulate acceptable ways of relating to health and illness.

In this chapter, communication will be introduced, not only as a feature of interpersonal involvement, but as an emerging social science discipline, one branch of which is concerned with illuminating the processes of creating, transmitting, receiving and acting upon health-relevant information. Having established this disciplinary perspective, the essential focus will be on the nature of the transaction between nurses, clients and carers in the community. Given the relative dearth of communication research specifically focused upon the community setting, however, literature from adjacent (but admittedly different) areas such as general nursing and community-based medicine will be included. The notion of interpersonal communication as skilled activity will be presented and a conceptual model of the undergirding mechanisms briefly explored. Recognized areas of skill deficit are exposed and possible reasons for poor standards proposed. Finally, implications for promoting this dimension of health care through improved training will be pursued and an approach to communication skill training sketched.

Before moving on to tackle this agenda some of the factors which have coalesced in the recognition of the importance of communication in health will be explored. (It is probably more accurate to use the word 're-recognition' since the nature of the practitioner–client relationship was regarded as an indispensable aspect of care and recovery in the days before 'germ theory' revolutionized medicine (Clare, 1993).)

4.1 Recognition of the importance of communication in health

It seems that the rediscovery of the crucial part which the nature of provider–recipient, person-to-person contact plays in quality care can be traced to several interrelated influencing factors, operating at different levels. These concern the changing face of present-day disease, conceptualizations of health and illness, general changes within the structure of society, policies of health care, and empirical findings on health worker communication and its effects on client outcomes.

Epidemiology has drawn attention to the dramatic changes this century in patterns of mortality and morbidity in Western Europe and the United States with consequent implications for primary health care (DiMatteo & DiNicola, 1982; Clear, 1993). Today's challenges are inherently different from the acute infectious epidemics of the nineteenth century which were ultimately controlled by means of vaccinations and antibiotics (Davis & Fallowfield, 1991). Proactive measures of prevention, health maintenance and promotion are undoubtedly the most effective means of tackling contemporary health problems such as HIV infection and AIDS, cardiovascular disease, cancer, cirrhosis of the liver, depression, etc.

Once contracted, health care intervention can at best hope to ameliorate rather than cure these conditions. Here success depends not upon the eradication of micro-organisms but the influencing of individuals in such a way as to bring about changes in values, attitudes, beliefs and ultimately habits and lifestyles. Indeed this was acknowledged when the White Paper *The Health of the Nation* (DOH, 1992a), launched in July 1992, was described as '... not about taking pills. It is about changing habits and behaviour – though it is stating the obvious to say that behaviour change is very much harder to achieve than taking tablets' (Bottomley, 1993). As such, the operational technology owes more to disciplines such as psychology, sociology and communication than to chemistry or microbiology.

The implications of this stance for the suitability of the traditional model of health care, the biomedical model, which draws its inspiration from the natural sciences, are increasingly becoming obvious. This disease-oriented 'body-as-machine' approach with its accompanying conceptualization of the patient as damaged structure or malfunctioning system, demands no great communicative ability on the part of the 'practitioner-as-expert' since the 'client-as-person' is scarcely recognized. The villification of the biomedical model, in the health literature, and its replacement with a more holistic biopsychosocial alternative is ongoing (Clare, 1993). In nursing, in particular, the shortcomings of the former as an acceptable basis for modern practice have been readily recognized (Kasch, 1986; McGinnis, 1987). Indeed in many aspects of contemporary community health care nursing, where there is neither 'disease' nor 'patient', it seems a particularly inappropriate framework upon which to base service intervention. Limitations of this model as a basis for both psychiatric (Shanley, 1984) and learning disability nursing (Benicki & Leslie, 1983), have been commented upon. There is evidence though that, despite such rhetoric, the biomedical model still persists in some quarters to inform nursing practice (Abraham & Shanley, 1992; Greenwood, 1993).

A more broadly-based and holistic, biopsychosocial alternative to this model which can additionally accommodate interpersonal and societal influences on health together with the expectations, beliefs and predispositions of the individuals concerned, has much to commend it. Caring for clients demands a recognition of the relationship of social and psychological phenomena to their health needs, a sensitivity to their particular circumstances in each case, and an ability to deal successfully with these phenomena at a number of levels (DiMatteo & DiNicola, 1982). Viewed in this light, effective communication between the health care professional, client, and informal carer in the community becomes an essential requirement (Llewelyn & Trent, 1987).

Changing views of health itself, from the mere absence of illness to more positive, holistic and dynamic notions of optimizing resources to maximize personal potential (Ewles & Simnett, 1992), should be appreciated as a further reason for the recent reinstatement of communication at the centre of health care. Working with those in the community in a spirit of active co-operation and participation so that, through empowerment, they are enabled to adapt to change, more successfully meet their needs and fulfil their potential for quality life obviously places a premium upon such communicative activities as informing, teaching, interviewing, influencing, persuading, negotiating and counselling (Llewelyn & Trent, 1987; Wasik, *et al.*, 1990; Seale, 1992).

Present health policy is decidedly directed towards increasing emphasis upon community-based care, and away from the established dependence on institutional care (Sines, 1988a). Effects on nursing provision have been quite profound (DHSS, 1986) and constitute a related influencing factor in the present emphasis upon good communication in health care delivery. The different patterns of contact with clients and families in the community, coupled with the often long-term involvement necessitated by chronic conditions, puts an added premium upon effective communication. The ramifications of these policy changes in this respect, though, need to be much more extensively researched (Sharf, 1993).

Additionally, the advent of consumerism in the NHS has cast the client as the consumer of a service with a set of attendant and now formalized rights and expectations (DOH, 1992b). This proposes a type of relationship between provider and recipient of care which is radically different from that which has traditionally prevailed, especially in medicine, and brings the need for improvements in communication with patients sharply to the fore. This aspect of care has consistently been criticized by recipients of health services (Ley, 1988; Meredith, 1993). (Methodological difficulties with much patient satisfaction research are recognized but will not be pursued. See, for example, Bond and Thomas (1992) for further elaboration.) Nevertheless, the Health Services Commissioner's Annual Report has consistently identified poor or inadequate communication between patient and health professional as the source of many of the grievances dealt with. The annual report for 1992–93, for example, places this category of complaint highest of the 15 categories established for acute hospital outpatients and mental health (HMSO, 1993). When considered by professional grouping, nursing, midwifery and health visiting, taken together, recorded the second highest number of communication complaints of the eight service groups mentioned. Only medical and dental recorded a higher incidence of complaint of this type. For nursing, midwifery and health visiting, communication issues represented the second highest category of upheld complaint, being almost a quarter of the total number brought against this group. The health services commissioner's conclusion was that 'Good oral and written communications are essential for the provision of a satisfactory service. Without failures in communications there would be a dramatic fall in the number of complaints to me – and to health authorities themselves' (HMSO, 1993). It would seem, however, that more complaints of this type stem from hospital than from community experiences. Nevertheless, if recipients' judgements of the quality of the service received are to be given credence, then improved communication is a daunting challenge currently facing all health workers.

Specific features of communication which cause dissatisfaction have been identified and reported (Maguire, 1984; Faulkner & Maguire, 1984; MacLeod Clark, 1985; Dickson, 1989; Abraham & Shanley, 1992). These tend to centre around inaccurate perceptions of patient needs leading to failure to detect or deal with psychosocial concerns, the adoption of a too socially dominant position, and failure to show respect for persons. The greatest bone of contention, however, would appear to revolve around information-giving – or rather the lack of it! The findings have been summarized by the Audit Commission (1993): 'A common complaint is that there is not enough information. Equally, information often exists, but the quality is poor...'. While the hospital setting was the focus of the Audit Commissioner's report, the accusation has also been levelled at other sectors of health care. A fairly consistent criticism of the community psychiatric nurse by both clients and family carers, although this branch of community health care nursing is not unique in this respect, is that not enough information is provided about such matters as the client's condition, medication and available community services (Munton, 1990; Allen, 1993).

Concern over client dissatisfaction is sharpened by the fact that there is now a growing body of empirical evidence that not only do patients demand more and better standards of communication from health carers but that they often actually benefit from them. While a comprehensive review of this work will not be undertaken, it is generally accepted that improved communication, usually in the form of adequate information, teaching and counselling, can lead to positive physical, psychological and behavioural changes (Hayward, 1975; Boore, 1978; Wilson-Barnett, 1984; Orth *et al.*, 1987; Feinberg, 1988; Ley, 1988; Davis & Fallowfield, 1991; Audit Commission, 1993).

The expression of a lack of satisfaction with health practitioner communication, together with demands for clients to be better informed of their condition, may, according to Dickson *et al.* (1989), reflect more basic structural changes in society. A less clearly differentiated class structure and the lowering of class barriers with corresponding adjustments to established norms, now mean that people are more insistent that their rights be acknowledged and respected and less willing to acquiesce unquestioningly in the face of authority. Consequently, and with medicine in mind, Badenoch (1986) wrote that the 'old doctor–patient relationship – half-father/half-child, half-master/half-servant – has already given way to a consultation where the doctor offers guidance and seeks the co-operation of the patient...'. Again, better education and increased knowledge of, and interest in, health matters have meant that many patients now insist on a collaborative, egalitarian relationship with their health practitioner. Within such an arrangement, patients can accept a greater responsibility for their health and play a more active part in its promotion. From a community health care nursing perspective in particular, of course, this change in outlook has distinct strategic potential (Luker & Orr, 1992).

Defining the nature of the relationship between client and community health care nurse in this way, not only accentuates its importance, but by implication, the processes of interpersonal communication which serve to initiate, sustain and indeed terminate such associations. Having considered at length some of the reasons for the increasing interest in, and emphasis upon, provider–recipient communication in health, it is now time to give more focused thought to communication *per se*.

4.2 Communication and health communication

The statement that communication is important to health care has two different meanings. Communication can refer merely to a dimension of practice or, more profoundly, to an emerging social science discipline. Those who write about communication from within the field of health, tend to restrict themselves to the former usage. The provision of a social sciences perspective on their work is left largely to psychology and sociology. From merely an area of common applied interest shared by these established sciences, and indeed by anthropology, ethology and linguistics, communication is now beginning to emerge as a discipline in its own right with its own acknowledged domain of study, distinct theories (albeit to an, as yet, limited extent), recognizable approaches to research and growing body of literature.

While many quite fundamental questions of identity still remain to be addressed (Levy, 1992), the mission statement of communication as science, according to Berger and Chaffee (1987), is with understanding

'... the production, processing, and effects of symbols and sign systems by developing testable theories, containing lawful generalizations, that explain phenomena associated with production, processing, and effects.'

Health is one of the specific areas of applied interest within the emerging discipline of communication. The establishment of the Health Communication Division of the International Communication Association in 1975 gave formal recognition to this area of specialism amongst those with a shared commitment to the study of '... the way we seek, process and share health information' (Kreps & Thornton, 1992). Elaborating upon this basic notion, Northouse and Northouse (1992) define health communication as

'... a subset of human communication that is concerned with how individuals deal with health-related issues. In health communication, the focus is on specific health-related transactions and factors that influence these transactions ... Transactions can be verbal or nonverbal, oral or written, personal or impersonal, and issue oriented or relationship oriented, to name a few of their characteristics.'

Four levels of involvement

Work on health communication issues has been ongoing at four levels of involvement: the intrapersonal, the interpersonal, the organizational/social network, and the macro-societal (Pettegrew & Logan, 1987). Only a perfunctory mention of any but the interpersonal level is possible within the scope of this chapter. For detailed mention of the other three see, for example, Kreps & Thornton (1992).

Briefly, intrapersonal explorations of health communication have focused largely upon patient or at-risk groups and have illuminated cognitive and affective processes, together with personality characteristics implicated in the production, receipt, processing and reaction to health messages. At the level of the organization or social network, researchers are interested in, for instance, identifying communication channels and practices within organizational structures which are part of a health service and assessing their contribution to the efficiency and effectiveness of the system (Hargie & Tourish, 1993). Alternatively, the ways in which communication operates within smaller health-care teams (Humphris, 1988) or self-help groups (Arntson, 1980) are legitimate matters of concern.

In discussing contrasting paradigms of health visiting, Twinn (1991) spoke positively of the emancipatory care approach where

'Networking with community groups is playing an increasingly important role in practice, and may prove to be a more effective way of working than the traditional individualistic approach, currently employed by many practitioners.'

The role of the mass media in the widespread public appreciation of issues of health and illness, together with concerted efforts to effect change in beliefs, attitudes and practices is of major interest amongst those working at the macro-societal level of health communication (e.g. Reeves *et al.*, 1991). Making use of the local media to increase exposure to health issues is one of the community initiatives developed by health visitors (Drennan, 1986). The effects of cultural variables on, let's say, the meanings attached to health-related concepts and practices, together with implications for the exchange of health messages would also be an example of the type of work undertaken at the macro-societal level.

Radio, television and the popular press are not, of course, the only forms of mediated communication of relevance to health care. Exciting new developments are presently taking place in the establishment of NHS-wide electronic information systems. Such networks will facilitate the development of 'electronic patient medical records which will in turn enable the "dream" of converting the NHS into a *proactive health* service, rather than a *reactive illness* service, to be realised' (NHS Information Management Group, 1993).

From survey evidence of publications in the field, it can be said that interpersonal communication – and particularly the study of practitioner–patient relations – consistently attracted more research interest between the years 1985 and 1995 than any other single category of application in the health field (Finnegan & Viswanath, 1990). Within this category, it is arguably the case that physician–patient interaction has dominated. Furthermore, research which is nurse–patient based has been conducted mainly in the hospital, rather than the community setting. The lack of research in this domain, voiced by Morse and Piland (1981) and McIntosh (1981), would seem to represent a still unmet need (Sellick, 1991). A concerted community-based research initiative in nurse–client communication is long overdue.

4.3 Interpersonal communication

As a concept, communication is notoriously difficult to pin down. Ellis and Beattie (1986) describes it as 'fuzzy', with boundaries that are blurred and not altogether certain. This understandably has created difficulties when it comes to matters of formal definition. Holli and Calabrese (1991) attribute the problem in part to the range of disparate activities subsumed under this label, some of which have already been mentioned. From the plethora of definitions of communication which have been mooted over the years, Hewes and Planalp (1987) distilled two central themes: intersubjectivity and impact. The former acknowledges the quest for shared meaning in the process of striving to understand others and being understood in turn. But, as pointed out by Fitzpatrick *et al.* (1992), '... the production of potentially meaningful behaviour does not guarantee impact'. Impact represents the extent to which a message brings about change in thoughts, feelings, or behaviour.

Interpersonal communication is a subset of the discipline which concentrates upon communication which is nonmediated (i.e. face-to-face) and takes place in a dyadic (one-to-one) setting or small group, with participants essentially unconstrained in the form and content of their interaction by other than normal personal characteristics and the dictates of the situation within which they find themselves (Hartley, 1993). In simple terms, it has been defined by Brooks and Heath (1985) as, 'the process by which information, meanings and feelings are shared by persons through the exchange of verbal and nonverbal messages'. Several features of interpersonal communication are intimated in this definition and will now be briefly pursued.

Features of interpersonal communication

A transactional process
The notion of process is one of the most commonly cited characteristics of interpersonal communication, accentuating the ongoing, dynamic quality of

the activity. Indeed, in a sense, once the process stops, communication ceases to exist (Cronkhite, 1976). This process involves at least two participants who individually act as source–receivers, i.e. they are simultaneously both senders and receivers of messages. Describing this process as transactional implies that an alteration to any one of the components brings about corresponding changes to others and affects the system as a whole. As each participant acts and reacts to the other(s) in a system of reciprocal influence they make ongoing adjustments to the communication which unfolds (Myers & Myers, 1985).

Purposeful

Interpersonal communication is purposeful. Those who enter into it, do so with some end in mind; they want to effect some desired outcome (Myers & Myers, 1985). It is this which both provides impetus and gives direction to the transaction.

Multidimensional

Interpersonal communication is multidimensional – messages exchanged are seldom unitary or discrete. Watzlawick *et al.* (1967) asserted that it takes place at two separate but nevertheless interrelated levels. One has to do with substantive content, the other with relational matters, helping to determine how participants define their association in terms of, for instance, extent of affiliation, balance of power, and degree of intimacy and trust. This bifurcation has been found to have broad validity in the field of health communication where Thompson (1990) stressed its importance in understanding nurse–client interaction.

Content is probably the more immediately recognizable dimension of interpersonal communication, dealing as it does with the subject matter of talk. But familiarity should not be allowed to conceal the often fraught nature of the activity. It is relevant here to mention the symbolic and code-based features of language. The relationship between words and the things they represent in the environment is quite arbitrary. Meanings have therefore been described as belonging to the people who use the words rather than to the words themselves (Burgoon *et al.*, 1994).

As a consequence of this inevitable degree of subjectivity, the same word has often radically different connotations for interactors; this can lead to confusion, misunderstanding and possible distress. To the client the description of his or her condition as 'chronic' may conjure up a whole set of quite different (and possibly alarming) images from those it would convey to the community health care nurse! Sutherland *et al.* (1991) produced evidence that cancer patients attach markedly differing interpretations to probabilistic information based upon words and phrases like 'common', 'occasionally', 'rarely', 'may occur', etc. Considerable diversity also appears to exist among health professionals, in the meanings attached to psychological terms (Hadlow & Pitts, 1991)! The implementation of the *terms project* in nursing, amongst other areas of health care delivery, should serve to afford greater commonality in the future use of clinical labels (NHS Information Management Group, 1993).

Through relational communication, interactors work at establishing where they stand with each other vis-à-vis, for instance, dominance, intimacy and liking. These matters are typically handled in indirect and subtle ways involving, although not exclusively, nonverbal behaviour such as eye contact, touch and interpersonal distance (Argyle, 1988). Forms of address and ways of conducting talk are also implicated (Hargie *et al.*, 1994). In an early study, Stein (1968) observed that it was unacceptable for nurses to offer doctors direct advice on treatment matters. They could, however, get their message across in a more veiled fashion by indirectly indicating their views.

Elaborating upon these notions, Wilmot (1987) highlighted the complexity of the interrelationship between these two facets of communication – the content and relationship. While relational issues are seldom explicitly confronted at the content level, the way in which discourse is conducted has inevitable relationship implications. This assertion was borne out in the study by Chalmers and Luker (1991) of the development of health-visitor–client relationships. Building the relationship was found to be a feature of the ongoing interactional process rather than being in some way separate and distinct from it. Even when the relationship became problematic it was uncommon for this to become a topic of conversation and be dealt with explicitly as part of the content of communication.

Communication has additionally an identity dimension. Personal, social and professional identities are projected, and in turn either confirmed or invalidated, in the types of topic chosen to form the content of talk, the linguistic codes used and accents revealed, along with nonvocal features of dress and general deportment. Implications for nursing practice can be drawn (Villard & Whipple, 1974). Some nurses, through self-presentation, seem to nurture an habitually 'busy' image in an attempt, it has been suggested, to avoid communication with patients. Pollock (1987) reported that perceived busyness was one of the characteristics of the community psychiatric nurse that carers found less helpful.

In addition to the projection of an image of self, the nurse can propose a particular patient identity in the ways in which the latter is related to. This may be grossly at odds with the 'face' being presented by the patient and reflecting his/her own sense of self. Simplified addressee registers, including 'secondary baby talk', are sometimes a feature of helper conversations with the elderly (Caporael & Culbertson, 1986) and people with learning disability (Sines, 1988b).

Finally, interactors can, in part, create the situation which they share in communicating. An assessment interview, let's say, can take on the trappings of a relaxed, friendly chat or something approaching an interrogation depending upon, amongst other features, the amount and types of questioning conducted.

Inevitable?

Interpersonal communication is inevitable. This is a contentious claim made by some theorists (e.g. Watzlawick *et al.*, 1967; Scheflen, 1974) who hold an extremely broad view of what constitutes the phenomenon. It is represented in the often-quoted maxim that under circumstances where people are aware of the presence of others in a social situation, 'one cannot *not* communicate' (Watzlawick *et al*, 1967). Others, including Ekman and Friesen (1969) and Burgoon *et al.* (1944), restrict communication to a particular subset of human behaviour on the basis of several criteria including intention. Interpersonal communication presupposes some degree of intentionality, they hold. Certainly when the idea of interpersonal communication as a skilled activity is considered, this notion takes on added significance.

4.4 Interpersonal skill

Communication as skill is based upon the use of contextually appropriate means of relating effectively and efficiently to others so as to accomplish warrantable outcomes (Dickson, 1988). Elaborating upon this line of thought, Dickson *et al.* (1993) explore four underlying themes:

(1) *Utility.* Communication which effectively and efficiently brings about a desired state of affairs is held, other things being equal, to be more skilled than that which fails (Argyle, 1983).
(2) *Behavioural facility.* Behaving skilfully implies that behaviour is conducted in a particular manner, e.g. controlled, co-ordinated, sequenced, etc.
(3) *Contextual propriety.* What counts as a skilled way of conducting oneself in one situation may be rather gauche in another. The social context matters.
(4) *Normativity.* This extends the previous point by introducing considerations not only of the acceptability of conduct but the warrantability of goals as projects worthy of pursuit according, perhaps, to recognized codes of professional conduct. It has been found that some nursing staff use blocking tactics with patients to cut off lines of conversation that nurses find uncomfortable (Bond, 1978; MacLeod Clark, 1982). While such conduct may be accomplished with considerable aplomb and satisfy at least the first two of the above criteria, it would not be acceptable as highly skilled nurse–client communication due to the violation of the normativity stipulation.

A theoretical model of the concepts and processes involved in skilled inter-action will now be briefly outlined. It draws upon Argyle's model of social skill (Argyle, 1983), as elaborated by Hargie and Marshall (1986) and Dickson *et al.* (1993). The latter have been applied to health communication (Dickson *et al.*, 1989; Skipper, 1992), including nursing in hospital (McCann & McKenna, 1993) and community settings (Crute, 1986).

A detailed consideration of Fig. 4.1 lies well beyond the scope of this chapter and the interested reader is directed to Dickson *et al.*, (1989) for further information. Briefly stated, however, the model depicts dyadic interactors as essentially goal-driven information processors, planners and decision-makers, influenced by their personal histories and characteristics, including emotional states and predispositions, and sensitive to each other, their social environment and the effects of their actions. This does not, however, deny that on many occasions, communication is what Langer *et al.* (1978) called 'mindless' when 'new information is not actually being pro-cessed. Instead prior scripts, written when similar information was once new, are stereotypically re-enacted'.

The multiple contextualization of interaction is also stressed. While the model fundamentally addresses interpersonal communication, it also reflects the impact on face-to-face involvement of broader organizational and cul-tural influences.

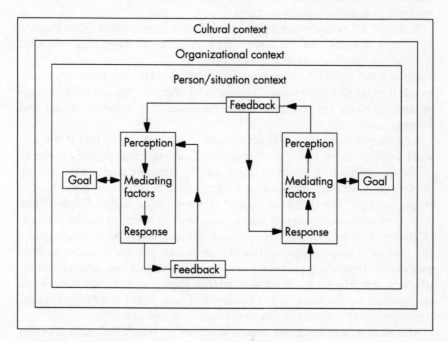

Fig. 4.1 Skill-based model of interpersonal communication.

Person/situation context

Communication is heavily context-bound. Interaction takes place within a person–situation context (Endler & Magnusson, 1976). Not only is what ensues a feature of personal characteristics such as the knowledge, beliefs, values, attitudes, emotions, expectations, predispositions, etc., of those involved but it is co-determined by situational factors such as roles enacted and the rules which pertain. Hargie and Marshall (1986) also discuss the potential effect which physical aspects of the environment such as decor can exert upon the communicative process.

This situational component of the model in Fig. 4.1 has, of course, particular significance for work in the community. Nursing in the client's home, for instance, brings with it an additional role not encountered in the hospital setting – that of guest (Baly *et al.*, 1987). The acceptance of this role is held by Trojan and Yonge (1993) to contribute to the initial phase of establishing a caring relationship when nursing the elderly in this setting. There is some evidence that situations can arise where community health care nurses are very aware of a certain conflict between this and the more traditional, dominant role of nurse (McIntosh, 1981). Resolution depends, in part, on the particular circumstances which prevail. It seems that mostly the role of guest predominates save where, for instance, there is an evident inability of the informal family carer to cope adequately with the patient, resulting in possible neglect or harm.

A range of sociodemographic attributes of interactors also exert a significant influence on the communicative process. Based upon detailed analyses of the audio-taped consultations of 537 patients and their 127 doctors, Roter *et al* (1991) discovered that compared to their male colleagues, female doctors had longer consultations in which both they and their patients engaged in more positive talk, partnership-building, question-asking and information-giving.

A further characteristic of interpersonal communication is that it is transacted between individuals in relationship. That relationship may be one of strangers, old friends, sworn enemies, etc. Community health care nursing involves providers and recipients in longer-term contact than is typical in the hospital setting. The relational context is, therefore, a further distinguishing feature of community nursing which may have an effect upon the communicative process between nurse, clients and informal carers. Sharf (1993) points out that little communication research in health has taken a longitudinal perspective. There is a great need, therefore, to investigate how communication affects, and is affected by, developing relationships. Perhaps some of the work on personal relationships (e.g. Gilmore & Duck, 1986) would be a useful starting point as a source of theories, hypotheses and procedures.

At a more macro level, the organization within which the nurse operates can be thought of as representing a further framework which can shape communication. Discussions can be found in the literature of organizational factors that create barriers to effective nurse–patient interaction (Lillie, 1985; May, 1990). More broadly still, cultural and subcultural variables have a bearing on the different features of the communicative process depicted in Fig. 4.1.

The influential relationship between communication and context is varyingly bidirectional. What transpires during interaction can bring about changes in the knowledge, beliefs, values, etc., of those involved. Indeed effective health education and counselling depend upon it (Ewles & Simnett, 1992). Relationships are shaped and altered through unfolding interaction. Likewise situational factors can be redefined, within limits, by those taking part, as already mentioned.

Goals

Within this person–situation framework, the communicative process is held to be essentially purposeful and goal-directed. The goals being pursued by interactors may be shared, complementary or conflicting. The importance in community health care nursing of maximizing the former is very much stressed (Orr, 1992). More generally, French (1983) observed that nurses engage in communication with patients in order to, for instance, collect information, give information, facilitate patient self-expression, provide reassurance, foster equality of the relationship, control behaviour and facilitate recovery. Other purposes of direct relevance to health practitioners have to do with offering emotional support and alleviating anxiety and distress (Stevens, 1975).

Nevertheless it would appear that customarily there has been something of an imbalance in the sorts of communicative goals pursued. Ruffner and Burgoon (1981) claim that, broadly speaking, goals may be instrumental or consummatory. The former are carried out as a means of achieving some further objective. The district nurse may ask the patient about pain experienced in order to reach a decision as to whether drug dosage should be increased. With consummatory goals, the objective is achieved in the act of communicating. Traditionally nursing has placed a premium upon the former, to the neglect of the latter, since the majority of communicative episodes with patients seem to have been, in fact, confined to providing physical care (MacLeod Clark, 1984).

Despite the move away from task-based hospital nursing practices, it would appear that in many cases the reality of nursing that students are still exposed to on the ward has little changed (Greenwood, 1993). Correspondingly, Morrison and Burnard (1989) reported that nurses seemed much more confident in their abilities to deal with clinical or community situations requiring essentially authoritative approaches such as informing, confronting or prescribing, compared with facilitative alternatives including supportive, catalytic or cathartic involvement. Paradoxically, it is just those approaches to care with which the nurse feels more comfortable that are regarded as essentially misapplied according to much contemporary thinking on community nursing practice (Orr, 1992).

Response

Regardless of the type of goal, in keeping with the model of skilled interaction presented in Fig. 4.1, particular strategies of action are decided upon and operationalized in verbal and nonverbal responses (Argyle, 1983).

Feedback

Adequate self-monitoring of performance seems to be an important component of feedback. Successful self-monitors are very much aware of their performance and control and adjust their behaviour in purposeful ways (Snyder, 1987). Relatedly, the importance of nurse self-awareness has been stressed in promoting effective interpersonal interaction (Ashworth, 1985). As mentioned by Benicki and Leslie (1983), it is only through this means that the community learning disability nurse can avoid conveying, for instance, unintended messages of, perhaps, disgust in inappropriate nonverbal cues given off. There is some evidence, though, to suggest a certain lack of sensitivity in this regard among nursing staff (MacLeod Clark, 1984). Thompson (1990), in her review of nurse–client interaction, wrote that nurses '... do not communicate as they profess they should nor as they think they do'.

In responding to each other, participants also make feedback available. Kreps (1988) accentuates the relational significance of this process: '...partners work at continually updating their awareness of mutual expectations by giving and seeking interpersonal feedback, enabling them to continue to act appropriately towards each other...'. Feedback also has a crucial substantive dimension enabling decisions to be taken as to the extent of goal attainment.

Perception

Person perception is fundamental to skilful interaction yet its essentially selective and inferential nature, which is heavily dependent upon the knowledge structures, expectations and attributional processes of the perceiver, results in many instances in perceptual inaccuracy and miscommunication (Forgas, 1985; Hinton, 1993). Based upon a review of research, Biley (1989) concluded that, '... the results of the studies on nurse perception quoted ... show that nurses are not accurate in perceiving worry, anxiety, and stress in patients'. Indeed, Johnson (1982) found that fellow patients were more accurate than staff in picking up patients' worries! Interestingly, nurses tended to err through overestimation of these concerns. On the other hand, they have also been accused of frequently failing to notice, or misconstruing emotional cues (Faulkner & Maguire, 1984). This led Hogstel (1987) to advocate that part of nurses' training should be explicitly concerned with sharpening their observation skills. Certainly the salience to the communication process of the community learning disability nurse being able to read 'the patient's individual body language; for example his facial expression, posture, and hand movements...', has been stressed (Benicki & Leslie, 1983).

Mediating factors

Information stemming from perceptions of self, the situation, and the other interactor is processed in accordance with a complex of mediating factors. Some of the intrapersonal components of interpersonal communication which operate at this stage are discussed by Kreps (1988) in terms of the organizing, processing and evaluation of information, decision-making and the selection of action strategies. Dickson *et al.* (1989) make reference to further cognitive and emotional factors involved. As already mentioned, the resulting plan of action which is deemed to maximize opportunities for goal attainment, under the prevailing circumstances, will consequently determine action.

Two final points which might not be obvious from what has been said deserve mention.

(1) Skilled communication invokes all the elements and processes encapsulated in the model presented and briefly discussed above. It does not only refer to what people say or do, although it is obviously at this response stage that skill is manifested in action.
(2) Potential barriers to effective communication exist at each of the different stages of the model (Trower *et al.*, 1978). This may be particularly so in a health-care context where, as Barnlund (1976) reminds us, the complexities of problems faced often militate against the successful sharing of messages, without ambiguity or information loss. The health-care worker, client and family carer may differ in the concepts, language and knowledge base with which they respectively make sense of these matters. This may be more problematic in doctor–patient than nurse–client encounters.

Bourhis *et al.* (1989) observed that doctors and nurses are 'bilingual' in that they are privy to a highly specialized register, 'medical language', in addition to 'everyday language'. Patients do not share this 'bilingualism'. Nonetheless, it was found that doctors typically persisted in using 'medical language' in medical settings with patients, while nurses switched from one register to the other as circumstances dictated. This often casts them in the role of 'communication broker' between patient and doctor.

4.5 Training in communication skills

There is no single answer to the question of why communication seems so problematic in health care. A number of contributory factors have been unearthed. These include the persistence of the biomedical model of care (Hunt, 1988; Abraham & Shanley, 1992), inadequate knowledge on the part of the nurse (Greenwood, 1993), emotional self-protection (Squire, 1990; Parathian & Taylor, 1993), inappropriate expectations of senior staff (Bebb, 1987), conflicting role demands (Faulkner, 1985) and other organizational aspects of care delivery (May, 1990; Bergen, 1991). Fielding & Llewelyn (1987) make the further intriguing point that there may be hidden benefits for members of organizations from sustaining poor communication!

A further widely accepted cause of poor communication is lack of skill (Maguire, 1985; Maguire & Faulkner, 1988; Sellick, 1991, Audit Commission, 1993). One of the findings to emerge recently from a major international study of patient information and education programmes in Japan, Europe, and North America is that 'Insufficient attention has been given to training the communication skills of health-care professionals, and to retaining these skills in continuing education programs' (International Medical Benefit/Risk Foundation, 1993). This practice deficit is often readily acknowledged by nurses (Noble, 1991; Crockford *et al.*, 1993; Greenwood, 1993). While much of this literature refers to nursing in the hospital setting, it does not seem to have exclusive relevance to that domain. Reynolds and Cormack (1987) concluded that '... there is little doubt from research findings that nurses in both hospital and community settings have serious difficulties in the structured utilization of interpersonal skills...'

Conceptualizing communication according to the model outlined in Fig. 4.1 has obvious implications for training to improve skill. Training, to be effective, must take on board the different features of interpersonal skill outlined. Put briefly, at a cognitive level participants must know what to do, when, and how to do it; perceptually, they must be alert to potentially significant features of their social surroundings; affectively, they must be aware of their own feeling states and those of the other, together with the effects that these can have on actions; and behaviourally they must be able to operationalize their thinking, perceiving and feeling in such a way as to achieve their goals in accordance with the defining criteria of skill already presented.

Two general strategies can be detected in approaches to interpersonal skill training. One focuses upon the process of interaction, the other upon the content. The first can be criticized for increasing knowledge of topics such as person perception, motivation, social cognition processes, etc., without actually providing much by way of insight into the techniques and tactics of, let's say, counselling or client education. The second, on the other hand, has been accused of merely programming stereotypical patterns of behaviour as if these particular patterns had some inherently skilled quality. A more satisfactory alternative synthesizes elements of both by providing trainees with an understanding of the nature and mechanisms of skilled interpersonal involvement together with some of the techniques and tactics of specific processes like interviewing, educating, negotiating, etc., which they can tailor to meet their own particular needs and circumstances. A training approach along these lines has been proposed which identifies four stages of operation (Hargie & Saunders, 1983; Dickson *et al.*, 1989). These stages are preparation, training, evaluation and feedback.

Preparation

This includes identifying the needs of trainees either individually or collectively (the former is recommended by Fielding and Llewelyn (1987)), establishing aims and objectives of training, identifying content and selecting training procedures. With more mature and experienced participants, this often becomes a collaborative enterprise leading to a negotiated programme.

Training

Here modes of instruction must be utilized which will enable the different aspects of interpersonal skill, noted above, to be addressed. These have been discussed in terms of *sensitization*, *practice* and *feedback*. Sensitization techniques are designed to enhance knowledge and awareness. They may include lectures, background reading, discussions, videotapes, audiotapes, films, role-play, and talks. While sensitization is necessary, it is not sufficient. Given the nature of skill, performative requirements must be met in training: practice is important. Trainees need to be provided with opportunities to implement their knowledge and understanding in action. Here again a range of techniques is available, e.g. simulation exercises and games. Role-play, if properly introduced, has much to commend it and is one way of subtly surfacing some of the affective issues surrounding nursing practice in emotionally difficult settings. But practice without feedback is sterile. Information on the process and outcome of practice attempts must be made available. This can be provided by tutors, peers and practice partners. In addition audio-taped, but particularly video-taped feedback can make an extremely illuminating contribution to the learning experience in respect of enhancing awareness of self and others. It represents a rich source of material in a form which is readily conducive to promoting further in-depth discussion and illustration of many of the features of skilled interaction which have been highlighted.

Evaluation

This includes evaluation of the effects of the training intervention as evidenced by changes in trainee understanding, sensitivity, and interactive behaviour. Some of these outcomes are easier to assess than others. Outcome effects of a different order, such as improvements in client/carer satisfaction, co-operation, etc., may be obtained. Feedback from participants on the learning experience *per se* may be sought, enabling an evaluation of the programme and its operation to be made.

Feedback

Based upon evaluation, subsequent modifications to the training intervention at each of the above stages can be contemplated.

Training of this general type is now used quite widely in health and caring settings to promote practitioner interpersonal skills. Where formal evaluations have been reported, the results have been essentially positive in respect of participants' reactions to the experience (Morrow & Hargie, 1987; Dickson & Maxwell, 1987), helping attitudes (Sellick, 1991), empathic sensitivity (Anderson & Gerrard, 1984) and enhanced performance (Crute, 1986; Gallagher, 1987; Daniels *et al.*, 1988).

4.7 Conclusion

It is now widely accepted in health circles that quality of care delivery can be raised through improved communication practices. There is less awareness of communication as an emerging social science discipline, one area of application of which directly addresses health matters at intrapersonal, interpersonal, organizational/social network, and macro-societal levels. While providing examples of the relevance of each to community health care nursing, this chapter has focused upon interpersonal communication between the nurse, on the one hand, and the client and informal community carer on the other. The essential nature of interpersonal communication was outlined and the notion of skill introduced. Lack of interpersonal skill in certain areas of professional involvement in one of several possible causes of the sorts of communication inadequacies identified. Pursuing this line of thought, a structured approach to communication skills training was presented.

Evaluative studies of such training interventions are encouraging. The criteria upon which such judgements have been based, however, are for the most part, second-order and proximal. Typically they involve measures of various aspects of functioning evinced by the trainee shortly after training. The extent to which such changes persist, generalize to a range of health care contexts and ultimately effect significant and positive outcomes in the health status of the client has yet to be conclusively determined. Evans *et al.* (1992) have found, though, that patients of doctors who had undergone a communication skills training programme were significantly more satisfied with their consultations than those of doctors without such training. Still, much needs to be done if communication standards in health care are to be improved. The general lack of community-based research in this area has been alluded to on several occasions. A concerted initiative is long overdue to illuminate the unique communicative demands which accompany nursing in this context.

4.8 References

Abraham, C. & Shanley, E. (1992) *Social Psychology for Nurses.* Edward Arnold, London.

Allen, C. (1993) Clients' needs, views and wishes. *Community Psychiatric Nursing Journal,* **13**, 6–12.

Anderson, M. & Gerrard, B. (1984) A comprehensive interpersonal skills program for nurses. *Journal of Nurse Education,* **23**, 353–5.

Argyle, M. (1983) *The Psychology of Interpersonal Behaviour.* Penguin, Harmondsworth.

Argyle, M. (1988) *Bodily Communication.* Methuen, London.

Arntson, P. (1980) *Professional–client communication: the narrative response in self-help groups.* Paper presented to the Health Communication Division of the International Communication Association Convention, Acapulco, Mexico.

Ashworth, P. (1985) Interpersonal skill issues arising from intensive care nursing contexts. In: *Interpersonal Skills in Nursing: Research and Application* (ed. C. Kagan). Croom Helm, London.

Audit Commission (1993) *What Seems to be the Matter? Communication Between Hospitals and Patients.* HMSO, London.

Badenoch, J. (1986) Communication skills in medicine: the role of communication in medical practice. *Journal of the Royal Society of Medicine,* **79**, 565–7.

Baly, M., Robottom, B. & Clark, J. (1987) *District Nursing.* Heinemann Nursing, London.

Barnlund, D. (1976) The mystification of meaning: doctor–patient encounters. *Journal of Medical Education,* **51**, 716–25.

Bebb, R. (1987) Care to talk? *Nursing Times,* **83**, 40–41.

Benicki, A. & Leslie, F. (1983) The mental handicap nurse's specialist role. In: *Nurses and the Mentally Handicapped* (ed A. Tierney). Wiley, Chichester.

Bergen, A. (1991) Nurses caring for the terminally ill: a review of the literature. *International Journal of Nursing Studies*, **28**, 89–101.

Berger, C. & Chaffee, S. (eds) (1987) *Handbook of Communication Science*. Sage Publications, Beverly Hills, California.

Biley, F. (1989) Nurses' perception of stress in preoperative surgical patients. *Journal of Advanced Nursing*, **14**, 575–81.

Bond, S. (1978) *Processes of communication about cancer in a radiotherapy department* PhD thesis, University of Edinburgh.

Bond, S. & Thomas, L. (1992) Measuring patients' satisfaction with nursing care. *Journal of Advanced Nursing*, **17**, 52–63.

Boore, J. (1978) *A Prescription for Recovery*. RCN, London.

Bottomley, V. (1993) *Department of Health Press Release*. H93/65, 29 March.

Bourhis, R., Roth, S. & MacQueen, G. (1989) Communication in the hospital setting: a survey of medical and everyday language use amongst patients, nurses and doctors. *Social Science and Medicine*, **28**, 339–89.

Brooks, W. & Heath, R. (1985) *Speech Communication*. W.C. Brown, Dubuque, Iowa.

Burgoon, M., Hunsaker, F. & Dawson, E. (1994) *Human Communication*. Sage Publications, Thousand Oaks, California.

Caporael, L. & Culbertson, G. (1986) Verbal response modes of baby talk and other speech at institutions for the aged. *Language and Communication*, **6**, 99–112.

Chalmers, K. & Luker, K. (1991) The development of the health visitor–client relationship. *Scandinavian Journal of Caring Science*, **5**, 33–41.

Clare, A. (1993) Communication in Health. *European Journal of Disorders of Communication*, **28**, 1–12.

Crockford, E., Holloway, I. & Walker, J. (1993) Nurses' perceptions of patients' feelings about breast surgery. *Journal of Advanced Nursing*, **18**, 1719–18.

Cronin-Stubbs, D. (1983) Interpersonal relationships in community health nursing practice. In: *Community Health Nursing* (ed. W. Burgess). Appleton-Century-Crofts, Norwalk, Connecticut.

Cronkhite, G. (1976) *Communication and Awareness*. Cummings, Menlo Park, California.

Crute, V. (1986) *Microtraining in health visitor education: an intensive examination of training outcomes, feedback processes and individual differences*. DPhil thesis, University of Ulster.

Daniels, T., Denny, A. & Andrews, D. (1988) Using microcounselling to teach RN nursing students skills of therapeutic communication. *Journal of Nurse Education*, **27**, 246–52.

Davis, H. & Fallowfield, L. (1991) Counselling and communication in health care: the current situation. In: *Counselling and Communication in Health Care* (eds H. Davis & L. Fallowfield). Wiley, Chichester.

DHSS (1986) Report of the Community Nursing review. *Neighbourhood nursing: a focus for care* (The Cumberlege Report). HMSO, London.

Dickson, D. (1988) *Improving the communication skill of health professionals: a structured approach to training.* Paper presented at the London Conference of the British Psychological Society, City University, London.

Dickson, D. (1989) Interpersonal communication in the health professionals: a focus on training. *Counselling Psychology Quarterly*, **2**, 345–66.

Dickson, D., Hargie, O. & Morrow, N. (1989) *Communication Skills Training for Health Professionals.* Chapman & Hall, London.

Dickson, D. & Maxwell, M. (1987) Comparative study of physiotherapy students' attitudes to social skills training undertaken before and after clinical placement. *Physiotherapy*, **73**, 60–64.

Dickson, D., Saunders, C. & Stringer, M. (1993) *Rewarding People.* Routledge, London.

DiMatteo, M. & DiNicola, D. (1982) *Achieving Patient Compliance: the psychology of the medical practitioner's role.* Pergamon, New York.

DOH (1992a) *The Health of the Nation.* HMSO, London.

DOH (1992b) *The Patient's Charter.* HMSO, London.

Drennan, V. (1986) Developments in health visiting. *Health Visitor*, **59**, 108–110.

Ekman, P. & Friesen, W. (1969) The repertoire of nonverbal behaviour: categories, origins, usage and coding. *Semiotics*, **1**, 49–98.

Ellis, A. & Beattie, G. (1986) *The Psychology of Language and Communication.* Weidenfeld & Nicholson, London.

Endler, N. & Magnusson, D. (eds) (1976) *Interactional Psychology and Personality.* Hemisphere, Washington.

Evans, B., Stanley, R. & Burrows, G. (1992) Communication skills training and patients' satisfaction. *Health Communication*, **4**, 155–70.

Ewles, L. & Simnett, I. (1992) *Promoting Health: a practical guide to health education.* Wiley, Chichester.

Faulkner, A. (1985) The organizational context of interpersonal skills in nursing. In: *Interpersonal Skills in Nursing: research and application* (ed. C. Kagan). Croom Helm, London.

Faulkner, A. (1992) *Effective Interaction with Patients.* Churchill Livingstone, Edinburgh.

Faulkner, A. & Maguire, P. (1984) Teaching Assessment Skills. In: *Recent Advances in Nursing, 7, Communication* (ed. A. Faulkner). Churchill Livingstone, Edinburgh.

Feinberg, J. (1988) The effect of patient–practitioner interaction on compliance: a review of the literature and application in rheumatoid arthritis. *Patient Education and Counselling*, **11**, 171–87.

Fielding, R. & Llewelyn, S. (1987) Communication training in nursing may damage your health and enthusiasm: some warnings. *Journal of Advanced Nursing*, **12**, 281–90.

Finnegan, J. & Viswanath, K. (1990) Health communication: medical and public health influences on the research agenda. In: *Communication and health: systems and applications* (eds E. Ray & L. Donohew). Lawrence Erlbaum, Hillsdale, New Jersey.

Fitzpatrick, M., Edgar, T. & Freimuth, V. (1992) Communication, language and health: an overview. *Journal of Language and Social Psychology*, **11**, 1–8.

Forgas, J. (1985) *Interpersonal Behaviour*. Pergamon Press, Oxford.

French, P. (1983) *Social Skills for Nursing Practice*. Croom Helm, London.

Gallagher, M. (1987) *The microskills approach to counsellor training: a study of counsellor personality, attitudes and skills*. DPhil thesis, University of Ulster.

Gilmore, R. & Duck, S. (eds) (1986) *The Emerging Field of Personal Relationships*. Lawrence Erlbaum, Hillsdale, New Jersey.

Greenwood, J. (1993) The apparent desensitization of student nurses during their professional socialization: a cognitive perspective. *Journal of Advanced Nursing*, **18**, 1471–9.

Hadlow, J. & Pitts, M. (1991) The understanding of common health terms by doctors, nurses and patients. *Social Science and Medicine*, **32**, 193–6.

Hargie, O. & Marshall, P. (1986) Interpersonal communication: a theoretical framework. In: *A Handbook of Social Skills* (ed. O. Hargie). Croom Helm, London.

Hargie, O. & Saunders, C. (1983) Training professional skills. In: *Using video: psychological and social applications* (eds P. Dowrick & S. Biggs). Wiley, Chichester.

Hargie, O., Saunders, C. & Dickson, D. (1994) *Social Skills in Interpersonal Communication*. Routledge, London.

Hargie, O. & Tourish, D. (1993). Assessing the effectiveness of communication in organisations: the communication audit approach. *Health Services Management Research*, **6**, 276–85.

Hartley, P. (1993) *Interpersonal Communication*. Routledge, London.

Hayward, J. (1975) *Information – a prescription against pain*. RCN, London.

Hewes, D. & Planalp, S. (1987) The individual's place in communication science. In: *Handbook of Communication Science* (eds C. Berger & S. Chaffee). Sage Publications, Beverly Hills, California.

Hinton, P. (1993) *The Psychology of Interpersonal Perception*. Routledge, London.

HMSO (1993) *Health Services Commissioner for England, for Scotland and for Wales; Annual Report for 1992–93*. HMSO, London.

Hogstel, M. (1987) Teaching students observational skills. *Nursing Outlook*, **35**, 89–91.

Holli, B. & Calabrese, R. (1991) *Communication and Education Skills: the dietician's guide*. Lea & Febiger, Philadelphia.

Humphris, D. (1988) Team working – breaking down the barriers. *Nursing*, 3, 999–1005.

Hunt, M. (1988) Talking to terminally ill patients at home. *Nursing Times*, 84, 58–9.

International Medical Benefits/Risk Foundation (1993) *Improving Patient Information and Education on Medicines: Report from the Foundation's Committee on Patient Information*. International Medical Benefits/Risk Foundation, Geneva.

Johnson, M. (1982) Recognition of patients' worries by nurses and by other patients. *British Journal of Clinical Psychology*, 21, 255–61.

Kasch, C. (1986) Toward a theory of nursing action: skills and competency in nurse–patient interaction. *Nursing Research*, 35, 226–30.

Kreps, G. (1988) The pervasive role of information in health and health care: implications for health care policy. In: *Communication Yearbook 11* (ed. J. Anderson). Sage Publications, Beverly Hills, California.

Kreps, G. & Thornton, B. (1992) *Health Communication: Theory and Practice*. Waveland Press, Prospect Heights, Illinois.

Langer, E., Blank, A. & Chanowitz, B. (1978) The mindlessness of ostensibly thoughtful action. *Journal of Personality and Social Psychology*, 36, 635–42.

Levy, M. (1992) Editor's Note. *Journal of Communication*, 42, 3–4.

Ley, P. (1988) *Communication with Patients: Improving Communication, Satisfaction and Compliance*. Croom Helm, London.

Lillie, F. (1985) The wider social context of interpersonal skills in nursing. In: *Interpersonal Skills in Nursing: Research and Application* (ed. C. Kagan). Croom Helm, London.

Llewelyn, S. & Trent, D. (1987) *Nursing in the Community*. The British Psychological Society and Methuen, London.

Long, A. & McGreevy, P. (1993) Advocating Advocacy. *Community Psychiatric Nursing Journal*, 13, 10–16.

Luker, K. & Orr, J. (1992) *Health Visiting: towards community health nursing*. Blackwell Science, Oxford.

MacLeod Clark, J. (1982) *Nurse–patient verbal interaction: an analysis of recorded conversations on selected surgical wards*. PhD thesis, University of London.

MacLeod Clark, J. (1984) Verbal communication in nursing. In: *Recent Advances in Nursing, 7, Communication* (ed. A. Faulkner). Churchill Livingstone, Edinburgh.

MacLeod Clark, J. (1985) The development of research in interpersonal skills in nursing. In: *Interpersonal Skills in Nursing: research and application*. (ed. C. Kagan). Croom Helm, London.

Maguire, P. (1984) Communication skills and patient care. In: *Health Care and Human Behaviour* (eds A. Steptoe & A. Mathews). Academic Press, London.

Maguire, P. (1985) Deficiencies in key interpersonal skills. In: *Interpersonal Skills in Nursing: research and application* (ed. C. Kagan). Croom Helm, London.

Maguire, P. & Faulkner, A. (1988) Improving the counselling skills of doctors and nurses in cancer care. *British Medical Journal*, **297**, 847–49.

May, C. (1990) Research on nurse–patient relationships: problems of theory, problems of practice. *Journal of Advanced Nursing*, **15**, 307–15.

McCann, K. & McKenna, H. (1993) An examination of touch between nurses and elderly patients in a continuing care setting in Northern Ireland. *Journal of Advanced Nursing*, **18**, 838–946.

McGinnis, P. (1987) Teaching nurses to teach. In: *Nursing Education: Research and Developments* (ed. B. Davis). Croom Helm, London.

McIntosh, J. (1981) Communicating with patients in their own homes. In: *Communication in Nursing Care* (eds W. Briggs & J. MacLeod Clark). HM&M Publications, Aylesbury.

Meredith, P. (1993) Patient satisfaction with communication in general surgery. *Social Science and Medicine*, **37**, 591–602.

Morrison, P. & Burnard, P. (1989) Students' and trained nurses' perceptions of their own interpersonal skills: a report and comparison. *Journal of Advanced Nursing*, **14**, 321–9.

Morrow, N. & Hargie, O. (1987) Effectiveness of a communication skills training course in continuing pharmaceutical education in Northern Ireland: a longitudinal study. *American Journal of Pharmaceutical Education*, **51**, 148–52.

Morse, B. & Piland, R. (1981) An assessment of communication competencies needed by intermediate level health care providers. *Journal of Applied Communication Research*, **9**, 30–41.

Munton, R. (1990) Client satisfaction with community psychiatric nursing. In: *Community Psychiatric Nursing* (ed. C. Brooker). Chapman & Hall, London.

Myers, G. & Myers, M. (1985) *The Dynamics of Human Communication*. McGraw-Hill, New York.

NHS Information Management Group (1993) *Read Codes and the Terms Projects: A Brief Guide*. DOH, London.

Noble, C. (1991) Are nurses good patient educators? *Journal of Advanced Nursing*, **16**, 1185–9.

Northouse, P. & Northouse, L. (1992) *Health Communication: strategies for health professionals*. Appleton & Lange, Norwalk, Connecticut.

Orr, J. (1992) The community dimension. In: *Health Visiting: towards community health nursing* (eds K. Luker & J. Orr). Blackwell Science, Oxford.

Orth, J., Stiles, W., Scherwitz, L., Hennrikus, D. & Vallbona, C. (1987) Patient exposition and provider explanation in routine interviews and hypertensive patients' blood pressure control. *Health Psychology*, **6**, 29–42.

Parathian, A. & Taylor, F. (1993) Can we insulate trainee nurses from exposure to bad practice? A study of role play in communicating bad news to patients. *Journal of Advanced Nursing*, **18**, 801–807.

Pettegrew, L. & Logan, R. (1987) The health care context. In: *Handbook of Communication Science* (eds C. Berger & S. Chaffee). Sage Publications, Beverly Hills, California.

Pollock, L. (1987) *Psychiatric nursing in the community: a study of a working situation*. PhD thesis, University of Edinburgh.

Raymond, E. (1983) The practice of health visiting. In: *Health Visiting* (ed. G. Owen). Ballière Tindall, London.

Reeves, B., Newhagen, J., Maibach, E., Basil, M. & Kurz, K. (1991) Negative and positive television messages: effects of message type and context on attention and memory. *American Behavioural Scientist*, **34**, 679–95.

Reynolds, W. & Cormack, D. (1987) Teaching psychiatric nursing: interpersonal skills. In: *Nursing Education: Research and Developments* (ed. B. Davis). Croom Helm, London.

Roter, D., Lipkin, M. & Korsgaard, A. (1991) Sex differences in patients' and physicians' communication during primary care medical visits. *Medical Care*, **29**, 1083–93.

Ruben, B. (1990) The health caregiver–patient relationship: pathology, aetiology, treatment. In: *Communication and Health: systems and applications* (eds E. Ray & L. Donohew). Lawrence Erlbaum, Hillsdale, New Jersey.

Ruffner, M. & Burgoon, M. (1981) *Interpersonal Communication*. Holt, Rinehart and Winston, New York.

Scheflen, A. (1974) *How Behaviour Means*. Anchor, Garden City, New Jersey.

Seale, C. (1992) Community nurses and the care of the dying. *Social Science and Medicine*, **34**, 375–82.

Sellick, K. (1991) Nurses' interpersonal behaviours and the development of helping skills. *International Journal of Nursing Studies*, **28**, 3–11.

Shanley, E. (1984) *Evaluation of mental nurses by their patients and charge nurses*. PhD thesis, University of Edinburgh.

Sharf, B. (1993) Reading the vital signs: research in health care communication. *Communication Monographs*, **60**, 35–41.

Sines, D. (1988a) Introduction: setting the scene. In: *Towards Integration: comprehensive services for people with mental handicap* (ed. D. Sines). Harper & Row, London.

Sines, D. (1988b) Maintaining an ordinary life. In: *Towards Integration: comprehensive services for people with mental handicap* (ed. D. Sines). Harper & Row, London.

Skipper, M. (1992) *Communication processes and their effectiveness in the management and treatment of dysphagia*. DPhil thesis, University of Ulster.

Snyder, M. (1987) *Public Appearances, Private Realities*. Freeman Press, New York.

Squire, R. (1990) A model of empathic understanding and adherence to treatment regimens in practitioner–patient relationships. *Social Science and Medicine*, **30**, 325–39.

Stein, L. (1968) The doctor/nurse game. *American Journal of Nursing*, **68**, 1–5.

Stevens, R. (1975) *Interpersonal Communication*. Open University Press, Milton Keynes.

Sutherland, H., Lochwood, G., Tritchler, D., Sem, F., Brooks, F. & Till, J. (1991) Communicating problematic information to cancer patients: is there 'noise' on the line? *Social Science and Medicine*, **32**, 725–31.

Thompson, T. (1990) Patient health care: issues in interpersonal communication. In: *Communication and Health: Systems and Applications* (eds E. Ray & L. Donohew). Lawrence Erlbaum, Hillsdale, New Jersey.

Trojan, L. & Yonge, O. (1993) Developing trusting, caring relationships: home acre nurses and elderly clients. *Journal of Advanced Nursing*, **18**, 1903–10.

Trower, P., Bryant, B. & Argyle, M. (1978) *Social Skills and Mental Health*. Methuen, London.

Twinn, S. (1991) Conflicting paradigms of health visiting: a continuing debate for professional practice. *Journal of Advanced Nursing*, **16**, 966–73.

Villard, K. & Whipple, L. (1974) *Beginnings in Relational Communication*. Wiley, New York.

Wasik, B., Bryant, D. & Lyons, C. (1990) *Home visiting: procedures for helping families*. Sage Publications, Newbury Park, California.

Watzlawick, P., Beavin, J. & Jackson, D. (1967) *Pragmatics of Human Communication*. W.W. Norton, New York.

Wilmot, W. (1987) *Dyadic Communication*. Random House, New York.

Wilson-Barnett, J. (1984) Interventions to alleviate patients' stress: a review. *Journal of Psychosomatic Research*, **28**, 63–72.

Chapter 5

Contribution of the Social Sciences

This Chapter aims to situate our understanding of everyday health and medical events in a social context. It opens and finishes by referring to some of the fundamental social, political and cultural changes which have impinged on the role of the community nurse during the last quarter of the twentieth century. The relevant changes are often described via the concepts of modernity and post-modernity and that is the framework which will be adopted here.

Following a discussion of modernity and medicine (Section 5.1), the concepts of disease, illness and sickness (Section 5.2) will be examined. Section 5.3 concentrates on the social contexts of illness, examining the ways in which social class, community and family life are commonly related to various aspects of health and disease.

Section 5.4 focuses on one of the most elemental changes which have occurred in the organization of health care systems during the twentieth century – the hospital to community transition. This section ends with a brief consideration of some health promotion issues and a glance at that relatively recent ideological shift which tends to locate the primary responsibility for health care in the personal (as opposed to the public) sphere.

5.1 Modernity and medicine

The social sciences and medicine are both products of modernity. Their development is testimony to a guiding and overarching faith in the virtues of rational investigation and the pursuit of truth. The very term social *sciences* is witness to this, and whether we think in terms of sociology or anthropology, psychology or economics, or even some mixture of all of these disciplines we are encouraged to believe in the existence of a rational, systematic and privileged route to true and accurate knowledge about the world. Indeed the social sciences were in many ways deliberately developed in order to provide superior knowledge to that which could be culled from common sense or the prejudices of both the powerful and the powerless alike. Thus, during the late nineteenth and early twentieth centuries it was assumed that the application of scientific method to human affairs could reveal the true and real facts about poverty, housing, inequality, prejudice, disadvantage and disease, and thereby lead us along the correct path to social reconstruction and social progress.

In the same way, of course, medicine – understood as the application of scientific principles to affairs of the human body – could also be regarded as a form of practice which was designed to deliver us from ignorance and misery. So scientific medicine as it emerged out of the nineteenth century was believed to hold the answers to our bodily problems in the same way that scientific studies of society were believed to hold answers to our social and economic problems. The palaces of scientific medicine were, of course, the hospitals rather than the universities, and during the nineteenth and twentieth centuries the hospital as a form of social organization came to dominate all forms of health care. The hospital thereby provided the space where bodily pathologies could be observed and studied, and where cures could be discovered and applied. Furthermore, and as we are now aware, the sacred knowledge of science was inevitably entrusted to the professions – medicine at first and later, during the twentieth century, nursing and then the various professions allied to medicine.

In this specialized domain of the medical the social scientist also had a role to play. That role was to add to the knowledge obtained by clinical and experimental medicine so as to build up a complete and total picture of the world, and especially a complete and total picture of the nature of diseases as they affected human populations. Thus the earliest social scientists searched for the causes and correlates of disease in much the same way as did the medical epidemiologists. And for such purposes social scientists adopted the language and assumptions of medicine, as well as its methods of inquiry (namely the various forms of experimental and quasi experimental design).

The primary aim was of course to discover how diseases were socially distributed and how the distribution of medical resources might help to alleviate human suffering. In medicine, however, the social causes and correlates of diseases were rarely to be regarded as anything but secondary to the primary causes of disease which, as one might expect, were seen first and foremost as biological and somatic in character. Nevertheless, social scientific and medical research proceeded on the assumption that the more facts that were accumulated about disease, and the more we came to know about the world of disease and illness in all its aspects, the more likely we were to be able to manipulate that world and mould it to our own purposes and designs.

In short, the problems associated with disease and illness were viewed almost exclusively as technical problems. Consequently, the training of nurses and other medical professionals tended to take a predominantly technical form. Thus, if one examines textbooks of nursing from the first half of the century, for example, one cannot fail to be struck by the manner in which the nurse is seen as, at best, a technician – applying the prescription of the scientifically trained doctor. And this reduction of medical (and other) problems to technical issues is one of the features which characterizes the condition which we refer to as modernity.

Naturally, we are also aware that as the century unfolded, a further perspective on disease and illness developed. This latter formed, in many ways, the perspective on which the work and the role of the community nurse was predicated, and it centred on a growing awareness that human health had a social as well as a biological dimension. That is to say, an awareness that there was much more to a disease and illness than could be found in the principles of hospital medicine and above all, a recognition that good health was linked in a myriad of ways to healthy interpersonal relationships.

In the sections which follow I shall outline the manner in which social science added to medical knowledge in terms of the modernist framework, and thereby illustrate the significance of social scientific data for an understanding of disease. But I also intend to demonstrate how the work of the community nurse fits into a new conceptualization of states of health and illness, and a new understanding of the role of the community in fostering or hindering personal well-being. Before I do so, however, it is necessary to take a brief glimpse at some features of what is nowadays called post-modernity, for it is in the state of post-modernity that we ordinarily live and work.

The logic of post-modernity impinges on medical practice in a number of ways, but in effect most of the implications can be traced back to the loss of faith in the possibilities of finding *the* truth about the world. This turning away from the possibility of discovering truth has been evident in philosophy and social science for most of the twentieth century, yet it is only during the 1980s and 1990s that such a tendency seems to have gained the upper hand. For in all their different ways, the philosophical pacesetters of the 1980s such as Derrida, Foucault, Heidegger and Rorty (as well as many others), have argued that the possibilities of gaining truth by discovering a correspondence between a scientific statement and a 'fact' is no longer plausible. Instead truth is that which is, in some way or another, socially and culturally manufactured. For those of us who believe in the solid factitious nature of the world, this is a difficult notion to accept. But difficult or not, it provides the key to understanding a number of fundamental and important developments in the organization of health care in the late twentieth century.

For example, as the old certainties of science begin to collapse we see various alternative ways of thinking and doing entering into the newly created spaces of doubt. Thus in the world of medicine we witness an increased availability of alternative therapies such as acupuncture, homoeopathy and chiropractice, together with a growing trust in their effectiveness. And these movements are, I suspect, testimony to a fundamental shift in twentieth century attitudes towards the scientific enterprise. For it is clear that among large sections of the lay public, science is no longer regarded as the keeper of the true or even the keeper of the good. On the contrary, science is often regarded with suspicion and distrust: part of an enterprise which carries with it risks and dangers which are seemingly never fully spelt out by scientific specialists themselves (Beck, 1992). So increasingly such things as vaccination programmes, the need for (animal) experimentation and new forms of medical engineering are regarded with ambivalence and often much criticism. Indeed scientific medicine often has to meet standards of proof which are rarely required of the acupuncturist, herbalist or homoeopath. And one offshoot of this concern with alternatives in the field of social science has been an increased awareness of lay interpretations of health and illness as valid and interesting sources of knowledge (e.g. Radley, 1993). Such an awareness is in large part based on the thesis that professional medical workers no longer have a monopoly on what should count as disease and illness – nor, indeed, on what should count as appropriate therapy. We shall examine some of the implications of these changes in later sections.

Related to this suspicion of science, we may also see in the post-modern world an indistinct but perceptible erosion in the role and status of the professional specialist – partly, perhaps, because professional knowledge is no longer firmly protected under a sacred canopy of unchallengeable truths. Indeed, the authority and knowledge of the professional can be, and often is, challenged. It is challenged both at the level of everyday interaction (in the clinic, the school, the hospital) and, more seriously, at the level of political discourse. Doctor, teacher, nurse (or whoever) no longer know best, and professional knowledge can therefore be subordinated to the will of the generalist and nonspecialist – the 'manager'. Health professionals are therefore no longer the only or even the most important figures in the design of health care programmes.

Consequently, we also see in the post-modern world a fragmentation of the system of care – which goes hand in hand with the fragmentation of knowledge systems to which I have just alluded. So, whereas modernity (in terms of health care, at least) was organized around the all-powerful hospitals, post-modernity is left without any identifiable centre of gravity. Instead we see only nodes of activity: some in the hospital, some under the aegis of a non-hospital-based health authority, some under the tutelage of the social services, and yet others spread out across that nebulous entity called the community. All of these changes have important and significant implications for the role of the community nurse, and it is our duty to understand something about why these changes came into existence and what their implications are for professional nursing practice. The study of such implications forms the backdrop for the sections which follow.

5.2 Disease, illness and sickness

'For us the human body defines, by natural right, the space of origin and of distribution of disease ... But this order of the solid, visible body is only one way – in all likelihood neither the first, nor the most fundamental – in which one spatializes disease. There have been, and will be, other distributions of illness.' (Foucault, 1973)

According to Michel Foucault the medicine of modernity was dominated by the notion that disease was to be defined and recognized in terms of lesions located inside the human frame. In that sense, disease could be understood as a thing which lodged itself firmly in any one of various bodily organs. So, for example, twentieth century hospital psychiatry came to regard the brain as the organ of the mind, and to assume that what were called mental diseases would show themselves up as lesions of the brain. With the rise of germ theory (from the 1870s onwards), it was also argued that the onset of each disease could probably be attributed to contact with a specific bacterium: tuberculosis with the tuberculosis bacterium, syphilis with its causative agent and so on.

In terms of psychiatry, of course, the paradigm case was taken to be that of General Paralysis of the Insane (GPI) which was assumed to be caused by *Treponema pallida* (the agent also linked to syphilis). This belief in a disease as a real thing with an identifiable cause was commonly referred to as the ontological theory of disease. Its influence lasted well into the twentieth century. In fact, it was only during the 1950s that faith in the ontological theory of disease began to collapse.

Even during the nineteenth century, of course, there had been alternative ways of understanding disease to that of the ontologists. A number of French theorists in particular (Comte, Broussais, Bernard) had, for example, argued that disease was not a 'thing' out there in the world at all, but merely a deviation from the normal state of affairs. The diseased heart, for example, was according to this view not so much as a different type of heart as one which was quantitatively different from the normal (perhaps it was heavier or contained more fatty tissue than normal). In a similar way the diseased liver or kidney was not to be regarded as a qualitatively different kind of organ but merely one which differed on some scale of measurable differences.

This second or quantitative vision of disease did not, however, gain general acceptance until the findings of various types of community surveys began to come on stream during and after the 1950s. Thus Armstrong (1983), for example, points out how community surveys of arterial blood pressure in the general population established that there was a very wide range of such pressures, and what was normal and abnormal could only be defined in relation to certain social and environmental contexts (age, type of work undertaken and so on). Given the results of such surveys medical writers began to suggest that perhaps the concept of 'disease' was outmoded, and that we ought instead to think in terms of syndromes.

Despite these arguments, of course, we know that even today the nosology of diseases is presented as if there were a limited number of tightly defined entities in the world which can kill or injure human beings. Thus the World Health Organization (WHO), for example, provides a nosology which is divided into many forms of disease, causes of death or sources of injury – bronchopneumonia, for example, is numbered 485 and coronary thrombosis 410 (WHO, 1993). These causes are generally subdivided into 18 large categories. When we look at the categories in detail we can see that they are built on anatomical subsystems – reflecting Foucault's argument which opened this section. Thus diseases of the circulatory system are sited next to diseases of the respiratory system and diseases of the nervous system are categorized separately from diseases of the genito-urinary system.

Yet despite the fact that people still speak of diseases in everyday language as if they were things, the practical reality is that diseases are better thought of as collections of (sometimes ill-defined) signs and symptoms. Indeed we might like to think of the problem in terms of J.K. Wing's remarks about psychiatric illness – in the context of which he claimed that diseases are best thought of as names for theories rather than names for things (Wing *et al.*, 1981).

As for the doctrine of specific aetiology – the notion that a disease could be defined in terms of a specific causal agent such as a bacterium or a virus – that, too, has undergone a number of changes. Probably the most forceful and interesting attack on this doctrine was that launched by Ludwig Fleck during the 1930s. Fleck was a pathologist by training and was interested in the historical details of the diagnostic test for syphilis – the Wassermann test. The story of the Wassermann reaction had been presented to Fleck as a story of medical discovery and scientific rigour. On tracing the historical detail, however, Fleck found that the process of discovery was as much a social and political one as a scientific one.

For example, Fleck argued that the bacterium which the Wassermann test was designed to reveal (*spirochaete pallida*) turned out to be only one of many of the 'causes' of syphilis and could never be regarded as *the* cause – even in Wassermann's own day. He held, moreover (Fleck, 1979), that Wassermann's test for syphilitic antibodies in patients' blood was only successful in a small percentage of cases – and that, strictly speaking, the test was only for the antibodies and not for the bacterium itself. And nor was the scientific basis for using a blood test to detect syphilis ever clear. Indeed, argued Fleck, the ways in which the Wassermann test came to be regarded as a test for syphilis, and the ways in which Wassermann alone came to be credited with the relevant scientific discovery, requires a social and political understanding of German medicine during the early twentieth century as much as an understanding of laboratory techniques. For Wassermann's work was advanced as much on political grounds as it was on scientific ones.

Not surprisingly, perhaps, Fleck concluded that scientific 'facts' in general are never simply observed or discovered, but are invariably constructed in terms of the social and political interests and beliefs of the age. It was an argument which was later taken up by Kuhn (1970) and applied to other fields of scientific discovery such as those of astronomy and chemistry – perhaps thereby fuelling that suspicion of scientific reasoning to which I referred in Section 5.1.

The current state of analysis, then, would suggest that it is basically fallacious to think in terms of diseases and their causes as precise and definite 'things in the world'. In fact, it is more or less clear that diseases have to be constructed in order to be recognized – and nurses play an important part in that process of construction. Consequently, the ways in which a disease comes to be defined and understood demands a social scientific as much as, say, a biological understanding of the world. This claim is perhaps relatively easy to demonstrate when we think of psychiatric illnesses, but the selfsame lessons can be applied to the analysis of physical disorders. Thus bronchopneumonia, for example, which is a quite commonly observed cause of death among the elderly, has changed in character and definition quite markedly during the twentieth century. So much so that its description in, say, a modern pathology text would have little parallel with the way in which it is recognized in general practice – in fact you would probably be hard pressed to find the term bronchopneumonia in a modern pathology text in the first place. For the pathologist defines the pneumonias in terms of their causative agents, whilst the general practitioner defines them in terms of their clinical symptoms – each specialist thereby categorizing and classifying the world according to their different practical interests.

This relationship between social interests and disease is even more striking when we come to consider the occupational diseases, for we know that many of the latter – asbestosis, pneumoconiosis, byssinosis and so on – were defined as much in the law courts as they were in the laboratory or the outpatients' clinic (Weindling, 1985). And more recently we have seen how the question as to whether Repetitive Strain Injury (RSI) is or is not a clinical entity is in large part settled by means of legal dispute rather than scientific adjudication. This is not to mention the relatively recent analyses of the relationship between HIV and AIDS – all of which serves to show how the establishment of definitions of a disease and its causes is a complex and intricate business which involves far more than laboratory analysis or straightforward clinical expertise.

Despite the fact that we have good grounds for questioning whether one can regard a disease solely as a biological entity, it continues to be the case that many medical anthropologists have chosen to draw a line between disease and illness in a way which overlooks the very complexities which we have just been considering. For example, Kleinman (1973) has argued that: 'Disease occurs as a natural process. It works upon biophysical reality and/or psychological processes, as the case may be. But the experience of illness is a cultural or symbolic reality.' In other words disease belongs to the realms of biology and medicine, whilst illness belongs to the realm of culture and anthropology (or sociology and psychology).

Whatever the merits of our original argument it is in fact the case that much social scientific work has concentrated on the study of illness in this sense. That is to say, it has concentrated upon how people in ordinary everyday life interpret their bodily feelings and disorders. It was the anthropologists who first followed this track – drawing our attention to the ways in which people from non-Western cultures understood and classified what we regard as forms of disease. More recently, however, the study of lay interpretations of illness – or lay representations of illness – has formed a subject of study in both social psychology and sociology (Radley, 1993). Studies in these latter disciplines tend to indicate that lay frameworks often interpret bodily disorder in terms of personal weakness or failing, and that illness for many individuals is often thought to be as much a moral as a biological event (Herzlich, 1973). In the same way it is clear that many people who regard themselves as 'healthy' view their condition as a consequence of some kind of moral worth: that they are healthy because they live life in moderation or live an active and fulfilling life or whatever. They regard their health as coming from within – in the spiritual or moral sense as it were.

Similarly when we look at the problem of causation, we discover that the lay public has quite intricate theories about how disease is caused and how illnesses are transmitted. For example, it is quite common for people to talk about certain forms of disease 'being in the family', or being caused by getting too wet or too hot, or too cold, and from sitting in draughts and so on. Not long ago social science, like medicine, would have dismissed such lay interpretations as mere instances of irrationality and error. These days, however, it is recognized that since lay (rather than professional) interpretations of disease and its aetiology directly affect the ways in which people organize their daily lives, it is lay knowledge rather than professional knowledge which ought to act as the starting point of professional practice (Blaxter, 1984; Helman, 1984). This is perhaps even more important when we think about how members of particular ethnic groups might interpret and report upon the various signs of bodily disorder. Indeed, this recognition of lay representations of illness and disease as constituting significant forms of knowledge is, of course, just one more instance of the manner in which the elements of post-modernity have impinged on academic thinking about such matters.

This question of morality brings us very firmly to the last concept of the trio with which we began: sickness. For if illness may be seen as a personal response to bodily disorder then sickness may be seen in terms of the cultural role which the sick person is expected to play. The importance of the cultural expectations which are imposed on the sick person was first underlined by Parsons during the early 1950s (Turner, 1987). Parsons argued that in

Western societies there was such a thing as the sick role in terms of which the ill were generally excused the normal round of social and economic activities; they were temporarily exempted from their social obligations, but equally they had placed on them an obligation to try to get better, and in line with this obligation they were expected to seek the best available professional help.

Parsons' formulation of the sick role is not, of course, beyond criticism but, whatever its weaknesses, its merits revolve around the way in which it underlines how sickness is every bit as much a social fact as it is a biological fact. The community nurse therefore ought to be sensitive to the cultural variations which may exist in the performance of the sick role. And the nurse, whether in community or institutional settings, should be aware that neither disease, nor illness nor sickness can be satisfactorily defined and understood in terms of human biology alone. In a similar vein, perhaps we can begin to see that an understanding of health beliefs which concentrates only on personal and individual perceptions (as in, say, the health belief model of Rosenstock (1974)) and which exempts any study of cultural factors is equally likely to be misleading.

5.3 The social context of illness: class, community and family

Studies of how people interpret the sick role, and how they understand illness and disease, form just one component of the social scientific contribution to nursing and other forms of medical practice. Most of the traditional forms of social scientific investigation, however, tended to adopt a rather different investigative tack to the ones mentioned above. That tack took the form indicated in Section 5.1: a search for the origins and causes of disease.

The publication in 1928 of a paper by Stevenson on infant mortality in this regard serves to mark off a turning point in twentieth century medicine (see also Prior, 1989). Stevenson indicated how rates of infant mortality varied by what he called social class. His definition of class was not particularly well thought out and his argument contained numerous loopholes, but his suspicion – that the very chances of life and death may be related to the distribution of social and economic advantages, as much as to any given inborn biological constitution – served as the backbone for a series of major research programmes which were executed throughout the twentieth century. There is not sufficient space here, of course, to discuss the full body of work available on the theme of social class and health, but suffice it to say that most of the arguments relating to this question were more than adequately summed up in the Black Report in 1980.

Sir Douglas Black and his associates were in part puzzled as to why – almost 40 years after the founding of the National Health Service –

inequalities in mortality and morbidity persisted. The extent of the inequalities themselves was relatively easy to document. For example, using 1971 Census data, Black demonstrated that mortality rates for adult males in social class V (England and Wales) were two and a half times greater than for adult males in social class I. And the social class gradient as it is often called, was especially marked in patterns of infant mortality and childhood mortality (Townsend *et al.*, 1988). There was also evidence that chronic illness was linked to social class, and that the usage which people from the different social sectors made of the health service varied.

In addition to class variations, of course, there was also evidence of strong gender variations and regional variations. Thus women were shown to have a distinct 'survival' advantage at almost every age, as compared to men. Whilst on the regional front, people in areas such as South Wales and the north of England were shown to experience higher mortality rates at any given age than people in the south-east of England. These divisions and patterns were further underlined in a second report published by the Health Education Council in 1987 (Townsend *et al.*, 1988).

One could fairly conclude, on the basis of the two publications, that forms of social and economic well-being were correlated with variations in personal health. What exactly the links were was, of course, another matter. Sir Douglas Black reviewed a number of possible explanations in his 1980 report, only some of which attributed the health inequalities directly to economic inequalities.

The understanding of the ways in which mortality and morbidity rates have been linked to social and economic factors has numerous parallels in psychiatric medicine. As with studies of the killer diseases, for example, it was long ago noted that rates of psychiatric illness and admission to hospital were linked to social class (or social status as the American researchers tended to call it). Links between social class and rates of psychiatric disorder were, for example, established in a whole series of US studies from the 1930s onwards. More interestingly from our point of view, however, is the fact that some of the earliest studies on the social distribution of psychiatric illness also pinpointed family and community patterns as being related to 'mental health' and illness.

Among the very first to investigate the role of social factors in the creation of mental illness were Faris and Dunham (1939) who examined the distribution of psychiatric illnesses in the Chicago Metropolitan Area during the 1930s (Prior, 1993). Although now rather an outdated piece of work, the Faris and Dunham study is of interest for the ways in which it attempted to link aspects of what the authors referred to as personal disorganization with aspects of social disorganization.

For example, they pointed out that mental illness was associated with social isolation; that its rates increased in areas of community instability; and that in all probability it was associated with forms of family instability. These findings were interesting mainly because, during the earlier part of this century, psychiatric illnesses (rather like identifiable forms of somatic disorder) were assumed to be caused by things in the body, rather than by social or economic conditions. By implication it was held that social and economic conditions only affected aspects of recovery and not aspects of causation (which is why the activities of psychiatric social workers were for so long restricted to the operation of 'after care' programmes).

In terms of daily social activity, of course, it was assumed that family life could only appear as a determinant of health and illness in so far as it acted as a mechanism for the hereditary transmission of disease. (The family was not theorized as a unit of interacting personalities until well into the 1920s and 1930s.) The focus on the family tended, therefore, to concentrate on the genetics of mental illness. Indeed, the notion of inherited defect dominated twentieth century psychiatry so much that the notion that mental illness and forms of handicap were transmitted through families was accepted as an axiom of psychiatric medicine. This was so even after biologists such as L.S. Penrose demonstrated that very few forms of mental handicap were actually inherited. In fact, Penrose argued that there was a difference between suggesting that a defect had a genetic component and saying that the genetic defect was directly transmitted through families. Indeed most of the people that Penrose studied (in the Colchester Asylum) did not procreate, and so he found it difficult to understand how people who failed to procreate in sizeable numbers could be responsible for the pool of 'amentias' (as they were called) in the population at large (Prior, 1993).

Dearly held theories are, however, rarely cast aside for want of facts (and in this respect the history of the thesis that mental illnesses were predominantly forms of inherited genetic defect holds some interesting lessons for the present day). Indeed, psychiatrists held firm to such a belief despite the absence of any rational evidence. For we must recall that during the first half of the twentieth century biologists were not even able to count the number of chromosomes in human tissue with any accuracy; nor were they able to differentiate between male and female tissue on the basis of chromosomal evidence until 1952 – still less identify a gene for schizophrenia or whatever. Yet despite such lacunae, medical texts persistently described forms of mental handicap and mental illness as genetic in origin and inherited through families. This vision of the family as a pool of genetic material more or less defined the only way in which the family entered into nursing and medical discourse during the period 1900–1950 (and it is a danger which seems to be resurfacing with the rise of the new genetics).

There were, of course, some psychiatrists who argued for a social as well as a biological psychiatry; Southard and Meyer were two such (Prior, 1993), but even they failed to theorize the family as anything but a biological and legal entity. It was only with the popularization of Freudian psychology and, later, when sociology began to analyse the family as an interactive social unit that the possibilities for tracing the effects of family life on individual health and well-being began to arise. In fact, it was only during the 1950s that social scientists – such as the aforementioned Parsons – began to argue that the ways in which families interacted could shape (for better or for worse) the personalities of their members.

In terms of social psychiatry these arguments reached their greatest popularity during the 1970s with the widely advertized work of Bateson and his colleagues, the work of R.D. Laing, and, in more rigorous form, the work of George Brown and his associates. By the 1990s, of course, and in the wake of formidable social policy changes, much of this research was set aside and the family was seen as a haven of care as well as an appropriate setting for treatment. The evidence of twentieth century social scientific research, however, suggested that family life was often far from benign.

The changing vision of the family is parallelled by changing visions of community. For whereas policy makers during the early twentieth century saw communities as groups enclosed in institutions (as was the case with asylums for the insane), by the late twentieth century communities were seen as noninstitutionalized groups linked to some locality or other. Naturally, in so far as illness and disease were interpreted solely as matters of the human body, the enclosed community-based forms of treatment made some sense, but once it was recognized that illness had a social component it became clear that aspects of health and illness could not be properly confined to institutions (i.e. hospitals). The consequent expansion of health care into 'the community' has, of course, occurred in both physical and psychiatric medicine and in each case it represents an organizational expression of the belief that health and illness have social correlates every bit as much as biological correlates. In terms of social sciences, however, the concept of community is somewhat old fashioned, and for some decades now sociologists have chosen to speak of social networks rather than communities.

The sociology of community is far too broad a topic to deal with in this chapter. Suffice it to say perhaps that social scientists never reached a consensus on what 'community' might be. For some, a community was an entity held together by a common culture (as defined by a common language or belief system, for example), whilst for others it was defined almost entirely in terms of a common locality or district.

Given the ambiguities and contradictions in the terminology, it is not so surprising that during the 1950s and 1960s, sociologists and anthropologists began to concentrate on the interactive links between specific individuals rather than an ill-defined collective of people, and to speak of social networks. More interestingly, in the field of health research it has since been established that the structure of social networks can be a key factor in determining such things as the onset of illness episodes and even treatment outcomes. Much social scientific work concerned with the onset of depression and florid symptoms in schizophrenia has, for example, implicated the significance of social networks for such processes (see, for example, Brown & Harris (1978)). And in the realm of 'care' the significance of such networks was underlined by the authors of the Barclay Report (1982) on social workers and their tasks – wherein a concentration on the development of networks rather than casework was said to mark the way forwards for social work in general.

In the UK, as well as many other western countries, these various technical issues and analyses have been carried out in the wake of changing ideological and political circumstances. And since 1979, in particular, there has been a political emphasis on the role of individuals rather than communities in fostering good health and good health care. The focus on individuals is, for example, especially apparent in documents such as *The Health of The Nation* (DOH, 1992), in which it is argued that health and illness are things which can be directly linked to aspects of personal lifestyle (such as smoking cigarettes and failing to take sufficient exercise). References to the role of the wider community – the impact of such things as unemployment and economic inequalities – in fostering good health, tend therefore to be placed on the sidelines. The underlining of personal responsibility is also apparent in many features relating to what is called the 'delivery' of health care. Thus the emphasis on patients as consumers, as well as such things as consumer choice and market forces has resulted in a radical shake-up of both local and national health care policies. In fact there is a sense in which nationwide health care provision has now been fragmented and fractured beyond repair – devolved to hospital trusts and fundholding GPs rather than to regional or district planning authorities.

The emphasis on markets and costs has further served to bring into the open a number of very serious (and previously disguised) moral problems relating to health care: how health care should be rationed, for example, and whether or not cigarette smokers and people over, say, 65 years old are entitled to the same amount of health resources as non-smokers and younger people. Indeed, these ethical debates highlight the ways in which a sense of communal responsibility for the health of all has, during the 1980s and 1990s, been replaced by an ethic of individualism and individual responsibility. This, too, is characteristic of post-modernist ideologies.

5.4 The social context of treatment: from hospital to community

Leaving aside political and ideological considerations for the moment, it is clear that the space in which medicine has operated has expanded. Thus medicine has moved out of the hospital and into the community, the family, the home and the school. And the twentieth century history of nursing shadows all the important developments. For as each new site of medical practice has arisen, a specialist nurse has been trained to cope with it. What is more, this expansion of nursing and other forms of medical practice into the family, the school, the workplace and the community has served to underline the ways in which we have come to recognize how health and illness are far from being things which can be segregated from the normal course of events. Indeed, they increasingly appear as states of existence which are best dealt with *in situ* – as familiar components of everyday life. It seems likely, therefore, that the idea that sickness is something which can be segregated in a hospital and treated by medical means alone has had its day.

This reassessment of the role of hospitals in health care systems is, of course, a particular feature of the last quarter of the twentieth century. It is especially apparent in the flight to community care for those with psychiatric and other chronic problems. This latter has been variously seen as a consequence of so-called monetarist economic policies, pharmacological advances in psychiatric medicine, and even the rise of libertarian attitudes during the 1960s and 1970s. Yet few of these arguments are in any way convincing when we examine the evidence. Indeed, it is likely that the shift in the centre of gravity of health care systems from hospital to community is best explained in terms of our reassessment of what health problems really are, i.e. the shift is truly a product of the growing twentieth century awareness that there is more to health and illness than can be found in biology and physiology alone.

This awareness of the role of the 'social' in health is also reflected in a number of other policy-related issues. And of the latter, perhaps the most important is to be found in the growing emphasis placed by health authorities on the subject of health promotion. Health promotion was, of course, not heard of as such before the 1970s, but from the 1970s onwards almost every Western government devised and advocated a health promotion programme (culminating in the 1978 WHO document *Health for All*).

However, as with programmes for community care, it would be wrong to think that the associated policies arose out of fresh air – without any links to the wider concerns of the societies in which they were devised. On the contrary, the emergence of health promotion programmes can in large part be linked to the appearance of other significant features of life in modern industrial societies. For example, they can be clearly linked to the modern Western obsession with the development of 'lifestyles' as a mode of self- and group identity. (In this regard it is interesting to note that a number of postmodern social theorists have claimed that styles of social consumption may have overtaken class as the predominant source of social distinction in the Western world.) And it is certainly the case that many health promotion documents such as *Prevention and Health, Everybody's Business* (DHSS, 1976), spoke specifically of lifestyles as a key to good health.

Equally one can begin to see how an emphasis on lifestyles links in with the politics of the personal (as opposed to the politics of class) which seems to loom large in many Western societies. One might even argue that the newly placed emphasis on health, as against illness, is itself indicative of a deep-seated ideological and social change. What is clear is that the general tenor of such documents as *The Health of The Nation* (DOH, 1992) suggest that the high road to health promotion and the prevention of illness lies in the field of social behaviour rather than in the field of what used to be called public health.

Finally we should note how the recognition of the importance of the social – and especially the importance of social relationships within families and other close-knit groups – has had a fundamental effect on the work of health care professionals themselves. For there has been a growing awareness since the 1960s that the interactional contexts in which doctors and nurses meet patients can also impede or progress treatment outcomes. Indeed, perhaps one of the few lessons to be derived from the work of the labelling theorists of the 1960s and 1970s is that professionals can make an impact on the self-image of patients. And that sometimes the very act of professional intervention can set the seal on a stigmatizing and labelling process which will have negative consequences for the individual patient.

In this respect professional health workers must be constantly aware of the possibility that what they say and do for patients may have a significance far beyond the transient moment of consultation or interview (Brown, 1989). Indeed, this is perhaps why the very notion of 'counselling' has developed with such force during the latter part of the twentieth century, and why models of nursing often underline the importance of dealing with the feelings and interpretations of the patient. And the introduction of counselling into almost every aspect of health care activity is in many ways testimony to the fact that health, illness and disease are nestled every bit as much in features of personal (social) interaction as they are in features of anatomical subsystems.

5.5 References

Armstrong, D. (1983) *The Political Anatomy of the Body*, Cambridge University Press, London.

Barclay Committee Working Party Report (1982) *Social Workers, Their Roles and Tasks*. Bedford Square Press, London.

Beck, U. (1992) *Risk Society. Towards a New Modernity*. Sage Publications, London.

Blaxter, M. (1984) The causes of disease: women talking. In: *Health and Disease. A Reader* (ed N. Black *et al.*), pp 34–43. Open University Press, Milton Keynes.

Brown, G. & Harris, T. (1978) *The Social Origins of Depression. A Study of Psychiatric Disorder in Women*. Tavistock, London.

Brown, P. (ed) (1989) *Perspectives in Medical Sociology*. Wadsworth, Belmont.

DHSS (1976) *Prevention and Health: Everybody's Business. A Reassessment of Public and Personal Health.* HMSO, London.

DHSS (1980) *Inequalities in Health: Report of a Research Working Group* (The Black Report). HMSO, London.

DOH (1992) *The Health of the Nation. A Strategy for Health in England.* HMSO, London.

Faris, R.E. & Dunham, H.W. (1939) *Mental Disorder in Urban Areas: an Ecological Study of Schizophrenia and other Psychoses.* Chicago University Press, Chicago.

Fleck, L. (1979) *Genesis and Development of a Scientific Fact.* University of Chicago Press, Chicago.

Foucault, M. (1973) *The Birth of the Clinic.* Tavistock, London.

Helman, C. (1984) Feed a cold, starve a fever. In: *Health and Disease. A Reader* (ed. N. Black *et al.*) pp. 10–16. Open University Press, Milton Keynes.

Herzlich, C. (1973) *Health and Illness. A Social–Psychological Analysis.* Academic Press, London.

Kleinman, A. (1973) Medicine's symbolic reality. On a central problem in philosophy of medicine. *Inquiry*, **16**, 206–13.

Kuhn, T.S. (1970) *The Structure of Scientific Revolutions*, 2nd edn. University of Chicago Press, Chicago.

Prior, L. (1989) *The Social Organization of Death.* Macmillan, London.

Prior, L. (1993) *The Social Organization of Mental Illness.* Sage Publications, London.

Radley, A. (ed.) (1993) *Worlds of Illness. Biographical and Cultural Perspectives on Health and Disease.* Routledge, London.

Rosenstock, I.M. (1974) The health belief model and preventative health behaviour. *Health Education Monographs* **2**, 328–35.

Stevenson, T.H.C. (1928) The vital statistics of wealth and poverty. *Journal of the Royal Statistical Society*, **91**, 207–30.

Townsend, P., Davidson, N. & Whitehead, M. (1988) *Inequalities in Health: the Black Report*, 3rd edn. Penguin, Harmondsworth.

Turner, B. (1987) *Medical Power and Social Knowledge.* Sage Publications, London.

Weindling, P. (ed) (1985) *The Social History of Occupational Health.* Croom Helm, London.

WHO (1978) *Health for all.* Declaration of WHO Conference on Health Care, Alma Ata. WHO, Geneva.

WHO (1993) *Manual of the International Statistical Classification of Diseases, Injuries and Causes of Death*, tenth revision. WHO, Geneva.

Wing, J.K., Bebbington, P. & Robins, L.N. (eds) (1981) *What is A Case? Problem of Definition in Psychiatric Community Surveys.* Grant McIntyre, London.

Chapter 6

Care Management

6.1 Central objectives of community core

The final implementation phase of the 1990 NHS and Community Care Act was witnessed in April 1993. Among the key tasks to be accomplished by this date was the requirement for local authority social service departments to make provision for care management arrangements for clients in need of community care and support in their locality.

The central objectives of the community care reforms are presented below (DHSS NI, 1990) to demonstrate the centrality of the care management process to government policy:

- to promote the development of domiciliary, day and respite services to enable people to live in their own homes wherever possible;
- to ensure that service providers make practical support for carers a high priority;
- to make a proper assessment of need and good care management the cornerstone of high quality care;
- to promote the development of a flourishing independent sector alongside good quality public services;
- to clarify the responsibilities of agencies and so make it easier to hold them to account for their performance;
- to secure better value for taxpayers' money by introducing a new funding structure for community care.

6.2 Principles of community care

Several principles underpin the government's approach to community care.

- Services should respond flexibly and sensitively to the needs of individuals and the relatives and friends who care for them.
- Services should, wherever practicable, offer users a range of options.
- Services should intervene no more than is necessary and thus foster independence.
- Services should concentrate on those with greatest needs.

The principal focus of care management is set within the context of a 'mixed economy of care', where the process of a consumer-led approach places major emphasis on the needs, wishes, ambitions and wants of people, their families and carers. This emphasis demands that service responses are planned from the consumer's perspective and that they are continuously monitored in respect of the extent to which they meet the actual (rather than the perceived) needs of service users.

Care management can be defined as the tool used by practitioners as they focus service provision on individual needs. Care management is essentially a way of ensuring that individuals are connected to all the services they require irrespective of the source. It is a model based on the principle of providing the widest range of choice possible to clients without reliance on any one service agency. In order for this to be achieved there will be a need to prepare nurses and social workers to work as care managers.

This chapter explores the care management process and provides a framework for the accomplishment of competence in the provision of this essential process.

6.3 Principles of care management

The consumer focus directs the whole process of care management from the initial stages of sharing information, through joint assessments of need and shared planning to the evaluation and monitoring of service delivery. Such a focused approach to consumer-led services may challenge conventional methods of care planning and delivery and will inevitably demand changes in current practice. On the other hand it might simply demand an extension of good practice which is to be witnessed in various forms throughout the health and social service care systems in the United Kingdom.

Central to the care management process will be concepts such as advocacy, representation, empowerment and client involvement and these will need to be pursued and evaluated in individual work practices. Preparation for care management practice will include specific instruction and demonstration of the care management process, the objectives of which might be presented as:

(1) demonstration of proficiency in the use of a variety of assessment procedures in to order identify client needs;

(2) utilization of a variety of care planning procedures in order to prepare detailed care plans for individuals;

(3) critical evaluation of the effectiveness of systems currently employed to identify and deploy resources for service users;

(4) demonstration of competence in co-ordinating services for clients;

(5) negotiation and agreement (in partnership with service users and others) of the provision of the optimum package of care (services) following critical appraisal of a variety of options;

(6) securing and facilitating service provision;

(7) providing opportunities for user and carer involvement and views in the process (by ensuring sensitivity, flexibility and choice);

(8) securing and maintaining service effectiveness and efficiency;

(9) evaluation and review of the outcomes and success of all care packages;

(10) identification and provision of advice to service planners and policy-makers of the results of all care plans including communication of all unmet needs.

The care management process is usually provided to persons with longer term or complex needs and is facilitated through the allocation of a named person, designated as a care manager. Care managers are usually social workers, specialist community health care nurses and other community workers but there is no conditional requirement that any one professional background is required. Care managers will be responsible for getting to know each individual consumer and his or her family and will 'map' their day-to-day needs and requirements and formulate a clear action or care plan to take account of their needs, wants and ambitions. Ideally, the care manager should be as independent from the statutory agencies as possible.

The principle aim of the care management process should be to provide services which are as fully integrated into local neighbourhoods as possible. Good practice should also emphasize the importance of involving service users in the planning of their lives and should aim to promote the concept of advocacy to encourage their participation in all decision-making processes.

The skills base must recognize the fundamental skills of communication; observation; negotiation; decision-making; contracting; engagement with clients, families and carers; risk management; advocacy; conflict resolution; change management; and promotion and maintenance of client empowerment. The value base should reflect a shared belief in the fundamental values of choice, privacy, dignity, independence, fulfilment and rights. The importance of antidiscriminatory practice is also emphasized.

6.4 The benefits of care management

The Care Management and Assessment: Managers' Guide (SSI, 1991) identifies ten key benefits:

(1) a needs-led approach to assessment and the use of resources tailoring services to individual requirements;
(2) a commitment to individual care planning, specifying desired outcomes;
(3) a clear division of responsibility between assessment/care management and service provision, separating the interests of service users and providers;
(4) more responsive services as a result of linking assessment and purchasing/commissioning;
(5) a wider choice of services across the statutory and independent sectors;
(6) a partnership in which users/carers play a more active part alongside practitioners in determining the nature of the services they receive;
(7) improved opportunities for representation and advocacy;
(8) a way of meeting the needs of individuals more effectively (demonstrating cost-efficiency, cost-effectiveness and 'value-for-money');
(9) greater continuity of care and accountability to users and carers;
(10) better integration of services within and between agencies.

6.5 Stages of care management

There are seven key stages in the care management process: providing information; screening; assessing need; care planning; and implementing, monitoring and reviewing the care plan.

Publishing and providing information

Prospective users and carers receive information about the needs for which care agencies accept responsibility to offer assistance, and the range and cost of services currently available. Information leaflets are available for each service and these provide a summary or profile of the service.

Determining the level of assessment – screening

Requests for additional information or advice result in the allocation of a generic care officer who is responsible for the provision of further information and for the acquisition of data relating to the nature of the user/carer request. This stage of the process is referred to as the 'screening stage' and a key aim is to determine the nature and extent of any detailed assessment that might be required in order to clarify client/user need.

Assessing needs

A practitioner is allocated as a 'named person' to assess the needs of the individual and of any carers, in a way that also recognizes their strengths and aspirations. In order to take account of all relevant needs, assessment may bring together contributions from a number of specialists or agencies. The purpose of the assessment is to define the individual's needs in the context of local policies and priorities and agree on the desired outcome of any involvement. If the assessment demonstrates eligibility for care management, a 'care manager' is allocated by the local social services department.

Planning care

The next step will be to consider the resources available from a range of potential providers (from the statutory, voluntary and independent sectors) that best meet the individual's requirements. The role of the 'named person' is to assist the user in making choices from these resources and explore the potential possibility for the provision of new solutions outwith the current range of services 'on offer'. A care plan will then be designed and presented to the 'care management' team for approval and costing. The plan will be costed and the user's agreement obtained. The plan will specify who will do what, at specific intervals and with predetermined outcomes and criteria for the measurement of 'successful outcomes'.

Implementing the care plan

The implementation phase of the process requires the securing of the necessary finance and confirmation of the availability of other identified resources. This may involve negotiation with a range of service providers, specifying the exact type and quality of the service required, and ensuring that services are co-ordinated with one another. The responsibility of practitioners at this stage will vary according to the level of their delegated professional and budgetary authority.

Monitoring

The plan is implemented and subjected to continuous monitoring. Adjustments to the care plan will be made by the care manager (in consultation with the user/carer) in order to ensure that users, carers and service providers achieve the desired outcomes specified in the written care plan/contractual agreement.

Reviewing

At specific intervals, the progress of the care plan will be formally reviewed with the user, carers and service providers to ensure that services remain relevant to needs and to evaluate services in the continuing quest for quality improvement. Such reviews should be conducted at six-monthly intervals.

The Care Management process is summarized in Fig. 6.1.

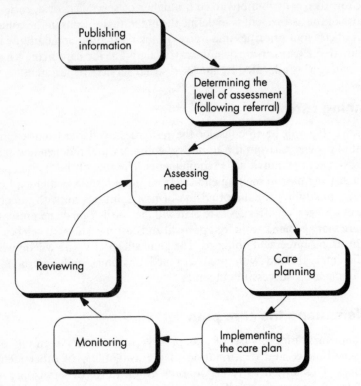

Fig. 6.1 The process of care management (SSI, 1991).

6.6 Models of care management

According to *The Managers' Guide* (SSI, 1991) the eventual goal of all care management processes is to enable all users and carers to benefit from some kind of care management arrangements. The models which may be adopted by social service departments to achieve this objective will vary across the country and it should not be assumed that there is a 'correct' way of implementing the process. However, it is generally acknowledged that care management arrangements can take the form of:

■ a single care manager performing all or most of the tasks of care management with varying degrees of budgetary responsibility;
■ an administrator co-ordinating a range of practitioners;
■ users acting as their own care managers;
■ different practitioners assuming responsibility for the various tasks involved in care management.

Care management is usually associated with the first of these models since it exemplifies the basic principle of arranging care on the basis of a contractual arrangement between a user and a practitioner (a relationship that develops over time). It has clear advantages over the other models described above which rely, to some considerable extent, on administrative and co-ordinating functions without necessarily requiring the implementation of all the care management principles outlined in Section 6.3.

However, it is now becoming abundantly clear that not all users will be able to benefit from the services of their own care manager. This means that, for the majority of users, the most likely option will be one in which skilled practitioners (community nurses and social workers) are used selectively for tasks such as assessment, with other tasks delegated to support staff. The following paragraphs are adapted from 'models' suggested by Papadopolous (1992) who further considers the issue of style and management of the care management process.

The broker model

In this system the care manager focuses on identifying user needs, selecting from a range of available services those most suited to meet these needs, negotiating contractual arrangements, and purchasing these services on behalf of the user, thereby facilitating positive choices to be made.

The therapist as care manager

The care manager has two roles in this model:

(1) A care management function, whereby a care manager seeks to identify the user's needs and co-ordinates services to meet those needs;
(2) A direct therapeutic function, which meets some of the user's needs.

The multidisciplinary team

This is an extension to the 'therapist as care manager' model; but in this model the outcomes of the care management process are influenced by professional inputs and individuals are likely to have particular care management tasks delegated to them by the care manager, whose role is to undertake mainly administrative duties and to co-ordinate team activities.

Informal networks acting as care manager

Users' informal networks undertake care management functions on behalf of the user and the professional team. The advantage of this method is that informal networks have the freedom to retain their autonomy in directing service inputs.

Care management in specific service contexts

While users may be receiving care in a particular context they may have additional needs that cannot be addressed within that context. In this model, care management occurs within the establishment itself and is carried out either by individuals or by a team. The role of the care manager in this model is to activate other service inputs from outside the direct confines of that organization.

In order to identify those greatest in need of care management, criteria must be established in each locality to assess the eligibility of requests for care management. The criteria will usually be determined by the complexity of need and the requirement for multi-agency co-ordination or for the provision of 'higher cost' packages of care. Care management will normally be provided for all users who require a residential care placement. Costs and complexity may, therefore, be regarded as specific criteria for acceptance to the care management programme. Conversely user needs that require uni-disciplinary assessments and action will rarely demand care management support. Examples of eligible cases are:

- exploration of residential care or home support for a person with Parkinson's Disease following the recent death of a home carer;
- design and development of an 'after-care' package for a person being discharged from long-term care from a mental health hospital;
- co-ordination of a day and home-based support package for a person with a learning disability to prevent long-term care admission to a social service residential care facility;
- co-ordination of a range of home-based health and social care services to support a person in their own home following a diagnosis of terminal illness.

Examples of ineligibility for care management are:

- requests for day services;
- home help assessment and service provision;
- applications for DSS benefits and home adaptations from the domiciliary occupational therapy service.

6.7 Empowerment and care planning

Two fundamental concepts that underpin the care management process are client autonomy and empowerment. The government's community care policy throughout the 1980s and 1990s was based on a strong sense of self-care and altruism on the part of the family and the community (Minford, 1984) and, indeed, it could be argued that the whole thrust of the 'Thatcherite' community care reforms have been socially engineered to exploit the caring capacity of the community while reducing dependence upon the public sector (McCarthy, 1989). Because of this, professional responses provided by both nursing and social work have been required to undergo radical change.

For example, in recent years there has been increased public demand for professional responses to be mediated through the development of a partnership with clients to determine shared action plans for care (Brechin & Swain, 1987). Self-reliance and self-care have also been regarded as ultimate goals by the nursing profession, and according to MacLeod Clark and Latter (1990) self-care should 'reflect a basic philosophical right of clients'.

These concepts are far from alien territory for nurses. For example, Martha Rogers, one of our contemporary nurse theorists, regards individuals as unitary beings, integrated within the energy fields of surrounding care environments and care providers. Her model is based upon the principle of dynamism which suggests that the nurse and the client maintain a 'healthy respect' for each other and that personal development and direction of life processes are characterized by phenomena such as integrity, continuity, dynamism and creative change (Rogers, 1970).

O'Brien (1987), a leading advocate and normalization theorist, has described a number of key accomplishments that he believes are essential if human care services are to respond to the needs of clients. In his model five principles are presented:

- choice
- relationships
- dignity and esteem
- participation and integration
- competence.

According to O'Brien, all professionals should measure the effectiveness of their interventions against specific criteria that enhance the quality of life for their clients in accordance with these five areas. The framework within which such principles are to be delivered must be coherent and consistent, thus requiring the provision of humanistic care values, user-directed routines and neighbourhood-focused care environments.

O'Brien's above-mentioned accomplishment framework offers scope for the provision of a new partnership in care for users. However, in order for this to be fully realized a new system of negotiated care or life planning is required. Many services have now responded to this challenge by introducing a series of mechanisms for determining the needs of clients. An individual programme planning process, care management and shared action planning (Brechin & Swain, 1987) are all examples of mechanisms or processes whereby professional staff have enabled their clients to assess their actual needs and to plan responsive services. The care planning system depends upon goal planning as a basic principle.

Goal planning underpins the essence of learning disability nursing and Imogene King, another contemporary nurse theorist, based her model for nursing upon the principles of goal realization and interaction (King, 1981). In her model, she suggests that interaction (or reciprocal influence) forms the foundation for the delivery of nursing care. This transactional model can be regarded as an agreement which relies upon the determination of targeted interactions which lead to goal realization. In King's theory, the joint determination and achievement of goals by way of perception, communication, interaction and transaction is essential to the process of nursing. Her model complements the care management process.

Some users will be unable to communicate through any conventional communication system and may rely on a range of idiosyncratic systems to communicate their needs. Nurses spend much of their direct care time engaged in the process of interaction with their clients and in so doing they are able to acquire both specific and general skills in needs assessment and diagnosis with their users. This function is not unique to professionals working with any one client group and the nurses' advocacy role is identified by the UKCC in the Code of Professional Conduct (UKCC, 1992) and requires that nurses act always to uphold their patients' interest. In a supplementary document, *Exercising Accountability*, the UKCC (1989) advises that 'Advocacy is concerned with promoting and safeguarding the well-being and interests of clients.'

The advocacy role is complex and demands that nurses should be prepared to undertake complex and sometimes controversial roles in support of the primacy of their patients'/clients' interests.

In so doing their role includes:

- upholding the rights of persons without prejudice or discrimination;
- acting always in the patient's best interests;
- acting as an intermediary between the person and those providing or seeking to provide services for that person.

Each of these functions is interdependent and requires the nurse to acquire and apply effective assertion and negotiation skills. A major component of the advocacy role is the extent to which the nurse succeeds in empowering her clients in order to enable them to take an active role in determining their own futures (which will include decisions about their health status and the provision of care). This may involve the development of self-advocacy skills which aim to enhance the person's ability to speak out and act on their own behalf.

Assessing user needs and implementing care plans challenges the skills of professional carers. Considerable skill and acute powers of observation will be required to validate 'initial observations' and assessments. New ideas will have to be tested and new opportunities provided and for each user a detailed analysis of needs and wants will be necessary.

Nurses will rely upon a symphony of skills (both formal and experiential) and the intuition to design and develop individual care plans; in addition a range of checks and balances should be employed in order to collect as many responses as possible from others involved in the person's life and thus extend understanding of the person's needs. Finally, all such changes must be enacted within a negotiated client-directed care plan and this will often require the support of other professional carers. This, then, is the main test for persons whose autonomy is impaired and it will require the promotion of equal power sharing between client and carer.

This process involves a number of practical considerations, e.g. the calculation of risk and the endorsement of a course of action chosen by clients themselves (which may not always be supported by professional carers).

Risk-taking is now recognized as a primary nursing function and may be described as an ethical principle. Beneficence, one of the key principles that govern nursing practice, requires that we should always provide 'good and well-intentioned consequences' for clients. Risk-taking is therefore a central feature of care management and demands that care managers are competent to assess and calculate risks and to apply risk-taking procedures during the course of their everyday work.

Essentially risk-taking involves the implementation of cost benefit analysis, taking account of the expressed preferences of users and the views of their carers, families and others involved in the delivery of service responses. Occasionally conflicts of interest may result in the formation of subjective judgements and the introduction of personal bias. Carer aspirations may also conflict with user requirements and care managers will need to possess advanced negotiation, problem-solving and conflict resolution skills. Consideration should also be given to seeking the opinion of an independent arbitrator whenever conflicts of interest are expressed or when the care manager considers that he or she is unable to remain objective.

Empowerment also demands that care managers listen to users and this requires the active involvement of front-line workers in this process. These will often be carers and families who have the opportunity of working closely with consumers to assist them in identifying the things that are important to them and to their health and social care status. User reports and user satisfaction surveys may also be employed to assess the extent to which users are satisfied with the services they receive.

This also requires us to provide users with better information about our services in order to enable them to make informed choices. This, then, is a key component of the empowerment process. Many established services have published information leaflets to inform clients/users of their rights and nurses have also introduced and facilitated self-advocacy groups. The introduction of individual programme planning processes and care management systems are further examples of mechanisms or processes whereby professional staff have engaged in active dialogue with clients to assess needs and plan services.

6.8 Levels of assessment

Statutory obligations to meet client needs have to be clarified or extended through agency policy and planning. The model of care management adopted locally will identify a referral system and screening criteria which define client eligibility for service delivery. At this stage the roles of the care manager must be clearly defined and their skills and knowledge base clarified. Challis *et al.* (1990) discuss the important distinction between the stages of assessment necessary in an effective care management model:

'... the history of long term social care ... is one where the task of assessment has often been performed in a perfunctory and narrow way (SSI, 1987). Indeed such assessments have often been more concerned with identifying whether the person is eligible for the provision of a service rather than the more general identification of their needs. As a consequence a great deal of what is passed for assessment should more rightly be defined as screening or judging eligibility. Hence a clear distinction between assessment and re-assessment is fundamental to understanding the care management process.'

The initial process of referral and screening within care management demands that all relevant care agencies agree how to refer to one another and to co-operate in the assessment of needs that are the responsibility of more than one agency. The arrangements for close multidisciplinary working present a challenge to current communication systems, recording of referrals and allocation of roles and responsibilities.

The primary responsibility of the care management team will be to determine the criteria for referral and screening procedures. In the first place this process will be governed by the legal structures and obligations of the agency for specific individuals and client groups. For example, the NHS and Community Care Act (1990) requires local authorities to provide informed assessments for all clients who require community care. Other responsibilities require social service departments to provide residential care and day care services and make provision for a variety of home support systems such as home help services, child care services and services for people with impaired sight and hearing.

The major priority in assessment within care management is the emphasis upon individual need. It may be argued that traditional assessment has been directed towards assessment for service provision. However, this principle is certainly not acceptable within the care management model which demands that user needs, wants and ambitions form the nucleus of the assessment process. The starting point must be to 'get to know' the user and familiarize yourself with the user's present care arrangements, assessing these in terms of the user's strengths and needs. The 'getting to know you' process is time intensive and will require the allocation of specific periods of time. Only when the care manager has acquired accurate insight into the actual needs of the user, can an attempt be made to develop an individual statement of need which will become the central tool against which to identify service responses.

Ideally the assessment of individual need should be conducted without dependence upon any specific forms of available service provision. However, in reality it will be difficult for professional staff to assess need without direct reference to service provision. This state of affairs is understandable but unacceptable since the assessment of needs should and must be separate from service delivery. Hoghughi (1980) defines assessment as 'a continuous process aimed at providing information about a person or situation as a guide to most appropriate action'.

As a process assessment is central to care management. Lunn (1991) reports on the implementation of care management in psychiatry and notes that assessments cover physical, emotional and social issues as well as detailed aspects of the user's mental health and well-being. Crucially, Lunn reports that the user's own perception of his or her needs are included in the assessment. Kent County Council (1991) reports similar findings in its review of care management in that county and notes the importance of holistic assessments. Kent has adopted a joint assessment model between health and social care agencies which serves to identify the overall needs of users and reduce unnecessary duplication of assessment and user time.

The key lesson arising from evaluations of care management (Pilling, 1992) demonstrates the need for holism in the assessment process and for the design of interagency assessment procedures and pro-formas.

The Kent County Council report (1992) recognizes the realities of conflict in assessment of need between the perceptions of individuals in need and carers and professional workers. It recommends that conflicts and differences of opinion must be recorded and suggests that the assessor must be honest and clear when giving explanations about services that are and are not available and reasons for unmet need.

Joint assessments require multidisciplinary and multi-agency sharing and agreement on procedures for collection, recording and sharing of information. It is recommended that shared care files and records are introduced in all agency teams with the aim of facilitating the transfer of client information and enabling access to essential data for all members of (the authorized) client team.

Finally, professional workers are reminded of the need to record their findings in an honest and jargon-free style. Records should also be shared and validated by users and maintained in a professional and confidential manner. Legislative requirements relating to client rights of access to health and social care records should be complied with.

Here is a summary of key headings to be included in assessment protocols:

- biographical details
- self-perceived needs
- self-care
- physical health
- mental/emotional health
- use of medicines
- abilities, attitudes and lifestyles
- race and culture
- personal history
- needs of carers
- social network and support
- housing
- care services
- finance
- transport
- risk.

The assessment process may be broken down into three phases.

First level assessment – screening

An initial 'pen picture' of the individual is often developed within the context of a prepared pro-forma. Details are recorded in respect of the declared area of need. The results from the screening exercise usually inform eligibility for care management or referral to another service or agency.

Second level assessment

Information is collected by a designated care manager in accordance with the criteria outlined above. The assessment provides sufficient detail to produce a first draft of the user's individual care plan. This stage involves a detailed analysis of the user's own perception of need and care/support circumstances.

Third level assessment

A range of detailed assessments is co-ordinated from a number of specialist practitioners and agencies involved in the care and support of an individual. The care manager collates information from various sources and as a result produces an holistic care assessment and care plan in consultation with the user and his/her primary carers.

The majority of care management services provide copies of outline assessment forms and have published eligibility criteria for acceptance for care management. Users will also be required to sign a consent form empowering the care manager to collect data on their behalf as part of the assessment and care management process.

6.9 Individual care planning

The next stage of the care management process may be achieved through the implementation of individual programme planning which is described by Wilcock (cited in Sines, 1987). This model emphasizes the importance of planning for people within the context of service management structures and supports:

'The increasing emphasis on providing individualised services for people demands the development of service systems that will help identify the person's needs and plan to meet them ... approaches are designed to ensure that staff make decisions that are relevant to a person's life.' (Wilcock, 1987).

Brechin and Swain (1987), in a rather more participative model, introduce the concept of 'shared action planning' which emphasizes the importance of relationships 'being the heart of the matter'. They start their analysis of the skills involved in the shared action planning process with the following quote:

'They are used in friendships, family living, relationships at work and in mutual helping and caring. Such skills grow and develop through and within personal relationships. Relationships are, in this sense, the heart of the matter.' (Brechin & Swain, 1987, p. 3)

These authors introduce a new dimension into the personal planning process which is based on the principle of the importance of the interactions that take place between the carer and the user (and his/her friends). They talk of compassionate and supportive caring relationships with reference to their place in determining the context of successful care planning and life experiences:

'Shared Action Planning happens when there is co-ordination, organisation and people know who is responsible for doing what.' (Brechin & Swain, 1987, p. 131)

Consequently individualized approaches to care should provide a framework for people to express their wishes and desires through a shared process with named workers, which in turn should lead to valued outcomes for the individual. Individual programme planning uses the same four stages as the nursing process (assessment, planning, action and evaluation) but it is not a purely nursing method, but builds in inputs from every relevant discipline and carer on the basis of equality. It pays particular attention to clarifying the client's unique needs as he/she sees them (evidence for the success of this approach may be found in Jenkins *et al.*, 1988).

The shared action planning model affords clients opportunities for empowerment which aim to ensure that maximum control is provided for self-determination and advocacy. However, increased choice may also be accompanied by exposure of 'vulnerable' clients to increased risks in the community. Risk-taking and risk analysis have formed a central part of the debate and it should be acknowledged that an environment which allows an appropriate degree of personal choice and privacy can never be risk free.

The delicate balance that must be forged between the provision of an overprotective (often the worst possible scenario which may be characterized by abuse factors) and a facilitative environment will require careful deliberation and this process might well involve multiprofessional decision-making. Individual case review (often using the shared action planning approach introduced above) is the most appropriate forum for seeking agreement on issues that might involve calculated risks. Services should ensure that negotiated risk-taking processes and guidelines are available to staff to support them whenever such decisions must be made.

Once the care manager has agreed a package of care with the user and potential providers to meet the needs of each individual, contracts will be assigned to one or more service providers who may be selected from statutory, voluntary or independent sector agencies. Contracts will identify the exact nature of services to be offered and delivered and clear statements of responsibility and accountability will be contained within them. Each care package will also be costed and paid for from a complex system of allowances which will be co-ordinated by the local authority social service department. In order to ensure that each service provider delivers the services outlined in the contract, each agency will be required to demonstrate that systems are in place to quantify the services that it is providing on a day-to-day basis. The systems to be used for this purpose will be determined by local social service departments in collaboration with other agencies. Independent inspection and audit will also operate to ensure that clients and public authorities receive the best value for money from service providers.

The concept of quality assurance is an essential component and agreed standards will be established by health and social service teams in order to ensure that services may be assessed and evaluated in respect of their ability to meet these standards in practice. Service users and their families will also be involved in the positive monitoring of the services they receive and will be encouraged to participate in service audits.

In practice the aim will be to provide individually tailored packages of care which will be subject to regular review and monitoring and which can be adapted as individual circumstances change. In some cases the community health care nurse may find that he or she acts in the capacity of representative or 'advocate' for clients – someone who speaks on behalf of those people who are unable to make decisions for themselves. This will be particularly true for those people with mental health needs who have traditionally relied on employed staff from statutory agencies to represent their needs (for example those people who have lived for some considerable time in long-stay hospital services).

This section has established the importance of care management as a process for the identification of care needs and for the formulation of responsive contracts for care provision. The community care nurse may act as a care manager or may be involved in direct service provision. In other cases nurses may co-ordinate a range of services between primary health care nurses (district nurses, public health nurses (health visitors) and social workers, etc) and in so doing they may be regarded as 'key workers'. On other occasions they may account for their work to other professionals who have similar responsibilities. The allocation of care manager or key worker responsibilities will depend on local arrangements between health and social work departments and will be determined by the actual needs of the clients involved and the skills and availability of participating professionals.

No matter which method of operation is adopted community mental health professionals will require a number of requisite processes to support them in the implementation of care management:

(1) a system of multi-agency personal planning based on common principles and understanding;
(2) a computerized database to identify each person's needs and wants and abilities;
(3) individually designed day and residential services;
(4) a flexible budget system with compatibility between health and social service agencies and which enables the transfer of money to follow clients and to meet each individual's needs;
(5) joint training packages to assist staff from different agencies in

acquiring the necessary skills, knowledge and competences required to encourage service users to become equal participants in the planning of their care and futures;

(6) systems to promote consumer awareness and advocacy;

(7) a common agreement on agency policies, procedures, systems and structures to promote good quality services;

(8) an agreement across agencies on individual responsibility and accountability in the formulation, placing and discharge of contract agreements;

(9) an agreed central policy on standards against which local services should be judged and monitored;

(10) an agreed system for service monitoring and evaluation.

The principles of care management suggest that service users are change agents themselves and must be involved in determining their own futures. Care management relies on promoting individually designed packages for people and replaces traditional models of life planning. It requires that a range of opportunities is provided to service users based on the principle of integration within normal communities and demands that people have the right to adopt and maintain an ordinary life, and have personal relationships and friendships.

Care management requires all service providers to evaluate their own performance in respect of the quality of service they are offering to consumers and clearly defines personal responsibility for each component of the service. Care management, therefore, recognizes the need for innovative planning and the skills of the care manager to involve appropriate service delivery to provide for cost-effective yet quality provision.

Finally once a care plan has been negotiated a summary of the 'shortfalls' in local service provision must be identified in order to inform future service planning.

6.10 Multidisciplinary and multi-agency relationships

The acquisition of effective teamworking and networking skills is essential for the implementation of effective care management. Effective multi-disciplinary and multi-agency working practices underpin this process and demand that formal arrangements are in place to manage, monitor and review the work of a range of teams and professional responses. However, despite the existence of positive partnerships between professional teams in the community, a number of prejudices and intra-professional attitudes continue to militate against the formation of genuine partnerships between health and social care staff. Much prejudice may stem from anxiety about changes to previously guarded roles, competences and professional autonomy but care management challenges professional staff to review their attitudes, feelings and values in order to enhance the quality of prospective multidisciplinary working.

Care in the community also demands greater co-ordination of services from a range of sectors. There is also a clear expectation that health and social care agencies promote service provision within the private, voluntary and 'not for profit' sectors of service delivery. Co-ordination of service delivery should aim to encourage diverse service provision which clearly meets individual needs and provides a service which meets clear defined outcome or quality standards.

Diversity in the community is a prerequisite for care management. Care managers and professional staff will often be united in their quest for the design and development of a range of new, innovative and creative responses to meet user needs. Community action and development have long been recognized as key functions of the community health care nursing team and these skills are of particular importance in the development of new service responses in care management.

Co-ordination of precious staff resources is also required if unnecessary duplication of effort is to be avoided. Staff should familiarize themselves with the roles, functions and responsibilities of formal and informal carers in their catchment area and should 'map' their respective contributions. A data base of local resources, human and physical, should be maintained with the aim of informing the design of creative solutions for the provision of individual care plans for users. Community profiling and epidemiological research are key tasks in this process.

The challenge of multidisciplinary teamwork has been well summarized by the Central Council for Education and Training in Social Work (CCETSW, 1989):

'Members of multidisciplinary teams walk on a tightrope between main-taining their professional identity on the one hand and sharing skills or blurring professional boundaries on the other hand ... consensus is not the goal of multi-disciplinary working. Rather, the process of creative conflicts is central to its success. It is only through honest dialogue that team members can share skills with others and expand the team horizons of what is possible in the helping process.'

The essential elements within any team have been defined by Woodcock (1988) in his definition of team building blocks. These act as an effective set of criteria against which to measure the functioning of any team. Effective leadership, arrangements for managerial and professional accountability and reporting systems must also be developed and implemented if the care management process is to be effective (and if multidisciplinary teamwork is to be achieved).

The team cannot exist in a vacuum and will also interact with other teams (such as the primary health care team or community mental health team) but there must be recognition of the need for the care management team to develop as an independent entity with its own dynamic identity.

In the context of care management the life of the team must be primarily determined by the needs of individual users. Membership of the team will therefore change and fluctuate depending upon the actual needs of users. Consequently different professionals will be involved in different teams as individual needs dictate. Effective teams require:

- balanced roles
- clear objectives and agreed goals
- openness and honesty
- support and trust
- co-operation
- sound procedures
- appropriate leadership
- regular review
- individual development
- sound inter-group relations
- effective information and communication systems.

The co-ordination and management of the interagency team process is complex but is a prerequisite for the care management process. Readers are referred to Øvretveit's text (1993) for further reading and information on this subject.

6.11 Information systems

Users, their carers and families have a right to expect service agencies to publish information about their services. This right has been enshrined within the Patient's Charter (DOH, 1992) and is recognized as a core component of the care management process.

A central theme of care management is user choice and involvement and this must commence with the provision of information from which positive and informed choices can be made. Bereford and Croft (1988) advise that:

'If agencies and practitioners are serious about participation and partnership with service users, then we would suggest some initial steps for making social service language and communication more consistent with such goals:

- Include as part of agency policy on access to records the use of accessible language in care notes.

- Listen to people's own preference for language, terms and definitions to describe themselves.
- Include language on the training agenda instead of taking it for granted.
- Begin constructing appropriate and accessible information in association with service users, carers and other people for whom it is intended.
- Stop using initials and acronyms in the presence of service users.
- Look again at how you think and talk about service users. How much do you find yourself seeing *them* as a separate entity and attaching generalised characteristics "to them"?
- Reconsider terms that internalise issues like, for instance, "attention seeking behaviour" – what neglect and desperation may make people seek such attention?
- Explore and develop ways of improving service users' access to agency information.

Then the dialogue that is part and parcel of greater user involvement and participation may begin to be more possible.'

Each local authority and health service is expected to produce its own information charter (as required by the Patient's Charter (DOH, 1992) and Citizen's Charter (DOH, 1991) initiatives). These must be written in such a way as to inform users of their rights. Care managers will often find that they are expected to act as brokers for the dissemination of information about local services and resources.

In order to facilitate this process computerized data bases will be required to store information about local services, their cost and availability. Matched to this will be the need to design and implement effective systems to record the outcome of individual care plans and agreements. There are many examples of local software packages that co-ordinate client information with local resources inventories and budgetary control systems. Such systems will become essential for the management and co-ordination of the care management process as local agencies develop competence in responding to user needs.

6.12 Monitoring and evaluating the effectiveness of care management systems

Quality control and quality assurance are considered essential to the care management process. Accordingly care managers must demonstrate proficiency in the evaluation and review of outcomes for users in accordance with goals and criteria specified in their individual care plan or contract. Contract compliance is a necessary feature of the process and requires that users and care managers engage in systematic and regular review of the effectiveness and appropriateness of the care responses identified in the care plan.

Care managers will need to develop a monitoring and review system within care management to promote accountability systems and quality assurance. This process involves:

- the setting of specific criteria against which the effectiveness of care responses may be measured (both quantitatively and qualitatively);
- the provision, within client contracts, for periodic review and monitoring of service responsiveness;
- the provision for user and carer feedback on their perception of the 'effectiveness and appropriateness' of the service;
- arrangements for the provision of written monitoring reports from service providers that identify measures of compliance with contract specifications;
- the design of strategies to counteract the impact of stigma and discrimination;
- the development of mechanisms to ensure that the care manager also reflects on his/her own values and engages in peer supervision;
- formulation of external review mechanisms and feedback mechanisms to identify areas of service deficiency with the aim of informing future service planning.

The concepts of quality assurance, quality control and quality management have become powerful tools in the search for excellence in a mixed economy of care. The Citizen's Charter has recognized the rights of users of public services to challenge the quality of service provision. Care itself, however, is a difficult concept to quantify for users and providers. Care management recognizes that the consumer must be central to the quality process and this demands that users must be afforded every opportunity to participate in evaluative exercises relating to the quality of their care plan. The role of the care manager in this process may be directed to that of broker or advocate. However, the role and status of the care manager may pose the question, 'Advocate for whom?' Purchaser, provider or consumer?

Papadopolous (1992) provides the following definition of monitoring and evaluation:

'Monitoring involves obtaining regular feedback at each stage of the case management process. This facilitates decision-making at the subsequent stages. Monitoring methods are likely to involve regular consultation and review between members of the case management team, service providers and service consumers. Data concerning progress to date of all process elements should be provided and assimilated.

Evaluation refers to the degree of congruence between programme objectives and final outcomes; that is, the extent to which the case management programme has fulfilled its desired objectives.'

The first stage in the review process will be to provide a systematic structure for the monitoring of service achievement. Reviews may be held at six-monthly intervals and may be chaired or facilitated by the care manager and the service user. Reviews are normally multidisciplinary and serve the purpose of measuring the quality of service delivery against criteria specified in the user care plan. A summary of outcomes is maintained and key tasks and criteria to measure their achievement are set for forward planning for the next review. This cyclic process is further informed by the provision of monthly written reports to the care manager from service providers. Such reports contain minimum data sets designed to inform the monitoring process.

There are many forms of quality control mechanism and these will be selected in accordance with specific user needs and local policy arrangements. However, specific quality assurance must be identified and employed as an integral part of care management. Cognisance must be taken of other legitimate quality assurance methods such as those used in the inspection and monitoring of residential care and nursing homes (as required by the NHS and Community Care Act (1990)).

6.13 Financial management

Care managers will be required to demonstrate proficiency at various levels of financial or budgetary management. The extent to which competence is demanded will be determined, in part, by the nature of the care management model implemented.

Deeley and Williams (1990) identify eight models of care management:

(1) *The care manager with budget model.* One individual takes responsibility for all the tasks required by a particular client from the point of referral through to the point of monitoring and review process, and has control of the budget. A variation of this is where the care managers have a budget limited to a certain proportion of the cost of residential care.

(2) *The care manager without budget model.* Similar to Model (1) above, except that, having planned the preferred service provision, the care manager negotiates with the budget holder who then decides what resources to follow.

(3) *The team leader/care manager with budget model.* The care manager is the person responsible for co-ordinating staff (from whatever background)

in the various tasks involved, and then deciding, once a care package has been planned, what resources can be made available.

(4) *The team leader/care manager without budget model.* Similar to Model (3) above, but the team manager's responsibility is simply to ensure that all the tasks are carried out and then to negotiate with the budget holder for all resources required.

(5) *The independent care manager model.* The social services department takes responsibility for the initial referral but, once it is clear that the person is going to need continuing support, an independent care manager is appointed to determine with the user the package required, to negotiate with the various agencies for its provision and with the social services for its financing, and to take responsibility for the ongoing monitoring and review.

(6) *The user as care manager model.* Users themselves assume responsibility for the care management function after the initial referral to social services.

(7) *The independent care manager or client care manager as budget holder.* Similar to Models (5) and (6) above, but this care/client manager also has responsibility for the budget.

(8) *The 'no-change' option.* Professional workers carry on in their usual way except that they identify more clearly the individual task they are undertaking as defined under the general terms of care management.

It becomes apparent that care management will create many changes within the present context of service planning and delivery. The financial controls for costing care have traditionally been centralized. One major objective for the community care reforms argues greater flexibility and transparency in the management of finances and costing of care packages. This has resulted in the devolution of budgetary control to local providers, and in some cases, to care managers.

Smith *et al.* (1992) have reviewed the links between care management and finance and discuss three models:

- '*Nominal budget.* The care manager works with a knowledge of the cost of the service, but the cash-limited allocation is held centrally.
- *Total budget.* The care manager directly purchases all services under individualized client contacts.
- *Partial budget.* The care manager directly purchases some services under individual client contacts, but accesses the remainder under terms of macro-contracts negotiated centrally.'

The model adopted by local agencies will have major implications for budgetary control and for issues of accountability. Care managers will therefore require access to personal training and development programmes to assist them in the acquisition of budgetary skills which range from costing care programmes/contracts to the monitoring of monthly budget statements and annual expenditure accounts.

6.14 Review systems and policy planning

The final stage in the care management process is the design and implementation of a review system that facilitates feedback to inform policy planning.

As a truly effective process care management must encourage an independent system of purchase and provision of services to meet individual needs. Changes in the economy, in societal laws and values and the range of user needs and characteristics constantly interact to demand regular policy and planning reviews in all provider and purchasing authorities. The effective care management system will feed forward the individual needs of users to ensure that future planning attempts to reduce the range of unmet needs. Review systems must also recognize the reality of restrictions in resources; they must also recognize and reward innovation by practitioners and users in meeting individual needs.

The review system employed within care management systems must be a recognition of the developmental nature of the assessment of individual needs. The review system must value the changing nature of human needs and must applaud innovative and flexible means to meet these needs. The review system must also operate within the realities of financial control on resource allocation. Care management has identified the need for multi-disciplinary and multi-agency collaboration in assessing and meeting individual need. A review system that shares and applauds good practice should encourage recognition of alternative and diverse methods of meeting needs through the resources available. The system should also be time and resource efficient and effective. Future planning should encourage diversification in complementing service provision and attempt to promote quality in the mixed economy of care.

6.15 Conclusion

The aims of the care management process are simple but the methods to be employed to achieve those aims are complex and challenge traditional service models and professional responses. The key test is the extent to which users, their carers and families believe that they have been empowered to direct their own care and to receive appropriate services that are responsive to their actual needs. These responses must be robust and flexible enough to meet the demands of evolving and changing care and support needs.

6.16 References

Bereford, P. & Croft, S. (1988) Language for service users. *Social Work Today*, **19**(49), 22.

Brechin, J. & Swain, A. (1987) *Changing Relationships – Shared Action Planning for People with a Mental Handicap.* Harper & Row, London.

CCETSW (1989) *Multi-disciplinary Working – Inter-disciplinary Association of Mental Health Workers.* CCETSW, London.

Challis, D., Chessum, R., Chesterman, J. & Traske, K. (1990) *Case Management in Social and Health Care.* Personal Social Services Research Unit (PSSRU), Canterbury.

Deeley, J. & Williams, C. (1990) Training for Case Management. In: *Journal of Training and Development*, **1**(2), 19–28.

Devenney, M. (1992) User Participation in Quality Assurance. In: *Quality Counts* (eds D. Kelly & B. Warr). SCA Education, London.

DHSS NI (1990) *People First: Community Care in Northern Ireland in the 1990s.* HMSO, Belfast.

DOH (1991) *The Citizen's Charter.* HMSO, London.

DOH (1992) *The Patient's Charter.* HMSO, London.

Hoghughi, M. (1980) *Assessing Problem Children.* Burnett Books, London.

Jenkins, J., Felce, D., Toogood, S., Mansell, D. & de Kock (1988) *Individual Programme Planning.* British Institute of Medical Handicap Publications, Kidderminster.

Kent County Council (1991) *Good Care: Care Management Practice Guide.*

King, I. (1981) *A Theory for Nursing.* John Wiley, New York.

Lunn, T. (1991) 'Teamspirit'. *Social Work Today*, **22**, 16–17.

MacLeod Clark, J. & Latter, S. (1990) Health promotion – working together. *Nursing Times*, **86**(48), 28–31.

McCarthy, M. (ed.) (1989) *The New Politics of Welfare – An Agenda for the 1990s* MacMillan, London.

Minford, P. (1984) State Expenditure: a study in waste. Economics Affairs, April/June. In: *The Politics of Greed: The New Right and the Welfare State* (M. Loney, 1986). State Pluto, London.

NHS and Community Care Act (1990). HMSO, London.

O'Brien, J. & Lyle, C. (1987) *Framework for Accomplishment.* Responsive Systems Associates, Decatur, Georgia.

Øvretveit, J. (1993) *Coordinating Community Care – Multidisciplinary Teams and Care Management.* Open University Press, Buckingham.

Papadopolous, A. (1992) *Case Management in Practice.* Winslow, Oxford.

Pilling, D. (1992) *Approaches to Case Management for People with Disabilities.* Jessica Kingsley, London.

Rogers, M. (1970) *An Introduction to the Theoretical Basis of Nursing.* F.A. Davis, Philadelphia.

Sines, D. (1987) *Towards Integration – Comprehensive Services for People with a Mental Handicap*. Harper & Row, London.

Smith, H., Peck, E. & Ritchie, P. (1992) *Case Management in Practice*. CCETSW, London.

SSI (1991) *Case Management and Assessment: Managers' Guide*. HMSO, London.

SSI (1991) *Case Management and Assessment: Practitioners' Guide*. HMSO, London.

UKCC (1989) *Exercising Accountability*. UKCC, London.

UKCC (1992) *Code of Professional Conduct for Nurses, Midwives and Health Visitors*. UKCC, London.

Wilcock, P. (1987) Life Planning. In: *Towards Integration – Comprehensive Services for People with a Mental Handicap* (ed. D. Sines). Harper & Row, London.

Woodcock, M. (1988) *Fifty Activities for Teambuilding*. Gower, London.

Chapter 7

Research Perspectives

Research is exciting. There is enormous potential, in all branches of community nursing, to gain greater insight into aspects of practice through research. While research itself does not change practice, it enlarges the database of information from which we can draw in order to make professional decisions. The strength of research is its objectivity and it is unsurprising, therefore, that there is a policy requirement for nursing practice to be research based (DHSS, 1972; NHS Management Executive, 1993).

To relate this requirement to your own area of expertise, ask yourself what are the current issues in your specialism within community nursing. What research questions might you ask about *your* practice? For example, you may be concerned about a particular clinical intervention: is one treatment more effective than a second, cheaper treatment? Perhaps you think clients' perceptions should be examined, to assess the needs of a specific group, such as carers or lone mothers, or – more generally – to discover the perceived health needs of a local community. You may feel that the current emphasis on management issues within the new NHS makes this an appropriate focus for research, with questions about the effectiveness of packages of care, the appropriateness of liaison procedures between hospital and community services, or measurement of the health gains within your client caseload or your practice population.

Whatever your focus, there are particular features of research that distinguish it from 'finding out'. Science – and by extension, scientific research – has been described as 'a way of thinking' and 'a process of inquiry' (Graziano & Raulin, 1993). The scientific way of thinking is logical, systematic and orderly, and the process of inquiry is outlined in a series of steps called the research process. Throughout the stages of the research process, measures are taken to eliminate the personal preferences of the researcher and any bias that might creep in as a result of, for example, poor sampling technique.

To further objectify research findings, only empirical evidence is used: empirical evidence is 'rooted in objective reality' (Polit & Hungler, 1989), which means it can be observed and/or recorded as occurring independently of the researcher, and this differentiates it from the subjective opinion of the researcher. In short, scientific research involves a series of controls designed to make it as objective as possible.

Despite these measures, we should be wary of attributing to research more authority than its merits. Research findings are not 'the truth', and research studies do not 'prove' anything. There is rarely a perfectly executed research study. However, research findings are the most accurate statements available to us at any given time about particular phenomena, and we should therefore use research as a means to providing high quality, consistent care.

Research can be a fascinating journey of discovery, and nursing research, in particular, is tremendously rewarding if you choose a topic related to your work. Hockey (1991) describes research as 'a precious jewel which gives opportunity for stimulating innovative activity'. On the other hand, there are times during the course of almost any project when despondency sets in – perhaps when anticipated time schedules are passed and the whole thing seems to be moving tortuously slowly. Reid (1993) is blunt:

> 'Research can be a lonely business at times ... and it may be gloomy. Progress can be sporadic – for weeks you do not appear to be achieving anything tangible. But then, suddenly, you move forward and all the misery is soon forgotten ... It can be fascinating, tantalising, addictive and rewarding.'

If you are ready for this tantalizing experience, read on! In the following sections, we shall look at approaches to research and the research process, before considering ethical issues and finishing with guidelines on how to carry out a critical evaluation of a research article.

7.1 Approaches to research

Historically, there are two approaches to research methodology, both relevant to community nursing. As an aide memoire (rather than an accurate representation of reality) you might like to visualize two caricatures: the first, a white-coated scientist in the laboratory, in complete control of a carefully designed experiment – this representing a positivist approach using quantitative data; the second, an anthropologist carrying out fieldwork in the bush, quietly observing people's daily lives and doing everything possible to keep the situation 'natural' – this representing an interpretive approach using qualitative data. These are now considered in more detail.

The positivist approach: 'scientific' quantitative methodology

Positivism in social science derives from the work of the sociologist Emile Durkheim who, during the latter part of the nineteenth and the first half of the twentieth century, claimed that belief systems, customs and institutions of society ('social facts') exist externally to the consciousness of individuals; therefore these aspects of social life can be observed and measured. Following the numerical recording of information (data) about selected aspects of social life, statistical tests can demonstrate correlations (associations) between them. Durkheim (1938) argued that it is the job of the researcher to seek causation – i.e. to discover which factor is the cause of a particular kind of behaviour, and which factor, or variable, is the effect. Durkheim himself carried out a major study of suicide demonstrating correlations between high rates of suicide and predominantly Protestant populations.

Research falling within this paradigm usually generates numbers or frequencies, and it 'quantifies or measures' (Hockey, 1991). There is close control by the researcher at each stage of the proceedings, and the whole exercise is underpinned by deductive theory. In deductive research, previous knowledge or theories form the starting point. Then a question or hypothesis is formulated, relating to the theory. A series of scientifically accepted operations is planned and systematically followed; thus the conclusion is deduced. In its purest form, the orthodox scientific approach consists of the experiment and, in medical research, this often takes the form of the randomized controlled trial.

The interpretive approach and qualitative methodology

A second early sociologist writing at this time, Max Weber, argued that 'social action' should be the focus for social science (Weber, 1958). To explain social action, social scientists need to understand the meanings and motives that underlie human behaviour. In order to discover these meanings and motives, you need to be able to imagine the situation from the point of view of those you are studying – an exercise that Weber called *verstehen*.

Following from this approach, Blumer (1969) and other symbolic interactionists focused on 'self-concept' as the key issue for social science. Consistently with Weber, they advocated that researchers should try to understand the world views of those studied by 'taking the role of' the subjects. At one step further along the interpretive continuum, phenomenologists such as Cicourel (1976) maintain that there is no such thing as objective reality; there are only interpretations of reality formed by individuals. According to this view there is no point in carrying out experiments or statistical procedures since these exercises have legitimacy only in the subjective world views of the scientists conducting them. Rather, the job of the social scientist is to make sense of the meanings that individuals attach to their actions.

In contrast with positivism, research using an interpretive framework tends to generate qualitative data in the form of words, ideas and theories. In this kind of research, the intention is not to control or manipulate situations – instead, the researcher aims to disturb existing behaviour as little as possible, in order to describe social life as it occurs and explain why people behave as they do. Inductive theory is employed: observed social behaviour forms the starting point, and from this there should follow ideas or theories which attempt to explain what is observed. In this respect, theory is induced from the empirical data.

Examples of methodologies consistent with interpretive approaches are interviews and participant observation (where the researcher observes and participates in the lives of those being studied). Arguably, the purest form of qualitative research is ethnography, which is an approach involving detailed description and analysis of the way of life of a people from their point of view, achieved by spending a considerable period of time with them. Ethnography is most commonly used by social anthropologists.

How do the two approaches relate to community nursing?

As Reid (1993) states: 'the historical dominance of the scientific [i.e. positivist] approach is evident in most scientific writings on health research'. The result is a perpetuation of the view that scientific research, experimentation and 'hard' numerical data are somehow superior to qualitative research. Given the traditional position of nursing as subordinate to medicine (which espouses positivism), it is unsurprising that, until quite recently, some nursing texts still presented quantitative methods as the only worthwhile tools for nurse researchers.

This, of course, is not the case. It is quite possible to use quantitative and qualitative methods sequentially or simultaneously (Field & Morse, 1991), with the advantage of combining the strengths of each. For example, you might use interviews (qualitative) to discover the possible needs of carers in your area, before constructing a larger survey (mainly quantitative) to assess the prevalence of these identified needs. Researchers in the field of community nursing have used a variety of approaches. Luker (1982), for example, adopted an experimental approach to assess whether a specific intervention with elderly clients resulted in health gain. Orr (1980) developed a questionnaire that yielded quantitative and qualitative data to reveal the experiences of mothers in Northern Ireland. Mason (1994) carried out participant observation in Northern Ireland and Jamaica to discover how mothers related to health professionals, while Cowley (1991) selected another interpretive approach – grounded theory – to reveal the complex nature of health visitor/client interactions. To return to Reid (1993):

'Today, the best professional researchers in health increasingly regard these different traditions as complementary, not competing, and they use the term triangulation to describe the concurrent use of more than one approach to a research problem.'

Finally, it is worth highlighting some similarities between one approach to community health care and one approach to research: community development and ethnography. Community development is based on notions of ownership and empowerment, taking as its starting point the collection of information about the health needs of local communities – as perceived and expressed by the people themselves. An important feature of the community development approach is the contextualization of health needs within their specific social settings.

Ethnography has been described as 'a generalized approach to understanding behaviours from an emic point of view' (Field & Morse, 1991), and as the 'documentation of a way of life' (Keesing, 1976). Here, too, there is an emphasis on social context and on understanding the world through the eyes of those being studied. Indeed, in these respects there is a general alignment between the range of qualitative methodologies and the ethos of community nursing as a whole, which is based on respect for clients' viewpoints and intimate knowledge of local communities. It would seem that there is great potential for community nurses to complement epidemiological and public health research with qualitatively oriented research which would reveal the motives and meanings behind the health behaviours already measured.

7.2 The research process – what is it?

The research process is the 'how to do it' of research: a series of practical steps that operate as guidelines, especially useful for novice researchers. You might find the term 'research process' comforting, given the obvious comparison with the familiar term 'nursing process'. Like the nursing process, the research process has a preparatory phase (assessing and planning), an action phase (implementation) and an analysis phase (evaluation). Furthermore, as in direct nursing care, the whole cycle can begin again if – as often happens – the project concludes by raising more research questions.

The steps of the research process are not meant to be rigidly prescriptive; for example, in some qualitative research a pilot study is unnecessary. A certain amount of flexibility is allowed, as one or two phases may persist beyond their allocated time slot. It is likely, for example, that you will continue to gather literature throughout the course of the project, and ethical issues remain important at every stage. Nevertheless, the steps of the research process are very useful guidelines and if your study is positivistic in orientation, each stage must be completed.

7.3 How to do research: the research process, step by step

This section gives an outline of the research process, while Sections 7.4, 7.5 and 7.6 provide details of the main activities involved at each stage.

(1) *Preparation: the 'think about it' or conceptual phase* (see Section 7.4).

- decide on a broad research problem area
- search the literature
- review the literature
- state the research problem, the research question or the research hypothesis
- decide on the research design and sample
- consider reliability and validity
- prepare a research proposal
- gain access to the research site.

(2) *Data collection: the 'go and do it' or empirical phase* (see Section 7.5)

- pilot study
- data collection
- data storage.

(3) *Analysis and presentation: the 'see what it all means' or interpretive phase* (see Section 7.6).

- data analysis
- present findings, conclusions, recommendations
- communicate results.

7.4 Preparation: the conceptual phase

Decide on a broad research problem area

What aspects of your practice do you find yourself asking questions about? For example, you may think that pressure damage would be an appropriate topic to look into, or the use of lay workers in community health nursing teams, or support for women following miscarriage. At this stage, you are identifying the broad subject area and thinking of key words that describe it. It is best to avoid subjects with which you, yourself, are heavily emotionally involved – it could be difficult, for example, to conduct and analyse research interviews on bereavement if you have recent personal experience of this.

Search the literature

Benton and Cormack (1991) recommend a 'systematic and unhurried' approach in searching the literature and, for new researchers, this will probably take at least two months (Mason, 1993). There are three main ways to search the literature: by manual search, computer search or personal communication.

To conduct a manual search you might start by checking the subject index in your library. If, for example, your topic is 'mastectomy', look up this word and you will obtain a list of all references in the library on that subject. Subject indexes were traditionally kept in stacked drawers, and are now generally available on computer terminals. This kind of search is limited to items stocked within the library.

An easy way to carry out a more wide-ranging manual search is to look through the contents pages of recent issues of reputable journals such as *The Journal of Advanced Nursing*, *The International Journal of Nursing Studies*, or *Qualitative Health Research*. When you find articles on your chosen subject, check the reference lists at the back, and search out the most relevant, using the inter-library loan system to obtain items that are unavailable in your library. While useful, this method needs to be supplemented by at least one or two of the following to comprise a comprehensive search.

Indexes, abstracts and bibliographies are easy-to-use manuals available in large libraries. Simply look up your key words (e.g. 'mastectomy', 'skill mix', 'pressure sores') and this will guide you to lists of references on the subject. In some cases, abstracts of the articles are also provided. Useful manuals to start with are the RCN's *Bibliography of Nursing Literature*, *The Index of Nursing Research* and the *Cumulative Index to Nursing and Allied Health Literature (CINAHL)*. You should move beyond purely nursing articles and examine the medical literature (through *Index Medicus*) and social science literature (through the *Social Science Citation Index*). A full list of indices and abstracts is provided by Polit and Hungler (1989).

Computer searches are more efficient than manual methods. On-line computerized searches make telephone contact with databases in the USA and Europe, and are usually carried out by a librarian. However, not all libraries offer this service to students. You can carry out your own computer search of major databases such as MEDLINE (for medical references) and CINAHL if you have access to a CD-ROM (compact disc read only memory) system. This is less complicated than it sounds: simply input your key words and, following a straightforward series of commands, obtain a printout of references and abstracts.

'Personal communication' means just that. Who are the experts in the field? Go and talk to them! Experts are usually very happy to provide offprints of their work (and to be quoted!). Finally, librarians are there to help, so feel comfortable when you need to ask for guidance. It can be exciting when you find just the 'right' article – enjoy the hunt!

Review the literature

A literature review is more than a listing of articles: it should be a concise, informative and structured critical review of the subject area. This means taking a step back and considering the research that has been done. Has it taken a particular slant? Is there one favoured method, and if so, might another approach provide new insights? You should consider the methodological strengths and weaknesses of previous studies, as this provides a basis for assessment of the validity of the findings. What are the main findings, and are there contradictions between different studies?

Most importantly, you should identify gaps in the literature, and use this as a justification for your proposed study. For example, there is a vast literature on breastfeeding, but very little on the influence of men on the breastfeeding practices of women: this, then, is an obvious focus for future research. A literature review should always have a message, and the main message should relate to the need for your piece of work.

State the research problem, the research question(s) or the research hypothesis

All research studies contain a research problem, most contain a research question, and some contain a hypothesis. Once you have reviewed the literature, you are in a position to state precisely what you intend to examine.

Problem

Regardless of approach or orientation, there must be a focus, and this is the research problem. Drawing on the examples cited at the beginning of this section, the research problem might relate to:

(1) the incidence of pressure sores and the frequency of district nurse visits;
(2) the opinions held by professional health workers about the involvement of lay workers; or
(3) the needs of women following miscarriage.

Question

Research questions derive from the research problem. Following the examples through, we obtain the following possible research questions:

(1) What is the relationship between the incidence of pressure sores and the frequency of district nurse visits?

(2) What are the opinions held by professional health workers about the involvement of lay workers?

(3) What are the needs of women following miscarriage?

Any one study can contain more than one research question, and although it is probably best to keep things simple (i.e. with just one or two questions), up to four or five questions are acceptable. Moral questions are not researchable, so you cannot ask: 'is it right to...?'

Finally in some qualitative studies the research questions are asked after the collection of data, on the grounds that preconceived notions (for example, that the appearance of lay workers is an issue for health professionals) influence the recording of data during participant observation.

Hypothesis

A hypothesis is a hunch or prediction about what is going to happen. In example (1), above, the hypothesis might be: frequency of district nurse visits affects the incidence of pressure sores. This is called a two-tailed hypothesis because district nurse visits (the independent variable, or IV) could influence the incidence of pressure sores (the dependent variable, or DV) in one of two ways – either by raising or lowering it. Expressed as a one-tailed hypothesis, the influence is clearly in one direction: 'it is hypothesized that frequent visits reduce the incidence of pressure sores'. For statistical reasons, it is usually better to produce one-tailed hypotheses. Experimental studies require a hypothesis or hypotheses, and descriptive studies may contain them. In example (2), above, a relationship may be hypothesized, for example, between age of respondent and opinions held. Hypotheses should be justified in some way, so you should cite relevant literature, direct observation or knowledge of the effects of the IV on the DV as a rationale for your prediction. Interpretive, qualitative studies do not generally begin with research hypotheses.

Decide on the research design and sample

The research design is 'the overall plan for collecting and analysing data' (Polit & Hungler, 1989). There are many possible plans and these are categorized into schemes in the research methods literature; unfortunately, different authors devise different schemes and this can be confusing. Almost universally, however, there is a distinction made between 'experimental' and 'non-experimental' designs. Castles (1987) further subdivides non experimental designs into 'descriptive' and 'exploratory' types.

Experimental design

Experimental designs are used to establish cause and effect, or, in medical terms, treatment intervention and outcome. True experiments have three characteristics: manipulation, control and randomization.

Manipulation

The researcher does something, or causes something to happen to one of the variables, the IV. Returning to our first example, the researcher would manipulate the variable 'frequency of district nurse visits' to discover its effect on the incidence of pressure sores. Ethical issues are an important consideration here: there may be a contradiction between the requirement of a true experiment to manipulate the frequency of district nurse visits in advance of data collection, and the ethical requirement to provide care according to need.

Control

The experiment is controlled by the researcher in terms of design, sampling technique and control of extraneous variables (i.e. variables which might confound the relationship between the IV and the DV, which – in our example – could be general health, morale or level of dependency). A 'control' group is included, which does not receive the treatment. In our example, one group of patients would receive more frequent district nurse visits (the experimental group) and one group would remain unchanged (the control group).

Randomization

Each study subject is randomly (i.e. with an equal chance) allocated to either the experimental group or the control group. The effect of randomization is to offer some control of extraneous variables.

An experiment lacking the characteristics of randomization or control is called a quasi-experiment. The true experimental design offers most control, quasi-experimental designs offer some control and non-experimental designs offer least control. In practice, quasi-experiments are most common in social and nursing research as true randomization is difficult to achieve. For example, rather than randomly allocating our district nurses' patients into two groups which will receive 'frequent visits' and 'occasional visits', we might observe all the patients of several district nurses and then divide them into groups according to the frequency of visits they received. This latter design is an example of a quasi-experiment. Tools used in experiments and quasi-experiments include structured non-participant observation checklists, and questionnaires. A useful outline of the characteristics of experiments and quasi-experiments is provided by Reid (1993).

Descriptive design

Descriptive designs 'are created by the investigator in order to make accurate statements about the characteristics of individuals, situations or groups' (Castles, 1987). Questionnaires are a common tool used in descriptive design, and for our second example we might select a descriptive design using questionnaires to make accurate statements about the opinions of professional health workers on the involvement of lay workers. This design presupposes prior knowledge of the problem, so that the researcher knows who to study and what to ask; once these decisions are made, the design is not flexible. Descriptive studies are likely to fall predominantly within the positivist, quantitative paradigm, although this may be complemented with, for example, open-ended (qualitative) questions on a questionnaire.

Exploratory design

An exploratory design is chosen when little is known about the variables of interest, or when in-depth information is sought about the world views of those being studied. 'The needs of women following miscarriage' is a topic that lends itself to this framework since little is known about it; furthermore, a detailed exploration of the lives of a few women is likely to yield the most thorough or 'rich' data. Research instruments appropriate to exploratory design include participant observation and interviews, and the design itself is flexible. Exploratory studies clearly fall within the interpretive, qualitative paradigm.

Sampling

The selection of study subjects, or sampling, is crucially important. There are two main kinds of sample used in research: probability samples and non-probability samples. The underlying principle for probability sampling is that each subject has an equal chance of being included; this eliminates bias and therefore it is possible to generalize findings to the wider population from which the sample was drawn. It is essential in experimental research to use probability samples, and highly desirable in descriptive research.

Non-probability samples are used in exploratory studies where the intention is 'to say a lot about a smaller number'. Study subjects, such as the women following miscarriage, might be selected on the grounds that they have had the experience, are available, articulate and willing to participate. This kind of sample could be biased if, for example, willing participants happened to be predominantly middle class. Therefore it is not possible to make generalizations from non-probability samples.

Consider reliability and validity

It is important that your research instrument – whether questionnaire, observation checklist or interview – should measure what you think it is measuring (or describe what you think it is describing in the case of interviews). This is called validity. A pilot study can help you assess the validity of the instrument: for example, if your questionnaire on skill mix baffles most of the respondents, you can be fairly sure that you are not obtaining a true measurement of their opinions on skill mix! There are different kinds of validity with which you should become familiar, and these are thoroughly explained in the literature (e.g. Castles, 1987; Cormack, 1991; Polit & Hungler, 1989).

Reliability concerns the consistency of an instrument. Just as a sphygmomanometer should consistently measure blood pressure correctly in the absence of any mechanical defect, so a questionnaire on skill mix should consistently measure respondents' attitudes in the absence of any 'instability' in the research instrument. Kerlinger (1973) says that reliability is whether, when we measure the same objects lots of times with the same or comparable instruments, we get the same or similar results. There are different tests of reliability, widely reported in the research methods literature. These tests are considered essential in experimental research and desirable for surveys and observational techniques. In most qualitative studies, the context and experience of each interview or episode of participant observation is unique, and therefore the issues surrounding reliability (if it is mentioned at all) are different (Field & Morse, 1991; Deatrick & Faux, 1991).

Prepare a research proposal

Having worked out the research design, you are now in a position to write a research proposal. Essentially, this is a concise statement about 'what you intend to do, why you want to do it, and how you will go about it' (Burnard & Morrison, 1990). Research proposals are often written to obtain funding, and in this case their main function is to justify and 'sell' the project. In any case, the writing of a proposal is an important exercise that forces you to think through each stage of the project, thereby clarifying your thoughts and methods, and allowing others to assess them. Bond (1991) maintains that a research proposal should contain:

- title
- summary
- justification for the study
- related research
- aims and objectives
- plan of investigation (research design and timescale)

- ethical considerations
- resources needed
- budget
- curriculum vitae.

Gain access to the research site

In order to gain access to health professionals or patients/clients, formal permission needs to be sought from the relevant employing authority or health authority, and possibly from the university ethics committee. It is likely that a short research proposal or summary of your intentions will be required. It is wise to seek access at an early stage, as it can take months, in some cases, for permission to be granted.

7.5 Data collection: the empirical phase

Carry out a pilot study

A pilot study is 'a small-scale version, or trial run, done in preparation for a major study' (Polit & Hungler, 1989). This is important in order to discover shortcomings in the research instruments and to gauge whether expectations about timescale, storage of data, etc., are realistic. Additionally, the pilot study can provide an opportunity to assess the reliability and validity of the research instruments. Respondents or subjects selected for the pilot study must not participate in the main study.

Data collection and storage

Students often remark that the preparatory stages of the project are most difficult, and it is a relief to get going! Interviewing can be a fascinating and intense experience, as you relate to respondents, gaining insight into how each one feels and thinks. However, this is a time-consuming process and it is unlikely, if the interviews are flexible in format and located in the homes of the informants, that you will be able to undertake more than two in one day. By contrast, postal questionnaires can be distributed and returned with relative ease and speed, thus allowing for much larger samples; however, response rates tend to be lower and they preclude the kind of in-depth understanding of respondents' perspectives achievable by means of qualitative techniques.

Whether you choose interviews, questionnaires, observation schedules or some other research instrument, it is important to have learned about the technique through reading, practice and discussion with an experienced researcher in advance of carrying it out. It is also important to acknowledge the limitations of the instrument.

Qualitative data are usually transcribed from tapes to paper, and both cassettes and pages of transcript are carefully stored. Photocopies of transcriptions are an important insurance against loss or damage of the originals. Quantitative data can be stored in its original form if the sample is small; for larger samples, the data will be coded and punched into a computer, in preparation for analysis.

7.6 Analysis and presentation: the interpretive phase

Data analysis

Decisions about data analysis will have been made during the preparatory phase and, again, it is important to be familiar with your chosen technique before reaching this point. You might be delighted to achieve a 90% response rate from your postal survey, but meaningful analysis can proceed only if questionnaire responses can be coded in a way that permits statistical analysis. Learn some basic statistics at an early stage! Analysis of qualitative data is more flexible; however, there are accepted protocols for qualitative analysis and useful guidelines are provided by Field and Morse (1991), Pollock (1991), and Polit and Hungler (1989). In either case, your method of data analysis should be quite explicitly justified and explained.

Present findings, conclusions and recommendations

In quantitative studies, 'presentation of findings' normally comprises an independent section that is entirely factual in the sense that it reports – without discussion or speculation – the results of the survey, observations or other data collection method. Quantitative studies then discuss results in a discussion section where the statistical findings are related to the research question or hypothesis, and evaluated with reference to the literature. Because qualitative studies are essentially interpretive, findings are often presented and discussed, or interpreted, in a single section which should contain quotations from respondents and an indication of the social context in which the fieldwork or interviews were conducted.

Conclusions should be a logical outcome of the findings, presented with clarity and conciseness. It is useful, at the concluding stage of any project, to refer back to the original research question and then, as far as possible, provide an answer. Do not despair, however, if there does not seem to be a clear-cut answer: research projects are notorious for raising more questions than they answer! Notwithstanding, in nursing research you should be in a position to make three or four main recommendations relevant to practice.

Communicate results

Since the raison d'etre of nursing research is to inform and influence practice, it is imperative to be proactive in disseminating the findings of your study as widely as possible. This could be in face-to-face situations such as research group sessions, workshops or conferences, by means of written reports to practitioners and managers, or articles in professional and academic journals. The most effective way to influence practice is by targeting groups of specialists at an early stage and keeping them informed and involved throughout (Agency for Health Care Policy and Research, 1992; Mittman *et al.*, 1992).

Before leaving this section on the research process, two points are worth emphasizing:

(1) The importance of matching the research question with the overall approach, the selected instrument(s) and the method of analysis. You should seek the opinion of an experienced researcher to verify that your project is successful in this respect.
(2) The need to develop and adhere to a realistic time schedule: while there are fewer steps in phases two and three of the research process, as presented above, this does not mean they are quicker.

7.7 Ethical issues in research

Is it right to carry out in-depth interviews for research purposes when these might cause emotional distress to respondents? If a potentially beneficial treatment is given to half the subjects in a randomized controlled trial, is it right to deny that treatment to the control group? Who owns the final report, maintaining control over its distribution: the researcher, nurse managers, the funding body or the research subjects?

Such questions do not always have straightforward answers, hence the creation of research ethics committees which vet projects at the proposal stage. Procedure for submission of projects to ethics committees is variable, and you need to check the protocol at your institution. At the very least, your supervisor and/or another experienced researcher should check your proposal for potential ethical problems.

Confidentiality is the first ethical issue with which you are likely to be concerned. Confidentiality means that while it is possible to attach the identity of a respondent to a particular statement, there is a guarantee that this connection will never be publicly divulged. Anonymity means that even the researcher is unaware of which respondents made which statements. You should be able to assure your research subjects at least of confidentiality.

Another major issue is that of consent. According to Field and Morse (1991), informed consent occurs when:

'... the person is knowledgeable, that is, has been informed about all procedures and no deceit or concealment has been used; has exercised voluntary choice, without coercion, and was competent to freely choose.'

While it is regarded as acceptable in some sociological and anthropological studies to work covertly, i.e. without the full knowledge of the subjects, informed consent is considered to be essential in nursing research (RCN, 1993).

A full set of ethical guidelines for nurse researchers has been produced by the RCN (1993). This short document promotes the highest ethical standards and highlights important issues that may not be anticipated at the outset. It is essential reading for nurse researchers at all levels.

7.8 Critical evaluation of a research article

A decision to alter practice in the light of research findings can be justified only if the research itself is of high quality. Therefore it is important to be able to evaluate research articles critically for their strengths, weaknesses and overall merit. It is useful, when critiquing an article, to have a conceptual scheme to structure your thinking, and several such schemes are presented in the literature (Treece & Treece, 1986; Castles, 1987; Polit & Hungler, 1989). The following suggested scheme is a modification of that provided by Polit and Hungler (1989), and it offers a checklist of items to be commented upon:

Substantive and theoretical dimensions

- Is the topic important for nursing?
- Is the research problem and question clearly presented?
- Is the choice of topic justified? Does the research question represent a logical next step in view of previous research?
- Is the theoretical framework explicit? If so, does it provide a suitable context for the study?

Methodological dimensions

- Is there a match between the research question, the overall approach, the instrument(s) and method of analysis – i.e. is there consistency within the research design?
- Was the sample appropriate?
- Were measures taken to assess the validity and reliability of the research instrument(s)?

- Was the research actually executed as planned, or was the original proposal compromised in any way?
- Has the author acknowledged the limitations of the study?

Ethical dimensions

- Was confidentiality maintained? Anonymity?
- Was informed consent obtained from the participants?
- Are there any other ethical issues – e.g. possible harm or emotional upset to participants, denial of an effective intervention to a control group – and are these addressed?

Interpretive dimensions

- Are the conclusions warranted by the empirical results?
- If statistical correlations are demonstrated, are these used, erroneously, to claim causation?
- If generalizations are made from the research sample to wider populations, is this justified?
- Is there logical consistency between the findings and the stated implications for practice?

Presentational and stylistic dimensions

- Is enough information provided to evaluate the various dimensions of the article?
- Is the language clear, concise and jargon free? Is it tentative, as befits research?
- Is the report well structured?
- Are subjective and loaded statements avoided?
- Is the title fully informative of the content of the article?
- Is the abstract fully informative of the content of the article?
- Is the report thoroughly referenced with an up-to-date list of articles and books?

The word 'critique' is misleading in its implied emphasis on critical comment, whereas a competent critical review should highlight both the strengths and weaknesses of the research article. Furthermore, a primary purpose of critical evaluation is to suggest ways in which the research could be improved, thus benefiting future researchers. The aim of the critique is to sharpen research awareness and technique for everyone concerned, not to decimate the author! As you write your critique, think – with each sentence – how you will feel when it is your article being assessed!

7.9 Blending of theory and practice

In the introduction to the NHS Management Executive document, *Research for Health* (1993), Professor Michael Peckham states:

'The prime objective is to see that Research and Development becomes an integral part of health (and social) care so that ... staff find it natural to rely on the results of research in their day-to-day decision making and longer term strategic planning.'

Thus, theory and practice should blend, as you use research findings routinely in your work.

Within the reformed NHS, purchasing authorities and providers need research-based 'intelligence' in three main areas; these are now briefly discussed.

Assessment of health needs

Purchasing authorities need to assess the health status of the people they serve (Waldegrave, 1992), in order to decide what health care to commission. This will involve the gathering of research information from a range of sources, including providers of health care. Descriptive research designs are appropriate for health needs assessment, including large scale surveys and statistical analysis of data to determine correlations between, for example, geographical location and health status.

Providers of health care also need information about the health status of their local populations in order to make decisions about distribution of resources and prioritization of services. At a more immediate level, ask yourself 'are the health needs of clients in my caseload significantly different from those in my colleagues' caseloads? Do I have evidence of this? If so, shouldn't my day-to-day work also be significantly different?

Finally, with relation to health needs assessment, the potential for qualitative approaches to complement surveys has been little exploited. Ethnographic accounts of local communities can provide a wealth of information about perceptions of health, health needs and the rationale for health behaviours.

Consumer attitudes and opinions

This is an open field for descriptive and exploratory research. At all levels, we need to know what clients want and think, and this can be achieved by research using questionnaires, telephone surveys, group or individual interviews and participant observation.

Outcomes

Evaluation of the outcomes of nursing care can be tricky, especially in health promotion and prevention: how can you measure something that does not occur? However, there is an increasing emphasis on the importance of outcome measures, and it is easier to see how this can be achieved in situations where nursing interventions would be expected to produce observable, recordable and measurable results. For example, the nursing intervention might consist of an extra daily social visit to the isolated elderly, and the expected outcome an improvement in morale. A hypothesis is formed: 'an extra daily visit improves the morale of isolated elderly people', and an experimental or quasi-experimental design required.

In order to evaluate innovations in practice, it is crucially important to have baseline measurements. You cannot assess the effectiveness of new practices unless you have clear information about the situation before implementation, as well as the situation afterwards. It has become so important for nurses, and in particular community nurses, to demonstrate their cost-effectiveness that the notion and practice of evaluation must become central to managers and practitioners alike.

7.10 Conclusion

Community nursing needs all kinds of research. Whether the focus is on topical issues such as skill mix or community care, or on more specific aspects of your own specialism, the goal is to provide cost-effective and research-based care. Individual practitioners may choose to participate in research activity to a greater or lesser degree, so that some initiate research projects while others help collect data as part of a research team. At the minimum, all community nurses should have easy access to relevant research-based articles. Once you have taken a course in research methods, you can enthusiastically evaluate these for the standard of the research, before using your professional judgement to decide whether the findings can be incorporated into your practice!

This chapter skims the surface of a wide and expanding field, representing a starting point for your research career. As you become increasingly familiar with the new concepts and language of research, you will find that it becomes more enjoyable and less intimidating. Whether you finally become an active researcher or a critical evaluator of the work of others, the outcome for your practice can only be positive.

Acknowledgement

I would like to acknowledge the invaluable critical comment provided by Ms Marcella Quinn on the first draft of this chapter.

7.11 References

Agency for Health Care Policy and Research (1992) *Effective Dissemination of Health and Clinical Information and Research Findings.* AHCPR, Rockville.

Benton, D.C. & Cormack, D.F.S. (1991) Reviewing and evaluating the literature. In: *The Research Process in Nursing* (ed. D.F.S. Cormack), 2nd edn. Blackwell Science, Oxford.

Blumer, H. (1969) *Symbolic Interactionism* Prentice-Hall, Hemel Hempstead.

Bond, S. (1991) Preparing a research proposal. In: *The Research Process in Nursing* (ed. D.F.S. Cormack), 2nd edn. Blackwell Science, Oxford.

Burnard, P. & Morrison, P. (1990) *Nursing Research in Action; Developing Basic Skills* Macmillan, Hampshire.

Castles, M.R. (1987) *Primer of Nursing Research.* W.B. Saunders Co, Philadelphia.

Cicourel, A.V. (1976) *The Social Organisation of Juvenile Justice.* Heinemann, London.

Cormack, D.F.S. (ed) (1991) *The Research Process in Nursing*, 2nd edn. Blackwell Science, Oxford.

Cowley, S. (1991) A symbolic awareness context identified through a grounded theory study of health visiting. *Journal of Advanced Nursing*, 16, 648–56.

Deatrick, J.A. & Faux, S.A. (1991) Conducting qualitative studies with children and adolescents. In: *Qualitative Research in Nursing; A Contemporary Dialogue* (ed. J.M. Morse). Revised edn, Sage Publications, London.

DHSS (1972) *Report of the Commission on Nursing.* HMSO, London.

Durkheim, E. (1938) *The Rules of Sociological Method.* The Free Press, New York.

Field, P.A. & Morse, J. (1991) *Nursing Research; The Application of Qualitative Approaches.* Chapman and Hall, London.

Graziano, A.M. & Raulin, M.L. (1993) *Research Methods; A Process of Inquiry*, 2nd edn. Harper Collins, New York.

Hockey, L. (1991) The nature and purpose of research. In: *The Research Process in Nursing*, (ed. D.F.S. Cormack), 2nd edn, pp. 3–12. Blackwell Science, Oxford.

Keesing, R.M. (1976) *Cultural Anthropology; A Contemporary Perspective.* Holt Reinhart and Winston, London.

Kerlinger, F.N. (1973) *Foundations of Behavioral Research*, 2nd edn. Holt, Reinhart and Winston, New York.

Luker, K. (1982) *Evaluating Health Visiting Practice.* RCN, London.

Mason, C. (1993) Doing a research literature review. *Nurse Researcher*, 1(1), 43–56.

Mason, C. (1994) Maternal and child health needs in Northern Ireland and Jamaica: official and lay perspectives. *Qualitative Health Research*, **4**(1), 74–94.

Mittman, B.S., Tonesk, X. & Jacobson, P.D. (1992) Implementing clinical practice guidelines: social influences strategies and practitioner behaviour change. *Quality Review Bulletin*, **18**(12), 413–22.

NHS Management Executive (1993) *Research for Health*. NHSME, Lancashire.

Orr, J. (1980) *Health Visiting in Focus*. RCN, London.

Polit, D.F. & Hungler, B.P. (1989) *Essentials of Nursing Research*, 2nd edn. J.B. Lippincott, London.

Pollock, L.C. (1991) Qualitative analysis. In: *The Research Process in Nursing* (ed. D.F.S. Cormack), 2nd edn. Blackwell Science, Oxford.

RCN (1993) *Ethics Related to Research in Nursing*. RCN, London.

Reid, N. (1993) *Health Care Research by Degrees*. Blackwell Science, Oxford.

Treece, E.W. & Treece, J.W. (1986) *Elements of Research in Nursing*. C.V. Mosby, St Louis.

Waldegrave, W. (1991) Forward in *The Health of the Nation*. Cm 1523. HMSO, London.

Weber, M. (1958) *The Protestant Ethic and the Spirit of Capitalism*. Charles Scribner's Sons, New York.

Part 2

Contemporary Community Health Care Nursing Practice

Chapter 8

Towards Public Health Nursing

The White Paper *Working for Patients* (DOH, 1989b) and the NHS and Community Care Act (1990) instigated profound changes in the NHS, most notably by the introduction of an internal market operated by distinct groups of purchasers and providers. Key features of the reformed NHS include assessment of health needs, strategic planning, targeted action and evaluation of effectiveness by outcome measurement.

The impact on health visiting is considerable. The supportive, empowering dimension of health visiting activity is hard to measure, and emergent self esteem builds slowly in individual clients. Primary prevention is a long-term enterprise, and success difficult to quantify. In short, the health service reforms pose special challenges for health visiting.

However, the current policy focus on public health is consistent with the historical ethos of health visiting, and it is in this arena that health visiting has, perhaps, the greatest potential for growth. The connection between health visiting and public health is highlighted by the UKCC (1994) in the draft PREP proposals, which envisage a specialist category of public health nursing embodying the practice of health visiting. The principles of health visiting (see Table 8.1) are consistent with a public health approach, and health needs assessment – the cornerstone of public health – forms a major component of health visitor education.

It is likely, therefore, that the public health dimension of health visiting work will receive an increasingly high profile, and it is partly in this expectation that the following chapter is written. However, the situation is fluid, so some of what follows is necessarily speculative. It is axiomatic in the modern health service that the only certainty is continuing change!

Table 8.1 The principles of health visiting.

(1) *The search for health needs*
Health visitors work proactively in their search for acknowledged and hidden health needs within communities and caseloads.

(2) *Stimulation of the awareness of health needs*
Having identified the health needs of the population, health visitors stimulate an awareness of these needs among individuals, families, lay organizations and community groups. The emphasis in work with individuals is on self-empowerment, while the stimulation of health needs awareness in communities might be achieved by the development of self-help groups, action groups and pressure groups.

(3) *The influence on policies affecting health*
Health visitors seek to influence policies affecting health at many levels, for example through pressure groups, consumer organizations, health authorities, MPs, national and international committees and the media.

(4) *The facilitation of health-enhancing activities*
Health visitors seek to facilitate healthy lifestyles for individuals by contributing to the creation of social–structural conditions that allow people to adopt health-enhancing behaviours, and by working in partnership with clients to enable them to make informed lifestyle choices.

(Sources: CETHV, 1977; Twinn & Cowley 1992)

8.1 Full circle: the development of health visiting from sanitary inspector to the new public health

Overcrowding, poverty and high infant mortality in the nineteenth century prompted the emergence of voluntary movements aiming to improve the moral, social and hygienic welfare of the urban poor. One such organization, the Ladies Sanitary Reform Association, was formed in Manchester and Salford in 1862, and this is generally acknowledged to be the start of health visiting. 'Respectable working women' were appointed to go 'from door to door among the poorer classes of the population, to teach and help them as the opportunity offered' (McCleary, 1933). They were to teach hygiene and child welfare, mental and moral health, and provide social support.

Co-existing with the voluntary lady visitors at the turn of the century, women sanitary inspectors carried out public health work, despite the prevailing feeling at the time that this latter work was unsuitable for women. The women sanitary inspectors aimed to increase their marketability by combining inspection duties with home visiting; they opposed the separation of sanitary inspection and home visiting as jobs, fearing that the latter would be demoted as 'female work' with lower status and lower pay. Eventually, however, this occurred, and a lower level qualification was devised for health visitors, as they were increasingly known (Robinson, 1982; Davies, 1988). Thus, health work for women was channelled into the private sphere of home and family, befitting the sex whose assumed qualities of tact and sympathy, it was argued, produced the most appropriate 'mother's friend' (Davies, 1988).

Through the first half of the twentieth century, health visiting activity focused on maternal and child health. Dramatic reductions in infant and child deaths seemed to vindicate the work; ironically, however, it also raised questions about the continued need for the service. Nevertheless, security for health visiting seemed assured with the inception of the NHS: the National Health Service Act specified that the health visiting function would involve: 'giving advice as to the care of persons suffering from illness ... to expectant mothers and nursing mothers, and to mothers and others with the care of young children' (MOH, 1946). The Act further stated that health visitors should be concerned with the health of 'the household as a whole', working closely with family doctors and not encroaching on the work of nurses or sanitary inspectors.

While succeeding legislation reiterated the 'family visitor' focus of health visiting (MOH, 1956), health visitors themselves became proactive in redefining their functions more widely to relate to the public sphere of health policy as well as the private sphere of family life (Council for the Education and Training of Health Visitors (CETHV) (1977)). The 1970s and 1980s were productive in terms of theoretical development and reassessment of the role and function of health visiting. The principles of health visiting were developed by the CETHV and the health visiting remit was reoriented to health needs assessment, awareness raising and health promotion in all possible settings and by a variety of means to individuals, families, communities and nationally (CETHV, 1977).

This reorientation proved far sighted in view of the profound changes to the NHS legislated in The NHS and Community Care Act (1990). Strategic planning for health care delivery is now supposed to begin with assessment of the health needs of local populations, and health targets are to be achieved through awareness raising and health promotion (DOH, 1992b) – precisely the activities highlighted by the CETHV. It would seem, therefore, that the adoption of a wider public health approach by health visitors represents an appropriate adaptation to the new situation. In another sense, however, health visitors evolved as described from the public health movements of the nineteenth century and by merging with the women public health inspectors of the early twentieth century. It may be that the apparently innovative drive towards public health is simply a return to the roots of the profession: health visiting has come full circle.

8.2 Public health and public health nursing

The concepts and activities of public health are familiar to health visitors, although their daily work has traditionally been constrained by a focus on the 'nought to fives' (Clark, 1981). In theory, the market NHS should free health visitors to translate this public health knowledge into practice, since other workers – as 'allies' of health visitors – now increasingly contribute to routine home visiting and child health surveillance.

The definition of public health in the King's Fund report, *The Nation's Health* (Jacobson *et al.*, 1991) reads, in part, like an outline of the work of the health visitor. The report says that public health involves:

'... the promotion of health, the prevention of disease, the treatment of illness, the care of those who are disabled and the continuous development of the technical and social means for the pursuit of these objectives.'

A useful RCN information leaflet on public health (RCN, 1994) defines it as:

'... a collective view of the health needs and health care of a population rather than an emphasis on an individual perspective. A central component of this collective approach is an emphasis on partnership at all stages and levels of the public health process. This means partnership with communities and clients within them as well as partnerships across and between professional groups. Teamwork is an essential prerequisite to effective public health work.'

Components of public health include, according to RCN (1994):

■ mortality and morbidity statistics and their associated factors;
■ socio-structural and environmental factors known to impact upon health:
■ service provision, including non-NHS services, such as clean water;
■ the knowledge, beliefs and perceptions about health and health care held by the general public;
■ specific client groups, particularly vulnerable groups such as the homeless and those living in poverty;
■ social policy measures, especially legal and fiscal measures;
■ a particular method of working using community development or community participation approaches.

Like public health, epidemiology is concerned with populations rather than individuals. Epidemiology is considered to be 'the basic science of public health' (Detels, 1991) because it describes relationships between health and disease and other factors in human populations – for example, the relationship between coronary heart disease (CHD) and smoking. This provides public health professionals with the information needed to implement effective intervention programmes.

Screening is an activity that contributes to the public health process by applying a relatively simple test to populations in order to detect preclinical disease. The objective of screening is to reduce mortality or morbidity or to improve the quality of life, and it is usually used to detect serious chronic disease (Hakama, 1991). While primary prevention (i.e. preventing disease from occurring) forms the main focus of health visiting activity, secondary prevention, including screening, is employed to reinforce other health promotion measures. For example, distraction hearing tests are used to detect hearing defects in children, and the Ortolani and Barlow tests are employed to detect congenital dislocation of the hip. Screening tests are not infallible and false positive results can be counterproductive by producing morbidity, in the form of anxiety, in otherwise healthy people. Screening is therefore a policy issue, and blanket screening of populations is introduced only after careful consideration of the benefits, adverse effects, and overall cost-effectiveness.

Two complementary approaches in public health are the population approach, which adopts blanket measures aiming to improve health throughout the community, and the high risk approach, which concentrates on those at greatest risk of ill health. The authors of *The Nation's Health* generally favour the broader population approach, quoting 'good evidence' that an exclusively high risk approach is unlikely to reduce the scale of CHD, alcohol-related harm or hypertension (Jacobson *et al.*, 1991). Another way of looking at public health activity is to consider it on three levels:

- Individual level;
- Total population, group or community level;
- Policy level, national and/or local campaigns (RCN, 1994).

The last-mentioned approach is likely to form a more useful framework for nursing practice.

What does all this mean for practising health visitors? How might the new emphasis on public health affect their day-to-day work?

The Strelley nursing development unit (NDU), located in a disadvantaged geographical area in Nottingham, provides a good example of public health nursing in action (Strelley Nursing Development Unit, 1993; Jackson, 1994). Health visitors working in Strelley found that the public health role worked successfully only when it was separated from generic health visiting, therefore a full-time post was made free for public health work. The first public health visitor compiled a community health profile to identify health needs, selecting accident prevention as one area to be targeted.

At community level, the public health visitor worked with local community groups and contacted the local accident investigation unit to establish traffic calming schemes in accident black spots. A multi-agency forum with representation from education, social services, housing, environmental health, the voluntary sector and the health service was set up to raise awareness, while a low-cost home safety equipment scheme made smoke alarms and other devices more accessible to residents. At an individual level, local people asked for basic first aid courses, which were subsequently run by the NDU and community workers. At policy level, the NDU successfully campaigned for more public telephones on the estate so that emergency services could be readily contacted, while further political pressure successfully secured a welfare rights advice session one day per week at the local library.

Follow-up projects included – at the request of local women – a Baby Drop-In, which 'is more like a group than a clinic', and a women's aid advice service launched in response to the known high incidence of domestic violence. The current challenge for each of these projects is to provide 'hard' outcome data for providers and purchasers.

An important influence on public health in the UK is the White Paper *Health of the Nation* (DOH, 1992b), which highlights five areas for health action: coronary heart disease (CHD) and strokes; cancers; mental illness; HIV/AIDS and sexual health; and accidents. In each case, numerical targets are set for reduction in incidence through individual behaviour change, changes in practice and delivery of care, and changes in the environment. The *Health of the Nation* has been criticized on the following grounds:

(1) overemphasis on behaviour change, neglecting social, economic and environmental influences on health (HVA, 1991; RCN, 1991; Charlton, 1992);
(2) the focus on secondary prevention and medical intervention rather than health promotion (HVA, 1991);
(3) neglect of issues of equity, access and partnership (HVA, 1991; RCN, 1991);
(4) demeaning individual variation in favour of generalizations at the level of populations (Caraher, 1994). Nevertheless, as a policy document, *Health of the Nation* is highly influential, and its focus on health gain has been universally welcomed.

Health visitors have an important contribution to make to each of the target areas, and innovative strategies for doing so are outlined in the DOH handbook, *Targeting Practice: the Contribution of Nurses, Midwives and Health Visitors* (DOH, 1993). For example, with relation to CHD, a group of health visitors in Surrey identified poor diet amongst low income families as a problem, evidenced by low birth weight, failure to thrive, obesity, high levels of dental caries and frequent referrals to speech therapy. A multidisciplinary group of health visitors, health promotion officers and a community dietician, in consultation with the HVA and The Health Promotion Unit, devised an intervention programme with inbuilt evaluation. This involved lunchtime group sessions with identified 'at risk' families in local pubs, community centres and church halls. Topics included preparing and sharing a meal, discussion about shopping and best value choices, budgeting for meals and nutritional labelling.

Evaluation is by means of a diet 'diary' completed before the group begins, immediately after, and six months later, in addition to a client satisfaction survey. The evaluation to date is positive, and success is further evidenced by the fact that clients have started to ask for recipe books, which are being prepared in a sensitive way in view of the above average rate of illiteracy. The health visitors hope that group members will join in the planning, running and evaluation of the group as it develops, and the project is providing a valuable learning experience for students of health visiting, district nursing, and Project 2000 students.

To summarize, it is clear that public health is high on the agenda for health visitors. Various models for the health visiting contribution to public health have been suggested, including an integration of generic health visiting duties with a public health function – as in the Surrey project described above (DOH, 1993). Alternatively, it is advocated that the two roles should be separated (Jackson, 1994), a view that is elaborated by Barker who argues that health visitors should specialize and work either as practice health visitors employed by general practice fundholders, or as 'all-community' health visitors employed by FHSAs or public health directorates (Barker, 1993). A third possibility is that all professions concerned with public health should establish 'a new common identity' (Watkins, 1992) with a joint register of public health practitioners. This, it is argued, would raise the profile of public health and facilitate a sharing of expertise in the interest of public health. Whichever model is chosen, it is clear that the remit of health visiting is expanding into the public sphere. This is a chance to put into action the principles of health visiting in the fullest possible way.

8.3 Health visiting in the market NHS

The NHS of the 1990s is modelled on business and underpinned by an ethos of competition. The rationale for the introduction of an internal market to health care is improvement of efficiency and effectiveness by having health care providers compete against one another for funds. The function of purchasing authorities, as 'champions of the people' (Waldegrave, 1991) – distinct from any vested professional interest – is to assess local health needs and buy appropriate health services, aiming to obtain value for money on behalf of the populations they represent. Evidence of value for money is sought by purchasers through outcome measures.

GPs form an increasingly powerful body within the reformed NHS, operating as both providers and purchasers of health care. GP Fundholding practices are allocated a budget according to the size and demographic structure of their practice population, putting them in a strong position to demand desired quality standards from the hospitals with which they place contracts. While GPs employ practice nurses directly, current NHS Management Executive guidelines forbid direct employment of community nurses by GPs (Cohen, 1994). Instead, health visitors and other community nurses are employed by community services units or trusts, to which they remain accountable. There is evidence that a substantial proportion of GP Fundholders are frustrated by having to contract their community services to an NHS community unit (Glennerster *et al.*, 1994), while the HVA (1991) defends this position as essential to the autonomy of the profession.

Deriving from the White Paper *Promoting Better Health* (DOH, 1989), the GP Contract came into effect on 1 April 1990. This provided a new emphasis on health promotion and disease prevention, with targets for vaccination, immunization and cervical cancer screening, as well as encouragement for the development of health promotion clinics and closer involvement with child health surveillance. The profile of health promotional activity has undoubtedly been raised as a consequence of *Promoting Better Health*. However, much of the additional activity is carried out by practice nurses, and some health visitors perceive this as a usurping of the health visiting role (Lightfoot, 1994).

Many health visitors criticize the market NHS on the grounds that the business ethos is inappropriate for a humanitarian organization, and health cannot be 'produced'. Moreover, as indicated earlier, health visiting focuses on the slow and difficult-to-quantify process of empowerment through confidence and esteem building: how can cost-effectiveness be demonstrated here? (Twinn & Cowley, 1992). It seems, however, that the market NHS is firmly established. Analysis of its deficiencies is no longer the priority for health visiting and, on the contrary, strategic thinking is. How can health visiting skills be used most cost-effectively in the market NHS? In what ways can health visitors meet client need by contributing – visibly – to the now-not-so-new contractual arrangements?

Important strategic focuses

Purchasing

A major area for growth potential in health visiting lies in its contribution to purchasing. The first function of purchasing authorities is assessment of health needs or 'intelligence gathering', and this calls for precisely the skills possessed by health visitors, who are experienced at local community health profiling. Goodwin (1992) found that many Public Health Directors 'seemed desperate for any help they could get in identifying needs and drawing up better service specifications'. The nursing contribution to needs assessment is formally promoted by the NHS Management Executive (1993b, cited in RCN, 1994) which states that:

'Purchasers have responsibility for public health and should ensure they make best use of nursing expertise. For example by contracting for the use of public health nursing input into health profiling.'

Moreover, community health profiles contain qualitative data (Orr, 1992) to usefully complement the broad statistical overviews often produced by public health departments. Health visiting skills can and should be used in this way, and, to provide the mechanism, 'service specifications should identify profile data as one of the kinds of information to be supplied by community nursing providers' (Goodwin, 1992). Already, in mid-Staffordshire, a purchaser and provider (a community trust) have collaborated on needs assessment, and community nurses play a large part in gathering data. In Oxfordshire, the results of community health profiling provide the basis for service agreements.

Nursing as a whole has been slow to recognize the importance of purchasing (King's Fund, 1993). Naish (1993) recommends that health visitors examine the contract specification documents from their purchasing authorities, returning constructive critical comment to the purchasers. Furthermore, community health profiles – an invaluable resource – should be sent directly to the purchasing authority's public health department.

Marketing

A second important strategic focus for health visitors should be marketing. While health visitors have always subtly marketed their service in negotiation with clients (De La Cuesta, 1994), marketing now has to be much more public, directed at potential purchasers of health visiting services (health authorities and GPs) as well as customers/clients. In the market NHS, the central question underpinning any action is: 'What is the health gain inherent in this activity?' (Carpenter, 1992), and the essence of marketing is to make this public. Edwards (1994) suggests that three questions are appropriate:

(1) How can the service best contribute to local health needs assessment?
(2) How is the impact of the service to be measured?
(3) How is the current position of the service to be described?

It is important that a description of the service concentrates on likely advantage to the client, rather than outlining a professional role.

Perhaps the most useful marketing suggestion, again from Edwards (1994), is to ask: 'What are the gold star features of the service?' If health visiting was to be marketed to a community which had not heard of the service, and where potential customers had to be persuaded to pay for it, how could it be recommended? As an individualized service offering personal attention in people's own homes? As a professional service offering skilled advice on childcare? Or as an outreach service facilitating the development of self-help groups on issues like smoking or weight reduction? Which would people buy? This approach validates the importance of the community health profile, which can be compared with market research in assessing unmet needs and the potential for 'custom'.

Evaluation

A third strategic focus for health visiting is evaluation. Since purchasers are interested in outcomes, outcome measures should, as far as possible, be built into all health visiting interventions. This may not be as difficult as it seems. Starting with the concept of effectiveness, we can say that effectiveness is demonstrated when an intervention achieves what it set out to achieve (Harrison, Hunter & Pollitt, 1990); therefore it is essential at the start of any project to set clear objectives, which act as a baseline against which to measure achievements. There are many examples in the literature which clearly demonstrate the effectiveness of health visiting:

- Home visiting by health visitors was related to a higher uptake of developmental assessments and hearing tests, and was a source of consumer satisfaction (While, 1990).
- Health visiting the over-70s in Powys was associated with reduced mortality and minor improvements in quality of life (Vetter, Jones & Victor, 1986).
- Health visiting support enabled women to breastfeed for longer than those not offered this support (Houston, 1981).
- Health visiting intervention strongly influenced individuals' willingness to make their home safer (Colver & Pearson, 1985).
- A four-year evaluation of health-visitor-run courses to assist people with stress showed reduced dependency on drugs and reduced demands on GPs' time (Tyler & Barnes, 1989).

An outstanding example of effective evaluation is incorporated in The Child Development Programme (CDP). The programme involves structured health visiting to first time mothers, with an emphasis on empowerment and participation. Outcomes are recorded manually by health visitors and fed into the computer programme MONITOR, which permits statistical analysis. This is a more powerful tool than other information systems which simply record numbers of visits by category, and it represents one of the best chances health visitors have to demonstrate the effectiveness of their work. It has been shown that health visiting input based on the CDP can improve the home environment and nutritional status of children, reduce the incidence of early hospitalization and language delay, increase immunization rates and produce 'a remarkable reduction' in the number of children on child abuse registers or sustaining child abuse injuries compared with children who are not receiving the programme (Barker & Anderson, 1988).

Cost-effectiveness

A further challenge is to demonstrate the cost-effectiveness of health visiting interventions. Cost-effectiveness is the ratio between inputs (e.g. staff time) and outcomes (e.g. improved quality of life) (Harrison, Hunter & Pollitt, 1990). User satisfaction surveys, breastfeeding and immunization uptake rates, changes in health behaviour such as eating habits, weight loss/gain, and attendances at group or clinic sessions are examples of outcome measures. It is now also important to register the volume and cost of health visiting input, and to ask whether the outcomes justify the inputs. This question is being asked by both GP and health authority purchasers, who want to know whether input costs could be reduced by the employment of lower grade staff.

This raises the contentious issue of skill mix, which can be defined as the balance between skilled and untrained, qualified and unqualified, supervisory and operative staff within a service area (Social Policy Research Unit, 1992). Since traditional health visiting is characterized by one-to-one relationships between mothers and health visitors, it has been argued by health visitors that any variant represents a dilution of the service. The introduction of skill mix teams into health visiting has therefore met with resistance in many instances.

However, this has the effect of making health visiting appear defensive and entrenched to purchasers. Skill mix is likely to increase, given tight spending regimes, pressures to cut staff costs, and the fall off in numbers of students of nursing and health visiting. Two models of skill mix have so far emerged:

(1) 'general' support by staff such as RGNs and nursery nurses who carry out a variety of tasks in an *ad hoc* way; and
(2) 'specific' support by similar staff, whose tasks are more clearly defined (Lightfoot, 1994).

It is suggested by Lightfoot (1994) that potential problems of role confusion might be averted by adoption of Model (2) above. A further important factor is acknowledged by The Audit Commission (1992), which emphasizes that skill mix does not mean a blanket prescription for basic tasks to be carried out by lower grade staff. The picture is more complex, since cost-effectiveness may be assured if a highly qualified nurse carries out a complex task along with several basic tasks, during one visit. This is frequently the case in health visiting where, in one visit, relatively basic skills are used to assess a child's hearing and general development, along with more complex supportive, listening and counselling skills directed towards the mother and the family as a whole.

Information technology

Finally, information technology (IT) is a resource increasingly used by purchasers to evaluate contract compliance (i.e. the extent to which negotiated contracts with providers are being met). Unfortunately, information systems throughout the UK are not currently compatible, so comparisons across regions cannot be made. Yet more unfortunately for health visiting, contracts often stipulate the number of client contacts to be achieved annually, with the implicit and erroneous assumption that 'more visits' means better health visiting. However, despite the limitations, it is crucially important that information forms are completed and returned; otherwise, in the absence of evidence to the contrary, purchasers will assume that contracts have been broken and are therefore not worth renewing. More promisingly, a new Community Information System for Providers (CISPS) is being developed, which aims to overcome problems of comparability and measurement of the quality of health visiting (NHS Management Executive, 1993b). In the meantime, assessment of health needs, influencing purchasers, marketing and evaluation are interlinked activities where imaginative thinking, confidence and innovation can help ensure that health visiting remains an important outreach service customized to the needs of clients.

8.4 Promoting health in the community

The principles of health visiting (CETHV, 1977) have proved an enduring framework for health promoting activities by health visitors. Application of the principles to current practice is outlined by Twinn and Cowley (1992) as follows:

(1) *The search for health needs.* This is achieved through partnership with, and empowerment of, clients, who then identify their own health needs. The search for health needs involves rigorous data collection, data analysis and use of empirical evidence.
(2) *Stimulation of an awareness of health needs.* Health visiting aims to enable people to become aware of their own health needs in the context of poverty, etc. Esteem building and self-empowerment form the starting point. Awareness raising is also achieved by use of the media, work with lay organizations and community groups, action, pressure- and self-help groups. Targets for awareness raising include clients, health service

managers (providers and purchasers), politicians and policy makers.

(3) *Influences on policies affecting health.* Health visitors are assessors of health need who participate in the public health policy process by contributing nursing advice. Targets for political pressure include local and government level councillors and politicians, pressure groups and consumer organizations. Health visitors provide a voice for women, and support community development approaches to health promotion.

(4) *The facilitation of health-enhancing activities.* Health visitors acknowledge that individuals may find it difficult to adopt a healthy lifestyle because of their circumstances; therefore empowerment is sought through personal confidence and esteem building. A wide range of health-enhancing activities is undertaken, including projects such as 'Cope Street' (Billingham, 1989) and participation in the Child Development Programme (Barker & Anderson, 1988). Other health-enhancing activities consistent with the spirit of empowerment include increasing client access to information by means of parent held records, action on road safety and environmental issues, and participation in the 'Healthy Cities' initiative (Ashton, 1988).

The strength of the principles lies in their acknowledgement of the socio-economic influences on health. A victim-blaming ideology is avoided and health promotion is conceived at a macro, political level, as well as through empowerment of individuals. The framework thus remains relevant to three approaches to promoting health in the community: those of participation, community development and the new public health.

A participation approach to health promotion

A good example of health visiting principles in action is the Cope Street project (Billingham, 1989; Rowe, 1993), which is based on a participation approach to health promotion. Recognizing that preventive services for young pregnant women and mothers needed to be offered in more acceptable ways, Nottingham Community Health rented an inner-city terraced house at 45 Cope Street. The nursing team consists of one full-time health visitor/ midwife, one part-time health visitor, two part-time nursery nurses, and one part-time midwife. The philosophy is clear (Rowe, 1993):

'... we respect the women who use our service. These young women strive against all odds to do their best for their children and often achieve high levels of success, even in situations of high economic or social stress. Our fundamental aim will always be to build their self-esteem, self-confidence and feeling of self worth.'

This is achieved by means of non-thematic groupwork, and other group sessions jointly planned by the women and the staff. A crèche is provided where women's wishes about the care of their children are respected, and underpinning all action is a sense of valuing the women as individuals. Evaluation consists of assessment of client satisfaction, and monitoring of outcomes. Both have been positive, and outcomes are illustrated by the following quotations from clients: 'I feel confident, not depressed any more'; 'I learnt a lot and had a good laugh'; and, 'I understand more about my child's behaviour and different ideas about how to handle it' (Rowe, 1993).

The essence of this approach is acknowledgement of the socio–economic and cultural context within which health is experienced. A focus on 'lifestyle' alone is considered inappropriate, since the health behaviour of individuals is constrained by factors such as unemployment, poverty, cultural beliefs and commercial pressures. As Goodwin (1992) argues with relation to the prevention of coronary heart disease, a national nutrition policy including healthy school meals and statutory food labelling, and the banning of all tobacco advertising, should accompany the screening of individuals. This is not to deny the evidence demonstrating relationships between behaviour and disease – rather, it is intended to highlight another relationship: that between behaviour and the socio-economic pressures to which individuals are subject. It is important that health messages take this wider context into account, lest they act counterproductively to disempower individuals by setting inappropriate and unattainable goals.

A community development approach

A second approach to promoting health in the community, also based on an empowerment model, is community development. Community development can be distinguished from participation approaches in the way that health problems are identified: in the former, a community defines its own health needs and makes these known to service providers in order to bring about change; in the latter, health problems are identified by professionals who then negotiate with community members for appropriate action. The overall goal of community development, in accordance with the World Health Organization's campaign *Health for all 2000* (WHO, 1978), is a reduction in inequalities in health through empowerment, participation, collaboration and local primary health care. The key features of community development are:

(1) holism, where the multidimensional nature of human experience is taken into account;
(2) it is done *with* people and not *to* them; the members of the group or community are involved at all stages;
(3) a community identifies its own needs, and these are viewed as inter-related;

(4) outcomes are unpredictable. 'If what you are doing is done in negotiation with a community, reflects that community's needs, and goes at the pace that the community determines, then you can't necessarily determine the outcome or even the time-scale with any reliability.' (Kennedy, 1992);
(5) lay/local perceptions are emphasized.

An example of health visiting involvement in community development is the Ancoats health initiative in north Manchester (Sutcliffe, 1994). The community identified as their principal health need the reopening of a full accident and emergency service at the local hospital. This could not be achieved, but by following protracted negotiations between the local action group, GPs and health authority representatives it was agreed that a self-contained community health clinic would be built, with comprehensive services including health visiting, district nursing, community midwifery and psychiatry, child developmental assessments, immunization, family planning and a women's health clinic. A philosophy of partnership prevails, and this has facilitated, for example, the introduction of a well woman's service run by local volunteers. Within the first six months of opening, 3800 people visited the treatment room, and clinic sessions have been increased to meet demand, going some way to fill the gap left in accident and emergency cover.

Public health approaches

As defined earlier, public health can incorporate community participation and community development as action strategies to meet the health needs of populations. In public health, too, there is emphasis on social policy measures to improve health, and this relates particularly to disadvantaged groups. In Great Britain, the major component of disadvantage is unemployment and low paid work, while the second largest component comprises single parent families, large families, the elderly, disabled and chronically sick (Illsley & Mullen, 1991). Incontrovertible evidence exists that such groups experience higher rates of mortality and morbidity (Carter & Peel, 1976; Townsend, 1979; Whitehead, 1987), and that disadvantage from one cause is rarely a discrete factor separate from other stresses and strains.

There is further evidence that many of the 'poor' do not take up their full entitlement to social security benefits (Illsley & Mullen, 1991), suggesting that appropriate action for health professionals and social workers would include campaigning for a simplification in procedures and initiation of schemes to provide positive assistance with claiming. There should also be calls for an increase in public assistance such as home helps, better crèche provision, and help with major expenses.

Finally, some preventive measures obtain particular significance for the disadvantaged, who are disproportionately affected. These include regulation of domestic, road and industrial accidents; controlled use of harmful substances (alcohol and drugs); promotion of healthy foods and eating habits; better working conditions; and reducing environmental pollution (Illsley & Mullen, 1991).

A list of documents which might be useful when planning a campaign to influence policy, is contained in Section 8.7.

The issue of disadvantage touches on the wider issue of human rights. The International Council for Nurses (ICN) supports the Geneva Convention and the UN Universal Declaration of Human Rights, providing formal espousal of a set of values implicitly accepted in health visiting. Work is currently in progress to develop a WHO declaration on patients' rights (Sheldon, 1994).

With respect to children's rights, the UN Convention on the Rights of the Child (United Nations Children's Fund, 1989) was ratified by the British government in 1991. The Convention highlights the paramountcy of the child's interests, and the right of children to have their views known and heard. This is consistent with the main message of The Children Act (1989), a major piece of British legislation which draws together previously patchy policies into a statement emphasizing the rights of children and the responsibilities of parents. Several useful publications outline the major points contained within The Children Act (1989, for example, The Children Act: An Introduction (HMSO, 1989); HVA, 1989; HMSO, 1992; DOH, 1992a), and all health visitors should be familiar with these.

To conclude Section 8.4, it seems that – in theory – there are endless possibilities for new and imaginative ways of promoting health in the community.

Alliances between health visitors and others are already generating creative projects on, for example, sexual health, psychological health after childbirth, well men clinics, smoking and breast cancer screening (DOH, 1993). Health stalls and open clinic days are being run jointly by health visitors, district nurses and practice nurses, while behaviour problem clinics and stress reduction clinics are organized by health visitors, community practice nurses and psychologists (Appleby, 1991). Castledine (1994) further recommends that nurses should work more closely with consumer organizations; with respect to health visiting this might involve liaising with women's groups, local councils, associations of ethnic minority groups, trade unions, or youth action organizations. Finally, and depending on local circumstances, health promotion activities could be negotiated with specific population groups, such as travellers, isolated rural communities, the homeless, or unemployed people.

Whichever approach is taken, the starting point is always listening, respect for people, and negotiation. While this might now be translated into the language of the market, the new healthspeak should not disguise the central focus of health visiting work, which is always the client as individual, family or community.

8.5 Conclusion

Professional life in the market NHS is a challenging experience. Change is a way of life, and the fixed structures of the traditional system have given way to more fluid, experimental and often more exciting ways of working. Ironically, however, new constraints have replaced the old; and limited resources, inappropriate information systems and reactive management sometimes leave health visitors rushing around to complete itemized checks on as many children as possible, thus excluding the very kind of imaginative, strategic health promotional work envisioned by the NHS Management Executive (1993) and the DOH (1993). To some extent, this may be a transitional stage and improved ways of measuring health visiting activity, together with proactive management, should free more health visitors to adopt the public health role for which they are so well prepared.

Given the expanding remit of health visiting from the traditional focus on the private sphere of family health to inclusion of a wider, collective, public health orientation, working models for health visiting need to be reassessed. Can the public health function be carried out alongside family visits by generic health visitors? Or should there be specialist health visitors for each, maybe with different employers (health authorities and GPs respectively) as suggested by Barker (1993)? Since there is now a mixed economy of care and mixed structures for the delivery of that care, it seems likely that a range of models for health visiting will emerge.

It is worthwhile reflecting on the history of health visiting, to contextualize the possible future. As described, health visiting emerged as a response to socio–economic conditions in the nineteenth century which clearly highlighted a role for home visitors to provide support and health advice to the poor. What do current socio–economic conditions indicate a need for? Presumably, the multifactorial nature of health, and the influences upon it, legitimate a 'broad brush' approach by health visitors to health promotion today. At the turn of the century, rigid notions about gender specific behaviour squeezed women out of the market for public health promotion. Almost one hundred years later, health visitors are again moving into the public sphere in a world which, it is to be hoped, is more open to the enormous contribution the profession can make.

Acknowledgement

I would like to thank Professor Jean Orr and Miss Gerry O'Sullivan for their invaluable comments on the first draft of this chapter.

8.6 References

Appleby, F. (1991) In pursuit of excellence. *Health Visitor* **64**(8), 254–6.

Ashton, J. (1988) *Healthy Cities, Concepts and Visions.* Department of Community Health, University of Liverpool.

Audit Commission (1992) *Homeward Bound: A New Course for Community Health.* HMSO, London.

Barker, W. (1993) Patch and practice: specialist roles for health visitors. *Health Visitor*, **66**(6), 200–203.

Barker, W. & Anderson, R. (1988) *The Child Development Programme. An Evaluation of Process and Outcomes.* Early Child Development Unit, Bristol.

Billingham, K. (1989) 45 Cope Street – working in partnership with parents. *Health Visitor*, **62**(5), 156–7.

Caraher, M. (1994) Health promotion: time for an audit. *Nursing Standard*, **8**(20), 33–5.

Carpenter, J. (1992) Public health medicine and the purchasing function: a public health physician's view. In: *Yorkshire Health Public Health Report.* University of York.

Carter, C.O. & Peel, J. (eds) (1976) *Equalities and Inequalities in Health.* Academic Press, London.

Castledine, G. (1994) Nurses should work more closely with consumer organisations. *British Journal of Nursing*, **3**(1), 31–2.

CETHV (Council for the Education and Training of Health Visitors) (1977) *An Investigation into the Principles of Health Visiting.* CETHV, London.

Charlton, B.G. (1992) Setting targets and 'The Health of the Nation'. *Medical Audit News*, **2**(11), 146–7.

The Children Act (1989). HMSO, London.

Clark, J. (1981) *What Do Health Visitors Do?* RCN, London.

Cohen, P. (1994) Chief nurse rules out GP management. In: *Health Visitor*, **67**(4), 117.

Colver, A.F. & Pearson, P. (1985) Safety in the home: how well are we doing? *Health Visitor*, **58**(2), 41–2.

Davies, C. (1988) The health visitor as mother's friend: a woman's place in public health, 1900–14. *The Social History of Medicine*, **1**, 38–57.

De La Cuesta (1994) Marketing: a process in health visiting. *Journal of Advanced Nursing*, **19**, 347–53.

Detels, R. (1991) Epidemiology: the foundation of public health. In: *Oxford Textbook of Public Health, Vol 2, Methods of Public Health* (eds W.W. Holland, R. Detels & G. Knox), pp. 285–91. Oxford University Press, Oxford.

DOH (1989a) *Promoting Better Health. The Government's Programme for Promoting Better Health Care.* Cm 2459. HMSO, London.

DOH (1989b) *Working for Patients.* HMSO, London.

DOH (1992a) *What Every Nurse, Health Visitor and Midwife Need to Know. The Children Act, 1989.* DOH, London.

DOH (1992b) *Health of The Nation: A Strategy for Health in England.* HMSO, London.

DOH (1993) *Targeting Practice: the Contribution of Nurses, Midwives and Health Visitors*. DOH, London.

Edwards, J. (1994) How to sell your services in the NHS. *Primary Health Care*, **4**(1), 6–8.

Glennerster, H., Matsaganis, M., Owens, P., & Hancock, S. (1994) GP Fundholding: wild card or winning hand? In: *Evaluating the NHS Reforms* (eds R. Robinson & J. Le Grand). King's Fund Institute, Berkshire.

Goodwin, S. (1992) Community nursing and the new public health. *Health Visitor*, **65**(3), 78–80.

Hakama, M. (1991) Screening. In: *Oxford Textbook of Public Health, Vol 3, Applications in Public Health* (eds W.W. Holland, R. Detels & G. Knox), pp. 91–105. Oxford University Press, Oxford.

Harrison, S., Hunter, D.J. & Pollitt, C. (1990) *The Dynamics of British Health Policy*. Routledge, London.

HMSO (1989) *The Children Act: An Introduction*. HMSO, London.

HMSO (1992) *Child Protection. Guidance for Senior Nurses, Health Visitors and Midwives*. HMSO, London.

Houston, M.J. (1981) Home support for the breastfeeding mother. *Midwife, Health Visitor and Community Nurse*, 378–82.

HVA (Health Visitors' Association) (1989) *The Children Act: Guidance on Professional Practice*. HVA, London.

HVA (Health Visitors' Association) (1991) 'The Health of the Nation.' The HVA responds. *Health Visitor*, **64**(11), 365–7.

Illsley, R. & Mullen, K. (1991) The health needs of disadvantaged client groups. In: *Oxford Textbook of Public Health, Vol 3, Applications in Public Health* (eds W.W. Holland, D. Detels & G. Knox), pp. 539–54. Oxford University Press, Oxford.

Jackson, C. (1994) Strelley: teamworking for health. *Health Visitor*, **67**(1), 28–9.

Jacobson, B., Smith, A. & Whitehead, M. (1991) *The Nation's Health. A Strategy for the 1990s*. King's Fund, London.

Kennedy, A. (1992) Why community development and health? In: *Community Development and Health Visiting*, Glasgow Healthy City Project, Glasgow District Council, Glasgow.

King's Fund (1993) *The Study on the Professional Nursing Contribution to Purchasing*. King's Fund, London.

Lightfoot, J. (1994) Demonstrating the value of health visiting. *Health Visitor*, **67**(1), 19–20.

McCleary, G.F. (1933) *The Early History of the Infant Welfare Movement*. H.K. Lewis and Co, London.

MOH (1946) *National Health Service Act. Health Services to be Provided by Local Health Authorities under Part III of the Act*. Circular 118/47. HMSO, London.

MOH (1956) *An Inquiry Into Health Visiting* (The Jameson Committee). HMSO, London.

Naish, J. (1993). The power of purchasers. *Primary Health Care*, **3**(7), 20–21.
The NHS and Community Care Act (1990). HMSO, London.
NHS Management Executive (1993a) *New World, New Opportunities. Nursing in Primary Health Care*. NHSME, Lancashire.
NHS Management Executive (1993b) *Community Information Systems for Providers: Describing Community Care*. NHSME, Lancashire.
Orr, J. (1992) Health visiting and the community. In: *Health Visiting. Towards Community Health Nursing* (eds K. Luker & J. Orr), 2nd edn. Blackwell Science, Oxford.
RCN (1991) *The Health of the Nation. A Response From The Royal College of Nursing*. RCN, London.
RCN (1994) *Public Health: Nursing Rises to the Challenge*. RCN, London.
Robinson, J. (1982) *An Evaluation of Health Visiting*. CETHV, London.
Rowe, A. (1993) Cope Street revisited. *Health Visitor*, **66**(10), 358–9.
Sheldon, T. (1994) Fighting back. *Health Service Journal*, **27**, 24–26.
Social Policy Research Unit (1992) *Nursing by Numbers?* Social Policy Research Unit and Centre for Health Economics, York.
Strelley Nursing Development Unit (1993) *The Public Health Post at Strelley: an interim report*. Strelley NDU, Nottingham.
Sutcliffe, P. (1994) Ancoats: community health initiative in action. *Health Visitor*, **67**(1), 30–32.
Townsend, P. (1979) *Poverty in the United Kingdom*. Penguin, Harmondswoth.
Twinn, S. & Cowley, S. (1992) *The Principles of Health Visiting: a re-examination*. HVA, London.
Tyler, M. & Barnes, S. (1989) A group approach to living with stress – four years on. *Health Visitor*, **62**(10), 309–11.
UKCC (1994) *The Future of Professional Practice –The Council's Standards for Education and Practice following Registration*. UKCC, London.
United Nations Children's Fund (UNICEF) (1989) *The United Nations Convention on the Rights of the Child*. Artisan, London.
Vetter, N., Jones, D. & Victor, C. (1986) Health visiting with the elderly in general practice. In: *Research in Preventive Community Nursing Care* (ed. A. While). John Wiley and Sons, Chichester.
Waldegrave, W. (1991) Introduction to *The Health of the Nation* (Green Paper). Cm 1523. HMSO, London.
Watkins, S.J. (1992) A route from two roots. *Health Visitor*, **65**(4), 111.
While, A. (1990) Health visiting practice with families with young children. In: *Directions in Nursing Research* (eds J. Wilson Barnett & S. Robinson). Scutari, London.
Whitehead, M. (1987) *The Health Divide: Inequalities in Health in the 1980s*. Health Education Authority, London.
WHO (1978) *Health for All*. Declaration of WHO Conference on Primary Health Care, Alma Ata. WHO, Geneva.

8.7 Further reading

Guide for RCN Members on Parliamentary Lobbying. RCN, London.
The Right to Petition the European Parliament. Pamphlet available from European Parliament, London or Dublin.
The European Convention on Human Rights, The European Social Charter plus work on equality between men and women, and other documents and information. Council of Europe, Point Information, Strasbourg, France.

Chapter 9

Identifying and Developing Competence in General Practice Nursing

Practice nursing encompasses a wide and varied range of activities which are undertaken by nurses working with, and mainly employed by, general medical practitioners. A wide range of factors – political, legal, ethical, financial, professional and others – influence employment in the general practice setting. There has been an escalation in the employment of practice nurses, both prior to and since the implementation of the 'new' GP contract with payment for health promotion activities (DOH, 1989; 1990a). Total numbers of practice nurses have been estimated at over 10 000 in 1992 and later at over 16 000 by the Audit Commission (1992; 1993) and at 18 000 by the Royal College of Nursing (RCN, 1992), compared with 567 in 1973 (RCN & RCGP, 1974). This trend seems likely to continue. Although practice nurses form a comparatively new occupational group they are becoming established and valued members of the primary health care team.

Employment in this setting offers considerable scope for increasing the contribution of nursing to primary health care with considerable potential to reduce the mortality and morbidity rates in a practice population, particularly with the increasing emphasis on health promotion. The nurse can provide health care consultations, clinical nursing care, advice and referrals on a direct access basis to the practice population as well as through referrals from other members of the team.

The NHS and Community Care Act (1990) led to the introduction of GP Fundholding and NHS Trusts, with general practitioners as 'purchasers' (DOH, 1990b; NHSME, 1993a). Glennerster et al. (1992), cited by Young (1992) note that, 'Fundholding by general practices is the most innovative and potentially far-reaching aspect of the NHS reforms'. This change offers potential for a nursing contribution to the commissioning of services for patients as the practice nurse will be in an influential position to contribute to the clinical and contractual decisions that are involved in the purchasing process in the community.

176

Another change in the pattern of health service provision which affects the general practice setting is an increased commitment to improved partnership with patients and clients with an emphasis on patient empowerment and patient-centred decision-making. This is reflected in documents like the Patient's Charter (DOH, 1992a) and in legislation pertaining to patients' rights of access to health records (Access to Health Records Act, 1990) (NHSME, 1991).

Nurses have to respond proactively not only to these changes but to many other wider social changes. An ability to initiate and promote changes which aim to improve health and the quality of health care provision is also required. Education plays a key role in this process. As a group, practice nurses bring diverse professional and educational experiences to their practice, with a corresponding variation in their personal educational requirements. This indicates that the nurse should be willing to identify, explore and develop his/her personal competencies and examine personal knowledge, values and skills in order to ensure that competencies are matched to the standards of professional practice for which he/she is accountable.

9.1 Functions of the practice nurse

Competencies may be assigned to the functions of the practice nurse which are enacted through various processes. Although overlapping, these functions can be considered separately in order to impose some order on the complexity of nursing in this setting and thus assist the nurse in the identification of the aspects of professional practice he/she needs to develop. The functions can be broadly described as teacher, researcher, communicator, manager and clinician.

Health promotion activities should permeate practice. Health education requires teaching skills which can range from the enhancement of self-reliance in clients to the dissemination of knowledge and practical skills. Research activities, which can range from informed reading and the application of research to practice to the production and dissemination of research findings, should underscore all aspects of practice. Interpersonal communication skills and a counselling approach appear essential for the development of competency in health promotion, health education and clinical work. As a clinician the nurse applies diagnostic, clinical and therapeutic skills. In order to engage effectively in professional and management processes the nurse must also be a manager who can control and co-ordinate his/her workload; demonstrate leadership; undertake care management; and accept personal accountability for the standard of nursing within his/her sphere of responsibility.

9.2 Defining competence

Competence-based approaches are in vogue for nursing education (English, 1993), but discussion of professional competence is not confined solely to nursing. Ellis and Whittington (1988) suggest it is popular because of the risk that if professionals do not assess competencies themselves, then, in the present economic climate it may be done by others, and that it is necessary also because of the 'complexity of the task confronting the educators of novice professionals.' This applies not only in the education of novitiates but also in continuing professional education and the nurse should be alert to his/her personal role in standard setting and in examining the evidence and methods for judging work against particular standards.

The competence model based on standards has been promoted by the National Council for Vocational Qualifications (NCVQ) and the Education and Training Agency of the UK (now the Training and Enterprise and Education Directorate of the Department of Employment – TEED). One of the many definitions notes that competence is:

> '... a broad concept, which embodies the ability to transfer skills and knowledge to new situations within an occupational area. It encompasses organisation and planning of work, innovation and coping with non-routine activities. It includes those qualities of personal effectiveness that are required in the workplace to deal with co-workers, managers and customers.' (Education and Training Agency of the UK, 1988)

This definition includes knowledge and interpersonal communication skills as well as the transferability of competence to new areas. In many nursing situations several activities may be combined and it may be useful to recognize competency as a repertoire of behaviours, and, as Race (1993) proposes, there may be 'shades of competence' which require more refined descriptors than 'can do'. The assessment of competence in hypothetical nursing situations, such as emergencies, which are not routinely encountered, may have to be simulated and/or assessed on knowledge base alone, and Whittington and Boore (1988) see knowledge as a central feature of competence. Whilst the term 'competence' is an ambiguous one which has been 'over-defined' rather than 'ill-defined' (Runciman, 1990), most definitions emphasize prespecified standards.

Predetermined lists of standards and criteria to measure competence do not reflect 'shades of competence' and could be seen as 'atomistic, individualistic and unable to cover all aspects of relevant behaviour and mental activity' (Ashworth & Saxton, 1990). But despite the limitations of 'lists', the involvement of practitioners in setting standards and in assessing their personal competencies, as well as the 'structure, process and outcomes' of interventions, could be seen to provide useful exercises which might help to structure professional and personal development. In the current context of change, the practice nurse has a key role in setting and monitoring his/her own standards, particularly when developing innovative practice. Barriball and Mackenzie (1992) suggest that community nurses need to undertake a critical analysis of practice which measures 'the impact of nursing interventions to ensure that their specialist skills are used efficiently and effectively.'

For the nurse who is immersed in carrying out his/her functions as a practice nurse, possibly at an 'intuitive level' (when 'the expert operates from a deep understanding of the total situation' (Benner, 1984)), taking the time and effort to analyse the competencies he/she brings to practice could be a daunting task. But with the current emphasis on accountability, it is an increasingly important task which can help the nurse structure a personal profile which includes the personal responses of the nurse to continuing educational needs. A reflective personal profile could include also 'the broad themes of trust, caring, communication and knowledge/adaptability...' which Girot (1993) refers to in her ward-based phenomenological study of competence.

9.3 Professional values and ethical aspects of practice

Knowledge of approaches to ethical issues and an ability to set standards of practice which include ethical aspects of practice are required by the practice nurse. The value base from which a nurse works is presented in the Code of Professional Conduct (UKCC, 1992a), which lays out the moral principles which govern nursing practice in the UK. Subscription to these values is prerequisite for competent practice. A keen appreciation of health as a value and of the WHO (1978) philosophy of primary health care, which is seen as 'essential health care' which should be available, accessible, equitable and acceptable, is especially applicable. The 'acceptability' of services should be based on humanitarian principles and on honest interpersonal interactions between the nurse and an individual patient, a family or a community. In the context of setting priorities and targets and the quest for cost-effectiveness, the traditional values of the NHS, like equity, could possibly be at risk but should not be compromised for the sake of expediency.

Confidentiality during, and indeed after, all client interactions and related record keeping should be maintained. The Code of Professional Conduct (UKCC, 1992a) includes the principles guiding the handling of confidential information. Other pertinent UKCC documents (UKCC, 1987; 1993b) deal specifically with confidentiality and with record keeping. Familiarity with, and adherence to, the legislation which has been enacted to deal with data protection and with the rights of patients/clients in regard to access to information and records must also be assured. Informed consent to investigations, treatments and research should be assured for all parties concerned.

9.4 Professional and management issues

A legal, written contract of employment and job description can help to define the initial parameters of professional practice and the structure in which they are enacted. This is important because much of that practice will be delegated by another profession, namely the general medical practitioner(s) by whom the nurse is employed.

The construction of a job description which is valid and relevant could be problematic. Attention needs to be given to the assessment of workload, identification of gaps in personal competence and arrangements for updating and/or acquisition of new skills. It is desirable that the contract should include a clear commitment to both post-basic and continuing education (RCN, 1991a). Caution is required, too, as it has been suggested that some GPs exert pressure on practice nurses to undertake procedures for which they have not been trained (Simon, 1992a), and clarity about the legal position of the nurse and appropriate education and training are crucial (Medical Defence Union, cited by Simon, 1992a). The contract and job description should be reviewed and updated at established intervals. Such reviews could help facilitate a smooth introduction of innovations, by either the nurse or the employer. Useful guidance about contracts and job descriptions can be obtained from professional bodies, such as the Royal College of Nursing (RCN, 1993).

Although general practice has always operated on business principles, with GPs as independent contractors, the advent of, first, the new GP contracts (DOH, 1989), and, secondly, fundholding practices has underlined this aspect of general practice. The costs of employing practice nurses are considerable, although 'Few practices would have achieved higher target payments for cervical cytology and immunization levels without substantial input from practice nurses' (Atkin & Hirst, 1994). It is important that business management principles are kept in mind and that 'value for money' is demonstrated by the nurse.

Participation by the nurse in regular team meetings which include the formulation of policies and written protocols on their agenda should help to formalize the boundaries of both established practice and new initiatives. Policy formulation by the practice team provides the general aims and direction for the practice, and is, of course, influenced by wider social changes and political developments. Protocols are derived from practice policies and can offer guidance on roles and responsibilities as well as laying a basis for the audit and evaluation of practice. It has been suggested that, as well as identifying roles, the formulation of protocols can help to improve the quality of care (RCN and South Glamorgan FHSA, 1991b). Team meetings offer an opportunity for the nurse to exercise interpersonal communication skills, such as those of leadership and negotiation.

9.5 Communication skills and practice

Effective interpersonal communication skills and a counselling approach are essential for work with individual persons and their carer(s) or with groups. The situations in which these skills are used can range from rapid relationship building in some clinical situations to the longer term relationships associated with formal health education sessions and with health maintenance for clients with long-term illness or disability. Specialist counselling requires more educational and experiential input than is normally available to most nurses; thus it is important that the nurse can recognize any personal limitations and be able to suggest appropriate referrals to another person or agency for clients.

Interpersonal communication skills, such as interviewing, listening, explaining, negotiating and contracting which are used in forming and maintaining relationships with clients, are also important in the teamwork and management contexts. Clearly a leadership style which values the contribution of all the team members should be cultivated. In managerial contexts the different power relationships may mean that the communication skills required for teamwork, leadership, delegation and change management may be associated more with assertive self-projection than the empathetic counselling approach which is appropriate in most nurse/patient interactions. This is not to say that empathy with colleagues will not be required, but that it may not always be appropriate.

It is arguable that in the past nurse education did not encourage nurses to develop their creative leadership and change management skills. In more recent years, the nursing process approach, which emphasizes systematic problem solving and decision-making skills during patient care planning, has been adopted by educators, managers and practitioners. Transfer of these skills to the managerial arena of practice could enhance practice.

An ability to collaborate and liaise with others is necessary not only within the primary health care team but also to work effectively with relevant statutory and voluntary agencies. Care management, as described in the government document *Caring for People* (DOH, 1990b), emphasizes co-operation and co-ordination between agencies which requires a wider view of teamwork than the primary health care team. Poulton (1991) has described professional teams, like health visiting teams; multidisciplinary teams, like the primary health care one; and multi-agency teams. Working in a variety of 'teams' may require more formal organization and different competencies than those used when working exclusively in the primary health care team.

For example, communicating by telephone, letter and/or a fax machine and attending case conferences may be necessary for a multi-agency approach to client care or when liaising with hospital-based colleagues.

Practice nurses are in a prime position to act as patient advocates and to facilitate empowerment of clients to make informed, autonomous choices about their health care choices. With the new marketing approach public relations are increasingly important and effective communication skills are required to facilitate client access to service. The dissemination of accurate information and advice through nursing participation in the formulation of practice information leaflets, efficient 'call–recall' systems and patient suggestion and complaint procedures could help to empower patients and clients.

9.6 Professional accountability

Employment in the general practice setting can involve advancement and expansion of the nurse's role beyond traditional boundaries. Debate has taken place about whether the responsibility for ensuring the nurse is adequately prepared for this role rests with the nurse or with the employing doctor. The situation is rarely clear-cut and professional boundaries are often blurred. Changes such as the possible extension of nurse prescribing to practice nurses and developments in the role of nurse practitioners seem likely to increase ambivalence and ambiguities. The Medical Defence Union advises practice nurses to be alert to medico-legal implications of delegated work (Simon, 1992a) and it has been suggested that the practice nurse's accountability to a GP employer places the nurse in a vulnerable position (Rowley, 1994).

Within the nursing profession it is widely accepted that an assessor of competence in nursing should be an appropriately qualified nurse (peer appraisal) and that professional accountability places a responsibility on the individual nurse to ensure that he/she is able to undertake a particular role and carry out delegated functions competently and with confidence. Wiles and Robinson (1994) note that practice nurses are 'very much under the control of GPs who employ them', but they also point out that 'challenge to the supremacy of the GP within the team' is most likely to come from practice nurses and nurse practitioners.

Professional judgement by the individual nurse, based either on personal opinion or through consultation with others, such as colleagues, nurse advisers, primary health facilitators or professional organizations must be brought to bear on decisions about role expansion. This means not just undertaking tasks whenever they are delegated by a doctor but accepting personal professional accountability, with primacy being given to the safety of the patients, in accordance with the values expressed in the Code of

Professional Conduct (UKCC, 1992a). Guidelines which accompany the Code (UKCC, 1989; 1992b; 1993b) lay the responsibility for clinical decision-making and role development on the individual nurse and challenge the formerly perceived need, by either nurses or their employers, for endorsement of competence by an 'official certificate'.

9.7 Roles and relationships in the primary health care team

Arguably roles and relationships between practice nurses and their nursing colleagues in the primary health care team have not been entirely harmonious. Up until the 1960s a few nurses had been employed by GPs. In 1965 the 'Doctor's Charter' (Gillie, 1963) was implemented. The Charter led to a burgeoning of health centres with community nursing attachments and introduced reimbursement of practice nurse salaries. The attachment of district nurses frequently included treatment room work and despite an increase the number of practice nurses remained relatively small. Initially treatment room work of practice nurses was mainly clinical but the recent emphasis has been on health promotion and groupwork which traditionally has been perceived as the preserve of health visitors. Also it has been reported that lack of communication and misundertstanding about practice nursing can sometimes lead to inappropriate referrals from GPs and district nurses, possibly because 'areas of responsibility were so varied and changing so quickly' for practice nurses (Wiles & Robinson, 1994).

But gradual adjustments are being made and practice nurses seem to be more readily accepted as integral members of the nursing team. This should help to reduce the potential risk of professional isolation identified by Martin (1987) and which has been presented as a greater risk for practice nurses than for nurses working within organizations or with colleagues (UKCC, 1990a). Practice nurses should be less marginalized relative to their colleagues when their status as specialist community practitioners is confirmed following implementation of community PREP proposals (UKCC, 1991; 1992c; 1994b).

As the practice nursing role has evolved, opportunities for specialist practice have been grasped by many practice nurses, especially in relation to health promotion and the care of persons with long-term or chronic illnesses or disabilities, such as diabetes, asthma, hypertension, stoma care or heart disease who are sufficiently fit to attend the surgery premises. A study of district nurses by Griffiths and Luker (1994) found that, although they valued the role of the clinical nurse specialists as a resource, the district nurses were very keen to develop their own skills in clinical areas. It appears that practice nurses have similar aspirations and although it remains important that the nurse has access to appropriate clinical nurse specialists for relatively rare conditions, particularly in children, there are clearly opportunities for specialist and advanced practice in practice nursing.

The development of nurse practitioners, 'might be regarded as a move towards gaining professional independence and equality with the general practitioner and away from the traditional portrayal of the nurse receiving delegated and trivial tasks from the doctor' (Bowling, 1981; cited by Mackenzie, 1989). The nurse practitioner role, as described by Stilwell (1985), envisages the nurse as available to patients for direct consultations and able to undertake physical assessments, screen for serious disease, treat minor injuries and 'self limiting diseases' and chronic illness and provide health education and counselling. Although Stilwell (1988) suggests this role can be safely undertaken and that it is acceptable to patients and to colleagues this move towards independence has not been smooth. Some nurses would contend they are working at this advanced level but not using this title. Apart from the confusion surrounding the title itself, some GPs have been reluctant 'to hand over more responsibility to potential nurse practitioners' (Simon, 1992b). But such independent practitioners have made innovative contributions to health care, for example for homeless men (Smith, 1992).

To develop further such innovative practices the nurse will need to be able to analyse critically the political, legal, ethical, financial and professional factors which influence employment in a general practice setting in order to influence changes, especially those within the professional domain. The nurse should have a sound understanding of historical perspectives; studies of practice nursing and of nurse practitioners; specialist nursing; key task analysis; job descriptions and contracts; initiatives and potential developments in practice nursing; and professional perceptions and responses to health care needs.

For the development of both professional and management expertise a knowledge of the legislative and professional framework for practice is required. This should include such factors as working in a 'mixed economy of care'; national, local and practice-based policies, structures and protocols; GP contracts and statements of fees and allowances; health and safety regulations and creating a safe working environment; issues in accountability and the scope of professional practice; ethical issues; legal aspects; and consumer perspectives and organizations.

9.8 Management functions

Four key management roles in general practice have been identified: those of managing services, finance, people and information (AHCPA, 1991). Resource management of finance, people and information is required in order to provide the 'service' of nursing care. Management skills are required in the organization of clinics, including 'call–recall' systems, in health promotion, screening and health education initiatives, and in clinical and teaching activities. Access to adequate resources, both within and outwith the practice area, are a prerequisite for safe, effective practice for which the individual nurse is accountable. External resources can be identified and recorded in a practice profile which should be regularly updated. Barriball and Mackenzie (1992) emphasize the importance of preparing health profiles, caseload and workload analysis for effective community nursing.

In order to manage and organize resources such as equipment and supplies the nurse needs to identify demand, suitability and practicality, quality, price and supply of products. Therefore purchases need to be monitored frequently. Purchasing decisions must be prioritized within an agreed budget. As well as decision-making skills, those of advocacy, negotiating and contracting with employers and other team members may be required if resources are to be obtained and used effectively.

Quality assurance approaches have become established as appropriate to health care provision. Such approaches involve setting standards and identifying or collating targets and performance indicators. A nursing standard has been defined (RCN, 1992) as:

'... a professionally agreed level of nursing service or care, which encapsulates a definition of good practice, expressed in the form of a statement against which current practice can be tested to see whether or not the standard has been achieved.'

Standards have to be achieved within financial allocations, so the acquisition of budgeting skills is required. Reference to nationally accredited standards for auditing can be useful. A range of tools and organizations is available to assist in standard setting and developing quality assurance programmes. These include the UKCC requirements and guidelines (UKCC, 1987; 1992d; 1993a), the RCN (1991a), the AHCPA (1991) standard setting exercises and the King's Fund Organizational Audit (King's Fund College, 1988).

Nursing care management for individuals and their carers, and for groups, as suggested earlier, can be implemented through a 'nursing process' approach allied to a model of nursing. This process includes an evaluation of outcomes and, provided standards are incorporated into health care plans, contracts and records, it is clearly appropriate for the application of a quality assurance approach.

9.9 Information technology and record-keeping

Succinct and comprehensive record-keeping is essential to provide continuity of care; to demonstrate accountability; for legal purposes; and to record the criteria set for the monitoring and evaluation of practice (Damant *et al.*,

1994). Skills in the use of management information systems, information technology (IT) and computerized data can be invaluable to help in the maintenance of accurate and comprehensive records. Also, sound records can provide an information base for research purposes. Damant *et al.* (1994) state that:

'The growth of alternative forms of record keeping, information technology and computers in the practice has the potential to revolutionise recording in the future.'

A change in emphasis from service activity to a focus on the effectiveness of care delivery has been recommended by the NHS Management Executive (1993b) who suggest that information management and technology can help to assess effectiveness and that 'community nurses can play a key part in realising the benefits of information management and technology'.

9.10 Health promotion activities

The practice nurse is accessible to the majority of a practice population and the role encompasses many aspects of health promotion including those of promoting healthy lifestyles for all age groups, screening for persons with risk factors or undetected disease, and the monitoring and support of persons with established disease. There are opportunities to participate in national, regional and local health promotion programmes, such as the health targets set by WHO (1978; 1985) and those set by the government (DOH, 1992b). These targets and the banding system of payment to GPs for health promotion activities can help give direction to health promotion initiatives.

Health promotion is linked closely to primary health care. The principles enshrined in the WHO Declaration at Alma Ata (1978) suggest that primary health care is an approach which extends beyond 'community health services or services provided by general practitioners' (RCN, 1992). The practice nurse is well situated to identify the primary health care needs of a community and furthermore:

'General practice populations offer an ideal base for the integration of public health and primary health care.' (Cernik & Wearne, 1994)

Although the current model of health promotion used by practice nurses appears to be mainly prescriptive and based on an 'educational' model rather than a social or primary health care one there may be a likelihood of gradual change over the next few years; and:

'Through increased health promotion training of practice nurses the advancement of health promotion, and with it the role of the practice nurse seems assured in general practice.' (Bradford & Winn, 1993)

The target-setting approach requires that indices of the health status and well-being of the practice population are developed, and such indices lay the basis for measurement of outcomes. Thus an understanding of the concepts of health, health care needs, health beliefs and approaches to health promotion and an ability to assess epidemiological information, public health data, the social factors which can affect health, and research evidence is required to evaluate the health care needs of the practice population.

The preparation and maintenance of a practice and neighbourhood profile in liaison with other members of the primary health care team – for example, health visitors – can provide an invaluable resource and lay the foundation for health promotion activities. The availability of resources from other health promotion agencies and from local facilities, such as leisure complexes, voluntary organizations and self-help groups can be included in the profile. In conjunction with effective IT information storage and retrieval the profile can help to monitor health status indicators and co-ordinate teamwork and liaison and referral processes.

Consumer views could add another dimension to a practice profile. Among the type of research which could be replicated to survey the perceived health care needs of a practice population is a study by Antonson and Robertson (1993). From a survey seeking information about unmet health care needs (sample size, 1770; response rate, 38%; $N = 672$) they suggest possible unmet needs include those related to health promotion activities and to education and guidance for informal carers. This survey indicates 'a possible need for more research relating to the kind of activities the public want, how to educate the public about health promotion to encourage more attendance at existing activities and specific targeting of educating messages and sessions to those most likely to attend' (Antonson & Robertson, 1993).

The profile could include details about any identified environmental risk factors; health assessments of local communities; and details of identified 'at-risk' groups (for example, homeless persons, families experiencing poverty and cigarette smokers); and individuals at risk of developing specific disorders, such as coronary heart disease (CHD) and/or strokes. Such information could be used to help provide appropriate information and advice to the community, groups and individuals. As well as a sound information base, the provision of health care programmes which are the most suitable for a particular local community requires managerial and educational skills. Well planned health promotion should include performance criteria which will facilitate auditing and evaluation of health gain outcomes. Health education and screening activities to reduce risks to health may be targeted at individuals, such as patients who are new to the practice or at risk of or experiencing particular health problems, or groups, such as women or persons who are aged 75 or older.

Competency in clinical investigations and procedures of a specialist nature is required to deal effectively with a range of health problems, disorders or conditions. It is necessary for the nurse to ensure that his/her physical examination and diagnostic skills are up to date and used appropriately. For example, the prevention of strokes by good control of blood pressure levels has proved to be an effective strategy, and monitoring of blood pressure levels is being improved by the use of ambulatory blood pressure monitors (Kemp, 1993). Similarly, through identifying persons at risk and supporting clients, the nurse may be able to help clients reduce the factors associated with CHD, the major cause of death in the UK (Hibbert, 1993). Health education for persons with specific health-related problems may be organized through national or local strategies, media campaigns, posters and/or leaflets on the clinic premises, through specified clinics and on an opportunistic basis.

Strategies to control infectious diseases, particularly those of childhood or for persons travelling abroad, include the administration of vaccines for immunization purposes. The administration of vaccines also provides an opportunity for general health education. Nurses undertaking this task require a knowledge of the cycle of infection, infectious diseases, preventive measures and/or the vaccines (including contra-indications, side effects and possible reactions) and immunization schedules, the control of equipment and the development of practice policies and protocols which address the issues surrounding responsibilities and accountability.

9.11 Clinical nursing care

The practice nurse has to respond to the immediate nursing care needs of patients and clients, whether they are 'self-referred' or referred by another team member or another agency. Expert nursing care depends to a large extent on the nurse's ability to formulate care plans based on accurate nursing diagnoses, appropriate clinical judgments and the use of a holistic model of care, and to work in partnership with patients and clients, families, lay carers and other team members and other agencies. A holistic approach can help the nurse undertake a full nursing assessment of a patient who may have been referred initially for technical or diagnostic investigations (RCN, 1992). In order to refine this process the nurse can choose from a range of nursing models that which best suits the client's health care needs and gives due regard to ethical, social and cultural issues.

Planning nursing care involves a process of establishing rapport, information gathering and interviewing, reviewing the client's past experience and current expectations, agreeing needs, outlining functions and drawing up an initial 'contract' of mutually agreed goals and specifying how these goals are to be addressed and evaluated. This may involve liaison and collaboration with a range of voluntary organizations, pressure groups and the private sector as well as with other members of the primary health care team.

A research-based rationale for clinical decision-making can help to define and clarify the parameters of the 'expert tasks' that the nurse undertakes and should help to avoid the risk of 'ritual procedure' based practice. A knowledge of the theories and concepts underlying the approaches to the prevention, management and treatment of the diseases and conditions commonly encountered in general practice is required. Such theories and concepts should be grounded in the application of research findings to practice, and conversely, research questions should arise from and be tested in practice. Hence the nurse should be able to evaluate existing research, conduct research projects and disseminate the findings of research in order to enhance the care of patients and clients.

The nurse may provide preparatory and post-operative nursing care for patients undergoing tests, investigations and surgical procedures, which can range from practice-based interventions to hospital day surgery or more complex operations, such as heart surgery. The nursing role can include interpretation and explanation of procedures and their results; provision of rehabilitation for individuals or groups; and the organization and management of facilities and equipment for practice-based procedures. A knowledge of the principles of wound healing and an ability to evaluate wound care products objectively are required in order to provide appropriate care to patients with specific wounds and/or prostheses, such as leg ulcers, pressure sores, stoma, breast or limb prostheses or ambulatory renal dialysis.

Emergencies, such as acute trauma, burns and medical emergencies may arise within the practice. Competency to prepare for and deal with these requires more than a reactive first aid service, and attention needs to be given to accident prevention and the legislative aspects of care, including that which is pertinent to the abuse of children. Participation in the preparation of protocols and procedures to deal with emergency situations is essential.

Opportunities for specialization and for the provision of information, support, and referrals when necessary, for persons with specific conditions, or their carers, are abundant in the general practice setting. Knowledge of (or an ability to find out about) the prevalence, effects, treatments and health educational aspects of selected disorders and health problems is needed. Examples of the more common, or important, conditions and health related problems include asthma; ischaemic heart disease; HIV infection and AIDS; cancer (especially of the cervix, breast, testes, bowel and skin); diabetes, blood dyscrasias; hypertension; smoking; obesity; incontinence; substance abuse, addictions and dependencies; and family violence.

Nursing interventions can range from health promotion and prevention of disease to treatment, rehabilitation, long-term care and palliative care.

Nursing care for groups with special needs, as well as persons with particular conditions, can be facilitated by the use of a practice profile/register, review systems and protocols. Assessment and care management for older people is an important area, especially since the introduction of assessment and screening for persons aged 75 and over in the practice population. Competence is required in pain control; stress management; drug therapies; nutrition and exercise programmes. Knowledge of the actions, side-effects and contra-indications to drugs commonly used in general practice, 'over-the-counter drugs' and complementary therapies is needed in order to monitor the effectiveness of drug regimes.

9.12 Education

The provision of a high-quality nursing service is premised upon the provision of appropriate education and skill acquisition (Whittington & Boore, 1988). Although bringing skills and knowledge based on prior experience and education to the post, it is likely that the nurse will need a systematic programme of personal professional development in order to acquire the competencies required to carry out his/her role, and to further develop the potential contribution of practice-based nursing to primary health care. Butterworth (1994) notes the importance of an effective educational and professional framework for the development of practice nursing at an advanced level and reminds us of the complications in the practice setting due to 'vicarious liability by employers' and 'the rise of a litigation minded public'.

Concern has been expressed about the lack of training for practice nurses, and that they may be 'very cheap labour' (Cumberlege, 1986). Indeed, education has been described as 'one of the most pressing issues' which faces practice nurses (Peachey, 1992). A study by Wade (1993) describes how about a third of practice nurse respondents who added comments to her questionnaires referred to education and training. In particular:

'Comments about taking responsibility for their own training needs by attending courses in their own time or about persuading GPs or practice managers of the value of training were quite common.'

Self assessment and knowledge of personal capabilities are integral components of professional education, whether formal or informal. Although the nurse may identify appropriate areas of practice for personal development, problems may arise in accessing courses because many practice nurses work part-time, or work alone, so a replacement is needed during study leave and funding for courses may not be readily available.

The recommendations of Post Registration Education and Practice framework (PREP) (UKCC, 1990a; 1993c; 1994a) aim to help practitioners maintain and develop their professional knowledge and competence, and should assist nurses in their efforts to obtain assistance with their educational needs. From April 1995, in order to maintain registration, nurses will be required to complete:

'... at least five days study every three years; a Notification of Practice form; a Statutory Return to Practice programme after a break in practice of five years or more and a personal professional profile.' (UKCC, 1994a)

The implementation of the proposals for 'Community PREP' (UKCC, 1991; 1994b), which are based on explicit standards for specialist community health care nursing, will become a statutory requirement from September 1995. This will provide a real opportunity for practice nurses to join their community nursing colleagues on educational programmes.

Educational initiatives such as modular courses with academic accreditation allied to a common core for all community nurses and part-time courses should help to strengthen opportunities for practice nurses to gain a formal professional qualification that is on a par with their community nursing colleagues. In the longer term it should strengthen educational support structures for practice nurses which have already been developed but to a limited extent. Such developments include joint appointments between educational institutions and practice areas and clinical supervision and teaching from experienced, educationally prepared practice nurses.

A framework of assessment and supervision of clinical competence has been developed for practice nurses in Enfield and Haringey. This Nurse Training Practice initiative:

'embraces a training policy for practice nursing, accreditation of practices for the purpose of practice nurse training and collaboration with colleges of nursing and higher education on the standard and content of practice nurse courses.' (Enfield & Haringey, 1992).

Placements are provided too for students on the adult branch of Project 2000 educational programmes. The practice nurses 'trainers' undertake a teaching and assessment course and their salaries are reimbursed by the FHSA at 100% for the first year and 90% thereafter. If family planning clinical training is provided the supervising nurse must hold an approved Family Planning (FP) Instructor qualification. Cervical cytology and pelvic examination training can be provided by the FP instructors or by nurses who have held the Marie Curie Certificate for at least one year.

Educational experiences, such as participation in seminars, workshops, tutorials and role play, encourage the exchange of ideas, views and experiences with colleagues and provide an opportunity to interact with other health care professionals. Such interactions may also provide mutual support and help to reduce the stress and anxiety associated with a return to study. Networking, membership of professional groups and attending conferences can provide support and learning opportunities. Purposeful reading from a wide range of authoritative sources and use of distance learning packages are useful strategies for professional development, although these do not always address assessment of competence in the work situation or offer opportunities to interact with other students.

Peer review (or appraisal) linked to supportive clinical supervision may help to maintain identified professional standards and improve and develop clinical expertise throughout professional life (Butterworth, 1994). Various models, such as study groups, interest groups, standard-setting groups and quality circles, could be tested. Clinical supervision from peers, supervisors, primary health care facilitators or 'practice nurse advisers' (Hoddincott and Martin, 1989) should be useful in helping nurses to identify, develop and evaluate learning strategies. Butterworth (1994) suggests that participation in case conferences could stimulate critical debate about practice activity and enrich professional practice. He further notes that clinical supervision requires time, energy and clinical expertise; to this might be added the possession of teaching skills and a commitment to teaching and learning.

From a review of the literature, Falchikov and Boud (1989) conclude that self-assessment can be as reliable as other forms of assessment, and that it improves when training is given – for example, when developing skills related to particular criteria, whether these criteria are self-set or from other sources. Record keeping, or 'profiling', of personal professional development could enhance the interpretative approach to nursing advocated by Benner (1984), and facilitate experiential learning from 'real-life practice', and help to link theory to practice. Other strategies to assist self-directed learning include diaries, the analysis of critical incidents and learning contracts. Such strategies are considered to facilitate 'reflection', that is, thinking about and building on experience in a constructive way, clarifying feelings and emotions (Hull *et al*, 1994). Sometimes claims for academic accreditation of prior educational or experiential learning (APEL) may depend on a self-assessment 'profile' which identifies relevant goals, personal attributes and past learning experiences (whether formal, in-service or work-based) and achievements; the 'profile' also provides some evidence that the learning being claimed has been attained.

When personal record-keeping is linked to purposeful reading then resource packages of educational material can be developed which are not only invaluable for self-directed learning but can also be useful for colleagues and students. Hammick (1994) suggests that critical reading improves with practice and that 'It encourages creativity and provides insight into the world of enquiry' and '... is an important element of capability in health-care practice'.

Practice nursing seems to offer nurses the opportunity for more control over organization of their workload and more flexibility in terms of employment, such as hours and conditions, while job satisfaction appears high within this professional group. A survey of over 220 practice nurses from four trusts found that practice nurses seem to be 'highly satisfied with their jobs' (Wade, 1993). This relatively high level of job satisfaction may be due to the degree of autonomy and independence, both about decisions on patient/client care and about expanding their role, outside a nursing management structure which has been noted by the RCN (1991a).

As the traditional roles of community nurses are being redefined and further radical changes in nursing have been forecast (DOH, 1994), it has been suggested that flexibility will be crucial for the advancement of nursing. Allied to policies and forecasts that in the future more care will be community based, then it seems that, providing an improved educational structure is ensured, practice nursing is well placed to demonstrate the competencies needed to face the health care challenges of the future.

9.13 References

Antonson, M.G. & Robertson, C.M. (1993) A study of consumer-defined need amenable to community nursing intervention. *Journal of Advanced Nursing*, **18**, 1617–25.

Ashworth, P. & Saxton, J. (1990). On competence. *Journal of Further and Higher Education*, **14**, 3–25.

AHCPA (1991) *Management Standards in Primary Care: An AHCPA Guide to Best Practice: Promoting the Best Quality of Patient Care: an Interim Report.* Association of Health Centre and Practice Administrators, London.

Atkin, K. & Hirst, M. (1994) *Costing Practice Nurses: Implications for Primary Health Care.* Centre for Health Economics, University of York.

The Audit Commission (1992) *Community Care: Managing the Cascade of Change.* HMSO, London.

The Audit Commission (1993) *Practice Makes Perfect: The Role of the Family Health Services Authority.* HMSO, London.

Barriball, K.L. & Mackenzie, A. (1992) The demand for measuring the impact of nursing interventions: a community perspective. *Journal of Clinical Nursing*, **1**, 207–12.

Benner, P. (1984) *From Novice to Expert: Excellence and Power in Clinical Nursing Practice.* Addison Wesley, London.

Bowling, A. (1981) *Delegation in General Practice. A Study of Doctors and Nurses.* Tavistock, London.

Bradford, M. & Winn, S. (1993) Practice Nursing and Health Promotion: A Case Study. In: *Research in Health Promotion and Nursing* (eds J. Wilson-

Barnett & J. Macleod Clark), pp. 119–31. The Macmillan Press, Basing-stoke.

Butterworth, T. (1994) *Concepts of Clinical Supervision.* Paper presented at a National Conference on Clinical Supervision, Centennial Centre, Birmingham, 24 February 1994.

Cernik, K. & Wearne, M. (1994) Promoting the integration of primary care and public health. *Nursing Times,* **90**(43), 44–5.

Cumberlege, J. (1986) Speeches to Royal Society of Health and to RCN Conference at St Bartholomews Hospital. *Nursing Times,* 17 September 1986, 6.

Damant, M., Martin, C. & Openshaw, S. (1994) *Practice nursing: stability and change.* Mosby, London.

DOH, (1989) *General Practice in the NHS. The 1990 Contract.* HMSO, London.

DOH (1990a) NHS/General Medical Services. *Statement of fees and allowances payable to general medical practitioners in England and Wales from 1 April 1990.* HMSO, London.

DOH (1990b) *Caring for people. Community care into the next decade and beyond.* HMSO, London.

DOH (1992a) *The Patient's Charter.* HMSO, London.

DOH (1992b) *The Health of the Nation: A Strategy for Health in England.* HMSO, London.

DOH (1994) *The Challenges for Nursing and Midwifery in the 21st century* (the 'Heathrow report'). DOH, London.

Education and Training Agency of the UK (1988) *Development of Assessable Standards for National Certification. Guidance Note 1. A Code of Practice and Development Model.* Education Training Agency, Sheffield.

Ellis, R. (ed.) (1988) *Professional Competence and Quality Assurance in the Caring Professions.* Chapman & Hall, London.

Ellis, R. & Whittington, D. (1988) Social Skills, Competence and Quality. In: *Professional Competence and Quality Assurance in the Caring Professions* (ed. R. Ellis), pp 263–95. Chapman & Hall, London.

Enfield and Haringey Family Health Services Authority (1992) *Nurse Training Practices.* Enfield and Haringey FHSA, North East Thames Regional Health Authority.

English, I. (1993) Intuition as a function of the expert nurse: A critique of Benner's novice to expert model. *Journal of Advanced Nursing,* **18**, 387–93.

Falchikov, N. & Boud, D. (1989) Student self-assessment in higher education; a meta-analysis. *Review of Educational Research,* **59**, 395–404.

Gillie, A. (1963) *The Work of the Family Doctor.* Report of a sub-committee of the Central Health Services Council ('The Doctors' Charter'). HMSO, London.

Girot, E.A. (1993) Assessment of competence in clinical practice: a phenomenological approach. *Journal of Advanced Nursing,* **18**, 114–19.

Glennerster, H., Latsaganis, M. & Owens, P. (1992) *A foothold for funding: A preliminary report on the introduction of GP fund holding.* King's Fund, London.

Griffiths, J. & Luker, K. (1994) Community nurse attitudes to the clinical nurse specialist. *Nursing Times*, **90**(17), 39–42.

Hammick, M. (1994) Reading and reviewing the literature. *British Journal of Therapy and Rehabilitation*, **1**(1), 43–6.

Hibbert, A. (1993) Coronary heart disease: Risk factors and the nurse's role. *Primary Health Care*, **3**(2), 9–10.

Hoddincott, D. & Martin, C. (1989) Practice nurse adviser: a new role. *Primary Health Care*, May 1989, 16–17.

Hull, C., Mangon, P. and Kershaw, B. (1994) Professional development – Unit 3, assessment. *Nursing Times*, **90**(16), 9–14.

Hunt, G. & Wainwright, P. (1994) *Expanding the role of the nurse: The scope of professional practice.* Blackwell Science, Oxford.

Kemp, F. (1993) Hypertension: ABPM in practice. *Primary Health Care*, **3**(2), 14–15.

King's Fund College (1988) *King's Fund Organizational Audit.* King's Fund College, London.

Mackenzie, A. (1989) *Key issues in District Nursing. Paper One: The District Nurse within the Community Context.* District Nursing Association UK, London.

Martin, C. (1987) Practice makes perfect? *Nursing Times*, **83**(17), 28–31.

The NHS and Community Care Act (1990). HMSO, London.

NHSME (1991) *Access to Health Records Act (1990): A guide for the NHS.* NHSME, London.

NHSME (1993a) *Guidance on the Extension of the Hospital and Community Health Services Elements of GP Fundholding Scheme from April 1993.* NHSME, London.

NHSME (1993b) *An Information Management and Technology Strategy for the NHS in England. A View for Community Nurses.* NHSME, London.

Peachey, M. (1992) Practice makes perfect. *Nursing Times*, **88**(11), 19–60.

Poulton, B. (1991) Does your team really work? *Primary Health Care*, **1**, 11–14.

Race, P. (1993) *Quality of Assessment in Introducing Innovations In Assessment.* Staff development package, enterprise in higher education. University of Ulster, Jordanstown and Coleraine.

RCN and RCGP Joint Working Party (1974) *Nursing in general practice in the re-organised National Health Service (1979–1984).* Report of the joint working party, Royal College of Nursing and Royal College of General Practitioners, London.

RCN (1991a) *Standards of Care for Practice Nursing.* RCN, London.

RCN and South Glamorgan FHSA (1991b) *Protocols for health promotion clinics.* RCN and South Glamorgan Family Service Authority.

RCN (1992) *Powerhouse for Change: Report of the Task Force on Community Nursing.* RCN, London.

RCN (1993) *Guidance on the Employment of Nurses in General Practice.* RCN, London.

Rowley, E. (1994) The role of the practice nurse. In: *Expanding the Role of the Nurse: The Scope of Professional Practice* (eds G. Hunt & P. Wainwright), pp. 132–48. Blackwell Science. Oxford.

Runcinan, P. (1990) *Competence-based education and the accreditation of work-based learning in the context of Project 2000 programmes of nurse education.* Scottish National Board for Nursing, Midwifery and Health Visiting, Edinburgh.

Simon, P. (1992a) GPs delegate too much to nurse colleagues. *Nursing Times,* **88**(17), 8.

Simon, P. (1992b) Pioneer spirit. *Nursing Times,* **88**(30), 16–17.

Smith, S. (1992) The rise of the nurse practitioner. *Community Outlook,* Nov/Dec 1992, 16–18.

Stilwell, B. (1984) The nurse in practice. *Nursing Mirror,* **158**(21), 17–19.

Stilwell, B. (1985) Prevention and health: the concern of nursing. *Journal of the Royal Society of Health,* **105**(1), 31–4.

Stilwell, B. (1988) Patient attitudes to a highly developed extended role – The nurse practitioner. *Recent Advances in Nursing,* **21**, 82–100.

UKCC (1987) *Confidentiality: an Elaboration of Clause 9 of the 2nd Edition of the UKCC's Code of Professional Conduct for the Nurse, Midwife and Health Visitor.* UKCC, London.

UKCC (1989) *Exercising accountability: A framework to Assist Nurses, Midwives and Health Visitors to Consider Ethical Aspects of Professional Practice.* UKCC, London.

UKCC (1990a) *Report of the Post-registration Education and Practice Project (PREPP).* UKCC, London.

UKCC (1990b) *Statement on Practice Nurses and Aspects of the GP Contract.* UKCC, London.

UKCC (1991) *Report on the Proposals for the Future of Community Education and Practice.* UKCC, London.

UKCC (1992a) *Code of Professional Conduct for the Nurse, Midwife and Health Visitor,* 3rd Edition. UKCC, London.

UKCC (1992b) *The Scope of Professional Practice for the Nurse, Midwife and Health Visitor.* UKCC, London.

UKCC (1992c) *Registrar's letter – Proposals for the Future of Community Education and Practice – the Council's Policy Following Consultation.* UKCC, London.

UKCC (1992d) *Standards for the Administration of Medicines.* UKCC, London.

UKCC (1993a) *Standards for Records and Record Keeping.* UKCC, London.

UKCC (1993b) *The Scope of Professional Practice: a Position paper*. UKCC, London.

UKCC (1993c) *Final Report on the Future of Professional Education and Practice*. UKCC, London.

UKCC (1994a) PREPP – government supports UKCC proposals. *Register*, No. 14, Spring 1994, pp. 4–5. UKCC, London.

UKCC (1994b) *The Future of Professional Practice: Council's Standards for Education and Practice following Registration*. UKCC, London.

Wade, B.E. (1993) The job satisfaction of health visitors, district nurses and practice nurses working in areas served by four trusts: year 1. *Journal of Advanced Nursing*, **18**, 992–1004.

Whittington, D. & Boore, J. (1988) Competence in nursing. In: *Professional Competence and Quality Assurance in the Caring Professions* (ed. R. Ellis), pp. 109–39. Chapman & Hall, London.

WHO (1978) *Health for all*. Declaration of WHO Conference on Primary Health Care, Alma Ata. WHO, Geneva.

WHO (1985) *Targets for health for all*. WHO Regional Office for Europe, Copenhagen.

Wiles, R. & Robinson, J. (1994) Teamwork in primary care: the views and experiences of nurses, midwives and health visitors. *Journal of Advanced Nursing*, **20**, 324–30.

Wilson-Barnett, J. & Macleod Clark, J. (eds) (1994) *Research in Health Promotion and Nursing*. The Macmillan Press, Basingstoke.

Young, L. (1992) GP Fundholding: A way forward for community health services. *Primary Health Care*, **2**(6), 8–9.

Chapter 10

Contemporary District Nursing Practice

The district nurse is:

'a qualified registered nurse who has also been especially trained to promote health, provide skilled nursing and health care to people in their own homes, wherever this may be. She/he leads a team of nursing staff and ensures that this care is appropriately planned and delivered to those who need it while at the same time making sure that other family members receive the help and support they need.' (James & Low, 1990)

The professional role and function of the district nurse is expressed through her ability to make independent professional judgements, while accepting responsibility for her actions and accountability for her decisions. This may be demonstrated through an established and highly developed standard of nursing skill and knowledge, a proactive response to nursing needs within the community, acceptance as an expert member of the primary health care team (PHCT) and commitment to the education and development of students with whom she is in contact.

District nursing falls under the umbrella of 'community health nursing', defined in *Powerhouse for Change* (RCN, 1992a) as:

'... professional nursing directed towards communities or population groups as well as individuals living in the community. It includes assessment of the environmental, social and personal factors which influence the health status of the targeted population. Its practice incorporates the identification of groups and individuals within the community who require help in maintaining or achieving optimal health.'

District nurses are, then, autonomous practitioners and members of multidisciplinary teams who work in collaboration with others to implement the nursing process, not only for individuals, but also groups and indeed their communities.

District nurses provide health care consultations, clinical nursing care advice and referrals on a direct access basis to practice and community populations, as well as through referrals from other members of the PHCT. In addition, with the introduction of GP Fundholding, the district nurse is in an influential position to contribute to the clinical and contractual decisions that will be involved in this process.

Within her professional role, the district nurse will encourage and promote health and the prevention of ill health for individuals in her care as well as the neighbourhood/community in which she works. In so doing she utilizes significant interpersonal skills in her capacity as counsellor, advocate and manager for her patients and her locality, and she controls and co-ordinates resources at her disposal with the explicit aim of promoting health gain and general well-being.

The district nurse will also recognize the importance of liaison mechanisms, and the contribution to be made by inter-agency networks, and ensure that services available are delivered both efficiently and effectively.

10.1 Current challenges and issues

District nurses care, and will continue to care, for increased numbers of chronically ill people in the community, despite a continued reduction in government spending in community care, and the dilution of qualified nursing skills through the increased usage of unqualified staff (Skidmore, 1992). It is also worth noting that the workload of the district nurse has increased fourfold since 1972 (Ross, 1987), but this increase has not been matched by an increase in qualified staff.

The implementation of a new skill mix in district nursing teams has often demanded that unqualified staff members require extra training and supervision from qualified (and busy) district nurses who are engaged in the maintenance of a heavy caseload whilst undertaking such supervision (Schroeder, 1992). This situation is exacerbated by shorter in-patient hospital stays and an increase in the number of acutely ill patients requiring access to nursing skills in the community.

Coupled with this, the government is implementing a strategy of resource rationing, assisted by the implementation of care management strategies, which makes it unlikely that everyone's needs will be met (Smith, 1993). It has been argued that health care has become service-driven rather than needs-directed (Laurent, 1993), although it must be said that many district nurses strive to meet the increasing demands of their patients, and these needs may be multiple and complex in nature. Healy (1993) argues that many patients believe that their needs are not being met, and this seems to

contradict the notion that the government is offering choice and empowerment for patients in order to improve their standards of care (Kelling, 1993).
As gatekeepers to local health care resources district nurses may well find
themselves faced with the dilemma of prioritizing casework.

Increasing numbers of chronically ill people are being cared for in the
community, in their own homes, but the district nurse is still obliged to meet
these needs at a time of reduced government spending. At the same time, the
nurse is encouraged to maintain and improve professional knowledge and
competence, and to 'endeavour always to achieve, maintain and develop
knowledge, skill and competence' to respond to the needs of those in her care
(UKCC, 1992b). Those wishing to develop their professional profile by
becoming qualified community nurses often do this by undertaking part-time
professional courses in universities and colleges in their own time and at their
own expense. There is obviously an ever-increasing need for nurses to keep
up-to-date and maintain standards, and district nurses are no exception to
this rule.

However, the need to train such people both academically and professionally necessitates the further enhancement of the educational role of
already stretched community staff. Qualified community nurses also
undertake additional courses to qualify them as teacher practitioners, but
this does not lead to monetary recompense in every case, nor to a reduction in
caseload numbers when the teacher practitioner undertakes to have a student
with her for a fixed period of time.

Instead of giving in to these problems, district nurses strive to expand and
develop their expertise in order to provide the best possible service (Barriball
& Mackenzie, 1993), and to meet the requirements of the *Citizen's Charter*
(DOH, 1992) which states that emergency visits will be carried out within 24
hours of request, and in all other cases a visit within one week from the date
help was first requested. The effectiveness of their care is demonstrated by
recorded evidence in an effort to demand further resources (Buchan, 1991),
no matter how infrequently these demands are met.

The conflict between education and service is often presented to newly
qualified nurses as a rude awakening and as such they may find it difficult to
integrate their education within their practice. This conflict would seem to
pervade the nursing profession, community nursing being no exception.
District nursing students often complain that they find it nearly impossible to
relate theory to practice, mainly because of the lack of adequate resource
allocation in the community.

One other contradiction faced by community nurses is that they are now
educated at a tertiary (or degree) level and are often subsequently employed
as staff nurses with a pay scale that does not reflect their abilities and training
or status as specialist practitioners.

Many prospective district nurses enter higher education as 'mature'
students, i.e. over 20 years of age, and enrol as part-time students. Many

often find it difficult to 'persuade' their employers to allocate them the time necessary to undertake the course with the result that many of these nurses rely upon the use of their own annual leave in order to advance their skills and professional competence.

The notion of holism is prevalent in nursing today, i.e. focusing on the needs of the whole person from a social, psychological, physical and spiritual viewpoint (Griffin, 1993). However as Buckle (1992) points out, there may have been an increase in holistic thinking, but this has not been echoed in practice, because the system in which nursing operates advocates fragmented care and institutionalized power, not holistic teamwork (a sentiment echoed by Owen & Holmes (1993) who have argued that holism is pure rhetoric). Nevertheless, district nurses are engaged in the provision of holistic care, as may be witnessed in the district-nursing-team-led multidisciplinary team approach to community care adopted in Tyneside (Harris, 1992).

Perhaps the most important challenge to the district nursing profession relates to the redefinition of skill mix. Skill mix is often defined within a conceptual framework which incorporates care management, GP Fund-holding and contracting and interprofessional teamwork.

It is within this framework that today's district nurse must redevelop her role and demonstrate skilled proficiency and diversity. Traynor (1993) found that this new working environment had aroused feelings of anxiety, uncertainty and a certain degree of alienation among community nurses in general. Many G-grade district nurses in Traynor's study felt that their futures were uncertain because they believed that their managers considered that 'they were too expensive', whilst health visitors expressed disillusionment in their profession as a result of constant change and a lack of direction. All community nurses highlighted their heavy workload and administrative duties as an additional cause for concern, which inevitably interfered with the amount of time they could spend with patients and clients. In contrast, managers were excited by the new challenge and the new organizational culture. This example perhaps highlights the ongoing difference of opinion held by managers and community nurses who are actively involved in the care of patients.

Skill mix has been described by the North East Thames Regional Health Authority as 'the balance between trained and untrained, qualified and unqualified, and supervisory and operative staff within a service area as well as different staff groups. The optimum skill mix is achieved when a desired standard of service is provided at the minimum of cost, which is consistent with the efficient deployment of trained, qualified and supervisory personnel and the maximization of contributions from all staff' (RCN, 1992b). As Gibbs *et al.* (1991) point out, the issues surrounding skill mix are 'contentious', and, despite the fact that most people would agree that change within the NHS is inevitable, 'skill mix has always been a thorny issue'.

The introduction of something new has always been greeted with a degree of suspicion and reluctance within the nursing profession, especially when practitioners feel, rightly or wrongly, that they have not been consulted by management in the implementation of such change. However, demographic changes alongside a possible shortage in nurses and an increase in demand for health care from the general public within a limited government budget have necessitated drastic change in health care provision in the United Kingdom.

Mix and Match: A Review of Nursing Skill (DHSS, 1986) highlighted the point that skill mix could be seen to represent a major ideological division between the professional nurse and the employing authority. For the employer, control over budget and other resources including skill mix and grade mix of local staff, are of paramount importance (Gibbs *et al.*, 1991), while the qualified specialist community nurse may view the situation as a threat to the amount of time and the quality of care given to patients.

Certainly today, a common complaint of many district nurses employed at G-grade is that their role relates more to administrative duties than actual care giving. This point is highlighted when the number of G-grade posts are cut back and replaced by staff nurses or nursing auxiliaries in the community setting. However the 1986 DHSS review did show that there was no clear relationship between a higher proportion of qualified nurses in long-stay hospital wards and the practice of individualized care. But in wards where the overall staffing level and proportion of qualified staff was low, only basic physical needs of patients were met. It must be borne in mind that the DHSS survey was a 1986 one, and in the acute hospital setting. In the 1990s, with governmental emphasis on day surgery, early discharge from hospital, closure of hospital beds, and community care, the fears of G-grade district nurses are justifiable, as more patients are discharged into the community – into the care of an already stretched health care workforce.

In 1992 the NHS Management Executive produced a report which recommended a radical shift in skill mix within district nursing, leading to the implementation of a proposed 26% threshold of the workforce at G/H grade and approximately 65% at D/E grade. The committee responsible for writing this report came to this decision by developing a series of tasks performed by district nurses and ascertaining how long each nursing task took to complete. They also analysed what level of expertise was required in order to complete these tasks satisfactorily (and to an agreed standard).

In its response to the NHSME report (also known as the *Value for Money* (VFM) Report) the RCN (1993) highlighted the fact that the report:

(1) 'failed to recognize any aspect of the psychological or therapeutic care' given by qualified nurses;
(2) failed to recognize the holistic quality of nursing care;
(3) ignored the team approach that is so very necessary for the successful delivery of patient care within district nursing; and

(4) did not acknowledgement the achievements gained by district nurses with their patients.'

The RCN stated quite clearly that the VFM report was simply a 'time and motion' study which would lead only to anger and frustration amongst nurses. They pointed out that although nursing activities can be delegated to many different grades of staff, there are certain activities that must be undertaken by an experienced and knowledgeable G- or H-grade nurse. These activities include the assessment and reassessment of health needs, evaluation of nursing care, health education and promotion, counselling, and referrals to other agencies.

However, not all managerial decisions are implemented without the consent of the community health care workforce. The North Mersey Community (NHS) Trust attempted to implement the recommendations of the VFM report in Liverpool, with the intention of reducing the district nursing workforce from 82 G- and H-grade nurses to 57, with all other staff being reduced to E-grades; this it did by inviting staff to apply for care management positions in the community (Jones, 1993).

District nurses in the area challenged this decision, and highlighted instead the shift in emphasis between the current role of the district nurse and the difficulties in a structure that would separate the management and delivery of care. They emphasized the fact that district nurses already managed their caseloads on a day-to-day basis, that 'the increased management burden in the new job description would remove managers from the bedside for a very high proportion of their working hours', and that this 'would result in care being delivered with less regular evaluation, and possibly with decreased health gain or less independence for the patient'.

The Liverpool district nurses won their case by emphasizing the clinical commitments and far-reaching responsibilities of their caseload, as well as the throughput of new patients, deprivation indicators and possible future developments in health promotion work. No members of staff were demoted, and management gave a commitment to provide short-term contracts to cover long-term planned leave; 74 G- and H-grade posts for district nursing were maintained.

The issues involved in the implementation of skill mix may be controversial, but it should be remembered that within the various arguments is the question of the real value of nursing (McKeown, 1994). Advocates of skill mix may argue for the reduction in numbers of qualified staff, but the need for quality of care and the maintenance of standards must always be influential in decision-making processes.

McKeown (1994) suggests that the values underpinning such views of nursing should include co-operation, mutuality, reciprocity and equality. Respect for other professionals' roles and functions should not be overlooked, and, if they were considered complementary and not contradictory, then the needs of the patient would be better served and job satisfaction levels increased. This can only be for the good of all concerned with the provisions of community health care.

10.2 Clinical competences

According to Baly (1985), the nature of district nursing is concerned with acting for the patient. This includes doing those things or assisting with those activities that patients are unable to carry out independently for themselves, providing an environment that encourages personal development and supporting the patient in his or her daily activities physically, psychologically and socially. This is not meant to imply that the average workload of the district nurse is task-oriented; a decade ago Baly might have suggested that district nursing care was occasionally disease-oriented, but this would not be regarded as acceptable today. District nurses, along with nursing professionals in other specialist areas, base their care on the nursing process and on an appropriate nursing model of care. Indeed, it is only by assessing, planning, implementing and evaluating care in such a manner that individualized care can be guaranteed.

The choice of nursing model will be made by the district nurse who carries out the initial assessment of the patient, in conjunction with that patient. It is vitally important for the professional to involve the patient in the choice of his or her care. If this collaboration is guaranteed, then the likelihood of subsequent patient compliance is heightened. It is recommended in *The Future of Professional Practice: The Council's Standards for Education and Practice Following Registration* (UKCC, 1994) that the nurse should be able to:

(1) assess the health and health-related needs of patients, clients, their families and other carers and identify and initiate appropriate steps for effective care for individuals and groups;
(2) assess, diagnose and treat specific diseases in accordance with agreed medical protocols; and
(3) assess, plan, provide and evaluate specialist clinical nursing care to meet care needs of individual patients in their own homes.

Thus it is clear that the district nurse not only cares for the patient in isolation, but care of patients includes the care and consideration of their families, friends and all their carers, be they lay or professional. The district nurse will provide skilled nursing care for any person living in the community, and she will often carry out this care in relation to other members of the PHCT.

One area of care that has become an increasingly important part of the workload of district nurses is that of terminal illness and bereavement, as increasingly the patient's right to choose where he will die is recognized and respected (Turton & Orr, 1985). With emphasis on community care, many more people are being discharged home to die, or choosing to be cared for at home. The reasons which may influence this choice are multiple and varied, but often include personal choice and the availability of care in the community. It is preferable for many to die in the familiar surroundings of their own homes, and relatives often find comfort in the knowledge that they were involved in the care of their loved ones until they died. However, caring for a patient dying at home can cause a several-fold increase in the workload of the district nurse. The patient's dependency increases, and as a result the time the nurse spends with that patient and his or her family also increases. This inevitably necessitates a flexible approach to time management, as it is difficult to judge accurately how long each visit to a person who is dying will actually take. As Turton and Orr (1985) point out, the district nurse must work particularly closely with the other members of the primary health care team in order to provide the best possible nursing care.

Nurses working in all areas of practice recognize the necessity for counselling some of the people in their care, but not all are fortunate enough to have sufficient time to utilize their skills adequately and efficiently. The British Association for Counselling (1983) defines counselling as 'giving the client an opportunity to explore, discover and clarify ways of living much more satisfyingly and resourcefully', and the Association believes that it is made up of three elements:

(1) The client and his problem, or his reason for seeking help;
(2) The counsellor and his skills; and
(3) The relationship between them.

In order to undertake this vital role, especially in the field of terminal care, district nurses must first understand the true nature of counselling and appreciate the amount of time and commitment the provision of such care entails.

Tschudin (1987) emphasizes that the difference between counselling and other forms of helping is that counselling involves listening to the person as a whole, and not just the words that are spoken nor the problem that is presented. She points out that 'as helpers we need more than just skill and information; we need to be willing to use ourselves in the process'. If this is the case, then the problems of providing an adequate and confidential counselling service within district nursing becomes obvious. With increasing staff shortages and a decrease in the numbers of professionally qualified district nurses employed in the community, combined with increasing numbers of patients cared for in the community setting, the opportunities for the provision of counselling by busy district nurses are few and far between. Despite this, anecdotal evidence would suggest that most district nurses include 'counselling' in their repertoire of nursing skills, and regard it as a necessary and worthwhile part of their daily work.

There is an increasing demand for counselling and psychotherapy these days, and this may be related to changing public attitudes to fitness and general health. However, in order to ensure that the true nature of counselling is appreciated by both the nurse and patient alike, it is necessary to ensure that enough time is set aside for active listening to the concerns and needs of the patient, and for the district nurse to be aware of the potential side effects of this particular kind of care on herself as an individual.

Turton and Orr (1985) point out that there are many times when a district nurse may have been very close to a family, giving support, or that she may experience a run of deaths or have unusually large numbers of terminally ill patients in her care. In situations like these it is necessary for the district nurse to recognize the warning signs of her own stress – fatigue, apathy, anxiety, irritability, insomnia, to name but a few. It is vitally important that the nurse is aware of and recognizes these signs before they become problematic; if this does occur, not only will the nurse herself suffer, but her patient care will begin to deteriorate and job satisfaction will disappear. Penson (1990) points out that some of the main features of counselling are that it is a two-way process, it is non-judgemental in approach and it focuses on problems identified by the patient or client, with implicit ideas of personal fulfilment and growth. Penson says that '"counselling" has become a jargon word much overused in professional circles. Sometimes it would seem to include almost any one-to-one communication and, in nursing, it can even be used to describe disciplinary activities!'

It is therefore very necessary that district nurses understand the true nature of counselling, and are aware of other professional and voluntary organizations that offer counselling services and help, and they are able to refer to them whenever necessary.

One of the most important things that the district nurse can do is to assure both the patient and his family and carers that death is very rarely an unpleasant experience. It is important that all those involved in the care of someone who is dying realise this, as often people's first exposure to death is as exemplified on the television or cinema screen, and they expect dying to be a painful and negative experience. There is a great need for the district nurse to be knowledgeable about pain and symptom control in terminal care, as she is often the main carer, and the main liaison between the patient and his general practitioner.

10.3 Health education

District nurses will have developed specialist clinical skills in order to meet a wide range of needs which may be found in the community. These skills will include the delivery of expert nursing care, exercising appropriate clinical judgements and demonstrating a team approach to care. In order to ensure that the nursing care delivered is at an optimum level and that all needs in the community are being met, it is necessary for the district nurse to be aware of changes in epidemiology or population in his or her particular area. It is important for district nurses to be aware of environmental and social factors that may influence the health and health needs of those in their care, and it may be necessary for a nurse to initiate or partake in health programmes, or national, regional or local health initiatives.

Many health education and health promotion programmes are aimed at the general public or particular groups of people. It is important to consider the benefits of health education on the individual level, especially as it is at this level that the district nurse will be most active. Health education and health promotion programmes require that we need to consider if we educate first and then develop, or if the two processes occur concurrently. Education and development are processes that are independent, but they are also interdependent. The verb 'to educate' can be described as 'to bring up, train and instruct, according to an accepted standard' (Chambers Dictionary, 1985), while 'to develop' can mean 'to unroll; to lay open by degrees; to bring to a more advanced or more highly organized state'. From these definitions it may be concluded that while to educate is a learning process which travels in a linear progression, according to the prescribed rules, the process of 'development' can also be interpreted as a learning process, but one which progresses in many directions. It may therefore be considered a gradual unravelling of the person's potential to maintain optimal health and to assume responsibility for his or her own health gain and maintenance.

The role of all nurses involves teaching and educating those in our care, and perhaps this is nowhere more important than in the community setting. District nurses are in the privileged position of working and caring for people in their own homes and in their own environment; they have first-hand experience of the social, economic and cultural values that influence the way in which patients understand and perceive their health needs. There is a great difference between teaching and learning, however, and it is important for district nursing practitioners to recognize this. When district nurses teach, be it in a formal or informal setting, they demonstrate, instruct and illustrate, but in order to educate, they must ensure that people understand the information given to them, and that such information has a meaning and purpose for them.

Many district nurses are involved in health education on a one-to-one basis, although they will also target their information at groups of people on occasion. However, as the bulk of their work is carried out in the homes of individuals, this is where their primary target lies. The use of an holistic nursing care model is an advantage in such circumstances, as it may involve emotional, spiritual, physical and psychological areas of people's lives.

The terms 'health education' and 'health promotion' are much in vogue today. Health has been defined as 'a state of complete physical, mental and social well-being and not merely the absence of disease or infirmity' (WHO, 1978), and this is the ideal that district nurses aim for. However, different people have different opinions as to what health education and promotion actually are, depending on their roles in health, or indeed whether they are at the receiving end of this information or not; there are even many differences held by members of the same profession.

According to Strehlow (1983), health education consists of 'health teaching at all levels, ages and stages, an activity carried out for the mutual benefit of those participating in teaching and learning activities'. She even goes as far as to say that the achievement of health should be fun! Illich (1977) believed that health 'designates a process of adaptation, the ability to accept damaged environments, to growing up, to ageing, to healing when damaged, to suffering and to the peaceful expectation of death'. Tones *et al.* (1990) argue that health education is an activity that 'promotes health-related learning, i.e. some relatively permanent change in an individual's competence or disposition'. Cohen (1981) laudably suggests that health education is the equivalent of a reduction in ignorance about health.

All these extremely well-meaning definitions of health and health education are remarkable if only for the fact that they are mainly held, or perhaps believed in, by health professionals. Experience will inform any doctor, nurse or teacher that the ordinary man or woman in the street will report that being 'healthy' to him or her means *not* being ill, or at least being able to carry on with normal everyday life for as long as possible. Many people also differentiate between the idea of being sick and that of being unwell, or ill:

'That health is something more than the absence of disease, has been suggested by the notion of good health as the power of overcoming disease which is actually present; ... although health is sometimes the absence of serious disease, it is also possible to refer to someone as healthy even though serious disease is said in the same breath to be present.' (Williams, 1983)

It can be seen, therefore, that health education and health promotion are inseparably linked. It is difficult to be involved with one and not the other, and it is important for district nurses to recognize this. Perry and Jolley (1991) believe that health education is a part of health promotion and that health promotion becomes 'a broader umbrella expression including other activities apart from the communication of health information to the public', a belief that Tones *et al.* (1990) would agree with, adding the proviso that the particular contributions made by education to health promotion are as follows:

(1) to influence individual choices;

(2) to influence the adoption of healthy public policies; and
(3) to raise public awareness of the issue in question.

It is in these three areas especially that district nurses may be particularly effective. They are particularly concerned with bringing about a healthier lifestyle for those in their care, but they need to be aware that their patients may only be concerned with maintaining a certain standard of living, carrying on their lives as normally as possible. It is therefore imperative that district nurses are aware of the relationships between environment, living conditions, lifestyles and local health problems, as well as knowledge of the full range of resources available in their particular area, in order to ensure that the best care possible is delivered to their patients. It is also imperative that the district nurse is aware of how patients feel about their situation, and whether they believe they have the ability to change their circumstances, if desired. The emphasis needs to remain on patient-centred goals and an assessment of their actual and potential goals, with the consent, co-operation and involvement of the patient concerned (Pearson & Vaughan, 1987). It is no longer acceptable (nor policy) for the nurse to decide alone as to what the patient should or should not do.

10.4 Conclusion

In *The Scope of Professional Practice* (UKCC, 1992a) it is stated that the nurse '... must honestly acknowledge any limits of personal knowledge and skill and take steps to remedy any relevant deficits in order effectively and appropriately to meet the needs of patients and clients'. This is obviously a wise precaution in order to prevent any harm being done to patients in receipt of nursing care, and one which every nurse should abide by. In the area of community nursing, with increasing workloads often accompanied by reductions in skill mix and staffing levels, it is sometimes difficult to keep up to date with changes within the profession and within the area of health generally. However, it is incumbent on each district nurse to be aware of his or her professional accountability and to keep up to date with current trends and changes, and ensure that they are acting in the patients' best interests.

Melia (1992) reminds us that one of the basic assumptions that we all make is that, within the limits of the law, we have the freedom to act as we choose, and that this freedom is based on the idea of 'autonomy' – 'our capacity to think and act on the basis of our own reasoning'. However, with reference to decision-making Melia (1992) cautions that there are occasions when nurses ignore a patient's autonomy, either in order to safeguard the patient's safety, or because it suits them to do so. The problem is knowing when and where to draw the line. All that nurses can safely do is to offer clients and patients advice and information, to guide them within the professional code of professional conduct, and allow them to make their own decisions based on this knowledge, and their needs and perceptions.

Realistically, there will be times when nurses are obliged to intervene in order to stop people damaging themselves or others. It is incumbent on those in positions of influence in the care of others to ensure that, in nursing, people are provided with an enhanced knowledge allowing them to become as self-caring as possible, while knowing that support and help are available (if and when required). Nurses themselves encounter so much stress in their daily working lives that they should be aware of their own needs and vulnerabilities, and district nurses are no exception. Until they can recognize and comprehend their own behaviours and realize they can bring about positive change in themselves they will be of limited benefit to their patients.

For example, in the field of bereavement, many nurses find the strain of constantly coping, when all around are sick or dying, too much to bear, and consequently the levels of short- and long-term absences from work increase. Nurses constantly state that they need more opportunities to discuss these and other sensitive areas (Hitch & Murgatroyd, 1983; Kelsey, 1992; Farrar, 1992); perhaps it could be argued that district nurses are especially in need of this facility, due to the partially solitary nature of their work, the degree of their autonomy, and the fact that they are often the main carer in the home.

District nurses continue to be concerned with people in their own homes and in their normal social settings with their families and carers, to provide a level of care that strives for excellence in all things, and to support and encourage patients to become as independent and self-sufficient as possible, and this care is successful when, as Gordon and Klouda (1989) point out, the care is set 'in the context of what people know, do and feel in the context of the reality of their lives'.

10.5 References

Baly, M. (ed.) (1985) *A New Approach to District Nursing*. Heinemann, London.

Barriball, K. & Mackenzie, A. (1993) Measuring the impact of nursing interventions in the community: a selective review of the literature. *Journal of Advanced Nursing*, **18**, 491–97.

British Association for Counselling (1983) *Code of Ethics*. BAC, Rugby.

Buchan, J. (1991) Assessing the cost of nursing. *Nursing Standard*, **6**(4), 40.

Buckle, J. (1992) Which lavender oil? *Nursing Times*, **88**(32), 31–2.

Cohen, D. (1981) Prevention as an economic good. In *Education for health* (1983) (ed. M.S. Strehlow). Harper & Row, London.

DHSS (1986) *Mix and Match: A Review of Nursing Skill*. DHSS, London.

DOH (1992) *Citizen's Charter*. HMSO, London.

Farrar, A. (1992) *Pathways to Wellness*. Life Enhancement Publications, Illinois.

Gibbs, I., McCaughan, D. & Griffiths, M. (1991) Skill mix in nursing: a selective review of the literature. *Journal of Advanced Nursing*, **16**, 242–9.

Gordon, G. & Klouda, T. (1989) *Preventing a Crisis: Aids and Family Planning*. Macmillan, London.

Griffin, A. (1993) Holism in nursing: its meaning and value. *British Journal of Nursing*, **2**(6), 8–10.

Harris, P. (1992) Top of the team. *Nursing Times*, **88**(47), 25–8.

Healy, P. (1993) Arrangements for care. *Nursing Times*, **89**(3), 48–50.

Hitch, P.J. & Murgatroyd, J.D. (1982) Professional Communications in Cancer Care – a Delphi survey of Hospital Nurses. *Journal of Advanced Nursing*, **8**, 413–22.

Illich, I. (1977) *Disabling Professions*. Marion Boyars, London.

James, E. & Low, H. (1990) *The District Nurse*. RCN District Nurses Forum, London.

Jones, P. (1993) Standing firm, gaining strength. *Primary Health Care*, **3**(9).

Kelling, K. (1993) The cost of caring. *Nursing Standard*, **7**(42), 21–2.

Kelsey, S. (1992) Can we care to the end? *Professional Nurse*, January, 1992, 216–9.

Laurent, C. (1993) Out in force. *Nursing Times*, **89**(3), 41–2.

McKeown, M. (1994) Skill-mix reviews: the need to be aware. *Nursing Standard*, **8**(32), 37–9.

Melia, K. (1992) *Everyday Nursing Ethics*. Macmillan, London.

NHS Management Executive (1992) *The Nursing skill mix in the District Nursing Service*, NHSME, London.

Owen, P. & Holmes, C. (1993) Holism in the discourse of nursing. *Journal of Advanced Nursing*, **20**, 1753–60.

Pearson, A. & Vaughan, B. (1987) *Nursing Models and the Nursing Process*. Lippincott, London.

Penson, J. (1990) *Bereavement: A Guide for Nurses*. Harper & Row, London.

Perry, A. & Jolley, M. (1991) *Nursing: A Knowledge Base for Practice*. Edward Arnold, London.

RCN (1992a) *Powerhouse for Change: Report of the task force on community nursing*. Royal College of Nursing, London.

RCN (1992b) *Skill Mix and Reprofiling: A Guide for RCN Members*. Royal College of Nursing, London.

RCN (1993) *District Nurses and Value for Money: An RCN Response*. Royal College of Nursing, London.

Ross, F. (1987) District Nursing. In: *Recent Advances in Nursing (15) – Community Nursing* (ed. J. Littlewood). Churchill Livingstone, Edinburgh.

Schroeder, J. (1992) Carers focus: community outlook. *Nursing Times*, **88**(45), 60–62.

Skidmore, D. (1992) Combining talents. *Nursing Times*, **88**(34), 16–18.

Smith, L. (1993) The art and science of nursing. *Nursing Times*, **89**(25), 26–7.

Strehlow, M.S. (1983) *Education for Health*. Harper & Row, London.

Tones, K., Tilford, S. & Robinson, Y. (1990) *Health Education*. Chapman & Hall, London.

Traynor, M. (1993) Community nurses: a culture of uncertainty. *Nursing Standard*, **7**(37), 38–40.

Tschudin, V. (1987) *Counselling Skills for Nurses*. Ballière Tindall, London.

Turton, P. & Orr, J. (1985) *Learning to Care in the Community*. Hodder & Stoughton, London.

UKCC (1992a) *The Scope of Professional Practice*. UKCC, London.

UKCC (1992b) *The Code of Professional Conduct*. UKCC, London.

UKCC (1994) *The Future of Professional Practice: The Council's Standards for Education and Practice Following Registration*. UKCC, London.

WHO (1978) *Health for All*. Declaration of WHO Conference on Primary Health Care, Alma Ata. WHO, Geneva.

Williams, R. (1983) Concepts of health: an analysis of lay logic. *Sociology*, **17**(2), 185–205.

Chapter 11

Competence for Community Health Care Nursing (Children)

Nursing a sick child in the community presents unique challenges and problems and demands the care and support of a specialist practitioner. That practitioner is the community child health care nurse, more commonly known as the paediatric community nurse (PCN). This chapter discusses paediatric community nursing and the role of these specialist practitioners by reflecting on their history, the current stage of their development and the way in which their interface with the secondary care services is evolving.

Reduced reliance on admission alongside the changing health care system is presenting a new and challenging wall for paediatric community nursing, prompting the emergence of the PCN as an independent practitioner. This role and that of the community neonatal nurse will be explored. Professional and personal competences together with the professional development of the PCN will be discussed and aspirations for the future care of sick children in the noninstitutional setting outlined.

Paediatric community nursing is developing rapidly as a branch of paediatric nursing; a new era has begun, and practice in the care of children in the community is subject to constant review and enhancement. The associated body of published knowledge is still small, references and research limited. Parts of this chapter will therefore be either anecdotal or based on current and previous experiences of practising PCNs.

11.1 Why paediatric community nurses?

Three case studies illustrate the role of the PCN, the nature of the nursing care they provide and the fact that children with life-threatening and life-limiting disorders can live as normal a life as possible at home with the family they love and trust caring for them.

Hannah is three years old. She has cystic fibrosis, is colonized with pseudomonas aeruginosa and requires two intravenous antibiotics three times a day, four or five times a year, for two weeks at a time. She has twin brothers aged 18 months, one of whom was on a ventilator for ten days following delivery. Lactose intolerance adds to her malabsorption problem associated with the cystic fibrosis. An implanted central venous line with a subcutaneous port called a Portacath was inserted when Hannah was 18 months and the twins six weeks old. All three children were admitted together to the local district hospital paediatric unit for one night as the twins were breast fed for their first 15 months. That was the only occasion on which Hannah was admitted. Her complex range of treatment, medications, intravenous schedules and care have all been undertaken by her family at home with the teaching support and advice of the PCN and GP who share care with the consultant paediatrician.

Amy is five years old and has had a tracheostomy and gastrostomy for two years. Five nights were spent in hospital at the time of their creation. She attended play school and now a mainstream infants school with a nurse (funded jointly by the local authority education and community nursing budgets) discreetly in attendance and working as a classroom helper. Equipment and supplies are provided either by GP prescription or the PCNs budget.

Alex died at home aged six weeks from a rare metabolic disorder which was incompatible with life. The PCN supported the parents both before and after his death. His death was difficult and required intensive care to ensure he died with comfort and dignity where his parents chose, at home with his two sisters. Alex was at home for most of his short life and during that time required continuous nasogastric feeding, oxygen, suction and increasing doses of oral, followed by subcutaneous, morphine via a parent-controlled analgesia pump.

These three children, like many others nationally, are enabled to live a normal life at home and in other community settings. Their diseases do not dictate their lifestyle but fit into it (Sidey, 1990). They do not reside in an acute ward, labelled as and feeling sick. Their family and associated life evolves almost normally. PCNs are educated to facilitate packages of care for children with a wide range of illnesses, ensuring that sick children live life to the full whatever the nature or prognosis of their illness.

PCNs possess unique knowledge and skills to respond to the needs of such chronically or acutely sick children and adolescents, at the same time identifying the associated special needs of parents and siblings as they provide flexible and dynamic quality care. A special role of the PCN is to act as the child's advocate and respond to the relevant advances in paediatric nursing care. PCNs understand how to use community networks to facilitate family-centred appropriate home care, by teaching, supporting, advising, counselling and liaising (RCN, 1993).

11.2 History

In 1973 James and Joyce Robertson, speaking at the annual conference of NAWCH (The National Association for the Welfare of Children in Hospital), now ASC (Action for Sick Children), pleaded that no child should be admitted to hospital without their mother or full time mother substitute. Little mention was made of sick children being nursed at home despite the fact that the Platt report (1959) recognized the psychological trauma of children spending time in hospital separated from those they loved and trusted (MOH, 1959).

Both the Platt report and, later, the Court report (DHSS, 1976), emphasized the need to look at community care for sick children, yet in 1973 very few such community schemes existed. Among them were schemes at Rotherham, established in 1949, Paddington (1954), Birmingham (1954) and Southampton (1969). Whiting (1988) showed that only 12.6% of health authorities in 1988 had a community child care nurse, with another 17.4% planning to introduce teams. The 1995 RCN Paediatric Society's Directory of Paediatric Community Nursing Services provides details of established schemes, now representing 50% of district purchasing authorities (RCN, 1995). This increase is set to continue, thereby showing a return to patterns of care of the early part of the century when most sick children were cared for by their family at home.

Hospital care only became the norm as the century progressed, and this was due to the misguided belief that such care reduced child mortality, whereas, in the early part of the century, such deaths had little to do with the locus of care and more to do with ignorance of how infectious diseases spread (Sidey, 1993). Now, once again, when PCNs are available, children need only be admitted to hospital when the care they require cannot be given at home without real disadvantage (DOH, 1991).

11.3 Current patterns of paediatric community nursing provision

Nationally, over the last 40 years, children's home care schemes or paediatric community nursing services have developed in a number of ways and may be placed in four broad categories:

- community based
- hospital based
- as resource nurses
- as specialist nurses.

These developments have been due to a variety of factors including local needs and priorities; resources, such as skill, funding and commitment; and past, present and anticipated communication and collaboration. Generic or specialist PCNs practise as part of well-staffed schemes (as witnessed in services in Southampton and Nottingham), providing 24-hour cover throughout the year. Partly-staffed schemes provide partial cover and single-handed or poorly staffed schemes provide limited weekday cover only.

Most sick children who require the support of a PCN are attached to district general hospitals where the least number of PCNs are to be found. Home care can only be offered or requested where PCNs are available and caseloads have to be determined and controlled in response to numbers of staff, skill mix, intensity of care required, geography and funding. Tatman (1994), in *Wise Decisions – Developing Paediatric Home Care Schemes*, provides comprehensive advice on many aspects of the setting up and monitoring of paediatric community nursing services.

11.4 Consumer, purchaser and provider expectations

'Improved survival of low weight births has led to increased levels of morbidity throughout childhood.' In addition, 'children are now treated as outpatients, day cases or in paediatric home nursing schemes ... Others are kept in hospital for shorter periods' (Woodroffe & Glideman, 1993). Many of these children have sophisticated care needs. These factors, together with increased consumer awareness and the sterling work of the voluntary group, Action for Sick Children, have increased the demand for more PCNs. The Children Act (1989), *Bridging the Gaps* (Action for Sick Children, 1993), *Children First* (Audit Commission, 1993) and *Welfare of Children and Young People in Hospital* (DOH, 1991) endorse the right of the child, family, and secondary and primary care services to expect appropriate nursing provision to be made for sick children in the community.

Such provision is not necessarily a cheap option but can be demonstrated to be cheaper than the cost of occupying acute hospital beds (Atwell & Gow, 1985; Whiting, 1994). Purchasers and providers of health care seek to negotiate the most appropriate and cost-effective packages of home care. Such packages have been evidenced as preferential targets in purchasing specifications and service provider contracts throughout the UK.

11.5 Community or acute based?

The majority of paediatric community nursing schemes are based according to their source of funding. Community care reduces the need for hospital care and The Audit Commission (1993) has suggested that money for home care could be released from hospital budgets. Ideally funding should be provided within the context of combined children's services directorates, but in practice, the separation of hospital and community services into different NHS Trusts (few of whom provide both in-patient and community nursing care) can lead to conflict over ownership and poor co-ordination of service provision. Ultimately home care for children will be purchased in the same way as other community nursing services, with purchasers ensuring that the main considerations are the needs of the sick child and family. Wherever based and however funded, care will be provided in conjunction with GPs and health visitors who have knowledge of the family, with the local paediatrician providing an umbrella of specialist knowledge as required and requested.

11.6 Communication

Established and effective lines of communication should exist between the PCN, the sick child and family and associated professionals from both primary and secondary care settings. These may be achieved in many ways: via mobile phones, message pagers, visiting cards, stickers for records, regular multidisciplinary team meetings, planned meetings with consultants and GPs, circulated service information folders containing caseload and allocation lists, patient summary lists and general information and summary cards for GPs to insert in their records. Office-based telephones with answerphones also assist family and professional communication, as does clerical support. For many years triage by telephone has been an accepted part of paediatric community nursing practice. Competent carers can accurately assess and relate details of their child's condition and associated changes by telephone. Reduction in home visits and long distance problem solving can be achieved by joint assessment with the PCN together with support and advice. Occasionally acute technical problems can be resolved by the provision of direct telephone instructions.

Records of care, actions and episodes of treatment are stored in the form of client-held records, computerized record systems and more traditional records; they may be maintained by the PCN, family or patient or a combination of these. They may consist of a one-off visit sheet or a comprehensive document which enhances family-centred care (Farrell, 1992; UKCC, 1991). Care plans are available either to accompany the patient or held in the paediatric community nursing office, which should ideally be situated adjacent to the in-patient paediatric ward or unit. Patient- and carer-held records, which accompany the patient and can be accessed by them and any professional involved, greatly facilitate communication and liaison, particularly when children have life-limiting or life-threatening disorders. Many professionals will be involved with these families and family-held records can enhance quality and continuity of care. Statistics harvested and stored by computer technology can produce valuable information to inform on the costing and planning of home care. A computerized thesaurus of terms for paediatric nursing is in preparation by the NHS Management Executive Centre for Coding and Classification.

11.7 A child's right to family-centred home care

It is now widely accepted that sick children who experience loss and separation while in hospital, especially the very young, suffer emotional trauma to a greater or lesser extent, which can be long-lasting (Bowlby, 1965; Robertson, 1989; Rutter, 1981). The effect of having an ill child in the family is unpredictable and will often vary (Douglas, 1993). The illness may be sudden in onset or may present as a chronic disorder punctuated by acute episodes. A single or ongoing life crisis may be punctuated by additional crises, resulting in ordinary but unique families coping with extraordinary circumstances. They are, however, the experts on their child, responding to that child's normal everyday physical, emotional and social needs, most of which remain unchanged when ill health occurs.

The shock, worry and guilt which accompany a child's illness threaten the integrity of the family unit, and this may be exacerbated if the locus of care moves from the home to a hospital setting. The carers' perceived and sometimes actual loss of control, autonomy and competence can compound feelings of grief, guilt and shock, resulting in a stressed family whose dynamics may become distorted and destabilized (Whiting, 1989; Muller *et al.*, 1992). Such experiences are far from helpful for a sick child and family confronted on admission by strangers in an unfamiliar place. Responses to these stressful experiences may be determined by factors such as previous life experiences and other current life events. Consequently each family member may be stressed in different ways.

One way of ameliorating stress is to focus on family-centred care at home; this can lead to parents, patients and siblings, where possible, being involved as active partners with health care professionals in management, decision-making, treatment and care during the child's illness. Parents who undertake such a role may demonstrate enhanced self esteem and coping mechanisms, the execution of the role helping them come to terms with such emotions as guilt and grief (Douglas, 1993; Muller *et al.*, 1992).

Children may feel guilty that they are ill and view their illness as a punishment for some past incident not even realized by an adult. Carers may express grief and guilt for the loss of their child's health, even in a minor disorder and especially in a major illness. These feelings are further compounded in the case of congenital disorders where parents are often observed to assume personal responsibility for the provision of the most complex care at home in their efforts to help their child.

Home care is not the best option for every family but the majority will either request it or can be led towards the acceptance of the concept by the provision of individual packages of care and support. It can provide families with mastery and a sense of control over the specific demands imposed by the illness, which may then decrease their anxiety and increase their confidence. Drawing on their own resources, families may feel less overwhelmed by the ongoing crisis generated by their child's illness and able to maintain equilibrium within their family dynamics. Thus the integrity of the family is preserved and the long-term emotional trauma experienced by the patient and siblings is ameliorated (Muller *et al.*, 1992).

11.8 Lessons learnt from past practice

In the absence of the provision of paediatric nursing support and advice, either in the community by PCNs or to the community by paediatric resource nurses, sick children either had to stay in hospital for too long, had to return regularly to paediatric wards for treatment or were discharged into the community under the care of inappropriately educated and/or experienced nurses. Parents were often faced with the conflict of neglecting either their sick child or their well child in an attempt to cater for the needs of other family members. Family stress was also compounded by the inadequate provision of home care which often resulted in inappropriate readmission.

It is not regarded as safe practice to expect district nurses, health visitors or general practice nurses who do not hold a paediatric qualification or do not practice under the guidance of a specialist PCN to care for sick children in the community. These children have specialist age-oriented needs. Similarly it is not safe practice to expect hospital-based nurses with little community experience, and unsupervised by a PCN, to move from the hospital to the community setting in order to care for sick children without appropriate further education and experience. PCNs with a recognized UKCC-recorded community qualification have experience of both settings and can effectively practise between the two.

The provision of specialist paediatric nursing support was advocated by the Allitt Inquiry (DOH, 1994) following an investigation into the care practised in one British hospital. The Inquiry found that the care practice of an inappropriately educated and inexperienced nurse resulted in tragic consequences for the children for whom she was responsible. It was reported that clinicians, managers and other staff did not always give sufficient attention to the needs and rights of children. Children have the same rights as any citizen to receive flexible access to health care services designed to meet their specific needs.

One recommendation of the Allitt inquiry was that the document *Welfare of Children and Young People in Hospital* (DOH, 1991) should be more closely observed. This document's first cardinal principle states that 'children are admitted to hospital only if the care they require cannot be as well provided at home, in a day clinic or on a day basis in hospital'. Implicit in this statement is that such care be provided by appropriately educated practitioners. Nurses who are inappropriately educated and experienced to nurse children in the community should not attempt to provide such care in the interests of early discharge or prevention of admission. Inappropriate or understaffed care provision may result in unsafe delivery of care (Hennessy, 1993).

11.9 Relationships and liaison with the primary health care team

Multidisciplinary teamwork is a prerequisite for the production of any home care package. Within this team will be a team leader, usually the PCN, GP, health visitor or other relevant team member involved with the family and with whom they most easily relate. The PCN, working between hospital and community, can provide the effective clinical liaison required for effective communication between professionals in both settings and supervise the necessary clerical liaison. Each member of the care team should respect, support and enhance the others' roles and skills in order to provide a comprehensive package of care to the sick child and family. The team may include school nurses, social workers, paediatric dieticians, speech therapists, physiotherapists, occupational therapists and general practice nurses. District nurses may also share in the provision of nursing care or provide care and liaise with a specialist paediatric nurse, but in such circumstances the PCN will usually fulfil the role of the child's primary nurse. Shared care may be desirable in specific situations and will be apparent to varying degrees where a specialist paediatric community nursing service is not adequately resourced.

11.10 Management models

Paediatric community nursing services are currently managed and co-ordinated in various ways by the NHS Trust or GP Fundholding practice that employs them. Appropriately staffed and funded schemes are most appropriately managed by a budget-holding senior PCN who has specific responsibility for the services budget. PCN managers will be accountable to a director within their trusts or clinical directorates. Managers in the hospital sector are unlikely to have community knowledge or experience and, at present, the majority of community nurse managers are unlikely to possess specialist knowledge or experience of paediatric nursing. PCNs can therefore be inappropriately managed, and their needs – and those of their patients – inadequately understood. The emergence of combined health directorates integrating care in both hospital and community settings will facilitate new management models which will prove to be more effective and efficient for the practising PCN.

11.11 Funding – past, present and future

Lack of funding, either due to poor resources or commitment, has, in some areas, prevented the development and growth of many paediatric community nursing schemes. However, some hospital sector managers have demonstrated foresight and commitment by closing beds in their hospitals with the aim of releasing revenue resources in order to fund home care. Community managers, in a minority of areas, have also funded services which have reduced or prevented hospital admission and yet received no transfer of funds from hospital sector budgets.

Community care reduces the demand for in-patient care, and, where care schemes are funded by the community services, the funding should follow the patient and be re-allocated from hospital sector budgets. Unlike district nursing or health visiting, some specialist nursing services, including paediatric community nursing, are not regarded as essential services. Funding is allocated via district health authority purchasers to local community and hospital budgets, and, in the absence of combined health directorate budgets, joint funding between hospital sector and community services may, and should, be negotiated.

Nursing children at home can be demonstrated to be cheaper than the cost of occupying an in-patient bed, although the former is not in itself considered to be a cheap option. However, future health strategies may exploit this cost benefit to the advantage of the sick child and family. Little work has yet been undertaken to develop accurate evaluation tools to assess the cost benefits of caring for sick children at home and similarly little has been done to design schemes for income generation (Anderson, 1993).

Supplies and equipment for home care should be budgeted for via medical loan departments and nursing supplies. Sick children at home need ready access to a range of specialist supplies and equipment to facilitate home care in the same way as provision is made for sick adults. No child of any age should have to stay in hospital because of inadequate resources at home.

Sadly, PCNs have sometimes found themselves involved in unnecessary, emotive and ethical battles as they aim to negotiate and secure adequate resources to facilitate home care.

Only a minority of PCNs have access to an adequate range of appropriate resources which are either provided or purchased from both stock and non-stock sources, as required. In addition, reliance is often placed upon voluntary organizations and local donations to provide extra resources. Contracts negotiated with independent sector home delivery companies such as Caremark can reduce a PCN's workload and provide a quality service for families by delivering the full range of supplies for patients receiving such treatment as intravenous cytotoxic, antibiotic, gamma globulin and analgesic therapy and enteral or parenteral feeding.

GPs may request or welcome advice from the PCN and/or paediatrician on the use and prescribing of some medications, dosages and routes, particularly where sliding scales of dose and time are required. Fundholding GPs may use this information to advise their family health service authority (FHSA) of potential expensive prescribing patterns. Such practice may assist the FHSA in the design of contingency plans to provide increased GP drug budgets. The FHSA does not expect the drug budget of nonfundholding GPs, once exhausted, to continue to pay for expensive medication, and transfers the additional cost to the local acute hospital budget once this has occurred. However, each FHSA has its own policy and these policies vary considerably.

In a situation where the GP feels unable, or refuses, to accept clinical responsibility for treatments undertaken at home, the cost is carried by the budget of the physician/surgeon who has clinical responsibility for the child's care. Modern therapy can be expensive, whether administered at home or in hospital: for example, a two-week course of intravenous antibiotic therapy via a self-infusion device delivered to the patient ready dispensed, can cost in excess of £3 000. But with hospital bed occupancy costs amounting to several hundred pounds a day, it can be shown that home care is consistently cheaper than hospital care.

Evidence suggests that deficits in financial resources interfere with discharge patterns, and patients and their families may be shielded from the actual reason for being detained in hospital (Caremark, 1994). Home care should not be a lottery depending on whether or not the patient's GP is a fundholder or upon the policy of a particular FHSA. Good liaison and the design of clinical protocols will facilitate appropriate discharge and prescribing patterns. Rudimentary costing indicates that a home visit by a PCN costs between £29.00 and £50.00. If one PCN, for example, saved 50 in-patient bed days per month (and this is a conservative estimate), at a cost of £150.00 per bed, a saving of £7 500.00 would be made. If the same PCN made 50 visits at a cost of £35.00 per visit, totalling £1750.00, even the extra costs of travelling, telephone calls, salary and administration would not add up to the

£7 500.00 of in-patient costs. Supplies and medication cost the same whether a patient is at home or in hospital.

Example

Acute bed savings
50 acute beds saved in 1 month
Cost of acute bed per day: £150.00
£150 × 50 = £7 500. 00

PCN Costs
50 PCN visits
Cost of each PCN visit: £35.00
£35 × 50 = £1 750.00

Salaries vary according to grade. The above example demonstrates that value for money will be achieved alongside value for the grade employed following further investment in PCN deployment.

11.12 Caseloads

Caseloads vary according to local needs, clinical and nursing resource constraint and interprofessional liaison methods between consultants and GPs.

The following example illustrates the caseload characteristics of one PCN service, staffed by two nurses (although the estimated number of nurses required is five). The service is funded by a local community NHS Trust and is attached to a district general hospital.

- Cystic Fibrosis: 14
- Gastrostomy: 7
- Tracheostomy: 2
- Oncology: 2
- Life-threatening inherited/metabolic disorders: 4
- Life-threatening birth induced accidents: 4
- Severe eczema: 1
- Central venous lines: 8
- Renal failure: 2
- Traction: 1
- Nasogastric feeding: 3
- Choanal atresia: 2

The following provides an example of equipment obtained for the clients receiving care and support in the above caseload example:

- Enteral feeding pumps: 10
- Suction machines: 9
- Drip stands: 1
- Intravenous pumps: 1
- Gallows traction: 1
- Nebulizers: 18
- Humidifiers: 2

11.13 Earlier discharge and prevention of admission

Experienced PCNs will assess, negotiate and facilitate home care in the majority of practice settings. It is suggested that home care should rarely be denied except in circumstances such as unresolvable carer anxiety or when the carer is shown to be unable or unwilling to understand the care required. However, adverse social circumstances rarely prevent the provision of home care (for example, the author has not experienced any infection in venous access routes during a ten year period among many patients receiving intravenous therapy). Home care settings which might be perceived as unsuitable by professionally determined criteria may be regarded as normal and satisfactory to some families but the PCN has a primary responsibility to assess all aspects of a family's motivation and ability to care for their sick child's needs at home. In so doing the nurse will have consideration for the principles of benevolence and respect for, firstly, the sick child and secondly the family (Whiting, 1989). The prime duty of care is to the child and his or her physical and emotional safety.

The design and implementation of unique patient- and family-led packages of care, negotiated for each family, bridge the gap between hospital and home and result in home care which is to the advantage of the whole family. Much teaching is undertaken – at home where possible – to facilitate easier learning, support and advice, especially in the initial stages before families acquire autonomy and the confidence to practise new skills. This autonomous process will develop at the family's own rate; families vary greatly in the time taken to acquire confidence in all aspects of their home care role. Once learned, the family may view their new skills as an extension of their usual caring role, and if they reach this point at a pace sensitively negotiated between themselves and their PCN, less input will be required from the latter except at planned times in the care process.

Reactive, as opposed to proactive, care, anticipated in a mutually trusting and supportive manner, produces a relaxed family and a happy child within the confines of the illness. The maintenance of positive morale for the child and family may lead to positive self-esteem which is invaluable to the sick child (Sidey, 1990). Ongoing support, information and the provision of a contact point reduce out-of-hours visiting, which is important to poorly-staffed schemes.

The Audit Commission (1993) found that, although some professionals thought that home care placed 'a great burden on parents', the contrary was true. The Commission interviewed 48 parents caring for quite ill children at home, and '... no resistance whatsoever was found' to assuming the home care role. However, the PCN needs to monitor carefully and evaluate the effectiveness and suitability of the home care package, and its development, seeking the advice, support and help of colleagues and associated staff (such as clinical psychologists) if required.

Occasionally additional support will be required at home but relief care for skilled parents practising sophisticated care at home is very limited. Hospice places are few in number and admission to hospital wards rarely provides appropriate relief for the child and family. As paediatric community nursing develops, the need for half-way houses providing family-controlled care in which they and their children have confidence, will become more evident, as will the need for domiciliary relief teams such as have evolved as part of the comprehensive service provided by the Nottingham Paediatric Community Nursing team. In our multicultural society, home care may be of even greater value to some ethnic minority groups. Care at home enables such families to continue to conduct their lives according to their beliefs. Sensitivity must be shown when visiting families in order to avoid offence by either dress, gender or attitude within their home (Black, 1989; Slater, 1993).

11.14 Generic versus specialist

Specialist nurses may be attached to regional or supraregional centres and reach out into the wider community that they serve, advising and liaising between clients and their families and other support systems. A specialist PCN may also be appointed as a resource nurse to a District General Hospital which may not possess other such advanced practitioners. In such instances earlier discharge of children may be facilitated from specialist children's hospitals so that their treatment and care can be continued at home (for example, in the case of a child with Childhood Leukaemia).

PCNs may attain specialist practitioner status through a process of further education, reflective practice and critical thinking (Muir, 1993; Lindsay, 1993). Generic PCNs may develop areas of special interest and expertise and, nationally, a mixed skill profile of generic and specialist paediatric nurses exists (for example, specialist paediatric nurses for children with cystic fibrosis). Ideally paediatric community nursing schemes should be managed by an experienced specialist PCN practitioner/manager whose primary responsibility will be to lead a multiskilled team of generic nurses developing individual areas of expertise and PCNs working as primary, specialist and advanced practitioners.

A comprehensive network of such services is required nationally to ensure that home care is available to all children in a manner comparable to the way in which home care is provided for adults. Appropriately skilled and educated specialist PCNs are emerging as independent practitioners in areas such as pain control, urology, diabetes, oncology, orthopaedics and neonatology. In some areas the voluntary sector funds link nurses who work from paediatric units. Closer liaison and evaluation of the contribution made by these nurses would enhance understanding of their roles and their contribution to caring for sick children, and facilitate common standards of practice.

11.15 Neonatal community nurses

In 1994 ten community neonatal services were identified in the *RCN Directory of Paediatric Community Nursing Services* (RCN, 1994), although neonates are discharged under the care of generic PCNs in other unspecified areas. Lindsay (1993) found that:

> 'Infants who have needed to stay in hospital for a long time after birth benefit from close observation and support when discharged and can be discharged earlier when such provision is made. Low birthweight infants may be discharged home irrespective of their weight provided they are feeling well'.

However, midwives and health visitors are rightly anxious about supporting these infants at home, especially when they may be sick as well as premature. Neonatal community nurses, who may be midwives or sick children's nurses and hold a neonatal qualification, provide a valuable link between the special care baby unit (SCBU) and the home, community midwife and health visitor. A nursing service comprising midwives and paediatric nurses, attached to both the SCBU and paediatric community nursing service, can provide midwifery support to the mother and neonatal and paediatric nursing skills to these premature and sometimes also sick infants at home. Such care should continue until their care becomes the province of the community midwife, health visitor and/or PCN (Kennelly & Collins, 1991).

11.16 Paediatric community nurses as independent practitioners

The emergence of PCNs as independent practitioners in their own right has been accompanied by a specific range of challenges, opportunities and skills. A client-led extended nursing role is leading the field in community nursing. PCNs have not sought such a role for its own sake, but have developed skills demanded by their clients' care and treatment needs (UKCC, 1992).

PCNs may possess skills hitherto considered the province of the medical practitioner and the paediatric unit, which may be far removed from the patient's home. Through the formation and implementation of agreed protocols, advanced competence and accountability have enabled PCNs to undertake complex infusion schedules based on variable dose and time scales; establish their own peripheral infusions; administer blood products; access and maintain implanted and tunnelled central venous lines for both blood sampling and other infusions; change gastrostomy and tracheostomy tubes; maintain ventilator-dependent children; supervise total parenteral nutrition; and set up tractions (Holden, 1991). Advanced nursing skills will be determined by the needs of their particular and vulnerable client group. Such roles are not without professional dilemmas, and the teaching and mentoring of less experienced practitioners must be conducted under the guidance of the leaders in the field of paediatric community nursing, many of whom are emerging as independent practitioners.

Acting as advocates for both the profession and their patients, they provide leadership through advocacy, negotiation and education – and by the example of their hands-on care practice. They are seen to be enablers, empowerers, facilitators and supporters of their peers and colleagues and are committed to the philosophy and value of home care. Ethical dilemmas and boundaries are continually evolving and challenge the quality and standards of care provided.

11.17 Stress

The content of a PCN's caseload and the nature of the role inevitably lead to stress. A PCN in a poorly-staffed scheme with little or no peer support is especially vulnerable. Such a scheme may comprise very ill children who would otherwise occupy the most hospital bed days; the majority of these children have life-limiting or life-threatening illnesses in the short, medium or long term. Inappropriate management and lack of support are encountered by some PCNs, who may also endure and function within unrealistic job descriptions. Stress is inevitable and most nurses are taught to handle it by trial-and-error learning. Burnout has been described as the disease of over-commitment. 'Sharing and discussing problems and potential solutions is not an admission of weakness but of strength' (Douglas, 1993). The management of personal stress levels must be effective and appropriate, and must be the responsibility of the PCNs themselves, or of those who work with or manage them (Douglas, 1993; Miller, 1992).

11.18 Education

Hospital is no longer regarded as the only primary learning environment for paediatric student nurses, whether they are registered sick children's nurses, Project 2000 child care nurses or community practitioner learners. Project 2000 child care nurses ostensibly have the skills needed to nurse children competently in the community but the majority have received very little practical experience with sick children in the community under the mentorship of qualified PCNs. Their syllabi reflect an interest in the subject but some of their reading lists lack relevant material and it is doubtful whether many of their tutors on this topic have a community and paediatric qualification. Placements with a PCN may vary from 4 days to 12 weeks.

The Project 2000 Child Branch does not as yet provide the theory, practice and rigour to enable the child care nurse to function effectively in a community nursing role, although evidence exists that it provides the foundation for the development of such expertise. PCNs are role models who should offer support and encouragement to enable students to develop the necessary expertise for competent practice. However, PCNs are not always equipped to facilitate student learning and support the student in an 'associate' role, as described by Muir (1993). Some PCNs do not hold a community qualification and very few have received formal instruction in teaching methods. Skeleton staffed schemes find that freeing time to support a student adds a further burden to their busy work schedule, and rarely is any extra staffing made available to release their time and skills.

Busy practitioners may be regularly requested to provide placements for students; this confronts them with the ethical dilemma of whether or not to take students repeatedly to visit key families where the student will gain the most valuable experience. This is in an attempt to compensate for short placements but places a burden on these already overstretched families. Families are sometimes only too willing to help, out of gratitude for their home care option, and must be protected from over-exposure to student placements. Students, whether Project 2000, shortened, conversion or traditional registered sick children's nurses, or (recently) degree or diploma entrants may therefore have brief and/or inadequate experience of paediatric community nursing.

PCNs require planned injections of resources to facilitate useful placements for students covering a time span which allows the student to gain a comprehensive overview together with 'hands on' experience (ENB, 1994).

PCNs have, as yet, only tenuous links with higher education but as the introduction of the UKCC's Standards for Education and Practice Following Registration (UKCC, 1994) become effective, these will be extended, as for other inclusive degree courses in community health care nursing, with inclusive paediatric modules.

Collaboration, imagination and cohesion between educational and service personnel have produced exciting courses enabling students to acquire posts in the community, and thus gain a credible and appropriate community nursing qualification. Until the existence of these courses, the only community qualification open to a paediatric nurse was the health visiting or district nursing certificate and diploma and neither of these provided education and clinical experience relevant to nursing sick children at home. Health visiting courses to not contain a sick child component and the majority of district nurse courses do not contain a paediatric component despite the recommendations contained within the ENB (1990) guidelines, which state that the structure and content of district nursing courses should 'allow registered sick children's nurses to pursue their particular interest in the care of sick children in both practical placements and theoretical study'. Many PCNs have obtained district nursing certificates and diplomas based on adult, and mainly elderly, care models. This road is still the only one available in many areas.

Future practitioners of paediatric community nursing will have access to a specialist education programme, but where does that leave the many RSCN nurses who have not had the opportunity to access such courses in their careers? How does this deficit assist associated health care professionals to develop a working understanding of the PCN which, it is hoped, will be achieved by the common core elements of the new community courses? How does the deficit help the necessary development of a skill mix within teams? This deficit will continue until a comprehensive national network of community children's nursing specialist courses with associated practice placements is facilitated. This in turn will produce a long-overdue national network of nurses caring for children in the community who are educated in paediatric and community care. In addition, practice nurses and mental handicap nurses undergoing community education require a paediatric input to ensure that children included in their caseload receive the appropriate care for their age group (Muir, 1993; Lindsay, 1993; Gastrell, 1993; UKCC, 1994; Sidey & Bent, 1994; ENB, 1990).

11.19 Professional development

Paediatric community nursing is specialist nursing designed to provide optimum and effective care and support for the sick child and the associated family. It is accepted as being beneficial for all involved, and as a uniquely developing service both in practice and education. PCNs have contributed to this development with their individuality, personalities and goodwill. Goodwill, however, is not enough in the absence of a corporate philosophy that ensures that paediatric community nursing does not fall into the traps of expansion at the price of extension or quantity at the cost of quality. Articulate, clinical leadership will channel the variety of developing schemes into a structural national network with common goals, whether they be community based or hospital sector based. Hospital based schemes, extending from the wards to the community, only succeed in the quality and value of their services if they are composed of appropriately educated, experienced, supervised and managed staff. Appropriately qualified PCN managers, while acknowledging service resource limits, will be the agents for change, supporting and leading their colleagues locally and nationally as this branch of paediatric nursing expands its research and education base.

Evolving lecturer/practitioner roles and established PCNs are at the forefront of the process of the design and implementation of skills and knowledge in the form of competences within accredited frameworks which rely on nationally recognized standards for practice. Political awareness by the profession will ensure that opportunities are seized within the new health care system and its community and child health services, to ensure that neither a two-tier nor a second rate service develops for children. Changing health care trends and needs demand proactive planning to determine skill and financial resources, appropriate grading, skill mix and staffing and realistic caseloads alongside income generation or funding strategies.

Associated Community Nurses and other professionals welcome integration, shared caring and mutually beneficial teaching programmes when facing and fearing the unknown. In some areas PCNs are working with their colleagues, particularly district nurses and health visitors, to provide teaching and shared care protocols. Nurse prescribing will be enhanced by such practice, ensuring that prescribing patterns for children are directed by or under the supervision of children's nurses.

11.20 Conclusion

The art and science of paediatric community nursing has had its cornerstone laid by the courage and commitment of sick children, their carers and their PCNs who had the vision and confidence to seek new horizons in paediatric nursing. PCNs are the practitioners and prescribers of care for the varying health care needs of this new population of sick children. Home care and treatment offer the patient quality of life when resources are used effectively. Children should be admitted to hospital only if the care they require cannot be provided at home (ENB, 1990).

11.22 References

Action for Sick Children (1993) *Caring for Children in the Health Services – Bridging the Gaps.* Action for Sick Children, London.

Anderson, P. (1993) European charter of children's rights. *Bulletin of Medical Ethics*, October 1993.

Atwell, J. & Gow, M. (1985) Paediatric trained district nurses in the community. *British Medical Journal*, **291**, 222–9.

Audit Commission (1993) *Children First.* HMSO, London.

Black, J. (1989) *Child Health in a Multicultural Society.* British Medical Association, London.

Bowlby, J. (1965) *Child Care and the Growth of Love.* Penguin Books, Harmondsworth.

Caremark (1994) *At Home* (sponsored by Caremark), Issue 7, February.

The Children Act (1989). DOH, HMSO, London.

Couriel, J. & Davies, P. (1988) Costs and benefit of a community special care baby service. *British Medical Journal*, **296**, 1043–6.

DHSS (1976) *The Court Report – Fit for the Future.* HMSO, London.

DOH (1991) *Welfare of Children and Young People in Hospital.* HMSO, London.

DOH (1994) *The Allitt Enquiry.* HMSO, London.

Douglas, J. (1993) *Psychology and Nursing Children.* Macmillan, London.

ENB (1990) *Regulations and guidelines for the approval of institutions and courses.* English National Board.

ENB (1994) Research Highlight. *An Evaluation of the Initial Preparation for Nurses Caring for Children in the Community in the Context of Services Needed and Provided.* English National Board for Nursing, Midwifery and Health Visiting, London.

Farrell, M. (1992) Partnership in care: paediatric nursing model. *British Journal of Nursing*, **1**(4).

Fradd, E. (1990) Setting up a paediatric community nursing service. *Senior Nurse*, **10**(7).

Gastrell, P. (1993) Diploma courses for paediatric community nurses. *Paediatric Nursing*, **5**(10), 13–14.

Hennessy, D. (1993) Purchasing paediatric community nursing care. *Paediatric Nursing*, **5**(2), 10–12.

Holden, C. (1991) Home parenteral nutrition. *Paediatric Nursing*, (supplement), April.

Kennelly, C. & Collins, P. (1991) Bridging the gaps. *Paediatric Nursing*, March, 9–10.

Lindsay, B. (1993) Fit for the community. *Paediatric Nursing*, **5**(2), 13–15.

Miller, S. (1992) The cost of caring. *Paediatric Nursing*, **4**(9), 15–16.

MOH (1959) *The Platt Report.* Central Health Services Council, HMSO, London.

Muir, J. (1993) Community based practice and education. *Paediatric Nursing*, **5**(7), 25–7.

Muller, D.J., Harris, P.J., Wattley, L. & Taylor, J.D. (1992) *Nursing Children. Psychology, Research and Practice.* Chapman and Hall, London.

RCN (1993) *Buying Paediatric Community Nursing.* RCN, London.

RCN (1995) *Directory of Paediatric Community Nursing Services.* RCN, London.

Robertson, J. (1989) *Separation and the very young.* Free Association Books, London.

Rutter, M. (1981) *Maternal Deprivation Reassessed.* Penguin Books, Harmondsworth.

Sidey, A. (1990) Co-operation in Care. *Paediatric Nursing,* 2(3), 10–12.

Sidey, A. (1993) *Paediatric community nursing.* Paper presented on 24 March 1993 at the Royal College of Nursing Conference in Northern Ireland.

Sidey, A. & Bent, J.E. (1994) *Paediatric community nursing. Making it happen.* Paper presented to National Association of Fundholding Practices/ Royal College of Nursing Conference, Brighton.

Slater, M. (1993) *Health for all our children.* Action for Sick Children, London.

Tatman, M. (1994) *Wise Decisions.* Scutari, Lodon.

UKCC (1992) *Standards of Record Keeping.* UKCC, London.

UKCC (1992) *The Scope of Professional Practice.* UKCC, London.

UKCC (1994) *The Future of Professional Practice – The Council's Standards for Education and Practice following Registration.* UKCC, London.

Whiting, M. (1988) *Community paediatric nursing in England in 1988.* MSc thesis, University of London.

Whiting, M. (1989) Community Care. In: *Ethics in Paediatric Nursing* (G.M. Brykczynska). Chapman & Hall, London.

Whiting, M. (1988) *Community paediatric nursing in England in 1988.* MSc thesis, University of London.

Whiting, M. (1994) Paediatric community nursing. Does it really save money. In: *At Home* (sponsored by Caremark), Issue 7, February.

Woodroffe, C. & Glideman, M. (1993) Trends in Child Health. *Children and Society,* 7(1), 49–63.

11.23 Further reading

British Paediatric Association (1992) *Community Child Health Services.* BPA, London.

Cleary, J. (1992) *Caring for Children in Hospital.* Scutari, London.

Davis, H. (1993) *Parents of Children with Chronic Illness or Disability.* British Psychological Society Books, Leicester.

DOH (1993) *A Vision for the Future.* HMSO, London.

DOH (1993) *The Health of the Nation.* HMSO, London.

Dryden, S. (1989) Professional respect. *Community care,* 2 February 1989.

Eiser, C. (1990) *Chronic Childhood Disease. An Introduction to Psychological Theory and Research.* Cambridge University Press, Cambridge.

Eiser, C. (1993) *Growing up with a chronic disease*. Jessica Kingsley Publishers, London.

Fradd, E. (1992) Working with Specialists. *Community Outlook*, June, 29–30.

Glasper, A. & Tucker, A. (1993) *Advances in Child Health Nursing*. Scutari, London.

McCarthy, F. (1986) A home discharge program for ventilator assisted children. *Paediatric Nursing*, **12**(5).

Miller, S. (1994) Disability in Asian communities. *Paediatric Nursing*, **6**(1), 16–18.

RCN Paediatric Community Nurses Forum (1991) Don't ignore the PCN. *Paediatric Nursing*, December, 21.

Richardson, J. & Edwards, J. (1993) Integrating services in community child care. *Nursing Standard*, **8**(7), 32–5.

Robottom, B. (1969) The contribution of the children's nurse to the home care of children. *British Journal of Medical Education*, **3**, 311–12.

Sidey, A. (1989) Intravenous home care. *Paediatric Nursing*, **1**(3), 14–15.

Sidey, A. (1991) The Management of Gastrostomies. *Paediatric Nursing*, **3**(7), 24–6.

UKCC (1991) *Report on Proposals for the Future of Community Education and Practice*. UKCC, London.

Wade, S. (1993) Making Sense of Models. *Journal of Community Nursing*, November, 20–26.

Whyte, D. (1992) A family approach to the care of a child with a chronic illness. *Journal of Advanced Nursing*, **17**, 317–27.

Chapter 12

Occupational Health Nursing

Occupational health nursing can be defined as the application of nursing principles in conserving the health of workers in all occupations. It has as its primary focus the health care and safety of the adult working population. Working adults are the essential backbone of the world's economy. Through organization and management of their labour, workers produce and distribute nearly all goods and services. Indeed, the years spent working cover the majority of most people's lives. Work starts on average at 16 years of age and finishes, again on average, when the worker reaches 60 plus. Occupational health nurses (OHNs), therefore, provide health care throughout a major part of a person's life.

To be an effective practitioner of occupational health nursing, it is necessary to reject some of the often-preconceived concepts of nursing and to adapt to the demands and constraints of a different discipline, operating in a very different environment. Many nurses have been educated within the ill-health and medical model continuum, and have been more concerned with the treatment of illness and cure rather than the prevention of ill health. Fortunately these concepts are changing and the nurse is now educated within the preventative health model. However, for many nurses entering occupational health for the first time, an almost 180° turn round in thinking has to be achieved, i.e. from the institutional model of patient care, treatment and cure to a workplace knowledge of occupation and the effects of that occupation on health. It follows, therefore, that an OHN's concerns must be the effect of work on health and the effect of health on work.

These concepts have been most effectively evoked within the Hanasaari Conceptual Model of occupational health nursing (see Fig. 12.1). This model was developed by senior occupational health nurses from both education and practice at a workshop in Hanasaari in the late 1980s. The four concepts of nursing combine to form a paradigm: the person receiving the care; the environment within which the person exists; the health/illness continuum

234

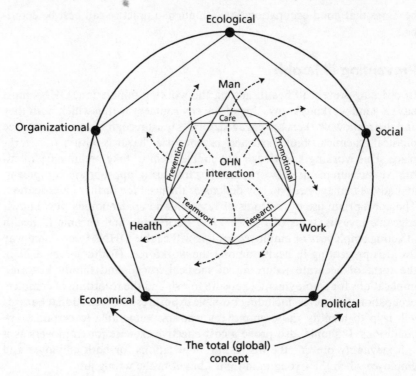

Fig. 12.1 The Hanasaari Model.

within which the person falls at the time of interaction with the nurse; and the nursing actions themselves. The relationship between man, work and health and the OHN, within the total global concept, is central to the philosophy of this model of nursing (Alston, 1990).

12.1 Contemporary practice

In the early 1990s the Society of Occupational Health Nursing of the Royal College of Nursing, established a working party to look at the key competencies and skills required for occupational health nursing. A series of leaflets under the *Good Health is Good Business* label have ensued, and the intention is that these will continue in order to encourage the occupational health nurse to initiate and maintain good practice. The first of the leaflets described the key elements of occupational health nursing as preventing ill-health; promoting health and safety; providing care; monitoring the environment; managing health provision and ensuring professionalism, quality and legal compliance (Forward Strategies Working Group, 1991). It is under these headings that good occupational health nursing practice can best be described.

Preventing ill health

In order to prevent ill health among the working population, OHNs must have a good working knowledge of the environment within which both they and their fellow workers are engaged. OHNs must recognize and evaluate the physical, chemical, biological and psychosocial hazards within the workplace. This working knowledge will enable them to take preliminary quantitative measurements of workplace hazards using appropriate equipment, and advise management on any deficits or the need for further investigation. The appropriate use of the tools of research and epidemiology plus knowledgeable investigations of outbreaks of both acute and chronic ill health affecting employees or employee groups will enable OHNs to go some way towards preventing ill health among the workforce. Health surveillance in the form of accurate recording of medical, social and family histories, implications for employment, exposure to risk and the recording of complete occupational histories, including possible exposures to occupational hazards will help to identify those employees who are vulnerable to certain work conditions. It should also prove a cost-effective exercise for employers as it will inevitably prevent the distressing implications for both employer and employee when the wrong man finds himself in the wrong job.

Providing OHNs have a good working knowledge of both working and environmental conditions within their sphere of work, they can provide individual employees with relevant health information on jobs or processes, the measures taken by employers to promote employees' health and the actions employees must take to protect their own health. In discussion with employees returning to work following sickness absence, the implications for employment, exposure to risks, fitness for special specified jobs and alternative jobs within the company can be explained and appropriate recommendations made to management.

Promoting health and safety

OHNs are advised to ensure they have the knowledge and ability to advise on the promotion of health and prevention of accidents and illness within the working population. It is essential that they are able to help employees to identify their own health needs and with the help of the occupational health team to develop appropriate programmes to meet these needs. The occupational health team, of which the nurse is an integral part, along with, for example, safety officers, hygienists, medical advisors, ergonomists and psychologists should, within the working environment, implement and evaluate health and safety policies and strategies and make recommendations to both employee and employer aimed at enhancing the quality and safety of the workplace.

Providing care

OHNs must ensure that they are competent in assessing the need for health surveillance and the planning, implementation and evaluation of health care programmes. In determining situations which may be hazardous to the health and well-being of workers, they must apply their knowledge in the provision of treatment for illness or injury. Counselling and support services for employees with problems are essential skills that OHNs must maintain. A knowledge of rehabilitation and help with resettlement into appropriate work, plus the co-ordination of occupational health care within the wider community's social and welfare provision, are also essential factors in the establishment and maintenance of efficient occupational health services.

Monitoring the environment

Part of the remit of OHNs is to assess and investigate the effects of the working environment on employees' health. In determining situations that may be hazardous to health, OHNs, within the remit of the occupational health team, must develop and implement programmes of appropriate control and evaluative measures in order to maintain an effective presence within the occupational health team. OHNs must also acquire the necessary knowledge to enable them to recognize those factors which contribute to and/or adversely affect the physical, mental and social well-being of employees.

Managing health provision

An employer who cares enough about the health and well-being of his workforce to provide an occupational health service has the right to expect that the OHN will provide effective management of the service. This will include the effective and efficient recording of data; awareness of the social and political factors relating to the health care of the working population and the confidential rights of clients; a knowledge of other professional groups and agencies that can assist employees with needs and problems; skills in enhancing effective communication and the fostering of interpersonal relationships and the application of those skills in the training of other occupational health personnel; the maintenance of effective and appropriate data systems which comply with Health and Safety legislation and the employer's legitimate policies/concerns and which enable research and epidemiological studies to ensue.

Ensuring professionalism, quality and legal compliance

OHNs must be able to analyse and interpret the law effectively in relation to occupational health care and practice and in so doing must ensure that professional responsibility and accountability are undertaken within the constraints and demands established by both legal and professional guidelines and statutes. They must ensure the provision of a quality occupational health service to employers and employees by the initiation and evaluation of health audits to determine needs in the assessment, formulation, planning and implementation of occupational health care programmes.

12.2 Job satisfaction

There are many settings within which OHNs work. One of the main attractions of occupational health nursing is its diversity of employment and employment situations. OHNs can find themselves working at one extreme in a heavy chemical or engineering factory and at another extreme in the large offices of an international banking organization, both of which are very different from the traditional role and location of nursing.

OHNs can find employment within public service industries such as health boards, NHS Trusts, the providers of electricity services or major airlines, for whom, on the same day, they can be caring for such diverse needs as those of office workers, flight personnel or aircraft maintenance employees. They can, for example, in the morning be wearing a duffle coat and hard hat while talking to mechanics, engineers and maintenance personnel on the shop floor, and in the afternoon, in more formal attire and surroundings, be discussing the problems of a 'sick building syndrome' with a group of office workers. One of the main attractions of occupational health nursing is that nurses are working for the major part of their day with well people. It is extremely important to have both job and role satisfaction while maintaining integrity and professionalism.

There have been many studies on the relationship between workroles, workrole values and job satisfaction and the subsequent implications for nurse retention. According to Geiger and Davit (1988) job satisfaction can be defined as the extent to which a nurse's felt needs are fulfilled by the job he or she performs. Kramer and Harper (1989) found that the greater the congruence in values the higher the nurse's participant scores were for job satisfaction and perceived productivity. Although no definitive research has been undertaken in job satisfaction and retention for OHNs, Lowis (1989) found that senior OHNs who had been in post for some time expressed satisfaction with their role, job and employer.

Lowis found that the nurses tended to remain in post with the same employer for longer periods than nurses working in the more traditional areas of nursing. While it was difficult to extract exact reasons for this phenomenon, those interviewed described feelings of being valued by both employer and employees and of finding real satisfaction in the esteem in which they were held mainly by the healthy working man. 'The satisfaction of preventing ill health amongst the well, rather than trying to effect a cure for the ill is immense,' said one senior occupational health nurse (Lowis, 1989).

12.3 Primary health care and the occupational health nurse

In 1974 the World Health Organization and UNICEF produced a joint report called *Primary Health Care* (WHO/UNICEF, 1974). This report defined primary health care as essential care based on practical, scientifically sound and acceptable methods in technology, made universally available to individuals and families in the community through their full participation and at a cost the community and country could afford and maintain at every stage of their development, in the spirit of self-reliance and self-determination. The definition went on to state that primary health care forms an integral part of both the country's health system, of which it is the central function and main focus, and of the overall social and economic development of that particular country. It is the first level of contact for individuals, the family and the community with the national health care systems, bringing health care as close as possible to where people live and work, and providing promotive, curative and rehabilitative services accordingly (WHO/UNICEF, 1974). The locus and focus of this definition was on where people live and work and suggests that primary care should be practised by health care professionals within the community, whether within the home or the workplace. The BMA Board of Science and Education suggested that the primary health care team (PHCT) should be composed of a nucleus of doctors, nurses, social workers and medical secretaries, with a conglomerate of experts supporting that nucleus (BMA, 1974).

The network needed to provide both formal and informal sources of help and support to meet health care needs is complex, but as the emphasis of the PHCT is on meeting the needs of the wider community both at work and within the home, it logically follows that GPs, occupational health physicians, health visitors, district nurses, community psychiatric nurses and OHNs should be part of the overall PHCT working together to care for the needs of the community.

It is universally accepted that a number of people presenting at GP surgeries or accident and emergency departments have the source of their illness/injury within the workplace. It is conceivable that many GPs, district nurses and health visitors have little or no idea of the conditions within which many of their clients spend most of their working lives. It therefore follows that when clients present with ill health, the health carers cannot expect to have a knowledge of the causes of that ill health if it is in fact work related. The revised syllabus of the General Medical Council for the education of student doctors now takes account of the working environment and includes a core module on occupational disease and the working environment. In 1992 the Health and Safety Executive explored the possibility of including occupational health advice as part of primary health care nursing education (Griffin, 1992). This advice has to a large extent been implemented in many community nursing programmes throughout the country and it is confidently expected that, as the move towards generic courses for community nurses with discipline specific integral modules proceeds, the PHCT focuses will expand to include those who care for people at work.

12.4 Management and professional development

To be effective an occupational health service must be, and be seen to be, independent of operational management and trade union industrial relation structures. This is not to imply that the service can operate irrespective of the needs and constraints of the organization, but rather that it must be seen to be divorced from the pressures leading to a 'bending of its advice to suit one side or the other in a confrontation' (Raper, 1991). At a time when industry is facing severe financial stresses, OHNs are under even more pressure than usual to prove their worth and survive in a company's climate that demands a payback and workplace effective deliverables.

OHNs must therefore provide the evidence that their contribution to the success of the company meets the bottom line cost of their department. This can only be achieved by effective management of an occupational health service by OHNs. There are numerous difficulties in proving the worth of the occupational health service; the inadequacy of systems of record keeping, inaccuracy in the compiling of statistics and the impossible task of evaluating perceived costs of absence all contribute to the dilemma. It is therefore essential to identify the value of the occupational health nursing service. This can only be achieved by demonstrating that it contributes to the organizational goals of the company and thereby ensures that the company's major functions are being fulfilled (for example, if a company uses a quality assurance philosophy, or complies with BS 5750, *British Standard Quality System Specification for Design/Development, Production, Installation and Service*, its occupational health nursing service must find a way of ensuring that its practice contributes to and features in the company's quality assurance programme). However, this is not without its problems. If an occupational health quality assurance programme is to be developed, it is committing itself to plan, monitor, evaluate and most importantly, report and declare its contribution to the company's organizational goals. Consequently, it is essential to develop quality assurance control and audit within an occupational health nursing service.

Quality assurance programmes must be introduced as a way of focusing the benefits of the Service to its organization. Kitson (1990) identified that no system can guarantee success, rather success has to be built in to the process of implementing and using a quality assurance system; and O'Mally (1992) stated that occupational health nursing has a solid base on which to construct quality assurance programmes, ie. the provision of its practice in industry is valued by the workforce. The quality journey from its concept to total quality management is inevitably a long one with many twists, turns and dead ends but OHNs with a consistency of purpose and the specialist knowledge that holds programmes together can succeed.

This paradigm has four constituents: communication, education, training and facilitation. O'Mally's conclusion is that the most essential of these is communication and if this is ineffective few initiatives will succeed (O'Mally, 1992). Professional development for OHNs must inevitably be linked to good management, which in turn is inevitably linked to good quality.

12.5 Legislation

OHNs must recognize that in many areas of their practice they have extended accountability. This responsibility and accountability is clearly identified in:

(1) the Health and Safety at Work Act 1974, which places a duty on an employer to ensure, so far as is reasonably practicable, the health, safety and welfare at work of all its employees; and
(2) the 1992 Code of Professional Conduct of the United Kingdom Central Council (UKCC), which states that each registered nurse, midwife and health visitor shall act always in such a way as to promote and safeguard the well-being and interests of patients and clients.

Professional accountability also has to be justified within an organization's culture, rules and regulations. It is essential therefore that OHNs develop policy related to their work within the organization. That policy gives licence to OHNs to explain and justify their actions.

The Royal College of Nursing, when commenting on occupational health nursing services, states that the role of OHNs is not a static one confined by a list of tasks or duties. The fundamental principles governing the role are concerned with prevention of disease and injury, promotion of health and the alleviation of suffering. The RCN goes on to state that, in discharging these responsibilities, OHNs must be conscious of the need to observe the codes of professional conduct and the guidance notes produced to accompany the various clauses, and to work within and to the various government acts intended to ensure the health, safety and welfare at work of all employees (RCN, 1991).

A sound working knowledge of nursing legislation is an integral part of basic nurse education that is reinforced in all post-registration courses. The UKCC regularly informs those nurses on its register of the necessity to have knowledge of, and adhere to, nursing legislation. However, OHNs must acquire the specialist work-related knowledge found within the various government Acts in order to practise in a safe, competent and professional manner. Knowledge of workplace Health and Safety legislation promotes and encourages the application of that legislation to occupational health nursing practice and provides opportunities for professional development. OHNs should be familiar with all workplace legislation but in particular a thorough knowledge of the following statutory instruments is essential to ensure safe practice.

Control of Substances Hazardous to Health Regulations (COSHH) (1988)

These regulations apply to virtually all work in which people are exposed, or are liable to be exposed, to substances hazardous to health. They seek to control exposure to hazardous substances which arise out of, or in connection with, work. They have seven principal aims:

- to maintain and improve existing standards of health and safety in relation to work involving substances hazardous to health;
- to simplify the existing law and consequently the task of employers and employees in complying with it and of inspectors enforcing it;
- to provide one set of regulations covering substances hazardous to health, including those not specifically covered by any existing provision or covered only where they occur in factories;
- to set clear objectives which will be cost-effective by matching precaution to the risk involved;
- to provide a suitable framework for implementing existing and future EC Directives on worker protection;
- to enable the government to ratify ILO Convention 139 on carcinogenic substances;
- to repeal or revoke wholly or partially legislation which is no longer relevant.

The main duties imposed on the employer and, where applicable, on OHNs by the COSHH Regulations are:

- assessment of risk;
- assessment of steps needed to meet the requirements of the Regulations;

- prevention or control of exposure;
- ensuring that controls are properly used and maintained;
- examination and testing of control measures;
- informing, instructing and training employers;
- monitoring the exposure of employees and ensuring the health surveillance of those employees at risk.

(Adapted from HSE–COSHH: An Open Learning Course, 1992.)

Reporting of Injuries, Diseases and Dangerous Occurrences Regulations (RIDDOR) (1985)

These regulations also apply to virtually all areas of work activity and represent the UK's system for incident reporting. Areas currently not covered by these Regulations, e.g. the offshore oil industry and British Rail, will be brought on-line in 1995 when revised Regulations are introduced.

The Regulations require the reporting 'in certain cases by the quickest practicable means, e.g. by telephone' to the authority responsible for enforcing the Health and Safety at Work Act 1974 at the premises where the incident occurred:

- for workplaces such as factories, building sites and farms – the Health and Safety Executive;
- for workplaces such as offices, shops and restaurants – the Environmental Health Department.

Any disease, injury or dangerous occurrence is covered under the Act and records of every incident reported must be maintained in accordance with RIDDOR regulations.

Management of Health and Safety Regulations (1992)

These Regulations set out broad duties which apply to almost all work activities in the UK. They are aimed mainly at improving health and safety management and can be seen as explicating what is required of employers under the Health and Safety at Work Act 1974. The main provisions are designed to encourage a more systematic and better organized approach to dealing with health and safety matters. OHNs would be advised to consider how best they can apply these regulations to better their practice and improve their professional development. Figure 12.2 shows a schematic approach to achieving these goals.

OHNs would also be advised, when studying how best to apply the total concepts of Health and Safety legislation to workplace mapping, to consider

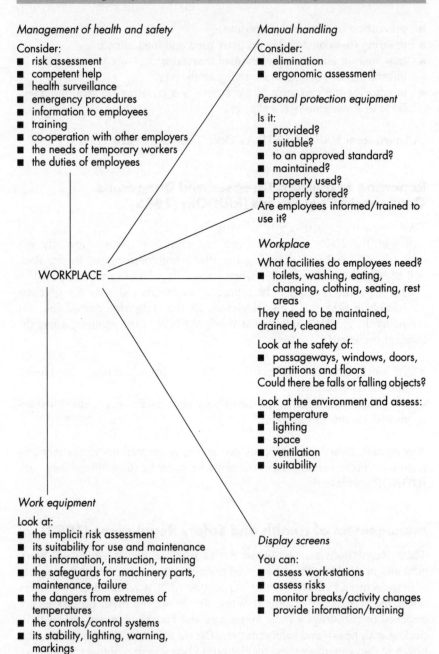

Management of health and safety

Consider:
- risk assessment
- competent help
- health surveillance
- emergency procedures
- information to employees
- training
- co-operation with other employers
- the needs of temporary workers
- the duties of employees

WORKPLACE

Manual handling

Consider:
- elimination
- ergonomic assessment

Personal protection equipment

Is it:
- provided?
- suitable?
- to an approved standard?
- maintained?
- property used?
- properly stored?

Are employees informed/trained to use it?

Workplace

What facilities do employees need?
- toilets, washing, eating, changing, clothing, seating, rest areas

They need to be maintained, drained, cleaned

Look at the safety of:
- passageways, windows, doors, partitions and floors

Could there be falls or falling objects?

Look at the environment and assess:
- temperature
- lighting
- space
- ventilation
- suitability

Work equipment

Look at:
- the implicit risk assessment
- its suitability for use and maintenance
- the information, instruction, training
- the safeguards for machinery parts, maintenance, failure
- the dangers from extremes of temperatures
- the controls/control systems
- its stability, lighting, warning, markings

Display screens

You can:
- assess work-stations
- assess risks
- monitor breaks/activity changes
- provide information/training

Fig. 12.2   A schematic approach to achieving health and safety goals. (Forward Strategies Working Group, 1993).

a hierarchical system of legislation. When studied in the manner presented in Fig. 12.3, the applications of preventative ill health and positive health promotion strategies to the care of those at work are simplified.

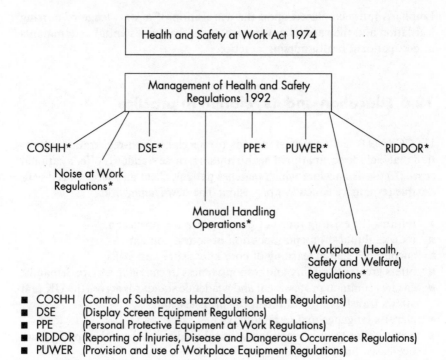

■ COSHH (Control of Substances Hazardous to Health Regulations)
■ DSE   (Display Screen Equipment Regulations)
■ PPE   (Personal Protective Equipment at Work Regulations)
■ RIDDOR (Reporting of Injuries, Disease and Dangerous Occurrences Regulations)
■ PUWER (Provision and use of Workplace Equipment Regulations)

* Examples of supporting acts/regulations

Fig. 12.3 Hierarchy of legislation

It therefore follows that within the field of practice, OHNs working within stated legislative procedures, are individually accountable for their decisions, actions and standards of practice. They can and should, therefore, be held liable for their activity if it can be demonstrated that they have failed to apply the expected skills or achieve the level of competence required, or have undertaken activities for which they are not trained. All OHNs must ensure that they have:

■ acquired the necessary occupational health nurse education and training, recognized by the Statutory Bodies for Nursing, Midwifery and Health Visiting (UK Central Council for Nursing, Midwifery and Health Visiting; and four National Boards for England, Scotland, Wales and Northern Ireland);

- acquired the appropriate skills for specialist practice; and
- ensured the maintenance of competence by periodic professional refreshment and retraining.

Emphasis must be placed upon the acquisition of a knowledge of nursing legislation and the various government Acts that are essential determinants of occupational health nursing practice.

12.6 Education and its relation to practice

UKCC (1994) has set new standards for specialist post-registration education that include occupational health nursing; these standards offer a rational cost-effective framework which matches patient, client and service need with flexible responsive education provision. The new framework:

- reforms the existing range of post-registration provision;
- reduces duplication and repetition of course content;
- encourages shared learning of core knowledge and skills;
- offers greater flexibility and responsiveness to changing service demands;
- ensures common professional and academic standards across the UK and allows transferability of credit for prior learning;
- clarifies language and terminology;
- ensures that teachers maintain clinical credibility through explicit practice-based links.

Within this general framework there is provision for very specific objectives that OHNs must achieve in order to become competent practitioners. Good practice must at all times drive education but in order to achieve a high degree of professional practice OHNs must have insight into those specific educational objectives that provide for a sound and safe practitioner.

Correct analysis of the theoretical content of occupational health nursing education and its application to clinical nursing practice is the core objective of the educative process. This is complemented by an understanding of the influence of social and cultural factors on life experiences and opportunities and a proper interpretation of social policy and theory to enhance the practice of nursing within the workplace.

In every workplace there exist special groups of people – e.g. ethnic minorities, the young, the elderly and the disabled. Along with everyone else, these workers have special needs. It is the OHNs duty to identify these health needs and design health promotion and ill health prevention programmes to suit the specific needs of individuals, cohort groups and workplace communities. These programmes should include:

- health screening – which must relate specifically to identified work-related hazards and generally to normal working requirements;
- disaster and emergency planning, including emergency treatment and evacuation procedures;
- health promotion related to the positive and negative determinants of health, both general lifestyle and work-related health hazards;
- the interpretation and application of Health and Safety legislation with particular regard for the environment and the well-being and protection of those who work, and the wider community.

Research is essential to good practice. Occupational health nursing currently lacks a sound reflective research base. Skills of critical evaluation are necessary to stimulate an enquiring, analytical and creative approach to occupational health nursing. In order to study health-related problems encountered in their working environment OHNs must learn and practise research skills. These will enable them to respond to changing health needs; assess, analyse and identify possible contributory factors to a problem; and critically evaluate the advantages and disadvantages of both epidemiological and clinical approaches to health disorders.

The standards which the nursing profession sets for its practitioners, both within education and practice, and the control which it exercises over their implementation are the means by which the quality of nursing is assured. This statement must be held true for all branches and avenues of nursing. Occupational health nursing is no exception.

12.7 References

Alston, R. (1990) The Hanasaari Conceptual Model. In: *Working at Health* (B. Friend), *Nursing Times*, **18**(16), 21.

BMA (1974) *Primary Health Care Teams*. British Medical Association Board of Science and Education, London.

Forward Strategies Working Group (1991) *Good Health is Good Business*. RCN, London.

Forward Strategies Working Group (1993) *Opportunities for Developing Professional Practice*. RCN, London.

Geiger, J.W. & Davit, J.S. (1988) Self-image and job satisfaction in varied settings. *Nursing Management*, **19**(2), 50–6.

Griffin, N. (1992) *Occupational Health Advice as Part of Primary Health Care Nursing*. Health and Safety Executive, London.

Health and Safety Executive (1992) *COSHH – An Open Learning Course*. HSE, London.

Kitson, A. (1990) One way to quality. *Nursing Standard Supplement – Quality Assurance Network Newsletter*, **5**(9), 57 (insert).

Kramer, M. & Harper, L.P. (1989) Shared values: impact on nurse job satisfaction and perceived productivity. *Nursing Research*, **38**, 172–7.

Lowis, C.A. (1989) *Expertise and attributes of occupational health nurses.* MEd thesis, University of Aberdeen.

Raper, J. (1991) *Professional accountability and the occupational health nurse.* Course Paper for the BA in Community Health Nursing–Occupational Health Nursing. The Robert Gordon University, Aberdeen.

RCN (1991) *Occupational Health Nursing Services: A Handbook for Employers and Nurses.* Scutari, London.

WHO/UNICEF (1974) *Primary Health Care: A Joint Report.* WHO, Geneva.

UKCC (1994) *The Future of Professional Practice – The Council's Standards for Education and Practice Following Registration.* UKCC, London.

Chapter 13

Community Mental Health Nursing

Once upon a time there was a strange creature called a 'keeper' who rattled keys, distributed cascara and looked after people in large, lock-up institutions called asylums. This mortal has been made redundant and been replaced by the cult of the supermodel, the community mental health nurse (CMHN) and his or her attendants, the promotion of mental health and the provision of psychotherapeutic care at individual, family, community and global levels.

CMHNs 'reside' in health clinics, voluntary organizations and accident and emergency departments. Indeed, they will work from any base giving them easy access to people who are suffering from mental health problems. They practise a wide variety of therapies ranging from behavioural psychotherapy and grief counselling to psychodynamic psychotherapy, relaxation and visualization.

One of the primary aims of this new model of CMHN must be political – though specifically non-aligned, and concerned only with advancing the twin causes of freedom and justice. CMHNs must have the courage to take on parties or institutions, irrespective of size or power, and confront key issues in the public arena. They must promote the cause of their clients. Their raison d'être is to represent the mentally ill (as well as issues about mental health), whose cause is routinely forgotten or swept under the rug.

There is no such a thing as an 'introverted' CMHN. They need to be heard, to stand up and be counted, and they must be almost vocational. They must be prepared to take risks and face ostracism. The new model of CMHN is brave, intellectual, articulate and moral; he or she cares.

The greatest enemy of this new model of CMHN is complacency. In order to maintain their integrity and viewpoint CMHNs must exercise superhuman vigilance. Community mental health nursing is essentially a matter of compromise. To enter the practice arena with fixed ideas is asking for trouble. The dangers of alignment to definitive dogmas related to the provision of care, specific models of nursing care or concrete practice methodologies threaten nurses at every turn. Steering between these obstacles is a lonely business.

Both society and the nursing profession need this new model of CMHN to demythologize mental ill health. CMHNs offer high quality therapeutic care founded on a code of professional practice (UKCC, 1992). Being accountable to that code gives nurses licence to enhance and own a personal practice methodology which is unique to each individual nurse's style and personhood.

The primary objectives of community mental health nursing are:

(1) to empower people and communities by restoring their sense of personal worth and dignity; and
(2) to take on authority by advocating proactively on behalf of a forgotten class: the mentally ill, and their carers.

Five defining characteristics underpin the professional practice of community mental health nursing:

■ a guiding paradigm;
■ therapeutic presence;
■ the therapeutic encounter;
■ the principles of community mental health nursing;
■ a systematic needs-based approach to practice.

The fundamental portrait of the CMHN as a reflective practitioner (Schön, 1983) is succinctly interwoven into each of the distinct characteristics. Moreover, these fundamental aspects are not displayed in order of priority. They are operationalized continuously and simultaneously. It is their dynamic combination in practice which illustrates the distinctive nature of community mental health nursing.

13.1 A guiding paradigm

The fundamental concepts involved in community mental health nursing are to respect, value and facilitate the self-propelling and self-generating growth unique within each individual (Rogers, 1990). For CMHNs the adoption of a person-valuing paradigm can serve as a means of utilizing systematically the powerful healing forces both within and between individuals, families, groups and nations.

This paradigm offers an invitation to expand and shift from the hierarchical models of nursing care that are currently in vogue. These models are based mainly on theoretical configurations of the notions of Menzies-Lyth

(1959) on institutional defence mechanisms and the concept of the nurse as a 'knowledgeable doer' (UKCC, 1988). A person-valuing paradigm necessitates the use of a co-participative, person-centred perspective of a nurse *being with* and *for* the individual who is in need of mental health care.

Utilizing this person-valuing paradigm as a therapeutic modality enables the psyche in its totality to be taken into account, including its innate and powerful potential for creativity, growth and healing. At individual level this therapeutic modality is grounded in the belief that the person/client holds the key to the healing process. At community level, the use of a person-valuing paradigm as a guide to practice is based on the ideology that the knowledge required for essential mental-health-giving properties and nutrients rests, sometimes dormant, within the residents of that community.

The three-dimensional nurse

The authors of Project 2000 (UKCC, 1988), the document which outlines proposed far-reaching changes in nurse education, emphatically stress that, while nurses must remain practical people, their practice must be based on more than the knowledge currently offered. While this emphasis on the two dimensions of *knowing* and *doing* seems to be a very reasonable foundation on which to build the future of nursing it also seems to explain very well the busyness in which nurses are so often involved. The externally imposed requirement to be busy is very soon internalized by many nurses, especially in today's political climate. It is also evident that by emphasizing the *knowing* and the *doing* in ideal, futuristic nursing, a third and most important therapeutic dimension of nursing, namely *being*, seems to have been entirely neglected.

Being as a therapeutic experience

At an individual level, *being with* and *caring for* the person is both a valuable and therapeutic experience (Travelbee, 1971; Leininger, 1978; Benner, 1984; Watson, 1985). It emphasizes the role of the nurse as caring for the person with an illness. The person-valuing paradigm demands that community mental health nurses understand and make sense of the self through listening, exploration, clarification and interpretation rather than by observing and explaining illnesses and behaviours. The person-valuing paradigm suggested here has its foundations in, and was developed from, a synthesis of Parse's theory of human becoming (Parse, 1992), Rogers' human science perspective of a unitary human being (Rogers, 1980) and existential phenomenology (Heidegger, 1987; Merleau-Ponty, 1974; Satre, 1969).

This paradigm advocates that nursing is a profession with a primary emphasis based on the concept of care and on valuing people. Working with and caring for another human being using this person-valuing paradigm also involves more than just *being with* and valuing the subjective and complex world of the person and therefore his or her problems and needs. CMHNs must be competent to encourage, motivate and facilitate individuals and groups to get in touch with their inner resources, strengths, potentials and beauty. Such inner qualities can invigorate and liberate tremendously powerful healing forces.

13.2 Therapeutic ambience

Healing work of this nature should be carried out within a therapeutic ambience marked by a high degree of emotional nourishment and containment for feelings (expressed and repressed), acceptance, genuine concern for and openness to sharing. The person-valuing paradigm paradoxically implies that mental health is also embroiled in the process of 'becoming' (Rogers, 1990). Mental health is engrained into each individual's chosen way of living, and cherished ideals; and into the way in which he or she works at becoming a free spirit, an autonomous person (Mills, 1986); and at the same time, of believing oneself to be part of and concerned for the general community and a wider universe of people.

Mental health, therefore, leads to a true value of life, people and all living species, including planetary health and the health of future generations (Long & Chambers, 1993). Mental health is profoundly featured in each person's own experience of both valuing and living in their internal and external world; and this can be made known to the nurse only by personal description. Herein lies the complexity, quality and richness of the process of community mental health nursing.

This intangible human richness rests mainly in the life experiences of those people potentially or actually in need of help. Richness is woven into the fabric of their perceptions of their life histories. It is evident in the pain of loss and abuse, and in people's capacity as human beings to hope for something better. It is observed in their struggle to achieve truth and to gain meaning for their very existence.

Personal profiles of the worst horrors of unhappy lives should not blind narrators to the enrichment that may occur in personal suffering, paining and distress. Given time, during therapy and between each therapeutic encounter, the client may come to recognize that mental ill health is frequently a teacher. Consequently, he or she may come to see the liberating effects of life's experiences and subsequently develop abilities to preserve the fruits of that liberation, whether in expanded creativity, enhanced insight or a subtle, internal reordering of personality.

It is imperative that CMHNs master the ability to show their clients that they value, and convey accurate empathy with, the latters' communicated expressions of woundedness, felt helplessness and experiences of pain and distress. Coupled with this, CMHNs must demonstrate the ability and confidence to listen authentically, explore, clarify and interpret the immediate experiencing that occurs during each therapeutic encounter (Rogers, 1977). This is an empowering process. The use of a person-valuing paradigm as a basis on which to build practice methodology demands that nurses actually believe that each person is a unique being within the social context of each experience as it is lived (Heidegger, 1992).

13.3 Becoming a mirror image for the person

The journey into and through mental ill health, the healing process and recovery have been needed by many well known human beings, for example St. Augustine (cited in Assagoli, 1977), and currently by others less famous, like ourselves, emphasizing the sometimes tenuous but quintessential connections to life's meaning and purpose (Rogers, 1961).

To achieve a successful outcome and recovery the client must observe descriptions of lived experiences and personal histories of paining and distress being validated in the caring eyes of a nonjudgemental nurse who demonstrates empathy with, mutuality, genuineness and concern for the other person, namely that client. This dynamic, circular, therapeutic encounter corresponds consistently with the move to finally understanding and accepting a person-valuing paradigm. Community mental health nursing begins from within the essence of the person/client. Moreover, as catalysts for healing and change, nurses must rely upon the client for the direction, pace and movement of the healing process (Rogers, 1961).

For community mental health nurses this 'paradigm shift' promotes an enlarged insight into and understanding of the quality of life or world view, from the person's perspective. It is also important to note the fundamental concept that people in general do not respond to reality but to their perceptions of reality, and that there are as many perceptions of reality as there are people (Rogers, 1990).

13.4 Providing a new focus of care: shifting the power base

Shifting to a new person-valuing paradigm as a guide to practice means more than adding to or replacing current ideologies. It presents a formula for changing the top-down theoretical force and direction of nursing models which underlie present-day mental health nursing practice (Reed & Robbins, 1991). Basically, such models attempt to give nursing care rationally by assessing patients' needs or problems and then planning nursing care to meet those needs. This method is now widespread. It can become highly ritualized, and it may bear little relationship to the person's actual needs as he or she perceives them. Indeed, occasionally nursing care planned as the result of using such models tries to pin nursing down and can bring completely inappropriate results. Completing a nursing care plan becomes more important than an exploration and interpretation of the dynamics that are going on in the 'here and now' encounter or the nurse/client relationship. An unacknowledged part of this sort of mechanical, 'professional knows best' form of nursing care is the way in which it is psychotherapeutic and also the way it can fail to be so.

The conventional relationship between the nurse and the 'patient' in Western culture in the last 40 years or so, has been that of parent/child; top dog/underdog; doer/receiver; knowledgeable/uninformed. The burden of nurses doing things to people bears its own stress sooner or later and results in nurses forming a psychological distance between themselves and clients. Some adaptive coping mechanisms used by nurses include withdrawal and noninvolvement; opting for an authoritarian point of view; repressing the emotions which accompany the development of a relationship; not allowing the dying process to occur as an expected phenomenon which should be as free from fear as possible; or taking a dehumanizing stance towards the patient who becomes the chronic 'schizophrenic' or the hopeless and hapless 'alcoholic' in Villa 15. Yet, if effective, high-quality mental health nursing and the promotion of mental health and well-being are to be embraced and mastered, practice methodology must be based on valid theories and an understandable paradigm which is grounded solidly in the experiences of both its enthusiasts and its 'naysayers'.

A person-valuing paradigm, because of its integral, unifying, community and global aspects, seems an ideal foundation on which to build the practice methodology of community mental health nursing. The Code of Professional Conduct (UKCC, 1992) allows nurses to develop a unique, individualized style of practice based on the person-valuing paradigm. This gives CMHNs the freedom to work in co-participation with clients and the community. Consequently, the top/down, nurse/patient relationship needs to be markedly altered. Indeed, it may even be true to say that mental health nursing is at a preparadigmatic stage of professional development.

Decision making

Some established practitioners may find difficulty accepting with comfort, much less enthusiasm, the decisions, questions, suggestions and feelings put forward by their clients. Others, having come to the new person-valuing relationship in one way or another, actually find it a relief as they are no longer alone in being responsible for, and making decisions about, their clients' lives and consequently their health and treatment. The participation of the client in the decision-making process has been helpful in changing the image of health practitioners as gods on pedestals holding the choices of life and death over patients.

Continuing with this line of reasoning, the argument for a change in direction to a person-valuing perspective which places the client and his or her world (as he or she perceives it) centre stage is advanced by the assertion (Phillips, 1987) that shifting paradigms produces a whole new view of the world and a whole new set of puzzles. This scholarship debate, however, enables theorists and practitioners alike, to explore what community mental health nursing is and, more importantly, what it could be.

13.5 Learning from the natural sciences

Kuhn (1970) eloquently portrays this shift through acknowledging changing paradigms in the natural sciences using Newton, Maxwell and Einstein, who moved outside the 'normal' parameters of science to explore and examine new theories and also to compete with other schools of thought. They all eschewed the treadmill in favour of their own egotistic, mercurial and assertive theoretical suppositions. Scientific thinking, however, does remain very valuable because it has served society and nursing so well.

Indeed, many of the professions' advances appear to be largely as a result of scientific thinking and the problem-solving technique. There are, however, limitations and weaknesses involved in over-adherence to the scientific method. Life becomes very dull when people, such as CMHNs and their clients, are afraid to take risks or to be spontaneous, and are denied the right to believe in anything, even themselves, unless such behaviours have been fully tested.

Mental health is not a theory; like life itself, it has to be lived. Moreover, if nurses are always looking for the causes, clinical features and diagnosis of certain mental health problems, this may hinder them from experiencing the reality and richness of clients' unique perceptions or exploring, clarifying and interpreting the meaning of the 'here and now' therapeutic encounter.

Furthermore, looking for one cause for a particular mental health problem or life experience can lead to simplistic thinking because there may in fact be more than one reason for any itemized behaviour. In the final analysis such erroneous thinking is hardly scientific. It is obvious, then, that scientific thinking can slip up on occasion and this may be especially evident when championing the need for a paradigm shift which shows that CMHNs actually do accept all individuals *as they are* and not as they, the nurses, would like them to be. Bartjes (1991), cited in Gray and Pratt (1991), asked the question:

'Do nurses see patients/clients as they really are and know them in their reality, or do nurses see patients/clients merely as a projection of their own theories of what human beings should be?'

CMHNs differ from other nurses in some fundamental ways. They do not *fix*. They do not *do* something to make things or people better. They do not talk *to* people. They are knowledgeable *beings*. As such, they respect and value each individual. They do this in the awareness that *being with* and *for* the person and valuing his or her perceptions of self-lived experiences is not a learned response but a process of *becoming* for both individuals concerned. This therapeutic approach takes time and emerges and develops incrementally as experience and knowledge are acquired and consolidated.

13.6 Self-monitoring

In view of these humanistic, esoteric, and essential health-giving and life-nurturing dimensions, CMHNs must come to believe that they, too, possess essential life-affirming and health-giving inner strengths and resources including the human quality to care. They too need to continue to develop and grow as persons and as professionals. Because of this, they should be facilitated to believe that they are self-actualizing people with a need to further enhance this human capacity to care (Heidegger, 1992).

In addition, they must be provided with the skills and opportunities to become open and genuine, self-monitoring, self-reflective and self-receptive people. This goal may be achieved through the belief in the adoption of structured, sensitive, clinical supervision. Supervision is not merely about choosing from a menu of approaches. It is important to have a unifying concept that integrates the supervisor's own approach and makes the supervision more than the application of a technique or methodology (Hawkins & Stohet, 1989).

The adoption of a new person-valuing paradigm challenges nurses to adopt a practice methodology which respects and prizes all people, their individual perceptions of their internal worlds and their lived experiences. CMHNs are primarily catalysts for healing and change.

This humanistic paradigm rejects logical positivism, the natural science perspective that previously informed nursing and was based on the notion that people can be reduced to components or 'sick parts' with the subsequent effect of labelling the patient with a medical diagnosis. Logical positivism purports that knowledge is derived from hypoticodeductive methods which are objective and verifiable and views the world from a cause-and-effect perspective. The influence of this knowledge was thought to enable nurses to understand how people functioned and consequently the practice of nursing based on this belief was mainly about 'fixing' those assessed, unwell components and doing procedures *on* and *to* patients. The reductionist approach advocated by logical positivism fails in its consideration of the whole person including the internal and external forces that impact on, and at times control, people's lives.

13.7 Therapeutic presence

Community mental health nursing in its uniqueness attributes precedence to the interpersonal, dynamic process of enabling individuals, families and nations to restore equilibrium between their internal and external worlds (Long & Chambers, 1993). Through therapeutic use of self the nurse embraces the concept of self to influence all therapeutic approaches to care (DHSS NI, 1993).

Implicit in this concept is the belief that a nurse's therapeutic presence has a complex role to play in the promotion of healing and in the recovery process – in liberating self-propelling growth and recovery in clients. The unique attributes of the CMHN, coupled with the salience of what he or she says, feels, thinks and believes, when accepted and introjected, can lead to clients internalizing a positive experience of self. *Being with* and *for* clients is the quintessential health-giving way in which CMHNs can meet the psychotherapeutic needs of clients.

It is obligatory, therefore, that CMHNs are afforded an opportunity for self-exploration about who and what the self is before coming to an appreciation of the nature and use of self as a therapeutic catalyst. Therapeutic presence is that personal knowledge, understanding and awareness of the self in the psychotherapeutic encounter. Being sensitive to and aware of these felt experiences can be used by nurses as barometers for feedback about self and also about the client with whom the nurse is interacting (Galyin, cited in Miller, 1989).

Personal reflections and thoughts about identified, internal feelings may enhance or inhibit the nurse's verbal response and capacity to *be* with the client. Consequently, the nurse either invites or suppresses the client's expression of painful thoughts, feelings and emotions.

Three critical incidents of such experiences are cited in order to humanize the very complex and fascinating concepts involved.

Critical Incident One

Nurse A had difficulty containing a client's painful thoughts and feelings about her mother, whom she then hated. Nurse A had no mother and envied the client for having one. In her mind she believed that if she did have a mother she certainly would not hate her.

Critical Incident Two

Nurse B listened very carefully to a woman saying she had just had an abortion. On reflection, Nurse B felt a personal sense of grief and sadness as he was gay and knew he would never father a child. He was angry with his client and wondered how she could do this when he could have fostered her child.

Critical Incident Three

Nurse C remained openly attentive while a woman informed her that she had been sexually abused by her father as a child. She had known that someday she would hear these words and had secretly speculated about how she would deal with them. That day arrived and because of her own paining she could not hear what the client had to say. Therefore she could not contain her client's painful feelings, nor could she respond appropriately.

Planning how to deal with disclosures through the medium of knowledge, wonder or speculation works only in the mind. Such mental scripts rarely work in the here-and-now encounter. Nurses are not thesbians. They cannot theorize or plan how to feel. Feelings do not lie.

Community mental health nursing is an interactive process and as such its primary purpose is to restore clients' dignity and worth as healthy, unique human beings. Both the CMHN and the client are human beings first. Both possess given, individual variances: all the characteristics and attributes of being human. In this very real sense, both the client and the nurse are equal, yet each is unique in individual expression of these characteristics. This has implications for the interactions that occur in the nurse/client relationship and also for the pace and direction of the healing work.

Watson (1985) believes that nurses are beginning to develop a new consciousness regarding the centrality of caring within the nurse/client relationship. Nursing is beginning to raise new questions about what it means to be a nurse; to be mentally ill; to approach death; to be caring; to appreciate and begin to understand the lived experience of clients with acute or chronic mental ill health.

The quintessential tenet of the nurse/client relationship is therapeutic communication. It is a two-way process. Communication embraces the notions of giving and receiving, opening up, reflecting and responding (Hargie & Dickson, 1989). Working within a therapeutic encounter, communication also involves *empathic being* and having an ability to invite, 'staying with', containing and interpreting a client's painful thoughts and emotions, and thus helping the person to work through distressing experiences. Keltner *et al.* (1991) believe that:

> 'Therapeutic communication relies on client disclosure of personal and sometimes painful feelings, with the professional at an emotional distance, near enough to be involved but objective enough to be helpful.'

Consequently, if nurses are to use the self as a therapeutic catalyst, it is essential that emotions and thoughts such as those highlighted in the critical incidents are identified and worked through. Self-awareness is essential in order to gain insight about whether clients in general, specific clients or isolated events trigger off the nurse's own unresolved experiences and feelings. Stuart and Sundeen (1983) have said that:

'Nurses' unresolved conflicts about authority, sex, assertiveness and independence will tend to create, rather than solve problems.'

Unexamined life histories, coupled with unexplored and unresolved feelings in nurses, may render them unable to stay with and contain clients' painful thoughts and feelings. When this happens, a nurse's presence is no longer that of a catalyst for healing and recovery. A potential therapeutic agent, she/he becomes instead contaminated and atherapeutic.

Moreover, when this occurs, nurses may begin to 'act out' their personal histories of 'paining and despair' through the experiences of their clients. It is important to realize that sometimes clients are more in touch with their feelings and thoughts than are nurses. Likewise, clients may quickly realize that the nurse is the one who cannot stay with and contain certain distressing emotions. The outcome is such for the client that he or she may, once again, withdraw into social isolation, refusing to open up and share painful experiences. This in turn, reinforces the concept of, perhaps lifelong, mistrust (Erikson, 1979). Clients who do this may continue to bottle up or repress painful feelings and thoughts, and literally cause additional suffering to themselves and to others.

Alternatively, roles may be reversed and clients may end up nursing the nurse, through guilt and in the knowledge that distressing, painful emotions have been stirred up in the nurse.

CMHNs must be clear in their own minds about what they expect and what they can realistically offer to clients in terms of therapeutic use of self. They may discover they are incapable of inviting and containing the in-depth sharing of distressing experiences and the verbal and nonverbal expressions of accompanying painful emotions. Moreover, they may regard such sharing as either too personally paining or feel that *they* have caused the client further suffering. In reality, however, the sharing, exploration and reflection on such experiences, thoughts and feelings will help clients accept that the expression and feeling of emotions is healing in itself (Wittenberg, 1970).

Therefore, CMHNs require an understanding and awareness of their own therapeutic presence in order that they may be able to stay with and contain their clients' innermost thoughts, feelings and emotions. Otherwise, they may find it impossible to integrate their therapeutic presence into the nurse/client relationship. Rogers (cited in Baldwin, 1987) has written:

'Recently I find that when I am closest to my inner intuitive self whatever I do seems to be full of healing, simply my presence is releasing and helpful.'

The nurse's therapeutic presence is fundamental to all therapeutic approaches to care and as such forms a crucial interpersonal bridge towards healing and recovery. The use of self as a therapeutic catalyst can be felt by clients as bearable. It is intrinsically bound by genuine concern for the client and it is knitted together with unconditional positive regard (Rogers, 1990).

Staying with and containing the frightening thoughts, feelings and emotions of clients allows the more mature parts of the individual to emerge. Working in this manner allows the client's vague, confusing and limitless feelings and thoughts to be borne by another, the nurse, and therefore become more manageable for the individual (Wittenberg, 1970). The therapeutic process challenges nurses to become competent in those health-giving skills which bring meaning to the individual's perceptions of lived experiences.

CMHNs do this by putting words to, clarifying and interpreting painful thoughts, feelings and emotions in an accepting and non-punitive way. Such co-participation in therapy expresses a belief in, and facilitates, the client's capacity for self-understanding and for working through and eventually integrating painful and frightening experiences. Wright and Giddey (1993) express the thought that:

'Nursing is not just about techniques, methods and models, primarily it is to do with being a person who works with other people at times when they are ill, distressed or anxious.'

The therapeutic encounter

Being and working with another human being is quintessential for the development and maintenance of a therapeutic relationship, which is the crux of community mental health nursing. Keltner *et al.* (1991) have said that:

'The therapeutic relationship can be described in terms of three stages of development, namely, orientation, working and termination.'

The essence of the therapeutic relationship is referred to by Buber (1937; 1987), as the *interhuman*. The interhuman is not owned by either the nurse or the client, it exists between them. Community mental health nursing is, therefore, located within the interhuman. The central tenet in Buber's philosophy is that to be human is to relate (Buber & Rogers, 1965; Buber, 1988). This rules out the use of any form of nursing model which suggests that the 'patient' becomes the focus of analysis, as though he or she could be reduced to a collection of parts, needs and problems.

Instead, the 'dynamic centre' of the other is *experienced* for the other cannot become the 'separate object of my contemplation or even observation' (Buber, 1937; 1987). Being present with the other is a total experience and each therapeutic encounter with a given individual is a new encounter.

This precludes the measurement or analysis of the actual therapeutic experience. To be with the other in this sense means to rule out all other considerations during the time of the interaction. 'True beings are lived in the present, the life of objects is lived in the past.' (Buber, 1937; 1987).

In community mental health nursing, then, the nurse client relationship takes centre stage as a therapeutic channel for healing and growth and as such it is an end in itself. Moreover, if nurses are encouraged to find out all about clients and use sophisticated classificatory systems or models, but fail to engage in establishing a meaningful relationship with clients in need, then those clients will be the poorer. When a nursing model becomes more important than clients' perceptions of reality, people are automatically reduced in dignity and as human beings.

The concept of presence indicates that changes occur in both the nurse and the client during the therapeutic encounter and that a nurse's 'openness' to enter into therapeutic dialogue or communion in relation to *being with and for* the client is of major importance to the processes of healing and recovery.

Each therapeutic encounter becomes a lived experienced for both the nurse and the client, during which the CMHN travels with and is the companion for the person on part of his or her journey through life. This is the caring aspect of community mental health nursing and it rests comfortably within the interhuman dimension (Buber, 1937; 1987).

Thus far it can be seen that clients hold the key to their own healing. Discovering the quintessential, invigorating, mental-health-giving ingredients is augmented by the therapeutic presence of a *being* CMHN and his or her attendant – the therapeutic encounter.

Community mental health nursing also aims to help clients to gain an awareness of the meaning of life and the purpose of living. In co-participation with clients, intentions are identified for achieving that aspiration by designing specific goals and plans. Thus, the promotion of such decision-making and decision-taking contributes greatly to empowerment and the totality of the healing process.

13.8 Professional practice

The UKCC (1991) has adopted *The Principles of Health Visiting* (CETHV, 1977) in a modified form for all community health care nurses in its proposals for the reform of community nurse education and practice. These principles have also been endorsed by the National Health Service Management Executive (NHSME, 1992) which has included them in its suggested model contract for fundholding GPs.

The principles are based on the belief that health is a *resource for life* and not the objective of living. Resources which contribute to positive mental health belong to a person's lived perceptions of his or her internal world and/

or the external world as experienced by the individual, from a social, family and community context.

Thus, community mental health nursing involves finding ways to formulate resources for clients and their carers by promoting mental health; creating and maintaining mental well-being; preventing mental ill health; offering therapeutic care to those people who suffer from acute and chronic mental ill health; and providing proactive community-based outreach services. This specific focus is testimony to the forward-looking nature of the work of CMHNs.

13.9 Principles

In its uniqueness, community mental health nursing recognizes the diversity and breadth of the role of CMHNs. They aim to offer a proactive outreach service which embraces a professional responsibility to seek out, challenge and influence public policy related to mental health. Their overall objective is to work in co-participation with clients, their carers and communities to maximize overall mental health potential.

The four principles of health visiting, as recommended by the UKCC (1991), are transubstantiated into five principles of community mental health nursing:

- the search for recognized and unrecognized mental health needs;
- the prevention of a disequilibrium in mental health;
- the facilitation of mental-health-enhancing activities;
- therapeutic approaches to mental health care;
- influences on policies affecting mental health.

These principles draw on the notion that 'principles state a relationship between two facts that may be used to explain, guide and predict action' (Chater, 1975).

The search for recognized and unrecognized needs

The search for and identification of recognized and unrecognized mental health needs is integral to the concept of a facilitative and empowering partnership with clients and communities. In order to practise this principle, CMHNs are required to research, analyse and audit detailed health and poverty profiles of the specific recognized and unrecognized needs they identify within the population for which they are responsible.

Poverty profiling is not radically different from health profiling. It is a specific attempt to identify the level and distribution of poverty and poverty-related health and social needs (current and potential) in a defined population (Blackburn, 1992). Mental health indicators range on a continuum from suicide, severe depression and phobia through to the whole range of identity, sexual, marital and human relationship problems for which it is both humane and realistic to offer high-quality nursing care (Long & Chambers, 1993).

Mental health cannot be divorced from the socio-economic and cultural context in which it is experienced (Anderson, 1984; Cowley, 1991). Consequently, many unresolved mental health needs are not addressed within the current purchaser/provider ideology of the NHS. CMHNs should use the commissioning process (Roy, 1990) to improve, change and expand services to meet the needs and preferences of service users, carers and communities.

A health and poverty profile is essentially a contextualizing profile. It assigns identified health information about recognized and unrecognized mental health needs into a social context. It offers CMHNs an overview of poverty and an awareness of how people's experience of poverty shapes their lives and affects their mental health.

A health and poverty profile acts as a base and information source for prioritizing, planning, implementing and evaluating practice (Twinn *et al.*, 1990). It also generates objective and comparable information and data that can be used by practitioners. However, despite the growing emphasis on health and poverty profiling in practice, there remains a great need for an informal network of identifying mental health needs at macro and micro levels, within the GP practice and within each CMHN's caseload.

At a wider level, the development and updating of a community mental health and poverty profile provides evidence for the evaluation of the effectiveness of mental health services by using approaches which are tailor-made to meeting clients' needs and perceptions rather than simply recording the activities and skills of each individual practitioner (Rowe & Mackeith, 1991).

Community mental health and poverty profiles are part of a cyclical process of ensuring the centrality of human concern and respect for individual and community mental health needs; this they do by identifying recognized and unrecognized mental health needs; planning and developing proactive and responsive mental health care services; enabling community mental health nurses to target their services more effectively; and evaluating service provision. The profiles also act as a tool to aid in the critical assessment and redistribution of resources within community mental health nursing and in the wider field of primary health care.

Thus CMHNs in co-participation with individual clients and community groups, empower people to identify their own mental health needs. They possess expert knowledge in epidemiology and research skills that can be used to facilitate an understanding of mental health needs, problems and current and potential mental health trends. At community level nurses may use empirical evidence to raise awareness of mental health issues and associated problems surrounding mental ill health.

The prevention of disequilibrium

The Caplan (1961) model of primary, secondary and tertiary prevention can be used as a practical guide to focus on this principle. Primary preventative measures are carried out by CMHNs through designing mental health promotion programmes and health education packages, e.g. the promotion and maintenance of healthy relationships (Duck, 1992; Kelley *et al.*, 1988); preconceptual mental health care; promoting healthy bonding (Bee, 1994; Sluckin & Sluckin, 1992); facilitating emotional health and well-being; healthy, non-shaming and non-punitive communication patterns (Dwindell & Middleton-Moz, 1986); human sexuality and education for love (Iven, 1994); and death, dying and letting go as natural experiences in living (Worden, 1982; Sherman, 1988; Gunzberg & Stewart, 1994). CMHNs are in a key position to inaugurate, develop, implement and research such health-promoting and life-enriching programmes. Such mental health activities challenge nurses to redirect their focus and promote positive mental health at a wider level.

Secondary prevention

Secondary preventative measures are conducted by CMHNs who offer individuals, families, groups and communities a diversity of health-promoting strengths and strategies for coping with identified disequilibrium in mental health. Some examples of such health-giving activities are anxiety and stress management (Gaylin, cited in Miller, 1989); dealing with rational fear (Beck, 1979); resolving anger, resentment and shame (Bradshaw, 1992); screening and identifying 'at risk' indicators for self-destructive and self-abusive behaviours (Beck *et al.*, 1974; Beck *et al.*, 1979); and planning a screening programme for the early identification and remediation of addictive behaviours (Long & Mullan, 1994). To put any of these programmes into action requires an advanced level of planning, educative, therapeutic and management skills (Cowley, 1991).

Tertiary prevention

Tertiary prevention involves planning current mental health care and preventing further deterioration in people who suffer from chronic mental ill health. To be successful in carrying out this role, CMHNs must be competent in the quintessential advanced skills and abilities to monitor client and carers satisfaction. They must also be competent to assess, monitor and evaluate therapeutic modalities and accompanying health-care skills. This principle also embraces the notion that CMHNs are proficient in assessing, monitoring and evaluating the uses, benefits and positive and negative side effects of drugs and other chemicals used in psychiatry (Healy, 1993) as well as in the field of addictions (Tether & Robinson, 1986).

Finally, this principle implies that CMHNs pursue further research into planning and monitoring appropriate health-giving regimes to meet the various stages of the healing process.

The facilitation of mental-health-enhancing activities

Respect for the autonomous person implies respect for both that person's goals and for his or her own way of pursuing them (assuming that they do not infringe on the autonomy of others) (Gore, 1984). Most people want to be healthy, both physically and mentally, although the pursuit of mental-health-enhancing behaviours is not always wholehearted. In truth, it may be fair to say that some people are not aware of what constitutes 'normal' mental health for them. Moreover, many individuals are unsure and uncertain about what steps they need to take in order to achieve a true sense of mental well-being.

Indeed, we may in fact live in a society that positively gives rise to mental ill health. There are also individual differences both within and between cultures as to what constitutes 'normal' behaviours and acceptable social norms and, consequently, sound mental health (Kaptein, 1993).

Long and Chambers (1993) have defined mental health as:

'A process of equilibrium both within and between the inner and outer Self, the social environment and the natural world in which people live. Within individuals it is manifest by self awareness; self acceptance; and the ability to cope with changing life circumstances; a personal recognition and acceptance of inner strengths and resources and a desire to aim for continuous personal potential and self development throughout life. Positive mental health leads to a true value of all people as unique individuals and, therefore, the awareness of the existence of one humanity in an evolving world.'

The facilitation of mental-health-enhancing activities can be promoted by designing health and self-awareness programmes. Such educative experiences should be designed and implemented in such a way as to empower people to believe in themselves as unique individuals; to enable them to come to know, understand and accept both self and others; to improve relationships; to increase their understanding of life's meaning and purpose; and to realize their creative potential.

At community level, to protect the individual's autonomy within defined limits, society imposes norms of behaviour on its members (Prior, 1993). In the most permissive range, compliance brings with it acceptance, social esteem, social status and material rewards. Alternatively it is difficult, if not impossible, for others to sustain and maintain mental health and retain their dignity in a climate where poverty and unemployment are paramount; where there is gross inequality and social injustice; where the young, the homeless, and those who are socially disadvantaged, including those who belong to minority groups, are undervalued and deprived of equitable opportunities and equal civil liberties for personal, social, educative and futuristic self-growth and development.

If society is organized in a mentally unhealthy and inhumane way, then individuals will naturally become disturbed. Many 'mental' illnesses and mental disabilities have been socially constituted. It is both immoral and futile to help these people to adjust without simultaneously changing the conditions that lead to their maladjustment (Bohart & Todd, 1988).

The person who chooses to go his or her own way, regardless of social class or culture, can do so only at the cost of appearing slightly odd or eccentric to others. Many, because of their unusual behaviours, are labelled 'mentally ill'. Over time, this non-compliance makes a difference to the individual and his or her mental health and so called autonomy and *freedom to be* (Kaptein, 1993).

Providing relaxation exercises may help in the short term to enable people to live in and adjust to a mentally sick society and also to comply with the norms of that society. Such helping may simply be another way of shoring up the status quo (Albee, 1986). The norms of health and sickness are social, legal and cultural norms; thus, the total concept of mental health is atrociously difficult to define. By offering certain relaxation classes and stress management courses CMHNs may in fact be reinforcing the notion that individuals are mentally ill rather than challenging the notion that mental health is inseparable from the whole individual and the socio-economic context in which it is experienced. Such superficial remedies have been described as immoral by theorists who point to the potential harm of a victim-blaming ideology (Anderson, 1984; Seedhouse, 1986). Indeed, for many individuals mental health looks like an impossible goal.

However, when it is overtly recognized, mental health is a realistic way of seeing the world, accompanied by inner peace and strength. Mental health is like a gyroscope that helps human beings to keep their balance, no matter what turbulence swirls around them. True mental health embodies the ideology of the whole being towards balance, creativity, joy, service to humanity and finally self-actualization (Maslow, 1987) and self-realisation (Rogers, 1990).

On this more positive note, mental health activities can be promoted and facilitated. Human beings can, in effect, use their enhanced mental capabilities to save as well as destroy relationships within and between self and others, groups or nations. Every individual effort to facilitate mental-health-enhancing activities and to promote mental health, peace and well-being must have a direct effect on collective mental health at family, community and global levels.

Mental-health-promoting activities are complex in their simplicity. Moreover, sometimes professionals and individuals are so caught up coping with needs and problems that they lose sight of all that is natural, pure and positive. Four, free and natural examples are illustrated in the following sections.

Nature as a healer

Community mental health nursing speaks to the synthesis of persons, groups and nations. Mental health is a universal concept which has no bounds. As such, it accepts the ideas of environmental and global mental health concerns more easily. Each individual benefits from creating comfortable settings because they reduce anxiety and selfconsciousness. Such healing settings may be found free and in abundance outside the ward and home environment. Nature itself provides a therapeutic climate which promotes mental health and generates an expectation for possible future mental health, truth, healing and recovery.

When using the natural environment for the promotion of mental health, individuals become more amenable to therapy, better able to focus, more playful and creative. Staff become less impersonal in dealing with human needs. Such sensory rich surroundings optimize the ability to perform by making perceived shortcomings less formidable and by minimizing mental disabilities aggravated by fear and tension. Most of all, by inviting clients to pause, attend and be nourished by the planet's richness, nature's settings promote mental health and well-being and help people to feel connected to humanity and to the universe. And yet to feel free. Insight such as this brings human beings closer to their innermost self, their ultimate source of mental health, healing and recovery.

Light

The nutritionist Wurtman (cited in Olds, 1985) asserts that light is the most important environmental input (after food) in controlling bodily function. Ott (1973) writes of a trend in which people spend increasing hours behind windows and windshields, eye- and sunglasses, in front of TV and display terminals and under the partial spectrum of fluorescent radiation interspersed by shadows. This unnatural habitat affects the incidence of headaches, diabetes, hormonal imbalance and criminal behaviour (Ott, 1973).

Thus time spent outdoors, or in the presence of sunlight through an open window, may indeed be critical for mental health. Lam (1977) highlighted a relationship between depression and increased positive ions in the air. This study also revealed a possible connection between depression and light. Lam suggests that on grey days, because of reduced exterior illumination, more artificial lights are used inside, thereby approximating night-time conditions in the daytime. The result is that people's biological clocks are thrown off balance and they may feel depressed. Mental health nurses must be aware that this effect also exists in interior places without windows.

In nature, by contrast, individuals are surrounded by luminousness. For biological and aesthetic reasons and for the promotion of mental health, lighting must become part of the architecture. Full spectrum lights which approximate the range of wavelengths provided by sunshine may reduce disturbances caused by inadequate exposure to the ultraviolet and infra-red ends of the spectrum (Ott, 1973). Thus they facilitate mental-health-enhancing activities. Beyond this, community mental health nurses should use every means possible to give clients access to natural light.

Privacy

Whether indoors or out, individuals who are in the process of mentally healing are usually symbolically depicted alone, walking, seated or lying (Gunzberg & Stewart, 1994). Occasionally a trusted friend is present as well. More often pets – a dog or a cat – are the person's only companion (Dewdney *et al.*, 1994). The striking absence of people and the aloneness contrast sharply with the togetherness and professional intervention mores of society. This suggests that perhaps privacy, expanded to include animals, is an essential mental-health-enhancing activity.

Wolfe and Laufer (1974) describe being alone or by oneself as one of four types of privacy essential for positive mental health. Feeling at one with, in private, nature's 'varied sameness' may enable people to achieve a personal centre or grounding that is a prerequisite for coping with self and the social domain. Keeping in touch with one's deeper sources of wholeness and individuality, and with the healing force of the universe, requires some privacy and solitude. Thus, in order to facilitate mental-health-enhancing activities, people should be given space, time and encouragement to be alone, both indoors and out.

Beauty

In *What We May Be* Ferrucci (1982) devotes an eloquent chapter to the regenerative, self-transcendent and revelatory effects of beauty. By contacting the aesthetic dimension, he argues, people seem to experience themselves as more beautiful. They also seem to be more open to the experience of beauty in the surrounding environment. Both sets of feelings in turn facilitate mental-health-enhancing activities and assist the healing process.

When people are afforded an opportunity to embrace nature's physical wholeness and harmony this experience can be transmitted to psychic wholeness and tranquillity. This in itself provides an argument for taking advantage of the beauty that nature provides and also for the therapeutic benefits of creating more loveliness around us.

While beautification of dwellings is a mental-health-enhancing activity for many homemakers at a family level, comparable consideration is rarely given to the urban landscape at community level. The same omission may be true for the neighbourhood, workplace, mental hospital, prison or shelter – all embracing the need for the creation of a therapeutic ambience. These settings, by virtue of their anonymous ownership, become an aesthetic no-man's-land, designed more to assist the custodians who maintain them than the users who must grow, live, heal and recover within them.

The facilitation of mental-health-enhancing activities at family and community levels means that the men and women of this generation should devote more energy to the creation of aesthetically pleasing homes, workplaces and communal places for the collective well-being of people, especially the children who are our future generation.

The subconscious images of nature as a primal source of mental health nourishment and rejuvenation are probably laid down in childhood when perceptions of the environment are immediate and holistic. Children have little sense of part/whole relationships, or of the self as a separate entity, and so they live according to the information provided by their senses, feasting upon the nuances of colour, light, sound and touch by which they come to know the world and make sense of self and their reality. As the Hindus claim, 'sarvam annam' [everything is food].

Thus, it is both illusionary and potentially harmful to assume that an environment can be neutral. Environments, like human beings and all other aspects of life, are potent purveyors of positive and negative mental health stimulation and information – be it the ill effects of neglect, poverty, abuse, dysfunction and disorder or the beneficial effects of mental-health-enhancing activities such as beauty, unity, creativity, peace, truth and justice. These bipolar teratogens make a tremendous impact on overall mental health and on the development of each and every individual's life.

To facilitate mental-health-enhancing activities, to be aware of, to influence, to cultivate and to refine beliefs are all part of the healing process. Using the natural environment contributes greatly to the promotion of a healing climate.

Therapeutic approaches

The Community Psychiatric Nurses' Association survey (CPNA, 1985) reported that the numbers of CPNs had grown in the period 1980–85 from 1 667 to 2 758, an increase of 65% (Brooker, 1986). By 1989 the number of CPNs within the UK had increased to 4 990 (White, 1993). If this rate of growth continues, it is projected that there will be some 12 000 CMHNs in the UK by the year 2000 (Brooker, 1986).

The role of the CMHN has undergone significant reclarification as community mental health care services have continued to expand and develop. During the 1960s the role of the CPN received attention because this new discipline had evolved to address the needs of people who were mentally ill in the community. Until then this role had been exclusively that of district nurses (Smith, 1970a). In an attempt to prevent role overlap a composite role for CPNs evolved (Mangeu & Griffiths, 1980). This role embraced the following functions: follow-up after discharge; attending to practical needs; giving support to families; administering medication; co-ordinating between hospital and community; and encouraging people to socialize in the community.

The activities of the CPN underwent further analysis and clarification throughout the 1970s as attempts were made to provide a clearer understanding of their role and function (Sharpe, 1975; Roberts, 1976; Greene, 1978; Martin & Kenny, 1979). The role of CPNs at that time was one that focused on social/environmentalist and interpersonal dimensions (Murphy, 1977).

The search for a more specialized role for CPNs continued as community mental health services became more sophisticated. Hunter (1974) purported that CPNs should be able to utilize a range of psychotherapeutic interventions. In addition, he suggested that behavioural therapy was the most important intervention required. This was probably due to the fact that the work of Skinner (1957) and other behaviourists just happened to be in vogue in that decade. It seems fair to say that this style of therapy deals only with certain aspects of a client's behaviour. This blinkered approach to community mental health care nursing indicated that there was a deficit in holistic approaches to care at individual client level. Needless to say, families, carers and communities received little mention in overall care plans.

Carr *et al.* (1980) were early in calling upon CPNs to develop a range of skills which would enable them to be recognized as clinical consultants, a term which has now been discussed at length by the Mental Health Nursing Review (1994).

The research of Skidmore and Friend (1984) revealed that there were many deficiencies in CPN practices which they identified as being primarily due to an inadequate education base. They indicated that CPNs were not being equipped in the essential skills to carry out their jobs effectively. Indeed, they highlighted the CPNs in their sample group as 'lacking in skills'! Their findings led to the authors' purporting that the inadequacies of CPNs led to their 'muddling through' client encounters and using specialism as a shield.

Yet the demand for greater specialism continued to grow throughout the 1980s. Brooker (1986) reported that one in five CPNs could be recognized as specialist practitioners. Most of the scholars at that time continued to argue that specialism was the way forward for CPNs (Carr *et al.*, 1980; Brooker, 1986; CPNA, 1985).

Others counter-argued that specialization was nothing more than a form of professional escapism. Skidmore and Friend (1984) indicated that specialization did little to improve the quality of nursing care offered by CPNs. Both authors cautioned against this developing trend. They contended that the needs of certain clients would be overlooked if particular clients and their needs did not match the appropriate speciality. More recently, Brooker and White (1993) have challenged the benefits of specialization on client-care outcomes.

In the present era, however, CMHNs care for and are interested in each and every member of the community in which they are based. They strive to promote the mental health of the nation. Hence, it is argued here that *all* CMHNs are specialist practitioners in that they are concerned with the totality of mental health care at individual, family, community, society and global levels. It is imperative, therefore, that they have a solid, eclectic and integrated theoretical grounding on a wide range of contemporary psychotherapeutic approaches to mental health care. After their initial education as CMHNs they may wish to further specialize in one particular therapeutic modality or with a certain client group. Meanwhile, in order to function holistically, they must become purists in community mental health care nursing and consultants in the provision of high quality mental health care. Consequently, they must be exposed to the whole gamut of current psychotherapeutic modalities. The extent of the clients' needs for specialist mental health nursing intervention, however, requires further research.

Suffice it to say that many people who are mentally ill have been passed about from one service to another and from one health professional to another for most of their 'sick careers' (Szasz, 1970). Some have encountered this brand of emotional abandonment even prior to entering the caring services. This form of seesawing about with an individual's emotions does little to facilitate the development of trust which is the most critical component of community mental health care nursing (Erikson, 1979; Rutter, 1987; Rutter & Durkin, 1987).

Being constantly referred to others for help leads clients to believe that they are 'hopeless cases' and perhaps beyond the zone of hope or the realm of recovery. Such referrals, if carried out without thought of the resulting health/ill health outcomes for the client, may actually prevent the initiation and maintenance of a therapeutic, health-giving bridge between the client and the nurse (Bradshaw, 1992).

Similarly, instead of offering therapy, mental health nurses may in fact be reinforcing a client's belief that human relationships do not last and therefore should not be given time, nor worked through. In addition, clients may feel they are being fobbed off or too sick or too bad to be cared for. Moreover, why would our clients place themselves in a position to be hurt once again by beginning to trust yet another professional who subsequently passes them on to someone else?

Literature suggests that we are experts at reading and writing about therapeutic relationships which are ultimately based on human qualities such as trust and care. Yet many of us fail to recognize and practise the necessary ingredients that are inherent in the formation of trust. Clients must *feel* the nurse's empathy. They must *feel* unique, prized, secure, safe, and worthy of care and emotional containment. They must realize that when they share a lived experience with the nurse, the nurse will not reject them but will continue to work with them until those experiences have been dealt with, worked through and finally integrated or discarded – hence enabling the person to become whole, empowered and mentally well. This type of healing work takes time.

It is important, therefore, that clients come to perceive the CMHN as the mental health professional with perseverance, true grit and tenacity coupled with the human capacity to care. They are the professionals who believe that each human being has the ability to heal, recover, develop and grow, even in the face of adversity and when all else fails. This practice ideology is founded on the belief that each individual is capable of achieving his or her full potential. Clients, therefore, are offered hope for the future. CMHNs may be their only human source of comfort and security. For many, they may be the only anchor person who remains constant in their lives, thus offering clients therapeutic contact on a planned, structured and sequential basis. This form of care is therapeutic in itself as clients learn across time that CMHNs are the professionals who are dependable and who genuinely care enough to *be there* for them. Certainly, referral to other acolyte agencies and different satellite specialists who deal with certain aspects of holistic health can be crucial, but the CMHN should remain the solid, pivotal professional in the community offering therapeutic care for clients who are mentally ill and their carers.

CMHNs are competent to work as autonomous practitioners, with clinical, supportive supervision (Butterworth & Faugier, 1992) and they also work as members of wider community mental health care teams. It is essential, therefore, that they become skilled and versed in a wide variety of therapeutic approaches to care during their community mental health nursing course, and that they are given an opportunity to specialize at a later date by being involved in the kind of further education they require. They should also play a prominent role in developing the type of service their clients require.

However, while an increasing number of CMHNs report specialization in respect to client caseload populations, a significantly smaller number have specialized in a specific therapeutic approach to care. White (1993) found that only one in seven of the total sample group that he studied ($n = 145$) reported that they had specialization in a therapeutic modality. White concluded that 36% of CMHNs approached their work generically.

Many academics have pooled their ideas, carried out research and nudged the community mental health nursing service to grow and develop into a dignified, highly respected, experienced, worthwhile and research-based profession. Some examples of high quality, methodologically sound research are to be found in Birchwood *et al.* (1993), Warner (1991), and in the volumes entitled *Community Psychiatric Nursing*, edited by Brooker (1990) and Brooker & White (1993). In addition, in the USA, high calibre research on the care of families of people who are mentally ill has been eloquently portrayed and edited by Hatfield and Lefley (1987).

Used with wisdom, scientific research may be integrated to enlighten and enhance practice; this leads to therapeutic excellence in the care of people who are mentally ill, their families and their carers. In so doing CMHNs touch the lives of every individual in the area for which they are responsible. This includes people like you and me.

Influences on policies affecting mental health

Mental health has been described as the dynamic process of maintaining an equilibrium between the individual's inner and outer self, the social environment and the natural world in which he or she lives (Action Plan for Mental Health Nursing, DHSS NI, 1993). It is essential that mental health be regarded in broad holistic terms. Despite having to grapple with the complexities of a swiftly evolving society and a rapidly changing NHS, it remains imperative that CMHNs retain their humanitarian principles. A fundamental belief in the integrity, value and dignity of health appears in stark opposition to the jargon of the marketeer and the market-based belief in health as a commodity. Crude statistics do not always tell the whole story. If compromises are to be made, it is important to ensure that they do not undermine the essential human concern and respect for persons upon which community mental health nursing is built and remains solidly standing.

13.10 Change

Mental health is political. It cannot be divorced from the decisions made in town halls or from policies created and legislated at government level. Historically, it is now more important than ever for CMHNs to be politically aware and to take actions where appropriate, through local networks.

Populations move, people are discharged from long-stay hospitals, mental health needs change; diseases such as TB and other infectious illnesses come and go. Health services have to change and adapt accordingly, and cannot be chained to the spot by health professionals who sometimes attempt to guard their own territory. Professionals are not always wrong but they must be aware that they do not always know best either. It is fundamentally important that people who are mentally ill should be cared for effectively and safely in the community.

13.11 Care programme approach

The care programme approach, introduced in April 1991, involves collaboration between health and social services in order to provide individually-tailored care programmes for all people with mental health problems. This includes all those people who will be, or have been, discharged from mental hospitals and other institutions and who are subsequently relocated into the community mental health services (see Chapter 6).

There are still problems, however, with the understanding and implementation of the 'key worker' principle in community mental health teams (DOH, 1994). These problems relate mainly to the areas of clinical leadership and effective prioritization of cases and resources. It is quintessential that the allocation of a key worker appropriately reflects the needs of individual clients and their carers and also ensures that different professional skills are utilized to best effect.

13.12 Supervised discharge planning

The Secretary of State for Health outlined a set of proposals which reinforce the need for safe and effective practice in the supervision and support for people when they leave hospital (DOH, 1993). These proposals incorporate the principles of the Care Programme Approach, and include the principal clause of a 'named' key worker for each patient (see Chapter 6). CMHNs are in the ideal position to act as key workers.

The notion of developing a concept of *supervised discharge*, and the action taken to ensure that CMHNs play a central role in the Care Programme Approach, is crucial for the advancement of community mental health services and a locally based approach to care.

Ten essential points have been addressed in the Mental Health Nursing Review (DOH, 1994) which, if implemented, will go a long way towards ensuring the safe and therapeutic preparation for and transition of patients from hospital to the community setting. Equal attention must be paid to the MIND publication, *Discharged from Mental Hospital* (Bean & Mounser, 1993).

As the reprovision programmes gather momentum against a background of growing public and media concern, greater emphasis will have to be placed on ensuring effective support systems and continuing holistic, psychotherapeutic care for people with serious and enduring mental illness. This includes promoting the mental health of, and providing care for, their families, their carers and the community in which they reside.

13.13 Proactive collaboration

Pressure groups and consumer organizations add an important dimension, as does the growth of community development work and the recognition of its importance in society. The mixed economy of care, with its plurality of statutory, voluntary and private providers, also stimulates a need for quality assurance and hopefully increases the choices available to individuals (NHSME, 1992). To ensure that services are proactive and client-led, as required by the Citizen's Charter (DOH, 1991a) and the Patient's Charter (DHSS NI, 1992), clients' perceptions of their needs should also be sought and cognisance taken of them.

CMHNs must work in the forefront of primary health care (NHSME, 1992). The principle of influence suggests that they may do this by working as consultants and as advocates.

Consultancy

Working in co-participation with local people, CMHNs have the knowledge and understanding of the community in which they are based (*A Review of Mental Health Nursing* (DOH, 1994)). They are the mental health consultants who have collected data and have also examined and synthesized scientific research on current and futuristic epidemiological mental health trends (Tunmore & Thomas, 1992). They are in an ideal situation to inform the planning of services to meet actual and potential mental health needs. The principle of influence must be perceived as being good for the health of individuals, their carers and the total community in which mental health nurses practise. Implicit in this principle is the need for CMHNs to search out, challenge and attempt to change those factors that adversely affect the mental health of the present and future population.

Advocacy

The advocacy role of CMHNs is to safeguard and represent the rights of their clients and to assist, enable and empower clients to ensure that their needs are expressed and met. The possession of rights enhances the dignity of the rights held and so exemplifies the idea of respect for persons (Campbell, 1988). People with a mental health problem have the right to liberty, equity of services with other citizens, acknowledgement of their mental illness, and access to survivor groups. They also have the right to refuse an assessment or treatment, and carers have the right to refuse to care (BMA, 1992). Parallel to this, both clients and carers have the right to complain about the services provided, including that of the 'named' CMHN (NHSME, 1992).

Thus, CMHNs have a duty to educate and empower clients and carers in the social and life skills necessary to enable them to make complaints and seek health and social justice. In this way clients are empowered to take decisions and so take control of their lives. Moreover, this enhances their self-advocacy skills.

Advocacy, therefore, is an essential component of mental health nursing. CMHNs are required to protect and defend the rights of their clients to ensure that their strengths and needs and not just their diagnoses are recognized.

13.14 Targets

The Health of the Nation (DOH, 1991b) set out a comprehensive strategy for health which has been adopted by the World Health Organization as a model for other countries to follow' (Yeo, 1993). DOH (1991b) focused initially on five priority areas and set three primary targets for reducing morbidity and mortality in the mental illness key areas. The targets are:

- to improve significantly the health and social functioning of people who are mentally ill;
- to reduce the overall suicide rate by at least 15%; and
- to reduce the rate of suicide in people with severe mental illness by at least one-third.

Risk assessment

The benefits to be achieved by real community care and concomitant increased normalization for people who are mentally ill and their carers have far outreached the deficits. This may be especially true for our future generations. However, there are real concerns about the dangers which a minority of people with serious mental illness may pose to the community. These concerns have been focused on a small, but tragic, number of high-profile incidents of violence and suicide, prompting an internal review by the government on the care of vulnerable people with mental health problems who might slip through the net of services.

To date, much of risk assessment undertaken by mental health nurses has been intuitive and informal. The implementation of the Care Programme Approach, involving the concept of a 'named' key worker, will require mental health nurses to offer more formal specifications of their risk assessment methods, including the criteria underpinning clinical judgements. There is an urgent need to review current practice and to define ways which help identify and protect individuals 'at risk', and also safeguard the community. Care programmes must be delivered which offer effective, safe and appropriate intervention strategies and proactive support systems.

Homeless and rootless people

It is also true to say that little attention has been given to the bulk of mentally ill individuals who generally have no home and few relatives (Bean & Mounser, 1993). Nevertheless, it is fair to say that some progress has been made in this area. There is less of the old talk of tramps, vagrants, down-and-outs, skippers and dossers. The new vocabulary of homelessness runs to scrounger, sponger, Johnny-go-home and so on. CMHNs have a role to play in working alongside the homeless and motivating them to experiment with ideas and learn social and life skills. This may involve street work. They may even encourage the homeless to get across the real experience of what it means to be a homeless person in a wealthy society (Dewdney *et al.*, 1994).

Business and advertising

CMHNs can make a difference to the lives of people with severe mental health problems at individual, family, community and global levels. They have the essential skills to influence mental health in the world of business and in the realm of advertising. Such domains are powerful in suggesting norms of happiness, friendship and sexual satisfaction and tend to create feelings of inadequacy among those who have not accomplished, and possibly will never achieve, those social and advertisers' norms. CMHNs have a pivotal role both as key workers and as team members.

The prevention of suicide

Statistics on suicide are a real cause for concern. Suicide is an avoidable form of mortality, yet accounts for 1% of deaths annually (Reid & Long, 1993). The number of people dying from suicide is on a par with those dying from road traffic accidents (Collee, 1992). Suicidal ideations produce features of both a private depression and a public failure where there is a need to come to terms with the split between sentimental and unrealistic ideals and the reality and pain of living. Hence, the act of suicide can be defined as a short-cut to dying. More work must be carried out in this area.

Therapist–client matching and multicultural community mental health care

Should clients and CMHNs be matched according to important characteristics such as gender or ethnic group? While this appears to be a question that can be empirically answered, it remains controversial. Nonetheless, the special needs of people who belong to ethnic groups and of women who are mentally ill must be identified and met under the principle of influence. There are those who argue that ethical practice necessitates therapist–client matching and others counter this, suggesting that successful therapeutic care touches universal themes meaningful to all groups.

Since many people who are mentally ill are female and from ethnic minorities and many CMHNs remain both white and male, the field of cross-cultural or multicultural community mental health care is a growing one. It is imperative, therefore, that CMHNs receive multicultural education and training. CMHNs working with different ethnic groups should be encouraged to examine their own values in relation to those of clients. Ethically, they are obliged to value client differences and learn from them. As part of their educational programme they learn specific communication skills effective in working with different groups. They are taught to avoid blaming the victim – to avoid, for example, seeing natural responses to racism, sectarianism and oppression as evidence of individual psychopathology (Logue, 1992). Multicultural CMHNs avoid stereotyping and encourage clients to explore their full potential, while realistically acknowledging social barriers to their aspirations.

A voice for women

Similarly, there is a need to critique and recast assumptions about the mental health of women in a way which elevates women's experiences. Women frequently find their views being undervalued or discounted. CMHNs provide a voice for women who are mentally ill. They can be instrumental in highlighting the real concerns of women's issues.

Gilligan (1977) and Benjamin (1984) suggest the importance of women, including health professionals, finding a balance between the extremes of self-definition: between autonomy (consideration of oneself) and connection (consideration of others). Mental health problems such as excessive dependency, anxiety and anger are subsequently explored as the consequences of narrow social and self definitions. The multifactorial dimensions of mental health services for women are explored and debated by Belle, 1982; Brodsky and Hare-Mussin, 1980; Carmen *et al.*, 1981; Kaplan, 1983; Walker, 1984; and the Mental Health Nursing Review, DOH, 1994.

The articulation of 'the feminine voice' in the moral domain is one piece of an evolving alternative perspective on women in society that has relevance for conceptualizations about women's mental health. There is little systematic information about differences in perceptions of female nurses' own mental health problems, and perceptions of the nature of help among groups of women, including poor women, minority women and lesbians. Nonetheless, it is assumed that there are important differences between men and women and among various groups of women (Burden & Gottlieb, 1987).

Moreover, CMHNs should be taught to identify and respect these differences. They must hear and value women's perceptions about where their concerns and problems are coming from. Subsequently, it is the role of the CMHN to represent females and help influence policies affecting the mental health of all women.

Rather than attempting an overview of the complex and multidimensional topic of women and mental health, this chapter has sought to exert influence by focusing on just a few points. It has not said how mental health services for women should be provided. Rather, it has offered a loosely woven perspective that may alter the tone and direction of curricula for all mental health services for women, and of the services themselves.

13.15 A systematic needs-based approach to practice

Community mental health nursing services should be organized in a way that will help to accomplish the vision expressed about 'mental health for all' throughout this chapter. CMHNs engage in and strive to enhance the full spectrum of nursing care which enables the creative potential of professional practice to be fulfilled. Five key features are essential for the delivery and evaluation of high quality community mental health care:

- The primacy of mental health promotion and prevention at individual, family, group, community and global levels must be upheld.
- The expertise of CMHNs and their unique and dynamic combination of therapeutic skills and psychotherapeutic approaches to care must be used to maximum effect at micro, median and macro levels.
- The service must be proactive and responsive to recognized and unrecognized mental health needs.
- A collaborative and flexible approach to practice must be adopted.
- The views and perceptions of service users, their advocates and their carers must be paramount.

These aspects have long been recognized as the crucial factors in delivering community mental health nursing services. Indeed, they were highlighted as important reasons for introducing the NHS and Community Care Act (1990). However, the ways in which this Act proposed to achieve these same health goals are markedly different from the ways put forward here.

The NHS Act presumes that the introduction of *competition* through the 'marketplace' NHS will lead to an improvement in the service, and ensure that these aims are achieved. This approach differs radically from the key features addressed in this chapter, which emphasize *empowerment* of clients, families, carers and communities and also of all practitioners who work in the field of mental health care. Implementation of the Act has created fundamental changes which need to be taken into account when considering the best way to plan community mental health nursing services.

CMHNs are employed in a wide range of provider units. They work in trusts and directly managed units, which vary widely in size, in scope of services covered and in the way they are managed and organized. Each provider unit may have its own philosophy or mission statement to guide the fulfilment of the services they provide. Overall, there is complexity and fragmentation throughout the health service (Long & McGreevy, 1993).

A number of different models are evolving in the organization, delivery and evaluation of the community mental health services. The fundamental principles of mental health for all, universal services for all and openness and availability for all remain unchanged. A needs-based approach is suggested here. This model is based on four key factors:

- health needs profiling;
- prioritizing mental health care;
- specification of mental health targets;
- identification of measurable mental health outcomes.

Health needs profiling

Service organization must be based on the needs of the population served by the CMHN using health profiling to identify recognized and unrecognized mental health needs. Individual client assessment should aim to identify a client's capacities as well as his or her incapacities and should include an overview of the client's internal world and also of his or her inner strengths and resources. In return, the service provided must be effective, proactive and appropriate.

Prioritizing

Practitioners will require the support of managers skilled in their area of professional practice if they are to draw up priorities and develop their work to the highest standard and effectively and efficiently deliver community mental health nursing care. Primary health care services must become the essence of future health care.

Specification of targets

The ways in which mental health services are commissioned need further development to ensure that resources and priorities reflect a planned approach and an overall strategy for promoting mental health, preventing mental ill health and ensuring the therapeutic care of people who are mentally ill and their carers. Services must be developed to ensure that all members of the community have equal access to health services.

Identification of measurable outcomes

Mental health outcomes/objectives must be identified and evaluated yearly to measure how effectively the objectives have been met. Contracts can be informed by the *needs profile* which will need annual updating. Partnership between government, local authorities, the voluntary and statutory services and community groups, both at national and local levels, is vital to improve the nation's health.

Finally, it is crucial that all doctors, nurses and others who serve in the community work collaboratively and collectively to promote the overall health of their community.

13.16 References

Albee, G. (1986) Towards a Just Society: Lessons from observation (the primary prevention of psychopathology). *American Psychologist*, **41**, 891–8.

Anderson, D. (1984) Health Promotion – An Overview. *European Monographs in Health Education Research*, **6**(4), 4–19.

Argyle, M. (1987) *The Psychology of Happiness*. Methuen, London.

Assagoli, R. (1977) *Psychosynthesis*. Penguin, New York.

Baldwin, M. (1987) The Use of Self in Therapy: An Introduction. *Journal of Psychology and the Family*, Spring edition, **3**(1).

Barker, P.J., Baldwin, S. (1991) *Ethical Issues in Mental Health*. Chapman and Hall, London.

Bartjes, A. (1991) Cited in *Towards a Discipline of Nursing* (eds G. Gray & R. Pratt). Churchill Livingstone, Edinburgh.

Bee, H. (1994) *The Developing Child*. Harper Collins College Publishers, New York.

Bean, P. & Mounser, P. (1993) *Discharged From Mental Hospital*. Macmillan Press, London.

Beck, A.T., Weissman, A., Lester, D. & Trexler, L. (1974) A measurement of pessimism: the hopelessness scale. *Journal of Consulting and Clinical Psychology*, **42**, 861–5.

Beck, A.T. (1979) *Cognitive Therapy and Emotional Disorders*. New American Library, New York.

Beck, A.T., Kovacs, M. & Weissman, A. (1979) Assessment of Suicidal Intention. The Scale for Suicidal Ideation. *Journal of Consulting and Clinical Psychology*, **47**, 343–52.

Belle, D. (1982) *Lives in Stress: Women and Depression*. Sage Publications, Beverly Hills, California.

Benjamin, L.S. (1984) Principles of Prediction Using Structural Analysis of Social Behaviour (SASB) In: *Personality and the Prediction of Behaviour* (eds R.A. Zucker, J. Aronoff & A.J. Rabin). Academic Press, New York.

Benner, P. (1984) *From Novice to Expert*. Addison-Wesley, Reading, Massachusetts.

Birchwood, M., Hallett, S. & Preston, M. (1993) *Schizophrenia: An Integrated Approach to Research and Treatment*. Longman, London.

Blackburn, C. (1992) *Poverty Profiling*. Health Visitors Association, London.

BMA (1992) *National Targets on Community Care: Targets for Service Provision*. BMA, London.

Bohart, A.L. & Todd, J. (1988) *Foundations of Clinical and Counselling Psychology*. Harper and Row Publishers, New York.

Bradshaw, J. (1992) *Healing the Shame That Binds You*. Health Communications Inc, Florida.

Brodsky, A.M. & Hare-Mussin, R. (eds) (1980) *Women and Psychotherapy*. Guildford Press, New York.

Brooker, C. & Brown, M. (1986) National Survey of Practising Nurse Therapists. In: *Readings in Psychiatric Nursing Research* (ed. J. Brooking). Wiley, Chichester.

Brooker, C. (1990) *Community Psychiatric Nursing. A Research Perspective*. Chapman and Hall, London.

Brooker, C. & White, E. (1993) *Community Psychiatric Nursing. A Research Perspective*, Vol 2. Chapman and Hall, London.

Buber, M. & Rogers, C. (1965) Transcriptions of dialogue held 18 April 1965. Ann Arbor, Michigan. Unpublished manuscript.

Buber, M. (1937) *I and Thou*. T & T Clark, Edinburgh.

Buber, M. (1988) *Knowledge of Man: Selected Essays*. Atlantic Highlands, Humanities Press, New York.

Buber, M. (1987) *I and Thou*. Translated by Walter Kaufmann. Scribners, New York.

Burden, D.S. & Gottlieb, N. (1987) *The Woman Client. Providing Human Services in a Changing world*. Tavistock, London.

Butterworth, C.A. & Faugier, J. (eds) (1992) Clinical supervision and mentorship. In: *Nursing*. Chapman & Hall, London.

Campbell, R. & Collinson, D. (1988) *Ending Lives*. Basil Blackwell, Oxford.

Campbell, T. (1988) *Justice*. Macmillan, London.

Caplan, G. (1961) *An Approach to Community Mental Health*. Tavistock Publications, London.

Carmen, E.H., Russo, N.F. & Miller, J.B. (1981) Inequality and Women's Mental Health. *American Journal of Psychiatry*, 138, 1319–30.

Carr, P.J., Butterworth, C. & Hodges, B. (1980) *Community Psychiatric Nursing*. Churchill Livingstone, Edinburgh.

CETHV (1977) *An Investigation into the Principles of Health Visiting*. Council for Education and Training of Health Visitors, London.

Chater, S. (1975) *Understanding Research in Nursing*. WHO, Geneva.

Collee, J. (1992) At the end of their rope. *The Observer*, 1 March, p. 66.

Community Psychiatric Nurses' Association (1985) *The National CPNA Survey Update*. CPNA, Bristol.

Cowley, S. (1991) *A grounded theory of situation and process of health visiting*. PhD thesis, University of Brighton.

Dewdney, A., Gray, C., Minnion, A. & the residents of Rufford Street Hostel (1994). *Down But Not Out*. Trentham Books, Stoke-on-Trent.

DHSS NI (1992) *The Patient's Charter*. HMSO, Belfast.

DHSS NI (1993) *An Action Plan for Mental Health Nursing*. HMSO, Belfast.

DOH (1989) *Caring for People*. HMSO, London.

DOH (1991a) *The Citizen's Charter*. HMSO, London.

DOH (1991b) *The Health of the Nation. A Consultative Document for Health in England*. HMSO, London.

DOH (1993) Secretary of State for Health announces ten point plan for developing successful and safe community care: Press release. DOH, H/93/908.

DOH (1994) *Working in Partnership. A Collaborative Approach to Care*. Report of the Mental Health Nursing Review Team. HMSO, London.

Duck, S. (1992) *Human Relationships*. Sage Publications, London.

Dwinell, L. & Middleton-Moz, J. (1986) *After the Tears*. Health Communications, Pompano Beach, Florida.

Erikson, E. (1979) *Childhood and Society*. Norwood, London.

Ferruci, P. (1982) *What We May Be*. Los Angeles Torcher, Psychosynthesis Trust.

Gaylin, W. (1989) Cited in Modelling awareness of feelings: a real tool in therapeutic communication workbox (ed. L. Miller). *Perspectives in Psychiatric Care*, **XX5**(2).

Gilligan, C. (1977) In a different voice: women's conceptions of self and of mortality. *Harvard Educational Review*, 47, 481–517.

Gore, P. (1984) J.S. Mill on obscenity law reform. *Politics*, 4, October, 3–7.

Greene, J. (1978) Discharge or be damned – The work of the CPN. *Royal Society Health Journal*, **98**, 104–7.

Gunzberg, J.C. & Stewart, W. (1994) *The Grief Counselling Casebook. A Student's Guide to Unresolved Grief*. Chapman and Hall, London.

Hargie, O.D.W. & Dickson, D. (1989) *The Psychology of Interpersonal Skills*. Croom Helm, London.

Hatfield, A.B. & Lefley, H.P. (1987) *Families of the mentally ill. Coping and adaptation*. Cassell, London.

Hawkins, P. & Stohet, R. (1989) *Supervision in the helping professions*. Open University Press, Milton Keynes.

Healy, D. (1993) *Psychiatric Drugs Explained*. Mosby Year Book, Europe.

Heidegger, M. (1987) *On Being and Acting: From Principles to Anarchy*. Translated by R. Shurmann. Indiana University Press, Bloomington.

Heidegger, M. (1992) *The concept of time from the 1924 German Edition* (translated by W. McNeil). Blackwell Publishers, Oxford.

Hunter, P. (1974) CPNs in Britain: an historical overview. *International Journal of Nursing Studies*, **2**, 223–33.

Iven, H. (1994) *Sex Education in Schools in Teaching Today, No. 8.* T. ASUW, London.

Kaplan, M. (1983) A Woman's View of DSM–111. *American Psychologist*, **38**, 786–92.

Kaptein, R. (1993) *On the Way to Freedom.* With the co-operation of Duncan Morrow; introduction by Rene Girand. The Columba Press, Dublin.

Kelley, H.H., Berscheid, E., Christensen, A., Harvey, J.H. & Houston, T.L. (1988) *Close Relationships.* W.H. Freeman, New York.

Keltner, I., Schroke, B. & Bostrom, M. (1991) *Psychiatric Nursing: A Psychotherapeutic Management Approach.* Mosby, London.

Kuhn, T. (1970) *The Structure of Scientific Revolutions*, 2nd edn. The University of Chicago Press.

Lam, W.M.C. (1977) *Perception and lighting as form givers for architecture.* McGraw Hill, New York.

Leininger, M. (1978) *Transcultural Nursing.* Wiley, New York.

Logue, K. (1992) *Anti-Sectarianism and the Voluntary and Community Sector.* Community Relations Council, Northern Ireland.

Long, A. & Chambers, M. (1993) Mental Health in Action. *Senior Nurse*, **13**(5), 7–9.

Long, A. & McGreevy, P. (1993) Advocating advocacy. *Community Psychiatric Nursing Journal*, October 1993, 11–14.

Long, A. & Mullen, B. (1994) An exploration of women's perceptions of the factors that contributed to their alcohol abuse. *Advanced Journal of Nursing*, **19**.

Mangeu, S. & Griffith, J. (1980) Community psychiatric nursing – a literature review. *International Journal of Nursing Studies*, **17**, 197–210.

Martin, F. & Kenny, W. (1980) *Patient or Client: A Study of Social Work and Community Nursing Services for the Mentally Ill in Scotland.* Department of Social Administration, University of Glasgow.

Maslow, A.H. (1987) *Motivation and Personality.* Harper & Row, New York.

Menzies-Lyth, I. (1959) The Functioning of Social Systems as a Defence Against Anxiety. Cited in I. Menzies-Lyth. *Containing Anxiety in Institutions. Selected Essays.* (1988). Free Association Books, London.

Merleau-Ponty, M. (1974) *Phenomenology of Perception.* Humanities Press, New York.

Mills, J.S. (1986) *On Liberty.* Penguin, London.

Murphy, J. (1977) Community Link. *Nursing Mirror*, **144**, 55–6.

NHS and Community Care Act (1990). HMSO, London.

NHSME (1992). *Guidance on the Extension of the Hospital and Community Health Services Elements of GP Fundholding Scheme from 1 April 1993.* EL 48 (92). NHSME, London.

Olds, A.R. (1985) Psychological considerations in humanising the physical environment of paediatric outpatient and hospital settings. In: *Psychosocial Aspects of Paediatric Care.* Stratton, New York.

Ott, J.N. (1973) *Health and Light*. Simon and Schuster, New York.

Parse, R.R. (1992) Human becoming: Parse's theory of nursing. *Nursing Science Quarterly*, **5**(35), 35–45.

Phillips, J.R. (1987) A critique of Parse's man–living–health theory. In: *Nursing Science* (ed. R. R. Parse). W.B. Saunders, Philadelphia.

Prior, L. (1993) *The Social Organisation of Mental Illness*. Sage Publications, London.

Reed, J. & Robbins, I. (1991) Models of nursing. *Journal of Advanced Nursing*, **16**(11), 1350–57.

Reid, W. & Long, A. (1993) The role of the nurse providing therapeutic care for the suicidal patient. *Journal of Advanced Nursing*, **18**, 1369–76.

Roberts, L. (1976) The CPN – early development and current role. *Nursing Times*, **72**, 2020–21.

Rogers, C.R. (1961) *On Becoming a Person*. Houghton-Mifflin, Boston.

Rogers, C.R. (1977) *Carl Rogers on Personal Power*. Constable, London.

Rogers, M. (1980) Nursing: a science of unitary man. In: *Conceptual Models for Nursing Practice* (eds A. Reihl & C. Ray), 2nd edn. Appleton-Century-Crofts, New York.

Rogers, C.R. (1990) *Client Centred Therapy*. Constable, London.

Rowe, A. & Mackeith, P. (1991) Is evaluation a dirty word? *Health Visitor*, **64**(9), 292–3.

Roy, S. (1990) *Nursing in the Community*. Report of a working group, North West Thames Regional Health Authority, Sheila Roy (Chair). HMSO, London.

Rutter, D.R. & Durkin, K. (1987) Turntaking in mother–infant interaction. An examination of vocalizations and gaze. *Developmental Psychology*, **23**, 54–61.

Rutter, M. (1987) Continuities and discontinuities from infancy. In: *Handbook of Infant Development* (ed. J.D. Osofsky) 2nd edn., pp. 1256–96. Wiley–Interscience, New York.

Satre, J.P. (1969) *Being and Nothing Less*. Routledge, London.

Schön, D.A. (1983) *The Reflective Practitioner: How Professionals Think in Action*. Basic Books, New York.

Seedhouse, D. (1986) *Health: The Foundations for Achievement*. John Wiley & Sons, Chichester.

Sharpe, D. (1975) Role of the CPN. *Nursing Mirror*, **141**, 60–2.

Sherman, K.L. (1988) Grief is more than crying. In: *Reading in Psychosynthesis: Theory, Process and Practice* (eds J. Weiser & T. Yeomans). Department of Applied Psychology: Institute of Education, Toronto.

Skidmore, D. & Friend, W. (1984) Community psychiatric nursing. *Nursing Times, Community Outlook*, 10 October, 369–71.

Skinner, B.F. (1957) *Verbal Behaviour*. Prentice Hall, New York.

Sluckin, W., Sluckin, A. & Herbert, M. (1992) *Maternal Bonding*. Basil Blackwell, Oxford.

Smith, B. (1970a) Mental illness and the district nurse: organic and neurotic reactions. *Nursing Times*, **66**, 1329–30.

Smith, B. (1970b) Mental illness and the district nurse. *Nursing Times*, **66**, 1363–4.

Smith, B. (1970c) Mental illness and the district nurse: preventative measures. *Nursing Times*, **66**, 1393–6.

Stuart, S. & Sundeen, T. (1983) *Principles and Practice of Psychiatric Nursing*, 2nd edn. C.V. Mosby, St Louis, Toronto, London.

Szasz, T. (1970) *The Manufacture of Madness*. Harper & Row, London.

Tether, P.L. & Robinson, D. (1986) *Preventing Alcohol Problems. A Guide to Local Action*. Tavistock, London.

Travelbee, J. (1971) *Interpersonal Aspects of Nursing*, 2nd edn. F.A. Davis, Philadelphia.

Tunmore, R. & Thomas, B. (1992) Models of psychiatric consultation liaison nursing. *British Journal of Nursing*, **1**(9), 447–51.

Twinn, S., Dancey, J. & Carnell, J. (1990) *The Process of Health Profiling*. Health Visitors Association, London.

Twinn, S., Dancey, J. & Buttigieg, M. (1992) Responding to the challenge – working with opportunities. *Health Visitor*, **65**(3), 84–5.

UKCC (1988) *Project 2000: A New Preparation for Practice*. UKCC, London.

UKCC (1991) *Community Education and Practice Report*. UKCC, London.

UKCC (1992) *Code of Professional Conduct for the Nurse, Midwife and Health Visitor*, 3rd edn. UKCC, London.

Walker, L.E. (1984) *Women and Mental Health Policy*. Sage Publications, Beverly Hills, California.

Warner, R. (1991) Creative programming. In: *Beyond Community Care: Normalisation and Integration Work* (ed. S. Ramon). Mind Publication, Macmillan, London.

Watson, J. (1985) *Nursing: Human Science and Human Care*. Appleton-Century-Crofts, New York.

White, E. (1993) *The 1990 National Quinquennial Community Psychiatric Nursing Survey*. Department of Nursing, University of Manchester.

Wittenberg, I. (1970) *Psychoanalytic Insight: A Kleinan Approach*. Routledge, London.

Wolfe, M. & Laufer, R. (1974) The Concept of Privacy in Childhood and Adolescence. In: *Man–Environment Interaction* (ed. D.H. Carson), EDRA, 6, 29–54, Milwaukee.

Worden, J.M. (1982) *Grief Counselling and Grief Therapy. A Handbook for the Mental Health Practitioner*. Springer, New York.

Wright, H. & Giddey, M. (1993) *Mental Health Nursing*. Chapman & Hall, London.

Yeo, Tim, Health Minister (1993) In: *Community Care and Mental Health: the Stanley Moore Memorial Lecture. Community Psychiatric Nursing Journal*, April 1993.

Chapter 14

Community Learning Disability Nursing

Community learning disability nursing emerged in the mid-1970s in direct response to the demands of service users and their families for the provision of a range of specialist professional support services outwith the traditional mental handicap hospital. Since that time commissioners and providers of health care services have contracted to provide community learning disability nursing care throughout the United Kingdom. The growth of this specialism within the family of nursing has been accelerated as community care programmes have shifted the locus of care away from the long-stay hospital and its associated services (Collins, 1994).

The implementation of the NHS and Community Care Act (1990) further emphasized the importance of care provision in the community and recommended the implementation of a range of non-institutionalized services within the context of 'the mixed economy of care'.

The community learning disability nurse (CLDN) may be regarded as the 'lynchpin' within an increasingly complex pattern of service responses, and works as an integral member of an interprofessional and multi-agency team. The advent of consumerism has also placed new demands for the development of enhanced competence amongst the workforce, with an emphasis on proficiency in the application of therapeutic skills and care management practices.

Specialist learning disability nurses must be able to respond to the generic and specialist health gain needs and expressed demands of their clients and their families. In order to achieve this objective they will be required to:

(1) stimulate a healthy lifestyle amongst service users and encourage self-reliance for personal health gain and maintenance;
(2) further educate service users, families, informal carers, the community and other care workers in order to maximize opportunities for community inclusion for people with learning disabilities;

288

(3) solve or assist in the solution of both individual and community health care needs and problems;

(4) orient their own efforts, and those of the community, for health promotion and for the amelioration of the effects of disability and the minimization of the consequences of secondary disability;

(5) work in, and with, community learning disability teams, and participate in the development and leadership of such teams;

(6) participate in the delivery of primary health care as equal partners with team members;

(7) demonstrate competence in the delivery of specialist therapeutic skills to enhance independence and to reduce the effects of disability;

(8) function as proficient care managers.

The practice of learning disability nursing has been further defined following the publication of a Chief Nursing Officer Letter (CNO PL (94) 7) (DOH, 1994a). In this circular, learning disability nursing was identified as a 'very important part of the family of nursing' and commissioners and providers of local services were urged to consider how best to ensure that the skills of these specialist nurses were made readily available to service users and their families.

The scope of professional practice for the community learning disability nursing service is therefore set to advance as new demands are placed on the health service to provide a range of alternatives for supported living for service users in the community. The role and function of the CLDN will, in turn, become increasingly challenged by social, political and economic influences and by the emergence of the 'contract culture'.

14.1 External influences

No informed discussion or debate on the provision of social or health care to clients in the community may be undertaken without due consideration of the policy context within which care is provided. There is a range of external social and policy issues that shapes and influences the pattern of service delivery, and these issues in turn will be influenced by societal attitudes and beliefs towards the more dependent members of our society. These have dictated the nature of the models of service delivery that have been provided over the last century and beyond. The deployment of staff skills, the philosophy of care applied and the environments within which people have been cared for are influenced by changes in public attitude, the allocation of resources and changes in social policy.

The challenge of change for the nursing profession as we aspire towards the end of this millennium has been outlined in a report commissioned by the four chief nurses of UK (DOH, 1994b). In this, their 'expert report', they identify the following 'drivers of change':

■ Different demands will be presented by service users who will, by far and large, seek to be supported in the community. However, shifts in society will influence how people relate to each other, their families and their work and these changes will, in turn, affect 'how able and willing families will be to support others, including the frail and vulnerable'.
■ Changes in career patterns and the distribution of wealth require people to live with increasing uncertainty.
■ More people are taking interest in assuming responsibility for their own health and well-being and in so doing are becoming more demanding consumers of health care services.
■ Scientific and technological knowledge have also driven change. The impact of genetic research will also be profound. As a result most admissions to hospital will be reserved only for those who require major surgery and treatment.
■ Ethical considerations are foremost in the health care agenda. Issues relating to euthanasia and genetic engineering will demand that nurses are involved at the 'cutting edge' of debates.
■ Policy initiatives have demanded that there is a shift of reliance away from institutions which will demand that more appropriate ways are found of providing support to people with learning disabilities.

The following paragraphs highlight a number of other key issues which have influenced the contract culture within which skills are transacted.

'Health for all'

In the Declaration of Alma Ata (WHO, 1978) the World Health Organisation stated that their aim of 'Health for All' by the year 2000 should be realized through the introduction of a range of targets for the promotion of health (and the prevention of ill-health) for the population. The government has adopted this aim within resource constraints as part of a Eurostrategy and, as a consequence, students must be provided with opportunities throughout the course of their educational programme to acquire competence as 'knowledgeable specialist practitioners' in the community.

Care in the community

The publication of the NHS and Community Care Act (1990) and its associated White Papers emphasizes the importance of caring for people in the community, which will be accompanied by reduced dependency on secondary health care service provision. The White Paper *Caring for People* (DOH,

1989a) noted that 'nurses working in the community are ideally placed to respond quickly to the needs of individuals and families'. Recent changes in child care legislation have also placed new demands on nurses (The Children Act, 1989).

Community nursing teams

The development of Community Learning Disability Teams has also provided an impetus for change. The importance of interprofessional teamwork and interagency co-operation is emphasized. Community nursing teams have a major contribution to make in the assessment of individual and community health needs and priorities for their local communities. Nurses must therefore be prepared to identify, communicate, influence and evaluate the development of community care plans to ensure the provision of access to a range of support services for clients and their families.

GP Fundholding and skill-mix reviews

The introduction of GP Fundholding has also influenced the purchase and provision of a range of differentiated community health care nursing services. Skill-mix reviews and increased attention to the provision of cost-effective (or 'value-for-money') packages of care will influence the deployment profile of community learning disability nurses in the future who must be able to compete within the context of an 'open economy' of care provision.

The nurse of the future

International perspectives on the provision of community care will also demand the preparation of a more responsive and informed nurse in the future.

The health of the nation

The targets set in *The Health of the Nation* (DOH, 1992) have resulted in an acceleration of activity in primary health care practice and health promotional activity.

The main proposals contained within the two government White Papers *Working for Patients* (DOH, 1989b) and *Caring for People* (DOH, 1989a) paved the way for the emergence of the 'contract culture'. They established the final scenario for the enactment of the Conservative Government's intention to introduce a more rational approach to resource allocation and resource management. The principles were to ensure that the resources available from the public purse would be focused on providing services that directly respond to service user needs and wants. Because of this, questions related to effectiveness, efficiency and value for money have predominated the health care agenda.

In order to achieve these aims a multiplicity of providers was necessary to encourage 'healthy competition' in the health care market. In the field of learning disability, the contract culture has been witnessed over the past decade as additional stimulus is provided to the nonstatutory sector (the private and voluntary) to become involved in the provision of care, hitherto regarded as the province of the NHS and Social Service Departments.

The emergence of new care providers has resulted in the provision of a matrix of residential and domiciliary services for users and their families. It is not surprising, therefore, that the CLDN has developed a key role in ensuring that these services are co-ordinated and effective in providing desired outcomes for clients and their families. In each of the White Papers referred to above the government emphasizes the importance of developing partnerships between consumers, their representatives and statutory agencies with the aim of promoting an open economy in care provision. As a result a new philosophy of care has emerged, based on the principle that care should be shared with consumers and that, wherever possible, care should be provided as close to people's homes as possible.

14.2 Philosophy of nursing care for people with a learning disability

The purpose of a specialist nursing service for people with a learning disability is to provide practical and responsive support to individuals and their families wherever they live, with the aim of enabling them to live valued and purposeful lives in homes of their choice. In so doing specialist advice and assistance is offered in association with family and other carers and other professionals in response to identified needs of service users, their carers and others working with them.

Nursing services should be provided in a way which respects the rights and wishes of individuals. Services should aim to offer a range of real choices and opportunities that assist individuals to participate in their own care and in the design of the services they require and receive, in order to widen their horizons and facilitate the development of their well-being and skills.

Learning disability nurses will practise as knowledgeable, safe, competent professionals. The following values underpin the provision of services.

■ People with a learning disability have the same rights as other members of society, and should have the opportunity to live in the same way as other people; individual rights and wishes should be paramount and the right to representation and confidentiality respected at all times.

- Services should be planned in partnership with service users to enable them to achieve their maximum potential and to lead full and purposeful lives, with the aim of preventing or reducing the effects of any presenting disability.
- The provision of specialist nursing care must respond to the expressed needs of individuals and should follow an interprofessional and multi-agency approach. Comprehensive services should cater for a wide variety of abilities and ages and should be 'seamless', co-ordinated, flexible and tailored to individual needs. They should be provided as close to the person's home as possible and when specialist professional responses are required, these should be accessible.
- Nursing care should be provided in such a way as to enhance the quality of life experienced by individuals; intervention should foster indepen-dence and be commensurate with the expressed needs of consumers.

Perhaps the most important guiding principle has been the acknowledgement by the nursing profession that learning disability is predominantly a social issue, conditioned by societal attitude and public reaction. The philosophy of present day nursing care is cased on the principle of normalization (Wol-fensberger, 1972). The characteristics of ordinary living underpin this approach, which aims to offer a range of choice and opportunities to people with learning disabilities from which they may be enabled to participate in real life experiences.

Community care is based on this principle and refers to the extent to which opportunities are provided for service users to be 'included' within their local communities and neighbourhoods. The majority of health and social services in the UK have adopted the following principles, adapted from Sines (1990) and Towell and Beardshaw (1991), as the foundation for service design and provision.

(1) People with a learning disability are entitled both to the same range and quality of services as those available to other citizens and to services designed to meet their special needs.
(2) Services for younger and older people should recognize their distinctive needs.
(3) In order to be effective the services must be readily available and acceptable to individuals and the families who need to use them.
(4) Services should be able to adapt to meet the needs of each individual.
(5) The philosophy must be to provide maximum opportunities for the residents to experience an ordinary lifestyle.
(6) Emphasis must be placed on encouraging the development of new skills, while staff are expected to allow or assist residents to experience life for themselves, rather than to 'do things for them'.
(7) Consumers should be encouraged to integrate within their local

communities and neighbourhoods; every opportunity is taken to encourage the use of local facilities for recreation, leisure, education, shopping and employment; people will therefore be supported in their contribution to the local community.

(8) Individuals should be encouraged to define their own lifestyle and individuality.

(9) People will be encouraged to develop friendships and to form personal relationships of their choice in order to enhance the quality of their lives.

Kinsella (1993) refers to a specific model of supported living in which people with learning disabilities receive appropriate support to enable them to live as integrated citizens in their own neighbourhoods (with appropriate, but discreetly provided, support). The principles required to achieve the aim of 'life sharing' are:

■ nurturing of a culture that diminishes rather than accentuates distinctions between staff and service users;
■ sharing of life space, activities, work and leisure;
■ demonstration of appropriate behaviours and attitudes that promote social acceptance and community integration;
■ reduction of professional barriers and inequitable power sharing between users of services and supporters.

14.3 Promoting shared care perspectives for practice

The principle aim of the service design and delivery should be to provide services which are as fully integrated into local neighbourhoods as possible. Good practice should also emphasize the importance of involving service users in the planning of their lives and should aim to promote the concept of advocacy to encourage their participation in all decision-making processes.

O'Brien and Lyle (1987) have identified five key determinants or accomplishments they consider necessary for the successful provision of quality based services:

■ choice for individuals;
■ opportunities for integration in the community;
■ opportunities for active participation as equal members of the community;
■ the acquisition of competence;
■ the formation of new friendships and relationships.

The 'accomplishments' framework of O'Brien and Lyle (1987) provides a most useful model for the assessment of needs and for the evaluation of service quality. However, in order to ensure that clients are involved in determining their own needs a systematic approach to care planning will be necessary.

During the past ten years a number of specific personal planning systems have been developed with the aim of co-ordinating needs assessment, service delivery and evaluation. These systems share a number of common principles and are based upon:

- a systematic framework and approach;
- an analytical method designed to assess and identify individual needs, wants and ambitions;
- the involvement of clients and their carers in the planning, implementation and evaluation of care programmes;
- a method of recording and evaluating outcomes;
- a system that ensures that people with learning disabilities are involved in planning their own futures;
- opportunities to plan desirable futures for service users;
- the inclusion of all people essential to the realization of objectives/outcomes identified in the personal plan;
- acknowledged support from commissioners and providers of local services as a legitimate forum for the identification of user needs;
- an inclusive system to identify and report service deficiencies in order to inform service planning processes.

Brechin and Swain (1987) introduced the concept of 'shared action planning' which emphasizes the importance of acknowledging the important role that relationships play in people's lives. This model enhances the personal planning approach and introduces a new dimension into the care programme process which is based on the principle of the importance of the interactions that take place between the service users and carers (and his or her friends). Brechin and Swain (1987) talk of compassionate and supportive caring relationships with reference to their place in determining the context of successful care planning and life experiences:

'Shared Action Planning happens when there is co-ordination, organization and people know who is responsible for doing what.'

Consequently individualized approaches to care should provide a framework for people to express their wishes and desires through a shared process with named workers which in turn should lead to valued outcomes for the individual.

The shared action planning model affords clients opportunities for empowerment; it aims to ensure that maximum control is provided for self-determination and advocacy. However, increased choice may be accompanied by exposure of 'vulnerable' clients to increased risks in the community. Risk-taking and 'risk analysis' have formed a central part of the debate and it should be acknowledged that an environment which allows an appropriate degree of personal choice and privacy can never be risk free. Issues relating to freedom of expression, 'whistle blowing', sexual freedom and 'refusal' to comply with medical instructions are but a few of those that might present themselves as challenges to professional carers and support staff (Brechin & Swain, 1987).

Learning Disability Nurses may find the shared action planning process of considerable assistance during the negotiation of care planning issues with users. It may enable staff to share delicate decision-making issues with users, carers and other professionals and facilitate meaningful deliberation when risk-taking or other ethical issues present. Consequently it would appear that the shared action planning approach is the most appropriate forum for seeking agreement on issues that might involve calculated risks. In support of this process, services should ensure that negotiated risk-taking processes and guidelines are available to staff to provide guidance whenever such decisions must be made.

14.4 Representing the rights of service users

The Patient's Charter (DOH, 1992a) has been the government's 'flagship' for the promotion of user rights in the UK, and applies to all public services. The Charter requires health authorities to provide consumers with information and means of representation to inform their judgements and evaluation of public sector provision.

Learning Disability nurses are often called upon to represent the needs and rights of service users. Through their specialist training and education and work experience with people with learning disabilities, they have acquired specific skills in consumer advocacy. Advocacy may be defined simply as the process of acting for, or on behalf of, another person who is unable to act for himself. Williams and Schoultz (1982) define advocacy as:

'... speaking or acting on behalf of oneself or another person or an issue, with self-sacrificing vigour and vehemence.'

Advocating for others is a controversial business and nurses may find themselves in compromising positions as they aim to uphold the interests of service users and maintain loyalty to their employers. It may, therefore, be said that nurses can never be independent advocates for their clients (Sutor, 1993). However, through formal education and experiential learning, they are able to share insights into consumer-related issues and represent the interests of their clients. In so doing their role involves:

- upholding the rights of persons without prejudice or discrimination;
- acting always in the consumer's best interests;
- acting as an intermediary between the person and those providing or seeking to provide services for that person.

Fowler (1989) describes four models of advocacy:

- guardian of patients' rights;
- preserver of patients' values;
- champion of social justice in the provision of health care;
- conservator of the patients' best interests.

Each of these functions is interdependent and requires the nurse to acquire and apply effective assertion and negotiation skills. A major component of the advocacy role is the extent to which the nurse succeeds in empowering her clients to take an active role in determining their own futures (which will include decisions about their health status and the provision of care). This may involve the development of self-advocacy skills enhancing the person's ability to speak out and act on his or her own behalf.

The nurse's role as advocate is identified in the *Code of Professional Conduct* (UKCC, 1992b) and requires that nurses act always to uphold the public interest. In a supplementary document, *Exercising Accountability*, the UKCC (1989) advices that:

'Advocacy is concerned with promoting and safeguarding the well-being and interests of clients. It is not concerned with conflict for its own sake.'

Examples involving conflict might include complaints about low staffing levels, inappropriate skill-mix, the imposition of treatment strategies on persons who are unable to provide informed consent or the premature discharge of a person from hospital care in the absence of acceptable community-care arrangements.

Such situations involve negotiation with doctors, managers and other members of the interdisciplinary team. Marshall (1991) notes that nurses often require the support and understanding of their professional colleagues. This may not always be achievable, particularly if other members of the multidisciplinary team are unwilling to consult or collaborate with their nursing colleagues.

Many issues confronting community nurses during everyday practice involve moral or ethical decisions. Ethics is primarily concerned with the question of how we ought to treat people and this must involve active deliberation of issues relating to truth-telling (veracity) and beneficence. The latter is one of the key principles that govern nursing practice and aims always to provide 'good and well intentioned consequences' for clients.

However, while this might seem to be a valued ideal it may, in practice, conflict with the philosophy of care offered in the work setting.

One specific challenge for learning disability nurses will be the extent to which they are able to involve users of services in everyday decisions relating to care planning and delivery. The NHS and Community Care Act (1990) recommends the involvement of consumers and their representative groups in all aspects of health care delivery and evaluation. The social care agenda also encourages partnership in care management and new complaints procedures have been published to advise consumers of their representation rights. Information leaflets have also been published to advise patients and clients of their expectations for accessing health and community services.

Nurses, too, have a specific role to play in representing the needs of consumers through involvement in the 'statementing' process concerning children with special needs (Education Act, 1981). Similarly the 1986 Disabled Persons (Consultation, Representation and Services) Act focuses attention on the need to involve consumers at all stages of the assessment and care delivery process through the involvement of appointees and advocates. The Children Act (1989) also emphasizes consultation and representation and its enactment will demand the acquisition of advocacy skills among nursing staff.

The process of listening to consumers requires the active involvement of front-line workers. These will often be nurses who have the opportunity of working closely with consumers at the 'coal-face' of service delivery. There are many ways of capturing the views of the public, and assisting them to identify the things that are important to them and their health care status. Personal communication and mutual respect would appear to be the most effective means of gaining insight into such issues.

Many people with learning disabilities are unable to engage in autonomous decision-making, and in such situations nurses must extend opportunities for consumer involvement; one method of facilitating the achievement of this objective is the establishment of self-advocacy groups. In so doing it should be noted that primary consumers are not the only ones who have an interest in the provision of care services. Secondary consumers such as parents, partners and other carers also have views and these must be heard. However, care should be taken to make a clear distinction between the wants, needs and views of each group (one group may occasionally be in conflict with the other).

Other methods, such as the use of individual programme planning processes, care management and shared action planning (see above), may be employed in order to maximize the involvement of users and serve as examples whereby professional staff have engaged in active dialogue with clients to assess needs and to plan services in active partnership.

The important role of voluntary organizations should also be noted and their ability to represent consumer interests has been well acknowledged by all government departments.

Putting the person first would appear to be an appropriate description of the primary aim of the advocacy process. Services must always focus first on the individual and should attempt to respond to the needs, wishes and preferences of the person as a whole. In order for this to be accomplished, individuals need to have the self-confidence and verbal ability to make their needs and views known. This is particularly important in formal meetings and with groups of people they do not know well. Membership of self-advocacy groups or the use of a citizen advocate (a person who agrees to represent the interests of a client without legal sanction or remuneration) may assist users to present their views independently of professional influence.

The extent to which nurses may act as effective advocates for consumers within the present professional and legal systems of the UK is somewhat limited. Despite major advances in the way in which nurses work to form equal partnerships with users of services, the extent to which nursing may be said to be truly representative of client interests remains questionable. However, nurses are certainly encouraged to advocate on behalf of their clients and their new educational curricula addresses the advocacy issue both critically and responsively.

14.5 Skills and competences

Community learning disability nursing has been identified as a specialist area of practice (UKCC, 1994). Courses leading to the award of the professional Community Learning Disability Nursing qualification are approved by the relevant National Board for Nursing, Midwifery and Health Visiting. Courses are provided flexibly to enable students to complete their studies (and to acquire the necessary practice competences to work as a CLDN) on a part-time basis or as full-time secondees; 50% of the course is theory based and the remainder is practice focused. Practice placements are provided for students throughout the course and students progress from taught practice placements to working as CLDNs under the supervision of a qualified practice teacher who also has the appropriate community qualification.

A maximum of two-thirds of the course is provided as common core modules which are shared by all community health nursing students prior to specialization in their chosen practice area. Students are expected to study together within the primary health team context and in association with their period of taught practice; the first half of the course will precede the specialist modules for preparation as a community learning disability nurse. The key elements for the core component of the course have been specified by the UKCC and fall into four areas: clinical nursing practice; care and programme management, clinical practice leadership; and clinical practice development.

Clinical nursing practice

This includes assessment, planning, implementation and evaluation techniques; the provision of informal care support for users and their families; counselling; nurse prescribing; interdisciplinary team working; management of the care process; and empowerment of clients.

Care and programme management

This includes health needs assessment and activity; dissemination of information; recognition of moral, ethical and legal issues; promotion of self-reliance for health care; initiation and contribution to health-care strategies designed to promote and improve health gain and maintenance strategies; design and implementation of epidemiological research and community profiles; and proficiency in care management.

Clinical practice leadership

This includes acting as a source of expert knowledge on behalf of the primary health care team; leading and directing a professional team; displaying expert clinical leadership skills; acting as an effective mentor and preceptor for students and novice staff; clinical supervision models; and resource management techniques.

Clinical practice development

This includes initiation and development of practice; application of research findings; design and implementation of quality assurance methods; and formulation and application of audit techniques.

Courses leading to the preparation of specialist community health-care nurses will be integrated within the higher education sector and will form an integral component of honours degree courses. Effective course delivery will be dependent on the integration of the course programme within a range of academic disciplines which will include:

- nursing
- philosophy and moral ethics
- psychology
- sociology
- social policy and administration
- communication sciences
- information technology
- research methods

- health economics
- education.

In applying their skills and practice in the community, students will need to assess a range of social risk factors that might emerge at different times to challenge the health status of individuals and groups. For example, child and adult abuse, victim abuse and deterioration in physical and mental health may challenge the diagnostic and problem-solving skills of practitioners. Social issues such as living with elderly carers and moving from hospital to live in the community will also demand particular responses and approaches. The legal context of care delivery must also be appreciated and observed.

During the course of the community health nursing programme students will be expected to participate in the assessment of individual and community care needs and to contribute to the formulation of strategies to address the identified health care needs of this client group. The compilation of neighbourhood profiles will assist students in the identification of local resources to enable the production of responsive community care plans and programmes for their clients and their families.

The organizational context of community nursing practice will demand the flexible application of a range of skills and nursing procedures in the community. Not only must the student aim to be personally acceptable to a client but he or she must understand the nature of the particular value system and culture of each individual in order to appreciate issues that might influence the delivery of health care.

The UKCC (1994) recommends that a minimum of two specific taught modules should be dedicated to preparing students to work proficiently in their chosen area of discrete (or specialist) practice:

'The programme for specialist preparation for Community Learning Disability Nursing is concerned with maximising the potential for independent living and minimising the effects of disability, among service users within a community setting. Specialist nursing for this client group also includes the provision of support, health education and health promotion to individuals, families, groups and communities. This involves a contribution to the wider health function.'

Entry into the community learning disability nursing programme is conditional upon the achievement of preregistration competence (and formal registration) as prescribed in accordance with Parts 5, 6, 7 and 14 of the UKCC Register.

The UKCC (1994) lists specific outcomes which must also be achieved for the award of the Community Learning Disability Nursing qualification:

(1) 'assess, plan, provide and evaluate specialist clinical nursing care to meet care needs for people with learning disabilities, their families and

carers in order to develop clients' personal capacities and their skills in self-advocacy and self-reliance for their health and social status;

(2) assess and manage clinical emergencies and critical events, including the management of challenging and violent behaviour, to ensure effective care and safety;

(3) play a key role in care management and identify and select from a range of health and social agencies, those which will assist and improve the care of individuals and groups; and

(4) initiate strategies to maximise the potential for independent living and minimise the effects of disability amongst people with learning disabilities living in the community.'

CLDNs will also be required to examine critically and analyse a range of management and leadership styles that influence the provision of community learning disability nursing practice. Consequently students will be expected to acknowledge the roles that management and political awareness play in directing clinical practice. Students will need to be conversant with a range of management, leadership and care philosophies relating to community learning disability nursing practice and demonstrate proficiency in the use of a range of management and leadership skills within a service that is in a process of consistent transformation and change.

More specifically CLDNs should:

(1) employ a range of scientifically validated assessment techniques to formulate a profile of a person's strengths, needs, wants and ambitions within the context of a care management framework;

(2) assume responsibility for the formulation, implementation and evaluation of various care planning methodologies for a group of clients for whom they are responsible;

(3) utilize consumer advocacy skills, experiential learning and specialist knowledge to represent and empower people with mental health needs within a shared action planning context;

(4) identify, through nursing diagnosis, a range of issues and problems that influence the emotional, spiritual, physical and social well-being of clients;

(5) recognize, assess and respond to the support needs of informal carers;

(6) investigate and monitor the effect that community learning disability nursing interventions have had on the health gains of individuals and their families;

(7) adopt and employ a range of qualitative and resource management measures and processes to evaluate the efficiency and effectiveness of community nursing practice;

(8) formulate and implement standards (in partnership with clients and other carers) in order to maintain high quality service delivery;

(9) engage in self- and peer review to evaluate the therapeutic effectiveness of nursing and other care delivered;

(10) lead and facilitate a multidisciplinary team to deliver comprehensive services to people with mental health needs and their families within a defined geographical area; act as a specialist health care resource within a multidisciplinary framework;

(11) recognize resource limitations and contribute to the collection and analysis of activity data to justify resource allocation;

(12) critically appraise the extent to which service providers meet the expressed needs of users and their families, and identify areas of deficiency;

(13) act as a peripatetic resource to residential care staff and lead a team of varying 'skill mix' as a specialist nurse leader;

(14) influence the process of change by encouraging the development of new community service responses by projecting personal and professional vision and by engaging in objective research.

14.6 Specialist therapeutic skills and practice

The importance of acquiring specialist therapeutic or interventionist skills is considered essential in community practice, and builds upon previously acquired competences. Increasing emphasis on noninstitutional approaches to care requires that those engaged in community learning disability nursing critically examine the scope of their practice and acquire competence in the provision of specialist nursing skills in a flexible and responsive manner (UKCC, 1992).

Specific competences relate to an ability to:

(1) apply and contract a range of appropriate specialist nursing interventions related to health gain areas for this client group in order to:

  ■ enhance the acquisition of self-help and social skills for people with learning disabilities;
  ■ enhance the successful integration (and where relevant the relocation) of people with special needs in the community;
  ■ reduce the effects of specific age-related disorders and presentations;
  ■ reduce the effects of symptoms related to multiple presentations, sensory impairments and other specific clinical conditions, and apply therapeutic approaches, e.g. alternative therapies;
  ■ reduce the effects of acute mental illness and promote positive mental health;
  ■ reduce the effects and presentation of challenging or antisocial behaviours;
  ■ reduce the effects of forensic behaviours and presentations;

(2) identify and respond to the needs of a wide range of people with special needs (irrespective of age or degree of learning disability) with the aim of developing personal capacity and encouraging self-reliance for their health and social status;

(3) critically analyse the theoretical basis of interventions deployed within the community learning disability nursing service, and select appropriate approaches to meet specified needs;

(4) apply advanced skills in:

■ the design, implementation and evaluation of behavioural therapies/ strategies;

■ meeting the interpersonal and emotional needs of clients through the use of a range of counselling and psychotherapeutic techniques, including group therapy;

■ clinical management of conditions such as epilepsy, physical disabilities, metabolic and neurological disorders and organic presentations;

(5) demonstrate through the formulation, implementation and evaluation of shared action plans (and care management packages) an ability to negotiate, cost and facilitate high quality care for individuals, families or groups, recognizing and articulating the ethical/moral implications of such actions;

(6) communicate effectively with other professionals and work as members of an interprofessional team;

(7) apply a range of strategies designed to promote positive health and well-being and prevent the presentation of disabling conditions (for example, through the acquisition of skills in prevention and crisis management);

(8) apply moral, legal and medico-legal aspects of care to practice and assume professional accountability for risk-taking and the management of care;

(9) work as integral members of resettlement teams and facilitate the smooth transition of service users from long-stay mental handicap hospitals to new homes in the community;

(10) employ a range of skills to educate the local community with the aim of encouraging meaningful integration;

(11) demonstrate through the use of case methodology an appreciation and understanding of the importance of evaluation and research within the therapeutic context contributing to the discovery of new knowledge.

CLDNs are also expected to analyse moral dilemmas involved in the provision (or withholding) of therapeutic care to a particular individual, and to challenge current methods of teamwork and service response. The promotion and articulation of the rights of people with learning disabilities to enjoy purposeful lives in their local communities (in accordance with ordinary life principles and government conventions, e.g. *The Patient's Charter* (DOH, 1992a)) must form the foundation of their nursing practice.

Finally, through the employment of dynamic leadership skills, CLDNs should be active participants in the design of new responses to meet changing consumer needs and apply nursing knowledge to evaluate the effectiveness of care provision.

14.7 Conclusion

During a time of intensive change in learning disability services there must be strong and effective nurse leadership and management if practitioners are to adapt to the many and varied challenges that lie ahead in the provision of health and social care proposed in recent government legislation (NHS and Community Care Act, 1990). This chapter ends with a summary of specific targets which are proposed for the effective management and leadership of community learning disability nursing services.

(1) Learning disability nursing services must develop a strategic vision relating to the management of nursing practice, workforce planning, education, leadership and resource management. Managers in all settings should agree a local strategy in partnership with clients, their families and carers and with other professionals to co-ordinate plans for effective service delivery and skill mix.

(2) As the business of large, specialist hospitals is redefined, nurse managers and leaders should be proactive in ensuring that the needs of service users and of the workforce are represented in order to ensure that the provision and accessibility of high quality services is maintained.

(3) Investment in the development and maintenance of effective communication channels between different parts of the nursing service (particularly between domiciliary and residential nursing care teams) should be regarded as a priority. Nurses working in the community, in residential care, in day services and in education and management should work together to create 'a seamless' service for the benefit of clients which aims to address and resolve all professional nursing matters.

(4) The highest possible financial and personnel skill and advice must be available to nurse managers.

(5) Senior nurses must continue to recruit and retain well-motivated and professionally committed nurses in sufficient numbers to maintain and improve services delivered to clients.

(6) A coherent learning disability nursing strategy, agreed by a cross-section of nurses and interested parties, should be developed in order to avoid unco-ordinated change.

(7) A framework should be introduced in each trust health authority which encourages all main stake holders to become involved in the design and development of change strategies aimed at improving the quality of care and life for people with a learning disability. Such strategies should seek to enable staff to assist in decisions relating to priority setting, the pace of change and implementation of timetables, resource allocation and the evaluation of service effectiveness.

(8) All staff should be encouraged to participate in different aspects of the management of care and local service delivery. The possibility of decentralization of certain management functions to ward and community team levels should be investigated in order to encourage the participation and involvement of front-line staff in decision-making processes.

(9) The allocation of nursing resources should be determined in response to the actual needs of service users following the introduction of care management processes, activity data analyses, care audits and quality assessments. This will also require the systematic use of a proven method of personal planning to accurately determine the skills required from qualified nurses and their support staff.

(10) Senior nurses, within general management arrangements, must determine the organizational and career structures in learning disability nursing within clinical practice, management, education and research.

(11) Senior nurses with others (including professionals from other disciplines and agencies), must determine workforce, grade, skill mix requirements and boundaries of practice to meet the needs of residents and clients in order to provide opportunities for supported living in the community.

(12) Senior nurses must determine the role, competences and training requirements of support staff and should encourage the recognition of their skills and contribution to the care process by facilitating access to vocational training opportunities.

(13) Specific consideration should be given to the skills demanded of those nurses working with clients who have additional needs such as challenging behaviours, multiple handicaps, mental health needs and sensory handicaps. Where appropriate, dual qualifications of RNMH (Registered Nurse for People with a Mental Handicap) and RMN (Registered Mental Nurse) should be obtained. Opportunities should be extended for reciprocal refreshment between specialities.

(14) Following experience gained from the implementation of the clinical grading process, nurses should be encouraged to engage in infinite experiment to provide a career structure based on recognition and positive reward for advanced clinical competences and ability, thus reducing dependence on traditional systems of promotion.

(15) Each workforce should engage in periodic review of workforce needs.

This should be integrated with an overall system of staff development and performance review and client need assessment/audit.

(16) Senior nurses must review and develop the potential of all staff for whom they are accountable. Those with specialist and advanced qualifications should be enabled to use their additional skills.

(17) Senior nurses must share responsibility for ensuring that the environment is conducive to delivery of high quality care.

(18) There should be identified policies for continuing education management training, career development and succession planning; nurses should make use of appropriate training to enable them to participate fully in all aspects and levels of management.

(19) Senior nurses must ensure that opportunities are available for nurses to train in research methods, undertake research projects and apply and disseminate the findings where appropriate.

(20) Flexible patterns of staff deployment should be encouraged which are responsive to the needs of service users.

(21) Independent counsellors should be provided to assist staff in sharing particular stresses acquired in the workplace. Such a service should be confidential, easily accessible and independent. It is particularly important in those areas where staff are working with people with challenging behaviour.

(22) Opportunities and encouragement should be extended to staff from nursing and social work backgrounds to transfer between traditional workplaces, and agencies employed whenever the needs of clients require the flexible deployment of skills and workforce resources. The role of nursing across service boundaries must be acknowledged and whenever nurses are employed outwith the NHS they should be extended the opportunity to practise as nurses with their accountability to the UKCC preserved. This approach would assist in the generation of a system of care characterized by a multiplicity of skills in partnership with informal carers.

(23) Each service must determine the standards and outcomes that it expects the workforce to attain. Information systems should be available to assist nurses in managing the nursing resource.

(24) Each service must introduce and publish policies and procedures which respect the rights of individuals and which reflect the philosophy of the service and its values.

(25) Nurse managers should set specific performance targets for all staff which should be reviewed annually.

(26) Each service should identify the standards of practice that it expects of its staff and should define the criteria by which outcomes/performance will be assessed and evaluated.

(27) Each service should design and implement a strategy which determines how quality will be measured and assured. Such strategies should be

published within the framework of each service contract/agreement and should be reflected in all management training courses and staff development modules.

(28) Each nurse should have access to a senior clinical practitioner/mentor to whom he or she should account in respect of personal professional practice as part of a negotiated and systematic supervision system.

(29) Each service should develop and publish/market a prospectus which includes the range of skills and services provided by the speciality for its service users. This should form the basis of a service agreement and should contain specific measures of quality and output.

(30) The increased emphasis on, and facility for, the collection and use of resident, client and workforce information must be matched by increased vigilance and determination to ensure privacy and confidentiality of personal data; staff should be trained in the use and application of information technology systems.

14.8 References

Brechin, A. & Swain, J. (1987) *Changing Relationships – Shared Action Planning for People with Mental Handicaps*. Harper & Row, London.

The Children Act (1989). HMSO, London.

Collins, J. (1994) *Still to be Settled – Strategies for the Resettlement of People from Mental Handicap Hospitals*. Values into Action, London.

The Disabled Persons (Consultation, Representation and Services) Act (1986). HMSO, London.

DOH (1989a) *Caring for People* (White Paper). HMSO, London.

DOH (1989b) *Working for Patients*. HMSO, London.

DOH (1992a) *The Patient's Charter*. HMSO, London.

DOH (1992) *The Health of the Nation*. HMSO, London.

DOH (1994a) *The Future of Learning Disability/Mental Handicap Nursing*, (CNO PL (94) 7), HMSO, London.

DOH (1994b) *The Challenges for Nursing and Midwifery in the 21st Century (The Heathrow Report)*. HMSO, London.

Education Act (1981). HMSO, London.

Fowler, D.M. (1989) Social advocacy. *Heart and Lung*, **1**,18.

Kinsella, P. (1993) *Supported Living – A New Paradigm*. National Development Team, Manchester.

The NHS and Community Care Act (1990). HMSO, London.

Marshall, M (1991) Advocacy within the multi-disciplinary team. *Nursing Standard*, **6**(10), 28–31.

O'Brien, J. & Lyle, C. (1987) *Framework for Accomplishment*. Responsive Service Systems and Associates, Georgia.

Sines, D.T. (1990) *Valuing the carers: an investigation of support systems* required by mental handicap nurses in residential services in the community. PhD thesis, University of Southampton.

Sutor, J. (1993) Can Nurses be Effective Advocates? *Nursing Standard,* 7(22), 30–33.

Towell, D. & Beardshaw, V. (1991) *Enabling Community Integration – the role of public authorities in promoting an ordinary life for people with learning disabilities in the 1990s.* King's Fund, London.

UKCC (1989) *Exercising Accountability.* UKCC, London.

UKCC (1992a) *The Scope of Professional Practice.* UKCC, London.

UKCC (1992b) *Code of Professional Conduct for Nurses, Midwives and Health Visitors.* UKCC, London.

UKCC (1994) *The Future of Professional Practice – The Council's Standards for Education and Practice Following Registration.* UKCC, London.

WHO (1978) *Health for all.* Declaration of WHO Conference on Primary Health Care, Alma Ata. WHO, Geneva.

Williams, P. & Schoultz, B. (1982) *We can Speak for Ourselves.* Condor Books, London.

Wolfensberger, W. (1972) *The Principles of Normalisation in Human Services.* National Institute on Mental Retardation, Toronto.

Part 3

The Measurement of Competence and Quality in Community Health Care Nursing

Chapter 15

Assessment of Competence to Practise

Courses leading to UKCC recordable or registerable qualifications in community health care nursing are offered within an educational framework which confers both academic awards and post-registration nursing qualifications (UKCC, 1994). Within this context each course is validated by an academic institution and is approved by the appropriate National Board for Nursing, Midwifery and Health Visiting. Though each course has a single purpose – to prepare registered nurses to work as specialist community health care nurses – the process of education must address two issues:

(1) how best to enable students to achieve satisfactory academic standards in subjects judged necessary and sufficient for completion of the programme of study; and
(2) how best to enable students to attain a standard of professional competence commensurate with effective community health care nursing practice.

If you have ever tried to juggle you'll appreciate that it is unlikely that you will learn to do something which involves skilful action simply by watching the performance of somebody who is already an expert. You will also realize that it is even less likely that juggling can be learned from reading about it. Of course, learning to practise as a community health care nurse is not exactly like learning to juggle. Juggling is simple; it involves the handling of inanimate objects and nobody gets hurt if you drop one of the objects. In contrast, community health care nursing is complex; it involves working with people and the consequences of a mistake can be dire. However, to become competent in either juggling or community health care nursing you need to learn, and to learn you need to practise.

In this chapter some of the issues associated with practice-based learning in community health care nursing courses are explored. More specifically, the

313

aim is to outline organizational aspects of practice-based study; discuss the relationship between practice-based and university-based course components and comment on conceptual frameworks which can be utilized to shape practice-based learning; highlight different approaches which are apparent in relation to competency-based education in the UK; and examine ways in which practice-based learning can be facilitated and assessed.

Sometimes the same term is used to describe different things and sometimes different terms are used to describe the same thing. This is evident when considering ways in which practice-based learning are discussed. The word 'practice' is used to refer to many different things (e.g. as an abbreviation for practice-based study, practice-based learning or practical knowledge). The phrases 'practice-based study' and 'practice-based learning' are not used interchangeably in this chapter. The former refers to activities intended to facilitate learning within practice-based components of a course and the latter refers to the student's learning which results from engagement in community health care nursing activities. The relevance of the term 'practical knowledge' is also discussed within the chapter. Phrases which are used synonymously with practice-based learning include 'learning in the clinical setting', 'work-based learning', 'fieldwork-based learning', 'practical work learning', 'skills acquisition' and 'experiential learning'.

Clarity of communication can also be compromised when the term 'theory' is used to refer to the opposite of 'practice' and for this reason the terms 'university-based study' and 'university-based learning' are preferred in this chapter. Of course, the types of activities which are associated with university-based study can take place outwith a university (e.g. by means of distance learning material). Use of the phrase 'university-based learning' in this context should be seen as broadly descriptive. It is also worth noting that Carr and Kemis (1986) have drawn attention to the dangers of an unsophisticated differentiation between 'theory' and 'practice', based on the notion that 'theory' is knowledge which students learn in the classroom and 'practice' is application of that knowledge somewhere else. Gauthier (1992) points out not only that there is a range of possible meanings for the terms 'theory' and 'practice' but also that relations between operationalized concepts will depend crucially on particular interpretations.

15.1 Organizational aspects of practice-based study

Very many people, not least service users and employers, have an interest in ensuring that student community health care nurses emerge from their courses of study as caring, skilful, knowledgeable and reflective practitioners. However, the people who are most directly involved in this process are students, practice supervisors and course lecturers. It may be helpful, therefore, to clarify organizational aspects of practice-based study by reference to each of these groups and by considering the responsibilities of National Boards in approving and auditing placement locations.

Students

As registered nurses, students who choose to undertake a course leading to the award of a community health care nursing qualification have already been assessed as competent with regard to their preregistration nursing practice. However, as Eraut (1992) points out:

'... the precise stage at which professionals are deemed to have qualified will depend on what they are expected to do, that is on the organisation of professional work. The appropriate question is "qualified to do what?" and the appropriate answer cannot be "qualified to do everything in the profession".'

As adult learners, students have the potential to draw on a wealth of personal and professional experience to help make sense of, and understand, new topics of study; and they are particularly well placed to contribute to the creation of an environment which promotes collaborative learning. For many students, however, preregistration nursing courses will have emphasized the development of expertise in relation to hospital-oriented nursing practice, though it is likely that an increasing number of students will have had experience of working in non-hospital settings following implementation of Project 2000 (UKCC, 1988) courses throughout the UK. For many students the community health care nursing course will offer exposure to higher education for the first time. These characteristics of the student group enable the design of community health care nursing courses to be underpinned by principles developed in relation to continuing education; they also highlight the need to include elements which are more characteristic of a preservice educational format. It is perhaps for this reason that community practice teachers and assessors have long been regarded as having essential roles to perform in the education of community health care nurses.

Practice supervisors

Practice-based study components normally consist of two sequential and integrated placements which are referred to as 'taught practice' and 'supervised practice'. In relation to taught practice the student is normally supervised by a 'community practice teacher', who is expected to formulate a study programme which will enable an individual student to develop confidence and competence in a particular branch of community health care nursing. Use of the title 'community practice teacher' to describe a practitioner whose work encompasses formal involvement in the education of individual community nurses has emerged fairly recently. In relation to community nursing in the home (district nursing) and public health nursing (health visiting) the traditional titles have been 'practical work teacher' and 'fieldwork teacher' respectively. Across-discipline titles such as 'teacher practitioner' and 'practitioner teacher' have also been adopted. Jarvis and Gibson (1985) note:

'The [community practice teacher's] role is not only highly skilled but one that requires preparation and it is also very significant because it lies at the interface of theory and practice and occupational preparation and practice'.

Within supervised practice the student will receive advice, guidance and assistance from an appropriately qualified nursing practitioner or nurse manager who acts as his or her 'community practice assessor' or 'assessor of supervised practice'. The role of the practice supervisor is considered to be vital in community health care nursing education as it is an effective means of ensuring that each student is exposed to situations which will enable incremental development of professional competences. This involves arranging the student's introduction to, and orientation within, the area of practice and providing information about local policies, procedures, systems and approaches. It also entails the allocation and review of caseload responsibilities and, crucially, the setting up of a framework for supervision and assessment.

Course lecturers

The organization of practice-based study constitutes an important part of the work of the course lecturer in community health care nursing. It involves taking the steps necessary to ensure that community practice teachers and assessors are included as full members of the course team and that links with employers and representatives of professional bodies are established, maintained and developed. Course lecturers must ensure that suitable procedures are in place to enable students and practitioners with whom the students will have contact during their placements to establish relationships which will promote learning. This entails organization of pre-placement briefings, matching students with practice supervisors, providing guidelines which highlight educational and administrative requirements, monitoring placements through contact with students and community practice teachers and/ or assessors and the organization of post-placement briefings. For students who already have experience of working in a community setting it is generally considered desirable that taught practice should be offered in a new location to ensure that he or she is able to adopt the role of a learner.

During supervised practice the student is required to carry out the full range of work activities associated with community health care nursing, albeit in relation to a smaller number of service users than would be the case for a qualified practitioner, and he or she will normally be required to complete additional course work. In instances where students know where they will be working following successful completion of the community health care nursing course it may be of advantage for supervised practice to be arranged in that location. This will not only help to ameliorate problems associated with service discontinuity but will also maximize the vocational utility of coursework.

Responsibilities of National Boards

As part of their role in approving community health care nursing programmes, National Board personnel work with course lecturers and practice supervisors to ensure that placement locations are audited and monitored. It is expected that each location will provide students with facilities suitable for undertaking practice-related activities and other coursework. It is also important that students have opportunities to participate in the range of activities necessary to develop an overview of the role required within a particular branch of specialist community health care nursing and learn to practise in an environment in which appropriate professional standards are maintained. Community practice teachers and assessors who supervise students undertaking courses leading to the award of particular community health care nursing qualifications (e.g. those of public health nursing or community nursing in the home) are normally required to have completed (or to be undertaking) a preparatory course.

Successful completion of an approved course is not yet a universal requirement within all branches of community health care nursing though, as the UKCC (1994) points out:

'Any student undertaking a programme leading to a registerable or recordable qualification must be supervised by someone who already has that qualification or who has the appropriate clinical or practical teaching experience.'

Individual community practice teachers and assessors are responsible for organizing a programme of study activities for each student, though other members of staff within the placement location will be able to contribute to the student's education. For this reason audit checklists which are developed by course staff and approved by the appropriate National Board are normally concerned with a wide range of factors (see Appendix 15.1) and are often incorporated within the framework of a joint clinical and educational audit.

15.2 Practice-based learning

In considering the relevance of practice-based learning it can be helpful to establish a distinction between 'theoretical knowledge' and 'practical knowledge'. There are several ways of conceptualizing the nature of knowledge but this distinction provides the rationale for the inclusion of a combination of academic and practical learning experiences in nursing courses (Alexander, 1983) and in a wide range of continuing education programmes for professionals (Cervero, 1988). Incorporation of university-based study within courses should mean that students are exposed to an environment which values and champions learning and learnedness. Moreover, students will have their attention directed to bodies of knowledge and methods of investigation which they can draw on to help make sense of complex issues. Within a higher education setting each student is expected not only to develop his or her capacity for critical analysis and creative synthesis but also to learn to construct coherent academic arguments in relation to particular topics or subject matter. Though important the learning which takes place during university-based study is not considered qualitatively sufficient to enable post-registration students to become competent to practise as specialist nurse practitioners or specialist community nursing practitioners. As the UKCC (1994) points out: 'The importance of practice-based learning must be emphasized as an integral part of a practice-based profession'.

Despite (or maybe because of) novel terminology, the work of Donald Schön has been seminal in opening up debate about the value of practical knowledge in the education of professionals. There is much evidence to suggest that Schön's ideas have been instrumental in shifting emphasis away from preoccupation with students' success in assimilating theoretical ('technical rational') knowledge and towards the development of their 'professional artistry'. Schön (1983) suggests that professional artistry can best be achieved by enabling students to develop their ability to act on the basis of their judgements ('knowing-in-action') which is '. . . the characteristic mode of ordinary practical knowledge', and by developing their capacity to re-frame and thus address problematic situations. For Schön, reflection-in-action is central to professional artistry as it is the process by which a situation is understood, problems set and action strategies determined. It also enables new practical knowledge to be generated by 'contributing to the practitioner's repertoire of exemplary themes from which, in the subsequent cases of his practice, he may compose new variations'. Schön (1987) proposes that the main purpose of continuing professional education programmes should be to create environments in which '. . . practitioners learn to reflect on their own tacit theories of the phenomena of practice, in the presence of representatives of those disciplines'.

The need to consider how best to develop the practitioner's capacity to exercise judgement, rather than just expecting him or her to learn and then apply certain techniques in particular situations, has served to emphasize the educational importance and relevance of practice-based study. It has also led to questioning of the balance between courses which focus on theoretical knowledge and those which emphasize the primacy of practical knowledge. Cervero (1992), for example, has commented: 'Although it would be inappropriate to use a model of learning from practice in all situations. It should become the dominant model when the goal is to develop practitioners who engage in wise practice'. Benner and Wrubel (1989) suggest that in nursing the relationship between theoretical knowledge and practical knowledge should be such that '... theory is derived from practice'.

Ideas about the best mix of components in a programme intended to facilitate learning in relation to both of these types of knowledge, and whether they could and/or should be integrated, are influenced by a wide range of factors – not least by ideology. Cervero (1992), for instance, has pointed out: '... for the better part of this century, our society has given legitimacy to knowledge that is formal, abstract and general, while devaluing knowledge that is local, specific and based in practice'. On the basis of an ethnographic study of practice-based components of community nursing in the home (district nursing), Mackenzie (1990) has noted that students are aware of 'different messages' during university-based and practice-based study which they try to reconcile by attempting to apply what they have learned in university to their nursing practice. When they find out that this doesn't work they will then '... develop strategies for coping with this "gap" and separate the two areas out, compartmentalising the two and working with them in parallel'. Mackenzie also found that '... students interpret the academic disciplines in order to make them usable in the practice situation', and are able to achieve integration towards the end of the course without being aware that this is happening.

Practice-based study is intended to enable students to learn through their engagement in a range of activities, and a variety of conceptual frameworks can be drawn upon to underpin, guide and/or inform curriculum design and to shape practice-based learning. One of the first issues which must be addressed in relation to course design is whether or not practice-based learning should be treated as essentially the same as, or essentially different from, university-based learning. Not unnaturally, different understandings which are apparent in how people respond to this issue reflect wider debates on the nature of knowledge and how best education can facilitate learning.

Regardless of course design, everyone involved in the educational process will have an idiosyncratic perspective from which he or she will consider how best to enable learning. Bassey (1992) has suggested that it is important for people involved in education '... from time to time to write down the platforms of their beliefs'. Unfortunately this is not normally a feature of current educational practice so it would be impossible to provide a comprehensive list of conceptual frameworks which underpin community health care nursing courses. Nevertheless, it is possible to mention some of the major influences by considering different ways in which practice-based learning is conceptualized. The following analysis of 'conceptions of learning' was facilitated by funding awarded to the author by the National Board for Nursing, Midwifery and Health Visiting for Scotland to carry out an exploratory study of practice-based learning in higher education accredited post-registration courses in Scotland (Kay, 1994).

Learning as behavioural change

Nurse education is currently moving away from the predominant influence of a 'behavioural objectives' approach which conceptualizes learning as behavioural change. This approach is associated with Tyler (1949) but, as Ormell (1992) points out, *A Taxonomy of Educational Objectives*, (Bloom, *et al.*, 1956; 1964) was also particularly influential as it '... invested the ideas of behavioural objectives with a degree of scientific credibility, visibility and curricular weight never previously quite achieved'. Though 'Bloom's Taxonomy' identifies three domains of learning (cognitive, affective and psychomotor), the original work concentrated on performance-derived cognitive attributes and the construction of a hierarchically conceived list of behaviours which could both describe learning and prescribe teaching strategies. An example of an essentially behaviourist approach in nurse education is provided by Donoghue and Pelletier (1991) who describe an '... ongoing search for an objective assessment tool for use by clinical teachers'.

Early criticisms of the 'objectives model' of curriculum (e.g. Stenhouse, 1975) and its corollary of evaluation by performance testing (Willis, 1988) have not always been heeded. It is still possible to find courses which only specify behaviours which students are expected to demonstrate by the end of their programme. Ormell (1992) has suggested that it is not the setting of goals within educational programmes which is the problem with this approach; rather it is the reduction of educational aims to statements of required behaviour. Within this context a course design which utilizes a 'domains of learning' approach by specifying aims in relation to knowledge–skills–attitudes or knowledge–skills–values need not restrict goals to 'behaviourally correct' criteria or determine relevance solely in terms of measurability.

Learning as conceptual change

The adoption of a *behavioural objectives* approach has been much less pervasive in higher education than in other educational settings. This is perhaps because of the influence of Ference Marton and Roger Saljö, whose work helped to ensure that UK research on student learning moved away from a primary concern with quantitative issues (e.g. how much can a student recall and what factors affect performance?) towards an exploration of the implications of qualitative differences (e.g. how does a student's understanding of a particular concept relate to the range of possible conceptions, and what factors influence conceptual change?) (Marton *et al.*, 1984). A consequence of this has been that attention has focused on 'learning outcomes' rather than behavioural objectives, and learning has been equated with conceptual change rather than behavioural change. Also, the introduction of qualitative research methods to investigate student learning in higher education has had other implications. As Saljö (1993) points out:

'Measurements provide the objective arguments for decisions to grant or deny people access to education and other social privileges. One of the more important contributions of qualitative research is that it may provide us with insights and conceptual tools that allow us to see the world from perspectives that are less fixed and ready-made'.

Learning as the creation of meaning

The idea of 'meaningful learning' has been around for some time. Recently, however, the influence of a much more radical conception of learning as 'the creation of meaning' has become apparent. Mezirow (1991), for instance, has pointed out that: '... our current frame of reference serves as the boundary condition for interpreting the meaning of an experience'. Many authors suggest that the development of 'critical thinking', with its implicit expectation that students will question meaning, is central to the process of education (e.g. Brookfield, 1987; McPeck, 1990). Perhaps the most radical alternative to traditional ideas about the nature of learning is to be found in the work of 're-conceptualists' such as William Pinar, whose ideas have been associated with reinterpretation of curriculum in the context of auto-biographical reconstruction (Pinar, 1986; Pinar & Reynolds, 1992). As Graham (1992) observes, this approach '... acknowledges the student's search for meaning as an interactive and reflective process undertaken in a social milieu'. A conception of learning as the creation of meaning is also evident in what has been described as 'the curriculum revolution' in American nurse education (Nelms, 1991).

Despite the very different emphases and implications which result from conceptions of learning as 'behavioural change', 'conceptual change' or 'the creation of meaning' each treats practice-based learning as essentially the same thing as university-based learning. Approaches which focus more specifically on practice-based learning include those which conceptualize learning as 'action change', 'skills acquisition' and 'transformation of experience'. This does not mean that they have no relevance for university-based learning but rather that they explicitly take into account practical knowledge. Before considering these frameworks it is worth noting that a growing body of research and literature is emerging from investigation into work-based learning. A particularly interesting development is to be found in the work of Lave and Wenger (1991), whose starting point was the study of apprenticeships. Introducing the notion of 'legitimate peripheral participation', they comment: '... learning through legitimate peripheral participation takes place no matter which educational form provides a context for learning, or whether there is any intentional educational form at all.'

Learning as action change

The notion of reflective practice as developed by Schön (1983; 1987) conceptualizes learning as change in the practitioner's actions and has influenced course design within many professions. As Jarvis (1992a) has pointed out, a number of writers have conceptualized learning in a similar way to Schön but their influence has been much less marked. In relation to reflective practice in nursing, Jarvis comments: '... it is no good seeking to make claims for nursing practice unless the structures are in place that encourage reflection in practice ...'. Fish *et al.* (1990; 1991) have outlined an approach to the education of public health nurses (health visitors), drawing directly on Schön's work to put in place organizational structures necessary to promote reflection in relation to practice. They comment (1991): 'The effectiveness of this process will depend on the supervisor's ability to set an appropriate agenda for the learning experience, but also on her ability to analyse, investigate, and theorise in the practice setting.'

Learning as skills acquisition

Though Harvey (1991) has highlighted the paucity of recent British research into 'skill', nursing in the UK has been heavily influenced by the work of the American nurse theorist Patricia Benner who has explored the relevance to nursing of the Dreyfus model of skills acquisition (Dreyfus & Dreyfus, 1986). In relation to the development of nurses' practical knowledge, Benner (1984) has suggested that a necessary prerequisite is to uncover and make explicit knowledge which is embedded in actual skilled nursing practice. This knowledge, which differentiates 'novice' and 'expert' nurses, can normally only be acquired through practice and requires that '... preconceived notions and expectations are challenged, refined or disconfirmed by the actual situation'. An important characteristic of the Dreyfus/Benner model of skills acquisition in nursing is rejection of the notion that behavioural criteria are sufficient to encompass the richness and variety of expert nursing practice.

Equally, through teaching or 'coaching' functions, expert practitioners can help less competent practitioners to develop skills.

Learning as the transformation of experience

The concept of 'experiential learning' is perhaps most often cited as an influence on the establishment of a framework which can facilitate work-based learning. Steinaker and Bell (1979) have developed a model which identifies five levels of experiential learning: exposure (where an individual is introduced to a new experience); participation (the individual decides to learn more about the experience); identification (the individual's views become altered because of the experience); internalization (the individual critically analyses and explores all aspects of the experience); and dissemination (the individual can express and describe the new experience). Kolb (1984) suggests that: '... the process of experiential learning can be described as a four-stage cycle involving four adaptive learning modes.' Both of these models have provided conceptual frameworks which are applied widely within the adult education. Additionally, experiential workshops are utilized to create conditions which promote learning as the transformation of experience. In discussing the running of a workshop to develop community health care nurses' helping skills, Rhys (1992) comments: '... learning is an ongoing process, for there is always more to discover as we each move along the path of our life.'

15.3 The context of competences

Learning is the means by which people develop knowledge, whether it be theoretical or practical. The conceptual frameworks outlined above are neither exhaustive nor mutually exclusive but are intended to provide an indication of educational influences which can underpin the design of practice-based study. Equally important are views on the outcomes of learning and within this context it is necessary to consider the relevance of competences. Though closely associated with government-led initiatives to establish a framework for vocational qualifications the idea of competence-based education has a separate history (Runciman, 1990) and is viewed variously as an exciting opportunity, a threat or an irrelevance.

Occupational competences are generally regarded as standards of performance required of people who fulfil a particular work role but can be defined broadly or narrowly (Winter, 1990). The introduction of a UK-wide framework for awarding vocational qualifications (Scottish Vocational Qualifications (SVQs) being equivalent to NVQs in the rest of the UK) has already had an impact on entry to preregistration nursing courses (UKCC, 1993). The framework identifies five levels of vocational qualification and it is likely that consideration will be given to the alignment of pre- and post-registration nursing qualifications within this system.

At the same time there have been a number of initiatives to improve links between higher education and employers (Employment Department Group, 1990). At present, however, there are considerable differences between the approach to competences which is apparent in higher education and the approach which has been adopted in relation to the NVQ/SVQ framework. This appears to reflect different points of view on the nature of competences as manifestations of practical knowledge. Competences can be considered to be either indicative or defining of practical knowledge for the purposes of designing vocational education. If teaching and learning strategies are based on the idea that competences are indicative of practical knowledge the approach to enabling their development will be very different to the one which will be adopted if they are considered to be defining.

Benner (1984) outlines a method of investigation which leads to explication of competences which are indicative of skilled nursing and illustrates how recognition of 'exemplars' and 'paradigm cases', which describe and explain significant nursing actions, can help to establish a theoretical knowledge base for nursing which is grounded in practice. By focusing on competences as indicative of practical knowledge this approach emphasizes the importance of judging professional effectiveness by what someone does in an actual situation. Of course, how an acknowledged expert functions will necessarily be defining of competences within a particular area of practice. However, competences which an expert practitioner develops will be the outcome of extensive learning. Elliott (1991) points out that if the aim is to develop expert practitioners it might be more appropriate to consider the process of learning which leads to an individual becoming an expert rather than assuming that competences can be decontextualized and transferred to other people. For this reason he suggests that action research can provide a useful framework for the development of professional expertise:

'... action research is the process by which the structure of abilities that define competent professional practice is most fully realized in those practitioners who aspire to develop their skills a stage beyond the advanced beginner.'

If education is based on the idea that competences are defining of practical knowledge then performance will be sufficient to indicate successful acquisition. Moreover, if successful acquisition is determined by performance then it becomes important to reduce complex activities into their component behaviours. This approach is apparent in the 'performance criteria', 'elements of competence' and 'units of competence' which are generated in very large numbers to define occupational competences and confer vocational qualifications within the SVQ/NVQ framework. Norris (1991) has pointed out: 'The most prevalent construct of competence is behaviourist.'

It is clear that the way in which competences (as the outcomes of practice-based learning) are understood will influence the content of practice-based study. It will also be an important factor in determining approaches to teaching and assessment. However, perhaps of even more direct concern for community health care nursing courses is the question of whether or not vocational education systems of the future will offer scope for different understandings. If all approaches to the development of vocational competences are based on the reduction of complex abilities to simple behaviours then it is likely that students will be expected to learn only what is specified and to learn in ways which appear most directly to achieve the desired behavioural objectives. This is likely to conflict with higher education traditions. As Ramsden (1992) points out:

'It is clear from several studies that the ideas expressed by teachers in higher education will usually embrace knowledge of procedures and familiarity with the basic facts of the subject, but they will invariably include what the lecturers describe as something more fundamental. These fundamentals can be summarized as an understanding of key concepts; an ability to go beyond the orthodox and the expected so that hitherto unmet problems can be tackled with spirit; a facility with typical methods of approaching a problem in the discipline; and – closely associated with the previous point – an awareness of what learning and understanding in the discipline consists of.'

Hager and Laurent (1990) suggest that the traditional divide between 'education' and 'training' has been bridged, commenting: '... in the modern vocational setting there really isn't any longer a useful distinction between terms'. Taking this on board, it is perhaps more appropriate to consider differences in approaches to the development of 'competences' in relation to the analysis of education models suggested by Jarvis (1985):

'... there are two models of education in the same way that there are two sociologies: "education from above" is a model that demonstrates that education is functional to the social system so that the individual is moulded to fit his niche in society through the educational process, whereas "education of equals" assumes that the individual is free, able to develop and fulfil his own potential and able to create a truly human social order as a result of this new found knowledge, skills and ability.'

There is no reason to suggest that vocational education should not be based on an 'education of equals' approach, though this is not often how it is viewed. In relation to the SVQ/NVQ approach Elliott (1991) comments: 'An underlying concern with prediction and control in the language employed is quite clear, as indeed is the atomistic approach to competency specification'.

15.4 Facilitating and assessing practice-based learning

Approaches to the facilitation and assessment of practice-based learning in community health care nursing are necessarily influenced (either explicitly or tacitly) by the ways in which conceptions of learning are operationalized and by ideas about competences. Of course, the question of how best to structure practice-based study is common to other forms of education in which learning outcomes encompass theoretical and practical knowledge. For example, in relation to social work education, the Central Council for the Education and Training of Social Workers (1992) comments: 'If students are learning for and from practice in order to achieve "competence to practise" it behoves us to assess whether this process is occurring satisfactorily.'

As other chapters make clear, the UKCC (1994) has specified learning outcomes for both core and discipline-specific elements of community health care nursing courses. These relate to clinical nursing practice; care programme management; clinical practice development; and clinical practice leadership. Practice supervisors have responsibility for creating programmes of study for individual students which take account of these factors but, as Mackenzie (1990) points out in relation to community nursing in the home (district nursing), information from course lecturers plays an important part in this process. Mackenzie notes that community practice teachers rely on objectives set by course learners to integrate theoretical and practical knowledge: '... all mention the objectives of the [university] programme as an important part of relating the [university] teaching and practice teaching'. This may be of advantage if it encourages innovation and enables flexibility in practice-based study arrangements. However, there is a danger that the provision of detailed guidance and direction may reduce the value that is attached to the relationship established between learner and practice supervisor and may inhibit the development of supervision arrangements.

Supervision can take many forms and may be viewed in different ways (Hawkins & Shohet 1991). As Butterworth (1993) points out:

'Supervision is often negatively associated with more traditional disciplinary dealings between managers and their staff. These dealings are seen as punitive and carry impressions born out of previous negotiations between superiors and novitiates, but this is a narrow definition and more generous interpretations are available.'

At its best, supervision can provide a safe environment for open discussion and is about formalization of the type of relationship which will best enable learning. Sessions should provide space for students to review their learning needs; highlight ways in which practice-based study can best be structured; and receive feedback with regard to progress and/or problems in achieving learning outcomes which have been identified by means of assessment strategies.

The purposes of assessment also vary considerably, being seen as a way of structuring and consolidating learning as well as recognizing and grading achievement (Beard & Hartley, 1984). Crooks (1988) identifies eight purposes for assessing students in tertiary education:

(1) Assisting in the selection or placement of students in relation to courses or course activities.
(2) Motivating students to work harder at their studies.
(3) Helping students to focus their learning on course aspects which are considered to be most important.
(4) Encouraging students to adopt active rather than passive approaches to learning, thereby helping them to consolidate and structure their learning.
(5) Providing feedback on students' progress and achievements, correcting misconceptions and guiding further development.
(6) Determining readiness to proceed to a new topic, level of complexity or course.
(7) Certifying or grading achievement in order to decide whether a student should pass a module or course, receive a particular grade or be judged to be competent.
(8) Evaluating the effectiveness of teaching strategies by considering group performance in relation to learning outcomes.

Clearly, strategies for assessment will reflect a range of understandings and influences. As Ramsden (1992) comments: 'No other aspect of instruction reveals more starkly the essential conception of teaching inherent in a course or in a lecturer's view of the education process.' In courses, or course components, where emphasis is on the development of students' theoretical knowledge, assessment is normally based on how students perform in exercises designed to test conceptual understanding of a particular topic or subject area. In course components which are intended to extend students' practical knowledge it is generally considered necessary to evaluate the student's actual performance.

Criteria for what constitutes competent community health care nursing practice will vary depending on learning outcomes and according to how 'competence' is construed. When considering this issue it can be useful to look at what competence doesn't mean. The opposite of competent is incompetent. If someone is competent it means that he or she is 'not incompetent'. Paradoxically, this double negative can illustrate how practice supervisors conceptualize their assessment roles. If asked, 'Under what circumstances would you judge that a student is not competent?' practice supervisors can generally explain the criteria upon which they would base this judgement. These include:

- if the student acts in a way which endangers people's safety;
- if the student treats people in a manner which is disrespectful or does not uphold the personal dignity and individual rights of service users; or
- if the student does not adhere to codes of professional conduct (e.g. with regard to confidentiality).

Opinions on what constitutes 'more competent' rather than 'less competent' community nursing practice vary much more and bring to mind Derek Rowntree's famous 'health warning': 'Relying too heavily on other people's opinions can seriously damage your sense of reality' (Rowntree, 1989).

Preliminary investigations by the author into practice-based learning in four branches of community health care nursing suggest that most of the information which practice supervisors gather in relation to a student's competence to practise is through informal rather than formal assessment methods. These include general discussions with the student, colleagues and service users; observing the student carrying out a wide range of tasks and projects; and interacting with the student in a variety of environments and with a large number of people. The practice supervisor is able to find out about the student's particular strengths and his or her limitations and will challenge, and be challenged by, the student's understanding of complex situations. By the end of taught practice the community practice teacher is required to judge whether or not the student has attained a level of competence commensurate with progression to supervised practice. By the end of supervised practice the assessor is required to judge whether or not the student has attained a level of competence commensurate with practising as an autonomous community health care nurse. In both of these situations assessment of competence to practise requires judgements to be made which need to take into account a wealth of perceptions and a myriad of criteria.

These preliminary investigations suggest that there is scope for the development of formal assessment methods in community health care nursing which can help to inform judgement of a student's practical abilities rather than his or her academic performance. Appendix 15.2 outlines some of the ways in which a practice supervisor can assess a student's practice. However, these methods are not always in general use and, though it may be appropriate to ask a practice supervisor who has had contact with a student over an extended period to assess whether that person is competent or not in relation to the work which he or she is expected to carry out, asking a practice supervisor to grade a student's performance in practice is fraught with difficulties. Within this context it appears to be the practice supervisor's judgement which is the means of safeguarding professional standards rather than the practice assessment document or 'tool'.

In some instances the practice supervisor is required to assess the student's performance of individual procedures which are considered to be essential in relation to a particular area of practice. In this context the supervisor is asked to observe the student carrying out the procedure and judge whether or not he or she is competent on the basis of his or her actions. The number of procedures which can be assessed in this sort of way are limited and even if a student were to be assessed as competent in relation to a wide range of specific procedures it would not automatically establish a practitioner's overall competence to practise. This approach (with feedback being provided) normally forms part of a practice supervisor's repertoire of strategies to enable the student to learn during practice-based study. However, it is not normally used as a means of testing whether the student should pass or fail a particular component of the course.

If the procedure is an essential requirement for effective practice, the practice supervisor will normally provide sufficient opportunities for learning (and sufficient instruction and guidance) to ensure that the student becomes competent. If a student is assessed by a practice supervisor as 'not competent' to carry out a specific procedure it would be as appropriate to question the effectiveness of the practice teaching as it would be to question the student's abilities. As Eisner (1993) points out, the functions of assessment can be reduced to: '... the assessment of the programme that is provided, the quality of teaching, and outcomes that result from the interaction of the first two.' Within this context, assessing a student's performance is not a straightforward matter.

In addition to assessment by the practice supervisor of the student's overall competence to practise and assessment of the student's performance with regard to specific procedures, post-registration courses incorporate assessed assignments which are intended to establish grading of a student's combined theoretical and practical knowledge. A wide range of assignments is in current use, including those which involve analysis of critical incidents, analysis of practice and analysis of care. Community health care nursing students are expected to be able to produce written coursework which entails description, explanation and analysis of their own practice, and to be able to discuss issues involved in evaluating its effectiveness. Formative assignments and summative assignments with component parts which lead to submission of a completed piece of written work provide opportunities for students to receive feedback. Moreover, they create opportunities for students to clarify their thinking and illustrate their understanding of issues and actions which are indicative of professional competence.

Written assignments are not only viewed as a means of monitoring the student's progress (and ultimately determining whether an individual should pass or fail a particular part of the course) but are also considered to be integral to learning, though there is variation in the extent to which practice supervisors are involved in setting and marking assignments. It is normally considered that there is a trade-off between consistency and inter-marker reliability on the one hand and authenticity and relevance to practice on the other. There are problems, however, in assuming that written assignments assess practical knowledge. In questioning the relevance of assessing nursing practice by indirectly assessing academic performance in written work, Shanley (1994) comments: 'Nurse educators have continued to use methods that are not only ineffective but are also misleading by failing to acknowledge that the system in operation does not clearly differentiate between competent and incompetent students.'

Beattie (1991) has called for innovation in assessment methods within Project 2000 courses, and, in relation to pre-registration nursing, Runciman (1990) outlines a number of assessment techniques for practice-based study. These include methods with written self-assessment components (including learning logs and profiling) which have been developed in relation to work-based learning. Jarvis (1992b) points out that a learning log is '... an analytical record that is kept of learning and practice', and suggests that this should form the basis for discussion with a 'learning partner'. The learning log is not normally used for assessing or grading performance but is a means of enabling learning. In relation to profiling, Runciman (1990) points out: 'The formative process is the "profiling"; the summative product is the "profile",' and cites Hitchcock who defines a profile as: '... a document which can record assessments of students across a wide range of abilities including skills, attitudes, personal achievements, personal qualities and subject attainments; it frequently involves the student in its formation. ...'

The use of profiles for assessment purposes is not without its critics. For instance, Stronach (1989) comments:

'... by constructing the student-centred, holistic and personalized profile, we de-individualize the learners by asking each of them at the same time to conform to a stereotype, and to be themselves. In that sense perhaps, there is no alienation more subtle than self-assessment.'

Issues of reliability and validity of assessment of work-based learning are generally viewed as problematic, though increasing demand for academic accreditation means that the development of more sophisticated assessment and self-assessment methods is likely to be a growth area for research (Williams, 1992; Benett, 1994).

Having commenced this chapter by highlighting similarities and differences between learning to juggle and learning to practise as a community health care nurse it may be appropriate to conclude by returning to this analogy. In both cases it is easier to learn if you have confidence that it is something which you can achieve. In both cases it will be easier to learn if you have a high level of motivation to succeed and receive encouragement to persevere. Perhaps most importantly, in both cases it will be easier to learn if you have someone to coach you who is already competent and who views the development of skilful action as something worthwhile. Whether learning which takes place during practice-based study is perceived to be qualitatively different from, or the same as, learning which takes place in other contexts, relationships which are established between the student and his or her practice supervisor will be of central importance. As Ramsden (1992) points out:

'The most important thing to keep in mind is that students adapt to the requirements they perceive teachers have of them. They usually try to please their lecturers. They do what they think will bring rewards in the system they work in. All learners, in all educational systems and at all levels, tend to act in the same way.'

15.5 References

Alexander, M.F. (1983) *Learning to Nurse: Integrating Theory and Practice.* Churchill Livingstone, Edinburgh.

Bassey, M. (1992) Creating education through research. *British Educational Research Journal*, **18**(1), 3–16.

Beard, R. & Hartley, J. (1984) *Teaching and Learning in Higher Education*, 4th edn. Paul Chapman Publishing, London.

Beattie, A. (1991) *Student Assessment. Preparation for Practice Occasional Papers*, **1**(6). National Board for Nursing, Midwifery and Health Visiting in Scotland, Edinburgh.

Benett, Y. (1994) The validity and reliability of assessments and self-assessments of work-based learning. *Assessment and Evaluation in Higher Education*, **18**(2), 83–94.

Benner, P. (1984) *From novice to expert: excellence and power in clinical nursing practice.* Addison-Wesley, California.

Benner, P. & Wrubel, J. (1989) The Primacy of Caring: Stress and Coping in Health and Illness. Addison-Wesley, California.

Bloom, B.S. (1956) *A Taxonomy of Educational Objectives: Handbook I, The Cognitive Domain.* Longmans, London.

Bloom, B.S. (1964) *A Taxonomy of Educational Objectives: Handbook II, Affective Domain.* Longmans, London.

Brookfield, S. (1987) *Critical Thinking.* The Open University, Milton Keynes.

Butterworth, T. (1993) Clinical supervision as an emerging idea in nursing. In: *Clinical Supervision and Mentorship in Nursing* (eds. T. Butterworth & J. Faugier). Chapman & Hall, London.

Carr, W. & Kemis, S. (1986) *Becoming Critical: Education, Knowledge and Action Research*. The Falmer Press, Lewes.

Central Council for the Education and Training of Social Workers (1992) *Assessing Students' Competence to Practise*. CCETSW, London.

Cervero, R.M. (1988) *Effective Continuing Education for Professionals*. Jossey-Bass, San Francisco.

Cervero, R.M. (1992) Professional practice, learning, and continuing education: an integrated perspective. *International Journal of Lifelong Education*, 11(2), 91–101.

Crooks, T. (1988) *Assessing Student Performance*. Higher Education Research and Development Society of Australia, New South Wales.

Donoghue, J. & Pelletier, S.D. (1991) An empirical analysis of a clinical assessment tool. *Nurse Education Today*, 11, 354–62.

Dreyfus, H.L. & Dreyfus, S.E. (1986) *Mind Over Machine: the Power of Human Intuition and Expertise in the Era of the Computer*. Basil Blackwell, Oxford.

Eisner, E. (1993) Reshaping assessment in education: some criteria in search of practice. *Journal of Curriculum Studies*, 25(3), 219–33.

Elliott, J. (1991) *Action Research for Educational Change*. Open University Press, Buckingham.

Employment Department Group (1990) *Higher Education Developments: The Skills Link*. Employment Department Group, Higher Education Branch, Sheffield.

Eraut, M. (1992) Developing the knowledge base: a process perspective on professional education. In: *Learning to Effect* (ed. R. Barnett). Open University Press, Buckingham.

Fish, D., Twinn, S. & Purr, B. (1990) *How to Enable Learning through Practice: A Cross-professional Investigation of the Supervision of Pre-service Practice. A pilot study – Report Number One*. West London Institute of Higher Education, Twickenham.

Fish, D., Twinn, S. & Purr, B. (1991) *Promoting Reflection: Improving the Supervision of Practice in Health Visiting and Initial Teacher Training. Report Number Two*. West London Institute of Higher Education, Twickenham.

Gauthier, C. (1992) Between crystal and smoke: or, how to miss the point in the debate about action research. In: *Understanding Curriculum as Phenomenological and Deconstructed text* (eds W.F. Pinar & W.M. Reynolds). Teachers College Press, New York.

Graham, R.J. (1992) *Currere* and reconceptualism: the progress of the pilgrimage 1975–1990. *Journal of Curriculum Studies*, 24(1), 27–42.

Hager, P. & Laurent, J. (1990) Education and training: is there any longer a useful distinction? *The Vocational Aspect of Education*, XLII (112), 53–60.

Harvey, N. (1991) British research into skill: what is going on? *The Psychologist*, 4(10), 443–8.

Hawkins, P. & Shohet, R. (1991) *Supervision in the Helping Professions: an Individual, Group and Organizational Approach.* Open University Press, Buckingham.

Jarvis, P. (1985) *The Sociology of Adult and Continuing Education.* Croom Helm, London.

Jarvis, P. (1992a) Reflective practice and nursing. *Nurse Education Today*, **12**, 174–81.

Jarvis, P. (1992b) Quality in practice: the role of education. *Nurse Education Today*, **12**, 3–10.

Jarvis, P. & Gibson, S. (1985) *The Teacher Practitioner in Nursing, Midwifery and Health Visiting.* Croom Helm, London.

Kay, A. (1994) *Bonus or Burden?: An exploratory Study of Practice Based Learning in Higher Education Accredited Post-registration Courses in Scotland.* Glasgow Caledonian University Department of Nursing and Community Health, Glasgow.

Kolb, D. (1984) *Experiential learning.* Prentice Hall, London.

Lave, J. & Wenger, E. (1991) *Situated learning: legitimate peripheral participation.* Cambridge University Press, Cambridge.

Mackenzie, A.E. (1990) *Learning from experience in the community: an ethnographic study of district nurse students.* PhD thesis, University of Surrey, Guildford.

Marton, F., Hounsell, D. & Entwistle, N. (eds) (1984) *The Experience of Learning.* Scottish Academic Press, Edinburgh.

McPeck, J.E. (1990) *Critical Thinking and Education.* Martin Robertson, Oxford.

Mezirow, J. (1991) *Transformative Dimensions of Adult Education.* Jossey-Bass, San Francisco.

Nelms, T.P. (1991) How has the curriculum revolution revolutionized the definition of curriculum? *Journal of Nursing Education*, **30**(1), 5–8.

Norris, N. (1991) The trouble with competence. *Cambridge Journal of Education*, **21**(3), 331–41.

Ormell, C. (1992) Behavioural objectives revisited. *Educational Research*, **34**(1), 23–33.

Pinar, W.F. (1986) 'Whole, bright, deep with understanding': issues in qualitative research and autobiographical method. In: *Recent Developments in Curriculum Studies* (ed. P.H. Taylor). NFER-Nelson, Windsor.

Pinar, W.F. & Reynolds, W.M. (eds) (1992) *Understanding curriculum as phenomenological and deconstructed text.* Teachers College Press, New York.

Ramsden, P. (1992) *Learning to Teach in Higher Education*, Routledge, London.

Rhys, S. (1992) Training student health visitors in helping skills. In: *Experiential Training: Practical Guidelines.* (ed. T. Hobbs). Tavistock/Routledge, London.

Rowntree, D. (1989) *Assessing Students. How shall we Know Them?* revised edn. Kogan Page, London.

Runciman, P. (1990) *Competence-based Education and the Assessment and Accreditation of Work-based Learning in the Context of Project 2000 Programmes of Nurse Education*. National Board for Nursing, Midwifery and Health Visiting for Scotland, Edinburgh.

Saljö, R. (1993) Preface. *International Journal of Educational Research*, **19**(3), 199–203.

Schön, D.A. (1983) *The Reflective Practitioner: How Professionals Think in Action*. Basic Books, New York.

Schön, D.A. (1987) *Educating the Reflective Practitioner: Towards a New Design for Teaching and Learning in the Professions*. Jossey-Bass, London.

Shanley, E. (1994) *Assessment of student nurses' performance – an exercise in futility?* Unpublished paper, University of Glasgow.

Steinaker, N. & Bell, R. (1979) *The Experiential Taxonomy: a New Approach to Teaching and Learning*. Academic Press, London.

Stenhouse, L. (1975) *An Introduction to Curriculum Research and Development*. Heinemann, London.

Stronach, I. (1989) A critique of the 'new assessment': from currency to carnival. In: *Rethinking appraisal and assessment* (eds H. Simons & J. Elliott). Open University Press, Buckingham.

Tyler, R.W. (1949) *Basic Principles of Curriculum and Instruction*. University of Chicago Press, Chicago.

UKCC (1993) *National Vocational Qualifications*. Register, Number 13, Autumn 1993.

UKCC (1988) *Project 2000: A New Preparation for Practice*. UKCC, London.

UKCC (1994) *The Future of Professional Practice – The Council's Standards for Education and Practice Following Registration*. UKCC, London.

Williams, E. (1992) Student attitudes towards approaches to learning and assessment. *Assessment and Evaluation in Higher Education*, **17**(1), 45–58.

Willis, G. (1988) The human problems and possibilities of curriculum evaluation. In: *The Curriculum: Problems Politics and Possibilities* (eds L.E. Beyer & M.W. Apple). State University of New York, Albany.

Winter, R. (1990) Competence and the idea of professionalism. In: *The Asset Programme, Volume 1: Professionalism and competence* (conference papers). Anglia Polytechnic, Essex.

Appendix 15.1
Auditing placement locations

Community health care nursing placements are discipline-specific, with each placement enabling the student to be involved in community health care nursing activities commensurate with his or her level of practice competence and under the supervision of an appropriately qualified practice supervisor. This appendix outlines some of the factors which need to be taken into account in the post-registration educational audit of community health care nursing placement locations.

Qualified nursing staff in post

Sufficient qualified staff are required to enable the student to observe and take part in an appropriate range of community health care nursing activities.

Practitioners available for teaching purposes

When a student is placed with a practitioner for teaching purposes this will alter the pattern of the practitioner's work. Within this context, arrangements need to be in place to ensure that service users are not disadvantaged because of student placements. All qualified nursing staff within the placement location can play a part in the student's education, though responsibility for the organization of the programme will rest with an appropriately qualified practice supervisor.

Appropriately qualified practice supervisors

It is normally considered appropriate that a practice supervisor will supervise one student at a time. When deciding on the number of students to be placed in an area at any one time account should be taken of the fact that practice supervisors have responsibility for students over a long period, even though the student may not be physically in the placement location at all times.

Learning experiences available within the placement location

All students in a community health care nursing placement location should have the opportunity to gain an understanding of the organization and management of services and the methods of working/networking used by community health care nurses.

Accommodation available for students and practice supervisors

Appropriate facilities should be available within the placement location to enable students and practice supervisors to work individually and jointly to fulfil the requirements of the programme.

The number of students from other courses utilizing the placement location

Contact between community health care nursing students and other students may be of mutual benefit but the overall teaching workload of the staff group within the placement location must be taken fully into account.

The extent to which a 'learning culture' is encouraged

All nursing staff have a professional responsibility to assist learners to develop their professional competence. Most nurses readily undertake this role but it may be that if staff in a placement location have experienced particular problems (e.g. staff absences) the needs of students will not be fully recognized and acted upon. Though difficult to evaluate, the extent to which a 'learning culture' is encouraged will be a crucial factor in determining the success or otherwise of a placement.

Appendix 15.2
Ways in which practice may be assessed

This appendix outlines a number of ways in which a practice supervisor can assess a student community health care nurse's practice.

Non-participating observation

Situations in which the practice supervisor can observe the student's practice may occur informally or may be arranged as a formal method of assessment. It must be remembered, however, that even a non-participating observer will exert an influence on a situation by his or her presence. Moreover, creating an unnatural situation whereby a student's performance can be assessed formally may be a source of tension for the service user, the student and the practice supervisor and may not represent 'normal' practice.

Observation of recordings

In some instances it will be possible for the student to secure the agreement of service user(s) to have a situation recorded by means of a video- or audio-tape. This will allow the student's practice supervisor to observe and comment on the student's performance in an actual situation. However, as with non-participating observation, a situation which is being recorded may well be experienced as unnatural by the people who are involved.

Live supervision

Live supervision, in which the student receives advice and guidance from the practice supervisor whilst practising, is normally considered to require the use of appropriate equipment (one-way screens, earphones, etc.). In certain situations, however, it is possible that particular tasks can be undertaken by the student with the practice supervisor present and participating as an advisor.

Setting and evaluating tasks

In formulating a programme of study, the practice supervisor is in a position to set the student tasks to carry out which represent various levels of vocational complexity and to evaluate the outcome of these tasks. As practice-based study components are intended to enable the student to develop his or her competence and confidence, it is important that the practice supervisor does not set tasks which are unrealistic.

Oral reflection and analysis

Discussion between the practice teacher and student on the events, situations and incidents which have been experienced by the student will take place informally. Equally, however, the practice supervisor should ensure that an appropriate formal framework for reflection and analysis is established as an integral part of the process of supervision. Presentation of care studies and practice exemplars with feedback and discussion will enable the student to develop his or her understanding of practice through dialogue with an experienced practitioner.

Written reflection and analysis

Written course assignments enable the student to demonstrate his or her theoretical knowledge. The use of learning logs and practice diaries provide opportunities for the student to offer written comments on events, situations and incidents and can provide a basis for discussion between the student and the practice supervisor. Additionally, asking a student to create written exemplars which explicate his or her practice competences may provide the means by which the practice supervisor can become aware of, and comment on, the student's practical knowledge.

Joint caseload management

Joint caseload management provides an opportunity for the practice supervisor and student to develop a framework for learning in relation to a wide range of practice situations. However, if there is joint responsibility for work activities it may be difficult for the practice supervisor to focus on assessment of the student's competence as something different from developmental supervision.

Others' views

To enable the practice supervisor to assess the student's competence it is possible for him or her to arrange for the student to co-work with another practitioner. In this way the practice supervisor can focus on evaluating the effectiveness of the student's practice by creating opportunities for separate and joint analysis of tasks undertaken. Equally, the practice supervisor will be able to assess how the student is perceived by service users by including their views on both the process and outcome of the student's practice. This can be carried out informally or formally (as a prearranged part of the practice-based study programme) and may take place with or without the student being present.

Chapter 16

Challenges and Opportunities in Education and Training

16.1 Reflecting on major change for community health practitioners

The exhausting process of coping with major organization/role change has been, and is likely to continue to be, a feature of career progression in community health nursing. The commercial logic of adopting a business type approach to meeting client need is paralleled in the type of qualifying courses accessible to nurses working in the wider community. While statutory bodies and professional organizations may still take a global approach to educational requirements, practitioners are likely to find that their employers are persuaded by alternative models which meet their own priorities and requirements.

In the past community nursing preparation has relied on the availability of courses of a certain duration and for practitioners to attend for the stated minimum time. The courses receiving formal or statutory recognition have been based on prescribed or outline curriculum, usually centrally determined and delivered by a variety of training and education institutions in diverse locations. While this training legacy remains, it is increasingly the case that community care organizations will seek a more appropriate strategy for education and training intended to meet their specific needs. Both health and social care agencies are now utilizing the critical incident or functional analysis methods of identifying priorities. When using these models the agencies do not seek to produce detailed and comprehensive lists of likely training needs based on prescribed courses. Instead, they identify and record those problems and staff activities which have a training solution and which have emerged as priorities in the view of the agency. This process, and in particular the way in which the priorities are determined, is likely to be constrained by factors associated with economics of scale, cost and budgetary consideration.

In health and social care the identification of training needs on the scale of that which a care provider unit requires demands sophisticated analytical, evaluative and communication skills. Over two decades ago Talbot and Ellis (1969) made the point that:

'. . . the provision of mere routine training answers to traditional problems will not be sufficient. The requirement is for a much more extensive diagnostic skill which looks beyond the learning processes of individuals and of groups and assesses the impact of this on the business needs for growth and adjustment.'

The context in which future community practitioners now have to work is, then, one of competing needs. They have to be willing to take a fresh view of the scope of their work and see what effect its structures, methods, policies and practices have in the optimum use of their previous experience, current abilities and potential for professional development. This process will include consideration of career paths, promotion plans, job opportunities within and across agencies, and what training is available to assist them to move along these paths. The backcloth against which all these things take place is one which is most challenging. In common with other professions, community health nursing has to monitor trends in the demand for its services. It also has to forecast likely threats and opportunities which may affect its survival or growth. This challenge has to include coping with critical factors, including the economic climate, central policies, new legislation, financial constraints, anticipated changes in the health and social care market, activities of provider competitors, changing demands of purchasers' contracts, conflicting statutory or professional bodies' demands, research and technology and developments, human resource issues and shifting expectations of clients and carers. From a community health care nurse's perspective all of these factors may mean that there can be a significant gap between what happens to community care strategies in theory and what actually happens in practice.

16.2 The evolving national scene for primary health care nursing

Any detailed review of the UK national scene reveals a complex situation. This complexity is the product of interactions among three major groups:

- employers within the health services, social services and independent sector, and in particular the degree of priority which the majority of these agencies give to staff development;
- employees, their professional organizations and trade unions, and the ambivalent attitude which may have been taken towards community training;

- the State, which has historically left responsibility for training in the hands of employing agencies but has, at times, intervened through legislation; in the 1980s the State itself became a significant provider of funds through grants for shared training in learning disabilities, research monies to the National Board for Nursing and funding to the NHS Training Directorate.

The historical perspective of employers of nurses, professional bodies and trade unions is important because the dilemma of community nursing has been paralleled by similar events in other occupations. This has meant that attitudes towards training for specialized work have had a direct influence on access, availability and quality of training in the UK. Knowledge of these events will help contemporary community practitioners understand how the current models of professional preparation have evolved. It is also helpful to develop an informed view of likely strengths and weaknesses inherent in the models, become familiar with bodies which have had a responsibility for standards of community education, and gain an appreciation of the some-times formidable obstacles which face those people within the health and social services who seek to make further reforms.

Progressive employers have for a long time agreed that service delivery should include a responsibility to provide training for the practitioners, and that this training, if it is to be meaningful, should be provided from within the service itself. However, the majority of employers in the UK 'provide neither the quantity nor the quality of training that is needed' (Kenney & Reid, 1987). The legacy is one of a paternalistic and indifferent attitude to training. Legislative attempts to reform training and education, particularly when aimed at specialized practice, have sometimes met obstruction from employing authorities who may see this as an uncalled-for intervention in the operation of their services.

The laissez-faire approach to specialized training by employers is not a recent phenomenon. Its roots are in the nineteenth century when divisions emerged within the field of academic education, vocational education, and training. Over 150 years the State has slowly accepted responsibilities for extending primary and secondary education. However, during this time it was left to voluntary groups to provide technical education which would be geared to supporting the diverse and expanding industries. Guilds and institutes emerged – and eventually technical colleges offering part-time education. The responsibility for these technical institutes was eventually taken by local education authorities, and under their stewardship the present system of further and higher education evolved.

This legacy of divided responsibilities has led to conflict between industries and services and education. This typical employer view of vocational education persists to this day. Nurses and other professionals will be aware of criticism made by employers, such as that teachers are 'out of touch' with the real world of vocational work. This often results in the view being taken that colleges fail to provide the required vocational skills and attitudes towards the work required by the service. At the other end of the scale is the educationalists' criticism that service employers are 'out of touch' with education values and aims and that true partnership is hard to establish.

Although trade unions and professional bodies can rightly claim to have made the case for specialized training this is a relatively recent phenomenon. Certainly, history has shown that the main efforts have been associated with pursuing parity with other occupations and professional groups, together with concerns about terms and conditions of service. There is little evidence of industrial action in support of training. The efforts of unions and bodies to improve training in the area of occupational competence, particularly for unqualified staff, have sometimes been hampered not just by employers but 'skilled' employees themselves.

The State has lent a hand in shaping specialist training either by indirect influence or legislation. An example of this – and a likely influence upon community health nursing – is the NHS and Community Care Act (1990), which was preceded by the Griffiths Report (DOH, 1988). An extract from the latter reinforces this point:

'An overriding impression on training is the insularity of training for each professional group. It may be over-ambitious to talk about common training in skills for everyone working in the community, but an understanding by each professional about the role of the other professions in the community could easily be achieved. Again this type of collaboration at local level in training matters should form part of the basic plan ...'

'... the functions of a 'community carer' should be developed into a new occupation, with appropriate training.'

The impetus and direction of the future preparation of community health care nurses can be detected by careful consideration of such policy statements. Whatever the organizational model within which the contemporary community health care nurse works, his or her future professional education will have to be compatible with key management principles. Therefore, effective curriculum planning will in the future support the translation of key principles into community action. A most useful report is *Nursing in the Community* (NWTHA, 1993), commissioned by the NHS Management Executive, which covers all community nursing services, including GP-based services. The key management principles highlighted in the report actually form the basis of national and local proposals for intended programmes of future preparation of community health workers. These include:

- a shared vision of care;
- joint assessment of population health needs;

- joint strategies;
- effective communications;
- commitment to quality.

The notion of sharing and joint action is high on the list but this activity has not been easily translated properly from the interprofessional view. Most progress in this direction has been made in the area of learning disabilities (Thompson & Mathias 1992).

The new momentum for shared training across all community settings appears particularly relevant in a climate of change. It is likely that future programmes of professional preparation will be designed to meet the challenge of shared learning. The strategy of a joint approach in purchasing and provision of services should accelerate shared learning and, if successful, could reinforce the potential of community nurses and practice nurses to become a primary workforce, able to respond quickly and accurately to demands within the changing arena of health care delivery. It is becoming increasingly likely, as the general management function grows, that in the future nurses and social workers may not be directly managed by their respective professions. If this is the case then it will become important that quality of supervision is examined and the preparation of clinical supervisors on shared programmes will become another challenge to be met by the appropriate agencies.

16.3 Features of programmes of preparation for community health care nurses

A characteristic feature of new models for educational and professional preparation programmes is that of being expressed in terms of intended outcomes linked to the vision of good practice. This is important because community health care nurses can and do develop skills which are necessary to underpin appropriate changes in service delivery. An effective programme designed by competent curriculum planners is likely to be capable of:

(1) assisting community health care nurses to focus on assessed needs of their local population;
(2) increasing effective communication between agencies and other workers;
(3) facilitating skills in developing accurate profiles of local health need;
(4) enhancing collaboration with associated agencies;
(5) extending the influence of primary health care nursing; and
(6) expanding skills in:

- direct client care;
- health promotion including mental health;

- therapy protocols;
- care management;
- scope of rehabilitation;
- palliative care;
- longer term specialist support.

Contemporary courses and programmes need to reflect the fact that in future community health care nurses will need to adapt to changes in function, role, professional relationships and caseloads. It is likely that the aims described will be met by a combination of the development of community practice together with continuing professional development.

16.4 Models of professional development

The education and training of all nurses has changed and accelerated in the past two decades. Changes in provision of health care and therapeutic intervention have led to radical alteration in the design of educational systems. The UKCC (1988) report, *Project 2000: A New Preparation for Practice*, proposed a strategy which was intended to support nursing education into the next century. The basis of this was the creation of a common foundation programme comprising an 18-month course including core studies which have to be undertaken by all candidates on the programme. This is followed by specialization in a branch of nursing, e.g. learning disabilities, mental health, children and adult.

Of equal importance to the pathway or structure was the notion of academic currency for the registrable qualification of professional preparation. This means that all courses based on the Project 2000 model offer a diploma level academic qualification. This has resulted in amalgamation or affiliation between colleges of nursing and midwifery and the higher education institutions. One advantage of this is that nurses now have increased access to higher level studies and a range of options become available in the post-qualifying field, including community health care nurses. The basis of access to professional development is the recognition and subsequent accreditation of prior learning (APL) and experience (APEL), and the acquisition of credits through a system of credit accumulation and transfer (CAT). Three levels, representing a typical course of study of 1, 2 and 3 years' duration, or certificate, diploma and degree level awards have 120 credits attached to each year, giving a total of 360 credits for an honours degree. Programmes can attract a variety of ratings or credits according to their design and recognition by awarding bodies. Modular programmes can carry partial credits and it is intended that this currency will enable access and mobility for practitioners pursuing continuing professional development.

16.5 The CATS tariff

The rationale for the CATS tariff is a system of credit points awarded at the specific levels which relate to standards of work. The credits are either *general* or *specific*, depending upon the nature of the subject area to be studied.

The *general credits* indicate a numerical value which represents credit points attached to quantifiable prior learning of a potential candidate, *without* this being considered in relation to a particular programme of study.

The *specific credits* indicate a numerical value which represents credit points attached to quantifiable prior learning for a potential candidate for a *prescribed* programme of study.

It is likely that professions such as community health care nurses will find any *general* credit awarded for a programme of study they have previously undertaken of particular use and value if it is matched with a course they wish to pursue, and a *specific* credit rating conferred.

Levels of study

The CATS levels which are awarded by universities relate to standards of work and not always to the year in which a course unit or module is taken during the study programme. The level is assigned to a course module or unit by considering the award to which the student's programme is leading. The student's prior knowledge (or the experience he or she requires) is also taken into account. The following Table 16.1 provides a broad guide to the levels likely to be considered by community health care nurses.

Table 16.1 Levels of study.

Award	Credits
Certificate of higher education:	120 *specific* credits at Level 1
Diploma of higher education:	120 *specific* credits at Level 1 and Level 2
Degree:	360 credits, of which the minimum to be acquired is 60 at Level 3 and the maximum 120 at Level 1
Honours degree:	360 *specific* credits, of which the minimum to be acquired is 120 at Level 3 and the maximum 120 at Level 1
Post-graduate diploma:	70 *specific* credits at Level M
Masters degree:	120 *specific* credits at Level M

APL

This is a process by which an individual can claim and gain credits towards awards based on evidence from assessed learning. Nurses may find that some of the many courses they may be interested in do not appear on a tariff list of specific credits towards programmes or modules of study. If this is the case they will need to seek *assessment of prior learning*. This is usually undertaken by submitting evidence to an APL advisor.

APEL

This is learning derived through experiences, and study of theory which may not be formally certified, e.g. a variety of short workshops or study days. The local APEL advisor will determine how best to support your case; this usually involves the compilation of a portfolio of evidence.

16.6 Increasing options

In order to show how the previously described concepts and models can be operationalized, two relevant national policies will be briefly described. One is the English National Board for Nursing, Midwifery and Health Visiting's *Framework* and *Higher Award* (ENB, 1991); the other is the proposed standards for post-registration education practice (PREP) (UKCC, 1990).

The ENB Framework and Higher Award

Following a commission research study in 1991 the ENB recognized that the organization of continuing professional education should be designed around the above-mentioned new concepts: *Framework* and *Higher Award*. A major feature was that the Higher Award element would give recognition for what had been achieved by the practitioner and minimize repetitious training.

Framework

This is a flexible system for organizing and delivering continuing education. It enables practitioners to plan their professional development and facilitates progression to the Higher Award if the practitioner wishes to do so. This can be used by *all* practitioners and allied professionals to meet their continuing professional development needs. It recognized *10 key characteristics* which represent skill areas together with knowledge components and attitudes.

Higher Award

This is accessed by practitioners who hold an effective registration with the UKCC. It is particularly pertinent to those engaged in direct practice. The integration of the 10 key characteristics is recognized by the Higher Award, which serves as both a professional and academic award. The ENB considers the academic level of the Higher Award is a minimum of an honours degree. It is conferred on nurses, midwives and health visitors who provide evidence of mastery of the 10 key characteristics.

The 10 key characteristics of advanced professional practice

(1) Professional accountability and responsibility.
(2) Clinical expertise with a specific client group.
(3) Using research to plan, implement and evaluate strategies to improve care.
(4) Team working and building, multidisciplinary team leadership.
(5) Flexible and innovative approaches to care.
(6) Use of health promotion strategies.
(7) Facilitating and assessing development in others.
(8) Handling information and making informed clinical decisions.
(9) Setting standards and evaluating quality of care.
(10) Instigating, managing and evaluating clinical change.

Figure 16.1 shows how one innovative college of nursing and midwifery has responded by designing a coherent programme for certificate level through to BSc (Hons) level in Advanced Professional Practice with the Higher Award. This will be expanded soon to include a Masters programme.

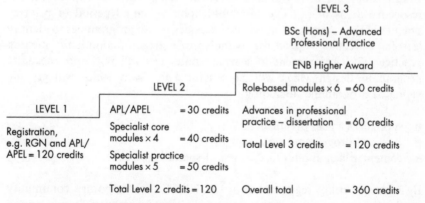

Additional modules can be taken to 'top up' credits, e.g. deficits after profiling for APL/APEL, or to gain additional credits for a particular award.

Fig. 16.1 Pathway to the ENB higher award. A typical example. Reproduced with the kind permission of Mid Trent College of Nursing and Midwifery.

16.7 UKCC PREP Proposals

The Post-Registration Education and Practice Project (PREP Report) (UKCC, 1990) and the Community Education and Practice Report (UKCC, 1991) were published with the aim of developing standards for post-registration nursing, midwifery and health-visiting education to meet effectively patient, client and service need.

A revision of the proposals based upon the results of the consultation exercise was undertaken in 1994 but the overall aim of determining standards of post-registration education and linking these to the professional register is to be maintained.

A description of standards for programmes leading to a community health care nursing qualification

The UKCC proposes that six areas of community practice are to be discussed in terms of standards of practice. These are:

(1) general nursing care of adults;
(2) general nursing care of children;
(3) nursing care of the mentally ill;
(4) nursing care of the mentally handicapped;
(5) nursing care of employees within the workplace;
(6) nursing contribution to the promotion of community health, child protection and health maintenance.

Future course curricula will need to reflect evidence that practitioners in the respective areas of practice can build upon an initial period of primary practice in the community. It will be necessary for all programmes to identify learning outcomes applied for to the specific areas of community nursing practice. The achievement of learning outcomes will rely upon accurate programme design which will be structured in a way which will provide validated programmes including:

■ specialist clinical practice;
■ care and programme management;
■ content which applies to the area of specialist practice.

By virtue of being registered with the UKCC, contemporary community heath care nurses will continue to have the right to practice. So any practitioner becomes subject to the regulation of the UKCC with respect to standards of practice. However, the patient or client who is prepared to accept care from such a practitioner is also conferring responsibility for acting in their best interests. The practitioner has, then, a dual responsibility:

primarily to the client and secondarily to the community he or she is responsible to if students under supervision fail to meet the requirements of the UKCC.

16.8 The wider context

Caring in the community involves a lot more than policy and practice guidance. The range of tasks, duties and obligations undertaken by practitioners requires skills, planning and training. These have to be underpinned by adequate resources. The challenge for education is to maximize the efficient and effective use of resources and development. The so-called 'caring professions' have not always been quick to engage in such activity, and, as Dingwall *et al.* (1988) recognize:

'... the shape of nursing cannot entirely be understood from within. Nursing is one interest in a division of labour where boundaries are in a constant state of flux ... Located as it is between a powerful profession jealous of its own freedom and prestige and the pervasive social concern of the economical management of deviance, the state of nursing is an early indicator of more profound social changes ... There are a number of options for the future of nursing. Purely on demographic grounds the status quo is not one of them.'

The future preparation of community health care nurses will have to realign the function and skills essential for such care in a proficient way which goes into the heart of wider social service provision. Such activity will be underpinned by radical changes both in community care provision and in educational service provision. Community health care nurses and their colleagues in the social services are seeking and achieving a more assertive voice in the form, content and outcomes of their programmes of preparation and the currency which these will hold in terms of transferrable skills.

16.9 Common denominators in health and social care

Forces are being exerted in health, social and educational services which affect policy development and wider opportunities for provision of service in new markets, together with a change in the expectations of service users. A common denominator is the pressure to raise standards, achieve clear and concise outcomes and develop work-based skills, together with designing assessment systems which attest to the achievement of all these things. A challenge has been set by central government support for new partnerships, new markets and links between employers and training and validating bodies.

A major feature has been support of the work of the National Council for Vocational Qualifications (NCVQ) by these partnerships. One result is that the care sector is defining competences required to undertake specific roles and functions. In turn, there is significant pressure to develop vocational systems in a cost-effective way which meet the needs of service user and worker regardless of circumstances.

Some aspects of community health care nursing have been closely associated with successful collaboration between agencies in relation to shared training (e.g. learning disabilities). The NCVQ initiatives are increasingly providing an anchor with which to maintain progress in the ever-changing public service scenario.

16.10 National Council for Vocational Qualifications (NCVQ)

The NCVQ was set up by the government in 1986 to introduce the National Vocational Qualification (NVQ) framework and to ensure that qualifications meet certain criteria and there is a broad comparability across different sectors. The equivalent body in Scotland is SCOTVEC. The NCVQ offers recognition or approval to standards designed by bodies representing the appropriate vocational sections – these are called *lead bodies* – and to assessments provided by awarding bodies. The NCVQ is not in itself an awarding body.

The lead bodies are being drawn together to form occupational standards councils. One of the councils is for Health and Social Care. It has a two-forum structure, one each for health and social care. The Council will be ultimately responsible for:

- overall strategy and direction;
- resource allocation;
- development work priorities;
- quality assurance mechanisms;
- representation of interests to government departments.

NVQ levels

Five levels of qualification are established, ranging from basic or foundation (Level 1) to degree standard equivalent (Level 5).

Level 1

Competence in a range of routine and predictable work activities.

Level 2

Competence in a variety of work activities, some complex and non-routine;

ability to work both alone and in collaboration with others in different situations.

Level 3

Competence in a variety of mainly complex and non-routine work activities in differing situations, often while controlling or guiding others.

Level 4

Competence in a wide range of complex, technical or professional work activities in differing situations, often with responsibility for both other staff and the allocation of resources.

Level 5

Competence involving the application of fundamental principles and complex techniques in a wide and often unpredictable range of work situations, together with responsibility for other people's work and the allocation of substantial resources.

The mechanism for checking that a person is competent is by a system of acquiring observable evidence in a range of circumstances verified by internal verifiers, external verifiers, principal verifiers and chief national verifiers. The systems are flexible. Unlike traditional training courses, there are no restrictions on access by age or training. Account is taken of prior learning and candidates can accumulate unit credits as they progress.

16.11 General National Vocational Qualifications (GNVQs)

GNVQs form part of the national framework. They are intended for post-16-year-old students in full time education and they offer a choice of routes at different levels. Currently there are three levels: foundation, intermediate and advanced. GNVQs have been devised to form an alternative route to those of GCSEs and A Levels. They are in five broad occupational areas one of which is Health and Social Care.

All the preceding facts speak of the tremendous challenge facing those curriculum planners who are to be concerned with preparing competent community practitioners. Competence appears to be a major component of success in meeting the challenge. This means performing to professional or occupational standards: there is no scope for 'second best' standards (Jessup, 1992). Unfortunately the history of both health and social care has produced evidence that second best has applied in relation to primary care.

The correct and diligent use of competences which are designed to achieve proficiency can form the basis of stronger partnership schemes between a variety of service and education providers. Somewhere within this maze of developments there lie new opportunities and options for progress. In community care the importance of interprofessional learning and training is increasingly seen as one way of bridging the many gaps in all systems.

16.12 Interprofessional education – a rationale

The gaps in both service and training provision referred to above have been identified by those practitioners and policy makers who are attempting with various degrees of success to meet the priorities of care as well as making community care a reality. The differing priorities of each locality usually reflect the progress which community health care practitioners and their respective colleagues have made in recent years towards meeting the challenge of community care development and training. The managerial and organizational agendas which are likely to be pursued and which will, therefore, need to be reflected in programmes of professional preparation include those identified by the Department of Health (DOH, 1993):

■ consolidation of basic systems around assessment, discharge, contracting and communication;
■ development of care management with the necessary components of budget and managerial devolution of responsibility taken into account;
■ enabling user and carer participation in decisions on planning, service delivery and quality control;
■ shifting the balance of care so that more resources are progressively made available for non-residential forms of care;
■ development of the purchasing and commissioning capability of organizations emphasizing cross-agency needs assessment and the development of joint commissioning;
■ the engagement of providers in the statutory and independent sectors in ways which will ensure more robust and creative market management;
■ ensuring that housing agencies are properly integrated into planning, purchasing and service delivery systems.

One of the major implications of such a comprehensive and complex agenda is that future education and training activities will need to include aspects of organizational changes as well as the acquisition of competence and skill. If community health care educationalists are to play their part in effectively contributing to the success of *Caring for People* (DOH, 1989) there will have to be accountable commitment at senior levels to service users' focus, interagency working and training. The evidence suggests that interagency working is easier to achieve where there is a history of working together, and where there are shared organizational statements of mission which have been developed for the work to be achieved together (Shaw, 1993a).

In order to be able to progress these aspects, agencies have to be prepared to spend time together, and share values, attitudes and views, thereby establishing a baseline and common language.

Barriers

This is not an easy process; it takes time, energy, creativity and the ability of personnel to establish networks across organizations. It is necessary for contemporary community programme educators to support operational development by overcoming specific barriers to progress. These barriers have formed part of the challenge associated with progress in interprofessional training in the learning disability field and have been identified in the research of Thompson and Mathias (1992), Shaw (1993b) and Brown and Thompson (1988). The barriers include:

- agency failure to release appropriate staff for training;
- inadequate financial backing for relevant training;
- lack of empathy and understanding between contributing agencies;
- insufficient involvement of service users and carers in the design of training programmes;
- mismatch of perception of genuine joint working;
- poor commitment to joint training by statutory bodies and managers.

It will be important that future community health practitioners expand to programmes of preparation which will assist in overcoming these barriers.

Clearly the government has seen community nurses as major figures of influence. This was reflected in the White Paper *Caring for People* (DOH, 1989). Community nursing staff play a vital role at present in the delivery of community care. The government proposals seek to build on their contribution. Nurses represent an important resource and it will be essential in future that health authorities, social services and validating bodies make best use of their time and skill.

So, collaborative working and training is now centre stage and programme designers now have to enhance such interprofessional collaboration in order to ensure accountable community care. The options available to them have increased dramatically in the past two years and have been described in outline in this chapter.

16.13 Conclusion

The nature of social policy, education and employment reforms is such that it is demanding new ways of thinking about preparing community health care practitioners. Increasingly, new qualification structures are emerging which link to the function of the practitioner rather than the traditional description of the role. There is an important yet changing agenda for the provision of community care and future education and training opportunities in community health nursing are expected to embrace these changing demands.

Similar demands are being made on colleagues in other disciplines and the common denominator is organizational and interprofessional competence. The requirement for competence has been identified in nearly all sectors of community practice and they hold the key to the implementation of policy on collaboration, joint production and partnerships in community care provision. The growth of options for community care provision in the independent sector and the evaluation of NHS Trusts have placed collaborative efforts in a complex context. Broader educational policy initiatives are having an impact on professional development. Chapter 16 has outlined current thoughts on educational preparation in vocational and academic arenas within a health and social care framework. Evidence of a process is emerging which links the identification of service user needs with community workforce profiles, which in turn will lead to a more accurate design of training and education programmes.

Professional competence has to incorporate knowledge, value systems and skills. Such competence may be demonstrated by community practitioners in a variety of contexts which can be embraced by a system of recognition of credit and transfer. This process should be able to accommodate the history of the development of community health courses which have been innovative and creative. This history includes the higher level of proficiency which is the ability of community health practitioners to transfer their learned skills to novel situations and to function in non-routine ways in a professionally effective manner.

16.14 References

Brown, J. & Thompson, A.R. (1988) *Quality and Care: A Positive Approach to the Future.* RCN/MHNA, London.

Dingwall, R., Rafferty, A. & Webster, C. (1988) *An Introduction to the Social History of Nursing.* Routledge, London.

DOH (1986) *Community Care: Agenda for Action* Report to the Secretary of State for Social Services (Chairman Sir Roy Griffiths). HMSO, London.

DOH (1989) *Caring for People: Community Care in the Next Decade and Beyond.* CM 849. HMSO, London.

DOH (1993) Training for the future, Training and Developmental Guidance and Support, the Implementation of the NHS and Community Care Act 1990, and the Full Range of Community Care Reforms. HMSO, London.

ENB (1991) *Framework for Continuing Professional Education for Nurses, Midwives and Health Visitors: Guide to Implementation.* English National

Board for Nursing, Midwifery and Health Visiting, London.

Jessup, S. (1992) *Outcomes, NVQs and the Emerging Model of Education and Training*. Falmer Press, London.

Kenney, J. & Reid, M. (1987) *Training Intervention – Institute of Personnel Management*. IPM House, London.

NHS and Community Care Act (1990). HMSO, London.

NWTHA (1993) *Nursing in the Community*. A Report of the North West Thames Regional Health Authority Working Group, London.

Shaw, I. (1993a) *Learning Together – Social Work and Nursing, Health and Social Care*. Department of Social Policy, University of York, pp. 255–262.

Shaw, I. (1993b) The Politics of Interprofessional Training – Lessons for Learning Disability. *Journal of Interprofessional Care*. 7(3).

Talbot, J.P. & Ellis, C.D. (1969) *Analysis and Costing of Company Training*. Gower Press, Aldershot.

Thompson, T. & Mathias, P. (1992) *Standards and Mental Handicap: Keys to Competence*. Baillière Tindall, London.

UKCC (1988) *Project 2000: A New Preparation for Practice*. UKCC, London.

UKCC (1990) *The Report of the Post-Registration Education and Practice Project*. UKCC, London.

UKCC (1991) *Report on Proposals for the future of Community Education and Practice*. UKCC, London.

Chapter 17

Measuring the Effectiveness of Community Health Care Nursing

Quality assurance and a profusion of related terms have rapidly become the buzz words of the new health services. Purchasers of health care are demanding higher standards and providers of services are trying to deliver them, often within a hugely restricted budget. Of all the services nursing is probably being scrutinized most keenly in terms of its cash-releasing potential, and nurses are finding themselves under increasing pressure to justify their consumption of public funds in terms of how their care actually benefits patients and clients.

Measuring the nature of this success, or the effectiveness of both nursing in general and community health care nursing in particular, may seem simple to anyone who has never tried it. It's not! It is a highly complex task and concerns capturing both qualitative and quantitative information about the relationship between the input to services and the outcome, in terms of health gain. Moreover, with the enhancement of post-registration education to produce a more competent and effective community health care nurse (UKCC, 1994a), the challenge of assessing the quality of increasingly complex nursing interventions, as well as maintaining and improving standards, is substantial.

This chapter provides an overview of current approaches to quality assurance, including the setting of standards, the auditing and measurement of performance and the evaluation of services. Examples drawn from community health care nursing are used to explore some of the questions raised when tackling this task. For example, what aspects of care will be examined in determining quality? What outcomes of care will be considered valid? And what tools are available to measure accurately the contribution of contemporary community health care nursing practice? The final section of the chapter is concerned with an examination of some of the issues surrounding the attainment of quality and places this process in the wider context of political change and the market economy.

17.1 Health care in the next century

The social and economic environment in which health care takes place is changing and significant refashioning of the health care system is now inevitable. The National Association of Health Authorities and Trusts (NAHAT) (1993) describes the forces for change as being about a new focus on positive health wherein at both individual and strategic levels public attitudes towards health have shifted. People now have a growing interest in and understanding of their own health due to improvements in education, access to increased information about health care and development of a new consumerism in response to the market orientation of the public services. People are now demanding to be informed about their health and be involved in choices made about their care. There is an increasing emphasis on the overall quality of care and the rights of health service users, as evidenced by government initiatives such as *The Citizen's Charter* and *The Patient's Charter*. Patient empowerment, patient choice and partnerships in care are key concepts for nursing both now and increasingly in the future.

Strategically, wellness rather than illness is being given greater prominence and national health policy is concerned increasingly with the development of targets for health improvement and health gain as well as more sensitive and accurate measurement of health status. Moreover as care in the community develops there is concern to link health and social care and provide better support for carers as well as for those being cared for. These policy directions open up opportunities for community nurses to demonstrate not only their real value as health promoters and educators but also how health gain can be achieved through nurse-led public health initiatives, community development schemes and the building of healthy alliances.

The community care legislation has also put pressure on community nurses to change and develop some of their ways of working. Assessing patient and client need is one of the key skills used in community nursing and this skill must be developed to ensure that community care means quality care. A discussion on nursing and midwifery in the next century, known as the Heathrow Report (DOH, 1994) places great emphasis on the care management role of nurses in the future – a role in which the nurse is key in co-ordinating and facilitating care and developing and maintaining pro-grammes of care.

Demographically the population is ageing and this will affect the needs and demands for care. Patterns of illness are changing – chronic degenerative diseases and cancers have replaced acute infectious diseases as the primary causes of morbidity and mortality in the UK. The management of disability is now as relevant as treatment. Technological changes in investigative and surgical procedures mean that people now experience shorter stays in hospital and have greater access to day surgery. The development of new drugs has shifted the management of certain conditions from surgery into primary care, for example peptic ulcer treatment. The trend towards a reduction in acute units and a massive growth in community-based services continues – specialist acute hospital provision is no longer appropriate for the wide range of health care needs that now exist. In the future many diagnostic and investigative procedures and much treatment and care will take place in primary and community settings, close to where people live. Nurses can manage and deliver much of this care, with contributions from medical and therapy staff only as required (King's Fund, 1992).

The purchaser/provider split and the managed market signal a move away from provider-driven services towards a system where purchasers/commissioners will seek increasingly to purchase interventions which maximize the individual's ability to stay healthy and minimize the need for treatment; and which can demonstrate effectiveness, appropriateness, value for money and high quality. Within purchasing contracts there is a new emphasis on outcomes, especially clinical outcomes, and how to achieve these in the most cost-effective manner. The government squeeze on public sector financing continues and systems of rationing within the new arrangements have become more explicit. It is therefore essential to involve patients, carers, staff and the wider public in priority setting at both individual and strategic levels if acceptable, effective and quality care is to be achieved (NAHAT, 1993).

17.2 The value of community health care nursing

For community health care nurses, determining the impact and demonstrating the value of the care they deliver can be fraught with problems. Put simply, this may be because what nurses do and the benefits of what they do are often not talked about in any coherent, public way. Their work is often a highly private, hidden activity, taking place behind people's front doors or with groups that society has tended to marginalize and ignore. Intervention can be very intimate and it's often associated with very degrading and debilitating circumstances. Some authors suggest that not only is it very difficult for either nurses or the public to share details of what has been a very private exchange but also that, precisely because it is not talked about, there is not yet a language that exists to be able to articulate and describe the nature of this work and the value of nursing care. Lawler (1991) argues that:

'... nurses' work is publicly and socially constructed on the basis of its invisibility. It is not highly visible work, some people prefer to remain ignorant about it, it has low status, it concerns things regarded with an element of smut and all of this is compounded by a reluctance of nurses to talk openly about their work.' (p. 219)

Moreover, the very nature of intervention in community health care nursing is often concerned with aspects of health promotion, disease prevention and social or psychological support – and these are notoriously difficult to measure in terms of impact and possible health gain. And yet, it is vitally important that precisely these aspects of community health care nursing are explained and their value articulated if nursing in this setting is to continue to provide a coherent service in the future. This responsibility must be taken on in creative and rigorous ways by community nurses themselves if the value of professional nursing within the health care system is to find its way into public debate and onto the public agenda. Nurses are the major providers of health care and must assume a leadership role in measuring the quality of their services as well as documenting their costs. If left to those without experience of, insight to or empathy for nursing activity the effectiveness of quality nursing care within the community arena may remain invisible and not awarded the priority it deserves (Naylor *et al.*, 1991).

17.3 Quality assurance

The measurement of the effectiveness and value of nursing care is part and parcel of a number of wider activities collectively called quality assurance – a term which has been extended to cover so many aspects of business, service and organizational work that it has become increasingly difficult to define. One way of grappling with this conceptual confusion is to break it down and define it in terms of its key elements. A vast literature on the subject suggests that quality assurance is fundamentally a cyclical process with three identifiable stages:

(1) agreeing expectations and establishing standards and goals;
(2) measuring what is happening and auditing performance;
(3) taking action to reconcile the differences between the reality and what should be.

By working through this cycle, quality of care is continuously maintained and improved (Shaw, 1986; Pearson, 1987; Redfern & Norman, 1990). It is useful to explore each of these stages in more detail in order to highlight the complexity of this cycle in relation to nursing care in general and community health care nursing in particular.

17.4 Establishing standards, goals and criteria for nursing care

Determining quality nursing care involves identifying *standards* and *criteria*. Pearson (1987) defines a standard as a measure to which others conform; the desired levels of achievement. In other words a standard for nursing care is the professionally agreed level of performance, suited to local practice, that is achievable, desirable and able to be monitored (Kitson, 1986). Criteria can be defined succinctly as those elements or statements within the standard, which are measurable and which reflect the intent, or the goal, of the standard (Pearson, 1987).

Self-care, immunity, health gain and wound healing are all examples of criteria relevant to community health care nursing intervention. If, for example, the criterion of immunity was agreed as the intent or goal of care, one type of standard that could be formulated by a primary health care team might read: *the practice population under five years old will have completed a course of pertussis immunization by the time they start school.*

Johns (1992) suggests that the process of standard-setting is fundamentally a problem-solving exercise which draws on a nurse's value orientation, professional judgement and relevant knowledge base. All of these elements are reflected in the standard of care statement given above. In terms of values, the nurse concerned with immunization will have to believe that immunity through immunization is desirable and that as a nurse she or he has a legitimate and recognizable right to encourage families to conform to this aspect of health care. Value stance will also play a role in how this service is offered and delivered. Will the nurse, for example, take an authoritarian, 'nurse knows best' approach? Or will immunization be tackled as an information-sharing, parent-choice, parent-empowering exercise within which the parents' wishes are respected and endorsed?

Professional judgement is underpinned by a composite of factors such as experience, intuition, education and socialization, which enable a nurse to choose appropriate interventions. Collectively, these factors constitute the relevant knowledge base which is the foundation of skilled performance and decision making. In respect of immunization, professional judgements, through the utilization of professional knowledge, may be made with regard to health promotion techniques and approach, contra-indications of immunization, clinical performance, side effects and so on.

Underpinning this entire process is a basic philosophy and collection of beliefs about the meaning of 'nursing'. It is impossible to determine standards and relevant criteria for any aspect of nursing care unless there is wide understanding of the nature and remit of the work and a belief that actions are valid and legitimate. Perceptions and definitions of nursing change over time and can be highly personal and individual, yet these have to be articulated if clear standards and criteria for measurement are to be negotiated and agreed (Johns, 1992).

Within the quality assurance literature (Donabedian, 1968; Jelinek *et al.*, 1974) the criteria of quality are usually divided into three broad categories:

■ those concerned with structure;

- those associated with process; and
- those related out outcomes.

Each of these categories will be explored in more detail.

Structural approaches

Pearson (1987) suggests that structural criteria are concerned with the prerequisites for patient and client care that enable an agreed level of performance to be achieved. These include physical resources and facilities, human resources and the organization of the unit or institution. Therefore, in respect of the standard for immunization given above, structural criteria would include such things as the availability and suitable storage of vaccine, supplies of sterile needles and syringes, a system of appointments and recall, availability of qualified nursing personnel and so on. Each of these criteria can be quantified and measured to determine whether the reality of care matches the level and intent of the standard.

Process approaches

Process criteria concern those things that need to be done in order to achieve defined goals and meet the agreed levels of performance. Process criteria are described in terms of action. For example, in respect of the standard for immunization, above, the criteria could be described in terms of nurses holding their own clinics to discuss and advise on immunizations and giving the immunizations, as appropriate. Another process criterion may concern the promotion of immunization through accessible, understandable and appropriate information. For example, in areas where English is not the first language of the population this may be achieved through the use of a link worker. Again, it is possible to see how these criteria may be monitored in terms of achieving a set standard.

Development of process criteria is dependent upon a number of fundamental issues. For example, a relevant knowledge base is essential in order to inform nursing actions. Community nurses need the competence, knowledge and skills concerned with promoting health, communication, pharmacology, biology, physiology and sociology, as well as practical skills in injection techniques, in order to achieve the stated standard for immunization. Likewise, criteria concerned with an understanding of the meaning of 'nursing', which is the raison d'être of how and why one delivers care and to whom, is a prerequisite to the process of high-quality nursing care. Additionally, wider aspects such as prevailing political ideology and the organizational form of health services also play their part in the development of process criteria. Consider, for instance, the way in which all nursing actions may have been affected by the adoption of market principles in the health care arena. Some of these issues are explored further later in the chapter.

Johns (1992) argues that, in terms of process, an effective practitioner is one who can synthesise knowledge gained from diverse disciplines, research findings and experience and apply this in practice. Argyris and Schön (1974) refer to this as matching 'theories-in-action' with 'theories-in-use' – a process which is dependent upon notions of reflective practice and the tenets of self-directed learning. This whole approach to practice links, in turn, into the degree of autonomy assumed by a nurse for her or his actions and the freedom of action allowed within any given organization. Community health care nurses, by the very independent, hidden and sometimes isolated nature of their work, are used to a high degree of autonomy and the process criteria identified to measure effectiveness of action will reflect this.

Outcome approaches

Outcome criteria are concerned with the results or impact of nursing intervention and can be measured in terms of health gain, change of health status, patient or client behaviours, patient or client satisfaction, accessibility, acceptability, readmission rates, mortality rates or other predetermined factors (Pearson, 1987). Outcome criteria, therefore, help to describe and identify elements of the end results of care. Measurement of these criteria helps to ascertain to what extent care is being provided effectively.

Within today's rapidly changing, market-oriented health services outcomes and outcome measures have come to be seen as the most valid indicators of quality care – especially in relation to notions of efficiency and effectiveness. These particular terms are frequently to be found littering the pages of policy documents and official reports and are often preceded by the word 'cost'. Cost-efficiency and cost-effectiveness would appear to be the new bywords of quality and they are presented regularly as the main features of success in relation to new services or ways of delivering care.

Drucker (1973) suggests that too much emphasis can be placed on being efficient, at the expense of being effective. For instance, if nurses are competent and diligent in their work but fail to respond flexibly and creatively to changing health needs, they may well be efficient at doing the wrong things. Drucker points out that quality is also dependent on being effective and it is effectiveness that is truly the foundation of success. Efficiency is about survival after success has been achieved.

From this perspective, efficiency criteria are concerned with doing things right, whilst effectiveness is about doing the right things. Ideally, a balance must be found between these two key elements of quality. Within the sometimes vicious world of market forces, cost cutting and value-for-money initiatives this fine balance may well be upset. If we are too concerned with efficiency, at the cost of being effective, overall quality of care is lost and it is the patient or client who is ultimately the loser.

These three categories of criteria – structure, process and outcome – constitute the classic triad used to define the quality of care. The three are fundamentally interdependent and cannot be separated in reality. In order to assess quality holistically, information about the resources available (structure), how they are used (process) and the end results (outcomes) all need to be considered before any judgements about quality can be made. (Pearson, 1987).

Problems exist, however, in embracing an approach that utilizes a range of criteria as they may compete with one another, especially in times of resource constraint. For example, Dalley (1990) points out that nursing care that is equitable and accessible may well be heavy on resources and therefore cost-inefficient. If services are rationed in order to cut cost and meet the demands for care of those in the direst need only, then the criteria of satisfaction or health gain across the given population may be minimized. Different criteria may well be given different priorities and awarded different value by the professionals who deliver the service, the patients and clients who use it, the employees or managers who are accountable for it and the government of the day who fund it. This issue of competing criteria is explored further in relation to community health care nursing and skill-mix later in the chapter.

17.5 Measuring and auditing performance

The next step of the quality assurance cycle is concerned with measuring or auditing performance. These activities are dependent upon the identification of clear criteria which reflect the intent of any standards of care and the construction of appropriate tools for measuring the stated criteria. Accurate, reliable and valid information about the health needs of the population and the services that are being provided by community health care nurses in response to these needs is essential to a quality service. Information, generated from audit, reflecting the value of good nursing care is a tool that can empower nurses by demonstrating whether they are working effectively and using their skills appropriately; the benefits of their interventions in respect of client and health gain; and their cost-effectiveness in the fact of cost-cutting exercises.

An information sheet published by the King's Fund (Hunt, undated) describes three approaches to nursing audit:

- *generic audit* (measuring overall quality of a unit, ward or clinical area);
- *problem specific audit* (measuring quality related to a clinical topic); and

■   *activity specific audit* (measuring quality of care provided by a person or group of people).

This is useful framework and it reflects and links into the structure, process and outcome approach described above.

For successful audit the nurses' own subjective attitudes and ideological beliefs must be explicitly acknowledged and explored and some degree of value consensus achieved within the team. Without this, agreement as to what the goals of care actually are and whether they have been achieved will not be possible.

Methodology

Whatever aspect of quality is being audited, the collection of accurate information is dependent upon the integrity of the measurement tools and the data collection instruments used. Any one criterion can be measured in a variety of different ways and there are many ways of assessing the reality, as well as the value, of nursing care. Audit and measurement should aim to be as valid and reliable as possible and in this respect the choice of methodology in constructing an audit or measurement tool is vitally important. Considera-tion should be given to what sort of information is required, the way it is to be collected and analysed and how the information is finally to be used. As discussed earlier, this often presents nursing with a number of difficulties, not least because nursing, and in particular community nursing, is such a complex and often hidden activity.

Just as criteria drawn from across the range of structure, process and outcome processes need to be identified to assess quality holistically, the same is true of measurement tools and audit strategies. The methodology for data generation, collection and analysis should be drawn from a broad range and reflect both the qualitative and quantitative paradigm in order to capture the multidimensional nature and therapeutic value of nursing.

Some of the context, process and outcome of nursing care can only be described in qualitative terms. Consider, for example, the collection of information concerned with the assessment of the social reality of people's lives – what it *means* to any one particular individual to live in poor housing or to be homeless – in order to plan appropriate care and level of interven-tion. This is not something that can easily be quantified. Similarly, measuring the effectiveness of care in these cases is not always straightforward. In situations where the nurse's intervention may be concerned with the raising of hope, self-esteem and confidence, or with working with families where children are at risk, this cannot be measured in any meaningful way in purely numerical terms nor can it be translated into results with hard statistical significance.

Different aspects of care, however, may well be more amenable to quantitative measurement and evaluation – for example, the rate of wound-healing, numbers of immunizations given, the number of people seen, the mortality rates associated with one particular area and so on.

Reliance on one type of measurement tool or information-gathering technique, or a narrow focus on only one type of criteria to the exclusion of other methods and other elements of quality, will provide unbalanced and partial information. Moreover, any action taken on the strength of narrow, one-dimensional findings may prove to be disastrous for the quality of care. Recent skill-mix exercises within nursing teams are a common example of this and, where managed badly, arguably reflect a downward pressure to constrain costs rather than an attempt to improve quality. In management initiatives of this type, the mix of skills required to meet the needs of a given community has often been based on narrow analyses of nursing activity. This data has tended to be derived from the use of quantitative measures, such as the Korner Data Sets, to gather information on numbers of home visits made, clinics held, client contacts made, tasks performed, etc., with little attention being focused on the nature of intervention involved, the process of care giving and the therapeutic effect of this care. The expedient use of reductionist, quantitative information of the type elicited from these systems may distort management perceptions of the true value of qualified nursing and its effect on the quality of care.

A recent government report of a study into nursing skill-mix in the district nursing services (NHSME, 1992a) recommended that the number of qualified G or H grade district nurses in the areas studied could effectively be halved and more D and E grade nurses employed instead. While most nurses, both practitioners and managers, support the need to ensure value for money within the nursing services and recognize the need to review the mix of the nursing workforce to achieve this aim, considerable concern was expressed that this was done by concentrating purely on nursing tasks (RCN, 1993a). The methodology utilized in the study relied on data being collected by ticking a checklist of tasks and noting their frequency and the time taken to do them. By taking into account only those parts of nursing which are visible and quantifiable and ignoring those less accessible or hidden aspects of care and their outcomes, the study demonstrated that the value and work of expert and appropriately qualified district nurses was not properly understood. As such the report was conceptually and methodologically flawed in that nursing was limited to a collection of observable tasks. Consequently, nursing skill and expertise may be lost or diluted and quality of patient care put at risk. Choice of appropriate tools for each situation, therefore, needs careful thought.

The York skill-mix study (Carr-Hill *et al.*, 1992), on the other hand, attempted to increase understanding of the relationship between grade-mix and the quality of care. This study concluded that the investment in employing qualified staff; providing access to post-registration education and training; and developing effective methods of organizing nursing care appeared to pay dividends in relation to good quality patient care and outcomes.

Techniques and tools for audit and measurement

Many 'off-the-shelf' audit tools created specifically for use with nursing are now available. Among those within regular use in the UK are *Monitor*, which has versions for use specifically within district nursing and health visiting (Goldstone & Lindsay, 1989; Whitaker & Goldstone, 1991); *Quality Patient Care Scale (QUALPACS)* (Wandelt & Ager, 1974); *Phaneuf* (Phaneuf, 1976); and *Criteria for Care* (Ball *et al.*, 1984). The effectiveness of these tools has been extensively researched (see, for example, Tomalin *et al.*, 1992; Redfern *et al.*, 1992) and they continue to provide in-depth ways of examining, measuring and describing the minutiae concerned for the most part with the structure and processes of nursing care.

Tools that concentrate specifically on the measurement of outcome criteria or the effectiveness of intervention, for example patient satisfaction surveys, have only recently become the focus for development – fuelled for the most part by a rush to embrace consumerism, as reflected in government initiatives such as *The Citizen's Charter* (DOH, 1991) and *The Patient's Charter* (DOH, 1992). These initiatives stress the importance of responding to consumer need and, together with the general NHS reforms, will have a profound influence on the manner in which community nursing care is delivered in the future.

In the recent push to develop research-based clinical practice a significant emphasis has been placed by government health departments on the identification and measurement of *clinical outcomes* and the need to set standards of care accordingly (NHSME, 1993a). These outcomes are developed from up-to-date and valid research findings and describe the best clinical outcome for any condition in respect of a particular treatment or intervention; the most recent example concerns the most effective treatment of varicose ulcers. In this way it is hoped that the effectiveness of clinical care can be improved. The government is keen to see these clinical outcomes start to influence quality components in purchasing contracts (NSHME, 1993a). Additionally, the establishment of the Clinical Standards Advisory Group by the NSHME is yet another initiative that will ultimately put the onus on nurses to provide services which are both effective and directed towards patient/client results.

Podgomy (1991) states correctly that historically indicators of nursing care have tended to focus on process issues. With the political and ideological shift of emphasis from process to outcome, the development of clinically based quality indicators – ones sensitive to the patient's response to nursing care in particular – has become imperative. Through the development and use of these nursing-focused quality assurance indicators, Podgomy asserts that the relationship of nursing care to patient outcomes will become increasingly defined.

The political- and market-oriented focus on clinical outcomes is, however, problematic for some aspects of community health care nursing. The question of how a clinical outcome is formulated for types of intervention such as public health work, health promotion activities or the provision of social support, for example, has not been addressed. For nurses concerned predominantly with these areas of intervention, e.g. health visitors, the political risks of being unable to account for their activities in clinical terms are potentially immense.

Other ways of measuring and auditing health and health care needs and demonstrating effectiveness in terms of response, without the emphasis being solely clinical, are however also receiving increasing attention. In particular, there is the *general practice or community population profile* (Twinn *et al.*, 1990; Hugman & McCready, 1993; RCN, 1993b). Since the NHS and Community Care Act (1990) this type of audit tool has become increasingly important as purchasers/commissioning agencies contract for services appropriate to their local population needs. Although not yet essential in non-fundholding general practices, directions from the government health department in England (NHSME, 1992b) state that fundholding practices must profile their practice population twice a year. RCN (1993b) guidance on practice profiling urges community nurses to take on this activity in order to determine priorities for both reactive and proactive care. The guidance suggests a practice population profile should compromise the following key elements:

- identification of the health and social needs of the population;
- the current service provision; and
- the skills, knowledge and expertise available in the team to meet the needs identified.

Information from a profile should enable a primary health care team to set shared objectives and target services accordingly. Hugman and McCready (1993) argue that in this way community nurses can set standards for care, target their skills more effectively and prove their worth to potential purchasers in the rapidly developing contract-based health service.

The setting of national *health targets* in each of the four countries of the UK also provides a useful framework for measurement and audit of health services in general and community nursing care in particular. As described earlier in the chapter, these targets mark an important shift in focus for the NHS away from the treatment of illness and disease and towards the promotion of health, and as such they provide many opportunities for community nurses to seize the initiative. These health targets are also consistent with the World Health Organization's *health for all* strategy

(WHO, 1978) which identifies nurses in primary health care as being the key professional group to take forward health initiatives at local level. Community nurses are ideally placed to develop local nursing strategies in response to each of the agreed government health targets concerned with HIV/AIDS and sexual health; mental health; preventing suicide; coronary heart disease and stroke; cancers; and accidents (RCN, 1993c).

Selection of appropriate tools for audit and measurement is vital to generating accurate and reliable information. Skills in audit and quality assurance techniques are now included in both Project 2000 (UKCC, 1988) curricula and the new post-registration courses leading to qualification as a specialist nurse (UKCC, 1994a). These skills are the passport to achieving and demonstrating high quality and effective community nursing health care.

17.6 Evaluation and enhancing the quality of care

The final stage of the quality assurance cycle concerns the evaluation of practice and the taking of action to reconcile the differences between the pragmatics of reality and what should be. The end result is the enhancement of quality, a better standard of care and assurance of effectiveness.

This stage of the cycle can only be completed once the stages described in previous sections have been completed, namely: criteria have been identified, i.e. a decision has been made about what to measure; sensitive and accurate tools to measure criteria have been devised; and appropriate and agreed standards have been set. The standard signifies what should be and appropriate measurement enables the evaluator to determine whether or not the reality of care meets that standard.

Many methods of evaluation of performance which feed into systems of audit and quality assurance are gathering momentum within nursing. These strategies assist in enhancing quality nursing care and may include individual performance review; peer review; clinical supervision; and personal professional profiling. These will be discussed briefly in relation to effectiveness and wider quality issues.

Individual performance review

The performance of individual practitioners contributes substantially to the overall quality of health services. Appraisal of staff by managers, with the emphasis on setting, achieving and reviewing performance targets in relation to effectiveness, is now firmly part and parcel of the management culture in the NHS and reinforces other approaches to enhancing quality of care. According to Rowland (1990) the intention of individual performance review (IPR) is to ensure that staff are clear about objectives they are to attain and know how their objectives relate to the work of others; and that staff get feedback and an explicit assessment of their performance. Because of this IPR should be a coherent and systematic way of identifying professional development needs and directions for training, and a way of promoting clear lines of responsibility and accountability.

Rowland (1990) goes on to suggest that appraisal through IPR can become part of an organization's change activity, particularly if it is conducted in a constructive, participative and transactional manner. However, she argues that IPR on its own is not a good indicator of quality in a holistic sense, as it focuses too heavily on results and outcomes and ignores structure or contextual issues and the process of performance. The most IPR can achieve in the quest for quality of service is to raise awareness of performance and assist in formulating the questions that need to be asked of individuals, professional groups, managers and service users in order for quality to become 'everybody's business'.

Peer review

Community health care nursing and care provided by other disciplines within the community setting are often provided by staff who may well work alone in an unsupervised environment. Managers may not have the opportunities or even the clinical knowledge to assess professional competence and compliance with agreed standards of care. Cutting (1994) argues that if managers become isolated from the processes of care for which they are responsible, then management becomes an empty exercise and creativity and innovation in care may dwindle. The result could be ineffective and poor quality nursing.

Cutting suggests the answer is independent peer review, based on clinical (multidisciplinary) auditing of packages of care, and describes a project set up in the Chester area to explore this. The project involved two primary health care teams who undertook an auditing programme of each other's care processes and packages of care in relation to a selected topic. The outcomes resulted in a major overhaul of clinical care.

Cutting (1994) suggests that a number of elements are essential for the success of peer review programmes:

(1) External facilitation of peer review sessions helps colleagues to confront one another as to aspects of care that need improvement.
(2) Work needs to be done on interprofessional communication if the review is to be meaningful.
(3) Training in the processes and approaches to audit is a prerequisite.

Clinical supervision

Peer review techniques can be closely linked to the concept of clinical supervision, which in recent years has attracted considerable attention. The

NHS Management Executive (NHSME, 1993b), in *A Vision for the Future*, recommended that clinical supervision be explored and further developed:

> '... so that it is integral throughout the lifetime of practice, thus enabling practitioners to accept personal responsibility for and be accountable for care and to keep that care under constant review.'

The value of clinical supervision lies not only in the way it can enable the development of clinical competence and thus ensure standards of care for patients but also in the support it offers to staff who work in complex and demanding situations (Kohner, 1994). Clinical supervision has also been highlighted as offering a way of enabling staff to develop their skills in response to patient or client need in line with *The Scope of Professional Practice* (UKCC, 1992). The UKCC has made the development of guidelines for effective clinical supervision a major tenet of its business plan for the Council term 1993 to 1998 (UKCC, 1994b). This will aim to encourage registered practitioners to reflect on the care they give and consider ways that this care can be developed and improved in line with the central requirement of being safe and effective.

Personal professional profiling

The maintenance of a record of individual personal and professional development is a major strand of the standards for maintaining an effective registration produced by the United Kingdom Central Council for Nursing, Midwifery and Health Visiting (UKCC, 1994a). The statutory requirement for all registered practitioners – and one which is aimed at the provision of competent, high quality and effective care – is that they maintain an up-to-date personal profile of their professional development which reflects on practice, identifies gaps in knowledge and makes known any steps that have been taken, or are being taken, to remedy any deficits in knowledge and skills.

Total quality management (TQM)

Any organization which is constantly striving to improve quality and effectiveness is likely to employ a number of the techniques of quality evaluation and enhancement described above. An approach which embraces and espouses a culture of continual quality enhancement and improvement is known as a total quality management (TQM) approach. TQM has been defined in a number of different ways but each definition includes the following elements:

■ a corporate approach to quality including pan-organizational goals of quality;

- development of a corporate culture of quality; and
- promotion of an enthusiasm for and commitment to quality as a continual process of improvement at all levels of the organization (Norman & Redfern, 1993).

In business parlance, TQM is a cycle of activity linked securely to the continuous assessment of the needs of customers. This is the only way forward for any organization which finds itself in a rapidly changing environment such as the one which represents community health care today and in the future. For community nursing a TQM approach to the delivery of care is the only way forward into the next century.

17.7 Conclusion

This chapter opened by stating that nurses are the major providers of health care and as such they must assume a leadership role in measuring the quality of their services and demonstrating the effectiveness of their care, as well as documenting the costs thereof. An overview has been provided of current approaches to quality assurance and there has been a discussion of those issues that are to be addressed if nurses are to seize this leadership role and take it seriously. Community nurses are vitally important to the success of care in the next century – the major challenge is to prove the value of their expert contribution.

17.8 References

Argyris, C. & Schön, D.A. (1974) *Theory in Practice: Increasing Professional Effectiveness*. Jossey-Bass, San Francisco.

Ball, J., Goldstone, L. & Collier, H. (1984) *Criteria for Care*. University of Newcastle, Newcastle upon Tyne.

Carr-Hill, R., Dixon, R., Gibbs, I., *et al.* (1992) *Skill-mix and the effectiveness of Nursing Care*. Centre for Health Economics, University of York.

Cutting, J. (1994) Assessing the quality of clinical processes within the primary health care team. *Primary Care Management* 4(2), 6–7.

Dalley, G. (1990) The impact of new community structures: an overview. In: *Enhancing the Quality of Community Nursing* (ed. J. Hughes), pp. 5–10. King's Fund Centre, London.

DOH (1991) *The Citizen's Charter*. HMSO, London.

DOH (1992) *The Patient's Charter*. HMSO, London.

DOH (1994) *The Challenges for Nursing and Midwifery in the 21st Century – The Heathrow Report*. HMSO, London.

Donabedian, A. (1968) Promoting quality through evaluating the process of patient care. *Medical Care*, 6(3), 181–201.

Drucker, P.F. (1973) *Management: Tasks, Responsibilities, Practices*. Harper & Row, New York.

Goldstone, L. & Lindsay, M. (1989) Introducing monitor. *Journal of District Nursing*, September, 24–25.

Hugman, J. & McCready, S. (1993) Profiles Make Perfect Practice. *Nursing Times*, **89**(27), 46–9.

Hunt, J. (undated) *Quality Assurance and Nursing* (Quality Assurance Programme Information Sheet No. 2). King's Fund Centre, London.

Jelinek, D., Haussman, R. & Hegyvary, S. (1974) *A Methodology for Monitoring Quality of Nursing Care*. US Department of Health, Education and Welfare, Bethesda.

Johns, C. (1992) Developing clinical standards. In: *Knowledge for Nursing Practice* (eds K. Robinson & B. Vaughn), pp. 156–71. Butterworth–Heinemann, Oxford.

King's Fund (1992) *London Health Care 2010: Changing the Future of Services in the Capital*. The Report of the King's Fund Commission. King's Fund, London.

Kitson, A. (1986) Indicators of quality nursing care – an alternative approach. *Journal of Advanced Nursing*, **11**, 133–44.

Kohner, N. (1994) *Clinical Supervision in Practice*. King's Fund, London.

Lawler, J. (1991) *Behind the Screens: Nursing, Somology and the Problem of the Body*. Churchill Livingstone, London.

NAHAT (1993) *Reinventing Healthcare: Towards a New Model*. National Association of Health Authorities and Trusts, London.

Naylor, M.D., Munro, B.H. & Brooten, D.A. (1991) Measuring the Effectiveness of Nursing Practice. *Clinical Nurse Specialist*, **5**(4), 210–15.

NHS and Community Care Act (1990), HMSO, London.

NHSME (1992a) *The Nursing Skill Mix in the District Nursing Service*. HMSO, London.

NSHME (1992b) *The Extension of GP Fundholding*. ELJ(92)48. National Health Service Management Executive, Leeds.

NSHME (1993a) *Improving Clinical Effectiveness*. EL(93)115. National Health Service Management Executive, Leeds.

NHSME (1993b) *A Vision for the Future. The nursing, midwifery and health visiting contribution to health and health care*. DOH, London.

Norman, I. & Redfern, S. (1993) The Quality of Nursing. *Nursing Times*, **89**(27), 40–43.

Pearson, A. (ed) (1987) *Measuring Quality Assessment: Quality Assurance Methods for Peer Review*. John Wiley & Sons, Chichester.

Phaneuf, M.C. (1976) *The Nursing Audit: Self-Regulations in Nursing Practice*, 2nd edn. Appleton-Century-Crofts, New York.

Podgomy, K.L. (1991) Developing nursing-focused quality indicators: a professional challenge. *Journal of Nursing Care Quality*, **6**(1), 47–52.

RCN (1993a) *District Nurses and Value for Money. An RCN Response.* RCN, London.

RCN (1993b) *The GP Practice Population Profile.* RCN, London.

RCN (1993c) *You're Nearer to a Nurse: Working for Change in the Community.* RCN, London.

Redfern, S.J. & Norman, I.J. (1990) Measuring the quality of nursing care: a consideration of different approaches. *Journal of Advanced Nursing*, **15**, 1260–71.

Redfern, S.J., Norman, I.J., Tomalin, D.A. & Oliver, S. (1992) The reliability and validity of quality assessment measures in nursing. *Journal of Clinical Nursing*, **1** 47–51.

Rowland, H. (1990) Staff performance reviews – indicators of quality? In: *Enhancing the Quality of Community Nursing* (ed. J. Hughes), pp. 85–9. King's Fund, London.

Shaw, C. (1986) *Introducing Quality Assurance.* King's Fund, London.

Tomalin, D.A., Redfern, S.J. & Norman, I.J. (1992) Monitor and Senior Monitor: problems of administration and some proposed solutions. *Journal of Advanced Nursing*, **17**, 72–82.

Twinn, S., Dauncey, J. & Carnell, J. (1990) *The Process of Health Profiling.* Health Visitors Association, London.

UKCC (1988) *Project 2000: A New Preparation for Practice.* UKCC, London.

UKCC (1992) *The Scope of Professional Practice.* UKCC, London.

UKCC (1994a) *Standards for Post-Registration Education.* UKCC, London.

UKCC (1994b) *Statement of Purpose and Values of the Council and Strategic Objectives and Business Plan of the Council for the Term 1993 to 1998.* UKCC, London.

Wandelt, M. & Ager, J. (1974) *Quality Patient Care Scale (QUALPACS).* Appleton-Century-Crofts, New York.

Whitaker, C. & Goldstone, L.A. (1991) *Health Visiting Monitor: an audit of the quality of Health Visiting Services.* Gale Publications, Essex.

WHO (1978) *Primary Health Care* (Health for All Series No. 1). WHO, Geneva.

Index